2013
北京统计年鉴
Beijing Statistical Yearbook

图书在版编目(CIP)数据

北京统计年鉴. 2013 ： 汉英对照 / 北京市统计局，国家统计局北京调查总队编. -- 北京 : 中国统计出版社，2013.7

ISBN 978-7-5037-6842-2

Ⅰ. ①北… Ⅱ. ①北… ②国… Ⅲ. ①统计资料－北京市－2013－年鉴－汉、英 Ⅳ. ①C832.1-54

中国版本图书馆CIP数据核字(2013)第140693号

北京统计年鉴-2013

作　　者/北京市统计局　国家统计局北京调查总队
责任编辑/郭　栋　　李　冲
封面设计/高　立
出版发行/中国统计出版社
通信地址/北京市丰台区西三环南路甲6号　邮政编码/100073
电　　话/邮购（010）63376909　书店（010）68783171
网　　址/http://csp.stats.gov.cn
印　　刷/北京画中画印刷有限公司
经　　销/新华书店
开　　本/880mm × 1230mm　1/16
字　　数/1216千字
印　　张/38印张　　彩插/1.75印张
版　　别/2013年8月第1版
版　　次/2013年8月第1次印刷
定　　价/350.00元

本书附同版本CD-ROM一张，光盘内容以书面文字为准。
如有印装差错，由本社发行部调换。

2012年，面对日趋严峻的国际经济形势，以及内部调整转型、自然灾害叠加等多重因素影响，全市人民在党中央、国务院和市委、市政府的坚强领导下，坚决贯彻落实党的十八大和市十一次党代会精神，紧密围绕主题主线，坚持“稳中求进”，积极推进各项宏观调控政策，全市经济持续健康发展，社会和谐稳定。

In 2012, facing the increasingly severe international economic situation, supplementing with internal adjustment and transformation, natural disasters and other factors, under the correct leadership of the CPC Central Committee, the State Council, the Beijing CPC municipal committee and the municipal government, the people of Beijing firmly implemented the main themes of the 18th CPC National Congress and the 11th Beijing CPC Municipal Committee, followed the general tone of making progress while ensuring the stability, actively carried out every macro-regulatory policy. The economy as a whole continued with stable growth, and the society maintained steady and harmonious development.

2012年的北京 Beijing in 2012

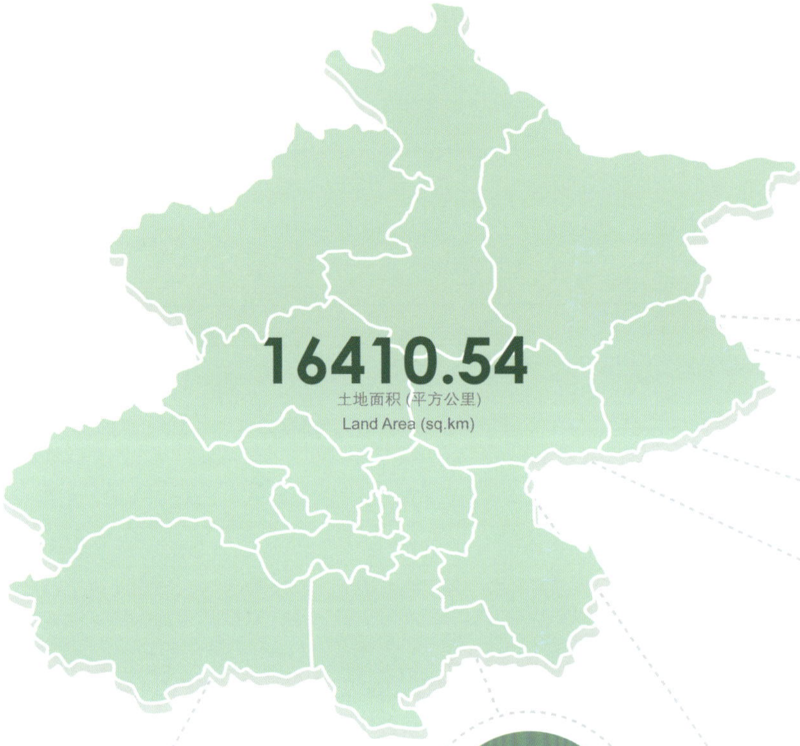

143
街道办事处(个)
Urban Subdistrict Office (unit)

3940
村民委员会(个)
Villagers' Committee (unit)

144
建制镇(个)
Organic Town (unit)

2816
社区居委会(个)
Community Neighborhood Committee (unit)

38
建制乡(个)
Organic Township (unit)

2069.3
常住人口(万人)
Permanent Population (10000 persons)

773.8
常住外来人口(万人)
Non-Natives permanent (10000 persons)

5.95
研究与试验发展(R&D)经费内部支出相当于地区生产总值比例(%)
Internal R&D Expenditure as Percentage of GDP(%)

2458.5
技术合同成交总额(亿元)
Total Amount of Technological Contracts Signed (100 million yuan)

17879.4
地区生产总值(亿元)
Gross Domestic Product
(100 million yuan)

13857
人均地区生产总值(美元)
Per Capita Gross Domestic Product
(USD/person)

76.5
第三产业比重(%)
Percentage of Tertiary
Industry (%)

6462.8
全社会固定资产投资额(亿元)
Total Investment in Fixed Assets
(100 million yuan)

3314.9
地方公共财政
预算收入(亿元)
Local Public
Budgetary Financial
Revenue
(100 million yuan)

7702.8
社会消费品零售总额(亿元)
Total Retail Sales of
Consumer Goods
(100 million yuan)

36469
城镇居民人均可支配收入(元)
Per Capita Annual
Disposable Income of Urban
Households (yuan)

16476
农村居民人均纯收入(元)
Per Capita Net
Income of Rural
Residents (yuan)

103.3
居民消费价格指数(%)
Consumer Price
Index (%)

3.97
每千常住人口执业医师(人)
Number of Licensed Doctors
per 1000 Permanent
Population (person)

4.60
每千常住人口
注册护士(人)
Number of Certified
Nurses per 1000
Permanent Population
(person)

4.48
每千常住人口
医院床位(张)
Number of Beds
of Hospital 1000
Permanent
Population (unit)

6.1
每十万常住人口
幼儿园数(个)
Number of Kindergartens
per 100000 Permanent
Population (unit)

29.7
每十万常住人口
体育场馆数(个)
Number of Sports Venues
per 100000 Permanent
Population (unit)

0.8
每十万常住人口博物馆数(个)
Number of Museums
per 100000 Permanent
Population (unit)

3.5
每十万常住人口银幕数(块)
Number of Projection
Screens per 100000
Permanent Population
(piece)

15.5
人均公园绿地面积
(平方米)
Per Capita Park
Green Areas
(sq.m/person)

520
机动车保有量(万辆)
Possession of Motor
Vehicles (10000 unit)

442
轨道交通运营线路
长度(公里)
Length of Subways
(km)

北京一日 A Day In Beijing

每日创造
Daily Production

2012
年 Year

- **123302.1** 地方财政收入(万元/日) Local Financial Revenue (10000 yuan/day)
- **131250.1** 地方财政支出(万元/日) Local Financial Expenditure (10000 yuan/day)
- **7945.9** 发电量(万千瓦时/日) Electricity (10000 kwh/day)
- **4564** 汽车生产量(辆/日) Output of Motor Vehicles(unit/day)
- **545064** 移动电话机生产量(台/日) Output of Mobile Telephone(unit/day)
- **27327.9** 服务贸易总额(万美元/日) Total Turnover of Service Trade (USD 10000/day)
- **1408.2** 公共电汽车客运量(万人次/日) Passengers Carried by Buses and Trolley Buses (10000 Person-times/day)
- **111504.7** 海关进出口总值(万美元/日) Total Value of Imports and Export at Customs (USD 10000/day)
- **672.6** 轨道交通客运量(万人次/日) Passengers Carried by Rail Transit (10000 Person-times/day)
- **90199.5** 国内旅游收入(万元/日) Earnings From Domestic Tourists (10000 yuan/day)
- **282** 期刊总印数(万册/日) Total Printed Copied of Magazines (10000 copies/day)

4103.8 第一产业(万元/日) Primary Industry(10000 yuan/day)

110909.8 第二产业(万元/日) Secondary Industry(10000 yuan/day)

373494.5 第三产业(万元/日) Tertiary Industry(10000 yuan/day)

488508.2 地区生产总值 (万元/日) Gross Domestic Product (10000 yuan/day)

- **61.8** 接待国内旅游者人数(万人次/日) Domestic Tourists (10000 Person-times/day)
- **1406.8** 旅游外汇收入(万美元/日) Foreign Exchange Earnings from Tourism (USD 10000/day)
- **1.4** 接待入境旅游人数(万人次/日) International Tourists (10000 Person-times/day)
- **616** 图书总印数(万册、万张/日) Total Printed Copied of Books (10000 copies/day)
- **2445** 报纸总印数(万份/日) Total Printed Copied of Newspapers (10000 pieces/day)

❶ 人均地区生产总值(美元/人)
Per Capita Gross Domestic Product(USD/person)

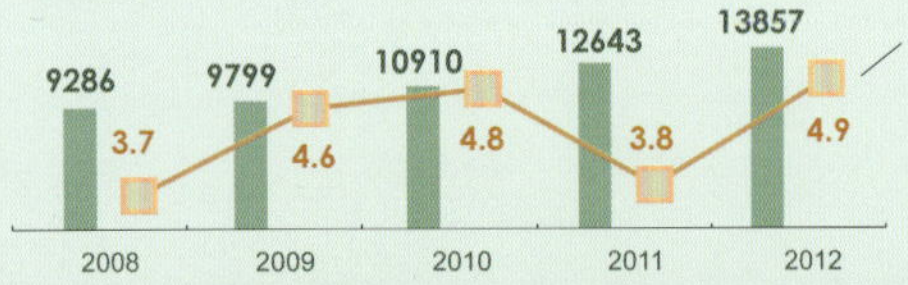

❷ 常住人口(万人)
Permanent Population (10000 persons)

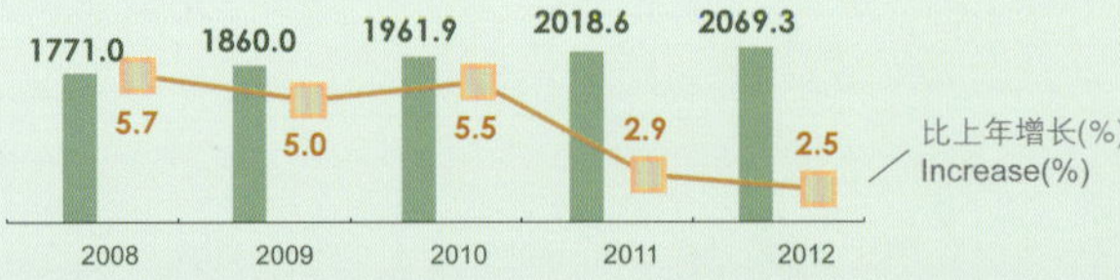

每日生活
Daily Life

505
出生人口(常住)
(人/日)
Birth Population
(Registered Residents)
(person/day)

241
死亡人口(常住)
(人/日)
Death Population
(Registered Residents)
(person/day)

476
登记结婚对数
(对/日)
Marriage Registered
(couple/day)

133
离婚对数
(对/日)
Registered Divorces
(couple/day)

36.3
医院诊疗人次
(万人次/日)
Patients Treated in
Hospitals
(10000 Person-times/day)

1522
首都机场飞机
起降次数(万件/日)
Takeoff and Landing
of Airplanes in Beijing
Capital International
Airport(unit/day)

99.6
城镇居民人均
可支配收入(元/日)
Per Capita Disposable
Income of Urban
Residents(yuan/day)

45876.9
吃类商品(万元/日)
Food
(10000 yuan/day)

19618.7
穿类商品(万元/日)
Clothing(10000 yuan/day)

127824.1
用类商品(万元/日)
Daily Supplies(10000 yuan/day)

17139.8
烧类商品(万元/日)
Fuel(10000 yuan/day)

210459.5
社会消费品零售总额 (万元/日)
Retail Sales of Consumer Goods
(10000 yuan/day)

345.4
污水处理量
(万立方米/日)
Disposal Volume of
Waste Water
(10000 cu.m/day)

65.7
城镇居民人均
消费性支出(元/日)
Per Capita Living
Expenditures of Urban
Residents(yuan/day)

1.77
生活垃圾清运量
(万吨/日)
Domestic Garbage
Cleaned and Transported
(10000 tons/day)

45.1
农村居民人均
纯收入(元/日)
Per Capita Net
Income of Rural
Residents(yuan/day)

4421.7
城乡居民生活用电量
(万千瓦时/日)
Electricity
for Living Use
(10000 kwh/day)

315.3
居民家庭用天然气
(万立方米/日)
Natural Gas
for Living Use
(10000 cu.m/day)

126.5
居民家庭用自来水
(万立方米/日)
Tap Water
for Living Use
(10000 cu.m/day)

3278
电影放映场次
(场次/日)
Film Show Times
(Times/day)

32.5
农村居民人均
生活消费支出(元/日)
Per Capita Living
Expenditures of Rural
Residents(yuan/day)

2012
年 Year

❸ 生活用水量(亿立方米)
Water Used for Living Use (100 million cu.m)

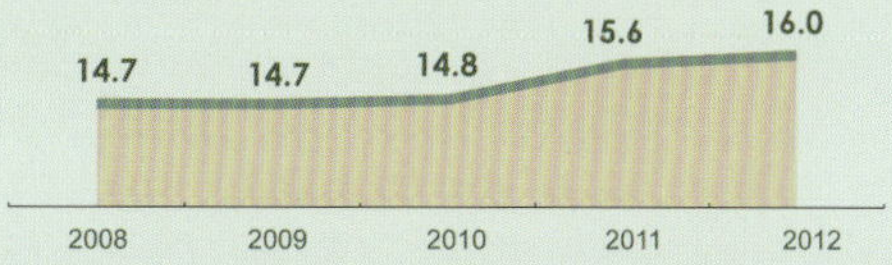

❹ 城乡居民生活用电量(亿千瓦时)
For Electricity Living Use (100 million kwh)

三大亮点支撑北京经济稳中求进

Three Highlights Supported the Steady Growth of Beijing's Economy

全市经济稳步回升
Beijing Experienced Stable Economic Recovery

地区生产总值 (亿元)
Gross Domestic Product (100 million yuan)

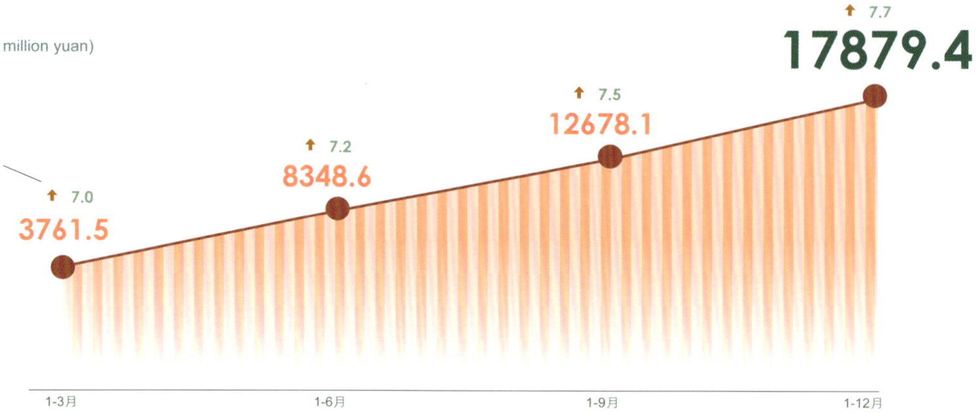

重点工业行业增加值增速加快
Added Value of Key Industrial Sectors Grew at Higher Rate

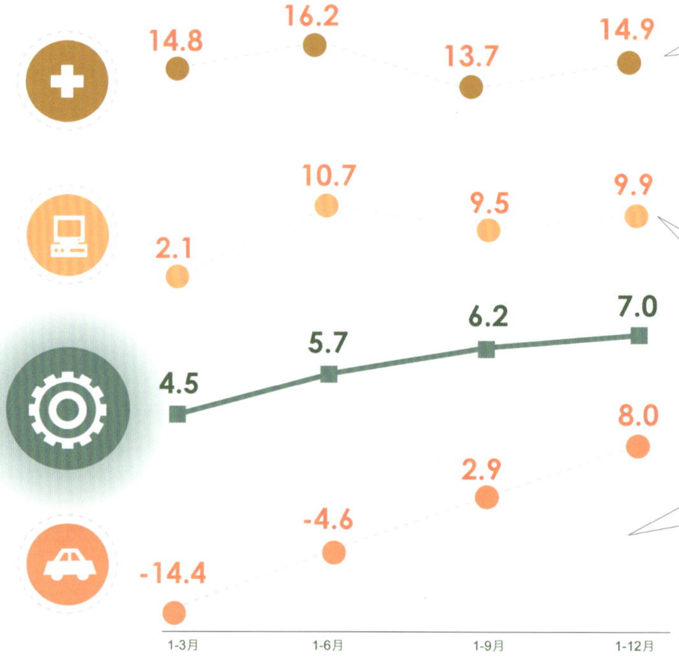

同仁堂科技、泰德制药、紫竹药业等生物医药企业快速发展。

Bio-pharmaceutical businesses such as Tongrentang Science & Technology, Beijing Tide Pharmaceutical, and Zizhu Pharmaceutical developed rapidly.

中芯国际、索尼手机、小米手机等电子企业增势较好。

Electronics businesses such as Semiconductor Manufacturing International Corp., Sony Mobile Phone and Xiaomi Mobile Phone also grew faster.

8代"索纳塔"、"朗动"、"新胜达"和"奔驰-GLK"的量产有效带动全市汽车制造业的增长。

Mass production of G-8 Sonata, Langdong, New-Santafe and Benz-GLK drove the growth of Beijing's automobile manufacturing effectively.

❶ 地区生产总值(亿元)
Gross Domestic Product (100 million yuan)

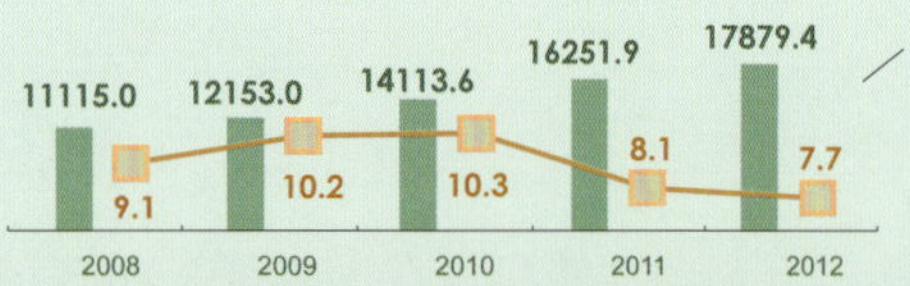

❷ 通信设备、计算机及其他电子设备制造业占全市规模以上工业增加值比重(%)
Communication Equipment, Computer and other Electronic Equipment Manufacturing as Percentage (%) of Added Value of Industrial Enterprises above Designated Size

医药制造业占全市规模以上工业增加值比重(%)
Medicine Manufacturing as Percentage (%) of Added Value of Industrial Enterprises above Designated Size

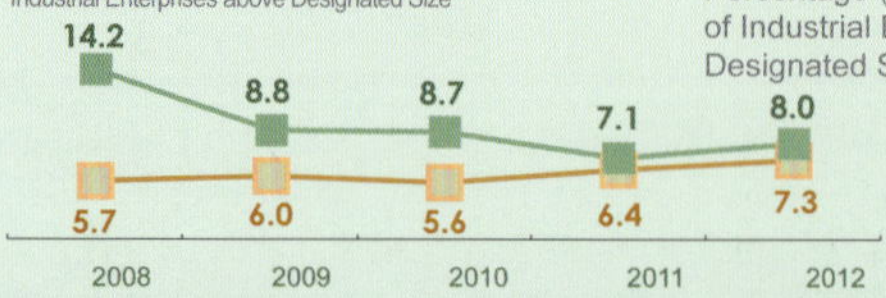

历史数据 Historical Data

中关村国家自主创新示范区创新驱动发展
Innovation-driven Growth of Zhongguancun National Innovation Demonstraplon Zone

中关村示范区经济高位平稳运行
Stable and Faster Economic Growth in Zhongguancun

中关村规模以上企业总收入
Total Revenues of Enterprises above Designated Size in Zhongguancun

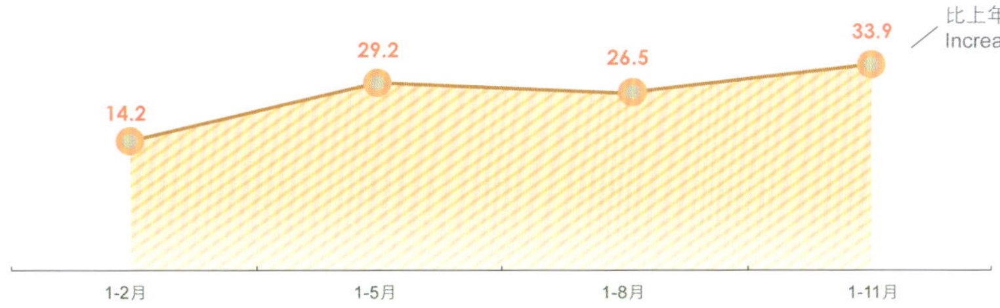

中关村规模以上企业技术收入
Technical Revenues of Enterprises above Designated Size in Zhongguancun

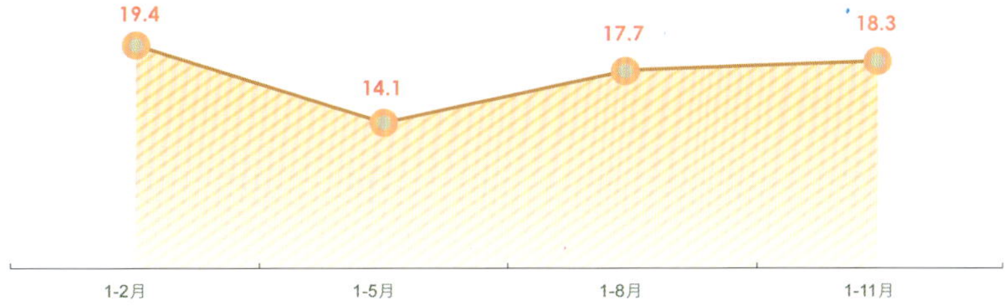

中关村规模以上企业专利申请量同比增加五成
Number of Patents Applied by Enterprises above Aesignated Size in Zhongguancun grew 50%

中关村规模以上企业专利申请量
Number of Patents Applied by Enterprises above Designated Size

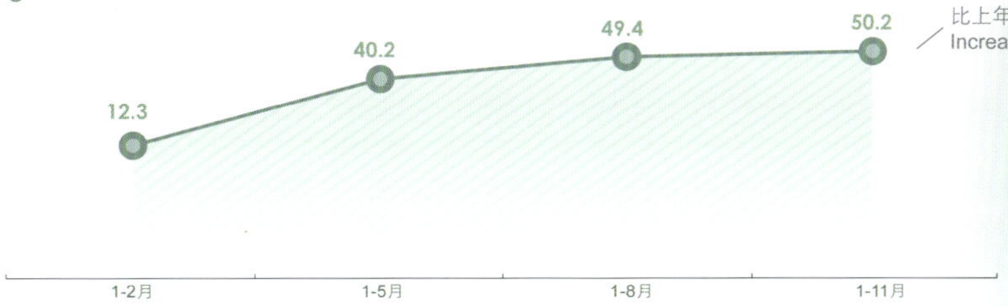

中关村规模以上企业发明专利申请量
Invention Patent Applications Filed by Enterprises above Designated Size in Zhongguancun

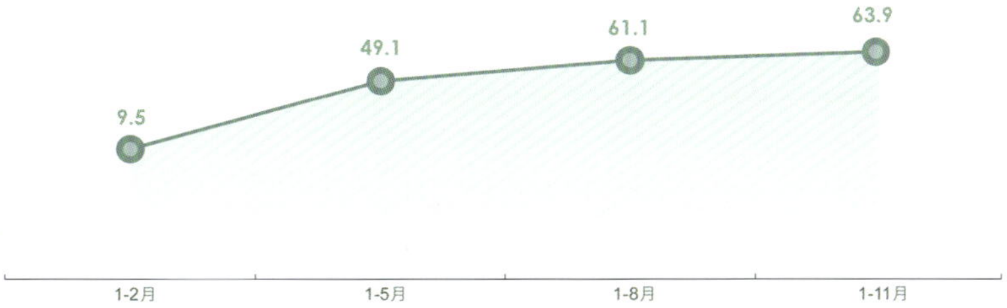

2012 年 Year

❸ 中关村示范区总收入(亿元)
Total Revenues of Zhongguancun National Innovation Demonstration Zone (100 million yuan)

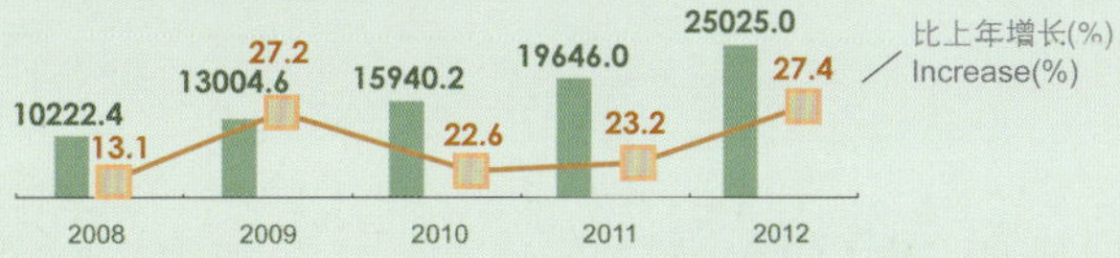

❹ 全市研究与试验发展（R&D）经费内部支出相当于地区生产总值比例(%)
Internal R&D Expenditure as Percentage of GDP in Beijing(%)

全市专利申请量(件)
Number of Patents Applied (unit)

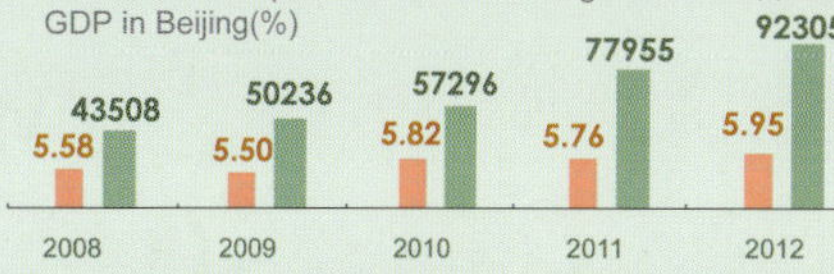

三大亮点支撑北京经济稳中求进

Three Highlights Supported the Steady Growth of Beijing's Economy

网上销售规模持续扩张 增长迅猛
Volume of Online Sales Expanded Continuously and Rapidly

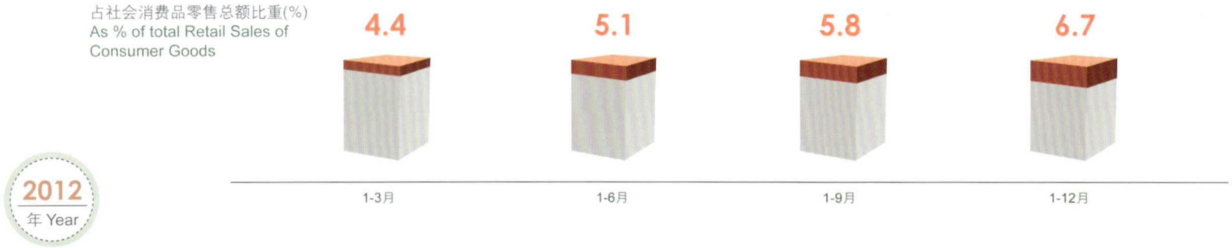

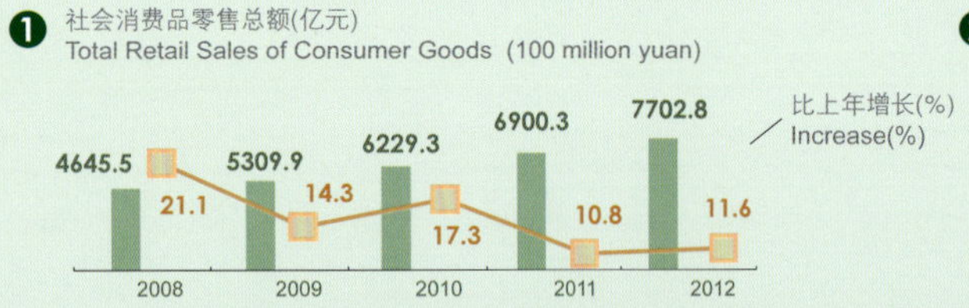

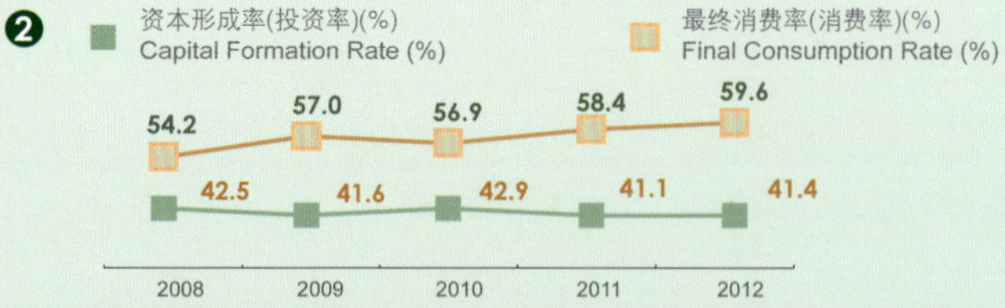

货物、服务进出口双双再创新高

Both Imports and Exports of Goods and Service Hit Another Record High

海关进出口总值首次突破4000亿美元
Gross Value of Imports and Exports at Customs Topped US$400 billion for the First Time

2012年，出口、进口及贸易逆差规模均为历史最高点；月度进出口总值均在300亿美元以上。

In 2012, imports, exports and trade deficit hit a record high; both of monthly imports and exports value exceeded US$30 billion.

服务贸易总额首次突破1000亿美元
Gross Value of Service Trade Topped US$100 billion for the First Time

2012年，北京地区服务贸易总额占全国的20.3%。
In 2012, the gross value of trade service in Beijing represented 20.3% of national total.

2012 年 Year

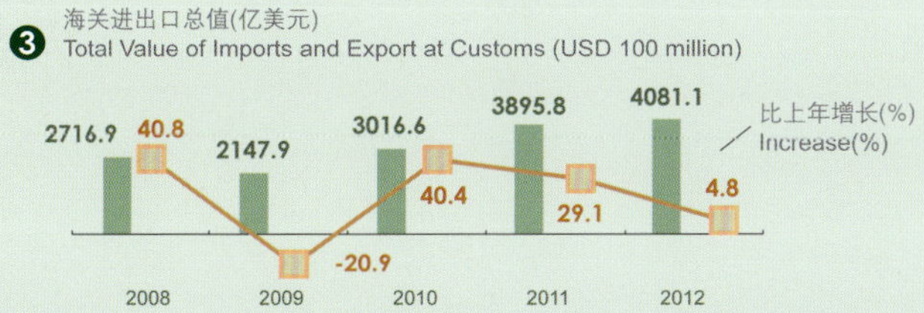

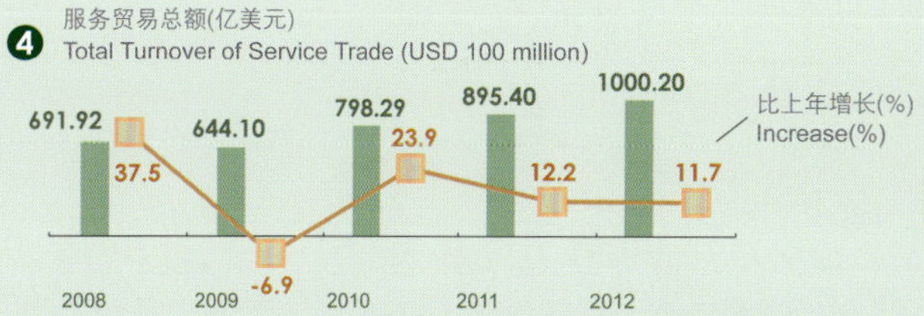

“转方式 调结构 提质量”见成效

Marked Progress in “Mode Transformation, Structure Adjustment, and Quality Improvement”

产业结构和就业结构优化
Industrial Structure and Employment Structure Optimized

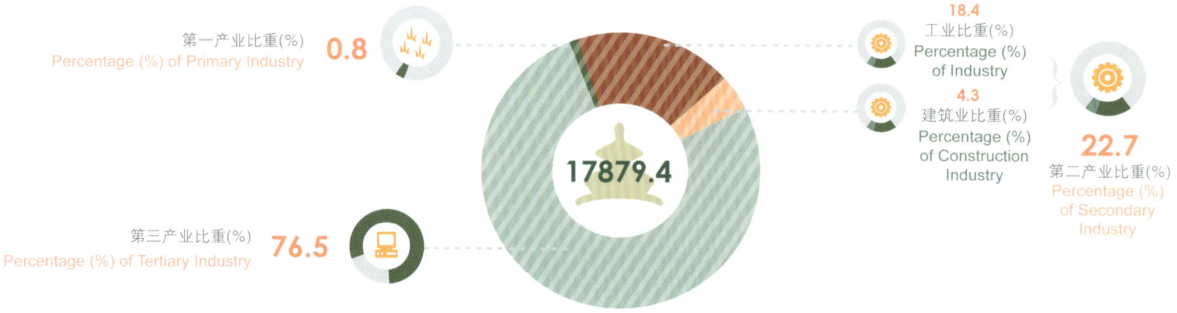

全市地区生产总值(亿元)
Gross Domestic Product in Beijing (100 million yuan)

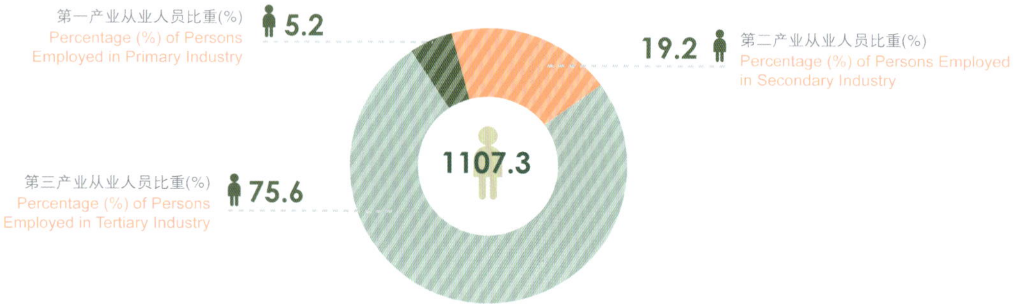

全市从业人员(万人)
Year-end Employed Persons in Beijing (10000 persons)

政策性住房建设稳步推进
Policy-Supported House Construction Progressed Steadily

❶ 三次产业结构变化(%)
Change to Composition of Three Industries (%)

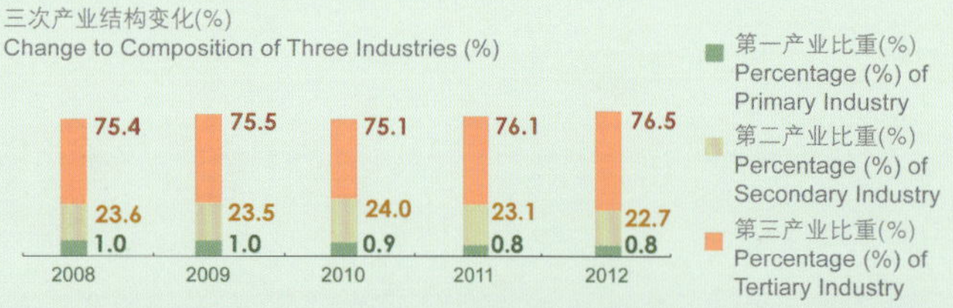

❷ 政策住房施工面积(万平方米)
Floor Space of Policy-supported House under Construction (10000 sq.m)

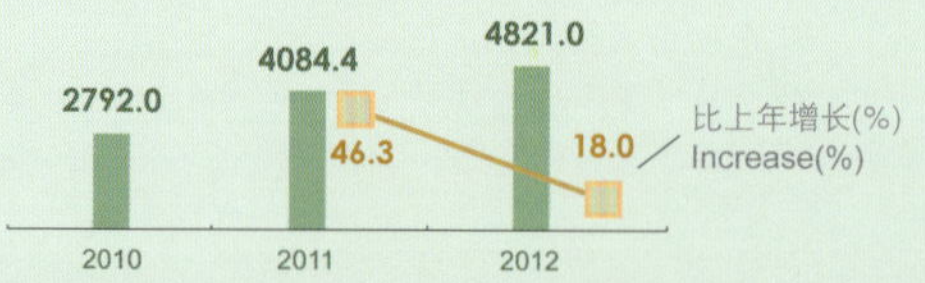

工业企业能耗继续下降 高耗能行业推动作用显著
Energy Consumption by Industrial Enterprises Continued to Decrease, which was Significantly Driven by High-energy-consuming Sectors.

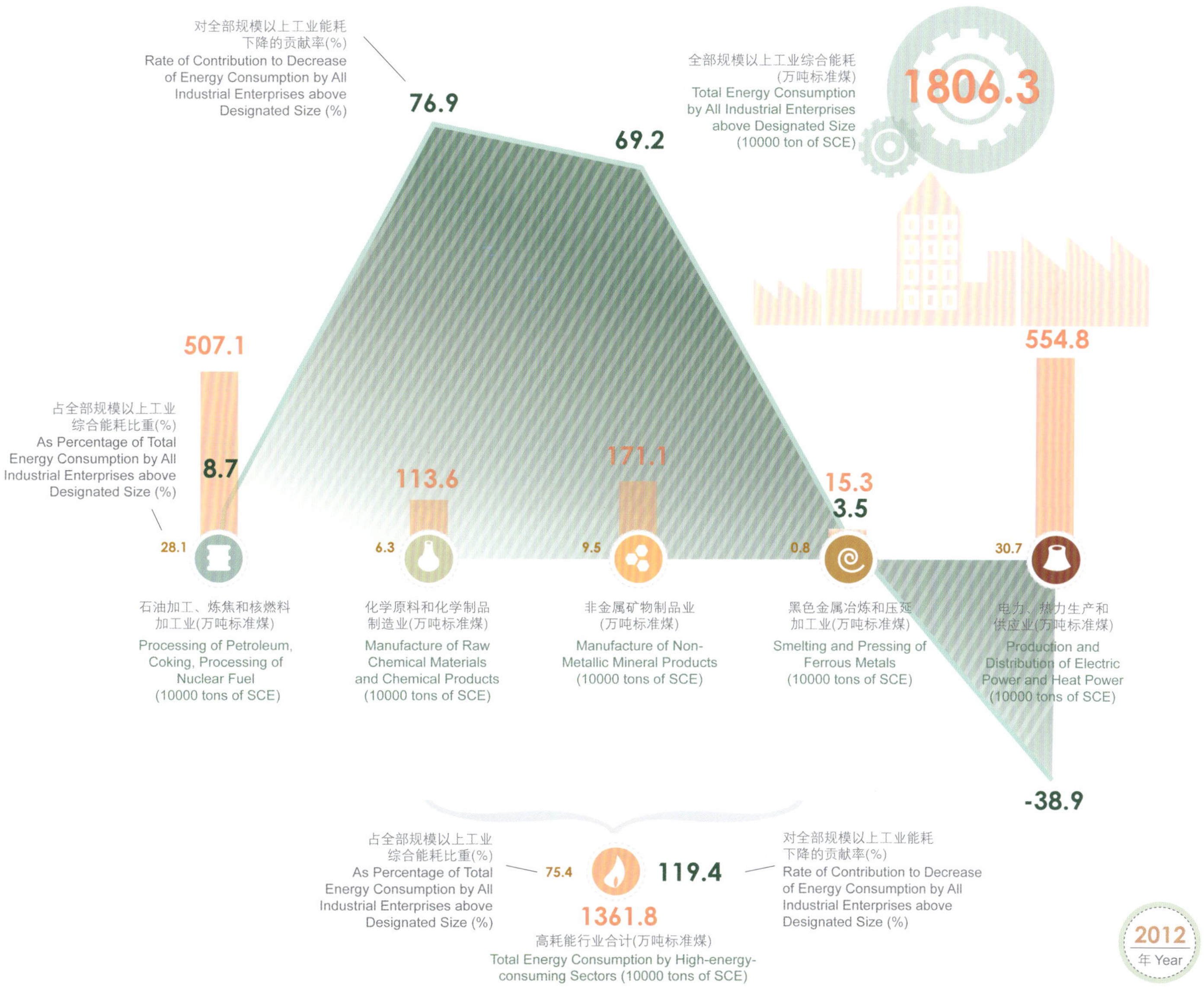

❸ 工业能源消费量(万吨标准煤)
Energy Consumption by Industry (10000 tons of SCE)

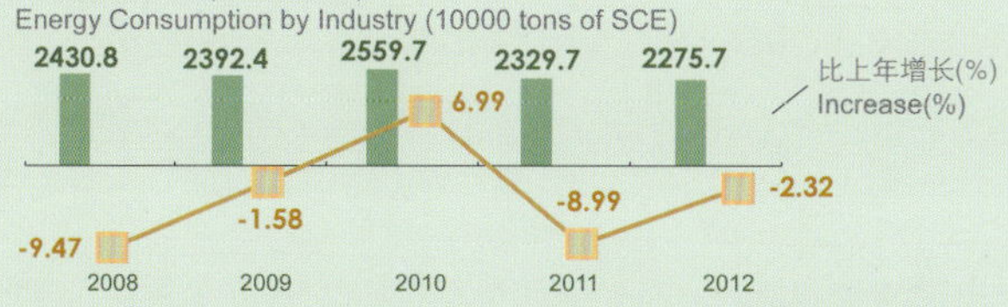

❹ 万元地区生产总值能耗下降率(%)
Decrease Rate of Energy Consumption per 10000 yuan GDP(%)

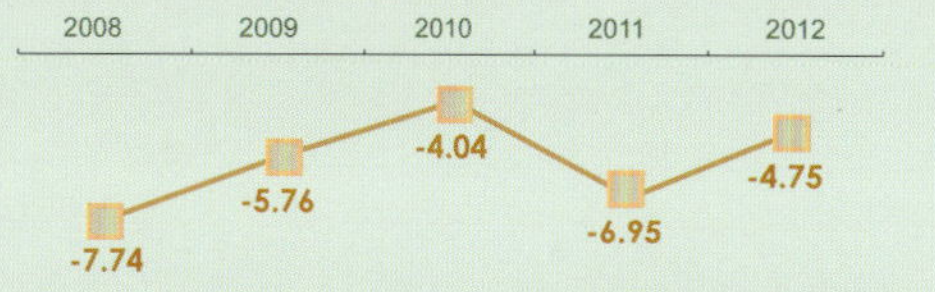

“转方式 调结构 提质量”见成效

Marked Progress in “Mode Transformation, Structure Adjustment, and Quality Improvement”

全社会劳动生产率持续上升
Overall labor Productivity Rose Continuously

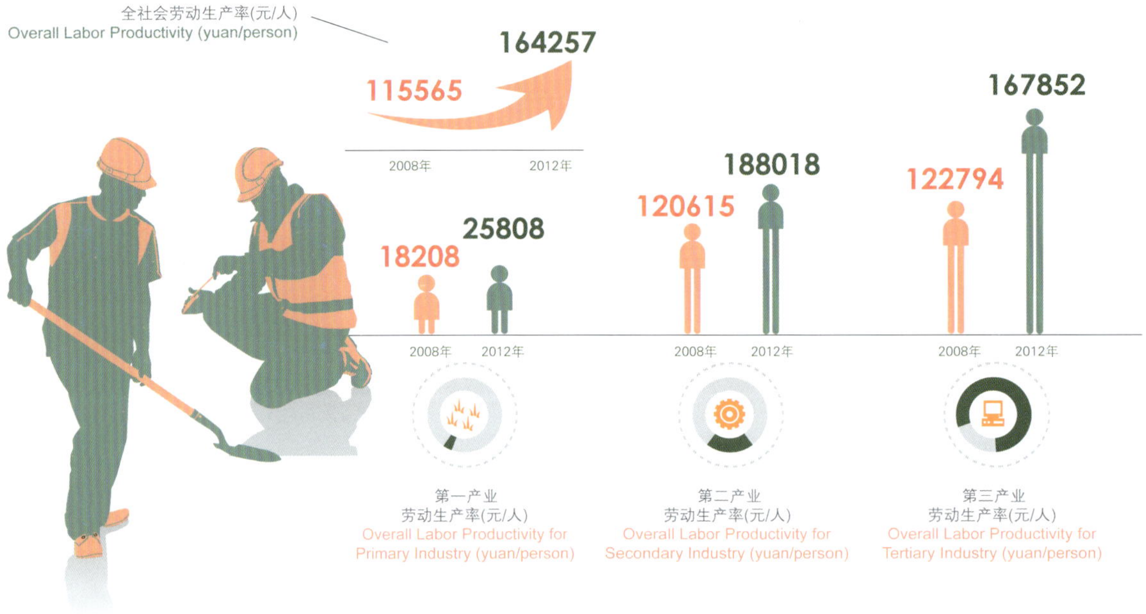

地方公共财政预算收入实现两位数增长
Local Public Budgetary Financial Revenue Grew at a Rate of more than 10%

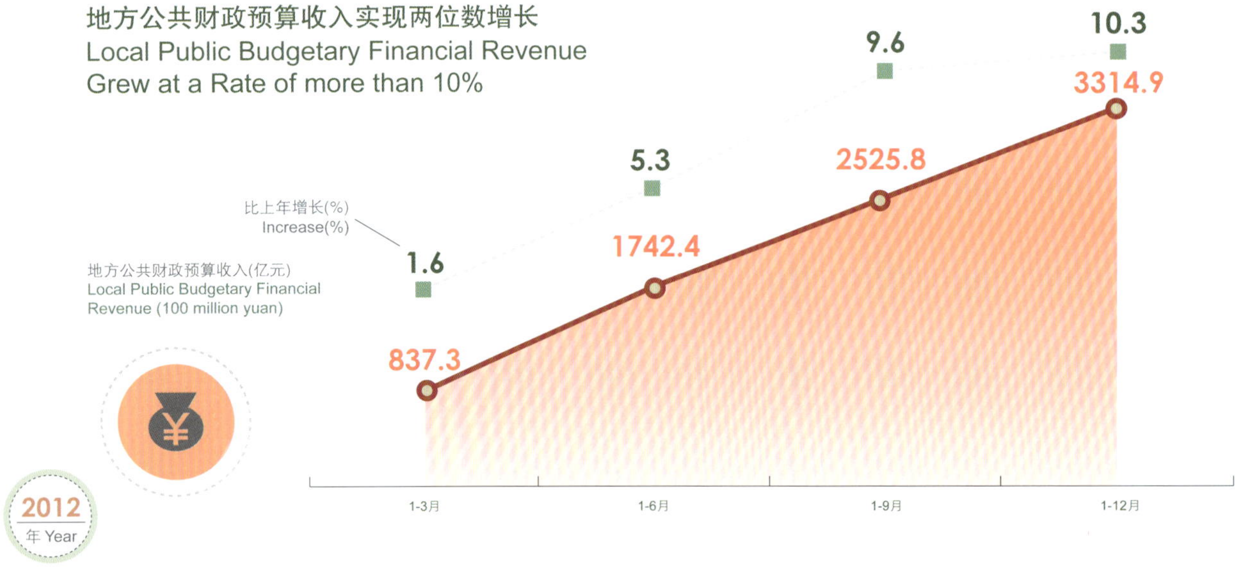

❶ 社会劳动生产率(元/人)
Overall Labor Productivity (yuan/person)

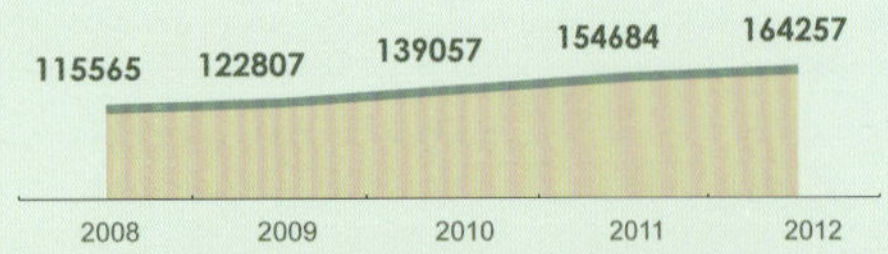

❷ 地方公共财政预算收入(亿元)
Local Public Budgetary Financial Revenue (100 million yuan)

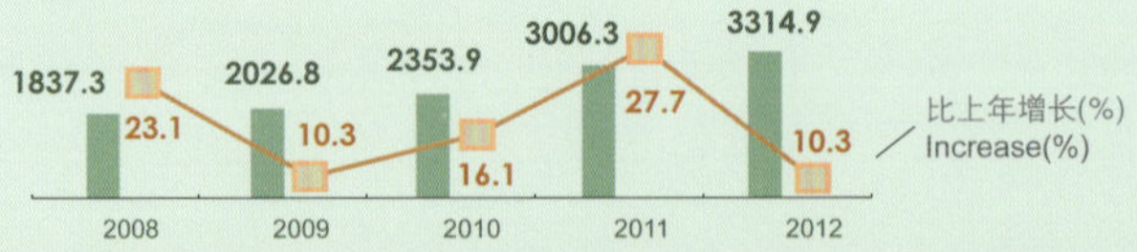

历史数据 Historical Data

城乡居民收入稳步增加
Urban and Rural Residents' Income Increased Steadily

城镇居民人均可支配收入(元)
Per Capita Disposable Income of Urban Residents(yuan)

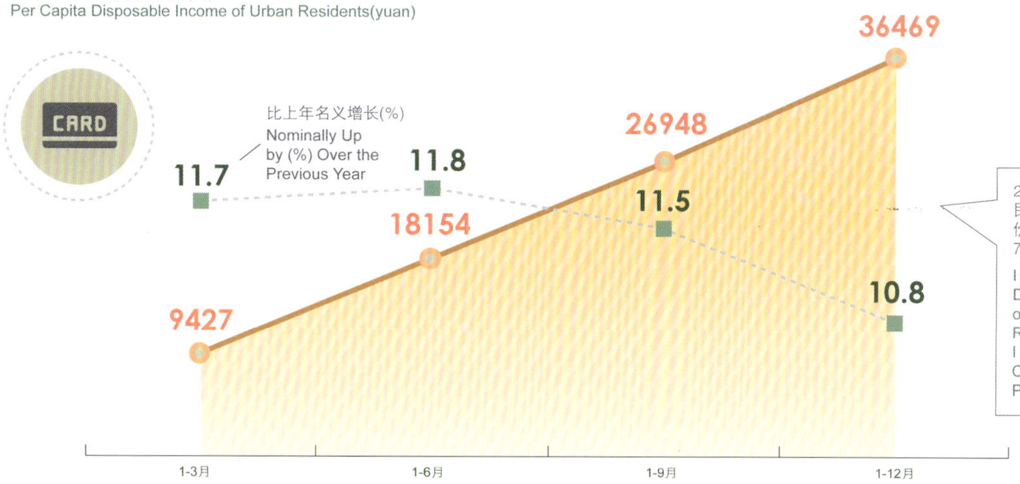

2012年，全市城镇居民人均可支配收入扣除价格因素后，实际增长7.3%。

In 2012, Per-capita Disposable Income of Urban and Rural Residents in Beijing Increased 7.3% Calculated at Constant Prices.

农村居民人均现金收入(元)
Per-capita Cash Income of Rural Residents (yuan)

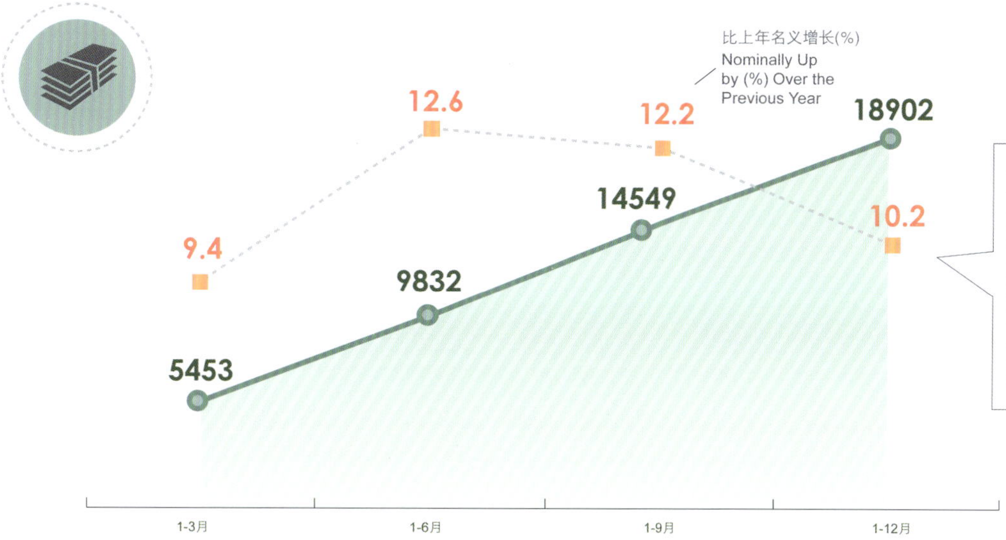

2012年，全市农村居民人均纯收入16476元，比上年名义增长11.8%，扣除价格因素后，实际增长8.2%。

In 2012, Per-capita Net Income of Rural Residents in Beijing was 16476 yuan, up by 11.8% Nominally, and 8.2% Calculated at Constant Prices.

2012 年 Year

❸ 城镇居民人均可支配收入(元)
Per Capita Disposable Income of Urban Residents(yuan)

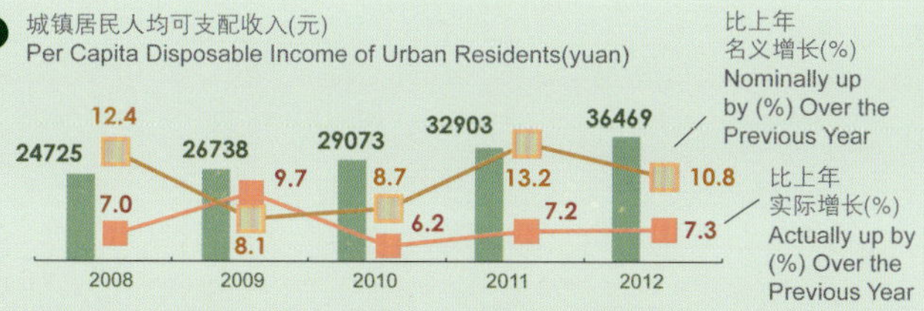

❹ 农村居民人均纯收入(元)
Per Capita Net Income of Rural Residents(yuan)

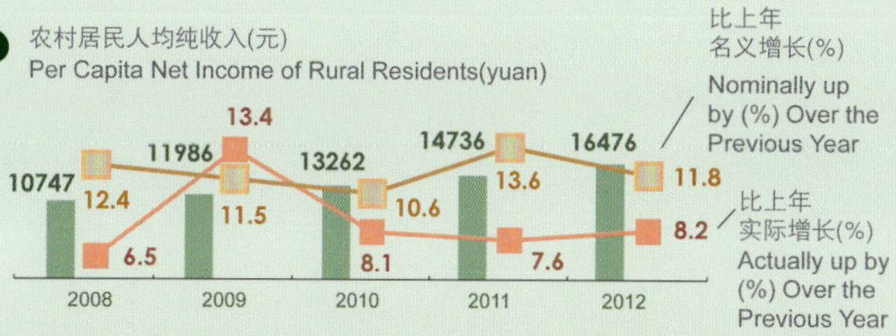

“转方式 调结构 提质量”见成效

Marked Progress in “Mode Transformation, Structure Adjustment, and Quality Improvement”

规模以上工业利润增长速度“低开走稳”
Growth of Profit of Industrial Enterprises above Designated Size “Recovered from Low Rate”

规模以上工业企业利润总额
Total Profits of Industrial Enterprises above Designated Size

2012年，汽车、医药行业有效带动工业利润增长。汽车制造业实现利润比上年增长11.1%，医药制造业实现利润增长12.9%。

In 2012, auto and medicine manufacturing industries drove the profit growth of industry effectively. Profit reaped by automobile manufacturing grew 11.1% as compared with the previous year, that by medicine manufacturing, 12.9%.

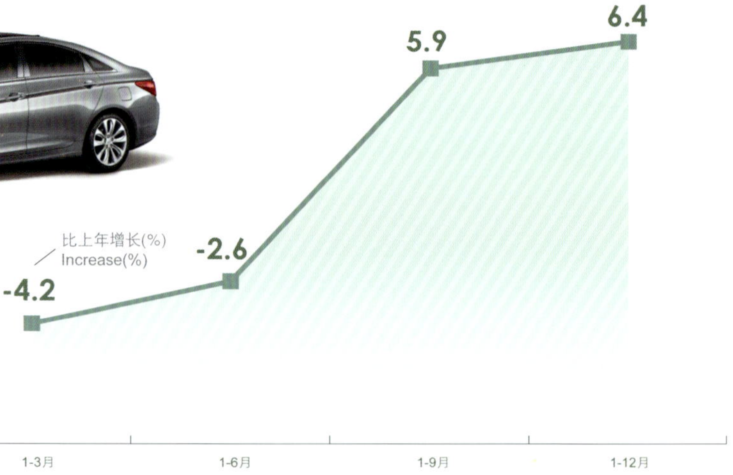

第三产业企业效益向好
Profit of Tertiary Industry Tended to be Better

限额以上第三产业利润总额
Total Profits of Enterprises in Tertiary Industry above Designated Size

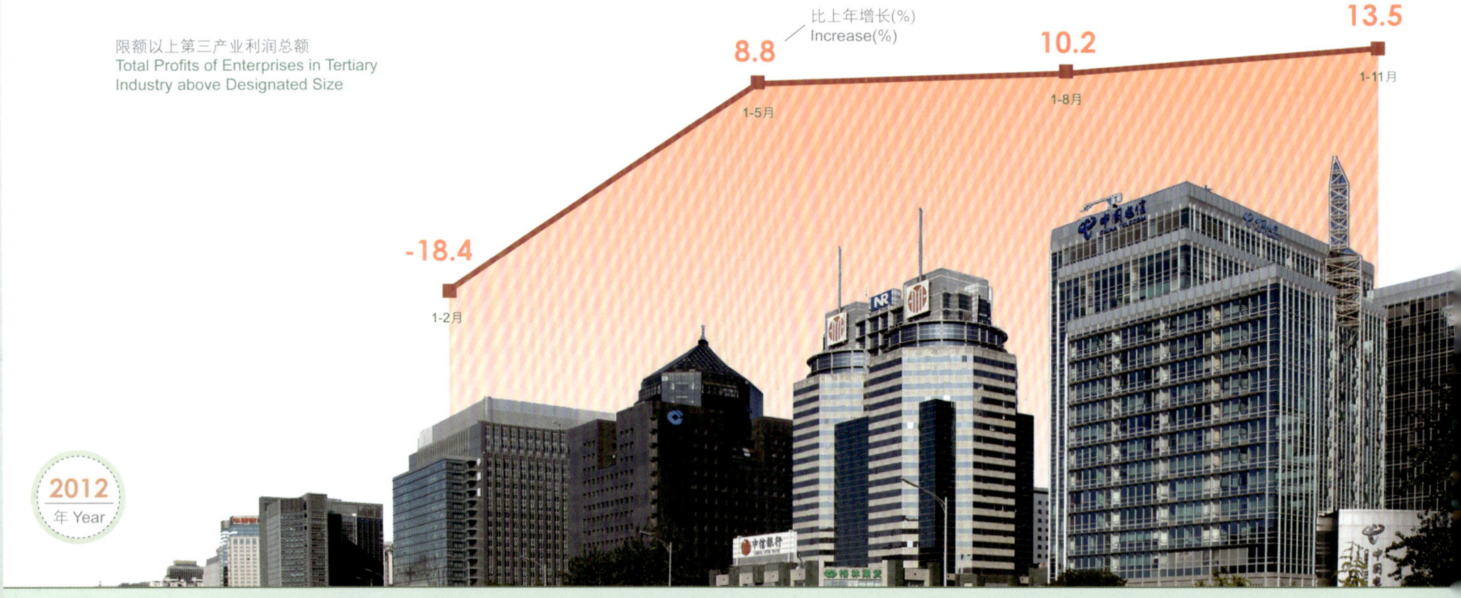

2012
年 Year

❶
■ 规模以上工业主营业务收入(亿元)
Main Business Income of Industrial Enterprises above Designated Size (100 million yuan)
■ 规模以上工业利润总额(亿元)
Total Profits of Industrial Enterprises above Designated Size (100 million yuan)

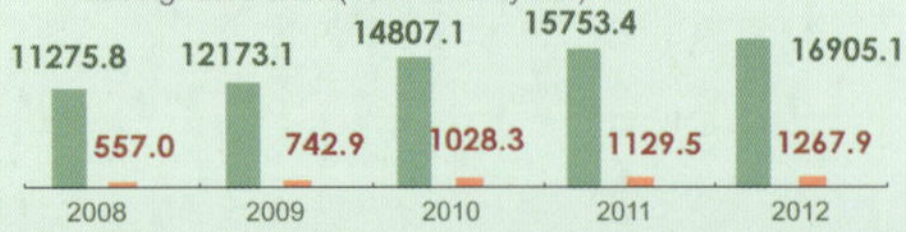

❷
■ 限额以上第三产业收入合计(亿元)
Industrial Enterprises above Designated Size (100 million yuan)
■ 限额以上第三产业企业利润总额(亿元)
Total Profits of Enterprises in Tertiary Industry above Designated Size (100 million yuan)

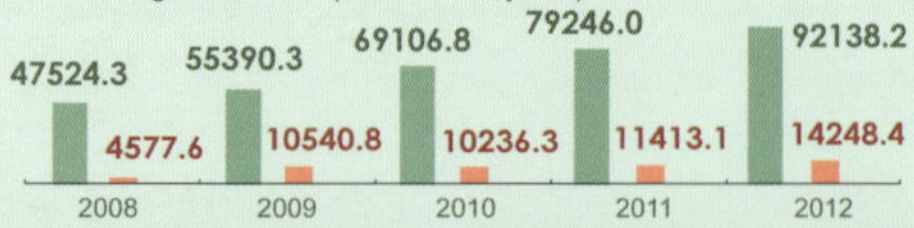

重点产业和重点领域发展态势稳健

Stable Growth in Key Industries and Key Areas

农业结构优化调整
Agricultural Structure was Optimized

农业生产运行平稳 平原造林工程拉动农业快速增长
Agricultural Production Ran Steadily. Afforestation Projects on Flatlands drove Fast Growth of Agriculture

2012年，全市启动“十二五”期间在平原地区实施百万亩造林工程，完成平原造林面积25.46万亩。

In 2012, the project of making one million mu of forest on flatlands during the 12th Five-year Plan was initiated in Beijing. 254,600 mu of forest were made on flatlands.

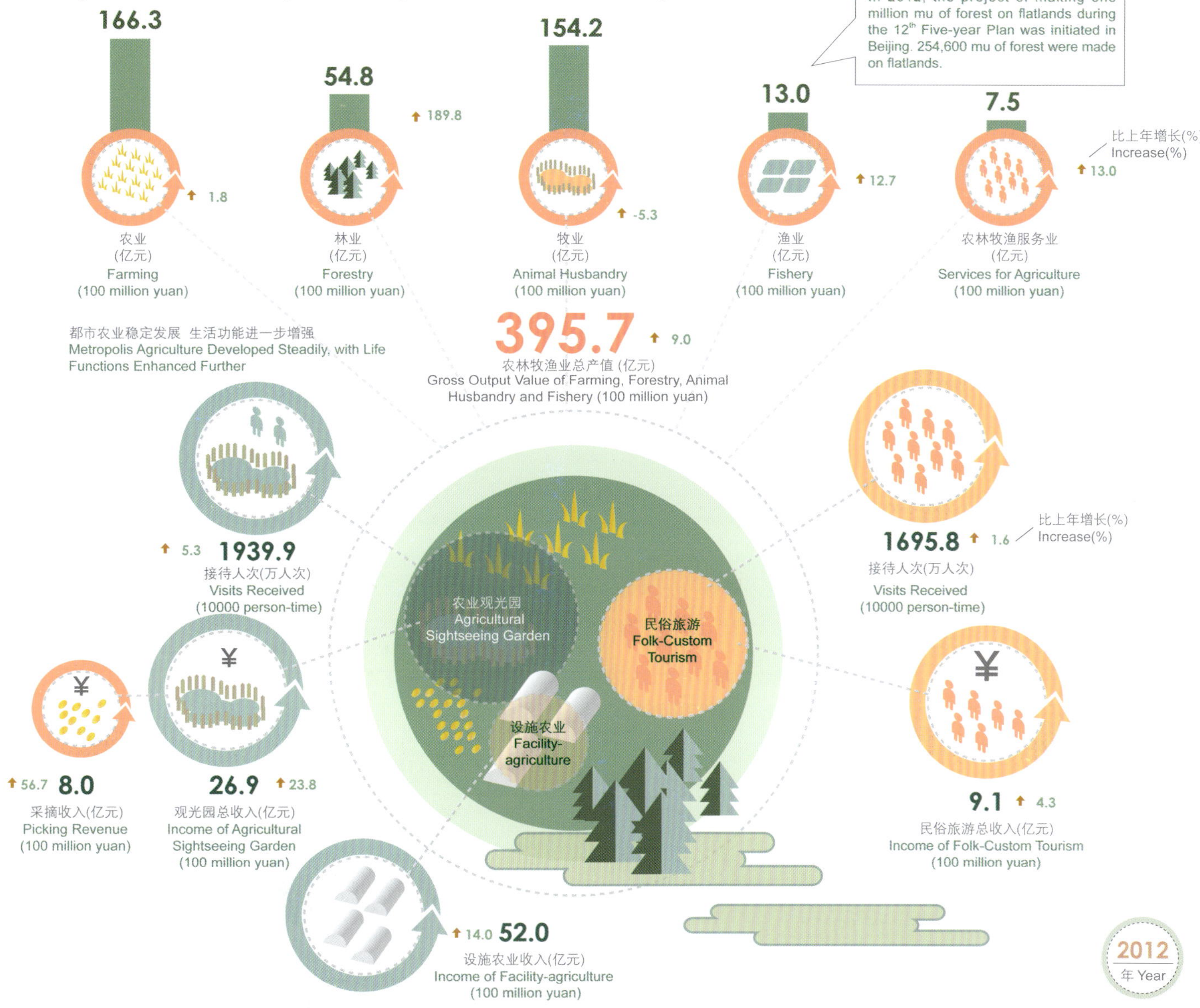

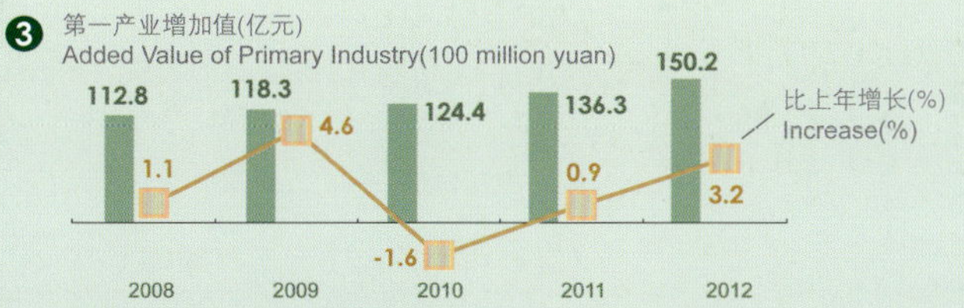

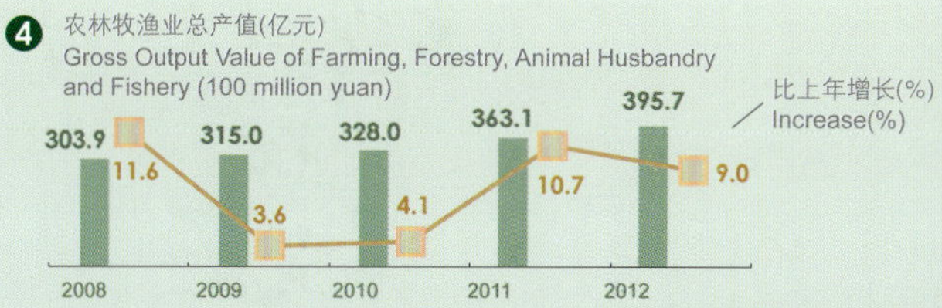

重点产业和重点领域发展态势稳健

Stable Growth in Key Industries and Key Areas

高端制造业发展平稳 科技创新能力有所增强
High-end Manufacturing Developed Steadily, with Scientific and Technological Innovation Capability Strengthened.

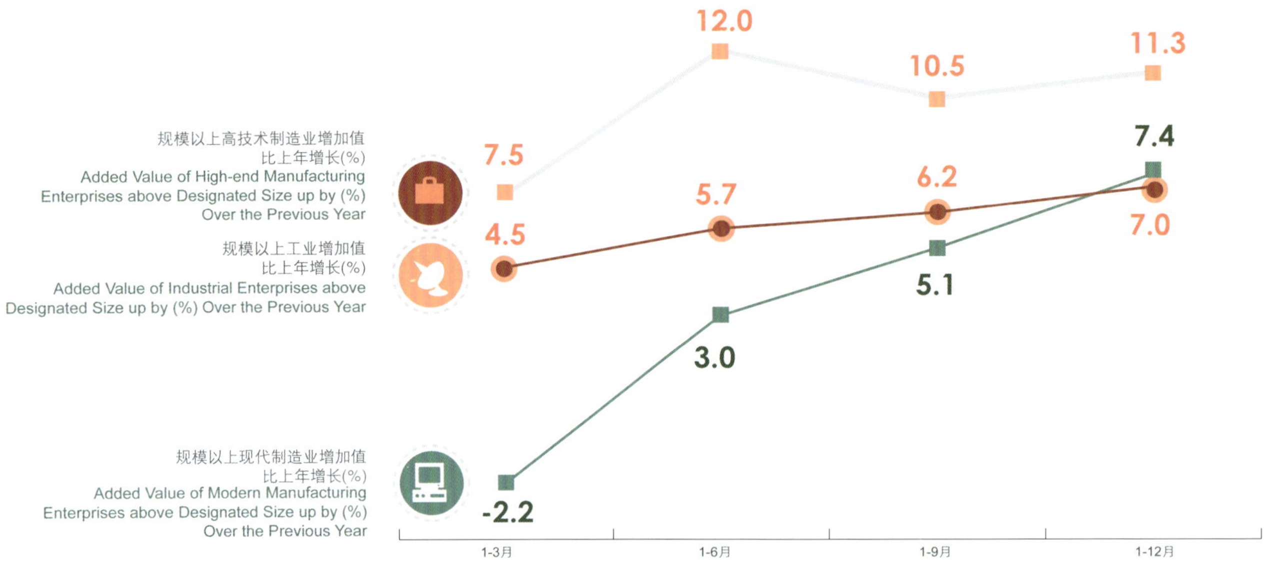

2012
年 Year

历史数据 Historical Data

❶ 高技术产业增加值(亿元)
Added Value of High-tech Industry (100 million yuan)

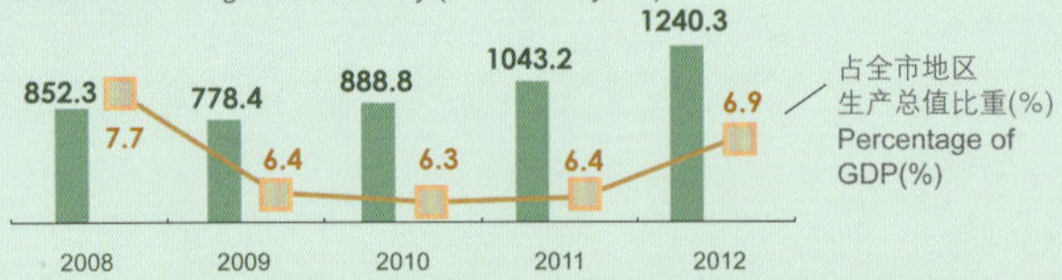

❷ 现代制造业增加值(亿元)
Added Value of Modern Manufacturing (100 million yuan)

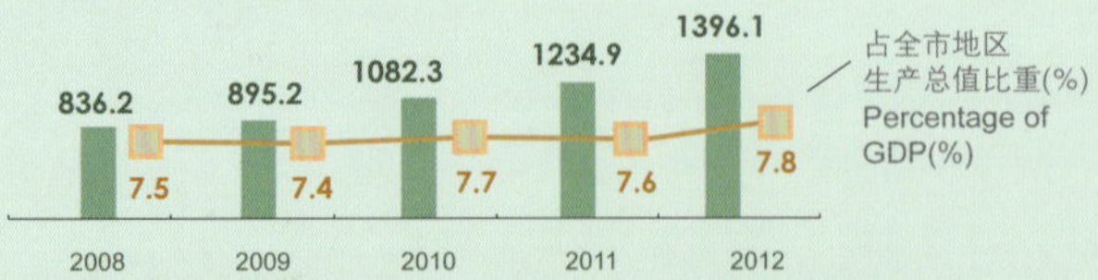

第三产业比重达到76.5%
Added Value of Tertiary Industry Represented 76.5%

行业 Industry	占全市地区生产总值比重(%) Percentage of GDP(%)	增加值(亿元) Added Value (100 million yuan)	比上年增长(%) Increase(%)
交通运输、仓储和邮政业 Transportation, Storage, Posts and Telecommunications	4.6%	816.3	6.9
信息传输、计算机服务和软件业 Information Transmission, Computer Servecis and Software	9.1%	1621.8	6.8
批发和零售业 Wholesale Trade and Retail Trade	12.5 %	2229.8	4.0
住宿和餐饮业 Accommodation and Catering	2.1%	373.1	-0.3
金融业 Finance	14.2 %	2536.9	12.7
房地产业 Real Estate	7.0%	1244.2	13.7
租赁和商务服务业 Tenancy and Commercial Servecis	7.5%	1340.6	9.5
科学研究、技术服务与地质勘查业 Scientific Studies, Technical Services and Geological Prospecting	7.1%	1268.4	7.1
水利、环境和公共设施管理业 Water, Environment and Municipal Engineering Conservancy	0.6%	101.3	6.7
居民服务和其他服务业 Resident Services and Other Services	0.7%	124.3	4.2
教育 Education	3.8%	681.8	5.2
卫生、社会保障和社会福利业 Health Care, Social Security and Social Welfare	2.0%	363.6	8.4
文化、体育与娱乐业 Culture, Art, Sports and Recreation	2.2 %	402.6	9.5
公共管理与社会组织 Public Manage and Social Organization	3.1 %	565.2	3.4

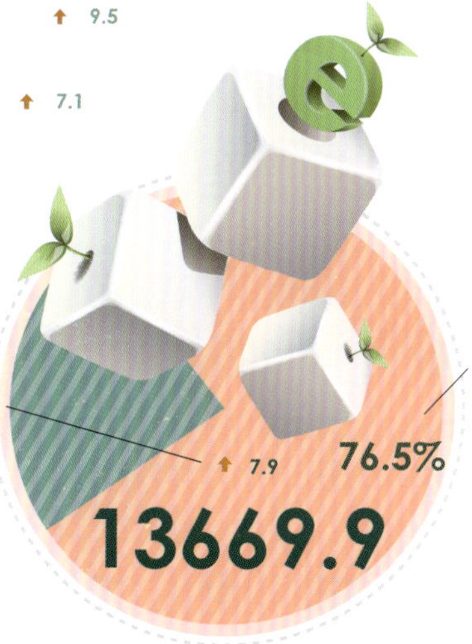

第三产业增加值(亿元)
Added Value of Tertiary Industry
(100 million yuan)

2012 年 Year

❸ 第三产业增加值(亿元) Added Value of Tertiary Industry (100 million yuan)

	2008	2009	2010	2011	2012
第三产业增加值(亿元) Added Value	8375.8	9179.2	10600.8	12363.1	13669.9
占全市地区生产总值比重(%) Percentage of GDP(%)	75.4	75.5	75.1	76.1	76.5
比上年增长(%) Increase(%)	12.5	10.2	9.3	8.7	7.9

❹

	2008	2009	2010	2011	2012
信息传输、计算机服务和软件业增加值占全市GDP比重(%) Added Value of Information Transmission, Computer Service and Software Sectors as % of Beijing's GDP	9.0	8.8	8.6	9.2	9.1
金融业增加值占全市GDP比重(%) Added Value of Finance Sector as % of Beijing's GDP	13.7	13.2	13.2	13.6	14.2
房地产业增加值占全市GDP比重(%) Added Value of Real Estate Sector as % of Beijing's GDP	7.6	8.7	7.1	6.6	7.0

重点产业和重点领域发展态势稳健

Stable Growth in Key Industries and Key Areas

生产性服务业、文化创意产业促进产业升级
Productive Services and Cultural Creativity Industry Promoted Industrial Upgrading

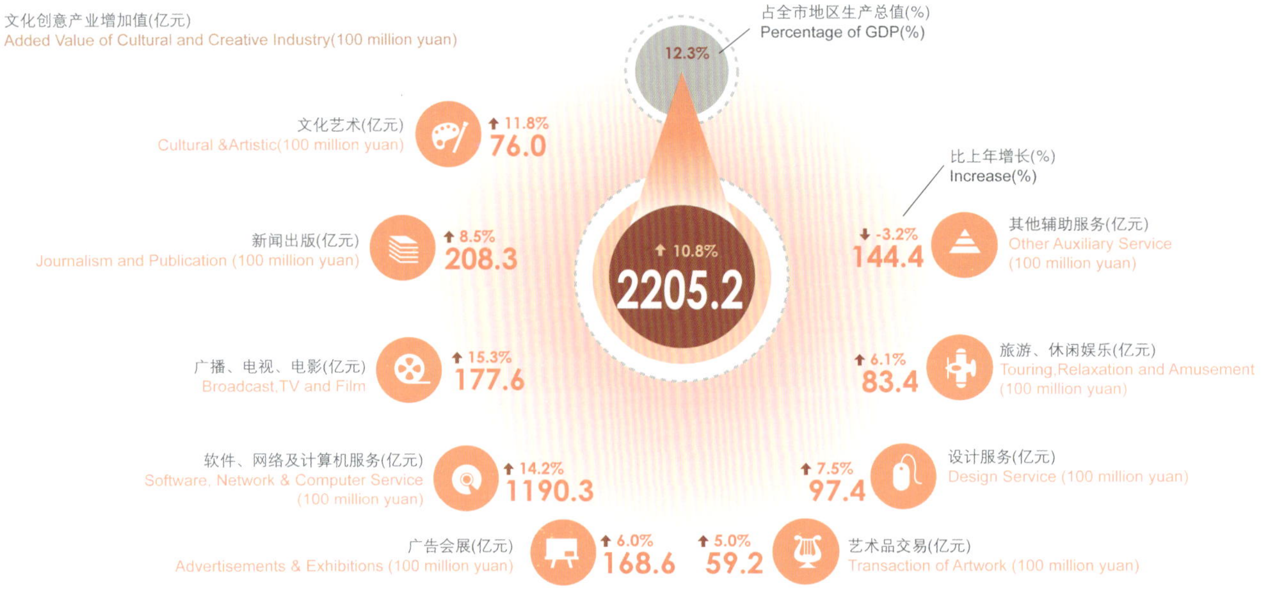

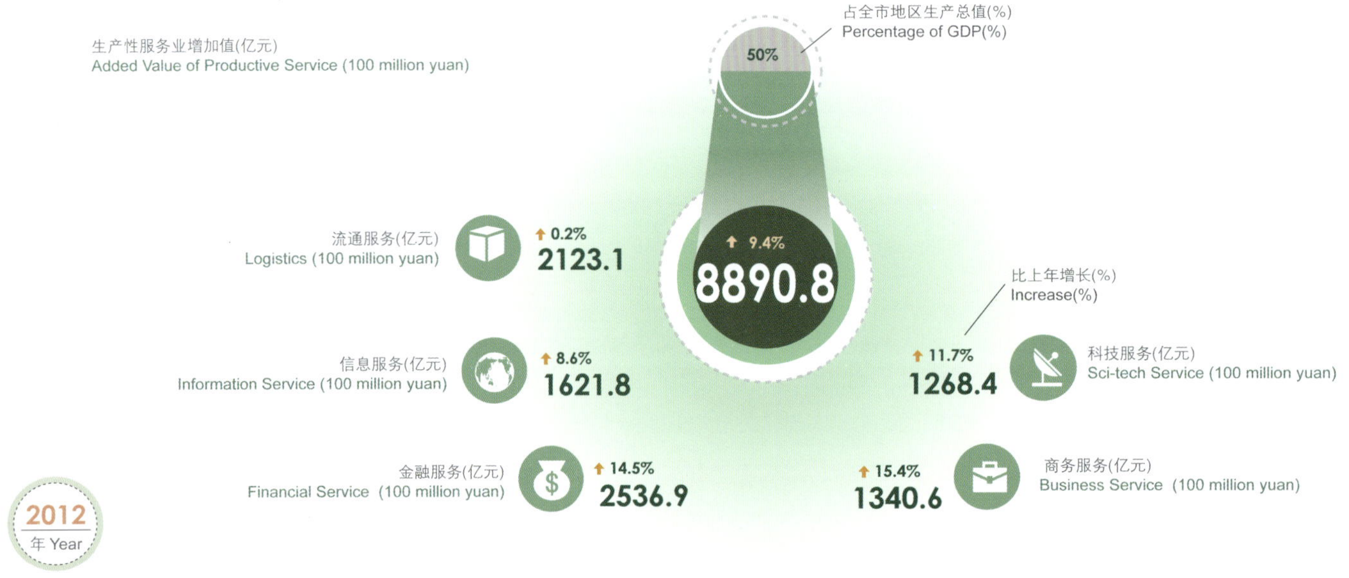

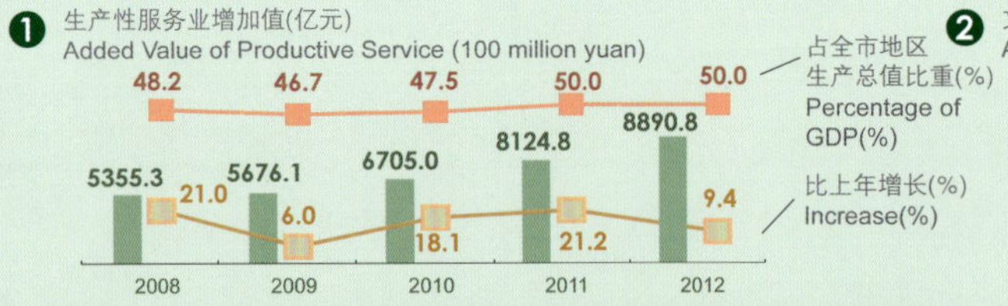

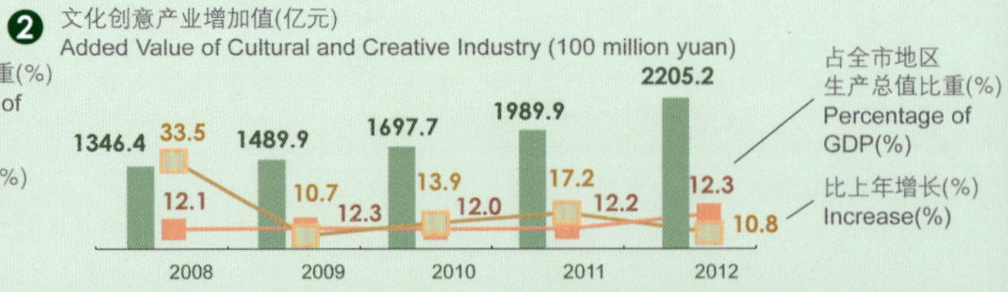

历史数据 Historical Data

旅游业支柱地位逐步确立
Pillar Position of Tourism was Established Step by Step

旅游总收入突破3600亿元
Total Tourism Revenues Topped 360 billion yuan

比上年增长(%)
Increase(%)

↑ 12.8%
3626.6
旅游总收入(亿元)
Total Tourism Revenues
(100 million yuan)

↓ -4.9%
51.5
旅游外汇收入(亿美元)
Tourism Foreign Exchange Earnings
(USD 100 million)

↑ 15.3%
3301.3
国内旅游收入(亿元)
Earnings Created by Domestic Tourists
(100 million yuan)

↑ 8.1%
23134.6
旅游总人数(万人次)
Total number of tourists
(10000 person-times)

↓ -3.8%
500.9
入境旅游人数(万人次)
International Tourists
(10000 person-times)

↑ 8.4%
22633.7
国内旅游者人数(万人次)
Domestic Tourists
(10000 person-times)

旅游业成为北京扩内需、调结构、促增长的重要力量。2012年，北京旅游购物与餐饮消费1894.3亿元，占社会消费品零售总额的24.6%；旅游相关产业投资681亿元，占全社会固定资产投资总额的10.5%。

Tourism became an important force for domestic demand expansion, structural adjustment and growth promotion in Beijing. In 2012, shopping, food and drink expenditures by tourists to Beijing registered 189.43 billion yuan, representing 24.6% of overall retail sales of consumer goods; investment in tourism-related industries was 68.1 billion yuan, representing 10.5% of total fixed assets investment of Beijing.

2012 年 Year

❸ ■ 入境旅游者人数(万人次) International Tourists (10000 person-times)
■ 旅游外汇收入(亿美元) Tourism Foreign Exchange Earnings (USD 100 million)

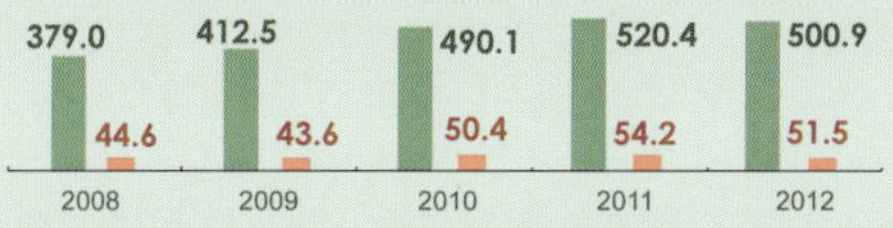

❹ ■ 国内旅游者人数(万人次) Domestic Tourists (10000 person-times)
■ 国内旅游收入(亿元) Earnings Created by Domestic Tourists (100 million yuan)

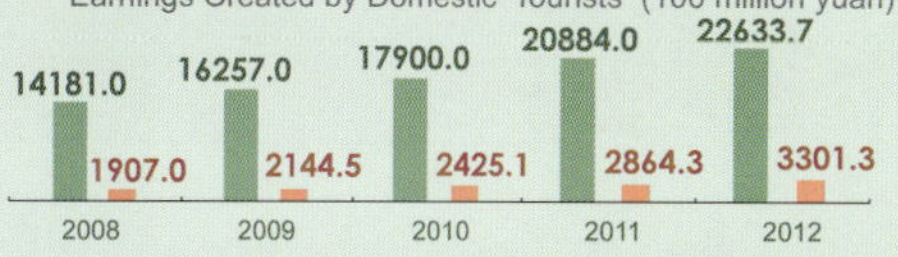

重点功能区发展对全市经济带动作用日益显著

key functional Zones Played an Increasingly Distinctive Role in Economy.

六大高端产业功能区经济保持平稳较快增长
Economy in Six Major High-end Industryl Functional Zones Kept Stable and Faster Growth

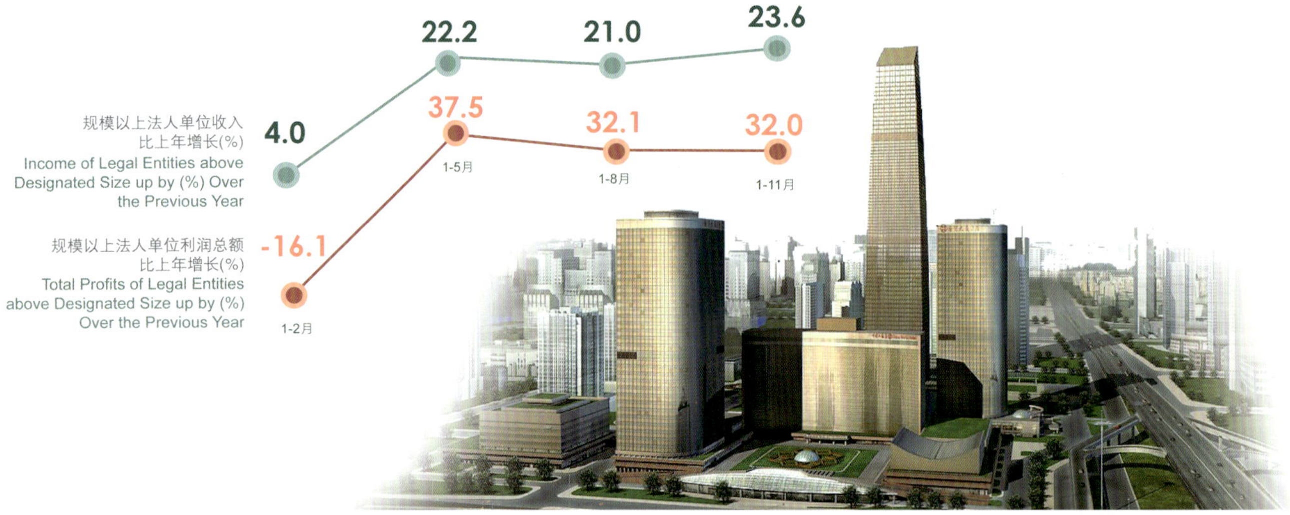

六大高端产业功能区产业发展势能持续增强
Constantly Strengthened Power Remained for Industrial Development in Six Major High-end Industry Functional Zones.

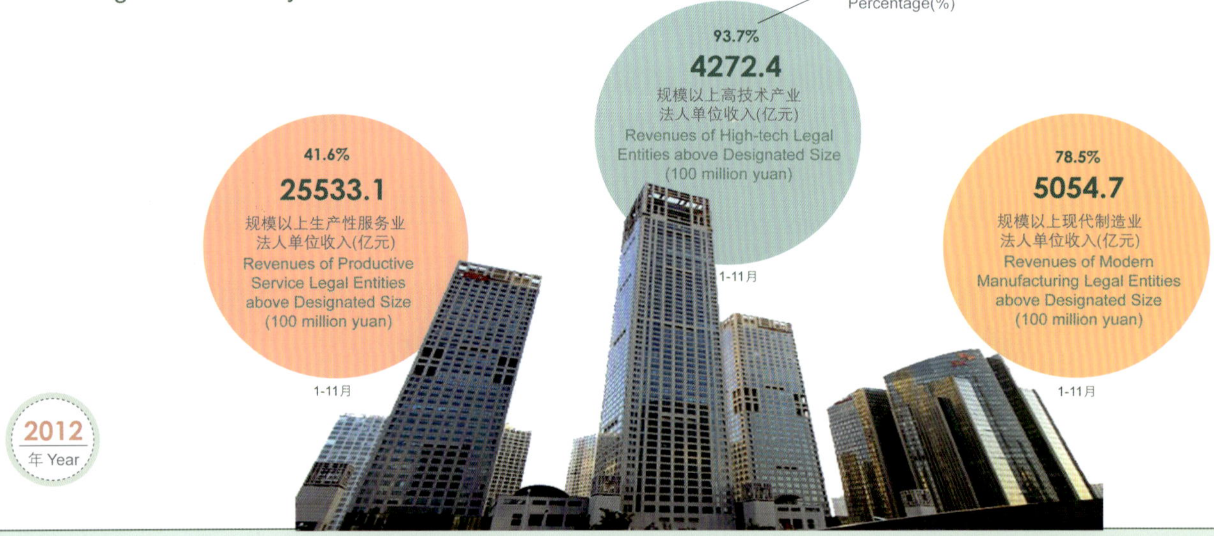

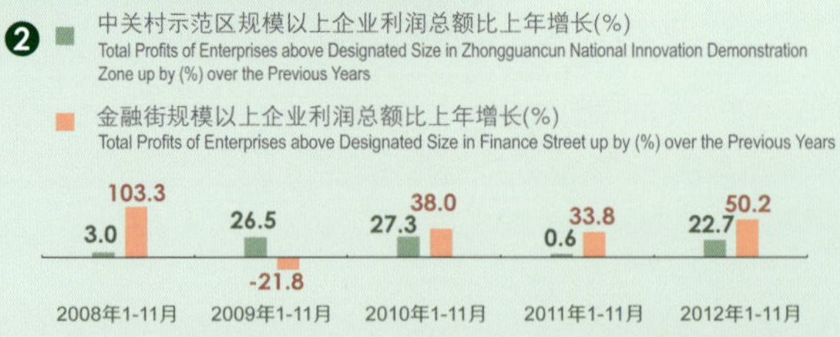

公共服务体系建设全面推进

Comprehensive Propress in Public Service System

投向公共服务领域的地方公共财政支出力度加大
More Public Fiscal Expenditures From Local Governments Went to the Field of Public Service

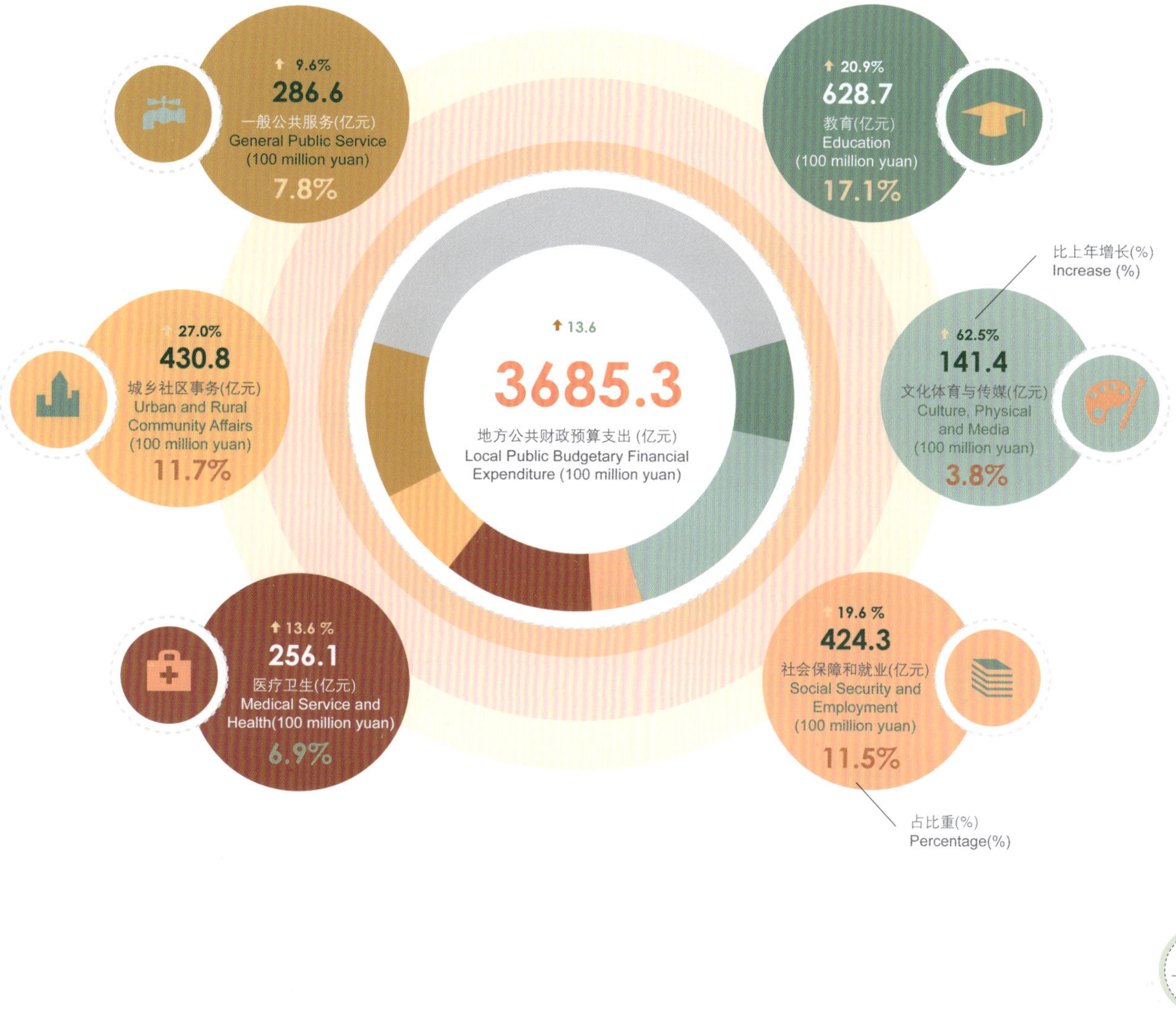

③ 一般公共服务支出(亿元)
General Public Service(100 million yuan)
教育支出(亿元)
Education(100 million yuan)
文化教育与传媒支出(亿元)
Culture, Physical and Media (100 million yuan)

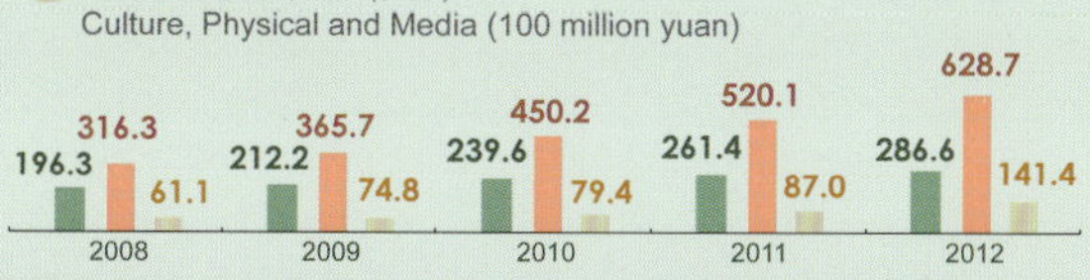

④ 社会保障和就业支出(亿元)
Social Security and Employment(100 million yuan)
医疗卫生支出(亿元)
Medical Service and Health(100 million yuan)
城乡社区事务支出(亿元)
Urban and Rural Community Affairs (100 million yuan)

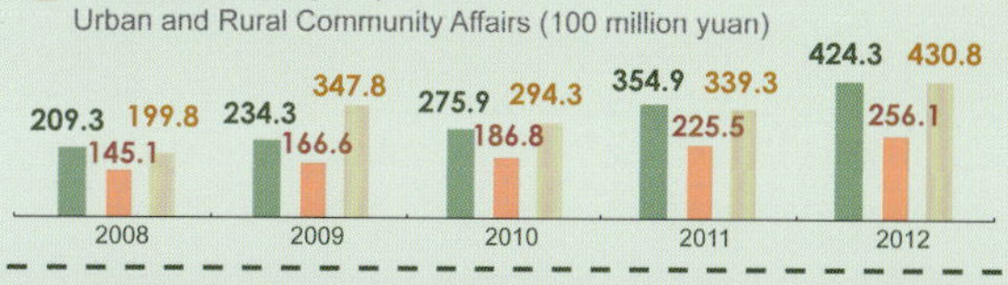

公共服务体系建设全面推进

Comprehensive Propress in Public Service System

各级各类教育均衡发展程度提高
All Types and Levels of Education Developed in a More Balanced Manner

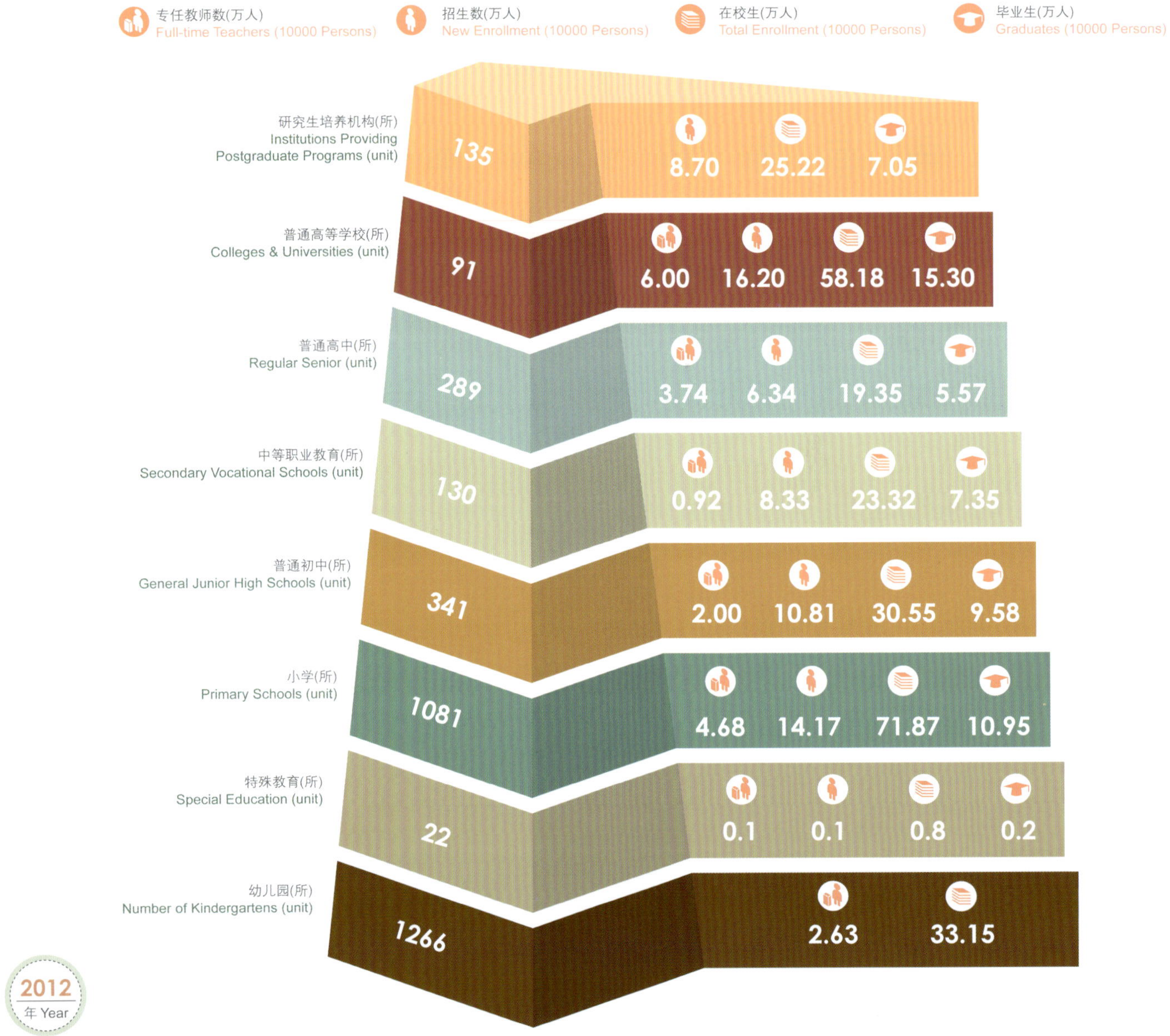

❶ 平均每一专任教师负担学生数(人)
Average Number of Students Instructed by a Full-time Teacher (person)

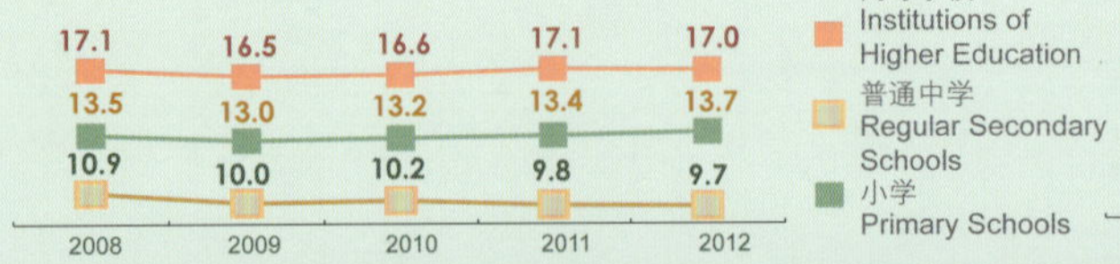

❷ 幼儿园园数(所) Number of Kindergartens (unit)　在园人数(万人) Children Enrollment (10000 person)

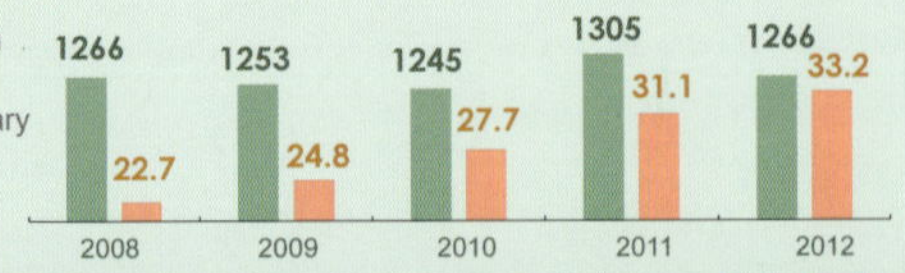

电影消费人次和票房收入保持较快增长
Film Viewers and Box Office Earnings Kept Faster Growth

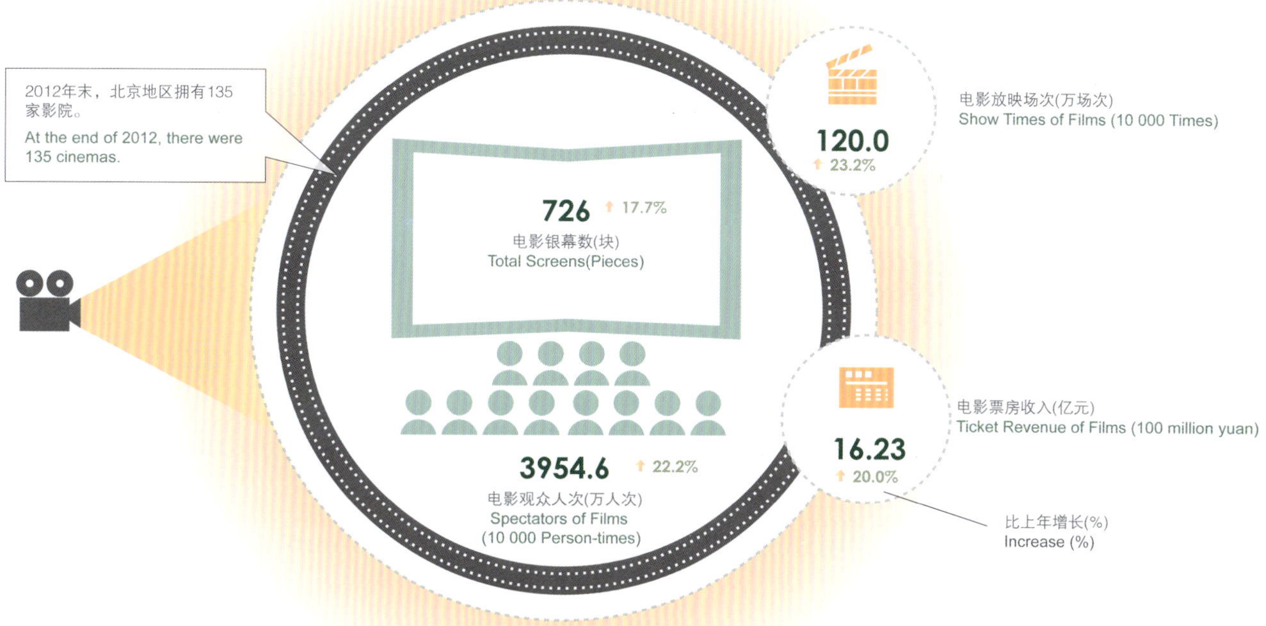

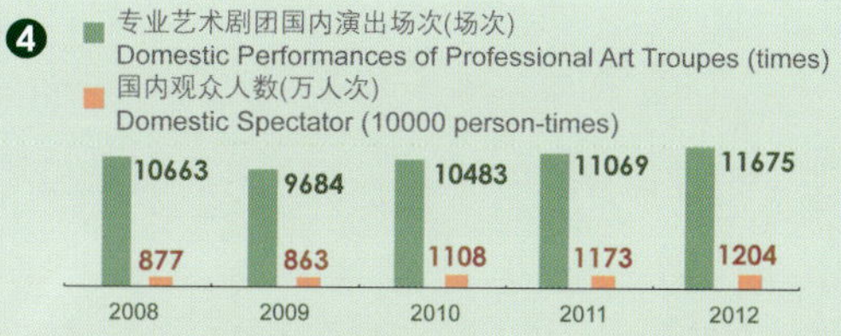

公共服务体系建设全面推进

Comprehensive Propress in Public Service System

就业保持稳定
Employment Remained Stablely

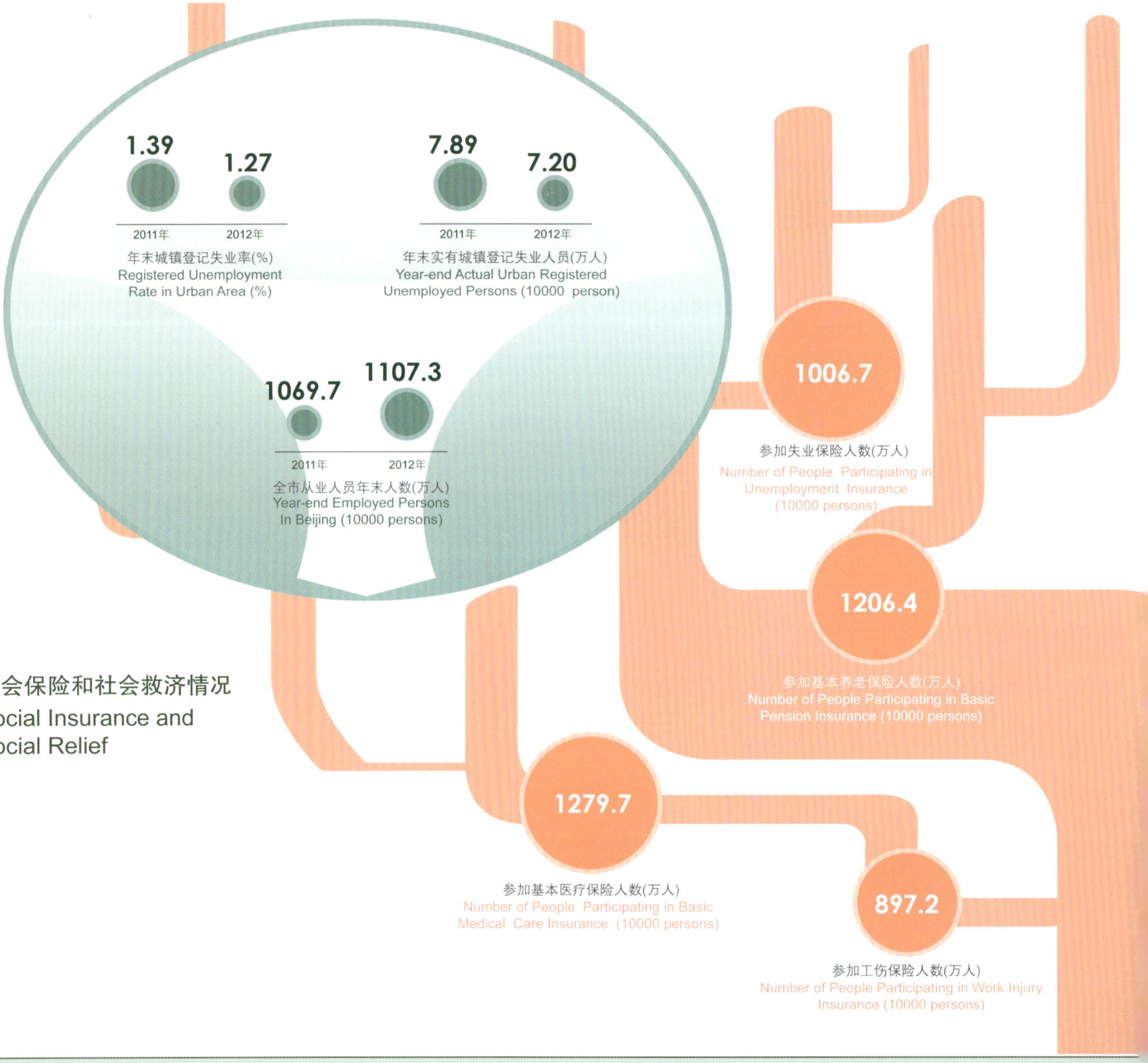

社会保险和社会救济情况
Social Insurance and Social Relief

2012
年 Year

❶ 全市从业人员年末人数(万人)
Year-end Employed Persons In Beijing (10000 persons)

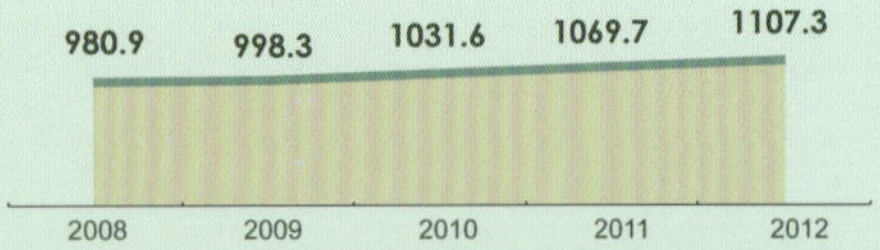

❷ 年末城镇登记失业率(%)
Registered Unemployment Rate in Urban Area (%)

社会保障待遇标准连续上调
Social Security Payment Increased Continuously

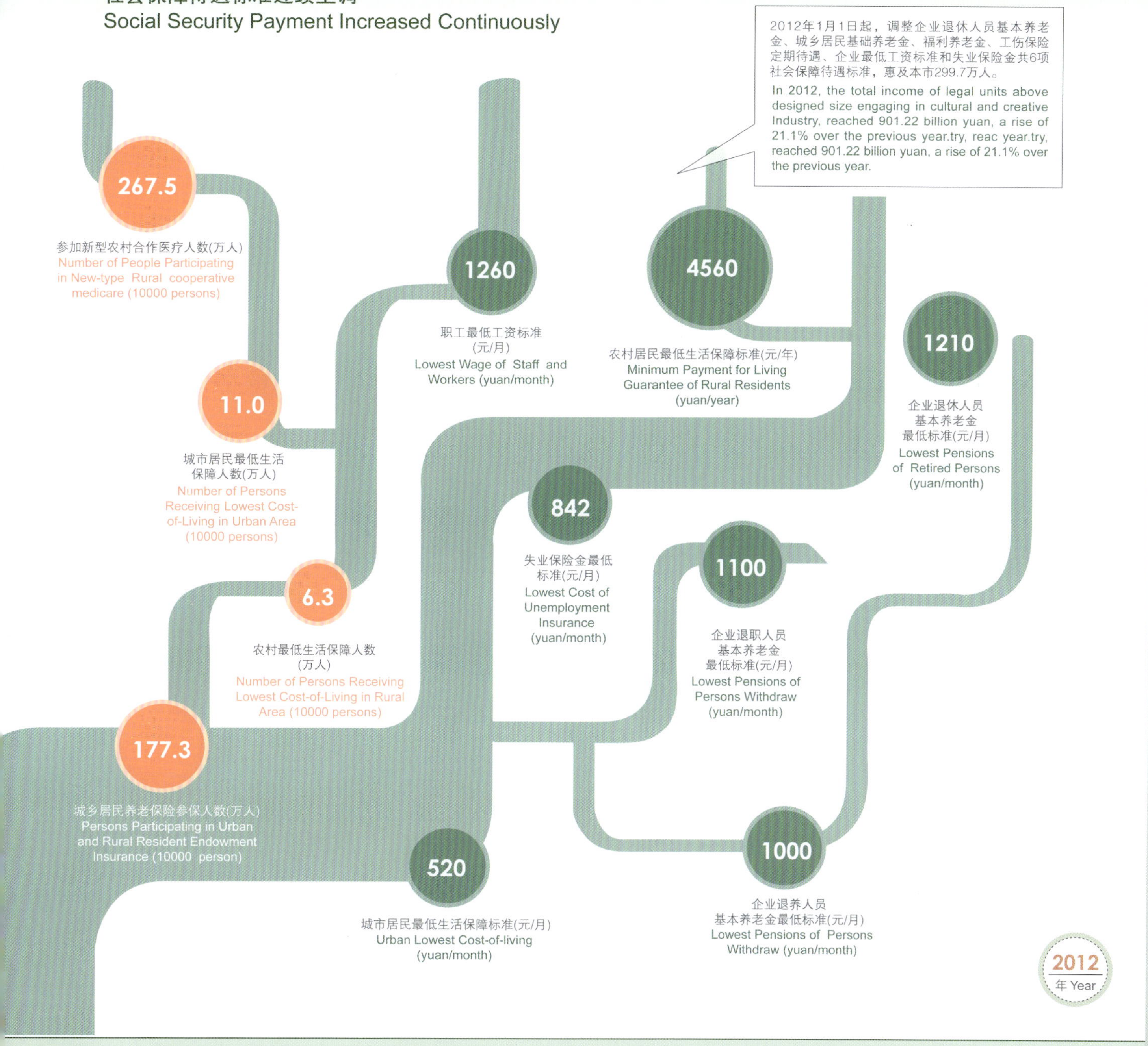

❸ 职工最低工资标准(元 / 月)
Lowest Wage of Staff and Workers (yuan/month)

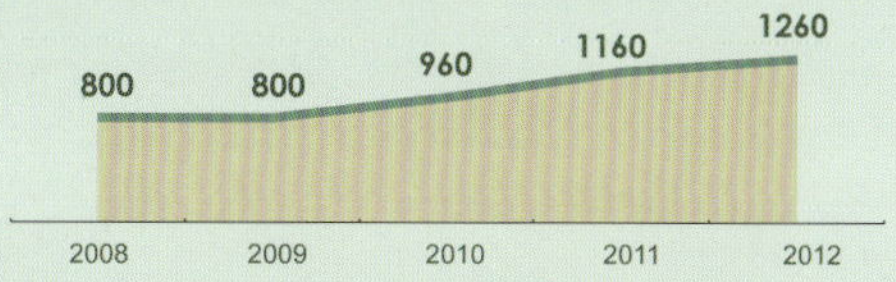

❹ 企业退休人员基本养老金最低标准(元 / 月)
Lowest Pensions of Retired Persons (yuan/month)

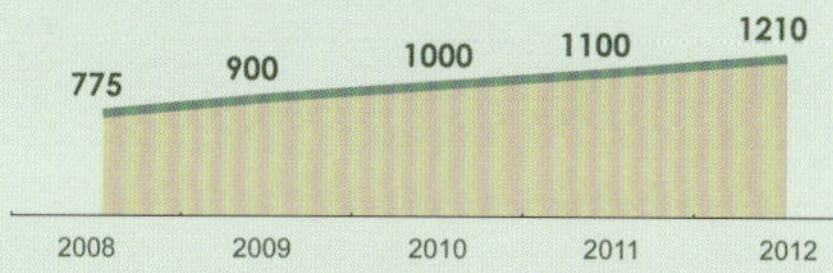

大力推进生态文明建设

Great Efforts to Promote Ecological Progress

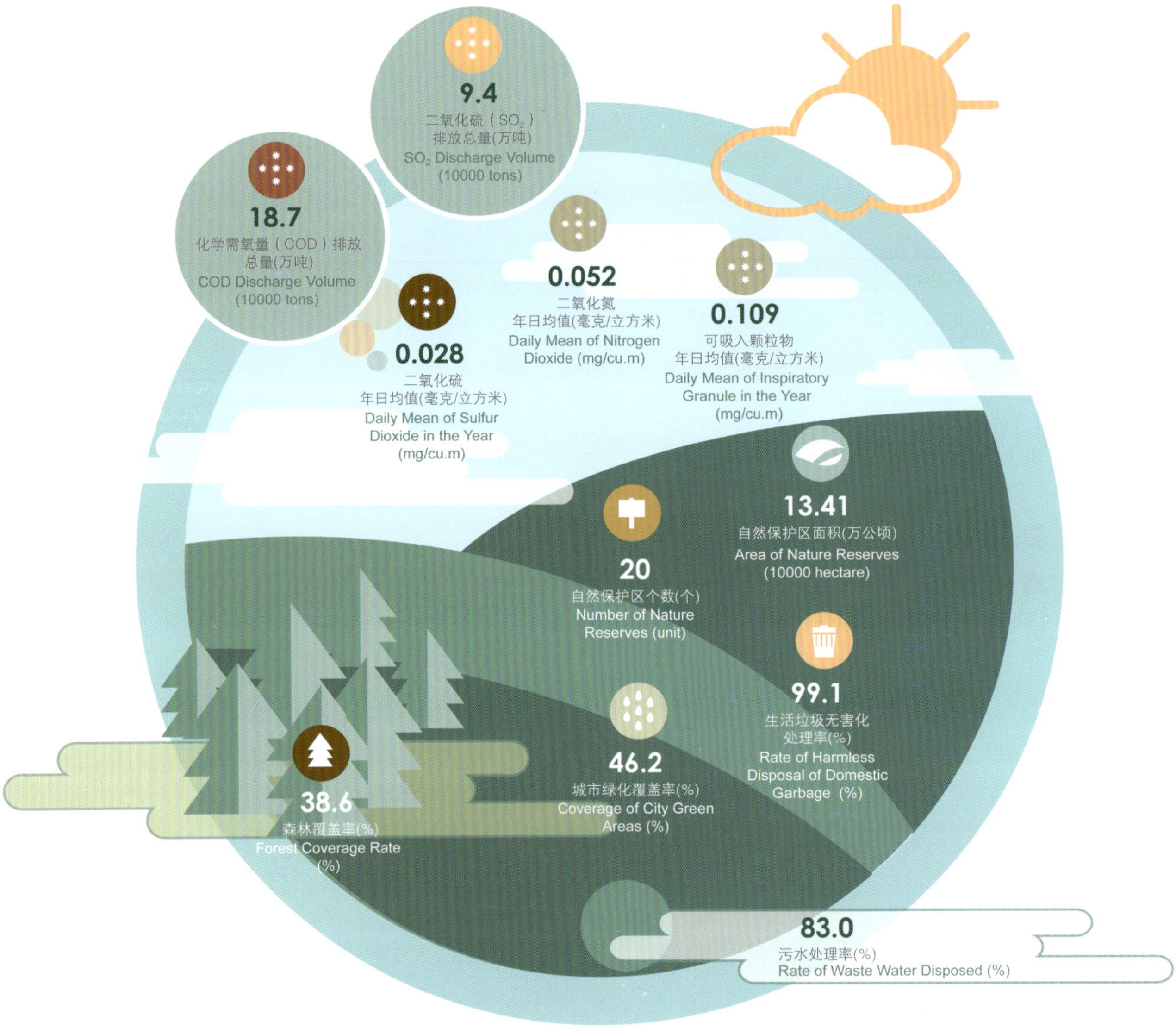

2012
年 Year

❶ 人均公园绿地面积(平方米/人)
Per Capita Park Green Areas(sq.m/person)

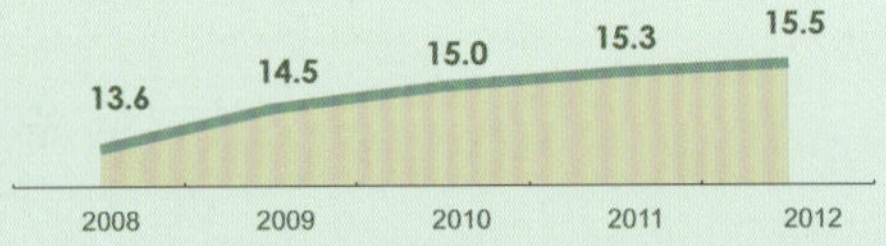

❷ 可吸入颗粒物年日均值(毫克/立方米)
Daily Mean of Inspiratory Granule in the Year (mg/cu.m)
二氧化硫年日均值(毫克/立方米)
Daily Mean of Sulfur Dioxide in the Year (mg/cu.m)
二氧化氮年日均值(毫克/立方米)
Daily Mean of Nitrogen Dioxide (mg/cu.m)

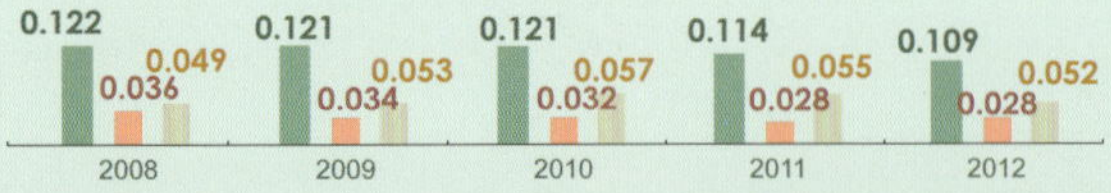

历史数据 Historical Data

《北京统计年鉴—2013》
编辑委员会及编辑工作人员

编委会

编辑工作人员

使用指南

《北京统计年鉴》是一部按年连续出版的大型统计资料。本年鉴通过大量的统计数据，真实地记录了北京市一年来经济社会发展变化情况，是国内外各界人士了解北京、认识北京的重要资料工具书。

一、关于框架结构

（一）总体结构

《北京统计年鉴》整体框架基本保持稳定，一般包括两部分：文章选编和统计表。

文章选编：主要登载各种大型普查或专项调查公报，例如，人口普查、经济普查、农业普查，以及 R&D 资源清查公报等。

统 计 表：包括 24 个章节，分别为综合，国民经济核算，人口与就业，能源、资源和环境，全社会固定资产投资和房地产开发，财政与税收，价格指数，人民生活，城市公用事业，农业及农村经济，工业，建筑业，交通运输邮电，批发和零售业、住宿和餐饮业，对外经济贸易，旅游业，金融和保险，教育、文化，科技，卫生、体育，社会福利、社区、政法及其他，第三产业，企业景气指数、消费者信心指数，开发区等 24 章。从多行业、多领域反映全市经济和社会发展情况。

（二）章节结构

章 节 设 置：主要是参照统计制度，排列顺序具有一定的内在逻辑，大体为先综合指标、后分行业或分领域；先经济领域、后社会领域。

章节内结构：每一章节由《简要说明》、《统计表》和《主要统计指标解释》三部分组成。《简要说明》在每一章节首页，主要介绍该章节的主要内容、资料来源、统计范围、指标口径和历史数据调整方法；《主要统计指标解释》在每章节页尾，主要对本章节内所涉及的主要指标、计算方法等做简要解释；《统计表》是各章节的核心内容。

统计表排列：每一章节注重从反映该领域主要情况出发，编排统计表内容。统计表的排列顺序一般先是主要指标历史数据表，后为当年数据表。

二、关于使用要领

（一）年份

按照惯例，书名中标注的年份为出版年份，年鉴中统计表内所表示的最新数据则为上一年数据。

统计表名中的“年份”大致会有三种标识方法，分别代表三种含义。一是统计表名为“******（1978-2012 年）”字样（其中，“******”代表该统计表反映的内容，下同），表示表内所列数据是从 1978 年到 2012 年；二是统计表名中未显示年份，表示表内所列数据为当年和上年两年数据；三是统计表名为“******（2012 年）”，表示表内所列数据为 2012 年的数据。

（二）符号

统计表中常见符号如下：

：代表表中的总量指标与分组指标呈依次缩进的格式。其中，有“#”号的分组指标表示其为总量指标的一部分；无“#”号的分组指标则反映全部分组指标数据之和为总指标数据。

‖ ：宾栏中的“‖”为分组符号，代表某个指标存在几种分组数据。

… ：表示该数据不足该表最小计量单位数。

空格：表示该项指标数据不详或没有数据。

*** ：表示为使个别单位的数据得以保密，该数据不予公布。

（三）文字说明

文字说明包括《使用指南》、《简要说明》和表下注解等。《使用指南》在《目录》之前，是对年鉴整体框架进行介绍，对主要调整内容进行说明；《简要说明》在每一章节首页，主要介绍该章节的主要内容、资料来源、统计范围、指标口径和历史数据调整方法等；统计表下的注释则是对部分统计指标口径、方法、范围等内容的说明。

（四）数据

一般情况下，每一章节的前几张表均为该专业或该领域核心指标的历史数据。历史数据如果按年份连续反映在一张表内的，一般是可以连续使用的，但也需要留意表下的注释，以便对指标内涵有更详尽的了解；如果历史数据分成若干张表显示，则表示相关指标统计有过重大调整，需要分段反映。

此外，最新出版的年鉴上发布的部分历史数据会与以往年鉴上的数据有调整，存在差异，因此，在查询和使用历史数据时应以最新出版的年鉴为准。

（五）电子光盘

《北京统计年鉴》配有电子光盘，包括中文版和英文版两种语言的版本，辅助用户对数据进行加工处理。

三、关于 2013 年版《北京统计年鉴》说明

与 2012 年版《北京统计年鉴》相比较，本年鉴在内容上主要做了如下修订：

1. 根据国家统计局规定，执行新行业划分标准和三次产业划分规定。一是本年鉴中，除国民经济核算和法人单位情况等内容外，其他涉及行业分组的数据均执行 2011 年《国民经济行业分类标准》(GB/T 4754-2011)；二是根据 2012 年国家统计局印发的《三次产业划分规定》(国统字[2012]108 号)，本年鉴中的劳动工资、固定资产投资和能源专业已经执行新的三次产业划分标准。

2. 调整或取消使用频率低、易引起混淆、易用错以及过时的统计表和指标。例如取消“商品房销售额”、“空气质量二级及二级以上天数比例”等指标，取消了《农村义务教育基本情况》和《全市 7 岁以下儿童系统管理情况》等统计表。

3. 根据新需求增加或补充有关内容。例如增加《卫生总费用》、《电影、电视剧、动画片制作情况》、《境外直接投资》、《限额以上信息传输、软件和信息技术服务业企业研究与试验发展(R&D)活动基本情况》等统计表；同时增加了“食品安全监测抽查合格率”、“药品抽验合格率”、“人口平均预期寿命”等指标，补充了《按行业分能源消费总量》、《外商投资企业实际利用外资情况》的历史数据。

4. 继续加强规范统一。包括对统计表格式规范和对各专业指标的规范，例如规范了各专业财务表中的“应交税金合计”口径范围。

USER GUIDE

Beijing Statistical Yearbook is a large statistical book published continuously on chronological basis. With a great deal of statistical data, this Yearbook gives a true reflection of the social and economic development and changes in Beijing over the past one year. It serves as an important reference book for domestic and foreign personnel in all circles to understand and know Beijing.

I. About the Overall Framework

(I) Overall Structure

The overall structure of Beijing Statistical Yearbook remains stable basically. Generally, it consists of two parts: article selections and statistical tables.

Article Selections: mainly include various large census and special investigation communiques, such as population census, economic census, agricultural census, as well as R&D resource check communique, etc.

Statistical Tables: include 24 chapters, i.e. general; national economic accounting; population and employment; energy; resource and environment; fixed assets investment and real estate development; finance and revenue; price index; people's living; urban public utilities; agriculture and rural economy; industry; construction industry; transport, post and telecommunication; wholesale and retail trades; accommodation and catering industry; foreign economic trade; tourism; finance and insurance; education and culture; science and technology; health and sports; social welfare and communities, politics and law and other; tertiary industry; enterprise prosperity index, consumer confidence index, and development zones, etc., 24 chapters in total, reflecting the economic and social development situation across the city through multiple industries and fields.

(II) Structure of Chapters

Setting of chapters: mainly refers to the statistical system, arranged in a sequence with certain inherent logics, roughly general indicators first, followed by different industries and fields; economic field first, then social field.

Inside structure of chapters: Each chapter is composed of the Brief Introduction, Statistical Tables and Explanatory Notes to Main Statistical Indicators. Brief Introduction appears on the first page of each chapter, mainly introducing the main content, source of data, statistical scope, indicator standards, method of adjustment to historical data in each chapter; Explanatory Notes to Main Statistical Indicators come on the last page of each chapter, mainly giving a brief explanation to main indicators calculation method involved in the chapter; Statistical Tables are the core content of each chapter.

Arrangement of statistical tables: In each chapter, the content of statistical tables is arranged with the focus on reflecting the main conditions in the said field. Generally, statistical tables are arranged as historical data tables of main indicators first, then tables of data in current year.

II. About Main Points in the Use

(I) Years

Conventionally, the year indicated in the book is the publication year. The latest data indicated in the statistical tables in the yearbook are data in the previous years.

"Years" in the statistical tables are marked in three ways roughly, representing three meanings respectively. First, the statistical table is named "******(1978-2012)" (of which, "******" represents the content reflected in the statistical table, the same below), indicating that the data listed in the table are those from 1978 to 2012; second, the statistical table contains no years, indicating that the data listed in the table are those for the current year and the previous year; third, the statistical table is named "****** (2012)", indicating that the data listed in the table are those for 2012.

(II) Symbols

There are kinds of common symbols in statistical tables:

#: represents the format of retractive gross indicators and grouped ones. Of which, a grouping indicator with the symbol "#" means that it is a part of the gross indicator; a grouped indicator without the symbol "#" shows that the sum of all figures of grouped indicators is the figure of gross indicator.

Blank: means no data are known or available for this indicator;

…: means this figure is less than the number of minimum measurement unit in the table;

‖: "‖" in the objective column is a grouping symbol, showing that there are several grouped figures in a indicator.

***: means this figure will not be published to keep the data of individual entities as secret.

(III) Literal Introductions

Literal Introductions include User Guide, Brief Introduction, and notes under the tables, etc. User Guide appears before the Table of Contents, giving an introduction to the overall framework of the yearbook, and explaining the main adjustments; Brief Introduction appears on the first page of each chapter mainly gives an introduction to the chapter's main content, source of data, statistical scope, standards of indicators, adjustment method of historical data, and the like; notes under the tables make an explanation on some indicator's standard, method, scope and the like.

(IV) Data

In general cases, the first tables in each chapter contain historical data of core indicators in the specialty or field. Generally, historical data that are shown in one table continuously by year can be used continuously. But it is also necessary to see about the notes under the table in order to have a more full understanding about the connation of indicators; historical data that are shown in several tables indicate that there were major adjustments to relevant indicators, and they need to be reflected by sections.

(V) Electronic CD-ROM

In addition, some historical data published in the latest yearbook may differ from those in the yearbooks in previous years. Therefore, the latest yearbook shall prevail in when users refer to and use any historical data.

Beijing Statistical Yearbook is provided with a CD-ROM made in two languages, Chinese and English, assisting users in working with and processing the data.

III. About Beijing Statistical Yearbook Version 2013

Compared with Beijing Statistical Yearbook Version 2012, this Yearbook mainly contains the following revisions:

1. According to provisions of National Bureau of Statistics, new standards for classification of new industiral sectors and three industries were implemented. First, in this yearbook, except for statistics on national economy accounting and corporate entities, other figures involving industrial grouping were calculated in line with the the Standard for Classification of National Economic Sectors 2011 (GB/T 4754-2011); second, according to the Provisions on Classification of Three Industries (GTZ [2012]No.108) printed and issued by the National Bureau of Statistics in 2012, labor wages, fixed assets investment and energy figures were calculated in line with the new standard for classificaiton of three industries.

2. Statistical tables and indicators that are less frequently used, easily confusable, easily misused and outdated were changed or cancelled. Fore example, such indicators as "sales of marketable houses", "percentage of days with air quality at grade two and above" were cancelled, and statistical tables such as Basic Statistics for Rural Compulsory Education, and Statistics for System Management of Children under 7 in Beijing were cancelld.

3. New contents were added or supplemented. For example, statistical tables such as Total Health Costs, Statistics for Production of Films, TV Plays and Cartoons, Foreign Direct Investment, and Basic Statistics for R&D of Information Transmission, Software and IT Service Enterprises Above Designated Size; at the same time, such indicators as "Food Security Monitoring and Sampling Check Pass Rate", "Drug Sampling Inspection Pass Rate", and "Average Life Expectancy of Population", and historical data for tables such as Total Energy Consumption by Industry, and Statistics for Foreign Fund Actually Utilized by Foreing-funded Enterrises were supplemented.

4. Continued efforts were made to regulating and consistence, including regulating the format of statistical tables and professional indicators. For example, the statistical scope of Total Tax Payable in professional financial statements was regulated.

目 录
Contents

一、综合
GENERAL SURVEY

二、国民经济核算
NATIONAL ACCOUNTS

三、人口与就业
POPULATION AND EMPLOYMENT

四、能源、资源和环境
ENERGY，RESOURCES AND ENVIRONMENT PROTECTION

五、全社会固定资产投资和房地产开发
TOTAL INVESTMENT IN FIXED ASSETS AND REAL ESTATE DEVELOPMENT

六、财政与税收

GOVERNMENT FINANCE AND REVENUES

七、价格指数
PRICE INDEX

八、人民生活
PEOPLE'S LIVELIHOOD

九、城市公用事业
PUBLIC UTILITIES

十、农业及农村经济
AGRICULTURE AND RURAL ECONOMY

十一、工业
INDUSTRY

十二、建筑业
CONSTRUCTION

十三、交通运输邮电
TRANSPORT, POST AND TELECOMMUNICATION SERVICES

十四、批发和零售业、住宿和餐饮业
WHOLESALE, RETAIL, HOUSING AND CATERING

十五、对外经济贸易
FOREIGN ECONOMY AND TRADE

十六、旅游业
TOURISM

十七、金融和保险
BANKING AND INSURANCE

十八、教育、文化
EDUCATION AND CULTURE

十九、科技
SCIENCE AND TECHNOLOGY

二十、卫生、体育
HEALTH AND SPORTS

二十一、社会福利、社区、政法及其他
SOCIAL WELFARE, COMMUNITY, POLITICS AND LAW AND OTHERS

二十二、第三产业
TERTIARY INDUSTRY

二十三、企业景气指数、消费者信心指数
PROSPERITY INDEX ON ENTERPRISES,CONSUMER CONFIDENCE INDEX

二十四、开发区
DEVELOPMENT ZONES

01

北京统计年鉴2013　BEIJING STATISTICAL YEARBOOK

综 合
GENERAL SURVEY

简要说明

一、本章资料的主要内容

本章主要包括北京市行政区划、法人及产业活动单位数、私营个体、非公经济、中小微型企业基本情况、全市社会经济发展的主要指标以及“十二五”时期监测指标等。

二、本章资料的数据来源

北京市行政区划情况来自北京市民政局；全市法人及产业活动单位情况来自北京市统计局；全市私营个体经济基本情况来自北京市工商行政管理局、北京市地方税务局、北京市国家税务局；非公经济数据和中小微型企业数据来自北京市统计局、国家统计局北京调查总队；全市社会经济主要指标及“十二五”时期主要监测指标资料由北京市统计局及国家统计局北京调查总队根据相关资料整理取得。

三、有关统计标准的变化说明

（一）《国民经济行业分类与代码》(GB/T 4754-2002 版）与原（GB/T 4754-1994 版）的主要框架结构变化:

增加的门类：a).信息传输、计算机服务和软件业 b).租赁和商务服务业 c).住宿和餐饮业 d).水利、环境和公共设施管理业 e).教育 f).国际组织

名称或范围进行调整的门类：a).农、林、牧、渔业 b).采矿业 c).制造业 d).交通运输、仓储和邮政业 e).批发和零售业 f).金融业 g).科学研究、技术服务和地质勘查业 h).居民服务和其他服务业 i).卫生、社会保障和社会福利业 j).文化、体育和娱乐业 k).公共管理和社会组织

取消的门类：a).地质勘查、水利管理 b).其它行业

（二）《国民经济行业分类》(GB/T 4754-2011 版）与原（GB/T 4754-2002 版）的主要框架结构变化:

门类名称调整：(1)“电力、燃气及水的生产和供应业”更名为“电力、热力、燃气及水生产和供应业”；(2)“信息传输、计算机服务和软件业”更名为“信息传输、软件和信息技术服务业”；(3)“科学研究、技术服务和地质勘查业”更名为“科学研究和技术服务业”；(4)“居民服务和其他服务业”更名为“居民服务、修理和其他服务业”；(5)“卫生、社会保障和社会福利业”更名为“卫生和社会工作”；(6)“公共管理和社会组织”更名为“公共管理、社会保障和社会组织”。

门类位次调整：(1)“批发和零售业”调至“建筑业”后面；(2)“住宿和餐饮业”调至“交通运输、仓储和邮政业”后面。

门类范围调整：A 农、林、牧、渔业；C 制造业；G 交通运输、仓储和邮政业；I 信息传输、软件和信息技术服务业；J 金融业；L 租赁和商务服务业；M 科学研究和技术服务业；O 居民服务、修理和其他服务业；P 教育；Q 卫生和社会工作；R 文化、体育和娱乐业；S 公共管理、社会保障和社会组织。

Brief Introduction

I. Main Content

Data in this chapter mainly show the basic information of administrative zoning of Beijing, number of corporate and industrial entities,non-public economy, small- and medium-sized enterprises, main indicators for social and economic development of the city, and monitoring indicators for the 12th Five-Year Plan, etc.

II. Source of Data

Data on administrative zoning of Beijing are from Beijing Bureau of Civil Affairs. Data on municipal corporate and industrial entities are from Beijing Municipal Bureau of Statistics. Data on private and self-employment economy in the city are from Beijing Administration for Industry and Commerce, Beijing Municipal Bureau of Local Tax and Beijing Municipal Bureau of State Tax. Data of non-public economy, small- and medium-sized enterprises are from National Bureau of Statistics Survey Office in Beijing and Beijing Municipal Bureau of Statistics. Data of social and economic indicators and main monitoring indicators for the 12th Five-Year Plan of the city are sorted out by Beijing Municipal Bureau of Statistics and National Bureau of Statistics Survey Office in Beijing on the basis of relevant data.

III. Adjustment to Historical Data According to New Industrial Standards

(I) Changes to the main framework of the Classification and Codes of Sectors in National Economy Version (GB/T 4754-2002) as compared with the former Version (GB/T 4754-1994):

Sectors added: a). information transmission, computer service and software sectors, b). leasing and business service sectors, c). accommodation, food and drink sector, d). water conservancy, environment, public facility management sectors, e). education, f). international organizations.

Sectors with name or range changed: a).agriculture, forestry, livestock raising, fishery, b). mining, c). manufacturing, d). transportation, warehouse storage, postal service, e). wholesale and retail trades, f). finance, g). scientific research, technical service, geologic survey, h). residents service and other service sectors, i). health, social security, and social welfare, j). culture, sports and entertainment, k). public management social organizations.

Sectors cancelled: a). geologic survey, water conservancy management, b). other sectors.

（II）Compared with the former (GB/T 4754-2002) version, the Industrial Classification for National Economic Activities (GB/T 4754-2011) mainly involves the following framework changes:

Changes to the name of category: (1) The “electric power, gas and water production and supply industry” is renamed “electric power, heating power, gas and water production and supply industry”; (2) the “information transmission, computer service and software industry” is renamed “information transmission, software and IT service industry”; (3) the “scientific research, technological service and geological surveying industry” is renamed “scientific research and technological service industry”; (4) the “residents service and other service industry” is renamed “residents service, repair and other service industry”; (5) the “health, social security and social welfare industry” is renamed “health and social work”; (6) “public management and social organization” is renamed “public management, social security and social organization”.

Changes to the place of category: (1) the “wholesale and retail industry” is put after the “construction industry”; (2) the “hotel and catering industry” is put after the “transportation, warehousing and post industry”.

Changes to the scope of category: A. Agriculture, Forestry, Husbandry, Fishery; C. Manufacturing; G. Transportation, Warehousing and Post Industry; I. Information Transmission, Software and IT Service industry; J. Financing; L. Leasing and Business Service; M. Scientific Research and Technological Service Industry; O. Residents Service, Repair and Other Service Industry; P. Education; Q. Health and Social Work; R. Culture, Sports and Entertainment Industry; S. Public Management, Social Security and Social Organization.

1-1 行政区划(2012年)
ADMINISTRATIVE DIVISIONS (2012)

单位：个 (unit)

地 区	District	街道办事处 Urban Subdistrict Office	建制镇 Organic Town	建制乡 Organic Township	社区居委会 Community Neighborhood Committee	村民委员会 Villagers' Committee
全 市	**Total**	**143**	**144**	**38**	**2816**	**3940**
首都功能核心区	**Core Districts of Capital Function**	**32**			**442**	
东 城 区	Dongcheng	17			187	
西 城 区	Xicheng	15			255	
城市功能拓展区	**Urban Function Extended Districts**	**70**	**9**	**22**	**1393**	**303**
朝 阳 区	Chaoyang	23		19	390	154
丰 台 区	Fengtai	16	2	3	297	65
石景山区	Shijingshan	9			142	
海 淀 区	Haidian	22	7		564	84
城市发展新区	**New Districts of Urban Development**	**28**	**72**	**7**	**672**	**2192**
房 山 区	Fangshan	8	14	6	123	461
通 州 区	Tongzhou	4	10	1	110	475
顺 义 区	Shunyi	6	19		91	426
昌 平 区	Changping	5	15		189	303
大 兴 区	Daxing	5	14		159	527
生态涵养发展区	**Ecological Preservation Development Districts**	**13**	**63**	**9**	**309**	**1445**
门头沟区	Mentougou	4	9		113	178
怀 柔 区	Huairou	2	12	2	32	284
平 谷 区	Pinggu	2	14	2	29	273
密 云 县	Miyun	2	17	1	89	334
延 庆 县	Yanqing	3	11	4	46	376

资料来源：北京市民政局。
Source: Beijing Civil Affairs Bureau.

1-2 全部法人、产业活动单位数(2012年)
TOTAL NUMBER OF JUDICIAL ENTITIES AND ESTABLISHMENTS (2012)

单位: 个 (unit)

项目	Item	法人单位数合计 Total Number of Judicial Entities	单产业法人 Single-sector Judicial Entities	多产业法人 Multi-sector Judicial Entities	多产业法人单位的产业活动单位数 Establishments of Multi-sector Judicial Entities
合计	**Total**	**406810**	**388883**	**17927**	**76472**
按登记注册类型分	**Grouped by Registration Status**				
内资	Domestically-funded Economy	391132	374867	16265	65381
国有	State-owned Units	21872	20356	1516	8036
集体	Collective-owned Units	14120	13548	572	1880
股份合作	Joint-stock Enterprises	15396	14818	578	1552
联营	Joint Ownership Units	506	483	23	97
有限责任公司	Limited-Liability Corporations	66174	61900	4274	20349
股份有限公司	Share Holding Corporations Ltd.	5125	4630	495	7423
私营	Private	255747	247607	8140	24132
其他	Others	12192	11525	667	1912
港澳台商投资	Units with Funds from Hongkong, Macao and Taiwan	5682	5063	619	4432
与港澳台商合资经营	Joint Venture with Hongkong, Macao and Taiwan	1367	1201	166	1118
与港澳台商合作经营	Cooperative with Hongkong, Macao and Taiwan	240	217	23	119
港澳台商独资	Hongkong, Macao and Taiwan Funded	4002	3590	412	3132
港澳台商投资股份有限公司	Hongkong, Macao and Taiwan Share Holding Corporations Ltd.	73	55	18	63
其他港澳台商投资	Others				
外商投资	Foreign Funded Units	9996	8953	1043	6659
中外合资经营	Chinese-Foreign Joint Venture	2465	2214	251	2143
中外合作经营	Chinese-Foreign Cooperative	305	274	31	133
外资企业	Wholly Foreign Funded	7073	6328	745	4271
外商投资股份有限公司	Foreign-funded Share Holding Corporation Ltd.	151	136	15	109
其他外商投资	Others	2	1	1	3
按隶属关系分	**Grouped by Administrative Relationship**				
中央	Central	10095	8841	1254	8894
地方	Local	396715	380042	16673	67578
按地理位置分	**Grouped by Geographic Location**				
二环路以内	Within the Second Ring Road	39468	36762	2706	15931
二环路至三环路	The Second-third Ring Road	61893	58412	3481	17599
三环路至四环路	The Third-Fourth Ring Road	79926	76626	3300	12653
四环路以外	Outside the Fourth Ring Road	225523	217083	8440	30289
按机构类型分	**Grouped by Organization Type**				
企业	Enterprises	375904	359560	16344	69153
事业单位	Institutions	11209	10768	441	1917
机关	Government Agencies and Organizations	2092	1881	211	1916
社会团体	Social Groups	4194	3822	372	2239
其他机构	Others	13411	12852	559	1247

注：本表为2013年5月31日名录库时点数据。
Note: Figures in this table are based on those at the directory library timepiont on May 31, 2013.

1-3　国民经济各行业法人和产业活动单位数(2012年)

NUMBER OF JUDICIAL ENTITIES AND ESTABLISHMENTS IN DIFFERENT SECTORS OF THE NATIONAL ECONOMY (2012)

单位：个 (unit)

行　业	Sector	法　人 单位数 合　计 Total Number of Judicial Entities	单产业法人 Single-sector Judicial Entities	多产业法人 Multi-sector Judicial Entities	多产业法人单位的产业活动单位数 Establishments of Multi-sector Judicial Entities
合　计	**Total**	**406810**	**388883**	**17927**	**76472**
农　业	Agriculture Farming	1357	1337	20	67
林　业	Forestry	476	471	5	13
畜牧业	Animal Husbandry	738	724	14	49
渔　业	Fishery	100	98	2	5
农、林、牧、渔服务业	Services for Agriculture	472	455	17	47
煤炭开采和洗选业	Mining and Washing of Coal	26	24	2	8
石油和天然气开采业	Extraction of Petroleum and Natural Gas	20	18	2	4
黑色金属矿采选业	Mining and Processing of Ferrous Metal Ores	21	19	2	9
有色金属矿采选业	Mining and Processing of Non-Ferrous Metal Ores	4	4		
非金属矿采选业	Mining and Processing of Nonmetal Ores	117	115	2	4
其他采矿业	Mining of Other Minerals	1	1		
农副食品加工业	Processing of Food from Agriculture Products	956	918	38	106
食品制造业	Manufacture of Foods	1084	1004	80	365
饮料制造业	Manufacture of Beverages	416	391	25	87
烟草制品业	Manufacture of Tobacco	1		1	2
纺织业	Manufacture of Textile	703	674	29	85
纺织服装、鞋、帽制造业	Manufacture of Textile Wearing Apparel, Foodware, and Caps	2454	2364	90	257
皮革、毛皮、羽毛(绒)及其制品业	Manufacture of Leather, Furs, Feather (Down) and Related Products	206	200	6	23
木材加工及竹、藤、棕、草制品业	Processing of Timber, Manufacture of Wood, Bamboo, Rattan, Palm, and Straw Products	689	672	17	37
家具制造业	Manufacture of Furniture	1407	1343	64	209
造纸及纸制品业	Manufacture of Paper and Paper Products	971	949	22	44
印刷业和记录媒介的复制	Printing, Reproduction of Recording Media	1712	1667	45	101
文教体育用品制造业	Manufacture of Articles for Culture, Education and Sports Activity	336	322	14	40
石油加工、炼焦及核燃料加工业	Processing of Petroleum, Coking, Processing of Nuclear Fule	211	200	11	23
化学原料及化学制品制造业	Manufacture of Raw Chemical Materials and Chemical Products	2265	2166	99	241
医药制造业	Manufacture of Medicines	628	581	47	133
化学纤维制造业	Manufacture of Chemical Fibers	42	38	4	10
橡胶制品业	Manufacture of Rubber	223	216	7	16
塑料制品业	Manufacture of Plastics	1518	1476	42	91
非金属矿物制品业	Manufacture of Non-metallic Mineral Products	2820	2735	85	222
黑色金属冶炼及压延加工业	Smelting and Pressing of Ferrous Metals	157	153	4	17

注：1. 本表为2013年5月31日名录库时点数据。
2. 本表行业划分执行2002年国民经济行业分类标准(GB/T 4754—2002)。

Note: a) Figures in this table are based on those at the directory library timepiont on May 31, 2013.
b) Sectors in this table are classified in accordance with the Standard for Classification of National Economic Sectors 2012 (GB/T 4754-2002).

1-3 续表 1 continued

单位：个 (unit)

行业	Sector	法人单位数合计 Total Number of Judicial Entities	单产业法人 Single-sector Judicial Entities	多产业法人 Multi-sector Judicial Entities	多产业法人单位的产业活动单位数 Establishments of Multi-sector Judicial Entities
有色金属冶炼及压延加工业	Smelting and Pressing of Non-ferrous Metals	243	236	7	14
金属制品业	Manufacture of Metal Products	3692	3576	116	294
通用设备制造业	Manufacture of General Purpose Machinery	3054	2923	131	444
专用设备制造业	Manufacture of Special Purpose Machinery	2517	2383	134	366
交通运输设备制造业	Manufacture of Transport Equipment	1465	1396	69	192
电气机械及器材制造业	Manufacture of Electrical Machinery and Equipment	2151	2058	93	234
通信设备、计算机及其他电子设备制造业	Manufacture of Communication Equipment, Computers, and Other Electronic Equipment	1468	1360	108	318
仪器仪表及文化、办公用机械制造业	Manufacture of Measuring Instruments and Machinery for Cultural Activity and Office Work	1264	1174	90	223
工艺品及其他制造业	Manufacture of Artwork and Other Manufacturing	794	758	36	101
废弃资源和废旧材料回收加工业	Recycling and Disposal of Waste	83	81	2	4
电力、热力的生产和供应业	Production and Distribution of Electric Power and Heat Power	317	298	19	93
燃气生产和供应业	Production and Distribution of Gas	43	36	7	39
水的生产和供应业	Production and Distribution of Water	115	109	6	49
房屋和土木工程建筑业	Construction of Buildings and Civil Engineering	2781	2392	389	2484
建筑安装业	Building Installation	2626	2444	182	657
建筑装饰业	Building Decoration	6779	6543	236	772
其他建筑业	Other Construction	965	923	42	103
铁路运输业	Railway Transport	36	29	7	150
道路运输业	Road Transport	4037	3852	185	731
城市公共交通业	Urban Public Transport	309	292	17	80
水上运输业	Waterway Transport	19	15	4	11
航空运输业	Air Transport	59	50	9	66
管道运输业	Transport Via Pipelines	7	7		
装卸搬运和其他运输服务业	Loading and Unloading and Other Transport Services	2245	2005	240	1266
仓储业	Storage	908	879	29	100
邮政业	Post	504	482	22	580
电信和其他信息传输服务业	Telecommunications and Other Information Transmission	3277	3008	269	1425
计算机服务业	Computer Services	6393	6133	260	1147
软件业	Software	12645	12153	492	1727

1-3 续表 2 continued

单位：个 (unit)

行 业	Sector	法 人 单位数 合 计 Total Number of Judicial Entities	单产业法人 Single-sector Judicial Entities	多产业法人 Multi-sector Judicial Entities	多产业法人单位的产业活动单位数 Establishments of Multi-sector Judicial Entities
批发业	Wholesale Trade	63731	60725	3006	8895
零售业	Retail Trade	58603	55761	2842	13611
住宿业	Hotels	4031	3696	335	1058
餐饮业	Restaurants	9247	8535	712	4931
银行业	Banks	115	65	50	3335
证券业	Security Activities	306	259	47	1126
保险业	Insurance	543	438	105	852
其他金融活动	Other Financial Activities	841	776	65	464
房地产业	Real Estate Business Services	14725	13439	1286	5254
租赁业	Leasing	2586	2506	80	409
商务服务业	Commercial Business Services	74975	73128	1847	7055
研究与试验发展	Research and Experimental Development	3275	3160	115	307
专业技术服务业	Professional Technical Services	12787	12316	471	1601
科技交流和推广服务业	Services of Science and Technology Exchanges and Promotion	22219	21861	358	974
地质勘查业	Geologic Prospecting	274	261	13	34
水利管理业	Management of Water Conservancy	275	270	5	14
环境管理业	Environmental Management	517	492	25	69
公共设施管理业	Management of Public Facilities	1702	1652	50	184
居民服务业	Services to Households	7040	6560	480	1530
其他服务业	Other Services	7781	7597	184	499
教 育	Education	8341	8081	260	946
卫 生	Health	2248	2046	202	1164
社会保障业	Social Securitiy	240	238	2	18
社会福利业	Social Welfare	604	594	10	70
新闻出版业	Journalism and Publishing Activities	1547	1474	73	186
广播、电视、电影和音像业	Broadcasting, Televisions, Movies, and Audio-Visual Activities	1859	1813	46	130
文化艺术业	Cultural and Art Activities	6631	6561	70	168
体 育	Sports Activities	917	890	27	96
娱乐业	Entertainment	1899	1806	93	296
中国共产党机关	Organs of Communist Party of China	333	331	2	6
国家机构	Government Agencies (C.P.P.C)	3228	3008	220	1949
人民政协和民主党派	People's Political Consultative Conference and Democratic Party	58	58		
群众团体、社会团体和宗教组织	Masses, Social Organizatuon and Religionary Body Social Organizations and Religion Organizations	4218	3847	371	2217
基层群众自治组织	Masses Autonomous Body	6187	5709	478	1039
国际组织	International Organization				

1-4 企业法人单位数(2012年)
NUMBER OF ENTERPRISES AS JUDICIAL ENTITIES (2012)

单位：个 (unit)

项 目	Item	法人单位合 计 Total Number of Judicial Entities
合 计	**Total**	**375904**
按营业状况分	**Grouped by Business Condition**	
营 业	Going on	315138
停 业	Closed	41963
筹 建	Preparation	6096
当年关闭	Closed in This Year	6039
当年破产	Bankruptcy in This Year	136
其 他	Others	6532
按开业时间分	**Grouped by Openning Time**	
1949年以前	Before 1949	62
1950-1965	Between 1950 and 1965	760
1966-1979	Between 1966 and 1979	880
1980-1989	Between 1980 and 1989	6628
1990年以后	After 1990	366475
按登记注册类型分	**Grouped by Registration Status**	
内资企业	Domestic Funded Enterprises	360265
国有企业	State-owned Units	7200
集体企业	Collective-owned Units	11720
股份合作企业	Cooperative Enterprises	15289
联营企业	Joint-owned Enterprises	424
有限责任公司	Limited-Liability Corporations	66084
股份有限公司	Share Holding Corporations Ltd.	5114
私营企业	Private	253914
其他内资企业	Other Domestically-funded Enterprises	520

项 目	Item	法人单位合 计 Total Number of Judicial Entities
港澳台商投资企业	Enterprises with Funds from Hongkong, Macao and Taiwan	5668
与港澳台商合资经营	Joint Venture with Hongkong, Maocao and Taiwan	1363
与港澳台商合作经营	Cooperative with Hongkong, Macao and Taiwan	237
港澳台商独资	Hongkong, Macao and Taiwan Funded	3995
港澳台商投资股份有限公司	Hongkong, Macao and Taiwan Share Holding Corporations Ltd.	73
其他港澳台商投资	Others	
外商投资企业	Foreign Funded Enterprises	9971
中外合资经营	Chinese-Foreign Joint Venture	2463
中外合作经营	Chinese-Foreign Cooperative	298
外资企业	Foreign Funded Enterprises	7057
外商投资股份有限公司	Foreign Share Holding Corporations Ltd.	151
其他外商投资	Others	2
按地理位置分	**Grouped by Geographic Location**	
二环路以内	Within the Second Ring Road	34427
二环路至三环路	Between the Second-third Ring Road	58433
三环路至四环路	Between the Third-Fourth Ring Road	77678
四环路以外	Outside the Fourth Ring Road	205366
按控股情况分	**Grouped by Share Holding Conditions**	
国有控股	State-owned Holding	17365
集体控股	Collectively Controlled	20674
私人控股	Privately Controlled	303987
港澳台商控股	Controlled by Companies from Hongkong, Macao and Taiwan	5471
外商控股	Controlled by Foreign Companies	9773
其 他	Others	18634

注：本表为2013年5月31日名录库时点数据。
Note: Figures in this table are based on those at the directory library timepiont on May 31, 2013.

1-5 全市私营个体经济基本情况
STATISTICS FOR INDIVIDUAL AND PRIVATE ECONOMY

单位：万元 (10000 yuan)

项目	Item	私营 Private 2012	私营 Private 2011	私营 Private 2012年为2011年% 2012 as % of 2011	个体 Individual 2012	个体 Individual 2011	个体 Individual 2012年为2011年% 2012 as % of 2011
工商登记注册 *	**Registered in Department of Industry and Commerce**						
户数 (户)	Number of Establishments (unit)	600354	544022	110.4	691066	762701	90.6
从业人员 (人)	Number of Employed Persons (person)	3710912	3435458	108.0	1066883	1110474	96.1
注册资本	Registered Capital	136694192	104919631	130.3	1712269	1586072	108.0
国税、地税入库税收合计	Taxes Put into Local and National Treasury	4640961	4339768	106.9	1339440	1122991	119.3

注：*为期末时点数。

资料来源：北京市工商行政管理局、北京市地方税务局、北京市国家税务局。

Note: Data with * indicates the accumulative data at the year-end.

Source: Beijing Administration for Industry and Commerce, Beijing Local Tax Bureau, Beijing State Tax Bureau.

1-6 规模以上非公经济主要指标(2012年)
MAIN STATUS OF NON-PUBLIC ECONOMICS ABOVE DESIGNATED SIZE (2012)

项目	Item	单位数 (个) Number of Enterprises (unit)	收入合计 (亿元) Total Income (100 million yuan)	利润总额 (亿元) Total Profits (100 million yuan)	应交税金合计 (亿元) Total Tax (100 million yuan)	从业人员平均人数 (万人) Average Number of Persons Employed (10000 persons)
合计	**Total**	**29059**	**37827.3**	**2879.8**	**1782.4**	**321.7**
按登记注册类型分	**Grouped by Registration Status**					
内资	Domestic Investment Economy	25032	19429.3	816.4	910.7	209.3
私营独资	Private Wholly-Funded	143	39.4	2.0	1.1	1.2
私营合伙	Private Partnership	355	141.9	70.4	15.5	2.2
私营有限责任公司	Private Limited Liability Companies	14601	8043.8	172.6	256.5	93.7
私营股份有限公司	Private Joint-Stock Companies	558	372.0	38.6	20.9	6.0
私人投资控股	Private Holding Companies	9375	10832.2	532.9	616.7	106.3
港澳台商投资	Units with Funds from Hongkong, Macao and Taiwan	1451	4585.8	419.7	302.9	39.8
港澳台商独资	Hongkong, Macao and Taiwan Enterprises	874	3349.4	262.5	165.9	24.8
港澳台商投资控股	Enterprises Funded and Controlled by Hongkong, Macaoand Taiwan Companies	577	1236.4	157.2	137.0	15.0
外商投资	Foreign Funded Units Funded Share Holding Corporations	2576	13812.2	1643.7	568.8	72.5
外商独资	Foreign Enterprises	1777	10964.4	1426.0	428.4	47.7
外商投资控股	Foreign Funded and Controlled Corporations	799	2847.8	217.7	140.4	24.9
按规模分	**Grouped by Size**					
#大型企业	Large-sized Enterprises	867	16984.1	1287.1	873.9	115.2
中小微型企业	Mini-, Small-, Mediume-sized Enterprises	27938	20709.6	1592.7	906.9	203.1
中型	Medium Size	5163	11722.5	1300.2	558.3	103.5
小型	Small Size	16511	7979.9	340.4	298.6	91.1
微型	Mini Size	6264	1007.2	-47.8	49.9	8.5
按行业分	**Grouped by Sector**					
#制造业	Manufacturing	2706	6781.2	439.0	298.9	62.5
建筑业	Construction	2822	1722.3	44.3	66.1	19.4
批发和零售业	Wholesale and Retail Trade	6573	16627.6	390.0	368.9	49.5
交通运输、仓储和邮政业	Transport, Storage and Post	749	717.2	30.5	25.3	16.0
住宿和餐饮业	Accommodation and Restaurants	2291	641.8	12.7	47.8	27.7
信息传输、软件和信息技术服务业	Information Transmission,Software and Information Technology Services	2303	3355.6	1084.5	243.4	45.5
金融业	Finance	1033	650.6	78.9	161.4	5.6
房地产业	Real estate	2946	1838.7	326.0	317.9	22.7
租赁和商务服务业	Renting and Leasing Activities and Business Services	4383	3681.2	321.3	157.0	37.2
科学研究和技术服务业	Scientific Research and Development, Technical Services	1867	956.3	89.6	56.4	16.1
水利、环境和公共设施管理业	Management of Water Conservancy, Environmen and Public Facilities	170	139.1	13.8	7.6	1.5
居民服务、修理和其他服务业	Resident Services, Repair and Other Services	335	131.0	3.1	7.4	6.4
教育	Education	250	141.8	7.3	6.6	6.0
卫生和社会工作	Health Care and Social Works	112	48.3	4.2	1.2	1.5
文化、体育和娱乐业	Culture, Sports and Entertainment	381	121.9	7.7	10.2	2.7
公共管理和社会组织	Pulic Administration, Social Security and Social Organizations	108	73.5		0.7	0.4

注：1. 本表私人投资控股包含内资中除私营独资、私营合伙、私营有限责任公司和私营股份有限公司以外的非公有经济，港澳台商投资控股包含除港澳台独资以外的港澳台商投资经济，外商投资控股包含除外商独资以外的外商投资经济。本表不包含个体经营户数据。

2. 2012年，规模以上非公经济实现增加值5839.9亿元，其中第二产业增加值1439.8亿元，第三产业增加值4400.1亿元。

3. 应交税金合计主要包括应交增值税、应交所得税、营业税金及附加和管理费用中的税金等。

4. 按规模分组中，各类型非公经济是指执行企业会计制度的非公企业数据，不包含执行事业会计制度的非公单位数据，因此，规模分组合计数不等于其他分组合计数。

Note: a) Private holding companies include non-public economies in domestically funded enterprises other than wholly private-funded, private cooperative, private liability limited and private joint-stock companies. Enterprises funded and controlled by Hongkong, Macao and Taiwan companies include economies funded by Hongkong, Macao and Taiwan companies other than those wholly funded by Hongkong, Macao and Taiwan companies. Foreign funded and controlled corporations include foreign funded economies other than wholly foreign-funded companies.

b) In 2012, the added value generated by non-public economies above designated size was 5839.9 million yuan, of which, the added value of secondary industry was 1439.8 million yuan, and that of tertiary industry, 4400.1 million yuan .

c) Total Tax mainly includes payable VAT,payable income tax, business tax and surtax, and tax in management expenses, etc.

d) In the group by size, figures of various types of non-public economies are those of non-public enterprises implementing enterprise accounting system, excluding those of non-public entities implementing public institution accounting system. Therefore, total amounts in the group by size are not equal to total amounts of other groups.

1-7 规模以上中小微型企业主要指标(2012年)
MAIN STATUS OF MINI- SMALL- AND MEDIUM-SIZED ENTERPRISES ABOVE DESIGNATED SIZE (2012)

项 目	Item	单位数 (个) Number of Enter-prises (unit)	收入合计 (亿元) Total Income (100 million yuan)	利润总额 (亿元) Total Profits (100 million yuan)	应交税金合计 (亿元) Total Tax (100 million yuan)	从业人员平均人数 (万人) Average Number of Persons Employed (10000 persons)
合 计	**Total**	**37166**	**50698.0**	**7638.7**	**1839.6**	**309.0**
按规模分	**Grouped by Size**					
中型	Medium Size	8124	33122.3	5195.5	1120.1	174.6
小型	Small Size	21254	13354.5	1101.9	546.6	123.0
微型	Mini Size	7788	4221.2	1341.3	172.9	11.4
按登记注册类型分	**Grouped by Registration Status**					
内 资	Domestic Investment Economy	33286	44729.6	6534.5	1488.7	259.5
港澳台商投资	Units with Funds from Hongkong, Macao and Taiwan	1407	2131.8	103.4	125.0	19.0
外商投资	Foreign Funded Economy	2473	3836.6	1000.8	225.9	30.5
按行业分	**Grouped by Sector**					
#制造业	Manufacturing	3421	5549.7	405.3	303.4	63.9
建筑业	Construction	3401	2198.0	89.8	83.0	25.4
批发和零售业	Wholesale and Retail Trade	7771	23003.1	272.5	315.1	35.6
交通运输、仓储和邮政业	Transport, Storage and Post	1028	961.7	-13.6	23.1	14.3
住宿和餐饮业	Accommodation and Restaurants	2971	513.1	-8.2	36.2	25.9
信息传输、软件和信息技术服务业	Information Transmission,Software and Information Technology Services	2530	1907.7	909.6	83.1	27.2
金融业	Finance	1678	5761.1	4647.7	265.9	6.3
房地产业	Real estate	4500	2487.8	410.5	377.3	27.0
租赁和商务服务业	Renting and Leasing Activities and Business Services	5477	4086.0	622.1	200.0	51.2
科学研究和技术服务业	Scientific Research and Development, Technical Services	2454	1872.0	179.6	84.0	15.9
水利、环境和公共设施管理业	Management of Water Conservancy, Environment and Public Facilities	294	151.9	12.1	6.9	1.8
居民服务、修理和其他服务业	Resident Services, Repair and Other Services	361	119.1	2.5	6.3	3.0
教育	Education	169	50.8	3.9	4.0	1.6
卫生和社会工作	Health Care and Social Works	111	34.3	2.2	0.7	1.1
文化、体育和娱乐业	Culture, Sports and Entertainment	895	409.8	47.9	30.9	6.1

注：1. 本表中的企业规模划型标准，依照《国家统计局关于印发统计上大中小微型企业划分办法的通知》〔国统字(2011)75号〕中关于《统计上大中小微型企业划分标准》规定。

2. 行业划分执行2011年国民经济行业分类标准（GB/T 4754-2011）。

Note: a) In this table, enterprise size is identified in accordance with the provisions concerning the Statistical Division Standards of Mini-, Small-, Mediume- and Large-sized Enterprises in the Notice of the National Bureau of Statistics Concerning Printing and Issuing Measures for Statistical Division of Mini-, Small-, Mediume- and Large-sized Enterprises (GTZ (2011)No.75).

b) Sectors in this table are classified in accordance with the Standard for Classification of National Economic Sectors 2011 (GB/T 4754-2011).

1-8 主要经济指标增长速度(1979-2012年)

单位：%

年份 Year	地区生产总值比上年增长 YoY Growth Rate of Gross Domestic Product	全社会固定资产投资比上年增长 YoY Growth Rate of Fixed Assets Investment	房地产开发投资比上年增长 YoY Growth Rate of Real Estate Development Investment	地方公共财政预算收入比上年增长 YoY Growth Rate of Local Public Budgetary Financial Revenue	社会消费品零售总额比上年增长 YoY Growth Rate of Sales of Consumer Goods	进出口总值比上年增长 YoY Growth Rate of Gross Amount of Imports & Exports
1979	9.7	17.3			20.6	
1980	11.8	25.3			17.8	
1981	-0.5	10.2			12.6	
1982	7.4	5.5			6.6	
1983	16.4	32.9			14.6	
1984	17.4	29.2			22.5	16.3
1985	8.7	41.8			27.0	-8.6
1986	8.0	13.0			15.3	-6.0
1987	9.6	28.2			21.9	-12.7
1988	12.8	19.7			35.5	11.9
1989	4.4	-14.4			15.2	-4.3
1990	5.2	28.5			17.1	-17.4
1991	9.9	7.1	6.7		18.3	2.5
1992	11.3	38.5	40.4		23.2	3.1
1993	12.3	54.3	73.3		21.5	11.7
1994	13.7	58.1	70.4		25.4	3.5
1995	12.0	29.7	254.6		24.0	28.2
1996	9.0	4.2	-7.0		11.7	-20.8
1997	10.1	9.6	0.6		13.8	3.7
1998	9.5	20.2	14.3	20.0	13.7	0.4
1999	10.9	1.3	11.7	22.6	9.9	12.6
2000	11.8	10.8	23.9	22.7	9.9	43.8
2001	11.7	18.0	50.1	31.6	10.4	4.2
2002	11.5	18.5	26.2	25.9	9.5	2.0
2003	11.1	18.9	21.5	18.2	14.5	30.5
2004	14.1	17.2	22.5	29.7	14.4	38.1
2005	12.1	11.8	3.5	23.5	10.9	32.7
2006	13.0	19.3	12.8	21.5	13.2	25.9
2007	14.5	17.6	16.0	33.6	16.4	22.1
2008	9.1	-3.0	-4.4	23.1	21.1	40.8
2009	10.2	26.2	22.5	10.3	14.3	-20.9
2010	10.3	13.1	24.1	16.1	17.3	40.4
2011	8.1	13.3	10.1	27.7	10.8	29.1
2012	7.7	9.3	3.9	10.3	11.6	4.8

注：1. 自2011年起全社会固定资产投资统计起点发生变化，但2011年全社会固定资产投资增长速度和房地产开发投资增长速度均按可比口径计算。
2. 2002-2004年地方公共财政预算收入增长速度是按可比口径计算。
3. 城镇居民人均可支配收入和农村居民人均纯收入实际增长速度是指扣除物价后的实际增长速度。

YOY GROWTH RATE OF MAIN INDICATORS (1979-2012)

农林牧渔业总产值比上年增长 YoY Growth Rate of Gross OutputValue of Farming,Forestry,Animal Husbandry and Fishery	规模以上工业总产值比上年增长 YoY Growth Rate of Gross Output Value of Industrial Enterprises Above Designated Size	居民消费价格指数(上年=100) Consumer Price Index (Preceding=100)	城镇居民人均可支配收入 Per-capita Disposable Income of Urban Household		农村居民人均纯收入 Per-capita Net Income of Rural Households	
			比上年名义增长 Growth Rate	比上年实际增长 Real Growth Rate	比上年名义增长 Growth Rate	比上年实际增长 Real Growth Rate
7.0		101.8	13.6	11.6	11.1	10.9
16.3		106.0	20.8	14.0	23.2	22.1
4.2		101.3	2.5	1.2	17.2	17.1
12.8		101.8	9.1	7.2	19.1	17.3
16.7		100.5	5.2	4.7	20.7	20.9
13.3		102.2	17.5	15.0	27.9	25.7
16.7	17.4	117.6	30.8	11.3	16.7	14.5
8.5	3.8	106.8	17.6	10.1	6.2	3.7
22.4	15.2	108.6	10.7	1.9	11.3	6.5
52.9	27.9	120.4	21.6	1.0	16.0	3.1
14.8	21.6	117.2	11.1	-5.2	15.8	2.2
16.2	3.8	105.4	11.9	6.2	5.4	2.1
9.0	16.7	111.9	14.2	2.1	9.6	1.7
10.5	17.8	109.9	15.8	5.4	10.3	2.0
18.8	35.7	119.0	39.4	17.1	18.2	5.1
43.7	35.1	124.9	43.5	14.9	30.6	9.1
13.9	-5.3	117.3	24.0	5.7	32.5	6.3
2.7	6.5	111.6	17.3	5.1	11.1	4.8
0.9	14.4	105.3	13.5	7.8	5.6	5.1
2.5	7.0	102.4	8.4	5.9	7.1	6.7
3.3	12.1	100.6	8.4	7.8	7.1	7.2
4.4	30.2	103.5	12.7	8.9	8.6	7.3
7.2	15.1	103.1	11.9	8.5	12.5	8.7
5.6	10.7	98.2	13.5	15.6	11.5	12.3
5.2	21.8	100.2	11.4	11.2	10.5	11.5
4.5	30.0	101.0	12.6	11.5	10.4	9.2
1.9	21.2	101.5	12.9	11.2	9.6	8.1
0.4	18.2	100.9	13.2	12.2	9.7	8.7
13.4	17.5	102.4	13.9	11.2	10.9	8.2
11.6	7.9	105.1	12.4	7.0	12.4	6.5
3.6	6.0	98.5	8.1	9.7	11.5	13.4
4.1	24.1	102.4	8.7	6.2	10.6	8.1
10.7	5.9	105.6	13.2	7.2	13.6	7.6
9.0	7.5	103.3	10.8	7.3	11.8	8.2

Note: a) The statistical starting point for Fixed Assets Investment in 2011 is changed. But the growth rate of Fixed Assets and Real Estate Development Investment in 2011 is calculated at fixed price. standard.

b) The growht rate of local public financial revenue in 2002-2004 is calculated at comparable price.

c) The growth rate of per-capita disposable income of urban households and per-capita net income of rural households means the real growth rate after the price influence is eliminated.

1-9 主要年份国民经济和社会发展总量与速度指标

项 目		Item		1990	1995
人口与就业		**Population and Employment**			
人 口		**Population**			
年末全市常住人口	(万人)	Year-end Total Population	(10000 persons)	1086.0	1251.1
按性别分		By Sex			
男性人口		Male		545.0	627.0
女性人口		Female		541.0	624.1
按城乡分		By Urban Area and Rural Area			
城镇人口		Urban Population		798.0	946.2
乡村人口		Rural Population		288.0	304.9
年末户籍人口	(万人)	Year-end Permanent Residents Registered	(10000 persons)	1032.2	1070.3
就 业		**Employment**			
从业人员年末人数	(万人)	Year-end Employment Persons	(10000 persons)	627.1	665.3
#城镇单位在岗职工人数		Fully Employed Staff and Workers		454.9	470.9
年末实有城镇登记		Number of Actual Jobless Persons among Regi			
失业人员	(万人)	Unemployed Persons in Urban Area	(10000 persons)	1.67	2.19
宏观经济		**Macro Economy**			
国民经济核算		**National Accounting**			
地区生产总值	(亿元)	Gross Domestic Product	(100 million yuan)	500.8	1507.7
第一产业		Primary Industry		43.9	73.5
第二产业		Secondary Industry		262.4	645.8
第三产业		Tertiary Industry		194.5	788.4
人均地区生产总值	(元/人)	Per Capita Gross Domestic Products	(yuan/person)	4635	12690
固定资产投资		**Investment in Fixed Assets**			
全社会固定资产投资	(亿元)	Total Investment in Fixed Assets	(100 million yuan)	179.2	841.5
#房地产开发投资		Real Estate Development		22.5	352.8
#国有单位		State-Owned Units		154.2	514.2
全社会房屋施工面积	(万平方米)	Floor Space of Houses under Construction	(10000 sq.m)	2864.9	5524.3
全社会房屋竣工面积	(万平方米)	Floor Space of Houses Completed	(10000 sq.m)	1081.2	1530.2
财 政		**Finance**			
地方财政收入	(亿元)	Local Financial Revenue	(100 million yuan)	74.0	115.3
#地方公共财政预算收入		Local Public Budgetary Financial Revenue			
地方财政支出	(亿元)	Local Financial Expenditures	(100 million yuan)	66.5	154.4
#地方公共财政预算支出		Local Public Budgetary Financial Expenditur			
价格指数(上年=100)		**Price Indices(Preceding Year=100)**			
居民消费价格指数	(%)	Consumer Price Index	(%)	105.4	117.3
商品零售价格指数	(%)	Retail Price Index	(%)	104.1	112.6
农产品生产价格指数	(%)	Indices of Producer's Prices of Farm Products	(%)	101.9	130.6
工业生产者出厂价格指数	(%)	Producer Price Index for Industrail products	(%)	107.9	107.3
工业生产者购进价格指数	(%)	Purchasing Price Index for Industrial Products	(%)	114.8	106.7
固定资产投资价格指数	(%)	Price Index for Investment in Fixed Assets	(%)		113.9
能源消费总量	**(万吨标准煤)**	**Total Energy Consumption**	**(10000 tons of SCE)**	**2709.7**	**3533.3**
产 业		**Industry**			
农村经济		**Rural Economy**			
耕地面积	(万公顷)	Cultivated Areas	(10000 hectare)	41.3	39.4
农林牧渔业总产值(现价)	(亿元)	Gross Output Value of Farming, Forestry, Animal Husbandry and Fishery (at current prices)	(100 million yuan)	70.2	164.4
主要农产品产量	(万吨)	Yield of Farm and Sideline Products	(10000 ton)		
粮 食		Grain		264.6	259.8
蔬菜及食用菌		Vegetables and Edible Mushrooms		356.1	397.3
禽 蛋		Poultry Eggs		25.8	28.5
牛 奶		Milk		21.7	20.6
肉 类		Meat		26.8	39.8

注：1. 地区生产总值绝对值按现价计算，发展速度按可比价格计算；2006-2010年人均地区生产总值根据第六次人口普查数据进行修正。
2. 2007年及以前在岗职工人数包括乡及乡以上独立核算法人单位，不包括乡镇企业、私营单位和个体工商户；2008年及以后包括乡镇企业。
3. 从2011年起，根据国家统计局相关规定，固定资产投资起点由50万元调整至500万元。

PRINCIPAL AGGREGATE INDICATORS ON NATIONAL ECONOMIC AND SOCIAL DEVELOPMENT AND THEIR RELATED INDICES AND GROWTH RATES IN MAIN YEAR

总量指标 Aggregate Data					速度指标(%) Indices (%)					
					指 数(2012年为以下各年) Index (2011 as Percentage of the Previous Years)					
2000	2005	2010	2011	2012	1990	1995	2000	2005	2010	2011
1363.6	1538.0	1961.9	2018.6	2069.3	190.5	165.4	151.8	134.5	105.5	102.5
710.9	778.7	1013.0	1040.7	1068.1	196.0	170.4	150.2	137.2	105.4	102.6
652.7	759.3	948.9	977.9	1001.2	185.1	160.4	153.4	131.9	105.5	102.4
1057.4	1286.1	1686.4	1740.7	1783.7	223.5	188.5	168.7	138.7	105.8	102.5
306.2	251.9	275.5	277.9	285.6	99.2	93.7	93.3	113.4	103.7	102.8
1107.5	1180.7	1257.8	1277.9	1297.5	125.7	121.2	117.2	109.9	103.2	101.5
619.3	878.0	1031.6	1069.7	1107.3	176.6	166.4	178.8	126.1	107.3	103.5
434.2	448.4	587.7	640.3	670.4	147.4	142.4	154.4	149.5	114.1	104.7
3.32	10.57	7.73	7.89	7.20	431.1	328.8	216.9	68.1	93.1	91.3
3161.7	6969.5	14113.6	16251.9	17879.4	1007.7	576.1	353.6	199.8	116.4	107.7
79.3	88.7	124.4	136.3	150.2	127.9	122.6	114.4	111.4	104.1	103.2
1033.3	2026.5	3388.4	3752.5	4059.3	814.1	486.0	309.6	180.8	114.7	107.5
2049.1	4854.3	10600.8	12363.1	13669.9	1357.1	675.9	383.0	209.5	117.3	107.9
24127	45993	73856	81658	87475	531.9	334.6	226.7	148.1	108.9	104.9
1297.4	2827.2	5493.5	5910.6	6462.8	3606.5	768.0	498.1	228.6	117.6	109.3
522.1	1525.0	2901.1	3036.3	3153.4	14015.1	893.8	604.0	206.8	108.7	103.9
765.8	897.7	1907.3	1903.3	2248.2	1458.0	437.2	293.6	250.4	117.9	118.1
6995.9	14096.2	15572.1	18065.2	20045.4	699.7	362.9	286.5	142.2	128.7	111.0
2358.2	4679.2	3908.4	4032.9	3723.5	344.4	243.3	157.9	79.6	95.3	92.3
398.4	1007.4	3810.9	4359.1	4512.9	6097.6	3915.4	1132.7	448.0	118.4	103.5
345.0	919.2	2353.9	3006.3	3314.9			960.9	360.6	140.8	110.3
490.3	1137.3	4065.0	4574.9	4803.8	7221.5	3111.2	979.7	422.4	118.2	105.0
443.0	1058.3	2717.3	3245.2	3685.3			831.9	348.2	135.6	113.6
103.5	101.5	102.4	105.6	103.3						
98.9	99.7	100.4	103.2	100.6						
95.0	102.9	106.5	110.7	104.7						
102.5	101.3	102.2	102.3	98.4						
100.0	111.4	110.5	108.4	98.7						
101.0	100.7	102.5	105.7	101.3						
4144.0	**5521.9**	**6954.1**	**6995.4**	**7177.7**	**264.9**	**203.1**	**173.2**	**130.0**	**103.2**	**102.6**
32.9	23.3									
188.6	239.3	328.0	363.1	395.7	563.7	240.7	209.8	165.4	120.6	109.0
144.2	94.9	115.7	121.8	113.8	43.0	43.8	78.9	119.9	98.4	93.4
466.3	373.1	303.0	296.9	279.9	78.6	70.5	60.0	75.0	92.4	94.3
16.0	16.0	15.1	15.1	15.2	58.9	53.3	95.0	95.0	100.7	100.6
30.3	64.2	64.1	64.0	65.1	299.7	316.0	214.6	101.4	101.6	101.7
50.5	53.3	46.3	44.4	43.2	161.1	108.6	85.6	81.1	93.3	97.2

Note: a) Figures in value terms on GDP are at current prices, whereas growth rates are at comparable prices.Per Capita Gross Domestic Product from 2006 to 2010 were adjusted from population census in 2010.

b) Urban entities in and before 2007 meant corporate entities keeping separate accounts at and above the township level, excluding township enterprises, private entities and self-employed operators. Urban entities in and after 2008 meant corporate entities keeping separate accounts excluding private entities and self-employed operators.

c) From 2011, the starting point of fixed assets is changed from RMB 500,000 to RMB 5 million according to relevant regulations of National Bureau of Statistics.

1-9 续表 1

项 目		Item		1990	1995
工 业		**Industry**			
工业增加值(现价,规模以上)	(亿元)	Added Value of Industry(at Current Prices,Above Designated Size)	(100 million yuan)		473.1
工业总产值(现价,规模以上)	(亿元)	Gross Output Value of Industry(at Current Prices, Above Designated Size)	(100 million yuan)	625.9	1493.3
轻工业		Light Industry		262.2	472.2
重工业		Heavy Industry		363.7	1021.1
工业企业主要经济指标(规模以上)		Main Indicators of Industrial Enterprises (Above Designated Size)			
资产总计	(亿元)	Total Assets	(100 million yuan)	498.3	2582.6
负债总额	(亿元)	Total Liabilities	(100 million yuan)		1528.8
主营业务收入	(亿元)	Operating Income	(100 million yuan)	610.5	1590.4
利润总额	(亿元)	Total Profits	(100 million yuan)	48.9	85.3
建 筑		**Construction**			
建筑业施工企业总产值	(亿元)	Gross Output Value	(100 million yuan)	94.7	426.6
建筑业施工企业年末从业人员	(万人)	Year-end Employed Persons	(10000 persons)	60.2	82.6
运 输		**Transportation**			
货物周转量	(亿吨公里)	Freight Ton-Kilometers	(100 million ton-km)	268.8	323.1
铁 路		Railway		206.7	239.3
公 路		Highway		57.5	76.2
民 航		Civil Aviation		4.5	7.5
管 道		Pipeline		0.2	0.07
旅客周转量	(亿人公里)	Passenger-kilometers	(100 million passenger-km)	119.8	207.7
邮 电		**Post and Telecommunication**			
邮电业务总量	(亿元)	Business Volume of Posts and Telecommunication	(100 million yuan)	11.9	56.1
固定电话用户	(万户)	Fixed Telephone Subscribers	(10000 subscribers)	33.3	150.5
固定电话主线普及率	(线/百人)	Widespreading Rate of Main Line	(lines/100 persons)	3.1	12.0
移动电话用户	(万户)	Mobile Telephone Subscribers	(10000 subscribers)	0.3	16.9
移动电话普及率	(户/百人)	Widespreading Rate of Mobile Telephone	(sets/100 persons)	0.0	1.4
商 业		**Commerce**			
社会消费品零售总额	(亿元)	Total Retail Sales of Consumer Goods	(100 million yuan)	345.1	950.4
吃类商品		Food		136.8	405.7
穿类商品		Clothing		45.6	138.9
用类商品		Daily Use Articles		154.6	387.9
烧类商品		Fuels		8.1	17.9
对外经济贸易和旅游		**Foreign Economy,Trade and Tourism**			
北京地区进出口总值	(亿美元)	Total Value of Imports and Export at Customs	(USD 100 million)	236.4	370.4
进口值		Imports		192.3	267.9
出口值		Exports		44.1	102.5
实际利用外商直接投资额	(亿美元)	Foreign Capital Auctually Used	(USD 100 million)	2.8	14.0
接待入境旅游者人数	(万人次)	International Tourists	(10000 person.times)	100.0	207.0
旅游外汇收入	(亿美元)	Foreign Exchange Earning from International Tourism	(USD 100 million)	6.6	21.8
金融保险		**Banking and Insurance**			
金融机构(含外资)本外币存款余额	(亿元)	Adding Deposit of Financial Institutions (Include Foreign Currency and Foreign Capital)	(100 million yuan)		
金融机构(含外资)本外币贷款余额	(亿元)	Adding Loan of Financial Institutions (Include Foreign Currency and Foreign Capital)	(100 million yuan)		
原保险保费收入	(亿元)	Premiums Income	(100 million yuan)		

注：1. 工业增加值按生产法计算。

2. 邮电业务总量2000年及以前按1990年不变价格计算，2010年及以前按2000年不变价格计算,从2011年开始按2010年不变价计算。

1-9 continued 1

总量指标 Aggregate Data					速度指标(%) Indices (%)					
					指 数(2012年为以下各年) Index (2012 as Percentage of the Previous Years)					
2000	2005	2010	2011	2012	1990	1995	2000	2005	2010	2011
776.0	1627.0	2751.7	2899.1	3033.3						
2842.0	6946.2	13699.8	14513.6	15596.2	2491.8	1044.4	548.8	224.5	113.8	107.5
719.3	1164.9	2000.0	2227.2	2402.1	916.1	508.7	334.0	206.2	120.1	107.9
2122.7	5781.3	11699.8	12286.4	13194.1	3627.7	1292.1	621.6	228.2	112.8	107.4
4612.7	12829.8	22750.6	25321.7	28613.2	5742.2	1107.9	620.3	223.0	125.8	113.0
2676.4	4706.7	11548.1	12648.6	14837.2		970.5	554.4	315.2	128.5	117.3
2821.4	7279.1	14807.1	15753.4	16905.1	2769.3	1063.0	599.2	232.2	114.2	107.3
127.1	413.5	1028.3	1129.5	1267.9	2590.9	1486.5	997.6	306.6	123.3	112.3
812.5	1894.0	5196.0	6046.3	6588.3	6957.0	1544.4	810.9	347.9	126.8	109.0
56.6	67.2	59.9	49.6	49.2	81.7	59.6	86.9	73.2	82.1	99.2
299.6	457.7	513.7	616.9	638.3	237.4	197.6	213.0	139.4	124.3	103.5
200.2	310.8	257.5	311.3	307.6	148.8	128.5	153.7	99.0	119.5	98.8
82.6	85.5	101.6	132.3	139.8	243.2	183.4	169.1	163.5	137.6	105.6
16.8	28.2	48.2	47.5	49.0	1096.8	653.6	292.1	173.9	101.5	103.2
0.04	33.3	106.4	125.8	141.9				426.7	133.4	112.8
314.0	838.1	1399.5	1528.7	1595.8	1332.0	768.3	508.2	190.4	114.0	104.4
214.7	413.0	1108.9	487.9	546.5						112.0
451.2	943.5	885.6	883.9	883.1	2652.4	586.7	195.7	93.6	99.7	99.9
33.1	61.3	45.1	43.8	42.7						
347.2	1459.8	2129.8	2575.9	3168.0			912.4	217.0	148.7	123.0
25.5	94.9	108.6	127.6	153.1						
1658.7	2911.7	6229.3	6900.3	7702.8	2232.1	810.5	464.4	264.5	123.7	111.6
471.4	751.0	1331.0	1561.4	1679.1	1227.4	413.9	356.2	223.6	126.2	107.5
198.8	282.4	548.4	665.2	718.0	1574.7	517.0	361.2	254.3	130.9	107.9
932.0	1643.7	3884.0	4080.1	4678.4	3026.1	1206.1	502.0	284.6	120.5	114.7
56.5	234.6	465.9	593.6	627.3	7744.6	3504.6	1110.3	267.4	134.7	105.7
494.0	1255.1	3016.6	3895.8	4081.1	1726.0	1101.9	826.1	325.2	135.3	104.8
374.3	946.4	2462.2	3305.9	3484.8	1812.0	1301.0	931.0	368.2	141.5	105.4
119.7	308.7	554.4	590.0	596.3	1351.1	581.8	498.2	193.2	107.6	101.1
24.6	35.3	63.6	70.5	80.4	2903.6	573.3	327.2	228.0	126.4	114.0
282.1	362.9	490.1	520.4	500.9	500.9	242.0	177.6	138.0	102.2	96.2
27.7	36.2	50.4	54.2	51.5	783.6	236.0	186.0	142.2	102.1	95.1
11526.0	28969.9	66584.6	75001.9	84837.3			736.1	292.8	127.4	113.1
6407.9	15335.5	36479.6	39660.5	43189.5			674.0	281.6	118.4	108.9
93.4	498.2	966.5	820.9	923.1			987.9	185.3	95.5	112.4

Note: a) Added value of industry calculated by production approach.

b) Business volumes of post and telecommunications before and 2000 were calculated at 1990's constant price and those since 2000 were calculated at 2000's constant price,since 2011 were calculated at 2010's constant price.

1-9 续表 2

项目		Item		1990	1995
教育、文化、科技、卫生		Education, Culture, Science and Technology and Health Care			
教育		Education			
在校学生数	(万人)	Students Enrollment	(10000 persons)		238.0
专任教师数	(万人)	Full-time Teachers	(10000 persons)		17.7
文化		Culture			
公共图书馆总藏数	(万册、万件)	Collection of Public Libraries	(10000 volumes)	2205	2629
专业艺术剧团国内演出场次	(场)	Times of Domestic Performance of Art Troup	(times)	7527	6728
科技		Science and Technology			
研究与试验发展经费内部支出	(亿元)	Expenditures on Internal Research and Development	(100 million yuan)		
技术合同成交总额	(亿元)	Volume of Transaction in Technical Bargain	(100 million yuan)	20.3	41.2
专利授权量	(件)	Grants for Patents	(unit)	2268	4025
卫生		Health			
卫生机构个数	(个)	Health Care Institutions	(unit)	4953	4955
卫生机构病床数	(万张)	Health Care Institutions Beds	(10000 units)	5.9	6.7
卫生技术人员数	(万人)	Medical Technical Personnel	(10000 persons)	11.2	11.6
#执业医师		Certified Doctors		5.1	5.4
注册护师(士)		Registered Nurses		3.5	3.7
生活与环境		People's Living and Environment			
婚姻		Marriages and Divorces			
登记结婚对数	(万对)	Register Number of Marriages	(10000 couples)	9.30	8.55
离婚对数	(万对)	Number of Divorces	(10000 couples)	1.47	2.02
居住		Housing			
城镇居民人均住房建筑面积	(平方米)	Per Capita Living Space in Urban Residents	(sq.m)		
农村居民人均住房面积	(平方米)	Per Capita Living Space in Rural Residents	(sq.m)	20.62	24.74
生活		People's livelihood			
城镇居民人均可支配收入	(元)	Per Capita Annual Disposable Income of Urban Households	(yuan)	1787.1	5868.4
农村居民人均纯收入	(元)	Per Capita Net Income of Rural Residents	(yuan)	1297.1	3208.5
金融机构(含外资)储蓄存款余额	(亿元)	Deposit and Loan Balance of Financial Institutions	(100 million yuan)		
工资		Wages and Welfare			
城镇单位在岗职工工资总额	(亿元)	Total Wages	(100 million yuan)	118.9	382.0
城镇单位在岗职工平均工资	(元)	Average wage of Staff and Workers	(yuan)	2653	8144
市政建设		City Construction			
全社会用电量	(亿千瓦时)	Total Electricity Consumption in Beijing	(100 million kwh)	150.5	222.6
自来水销售总量	(亿立方米)	Sales of Tap Water	(100 million cu.m)	5.3	6.8
居民燃气用户	(万户)	Households of Access to Gas	(10000 households)	176.1	219.8
城市公共交通客运量	(亿人次)	Passengers Carried of City Public Transport	(100 million person-times)	33.5	37.2
环境		Environment			
城市绿化覆盖率	(%)	Coverage Rate of Urban Green Area	(%)	28.0	32.7
污水处理率	(%)	Dispose Rate of Sewage	(%)	7.3	19.4

注：1. 北京地区用电量来源于北京市电力公司，2000年以前工业用电量不包含输配损失和发电企业自产自用电量。
2. 从2001年开始，有关职工的指标调整为在岗职工的指标。2007年及以前城镇单位在岗职工工资包括乡及乡以上独立核算法人单位，不包括乡镇企业、私营单位和个体工商户；2008年及以后包括乡镇企业。
3. 离婚对数包括在民政部门登记的对数和经法院调离和判离的对数。
4. 2010年起，卫生机构中的卫生院数据并入到社区卫生服务中心(站)等其他卫生机构。2011年起,卫生机构中包括村卫生室。
5. 城镇居民人均住房建筑面积改为城镇住户抽样调查数据。

1-9 continued 2

总量指标 Aggregate Data					速度指标(%) Indices (%) 指 数(2012为以下各年) Index (2012 as Percentage of the Previous Years)					
2000	2005	2010	2011	2012	1990	1995	2000	2005	2010	2011
229.9	226.4	330.0	342.6	356.8		149.9	155.2	157.6	108.1	104.2
16.7	17.5	20.7	20.0	20.5		116.0	122.6	117.3	99.1	102.5
3020	3626	4613	5049	5556	251.9	211.3	184.0	153.2	120.4	110.0
7610	8934	10483	11069	11675	155.1	173.5	153.4	130.7	111.4	105.5
155.7	379.5	821.8	936.6	1063.4			683.0	280.2	129.4	113.5
140.3	434.4	1579.5	1890.3	2458.5	12128.8	5971.6	1752.4	566.0	155.7	130.1
5905	10100	33511	40888	50511	2227.1	1254.9	855.4	500.1	150.7	123.5
6176	4818	6539	9699	9974	201.4	201.3	161.5	207.0	152.5	102.8
7.1	7.9	9.3	9.5	10.0	169.7	149.7	140.6	126.7	107.9	105.7
11.6	12.0	17.1	18.2	22.0	196.9	189.5	190.2	183.3	128.4	120.8
5.2	5.1	6.6	7.0	8.2	161.4	151.9	159.4	162.4	124.6	117.8
4.0	4.3	6.7	7.3	9.5	275.4	259.3	238.6	221.9	141.4	130.8
8.02	9.66	13.81	17.32	17.41	187.2	203.6	217.1	180.2	126.1	100.5
2.66	3.42	4.40	4.35	4.86	329.4	240.9	182.5	141.8	110.5	111.6
	22.03	28.94	29.38	29.26				132.8	101.1	99.6
28.91	36.94	40.62	48.63	49.08	238.0	198.4	169.8	132.9	120.8	100.9
10350	17653	29073	32903	36469	2040.7	621.4	352.4	206.6	125.4	110.8
4687	7860	13262	14736	16476	1270.2	513.5	351.5	209.6	124.2	111.8
	8315.8	17585.2	19690.6	22298.6				268.1	126.8	113.2
695.5	1520.1	3789.1	4778.6	5657.9	4758.5	1481.1	813.5	372.2	149.3	118.4
15726	34191	65683	75834	85307	3215.5	1047.5	542.5	249.5	129.9	112.5
384.4	570.5	809.9	821.7	874.3	581.0	392.8	227.4	153.2	107.9	106.4
7.5	7.2	8.9	9.5	9.4	178.0	138.2	124.5	131.0	105.2	99.2
291.9	462.6	634.2	644.1	713.5	405.2	324.6	244.4	154.2	112.5	110.8
40.7	51.8	69.0	72.3	76.2	227.6	205.0	187.3	147.1	110.4	105.4
36.5	42.0	45.0	45.6	46.2						
39.4	62.4	81.0	81.7	83.0						

Note: a) Figures of electricity eonsumption are provided by Beijing Electric Power Corporation. Before 2000, electricity consumption by industry excluded transmission and distribution losses and electricity generated and consumed by power generating enterprises.

b) From 2001, indicators related to the "staff and workers " have been changed to those of "fully employed staff and workers". In and before 2007, figures of wages of urban fully employed staff and workers covered corporate entities keeping separate accounts at and above the township level, excluding township enterprises, private entities and self-employed operators; in and after 2008, such figures included township enterprises.

d) Registered divorces include those registered with civil affair authorities and those mediated and judged in courts.

e) From 2010, data on health centers were involved into other health institutions such as community health service centers (stations).From 2011, health care institutions include village health centers.

f) Figures of per-capita floor space of houses in urban areas are from spot check data of urban households.

1-10 主要年份国民经济和社会发展结构指标
STRUCTURAL INDICATORS ON NATIONAL ECONOMIC AND SOCIAL DEVELOPMENT IN MAIN YEAR

单位: % (%)

项 目	Item	1990	1995	2000	2005	2010	2011	2012
人口与就业	**Population and Employment**							
常住人口	**Population**							
按性别分	By Sex							
男	Male	50.2	50.1	52.1	50.6	51.6	51.6	51.6
女	Female	49.8	49.9	47.9	49.4	48.4	48.4	48.4
按城乡分	By Urban Area and Rural Area							
城 镇	Urban	73.5	75.6	77.5	83.6	86.0	86.2	86.2
乡 村	Rural	26.5	24.4	22.5	16.4	14.0	13.8	13.8
就 业	**Employment**							
从业人员年末人数	Year-end Employed Persons							
第一产业	Primary Industry	14.5	10.6	11.8	7.1	6.0	5.5	5.2
第二产业	Secondary Industry	44.9	40.7	33.6	26.3	19.6	20.5	19.2
第三产业	Tertiary Industry	40.6	48.7	54.6	66.6	74.4	74.0	75.6
宏观经济	**Macro Economy**							
国民经济核算	**National Accounting**							
地区生产总值	Gross Domestic Product							
第一产业	Primary Industry	8.8	4.9	2.5	1.3	0.9	0.8	0.8
第二产业	Secondary Industry	52.4	42.8	32.7	29.1	24.0	23.1	22.7
第三产业	Tertiary Industry	38.8	52.3	64.8	69.6	75.1	76.1	76.5
投 资	**Investment**							
全社会固定资产投资	Structure of Total Investment in Fixed Assets							
城 镇	Urban	88.2	94.4	91.9	91.8	91.1	92.4	90.6
农 村	Rural	9.7	4.8	6.5	8.2	8.9	7.6	9.4
资金来源结构	Structure of Funded Sources							
国家预算内资金	State Budgetary Appropriation	25.3	7.7	7.4	2.8	1.2	0.9	1.7
国内贷款	Domestic Loans	16.7	13.4	26.0	23.2	26.6	22.5	23.9
利用外资	Foreign Investment	11.2	20.5	3.6	1.6	0.5	0.4	0.3
债券、自筹和其他资金	Securities,Fundraising and Others Investment	46.8	58.4	63.0	72.4	71.6	76.2	74.1
财 政	**Government Finance**							
地方公共财政预算 收入主要税种	General Budgetary Financial Revenue Items							
#增值税	Value Added Tax			13.3	10.6	8.9	7.9	9.5
营业税	Business Tax			43.2	41.7	36.3	35.6	34.8
企业所得税	Enterprise Income Tax			16.8	17.9	21.8	22.7	22.7
个人所得税	Private Income Tax			16.3	9.2	9.1	9.1	8.5
能源消费总量	**Consumption of Energy**							
第一产业	Primary Industry	3.9	3.4	2.5	1.6	1.4	1.4	1.4
第二产业	Secondary Industry	63.5	65.9	58.5	49.0	39.2	35.6	33.8
第三产业	Tertiary Industry	19.0	17.9	26.1	34.8	41.7	44.3	45.3
生活消费	Living Consumption	13.6	12.8	12.9	14.7	17.7	18.7	19.5

注：2012年的从业人员年末人数和能源消费总量三次产业分组口径根据国家统计局规定进行了调整。

Note: The grouping standard of 2012 Year-end Employed Persons and Consumption of Energy by three industries was changed according to provisions of National Bureau of Statistics.

1-10 续表 1 continued

单位：% (%)

项 目	Item	1990	1995	2000	2005	2010	2011	2012
产 业	**Industry**							
农 业	**Agriculture**							
农林牧渔业产值结构	Structure of Gross Output Value of Agriculture							
农 业	Farming	55.6	52.8	46.7	38.0	47.0	45.0	42.0
林 业	Forestry	1.3	1.7	2.8	5.2	5.1	5.2	13.8
牧 业	Animal Husbandry	39.8	41.8	46.4	50.5	42.6	44.8	39.0
渔 业	Fishery	3.3	3.7	4.1	3.6	3.5	3.2	3.3
农林牧渔服务业	Services for Agriculture				2.7	1.8	1.8	1.9
工 业	**Industry**							
规模以上工业主要行业增加值结构	Structure of Added Value of Industry by Sector (Above Designated Size)							
#医药制造业	Manufacture of Medicines		1.6	3.6	3.0	5.6	6.4	7.3
黑色金属冶炼和压延加工业	Smelting and Pressing of Ferrous Metals		20.1	8.9	14.0	1.1	0.1	0.2
汽车制造业	Manufacture of Motor Vehicles		9.4	3.7	8.7	16.6	19.4	16.9
计算机、通信和其他电子设备制造业	Manufacture of Computers Communication Equipmentand Other Electronic Equipment		9.9	24.7	16.7	8.7	7.1	8.0
电力、热力的生产和供应业	Production and Supply of Electric Power Heat Power and Heat Power		7.0	6.4	11.8	14.9	15.5	17.7
建筑业	**Construction**							
建筑业总产值结构	Stucture of Gross Output Value of Construction Industry							
#国有企业	State-Owned	68.7	69.1	44.8	27.4	6.3	6.3	5.7
集体企业	Collective Owned	31.3	26.4	21.7	4.7	2.0	2.0	1.8
港澳台商投资企业	Hongkong, Macao and Taiwan		1.4	1.4	1.2	1.8	1.7	1.5
外商投资企业	Foreign Funded Enterprises		1.2	2.0	1.7	1.0	0.8	0.8
交通运输业	**Transportation**							
货运量结构(按运输方式分)	Structure of Freignt (By Means of Transportation)							
铁 路	Railways	11.4	9.2	8.5	6.1	6.6	5.1	4.3
公 路	Highways	87.5	90.4	91.2	92.4	85.1	86.7	87.0
民 航	Civil Aviation	0.04	0.05	0.1	0.2	0.5	0.5	0.5
管 道	Pipelines	1.0	0.3	0.2	1.2	7.7	7.7	8.2
客运量结构(按运输方式分)	Structure of Passenger (By Means of Transportation)							
铁 路	Railways	50.4	45.1	24.2	9.5	6.3	6.7	6.9
公 路	Highways	46.7	47.7	70.7	85.3	89.7	89.1	88.8
民 航	Civil Aviation	2.9	7.2	5.1	5.2	4.0	4.2	4.3
国内贸易	**Domestic Trade**							
社会消费品零售总额结构	Retail Sales of Consumer Goods							
吃类商品	Food	39.6	42.7	28.4	25.8	21.4	22.6	21.8
穿类商品	Clothing	13.2	14.6	12.0	9.7	8.8	9.6	9.3
用类商品	Daily Use Articles	44.8	40.8	56.2	56.5	62.4	59.1	60.7
烧类商品	Fuels	2.4	1.9	3.4	8.1	7.5	8.6	8.1
对外贸易	**Foreign Trade**							
地区出口商品结构	Local Exports Goods							
#一般贸易	General Trade		70.6	65.9	54.5	45.0	50.6	48.0
加工贸易	Process Trade		21.3	29.6	39.6	42.1	35.0	37.5
地区进口商品结构	Local Imports Goods							
#一般贸易	General Trade		84.4	87.3	85.2	88.7	90.0	89.4
加工贸易	Process Trade		5.2	3.5	8.2	5.9	4.5	4.8
国际旅游	**International Tourism**							
接待海外旅游人数结构	Number of Tourists from Abroad							
外国人	Foreigners	63.7	80.5	84.4	85.9	86.0	86.0	86.7
港澳台同胞	Compatriots from Hongkong, Macao and Taiwan	34.6	17.6	15.6	14.1	14.0	14.0	13.3

1-10 续表 2 continued

单位：% (%)

项 目	Item	1990	1995	2000	2005	2010	2011	2012
教育、科技、文化、卫生	**Education, Science, Culture, Health Care**							
教 育	**Education**							
在校学生结构	Structure of Student Enrollment							
#高等教育	Higher Education	8.3	9.0	14.0	46.2	49.5	50.0	49.8
中等教育	Secondary Education	32.5	41.0	48.7	29.7	22.1	20.8	20.5
小学教育	Primary School	59.0	49.6	36.8	16.9	19.8	19.9	20.1
专任教师结构	Full-time Teachers by Type							
#高等教育	Higher Education	24.6	22.7	22.2	32.7	35.9	31.5	31.3
中等教育	Secondary Education	38.3	38.6	40.5	33.6	29.1	33.0	32.5
小学教育	Primary School	36.7	37.9	36.8	25.3	23.9	22.9	22.8
科 技	**Science and Technology**							
研究与试验发展(R&D)人员折合全时当量结构	Structure of Full-time Personnel Equivalent R&D Personnel							
基础研究	Basic Research				12.9	15.2	14.6	14.7
应用研究	Applied Research				29.8	27.1	25.2	24.6
试验发展	Expenditure Development				57.3	57.7	60.2	60.8
研究与试验发展(R&D)经费内部支出结构	Structure of Intrnal Expenditures on Scientific Expenditure							
基础研究	Basic Research				10.1	11.6	11.6	11.8
应用研究	Applied Research				27.8	26.4	24.3	22.7
试验发展	Expenditure Development				53.1	62.0	64.1	65.4
卫 生	**Health Care**							
卫生技术人员结构	Doctors by Types							
#执业医师	Certified Doctors	45.6	46.7	44.6	42.2	38.5	38.3	37.4
注册护士	Registered Nurses	31.0	31.7	34.5	35.8	39.3	40.1	43.3
生活、环境	**People's Livelihood and Environment**							
生 活	**People's Livelihood**							
城镇居民消费结构	Consumption Structure of Urban Residents							
食品(恩格尔系数)	Food (Engel Coefficient)	54.2	48.5	36.3	31.8	32.1	31.4	31.3
衣 着	Clothing	14.8	15.1	8.9	8.9	10.4	10.3	11.0
居 住	Housing	3.5	4.5	6.9	7.9	7.9	8.8	8.2
家庭设备用品及服务	Household Appliances and Service	10.4	8.8	12.9	6.4	6.9	7.1	6.7
医疗保健	Health Care and Medical Services	1.4	2.9	6.9	9.8	6.7	6.9	6.9
交通和通信	Transport and Communications	1.5	4.7	7.1	14.7	17.2	16.0	15.7
教育文化娱乐服务	Education, Cultural and Recreation Services	11.5	10.2	15.1	16.5	14.6	15.0	15.4
其他商品和服务	Miscellaneous Goods and Services	2.7	5.2	5.8	4.0	4.2	4.4	4.8
农村居民消费结构	Consumption Structure of Rural Residents							
食品(恩格尔系数)	Food (Engel Coefficient)	50.7	49.6	36.7	32.8	30.9	32.4	33.2
衣 着	Clothing	9.5	10.9	7.6	7.8	7.7	7.8	8.0
居 住	Housing	19.2	9.7	15.7	16.2	21.8	21.2	18.5
家庭设备用品及服务	Household Appliances and Service	8.0	7.6	7.3	6.2	5.6	6.5	6.5
医疗保健	Health Care and Medical Services	3.8	4.8	8.0	9.0	8.9	9.3	9.5
交通和通信	Transport and Communications	1.7	4.1	6.3	11.0	13.1	11.1	11.8
文教娱乐用品及服务支出	Education, Cultural and Recreation Services	6.6	10.6	14.4	15.1	9.7	9.1	9.7
其他商品和服务	Miscellaneous Goods and Services	0.6	2.8	4.0	1.9	2.4	2.6	2.8
环 境	**Environment**							
林木绿化率	Coverage of City Forest	28.3	36.3	42.0	50.5	53.0	54.0	55.5

1-11 国民经济和社会发展比例和效益指标
INDICATORS ON PROPORTIONS AND EFFICIENCY IN NATIONAL ECONOMIC AND SOCIAL DEVELOPMENT

项 目		Item		2012	2011
人口与就业		**Population and Employment**			
人 口		**Population**			
常住人口出生率	(‰)	Birth Rate of Permanent Population	(‰)	9.05	8.29
常住人口死亡率	(‰)	Death Rate of Permanent Population	(‰)	4.31	4.27
常住人口自然增长率	(‰)	Natural Growth Rate of Permanent Population	(‰)	4.74	4.02
就 业		**Employment**			
城镇登记失业率	(%)	Unemployment Rate in Urban Areas	(%)	1.27	1.39
就业弹性系数		Elasticity Coefficient of Employment		0.45	0.46
宏观经济		**Macro Economy**			
国民经济核算		**National Accounting**			
地区生产总值构成	(%)	Gross Domestic Product	(%)	100.0	100.0
第一产业		Primary Industry		0.8	0.8
第二产业		Secondary Industry		22.7	23.1
第三产业		Tertiary Industry		76.5	76.1
全社会劳动生产率	(元/人)	Overall Labor Productivity	(yuan/person)	164257	154684
第一产业		Primary Industry		25808	22622
第二产业		Secondary Industry		188018	177886
第三产业		Tertiary Industry		167852	158613
固定资产投资		**Investment in Fixed Assets**			
全社会固定资产投资相当于地区生产总值比例	(%)	Proportion of Investment in Fixed Assets to GDP	(%)	36.1	36.4
财 政		**Finance**			
地方财政收入相当于地区生产总值比例	(%)	Proportion of Government Revenue to GDP	(%)	25.2	26.8
地方财政支出相当于地区生产总值比例	(%)	Proportion of Government Expenditures to GDP	(%)	26.9	28.2
能源消费		**Energy Consumption**			
能源消费弹性系数		Elasticity Ratio of Energy Consumption		0.34	0.07
电力消费弹性系数		Elasticity Coefficient of Electricity Consumption		0.88	0.34
万元地区生产总值能耗（可比价）	(吨标准煤)	Energy Consumption per 10000 yuan GDP (Fixed Price)	(ton of SCE)	0.436	0.458
万元地区生产总值水耗（现价）	(立方米)	Water Consumption per 10000 yuan GDP (Current Price)	(cu.m)	20.07	22.13
产 业		**Industry**			
规模以上工业企业效益		**Economic Efficiency of Industrial Enterprises Above Designated Size**			
综合效益指数	(%)	Aggregate Index of Industrial Economic Deficiency	(%)	253.53	250.11
总资产贡献率	(%)	Contribution Rate of Total Assets	(%)	7.98	8.06
资产保值增值率	(%)	Changing Rate of Net Assets	(%)	109.67	113.13

1-11 续表 continued

项目		Item		2012	2011
资产负债率	(%)	Asset-Liability Ratio	(%)	51.85	49.95
流动资产周转率	(次)	Turnover Rate of Current Assets	(times)	1.59	1.71
成本费用利润率	(%)	Ratio of Profits to Industrial Cost	(%)	7.91	7.60
全员劳动生产率	(元/人)	Overall Labor Productivity	(yuan/person)	252465	245951
产品销售率	(%)	Proportion of Products Sold	(%)	99.04	98.92
建筑业		**Construction**			
产值竣工率	(%)	Ratio of Output Value Completed to Total	(%)	49.8	43.6
面积竣工率	(%)	Ratio of Follr Space of Building Completed	(%)	20.2	17.7
邮电通信业		**Post and Communications**			
移动电话普及率	(户/百人)	Population Rate of Mobil Telephone	(sets/100 persons)	153.1	127.6
固定电话主线普及率	(线/百人)	Population Rate of Main Line	(line/100 persons)	42.7	43.8
国内贸易		**Domestic Trade**			
人均社会消费品零售总额	(元)	Per Capita Retail Sales of Consumer Goods	(yuan)	37686	34671
教育、科技、文化、卫生		**Education, Science and Technology, Culture and Health Care**			
教　育		**Education**			
学龄儿童入学率	(%)	Enrollment Rate of Children at School-Age Junior Secondary Schools	(%)	99.99	99.99
平均每一专任教师负担学生数		Average Number of Students Instructed by a Full-time Teacher			
高等学校	(人)	Instiutions of Higher Education	(person)	17.0	17.1
普通中学	(人)	Regular Secondary School	(person)	9.7	9.8
小学学校	(人)	Primary Schools	(person)	13.7	13.4
科　技		**Science and Technology**			
研究与试验发展经费内部支出相当于地区生产总值比例	(%)	R&D Expenditures as Percentage of GDP	(%)	5.95	5.76
文　化		**Culture**			
每万人拥有公共图书馆	(个)	Number of Public Libraries per Million Persor	(unit)	0.01	0.01
每万人拥有博物馆	(个)	Number of museums per Million Persons	(unit)	0.08	0.08
卫　生		**Health Care**			
婴儿死亡率	(‰)	Infant Mortality Rate	(‰)	2.87	2.84
孕产妇死亡率	(1/10万)	Maternal Mortality Rate	(1/100000)	6.05	9.09
平均每千人口拥有执业医师数(常住人口)	(人)	Certified Doctors per 1000 Persons (Registered Permanent Residence)	(person)	3.97	3.46
平均每千人口拥有医院床位数(常住人口)	(张)	Beds per 1000 Persons (Registered Permanent Residence)	(Nos.)	4.48	4.34
家庭、生活、环境、灾害		**Household, Living, Environment and Accident**			
家　庭		**Household**			
少儿抚养比(常住人口)	(%)	Children Support Coefficient (Total Populatior	(%)	11.55	11.11
老年抚养比(常住人口)	(%)	Elder Support Coefficient (Total Population)	(%)	11.31	10.99
生　活		**Living**			
城镇与农村居民收入比例(以农村居民收入为1)		Ratio of Urban and Rural Residents' Income (Rural Residents' Income = 1)		2.21	2.23
城镇居民人均住房建筑面积	(平方米)	Per Capita Using Space of Urban Residents	(sq.m)	29.26	29.38
农村居民人均住房面积	(平方米)	Per Capita Living Space in Rural Residents	(sq.m)	49.08	48.63
环境、灾害		**Environment and Accidents**			
人均公园绿地面积	(平方米)	Per Capita Park Green Areas	(sq.m)	15.50	15.30
平均每起火灾直接经济损失	(元)	Average Direct Pecuniary Losses per Fire Acci	(yuan)	8686	12450
平均每起交通事故直接经济损失	(元)	Average Direct Pecuniary Losses per Traffic A	(yuan)	9443	4949
食品安全监测抽查合格率(含烟酒等)	(%)	Food security monitor spot check up-to-standard rate (tobacco and wine included)	(%)	95.29	95.51
药品抽验合格率	(%)	Drug spot check up-to-standard rate	(%)	99.71	99.32

1-12 北京一日
A DAY IN BEIJING

项 目		Item		2012	2011
每天创造的财富		**Daily Production**			
地区生产总值	(万元)	Gross Domestic Product	(10000 yuan)	488508.2	445257.5
第一产业		Primary Industry		4103.8	3734.2
第二产业		Secondary Industry		110909.8	102808.2
工 业		Industry		90008.2	83528.8
建筑业		Construction		20901.6	19279.5
第三产业		Tertiary Industry		373494.5	338715.1
#交通运输、仓储和邮政业		Transportation, Storage Posts and Telecommunications		22303.3	22164.4
地方财政收入	(万元)	Local Financial Revenue	(10000 yuan)	123302.1	119427.4
地方财政支出	(万元)	Local Financial Expenditure	(10000 yuan)	131250.1	125340.8
发电量	(万千瓦时)	Electricity	(10000 kwh)	7945.9	7200.9
汽车生产量	(辆)	Output of Motor Vehicles	(unit)	4564	4123
移动电话机生产量	(台)	Output of Mobile Telephone	(unit)	545064	711296
每天收入与消费量		**Daily Income and Consumption**			
城镇居民人均可支配收入	(元)	Per Capita Disposable Income of Urban Residents	(yuan)	99.6	90.1
城镇居民人均消费性支出	(元)	Per Capita Living Expenditures of Urban Residents	(yuan)	65.7	60.2
农村居民人均纯收入	(元)	Per Capita Net Income of Rural Residents	(yuan)	45.1	40.4
农村居民人均生活消费支出	(元)	Per Capita Living Expenditures of Rural Residents	(yuan)	32.5	30.4
城镇单位在岗职工平均工资	(元)	Average Wage of Fully Employed Staff and Workers	(yuan)	233.1	207.8
社会消费品零售总额	(万元)	Retail Sales of Consumer Goods	(10000 yuan)	210459.5	189049.3
机动车销售量	(辆)	Sales of Motor Vehicles	(unit)	3511	2184
居民生活用电量	(万千瓦时)	For Living Use Electricity	(10000 kwh)	4421.7	3965.4
居民家庭用自来水	(万立方米)	For Living Use Tap Water	(10000 cu.m)	126.5	131.5
每天其他活动		**Other Daily Activities**			
地区出口值	(万美元)	Exports of Local Enterprises	(USD 10000)	16292.9	16163.8
旅游外汇收入	(万美元)	Foreign Exchange Earning from Tourism	(USD 10000)	1406.8	1483.8
国内旅游收入	(万元)	Domestic Tourism Earnings	(10000 yuan)	90199.5	78474.0
接待入境旅游人数	(人次)	International Tourists Arrival to Beijing	(person-time)	13686	14258
接待国内旅游者人数	(人次)	Domestic Tourists	(person-time)	618415	572164
市内公共交通客运量	(万人次)	Urban Passenger Traffic	(10000 person-times)	2080.8	1979.6
报刊、图书印数量	(万份、万册、万张)	Printed Copies of Newspaper, Magazines and Books	(10000 copies)	3342.8	3174.2
每天人口和婚姻变动		**Daily Population and Marriage Changes**			
出生人口(常住人口)	(人)	Birth Population (Registered Permanent Residence)	(person)	505	452
死亡人口(常住人口)	(人)	Death Population (Registered Permanent Residence)	(person)	241	233
登记结婚对数	(对)	Marriage Registered	(couple)	476	475
离婚对数	(对)	Registered Divorces	(couple)	133	119

注：离婚对数包括在民政部门登记的对数和经法院调离和判离的对数。
Note: Registered divorces include those registered with civil affair authorities and those mediated and judged in courts.

1-13 "十二五"时期经济社会发展主要监测指标
MAIN MONITORING INDICATORS OF SOCIAL AND ECONOMIC DEVELOPMENT IN THE 12TH FIVE-YEAR PLAN

项　　目	Item	2012	2011
地区生产总值比上年增长 (%)	Annual Growth Rate of GDP of Beijing (%)	7.7	8.1
第三产业占地区生产总值比重 (%)	Service as % of GDP of Beijing (%)	76.5	76.1
最终消费率 (%)	End Consumption Rate (%)	59.6	58.4
地方公共财政预算收入比上年增长 (%)	Annual Growth Rate of Local Government General Budgetary Financial Revenue (%)	10.3	27.7
城镇居民人均可支配收入实际增长 (%)	Annual Growth Rate of Per-capita Disposable Income of Urban Residents (%)	7.3	7.2
农村居民人均纯收入实际增长 (%)	Annual Growth Rate of Per-capita Disposable Income of Rural Residents (%)	8.2	7.6
城镇登记失业率 (%)	Urban Registered Unemployment Rate (%)	1.27	1.39
食品安全监测抽查合格率 (%)	Pass Rate of Spot Check for Key Food Safety Monitoring (%)	95.29	95.51
药品抽验合格率 (%)	Pass Rate of Drug Spot Check (%)	99.71	99.32
全社会研究与试验发展经费支出占地区生产总值的比例 (%)	R&D Expenditure as % of GDP (%)	5.95	5.76
万元地区生产总值能耗降低 (%)	Decrease of Energy Consumption per 10000 yuan GDP (%)	4.75	6.95
万元地区生产总值水耗降低 (%)	Decrease of Water Consumption per 10000 yuan GDP (%)	7.38	5.49
全市林木绿化率 (%)	Forest Coverage Rate in the City (%)	55.5	54.0

主要统计指标解释

法人单位 指有权拥有资产、承担负债，并独立从事社会经济活动（或与其他单位进行交易）的组织。法人单位应同时具备以下条件：（1）依法成立，有自己的名称、组织机构和场所，能够独立承担民事责任；（2）独立拥有（或授权使用）资产或者经费，承担负债，有权与其他单位签订合同；（3）具有包括资产负债表在内的账户，或者能够根据需要编制账户。

产业活动单位 指位于一个地点，从事一种或主要从事一种社会经济活动的组织或组织的一部分。产业活动单位应同时具备以下条件：（1）在一个场所从事一种或主要从事一种社会经济活动；（2）相对独立地组织生产活动或经营活动；（3）能提供收入、支出等相关资料。

单产业法人 指仅包含一个产业活动单位的法人单位，该法人单位同时也是一个产业活动单位。

多产业法人 指由两个及以上产业活动单位组成的法人单位，这些产业活动单位接受法人单位的管理和控制。

登记注册类型 企业法人或企业产业活动单位的登记注册类型，按其在工商行政管理机关登记注册的类型填写。如企业登记注册类型发生变化，但未及时到工商部门变更登记，企业应根据变化后的实际情况填写。其他法人和产业活动单位的登记注册类型，按其主要经费来源和管理方式，根据实际情况，比照《企业登记注册类型与代码》填写。

国有企业 指企业全部资产归国家所有，并按《中华人民共和国企业法人登记管理条例》规定登记注册的非公司制的经济组织。不包括有限责任公司中的国有独资公司。

集体企业 指企业资产归集体所有，并按《中华人民共和国企业法人登记管理条例》规定登记注册的经济组织。

股份合作企业 指以合作制为基础，由企业职工共同出资入股，吸收一定比例的社会资产投资组建，实行自主经营，自负盈亏，共同劳动，民主管理，按劳分配与按股分红相结合的一种集体经济组织。

联营企业 指两个及两个以上相同或不同所有制性质的企业法人或事业单位法人，按自愿、平等、互利的原则，共同投资组成的经济组织称为联营企业。联营企业包括国有联营企业、集体联营企业、国有与集体联营企业和其他联营企业。

有限责任公司 指根据《中华人民共和国公司登记管理条例》规定登记注册，由两个以上，五十个以下的股东共同出资，每个股东以其所认缴的出资额对公司承担有限责任，公司以其全部资产对其债务承担责任的经济组织。有限责任公司包括国有独资公司、其他有限责任公司。

私营企业 指由自然人投资设立或由自然人控股，以雇佣劳动为基础的营利性经济组织。包括按照《公司法》、《合伙企业法》、《私营企业暂行条例》、《个人独资企业法》规定登记注册的私营独资企业、私营合伙企业、私营有限责任公司、私营股份有限公司和个人独资企业。

其他企业 指上述类型之外的其他内资经济组织。

港澳台商投资企业 指港澳台地区投资者依照中华人民共和国有关涉外经济的法律、法规成立的企业，包括与港澳台商合资经营企业、与港澳台商合作经营企业、港澳台商独资经营企业、港澳台商投资股份有限公司、其他港澳台商投资企业。

外商投资企业 指外国企业或外国人依照中华人民共和国有关涉外经济的法律、法规成立的企业，包括中外合资经营企业、中外合作经营企业、外资企业、外商投资股份有限公司、其他外商投资企业。

就业弹性系数 是研究经济发展与就业增长数量关系的函数，是指劳动力就业的增长率与经济增长率之间的比率。其经济含义：经济每增长 1%，就业能增长多少个百分点。

非公经济 指资产由我国私人控股、港澳台商控股、外商控股的“非公有控股”的企业法人单位，以及主要经费来源于私人、港澳台资和外资的非企业法人单位和个体工商户。其中，私人、港澳台及外商控股是指由其绝对控股和相对控股的经济成分。

Explanatory Notes on Main Statistical Indicators

Corporate Unit refers to any organization having the right to own assets and bear liabilities, and conduct social and economic activities independently (or conduct transactions with other units). A corporate unit shall meet all of such conditions as: (1) established according to law, having its own name, organization and site, capable of assuming civil responsibilities independently; (2) independently owning and using (or using under authority) assets or outlays, assuming liabilities, having the right to signing contracts with other units; (3) maintaining accounts including balance sheet, or capable of preparing accounts as needed.

Industrial Activity Unit refer to any organization of part of an organization located at one site and conducting one or mainly conducting one social and economic activity. An industrial activity unit shall meet all of such conditions as: (1) conducting one or mainly conducting one economic activity at one site; (2) organizing production, operation or business activities in a relatively independent manner; (3) capable of providing relevant data such as income and payment.

Single-industry Corporate Unit refers any corporate unit including only one industrial activity. Such corporate unit is also an industrial activity unit.

Multi-industry Corporate Unit refers to any corporate unit composed of two or more industrial activity units which are managed and controlled by the corporate unit.

Type of Registration The type of registration of an enterprise as legal person or enterprise as industrial activity unit shall be completed according to the type registered in the administration for industry and commerce. In the event of any change in the type of registration, with no registration alteration made with administration for industry and commerce in good time, the type of registration shall be completed according to the facts changed. The type of registration for other legal persons and industrial activity units shall be completed according to the main source of outlays and management manner, pursuant to the actual conditions, and by referring to the Type of Enterprise Registration and Code.

State-owned Enterprises refer to non-corporation economic organizations where the entire assets are owned by the state and which have registered in accordance with the Regulation of the People's Republic of China on the Management of Registration of Corporate Enterprises, excluding sole state-funded corporations in the limited liability corporations.

Collective-owned Enterprises refer to economic organizations where the assets are owned collectively and which have registered in accordance with the Regulation of the People's Republic of China on the Management of Registration of Corporate Enterprises.

Joint-stock Cooperative Enterprises refer to a form of collective economic organizations based on cooperation system, where capitals come mainly from employees as their shares, with certain proportion of capital from the public, where production is organized on the basis of independent operation, independent accounting for profits and losses, joint work, democratic management, a distribution system that integrates distribution according to work with distribution according to capital share.

Jointly Operated Enterprises refer to economic organizations established by two or more corporate enterprises or corporate institutions of the same or different ownership, through joint investment on the basis of equality, voluntary participation and mutual benefits. They include state-owned jointly operated enterprises, collective-owned jointly operated enterprises, state-collective jointly operated enterprises and other jointly operated enterprises.

Limited Liability Corporations refer to economic organizations established with investment from 2-50 shareholders and registered in accordance with the Regulation of the People's Republic of China on the Management of Registration of Corporations, each shareholder bearing limited liability to the corporation depending on its share of investment, and the corporation bearing liability to its debt to the maximum of its total assets. Limited liability corporations include sole state-funded limited liability corporations and other limited liability corporations.

Private Enterprises refer to profit-making economic organizations established by natural persons or controlled by natural persons using employed labor. Private enterprises include private solely-funded enterprises, private partnership enterprises, private limited liability companies, private joint-stock companies limited, and private-funded enterprises registered in accordance with provisions in the Corporation Law, Partnership Enterprises Law, Interim Regulations on Private Enterprises and Sole Proprietorship Enterprise Law.

Other Enterprises refer to domestic-funded economic organizations other than those mentioned above.

Enterprises funded by Hong Kong, Macao and Taiwan Investors refer to enterprises established by investors from Hong Kong, Macao and Taiwan in accordance with laws and rules of the People's Republic of China on foreign-related economy. They include joint ventures with merchants from

Hong Kong, Macao and Taiwan, cooperative enterprises with merchants from Hong Kong, Macao and Taiwan, enterprises wholly funded by merchants from Hong Kong, Macao and Taiwan, joint-stock companies limited funded by merchants from Hong Kong, Macao and Taiwan, and other enterprise funded by merchants from Hong Kong, Macao and Taiwan.

Foreign-funded Enterprises refer to enterprises established by foreign enterprises or foreigners in accordance with laws and rules of the People's Republic of China on foreign-related economy. They include Sino-foreign joint ventures, Sino-foreign cooperative enterprises, foreign wholly-funded enterprises, foreign-funded joint-stock companies limited, and other foreign-funded enterprises.

Employment Elasticity Factor is a function for the research of the relationship between economic development and job increase. It refers to a ratio of labor employment growth rate to economic growth rate. Economically, it means: how many percentage points will be brought for the growth of jobs by every one percent of economic growth.

Non-public Economy means enterprises as corporate units whose shares are controlled by "non-public entities" and whose assets are controlled by individuals, investors from Hong Kong, Macao and Taiwan, and foreign investors, along with enterprises not as corporate units and self-employed operators whose main funds are from individuals, investors from Hong Kong, Macao and Taiwan, and foreign investors. Of which, enterprises controlled by individuals, investors from Hong Kong, Macao and Taiwan, and foreign investors mean economic sectors absolutely controlled or relatively controlled by such companies.

02

国民经济核算
NATIONAL ACCOUNTS

简要说明

一、本章资料的主要内容

本章主要包括历年北京市地区生产总值、部分新兴产业增加值、各行业增加值、居民消费水平、全社会劳动生产率、三次产业的贡献率、投入产出数据等资料。其中，地区生产总值是由北京市统计局根据不同产业部门、不同支出构成的特点和资料来源情况而采用不同方法核算。

二、本章中关于历史数据调整的问题

本章中 1997-2008 年地区生产总值的数据及其分组资料，按照国家统一规定，根据“北京市第二次全国经济普查”和“北京市第二次全国农业普查”的数据结果进行了修正。

三、关于按照新行业标准调整历史数据的问题

2002 年 10 月，国家统计局新修订的《国民经济行业分类》(GB/T 4754-2002) 经国家质量监督检验检疫总局批准正式实施。本章中凡涉及行业及三次产业分组的数据（含历史资料）均已按新行业标准做出调整。

本章中人均地区生产总值按年平均常住人口计算。同时，根据全国第六次人口普查数据对 2006-2010 年人均地区生产总值数据进行了修正。

Brief Introduction

I. Main Content

Statistics in this chapter include the GDP of Beijing, added value of some emerging sectors, added value of different sectors, residents' consumption level, total productivity, contribution rate of three industries in previous years, as well as the input and output data. Among them, the GDP of Beijing is calculated by Beijing Municipal Bureau of Statistics according to the characteristics and source of data in different sectors and different compositions of payment.

II. Adjustment to Historical Data

Data of GDP 1997-2008 and grouping data have been corrected in accordance with the national uniform regulation and the results of Beijing 2nd National Economic Census and Beijing National 2nd Agricultural Census.

III. Adjustment to Historical Data According to New Industrial Standards

In October 2010, the Classification of National Economic Sectors revised by the National Bureau of Statistics of PRC (GB/T 4754-2002) became formally authorized by the State Administration for Quality Supervision, Inspection and Quarantine. In this chapter, all data related to sectors and grouping of three industries (including historical data) have been adjusted according to the new industrial standards.

Per- capita Gross Domestic Product are calculated at the annual permanent population. And 2006-2010 per-capita GDP figures were adjusted according to data from the national 6th census.

2-1 地区生产总值(1978-2012年)
GROSS DOMESTIC PRODUCT (1978-2012)

单位：亿元 (100 million yuan)

年 份 Year	地区生产总值 Gross Domestic Product	第一产业 Primary Industry	第二产业 Secondary Industry	工业 Industry	建筑业 Construction	第三产业 Tertiary Industry	人均地区生产总值(元/人) Per Capita Gross Domestic Product (yuan/person)	人均地区生产总值(美元/人) Per Capita Gross Domestic Product (USD/person)
1978	108.8	5.6	77.4	70.2	7.2	25.8	1257	797
1979	120.1	5.2	85.2	77.4	7.8	29.7	1358	908
1980	139.1	6.1	95.8	86.9	8.9	37.2	1544	1009
1981-1985	**950.9**	**62.3**	**589.4**	**515.5**	**73.9**	**299.2**		
1981	139.2	6.6	92.5	82.7	9.8	40.1	1526	895
1982	154.9	10.3	99.8	89.3	10.5	44.8	1671	883
1983	183.1	12.8	112.7	98.8	13.9	57.6	1943	983
1984	216.6	14.8	130.7	114.0	16.7	71.1	2262	972
1985	257.1	17.8	153.7	130.7	23.0	85.6	2643	900
1986-1990	**1978.7**	**162.9**	**1084.3**	**917.3**	**167.0**	**731.5**		
1986	284.9	19.1	165.8	141.2	24.6	100.0	2836	821
1987	326.8	24.3	182.6	154.5	28.1	119.9	3150	846
1988	410.2	37.1	221.3	189.5	31.8	151.8	3892	1046
1989	456.0	38.5	252.2	212.8	39.4	165.3	4269	1134
1990	500.8	43.9	262.4	219.3	43.1	194.5	4635	969
1991-1995	**4847.2**	**289.6**	**2220.4**	**1833.5**	**386.9**	**2337.2**		
1991	598.9	45.8	291.5	255.6	35.9	261.6	5494	1032
1992	709.1	49.1	345.9	293.0	52.9	314.1	6458	1171
1993	886.2	53.7	419.6	339.2	80.4	412.9	8006	1389
1994	1145.3	67.5	517.6	417.9	99.7	560.2	10240	1188
1995	1507.7	73.5	645.8	527.8	118.0	788.4	12690	1520
1996-2000	**12084.0**	**387.8**	**4277.7**	**3450.5**	**827.2**	**7418.5**		
1996	1789.2	75.0	714.7	576.2	138.5	999.5	14254	1714
1997	2077.1	77.2	781.8	635.9	145.9	1218.1	16621	2005
1998	2377.2	77.9	840.6	670.4	170.2	1458.7	19128	2310
1999	2678.8	78.4	907.3	724.0	183.3	1693.1	21407	2586
2000	3161.7	79.3	1033.3	844.0	189.3	2049.1	24127	2915
2001-2005	**26032.9**	**423.4**	**7759.7**	**6446.2**	**1313.5**	**17849.8**		
2001	3708.0	80.8	1142.4	938.8	203.6	2484.8	26980	3260
2002	4315.0	82.4	1250.0	1021.2	228.8	2982.6	30730	3713
2003	5007.2	84.1	1487.2	1224.5	262.7	3435.9	34777	4202
2004	6033.2	87.4	1853.6	1554.7	298.9	4092.2	40916	4943
2005	6969.5	88.7	2026.5	1707.0	319.5	4854.3	45993	5615
2006-2010	**55346.2**	**545.6**	**13571.1**	**11103.4**	**2467.7**	**41229.5**		
2006	8117.8	88.8	2191.4	1821.8	369.6	5837.6	51722	6488
2007	9846.8	101.3	2509.4	2082.8	426.6	7236.1	60096	7903
2008	11115.0	112.8	2626.4	2131.7	494.7	8375.8	64491	9286
2009	12153.0	118.3	2855.5	2303.1	552.4	9179.2	66940	9799
2010	14113.6	124.4	3388.4	2764.0	624.4	10600.8	73856	10910
2011	16251.9	136.3	3752.5	3048.8	703.7	12363.1	81658	12643
2012	17879.4	150.2	4059.3	3294.3	765.0	13669.9	87475	13857

注：1．本表按当年价格计算。
2．本表中地区生产总值三次产业数据按国家2002年版国民经济行业分类标准核算。
3．根据全国第二次农业普查和全国第二次经济普查结果对1997-2008年数据进行了修订(下同)。
4．人均地区生产总值按年平均常住人口计算。同时，根据全国第六次人口普查数据对2006年至2010年人均地区生产总值进行了调整(下同)。

Note: a) Data in this table are calculated at current prices.
b) Figures in this table on three industries in GDP were calculated with the national classification standard of nationaleconomy sectors 2002 edition.
c) Figures for 1997-2008 were revised according to results from the National 2nd Agricultural Census and National 2nd Economic Census (the same below).
d) Per Capita Gross Domestic Product are calculated at the annual permanent population of Beijing.And Per Capita Gross Domestic Productare from 2006 to 2010 are revised according to the resullts of the Sixth National Population Census,Beijing (the same below).

2-2 地区生产总值指数(上年=100)(1978-2012年)
INDICES OF GROSS DOMESTIC PRODUCT (PRECEDING YEAR=100) (1978-2012)

单位：% (%)

年份 Year	地区生产总值 Gross Domestic Product	第一产业 Primary Industry	第二产业 Secondary Industry	工业 Industry	建筑业 Construction	第三产业 Tertiary Industry	人均地区生产总值 Per Capita Gross Domestic Product
1978	110.5	109.0	115.1	112.4	153.0	97.7	109.1
1979	109.7	105.0	109.2	110.1	108.4	113.2	107.4
1980	111.8	109.3	110.1	110.1	110.3	118.5	109.8
1981	99.5	109.1	96.3	95.3	106.4	106.0	98.3
1982	107.4	113.4	105.8	105.8	106.1	109.9	105.6
1983	116.4	107.5	113.6	111.5	132.3	124.2	114.5
1984	117.4	106.8	116.1	115.7	118.8	121.8	115.6
1985	108.7	106.3	111.0	109.1	124.7	104.4	106.9
1986	108.0	100.1	104.8	105.0	103.7	115.7	104.6
1987	109.6	113.4	105.6	105.5	106.3	116.7	106.1
1988	112.8	111.2	112.1	113.0	106.5	114.1	111.0
1989	104.4	101.1	108.9	108.4	112.2	97.3	103.1
1990	105.2	103.3	101.1	101.9	95.6	113.3	104.0
1991	109.9	103.7	107.5	112.6	81.6	114.5	108.9
1992	111.3	103.1	112.2	110.3	125.7	111.9	110.5
1993	112.3	103.2	113.0	110.5	128.5	113.1	111.4
1994	113.7	102.8	114.1	113.5	117.0	115.0	112.5
1995	112.0	92.0	107.7	107.7	107.6	120.5	105.4
1996	109.0	97.2	106.2	106.1	107.0	113.4	103.1
1997	110.1	102.9	108.1	108.7	105.1	113.2	110.6
1998	109.5	101.1	109.6	108.7	114.2	110.1	110.1
1999	110.9	102.8	112.0	112.8	108.0	110.6	110.1
2000	111.8	103.1	111.4	113.2	102.1	112.9	106.8
2001	111.7	103.7	109.5	110.2	106.6	113.1	106.5
2002	111.5	102.7	108.4	107.8	110.9	113.3	109.1
2003	111.1	98.9	112.0	112.2	110.7	111.2	108.3
2004	114.1	99.4	117.0	119.3	106.3	113.1	111.4
2005	112.1	98.1	110.1	110.9	106.3	113.4	109.1
2006	113.0	100.6	110.5	109.5	116.0	114.3	109.1
2007	114.5	102.2	112.7	113.1	110.9	115.4	109.7
2008	109.1	101.1	100.8	100.2	103.7	112.5	103.7
2009	110.2	104.6	110.4	108.8	118.5	110.2	104.6
2010	110.3	98.4	113.7	114.9	108.3	109.3	104.8
2011	108.1	100.9	106.7	107.5	102.9	108.7	103.8
2012	107.7	103.2	107.5	107.0	109.7	107.9	104.9

注：本表按可比价格计算。

Note: Data in this table are calculated at comparable prices.

2-3 地区生产总值指数(1978年=100)(1978-2012年)
INDEX OF GROSS DOMESTIC PRODUCT (YEAR OF 1978=100) (1978-2012)

单位：% (%)

年份 Year	地区生产总值 Gross Domestic Product	第一产业 Primary Industry	第二产业 Secondary Industry	工业 Industry	建筑业 Construction	第三产业 Tertiary Industry	人均地区生产总值 Per Capita Gross Domestic Product
1978	100.0	100.0	100.0	100.0	100.0	100.0	100.0
1979	109.7	105.0	109.2	110.1	108.4	113.2	107.4
1980	122.6	114.8	120.2	121.2	119.6	134.1	117.9
1981	122.0	125.2	115.8	115.5	127.2	142.2	115.9
1982	131.1	142.0	122.5	122.2	135.0	156.3	122.4
1983	152.6	152.6	139.2	136.3	178.6	194.1	140.2
1984	179.1	163.0	161.6	157.7	212.1	236.4	162.0
1985	194.7	173.3	179.3	172.0	264.5	246.8	173.2
1986	210.3	173.5	187.9	180.6	274.3	285.5	181.2
1987	230.4	196.7	198.5	190.6	291.6	333.2	192.2
1988	259.9	218.7	222.5	215.3	310.6	380.2	213.4
1989	271.4	221.1	242.3	233.4	348.5	369.9	220.0
1990	285.5	228.4	244.9	237.9	333.1	419.2	228.8
1991	313.8	236.9	263.3	267.8	271.8	479.9	249.1
1992	349.2	244.2	295.4	295.4	341.7	537.0	275.3
1993	392.2	252.0	333.8	326.4	439.1	607.4	306.7
1994	445.9	259.1	380.9	370.5	513.7	698.5	345.0
1995	499.4	238.4	410.2	399.0	552.8	841.7	363.7
1996	544.3	231.7	435.7	423.4	591.5	954.5	374.9
1997	599.3	238.4	471.0	460.2	621.7	1080.5	414.6
1998	656.2	241.0	516.2	500.2	710.0	1189.6	456.5
1999	727.7	247.7	578.1	564.2	766.8	1315.7	502.8
2000	813.6	255.4	644.0	638.7	782.9	1485.4	536.8
2001	908.8	264.8	705.2	703.8	834.6	1680.0	571.7
2002	1013.3	271.9	764.4	758.7	925.6	1903.4	623.9
2003	1125.8	268.9	856.1	851.3	1024.6	2115.9	676.0
2004	1284.5	267.3	1001.6	1015.6	1089.1	2393.1	753.1
2005	1440.3	262.2	1102.8	1126.3	1157.7	2714.9	821.5
2006	1627.5	263.8	1218.6	1233.3	1342.9	3102.0	896.3
2007	1863.3	269.6	1373.4	1394.9	1489.3	3580.0	983.2
2008	2033.0	272.6	1384.4	1397.7	1544.4	4027.6	1019.6
2009	2240.4	285.2	1528.7	1520.8	1829.4	4437.6	1066.5
2010	2471.2	280.6	1738.1	1747.4	1981.2	4850.3	1117.7
2011	2671.4	283.1	1854.6	1878.5	2038.7	5272.3	1160.2
2012	2877.1	292.2	1993.7	2010.0	2236.5	5688.8	1217.0

注：本表按可比价格计算。
Note: Data in this table are calculated at comparable prices.

2-4 地区生产总值构成(1978-2012年)
COMPOSITION OF GROSS DOMESTIC PRODUCT (1978-2012)

单位: % (%)

年份 Year	地区生产总值 Gross Domestic Product	第一产业 Primary Industry	第二产业 Secondary Industry	工业 Industry	建筑业 Construction	第三产业 Tertiary Industry
1978	100.0	5.2	71.1	64.5	6.6	23.7
1979	100.0	4.3	70.9	64.4	6.5	24.8
1980	100.0	4.4	68.9	62.5	6.4	26.7
1981	100.0	4.7	66.5	59.4	7.1	28.8
1982	100.0	6.7	64.4	57.6	6.8	28.9
1983	100.0	7.0	61.5	53.9	7.6	31.5
1984	100.0	6.9	60.3	52.6	7.7	32.8
1985	100.0	6.9	59.8	50.8	9.0	33.3
1986	100.0	6.7	58.2	49.6	8.6	35.1
1987	100.0	7.4	55.9	47.3	8.6	36.7
1988	100.0	9.0	54.0	46.2	7.8	37.0
1989	100.0	8.5	55.3	46.7	8.6	36.2
1990	100.0	8.8	52.4	43.8	8.6	38.8
1991	100.0	7.6	48.7	42.7	6.0	43.7
1992	100.0	6.9	48.8	41.3	7.5	44.3
1993	100.0	6.1	47.3	38.3	9.0	46.6
1994	100.0	5.9	45.2	36.5	8.7	48.9
1995	100.0	4.9	42.8	35.0	7.8	52.3
1996	100.0	4.2	39.9	32.2	7.7	55.9
1997	100.0	3.7	37.6	30.6	7.0	58.7
1998	100.0	3.3	35.4	28.2	7.2	61.3
1999	100.0	2.9	33.9	27.0	6.9	63.2
2000	100.0	2.5	32.7	26.7	6.0	64.8
2001	100.0	2.2	30.8	25.3	5.5	67.0
2002	100.0	1.9	29.0	23.7	5.3	69.1
2003	100.0	1.7	29.7	24.5	5.2	68.6
2004	100.0	1.4	30.8	25.8	5.0	67.8
2005	100.0	1.3	29.1	24.5	4.6	69.6
2006	100.0	1.1	27.0	22.4	4.6	71.9
2007	100.0	1.0	25.5	21.2	4.3	73.5
2008	100.0	1.0	23.6	19.2	4.4	75.4
2009	100.0	1.0	23.5	19.0	4.5	75.5
2010	100.0	0.9	24.0	19.6	4.4	75.1
2011	100.0	0.8	23.1	18.8	4.3	76.1
2012	100.0	0.8	22.7	18.4	4.3	76.5

2-5 地区生产总值指数(2000年=100)(2000-2012年)
INDEX OF GROSS DOMESTIC PRODUCT (YEAR OF 2000=100) (2000-2012)

单位：% (%)

年份 Year	地区生产总值 Gross Domestic Product	第一产业 Primary Industry	第二产业 Secondary Industry	工业 Industry	建筑业 Construction	第三产业 Tertiary Industry	人均地区生产总值 Per Capita Gross Domestic Product
2000	100.0	100.0	100.0	100.0	100.0	100.0	100.0
2001	111.7	103.7	109.5	110.2	106.6	113.1	106.5
2002	124.5	106.5	118.7	118.8	118.2	128.1	116.2
2003	138.3	105.3	132.9	133.3	130.8	142.4	125.9
2004	157.8	104.7	155.5	159.0	139.0	161.1	140.3
2005	176.9	102.7	171.2	176.3	147.8	182.8	153.0
2006	199.9	103.3	189.2	193.0	171.4	208.9	166.9
2007	228.9	105.6	213.2	218.3	190.1	241.1	183.1
2008	249.8	106.8	214.9	218.7	197.1	271.2	189.9
2009	275.3	111.7	237.3	238.0	233.5	298.8	198.6
2010	303.7	109.9	269.8	273.5	252.9	326.6	208.1
2011	328.3	110.9	287.9	294.0	260.2	355.0	216.0
2012	353.6	114.4	309.5	314.6	285.4	383.0	226.6

注：本表按可比价格计算。

Note: Data in this table are calculated at comparable prices.

2-6 按行业分地区生产总值(2000-2012年)

单位：亿元

项　目	Item	2000	2001
地区生产总值	**Gross Domestic Product**	**3161.7**	**3708.0**
第一产业	**Primary Industry**	**79.3**	**80.8**
第二产业	**Secondary Industry**	**1033.3**	**1142.4**
工　业	Industry	844.0	938.8
建筑业	Construction	189.3	203.6
第三产业	**Tertiary Industry**	**2049.1**	**2484.8**
交通运输、仓储和邮政业	Transportation, Storage, Posts and Telecommunications	220.6	254.2
信息传输、计算机服务和软件业	Information Transmission, Computer Servecis and Software	164.4	210.1
批发与零售业	Wholesale Trade and Retail Trade	372.5	424.1
住宿和餐饮业	Accommodation and Catering	81.2	97.2
金融业	Finance	425.2	487.5
房地产业	Real Estate	144.0	203.6
租赁和商务服务业	Tenancy and Commercial Servecis	118.8	137.0
科学研究、技术服务与地质勘查业	Scientific Studies, Technical Services and Geological Prospecting	123.0	178.7
水利、环境和公共设施管理业	Water, Environment and Municipal Engineering Conservancy	23.4	25.2
居民服务和其他服务业	Resident Services and Other Services	36.2	42.2
教　育	Education	102.3	148.8
卫生、社会保障和社会福利业	Health Care, Social Security and Social Welfare	55.3	67.7
文化、体育与娱乐业	Culture, Art, Sports and Recreation	84.5	96.9
公共管理与社会组织	Public Manage and Social Organization	97.7	111.6

注：本表按当年价格计算；行业按国家2002年版国民经济行业分类标准核算。

2-7 按行业分地区生产总值指数(上年=100)(2000-2012年)

单位：%

项　目	Item	2000	2001
地区生产总值	**Gross Domestic Product**	**111.8**	**111.7**
第一产业	**Primary Industry**	**103.1**	**103.7**
第二产业	**Secondary Industry**	**111.4**	**109.5**
工　业	Industry	113.2	110.2
建筑业	Construction	102.1	106.6
第三产业	**Tertiary Industry**	**112.9**	**113.1**
交通运输、仓储和邮政业	Transportation, Storage, Posts and Telecommunications		103.8
信息传输、计算机服务和软件业	Information Transmission, Computer Servecis and Software		112.3
批发与零售业	Wholesale Trade and Retail Trade		112.4
住宿和餐饮业	Accommodation and Catering		109.0
金融业	Finance		113.1
房地产业	Real Estate		131.1
租赁和商务服务业	Tenancy and Commercial Servecis		104.5
科学研究、技术服务与地质勘查业	Scientific Studies, Technical Services and Geological Prospecting		130.1
水利、环境和公共设施管理业	Water, Environment and Municipal Engineering Conservancy		94.8
居民服务和其他服务业	Resident Services and Other Services		102.9
教　育	Education		125.0
卫生、社会保障和社会福利业	Health Care,Social Security and Social Welfare		115.6
文化、体育与娱乐业	Culture, Art, Sports and Recreation		104.3
公共管理与社会组织	Public Manage and Social Organization		105.3

注：本表按可比价格计算；行业按国家2002年版国民经济行业分类标准核算。

GROSS DOMESTIC PRODUCT BY SECTOR (2000-2012)

(100 million yuan)

2002	2003	2004	2005	2006	2007	2008	2009	2010	2011	2012
4315.0	**5007.2**	**6033.2**	**6969.5**	**8117.8**	**9846.8**	**11115.0**	**12153.0**	**14113.6**	**16251.9**	**17879.4**
82.4	**84.1**	**87.4**	**88.7**	**88.8**	**101.3**	**112.8**	**118.3**	**124.4**	**136.3**	**150.2**
1250.0	**1487.2**	**1853.6**	**2026.5**	**2191.4**	**2509.4**	**2626.4**	**2855.5**	**3388.4**	**3752.5**	**4059.3**
1021.2	1224.5	1554.7	1707	1821.8	2082.8	2131.7	2303.1	2764.0	3048.8	3294.3
228.8	262.7	298.9	319.5	369.6	426.6	494.7	552.4	624.4	703.7	765.0
2982.6	**3435.9**	**4092.2**	**4854.3**	**5837.6**	**7236.1**	**8375.8**	**9179.2**	**10600.8**	**12363.1**	**13669.9**
281.1	309.0	356.8	403.3	455.2	497.5	498.9	556.6	712.0	809.0	816.3
278.6	378.0	449.6	586.6	696.4	870.5	999.1	1066.5	1214.1	1493.4	1621.8
463.0	515.5	587.7	704.3	872.0	1098.2	1426.7	1525.0	1888.5	2139.7	2229.8
122.0	112.6	163.3	182.3	218.4	245.0	274.4	262.5	317.3	348.4	373.1
561.9	635.6	713.8	840.2	982.4	1302.8	1519.2	1603.6	1863.6	2215.4	2536.9
298.0	341.9	436.1	493.7	658.3	821.5	844.6	1062.5	1006.5	1074.9	1244.2
214.2	231.6	276.6	360.7	447.1	623.6	765.3	809.6	953.2	1162.1	1340.6
209.2	246.2	276.5	347.4	438.6	566.2	706.7	816.9	941.1	1135.5	1268.4
27.3	30.5	34.6	40.5	47.0	51.8	59.1	67.2	75.3	86.3	101.3
54.7	64.1	79.6	80.2	85.3	82.1	74.9	73.9	99.3	112.1	124.3
159.6	206.2	267.4	289.4	320.6	365.2	402.1	444.1	516.2	605.9	681.8
73.7	87.2	105.9	118.2	140.3	162.6	187.8	213.0	254.5	311.5	363.6
111.6	125.0	142.7	170.2	189.0	223.1	247.4	259.0	294.6	339.4	402.6
127.7	152.5	201.6	237.3	287.0	326.0	369.6	418.8	464.6	529.5	565.2

Note: Data in this table are calculated at current prices.This table follows the classification standard of national economy sectors 2002 edition.

GROSS DOMESTIC PRODUCT BY SECTOR (PRECEDING YEAR=100) (2000-2012)

(%)

2002	2003	2004	2005	2006	2007	2008	2009	2010	2011	2012
111.5	**111.1**	**114.1**	**112.1**	**113.0**	**114.5**	**109.1**	**110.2**	**110.3**	**108.1**	**107.7**
102.7	**98.9**	**99.4**	**98.1**	**100.6**	**102.2**	**101.1**	**104.6**	**98.4**	**100.9**	**103.2**
108.4	**112.0**	**117.0**	**110.1**	**110.5**	**112.7**	**100.8**	**110.4**	**113.7**	**106.7**	**107.5**
107.8	112.2	119.3	110.9	109.5	113.1	100.2	108.8	114.9	107.5	107.0
110.9	110.7	106.3	106.3	116.0	110.9	103.7	118.5	108.3	102.9	109.7
113.3	**111.2**	**113.1**	**113.4**	**114.3**	**115.4**	**112.5**	**110.2**	**109.3**	**108.7**	**107.9**
104.1	104.0	108.7	105.9	107.6	108.0	104.1	103.0	111.7	106.2	106.9
119.2	126.3	111.2	121.2	113.1	116.8	114.9	106.8	110.6	122.9	106.8
109.1	111.2	112.0	117.7	118.3	122.3	124.9	109.3	120.9	108.9	104.0
117.2	90.7	136.6	106.9	115.5	107.6	98.0	96.7	115.2	102.3	99.7
112.4	110.6	107.1	113.2	111.4	121.4	107.8	106.4	108.6	107.6	112.7
130.4	110.8	119.2	108.3	121.9	105.2	94.8	122.0	85.8	93.2	113.7
132.2	103.2	110.1	121.6	117.3	123.8	123.3	111.6	110.0	118.3	109.5
111.5	112.4	108.9	117.4	119.4	121.1	125.6	121.9	107.9	110.4	107.1
102.0	103.8	104.7	113.0	110.3	104.3	114.5	119.9	104.7	105.5	106.7
111.8	108.6	115.0	97.4	100.6	91.9	91.7	104.1	125.5	112.3	104.2
108.8	129.0	125.2	106.3	107.4	111.2	110.5	109.0	108.5	103.6	105.2
106.4	112.1	116.7	111.2	113.1	108.7	113.9	113.6	111.6	107.9	108.4
107.7	106.7	108.6	115.4	107.8	109.7	113.6	107.3	106.2	106.1	109.5
108.1	112.4	125.0	113.6	116.6	109.6	108.3	110.9	105.3	102.1	103.4

Note: Growth rates in this table are at comparable prices. This table follows the classification standard of national economy sectors 2002 edition.

2-8 部分新兴产业增加值(2004-2012年)
ADDED VALUE OF CULTURAL AND CREATIVE INDUSTRY AND OTHER INDUSTRY (2004-2012)

单位：亿元 (100 million yuan)

项　　目	Item	2004	2005	2006	2007	2008
地区生产总值	**Gross Domestic Product**	**6033.2**	**6969.5**	**8117.8**	**9846.8**	**11115.0**
文化创意产业	**Cultural and Creative Industry**	**573.0**	**674.1**	**823.2**	**1008.3**	**1346.4**
文化艺术	Cultural & Artistic	22.6	32.2	35.3	38.8	42.7
新闻出版	Journalism and Publication	108.1	106.8	135.3	142.2	153.7
广播、电视、电影	Broadcast, TV & Film	54.9	78.0	73.5	102.7	120.1
软件、网络及计算机服务	Software, Network, & Computer Service	229.2	266.6	375.5	483.4	703.1
广告会展	Advertisements & Exhibitions	47.8	51.0	52.2	64.9	112.2
艺术品交易	Transaction of Artwork	11.5	7.1	10.1	13.8	20.5
设计服务	Design Service	29.9	31.6	40.2	49.2	52.8
旅游、休闲娱乐	Touring, Relaxation & Recreation	27.0	37.6	48.4	50.2	58.4
其他辅助服务	Other Auxiliary Service	42.0	63.2	52.7	63.1	82.9
信息产业	**Information Industry**	**867.3**	**1152.7**	**1344.5**	**1668.3**	**1759.8**
电子信息设备制造	Electronic Information Equipment Manufacturing	216.6	303.5	343.5	391.6	331.5
电子信息设备销售和租赁	Electronic Information Equipment Sale and Lease	87.7	127.7	157.2	229.7	233.1
电子信息传输服务	Electronic Information Transmission Service	285.7	355.6	381.7	462.8	382.6
计算机服务和软件业	Computer Service and Software	163.9	231.0	314.7	407.8	616.5
其他信息相关服务	Other Information-related Service	113.4	134.9	147.4	176.4	196.1
高技术产业	**High-tech Industry**	**370.6**	**504.4**	**606.4**	**729.6**	**852.3**
核燃料加工	Nuclear Fuel Processing	0.2	0.2		-0.4	
信息化学品制造	Information Chemicals Manufacturing	1.5	1.1	1.7	1.7	2.7
医药制造业	Pharmaceutics	46.2	49.7	56.4	78.1	114.4
航空航天器制造	Aircraft Manufacturing	16.8	17.7	23.8	25.2	27.0
电子及通信设备制造业	Electronic & Communication Equipment Manufacturing	144.3	214.8	248.3	265.9	234.1
电子计算机及办公设备制造业	Electronic Computer & Office Equipment Manufacturing	48.4	65.3	63.6	88.2	64.8
医疗设备及仪器仪表制造业	Medical Equipment, Device & Instrument Manufacturing	53.3	52.0	73.5	82.7	86.6
公共软件服务	Public Software Service	59.9	103.6	139.1	188.2	322.7
现代制造业	**Modern Manufacturing**		**602.7**	**679.7**	**779.3**	**836.2**
电子类	Electronics		260.5	289.1	323.0	268.8
机电类	Electromechanical		132.6	154.2	169.6	212.0
交通类	Communications		130.0	142.7	178.3	206.5
医药类	Pharmaceutical		55.0	66.1	84.6	124.1
其他类	Other		24.6	27.6	23.8	24.8
现代服务业	**Modern Service Industry**	**2669.6**	**3206.8**	**3870.0**	**4933.1**	**5660.0**
信息传输、计算机服务和软件业	Information Transmission, Computer Service and Software	449.6	586.6	696.4	870.5	999.1
金融业	Finance	713.8	840.2	982.4	1302.8	1519.2
科学研究、技术服务和地质勘查业	Scientific Research, Technical Service and Geological Prospecting	276.5	347.4	438.6	566.2	706.7
卫生和社会保障业	Health and Social Security	100.7	112.9	133.8	155.1	171.2
文化、体育和娱乐业	Culture, Sports and Entertainment	142.7	170.2	189.0	223.1	247.4
房地产业	Real Estate	436.1	493.7	658.3	821.5	844.6
商务服务业	Commercial Service	268.7	350.4	434.1	608.8	748.7
环境管理业	Environmental Management	14.1	16.0	16.8	19.9	21.0
教　育	Education	267.4	289.4	320.6	365.2	402.1
生产性服务业	**Productive Service**	**2261.0**	**2802.1**	**3409.4**	**4425.2**	**5355.3**
流通服务	Logistics	544.5	667.2	844.9	1062.1	1365.0
信息服务	Information Service	449.6	586.6	696.4	870.5	999.1
金融服务	Financial Service	713.8	840.2	982.4	1302.8	1519.2
商务服务	Business Service	276.6	360.7	447.1	623.6	765.3
科技服务	Sci-tech Service	276.5	347.4	438.6	566.2	706.7
信息服务业	**Inforamtion Service**		**721.5**	**843.8**	**1047.0**	**1195.2**
信息传输服务	Inforamtion Transmission Service		308.4	309.4	375.6	265.7
信息技术服务	Information Technology Service		231.0	314.7	407.8	616.5
信息内容服务	Information Content Service		182.1	219.7	263.6	313.0
物流业	**Logistics Sector**			**368.0**	**383.5**	**423.4**
交通运输、邮政、仓储业	Transportation, Post, Storage			306.2	318.1	324.2
流通加工、配送、包装业	Circulation and Processing, Delivery, Packaging			61.8	65.4	99.2

2-8 续表 continued

单位：亿元 (100 million yuan)

项目	Item	2009	2010	2011	2012
地区生产总值	**Gross Domestic Product**	**12153.0**	**14113.6**	**16251.9**	**17879.4**
文化创意产业	**Cultural and Creative Industry**	**1489.9**	**1697.7**	**1989.9**	**2205.2**
文化艺术	Cultural & Artistic	48.8	53.7	68.0	76.0
新闻出版	Journalism and Publication	159.8	171.8	191.9	208.3
广播、电视、电影	Broadcast, TV & Film	124.5	138.6	154.0	177.6
软件、网络及计算机服务	Software, Network, & Computer Service	710.5	847.1	1042.2	1190.3
广告会展	Advertisements & Exhibitions	98.5	127.4	159.0	168.6
艺术品交易	Transaction of Artwork	30.9	43.0	56.4	59.2
设计服务	Design Service	76.4	84.2	90.6	97.4
旅游、休闲娱乐	Touring, Relaxation & Recreation	60.7	69.5	78.6	83.4
其他辅助服务	Other Auxiliary Service	179.8	162.4	149.2	144.4
信息产业	**Information Industry**	**1762.9**	**1989.2**	**2377.7**	**2560.7**
电子信息设备制造	Electronic Information Equipment Manufacturing	260.2	282.5	297.0	374.6
电子信息设备销售和租赁	Electronic Information Equipment Sale and Lease	235.1	261.4	320.5	245.2
电子信息传输服务	Electronic Information Transmission Service	445.6	480.0	613.5	661.5
计算机服务和软件业	Computer Service and Software	620.8	734.1	879.9	960.7
其他信息相关服务	Other Information-related Service	201.2	231.2	266.8	318.7
高技术产业	**High-tech Industry**	**778.4**	**888.8**	**1043.2**	**1240.3**
核燃料加工	Nuclear Fuel Processing				
信息化学品制造	Information Chemicals Manufacturing	2.0	3.3	2.2	1.5
医药制造业	Pharmaceutics	127.2	150.1	175.8	221.3
航空航天器制造	Aircraft Manufacturing	28.6	34.6	41.3	46.8
电子及通信设备制造业	Electronic & Communication Equipment Manufacturing	189.4	204.3	199.1	257.5
电子计算机及办公设备制造业	Electronic Computer & Office Equipment Manufacturing	33.2	36.4	44.3	56.1
医疗设备及仪器仪表制造业	Medical Equipment, Device & Instrument Manufacturing	89.0	88.3	105.6	116.0
公共软件服务	Public Software Service	309.0	371.8	474.9	541.1
现代制造业	**Modern Manufacturing**	**895.2**	**1082.3**	**1234.9**	**1396.1**
电子类	Electronics	202.9	222.9	226.6	295.7
机电类	Electromechanical	243.5	263.3	279.6	288.0
交通类	Communications	279.0	400.7	494.6	533.0
医药类	Pharmaceutical	141.6	165.7	200.8	244.1
其他类	Other	28.2	29.7	33.3	35.3
现代服务业	**Modern Service Industry**	**6264.7**	**7026.3**	**8311.3**	**9435.3**
信息传输、计算机服务和软件业	Information Transmission, Computer Service and Software	1066.5	1214.0	1493.4	1621.8
金融业	Finance	1603.6	1863.6	2215.4	2536.9
科学研究、技术服务和地质勘查业	Scientific Research, Technical Service and Geological Prospecting	816.9	941.1	1135.5	1268.4
卫生和社会保障业	Health and Social Security	192.9	226.3	286.0	335.2
文化、体育和娱乐业	Culture, Sports and Entertainment	259.0	294.6	339.4	402.6
房地产业	Real Estate	1062.5	1006.5	1074.9	1244.2
商务服务业	Commercial Service	791.7	930.9	1126.6	1302.2
环境管理业	Environmental Management	27.5	33.1	34.2	42.2
教育	Education	444.1	516.2	605.9	681.8
生产性服务业	**Productive Service**	**5676.1**	**6705.0**	**8124.8**	**8890.8**
流通服务	Logistics	1379.5	1733.0	2118.4	2123.1
信息服务	Information Service	1066.5	1214.1	1493.4	1621.8
金融服务	Financial Service	1603.6	1863.6	2215.4	2536.9
商务服务	Business Service	809.6	953.2	1162.1	1340.6
科技服务	Sci-tech Service	816.9	941.1	1135.5	1268.4
信息服务业	**Inforamtion Service**	**1267.6**	**1445.3**	**1760.2**	**1940.9**
信息传输服务	Inforamtion Transmission Service	319.6	309.4	371.3	355.0
信息技术服务	Information Technology Service	620.8	734.1	879.9	960.7
信息内容服务	Information Content Service	327.2	401.8	509.0	625.2
物流业	**Logistics Sector**	**427.7**	**493.7**	**562.5**	**598.5**
交通运输、邮政、仓储业	Transportation, Post, Storage	326.1	382.9	429.9	452.7
流通加工、配送、包装业	Circulation and Processing, Delivery, Packaging	101.6	110.8	132.6	145.8

2-9 收入法地区生产总值(1978-2012年)
INCOME APPROACH COMPONENTS OF GROSS DOMESTIC PRODUCT (1978-2012)

单位：亿元 (100 million yuan)

年 份 Year	地区生产总值 Added Value	劳动者报酬 Compensation for Labors	生产税净额 Net Taxes on Production	固定资产折旧 Depreciation of Fixed Assets	营业盈余 Operating Surplus
1978	108.8	37.1	16.5	11.5	43.7
1979	120.1	42.0	18.3	13.4	46.4
1980	139.1	48.9	21.0	15.4	53.8
1981-1985	**950.9**	**350.9**	**142.8**	**111.0**	**346.2**
1981	139.2	52.9	22.0	16.9	47.4
1982	154.9	57.4	23.2	17.7	56.6
1983	183.1	66.0	26.8	20.7	69.6
1984	216.6	79.1	31.8	25.4	80.3
1985	257.1	95.5	39.0	30.3	92.3
1986-1990	**1978.7**	**773.7**	**290.5**	**244.9**	**669.6**
1986	284.9	107.8	43.4	34.9	98.8
1987	326.8	125.4	48.0	40.9	112.5
1988	410.2	153.9	59.7	49.9	146.7
1989	456.0	179.3	66.5	57.1	153.1
1990	500.8	207.3	72.9	62.1	158.5
1991-1995	**4847.2**	**2102.6**	**717.3**	**608.1**	**1419.2**
1991	598.9	254.2	86.4	75.7	182.6
1992	709.1	304.7	103.3	89.5	211.6
1993	886.2	387.7	131.4	109.0	258.1
1994	1145.3	508.1	168.9	140.2	328.1
1995	1507.7	647.9	227.3	193.7	438.8
1996-2000	**12084.0**	**5112.5**	**1761.0**	**1664.8**	**3545.7**
1996	1789.2	760.9	264.9	236.9	526.5
1997	2077.1	880.1	302.6	275.0	619.4
1998	2377.2	1008.5	341.3	319.6	707.8
1999	2678.8	1135.3	388.1	375.3	780.1
2000	3161.7	1327.7	464.1	458.0	911.9
2001-2005	**26032.9**	**11244.4**	**3999.7**	**4091.6**	**6697.2**
2001	3708.0	1538.7	549.8	559.7	1059.8
2002	4315.0	1810.6	643.0	680.3	1181.1
2003	5007.2	2119.7	753.1	791.5	1342.9
2004	6033.2	2595.5	960.4	960.5	1516.8
2005	6969.5	3179.9	1093.4	1099.6	1596.6
2006-2010	**55346.2**	**26740.5**	**8959.8**	**7893.4**	**11752.5**
2006	8117.8	3657.3	1286.7	1268.3	1905.5
2007	9846.8	4405.8	1625.8	1383.0	2432.2
2008	11115.0	5615.8	1896.6	1608.4	1994.2
2009	12153.0	6141.6	1953.5	1707.7	2350.2
2010	14113.6	6920.0	2197.2	1926.0	3070.4
2011	16251.9	7992.4	2566.1	2155.8	3537.6
2012	17879.4	9102.6	2894.6	2269.6	3612.6

2-10 收入法地区生产总值(2012年)
INCOME APPROACH COMPONENTS OF GROSS DOMESTIC PRODUCT (2012)

单位：亿元 (100 million yuan)

项　目	Item	地区生产总值 Added Value	劳动者报酬 Compensation for Labors	生产税净额 Net Taxes on Production	固定资产折旧 Depreciation of Fixed Assets	营业盈余 Operating Surplus
地区生产总值	**Gross Domestic Product**	**17879.4**	**9102.6**	**2894.6**	**2269.6**	**3612.6**
第一产业	**Primary Industry**	**150.2**	**102.8**	**1.1**	**24.2**	**22.1**
第二产业	**Secondary Industry**	**4059.3**	**1731.9**	**901.1**	**635.0**	**791.3**
工　业	Industry	3294.3	1312.1	692.0	560.8	729.4
建筑业	Construction	765.0	419.8	209.1	74.2	61.9
第三产业	**Tertiary Industry**	**13669.9**	**7267.9**	**1992.4**	**1610.4**	**2799.2**
交通运输、仓储和邮政业	Transportation, Storage, Posts and Telecommunications	816.3	469.4	76.1	289.9	-19.1
信息传输、计算机服务和软件业	Information Transmission, Computer Services and Software	1621.8	867.7	176.5	203.8	373.8
批发与零售业	Wholesale Trade and Retail Trade	2229.8	859.2	761.0	114.4	495.2
住宿和餐饮业	Stay Place and Catering	373.1	255.6	60.6	43.1	13.8
金融业	Finance	2536.9	689.2	261.2	80.2	1506.3
房地产业	Real Estate	1244.2	346.6	278.9	375.4	243.3
租赁和商务服务业	Tenancy and Commercial Services	1340.6	1083.6	132.1	170.7	-45.8
科学研究、技术服务与地质勘查业	Scientific Research, Technical Services and Geological Prospecting	1268.4	839.2	148.4	110.6	170.2
水利、环境和公共设施管理业	Water Conservancy, Environment and Public Facilities	101.3	71.7	8.0	11.7	9.9
居民服务和其他服务业	Resident Services and Other Services	124.3	105.1	10.8	6.6	1.8
教　育	Education	681.8	582.1	11.7	73.2	14.8
卫生、社会保障和社会福利业	Health Care, Social Security and Social Welfare	363.6	327.8	1.1	29.3	5.4
文化、体育与娱乐业	Culture, Art, Sports and Recreation	402.6	271.3	61.6	40.1	29.6
公共管理与社会组织	Public Manage and Social Organization	565.2	499.4	4.4	61.4	

2-11 支出法地区生产总值(1978-2012年)
GROSS DOMESTIC PRODUCT BY EXPENDITURE APPROACH (1978-2012)

单位：亿元 (100 million yuan)

年份 Year	地区生产总值 Gross Domestic Product	最终消费支出 Final Consumption Expenditure	居民消费 Households	政府消费 Government Consumption	资本形成总额 Gross Capital Formation	固定资本形成总额 Completed Fixed Assets	存货增加 Changes in Inventories	货物和服务净流出 Net Export of Goods and Services	最终消费率(消费率) (%) Final Consumption Rate (%)	资本形成率(投资率) (%) Capital Formation Rate (%)
1978	108.8	53.0	28.6	24.4	31.7	24.9	6.8	24.1	48.7	29.1
1979	120.1	55.4	31.5	23.9	37.0	29.1	7.9	27.7	46.1	30.8
1980	139.1	57.3	39.6	17.7	45.1	36.5	8.6	36.7	41.2	32.4
1981	139.2	61.8	44.2	17.6	50.5	40.2	10.3	26.9	44.4	36.3
1982	154.9	68.6	48.8	19.8	51.8	42.3	9.5	34.5	44.3	33.4
1983	183.1	77.6	54.6	23.0	62.9	56.1	6.8	42.6	42.4	34.4
1984	216.6	96.5	64.8	31.7	84.7	72.5	12.2	35.4	44.6	39.1
1985	257.1	127.1	88.7	38.4	150.6	102.7	47.9	-20.6	49.4	58.6
1986	284.9	161.1	109.9	51.2	178.8	116.0	62.8	-55.0	56.5	62.8
1987	326.8	181.5	124.3	57.2	201.2	148.6	52.6	-55.9	55.5	61.6
1988	410.2	222.6	161.9	60.7	251.1	177.7	73.4	-63.5	54.3	61.2
1989	456.0	244.0	176.1	67.9	271.5	151.9	119.6	-59.5	53.5	59.5
1990	500.8	269.7	194.1	75.6	296.5	195.0	101.5	-65.4	53.9	59.2
1991	598.9	302.6	225.7	76.9	327.3	208.8	118.5	-31.0	50.5	54.7
1992	709.1	341.5	260.7	80.8	414.6	289.0	125.6	-47.0	48.2	58.5
1993	886.2	445.6	354.9	90.7	535.0	445.5	89.5	-94.4	50.3	60.4
1994	1145.3	614.1	504.2	109.9	787.5	703.8	83.7	-256.3	53.6	68.8
1995	1507.7	844.2	672.8	171.4	1036.0	912.0	124.0	-372.5	56.0	68.7
1996	1789.2	1022.7	815.5	207.2	1034.8	949.6	85.2	-268.3	57.2	57.8
1997	2077.1	1215.5	927.0	288.5	1235.1	1040.1	195.0	-373.5	58.5	59.5
1998	2377.2	1335.5	988.5	347.0	1360.3	1249.4	110.9	-318.6	56.2	57.2
1999	2678.8	1510.4	1075.9	434.5	1533.9	1264.6	269.3	-365.5	56.4	57.3
2000	3161.7	1688.0	1155.8	532.2	1697.4	1400.4	297.0	-223.7	53.4	53.7
2001	3708.0	1911.7	1244.8	666.9	1936.5	1602.1	334.4	-140.2	51.6	52.2
2002	4315.0	2300.3	1528.0	772.3	2332.7	1951.9	380.8	-318.0	53.3	54.1
2003	5007.2	2636.5	1729.7	906.8	2737.8	2437.9	299.9	-367.1	52.7	54.7
2004	6033.2	3085.3	1979.5	1105.8	3167.5	2844.3	323.2	-219.6	51.1	52.5
2005	6969.5	3486.5	2221.8	1264.7	3580.9	3204.7	376.2	-97.9	50.0	51.4
2006	8117.8	4138.5	2587.6	1550.9	3936.7	3551.2	385.5	42.6	51.0	48.5
2007	9846.8	5108.7	3040.0	2068.7	4469.3	4022.6	446.7	268.8	51.9	45.4
2008	11115.0	6026.4	3466.5	2559.9	4722.9	3989.5	733.4	365.7	54.2	42.5
2009	12153.0	6930.4	3998.2	2932.2	5049.9	4435.0	614.9	172.7	57.0	41.6
2010	14113.6	8032.8	4774.0	3258.8	6059.7	5342.4	717.3	21.1	56.9	42.9
2011	16251.9	9488.2	5525.0	3963.2	6683.6	5953.9	729.7	80.1	58.4	41.1
2012	17879.4	10655.1	6203.3	4451.8	7409.6	7032.8	376.8	-185.3	59.6	41.4

注：根据全国第六次人口普查数据对2006年-2010年的数据进行了调整(2-12、2-13、2-14、2-17同此)。
Note: Figures for 2006-2011 are revised according to the results of the Sixth National Population Census,Beijing (the same to 2-12、2-13、2-14、2-17).

2-12 支出法地区生产总值
GROSS DOMESTIC PRODUCT BY EXPENDITURE APPROACH

单位：亿元 (100 million yuan)

项目	Item	2012	2011	2012年为2011年% 2012 as % of 2011
地区生产总值	**Gross Domestic Product**	**17879.4**	**16251.9**	**107.7**
最终消费支出	**Final Consumption Expenditure**	**10655.1**	**9488.2**	**109.6**
居民消费	Household Consumption	6203.3	5525.0	109.5
城镇居民	Urban Households	5790.1	5147.1	109.5
农村居民	Rural Households	413.2	377.9	108.7
政府消费	Government Consumption	4451.8	3963.2	109.8
资本形成总额	**Gross Capital Formation**	**7409.6**	**6683.6**	**108.3**
固定资本形成总额	Completed Fixed Assets	7032.8	5953.9	115.0
存货增加	Changes in Inventories	376.8	729.7	53.1
货物和服务净流出	**Net Export of Goods and Services**	**-185.3**	**80.1**	

注：发展速度按可比价格计算。
Note: Date of 2012 as % of 2011 are calculated at comparable prices.

2-13 三大需求对地区生产总值增长的拉动(2001-2012年)
CONTRIBUTION OF THREE COMPONENTS TO GROWTH OF GDP (2001-2012)

年份 Year	最终消费支出 Final Consumption Expenditures		资本形成总额 Gross Capital Formation		货物和服务净流出 Net Exports of Goods and Services	
	贡献率(%) Contribution Rate(%)	拉动(百分点) Impetus (Percentage Points)	贡献率(%) Contribution Rate(%)	拉动(百分点) Impetus (Percentage Points)	贡献率(%) Contribution Rate(%)	拉动(百分点) Impetus (Percentage Points)
2001	32.4	3.8	43.2	5.1	24.4	2.8
2002	77.0	8.8	61.6	7.1	-38.6	-4.4
2003	40.7	4.5	66.3	7.4	-7.0	-0.8
2004	40.2	5.7	37.3	5.3	22.5	3.1
2005	37.2	4.5	45.7	5.5	17.1	2.1
2006	60.0	7.8	24.6	3.2	15.4	2.0
2007	61.1	8.9	21.0	3.0	17.9	2.6
2008	81.6	7.4	9.0	0.8	9.4	0.9
2009	76.4	7.8	39.0	4.0	-15.4	-1.6
2010	65.8	6.8	47.7	4.9	-13.5	-1.4
2011	83.4	6.8	12.7	1.0	3.9	0.3
2012	73.0	5.6	43.8	3.4	-16.8	-1.3

注：1．三大需求指支出法国内生产总值的三大构成项目，即最终消费支出、资本形成总额、货物和服务净流出。
2．贡献率指三大需求增量与支出法国内生产总值增量之比。
3．拉动指国内生产总值增长速度与三大需求贡献率的乘积。
4．本表按可比价格计算。

Note: a) Three components of GDP by expenditure approach are final consumption expenditure,gross capital formation and net exports of goods and services.
b) Contribution share of the three components to the increase of GDP refers to the proportion of the increment of the each component of GDP by expenditure approach to the increment of GDP.
c) Contribution of the three components to GDP growth refers to the growth rate of GDP multiplied by the contribution share of the three components.
d) Data in this table are calculated at comparable prices.

2-14 居民消费水平(1978-2012年)
HOUSEHOLD CONSUMPTION EXPENDITURE(1978-2012)

年份	居民消费水平(元) Level(yuan)			城乡消费水平对比(农村居民=1)	指数(1978年=100) Index(1978=100)			指数(上年=100) Index(Preceding=100)		
Year	全市 All Households	城镇居民 Urban Household	农村居民 Rural Household	Uban/Rural Consumption Ratio(Rural Households=1)	全市 All Households	城镇居民 Urban Household	农村居民 Rural Household	全市 All Households	城镇居民 Urban Household	农村居民 Rural Household
1978	330	451	185	2.4	100.0	100.0	100.0	112.3	110.1	122.6
1979	356	464	221	2.1	117.5	114.5	120.8	117.5	114.5	120.8
1980	440	562	280	2.0	147.6	140.0	159.0	125.6	122.1	131.5
1981	485	590	338	1.7	160.3	144.8	189.4	108.6	103.6	119.2
1982	526	622	384	1.6	170.6	149.7	211.2	106.4	103.4	111.5
1983	579	674	432	1.6	175.4	151.2	222.6	102.8	101.0	105.4
1984	677	789	494	1.6	201.4	173.9	250.4	114.8	115.0	112.5
1985	912	1101	585	1.9	263.2	235.3	289.2	130.7	135.3	115.5
1986	1094	1284	749	1.7	312.9	272.0	365.8	118.9	115.6	126.5
1987	1198	1391	827	1.7	316.7	272.0	375.3	101.2	100.0	102.6
1988	1536	1779	1046	1.7	367.7	313.3	435.7	116.1	115.2	116.1
1989	1648	1874	1169	1.6	398.2	337.1	472.7	108.3	107.6	108.5
1990	1797	2045	1186	1.7	466.7	393.4	527.5	117.2	116.7	111.6
1991	2071	2330	1345	1.7	528.3	440.2	587.1	113.2	111.9	111.3
1992	2375	2696	1456	1.9	553.7	465.3	583.0	104.8	105.7	99.3
1993	3206	3743	1634	2.3	619.6	529.0	588.8	111.9	113.7	101.0
1994	4508	5307	2114	2.5	717.5	618.4	630.6	115.8	116.9	107.1
1995	5663	6497	3101	2.1	774.2	656.7	737.2	107.9	106.2	116.9
1996	6497	7477	3420	2.2	814.5	693.5	742.4	105.2	105.6	100.7
1997	7418	8594	3638	2.4	928.5	795.4	791.4	114.0	114.7	106.6
1998	7954	9195	3874	2.4	949.9	812.9	797.7	102.3	102.2	100.8
1999	8598	9916	4163	2.4	1025.9	876.3	855.1	108.0	107.8	107.2
2000	8820	10145	4277	2.4	1031.0	878.9	860.2	100.5	100.3	100.6
2001	9057	10301	4695	2.2	1026.9	865.7	915.3	99.6	98.5	106.4
2002	10882	12505	5020	2.5	1204.6	1026.7	952.8	117.3	118.6	104.1
2003	12014	13826	5275	2.6	1267.2	1082.1	954.7	105.2	105.4	100.2
2004	13425	15438	5713	2.7	1371.1	1169.8	1000.5	108.2	108.1	104.8
2005	14662.0	16478.0	6602.0	2.5	1442.4	1202.6	1105.6	105.2	102.8	110.5
2006	16487	18185	7580	2.4	1579.4	1292.8	1236.1	109.5	107.5	111.8
2007	18553	20320	8984	2.3	1691.5	1375.5	1389.4	107.1	106.4	112.4
2008	20113	21872	10375	2.1	1777.8	1436.0	1547.8	105.1	104.4	111.4
2009	22023	23812	11917	2.0	1928.9	1550.9	1742.8	108.5	108.0	112.6
2010	24982	26949	13392	2.0	2116.0	1696.7	1896.2	109.7	109.4	108.8
2011	27760	30037	13659	2.2	2243.0	1805.3	1835.5	106.0	106.4	96.8
2012	30350	32857	14664	2.2	2391.0	1922.6	1958.5	106.6	106.5	106.7

2-15 社会劳动生产率(1978-2012年)
OVERALL LABOR PRODUCTIVITY (1978-2012)

单位：元/人 (yuan/person)

年 份 Year	社会劳动生产率 Overall Labor Productivity	第一产业 Primary Industry	第二产业 Secondary Industry	第三产业 Tertiary Industry
1978	2504	444	4496	1896
1979	2626	421	4567	2019
1980	2914	510	4760	2379
1981	2795	561	4325	2408
1982	2959	887	4445	2451
1983	3368	1102	4808	2983
1984	3909	1296	5355	3630
1985	4580	1680	6048	4253
1986	5002	1942	6339	4769
1987	5669	2580	6932	5479
1988	7046	4106	8324	6718
1989	7742	4292	9447	7114
1990	8203	4832	9578	7916
1991	9498	5047	10387	10095
1992	11051	5602	12325	11491
1993	13878	7179	14959	14577
1994	17728	9761	18767	18605
1995	22679	10223	23778	24538
1996	26997	10482	26914	30692
1997	31567	10760	30203	37205
1998	37202	10933	34764	44752
1999	43179	10740	41036	51888
2000	51082	10760	48695	61525
2001	59414	11214	53874	73082
2002	65974	11873	55408	83069
2003	72437	12909	64507	86864
2004	77478	14074	80837	83977
2005	80475	14341	87368	84828
2006	90313	14498	96009	95800
2007	105743	16716	110668	112388
2008	115565	18208	120615	122794
2009	122807	18898	140319	126872
2010	139057	20129	168451	140968
2011	154684	22622	177886	158613
2012	164257	25808	188018	167852

注：本表按当年价格计算。
Note: Data in this table are calculated at current prices.

2-16 三次产业贡献率(2001-2012年)
CONTRIBUTION SHARE OF THREE STRATA INDUSTRIES TO THE INCREASE OF GDP (2001-2012)

单位：% (%)

年份 Year	地区生产总值 Gross Domestic Product	第一产业 Primary Industry	第二产业 Secondary Industry	工业 Industry	建筑业 Construction	第三产业 Tertiary Industry
2001	100.0	0.8	26.7	23.3	3.4	72.5
2002	100.0	0.5	23.4	18.0	5.4	76.1
2003	100.0	-0.2	33.4	28.0	5.4	66.8
2004	100.0	-0.1	37.9	35.4	2.5	62.2
2005	100.0	-0.3	26.9	24.1	2.8	73.4
2006	100.0	0.1	23.5	17.9	5.6	76.4
2007	100.0	0.2	24.9	21.4	3.5	74.9
2008	100.0	0.1	2.4	0.6	1.8	97.5
2009	100.0	0.4	26.5	18.6	7.9	73.1
2010	100.0	-0.1	34.4	30.7	3.7	65.7
2011	100.0	0.1	19.7	18.1	1.6	80.2
2012	100.0	0.3	22.9	17.6	5.3	76.8

注：1. 产业贡献率指各产业增加值增量与GDP增量之比。
2. 本表按可比价格计算。

Note: a) Share of the contributions of the three strata of industry to the increase of the GDP refers to the proportion of the increment of the value-added of each industry to the increment of GDP.
b) Data in this table are calculated at comparable prices.

2-17 三次产业对地区生产总值增长的拉动(2001-2012年)
CONTRIBUTION OF THE THREE STRATA OF INDUSTRY TO GDP GROWTH (2001-2012)

单位：百分点

年份 Year	地区生产总值 Gross Domestic Product	第一产业 Primary Industry	第二产业 Secondary Industry	工业 Industry	第三产业 Tertiary Industry
2001	11.7	0.1	3.1	2.7	8.5
2002	11.5	0.1	2.7	2.1	8.7
2003	11.1	…	3.7	3.1	7.4
2004	14.1	…	5.3	5.0	8.8
2005	12.1	…	3.2	2.9	8.9
2006	13.0	…	3.1	2.3	9.9
2007	14.5	…	3.6	3.1	10.9
2008	9.1	…	0.2	0.1	8.9
2009	10.2	…	2.7	1.9	7.5
2010	10.3	…	3.5	3.2	6.8
2011	8.1	…	1.6	1.5	6.5
2012	7.7	…	1.8	1.4	5.9

注：1. 三次产业拉动指GDP增长速度与各产业贡献率之乘积。
2. 本表按可比价格计算。

Note: a) Contribution of the three strata of industry to GDP growth refers to the growth rate of GDP multiplied by the industrial shares.
b) Data in this table are calculated at comparable prices.

主要统计指标解释

地区生产总值 是按市场价格计算的地区生产总值的简称。它是一个地区所有常住单位在一定时期内生产活动的最终成果。地区生产总值有三种表现形式，即价值形态、收入形态和产品形态。从价值形态看，它是所有常住单位在一定时期内所生产的全部货物和服务价值超过同期投入的全部非固定资产货物和服务价值的差额，即所有常住单位的增加值之和；从收入形态看，它是所有常住单位在一定时期内所创造并分配给常住单位和非常住单位的初次分配收入之和；从产品形态看，它是最终使用的货物和服务减去进口货物和服务。在实际核算中，地区生产总值的三种表现形态表现为三种计算方法，即生产法、收入法和支出法。三种方法分别从不同的方面反映地区生产总值及其构成。

三次产业 根据社会生产活动历史发展的顺序对产业结构的划分，产品直接取自自然界的部门称为第一产业，对初级产品进行再加工的部门称为第二产业，为生产和消费提供各种服务的部门称为第三产业。它是世界上通用的产业结构分类，但各国的划分不尽一致。我国 2002 年版国民经济行业分类标准：

第一产业：农、林、牧、渔业（包括农业、林业、畜牧业、渔业和农、林、牧、渔服务业）。

第二产业：工业（包括采矿业、制造业、电力、燃气及水的生产及供应业）和建筑业。

第三产业：除第一、第二产业以外的其他各业。

最终消费率(消费率)

$$最终消费率(消费率)=\frac{最终消费支出}{地区生产总值}\times 100$$

资本形成率(投资率)

$$资本形成率(投资率)=\frac{资本形成总额}{地区生产总值}\times 100$$

部分新兴产业统计划分标准

1.文化创意产业 北京市文化创意产业指以创作、创造、创新为根本手段，以文化内容和创意成果为核心价值，以知识产权实现或消费为交易特征，为社会公众提供文化体验的具有内在联系的行业集群。北京市文化创意产业标准是在《国民经济行业分类》(GB/T 4754-2002）的基础上，根据文化创意活动的特点将行业分类中相关的类别重新进行的组合。适用于统计及政策管理中对文化创意相关活动的分类。内容上主要包括 9 个行业大类、27 个中类、88 个小类。

2.信息产业 信息相关产业主要是指与电子信息相关联的各种活动的集合。信息产业标准是国家统计局在《国民经济行业分类》(GB/T 4754-2002）的基础上，参考了联合国的《全部经济活动的国际标准产业分类》，并结合我国的实际情况制定的。北京市从 2004 年开始执行国家信息产业统计标准。

3.高技术产业 高技术产业主要是指与高技术产品相关联的各种活动的集合。高技术产业标准是国家统计局在《国民经济行业分类》(GB/T4754-2002）的基础上，根据高技术产业的特性，结合我国的实际情况制定的。北京市从 2006 年开始执行国家高技术产业统计标准。

4.现代制造业 现代制造业是指用现代科学技术武装起来的制造业，是现代科学技术与制造业相结合的产物。现代制造业是应用现代制造技术、现代生产组织系统和现代管理理念所进行的以现代集成制造为特征、知识密集为特色、高效制造为特点的技术含量高、附加值大、产业链长的产业组织体系。现代制造业产业标准是北京市统计局在《国民经济行业分类》(GB/T4754-2002）的基础上，根据现代制造业的特性，将符合基本要求的行业归并，结合北京市的实际情况制定的。北京市从 2005 年开始执行现代制造业统计标准。

5.现代服务业 现代服务业是相对于传统服务业而言，是适应现代人和现代城市发展的需求，而产生和发展起来的具有高技术含量和高文化含量的服务业。现代服务业有新服务领域、新服务模式、高文化品位和高技术含量的特征。现代服务业标准是北京市统计局在《国民经济行业分类》（GB/T4754-2002）的基础上，根据现代服务业的特性，将符合基本要求的行业归并，结合北京市的实际情况制定的。北京市从 2005 年开始执行现代服务业统计标准。

6．生产性服务业 指以市场化的中间投入服务为主导的行业，生产性服务业具有经营性和可贸易性的特点，不仅为制造业提供中间投入服务，也为第一产业和第三产业提供中间投入服务。北京市生产性服务业分类标准涉及《国民经济行业分类》(GB/T 4754-2002) 中交通运输、仓储和邮政业，信息传输、计算机服务和软件业，批发与零售业，金融业，租赁和商务服务业，科学研究、技术服务和地质勘查业等 6 个行业门类、22 个行业大类，共包括 148 个行业小类，根据业务活动特点将生产性服务业划分为流通服务、信息服务、金融服务、商务服务、科技服务五大类别。

7．信息服务业 指以信息资源为基础，利用现代信息技术，对信息进行生产、收集、处理、输送、存储、传播、使用并提供信息产品和服务的产业。本分类涉及《国民经济行业分类》(GB/T 4754-2002)中信息传输、计算机服务和软件业，文化、体育和娱乐业 2 个行业门类、6 个行业大类、17 个行业中类和 28 个行业小类。根据信息服务业的概念和活动性质，将信息服务业划分为信息传输服务、信息技术服务和信息内容服务三大领域。

8．**物流业** 指为物品及其信息流动提供相关服务的经济活动。按照国家发改委、国家统计局、中国物流与采购联合会联合制定的《社会物流统计核算与报表制度（试行方案)》中的相关规定，物流业统计范围为：在工商登记注册时企业（单位）名称中具有“物流”、“配送”“快运”、“储运”、“货运”等物流功能，且业务经营范围以配送、流通加工、包装、仓储、运输等物流业务为主的单位。

Explanatory Notes on Main Statistical Indicators

Gross Domestic Product is a short name for the GDP calculated at market prices. It represents the final results of all resident units in an area from their productive activities over a given period of time. It is expressed in three different perspectives, namely value, income, and products respectively. GDP in its value perspective refers to the total value of all goods and services produced by all resident units during a certain period of time, minus the total value of input of goods and services of the nature of non-fixed assets; in other words, it is the sum of added value of all resident units. GDP from the perspective of income is the sum of primary incomes created by all resident units and distributed to resident and non-resident units. GDP from the perspective of products means the finally used goods and services minus the imported goods and services. In the practice of national accounting, gross domestic product is calculated with three approaches, namely production approach, income approach and expenditure approach, which reflect the gross domestic product and its composition from different angles.

Three Strata of Industry means the division of industrial structure according to the historical sequence of social productive activities. The sector which receives products directly from the nature is called the primary industry. The sector which re-processes primary products is called the secondary industry. The sector which offers various services for production and consumption is called the tertiary industry. This is a world universal classification of industrial structure. But it is different in different countries. As stated in China's standards on Classification of Sectors in National Economy Version 2002:

Primary Industry: agriculture, forestry, animal husbandry and fishery (including agriculture, forestry, animal husbandry and fishery sectors and services in support of these industries.

Secondary Industry: industry (including mining, manufacturing, production and supply of electricity, water and gas) and construction.

Tertiary Industry: any sector other than the primary or secondary industries.

Final Consumption Rate (Consumption Rate)

Final Consumption Rate (Consumption Rate) = Final Consumption / GDP × 100%

Capital Formation Rate (Investment Rate)

Capital Formation Rate (Investment Rate) = Total Capital Formation /GDP ×100%

Statistical Classification of some new Industries

1. **Cultural Creation Industry** The cultural creation sector in Beijing means an internal correlative cluster of sectors with invention, creation and innovation as fundamental means, cultural content and creative fruits as core value, realization and consumption of intellectual property rights as transaction features, which provide cultural experience for the public. It is a new combination of related sectors in the industrial classification according to the characteristics of cultural creation activities on the basis of Classification of Sectors in National Economy (GB/T 4754-2002). It consists of 88 small categories, 27 middle categories and 9 major categories of sector.

2. **Information Industry** Information industry mainly means the set of activities related to electronic information. It is classified by the National Bureau of Statistics on the basis of Classification of Sectors in National Economy (GB/T 4754-2002) by reference to the International Standard Classification of Industries for All Economic Activities of the United Nations, combining the actual situation of China. The national statistical standard for information industry was effective in 2004 in Beijing.

3. **High-tech Industry** High-tech Industry mainly means the set of activities related to high-tech products. It is classified by the National Bureau of Statistics on the basis of Classification of Sectors in National Economy (GB/T 4754-2002) pursuant to the features of high-tech industry and combining the actual situation of China. The national statistical standard for information industry was effective in 2006 in Beijing.

4. **Modern Manufacturing Industry** Modern manufacturing industry mainly means the manufacturing industry equipped with modern sciences and technologies. Modern manufacturing is an industrial organization system with large content of technology, great added value and long industrial chain, with features of modern integrated manufacturing, intensive knowledge, efficient manufacturing, using modern manufacturing technologies, modern production organization system and modern management concepts. It is a combination of modern sciences, technologies and manufacturing. It is classified by the Beijing Municipal Bureau of Statistics on the basis of Classification of Sectors in National Economy (GB/T 4754-2002) pursuant to the features of modern manufacturing industry, merging the sectors meeting basic requirements and combining the actual situation of Beijing. The national statistical standard for information industry was effective in 2005 in Beijing.

5. **Modern Service Industry** Modern service is relative to conventional service. It is a service sector with great content of high technology and great content of culture, which has occurred and evolved to meet the need of modern people and modern cities' development. Modern service industry has new service fields, new service modes, high-grade culture and great content of high technology. It is classified by the Beijing Municipal Bureau of Statistics on the basis of Classification of Sectors in National Economy (GB/T 4754-2002) pursuant to the features of modern service industry, merging the sectors meeting basic requirements and combining the actual situation of Beijing.

The national statistical standard for modern service industry was effective in 2005 in Beijing

6. **Productive Service Sector** means the sector dominant with intermediate input services. Productive service is operating and tradable. It offers intermediate input services for manufacturing industry, and for the primary and secondary industries. The productive service sector of Beijing covers 148 small categories, 22 major categories, 6 sectors in the Classification of Sectors in National Economy (GB/T 4754-2002), including transport, warehouse storage, post and telecom service, information transmission, computer service and software, wholesale and retail trades, financing, leasing and business service, scientific research, technical service, and geological survey. By the features of business activities, productive service falls into five categories, i.e. circulation service, information service, financial service, business service, science and technology service.

7 . **Information Service Sector** means the sector producing, collecting, processing, delivering, storing, transmitting and using information, and providing information products and services on the basis of information resource and by using modern IT. This sector involves 28 small categories, 17 middle categories, 6 major categories, and 2 industries in the Classification of Sectors in National Economy (GB/T 4754-2002), including information transmission, computer service and software, culture, sports and entertainment. Pursuant to the concept and nature of activities, the information service sector consists of three fields, i.e. information transmission service, information technology service, and information content service.

8. **Logistics Sector** means economic activities offering relevant services for goods and information movement. Under relevant provisions in the Statistical Calculation and Reporting System (Tryout) for Social Logistics developed jointly by the State Development and Reform Commission, National Bureau of Statistics, China Federation of Logistics and Procurement, logistics statistics apply for: companies specializing in delivery, circulation processing, package, storage, transport and other logistics service, with their names registered for industry and commerce containing such terms as "logistics", "delivery", "fast transport", "storage and transport", "cargo transport", and so on.

03

人口与就业
POPULATION AND EMPLOYMENT

简要说明

一、本章资料的主要内容

本章人口部分包括历年北京市户籍人口资料；1953 年、1964 年、1982 年、1990 年、2000 年及 2010 年共六次全国人口普查的北京市人口数据；1990 年以后的人口变动情况抽样调查数据；北京市计划生育数据。

本章劳动力部分包括北京市三次产业从业人员情况；法人单位从业人员及平均工资情况；城镇单位在岗职工人数及工资情况；分行业城镇单位在岗职工人数、在岗职工工资总额、在岗职工平均工资情况等。

二、本章数据资料的来源

本章人口部分中，“户籍人口”数据来自于北京市公安局；“土地面积”数据来自于北京市国土资源局；计划生育情况来自于北京市人口和计划生育委员会；其余资料均来自北京市统计局。

本章劳动力部分中，城镇登记失业情况由北京市人力资源和社会保障局提供，其他资料来源于北京市统计局。

三、有关统计标准的变化说明

（一）关于行业划分。根据国家统计局规定，自 2012 年开始执行《国民经济行业分类》（GB/T 4754-2011）标准。

（二）关于三次产业划分。根据国家统计局《三次产业划分规定》（国统字[2012]108 号），该规定对三次产业的范围进行了调整。其中第一产业是指农、林、牧、渔业（不含农、林、牧、渔服务业）；第二产业是指采矿业（不含开采辅助活动），制造业（不含金属制品、机械和设备修理业），电力、热力、燃气及水生产和供应业，建筑业；第三产业是指除第一产业、第二产业以外的其他行业。2012 年本章数据根据此规定进行了调整。

（三）关于统计上城乡划分标准

2008 年 7 月，国务院批复了国家统计局与民政部、住房城乡建设部、公安部、财政部、国土资源部、农业部共同制定的《关于统计上划分城乡的规定》。人口部分的 2009 年、2010 年、2011 年、2012 年“城镇人口”和“乡村人口”按新标准执行，具体划分标准请查阅国函[2008]60 号文件和国家统计局令第 14 号。

Brief Introduction

I. Main Content

Population data in this chapter include household registered population in Beijing in previous years; data of population in Beijing from six national population censuses in 1953, 1964, 1982, 1990, 2000 and 2010; data from National Sample Survey on Population Changes after 1990 and data on Beijing Family Planning.

Labors statistics in this chapter include the information on employees in three industries in Beijing; employees and average wage in corporate entities; number and wage of on-the-job employees in urban entities; number, total wage and average wage of on-the-job employees in urban entities by sector, etc.

II. Source of Data

In the population section of this chapter, data on “household registered population” are from Beijing Public Security Bureau; data on “land area” are from Beijing Land Resource Bureau; family planning data are from Beijing Population and Family Planning Commission; other data are from Beijing Municipal Bureau of Statistics.

In the section of labors in this chapter, urban registered unemployment data are from Beijing Human Resource and Social Security Bureau; other data are from Beijing Municipal Bureau of Statistics.

III. Changes in Relevant Statistical Standards

(I) Classification of Sectors. According to relevant provisions of National Bureau of Statistics, the Standard for Classification of National Economic Sectors (GB/T4754-2011) became effective in 2012.

(II) Classification of Three Industries. According to the provision of National Bureau of Statistics on Classification of Three Industries (GTZ[2012]No.108), the scope of three industries has changed. The primary industry means agriculture, forestry, animal husbandry and fishery (excluding agricultural, forestry, animal husbandry and fishery services); the secondary industry means mining (excluding auxiliary activities), manufacturing (excluding metal products, machinery and equipment repair), electrical power, thermal power, fuel gas and water production and service sectors, and construction industry; the tertiary industry means industries other than the primary and secondary industries. In this chapter, figures for 2012 were adjusted according to this provision.

(III) Urban-Rural Statistical Definition

In July 2008, the State Council approved the Regulations on Urban-Rural Statistical Definition jointly developed by the National Bureau of Statistics, Ministry of Civil Affairs, Ministry of Housing and Urban and Rural Construction, Ministry of Public Security, Ministry of Finance, Ministry of Land Resource and Ministry of Agriculture. In the population section, new definition applies for the figures of “urban population” and “rural population” in 2009, 2010, 2011 and 2012. Refer to Document Guohan [2008] No.60 and Decree 14 of National Bureau of Statistics for specific standard of definition.

3-1 六次人口普查人口基本情况
BASIC STATISTICS ON POPULATION CENSUS IN 1953, 1964, 1982, 1990, 2000 AND 2010

项　　目	Item	1953	1964	1982	1990	2000	2010
常住人口　（万人）	**Permanent Population (10000 persons)**	**276.8**	**759.7**	**923.1**	**1081.9**	**1356.9**	**1961.2**
男	Male	159.8	391.1	467.1	559.3	707.4	1012.6
女	Female	117.0	368.6	456.0	522.6	649.5	948.6
性别比(女=100)	Sex Ratio(Female=100)	136.5	106.1	102.4	107.0	108.9	106.8
家庭户规模　（人/户）	**Average Family Size (person/household)**			**3.7**	**3.2**	**2.9**	**2.5**
各年龄组人口比重　(%)	**Composition by Age Group (%)**						
0-14	Age 0-14	30.1	41.5	22.4	20.2	13.6	8.6
15-64	Age15-64	66.6	54.4	72.0	73.5	78.0	82.7
65岁及以上	Age 65 and Over	3.3	4.1	5.6	6.3	8.4	8.7
总抚养比　(%)	**Gross Dependency Ratio (%)**	**50.2**	**83.8**	**38.9**	**36.1**	**28.2**	**20.9**
老年抚养比	Old Dependency Ratio	5.0	7.5	7.8	8.6	10.8	10.5
少儿抚养比	Children Dependency Ratio	45.2	76.3	31.1	27.5	17.4	10.4
民族人口	**Nationality Population**						
汉族　(万人)	Han Nationality (10000 persons)	260.0	731.2	890.8	1040.5	1298.4	1881.1
占常住人口比重　(%)	Percentage to Permanent Populatioı (%)	93.9	96.2	96.5	96.2	95.7	95.9
少数民族　(万人)	Minority Nationalities (10000 persons)	16.8	28.5	32.3	41.4	58.5	80.1
占常住人口比重　(%)	Percentage to Permanent Populatioı (%)	6.1	3.8	3.5	3.8	4.3	4.1
每十万人口拥有的各种受教育程度人口　(人)	**Population with Various Education Attainment Per 100000 Population (person)**						
大专及以上	Junior College and Above		4359	4866	9300	16839	31499
高中和中专	Senior Secondary/Secondary Technical School		4513	17646	18978	23165	21220
初　中	Junior Secondary School		11768	29086	30551	34380	31396
小　学	Primary School		31883	26197	22579	16963	9956
文盲人口及文盲率	**Illiterate Population and Illiterate Rate**						
文盲人口　(万人)	Illiterate Population (10000 persons)		168.9	114.7	94.3	57.8	33.3
文盲率　(%)	Illiterate Rate (%)		34.2	16.0	10.9	4.9	1.9
平均受教育年限　(年)	**Average Education Years (year)**		**5.3**	**7.8**	**8.6**	**10.0**	**11.5**
城乡人口　(万人)	**Population by Residence (10000 persons)**						
城镇人口	Urban Population	205.8	425.8	597.0	794.5	1052.2	1685.9
乡村人口	Rural Population	71.0	333.9	326.1	287.4	304.7	275.3
人口平均预期寿命　(岁)	**Population Life Expectancy (year)**			**71.9**	**72.9**	**76.1**	**80.2**

注：1. 1964年的文盲人口数为12周岁及以上文盲和半文盲人口，1982年、1990年、2000年、2010年的文盲人口数为15周岁及以上文盲和半文盲人口。文盲率是指15周岁及以上人口中，文盲人口和半文盲人口所占比重。

2. 本表与表3-2相同的指标数据不同，是因为本表数据为普查时点数，表3-2为年末时点数。1953年普查时点为7月1日零时；1964年普查时点为7月1日零时；1982年普查时点为7月1日零时；1990年普查时点为7月1日零时；2000年普查时点为11月1日零时；2010年普查时点为11月1日零时。

Note: a) Statistics on illiterate and Semi-illiterate people in 1964 were about the population at 12 and over, that in 1982, 1990,2000,and 2010, about the illiterate and semi-illiterate population at 15 and over. Illiterate rate means the share of illiterate people of the population at 15 and over.

b) This table has the same indicators but different figures from Table 3-2, because this table uses the census time point, and Table 3-2 uses the year end as the time point. Census time point in 1953 was 12 o'clock midnight, July 1; Census time point in 1964 was 12 o'clock midnight, July 1; Census time point in 1982 was 12 o'clock midnight, July 1; Census time point in 1990 was 12 o'clock midnight, July 1; Census time point in 2000 was 12 o'clock midnight, November 1;Census time point in 2010 was 12 o'clock midnight, November 1.

3-2 常住人口(1978-2012年)
PERMANENT POPULATION (1978-2012)

年份 Year	常住人口(万人) Permanent Population (10000 persons)	#常住外来人口 Non-Natives	按性别分 By Sex 男 Male	女 Female	按城乡分 By Urban Area and Rural Area 城镇人口 Urban Population	乡村人口 Rural Population	常住人口出生率(‰) Birth Rate (‰)	常住人口死亡率(‰) Death Rate (‰)	常住人口自然增长率(‰) Natural Growth Rate (‰)
1978	871.5	21.8	443.2	428.3	479.0	392.5	12.93	6.12	6.81
1979	897.1	26.5	454.6	442.5	510.3	386.8	13.67	5.92	7.75
1980	904.3	18.6	457.8	446.5	521.1	383.2	15.56	6.30	9.26
1981	919.2	18.4	465.9	453.3	533.3	385.9	16.93	6.02	10.91
1982	935.0	17.2	474.0	461.0	544.0	391.0	20.04	5.68	14.36
1983	950.0	16.8	483.0	467.0	557.0	393.0	15.63	5.49	10.14
1984	965.0	19.8	491.0	474.0	570.0	395.0	16.74	5.53	11.21
1985	981.0	23.1	500.0	481.0	586.0	395.0	15.45	5.75	9.70
1986	1028.0	56.8	524.0	504.0	621.0	407.0	15.82	4.47	11.35
1987	1047.0	59.0	525.0	522.0	637.0	410.0	17.29	5.40	11.89
1988	1061.0	59.8	534.0	527.0	650.0	411.0	14.43	5.08	9.35
1989	1075.0	53.9	538.0	537.0	664.0	411.0	12.84	5.35	7.49
1990	1086.0	53.8	545.0	541.0	798.0	288.0	13.04	5.81	7.23
1991	1094.0	54.5	547.0	547.0	808.0	286.0	8.03	5.82	2.21
1992	1102.0	57.1	554.0	548.0	819.0	283.0	9.22	6.11	3.11
1993	1112.0	60.8	559.0	553.0	831.0	281.0	9.35	6.16	3.19
1994	1125.0	63.2	564.0	561.0	846.0	279.0	8.96	5.76	3.20
1995	1251.1	180.8	627.0	624.1	946.2	304.9	7.92	5.12	2.80
1996	1259.4	181.7	639.0	620.4	957.9	301.5	8.02	5.34	2.68
1997	1240.0	154.5	628.7	611.3	948.3	291.7	7.91	6.02	1.89
1998	1245.6	154.1	630.6	615.0	957.7	287.9	6.00	5.30	0.70
1999	1257.2	157.4	636.4	620.8	971.7	285.5	6.50	5.60	0.90
2000	1363.6	256.1	710.9	652.7	1057.4	306.2	6.20	5.30	0.90
2001	1385.1	262.8	722.1	663.0	1081.2	303.9	6.10	5.30	0.80
2002	1423.2	286.9	743.1	680.1	1118.0	305.2	6.60	5.73	0.87
2003	1456.4	307.6	761.2	695.2	1151.3	305.1	5.06	5.15	-0.09
2004	1492.7	329.8	779.9	712.8	1187.2	305.5	6.13	5.39	0.74
2005	1538.0	357.3	778.7	759.3	1286.1	251.9	6.29	5.20	1.09
2006	1601.0	403.4	817.6	783.4	1350.2	250.8	6.22	4.94	1.28
2007	1676.0	462.7	850.8	825.2	1416.2	259.8	8.16	4.83	3.33
2008	1771.0	541.1	900.2	870.8	1503.6	267.4	7.89	4.59	3.30
2009	1860.0	614.2	949.8	910.2	1581.1	278.9	7.66	4.33	3.33
2010	1961.9	704.7	1013.0	948.9	1686.4	275.5	7.27	4.29	2.98
2011	2018.6	742.2	1040.7	977.9	1740.7	277.9	8.29	4.27	4.02
2012	2069.3	773.8	1068.1	1001.2	1783.7	285.6	9.05	4.31	4.74

注：1. 1978-1981年为户籍统计数，含暂住人口；1982-1989年数据是根据1982、1990年两次人口普查数据调整的；1990年以后数据为人口变动情况抽样调查推算数,其中1995、2005年为1%人口抽样调查推算数；2000年为第五次人口普查快速汇总推算数；2010年为第六次人口普查推算数。2006-2009年常住人口、出生率、死亡率等数据又根据2010年人口普查数据进行了调整。

2. "按城乡分"栏包括的"城镇人口"和"乡村人口"，1978-1989年数据为户籍管理统计中的"非农业人口"和"农业人口"口径；1990-1999年数据是根据1990年、2000年两次人口普查数据调整的；2000年数据为国家统计局1999年发布的《关于统计上划分城乡的规定(试行)》中的"城镇人口"和"乡村人口"口径，2001-2005年数据为该口径的推算数；2006-2008年数据为国家统计局2006年发布的《关于统计上划分城乡的暂行规定》中的"城镇人口"和"乡村人口"口径的推算数；2009-2012年数据为《国务院关于统计上划分城乡规定的批复》中的"城镇人口"和"乡村人口"口径的推算数。

Note: a) Data 1978-1981 were statistics of registered permanent residents, include temporary residents; data 1982-1989 were adjusted from population census in 1982 and 1990. Data after 1990 were estimated from sample check of population changes; data for 1995 and 2005 were estimated from 1% population sample check. Data 2000 were estimated from fast summarizing of the fifth population census,Data 2010 were estimated from fast summarizing of the 6th population census. Data of Population,Birth rate ,Death rate and Natural Growth rate from 2006 to 2009 were adjusted from population census in 2010.

b) In classification by rural and urban areas, the "urban population" and "rural population" from 1978 to 1989 were those in the household register statistics, data from 1990-1999 were adjusted from census conducted in 1990 and 2000, those in 2000 were on the basis of statistical classification of rural and urban population stated by the State Statistical Bureau, and those from 2001 to 2005 were estimated on such basis. Figures from 2006 to 2008 were estimated figures of "urban population" and "rural population" in Provisional Regulations on Statistical Division of Rural and Urban Areas issued by the State Statistics Bureau. Figures for 2009 and 2012 were estimated figures of "urban population" and "rural population" in Provisional Regulations on Statistical Division of Rural and Urban Areas issued by the State Statistics Bureau.

3-3 常住人口总量(2012年)
TOTAL NUMBER OF PERMANENT POPULATION (2012)

单位：万人 (10000 persons)

地区	District	常住人口 Permanent Population	#常住外来人口 Non-permanent Natives	城镇人口 Urban Population	乡村人口 Rural Population
全市	**Total**	**2069.3**	**773.8**	**1783.7**	**285.6**
首都功能核心区	**Core Districts of Capital Function**	**219.5**	**54.5**	**219.5**	
东城区	Dongcheng	90.8	21.2	90.8	
西城区	Xicheng	128.7	33.3	128.7	
城市功能拓展区	**Urban Function Extended Districts**	**1008.2**	**413.0**	**999.2**	**9.0**
朝阳区	Chaoyang	374.5	169.5	373.8	0.7
丰台区	Fengtai	221.4	83.7	220.1	1.3
石景山区	Shijingshan	63.9	21.4	63.9	
海淀区	Haidian	348.4	138.4	341.4	7.0
城市发展新区	**New Districts of Urban Development**	**653.0**	**275.1**	**449.0**	**204.0**
房山区	Fangshan	98.6	22.8	67.2	31.4
通州区	Tongzhou	129.1	50.7	81.6	47.5
顺义区	Shunyi	95.3	34.5	52.0	43.3
昌平区	Changping	183.0	95.7	146.6	36.4
大兴区	Daxing	147.0	71.4	101.6	45.4
生态涵养发展区	**Ecological Preservation Development Districts**	**188.6**	**31.2**	**116.0**	**72.6**
门头沟区	Mentougou	29.8	4.9	25.5	4.3
怀柔区	Huairou	37.7	10.3	25.8	11.9
平谷区	Pinggu	42.0	5.2	22.8	19.2
密云县	Miyun	47.4	7.1	26.2	21.2
延庆县	Yanqing	31.7	3.7	15.7	16.0

注：本表数据为2012年人口抽样调查推算数据。
Note: Figures in this table are estimated figures in 2012 sample survey on population change.

3-4 常住人口密度(2012年)
PERMANENT POPULATION DENSITY (2012)

地 区	District	土地面积 (平方公里) Land Area (sq.km)	常住人口 (万人) Permanent Population (10000 persons)	常住人口密度 (人/平方公里) Population Density (Permanent Population) (person/sq.km)
全 市	**Total**	**16410.54**	**2069.3**	**1261**
首都功能核心区	**Core Districts of Capital Function**	**92.39**	**219.5**	**23758**
东城区	Dongcheng	41.86	90.8	21691
西城区	Xicheng	50.53	128.7	25470
城市功能拓展区	**Urban Function Extended Districts**	**1275.93**	**1008.2**	**7902**
朝阳区	Chaoyang	455.08	374.5	8229
丰台区	Fengtai	305.80	221.4	7240
石景山区	Shijingshan	84.32	63.9	7578
海淀区	Haidian	430.73	348.4	8089
城市发展新区	**New Districts of Urban Development**	**6295.57**	**653.0**	**1037**
房山区	Fangshan	1989.54	98.6	496
通州区	Tongzhou	906.28	129.1	1425
顺义区	Shunyi	1019.89	95.3	934
昌平区	Changping	1343.54	183.0	1362
大兴区	Daxing	1036.32	147.0	1418
生态涵养发展区	**Ecological Preservation Development Districts**	**8746.65**	**188.6**	**216**
门头沟区	Mentougou	1450.70	29.8	205
怀柔区	Huairou	2122.62	37.7	178
平谷区	Pinggu	950.13	42.0	442
密云县	Miyun	2229.45	47.4	213
延庆县	Yanqing	1993.75	31.7	159

注：本表人口数据为2012年人口抽样调查推算数据。
资料来源：本表"土地面积"由北京市国土资源局提供。
Note: Figures of populationg in this table are estimated figures in 2012 sample survey on population change.
Source: Date of land area are provided by Beijing Land and Resources Bureau.

3-5 常住人口自然变动(2012年)
NATURAL CHANGE OF PERMANENT POPULATION (2012)

地　　区	District	出生人数(人) Number of Birth (persons)	死亡人数(人) Number of Death (persons)	自然增加人数(人) Natural Increase of Population (persons)	出生率(‰) Birth Rate (‰)	死亡率(‰) Death Rate (‰)	自然增长率(‰) Natural Growth Rate (‰)
全　　市	**Total**	**184899**	**88160**	**96739**	**9.05**	**4.31**	**4.74**
首都功能核心区	**Core Districts of Capital Function**	**19363**	**12768**	**6595**	**8.91**	**5.88**	**3.03**
东 城 区	Dongcheng	7296	4551	2745	8.03	5.01	3.02
西 城 区	Xicheng	12067	8217	3850	9.55	6.50	3.05
城市功能拓展区	**Urban Function Extended Districts**	**87903**	**36854**	**51049**	**8.81**	**3.70**	**5.11**
朝 阳 区	Chaoyang	31842	13692	18150	8.60	3.70	4.90
丰 台 区	Fengtai	18376	7895	10481	8.38	3.60	4.78
石景山区	Shijingshan	6118	2884	3234	9.61	4.53	5.08
海 淀 区	Haidian	31567	12383	19184	9.17	3.60	5.57
城市发展新区	**New Districts of Urban Development**	**60664**	**25576**	**35088**	**9.46**	**3.99**	**5.47**
房 山 区	Fangshan	9322	5142	4180	9.55	5.27	4.28
通 州 区	Tongzhou	10447	5155	5292	8.22	4.06	4.16
顺 义 区	Shunyi	10157	4905	5252	10.87	5.25	5.62
昌 平 区	Changping	16683	5837	10846	9.35	3.27	6.08
大 兴 区	Daxing	14055	4537	9518	9.70	3.13	6.57
生态涵养发展区	**Ecological Preservation Development Districts**	**16969**	**12962**	**4007**	**9.03**	**6.90**	**2.13**
门头沟区	Mentougou	2659	2257	402	8.98	7.63	1.35
怀 柔 区	Huairou	3293	2131	1162	8.80	5.70	3.10
平 谷 区	Pinggu	4315	2848	1467	10.30	6.80	3.50
密 云 县	Miyun	4212	3520	692	8.91	7.45	1.46
延 庆 县	Yanqing	2490	2206	284	7.83	6.94	0.89

注：本表数据为2012年人口抽样调查推算数据。
Note: Figures in this table are estimated figures in 2012 sample survey on population change.

3-6 常住人口年龄构成(2012年)
PERMANENT POPULATION BY AGE COMPOSITION (2012)

年龄组 Age Group	常住人口数(万人) Permanent Population (10000 persons)	比重(%) Percentage(%)
总计 Total	**2069.3**	**100.0**
0-4	81.5	3.9
5-9	59.3	2.9
10-14	53.7	2.6
15-19	99.6	4.8
20-24	254.4	12.3
25-29	243.2	11.8
30-34	198.5	9.6
35-39	166.6	8.1
40-44	178.7	8.6
45-49	173.5	8.4
50-54	134.5	6.5
55-59	139.0	6.7
60-64	96.4	4.7
65-69	61.8	3.0
70-74	49.6	2.4
75-79	42.4	2.0
80-84	23.4	1.1
85岁及以上 85 and over	13.2	0.6

注：本表数据为2012年人口抽样调查推算数据。
Note: Figures in this table are estimated figures in 2012 sample survey on population change.

3-7 常住人口受教育程度(2012年)
EDUCATION ATTAINMENT OF PERMANENT POPULATION (2012)

单位：人 (persons)

项目	Item	调查人口合计 Total	男 Male	女 Female
6岁及以上人口	**Population at 6 and above**	**351300**	**179064**	**172236**
#小学	Elmentary School Education	38844	18127	20717
初中	Junior High School Education	114137	61696	52441
高中	Senior High School Education	78479	39786	38693
大学专科	Junior College	44736	21801	22935
大学本科	4-year Unversity Education	56988	29410	27578
研究生	Postgraduate	10899	6557	4342

注：本表数据为2012年人口抽样调查样本数据。
Note: Figures in this table are sample figures in 2012 sample survey on population change.

3-8 常住人口家庭户规模(2012年)
FAMILY SIZE OF PERMANENT POPULATION (2012)

地区	District	调查家庭总户数(户) Total Number of Households (households)	家庭户规模所占比重(%) Percentage of Various Sized Family(%) 一人户 One Person	二人户 Two Persons	三人户 Three Persons	四人户 Four Persons	五人及以上户 Five Persons and above
全市	**Total**	**126252**	**22.0**	**30.9**	**29.8**	**9.9**	**7.4**
城镇	Urban	102784	22.4	30.8	30.9	9.3	6.6
乡村	Rural	23468	20.0	31.3	25.3	12.7	10.7

注：本表数据为2012年人口抽样调查样本数据。
Note: Figures in this table are sample figures in 2012 sample survey on population change.

3-9 户籍人口(1978-2012年)
REGISTERED POPULATION (1978-2012)

单位：万人 (10000 persons)

年 份 Year	户籍户数(万户) Registered Household (10000 households)	户籍人口 Registered Permanent Residents	#60岁及以上人口 Population at 60 and over	按性别分 By Sex 男 Male	女 Female	按户籍性质分 By Type of Household Register 非农业户 Non-Agricultural	农业户 Agricultural	户籍人口出生人数 Births of Permanent Population	户籍人口死亡人数 Deaths of Permanent Population	户籍人口自然增加人数 Natural Increase of Permanent Population	暂住人口 Temporary Residents
1978	205.5	849.7		432.1	417.5	467.0	382.6	10.9	5.2	5.7	21.9
1979	214.6	870.6		441.1	429.4	495.2	375.4	11.8	5.1	6.7	26.5
1980	223.2	885.7		448.4	437.3	510.4	375.3	13.7	5.5	8.2	18.6
1981	234.8	900.8		456.6	444.2	522.6	378.2	15.1	5.4	9.7	18.3
1982	245.0	917.8		465.5	452.3	534.0	383.8	18.2	5.2	13.1	18.0
1983	255.1	933.2		474.7	458.5	547.1	386.0	14.5	5.1	9.4	20.9
1984	263.1	945.2		481.2	464.0	558.1	387.0	13.2	5.1	8.1	21.4
1985	274.1	957.9		488.0	469.9	572.5	385.4	11.8	5.2	6.6	31.2
1986	284.6	971.2		495.5	475.7	586.8	384.4	12.9	5.2	7.8	61.2
1987	299.4	988.0		504.1	483.9	601.0	387.0	16.9	5.3	11.6	78.8
1988	310.8	1001.2		510.4	490.8	614.3	387.0	15.3	5.5	9.8	79.7
1989	322.5	1021.1		520.3	500.8	630.6	390.5	19.0	5.7	13.3	64.7
1990	335.0	1032.2		525.3	507.0	640.2	392.1	14.0	6.3	7.7	71.3
1991	343.1	1039.5		528.5	511.1	648.4	391.2	9.2	5.7	3.5	76.1
1992	349.3	1044.9		530.8	514.1	656.3	388.6	8.3	6.2	2.2	79.9
1993	354.6	1051.2		533.9	517.3	668.7	382.5	7.9	6.3	1.6	86.1
1994	360.3	1061.8		538.9	522.8	683.8	377.9	8.5	6.3	2.2	102.6
1995	365.7	1070.3		543.0	527.3	696.9	373.5	8.5	6.2	2.3	100.2
1996	370.9	1077.7		546.8	530.9	709.7	368.0	7.8	6.7	1.2	106.3
1997	375.7	1085.5		550.4	535.1	722.7	362.9	7.6	6.7	0.9	131.2
1998	383.4	1091.5		552.6	538.9	733.6	357.8	6.7	7.5	-0.8	131.9
1999	390.3	1099.8		556.7	543.1	747.2	352.6	6.3	6.2	0.1	150.1
2000	397.9	1107.5		560.1	547.4	760.7	346.8	7.2	7.8	-0.5	170.4
2001	405.3	1122.3		567.3	555.0	780.2	342.2	6.0	5.3	0.7	244.3
2002	416.3	1136.3		574.7	561.6	806.9	329.4	6.0	5.2	0.8	358.9
2003	427.6	1148.8		581.0	567.9	830.8	318.0	4.5	5.8	-1.3	332.6
2004	439.8	1162.9		587.2	575.7	854.7	308.2	6.6	6.2	0.4	341.5
2005	451.7	1180.7		596.0	584.7	880.2	300.5	7.5	7.0	0.5	355.1
2006	463.7	1197.6		604.2	593.4	905.4	292.2	7.7	5.1	2.6	516.9
2007	473.0	1213.3	210.3	612.0	601.3	929.0	284.3	9.9	5.2	4.8	554.9
2008	481.2	1229.9	218.6	620.0	609.9	950.7	279.2	10.6	5.1	5.5	748.3
2009	488.7	1245.8	228.7	627.5	618.9	971.9	273.9	10.9	6.2	4.7	874.9
2010	496.1	1257.8	237.2	632.8	625.0	989.5	268.3	10.2	9.1	1.1	886.1
2011	503.1	1277.9	250.5	642.4	635.6	1013.8	264.2	12.5	5.3	7.2	825.8
2012	509.2	1297.5	266.1	651.7	645.8	1039.3	258.2	14.5	5.7	8.8	784.2

资料来源：北京市公安局。
Source: Beijing Municipal Public Security Bureau.

3-10 户籍户数及人口数(2012年)
REGISTERED HOUSEHOLD AND POPULATION (2012)

地区	District	户籍户数及人口 Registered Household and Population						暂住人口(万人) Temporary Residents (10000 persons)
		户数（万户）Households (10000 households)			人口数(万人) Population (10000 persons)			
		合计 Total	非农业户 Non-Agricultural	农业户 Agricultural	合计 Total	非农业户 Non-Agricultural	农业户 Agricultural	
全市	**Total**	**509.2**	**396.2**	**113.0**	**1297.5**	**1039.3**	**258.2**	**784.2**
首都功能核心区	**Core Districts of Capital Function**	**81.7**	**81.7**		**235.3**	**235.3**		**42.8**
东城区	Dongcheng	34.5	34.5		96.8	96.8		21.1
西城区	Xicheng	47.2	47.2		138.5	138.5		21.7
城市功能拓展区	**Urban Function Extended Districts**	**205.4**	**188.8**	**16.7**	**574.9**	**540.9**	**34.1**	**428.3**
朝阳区	Chaoyang	76.5	69.8	6.7	197.4	183.6	13.8	174.0
丰台区	Fengtai	45.4	39.6	5.8	109.7	97.8	11.8	108.4
石景山区	Shijingshan	14.0	14.0		37.1	37.1		14.6
海淀区	Haidian	69.5	65.3	4.2	230.7	222.3	8.4	131.3
城市发展新区	**New Districts of Urban Development**	**145.8**	**85.9**	**59.9**	**323.9**	**181.2**	**142.7**	**280.8**
房山区	Fangshan	36.1	21.0	15.1	78.0	43.7	34.2	20.8
通州区	Tongzhou	33.2	18.9	14.3	68.3	36.0	32.2	67.7
顺义区	Shunyi	26.5	15.5	11.0	59.4	32.7	26.7	25.4
昌平区	Changping	24.7	15.7	9.0	56.1	36.2	19.8	91.6
大兴区	Daxing	25.3	14.9	10.4	62.2	32.4	29.8	75.4
生态涵养发展区	**Ecological Preservation Development Districts**	**76.3**	**39.8**	**36.5**	**163.4**	**82.0**	**81.4**	**32.3**
门头沟区	Mentougou	11.9	8.9	3.0	24.8	19.3	5.5	6.7
怀柔区	Huairou	13.4	6.1	7.2	27.8	12.6	15.3	11.0
平谷区	Pinggu	16.8	9.2	7.6	39.8	20.4	19.4	5.2
密云县	Miyun	20.5	9.1	11.4	43.0	17.7	25.3	6.4
延庆县	Yanqing	13.8	6.5	7.2	28.0	12.0	15.9	3.0

资料来源：北京市公安局。
Source: Beijing Municipal Public Security Bureau.

3-11 户籍人口年龄构成(2012年)
REGISTERED POPULATION BY AGE COMPOSITION (2012)

年龄组 Age Group	户籍人口(万人) Permanent Population (10000 persons)			占人口比重(%) Percentage(%)		
	合计 Total	男 Male	女 Female	合计 Total	男 Male	女 Female
总计 Total	**1297.5**	**651.7**	**645.8**	**100.0**	**50.2**	**49.8**
0-4	54.1	27.9	26.2	4.2	2.2	2.0
5-9	37.9	19.6	18.3	2.9	1.5	1.4
10-14	35.7	18.4	17.3	2.8	1.4	1.3
15-19	52.6	26.6	26.0	4.1	2.0	2.0
20-24	99.5	50.5	48.9	7.7	3.9	3.8
25-29	114.2	58.4	55.8	8.8	4.5	4.3
30-34	110.2	55.8	54.3	8.5	4.3	4.2
35-39	80.1	40.5	39.6	6.2	3.1	3.1
40-44	107.7	54.8	53.0	8.3	4.2	4.1
45-49	115.1	58.7	56.4	8.9	4.5	4.3
50-54	111.6	56.9	54.7	8.6	4.4	4.2
55-59	112.7	55.6	57.1	8.7	4.3	4.4
60-64	78.3	38.3	40.0	6.0	3.0	3.1
65-69	50.7	24.3	26.4	3.9	1.9	2.0
70-74	46.1	21.3	24.8	3.6	1.6	1.9
75-79	45.3	21.9	23.4	3.5	1.7	1.8
80-84	27.3	13.4	13.9	2.1	1.0	1.1
85-89	12.4	5.9	6.5	1.0	0.5	0.5
90岁及以上 90 and above	6.1	2.8	3.3	0.5	0.2	0.3

资料来源：北京市公安局。
Source: Beijing Municipal Public Security Bureau.

3-12 户籍人口性别构成及性别比(2012年)
SEX COMPOSITION AND SEX RATIO OF REGISTERED POPULATION (2012)

地　区	District	户籍人口(万人) Registered Permanent Residents (10000 persons)			性别比 (女=100) Sex Ratio (female=100)
		合　计 Total	男 Male	女 Female	
全　市	**Total**	**1297.5**	**651.7**	**645.8**	**100.9**
首都功能核心区	**Core Districts of Capital Function**	**235.3**	**117.0**	**118.2**	**98.9**
东城区	Dongcheng	96.8	47.9	48.9	97.9
西城区	Xicheng	138.5	69.1	69.4	99.7
城市功能拓展区	**Urban Function Extended Districts**	**574.9**	**290.4**	**284.5**	**102.1**
朝阳区	Chaoyang	197.4	99.1	98.3	100.9
丰台区	Fengtai	109.7	55.7	54.0	103.0
石景山区	Shijingshan	37.1	19.2	17.9	106.9
海淀区	Haidian	230.7	116.4	114.3	101.9
城市发展新区	**New Districts of Urban Development**	**323.9**	**161.8**	**162.1**	**99.9**
房山区	Fangshan	78.0	39.1	38.8	100.7
通州区	Tongzhou	68.3	33.9	34.4	98.6
顺义区	Shunyi	59.4	29.4	30.0	98.2
昌平区	Changping	56.1	28.3	27.8	102.0
大兴区	Daxing	62.2	31.1	31.1	99.8
生态涵养发展区	**Ecological Preservation Development Districts**	**163.4**	**82.4**	**81.0**	**101.7**
门头沟区	Mentougou	24.8	12.7	12.1	105.0
怀柔区	Huairou	27.8	14.0	13.9	100.7
平谷区	Pinggu	39.8	20.0	19.7	101.5
密云县	Miyun	43.0	21.5	21.5	100.4
延庆县	Yanqing	28.0	14.1	13.8	102.3

资料来源：北京市公安局。
Source: Beijing Municipal Public Security Bureau.

3-13 户籍人口变动情况
POPULATION CHANGE REGISTERED RESIDENTS

单位：人 (person)

项 目	Item	2012	2011
自然变动	**Natural Change**		
自然增加	Natural Increase	88200	71528
非农业人口	Non-agricultural Population	94812	76699
农业人口	Agricultural Population	-6612	-5171
出 生	Birth	145067	124837
非农业人口	Non-agricultural Population	129071	108035
农业人口	Agricultural Population	15996	16802
死 亡	Death	56867	53309
非农业人口	Non-agricultural Population	34259	31336
农业人口	Agricultural Population	22608	21973
机械变动	**Non-natural Change**		
机械增加	Non-natural Increase	107072	129313
非农业人口	Non-agricultural Population	97875	118836
农业人口	Agricultural Population	9197	10477
市外迁入	Move in from outside	190510	211447
非农业人口	Non-agricultural Population	180355	200022
农业人口	Agricultural Population	10155	11425
迁往市外	Move out	83438	82134
非农业人口	Non-agricultural Population	82480	81186
农业人口	Agricultural Population	958	948

资料来源：北京市公安局。
Source: Beijing Municipal Public Security Bureau.

3-14 户籍人口自然变动情况
NATURAL CHANGE OF REGISTERED RESIDENTS

单位：人 (person)

地 区	District	出生人数 Number of Birth		死亡人数 Number of Death		自然增加人数 Number of Natural Growth	
		2012	2011	2012	2011	2012	2011
全 市	**Total**	**145067**	**124837**	**56867**	**53309**	**88200**	**71528**
东城区	Dongcheng	9838	8359	3685	3406	6153	4953
西城区	Xicheng	14864	12331	5121	4990	9743	7341
朝阳区	Chaoyang	23581	20490	7324	6646	16257	13844
丰台区	Fengtai	11691	10122	4732	4397	6959	5725
石景山区	Shijingshan	3882	3268	1460	1397	2422	1871
海淀区	Haidian	23787	20523	5403	5256	18384	15267
门头沟区	Mentougou	2358	2050	1760	1473	598	577
房山区	Fangshan	8623	7468	4653	4261	3970	3207
通州区	Tongzhou	8370	7310	4099	3983	4271	3327
顺义区	Shunyi	7514	6292	3750	3482	3764	2810
昌平区	Changping	7856	6804	2796	2615	5060	4189
大兴区	Daxing	8696	7564	3019	2806	5677	4758
怀柔区	Huairou	3160	2753	2019	1739	1141	1014
平谷区	Pinggu	4100	3528	2504	2281	1596	1247
密云县	Miyun	4223	3672	2742	2617	1481	1055
延庆县	Yanqing	2524	2303	1800	1960	724	343

资料来源：北京市公安局。
Source: Beijing Municipal Public Security Bureau.

3-15 计划生育状况
FAMILY PLANNING

项　　目	Item	2012	2011	2012年比2011年增、减 Increase/decrese in 2012 over 2011
已婚育龄妇女人数（户籍）（人）	**Number of Married Women of Child-bearing Age (registered) (person)**	**2063395**	**2050779**	**12616**
非农业户口	Non-agricultural Population	1488644	1451963	36681
农业户口	Agricultural Population	574751	598816	-24065
实际采取节育措施人数(户籍)（人）	**Number of Women Actually Taking Birth Control Measures (registered) (person)**	**1735866**	**1766491**	**-30625**
非农业户口	Non-agricultural Population	1224668	1230896	-6228
农业户口	Agricultural Population	511198	535595	-24397
计划内生育（户籍）（人）	**Planned Bearing (registered) (person)**	**123364**	**104286**	**19078**
计划生育率（户籍）（%）	**Non-planned Bearing (registered) (%)**	**98.31**	**98.18**	**0.13**
非农业户口	Non-agricultural Population	98.84	98.75	0.09
农业户口	Agricultural Population	95.07	95.38	-0.31
独生子女领证率（户籍）（%）	**Acceptance Rate of Only-child Certificate (registered) (%)**	**53.09**	**55.06**	**-1.97**
非农业户口	Non-agricultural Population	50.06	52.95	-2.89
农业户口	Agricultural Population	60.95	60.18	0.77

资料来源：北京市人口和计划生育委员会。
Source: Beijing Municipal Commission of Population and Family Planning.

3-16 三次产业从业人员及构成(1978-2012年)

PERSONS EMPLOYED IN THREE INDUSTRIES AND THEIR COMPOSITION (1978-2012)

年 份 Year	从业人员年末人数 (万人) Year-end Employed Persons (10000 persons)				构 成(%)(合计=100) Composition (Total=100)		
		第一产业 Primary Industry	第二产业 Secondary Industry	第三产业 Tertiary Industry	第一产业 Primary Industry	第二产业 Secondary Industry	第三产业 Tertiary Industry
1978	444.1	125.9	177.9	140.3	28.3	40.1	31.6
1979	470.5	121.4	195.2	153.9	25.8	41.5	32.7
1980	484.2	118.0	207.3	158.9	24.4	42.8	32.8
1981	511.7	117.2	220.4	174.1	22.9	43.1	34.0
1982	535.2	115.1	228.6	191.5	21.5	42.7	35.8
1983	552.0	117.1	240.2	194.7	21.2	43.5	35.3
1984	556.2	111.3	247.9	197.0	20.0	44.6	35.4
1985	566.5	100.6	260.4	205.5	17.7	46.0	36.3
1986	572.7	96.1	262.7	213.9	16.8	45.9	37.3
1987	580.2	92.3	264.1	223.8	15.9	45.5	38.6
1988	584.1	88.4	267.6	228.1	15.1	45.8	39.1
1989	593.9	91.0	266.3	236.6	15.3	44.9	39.8
1990	627.1	90.7	281.6	254.8	14.5	44.9	40.6
1991	634.0	90.8	279.7	263.5	14.3	44.1	41.6
1992	649.3	84.5	281.6	283.2	13.0	43.4	43.6
1993	627.8	65.1	279.4	283.3	10.4	44.5	45.1
1994	664.3	73.2	272.2	318.9	11.0	41.0	48.0
1995	665.3	70.6	271.0	323.7	10.6	40.7	48.7
1996	660.2	72.5	260.1	327.6	11.0	39.4	49.6
1997	655.8	71.0	257.6	327.2	10.8	39.2	50.0
1998	622.2	71.5	226.0	324.7	11.5	36.3	52.2
1999	618.6	74.5	216.2	327.9	12.1	34.9	53.0
2000	619.3	72.9	208.2	338.2	11.8	33.6	54.6
2001	628.9	71.2	215.9	341.8	11.3	34.3	54.4
2002	679.2	67.6	235.3	376.3	10.0	34.6	55.4
2003	703.3	62.7	225.8	414.8	8.9	32.1	59.0
2004	854.1	61.5	232.8	559.8	7.2	27.3	65.5
2005	878.0	62.2	231.1	584.7	7.1	26.3	66.6
2006	919.7	60.3	225.4	634.0	6.6	24.5	68.9
2007	942.7	60.9	228.1	653.7	6.5	24.2	69.3
2008	980.9	63.0	207.4	710.5	6.4	21.2	72.4
2009	998.3	62.2	199.6	736.5	6.2	20.0	73.8
2010	1031.6	61.4	202.7	767.5	6.0	19.6	74.4
2011	1069.7	59.1	219.2	791.4	5.5	20.5	74.0
2012	1107.3	57.3	212.6	837.4	5.2	19.2	75.6

注：1. 2010年及以前，劳务派遣人员按照“谁发工资谁统计”进行统计。2011年，劳务派遣人员按照“谁用工谁统计”进行统计。
2. 2012年根据国家统计局关于三次产业口径的有关规定，对数据进行了相应调整。

Note: a) In 2010 and before, dispatched personnel of labor service were calculated by "wage payers". In 2011, dispatched personnel of labor service were calculated by "employers".
b) The grouping standard of 2012 Year-end Employed Persons and Consumption of Energy by three industries was changed according to provisions of National Bureau of Statistics.

3-17 按登记注册类型分从业人员年末人数(1978-2012年)
EMPLOYEES BY REGISTRATION STATUS (1978-2012)

单位：万人 (10000 persons)

年份 Year	合计 Total	#城镇 Urban	#国有单位 State-Owned	#集体单位 Collective-Owned	#联营单位 Joint Owned	#有限责任公司 Limited Liability Corporations	#股份有限公司 Share Holding Corporations Ltd.	#外商投资 Foreign Funded	#港澳台商投资 Hongkong, Macao and Taiwan Funded	#私营 Private	#个体 Individual
1978	444.1	291.6	240.9	50.7							
1979	470.5	311.9	254.2	57.8							
1980	484.2	326.8	269.4	57.1							0.3
1981	511.7	345.2	283.1	61.3							
1982	535.2	361.1	293.0	67.1							
1983	552.0	373.8	303.4	68.5							
1984	556.2	377.6	302.5	71.6				1.3			
1985	566.5	392.6	308.1	72.6				1.6			2.5
1986	572.7	400.5	324.4	71.1				2.4			2.6
1987	580.2	408.3	331.8	70.7				2.8			3.1
1988	584.1	413.9	336.4	69.9	0.2			3.4			3.5
1989	593.9	424.0	343.8	67.4	3.4			3.7			5.6
1990	627.1	461.2	357.9	86.8	5.1			4.6			6.3
1991	634.0	477.2	367.8	89.0	0.5			7.7	0.2		7.2
1992	649.3	490.6	371.5	90.5	0.4			11.4	0.2		14.0
1993	627.8	481.4	362.3	79.7	2.8			11.0	6.4		14.0
1994	664.3	492.7	363.5	73.3	3.5			15.0	9.4		20.9
1995	665.3	492.7	358.2	72.1	3.7			17.4	10.0		21.9
1996	660.2	495.7	355.1	68.6	3.4			20.7	10.1		22.9
1997	655.8	498.7	354.7	68.5	3.2			21.2	10.2		21.2
1998	622.2	463.2	308.1	51.0	5.2	13.7	10.8	21.2	13.1		20.1
1999	618.6	456.1	287.6	49.7	4.8	24.0	12.2	20.6	13.5		23.7
2000	619.3	456.3	266.2	48.3	4.0	34.2	14.0	23.8	14.2		24.4
2001	628.9	464.2	246.3	45.8	4.1	50.6	17.3	22.4	12.9		24.8
2002	679.2	513.6	224.8	36.8	4.1	85.0	27.1	29.2	17.0	4.8	33.1
2003	703.3	533.7	212.8	30.1	3.8	102.3	33.4	31.5	17.3	5.2	37.2
2004	854.1	682.7	199.5	28.2	3.5	134.5	37.9	45.0	18.3	134.2	45.7
2005	878.0	694.0	195.0	23.8	2.4	149.4	36.4	49.6	21.7	131.2	57.2
2006	919.7	734.2	189.3	18.8	2.1	165.1	35.5	57.3	23.5	154.8	65.6
2007	942.7	745.4	189.3	17.3	1.9	179.5	38.7	69.3	28.8	133.8	67.2
2008	980.9	813.7	187.8	24.8	2.2	196.4	46.4	72.9	33.5	159.6	65.1
2009	998.3	856.6	185.7	24.3	0.9	215.7	58.4	71.2	36.6	172.2	67.5
2010	1031.6	905.4	189.0	22.7	0.9	228.2	64.7	74.9	42.4	193.5	65.3
2011	1069.7	955.8	188.8	20.1	0.7	243.0	75.9	90.1	50.6	210.6	59.3
2012	1107.3	996.1	188.3	19.8	0.7	261.6	83.2	92.7	54.3	227.9	50.8

资料来源：表中私营和个体从业人员数据来源于北京市工商行政管理局。

Source: Figures of private and individual employees in the table come from Beijing Administration for Industry and Commerce.

3-18 全市法人单位从业人员和平均工资
EMPLOYEES IN ENTITIES AS LEGAL PERSONS IN THE CITY AND AVERAGE EARNING

项目	Item	从业人员年末人数（万人）Year-end Employed Persons (10000 persons)		从业人员平均工资（元）Average Earning (yuan)	
		2012	2011	2012	2011
合 计	**Total**	**951.4**	**907.7**	**74464**	**65294**
按登记注册类型分	**Grouped by Registration Status**				
内 资	Domestic Investment Economy	804.4	767.0	67876	59091
国 有	State-owned Units	188.3	188.8	87299	78270
集 体	Collective-owned Units	19.8	20.1	38552	32574
股份合作	Share Holding	7.2	7.7	34146	29218
联 营	Joint Ownership Units	0.7	0.7	63030	52697
有限责任公司	Limited-Liability Corporations	261.6	243.0	67006	60095
股份有限公司	Share Holding Corporations Ltd.	83.2	75.9	109537	95485
私 营	Private	234.0	221.8	42882	34235
其 他	Others	9.6	9.0	44253	34027
港、澳、台商投资	Units with Funds from Hongkong, Macao and Taiwan	54.3	50.6	96608	88037
外商投资	Foreign Funded Economy	92.7	90.1	118777	105793
按行业分	**Grouped by Sector**				
农、林、牧、渔业	Farming, Forestry, Animal Husbandry and Fishery	3.1	3.0	37156	31007
采矿业	Mining	6.9	6.8	78038	73826
制造业	Manufacturing	136.3	138.6	58839	50863
电力、热力、燃气及水生产和供应业	Production and Ddistribution of Electricity,Heating Power, Gas and Water	9.2	9.3	90345	81785
建筑业	Construction	58.5	58.7	54924	45814
批发和零售业	Wholesale and Retail Trade	124.6	113.5	60593	53175
交通运输、仓储和邮政业	Transport, Storage and Post	64.4	63.3	63064	56682
住宿和餐饮业	Hotel and Restaurants	47.7	44.7	38725	33482
信息传输、软件和信息技术服务业	Information Transmission,Software and Information Ttechnology Sservices	73.2	66.7	113390	100216
金融业	Financial Intermediation	39.5	33.4	181886	170209
房地产业	Real Estate	47.6	46.4	60767	52552
租赁和商务服务业	Leasing and Business Services	101.1	95.9	74710	65827
科学研究和技术服务业	Scientific Rresearch and Development, Technical Services	73.9	67.9	90514	82043
水利、环境和公共设施管理业	Management of Water Conservancy, Environment and Public Facilities	10.7	10.2	52287	46012
居民服务、修理和其他服务业	Resident Services, Repair and Other Services	16.4	15.7	35752	28193
教 育	Education	48.0	46.9	80447	70994
卫生和社会工作	Health Care and Social Works	24.3	23.9	94796	79700
文化、体育和娱乐业	Culture, Sports and Entertainment	21.2	19.7	92424	82726
公共管理、社会保障和社会组织	Pulic Administration,Social Security and Social Oorganizations	44.8	43.1	70272	66020
国际组织	International Organization				

注：1. 2010年及以前，劳务派遣人员按照“谁发工资谁统计”进行统计。2011年，劳务派遣人员按照“谁用工谁统计”进行统计。
2. 行业划分执行2011年国民经济行业分类标准（GB/T 4754-2011）。

Note: a) In 2010 and before, dispatched personnel of labor service were calculated by "wage payers". In 2011, dispatched personnel of labor service
b) Sectors in this table are classified in accordance with the Standard for Classification of National Economic Sectors 2011 (GB/T 4754-2011).

3-19 城镇单位在岗职工人数及工资总额(1978-2012年)
NUMBER AND WAGE OF FULLY EMPLOYED STAFF AND WORKERS IN URBAN ENTITIES (1978-2012)

年份 Year	在岗职工年末人数(万人) Fully Employed Staff and Workers of Year-end (10000 persons)	国有单位 State-Owned	集体单位 Collective Owned	其他单位 Others	在岗职工工资总额(亿元) Total Wages of Fully Employed (100 million yuan)	国有单位 State-Owned	集体单位 Collective Owned	其他单位 Others
1978	291.6	240.9	50.7		18.7	16.2	2.5	
1979	311.9	254.2	57.7		22.4	19.4	3.0	
1980	326.5	269.4	57.1		26.9	23.3	3.6	
1981-1985					**183.7**	**153.7**	**29.6**	**0.4**
1981	344.4	283.1	61.3		28.3	24.2	4.1	
1982	360.1	293.0	67.1		30.5	25.9	4.6	
1983	371.9	303.4	68.5		33.8	28.5	5.3	
1984	375.4	302.5	71.6	1.3	40.4	33.7	6.6	0.1
1985	382.3	308.1	72.6	1.6	50.7	41.5	9.0	0.3
1986-1990					**421.1**	**349.7**	**64.4**	**7.0**
1986	397.9	324.4	71.1	2.4	58.0	48.5	9.1	0.4
1987	405.2	331.8	70.7	2.7	66.7	56.0	10.1	0.6
1988	410.4	336.4	69.9	4.1	81.2	68.1	12.1	1.0
1989	418.4	343.8	67.4	7.2	96.3	81.0	13.4	1.9
1990	454.9	357.9	86.8	10.2	118.9	96.1	19.7	3.1
1991-1995					**1198.1**	**950.3**	**156.6**	**91.2**
1991	470.0	367.8	89.0	13.2	132.2	106.1	21.5	4.6
1992	476.6	371.5	90.5	14.6	158.5	128.6	23.9	6.0
1993	467.3	362.3	79.6	25.4	218.9	176.6	28.5	13.8
1994	471.8	363.5	73.4	34.9	306.5	243.4	36.2	26.9
1995	470.9	358.2	72.1	40.6	382.0	295.6	46.5	39.9
1996-2000					**2825.4**	**1988.5**	**236.5**	**600.4**
1996	460.6	349.0	64.8	46.8	442.4	339.4	46.2	56.8
1997	465.3	348.7	65.0	51.6	514.8	383.6	53.8	77.4
1998	450.1	321.7	50.8	77.6	558.2	391.9	45.0	121.3
1999	438.0	303.0	49.6	85.4	614.5	420.0	44.8	149.7
2000	434.2	283.0	46.0	105.2	695.5	453.6	46.7	195.2
2001-2005					**5662.3**	**2872.7**	**184.6**	**2605.0**
2001	400.3	235.9	40.0	124.4	777.3	477.8	44.8	254.7
2002	434.2	212.6	32.7	188.9	950.9	508.8	40.0	402.1
2003	436.3	197.6	26.1	212.6	1098.9	565.5	35.0	498.4
2004	446.4	183.7	24.8	237.9	1315.1	625.7	34.0	655.4
2005	448.4	178.5	20.7	249.2	1520.1	694.9	30.8	794.4
2006-2010					**13890.4**	**4904.7**	**219.9**	**8765.8**
2006	453.1	172.9	16.4	263.8	1805.5	738.0	30.5	1037.0
2007	478.9	172.7	15.4	290.8	2194.3	862.4	31.2	1300.7
2008	526.1	171.0	22.7	332.4	2874.3	1008.8	48.2	1817.3
2009	560.4	170.9	22.4	367.1	3227.2	1074.3	53.3	2099.6
2010	587.7	175.1	21.1	391.5	3789.1	1221.2	56.7	2511.2
2011	640.3	177.1	18.7	444.5	4778.6	1421.1	62.3	3295.2
2012	670.4	177.3	18.6	474.5	5657.9	1582.5	71.6	4003.8

注：1. 2007年及以前城镇单位是指乡及乡以上独立核算法人单位，不包括乡镇企业、私营单位和个体工商户。2008年及以后城镇单位是指不包括私营单位和个体工商户的独立核算法人单位(表3-20至3-24同)。

2. 表中2000年及以前数据为职工口径，职工包括在岗职工和不在岗职工(表3-20同)。

Note: a) Urban entities in and before 2007 meant corporate entities keeping separate accounts at and above the township level, excluding township enterprises, private entities and self-employed operators. Urban entities in and after 2008 meant corporate entities keeping separate accounts excluding private entities and self-employed operators (the same to Table 3-20 to 3-24).

b) Figures before 2001 were for employees including on-the-job and off-the-job ones (the same to table 3-20).

3-20 城镇单位在岗职工平均工资(1978-2012年)
AVERAGE WAGE AND INDEX OF FULLY EMPLOYED STAFF AND WORKERS IN URBAN ENTITIES (1978-2012)

单位：元 (yuan)

年份 Year	在岗职工平均工资 Average Wage of Fully Employed	国有单位在岗职工平均工资 Average Wage of Fully Employed of State-Owned	集体单位在岗职工平均工资 Average Wage of Fully Employed of Collective Owned	其他单位在岗职工平均工资 Average Wage of Fully Employed of Others
1978	673	703	471	
1979	742	778	556	
1980	848	889	635	
1981	837	880	685	
1982	863	896	715	
1983	931	964	785	
1984	1086	1127	946	1170
1985	1343	1367	1231	1768
1986	1488	1530	1287	2080
1987	1670	1712	1449	2267
1988	2000	2048	1738	2661
1989	2312	2366	1992	2761
1990	2653	2713	2334	3243
1991	2877	2937	2504	3713
1992	3402	3500	2828	4289
1993	4780	4920	3834	5469
1994	6540	6695	5009	8179
1995	8144	8237	6516	10278
1996	9579	9645	7133	13851
1997	11019	10917	8259	15370
1998	12285	11971	8800	15989
1999	13778	13483	8928	17748
2000	15726	15483	9844	19165
2001	19155	19776	11063	20594
2002	21852	23754	11997	21432
2003	25312	28464	13580	23769
2004	29674	34009	13422	28026
2005	34191	39067	14695	32324
2006	40117	43298	17781	39513
2007	46507	50524	20379	45508
2008	54913	59361	20990	54983
2009	58140	63239	23553	57911
2010	65683	70320	26607	65755
2011	75834	81215	32469	75584
2012	85307	90456	38596	85234

3-21 城镇单位在岗职工年末人数
NUMBER OF FULLY EMPLOYED STAFF AND WORKERS IN URBAN ENTITIES

单位：人 (person)

项 目	Item	2012	2011	2012年为2011年% 2012 as % of 2011
合 计	**Total**	**6703514**	**6403484**	**104.7**
按登记注册类型分	**Grouped by Registration Status**			
内 资	Domestic Investment Economy	5322816	5073039	104.9
国 有	State-owned Units	1772818	1770626	100.1
集 体	Collective-owned Units	185642	187587	99.0
股份合作	Share Holding	67876	72820	93.2
联 营	Joint Ownership Units	6073	6581	92.3
有限责任公司	Limited-Liability Corporations	2473332	2292940	107.9
股份有限公司	Share Holding Corporations Ltd.	741926	672601	110.3
其 他	Others	75149	69884	107.5
港、澳、台商投资	Units with Funds from Hongkong,Macao and Taiwan	517641	487439	106.2
外商投资	Foreign Funded Units	863057	843006	102.4
按行业分	**Grouped by Sector**			
农、林、牧、渔业	Farming,Forestry,Animal Husbandry and Fishery	24804	23156	107.1
#农 业	Agriculture	6536	6833	95.7
采矿业	Mining	68613	65967	104.0
制造业	Manufacturing	1050690	1047638	100.3
电力、热力、燃气及水生产和供应业	Production and Distribution of Electricity,Heating Power, Gas and Water	88135	89107	98.9
建筑业	Construction	400995	391999	102.3
批发和零售业	Wholesale and Retail Trade	646861	604255	107.1
批发业	Wholesale Trade	347716	318490	109.2
零售业	Retail Trade	299145	285765	104.7
交通运输、仓储和邮政业	Transport,Storage and Post	555438	550454	100.9
#铁路运输业	Railway Transport	99876	107990	92.5
道路运输业	Road Transport	265648		
邮政业	Post	65327	61969	105.4
住宿和餐饮业	Hotel and Restaurants	279594	262983	106.3
住宿业	Hotel	143891	143061	100.6
餐饮业	Restaurant	135703	119922	113.2
信息传输、软件和信息技术服务业	Information Transmission,Software and Information Technology services	512081	476871	107.4
金融业	Financial Intermediation	308109	266538	115.6
房地产业	Real Estate	343734	324241	106.0
租赁和商务服务业	Leasing and Business Services	580253	556866	104.2
租赁业	Leasing	7955	6670	119.3
商务服务业	Business Services	572298	550196	104.0
科学研究和技术服务业	Scientific Research and Development, Technical Services	495463	458786	108.0
水利、环境和公共设施管理业	Management of Water Conservancy, Environment and Public Facilities	88906	85461	104.0
居民服务、修理和其他服务业	Resident Services, Repair and Other Services	79999	66259	120.7
#居民服务业	Services to Households	26660	26235	101.6
教 育	Education	396645	379183	104.6
卫生和社会工作	Health Care and Social Works	216540	209738	103.2
#卫 生	Health	207332	196709	105.4
文化、体育和娱乐业	Culture,Sports and Entertainment	160205	154674	103.6
#文化艺术业	Culture and Arts	29536	30991	95.3
体 育	Sports	22693		
公共管理、社会保障和社会组织	Pulic Administration,Social Security and Social Organizations	406449	389308	104.4
国际组织	International Organization			

注：根据国家统计局规定，2012年起执行2011年国民经济行业分类标准（GB/T 4754-2011）。受行业划分标准变化影响，有些行业缺少2011年同口径数据。

Note: According to provisions of the National Bureau of Statistics, from 2012 the Standard for Classification of Sectors in National Economy 2011 (GB/T 4754-2011) is implemented. Due to changes in the sector classification standard, there may be no comparable figures in 2011 for some sectors.

3-22 城镇单位在岗职工工资总额
TOTAL WAGES OF FULLY EMPLOYED STAFF AND WORKERS IN URBAN ENTITIES

单位：万元 (10000 yuan)

项目	Item	2012	2011	2012年为2011年% 2012 as % of 2011
合计	**Total**	**56579220**	**47786423**	**118.4**
按登记注册类型分	**Grouped by Registration Status**			
内资	Domestic Investment Economy	42264987	35678615	118.5
国有	State-owned Units	15825113	14210741	111.4
集体	Collective-owned Units	716187	623215	114.9
股份合作	Share Holding	230019	215401	106.8
联营	Joint Ownership Units	39769	36351	109.4
有限责任公司	Limited-Liability Corporations	16638129	13747282	121.0
股份有限公司	Share Holding Corporations Ltd.	8511668	6619986	128.6
其他	Others	304102	225639	134.8
港、澳、台商投资	Units with Funds from Hongkong,Macao and Taiwan	4867678	3981722	122.3
外商投资	Foreign Funded Units	9446555	8126086	116.2
按行业分	**Grouped by Sector**			
农、林、牧、渔业	Farming,Forestry,Animal Husbandry and Fishery	99564	79176	125.8
#农业	Agriculture	23189	20237	114.6
采矿业	Mining	543038	489410	111.0
制造业	Manufacturing	6647951	5851367	113.6
电力、热力、燃气及水生产和供应业	Production and Distribution of Electricity,Heating Power, Gas and Water	811538	736889	110.1
建筑业	Construction	2448888	2092268	117.0
批发和零售业	Wholesale and Retail Trade	4953977	4029320	122.9
批发业	Wholesale Trade	3438786	2807505	122.5
零售业	Retail Trade	1515191	1221815	124.0
交通运输、仓储和邮政业	Transport,Storage and Post	3592690	3184968	112.8
#铁路运输业	Railway Transport	763203	695029	109.8
道路运输业	Road Transport	1078562		
邮政业	Post	432496	370464	116.7
住宿和餐饮业	Hotel and Restaurants	1223503	1010921	121.0
住宿业	Hotel	670818	597594	112.3
餐饮业	Restaurant	552685	413327	133.7
信息传输、软件和信息技术服务业	Information Transmission,Software and Information Technology Services	6383564	5174208	123.4
金融业	Financial Intermediation	6278276	5073934	123.7
房地产业	Real Estate	2198063	1844229	119.2
租赁和商务服务业	Leasing and Business Services	4945253	4244158	116.5
租赁业	Leasing	36442	29578	123.2
商务服务业	Business Services	4908811	4214580	116.5
科学研究和技术服务业	Scientific Research and Development, Technical Services	5330821	4469907	119.3
水利、环境和公共设施管理业	Management of Water Conservancy,Environment and Public Facilities	480722	422093	113.9
居民服务、修理和其他服务业	Resident Services, Repair and Other Services	315273	232925	135.4
#居民服务业	Services to Households	103661	103343	100.3
教育	Education	3436122	2901569	118.4
卫生和社会工作	Health Care and Social Works	2119431	1739247	121.9
#卫生	Health	2072759	1669259	124.2
文化、体育和娱乐业	Culture,Sports and Entertainment	1725996	1465532	117.8
#文化艺术业	Cultural and Art Activities	229944	221386	103.9
体育	Sports Activities	126214		
公共管理、社会保障和社会组织	Pulic Administration,Social Security and Social Organizations	3044550	2744302	110.9
国际组织	International Organization			

注：根据国家统计局规定，2012年起执行2011年国民经济行业分类标准（GB/T 4754-2011）。受行业划分标准变化影响，有些行业缺少2011年同口径数据。

Note: According to provisions of the National Bureau of Statistics, from 2012 the Standard for Classification of Sectors in National Economy 2011 (GB/T 4754-2011) is implemented. Due to changes in the sector classification standard, there may be no comparable figures in 2011 for some sectors.

3-23 城镇单位在岗职工平均工资
AVERAGE WAGES OF FULLY EMPLOYED STAFF AND WORKERS IN URBAN ENTITIES

单位：元 (yuan)

项 目	Item	2012	2011	2012年为2011年% 2012as % of 2011
合 计	**Total**	**85307**	**75834**	**112.5**
按登记注册类型分	**Grouped by Registration Status**			
内 资	Domestic Investment Economy	80266	71394	112.4
国 有	State-owned Units	90456	81215	111.4
集 体	Collective-owned Units	38596	32469	118.9
股份合作	Share Holding	33876	29210	116.0
联 营	Joint Ownership Units	65658	54133	121.3
有限责任公司	Limited-Liability Corporations	68004	61024	111.4
股份有限公司	Share Holding Corporations Ltd.	115693	101308	114.2
其 他	Others	40967	32699	125.3
港、澳、台商投资	Units with Funds from Hongkong,Macao and Taiwan	93616	83927	111.5
外商投资	Foreign Funded Units	111542	97952	113.9
按行业分	**Grouped by Sector**			
农、林、牧、渔业	Farming,Forestry,Animal Husbandry and Fishery	39664	34439	115.2
#农 业	Agriculture	33941	29690	114.3
采矿业	Mining	78460	73946	106.1
制造业	Manufacturing	63148	55674	113.4
电力、热力、燃气及水生产和供应业	Production and Distribution of Electricity,Heating Power, Gas and Water	92489	83581	110.7
建筑业	Construction	62079	53419	116.2
批发和零售业	Wholesale and Retail Trade	76642	68072	112.6
批发业	Wholesale Trade	98978	90183	109.8
零售业	Retail Trade	50684	43541	116.4
交通运输、仓储和邮政业	Transport,Storage and Post	65321	59113	110.5
#铁路运输业	Railway Transport	76960	68472	112.4
道路运输业	Road Transport	40830		
邮政业	Post	68579	61921	110.8
住宿和餐饮业	Hotel and Restaurants	43517	38592	112.8
住宿业	Hotel	46166	41583	111.0
餐饮业	Restaurant	40685	34956	116.4
信息传输、软件和信息技术服务业	Information Transmission,Software and Information Technology Services	127707	114168	111.9
金融业	Financial Intermediation	209483	198409	105.6
房地产业	Real Estate	64696	57544	112.4
租赁和商务服务业	Leasing and Business Services	88054	77782	113.2
租赁业	Leasing	47333	42730	110.8
商务服务业	Business Services	88620	78232	113.3
科学研究和技术服务业	Scientific Research and Development, Technical Services	109302	101033	108.2
水利、环境和公共设施管理业	Management of Water Conservancy,Environment and Public Facilities	53840	48674	110.6
居民服务、修理和其他服务业	Resident Services, Repair and Other Services	39186	34874	112.4
#居民服务业	Services to Households	38886	38268	101.6
教 育	Education	87579	77566	112.9
卫生和社会工作	Health Care and Social Works	100081	84897	117.9
#卫 生	Health	102295	86956	117.6
文化、体育和娱乐业	Culture,Sports and Entertainment	108910	95332	114.2
#文化艺术业	Cultural and Art Activities	78875	73171	107.8
体 育	Sports Activities	56376		
公共管理、社会保障和社会组织	Pulic Administration,Social Security and Social Organizations	75242	71272	105.6
国际组织	International Organization			

注：根据国家统计局规定，2012年起执行2011年国民经济行业分类标准(GB/T 4754-2011)。受行业划分标准变化影响，有些行业缺少2011年同口径数据。

Note: According to provisions of the National Bureau of Statistics, from 2012 the Standard for Classification of Sectors in National Economy 2011 (GB/T 4754-2011) is implemented. Due to changes in the sector classification standard, there may be no comparable figures in 2011 for some sectors.

3-24 国民经济各行业城镇单位在岗职工平均工资(2012年)

AVERAGE WAGES OF URBAN ENTITIES FULLY EMPLOYED STAFF AND WORKERS IN DIFFERENT SECTORS OF NATIONAL ECONOMY (2012)

单位：元 (yuan)

行业	Sector	平均工资 Average Wage	国有单位 State-owned	集体单位 Collective-Owned	其他单位 Others
合　计	**Total**	**85307**	**90456**	**38596**	**85234**
农、林、牧、渔业	**Farming, Forestry, Animal Husbandry and Fishery**	**39664**	**47384**	**23855**	**38374**
#农、林、牧、渔服务业	FFAF Services	40929	60150	30592	32863
采矿业	**Mining**	**78460**		**58386**	**78707**
煤炭开采和洗选业	Mining and Washing of Coal	70312			70312
石油和天然气开采业	Extraction of Petroleum and Natural Gas	72157			72157
黑色金属矿采选业	Mining and Processing of Ferrous Metal Ores	71031		68911	71093
有色金属矿采选业	Mining and Processing of Non-Ferrous Metal Ores	36000			36000
非金属矿采选业	Mining and Processing of Nonmetal Ores	41649		34293	49242
开采辅助活动	Mining Support Service Activities	88371			88371
其他采矿业	Mining of Other Ores				
制造业	**Manufacturing**	**63148**	**76688**	**31729**	**63390**
农副食品加工业	Processing of Food from Agricultural Products	43122	44525	21794	43501
食品制造业	Manufacture of Foods	52485	36897	22965	52710
酒、饮料和精制茶制造业	Manufacture ofWines,Beverage and Refined Tea	54992	56358	23418	54931
烟草制品业	Manufacture of Tobacco	164117	164117		
纺织业	Manufacture of Textile	37931	53156	24169	37617
纺织服装、服饰业	Manufacture of Textile Wearing Apparel and Ornament	36062	33174	29935	36464
皮革、毛皮、羽毛及其制品和制鞋业	Manufacture of Leather, Fur, Feather and its Products	35910		44982	34549
木材加工和木、竹、藤、棕、草制品业	Processing of Timber, Manufacture of Wood, Bamboo, Rattan, Palm and Straw Products	36640	62846	20994	37545
家具制造业	Manufacture of Furniture	38984	42111	21381	39317
造纸和纸制品业	Manufacture of Paper and Paper Products	38791	41594	24479	41338
印刷和记录媒介复制业	Printing,Reproduction of Recording Media	50686	54158	42625	50804
文教、工美、体育和娱乐用品制造业	Manufacture of Articles for Culture,Education, Artwork, Sport and Entertainment Activity	43522	42957	34916	43810
石油加工、炼焦和核燃料加工业	Processing of Petroleum, Coking, Processing of Nuclear Fuels	71284	47186	22633	71749
化学原料和化学制品制造业	Manufacture of Raw Chemical Materials and Chemical Products	59468	49515	30055	60985
医药制造业	Manufacture of Medicines	103875	72980	32874	105082
化学纤维制造业	Manufacture of Chemical Fibers	41772			41772
橡胶和塑料制品业	Manufacture of Rubber and Plastics Products	41393	44161	32198	42087
非金属矿物制品业	Manufacture of Non-metallic Mineral Products	47961	46670	28078	49018
黑色金属冶炼和压延加工业	Smelting and Pressing of Ferrous Metals	51929	69727	30916	52646

注：根据国家统计局规定，2012年起执行2011年国民经济行业分类标准（GB/T 4754-2011）。受行业划分标准变化影响，有些行业缺少2011年同口径数据。

Note: According to provisions of the National Bureau of Statistics, from 2012 the Standard for Classification of Sectors in National Economy 2011 (GB/T 4754-2011) is implemented. Due to changes in the sector classification standard, there may be no comparable figures in 2011 for some sectors.

3-24 续表 1 continued

单位：元 (yuan)

行业	Sector	平均工资 Average Wage	国有单位 State-owned	集体单位 Collective-Owned	其他单位 Others
有色金属冶炼和压延加工业	Smelting and Processing of Nonferrous Metals	47602	69637	26606	47643
金属制品业	Manufacture of Metal Products	47790	74594	29874	47887
通用设备制造业	Manufacture of General Purpose Machinery	65872	88571	30753	66539
专用设备制造业	Manufacture of Special Purpose Machinery	70357	102373	36761	68712
汽车制造业	Manufacture of Motor Vehicles	63855		32153	64120
铁路、船舶、航空航天和其他运输设备制造业	Manufacture of Railway Locomotives, Building of Ships and Boats, Manufacture of Air and Spacecrafts and Other Transportation equipments	82230	112144	35856	70061
电气机械和器材制造业	Manufacture of Electrical Machinery and Equipment	67848	61846	32751	68705
计算机、通信和其他电子设备制造业	Manufacture of Computer, Communication Equipment and Other Electronic Equipment	74368	55252	36246	74940
仪器仪表制造业	Manufacture of measuring instrument and meter	76275	67243	37554	77526
其他制造业	Other manufacturing	74000	97069	26788	70022
废弃资源综合利用业	Waste Rrecycling and Recovery	51598	85290	25406	53035
金属制品、机械和设备修理业	Repair of Fabricated Metal Products, Machinery and Equipment	101840	44573	31017	104159
电力、热力、燃气及水生产和供应业	**Production and Distribution of Electricity, Heating Power, Gas and Water**	**92489**	**94263**	**27295**	**92509**
电力、热力生产和供应业	Production and Distribution of Electric Power and Heat Power	98247	98014	27089	99276
燃气生产和供应业	Production and Distribution of Gas	82910	58742	22000	87081
水的生产和供应业	Production and Distribution of Water	67079	59931	28450	68185
建筑业	**Construction**	**62079**	**65065**	**50794**	**62444**
房屋建筑业	Construction of Building	64284	53021	41331	66968
土木工程建筑业	Civil engineering Construction	67918	80750	71571	65940
建筑安装业	Construction Installation	55677	40345	72566	55116
建筑装饰和其他建筑业	Building Completion,Finishing and Other Construction	49125	55640	39106	49348
批发和零售业	**Wholesale and retail trade**	**76642**	**101886**	**42606**	**75951**
批发业	Wholesale	98978	124816	50680	98079
零售业	Retail Trade	50684	55840	35268	50848
交通运输、仓储和邮政业	**Transport, Storage and post**	**65321**	**73713**	**27031**	**63885**
铁路运输业	Transport Via railway	76960	79021		70778
道路运输业	Transport Via road	40830	24969	19863	41400
水上运输业	Water Transport	173990			173990
航空运输业	Air Transport	150654	41889		150670
管道运输业	Transport Via Pipeline	75117			75117
装卸搬运和运输代理业	Loading,Unloading, Portage and Other Transport Services	70308	58045	45298	71580
仓储业	Storage	50298	56165	29815	48956
邮政业	Post	68579	68256		68792
住宿和餐饮业	**Hotel and Restaurants**	**43517**	**46357**	**33038**	**43368**
住宿业	Hotel	46166	46400	34851	46868
餐饮业	Restaurant	40685	45679	28599	40832
信息传输、软件和信息技术服务业	**Information Transmission,Software and Information Technology Services**	**127707**	**106542**	**32643**	**128260**
电信、广播电视和卫星传输服务	Telecommunications, Broadcasting,Television and Satellite Transmission services	131028	122643	27181	131280
互联网和相关服务	Internet and Related Services	97547	87837		97823
软件和信息技术服务业	Software and Information Technology Services	132038	107432	35181	132685

3-24 续表 2 continued

单位：元 (yuan)

行业	Sector	平均工资 Average Wage	国有单位 State-owned	集体单位 Collective-Owned	其他单位 Other
金融业	**Finance**	**209483**	**151115**	**162500**	**213228**
货币金融服务	Monetary Financial Services	230219	149067		237823
资本市场服务	Capital Market Services	204993	123307		208970
保险业	Insurance	142778	224294		141559
其他金融业	Other Financial Activities	230698	258608	162500	230308
房地产业	**Real Estate**	**64696**	**61780**	**39002**	**66330**
租赁和商务服务业	**Leasing and Business Services**	**88054**	**71652**	**24736**	**101931**
租赁业	Leasing	47333	73052	26392	45991
商务服务业	Business Services	88620	71646	24722	102965
科学研究和技术服务业	**Scientific Research and Development, Technical Services**	**109302**	**117745**	**71704**	**104414**
研究和试验发展	Research and Experimental Development	111794	112644	105351	108850
专业技术服务业	Professional Technical Services	110038	130486	55520	104447
科技推广和应用服务业	Services of Science and Technology Exchanges and Promotion	102909	110029	51271	102437
水利、环境和公共设施管理业	**Management of Water Conservancy, Environment and Public Facilities**	**53840**	**56982**	**24488**	**50021**
水利管理业	Management of Water Conservancy	69333	69292	50039	74647
生态保护和环境治理业	Environmental Management	87008	79525	21727	95165
公共设施管理业	Management of Public Facilities	50351	54573	22266	44377
居民服务、修理和其他服务业	**Resident Services, Repair and Other Services**	**39186**	**50640**	**27006**	**38571**
居民服务业	Services to Households	38886	50332	30050	35470
机动车、电子产品和日用产品修理业	Repair of Motor Vehicles, Electronics and Household Appliances	44120	49739	28395	45392
其他服务业	Other Services	36299	51916	21835	36016
教育	**Education**	**87579**	**94861**	**59553**	**54803**
卫生和社会工作	**Health Care and Social Works**	**100081**	**106453**	**67509**	**56093**
卫生	Health Care	102295	107982	72718	58876
社会工作	Social Work Activities	51030	62149	27795	29856
文化、体育和娱乐业	**Culture, Sports and Entertainment**	**108910**	**124131**	**38943**	**78211**
新闻和出版业	Journalism and Publishing Activities	113727	113840	62117	114661
广播、电视、电影和影视录音制作业	Broadcasting, Televisions, Movies and Audiovisual Activities	171047	204405	46943	92563
文化艺术业	Cultural and Art Activities	78875	81414	38831	68759
体育	Sports Activities	56376	82904	22537	44927
娱乐业	Entertainment	55329	84297	25470	50038
公共管理、社会保障和社会组织	**Pulic administration,social security and social organizations**	**75242**	**81402**	**37090**	**26838**
中国共产党机关	Organs of Communist Party of China	79099	79099		
国家机构	Government Agencies	81118	81118		
人民政协、民主党派	Peole's Political Consultative Conference and Democratic Parties	97045	97045		
社会保障	Social Security	71004	70660	69133	78766
群众团体、社会团体和其他成员组织	Mass Communities, Social Organizations and Other Membership Organizations	86437	88922	35637	83494
基层群众自治组织	Grass Roots Self-Government Organizations	16087			16087
国际组织	**International Organization**				

3-25 城镇登记失业人员和新增就业人数(1979-2012年)
NUMBER OF REGISTERED UNEMPLOYED PERSONS AND ADDITIONAL EMPLOYED PERSONS IN URBAN AREA (1979-2012)

单位：万人 (10000 persons)

年 份 Year	年末实有城镇登记失业人员 Number of Actual Jobless Persons among Registered Unemployed Persons in Urban Area	城镇登记失业率(%) Registered Unemployment Rate in Urban Area	城镇新增就业人数 Additional Employed Persons in Urban Area
1979	4.96	1.60	
1980	8.67	1.60	
1981	8.36	1.28	
1982	7.03	1.62	
1983	4.20	1.09	
1984	2.03	0.54	
1985	1.61	0.40	
1986	1.25	0.30	
1987	2.24	0.45	
1988	1.58	0.40	
1989	1.71	0.40	
1990	1.67	0.30	
1991	1.92	0.40	
1992	1.72	0.36	
1993	1.92	0.41	
1994	1.91	0.41	
1995	2.19	0.46	
1996	2.80	0.58	
1997	3.29	0.73	
1998	2.95	0.66	
1999	2.80	0.62	
2000	3.32	0.76	
2001	5.19	1.18	
2002	6.02	1.35	
2003	6.96	1.43	
2004	6.46	1.30	
2005	10.57	2.11	31.50
2006	10.40	1.98	34.39
2007	10.63	1.84	40.71
2008	10.33	1.82	41.97
2009	8.16	1.44	42.44
2010	7.73	1.37	44.64
2011	7.89	1.39	44.69
2012	7.20	1.27	43.89

资料来源：北京市人力资源和社会保障局。
Source: Beijing Human Resource and Social Security Bureau.

主要统计指标解释

户籍人口 指公民依照《中华人民共和国户口登记条例》已在其经常居住地的公安户籍管理机关登记了常住户口的人。

暂住人口 公安机关掌握的本市行政区域内，无本市常住户口，来自外省（市），在京暂住三日以上，并向公安机关申报暂住登记以及领取暂住证的人员。

常住人口 指在某地区实际居住半年以上的人口。

常住外来人口 指不具有本市户籍户口，来自北京市行政区划以外的省、自治区、直辖市，且在京居住半年以上的人口。

出生率 指在一定时期内（通常为一年）出生人数与同期平均人数(或期中人数)之比，一般用千分比表示。计算公式:

$$\text{出生率}=\frac{\text{年出生人数}}{\text{年平均人数}}\times 1000‰$$

出生人数是指活产，即脱离母体时（不管怀孕月数），有过呼吸或其他生命现象的活婴儿总和。年平均人数是年初、年底人口数的平均数，也可用年中人口数代替。

死亡率 指在一定时期内（通常为一年）死亡人数与同期平均人数（或期中人数）之比，一般用千分比表示。计算公式:

$$\text{死亡率}=\frac{\text{年死亡人数}}{\text{年平均人数}}\times 1000‰$$

自然增长率 指在一定时期内（通常为一年）人口自然增加数（出生人数减死亡人数）与该时期内平均人数（或期中人数）之比，一般用千分比表示。计算公式:

$$\text{自然增长率}=\frac{\text{年出生人数}-\text{年死亡人数}}{\text{年平均人数}}\times 1000‰$$

人口自然增长率=人口出生率－人口死亡率

从业人员 指在各级国家机关、党政机关、社会团体及企业、事业单位中工作，取得工资或其他形式的劳动报酬的全部人员。包括：在岗职工、聘用的离退休人员以及在单位中工作的港澳台及外籍人员、兼职人员、借用的外单位人员和第二职业者。不包括本单位的不在岗职工。

在岗职工 指在本单位工作并由单位支付工资的人员，以及有工作岗位，但由于学习、病伤产假（六个月以内）等原因暂未工作，仍由单位支付工资的人员。

在岗职工工资总额 与“在岗职工”指标相对应，根据1990年1月1日的国家统计局令（一号）修订，指单位在报告期内直接支付给本单位在岗职工的劳动报酬总额。包括基础工资、职务工资、级别工资、工龄工资、计件工资、奖金、各种津贴和补贴、交通补贴、洗理费、书报费、旅游费、过节费、伙食补助、住房补贴、住房提租补贴、由单位从个人工资中直接为其代扣或代缴的个人所得税、房水电费以及住房公积金和社会保险基金个人缴纳部分等。

在岗职工平均工资 指企业、事业、机关等单位的在岗职工在一定时期内的人均劳动报酬。它表明一定时期在岗职工工资收入的高低程度，是反映在岗职工工资水平的主要指标。计算公式为:

$$\text{在岗职工平均工资}=\frac{\text{报告期实际支付的全部在岗职工工资总额}}{\text{报告期全部在岗职工平均人数}}$$

从业人员平均工资 指企业、事业、机关等单位的从业人员在一定时期内的人均劳动报酬。计算公式为:

$$\text{从业人员平均工资}=\frac{\text{报告期实际支付的全部从业人员劳动报酬总额}}{\text{报告期全部从业人员平均人数}}$$

年末实有城镇登记失业人员 指年末实有的城镇登记失业人员数（包括全部正在领取失业保险金的失业人员）。

城镇登记失业率 指城镇登记失业人数与城镇从业人数和城镇登记失业人数二者之和的比。计算公式如下:

$$\text{城镇登记失业率}=\frac{\text{年末实有登记失业人数}}{\text{城镇从业人数}+\text{年末实有登记失业人数}}\times 100\%$$

Explanatory Notes on Main Statistical Indicators

Registered Population refers to the citizens who have registered their permanent residence with the public security household register authority of the location where they often live.

Temporary Population refers to persons known by the public security authority who are in administrative areas of Beijing, with no household register in the city, from provinces, autonomous regions and municipalities outside of the city, living in Beijing temporarily for more than three days, registered with the public security authority and having a Certificate for Temporary Resident.

Resident Population refers to the population actually living for more than half a year at a place.

Migrant Population refers to the population with no household registered in Beijing, from provinces, autonomous regions and municipalities outside of administrative areas of Beijing, and living in Beijing for more than half a year.

Birth Rate refers to the ratio of the number of births to the average population (or mid-period population) during a certain period of time (usually a year), which is often expressed in ‰. The following formula is used:

Birth Rate = Annual Number of Births/Annual Average Number of Population×1000‰

Number of births refers to live births i.e. the births when babies had shown any vital phenomena regardless of the length of pregnancy.

Annual Average Number of Population is the average of the number of population at the beginning of the year and that at the end of the year. Sometimes it is substituted with the mid-year population.

Death Rate refers to the ratio of the number of deaths to the average population (or mid-period population) during a certain period of time (usually a year) which is often expressed in ‰. The following formula is used:

Death Rate= Annual Number of Deaths/Annual Average Number of Population×1000‰

Natural Growth of Population refers to the ratio of the natural growth of population (births minus deaths) to the average population (or mid-period population) during a certain period of time (usually a year) which is often expressed in ‰. The following formula is used:

Natural Growth of Population = (Annual Number of Births - Annual Number of Deaths)/Annual Average Number of Population×1000‰

Natural Growth Rate of Population = Birth Rate - Death Rate

Employed Persons refer to all persons working in national government agencies, Party and political organs, social groups, enterprises and public institutions at all levels, receiving wages or labor remuneration in other forms. They include: on-the-job employees, retired persons employed, persons from Hong Kong, Macao, Taiwan and foreign countries who are employed, part-time employees, employees transferred from other entities, and employees with a second job. They exclude employees not on-the-job in the entity.

On-the-job Employees refer to persons working in the entity and paid by the entity, together with persons having a job in the entity, but not working temporarily due to study, illness, injury or maternity leaves (less than 6 months) and other reasons, and still paid by the entity.

Total Wages of On-the-job Employees correspond to the indicator On-the-job Employees, revised in accordance with Decree 1 of the National Bureau of Statistics of PRC dated January 1, 1990, referring to the total wages directly paid by an entity to on-the-job employees of the entity during the reporting period.

They consist of basic wage, position-based wage, post wage, wage of a rank, piece rate wage, bonus, allowances and subsidies, traffic subsidy, washing and haircutting allowance, books and newspaper allowance, travel benefit, festival bonus, food subsidy, housing subsidy, subsidy for incremental house rent, as well as personal income tax, water and electricity fees and the personally payable portion of housing accumulation fund and social security fund withheld directly by the employer from the employee's wage.

Average Wage of On-the-job Employees refers to the per-capita labor remuneration of on-the-job employees in enterprises, public institutions and government agencies within a given period of time. It shows the level of wage income of on-the-job employees within a given period of time, serving as a main indicator reflecting the level of wage of on-the-job employees. The following formula is used:

Average Wage of on-the-job Employees = Total Wages of All on-the-job Employees Actually Paid in the Reporting Period / Total Number of on-the-job Employees in the Reporting Period

Average Wage of Employed Persons refers to the per-capita labor remuneration of employed persons in enterprises and government agencies within a given period of time. The following formula is used:

Average Wage of on-the-job Employees = Total Wages of All Employed Persons Actually Paid in the Reporting Period / Total Number of Employed Persons in the Reporting Period

Year-end Actual Number of Urban Registered Unemployed Persons refers to the actual number of unemployed persons registered at the year end (including all unemployed persons receiving unemployment insurance benefit).

Urban Registered Unemployment Rate refers to the ratio of urban registered unemployed persons to the sum of urban employed persons and urban registered unemployed persons. The following formula is used:

Urban Registered Unemployment Rate

= Year-end Actual Registered Unemployed Persons / (Urban Employed Persons + Year-end Actual Registered Unemployed Persons) × 100%

04

能源、资源和环境
ENERGY, RESOURCES AND ENVIRONMENT PROTECTION

简要说明

一、本章资料的主要内容

本章包括的主要内容有：北京市能源生产量、能源消费量、万元地区生产总值能耗、能源消费的行业构成和品种构成、能源平衡表、能源消费弹性系数、人均及日均能源消费量和北京地区用电量情况；土地面积及利用情况；气象情况、水资源情况、排水及节水情况；园林绿化及森林情况；大气环境、固体废物处置情况等环境保护资料。

二、本章资料的统计范围

本章能源部分统计范围为全社会口径。

三、本章资料的数据来源

本章能源部分由北京市统计局、国家统计局北京调查总队提供；土地面积及利用由北京市国土资源局提供；气象资料由北京市气象局提供；水资源、排水及节水情况由北京市水务局提供；城市环境卫生由北京市市政市容管理委员会提供；其他资料由北京市环境保护局提供。

四、本章中关于历史数据调整的问题

按照国家统计局统一要求和统一方法，本章中 1995 至 2003 年的能源消费总量数据已根据"北京市第一次全国经济普查"的数据结果，采用"趋势离差法"进行修正。2004 年能源消费总量为第一次经济普查数据。

本章中 1997-2007 年的万元地区生产总值能耗及下降率、万元地区生产总值水耗及下降率、能源消费弹性系数、平均每万元地区生产总值能源消费量中使用的地区生产总值数据，已根据第二次经济普查和第二次农业普查结果进行了修正。

本章中人均生活用能、人均水资源按年平均常住人口计算；同时，根据全国第六次人口普查数据对 2006-2010 年的人均指标数据进行了修正。

五、有关统计标准的变化说明

（一）关于行业划分。根据国家统计局规定，自 2012 年开始执行《国民经济行业分类》GB/T 4754-2011 标准。

（二）关于三次产业划分。根据国家统计局《三次产业划分规定》（国统字[2012]108 号），对三次产业的范围进行了调整。其中第一产业是指农、林、牧、渔业（不含农、林、牧、渔服务业）；第二产业是指采矿业（不含开采辅助活动），制造业（不含金属制品、机械和设备修理业），电力、热力、燃气及水生产和供应业，建筑业；第三产业是指除第一产业、第二产业以外的其他行业。2012 年本章数据根据此规定进行了调整。

六、全市能源统计的内容及能源消费量的测算方法

全市能源统计主要内容包括第二、三产业限额以上法人单位能源消费情况全面调查；限额以下法人单位能源消费情况抽样调查；农业生产能源消费统计；居民生活能源消费情况抽样调查；能源供应部门的能源供应情况等。

全市能源消费总量包括三次产业能源消费量（生产消费）和居民生活能源消费量。其中，三次产业能源消费量根据各产业能源统计资料分别测算，居民生活能源消费量根据居民能源消费抽样调查资料测算。

从全市范围看，各能源品种的生产量、供应量和消费量应存在平衡关系。因此，在利用上述方法进行生产和居民生活的能源消费量测算时，还应根据全市各能源品种的生产量、供应量和供应结构进行平衡修正。

Brief Introduction

I. Main Content

This chapter consists of statistics for: volume of energy production and energy consumption in Beijing, energy consumption per 10000 Yuan GDP of Beijing, composition of energy consumption by sector and by type, energy balance sheet, energy consumption elasticity coefficient, per-capita and daily energy consumption and electricity consumption in Beijing; land area and land utilization; meteorology, water resource, water drainage and water saving; gardening and forest; atmospheric environment, solid waste disposal and other environmental protection data.

II. Scope of Statistics

In this chapter, statistics for energy cover the entire society.

III. Source of Data

Energy data are from Beijing Municipal Bureau of Statistics, and National Bureau of Statistics Survey Office in Beijing; data on land area and land utilization are from Beijing Municipal Bureau of Land Resource; meteorology data are from Beijing Municipal Bureau of Meteorology; water resource, water drainage and water saving data are from Beijing Water Authority; urban environment and sanitation data are from Beijing Municipal Administration Commission; other data are from Beijing Municipal Bureau of Environmental Protection.

IV. Adjustment to Historical Data

In accordance with requirements and uniform method of the National Bureau of Statistics, total energy figures 1995-2003 in this chapter have been corrected with a "trend deviation method" based on the results for Beijing from the "first national economic census". Data of total energy consumption 2004 are those of the first economic census.

Figures of GDP of Beijing used in the 1997-2007 energy consumption per 10000 Yuan GDP of Beijing, water consumption per 10000 Yuan GDP of Beijing and decrease rate, energy consumption elasticity coefficient, and energy consumption per 10000 Yuan GDP by different energy of Beijing have been corrected in accordance with results from the second economic census and the second agricultural census.

In this chapter, the per-capita energy consumption for living, per-capita water resource are calculated by average permanent population; at the same time, per-capita figures 2006-2010 have been corrected in accordance with the sixth census.

V. Changes in Relevant Statistical Standards

(I) Classification of Sectors. According to relevant provisions of National Bureau of Statistics, the Standard for Classification of National Economic Sectors (GB/T4754-2011) became effective in 2012.

(II) Classification of Three Industries. According to the provision of National Bureau of Statistics on Classification of Three Industries (GTZ[2012]No.108), the scope of three industries has changed. The primary industry means agriculture, forestry, animal husbandry and fishery (excluding agricultural, forestry, animal husbandry and fishery services); the secondary industry means mining (excluding auxiliary activities), manufacturing (excluding metal products, machinery and equipment repair), electrical power, thermal power, fuel gas and water production and service sectors, and construction industry; the tertiary industry means industries other than the primary and secondary industries. In this chapter, figures for 2012 were adjusted according to this provision.

Ⅵ .Content of Energy Statistics in the City and Calculation Method of Energy Consumption

Energy statistics for Beijing include complete survey on energy consumption in entities above designated size in the secondary and tertiary industries; sample survey on energy consumption in entities below designated size; statistics for energy consumption in agricultural production; sample survey on energy consumption in residents' life and energy supply in energy supply departments, etc.

Total energy consumption in Beijing includes energy consumption in three industries (in production) and residents' life. Of which, the energy consumption in three industries is calculated according to energy statistics for each industry, and that in residents' life is calculated according to data from sample survey on residents' energy consumption.

In terms of the whole city, the volume of production, supply and consumption shall be balanced among all types of energy. Therefore, in the calculation of energy consumption in production and residents' life by using above method, a correction shall be made for balance according to the volume of production, supply and consumption of all types of energy in the city.

4-1 能源生产量(2000-2012年) PRODUCTION OF ENERGY (2000-2012)

项 目	Item	2000	2001	2002	2003	2004	2005	2006
一次能源 （万吨标准煤）	**Primary Energy (10000 tons of SCE)**	**523.7**	**597.4**	**632.1**	**686.3**	**765.0**	**679.5**	**460.6**
#原 煤 (万吨)	Coal (10000 tons)	690.0	831.9	881.0	957.3	1067.9	945.2	642.1
二次能源 （万吨标准煤）	**Secondary Energy (10000 tons of SCE)**	**2461.4**	**2362.0**	**2388.6**	**2470.5**	**2850.8**	**2832.1**	**2714.4**
#汽 油 (万吨)	Gasoline (10000 tons)	146.2	146.7	154.1	151.4	169.8	156.5	159.3
煤 油 (万吨)	Kerosene (10000 tons)					8.1	12.4	11.6
柴 油 (万吨)	Diesel Oil (10000 tons)	183.9	186.7	174.1	170.2	180.7	176.8	185.9
燃料油 (万吨)	Fuel Oil (10000 tons)	78.6	67.4	64.4	64.5	68.2	68.9	64.0
液化石油气 (万吨)	Liquefied Petroleum Gas (10000 tons)	40.0	39.7	41.7	38.4	43.3	47.3	40.5
热 力 (万百万千焦)	Heat (10 billion kilo-joules)	8758.8	8608.2	9064.0	9616.6	10973.9	11335.7	12181.6
电 力 (亿千瓦时)	Electricity (100 million kwh)	180.7	174.5	180.3	188.3	200.4	209.8	209.7

4-1 续表 continued

项 目	Item	2007	2008	2009	2010	2011	2012
一次能源 （万吨标准煤）	**Primary Energy (10000 tons of SCE)**	**466.1**	**414.2**	**475.7**	**481.1**	**482.0**	**501.8**
#原 煤 (万吨)	Coal (10000 tons)	648.8	578.5	641.3	500.1	500.1	493.1
二次能源 （万吨标准煤）	**Secondary Energy (10000 tons of SCE)**	**2895.2**	**3213.3**	**3346.7**	**3457.3**	**3209.1**	**3267.2**
#汽 油 (万吨)	Gasoline (10000 tons)	176.5	215.5	272.6	257.1	251.2	261.9
煤 油 (万吨)	Kerosene (10000 tons)	36.4	85.2	111.6	116.1	126.4	132.9
柴 油 (万吨)	Diesel Oil (10000 tons)	268.2	373.3	364.2	350.4	355.7	319.1
燃料油 (万吨)	Fuel Oil (10000 tons)	41.9	42.1	29.6	34.9	21.4	24.0
液化石油气 (万吨)	Liquefied Petroleum Gas (10000 tons)	66.2	50.0	40.3	32.9	30.2	35.0
热 力 (万百万千焦)	Heat (10 billion kilo-joules)	12951.1	13846.2	14476.1	15710.9	15127.7	15632.4
电 力 (亿千瓦时)	Electricity (100 million kwh)	224.4	244.9	242.0	263.3	257.3	284.7

4-2 能源消费总量及万元地区生产总值能耗(1980-2012年)
TOTAL ENERGY CONSUMPTION AND ENERGY CONSUMPTION PER 10000 YUAN GDP (1980-2012)

单位：万吨标准煤 (10000 tons of SCE)

年份 Year	能源消费总量 Total Energy Consumption	第一产业 Primary Industry	第二产业 Secondary Industry	#工业 Industry	第三产业 Tertiary Industry	生活消费 Residential Consumption	万元地区生产总值能耗（吨标准煤） Energy Consumption per 10000 yuan GDP (ton of SCE)	万元地区生产总值能耗下降率(%) Decrease Rate of Energy Consumption per 10000 yuan GDP(%)
1980	1907.7	66.8	1400.3	1385.0	297.6	143.0	13.715	
1981	1902.6	53.3	1339.4	1326.1	334.9	175.0	13.668	-0.23
1982	1920.4	55.7	1346.2	1330.8	338.0	180.5	12.398	6.02
1983	1984.7	73.4	1379.4	1359.5	313.6	218.3	10.839	11.22
1984	2144.1	85.8	1470.9	1451.6	347.3	240.1	9.899	7.98
1985	2211.4	90.7	1488.3	1463.9	351.6	280.8	8.601	5.12
1986	2400.0	95.7	1612.0	1586.5	380.4	311.9	8.424	-0.49
1987	2475.8	89.0	1647.8	1619.8	424.7	314.3	7.576	5.88
1988	2612.6	111.7	1748.1	1719.7	412.2	340.6	6.369	6.45
1989	2653.2	114.4	1735.9	1700.0	427.0	375.9	5.818	2.73
1990	2709.7	105.7	1720.1	1686.4	515.3	368.6	5.411	2.92
1991	2872.0	126.7	1807.6	1773.7	542.0	395.7	4.795	3.56
1992	2987.5	143.6	1888.1	1851.6	552.4	403.4	4.213	6.54
1993	3264.6	133.6	2150.9	2106.9	561.0	419.1	3.684	2.69
1994	3385.9	143.6	2234.1	2198.1	574.8	433.4	2.956	8.78
1995	3533.3	120.4	2328.4	2282.4	632.7	451.8	2.344	6.83
1996	3734.5	110.8	2477.0	2430.7	698.1	448.6	2.087	2.75
1997	3719.2	95.7	2369.6	2312.3	799.8	454.1	1.792	9.55
1998	3808.1	96.2	2400.5	2343.1	856.4	455.0	1.603	6.49
1999	3906.6	86.9	2370.7	2308.5	971.8	477.2	1.459	7.49
2000	4144.0	104.8	2424.8	2356.4	1080.9	533.5	1.311	5.12
2001	4229.2	105.4	2366.6	2287.7	1196.2	561.0	1.198	8.62
2002	4436.1	103.0	2414.6	2325.4	1334.5	584.0	1.127	5.93
2003	4648.2	99.9	2476.7	2380.2	1391.0	680.6	1.062	5.73
2004	5139.6	85.6	2664.2	2550.2	1638.0	751.8	1.029	3.09
2005	5521.9	86.3	2702.5	2599.1	1918.7	814.4	0.986 (0.792)	4.17
2006	5904.1	92.3	2773.1	2670.1	2129.3	909.4	0.750	5.37
2007	6285.0	96.4	2793.8	2685.0	2389.5	1005.3	0.697	7.02
2008	6327.1	96.9	2550.5	2430.8	2610.5	1069.2	0.643	7.74
2009	6570.3	99.0	2544.2	2392.4	2760.3	1166.8	0.606	5.76
2010	6954.1	100.3	2726.7	2559.7	2897.4	1229.7	0.581 (0.493)	4.04
2011	6995.4	100.3	2488.7	2329.7	3100.5	1305.9	0.458	6.95
2012	7177.7	100.8	2426.1	2275.7	3252.1	1398.7	0.436	4.75

注：1. 本表能源消费量指标按等价值计算,万元地区生产总值能耗下降率按可比价计算。
2. 2000年及以前万元地区生产总值能耗按当年价格计算；2000年以后按可比价格计算，可比价格每五年调整一次基期，更换基期年份计算两个可比价数据，括号内数据是按新基期价格计算。

Note: a) The index of enery consumption in this table is at equalance prices.Rate of Energy Consumption per 10000 yuan GDP were calculated at comparable prices.

b) Energy Consumption per 10000 yuan GDP befor 2000 was calculated at the price of that year; figures after 2000 were calculated at comparable price. The base period of comparable price is changed every five years. Two figures at comparable price were calculated for the year in which the base period is changed.Figures in brackets were calculated at the price of new base period.

4-3 按行业分能源消费总量(2005-2012年)
TOTAL ENERGY CONSUMPTION (2005-2012)

单位：万吠标准煤 (10000 ton of SCE)

项　　目	Item	2005	2006	2007	2008	2009	2010	2011	2012
能源消费总量	**Total Energy Consumption**	**5521.9**	**5904.1**	**6285.0**	**6327.1**	**6570.3**	**6954.1**	**6995.4**	**7177.7**
第一产业	**Primary Industry**	**86.3**	**92.3**	**96.4**	**96.9**	**99.0**	**100.3**	**100.3**	**100.8**
第二产业	**Secondary Industry**	**2702.5**	**2773.1**	**2793.8**	**2550.5**	**2544.2**	**2726.7**	**2488.7**	**2426.1**
工业	Industry	2599.1	2670.1	2685.0	2430.8	2392.4	2559.7	2329.7	2275.7
建筑业	Construction	103.4	103.0	108.8	119.7	151.8	167.0	159.0	150.4
第三产业	**Tertiary Industry**	**1918.7**	**2129.3**	**2389.5**	**2610.5**	**2760.3**	**2897.4**	**3100.5**	**3252.1**
批发和零售业	Wholesale Trade and Retail Trade	157.6	162.7	202.9	195.2	206.9	192.7	211.5	221.7
交通运输、仓储和邮政业	Transportation, Storage, Posts and Telecommunications	563.4	717.6	840.8	993.9	1025.2	1104.8	1185.9	1235.1
住宿和餐饮业	Accommodation and Catering	199.9	202.5	249.7	218.0	220.8	239.4	253.1	262.3
信息传输、软件和信息技术服务业	Information transmission,software and information technology services	52.3	59.0	73.2	88.3	96.0	107.5	124.0	129.6
金融业	Finance	27.5	28.1	34.0	39.1	40.8	43.3	50.9	54.3
房地产业	Real Estate	306.7	308.9	318.4	346.0	364.2	389.6	391.2	411.5
租赁和商务服务业	Tenancy and Commercial Servecis	115.3	121.9	127.8	165.5	191.2	182.5	182.6	196.3
科学研究和技术服务业	Scientific research and development, technical services	85.5	94.1	101.7	116.9	123.1	122.7	144.7	163.9
水利、环境和公共设施管理业	Water, Environment and Municipal Engineering Conservancy	23.4	27.4	38.7	35.7	37.8	40.2	47.0	46.5
居民服务、修理和其他服务业	Resident services, repair and other services	64.9	72.5	58.7	31.9	33.6	34.2	46.2	47.1
教　育	Education	143.7	153.7	157.9	165.1	183.0	199.6	205.8	222.9
卫生和社会工作	Health care and social works	52.4	54.6	52.6	58.0	64.6	66.9	71.7	74.1
文化、体育和娱乐业	Culture, Art, Sports and Recreation	43.8	45.3	45.1	53.5	59.3	60.1	69.8	71.5
公共管理、社会保障和社会组织	Pulic administration,social security and social organizations	82.3	81.0	88.0	103.4	113.8	114.0	116.1	115.3
生活消费	**Residential Consumption**	**814.4**	**909.4**	**1005.3**	**1069.2**	**1166.8**	**1229.7**	**1305.8**	**1398.7**

注：1. 行业划分执行《国民经济行业分类》(GB/T 4754—2011)标准（下同）。
2. 2012年开始执行国家统计局《三次产业划分规定》，具体调整内容见本章简要说明（下同）。

Note: a) Sectors in this table are classified in accordance with the Standard for Classification of National Economic Sectors 2011 (GB/T 4754-2011) (the same to follow).

b) From 2012, the provisions of National Bureau of Statistics on Classification of Three Industires became effective. See Brief Introduction of this chapter for detailed changes(the same to follow).

4-4 按三次产业分万元地区生产总值能耗及能耗下降率(2001-2012年)

ENERGY CONSUMPTION PER 10000 YUAN GDP AND DECREASE RATE (2001-2012)

单位：吨标准煤 (ton of SCE)

项 目 Item	万元地区生产总值能耗 Energy Consumption per 10000 yuan GDP	第一产业 Primary Industry	第二产业 Secondary Industry	#工业 Industry	第三产业 Tertiary Industry
2001	1.198	1.282	2.091	2.460	0.516
2002	1.127	1.220	1.968	2.318	0.508
2003	1.062	1.196	1.803	2.114	0.476
2004	1.029	1.031	1.658	1.898	0.496
2005	0.986	1.060	1.527	1.745	0.512
	(0.792)	(0.973)	(1.334)	(1.523)	(0.395)
2006	0.750	1.035	1.238	1.429	0.384
2007	0.697	1.058	1.107	1.271	0.373
2008	0.643	1.052	1.002	1.148	0.362
2009	0.606	1.028	0.906	1.038	0.348
2010	0.581	1.058	0.853	0.967	0.334
	(0.493)	(0.806)	(0.805)	(0.926)	(0.273)
2011	0.458	0.799	0.689	0.784	0.269
2012	0.436	0.778	0.624	0.716	0.262

4-4 续表 continued

单位：% (%)

项 目 Item	万元地区生产总值能耗下降率 Decrease Rate of Energy Consumption per 10000 yuan GDP	第一产业 Primary Industry	第二产业 Secondary Industry	#工业 Industry	第三产业 Tertiary Industry
2001	8.62	2.98	10.90	11.91	2.13
2002	5.93	4.83	5.88	5.75	1.56
2003	5.73	1.96	8.39	8.80	6.23
2004	3.09	13.79	8.04	10.22	-4.08
2005	4.17	-2.80	7.89	8.07	-3.25
2006	5.37	-6.35	7.15	6.17	2.87
2007	7.02	-2.26	10.61	11.06	2.76
2008	7.74	0.57	9.43	9.67	2.89
2009	5.76	2.29	9.66	9.55	4.03
2010	4.04	-2.96	5.74	6.88	3.96
2011	6.95	0.89	14.46	15.34	1.55
2012	4.75	2.61	9.30	8.71	2.75

注：1. 万元地区生产总值能耗按可比价格计算，可比价格每五年调整一次基期，更换基期年份计算两个可比价数据，括号内数据是按新基期价格计算。
2. 表内万元地区生产总值能耗下降率按可比价格计算。

Note: a) Energy Consumption per 10000 yuan GDP were calculated comparable price. The base period of comparable price is changed every five years. Two figures at comparable price were calculated for the year in which the base period is changed.Figures in brackets were calculated at the price of new base period.
b) Energy consumption per 10000 yuan GDP decrease rate is at comparable prices.

4-5 电力平衡表(2004-2012年)
ELECTRICITY BALANCE (2004-2012)

单位：亿千瓦时 (100 million kwh)

项目	Item	2004	2005	2006	2007	2008	2009	2010	2011	2012
可供本地区消费的能源量	**Total Energy Available for Local Consumption**	**308.50**	**358.26**	**409.33**	**449.46**	**462.09**	**512.97**	**558.13**	**596.49**	**627.21**
加工转换投入(-)产出(+)量	**Input(-) or Output(+) in Processing and Transformation**	**200.40**	**209.80**	**209.65**	**224.43**	**244.86**	**242.02**	**263.34**	**257.28**	**284.73**
火力发电	Thermal Power	200.40	209.80	209.65	224.43	244.86	242.02	263.34	257.28	284.73
供热	Heating									
煤炭洗选	Washing-dressing Coal									
炼焦	Coking									
炼油及煤制油	Petroleum Refining									
#油品再投入量(-)										
制气	Gas Production									
#焦炭再投入量(-)	Coke Re-input(-)									
煤制品加工	Coal Products Processing									
回收能	**Energy Recycled**									
损失量	**Losses**	**40.65**	**41.23**	**43.64**	**46.85**	**47.36**	**54.86**	**49.68**	**46.82**	**51.02**
#运输和输配损失	In Transportation and Transmission	40.65	41.23	43.64	46.85	47.36	54.86	49.68	46.82	51.02
终端消费量	**Final Consumption Industry**	**469.46**	**525.81**	**575.35**	**628.24**	**660.79**	**703.99**	**781.22**	**806.86**	**860.92**
第一产业	Primary Industry	10.42	11.43	12.26	13.36	13.61	15.73	16.89	17.04	18.14
第二产业	Secondary Industry	216.39	224.57	242.19	249.60	247.09	248.09	279.70	265.56	272.01
工业	Industry	196.18	209.91	227.49	234.08	230.18	227.99	256.15	240.42	246.12
#用作原料、材料	Use in Materials									
建筑业	Construction	20.21	14.66	14.70	15.52	16.91	20.10	23.55	25.14	25.89
第三产业	Tertiary Industry	162.11	200.89	225.03	258.6	283.79	311.37	345.30	379.53	408.93
生活消费	Residential Consumption	80.54	88.92	95.87	106.68	116.30	128.80	139.33	144.74	161.83
城镇	Urban	64.75	70.64	76.89	86.26	95.01	98.32	95.38	95.48	137.09
乡村	Rural	15.79	18.28	18.98	20.42	21.29	30.47	43.95	49.26	24.74
平衡差额	Balance	-1.21	1.02	-0.01	-1.20	-1.20	-3.86	-9.44	0.09	
消费量合计	**Total Energy Consumption**	**510.11**	**567.04**	**618.99**	**675.09**	**708.15**	**758.85**	**830.90**	**853.68**	**911.94**

4-6 综合能源平衡表(标准量)(2004-2012年)
COMPREHENSIVE ENERGY BALANCE (STANDARD VOLUME) (2004-2012)

单位：万吨标准煤 (10000 tons of SCE)

项目	Item	2004	2005	2006	2007	2008	2009	2010	2011	2012
可供本地区消费的能源量	**Total Energy Available for Consumption**	**5169.57**	**5481.04**	**5650.63**	**5984.79**	**6144.99**	**6412.80**	**6777.08**	**6934.04**	**7179.42**
加工转换投入(-)产出(+)量	**Input(-) or Output(+) in Processing and Transformation**	**-35.52**	**-15.29**	**-27.81**	**-31.99**	**-24.24**	**-31.69**	**-73.50**	**-121.51**	**-119.05**
火力发电	Thermal Power				-1.60	-2.08	-3.20			
供热	Heating							-48.71	-99.05	-106.65
煤炭洗选	Coal Washing-dressing					-1.08	-0.55	-1.12	-1.10	-1.15
炼焦	Coking	-35.24	-15.29	-12.82	-3.73	-3.10	-1.06	-2.12		
炼油及煤制油	Oil Refining and Coal Liquification	-0.05		-13.62	-24.00	-16.45	-24.33	316.11	324.79	325.94
#油品再投入量(-)	Re-inputs of Oil Products							-335.89	-345.08	-344.14
制气	Gas Production	139.97	131.64	116.98	113.55	69.01	67.54	-0.43	-0.41	-0.36
#焦炭再投入量(-)	Coke Re-input(-)	-139.97	-131.64	-116.98	-113.55	-69.01	-67.54			
煤制品加工	Coal Products Processing	-0.23		-1.37	-2.65	-1.53	-2.56	-1.35	-0.66	-1.01
回收能	**Energy Recycled**							**92.14**		**8.33**
损失量	**Losses**	**176.05**	**183.59**	**194.09**	**175.54**	**184.47**	**211.23**	**211.77**	**202.87**	**218.91**
#运输和输配损失	in Transportation and Transmission	176.05	183.18	194.09	175.54	184.47	211.23	207.70	192.22	211.17
终端消费量	**Final Consumption Industry**	**4927.98**	**5323.07**	**5682.22**	**6077.51**	**6118.42**	**6327.41**	**6668.79**	**6671.01**	**6839.73**
第一产业	Primary Industry	85.60	86.35	92.30	96.44	96.90	99.01	100.25	100.33	100.75
第二产业	Secondary Industry	2476.85	2556.15	2606.52	2620.85	2383.95	2348.86	2501.93	2217.68	2149.53
工业	Industry	2362.78	2452.70	2503.80	2512.05	2264.18	2196.98	2334.92	2058.62	1999.08
#用作原料、材料	Use in Materials	444.59	454.24	439.20	377.89	395.56	355.47	346.53	418.89	365.08
建筑业	Construction	114.07	103.45	102.72	108.80	119.77	151.88	167.01	159.06	150.45
第三产业	Tertiary Industry	1613.80	1866.20	2073.96	2354.96	2568.34	2712.74	2836.90	3047.16	3190.70
生活消费	Residential Consumption	751.73	814.37	909.44	1005.26	1069.23	1166.81	1229.71	1305.84	1398.75
城镇	Urban	564.38	630.67	682.11	764.67	864.95	904.59	921.67	959.49	1115.45
乡村	Rural	187.35	183.70	227.33	240.59	204.28	262.22	308.04	346.35	283.31
平衡差额	Balance	30.02	-40.91	-253.49	-300.25	-182.14	-157.55	-84.83	-61.36	1.74
消费量合计	**Total Energy Consumption**	**5139.55**	**5521.94**	**5904.11**	**6285.04**	**6327.13**	**6570.34**	**6954.05**	**6995.40**	**7177.68**

注：2004-2009年，热力按等价热值计算，“加工转换投入产出量”中的供热没有损失量；从2010年起热力按当量热值计算，“加工转换投入产出量”中的供热有损失量。

Note: Heating power 2004-2009 was calculated as equivalent heat value. There were no losses of heating in the "input or output in processing and transformation" . Heating power in 2010 was calculated as equivalent heat value. There were losses of heating in the "input or output in processing and transformation" .

4-7 能源平衡表(实物量简表)(2012年)
ENERGY BALANCE (PHYSICAL VOLUME) (ABRIDGED EDITION) (2012)

单位：万吨 (10000 tons)

项目	Item	原煤 Coal	洗精煤 Clean Coal	其他洗煤 Other Washing Coal	煤制品 Coal Products	煤矸石 Coal Slack	焦炭 Coke	焦炉煤气(亿立方米) Coking Gas (100 million cu.m)
可供本地区消费的能源量	**Total Energy Available for Local Consumption**	**2264.79**	**1.77**		**3.32**		**32.26**	**3.58**
加工转换投入(-)产出(+)量	**Input(-) or Output(+) in Procesing and Transformation**	**-1256.90**	**-1.70**		**2.25**			
火力发电	Thermal Power	-649.56			-1.48			
供　热	Heating	-586.16			-20.18			
煤炭洗选	Coal Washing-dressing	-17.44	12.57					
炼　焦	Coking							
炼油及煤制油	Oil Refining and Coal Liquification							
#油品再投入量(-)	Re-inputs of Oil Products							
制　气	Gas Production	-1.60						
#焦炭再投入量(-)	Coke Re-input(-)							
煤制品加工	Coal Products Processing	-2.14	-14.27		23.91			
回收能	**Energy Recycled**							
损失量	**Losses**							
#运输和输配损失	In Transportation and Transmission							
终端消费量	**Final Consumption Industry**	**1007.89**	**0.06**		**5.59**		**32.27**	**3.58**
第一产业	Primary Industry	44.60						
第二产业	Secondary Industry	407.46	0.06		1.06		32.27	3.58
工　业	Industry	395.97	0.06		0.70		32.26	3.58
#用作原料、材料	Use in Materials	0.09						
建筑业	Construction	11.49			0.36			
第三产业	Tertiary Industry	283.60			4.53			
生活消费	Residential Consumption	272.23						
城　镇	Urban	62.23						
乡　村	Rural	210.00						
平衡差额	Balance	-0.004	0.01		-0.02		-0.01	
消费量合计	**Total Energy Consumption**	**2264.79**	**14.34**		**27.25**		**32.27**	**3.58**

4-7 续表 1 continued

单位：万吨 (10000 tons)

项 目	Item	高炉煤气（亿立方米） Blast Furnace Gas (100 million cu.m)	转炉煤气（亿立方米） Converter Gas (100 million cu.m)	其它煤气（亿立方米） Other Gas (100 million cu.m)	其它焦化产品 Other Carbonized Products	原油 Crude Oil	汽油 Gaso-line	煤油 Kero-sene
可供本地区消费的能源量	**Total Energy Available for Local Consumption**	**1.39**				**1075.77**	**154.04**	**310.44**
加工转换投入(-)产出(+)量	**Input(-) or Output(+) in Processing and Transformation**			**0.64**		**-1075.01**	**261.86**	**132.92**
火力发电	Thermal Power							
供 热	Heating							
煤炭洗选	Coal Washing-dressing							
炼 焦	Coking							
炼油及煤制油	Oil Refining and Coal Liquification					-1075.01	261.86	132.92
#油品再投入量(-)	Re-inputs of Oil Products							
制 气	Gas Production			0.64				
#焦炭再投入量(-)	Coke Re-input(-)							
煤制品加工	Coal Products Processing							
回收能	**Energy Recycled**							
损失量	**Losses**					**0.76**		
#运输和输配损失	In Transportation and Transmission							
终端消费量	**Final Consumption Industry**	**1.39**		**0.64**			**415.90**	**443.33**
第一产业	Primary Industry						5.05	
第二产业	Secondary Industry	1.39		0.64			28.99	0.13
工 业	Industry	1.39		0.64			19.38	0.13
#用作原料、材料	Use in Materials						0.20	0.04
建筑业	Construction						9.61	
第三产业	Tertiary Industry						121.58	443.21
生活消费	Residential Consumption						260.27	
城 镇	Urban						252.35	
乡 村	Rural						7.92	
平衡差额	Balance							0.02
消费量合计	**Total Energy Consumption**	**1.39**		**0.64**		**1075.77**	**415.90**	**443.33**

4-7 续表 2 continued

单位：万吨 (10000 tons)

项　　目	Item	柴油 Diesel Oil	燃料油 Fuel Oil	石脑油 Naphtha	润滑油 Grease Oil	石蜡 Oilfin	溶剂油 Solvent Oil	石油沥青 Oil Asphalt	石油焦 Petroleum Coal
可供本地区消费的能源量	**Total Energy Available for Local Consumption**	**-102.98**	**54.15**	**61.26**	**25.11**	**-9.42**	**0.10**	**10.57**	**-25.68**
加工转换投入(-)产出(+)量	**Input(-) or Output(+) in Processing and Transformation**	**318.59**	**-45.10**	**-0.08**		**9.60**		**8.95**	**25.81**
火力发电	Thermal Power	-0.10	-0.13						-5.69
供　热	Heating	-0.38	-1.86						-20.15
煤炭洗选	Coal Washing-dressing								
炼　焦	Coking								
炼油及煤制油	Oil Refining and Coal Liquification	319.08	24.01	114.82		9.60		8.95	51.65
#油品再投入量(-)	Re-inputs of Oil Products		-67.12	-114.90					
制　气	Gas Production								
#焦炭再投入量(-)	Coke Re-input(-)								
煤制品加工	Coal Products Processing								
回收能	**Energy Recycled**								
损失量	**Losses**								
#运输和输配损失	In Transportation and Transmission								
终端消费量	**Final Consumption Industry**	**215.34**	**9.05**	**61.18**	**25.22**	**0.18**	**0.10**	**19.52**	
第一产业	Primary Industry	3.81			0.10				
第二产业	Secondary Industry	71.53	6.79	61.18	25.12	0.18	0.10	19.52	
工　业	Industry	44.73	6.79	61.18	25.12	0.18	0.10	19.52	
#用作原料、材料	Use in Materials	0.24	3.50	61.18	25.12	0.18	0.10	19.52	
建筑业	Construction	26.80							
第三产业	Tertiary Industry	139.45	2.27						
生活消费	Residential Consumption	0.56							
城　镇	Urban								
乡　村	Rural	0.56							
平衡差额	Balance	0.27			-0.11				0.13
消费量合计	**Total Energy Consumption**	**215.82**	**78.16**	**176.08**	**25.22**	**0.18**	**0.10**	**19.52**	**25.84**

4-7 续表 3 continued

单位：万吨 (10000 tons)

项　　目	Item	液　化 石油气 Liquefied Petroleum Gas	炼厂 干气 Net Gas of Plant	其它 石油 制品 Other Petroleum Products	天然气 (亿立方米) Natural Gas (100 million cu.m)	热力 (万百万千焦) Heat (10000 million kilo-joule)	电力 (亿千瓦时) Electricity (100 million kwh)	其它能源 (万吨标准煤) Others (10000 tons of SCE)
可供本地区消费的能源量	**Total Energy Available for Local Consumption**	**10.60**		**-29.38**	**92.07**	**1433.55**	**627.21**	**33.73**
加工转换投入(-)产出(+)量	**Input(-) or Output(+) in Processing and Transformation**	**32.32**	**75.02**	**216.17**	**-34.78**	**15632.37**	**284.73**	**-11.34**
火力发电	Thermal Power		-0.48	-0.60	-21.22		284.73	-19.67
供　热	Heating	-0.04	-4.55	-7.19	-13.56	15632.37		
煤炭洗选	Coal Washing-dressing							
炼　焦	Coking							
炼油及煤制油	Oil Refining and Coal Liquification	34.99	80.05	283.00				
#油品再投入量(-)	Re-inputs of Oil Products	-2.63		-59.03				
制　气	Gas Production							
#焦炭再投入量(-)	Coke Re-input(-)							
煤制品加工	Coal Products Processing							
回收能	**Energy Recycled**							**8.33**
损失量	**Losses**	**3.88**			**4.68**		**51.02**	
#运输和输配损失	In Transportation and Transmission				4.68		51.02	
终端消费量	**Final Consumption Industry**	**39.12**	**74.09**	**186.80**	**52.61**	**17065.92**	**860.92**	**22.39**
第一产业	Primary Industry	0.07			0.01		18.14	
第二产业	Secondary Industry	2.59	74.09	186.80	10.89	5016.16	272.01	3.64
工　业	Industry	1.88	74.09	186.80	10.40	4890.54	246.12	3.47
#用作原料、材料	Use in Materials	0.23	3.21	164.39				
建筑业	Construction	0.71			0.49	125.62	25.89	0.16
第三产业	Tertiary Industry	17.37			30.18	8648.76	408.93	11.75
生活消费	Residential Consumption	19.10			11.54	3401.00	161.83	7.00
城　镇	Urban	11.21			11.27	3401.00	137.09	
乡　村	Rural	7.89			0.27		24.74	7.00
平衡差额	Balance	-0.08	0.93					
消费量合计	**Total Energy Consumption**	**45.67**	**79.12**	**253.62**	**92.07**	**17065.92**	**911.94**	**42.06**

4-8 能源平衡表(标准量简表)(2012年)
ENERGY BALANCE (STANDARD VOLUME) (ABRIDGED EDITION) (2012)

单位：万吨标准煤 (10000 tons of SCE)

项目	Item	合计 Total	原煤 Coal	洗精煤 Clean Coal	其他洗煤 Other Washing Coal	煤制品 Coal Products	煤矸石 Coal Slack	焦炭 Coke	焦炉煤气 Coking Gas
可供本地区消费的能源量	**Total Energy Available for Local Consumption**	**7179.42**	**1765.39**	**1.75**		**2.14**		**31.34**	**21.98**
加工转换投入(-)产出(+)量	**Input(-) or Output(+) in Processing and Transformation**	**-119.05**	**-962.18**	**-1.68**		**0.68**			
火力发电	Thermal Power		-525.43			-0.96			
供热	Heating	-106.65	-420.12			-12.99			
煤炭洗选	Coal Washing-dressing	-1.15	-13.57	12.42					
炼焦	Coking								
炼油及煤制油	Oil Refining and Coal Liquification	325.94							
#油品再投入量(-)	Re-inputs of Oil Products	-344.14							
制气	Gas Production	-0.36	-1.51						
#焦炭再投入量(-)	Coke Re-input(-)								
煤制品加工	Coal Products Processing	-1.01	-1.53	-14.10		14.63			
回收能	**Energy Recycled**	**8.33**							
损失量	**Losses**	**218.91**							
#运输和输配损失	In Transportation and Transmission	211.17							
终端消费量	**Final Consumption Industry**	**6839.73**	**803.21**	**0.06**		**2.82**		**31.34**	**22.01**
第一产业	Primary Industry	100.75	34.17						
第二产业	Secondary Industry	2149.53	318.05	0.06		0.54		31.34	21.98
工业	Industry	1999.08	309.01	0.06		0.35		31.34	21.98
#用作原料、材料	Use in Materials	365.08	0.07						
建筑业	Construction	150.45	9.04			0.18			
第三产业	Tertiary Industry	3190.70	218.18			2.29			0.03
生活消费	Residential Consumption	1398.75	232.81						
城镇	Urban	1115.45	58.67						
乡村	Rural	283.31	174.14						
平衡差额	Balance	1.74		0.01		-0.01		-0.01	-0.03
消费量合计	**Total Energy Consumption**	**7177.68**							

注：从2010年起，热力调整为按当量热值计算，电力仍然按等价热值计算。
Note: From 2010, heat power is calculated as equivalent heat value. Electric power is still calculated as equal in heat value.

4-8 续表 1 continued

单位：万吨标准煤 (10000 tons of SCE)

项目	Item	高炉煤气(亿立方米) Furnace Gas (100 million cu.m)	转炉煤气(亿立方米) Converter Gas (100 million cu.m)	其它煤气 Other Gas	其它焦化产品 Other Carbonized Products	原油 Crude Oil	汽油 Gaso-line	煤油 Kero-sene
可供本地区消费的能源量	**Total Energy Available for Local Consumption**	**1.55**				**1536.85**	**226.65**	**456.78**
加工转换投入(-)产出(+)量	**Input(-) or Output(+) in Processing and Transformation**			**1.15**		**-1535.76**	**385.30**	**195.57**
火力发电	Thermal Power							
供热	Heating							
煤炭洗选	Coal Washing-dressing							
炼焦	Coking							
炼油及煤制油	Oil Refining and Coal Liquification					-1535.76	385.30	195.57
#油品再投入量(-)	Re-inputs of Oil Products							
制气	Gas Production			1.15				
#焦炭再投入量(-)	Coke Re-input(-)							
煤制品加工	Coal Products Processing							
回收能	**Energy Recycled**							
损失量	**Losses**					**1.08**		
#运输和输配损失	In Transportation and Transmission							
终端消费量	**Final Consumption Industry**	**1.55**		**1.15**			**611.95**	**652.32**
第一产业	Primary Industry						7.44	
第二产业	Secondary Industry	1.55		1.15			42.66	0.19
工业	Industry	1.55		1.15			28.52	0.19
#用作原料、材料	Use in Materials						0.29	0.05
建筑业	Construction						14.15	
第三产业	Tertiary Industry						178.90	652.13
生活消费	Residential Consumption						382.96	
城镇	Urban						371.31	
乡村	Rural						11.65	
平衡差额	Balance							0.03
消费量合计	**Total Energy Consumption**							

4-8 续表 2 continued

单位：万吨标准煤 (10000 tons of SCE)

项 目	Item	柴油 Diesel Oil	燃料油 Fuel Oil	石脑油 Naphtha	润滑油 Grease Oil	石蜡 Oilfin	溶剂油 Solvent Oil	石油沥青 Oil Asphalt	石油焦 Petroleum Coal
可供本地区消费的能源量	**Total Energy Available for Local Consumption**	**-150.05**	**77.36**	**91.89**	**35.51**	**-12.86**	**0.15**	**14.07**	**-28.04**
加工转换投入(-)产出(+)量	**Input(-) or Output(+) in Processing and Transformation**	**464.22**	**-64.38**	**-0.12**		**13.11**		**11.91**	**28.17**
火力发电	Thermal Power	-0.14	-0.18						-6.20
供 热	Heating	-0.56	-2.61						-21.97
煤炭洗选	Coal Washing-dressing								
炼 焦	Coking								
炼油及煤制油	Oil Refining and Coal Liquification	464.93	34.30	172.23		13.11		11.91	56.34
#油品再投入量(-)	Re-inputs of Oil Products		-95.89	-172.35					
制 气	Gas Production								
#焦炭再投入量(-)	Coke Re-input(-)								
煤制品加工	Coal Products Processing								
回收能	**Energy Recycled**								
损失量	**Losses**								
#运输和输配损失	In Transportation and Transmission								
终端消费量	**Final Consumption Industry**	**313.78**	**12.98**	**91.76**	**35.67**	**0.25**	**0.15**	**25.98**	
第一产业	Primary Industry	5.55			0.14				
第二产业	Secondary Industry	104.23	9.73	91.76	35.53	0.25	0.15	25.98	
工 业	Industry	65.17	9.73	91.76	35.53	0.25	0.15	25.98	
#用作原料、材料	Use in Materials	0.35	5.02	91.76	35.53	0.25	0.15	25.98	
建筑业	Construction	39.05							
第三产业	Tertiary Industry	203.19	3.25						
生活消费	Residential Consumption	0.81							
城 镇	Urban								
乡 村	Rural	0.81							
平衡差额	Balance	0.40		0.01	-0.15			-0.01	0.13
消费量合计	**Total Energy Consumption**								

4-8 续表 3 continued

单位：万吨标准煤 (10000 tons of SCE)

项　目	Item	液　化石油气 Liquefied Petroleum Gas	炼厂干气 Net Gas of Plant	其它石油制　品 Other Petroleum Products	天然气 Natural Gas (100 million cu.m)	热力 Heat	电力 Electricity	其它能源 Others
可供本地区消费的能源量	**Total Energy Available for Local Consumption**	**18.17**		**-33.04**	**1197.83**	**48.88**	**1841.38**	**33.73**
加工转换投入(-)产出(+)量	**Input(-) or Output(+) in Processing and Transformation**	**55.41**	**117.88**	**260.48**	**-446.46**	**533.06**	**835.90**	**-11.34**
火力发电	Thermal Power		-0.75	-0.79	-281.78		835.90	-19.67
供　热	Heating	-0.06	-7.15	-9.57	-164.68	533.06		
煤炭洗选	Coal Washing-dressing							
炼　焦	Coking							
炼油及煤制油	Oil Refining and Coal Liquification	59.99	125.79	342.23				
#油品再投入量(-)	Re-inputs of Oil Products	-4.51		-71.38				
制　气	Gas Production							
#焦炭再投入量(-)	Coke Re-input(-)							
煤制品加工	Coal Products Processing							
回收能	**Energy Recycled**							**8.33**
损失量	**Losses**	**6.65**			**61.38**		**149.80**	
#运输和输配损失	In Transportation and Transmission				61.38		149.80	
终端消费量	**Final Consumption Industry**	**67.07**	**116.43**	**227.45**	**689.96**	**581.95**	**2527.49**	**22.39**
第一产业	Primary Industry	0.12			0.08		53.25	
第二产业	Secondary Industry	4.44	116.43	227.45	142.80	171.05	798.57	3.64
工　业	Industry	3.23	116.43	227.45	136.43	166.77	722.57	3.47
#用作原料、材料	Use in Materials	0.39	5.05	200.17				
建筑业	Construction	1.21			6.37	4.28	76.00	0.16
第三产业	Tertiary Industry	29.78			395.73	294.92	1200.55	11.75
生活消费	Residential Consumption	32.74			151.34	115.97	475.12	7.00
城　镇	Urban	19.22			147.80	115.97	402.48	
乡　村	Rural	13.52			3.55		72.64	7.00
平衡差额	Balance	-0.14	1.46		0.04		-0.01	
消费量合计	**Total Energy Consumption**							

4-9 分行业能源消费总量和主要能源品种消费量(2012年)

单位：万吨

项 目	Item	能源消费总量(万吨标准煤) Total Energy Consumption (10000 tons of SCE)	煤 炭 Coal	焦 炭 Coke
合 计	**Total**	**7177.68**	**2269.89**	**32.27**
农、林、牧、渔业	Farming, Forestry, Animal Husbandry and Fishery	100.75	44.60	
采矿业	Mining	195.12	47.34	27.73
煤炭开采和洗选业	Mining and Washing of Coal	6.44	1.34	
石油和天然气开采业	Extraction of Petroleum and Natural Gas	0.77		
黑色金属矿采选业	Mining and Processing of Ferrous Metal Ores	150.94	44.53	27.73
有色金属矿采选业	Mining and Processing of Non-Ferrous Metal Ores			
非金属矿采选业	Mining and Processing of Nonmetal Ores	1.81	0.14	
开采辅助活动	Mining Support Service Activities	35.16	1.33	
其他采矿业	Mining of Other Ores			
制造业	Manufacturing	1640.46	391.77	4.54
农副食品加工业	Processing of Food from Agriculture Products	30.85	17.66	
食品制造业	Manufacture of Foods	32.70	7.89	
酒、饮料和精制茶制造业	Manufacture of Wines, Beverage and Refined Tea	46.09	30.76	
烟草制品业	Manufacture of Tobacco	2.40	0.01	
纺织业	Manufacture of Textile	8.86	4.30	
纺织服装、服饰业	Manufacture of Textile Wearing Apparel and Ornament	22.65	13.83	
皮革、毛皮、羽毛及其制品和制鞋业	Manufacture of Leather, Fur, Feather and Its Products	1.39	0.38	
木材加工和木、竹、藤、棕、草制品业	Processing of Timbers, Manufacture of Wood, Bamboo, Rattan, Palm, and Straw Products	5.49	0.66	
家具制造业	Manufacture of Furniture	8.52	2.12	
造纸和纸制品业	Manufacture of Paper and Paper Products	15.31	8.66	
印刷和记录媒介复制业	Printing, Reproduction of Recording Media	30.29	3.80	
文教、工美、体育和娱乐用品制造业	Manufacture of Articles for Culture, Education, Artwork,Sport and Entertainment Activity	5.89	1.76	
石油加工、炼焦和核燃料加工业	Processing of Petroleum, Coking, Processing of Nuclear Fuel	564.68	3.29	
化学原料和化学制品制造业	Manufacture of Raw Chemical Materials and	158.36	71.24	0.01
医药制造业	Manufacture of Medicines	33.05	11.95	
化学纤维制造业	Manufacture of Chemical Fibers	1.72	0.03	
橡胶和塑料制品业	Manufacture of Rubber and Plastics	34.65	8.21	
非金属矿物制品业	Manufacture of Non-Metallic Mineral Products	235.20	152.13	2.15

注：各行业能源总消费量为各行业终端消费量与各行业分摊的损失量和加工转换损失量之和，不等于分品种能源消费量(标准煤)的合计。

CONSUMPTION OF TOTAL ENERGY AND ITS MAIN VARIETIES BY SECTOR (2012)

(10000 tons)

汽 油 Gasoline	煤 油 Kerosene	柴 油 Diesel Oil	燃料油 Fuel Oil	液 化 石油气 Liquefied Petroleum Gas	天然气 (亿立方米) Natural Gas (100 million cu.m)	热 力 (万百万千焦) Heat (10 billion kilo-joule)	电 力 (亿千瓦时) Electricity (100 million kwh)
415.90	**443.33**	**215.82**	**78.16**	**45.67**	**92.07**	**17065.92**	**911.94**
5.05		3.81		0.07	0.01		18.14
0.91		25.88	0.01	0.04	0.32	165.57	19.40
0.07		0.10				1.16	1.72
0.01					0.06		0.26
0.13		4.41	0.01		0.24	162.85	16.34
0.03		0.56				1.51	0.24
0.67		20.81		0.04	0.02	0.05	0.84
16.71	0.13	18.25	73.90	4.45	9.88	4439.60	175.62
0.54		0.46	0.03	0.05	0.12	47.06	3.97
0.62		0.53		0.25	0.45	101.72	4.86
0.36		0.59		0.01	0.09	102.38	5.46
0.01					0.12		0.26
0.12		0.03		0.02	0.03	18.97	1.35
0.80		0.23		0.03	0.03	35.25	2.09
0.08		0.01				1.96	0.19
0.14		0.08			0.02	1.05	1.11
0.50		0.10	0.01	0.02	0.01	14.32	1.38
0.36		0.19	0.01	0.02	0.06	8.71	1.95
0.90	0.01	0.23		0.03	0.30	75.78	5.92
0.19		0.04		0.02	0.04	26.88	0.71
0.05		0.08	67.12	2.66	2.62	1594.33	17.38
0.98		0.86	3.51	0.25	0.29	1113.76	17.02
0.53		0.30		0.02	0.35	113.07	4.87
0.02					0.02	9.52	0.37
0.62		0.25		0.11	0.09	84.78	7.25
0.98		10.00	3.18	0.11	0.98	33.17	21.45

Note: Total energy consumption in each sector is the end consumption of each sector plus losses shared by each sector and losses from processing in each sector, but not equal to sum of consumption (SCE equivalent) of all sorts of energy.

4-9 续表

单位：万吨

项　　目	Item	能源消费总量(万吨标准煤) Total Energy Consumption (10000 tons of SCE)	煤　炭 Coal	焦　炭 Coke
黑色金属冶炼及压延加工业	Smelting and Pressing of Ferrous Metals	32.23	1.31	0.79
有色金属冶炼及压延加工业	Smelting and Pressing of Non-Ferrous Metals	8.47	1.32	0.06
金属制品业	Manufacture of Metal Products	37.66	6.78	0.06
通用设备制造业	Manufacture of General Purpose Machinery	38.37	6.65	0.91
专用设备制造业	Manufacture of Special Purpose Machinery	26.03	5.14	0.03
汽车制造业	Manufacture of motor vehicles	98.84	9.15	0.46
铁路、船舶、航空航天和其他运输设备制造业	Manufacture of railway locomotives, building of ships and boats, manufacture of air and spacecrafts and other transportation equipments	17.46	11.48	0.02
电气机械和器材制造业	Manufacture of Electrical Machinery and Equipment	28.95	6.65	0.02
计算机、通讯和其他电子设备制造业	Manufacture of computer, communication equipment and other electronic equipment	82.79	0.68	
仪器仪表制造业	Manufacture of measuring instrument and meter	8.97	0.65	
其他制造业	Other manufacturing	6.52	0.08	
废弃资源综合利用业	Waste recycling and recovery	1.59	0.38	
金属制品、机械和设备修理业	Repair of fabricated metal products, machinery and equipment	14.48	2.82	0.03
电力、燃气及水的生产和供应业	Production and Distribution of Electricity, Gas and Water	440.08	1213.97	
电力、热力生产和供应业	Production and Distribution of Electric Power and Heat Power	400.38	1213.53	
燃气生产和供应业	Production and Distribution of Gas	10.92		
水的生产和供应业	Production and Distribution of Water	28.78	0.44	
建筑业	Construction	150.45	11.85	
批发和零售业	Wholesale Trade and Retail Trade	221.68	11.53	
交通运输、仓储和邮政业	Transportation, Storage, Posts and Telecommunications	1235.05	15.86	
住宿和餐饮业	Hotel and Restaurants	262.34	27.77	
信息传输、软件和信息技术服务业	Information transmission,software and information technology services	129.64	1.14	
金融业	Finance	54.26	0.96	
房地产业	Real Estate Trade	411.54	90.02	
租赁和商务服务业	Tenancy and Commercial Servecis	196.26	44.50	
科学研究和技术服务业	Scientific research and development, technical services	163.92	14.48	
水利、环境和公共设施管理业	Water, Environment and Municipal Engineering Conservancy	46.51	4.16	
居民服务、修理和其他服务业	Resident services, repair and other services	47.13	16.84	
教　育	Education	222.87	33.30	
卫生和社会工作	Health care and social works	74.05	10.26	
文化、体育和娱乐业	Culture, Art, Sports and Recreation	71.47	2.60	
公共管理、社会保障和社会组织	Pulic administration,social security and social organizations	115.35	14.71	
生活消费	Residential Consumption	1398.75	272.23	
城　镇	Urban	1115.44	62.23	
乡　村	Rural	283.31	210.00	

4-9 continued

(10000 tons)

汽　油 Gasoline	煤　油 Kerosene	柴　油 Diesel Oil	燃料油 Fuel Oil	液　化 石油气 Liquefied Petroleum Gas	天然气 (亿立方米) Natural Gas (100 million cu.m)	热　力 (万百万千焦) Heat (10 billion kilo-joule)	电　力 (亿千瓦时) Electricity (100 million kwh)
0.09		0.39		0.02	0.91	13.13	5.86
0.11		0.05		0.01	0.01	19.41	2.05
1.13		0.48		0.51	0.44	46.43	6.56
1.16	0.02	0.56		0.10	0.19	143.71	6.16
1.03		0.31	0.01	0.01	0.12	106.44	4.54
1.78	0.03	1.71	0.03	0.12	1.88	185.36	18.15
0.22		0.23		0.01	0.05	112.74	2.24
1.18		0.09		0.03	0.15	95.12	4.86
0.70		0.09		0.02	0.28	217.16	23.37
0.62		0.04			0.06	55.16	1.27
0.13		0.10		0.01	0.02	37.11	0.90
0.02		0.05				1.42	0.35
0.74	0.07	0.17		0.01	0.15	23.70	1.72
1.77		1.07	1.99	3.94	34.98	285.37	102.13
1.35		0.91	1.99	0.05	34.49	253.71	92.42
0.23		0.06		3.88	0.43	6.68	0.80
0.19		0.10		0.01	0.06	24.98	8.91
9.61		26.80		0.71	0.49	125.62	25.89
26.00		6.09	0.03	0.63	0.62	690.58	45.27
44.03	442.79	117.34	1.28	0.34	8.22	663.38	69.11
1.77		0.94	0.03	14.07	4.67	653.59	43.62
3.96		0.44		0.04	0.14	317.93	37.24
2.54		0.24		0.04	0.10	254.27	13.42
4.46		1.45	0.89	0.37	8.21	1332.85	60.29
10.61		2.92	0.01	0.20	2.03	722.34	30.63
9.40	0.41	1.49		0.13	3.07	782.88	23.40
2.05		4.42		0.15	0.20	41.03	9.88
1.50		0.84	0.01	0.15	0.91	110.15	5.04
3.45		1.76		0.47	3.97	1618.13	27.02
1.07		0.23		0.18	1.14	379.87	11.59
2.03		0.40		0.23	0.85	393.30	13.76
8.71		0.89	0.01	0.36	0.72	688.46	18.66
260.27		0.56		19.10	11.54	3401.00	161.83
252.35				11.21	11.27	3401.00	137.09
7.92		0.56		7.89	0.27		24.74

4-10 能源消费弹性系数(2000-2012年)
ELASTICITY COEFFICIENT OF ENERGY CONSUMPTION (2000-2012)

项 目 Item	能源消费比上年增长 (%) Growth Rate of Energy Consumption over Preceding Year	电力消费比上年增长(%) Growth Rate of Electricity Consumption over Preceding Year	地区生产总值比上年增长(%) Growth Rate of Gross Domestic Product(GDP) over Preceding Year	能源消费弹性系数 Elasticity Coefficient of Energy Consumption	电力消费弹性系数 Elasticity Coefficient of Electricity Consumption
2000	6.08	9.53	11.8	0.51	0.81
2001	2.06	5.68	11.7	0.18	0.49
2002	4.89	9.54	11.5	0.43	0.83
2003	4.78	5.71	11.1	0.43	0.51
2004	10.57	10.60	14.1	0.75	0.75
2005	7.44	11.16	12.1	0.61	0.92
2006	6.92	9.16	13.0	0.53	0.71
2007	6.45	9.06	14.5	0.45	0.63
2008	0.67	4.90	9.1	0.07	0.54
2009	3.84	7.15	10.2	0.38	0.70
2010	5.84	9.49	10.3	0.57	0.92
2011	0.59	2.74	8.1	0.07	0.34
2012	2.61	6.82	7.7	0.34	0.88

注：地区生产总值增长速度按可比价计算。
Note: The groth rates of GDP are calculated at comparable prices.

4-11 平均每万元地区生产总值能源消费量(2001-2012年)
ENERGY CONSUMPTION PER 10000 YUAN GROSS DOMESTIC PRODUCT (2001-2012)

项　目 Item	能源总消费量 (吨标准煤) Total (ton of SCE)	煤　炭 (吨) Coal (ton)	电　力 (千瓦时) Electricity (kwh)	石　油 (吨) Petroleum (ton)
2001	1.20	0.77	1127.91	0.23
2002	1.13	0.66	1108.09	0.25
2003	1.06	0.63	1053.83	0.22
2004	1.03	0.59	1021.65	0.20
2005	0.99	0.55	1012.86	0.20
	(0.79)	(0.44)	(813.60)	(0.16)
2006	0.75	0.39	786.01	0.15
2007	0.70	0.33	748.74	0.15
2008	0.64	0.28	719.84	0.14
2009	0.61	0.25	700.03	0.13
2010	0.58	0.22	694.69	0.12
	(0.49)	(0.19)	(588.72)	(0.10)
2011	0.46	0.15	559.28	0.10
2012	0.44	0.14	554.57	0.09

注：本表中每万元地区生产总值能源消费量按可比价格计算，可比价格每五年调整一次基期，更换基期年份计算两个可比价数据，括号内数据是按新基期价格计算。

Note: Energy Consumption per 10000 yuan GDP were calculated comparable price. The base period of comparable price is changed every five years. Two figures at comparable price were calculated for the year in which the base period is changed.Figures in brackets were calculated at the price of new base period.

4-12 人均生活用能源(2000-2012年)
PER CAPITA ENERGY CONSUMPTION FOR NON-PRODUCTION PURPOSE(2000-2012)

年份 Year	合计 (千克标准煤) Total (kg of SCE)	煤炭 (千克) Coal (kg)	电力 (千瓦时) Electricity (kwh)	液化石油气 (千克) Liquefied Petroleum Gas(kg)	天然气 (立方米) Natural Gas (cu.m)	汽油 (升) Gasoline (liter)
2000	407.1	223.6	363.6	13.7	16.4	31.4
2001	408.2	209.6	392.5	13.1	18.7	38.4
2002	415.8	156.0	445.8	16.3	24.1	50.7
2003	472.7	187.8	488.2	20.2	28.4	61.8
2004	509.8	167.6	546.2	22.2	32.9	72.2
2005	537.4	154.1	586.8	20.8	37.4	93.5
2006	579.4	169.9	610.8	15.2	53.5	113.5
2007	613.5	169.1	651.1	16.8	54.8	136.5
2008	620.4	148.4	674.8	12.8	53.1	153.8
2009	642.7	150.7	709.4	12.5	54.3	162.1
2010	643.5	145.9	729.1	11.3	53.1	164.9
2011	656.1	140.5	727.2	10.7	52.7	167.6
2012	684.3	133.2	791.8	9.3	56.5	174.4

注：本表人均生活用能源按常住人口年平均数计算。2006-2010年数据根据全国第六次人口普查进行了修正。

Note: Per-capita energy consumption for non-production prupose are calculated by average permanent population.The figures per-capita energy have been revised in accordance with the 6th national population census.

4-13 主要能源日均消费量(2000-2012年)
AVERAGE DAILY ENERGY CONSUMPTION BY VARIETY(2000-2012)

年 份 Year	合 计 (万吨标准煤) Total (10000 tons of SCE)	煤 炭 (吨) Coal (tons)	焦 炭 (吨) Coke (tons)	原 油 (吨) Crude Oil (tons)	汽 油 (吨) Gasoline (tons)	煤 油 (吨) Kerosene (tons)	柴 油 (吨) Diesel Oil (tons)	燃料油 (吨) Fuel Oil (tons)	电 力 (万千瓦时) Electricity (10000 kwh)	天然气 (万立方米) Natural Gas (10000 cu.m)
2000	11.3	76598.4	12270.5	20620.2	3046.4	3213.1	2303.3	2448.1	10297.8	352.5
2001	11.6	74331.5	11769.9	19191.8	3997.3	3542.5	2972.6	2147.9	10912.3	457.5
2002	12.2	70726.0	10353.4	20501.4	4380.8	3978.1	3145.2	1950.7	11953.4	569.9
2003	12.7	75274.0	12008.2	19909.6	4772.6	3778.1	3194.5	1811.0	12635.6	580.8
2004	14.0	80404.4	12451.6	22114.8	5420.8	4994.5	3603.8	1830.6	13937.2	737.7
2005	15.1	84081.4	10887.7	21906.8	6444.7	5187.9	3859.2	1804.9	15535.3	877.8
2006	16.2	83717.0	9551.2	21811.5	7620.8	6407.1	4862.7	1316.4	16958.6	1113.7
2007	17.2	81771.8	9813.4	26052.3	8896.4	7591.8	5260.8	1174.0	18495.6	1277.8
2008	17.3	75073.8	6363.4	30513.7	9314.2	8699.5	6207.7	699.5	19349.7	1658.5
2009	18.0	73005.5	5807.4	31861.1	9961.9	9367.9	6580.3	1161.6	20790.4	1901.4
2010	19.1	72181.1	6039.7	30583.3	10178.9	10757.0	6504.4	1826.8	22764.4	2048.8
2011	19.2	64809.3	911.8	30276.2	10679.2	11503.6	6605.8	2045.2	23388.5	2015.3
2012	19.6	62018.9	881.7	29392.6	11363.4	12112.8	5896.7	2135.5	24916.4	2515.6

4-14 全社会用电量(1978-2012年)
TOTAL ELECTRICITY CONSUMPTION IN BEIJING (1978-2012)

单位：万千瓦时 (10000 kwh)

年份 Year	全社会用电量 Electricity Consumption	第一产业 Primary Industry	第二产业 Secondary Industry			第三产业 Tertiary Industry	城乡居民生活用电 Electricity Consumption by Households		
				工业 Industry	建筑业 Construction			城市 Urban	乡村 Rural
1978	735000	48993	570621	570621		94555	20831	11022	9809
1979	802317	52134	620262	620262		107437	22484	11495	10989
1980	854638	65283	648496	648496		116947	23912	12441	11471
1981	867153	80027	643976	643976		121883	21267	9452	11815
1982	925700	104842	657060	657060		139403	24395	10820	13575
1983	956293	92601	687937	687937		151290	24465	12320	12145
1984	1029420	105234	716653	716653		177455	30078	16025	14053
1985	1106255	111110	746324	746324		210622	38199	22479	15720
1986	1181155	105688	851519	835725	15794	175090	48858	31008	17850
1987	1285023	77909	923797	899760	24037	224747	58570	35063	23507
1988	1378574	83809	970885	943383	27502	248446	75434	48624	26810
1989	1421817	100151	979216	949629	29587	258067	84383	56120	28263
1990	1504785	93049	1014037	986356	27681	302775	94924	65262	29662
1991	1613977	93256	1061207	1032064	29143	348769	110745	77575	33170
1992	1759611	101985	1155514	1123835	31679	375874	126238	88621	37617
1993	1924978	107010	1243115	1206001	37114	429835	145018	103579	41439
1994	2054504	101134	1307898	1262961	44937	479679	165791	119025	46766
1995	2225922	102099	1403864	1341398	62466	538936	181022	130897	50125
1996	2443709	111904	1496968	1422590	74378	617286	217551	158474	59077
1997	2636078	120444	1529201	1449129	80072	721774	264659	196641	68018
1998	2762080	108267	1548485	1457149	91336	811283	294045	220543	73502
1999	2972629	121242	1581977	1478523	103454	912834	356576	276642	79934
2000	3844266	130865	2172604	2066892	105712	1064322	476475	385396	91079
2001	3999415	131811	2105819	1978673	127146	1222471	539314	439058	100256
2002	4399637	137370	2293735	2145292	148443	1342490	626042	517386	108656
2003	4676056	107372	2418419	2250525	167894	1447344	702921	574623	128298
2004	5131804	104234	2593504	2391414	202090	1628731	805335	647474	157861
2005	5705364	114308	2795753	2605832	189921	1906093	889210	706405	182805
2006	6115719	122550	2943550	2744127	199423	2090888	958731	768884	189847
2007	6670089	133557	3091374	2881807	209567	2378399	1066759	862604	204155
2008	6897189	136065	2943893	2763399	180494	2654140	1163091	949878	213213
2009	7391465	157310	3027974	2853018	174956	2918229	1287952	982720	305232
2010	8099029	168992	3278682	3081364	197319	3258009	1393346	951811	441535
2011	8217055	170368	3109174	2894464	214708	3490143	1447370	945588	501782
2012	8742835	181391	3209078	2980645	228430	3734022	1618344	1370932	247412

注：1. 1985年以前农、林、牧、渔和水利业用电量中，只包含农业排灌、农副业和社队企业的用电量。
2. 1980年以前的城市居民用电量以全市市政用电量的 1/10计算。
3. 2000年以前工业用电量不包含输配损失和发电企业自产自用电量。

资料来源：北京市电力公司。

Note: a) Before 1985, electricity consumption by agriculture, forestry, stock-raising, fishery and water conservancy only included the electricity consumption by farming irrigation, agricultural sideline, and village enterprises.
b) Before 1980, electricity consumption by urban residents was one-tenth of the total public work electricity consumption in Beijing.
c) Before 2000, electricity consumption by industry excluded transmission and distribution losses and electricity generated and consumed by power generating enterprises.

Source: Beijing Electric Power Corporation.

4-15 土地面积及利用状况(2008年)
LAND AREA AND UTILIZATION (2008)

单位：平方公里 (sq.km)

地 区	District	土地面积 Land Area	农用地 Farming Land	#耕 地 Plowland	建设用地 Constructive Land	未利用地 Non-Utilize Land
全 市	**Total**	**16410.54**	**10959.81**	**2316.88**	**3377.15**	**2073.58**
东城区	Dongcheng	25.34			25.34	
西城区	Xicheng	31.62			31.62	
崇文区	Chongwen	16.52			16.52	
宣武区	Xuanwu	18.91			18.91	
朝阳区	Chaoyang	455.08	137.25	47.26	308.93	8.89
丰台区	Fengtai	305.80	78.75	31.61	203.26	23.80
石景山区	Shijingshan	84.32	31.79	2.14	49.44	3.10
海淀区	Haidian	430.73	194.89	26.90	229.24	6.60
门头沟区	Mentougou	1450.70	1091.28	18.17	95.35	264.07
房山区	Fangshan	1989.54	1159.06	282.78	350.55	479.94
通州区	Tongzhou	906.28	561.87	350.35	309.02	35.39
顺义区	Shunyi	1019.89	603.97	310.31	328.24	87.69
昌平区	Changping	1343.54	921.67	117.76	365.20	56.68
大兴区	Daxing	1036.32	667.75	381.17	311.94	56.63
怀柔区	Huairou	2122.62	1568.02	97.51	133.37	421.23
平谷区	Pinggu	950.13	713.84	123.67	126.98	109.31
密云县	Miyun	2229.45	1540.66	229.33	329.52	359.27
延庆县	Yanqing	1993.75	1689.03	297.92	143.73	160.99

注：1．1平方公里=100公顷=1500亩。
2．由于全国第二次土地调查结果尚未正式发布，本表中土地面积数据截止到2008年。
资料来源：北京市国土资源局。
Note: a) 1sq.km =100 hectare =1500 mu
b) As the results of national 2nd land investigation haven't been formally released, land area figures in this table were those ending 2008.
Source: Beijing Land and Resources Bureau.

4-16 水资源情况(2001-2012年)

单位：亿立方米

项　目	Item	2001	2002	2003	2004	2005	2006
全年水资源总量	**Total Volume of Water Resource in the Year**	**19.2**	**16.1**	**18.4**	**21.4**	**23.2**	**22.1**
地表水资源量	Volume of Surface Water Resource	7.8	5.3	6.1	8.2	7.6	6.7
地下水资源量	Volume of Underground Water Resource	15.7	14.7	14.8	16.5	15.6	15.4
人均水资源(立方米)	**Per-capita Water Resource(cu.m)**	**139.7**	**114.7**	**127.8**	**145.1**	**153.1**	**140.6**
全年供水(用水)总量	**Total Volume of Water Supplied and Consumed in the Year**	**38.9**	**34.6**	**35.8**	**34.6**	**34.5**	**34.3**
按来源分	By Source						
地表水	Surface Water	11.7	10.4	8.3	5.7	6.4	5.7
地下水	Underground Water	27.2	24.2	25.4	26.8	23.1	22.2
再生水	Recycled Water			2.1	2.0	2.6	3.6
南水北调	Water Transit from South to North						
应急供水	Emergent Water Supply					2.5	2.8
按用途分	By Purpose						
农业用水	Water Used by Farming	17.4	15.5	13.8	13.5	13.2	12.8
工业用水	Water Used by Industry	9.2	7.5	8.4	7.7	6.8	6.2
生活用水	Water Used by Households	12.0	10.8	13.0	12.8	13.4	13.7
环境用水	Water Used by Environment	0.3	0.8	0.6	0.6	1.1	1.6
万元地区生产总值水耗(立方米)	**Water Consumption per 10000 yuan GDP (cu.m)**	**104.91**	**80.19**	**71.50**	**57.35**	**49.50**	**42.25**
万元地区生产总值水耗下降率(%)	**Decrease Rate of Water Consumption per 10000 yuan GDP (%)**	**13.79**	**20.22**	**6.91**	**15.29**	**11.07**	**12.01**

注：1. 万元地区生产总值水耗按现价计算，下降率按可比价计算。按可比价计算，2012年万元地区生产总值水耗为21.82立方米。
　　2. 本表人均水资源按常住人口年平均数计算。2006-2010年数据根据全国第六次人口普查进行了修正。

资料来源：除人均数据和万元地区生产总值水耗以外其它数据来自北京市水务局。

STATISTICS ON WATER RESOURCE (2001-2012)

(100 million cu.m)

2007	2008	2009	2010	2011	2012
23.8	**34.2**	**21.8**	**23.1**	**26.8**	**39.5**
7.6	12.8	6.8	7.2	9.2	18.0
16.2	21.4	15.1	15.9	17.6	21.6
145.3	**198.5**	**120.3**	**120.8**	**134.7**	**193.3**
34.8	**35.1**	**35.5**	**35.2**	**36.0**	**35.9**
5.0	4.7	3.8	3.9	4.8	4.4
21.6	20.5	19.7	19.1	18.8	18.3
5.0	6.0	6.5	6.8	7.0	7.5
	0.7	2.6	2.6	2.6	2.8
3.2	3.2	2.9	2.9	2.7	2.9
12.4	12.0	12.0	11.4	10.9	9.3
5.8	5.2	5.2	5.1	5.0	4.9
13.9	14.7	14.7	14.8	15.6	16.0
2.7	3.2	3.6	4.0	4.5	5.7
35.34	**31.58**	**29.92**	**24.94**	**22.13**	**20.07**
11.38	**7.56**	**8.12**	**10.14**	**5.49**	**7.38**

Note: a) Water consumption per 10000 yuan GDP is at current prices,and decrease rate is at comparable prices.Caculated at comparable pri
2010, the water consumption per 10000 yuan GDP in 2012 is 21.82 cubic metres.
b) Per-capita water resource are calculated by average permanent population.Per-capita figures
2006-2010 have been corrected in accordance with the Sixth Population Census.

Source: Except for per-capita figures and water consumption per 10000 yuan GDP,other figures are from Beijing Water Authority.

4-17 气象情况(1978-2012年)
METEOROLOGY (1978-2012)

年 份 Year	降水量 (毫米) Precipitation (mm)	平均气温(℃) Average Temperature (℃)	最高 Highest	最低 Lowest	日照时数(时) Hours of Sunshine (hours)	平均风速(米/秒) Average Wind Speed (meter/second)	平均气压(百帕) Average Air Pressure (100 pa)	大风日数(日) Days of Strong Wind (day)	雨日数(日) Days of Rain (day)
1978	664.8	11.6	37.5	-14.4	2865.4	2.6	1012.8	35	64
1979	718.4	11.1	35.9	-15.4	2667.4	2.5	1012.2	33	63
1980	380.7	11.0	35.1	-15.4	2920.8	2.5	1012.7	29	83
1981	393.2	12.3	38.1	-14.0	2803.9	2.5	1010.8	15	92
1982	544.4	12.8	37.3	-14.3	2825.1	2.6	1010.5	26	92
1983	489.9	13.0	37.2	-15.0	2844.3	2.4	1010.3	29	100
1984	488.8	11.9	36.1	-14.9	2767.6	2.4	1010.6	18	90
1985	721.0	11.5	35.1	-15.2	2511.9	2.2	1010.4	12	104
1986	665.3	12.1	38.5	-15.4	2804.1	2.3	1010.7	21	96
1987	683.9	12.3	36.1	-15.5	2631.9	2.4	1010.3	23	102
1988	673.3	12.7	38.1	-13.2	2558.1	2.4	1010.8	17	96
1989	442.2	13.2	35.8	-11.0	2626.2	1.9	1011.1	3	78
1990	697.3	12.7	37.5	-14.8	2325.0	1.9	1010.6	12	113
1991	747.9	12.5	35.7	-12.6	2536.6	2.1	1010.8	8	98
1992	541.5	12.8	37.5	-8.7	2712.5	2.2	1011.0	6	100
1993	506.7	13.0	35.8	-13.0	2669.8	2.6	1010.8	12	91
1994	813.2	13.7	37.2	-11.5	2470.5	2.5	1010.1	9	92
1995	572.5	13.3	35.0	-9.2	2519.1	2.6	1010.3	16	89
1996	700.9	12.7	36.0	-10.0	2418.7	2.6	1011.0	16	103
1997	430.9	13.1	38.2	-14.0	2596.5	2.5	1012.9	11	76
1998	731.7	13.1	37.2	-14.2	2420.7	2.3	1012.5	10	93
1999	266.9	13.1	41.9	-12.2	2594.0	2.4	1012.5	7	86
2000	371.1	12.8	39.4	-15.0	2667.2	2.5	1012.7	10	83
2001	338.9	12.9	39.6	-17.0	2611.7	2.4	1012.9	10	78
2002	370.4	13.2	41.1	-12.8	2588.4	2.3	1012.7	15	84
2003	444.9	12.9	37.6	-15.0	2260.2	2.5	1013.3	6	93
2004	483.5	13.5	38.9	-12.9	2515.4	2.4	1012.6	12	94
2005	410.7	13.2	38.9	-11.5	2576.1	2.4	1012.8	5	79
2006	318.0	13.4	37.3	-14.7	2192.7	2.2	1012.5	5	86
2007	483.9	14.0	37.3	-11.7	2351.1	2.2	1012.6	5	78
2008	626.3	13.4	36.3	-13.5	2391.4	2.2	1012.6	8	100
2009	480.6	13.3	39.6	-12.2	2511.8	2.2	1011.9	15	86
2010	522.5	12.6	40.6	-16.7	2382.9	2.3	1012.2	14	88
2011	720.6	13.4	35.9	-11.6	2485.7	2.2	1013.2	3	82
2012	733.2	12.9	38.0	-13.7	2450.2	2.2	1012.2	3	85

资料来源：北京市气象局。
Source: Beijing Meteorological Bureau.

4-18 气象(2012年)
METEOROLOGY (2012)

月 份 Month	降水量 (毫米) Precipitation (mm)	平均气温(℃) Average Temperature (℃)	日照时数(时) Hours of Sunshine (hours)	平均风速(米/秒) Average Wind Speed (meter/second)	平均气压(百帕) Average Air Pressure (100 pa)	大风日数(日) Days of Strong Wind (day)	雨日数(日) Days of Rain (day)
全 年 Total	**733.2**	**12.9**	**2450.2**	**2.2**	**1012.2**	**3**	**85**
1	0.1	-3.6	168.6	2.2	1025.5		
2		-1.3	218.8	2.4	1022.2		
3	9.2	5.9	222.6	2.6	1017.9	1	5
4	53.5	16.2	235.8	2.7	1006.5		6
5	31.3	22.8	265.7	2.3	1004.8		8
6	103.9	25.0	172.1	2.3	999.3	2	16
7	284.0	27.4	166.3	2.0	998.6		16
8	59.9	26.0	214.3	1.9	1004.5		9
9	81.2	21.1	233.9	2.0	1010.7		12
10	21.4	14.6	231.0	1.9	1014.4		7
11	81.1	4.3	187.3	2.3	1017.1		5
12	7.6	-4.2	133.8	2.3	1024.3		1

注：1. 无霜期209天。
2. 年极端最高气温38℃，出现日期 6月17日。
3. 年极端最低气温 -13.7 ℃，出现日期 12月24日。
资料来源：北京市气象局。
Note: a) Annual frost-free period is 209 days.
b) Annual utmost highest air temperature is 38℃, seen on the 17th of June.
c) Annual utmost lowest air temperature is -13.7℃, seen on the 24th of December.
Source: Beijing Meteorological Bureau.

4-19 污水处理及环境卫生(1978-2012年)
SEWAGE DISPOSAL AND ENVIRONMENTAL SANITATION (1978-2012)

年份 Year	污水管道长度(公里) Length of Sewage Pipes (km)	污水处理能力(万立方米/日) Disposal Capacity (10000 cu.m/day)	污水处理率(%) Rate of Waste Water Disposed (%)	生活垃圾无害化处理能力(吨/日) Capacity of Harmless Disposal of Garbage (ton/day)	生活垃圾产生量(万吨) Output of Domestic Garbage (10000 tons)	生活垃圾清运量(万吨) Domestic Garbage Cleared and Transported (10000 tons)	生活垃圾无害化处理率(%) Rate of Harmless Disposal of Domestic Garbage (%)	粪便清运量(万吨) Volume of Excrement and Urine Disposal (10000 tons)
1978	290	23	7.6			107.20		88.9
1979	309	23	10.2			128.00		89.4
1980	334	23	9.4			147.00		95.1
1981	347	25	10.8			174.00		97.6
1982	365	25	10.9			204.70		99.3
1983	411	25	10.2			221.40		99.5
1984	568	25	10.0			235.40		98.8
1985	706	25	10.0			248.10		142.2
1986	747	26	8.9			274.40		167.5
1987	805	26	7.7			298.30		181.0
1988	770	26	7.4			319.90		190.0
1989	860	26	6.6			337.00		196.0
1990	904	30	7.3			384.10		210.0
1991	968	30	6.6			397.10		210.3
1992	1036	5	1.2			430.90		216.0
1993	1064	5	3.1			446.30		220.6
1994	1122	25	9.6			467.20		238.1
1995	1065	59	19.4			483.90		258.4
1996	1597	59	21.2			483.00		268.0
1997	1635	59	22.0			490.00		279.0
1998	1712	59	22.5			495.10		295.6
1999	1754	59	25.0			505.00		298.0
2000	1852	129	39.4	6550		295.56	56.4	274.0
2001	2163	144	42.0	6750		309.27	82.2	301.0
2002	2658	181	45.0	8750		321.35	86.4	311.7
2003	2903	215	50.1	9400		361.36	91.3	268.0
2004	2909	255	53.9	10050	495.46	405.86	93.8	175.0
2005	2521	324	62.4	10350	536.93	454.59	96.0	171.7
2006	3398	331	73.8	10350	585.13	538.32	92.5	175.7
2007	4357	348	76.2	10350	619.49	600.93	95.7	189.1
2008	4458	329	78.9	12148	672.82	656.61	97.7	206.8
2009	4495	356	80.3	13680	669.13	656.12	98.2	211.2
2010	4479	365	81.0	16680	634.86	632.98	96.9	194.4
2011	4765	369	81.7	16930	634.35	634.35	98.2	207.5
2012	5735	389	83.0	17530	648.31	648.31	99.1	207.2

注：1. 污水处理能力等指标1992年及以后为污水无害化处理情况，1992年以前为污水简易处理情况。
2. 生活垃圾无害化处理率按清运量计算。

资料来源：北京市水务局、北京市市政市容管理委员会。

Note: a) Disposal capacity and other indicators were about harmless disposal in and after 1992, and simple disposal before 1992.
b) The harmless disposal rate of domestic garbage is calculated with the volume of garbage cleared and transported.

Source: Beijing Water Authority，Beijing Municipal Commission of City Administration and Environment.

4-20 排水及节水
WATER DRAINAGE AND SAVING

项　目		Item		2012	2011
排　水		**Water Drainage**			
污水处理能力	(万立方米/日)	Disposal Capacity of Waste Water	(10000cu.m/day)	389	369
#二三级	(万立方米/日)	Grade-II and III Disposal	(10000cu.m/day)	389	323
污水年处理量	(万立方米)	Annual Disposal Volume of Waste Water	(10000 cu.m)	126411	118884
#污水厂	(万立方米)	Disposed by Waste Water Disposal Plants	(10000 cu.m)	124655	117365
#二三级	(万立方米)	Grade-II and III Disposal	(10000 cu.m)	124655	104165
污水处理率	(%)	Rate of Waste Water Disposed	(%)	83.0	81.7
#集中处理率	(%)	Rate of Concentrated Disposal	(%)	83.0	80.6
污水排放总量	(万立方米)	Total Volume of Waste Water Drainage	(10000 cu.m)	152010	145543
排水管道长度	(公里)	Length of Drainage Pipelines	(km)	12665	11085
污水管	(公里)	Sewage Pipes	(km)	5735	4765
雨水管	(公里)	Storm Sewer	(km)	4808	4444
雨污合流管	(公里)	Storm-sewage Sewer	(km)	2122	1876
再生水利用量	(万立方米)	Volume of Reusable Water Reused	(10000 cu.m)	75003	71012
节　水		**Water Saving**			
节水量	(万立方米)	Volume Saved	(10000 cu.m)	11311	8951
节水措施	(项)	Water Saving Measures Implemented	(unit)	123	205

资料来源：北京市水务局。
Source: Beijing Water Authority.

4-21 环境卫生
MUNICIPAL ENVIRONMENT AND SANITATION

项　目		Item		2012	2011
工作量		**Work Load**			
清扫街道面积	(万平方米/日)	Area Under Cleaning Program	(10000 sq.m/day)	14346	13701
生活垃圾无害化处理能力	(吨/日)	Capacity of Harmless Disposal of Garbage	(ton/day)	17530	16930
生活垃圾产生量	(万吨)	Output of Domestic Garbage	(10000 tons)	648.3	634.3
生活垃圾清运量	(万吨)	Domestic Garbage Cleared and Transported	(10000 tons)	648.3	634.3
生活垃圾无害化处理量	(万吨)	Volume of Harmless Disposal of Garbage	(10000 tons)	642.6	623.2
生活垃圾无害化处理率 (按清运量计算)	(%)	Rate of Harmless Disposal of Domestic Garbage (Calculated by Volume of Waste Cleared and Transported)	(%)	99.1	98.2
粪便清运量	(万吨)	Volume of Excrement and Urine Disposal	(10000 tons)	207.2	207.5
环卫机械数量	**(辆)**	**Number of Environmental Sanitation**	**(unit)**	**9384**	**7991**
环卫设施		**Environmental Sanitation Facilities**			
公共厕所	(座)	Lavatories	(unit)	5773	5843

资料来源：北京市市政市容管理委员会。
Source: Beijing Municipal Commission of City Administration and Environment.

4-22 环境保护(2000-2012年)
ENVIRONMENT PROTECTION (2000-2012)

年份 Year	可吸入颗粒物年日均值(毫克/立方米) Daily Mean of Inspiratory Granule in the Year (mg/cu.m)	二氧化硫年日均值(毫克/立方米) Daily Mean of Sulfur Dioxide in the Year (mg/cu.m)	二氧化氮年日均值(毫克/立方米) Daily Mean of Nitrogen Dioxide (mg/cu.m)	化学需氧量(COD)排放量(万吨) COD Discharge Volume (10000 tons)	二氧化硫(SO_2)排放量(万吨) SO_2 Discharge Volume (10000 tons)	区域环境噪声平均值(分贝) Environment Noise Mean in 6 Districts (db)	道路交通干线噪声平均值(分贝) Traffic Trunk Noise Mean in 6 Districts (db)
2000	0.162	0.071	0.071	17.9	22.4	53.9	71.0
2001	0.165	0.064	0.071	17.0	20.1	53.9	69.6
2002	0.166	0.067	0.076	15.3	19.2	53.5	69.5
2003	0.141	0.061	0.072	13.4	18.3	53.6	69.7
2004	0.149	0.055	0.071	13.0	19.1	53.8	69.6
2005	0.142	0.050	0.066	11.6	19.1	53.2	69.5
2006	0.161	0.053	0.066	11.0	17.6	53.9	69.7
2007	0.148	0.047	0.066	10.7	15.2	54.0	69.9
2008	0.122	0.036	0.049	10.1	12.3	53.6	69.6
2009	0.121	0.034	0.053	9.9	11.9	54.1	69.7
2010	0.121	0.032	0.057	9.2	11.5	54.1	70.0
2011	0.114	0.028	0.055	19.3	9.8	53.7	69.6
2012	0.109	0.028	0.052	18.7	9.4	54.0	69.2

注：化学需氧量(COD)排放量和二氧化硫排放量(SO_2)指标自2011年起调整统计口径和核算方法。
资料来源：北京市环境保护局。
Note: From 2011, statistical standard and calculation method are adjusted for COD emission and SO_2 emission.
Source: State Environmental Protection Administration of Beijing.

4-23 环境保护
ENVIRONMENT PROTECTION

项 目		Item		2012	2011
水环境		**Water Environment**			
废水排放总量	(万吨)	Total Discharge of Waste Water	(10000 tons)	140273.59	145468.95
#工业废水排放量		Industrial Waste Water Discharge Volume		9189.93	8632.72
化学需氧量(COD)排放量	(吨)	COD Discharge Volume	(ton)	186501	193184
#工业废水中COD排放量		Discharge of COD in Industrial Waster Water		6266	7118
氨氮排放量	(吨)	Ammonia Nitrogen Discharge		20483	21325
#工业废水中氨氮排放量		Ammonia Nitrogen Discharge in Industrial Waster Water	(ton)	352	434
大气环境		**Atmosphere Environment**			
二氧化硫(SO_2)排放量	(吨)	SO_2 Discharge Volume	(ton)	93849	97883
#工业二氧化硫排放量		Emission of Industrial SO_2		59330	61299
氮氧化物排放量	(吨)	Smoke and Dust Discharge Volume	(ton)	177495	188325
#工业氮氧化物排放量		Emission of Industrial Smoke and Dust		85331	90317
烟（粉）尘排放量	(吨)	Smoke and Dust Discharge Volume	(ton)	66829	65848
#工业烟（粉）尘排放量		Emission of Industrial Smoke and Dust		30844	29405
固体废物		**Solid Waste**			
一般工业固体废物产生量	(万吨)	General Industrial Solid Waste Generated	(10000 tons)	1104.05	1125.59
一般工业固体废物综合利用量	(万吨)	General Industrial Solid Waste Reused	(10000 tons)	871.73	748.70
一般工业固体废物处置量	(万吨)	General Industrial Solid Waste Disposed	(10000 tons)	219.49	348.61
危险废物产生量	(吨)	Hazardous Wastes Generated	(ton)	134130	119190
危险废物综合利用量	(吨)	Hazardous Wastes Reused	(ton)	44990	50545
危险废物处置量	(吨)	Hazardous Wastes Disposed	(ton)	89130	68645
生态环境		**Ecological Environment**			
自然保护区个数	(个)	Number of Nature Reserves	(unit)	20	20
#国家级自然保护区		State-level Nature Reserves		2	2
自然保护区面积	(万公顷)	Area of Nature Reserves	(10000 hectare)	13.41	13.41

注：2011年起水环境和大气环境调整了统计口径和核算方法。
数据来源：北京市环境保护局。
Note: From 2011, statistical standard and calculation method are adjusted for Water Environment and Atmosphere Environment.
Source: State Environmental Protection Administration of Beijing.

4-24 园林绿化及森林情况(1978-2012年)

年 份 Year	年末公园绿地面积(公顷) Park Green Areas (year-end) (hectare)	人均公园绿地面积(平方米/人) Per Capita Park Green Areas (sq.m/person)	城市绿化覆盖率(%) Coverage of City Green Areas (%)	林木绿化率(%) Coverage of City Forest (%)	年末园林绿地面积(公顷) Green Areas (year-end) (hectare)	森林面积(公顷) Forest Area (hectare)
1978	2693	5.07	22.30			
1979	2693	5.07	22.30			
1980	2746	5.14	20.10	16.6		
1981	2751	5.14	20.10	16.6		
1982	2779	5.14	20.10	16.6		
1983	2823	5.14	20.10	16.6		
1984	2878	5.14	20.10	16.6		
1985	3263	4.94	22.10	16.6		
1986	3606	5.07	22.86	16.6		
1987	3570	5.07	22.90	16.6		
1988	4074	5.80	25.00	16.6		
1989	6910	6.00	26.00	16.6		
1990	7110	6.14	28.00	28.3		
1991	4279	6.41	28.43	28.3		
1992	4213	6.65	30.33	28.3		
1993	4452	7.76	31.33	28.3		
1994	5221	7.89	32.39	28.3		
1995	5017	7.48	32.68	36.3		
1996	5147	7.54	33.24	36.3		
1997	5408	7.80	34.22	36.3		
1998	6351	9.00	35.60	36.3		
1999	6457	9.10	36.30	36.3		
2000	7140	9.66	36.50	42.0	26680	
2001	7554	10.07	38.78	44.0	30224	
2002	7907	10.66	40.57	45.5	32572	
2003	9115	11.43	40.87	47.5	38475	
2004	10446	11.45	41.91	49.5	36755	
2005	11365	12.00	42.00	50.5	38877	619243.2
2006	11788	12.00	42.50	51.0	45495	626006.3
2007	12101	12.60	43.00	51.6	46320	636565.7
2008	12316	13.60	43.50	52.1	46993	641368.3
2009	18070	14.50	44.40	52.6	61695	658914.1
2010	19020	15.00	45.00	53.0	62672	666050.7
2011	19728	15.30	45.60	54.0	63541	673411.8
2012	21178	15.50	46.20	55.5	65540	691341.1

资料来源：北京市园林绿化局。

GARDENS, PLANTED AREAS AND FOREST STATISTICS (1978-2012)

森林覆盖率 (%) Forest Coverage Rate (%)	活立木蓄积量 (万立方米) Amount of Growing Stock (10000 cu.m)	森林蓄积量 (万立方米) Amount of Forest (10000 cu.m)	森林火灾次数 (次) Number of Forest Fires (unit)	森林火灾经济损失 (万元) Economic Loss of Forest Fires (10000 yuan)
	1521.4	1295.3	9	11.4
35.9	1521.4	1295.3	13	96.7
36.5	1559.5	1368.9	8	28.1
36.5	1574.0	1394.4		
36.7	1810.3	1406.2	2	…
37.0	1854.7	1435.4	4	1.4
37.6	1899.4	1468.7	3	1.7
38.6	1943.3	1499.0	1	

Source: Beijing Municipal Bureau of Landscape and Forestry.

主要统计指标解释

能源生产量 能源生产量是反映能源生产规模、构成、生产成果的重要指标。按能源的成因分为一次能源（亦称天然能源）生产量和二次能源（亦称人工能源）生产量。

一次能源生产量 指报告期内生产一次能源的企业将自然界现存的能源资源经过开采而产出的合格产品，主要包括原煤、原油、天然气、水电等。

二次能源生产量 指报告期内将一次能源经过各种加工转换设备生产出的另一种形式的各种合格的能源产品。如火电、热力、洗煤、焦炭、各种石油制品、焦炉煤气、其他煤气等。

能源消费总量 指一定地域（行政或地理区域）内，国民经济各行业和居民家庭在一定时期所消费的各种能源的总和。能源消费总量包括终端能源消费量、能源加工转换损失量、能源运输和管理过程的损失量三部分。

能源消费总量（等价值） 是电力、热力按等价热值计算的能源消费总量。等价热值是能源统计中经常使用的一个热值概念，是指加工转换产出的某种二次能源所投入的一次能源的量，即获得一个度量单位的某种二次能源所消耗的以热值表示的一次能源。

能源加工转换投入产出量 能源具有由一种能量形式转换为另一种能量形式及耗用过程中可用一种能源替代另一种能源的特征。为提高能源的利用价值和效率，对能源进行加工、转换，产出适合生产和生活需要的更高级的能源产品。在加工转换投入(-)产出(+)量中，“-”表示能源加工转换的投入量，“+”表示二次能源的产出量。

投入量 是指为生产二次能源产品，所投入到能源加工转换设备的各种能源数量。在表中以负数表示。

产出量 是指各种能源（一次能源或少量再投入的二次能源）经过加工转换后，产出的各种二次能源产品（包括不作为能源使用的副产品，联产品）数量。

加工转换损失量 是指在能源加工、转换过程中损失的能量（能源），即能源加工、转换过程中投入的能源和产出的二次能源之间的差额。

损失量 指能源在经营管理和生产、输送、分配、储存等过程中发生的损失以及由于自然因素等原因造成的损失数量。不包括加工转换损失量。

终端消费量 是指能源消费环节的最后一个环节的能源消费，包括直接用作燃料、原材料和动力的各种能源的消费。它们的消费过程体现了能源消费的终止，不会再重新作为能源投入使用。终端消费量不包括用于能源加工转换投入量、加工转换损失量和损失量。

能源消费弹性系数 指能源消费总量增长率与地区生产总值增长率的比值。

电力消费弹性系数 指电力消费量增长率与地区生产总值增长率的比值。

平均每万元地区生产总值能源消费量 能源总消费量或分品种能源消费量与地区生产总值之比。

人均生活用能量 指用于生活消费的各种能源数量与人口总数之比。

日均能源消费量 指各品种能源源消费量与当年实际天数之比。

垃圾无害化处理能力 指垃圾无害化处理场（厂）按工艺设计每天所能处理生活垃圾的数量。垃圾无害化处理场（厂）必须是按照有关技术、环境、卫生标准和规范进行设计、建设、运行、维护和管理的各种生活垃圾处理设施，主要包括卫生填埋场、堆肥厂和焚烧厂等。

水资源总量 指降水形成的地表和地下水总量，不包括过境水量。

排水管道长度 指所有排水总管、干管、支管、检查井及连接井进出口等长度之和。计算时应按单管计算，即在同一条街道上如有两条或两条以上并排的排水管道时，应按每条排水管道的长度相加计算。

污水处理能力 指污水处理厂（或处理装置）每昼夜处理污水量的设计能力。

按污水处理的程度，一般可分为一级处理、二级处理和三级处理。

一级处理是以沉淀为主体的处理工艺。指去除污水中的漂浮物和悬浮物的净化过程，主要为沉淀。

二级处理是以生物处理为主体的处理工艺。指污水经一级处理后，用生物处理方法继续除去污水中胶体和溶解性有机物的净化过程。

三级处理也称高级处理或深度处理。指进一步去除二级处理不能完全去除的污水中的污染物的处理工艺。

污水处理量 指污水处理厂和处理装置实际处理的污水量。包括物理处理量、生物处理量和化学处理量。

污水处理率 指污水处理量与污水排放总量的比率。计算公式：

$$\text{污水处理率} = \frac{\text{污水处理量}}{\text{污水排放总量}} \times 100\%$$

生活垃圾清运量 指报告期内收集和运送到各垃圾处理场（厂）的垃圾的数量。

粪便清运量 指报告期内收集和运送到各粪便处理场（厂）的粪便的数量。

生活垃圾无害化处理量 指报告期内简易处理场和各

种垃圾无害化处理场（厂）处理垃圾的总量。垃圾简易处理量指垃圾简易填埋场所处理的垃圾总量。垃圾无害化处理量指垃圾无害化处理场（厂）所处理的垃圾总量。

生活垃圾无害化处理率 指报告期垃圾无害化处理量与垃圾产生量的比率。计算公式:

$$垃圾无害化处理率=\frac{垃圾无害化处理量}{垃圾产生量}\times 100\%$$

在统计时，如果生活垃圾产生量不易取得，可用清运量代替。

化学需氧量（COD）排放量 指工业废水中COD排放量与生活污水中COD排放量之和。指用化学氧化剂氧化水中有机污染物时所需的氧量。COD值越高，表示水中有机污染物污染越重。

二氧化硫（SO_2）排放量 指报告期内工业SO_2排放量与生活SO_2排放量之和。

工业固体废物综合利用量 指报告期内企业通过回收、加工、循环、交换等方式，从固体废物中提取或者使其转化为可以利用的资源、能源和其他原材料的固体废物量（包括当年利用的往年工业固体废物贮存量）。如用做农业肥料、生产建筑材料、筑路等。

公园绿地 指向公众开放，以游憩为主要功能，兼具生态、美化、防灾等作用，其绿地率达到65%以上，配有多种乔灌木及地被植物，有一定设施和艺术布局的绿地。包括公园、社区公园、街旁绿地、其他公园绿地。人均公园绿地面积计算口径为户籍非农业人口。

绿化覆盖率 指报告期末区域内绿化覆盖面积与区域面积的比率。

计算公式:

$$绿化覆盖率=\frac{区域内绿化覆盖面积}{区域面积}\times 100\%$$

森林面积 指由乔木树种构成，郁闭度0.20以上(含0.20)的林地或冠幅宽度10米以上的林带的面积，即有林地面积。它是反映森林资源总面积的重要指标。森林面积包括天然起源和人工起源的针叶林面积、阔叶林面积、针阔混交林面积和竹林面积。

活立木蓄积量 指一定范围土地上全部树木蓄积的总量，包括森林蓄积、疏林蓄积、散生木蓄积和四旁树蓄积。

森林蓄积量 指一定森林面积上存在着的林木树干部分的总材积，以立方米为计量单位。

森林火灾次数 指发生在城市市区外的一切森林、林木和林地的火灾次数，包括森林火警、一般灾害、重大灾害和特大灾害。

Explanatory Notes on Main Statistical Indicators

Energy Production is an important indicator reflecting the energy production size, composition and production results. By the cause of formation, it consists of the production of primary energy (also known as natural energy) and that of secondary energy (also known as artificial energy).

Production of Primary Energy means up-to-grade products produced by primary energy producers in the reporting period through extraction of existing energy in the nature, mainly including crude coal, crude oil, natural gas, water and electricity, etc.

Production of Secondary Energy means various up-to-grade energy products in another form that are made from primary energy with various processing and converting equipments in the reporting period, including thermal power, heating power, washed out, coke, various petroleum products, coke oven gas and other gas, etc.

Total Energy Consumption means the total consumption of various energies by national economic sectors and resident households in a specific region (administrative or geographic). Total energy consumption can be divided into three parts: end-use energy consumption, loss during energy processing and conversion and loss during energy transport and management.

Total Energy Consumption (in Equivalent Caloricity) means the total consumption of electric power and heating power calculated in equivalent caloricity. Equivalent caloricity is a caloricity concept frequently used in statistics of energy. It means the quantity of primary energy input for a secondary energy produced through processing and conversion, i.e. the primary energy in terms of caloricity which is consumed to produce one measuring unit of a secondary energy.

Input and Output of Energy Processing and Conversion One form of energy can be converted into another form of energy. And in the consumption, one sort of energy can be replaced with another. In order to improve the energy use value and efficiency, energy is processed and converted to produce energy products at higher levels which are suitable for productive and living needs. In the processing and conversion input (-) and output (+), "-" means the input for energy processing and conversion. And "+" means the output from energy processing and conversion.

Input means the volume of energy put into the energy processing and converting equipment in order to produce secondary energy products.

Output means the volume of secondary energy products (including byproducts and multi-products not used as energy generated) from processing and conversion of energy sources (primary energy or a small amount of secondary energy re-input).

Loss during Processing and Conversion means the energy lost in the processing and conversion of energy, namely the difference between the energy input and the secondary energy output during energy processing and conversion.

Energy Loss means the loss of energy during operation, management, production, transportation, distribution and storage, as well as the loss due to natural factors and other reasons. It excludes the loss during processing and conversion.

End-use Energy Consumption means the energy consumption in the last section of energy consumption, including the consumption of various energy sources used as fuel, raw materials and power. Such consumption represents the end of energy consumption, and the energy will not be put into use again as energy. End-use energy consumption does not include the input for energy processing and conversion, loss during the processing and conversion of energy, and energy loss.

Elasticity Coefficient of Energy Consumption means the ratio of growth rate of total energy consumption to the growth rate of GDP of Beijing.

Elasticity Coefficient of Electric Power Consumption means the ratio of growth rate of electric power consumption to the growth rate of GDP of Beijing.

Average Energy Consumption per RMB10000 GDP means the ratio of total energy consumption or energy consumption by variety to the GDP of Beijing.

Per-capital Energy Consumption by Households means the ratio of quantity of energy consumed by households to the total population.

Daily Energy Consumption means the ratio of energy consumption to the actual days in the same year.

Harmless Disposal Capacity of Waste means the quantity of domestic waste that can be disposed at harmless disposal facilities (sites) according to the process designed. Harmless disposal facilities (sites) must be domestic waste disposal facilities, including landfills, manure yards, incineration facilities and so on, which are designed, built, operated and managed in accordance with relevant technological, environmental, and sanitary standards and criterion.

Total Water Resources means the total volume of surface water and underground water caused by rainfall, excluding passing-by water.

Length of Drainage Pipelines means the total length of all main drain piles, trunk pipes, branch pipes, access manholes, and connector well entrances and exits, and so on. The length of single pipes shall be included. Namely, if there are two or more drain pipes parallel on a street, the length of every pipe shall be summed.

Waste Water Disposal Capacity means the designed capacity of waste water disposal for a waste water disposal plant (or facility).

In terms of extent, waste water disposal consists of the primary disposal, secondary disposal and tertiary disposal.

Primary Disposal is a disposal process focusing on deposition. It means a purification process removing the floating and suspended substances in waste water, mostly deposition.

Secondary Disposal is a disposal process focusing on biological disposal. It means a purification process further removing the colloids and resolvable organic substances in waste water after the process of primary disposal.

Tertiary Disposal is also known as senior or deep disposal. It means a disposal process further removing any pollutants that cannot be removed completely in the process of secondary disposal.

Volume of Waste Water Disposed means the volume of waste water actually disposed by waste water disposal plants and facilities, consisting of physical volume, biological volume and chemical volume of waste water disposed.

Rate of Waste Water Disposed means the ratio of waste water disposed to the total discharge of waste water. The formula is:

Rate of Waste Water Disposed = Waste Water Disposed / Total Discharge of Waste Water × 100%

Domestic Waste Removed and Transported means the quantity of waste collected and transported to waste treatment sites (plants) in the reporting period.

Excrement Removed and Transported means the quantity of excrement collected and transported to waste treatment sites (plants) in the reporting period.

Harmless Disposal of Domestic Waste means the total volume of waste disposed by simple disposal sites and harmless waste disposal sits (plants) in the reporting period. Simple disposal of waste means the total volume of waste by simple landfills. Harmless waste disposal means the total volume of waste disposed by harmless waste disposal sites (plants).

Rate of Harmless Disposal of Domestic Waste means the ratio of harmless waste disposal to the waste produced in the reporting period. The formula is:

Rate of Harmless Disposal of Domestic Waste = Harmless Waste Disposal / Waste Produced × 100%

In practical statistics, if it is hard to get data on the volume of domestic waste produced, the volume removed and transported may be used.

Chemical Oxygen Demand (COD) means the sum of COD emission in industrial waste water and the COD emission in domestic waste water. It means the amount of oxygen required when chemical oxidants are used to oxidize organic pollutants in water. A higher value of COD corresponds to more serious pollution by organic pollutants.

SO_2 Emission means the sum of industrial SO_2 emission and domestic SO_2 emission in the reporting period.

Industrial Solid Wastes Utilized means the volume of solid wastes from which useful materials can be extracted or which can be converted into usable resources, energy or other materials by means of reclamation, processing, recycling and exchange (including utilizing in the year the stocks of industrial solid wastes of the previous year). Examples of such utilizations include fertilizers, building materials and road materials.

Green Land in Parks means the green land open to the public, with main function of strolling and relaxation, together with ecological, landscaping and disaster preventing functions, and with more than 65% green coverage, provided with multiple arbors, shrubs and ground-cover plants, along with certain facilities and artistic layouts. They include parks, community parks, street-side green land and other green land in gardens.

Green Land Coverage Rate means the ratio of area of green land in a region to the area of the region in the reporting period. The formula for calculating forest coverage rate is as follows:

Green Land Coverage Rate = Area of Green Land in a Region / Area of the Region × 100%

Forest Area means the area of forest where arbor trees grow with canopy density above 0.2 (and at 0.2) or forest area with crown width more than 10m, i.e. the area of land with forest. It is an important indicator reflecting the total area of forest resources. Forest Area includes the area of coniferous forest, broad leaf forest, mixed coniferous-broad-leaf forest and bamboo forest from both natural and artificial origins.

Live Stumpage Reserves mean the total reserves volume of all trees on specific area of land, including trees in forest, trees in sparse forest, scattered trees and trees planted by the side of villages, farm houses and along roads and rivers.

Forest Reserves mean to the total volume of timber of forest tree trunks growing on specific area of forest, which are measured with cubic meters.

Number of Forest Fires means the number of all fires occurring in forests, woods, woodlands in and outside the urban districts, including forest fires, general fires, severe fires and super fires.

05

全社会固定资产投资和房地产开发

TOTAL INVESTMENT IN FIXED ASSETS AND REAL ESTATE DEVELOPMENT

简要说明

一、本章资料的主要内容

本章资料包括历年北京市全社会固定资产投资及其主要分组数据、保障性安居工程建设等情况。

二、本章资料的统计范围

1996 年及以前固定资产投资统计起点为 5 万元以上，1996 年以后调整为 50 万元及以上，从 2011 年开始调整为 500 万元及以上。

三、有关统计标准的变化说明

（一）关于行业划分。根据国家统计局规定，自 2012 年开始执行《国民经济行业分类》GB/T 4754-2011 标准。

（二）关于三次产业划分。根据国家统计局《三次产业划分规定》(国统字[2012]108 号)，该规定对三次产业的范围进行了调整。其中第一产业是指农、林、牧、渔业（不含农、林、牧、渔服务业）；第二产业是指采矿业（不含开采辅助活动），制造业（不含金属制品、机械和设备修理业），电力、热力、燃气及水生产和供应业，建筑业；第三产业是指除第一产业、第二产业以外的其他行业。2012 年本章数据根据此规定进行了调整。

四、本章资料的数据来源

本章资料来源于北京市统计局、国家统计局北京调查总队。

五、本章的统计调查方法

除农户固定资产投资统计采用抽样调查方法外，其他均为全面调查。

Brief Introduction

I. Main Content

Statistics in this chapter include data on fixed assets investment in Beijing and main grouped data; Construction of Guaranteed Housing Projects etc.

II. Scope of Statistics

Before and in 1996, the starting point of fixed assets is RMB 50,000; After 1996 the starting point of fixed assets is changed to RMB 500,000; From 2011, the starting point of fixed assets is changed to RMB 5 million .

III. Changes in Relevant Statistical Standards

(I) Classification of Sectors. According to relevant provisions of National Bureau of Statistics, the Standard for Classification of National Economic Sectors (GB/T4754-2011) became effective in 2012.

(II) Classification of Three Industries. According to the provision of National Bureau of Statistics on Classification of Three Industries (GTZ[2012]No.108), the scope of three industries has changed. The primary industry means agriculture, forestry, animal husbandry and fishery (excluding agricultural, forestry, animal husbandry and fishery services); the secondary industry means mining (excluding auxiliary activities), manufacturing (excluding metal products, machinery and equipment repair), electrical power, thermal power, fuel gas and water production and service sectors, and construction industry; the tertiary industry means industries other than the primary and secondary industries. In this chapter, figures for 2012 were adjusted according to this provision.

Ⅳ. Source of Data

Data in this chapter are from Beijing Municipal Bureau of Statistics and National Bureau of Statistics Survey Office in Beijing.

Ⅴ. Method of Statistical Survey

Except for statistics for farmers' fixed assets investment using sample survey, other statistics use the complete survey.

5-1 全社会固定资产投资和增长速度情况(1978-2012年)
TOTAL INVESTMENT IN FIXED ASSETS AND GROWTH RATE (1978-2012)

单位：亿元 (100 million yuan)

年份 Year	全社会固定资产投资 Total Investment in Fixed Assets	城镇固定资产投资 Urban Fixed Assets	#房地产开发投资 Real Estate Development Investment	农村固定资产投资 Rural Fixed Assets	#基础设施投资 Infrastructure Investment	#建筑安装投资 Building Installation Investment	新增固定资产 Incremental Fixed Assets
1978	22.6	22.6			5.4		16.9
1979	26.5	26.5			5.8		21.2
1980	33.2	33.2			6.0		23.2
1981-1985	**286.8**	**234.4**		**50.8**	**40.6**		**184.4**
1981	36.6	31.4		5.2	5.8		30.9
1982	38.6	34.5		4.1	6.1		26.3
1983	51.3	38.5		12.8	6.7		32.5
1984	66.3	52.2		14.1	8.8		47.1
1985	94.0	77.8		14.6	13.2		47.6
1986-1990	**724.1**	**634.9**	**22.5**	**76.5**	**117.9**		**417.4**
1986	106.2	94.5		10.4	14.5		58.5
1987	136.2	121.4		12.7	22.1		79.9
1988	163.0	138.7		21.3	23.2		77.3
1989	139.5	122.2		14.7	26.5		79.6
1990	179.2	158.1	22.5	17.4	31.6		122.1
1991-1995	**2358.7**	**2181.5**	**568.4**	**154.1**	**494.9**	**1297.1**	**1229.1**
1991	192.0	168.4	24.0	21.0	35.2	107.3	139.0
1992	266.0	234.7	33.7	27.2	58.8	136.2	157.8
1993	410.4	376.6	58.4	30.0	91.4	232.0	201.6
1994	648.8	607.4	99.5	35.7	153.4	362.6	356.0
1995	841.5	794.4	352.8	40.2	156.1	459.0	374.7
1996-2000	**5461.7**	**5063.8**	**1979.5**	**322.7**	**1382.1**	**3069.5**	**4051.2**
1996	876.9	825.6	328.2	43.6	188.8	515.8	592.5
1997	961.2	912.4	330.3	40.6	218.3	546.2	637.9
1998	1155.6	1060.3	377.4	75.8	320.4	626.9	759.3
1999	1170.6	1072.9	421.5	78.2	302.7	679.1	949.5
2000	1297.4	1192.6	522.1	84.5	351.9	701.5	1112.0
2001-2005	**10857.4**	**10033.6**	**5974.0**	**755.4**	**2260.0**	**5926.2**	**6897.4**
2001	1530.5	1417.1	783.8	93.7	356.4	801.6	1177.0
2002	1814.3	1688.2	989.4	102.5	411.9	964.9	1251.0
2003	2157.1	1999.9	1202.5	132.1	417.8	1151.3	1165.9
2004	2528.3	2333.0	1473.3	195.3	463.2	1438.9	1455.1
2005	2827.2	2595.4	1525.0	231.8	610.7	1569.5	1848.4
2006-2010	**21538.5**	**19678.6**	**10863.2**	**1859.9**	**6137.3**	**9860.6**	**11666.8**
2006	3371.5	3086.3	1719.9	285.2	935.3	1836.0	1972.1
2007	3966.6	3656.7	1995.8	309.9	1175.8	2117.9	2004.9
2008	3848.5	3554.8	1908.7	293.7	1160.7	1798.8	2666.8
2009	4858.4	4378.2	2337.7	480.2	1462.0	1983.0	2457.2
2010	5493.5 (5218.3)	5002.6	2901.1	490.9	1403.5	2124.9	2565.8
2011	5910.6	5463.9	3036.3	446.7	1400.2	2585.3	2382.0
2012	6462.8	5853.1	3153.4	609.8	1789.2	3076.6	2570.4

注：1. 根据国家统计局有关规定，从2004年起，全社会固定资产投资中不包括零星购置投资。
2. 2004年起,新增固定资产、基础设施投资、建筑安装投资中包含农村投资。
3. 根据国家统计局有关规定，2011年起投资统计起点调整为500万元，为便于比较2010年的相应数据也作了调整，未加括号的为原口径数，括号内为调整后的数据，当年固定资产投资等增长速度均按可比口径计算。

Note: a) National Bureau of statistics of china prescribed,from 2004,total investment in fixed assets excluded building and purchase of odd fixed assets.
b) Incremental fixed assets,infrastructure investment and building installation investment included rural investment from 2004.
c) According to related provisions of National Bureau of Statistics,the statistical starting point of investment was changed to 5 million yuan in 2011. To facilitate comparison, relevant figures in 2010 were changed.Figures with no brackets were based on former standard. Figures in brackets were adjusted Growth rates of fixed assets investment in respective years were on comparable basis.

5-1 续表 continued

单位：% (%)

年份 Year	全社会固定资产投资比上年增长 Growth rate of Investment in Fixed Assets	城镇固定资产投资 Growth rate of Urban Fixed Assets	#房地产开发投资 Growth rate of Real Estate Development Investment	农村固定资产投资 Growth rate of Rural Fixed Assets	#基础设施投资 Growth rate of Infrastructure Investment	#建筑安装投资 Growth rate of Building Installation Investment
1978						
1979	17.3	17.3			7.4	
1980	25.3	25.3			3.4	
1981-1985	**18.8**	**11.7**			**10.3**	
1981	10.2	-5.4			-3.3	
1982	5.5	9.9		-21.2	5.2	
1983	32.9	11.6		212.2	9.8	
1984	29.2	35.6		10.2	31.3	
1985	41.8	49.0		3.5	50.0	
1986-1990	**14.8**	**16.8**		**1.5**	**20.0**	
1986	13.0	21.5		-28.8	9.8	
1987	28.2	28.5		22.1	52.4	
1988	19.7	14.3		67.7	5.0	
1989	-14.4	-11.9		-31.0	14.2	
1990	28.5	29.4		18.4	19.2	
1991-1995	**34.2**	**36.0**	**59.9**	**19.7**	**40.8**	
1991	7.1	6.5	6.7	20.7	11.4	
1992	38.5	39.4	40.4	29.5	67.0	26.9
1993	54.3	60.5	73.3	10.3	55.4	70.3
1994	58.1	61.3	70.4	19.0	67.8	56.3
1995	29.7	30.8	254.6	12.6	1.8	26.6
1996-2000	**8.9**	**8.2**	**3.9**	**16.2**	**19.7**	**9.9**
1996	4.2	3.9	-7.0	8.5	20.9	12.4
1997	9.6	10.5	0.6	-6.9	15.6	5.9
1998	20.2	16.2	14.3	86.7	46.8	14.8
1999	1.3	1.2	11.7	3.2	-5.5	8.3
2000	10.8	11.2	23.9	8.1	16.3	3.3
2001-2005	**17.7**	**17.9**	**29.0**	**20.1**	**8.5**	**18.0**
2001	18.0	18.8	50.1	10.9	1.3	14.3
2002	18.5	19.1	26.2	9.4	15.6	20.4
2003	18.9	18.5	21.5	28.9	1.4	19.3
2004	17.2	16.7	22.5	47.8	10.9	25.0
2005	11.8	11.2	3.5	18.7	31.8	9.1
2006-2010	**14.4**	**14.2**	**12.0**	**16.2**	**24.2**	**7.7**
2006	19.3	18.9	12.8	23.0	53.2	17.0
2007	17.6	18.5	16.0	8.7	25.7	15.4
2008	-3.0	-2.8	-4.4	-5.2	-1.3	-15.1
2009	26.2	23.2	22.5	63.5	26.0	10.2
2010	13.1	14.3	24.1	2.2	-4.0	7.2
2011	13.3	14.8	10.1	-2.9	0.3	22.4
2012	9.3	7.1	3.9	36.5	27.8	19.0

5-2 按登记注册类型分全社会固定资产投资(1978-2012年)
TOTAL INVESTMENT IN FIXED ASSETS BY REGISTRATION STATUS (1978-2012)

单位：亿元 (100 million yuan)

年份 Year	全社会固定资产投资 Total Investment in Fixed Assets	国有 State-Owned	集体 Collective-Owned	股份制 Share Holding	港澳台商 Hongkong, Macao and Taiwan	外商 Foreign Funded	私营个体 Private	其他 Others
1978	22.6							
1979	26.5							
1980	33.2							
1981-1985	**286.8**	**223.8**	**22.6**				**40.4**	
1981	36.6	30.1	1.3				5.2	
1982	38.6	33.0	1.5				4.1	
1983	51.3	37.1	1.4				12.8	
1984	66.3	50.0	2.2				14.1	
1985	94.0	73.6	16.2				4.2	
1986-1990	**724.1**	**609.6**	**83.1**				**31.4**	
1986	106.2	88.7	13.3				4.2	
1987	136.2	115.8	15.2				5.2	
1988	163.0	133.2	21.4				8.4	
1989	139.5	117.7	15.1				6.7	
1990	179.2	154.2	18.1				6.9	
1991-1995	**2358.7**	**1764.2**	**188.7**				**24.8**	
1991	192.0	165.0	20.2				6.8	
1992	266.0	230.1	27.3				8.6	
1993	410.4	340.1	37.4				2.0	
1994	648.8	514.8	44.6				3.1	
1995	841.5	514.2	59.2				4.3	
1996-2000	**5461.7**	**3380.8**	**261.8**				**155.3**	
1996	876.9	545.7	57.6				4.8	
1997	961.2	605.7	54.7				4.0	
1998	1155.6	727.9	48.7				30.9	
1999	1170.6	735.7	55.8				36.1	
2000	1297.4	765.8	45.0				79.5	
2001-2005	**10857.4**	**3922.4**	**303.3**				**809.4**	
2001	1530.5	752.6	45.8				110.9	
2002	1814.3	771.5	53.9				150.6	
2003	2157.1	745.1	62.4				201.3	
2004	2528.3	755.5	69.5	1063.8	204.5	198.8	176.4	59.8
2005	2827.2	897.7	71.7	1211.8	164.1	274.1	170.2	37.6
2006-2010	**21538.5**	**8162.9**	**398.0**	**9206.8**	**903.8**	**1480.8**	**1121.2**	**265.0**
2006	3371.5	1207.2	69.3	1384.5	180.9	315.9	174.9	38.8
2007	3966.6	1343.0	80.4	1679.0	236.4	378.9	209.0	39.9
2008	3848.5	1388.6	66.8	1688.5	145.3	274.9	242.2	42.2
2009	4858.4	2316.8	68.9	1728.5	172.2	273.0	233.0	66.0
2010	5493.5	1907.3	112.6	2726.3	169.0	238.1	262.1	78.1
2011	5910.6	1903.3	99.4	3053.2	224.1	266.8	278.4	85.4
2012	6462.8	2248.2	106.8	3280.9	208.8	300.2	231.7	86.1

注：1. 根据国家统计局有关规定，从2004年起，全社会固定资产投资中不包括零星购置投资。
2. 国有包括登记注册类型为国有、国有联营及国有独资公司的单位。
3. 集体包括登记注册类型为集体和集体联营的单位。

Note: a) National Bureau of statistics of china prescribed, from 2004, Total investment in fixed assets excluded building and purchase of odd fixed assets.
b) State-owned units include state-owned companies,state-owned affilates and wholly state-owned companies.
c) Collective-owned units include collective companies and collective affilates.

5-3 按产业分全社会固定资产投资(1978-2012年)
INVESTMENT IN FIXED ASSETS BY INDUSTRY (1978-2012)

单位：亿元 (100 million yuan)

年 份 Year	全社会固定资产投资 Total Investment in Fixed Assets	第一产业 Primary Industry	第二产业 Secondary Industry	#工业 Industry	第三产业 Tertiary Industry	#运输邮电业 Transportation, Post and Telecommunications
1978	22.6	1.4	10.8	10.1	10.4	2.1
1979	26.5	1.0	12.0	10.2	13.5	2.1
1980	33.2	0.7	15.7	14.6	16.8	2.7
1981-1985	**286.8**	**5.9**	**98.1**	**89.4**	**130.4**	**16.3**
1981	36.6	0.6	13.6	12.1	17.2	2.2
1982	38.6	1.2	15.4	14.2	17.9	2.2
1983	51.3	1.2	16.4	15.4	20.9	3.2
1984	66.3	1.3	20.3	18.9	30.6	3.4
1985	94.0	1.6	32.4	28.8	43.8	5.3
1986-1990	**724.1**	**9.4**	**218.8**	**209.1**	**384.2**	**47.7**
1986	106.2	1.5	41.4	38.8	51.6	6.6
1987	136.2	1.6	46.9	44.3	72.9	9.7
1988	163.0	2.0	48.8	47.2	87.9	7.8
1989	139.5	1.9	38.4	37.0	81.9	10.0
1990	179.2	2.4	43.3	41.8	89.9	13.6
1991-1995	**2358.7**	**15.5**	**624.1**	**585.1**	**973.5**	**256.2**
1991	192.0	2.7	51.3	49.3	90.4	13.0
1992	266.0	3.9	82.9	80.2	114.2	28.4
1993	410.4	2.1	150.4	134.6	165.7	51.7
1994	648.8	3.7	185.8	175.9	318.4	81.2
1995	841.5	3.1	153.7	145.1	284.8	81.9
1996-2000	**5461.7**	**9.9**	**914.3**	**866.6**	**2160.2**	**615.3**
1996	876.9	2.8	174.9	167.3	319.7	99.5
1997	961.2	0.9	201.1	192.1	380.1	113.4
1998	1155.6	1.5	201.7	192.6	479.7	169.8
1999	1170.6	1.7	179.4	166.6	470.4	108.2
2000	1297.4	3.0	157.2	148.0	510.3	124.4
2001-2005	**10857.4**	**63.4**	**1410.6**	**1249.9**	**9383.4**	**1085.7**
2001	1530.5	8.4	154.2	137.5	1367.9	148.3
2002	1814.3	7.5	185.0	166.3	1621.8	194.1
2003	2157.1	21.0	260.7	244.4	1875.4	215.7
2004	2528.3	14.6	401.0	318.3	2112.7	218.8
2005	2827.2	11.9	409.7	383.4	2405.6	308.8
2006-2010	**21538.5**	**159.9**	**2172.8**	**2145.0**	**19205.8**	**3474.3**
2006	3371.5	14.5	363.2	358.0	2993.8	523.6
2007	3966.6	16.7	484.1	477.7	3465.8	631.3
2008	3848.5	28.1	386.0	380.8	3434.4	701.3
2009	4858.4	57.4	411.4	406.2	4389.5	827.9
2010	5493.5	43.2	528.1	522.3	4922.3	790.2
2011	5910.6	47.2	762.2	751.9	5101.3	739.7
2012	6462.8	145.4	719.8	707.8	5597.5	804.1

注：1. 根据国家统计局有关规定，从2004年起，全社会固定资产投资中不包括零星购置投资。
2. 2000年及以前按产业划分中，不含房地产开发投资及农村投资。2000年以后含房地产开发投资及农村固定资产投资。

Note: a) National Bureau of statistics of china prescribed, from 2004,total investment in fixed assets excluded building and purchase of odd fixed assets.

b) Data of investment in fixed affets grouped by industry excluded real estate development investment in fixed in rural assets on 2000 and before. After 2000, data of investment in fixed assets included real estate development investment and rural fixed assets.

5-4 全社会固定资产投资资金来源情况(1978-2012年)
INVESTMENT IN FIXED ASSETS BY SOURCE OF FUNDS (1978-2012)

单位：亿元 (100 million yuan)

年 份 Year	上年末 结余资金 Balance of Last Year End	本年资金 来源小计 Subtotal This Year	国家预算内资金 State Budgetary Funds	国内贷款 Domestic Loans	债 券 Securities	利用外资 Foreign Investment	自筹资金 Self-raising Funds	其他资金 Other Funds
1978		22.5	16.9					
1979		26.5	19.2					
1980		33.2	18.5					
1981		31.4	15.4					
1982		34.5	14.1					
1983		38.5	16.0					
1984		52.2	22.5					
1985		77.8	30.4					
1986		94.5	33.0					
1987		126.2	43.1					
1988		149.4	37.4					
1989		123.1	35.0	12.8		18.2	44.5	12.6
1990		136.2	34.4	22.8		15.2	52.3	11.5
1991		151.1	35.5	28.2		13.9	65.5	8.0
1992		216.7	42.2	40.1		14.9	109.9	9.6
1993	54.3	425.2	47.1	79.2	1.6	28.0	205.2	64.1
1994	71.1	695.7	64.1	91.5	0.8	96.9	331.2	111.2
1995	200.8	915.8	70.3	122.7	1.1	187.3	339.8	194.6
1996	204.9	926.1	76.7	152.8	1.0	161.2	330.5	203.9
1997	183.1	1016.7	86.3	194.3		139.2	383.4	213.5
1998	207.1	1140.1	98.4	223.8	17.0	132.1	450.2	218.6
1999	212.1	1183.8	136.2	262.2	1.4	82.7	461.3	240.0
2000	293.1	1439.1	107.0	373.8	0.6	51.5	505.6	400.6
2001	325.5	1796.8	136.7	429.4	2.5	35.6	595.6	597.0
2002	433.2	2075.3	108.5	543.8	1.9	41.5	672.8	706.8
2003	542.7	2674.0	78.4	755.2		52.6	887.9	899.9
2004	654.6	3712.8	118.6	804.7		120.5	1245.7	1423.3
2005	924.4	4553.7	128.8	1055.8		70.9	1452.8	1845.4
2006	1043.8	4927.3	126.4	1347.5	32.7	76.2	1532.2	1812.3
2007	1202.2	6193.0	102.2	1513.3	22.4	82.8	2195.6	2276.7
2008	1469.5	5184.7	104.2	1394.2	35.5	80.0	2016.4	1554.5
2009	1321.7	8702.2	118.1	3038.5	17.5	39.3	2441.3	3047.4
2010	2109.1	8327.8	99.5	2218.7	4.3	43.8	3209.1	2752.4
2011	2341.4	8235.4	71.7	1853.6	85.4	29.8	3588.6	2606.3
2012	2830.7	9156.0	156.1	2186.3	12.7	24.9	3478.4	3297.6

注：1978-1992年不含房地产开发和农村投资；1993-2003年不含农村投资。
Note: Figures for 1978-1992 excluded real estate development and rural investment, figures for 1993-2003 excluded rural investment.

5-5 全社会基础设施投资(1978-2012年)

单位：亿元

年份 Year	基础设施投资 Amount of Infrastructure Investment	#能源 Energy	电力 Electric Power	供热 Heating	供气 Gas Supply	供水 Water Supply	#公共服务业 Public Service	#园林绿化 Gardening	#环境卫生 Environmental Sanitation	#市政工程管理 Public Works Management
1978	5.4	1.4	0.7				0.6			
1979	5.8	1.1	0.4				1.3			
1980	6.0	0.9	0.6				2.3			
1981-1985	**40.6**	**9.4**	**5.4**				**11.2**			
1981	5.8	1.3	0.6				2.0			
1982	6.1	1.4	0.9				1.9			
1983	6.7	1.5	0.9				1.9			
1984	8.8	1.4	0.7				3.0			
1985	13.2	3.8	2.3				2.5			
1986-1990	**117.9**	**39.8**	**21.1**				**25.3**			
1986	14.5	4.8	2.3				2.1			
1987	22.1	8.0	4.1				3.1			
1988	23.2	8.8	4.1				5.3			
1989	26.5	9.2	5.2				6.6			
1990	31.6	9.0	5.3				8.3			
1991-1995	**494.9**	**134.1**	**84.6**	**12.3**	**15.2**	**22.0**	**62.9**	**2.9**		**57.3**
1991	35.2	12.4	6.4	2.0	1.3	2.7	7.5	0.3		6.8
1992	58.8	17.7	9.0	4.0	2.6	2.1	8.2	0.4		7.2
1993	91.4	19.3	11.4	1.4	2.6	3.9	4.1	1.6		1.7
1994	153.4	38.0	22.7	2.5	5.0	7.8	27.2	0.3		26.5
1995	156.1	46.7	35.1	2.4	3.7	5.5	15.9	0.3		15.1
1996-2000	**1382.1**	**363.4**	**239.7**	**45.2**	**41.4**	**37.1**	**321.0**	**14.2**	**27.1**	**275.9**
1996	188.8	59.2	48.2	3.4	4.1	3.5	29.1	2.3	0.1	25.4
1997	218.3	75.6	52.1	10.3	7.8	5.4	24.3	1.7	2.8	19.8
1998	320.4	85.1	54.2	14.2	6.7	10.0	38.0	3.0	1.9	33.1
1999	302.7	90.3	58.6	11.2	10.3	10.2	75.0	5.4	2.9	64.7
2000	351.9	53.2	26.6	6.1	12.5	8.0	154.6	1.8	19.4	132.9
2001-2005	**2260.0**	**301.7**	**165.2**	**52.7**	**53.9**	**29.9**	**668.6**	**23.1**	**79.9**	**511.4**
2001	356.4	40.8	19.3	7.2	11.0	3.3	114.6	6.7	22.4	85.4
2002	411.9	49.5	26.0	7.2	13.2	3.0	101.6	3.5	17.0	81.1
2003	417.8	36.1	10.6	11.3	10.8	3.4	152.8	1.9	17.0	103.6
2004	463.2	73.0	39.3	14.8	6.9	12.0	139.3	5.5	16.3	100.8
2005	610.7	102.3	70.0	12.2	12.0	8.1	160.3	5.5	7.2	140.6
2006-2010	**6137.3**	**780.3**	**443.6**	**176.9**	**57.6**	**102.1**	**1640.0**	**44.8**	**349.4**	**1117.7**
2006	935.3	113.4	72.8	18.7	11.0	10.9	265.3	3.4	55.4	194.8
2007	1175.8	200.2	121.0	43.0	11.2	25.0	289.5	8.0	75.7	187.3
2008	1160.7	144.1	88.4	25.9	8.1	21.7	291.6	8.0	82.2	188.7
2009	1462.0	165.4	88.9	40.1	10.5	25.8	434.5	15.9	77.7	314.0
2010	1403.5	157.2	72.5	49.2	16.8	18.7	359.1	9.5	58.4	232.9
2011	1400.2	171.1	90.1	25.3	17.0	38.8	379.4	8.1	40.5	267.8
2012	1789.2	231.9	106.3	64.8	27.3	33.5	508.1	22.0	23.5	361.6

注：2004年及以后基础设施投资包括农村基础设施投资。

TOTAL INFRASTRUCTURE INVESTMENT (1978-2012)

(100 million yuan)

#交通运输 Transportation	#铁路 Railway	#公路 Highway	#城市公共交通业 Public Transit in the City	#航空 Aviation	#邮政电信 Post & Telecom	邮政 Post	电信 Telecom	基础设施投资占全社会固定资产投资比重(%) Infrastructure Investment as Percentage of Total Fixed Assets Investment (%)
1.7	0.8	0.4		0.5	0.4			23.9
1.7	0.4	0.4		0.8	0.4			21.9
2.3	1.1	0.7		0.5	0.5			17.9
11.1	**3.9**	**5.5**		**1.7**	**5.2**			
1.8	0.6	0.9		0.3	0.4			15.8
1.9	0.8	0.8		0.3	0.4			15.8
2.6	1.2	1.0		0.4	0.6			13.1
2.3	0.7	1.3		0.3	1.1			13.3
2.6	0.7	1.6		0.4	2.7			14.0
28.3	**5.0**	**19.3**		**4.0**	**20.3**			
3.1	1.0	1.5		0.6	3.5			13.7
6.6	1.2	4.0		1.3	3.2			16.2
4.7	1.4	3.0		0.4	3.0			14.2
5.2	0.7	3.9		0.6	5.2			19.0
8.7	0.7	6.9		1.1	5.4			17.6
123.0	**50.8**	**30.6**	**22.4**	**4.6**	**137.3**	**9.5**	**127.8**	
9.3	0.8	5.6	2.3	0.5	5.8	5.0	0.8	18.3
20.1	4.7	10.7	4.0	0.7	12.3	1.1	11.2	22.1
29.4	11.2	4.7	4.7	1.1	24.2	1.7	22.5	22.3
30.0	13.6	3.6	5.7	1.0	48.6	0.9	47.7	23.6
34.2	20.5	6.0	5.7	1.3	46.4	0.8	45.6	18.6
337.4	**26.0**	**131.3**	**80.0**	**3.2**	**299.6**	**6.0**	**293.6**	
54.0	11.7	15.8	6.0	1.2	44.1	0.9	43.2	21.5
51.2	6.0	11.1	9.1	0.2	60.3	2.1	58.2	22.7
104.6	8.0	42.1	24.4		77.5	1.8	75.7	27.7
63.0		30.1	20.7		54.0	0.4	53.6	25.9
64.6	0.3	32.2	19.8	1.8	63.7	0.8	62.9	27.1
766.2	**23.2**	**294.0**	**302.8**	**137.6**	**384.0**	**6.2**	**377.9**	
104.4	1.5	52.8	45.1	2.0	84.8	2.2	82.6	23.3
159.7	1.4	107.0	44.6	1.4	78.7	1.6	77.1	22.7
129.2	9.3	55.3	48.8	15.8	82.2	0.9	81.3	19.4
148.8	7.2	38.2	51.1	52.3	68.5	1.0	67.5	18.3
224.1	3.9	40.7	113.2	66.2	69.9	0.5	69.4	21.6
3010.9	**358.7**	**732.8**	**1456.7**	**457.7**	**462.9**	**8.2**	**454.4**	
439.6	25.1	140.6	201.0	72.2	72.3	1.2	71.1	27.7
548.0	65.7	189.6	202.4	87.5	84.8	…	84.7	29.6
604.2	75.9	170.5	215.8	141.8	86.7	0.3	86.3	30.2
698.6	114.9	134.8	426.7	21.9	124.9	3.3	121.5	30.1
720.5	77.1	97.3	410.8	134.3	94.2	3.4	90.8	25.5
680.7	43.6	107.7	351.3	176.6	82.3	2.7	79.6	23.7
712.0	43.0	98.2	391.0	178.1	122.0	4.6	117.4	27.7

Note: Infrastructure investment in and after 2004 included rural infrastructure investment.

5-6 全社会基础设施投资(2012年)
TOTAL MUNICIPAL INFRASTRUCTURE INVESTMENT (2012)

项目	Item	投资额(万元) Investment (10000 yuan) 全市 Total	#城镇 Town	比重(%) Proportion (%) 全市 Total	#城镇 Town
合计	**Total**	**17892183**	**15491680**	**100.0**	**100.0**
能源	**Energy**	**2319432**	**2227318**	**13.0**	**14.4**
电力	Electricity	1063413	1019998	5.9	6.6
供热	Heat	648311	641862	3.6	4.1
供气	Gas	272588	263545	1.5	1.7
供水	Water	335120	301913	1.9	1.9
公共服务业	**Public Services**	**5081091**	**3855834**	**28.4**	**24.9**
园林绿化	Parks and Green Areas	219777	104970	1.2	0.7
环境卫生	Environmental Sanitation	235159	143336	1.3	0.9
市政工程管理	Municipal Construction	3616284	3367021	20.2	21.7
其他公共服务业	Others	1009871	240507	5.6	1.6
交通运输	**Transportation**	**7119624**	**6817514**	**39.8**	**44.0**
铁路	Railway	430083	427083	2.4	2.8
公路	Highway	982040	726678	5.5	4.7
管道运输	Pipelines	3053			
城市公共交通业	Public Traffic	3910115	3875720	21.9	25.0
#公交电汽车客运	Buses and Trolleys	86332	81832	0.5	0.5
出租汽车	Taxies	104644	95573	0.6	0.6
航空	Aviation	1781473	1781473	10.0	11.5
其他	Others	12860	6560	0.1	
邮政电信	**Post and Telecommunications**	**1220000**	**1185056**	**6.8**	**7.6**
邮政	Post	46065	35731	0.3	0.2
电信	Telecommunications	1173935	1149325	6.6	7.4
其他	**Other**	**2152036**	**1405958**	**12.0**	**9.1**
#水利	Water Conservancy	1088646	851548	6.1	5.5

5-7 全社会固定资产投资及新增固定资产(按行业分)(2012年)
INVESTMENT IN FIXED ASSETS AND ITS INCREMENTAL FIXED ASSETS (BY SECTOR) (2012)

单位：万元 (10000 yuan)

行业	Sector	投资额 Investment			新增固定资产 Incremental Fixed Assets		
		合计 Total	中央 Central	地方 Local	合计 Total	中央 Central	地方 Local
合计	**Total**	**64628134**	**8922657**	**55705477**	**25703729**	**3913678**	**21790051**
农、林、牧、渔业	**Agriculture, Forestry, Animal Production and Hunting, Fishing**	**1380302**	**8047**	**1372255**	**842039**	**5000**	**837039**
农业	Farming	228936	8047	220889	176706	5000	171706
林业	Forestry	1011956		1011956	555706		555706
畜牧业	Stockraising	50452		50452	28439		28439
渔业	Fishery	3727		3727	2016		2016
农、林、牧、渔服务业	Service Activities for Agriculture, Forestry, Animal Husbandry and Fishing	85231		85231	79172		79172
采矿业	**Mining**	**61915**		**61915**	**80244**		**80244**
煤炭开采和洗选业	Mining and Washing of Coal	12052		12052	9844		9844
黑色金属矿采选业	Mining and Processing of Ferrous Metal Ores	49863		49863	70400		70400
制造业	**Manufacturing**	**4696545**	**704797**	**3991748**	**2192352**	**231052**	**1961300**
农副食品加工业	Processing of Food from Agriculture Products	72732		72732	82161		82161
食品制造业	Manufacture of Foods	112968	21366	91602	127386		127386
酒、饮料和精制茶制造业	Manufacture of Wines, Beverage and Refined Tea	73565		73565	76922		76922
烟草制品业	Tobacco Manufacturing	1349	1349				
纺织业	Manufacture of Textile	5540		5540			
纺织服装、服饰业	Manufacture of Textile Wearing Apparel and Ornament	36875		36875	742		742
皮革、毛皮、羽毛及其制品和制鞋业	Manufacture of Leather, Fur, Feather and Its Products	5529		5529			
木材加工及木、竹藤、棕、草制品	Timber Processing and Wood, Bamboo/Ratan, Palm, Straw Products	3275		3275	2860		2860
家具制造业	Manufacture of Furniture	22767		22767	47744		47744
造纸及纸制品业	Manufacture of Paper and Paper Products	11318		11318	17871		17871
印刷和记录媒介复制业	Printing Reproduction of Recording	73673	13260	60413	47049	24272	22777
文教、工美、体育和娱乐用品制造业	Manufacture of Articles for Culture, Education and Sports Activity	3395		3395	1650		1650
石油加工、炼焦及核燃料加工业	Processing of Petroleum, Coking, Processing of Nuclear Fuel	91696	76631	15065	80804	62169	18635
化学原料及化学制品制造业	Manufacture of Raw Chemical Materials and Chemical Products	285196	219592	65604	104088	54778	49310
医药制造业	Manufacture of Medicines	439052	125706	313346	114083	5632	108451
化学纤维制造业	Chemical Fibre Manufacturing	4719		4719	815		815
橡胶和塑料制品业	Manufacture of Rubber and Plastics Products	19753		19753	16387		16387
非金属矿物制品业	Manufacture of Non-metal Mineral Products	126021	1616	124405	48853	8746	40107
黑色金属冶炼及压延加工业	Smelting and Processing of Ferrous Metals	15183		15183	21620		21620
有色金属冶炼及压延加工业	Smelting and Processing of Non-ferrous Metals	4631		4631	1970		1970
金属制品业	Manufacture of Metal Products	90145	21026	69119	75121	22937	52184
通用设备制造业	Manufacture of General Purpose Machinery	123117		123117	148104		148104

注：1. 本表分行业数据不含农户投资。
2. 行业划分执行2011年国民经济行业分类标准（GB/T 4754-2011）。

Note: a) The figures of grouping exclude investment of rural farmers.
b) Sectors are classified in accordance with the Standard for Classification of National Economic Sectors 2011 (GB/T 4754-2011).

5-7 续表 1 continued

单位：万元 (10000 yuan)

行业	Sector	投资额 Investment			新增固定资产 Incremental Fixed Assets		
		合计 Total	中央 Central	地方 Local	合计 Total	中央 Central	地方 Local
专用设备制造业	Manufacture of Special Purpose Machinery	200545	25320	175225	199027	50889	148138
汽车制造业	Manufacture of Motor Vehicles	1718331	138007	1580324	317688		317688
铁路、船舶、航空航天和其他运输设备制造业	Manufacture of Railway Locomotives, Building of Ships and Boats, Manufacture of Air and Spacecrafts and Other Transportation Equipments	102803	48917	53886	18562	1629	16933
电气机械及器材制造业	Manufacture of Electrical Machinery and	128095		128095	43828		43828
计算机、通信和其他电子设备制造业	Manufacture of Computer, Communication Equipment and Other Electronic Equipment	814793	7436	807357	525639		525639
仪器仪表制造业	Manufacture of Measuring Instrument and Meter	71551	2700	68851	54389		54389
其他制造业	Other Manufacturing	36046	1441	34605	14137		14137
废弃资源综合利用业	Waste Recycling and Recovery	452		452	452		452
金属制品、机械和设备修理业	Repair of Fabricated Metal Products, Machinery and Equipment	1430	430	1000	2400		2400
电力、热力、燃气及水生产和供应业	**Production and Distribution of Electricity, Heating Power, Gas and Water**	**2319535**	**210479**	**2109056**	**914638**	**1433**	**913205**
电力、热力的生产和供应业	Production and Supply of Electric Power and Heat Power	1711794	210479	1501315	773160	1433	771727
燃气生产和供应业	Production and Distribution of Gas	272619		272619	55830		55830
水的生产和供应业	Production and Distribution of Water	335122		335122	85648		85648
建筑业	**Construction**	**120227**	**40956**	**79271**	**145830**	**98194**	**47636**
房屋建筑业	Construction of Building	35220	24528	10692	44152	39877	4275
土木工程建筑业	Civil Engineering Construction	46496	2000	44496	40707	8485	32222
建筑安装业	Construction Installation	20507	14428	6079	54792	49832	4960
建筑装饰和其他建筑业	Building Completion, Finishing and Other Construction	18004		18004	6179		6179
批发和零售业	**Wholesale and Retail Trade**	**309248**	**25836**	**283412**	**118234**	**23273**	**94961**
批发业	Wholesale Trade	109173	25836	83337	51856	11359	40497
零售业	Retail Trade	200075		200075	66378	11914	54464
交通运输、仓储和邮政业	**Transport, Storage and Post**	**7347423**	**2091709**	**5255714**	**2430095**	**1655052**	**775043**
铁路运输业	Railway Transport	430083	420315	9768	26707	22507	4200
道路运输业	Road Transport	4990680	6278	4984402	554783		554783
水上运输业	Urban Public Transport						
航空运输业	Air Transport	1781548	1643104	138444	1725035	1618253	106782
管道运输业	Pipeline Transport	3053		3053			
装卸搬运和运输代理业	Loading, unloading, Portage and Other Transport Services	13060	1849	11211	27269	1849	25420
仓储业	Storage	82934	6846	76088	72886	12442	60444
邮政业	Post	46065	13317	32748	23415	1	23414
住宿和餐饮业	**Accommodation and Restaurants**	**579555**	**176264**	**403291**	**239101**	**3378**	**235723**
住宿业	Accommodation	487528	176264	311264	166732	3378	163354
餐饮业	Restaurants	92027		92027	72369		72369
信息传输、软件和信息技术服务业	**Information Transmission,Software and Information Technology Services**	**1654024**	**333613**	**1320411**	**1495288**	**153151**	**1342137**
电信、广播电视和卫星传输服务	Telecommunications, Broadcasting, Television and Satellite Transmission Services	1024287	247543	776744	882876	144160	738716
互联网和相关服务	Internet and Related Services	151640		151640	79037		79037
软件和信息技术服务业	Software and Information Technology Services	478097	86070	392027	533375	8991	524384
金融业	**Financial Intermediation**	**528919**	**418401**	**110518**	**422462**	**279881**	**142581**
货币金融服务	Banks	384558	384558		275229	275229	
资本市场服务	Security Activities	6120		6120	1004		1004
保险业	Insurance	85126	33843	51283	7997	4652	3345
其他金融业	Other Financial Activities	53115		53115	138232		138232

5-7 续表 2 continued

单位：万元 (10000 yuan)

行业	Sector	投资额 Investment			新增固定资产 Incremental Fixed Assets		
		合计 Total	中央 Central	地方 Local	合计 Total	中央 Central	地方 Local
房地产业	**Real Estate**	**34680819**	**2597710**	**32083109**	**11401311**	**213158**	**11188153**
租赁和商务服务业	**Renting and Leasing Activities and Business Services**	**401598**	**27654**	**373944**	**233261**		**233261**
租赁业	Leasing	50861		50861	9249		9249
商务服务业	Business Services	350737	27654	323083	224012		224012
科学研究和技术服务业	**Scientific Research, Technical Services**	**1330368**	**1149774**	**180594**	**549993**	**499655**	**50338**
研究与试验发展	Research and Experimental Development	915771	843060	72711	185251	163286	21965
专业技术服务业	Professional Technical Services	130906	76864	54042	146597	146126	471
科技推广和应用服务业	Services of Science and Technology	283691	229850	53841	218145	190243	27902
水利、环境和公共设施管理业	**Water,Environment and Municipal Engineering Conservancy**	**4941656**	**78944**	**4862712**	**1778492**		**1778492**
水利管理业	Management of Water Conservancy	1088648	15825	1072823	480701		480701
生态保护和环境治理业	Ecological Protection and Environmental Control	74106		74106	59475		59475
公共设施管理业	Management of Public Facilities	3778902	63119	3715783	1238316		1238316
居民服务、修理和其他服务业	**Resident Services, Repair and Other Services**	**205585**		**205585**	**120910**		**120910**
居民服务业	Resident Services	83778		83778	87001		87001
机动车、电子产品和日用产品修理业	Repair of Motor Vehicles, Electronics and Household Appliances	7372		7372	4727		4727
其他服务业	Other Services	114435		114435	29182		29182
教育	**Education**	**1083023**	**359950**	**723073**	**846079**	**249212**	**596867**
卫生和社会工作	**Health Care and Social Works**	**495850**	**129230**	**366620**	**341522**	**53120**	**288402**
卫生	Health Care	423845	128201	295644	306625	53120	253505
社会工作	Social Work Activities	72005	1029	70976	34897		34897
文化、体育和娱乐业	**Culture, Sports and Entertainment**	**972924**	**387192**	**585732**	**658577**	**403634**	**254943**
新闻出版业	Journalism and Publishing	85055	70551	14504	13329	13329	
广播、电视、电影和音像业	Radio Broadcasting, Television, Movies, Videos and Sound Recording	108300	100941	7359	4603	2474	2129
文化艺术业	Cultures and Arts	479512	99377	380135	465632	273604	192028
体育	Sports Activities	36974	2696	34278	22485	600	21885
娱乐业	Entertainment	263083	113627	149456	152528	113627	38901
公共管理、社会保障和社会组织	**Pulic Administration, Social Security and Social Organizations**	**1056279**	**182101**	**874178**	**455527**	**44485**	**411042**
中国共产党机关	Organs of Communist Party of China	23120	23120				
国家机构	Organs of State	594658	22157	572501	297161	32795	264366
社会保障	Social Security	141702	128308	13394	15594	11690	3904
群众团体、社会团体和其他成员组织	Mass Communities, Social Organizations and Other Membership Organizations	142505	8516	133989	17710		17710
基层群众自治组织	Grass Roots Self-government Organizations	154294		154294	125062		125062

5-8 全社会房屋建筑施工及竣工面积(1978-2012年)
FLOOR SPACE OF BUILDINGS UNDER CONSTRUCTION AND COMPLETED (1978-2012)

单位: 万平方米 (10000 sq.m)

年份 Year	施工面积 Floor Space of Buildings under Construction	#住宅 Residential Buildings	竣工面积 Floor Space of Buildings Completed	#住宅 Residential Buildings	中央 Central	地方 Local
1978	956.3	456.8	407.0	190.4	158.7	248.3
1979	1340.6	780.2	537.6	304.9	235.2	302.4
1980	1704.1	1037.0	648.4	396.9	315.8	332.6
1981-1985			**3941.6**	**2383.4**	**1723.2**	**2218.4**
1981	1875.8	1189.9	726.9	462.6	327.2	399.7
1982	1938.6	1210.1	728.3	463.8	303.7	424.6
1983	1952.1	1163.6	775.5	514.0	312.3	463.2
1984	2351.9	1327.1	818.7	437.6	352.7	466.0
1985	2802.7	1599.2	892.2	505.4	427.3	464.9
1986-1990			**5142.4**	**2939.9**	**2635.1**	**2507.3**
1986	2760.7	1557.4	906.5	532.7	424.5	482.0
1987	2578.0	1273.2	1042.2	608.9	507.8	534.4
1988	2642.2	1226.2	1065.6	623.5	499.6	566.0
1989	2450.8	1167.8	1046.9	601.8	565.8	481.1
1990	2864.9	1561.9	1081.2	573.0	637.4	443.8
1991-1995			**6206.7**	**3707.2**	**1869.2**	**4337.5**
1991	2818.0	1612.0	1036.4	601.8	396.2	640.2
1992	3126.8	1784.7	1111.4	681.2	399.3	712.1
1993	3607.5	1866.4	1158.0	654.8	320.5	837.5
1994	4460.9	2315.1	1370.7	832.1	366.8	1003.9
1995	5524.3	2897.6	1530.2	937.3	386.4	1143.8
1996-2000			**9644.3**	**5979.9**	**2726.7**	**6917.6**
1996	5633.2	2696.9	1517.5	870.4	452.0	1065.5
1997	5819.4	2881.3	1625.7	996.8	492.2	1133.5
1998	6496.1	3473.7	1821.5	1093.1	508.4	1313.1
1999	6556.5	3754.8	2321.4	1519.9	655.3	1666.1
2000	6995.9	4083.3	2358.2	1499.7	618.8	1739.4
2001-2005			**17781.6**	**11992.2**	**1733.0**	**16048.6**
2001	8203.3	5226.4	2554.6	1804.9	490.6	2064.0
2002	9697.7	6193.3	3121.8	2191.4	441.8	2680.0
2003	11262.2	7011.3	3222.8	2322.3	242.1	2980.7
2004	13121.9	7513.1	4203.2	2649.5	301.9	3901.3
2005	14096.2	8043.2	4679.2	3024.1	256.6	4422.6
2006-2010			**20059.1**	**10993.8**	**2002.6**	**18056.4**
2006	14069.2	7113.0	4191.0	2391.6	388.6	3802.4
2007	14146.7	6788.8	3866.4	2098.0	399.6	3466.8
2008	14145.3	6656.3	3840.7	1871.1	496.8	3343.9
2009	14380.6	7058.4	4252.6	2369.6	388.4	3864.2
2010	15572.1	7932.9	3908.4	2263.5	329.2	3579.1
2011	18065.2	8817.1	4032.9	2121.8	425.5	3607.4
2012	20045.4	9217.8	3723.5	1992.5	216.9	3506.6

注：2007年及以前，表中数据不包含农村农户房屋施工和竣工面积。
Note: Figures in and before 2007 excluded rural farmers' floor space of buildings under construction and completed.

5-9 全社会房屋建筑施工及竣工面积
FLOOR SPACE OF BUILDINGS UNDER CONSTRUCTION AND COMPLETED

单位：万平方米 (10000 sq.m)

项 目	Item	2012	2011	占竣工面积比重(%) Proportion in Floor Space Completed (%)	
				2012	2011
施工总面积	**Floor Space of Buildings under Construction**	**20045.4**	**18065.2**		
竣工总面积	**Floor Space of Buildings Completed**	**3723.5**	**4032.9**	**100.0**	**100.0**
按隶属关系分	**Grouped by Administrative Relationship**				
中 央	Central	216.9	425.5	5.8	10.6
地 方	Local	3506.6	3607.4	94.2	89.4
#国 有	State-owned	471.1	495.7	12.7	12.3
集 体	Collective-owned	67.5	120.8	1.8	3.0
按功能区分	**Grouped by Function**				
首都功能核心区	Core Districts of Capital Function	153.3	278.3	4.1	6.9
城市功能拓展区	Urban Function Extended Districts	1352.5	1840.5	36.4	45.6
城市发展新区	New Districts of Urban Development	1710.1	1466.3	45.9	36.4
生态涵养发展区	Ecological Preservation Development Districts	507.6	447.8	13.6	11.1

5-10 房地产开发情况(1990-2012年)

年份 Year	房地产开发企业个数(个) Number of Real Estate Development Enterprises (unit)	本年完成的土地开发面积(万平方米) Land Space Developed This Year (10000 sq.m)	房地产开发投资额(亿元) Real Estate Development Investment (100 million yuan)	#土地开发投资 Investment in Land Development	#土地购置费 Land Purchase Cost
1990			22.5		
1991-1995		**2169.9**	**568.4**		
1991	40	305.9	24.0		
1992	42	590.0	33.7		
1993	74	182.5	58.4	4.6	2.5
1994	81	382.5	99.5	11.6	4.0
1995	623	709.0	352.8	58.7	52.4
1996-2000		**1501.9**	**1979.5**	**131.8**	**161.5**
1996	554	239.8	328.2	33.0	15.0
1997	601	419.8	330.3	22.2	23.9
1998	585	195.0	377.4	22.7	28.4
1999	716	187.2	421.5	24.6	36.6
2000	893	460.1	522.1	29.3	57.6
2001-2005		**4124.3**	**5974.0**	**177.6**	**993.6**
2001	1142	1162.7	783.8	38.1	115.6
2002	1508	925.0	989.4	44.0	149.2
2003	1546	1088.2	1202.5	39.5	213.2
2004	2704	634.2	1473.3	36.5	275.8
2005	3123	314.2	1525.0	19.4	239.8
2006-2010			**10863.2**	**125.5**	**3642.0**
2006	2882	840.5	1719.9	35.7	477.9
2007	2688	248.7	1995.8	25.6	644.7
2008	3433	351.5	1908.7	24.0	639.0
2009	3171	364.0	2337.7	28.7	587.7
2010	3190		2901.1	11.5	1292.7
2011	3069		3036.3	4.9	1301.2
2012	2960		3153.4	4.5	1102.7

注：1. 2005年及以前的商品房销售面积为竣工后的全部商品房销售面积，2006年及以后为期房与现房销售面积之和。
2. 2010年起，商品房销售面积中包含定向安置房数据(下表同)。

STATISTICS FOR REAL ESTATE DEVELOPENT (1990-2012)

按用途分 Grouped by Purpose of Investment			按投资构成分 Grouped by Use of Funds		商品房销售面积(万平方米) Area of Marketable Houses Sold (10000 sq.m)	
#住 宅 Residential Buildings	#写字楼(办公楼) Office Buildings	#商业营业用房 Business Houses	#建筑安装工程 Building and Installation Projects	#设备工器具购置 Purchase of Equipment, Tools and Devices		#住 宅 Residential Buildings
12.3			18.4		142.2	
264.8			**341.9**		**855.6**	**816.5**
14.0			16.8		154.0	152.5
20.0			20.7		159.1	153.0
38.1			43.4	0.4	182.0	182.0
50.3			69.3	0.9	168.6	149.0
142.4	71.5	35.2	191.7	8.4	191.9	180.0
950.7	**351.5**	**161.3**	**1280.6**	**95.5**	**2416.7**	**2199.2**
124.9	84.2	35.2	222.0	17.0	215.3	183.1
132.9	91.1	29.2	208.0	19.8	290.9	256.2
168.0	78.5	36.1	250.7	20.7	409.2	377.0
236.6	52.5	30.2	278.6	16.8	544.4	484.7
288.3	45.2	30.6	321.3	21.2	956.9	898.2
3239.5	**696.1**	**368.3**	**3498.9**	**137.8**	**10084.3**	**9354.8**
464.2	72.0	41.7	438.0	22.3	1205.0	1127.5
586.7	97.3	57.6	572.7	31.5	1708.3	1604.4
633.0	142.7	61.3	716.2	24.3	1895.8	1771.1
776.0	187.9	94.8	872.1	35.4	2472.0	2285.8
779.5	196.2	112.9	881.8	42.3	2803.2	2566.0
5211.5	**1055.2**	**1270.8**	**4550.5**	**255.0**	**10121.4**	**8049.8**
863.6	216.7	226.0	953.2	55.5	2607.6	2205.0
991.7	242.2	267.4	1015.3	58.9	2176.6	1731.5
940.6	170.5	240.4	829.6	48.6	1335.4	1031.4
906.6	166.7	200.7	841.6	45.7	2362.3	1880.5
1509.0	259.1	336.3	910.8	46.3	1639.5	1201.4
1778.3	363.8	296.7	1235.1	38.5	1440.0	1035.0
1628.0	384.8	275.9	1383.1	65.7	1943.7	1483.4

Note: a) Space of marketable buildings sold in 2005 and before is the floor space of marketable buildings completed, and after 2006, is the sum of future and stock houses sold.

b) From 2010, marketable house sales include figures of oriented resettlement houses(the same below).

5-11 房地产开发面积(1990-2012年)

单位：万平方米

项目 Item	商品房施工面积 Construction Area of Marketable Houses	#本年新开工面积 New Construction Area in Current Year	#商业营业用房 Houses for commercial Operation	#办公楼(写字楼) Office Building	#住宅 Residential Houses	#经济适用房 Affordable Houses	#公寓别墅 Apartments & Villas	商品房竣工面积 Area of Marketable Houses Completed	#商业营业用房 Houses for Commercial Operation	#办公楼(写字楼) Office Building	#住宅 Residential Houses
1990	774.0	249.1	41.2	17.4	643.4			271.6	13.3	9.7	226.5
1991	815.1	317.6	57.6	2.1	692.1			275.2	10.9	0.9	240.4
1992	1021.1	508.6	54.8	7.6	865.4			331.4	8.3	2.7	300.8
1993	1262.0	524.8			887.6			356.4			280.6
1994	1593.2	659.4			1107.6			445.7			385.6
1995	2810.2	1012.2	252.6	462.7	1728.7		334.8	653.0	43.5	27.9	506.3
1996	2824.6	578.7	283.9	638.7	1520.7		316.8	663.4	38.3	79.0	470.8
1997	2869.6	848.4	260.8	637.7	1541.1		335.7	682.3	42.4	80.9	478.3
1998	3499.1	1193.4	297.7	590.7	2107.2		368.3	842.8	69.8	92.3	588.7
1999	3784.0	1061.8	281.3	484.4	2447.9	301.4	390.7	1208.5	43.1	108.8	908.3
2000	4455.0	1676.9	281.3	449.1	2971.6	296.6	537.8	1365.6	48.7	97.2	1013.7
2001	5966.7	2789.8	330.6	495.5	4349.6	563.1	494.4	1707.4	48.2	98.0	1393.4
2002	7510.7	3206.0	400.3	672.5	5397.5	660.2	550.8	2384.4	82.9	97.4	1926.2
2003	9070.7	3433.8	557.7	901.3	6352.9	802.5	705.0	2593.7	117.5	94.0	2080.8
2004	9931.3	3054.3	641.8	1122.4	6759.4	793.2	776.0	3067.0	225.3	153.9	2343.9
2005	10748.5	2965.9	809.2	1209.8	7283.4	783.4	1023.5	3770.9	180.9	287.8	2841.4
2006	10483.5	3179.4	1403.0	1245.8	6311.3	551.9	913.8	3193.9	289.2	304.4	2193.3
2007	10438.6	2557.4	1482.1	1364.6	5914.5	440.1	1009.2	2891.7	315.1	314.8	1854.0
2008	10014.3	2337.2	1429.8	1287.2	5538.2	544.9	954.7	2558.0	313.1	364.6	1399.3
2009	9719.1	2246.6	1323.4	1132.2	5551.9	628.7	840.9	2678.6	322.4	316.6	1613.2
2010	10300.9	2974.2	1229.3	1054.8	6176.0	572.7	830.0	2386.7	271.9	198.4	1498.5
2011	12065.4	4246.1	1187.5	1422.7	7168.1	444.8	754.8	2245.2	232.4	245.2	1316.1
2012	13122.5	3224.2	1236.9	1711.9	7510.4	435.1	642.2	2390.9	240.1	226.8	1522.7

注：2005年及以前的商品房销售面积为竣工后的全部商品房销售面积，2006年及以后为期房与现房销售面积之和。

REAL ESTATE DEVELOPMENT AREA (1990-2012)

(10000 sq.m)

		商品房销售面积						年末商品房待售面积			
#经济适用房 Affordable Houses	#公寓别墅 Apartments & Villas	Area of Marketable Houses Sold	#商业营业用房 Houses for Commercial Operation	#办公楼（写字楼） Office Building	#住宅 Residential Houses	#经济适用房 Affordable Houses	公寓别墅 Apartments & Villas	Year-end Area of Vacant Marketable Houses	#住宅 Residential Houses	#一年以内 Less than One Year	#三年以上 Three Years Over
		142.2									
		154.0			152.5						
		159.1			153.0						
		182.0			182.0						
		168.6	1.1	17.2	149.0						
	55.6	191.9	4.5	4.0	180.0		16.7	81.5			
	43.3	215.3	14.4	13.7	183.1		24.9	214.8	179.6		
	99.8	290.9	8.0	18.8	256.2		53.5	298.3	258.9		
	57.0	409.2	7.0	23.2	377.0		40.0	334.8	262.9		
114.1	93.2	544.4	6.8	48.0	484.7	45.8	55.1	624.3	529.1		
184.9	164.2	956.9	6.1	41.2	898.2	166.5	107.6	627.4	515.1		
214.0	150.8	1205.0	17.4	49.8	1127.5	185.2	120.8	774.0	634.1	429.4	84.6
228.4	161.9	1708.3	32.9	44.0	1604.4	220.7	153.6	919.0	763.2	557.9	96.4
322.8	127.9	1895.8	50.8	38.1	1771.1	320.0	131.9	1123.4	896.9	745.5	109.8
298.8	153.2	2472.0	60.2	92.5	2285.8	306.3	172.7	1044.1	723.8	744.4	72.9
325.6	342.7	2803.2	66.9	131.2	2566.0	304.0	302.1	1374.2	799.7	993.5	75.8
270.1	255.6	2607.6	108.6	260.3	2205.0	176.3	276.9	1039.7	494.1	628.3	106.9
188.6	239.6	2176.6	134.8	265.7	1731.5	100.1	319.3	1136.2	411.8	697.2	203.1
101.1	233.0	1335.4	112.4	139.4	1031.4	108.3	164.6	1438.3	522.7	945.1	209.8
98.2	213.7	2362.3	157.1	255.8	1880.5	82.2	339.8	1351.4	426.8	768.0	229.9
144.6	183.2	1639.5	142.1	208.1	1201.4	49.5	175.9	1482.7	511.9	810.4	239.7
74.6	133.0	1440.0	108.7	211.4	1035.0	39.4	93.3	1792.6	699.8	1021.5	298.3
188.5	135.1	1943.7	114.0	253.5	1483.4	85.9	116.9	1911.8	789.5	958.7	309.0

Note: Space of marketable buildings sold in 2005 and before is the floor space of marketable buildings completed, and after 2006, is the sum of future and stock houses sold.

5-12 房地产开发企业经营(2012年) BASIC INFORMATION OF REAL ESTATE DEVELOPMENT ENTERPRISES (2012)

项　目	Item	企业单位个数(个) Number of Enterprises (unit)	实收资本合计(万元) Contributed Capital (10000 yuan)	资产总计(万元) Total Assets (10000 yuan)	主营业务收入(万元) Income (10000 yuan)	利润总额(万元) Total Profits (10000 yuan)	年末从业人员(人) Staff and Workers (year-end) (person)
合　计	**Total**	**2960**	**44722802**	**342594115**	**30677877**	**6644707**	**91912**
按企业登记注册类型分	**Grouped by Registration Status**						
内资企业	Domestic Investment Enterprises	2689	36611486	291973090	25856489	4877534	77552
国有企业	State-owned	74	2602014	13779153	765018	91357	3366
集体企业	Collective-owned	20	69688	1429036	127446	31995	475
私营企业	Private	624	2097050	18437873	1335706	13247	10130
股份合作企业	Share Holding	2	13000	88566	361	-2569	107
股份有限公司	Share Holding Corporations Ltd.	75	5169853	26498311	1014526	621803	3706
有限责任公司	Limited Liability Corporations	1894	26659881	231740151	22613432	4121701	59768
港澳台商投资企业	Hongkong, Macao and Taiwan Funded Enterprises	164	5126680	31106907	3644466	1159778	8296
港澳台合资经营	Joint Venture	59	1358128	7093787	736771	98391	2672
港澳台合作经营	Cooperative	67	1244914	9601364	1874558	637102	3290
港澳台商独资企业	Hongkong, Macao and Taiwan Enterprises	38	2523638	14411756	1033137	424285	2334
港澳台商投资股份有限公司	Hongkong, Macao and Taiwan Share Holding Corporations Ltd.						
外商投资企业	Foreign Funded Enterprises	107	2984636	19514118	1176922	607395	6064
中外合资经营	Joint Venture	41	909769	8089317	390106	216872	1752
中外合作经营	Cooperative	42	716349	4469694	397671	151853	2762
外资(独资)企业	Foreign Enterprises	21	1021418	4217076	255584	166647	1119
外商投资股份有限公司	Foreign Share Holding Corporation Ltd.	3	337100	2738031	133561	72023	431
按隶属关系分	**Grouped by Administrative Relationship**						
中　央	Central	111	4490478	26400152	1615147	536347	3921
地　方	Local	2849	40232324	316193963	29062730	6108360	87991
按资质等级分	**Grouped by Grade**						
一　级	First-grade	124	7736475	73503281	5949506	2511704	13558
二　级	Second-grade	216	4760997	51148483	4690051	1105312	15711
三　级	Third-grade	296	4088137	39071482	4231640	1005616	10384
四　级	Fourth-grade	1159	12340595	93122005	9276372	1154500	30181
暂　定	Provisional	607	10114310	60552152	5745531	746838	13544
其　他	Other	558	5682288	25196712	784777	120737	8534
按营业状况分	**Grouped by Business Condition**						
营　业	Going on	2679	43105394	335576054	30383224	6629776	90173
停　业	Closed down	249	1378415	6059058	255734	6259	1376
筹　建	Preparatory	1	3000	71734		-707	31
当年关闭	Closed in the year	9	35000	94409	229	574	10
当年破产	Bankrupted in the year	1	1000	453		-330	30
其　他	Other	21	199993	792407	38690	9135	292

5-13 房地产开发企业开发建设(2012年)
REAL ESTATE DEVELOPMENT (2012)

单位：万元、平方米 (10000 yuan,sq.m)

项目	Item	全市合计 Total	#国有企业 State-Owned	#三资企业 Foreign Funded	按隶属关系分 Grouped by Administrative Relationship 中央 Central	地方 Local
计划总投资	**Total Planned Investment**	**207490584**	**15625548**	**19189793**	**9837689**	**197652895**
开始建设至本年度累计	**Accumulative Investment Completed**					
完成投资	**from Beginning to the End of This Year**	**140489765**	**10185100**	**13592600**	**7170068**	**133319697**
本年完成投资合计	**Investment Completed This Year**	**31534419**	**2465126**	**2121741**	**1837868**	**29696551**
#土地开发投资	Land Development	44813	151	1703	151	44662
土地购置费	Purchase of Land	11026870	454008	535669	1047791	9979079
本年完成投资按用途分	Grouped by Purpose of Investment Completed This Year					
住宅	Residential Buildings	16279851	1291897	827595	1152625	15127226
#普通住房	Ordinary Residential Houses	7899923	737634	231636	656109	7243814
别墅、高档公寓	Villas, High-grade Apartments	1815421	64812	283634	52485	1762936
办公楼(写字楼)	Office Buildings	3848067	104222	487331	43624	3804443
商业营业用房	Business Houses	2758685	99958	492434	243162	2515523
其他	Other	8647816	969049	314381	398457	8249359
本年购置土地面积	**Land Space Purchased This Year**	**3059890**	**284612**		**146053**	**2913837**

5-14 保障性安居工程建设情况
CONSTRUCTION OF GUARANTEED HOUSING PROJECTS

单位：亿元、万平方米 (100 million yuan,10000sq.m)

项　目	Item	2012	2011	2012年为2011年% 2012as % of 2011
完成投资额	**Investment Completed**	**857.5**	**746.1**	**114.9**
经济适用房	Affordable House	61.2	71.9	85.1
限价房	Price-restricted House	153.9	140.8	109.3
公租(廉租)房	Public-lease(low-rent) House	49.3	38.7	127.5
定向安置房	Positioned Resettlement House	593.1	494.8	119.9
施工面积	**Construction Area**	**4821.0**	**4084.4**	**118.0**
经济适用房	Affordable House	557.7	596.1	93.6
限价房	Price-restricted House	689.6	705.2	97.8
公租(廉租)房	Public-lease(low-rent) House	296.3	269.0	110.1
定向安置房	Positioned Resettlement House	3277.4	2514.1	130.4
竣工面积	**Area of Completed Construction Works**	**752.6**	**513.8**	**146.5**
经济适用房	Affordable House	241.0	113.7	212.0
限价房	Price-restricted House	197.7	155.7	127.0
公租(廉租)房	Public-lease(low-rent) House	37.8	83.4	45.3
定向安置房	Positioned Resettlement House	276.1	161.0	171.5
本年新开工面积	**Area of Construction Works Newly Started in Current Year**	**1112.3**	**1726.8**	**64.4**
经济适用房	Affordable House	74.8	96.1	77.8
限价房	Price-restricted House	142.2	278.8	51.0
公租(廉租)房	Public-lease(low-rent) House	109.8	106.3	103.3
定向安置房	Positioned Resettlement House	785.5	1245.6	63.1

主要统计指标解释

全社会固定资产投资 包括城镇固定资产投资（含房地产开发投资）和农村固定资产投资。

城镇固定资产投资 是指城镇各种登记注册类型的企业、事业、行政单位及个体户进行的计划总投资在500万元及以上的建设项目投资。镇及镇以上各级政府及主管部门直接领导、管理的建设项目和企事业单位的投资均为城镇固定资产投资。

农村固定资产投资 农村投资统计以投资项目建设地址所在的地域为界定农村投资统计的范围，即农村投资是指各种投资主体建设的建设项目地址在农村区域范围内的、以满足农村居民生产、生活需要为主要目的的各种投资活动。农村固定资产投资包括农户和非农户固定资产投资。

新增固定资产投资 是指报告期内交付使用的固定资产价值。包括本年内建成投入生产或交付使用的工程投资和达到固定资产标准的设备、工具、器具的投资及有关应摊入的费用。属于增加固定资产价值的其他建设费用，应随同交付使用的工程一并计入新增固定资产。

基础设施投资 是指能够为企业提供作为中间投入用于生产的基本需求；能够为消费者提供所需的基本消费服务；能够为社区提供用于改善不利的外部环境的服务等建设的投资，包括固定资产投资中用于市政工程、电信工程、公共设施和水利环保等建设的投资。具体包括：电力、燃气和水的生产和供应业；交通运输业；邮政业；信息传输业；水利、环境和公共设施管理业等。

上年末结余资金 是指上年资金来源中没有形成固定资产投资额而结余的资金。包括尚未用到工程上去的材料价值、未开始安装的需要安装设备价值及结存的现金和银行存款等。

本年资金来源小计 是指固定资产投资单位在报告期收到的，用于固定资产投资的各种货币资金。包括国家预算内资金、国内贷款、债券、利用外资、自筹资金和其他资金。

国家预算内资金 分为财政拨款和财政安排的贷款两部分。包括中央财政的基本建设基金(分经营性基金和非经营性基金两部分)、专项支出(如煤代油专项等)、收回再贷、贴息资金，财政安排的挖潜改造和新产品试制支出、城建支出、商业部门简易建筑支出、不发达地区发展基金等资金中用于固定资产投资的资金；地方财政中由国家统筹安排的资金等。

国内贷款 是指报告期固定资产投资项目单位向银行及非银行金融机构借入的用于固定资产投资的各种国内借款，包括银行利用自有资金及吸收存款发放的贷款、上级主管部门拨入的国内贷款、国家专项贷款(包括煤代油贷款、劳改煤矿专项贷款等)，地方财政专项资金安排的贷款、国内储备贷款、周转贷款等。

利用外资 是指报告期收到的用于固定资产建造和购置投资的境外资金(包括设备、材料、技术在内)。包括外商直接投资、对外借款(外国政府贷款、国际金融组织贷款、出口信贷、外国银行商业贷款、对外发行债券和股票)及外商其他投资(包括利用外商投资收益在国内进行固定资产再投资活动的资金)。不包括我国自有外汇资金(包括国家外汇、地方外汇、留成外汇、调剂外汇和国内银行自有资金发行的外汇贷款等)。

自筹资金 指固定资产投资单位报告期收到的，由各地区、各部门及企业、事业单位筹集用于固定资产投资的预算外资金，包括中央各部门、各级地方和企业、事业单位的自有资金。

其他资金来源 是指在报告期收到的除以上各种资金之外其他用于固定资产投资的资金。包括社会集资、个人资金、无偿捐赠的资金及其他单位拨入的资金等。

住宅建设投资 是指专供居住使用的房屋，包括职工家属宿舍、职工单身宿舍、学生宿舍和经济适用房等房屋建造的投资，不包括购置的商品住宅。

建筑安装工程投资（建筑安装工作量） 是指各种房屋、建筑物的建造工程，各种设备、装置的安装工程，又称建筑安装工作量。建筑工程投资必须经过兴工动料，通过施工活动才能实现。在安装工程中，不包括被安装设备本身价值。

设备工器具购置 是指建设单位或企、事业单位购置或自制的，达到固定资产标准的设备、工具、器具的价值。

房地产开发投资 指从本年1月1日起至本年最后一天止完成的全部用于房屋建设工程和土地开发工程的投资额，以及公益性建筑和土地购置费等投资。

土地购置费 通过各种方式取得土地使用权而支付的费用（包括开发补偿费）。土地购置费包括：（1）通过“划拨”方式取得的土地使用权所支付的土地补偿费、附着物和青苗补偿费、安置补偿费及土地征收管理费等；竣工后计入新增固定资产。（2）通过“出让”方式（包括协议出让、招、拍、挂出让）取得的土地使用权所支付的费用；竣工后不计入新增固定资产。土地购置费按当期实际发生额计入投资。土地购置费为分期付款的，应分期计入投资。

经济适用住房 指政府提供政策优惠，限定套型面积和销售价格，按照合理标准建设，面向城镇低收入住房困难家庭供应的具有保障性质的政策性住房。

限价商品住房 指政府控制土地出让价格，限定销售价格和套型面积，向城镇中等收入家庭供应的普通商品住房。

公共租赁住房 指政府提供财政投入和政策支持，限定套型建筑面积标准，按照合理标准组织建设，或通过长期租赁等方式筹集，按照当地政府规定的供应标准，面向城镇中等偏下收入住房困难家庭、新就业职工和有稳定职业并在城镇居住一定年限的外来务工人员供应的保障性住房。

廉租住房 指政府提供财政投入和政策支持，限定套型建筑面积标准，按照合理标准组织建设，或通过购买、改建和租赁等方式筹集，按照当地政府规定的供应标准，面向城镇低收入住房困难家庭供应的具有保障性质的住房。

房屋施工面积 是指报告期内施工的全部房屋建筑面积。包括本期新开工的面积和上年开工跨入本期继续施工房屋面积，以及上期已停建在本期恢复施工的房屋面积。本期竣工和本期施工后又停建、缓建的房屋面积仍包括在施工面积中，多层建筑应填各层建筑面积之和。

房屋竣工面积 是指报告期内房屋建筑按照设计要求已全部完工，达到住人和使用条件，经验收鉴定合格（或达到竣工验收标准），可正式移交使用的各栋房屋建筑面积的总和。

待售面积 指报告期末已竣工的可供销售或出租的商品房屋建筑面积中，尚未销售或出租的商品房屋建筑面积，包括以前年度竣工和本期竣工的房屋面积，但不包括报告期已竣工的拆迁还建，统建代建，公共配套建筑、房地产公司自用及周转房等不可销售或出租的房屋面积。

Explanatory Notes on Main Statistical Indicators

Total Investment in Fixed Assets in the City includes the urban investment in fixed assets (including the investment in real estate development) and rural investment in fixed assets.

Urban Investment in Fixed Assets refers to construction projects involving a total planned investment of 5000,000 Yuan and over by enterprises of various types of registration, institutions, administrative units and individuals in urban areas. The investment in construction projects under the direct leadership and management of government agencies at and above town levels and investment by enterprises and public institutions are included in urban investment in fixed assets.

Rural Investment in Fixed Assets Rural investment statistics cover the area where the construction sites of investment projects are located, namely, rural investment means all investment activities of construction projects conducted by various investment players in rural area which mainly aim to rural residents' production and living needs. Rural investment in fixed assets consists of investment in fixed assets by farmers and non-farmers.

Newly-Added Investment in Fixed Assets means the value of fixed assets put into use in the reporting period, including investment in projects completed and put into production or use in the year, and investment in equipment, tools and apparatus which reach the specified amount of fixed assets, together with apportioned costs. Other construction costs adding value to fixed assets shall be involved in the newly added investment of fixed assets together with the projects put into use.

Investment in Infrastructures means the investment in any construction that can provide intermediate inputs for enterprise to meet their basic production needs; that can provide consumers with basic consumer services needed; that can provide with communities with services used for improving any unfavorable external environment. It includes the investment in public works, telecom works, public facilities, water conservancy and environmental protection works, which is of the investment in fixed assets. In details, these infrastructures include: production and supply of electric power, fuel gas, and water; traffic and transport; postal service; information transmission; water conservancy, environment, and public facility management, etc.

Funds Carried Forward from the End of Previous Year means any money in the previous-year fund sources that did not form investment in fixed assets and is carried forward, including the value of materials not used for projects, value of equipment to be installed but not installed, and balance of cash and bank deposits.

Subtotal of Fund Sources in the Year means various monetary capital received by investors of fixed assets in the reporting period and to be used for investment in fixed assets, including fund from State budget, domestic loans, bonds, foreign investment, self-raised funds and other funds.

Fund from State Budget consists of budgetary appropriation and loans from the State budget. More specifically, it includes, from the budget of the central government, capital construction fund (operating fund and non-operating fund), special expenses (e.g. expenses on substituting petroleum with coal), loans from repayment, discount fund, expenses on innovation and trial production of new products, expenses on urban construction, expenses on temporary construction from business departments, development fund for less developed areas, as well as local budgetary fund transferred from the central budget.

Domestic loans refer to loans of various forms borrowed by fixed assets investment project entities from banks and non-bank financial institutions during the reference period for the purpose of investment in fixed assets, including loans issued by banks from their self-owned funds and deposit, loans appropriated by higher authorities, special loans by government (including loans for substituting petroleum with coal, and special loans for work coal mines), loans arranged by local government from special funds, domestic reserve loan and working loan, etc.

Foreign investment refers to foreign funds received during the reporting period for the construction and purchase of investment in fixed assets (including equipment, materials and technology), including foreign direct investment, foreign borrowings (loans from foreign governments and international financial institutions, export credit, commercial loans from foreign banks, issue of bonds and stocks overseas), and other foreign investments (including funds for domestic re-investment in fixed assets by using the earnings from foreign investment). Excluded from this category is capital in foreign exchanges owned by China (foreign exchanges owned by the central and local governments, foreign exchanges retained by enterprises, foreign exchanges by enterprises through the regulating mechanism, loans in foreign exchanges issued by the domestic banks with their own funds, etc.).

Self-raised funds refer to non-budgetary funds for investment in fixed assets received during the reporting period by investing units and raised from different places, sectors, enterprises and public institutions, including their own funds.

Other funds refer to funds for investment in fixed assets received from sources other than those listed above, including funds raised from individuals, personal funds, funds donated and funds transferred from other units.

Holding of Shares falls into State holding, collective holding, private holding, holding by Hong Kong, Macao, and Taiwan investors, and holding by foreign investors, with enterprise legal persons as the target of classification, and classified by the actual investment from contributors of certain economic sector in the paid-up capital, or the actual extent of holding and controlling of enterprise assets by contributors.

Investment in Construction of Residential Houses means the investment in houses specially used for residence, including employee family's dormitories, single employees' dormitories, student dormitories, and affordable houses, and so on, excluding commercialized residences purchased.

Investment in Construction and Installation Projects (Workload of Construction and Installation) means the investment in construction projects of various houses and buildings, installation projects of various equipment and devices, also known as the workload of construction and installation. It can only be realized through construction work and consumption of materials. For installation projects, the value of equipment installed is not included.

Purchase of Equipment, Tools and Apparatus means the value of equipment, tools and apparatus purchased or made by construction companies, enterprises or public institutions, which reach the specified amount of fixed assets.

Investment in Real Estate Development refers to all investment used for house construction projects and land development projects, together with public welfare buildings and land purchase costs spent from January 1st to the last day of the year.

Affordable Houses refer to policy-based houses that are supplied to urban low-income households with insufficient house, of guarantee nature, built in line with reasonable standards, with restricted house size and restricted selling price, with preferential policy from the government.

Marketable Houses at Restricted Price are general marketable houses supplied to urban middle-income households, of which the land transfer price is controlled by the government, with restricted house size and restricted selling price.

Public Houses for Lease refer to guaranteed houses supplied to urban lower middle-income households with insufficient house, new employed works, and migrant workers with stable job and living in certain number of years in a city or town, in line with supply standards stated by local governments, with financial input and policy support from the government, with restricted house size and building area, constructed in line with reasonable standards, raised in such manners as long-term lease.

Low-rent Houses refer to houses of guarantee nature, supplied to urban low-income households with insufficient house, in line with supply standards stated by local governments, with financial input and policy support from the government, with restricted house size and building area, constructed in line with reasonable standards, or raised in such manners as purchase, reconstruction or lease.

Floor Space under Construction refers to the total floor space of all houses and buildings under construction during the reporting period, including floor space of newly started buildings in current period, floor space of construction extended from the previous period to the current period, and floor space of construction suspended during the previous period and resumed in the current period. Floor space of construction completed in the current period, and floor space of construction started and then suspended in the current period are also included in the floor space under construction. For multi-storey buildings, the sum of floor space of all floors shall be calculated.

Floor Space of Houses Completed refers to the total floor space of all houses and buildings fully completed as required in the design in the reporting period, which meet the conditions for living and use, have been satisfactorily accepted (or meet the standards for completion and acceptance) and that can be handed over and put into use.

Area of Marketable Houses Sold refers to total contracted area of marketable houses (i.e. area of floor space as specified in formal contracts signed by both parties) sold in the reporting period. It consists of the floor space of completed houses and future houses.

06

北京统计年鉴2013　　BEIJING STATISTICAL YEARBOOK

财政与税收
GOVERNMENT FINANCE AND REVENUES

简要说明

一、本章资料的主要内容

本章资料包括北京市财政收支情况，北京市国税、地税税收(费)收入情况。其中财政收支包括历年财政收入、支出及相当于地区生产总值比例等情况；税收（费）包括历年国税、地税税费收入情况，国税、地税税收（费）收入分组情况。

二、本章资料的数据来源

本章财政收支数据由北京市财政局提供；税收（费）数据由北京市国家税务局、北京市地方税务局提供。

Brief Introduction

I. Main Content

Statistics in this chapter include fiscal revenues and payments in Beijing, income of state and local tax (fees) in Beijing. Of which, figures of fiscal revenues and payments include fiscal revenues, payments and as percentage of GDP of Beijing in previous years; figures of income of tax (fees) include income of state and local tax (fees) in previous years, as well as grouping of state and local tax (fees) .

II. Source of Data

Data of fiscal revenues and payments are from Beijing Municipal Bureau of Finance; data of tax (fees) are from Beijing Municipal Bureau of State Tax and Beijing Municipal Bureau of Local Tax.

6-1 地方财政收支(1978-2012年)
LOCAL FINANCIAL REVENUE AND EXPENDITURE (1978-2012)

单位：亿元 (100 million yuan)

年 份 Year	地方财政收入 Local Financial Revenue	地方公共财政预算收入 Local Public Budgetary Financial Revenue	税收收入 Tax Revenue	#增值税 Value-added Tax	#营业税 Operation Tax	#个人所得税 Individual Income Tax	#企业所得税 Company Income Tax	#城市维护建设税 Tax on City Maintenance and Construction	非税收入 Non-tax Revenue	基金预算收入 Fund Budgetary Income
1978	50.46		18.25							
1979	47.75		19.41							
1980	51.29		21.22							
1981-1985	**234.27**		**191.96**	**8.34**	**11.46**	**0.61**	**43.77**	**2.16**		
1981	49.12		24.22			0.02	1.76			
1982	47.25		25.81	0.05		0.05	1.43			
1983	39.84		38.03	1.30		0.07	11.70			
1984	45.62		43.91	2.20	1.23	0.13	12.70			
1985	52.44		59.99	4.79	10.23	0.34	16.18	2.16		
1986-1990	**337.13**		**397.96**	**65.02**	**103.00**	**7.29**	**116.89**	**16.67**		
1986	60.34		60.83	7.61	13.19	0.97	20.46	2.51		
1987	63.62		67.77	9.09	15.42	1.54	21.87	2.70		
1988	68.11		84.04	15.10	21.11	1.23	27.70	3.37		
1989	71.05		91.09	16.75	25.33	1.53	24.31	3.74		
1990	74.01		94.23	16.47	27.95	2.02	22.55	4.35		
1991-1995	**456.48**		**643.24**	**136.88**	**228.80**	**35.46**	**105.24**	**34.07**		
1991	77.02		100.58	19.53	30.78	2.56	20.59	4.77		
1992	80.25		110.54	22.29	35.86	3.15	19.08	5.13		
1993	84.10		148.19	42.30	52.07	4.30	14.20	6.57		
1994	99.85		120.53	25.54	45.63	9.24	21.70	7.18		
1995	115.26		163.40	27.22	64.46	16.21	29.67	10.42		
1996-2000	**1341.65**		**1397.26**	**185.46**	**570.06**	**190.18**	**223.71**	**70.84**		
1996	150.90		201.32	29.53	81.61	22.67	37.22	11.36		
1997	209.91	182.32	235.82	32.67	97.54	28.76	41.05	12.74	-53.50	27.59
1998	262.01	229.45	272.23	37.58	113.00	36.49	41.42	14.12	-42.78	32.56
1999	320.44	281.37	315.10	39.72	128.86	45.88	45.99	15.27	-33.74	39.07
2000	398.39	345.00	372.79	45.96	149.05	56.38	58.03	17.35	-27.79	53.39
2001-2005	**3611.96**	**3244.40**	**3216.46**	**367.43**	**1389.75**	**355.88**	**566.23**	**147.84**	**27.94**	**367.57**
2001	507.68	454.17	475.00	59.00	181.35	79.52	86.07	20.53	-20.83	53.51
2002	600.96	533.99	539.87	66.69	227.79	61.29	100.00	24.91	-5.88	66.97
2003	665.94	592.54	588.96	75.26	263.69	57.21	93.70	28.85	3.58	73.40
2004	830.03	744.49	726.50	68.88	333.16	73.34	121.70	34.72	17.99	85.55
2005	1007.35	919.21	886.13	97.60	383.76	84.52	164.76	38.83	33.08	88.14
2006-2010	**11889.54**	**8827.85**	**8453.62**	**800.72**	**3321.83**	**801.97**	**1965.28**	**317.03**	**374.23**	**3061.69**
2006	1235.78	1117.15	1076.82	117.80	460.99	102.28	213.86	45.17	40.33	118.63
2007	1882.04	1492.64	1435.67	134.84	601.06	135.20	309.34	56.63	56.97	389.40
2008	2282.04	1837.32	1775.58	158.34	651.78	171.33	497.52	63.95	61.75	444.71
2009	2678.77	2026.81	1913.97	179.73	752.60	177.84	430.42	71.28	112.84	651.96
2010	3810.91	2353.93	2251.59	210.01	855.40	215.33	513.09	80.00	102.34	1456.98
2011	4359.10	3006.28	2854.63	237.76	1071.51	272.90	683.71	145.65	151.65	1352.82
2012	4512.86	3314.93	3124.75	314.00	1152.74	281.49	752.47	160.34	190.18	1197.92

注：1. 地方财政收支数为决算数。
2. 2011年开始，原指标“地方一般预算收入”和“地方一般预算支出”更名为“地方公共财政预算收入”和“地方公共财政预算支出”(下同)。

资料来源：北京市财政局。

Note: a) Local financial revenue and expenditure figures are final.
b) From 2011, local financial revenue and local financial revenue expenditure is renamed local public financial budgetary revenue and local public financial budgetary expenditure(similarly following tables).

Source: Beijing Finance Bureau.

6-1 续表

单位：亿元

年份 Year	地方财政支出 Local Financial Expenditure	#地方公共财政预算支出 Local Public Budgetary Financial Expenditure	#一般公共服务 General Public Service	#教育 Education	#科学技术 Science and Technology	#文化体育与传媒 Culture, Physical and Media	#社会保障和就业 Social Security and Employment
1978	20.38						
1979	20.06						
1980	14.87						
1981-1985	**111.40**						
1981	14.85						
1982	16.80						
1983	19.61						
1984	27.15						
1985	32.99						
1986-1990	**272.89**						
1986	44.27						
1987	49.67						
1988	52.93						
1989	59.50						
1990	66.52						
1991-1995	**473.64**						
1991	67.98						
1992	71.74						
1993	80.99						
1994	98.53						
1995	154.40						
1996-2000	**1646.07**						
1996	187.45						
1997	262.20	236.39					
1998	307.55	280.68					
1999	398.53	355.19					
2000	490.34	443.00					
2001-2005	**4219.74**	**3878.85**					
2001	614.92	559.11					
2002	683.98	628.35					
2003	809.39	734.80					
2004	974.17	898.28					
2005	1137.28	1058.31					
2006-2010	**12765.99**	**9942.31**	**987.56**	**1604.40**	**578.30**	**309.36**	**1048.02**
2006	1411.58	1296.84	159.95	209.21	70.14	40.51	149.22
2007	2067.65	1649.50	179.56	263.00	90.74	53.62	179.28
2008	2400.93	1959.29	196.27	316.30	112.19	61.11	209.33
2009	2820.86	2319.37	212.21	365.67	126.31	74.75	234.29
2010	4064.97	2717.32	239.57	450.22	178.92	79.36	275.90
2011	4574.94	3245.23	261.38	520.08	183.07	87.01	354.88
2012	4803.75	3685.31	286.57	628.65	199.94	141.37	424.31

continued

(100 million yuan)

#医疗卫生 Medical Service and Health	#节能环保 Energy Saving and Environ-mental Protection	#交通运输 Transport-ation Expenditure	#城乡社区事务 Urban and Rural Community Affairs	#农林水事务 Farming, Forest and Water Affairs
718.40	**199.77**	**422.53**	**1182.65**	**613.55**
100.95	20.14	7.05	153.26	88.62
118.95	29.27	33.09	187.43	102.51
145.05	35.47	80.35	199.84	121.77
166.63	54.04	147.07	347.82	142.01
186.82	60.85	154.99	294.30	158.64
225.49	94.51	199.12	339.27	187.34
256.06	113.54	243.76	430.76	222.69

6-2 地方财政收支增长速度及相当于地区生产总值比例(1978-2012年)
GROWTH RATE OF LOCAL FINANCIAL REVENUES AND EXPENDITURES AND AS PERCENTAGE OF LOCAL GDP (1978-2012)

单位：% (%)

年份 Year	增长速度(上年=100) Growth Rate (Preceding Year=100)				相当于地区生产总值比例 As Percentage of GDP			
	地方财政收入 Local Financial Revenue	#地方公共财政预算收入 Local Government General Budgetary Financial Revenue	地方财政支出 Local Financial Expenditure	#地方公共财政预算支出 Local Government General Budgetary Financial Expenditure	地方财政收入 Local Financial Revenue	#地方公共财政预算收入 Local Government General Budgetary Financial Revenue	地方财政支出 Local Financial Expenditure	#地方公共财政预算支出 Local Government General Budgetary Financial Expenditure
1978	18.0		27.6		46.4		18.7	
1979	-5.4		-1.6		39.8		16.7	
1980	7.4		-25.9		36.9		10.7	
1981-1985					**24.6**		**11.7**	
1981	-4.2		-0.1		35.3		10.7	
1982	-3.8		13.1		30.5		10.8	
1983	-15.7		16.7		21.8		10.7	
1984	14.5		38.4		21.1		12.5	
1985	14.9		21.5		20.4		12.8	
1986-1990					**17.0**		**13.8**	
1986	15.1		34.2		21.2		15.5	
1987	5.4		12.2		19.5		15.2	
1988	7.1		6.6		16.6		12.9	
1989	4.3		12.4		15.6		13.0	
1990	4.2		11.8		14.8		13.3	
1991-1995					**9.4**		**9.8**	
1991	4.1		2.2		12.9		11.4	
1992	4.2		5.5		11.3		10.1	
1993	4.8		12.9		9.5		9.1	
1994	9.9		21.7		8.7		8.6	
1995	21.8		56.7		7.6		10.2	
1996-2000					**11.1**		**13.6**	
1996	30.9		21.4		8.4		10.5	
1997	25.5		39.9		10.1	8.8	12.6	11.4
1998	24.8	20.0	17.4	18.7	11.0	9.7	12.9	11.8
1999	22.3	22.6	29.6	26.5	12.0	10.5	14.9	13.3
2000	24.3	22.7	23.0	24.7	12.6	10.9	15.5	14.0
2001-2005					**13.9**	**12.5**	**16.2**	**14.9**
2001	27.4	31.6	25.4	26.2	13.7	12.2	16.6	15.1
2002	25.8	25.9	11.2	12.4	13.9	12.4	15.9	14.6
2003	17.2	18.2	18.3	16.9	13.3	11.8	16.2	14.7
2004	28.3	29.7	20.4	22.3	13.8	12.3	16.1	14.9
2005	21.4	23.5	16.7	17.8	14.5	13.2	16.3	15.2
2006-2010					**21.5**	**16.0**	**23.1**	**18.0**
2006	22.7	21.5	24.1	22.5	15.2	13.8	17.4	16.0
2007	52.3	33.6	46.5	27.2	19.1	15.2	21.0	16.8
2008	21.3	23.1	16.1	18.8	20.5	16.5	21.6	17.6
2009	17.4	10.3	17.5	18.4	22.0	16.7	23.2	19.1
2010	42.3	16.1	44.1	17.2	27.0	16.7	28.8	19.3
2011	14.4	27.7	12.5	19.4	26.8	18.5	28.2	20.0
2012	3.5	10.3	5.0	13.6	25.2	18.5	26.9	20.6

注：2002-2004年地方财政收入增长速度按可比口径计算。

Note: The growht rate of local public financial revenue in 2002-2004 is calculated at comparable price.

资料来源：北京市财政局。

Source: Beijing Finance Bureau.

6-3 地方财政收入
LOCAL FINANCIAL REVENUE

项　目	Item	绝对数(万元) Value (10000 yuan) 2012	2011	2012年为2011年% 2012as % of 2011	构　成(%) Composition (%) 2012	2011
合　计	**Total**	**45128578**	**43590993**	**103.5**	**100.0**	**100.0**
地方公共财政预算收入	**Local Public Budgetary Financial Revenue**	**33149340**	**30062751**	**110.3**	**73.5**	**69.0**
#增值税	Value-added Tax	3139994	2377647	132.1	7.0	5.5
营业税	Business Tax	11527384	10715081	107.6	25.5	24.6
个人所得税	Personal Income Tax	2814872	2728954	103.1	6.2	6.3
城市维护建设税	Tax on City Maintenance and Construction	1603445	1456499	110.1	3.6	3.3
固定资产投资方向调节税	Tax on the Adjustment of the Investment in the Fixed Assets	107				
耕地占用税	Tax on Cultivated Land Occupation	102719	115661	88.8	0.2	0.3
企业所得税	Company Income Tax	7524673	6837116	110.1	16.7	15.7
国有资本经营收入	State-owned Assets income	-305024	-298797			
罚没收入	Penalty and Confiscatory Income	430571	337461	127.6	1.0	0.8
行政事业性收费收入	Administrative Fees	458964	436096	105.2	1.0	1.0
基金预算收入	**Fund Budgetary Income**	**11979238**	**13528242**	**88.5**	**26.5**	**31.0**

资料来源：北京市财政局。
Source: Beijing Finance Bureau.

6-4 地方财政支出
LOCAL FINANCIAL EXPENDITURE

项 目	Item	绝对数(万元) Value(10000 yuan)		2012年为2011年% 2012as % of 2011	构 成(%) Composition(%)	
		2012	2011		2012	2011
合 计	**Total**	**48037548**	**45749405**	**105.0**	**100.0**	**100.0**
地方公共财政预算支出	**Local Public Budgetary Financial Expenditure**	**36853076**	**32452264**	**113.6**	**76.7**	**70.9**
#一般公共服务	General Public Service	2865685	2613757	109.6	6.0	5.7
教 育	Education	6286510	5200778	120.9	13.1	11.4
科学技术	Science and Technology	1999444	1830745	109.2	4.2	4.0
文化体育与传媒	Culture, Physical and Media	1413733	870080	162.5	2.9	1.9
社会保障和就业	Social Security and Employment	4243122	3548827	119.6	8.8	7.8
医疗卫生	Medical Service and Health	2560626	2254853	113.6	5.3	4.9
节能环保	Environmental Protection	1135370	945135	120.1	2.4	2.1
交通运输	Transportation Expenditure	2437624	1991209	122.4	5.1	4.4
城乡社区事务	Urban and Rural Community Affairs	4307560	3392685	127.0	9.0	7.4
农林水事务	Farming, Forest and Water Affairs	2226932	1873372	118.9	4.6	4.1
政府性基金支出合计	**Funds Expenditure**	**11184472**	**13297141**	**84.1**	**23.3**	**29.1**

资料来源：北京市财政局。
Source: Beijing Finance Bureau.

6-5 地税、国税税收(费)收入情况(1994-2012年)
INCOME OF LOCAL AND STATE TAX (1994-2012)

单位：亿元 (100 million yuan)

年份 Year	地税、国税税收(费)收入合计 Total Tax Revenues	中央级 Central	地方级 Local	地税税费收入 Local Tax Income	中央级 Central	地方级 Local	国税收入合计 State Tax Income	中央级 Central	地方级 Local
1994	340.1	169.6	170.5	62.7		62.7	277.4	169.6	107.8
1995	357.6	186.8	170.8	95.8		95.8	261.8	186.8	75.0
1996-2000	**3120.9**	**1685.0**	**1435.9**	**1102.6**	**9.0**	**1093.6**	**2018.3**	**1676.0**	**342.3**
1996	402.5	193.2	209.3	133.1		133.1	269.4	193.2	76.2
1997	463.7	218.4	245.3	187.5	1.5	186.0	276.2	216.9	59.3
1998	570.4	286.8	283.6	222.4	2.3	220.1	348.0	284.5	63.5
1999	742.0	418.4	323.6	259.1	2.4	256.7	482.9	416.0	66.9
2000	942.3	568.2	374.1	300.5	2.8	297.7	641.8	565.4	76.4
2001-2005	**8985.8**	**5668.2**	**3317.6**	**2994.7**	**504.4**	**2490.3**	**5991.1**	**5163.8**	**827.3**
2001	1264.7	770.3	494.4	391.7	3.0	388.7	873.0	767.3	105.7
2002	1437.8	884.0	553.8	480.2	77.9	402.3	957.6	806.1	151.5
2003	1641.9	1038.7	603.2	566.9	113.7	453.2	1075.0	925.0	150.0
2004	2004.2	1244.3	759.9	717.5	142.0	575.5	1286.7	1102.3	184.4
2005	2637.2	1730.9	906.3	838.4	167.8	670.6	1798.8	1563.1	235.7
2006-2010	**26136.7**	**17460.4**	**8676.3**	**7824.7**	**1622.0**	**6202.6**	**18312.2**	**15838.4**	**2473.7**
2006	3437.9	2331.5	1106.4	1003.6	196.7	806.9	2434.3	2134.8	299.5
2007	4460.3	2982.5	1477.8	1366.2	281.2	1085.0	3094.1	2701.3	392.8
2008	5444.4	3620.5	1823.9	1578.0	350.7	1227.3	3866.4	3269.8	596.6
2009	6337.4	4379.6	1957.8	1771.9	355.4	1416.4	4565.7	4024.2	541.4
2010	6456.7	4146.3	2310.4	2105.0	438.0	1667.0	4351.7	3708.3	643.4
2011	8004.7	5072.8	2931.9	2666.6	548.7	2117.9	5338.1	4524.1	814.0
2012	9220.4	5973.6	3246.8	2865.2	571.6	2293.7	6355.1	5402.0	953.1

资料来源：北京市地方税务局、北京市国家税务局。
Source: Beijing Local Tax Bureau, Beijing State Tax Bureau.

6-6 地税税费收入分税种、分行业完成情况(2007-2012年)
LOCAL TAX REVENUE BY CATEGORY AND INDUSTRY (2007-2012)

单位：亿元 (100 million yuan)

项目	Item	2007	2008	2009	2010	2011	2012
各项税费收入合计	**Total Tax Revenues**	**1366.14**	**1578.02**	**1771.87**	**2104.89**	**2666.62**	**2865.25**
按税种分	**By Category**						
#营业税	Sales Tax	601.06	651.78	749.90	855.40	1071.51	1152.74
企业所得税	Coporate Income Tax	150.64	161.06	142.24	173.18	210.52	221.02
个人所得税	Personal Income Tax	308.24	409.62	436.49	536.27	681.27	703.48
按行业分	**By Sector**						
第一产业	Primary Industry	1.66	2.05	2.57	3.67	3.90	4.94
第二产业	Secondary Industry	198.90	216.00	209.91	235.20	303.14	326.20
#制造业	Manufacturing	74.52	94.87	88.62	101.75	138.36	150.45
电力、燃气及水的生产和供应业	Production and Distribution of Electricity, Gas and Water	12.00	14.96	15.46	15.69	19.37	21.18
建筑业	Construction	108.51	97.19	98.64	109.88	134.37	144.65
第三产业	Tertiary Industry	1165.57	1359.97	1559.39	1866.00	2359.58	2534.11
#交通、运输仓储及邮政业	Transportation, Storage, Posts and Telecommunications	37.78	45.90	46.43	51.41	63.95	60.58
信息传输、计算机服务和软件业	Information Transmission, Computer Servicesand Software	64.63	82.03	85.87	98.02	125.48	132.76
批发和零售业	Wholesale Trade and Retail Trade	66.80	85.20	89.24	111.40	159.35	169.30
金融业	Finance	142.17	211.13	228.57	276.40	366.35	446.67
房地产业	Real Estate	317.19	282.32	371.28	437.40	520.36	525.44

资料来源：北京市地方税务局。
Source:Beijing Local Tax Bureau.

6-7 国税税收收入分税种、分行业完成情况(2007-2012年)
STATE TAX REVENUE BY CATEGORY AND INDUSTRY (2007-2012)

单位：亿元 (100 million yuan)

项目	Item	2007	2008	2009	2010	2011	2012
国内税收收入合计	**Total Domestic Tax Revenues**	**3030.6**	**3861.7**	**4561.1**	**4346.8**	**5332.5**	**6339.4**
按税种分	**By Category**						
#增值税	Value-added Tax	574.1	652.4	749.7	868.3	961.7	1096.0
营业税	Coporate Income Tax	196.6	225.3	160.6	145.4	161.3	191.3
企业所得税	Personal Income Tax	1874.9	2526.3	3116.5	2642.0	3506.5	3609.4
按行业分	**By Sector**						
第一产业	Primary Industry	0.4	1.0	4.0	5.8	0.7	0.3
第二产业	Secondary Industry	684.8	602.6	627.8	779.1	881.1	843.8
#制造业	Manufacturing	402.4	419.3	563.6	623.2	709.2	764.6
电力、燃气及水的生产和供应业	Production and Distribution of Electricity, Gas and Water	76.4	124.1	84.3	105.2	103.5	131.0
建筑业	Construction	7.4	14.6	20.4	30.1	45.3	54.8
第三产业	Tertiary Industry	2345.4	3258.1	3929.3	3561.9	4450.8	5495.3
#交通、运输仓储及邮政业	Transportation, Storage, Posts and	151.6	173.2	134.2	157.9	209.2	212.1
信息传输、计算机服务和软件业	Telecommunications Information Transmission, Computer Services and Software	116.6	126.2	208.4	30.8	105.9	245.9
批发和零售业	Wholesale Trade and Retail Trade	719.2	842.8	820.5	1081.6	1410.8	1314.6
金融业	Finance	1090.5	1768.6	2396.0	1831.2	2158.0	3034.0
房地产业	Real Estate	67.3	106.3	77.0	107.6	122.3	111.6

资料来源：北京市国家税务局。
Source: Beijing State Tax Bureau.

主要统计指标解释

财政部分

地方财政收入 指国家财政参与社会产品分配所得的收入，是实现国家职能的财力保证。包括地方公共财政预算收入和基金预算收入。

地方公共财政预算收入 是通过一定的形式和程序，由各级财政部门组织并纳入预算管理的各项收入。

基金预算收入 是按规定收取，转入或通过当年财政安排，由财政管理并具有指定用途的政府性基金预算收入等。

税收收入 包括增值税、营业税、企业所得税、个人所得税、资源税、城市维护建设税、房产税、印花税、城镇土地使用税、土地增值税、车船税、耕地占用税、契税等。

非税收收入 包括专项收入、行政事业性收费、罚没收入和其他收入。

地方财政支出 是以国家为主体，以财政的事权为依据进行的一种财政资金分配活动，集中反映了国家的职能活动范围及其所发生的耗费，包括地方公共财政预算支出和基金预算支出。

地方公共财政预算支出 是各级财政部门对集中的一般预算收入有计划地分配和使用而安排的支出。

基金预算支出 是各级财政部门用基金预算收入安排的支出。

一般公共服务支出 指政府提供基本公共管理与服务的支出，包括人大事务、政协事务、政府办公厅（室）及相关机构事务、发展与改革事务、统计信息事务、财政事务、税收事务、审计事务、海关事务、人力资源事务、纪检监察事务、人口与计划生育事务、商贸事务、知识产权事务、工商行政管理事务、国土资源事务、海洋管理事务、测绘事务、地震事务、气象事务、民族事务、宗教事务、港澳台侨事务、档案事务、共产党事务、民主党派事务及工商联事务、群众团体事务、彩票事务等。

教育支出 指政府教育事务支出，包括教育行政管理、学前教育、小学教育、初中教育、普通高中教育、普通高等教育、初等职业教育、中专教育、技校教育、职业高中教育、高等职业教育、广播电视教育、留学生教育、特殊教育、干部继续教育、教育机关服务等。

科学技术支出 指用于科学技术方面的支出，包括科学技术管理事务、基础研究、应用研究、技术研究与开发、科技条件与服务、社会科学、科学技术普及、科技交流与合作等。

文化教育与传媒支出 指政府在文化、文物、体育、广播影视、新闻出版等方面的支出。

社会保障和就业支出 指政府在社会保障与就业方面的支出，包括社会保障和就业管理事务、民政管理事务、财政对社会保险基金的补助、补充全国社会保障基金、行政事业单位离退休、企业改革补助、就业补助、抚恤、退役安置、社会福利、残疾人事业、城市居民最低生活保障、其他城镇社会救济、农村社会救济、自然灾害生活救助、红十字事务等。

医疗卫生支出 指政府医疗卫生方面的支出，包括医疗卫生管理事务支出、医疗服务支出、医疗保障支出、疾病预防控制支出、卫生监督支出、妇幼保健支出、农村卫生支出等。

节能环保支出 指政府环境保护支出，包括环境保护管理事务支出、环境监测与监察支出、污染治理支出、自然生态保护支出、天然林保护工程支出、退耕还林支出、风沙荒漠治理支出、退牧还草支出、已垦草原退耕还草、能源节约利用、污染减排、可再生能源和资源综合利用等支出。

交通运输支出 指政府交通运输和邮政业方面的支出，包括公路运输支出、水路运输支出、铁路运输支出、民用航空运输支出、邮政业支出等。

城乡社区事务支出 指政府城乡社区事务支出，包括城乡社区管理事务支出、城乡社区规划与管理支出、城乡社区公共设施支出、城乡社区住宅支出、城乡社区环境卫生支出、建设市场管理与监督支出等。

农林水事务支出 指政府农林水事务支出，包括农业支出、林业支出、水利支出、扶贫支出、农业综合开发支出等。

税收部分

税费收入 指由各级地方税务局征缴的各项税收收入和罚没收入。包括营业税、企业所得税、个人所得税、资源税、房产税、契税、城市维护建设税等。

税收收入 指由各级国家税务局征缴的各项税收收入和罚没收入。包括增值税、消费税、营业税、企业所得税、个人所得税、城市维护建设税等。

营业税 是对在中华人民共和国境内提供应税劳务、转让无形资产或者销售不动产的单位和个人，就其取得营业额征收的一种税。

企业所得税 是对中国境内全部企业的生产经营所得和其他所得征收的一种税。

增值税 指以商品或劳务销售额为计税依据并实行扣除已征税款制度的一种流转税。

个人所得税 是对个人（自然人）取得的各项应税所得征收的一种税。

Explanatory Notes on Main Statistical Indicators

Finance

Local Government Revenue refer to the revenue from participation of national finance in social product allocation. It is a financial guarantee to realize national functions, and includes local public budgetary financial revenue and fund budget revenue.

Local Public Budgetary Financial Revenue refers to the revenue organized by finance authorities at all levels in certain form and through certain procedures and involved in budgetary management.

Fund Budget Revenue refers to governmental fund budget revenues collected, transferred in or arranged by government finance in the same year in accordance with regulations, governed by government finance and for specific use of purpose.

Tax Revenue includes value-added tax, business tax, corporate income tax, individual income tax, resource tax, urban maintenance and construction tax, house property tax, stamp tax, urban land use tax, land value-added tax, tax on vehicles and boat operation, arable land occupation tax, deed tax, etc.

Non-tax Revenue includes special revenues, administrative charges, fines, and other revenues.

Local Financial Expenditure refers to a sort of allocation activity of financial funds by the state based on the position of finance. It is a concentrated reflection of the functional activity scope of the state and the expenditure incurred by it. It includes local public budgetary financial expenditure and fund budget expenditure.

Local Public Budgetary Financial Expenditure refers to the expenditure arranged by finance authorities at all levels during their planned distribution and use of the general budgetary revenue gathered.

Fund Budget Expenditure refers to the expenditure arranged by finance authorities at all levels with the fund budget revenue.

Expenditure for General Public Services refers to the spending on the basic public management and services provided by governments, including the expense on affairs of People's Congress, affairs of People's Political Consultative Conference, affairs of government general offices and relative institutions, affairs of development and reform, affairs of statistical information, affairs of finance, affairs of taxation, affairs of audit, affairs of customs, affairs of human resources, affairs of discipline inspection and supervision, affairs of population and family planning, affairs of commerce and trade, affairs of intellectual property, affairs of administration for industry and commerce, affairs of land and resources, affairs of oceanic administration, affairs of surveying and mapping, affairs of earthquake, weather affairs, ethnic affairs, religious affairs, affairs of Hong Kong, Macao, Taiwan, and Overseas Chinese, affairs of archives administration, affairs of Chinese Communist Party, affairs of democratic parties and federation of industry and commerce, affairs of mass organizations, and affairs of lottery tickets, etc.

Expenditure for Education refers to the spending of government on education, including the expense on the administration of education, pre-school education, primary education, junior high school education, senior high school education, regular higher education, primary vocational education, secondary vocational education, technical school education, vocational senior high school education and higher vocational education, radio and television education, student abroad education, special education, continuing education for management personnel, and services for education authorities, etc.

Expenditure for Science and Technology refers to the spending on science and technology (S&T), including the expense on the administration of S&T, basic research, applied research, research and development, conditions and services of S&T, popularization of social science and S&T, exchanges and cooperation of S&T, etc.

Expenditure for Cultural Education and Media refers to the spending on culture, cultural relics, sports, radio, film, television, press and publication, etc.

Expenditure for Social Security and Employment refers to the spending on social security and employment, including the expense on social security and employment administration affairs, civil affairs, budgetary subsidy on the social insurance funds, subsidy on National Social Security Fund, retirees of administrative units and institutions, subsidy on enterprise reform, subsidy on employment effort, pension, placement of ex-serviceman, social welfare, the handicapped undertakings, the system of cost of living allowances for urban residents, other urban social relief, rural social relief, living relief of natural disasters, affairs of Red Cross, etc.

Expenditure for Medical Service and Health Care refers to the spending on medical service and health care, including the expense on affairs of medical and health administration, medical services, medical guarantee, disease prevention and control, health inspection and supervision, women and children's health care, rural health care, etc.

Expenditure for Energy Saving and Environmental Protection refers to the spending of government on environmental protection, including the expense on administration of environmental protection, environment monitoring and supervision, pollution control, natural ecology protection, project of virgin forest protection, reforesting farmland, control of sources of dust storms, returning pastureland to grassland, returning cultivated land to grassland, energy conservation and utilization, emissions reduction, comprehensive utilization of renewable energy and resources, etc.

Expenditure for Transportation refers to the spending of government on transportation and postal services, including the expense on highway transportation, waterway transportation, railway transportation, civil aviation transportation and postal services, etc.

Expenditure for Urban and Rural Community Affairs refers to the spending of government on urban and rural community affairs, including the expense on administration of urban and rural communities, planning and management of urban and rural communities, public facilities in urban and rural communities, residential houses in urban and rural communities, sanitation in urban and rural communities, management and supervision of construction markets, etc.

Expenditure for Agriculture, Forestry and Water Conservancy Affairs refers to the spending of government on agriculture, forestry and water conservancy affairs, including the expense on agriculture affairs, forestry affairs, water conservancy affairs, poverty alleviation and comprehensive agricultural development, etc.

Revenues

Tax and Fees Revenue refers to the revenue of tax and fines levied and collected by local tax bureaus at all levels, including business tax, corporate income tax, individual income tax, resource tax, house property tax, deed tax, urban maintenance and construction tax, etc.

Tax Revenue refers to the revenue of tax and fines levied and collected by state tax bureaus at all levels, including value-added tax, excise tax, business tax, corporate income tax, individual income tax, urban maintenance and construction tax, etc.

Business Tax is a kind of tax levied against the business income of entities and individuals providing taxable labor services, transferring intangible assets or selling real estate within the territory of PRC.

Corporate Income Tax is a sort of tax levied against income of China domestic enterprises from their production and operation and other income.

Value-Added Tax is a sort of commodity turnover tax based on commodity and service sales, with a system of deduction of tax levied.

Individual Income Tax is a sort of tax levied against taxable income earned by individuals (natural persons).

07

价格指数
PRICE INDEX

简要说明

一、本章资料的主要内容

本章价格指数资料，反映生产、流通、消费与投资的价格变动趋势和变动幅度。主要包括居民消费价格指数；商品零售价格指数；农业生产资料价格指数；农产品生产价格指数；工业生产者出厂价格指数；工业生产者购进价格指数；固定资产投资价格指数；住宅销售价格指数。

二、本章资料的数据来源

本章资料由国家统计局北京调查总队、北京市统计局提供。

三、调查方法

（一）居民消费价格指数和商品零售价格指数

编制居民消费价格指数、商品零售价格指数的资料采用抽样调查和重点调查相结合的方法取得，即在全市选择不同的区域，按照布局合理的原则抽选价格调查点，由国家确定调查商品和服务项目，在此基础上按照消费量大、价格变动趋势有较强代表性的原则选择调查样本，对其市场价格进行定期调查，以样本推算总体。现将指数编制过程按下列几个步骤进行说明。

抽选价格调查点。按照布局合理等原则，将不同区域各种类型的商场、农贸市场、服务网点分别按销售额、成交额和经营规模为标志，从高到低排队，依据所需调查点的数量进行等距抽样。

选择代表规格品。代表商品和服务项目由国家确定，代表规格品由各省市按照有关原则选择。选择原则：（1）消费量较大；（2）价格变动趋势和变动程度有较强的代表性，即选中规格品的价格变动特征与未选中规格品之间价格变动的相关性愈高愈好；（3）选中的规格品之间，性质相隔愈远愈好，价格变动特征的相关性愈低愈好；选中的工业消费品必须是合格产品，产品包装上有注册商标、产地、规格等级等标识。

目前，居民消费价格调查按用途划分为8大类，262个基本分类，国家规定大城市调查规格品数量应在600种左右，北京市由于编制分收入层居民消费价格指数，代表规格品数量增加到1508种。商品零售价格指数划分为16个大类，229个基本分类，北京市代表规格品数量为1275种。

价格资料的采集。采取定人、定点、定时直接调查的方法采集价格资料。

权数资料来源与计算。居民消费价格指数的权数根据城市居民家庭生活消费支出调查资料整理计算。商品零售价格指数的权数根据商业统计中社会消费品零售额计算。

（二）工业生产者出厂价格指数（原指标为“工业品出厂价格指数”）和工业生产者购进价格指数（原指标为“原材料、燃料、动力购进价格指数”）

工业生产者出厂价格是工业品第一次出售时的出厂价格。该项调查采用重点调查与典型调查相结合的调查方法。重点调查对象为选中的全年主营业务收入2000万元及以上的工业法人样本单位及部分生产特定产品的全年主营业务收入2000万元以下的工业法人样本单位。

工业生产者购进价格是工业企业作为中间投入的价格。调查对象从填报工业生产者出厂价格的企业中选择。

选择代表企业的原则：(1)按工业行业选择调查企业，各中类行业原则上都要有调查企业；(2)大型企业应尽量都选占相当大比重企业；(3)选择生产正常、稳定的企业作为调查对象；(4)选择企业时要兼顾不同所有制形式。

选择代表产品的原则：(1)按工业行业选择代表产品；(2)选择对国计民生影响大的产品；(3)选择生产较为稳定的产品；(4)选择有发展前景的产品；(5)选择具有地方特色的产品。

除了以上原则及方法外，工业生产者购进价格调查还要考虑到特殊性，即调查企业要填报其生产中消耗的主要原材料、燃料、动力，不填报消耗较少、在生产投入中比重较小的原材料、燃料、动力。

权数的确定。编制工业生产者出厂价格指数所用的权数，用工业品销售额计算。计算资料来自于经济普查的工业数据。若近期没有经济普查，采用工业统计年度资料计算。编制工业生产者购进价格指数所用的权数来自工业部门各种物质消耗额，计算资料为经济普查资料结合一次性产品调查数据。权数一般五年更换一次。

（三）固定资产投资价格指数

固定资产投资价格调查采用重点调查与典型调查相结合的方法。固定资产投资价格调查所涉及的价格是构成固定资产投资额实体的实际购进价格（或结算价格）。调查的内容包括构成当年建筑工程实体的钢材、木材、水泥、地方建筑材料、电料、化工材料等主要建筑材料价格；投入的劳动力价格（单位工资）和各种施工机械使用费用；设备工器具购置和其他费用投资价格。

选择建筑安装工程调查点的原则：(1)样本单位应具有一定覆盖面；(2)投资经济活动代表性强；(3)兼顾不同经济类型；(4)选择重点工程；(5)兼顾不同工程类别。

选择其他费用调查点的原则：在选择其他费用调查点时，所遵循的原则与建筑安装工程调查点的原则基本相同，特别是要注意选择那些投资额大的工程。但由于其他费用不易取得，所以在实际操作过程中，应同时在建设单位、施工单位开展重点调查，并辅以典型调查(从有关管理部门取得资料)。

权数的确定。固定资产投资价格指数的计算权数是建筑安装工程、设备工器具购置和其他费用三者前三年投资完成额的平均比重。

（四）住宅销售价格指数是反映住宅销售价格总水平变动趋势和程度的相对数。包括新建住宅销售价格指数和二手住宅销售价格指数。

新建住宅销售价格的调查方法：目前我国住宅销售价格调查在 70 个大中城市开展。新建住宅销售价格、面积、金额等资料直接采用当地房地产管理部门的网签数据。新建住宅的网签数据内容主要包括：住宅在建项目（楼盘）名称、项目地址、幢号、总层数、所在层数、住宅结构、建筑面积、成交总价（合同金额）、签约时间等。

二手住宅销售价格的调查方法：二手住宅销售价格调查为非全面调查，采用重点调查与典型调查相结合的方法，按照房地产经纪机构上报、房地产管理部门提供与调查员实地调查相结合的方式收集基础数据。

（五）农产品生产价格指数

农产品生产价格调查采取抽样调查和重点调查相结合的调查方法。抽取 323 个农产品生产和出售的农业生产经营单位和行政村作为调查对象。对一些区域性比较强的农产品采取在主产区主观选样的方法选择农业生产经营单位和行政村作为调查对象。

被调查单位及行政村在辅助调查员的指导下将在报告期出售的农产品的名称、出售数量、价格、金额即时记入农产品生产价格调查台账，并上报，由市级超级汇总。

（六）农业生产资料价格指数

农业生产资料价格调查同农产品生产价格调查方法。

Brief Introduction

I. Main Content

Price index data in this chapter reflect the trend and rate of changes in prices of production, circulation, consumption and investment, mainly consisting of consumer's price index (CPI), retail price index (RPI), agricultural production materials price index, producer's price index for agricultural products, producer price index for manufactured products (PPI); Purchasing price for Industrial Sector ; House Selling Price Index.

II. Source of Data

Data in this chapter are from National Bureau of Statistics Survey Office in Beijing and Beijing Municipal Bureau of Statistics.

III. Survey Methods

1. Consumer price index (CPI) and retail price index (RPI)

Combined method of sample survey and key survey was used for developing the consumer price index and retail price index. Different areas were selected across the city. Price survey sites were selected in a principle of reasonable layout. Commodities and service items were identified by the country. Samples were selected from those with large quantity of consumption, and strongly representative trend of price changes. Their market prices were investigated on regular basis. The overall resulted was extrapolated from the samples. The process of CPI development was described as the following steps:

Selection of price survey sites. In such principles as reasonable layout, an equidistant sampling was conducted for department stores, agricultural product trade markets and service outlets in different types and in different areas by their sales value, transaction value and operational scale, which were ranked in a descending order, based on the number of survey sites required.

Selection of representative items. Representative commodities and service items are identified by the country. Representative items are selected by provinces and cities in relevant principles. Principles for selection: (1) Large quantity of consumption; (2) strongly representative trend and extent of price changes, namely, the characteristics of price changes of selected items shall be highly correlated with price changes of those not selected; (3) selected items shall be sharply different in their nature and poorly correlated in the characteristics of price changes; the selected industrial products must be up to grade, with registered trademark, origin, specifications, grade and other marks on the their package.

At present, CPI is composed of 8 major categories and 262 basic sorts. The country specifies that there should be 600 sorts of representative items for survey in a metropolis. In Beijing, due to the development of CPI by income class, representative items have increased to 1508 sorts. Retail price index consists of 16 categories and 229 basic sorts. In Beijing, there are 1275 sorts of representative items.

Collection of price data. Price data were collected through direct survey by designated persons at designated sites on periodic basis.

Source and calculation of weight data. CPI weights were calculated according to survey information on living consumption expenditures of urban residents. RPC weights are calculated according to consumer goods retail value in commercial statistics.

2. Producer Price Index for industrial products (PPI) （the original indicator "Ex-factory Price Index of Industrial Products"）; Purchasing Price Index for Industrial Producer (the original indicator "Raw Material, Fuel and Power Purchase Price Index"

The producer price index for industrial products means the ex-factory price of a manufactured products when it is sold for the first time. A combined surveys of key businesses and typical businesses. Starting from 2011, the key businesses are those with their annual turnover from primary activities over RMB20 million yuan, and the typical businesses are those with less than RMB20 million yuan .

Purchasing price for Industrıal Producer means the price of intermediate inputs in industrial enterprise. Enterprises for survey were selected among those reporting ex-factory prices of industrial products.

Principles in selecting representative enterprises: (1) Enterprises under survey shall be selected from each sector; (2) all (or a quite large portion of) large-sized enterprises shall be selected; (3) enterprises with normal and stable production shall be selected as survey targets; (4) different ownership enterprises shall be selected.

Principles in selecting representative products: (1) Representative products shall be selected from each industrial sector; (2) products having significant effect on national policy and people's livelihood shall be selected; (3) products with relatively stable production shall be selected; (4) products with promising development shall be selected; (5) products with local characteristics shall be selected.

In addition to the above mentioned principles, particularity shall be taken into account in the survey of price of raw materials, fuel and power. Namely, enterprises under survey shall report main raw materials, fuel and power consumed in production, without reporting those consumed less in production and taking a smaller percentage of productive inputs.

Determination of weights. Weights used for preparing producer price index for industrial products (PPI) are calculated with sales value of manufactured products. Data for calculation are industrial data from economic census. If no economic census was conducted recently, data from annual industrial statistics are used. Weights for preparing the purchasing index price for Industrial producer are from consumption value of different materials. Data for calculation are data from economic census combined with data from primary product survey; weights are generally changed every five years.

3. Price index for investment in fixed assets

A combined method of key survey and typical survey is used for the survey of Price index for investment in fixed assets Prices involved in the survey of fixed assets investment prices are actual purchase prices (or settlement prices) constituting the real part of values of fixed assets investment. The survey covers the prices of main building materials such as steel, timber, cement, local building materials, electric parts and chemical materials in building projects; prices of labor input (unit wage) and costs of use of construction machines; prices of purchase of equipment, tools and devices as well as other expenditures.

Principles for selecting survey sites of building and installation projects: (1) the sample unit shall have certain coverage; (2) have strongly representative economic activities of investment; (3) be in different ownership types of economy; (4) key projects shall be selected; (5) projects in different types shall be selected.

Principles for selecting survey sites of other expenditures: in the selection of survey sites of other expenditures, the same principles shall be followed as in the selection of survey sites of building and installation projects. Especially, projects with larger amount of investment shall be selected. As it is hard to obtain data of other expenditures, key survey shall be conducted simultaneous in building entities and construction entities in actual operations, supported with typical survey (data are obtained from relevant management authorities).

Determination of weights. Weights used for calculating the fixed assets investment price index are the average proportion of investment amount of building and installation projects, equipment, tools and devices purchase prices and other expenditures completed in the previous three years.

4. House Selling Price Index is a relative number reflecting the changing trend and extent of overall level of house selling price. It includes new house selling price index and second-hand house selling price index.

Survey method of new house selling price:

At present, real estate price survey is conducted in 70 medium or large sized cities across the country. For new house selling price, area, amount and other data, online data signed by local real estate management departments are directly used. Online signed data of new house transaction mainly consist of the name of construction project in process, project location, building number, total number of floors, floor number, house structure, building area, total price of transaction (contractual amount), and date of contract signing, etc.

Survey method of second-hand house selling price:

Survey of second-house selling price is non-complete survey conducted with combined method of key survey and typical survey. Basic data are collected in a combined manner of reporting by real estate broker agency, real estate management department and field survey by surveyors.

5. Producer price index of agricultural products

A combined method of sample survey and key survey was used for the survey of producer's prices of agricultural products. 300 agricultural entities and administrative villages producing and selling agricultural products were sampled. For some highly local agricultural products, agricultural entities and administrative villages were sampled with the method of subjective sampling in main production areas.

Under the instruction of assistant surveyors, the surveyed entities and administrative villages recorded instantly the name, quantity, price and amount of agricultural products sold in the reporting period onto the log book and reported them for summarizing at the municipal level.

6. Price index of agricultural Capital Good

The survey of agricultural production materials price was the same as that of producer's price index for agricultural products.

7-1 各种价格指数(1978-2012年)
PRICE INDICES (1978-2012)

(上年=100) (preceding year=100)

年 份 Year	居民消费价格指数 Consumer Price Index	商品零售价格指数 Retail Price Index	农业生产资料价格指数 Price Index of Agricultural Capital Goods	农产品生产价格指数 Index of Producers' Price of Farming Products	工业生产者出厂价格指数 Producer Price Index for Industrial Products (PPI)	工业生产者购进价格指数 Purchasing Price Index for Industrial Producer	固定资产投资价格指数 Price Index for Investment in Fixed Assets
1978	100.6	100.6	98.8				
1979	101.8	101.8	100.0	109.5			
1980	106.0	106.7	100.3	105.5			
1981	101.3	101.4	100.1	109.4			
1982	101.8	102.0	100.1	101.9			
1983	100.5	100.6	101.6	101.8			
1984	102.2	102.1	109.7	102.3			
1985	117.6	118.6	100.9	117.6			
1986	106.8	106.7	102.7	108.1			
1987	108.6	108.7	110.8	116.1			
1988	120.4	121.9	117.6	123.2			
1989	117.2	118.5	121.5	106.8			
1990	105.4	104.1	102.1	101.9	107.9	114.8	
1991	111.9	108.5	102.5	101.7	105.8	111.7	107.3
1992	109.9	108.3	103.6	102.4	100.9	103.3	112.2
1993	119.0	116.9	109.1	107.0	121.8	133.2	126.6
1994	124.9	117.9	120.1	133.4	112.9	118.7	116.2
1995	117.3	112.6	133.2	130.6	107.3	106.7	113.9
1996	111.6	107.3	106.8	101.5	100.7	100.3	108.2
1997	105.3	103.8	100.4	92.8	101.1	103.4	102.7
1998	102.4	98.3	102.6	93.6	95.1	98.1	100.8
1999	100.6	98.8	94.2	97.5	97.7	95.8	99.9
2000	103.5	98.9	101.7	95.0	102.5	100.0	101.0
2001	103.1	98.8	100.2	102.0	99.4	100.5	100.6
2002	98.2	98.4	102.9	92.4	96.6	97.1	100.4
2003	100.2	98.2	98.5	102.5	101.5	104.7	102.2
2004	101.0	99.2	114.3	106.2	103.0	114.2	104.3
2005	101.5	99.7	101.4	102.9	101.3	111.4	100.7
2006	100.9	100.2	103.7	99.1	99.1	105.5	100.4
2007	102.4	100.8	111.2	114.4	99.7	105.0	102.8
2008	105.1	104.4	117.4	112.3	103.3	115.8	107.8
2009	98.5	97.8	106.2	98.3	94.4	88.6	97.1
2010	102.4	100.4	106.9	106.5	102.2	110.5	102.5
2011	105.6	103.2	107.2	110.7	102.3	108.4	105.7
2012	103.3	100.6		104.7	98.4	98.7	101.3

注：工业生产者出厂价格指数原指标为“工业品出厂价格指数”；工业生产者购进价格指数原指标为“原材料、燃料、动力购进价格指数”(下同)。

Note: Producer Price Index for Industrial products (PPI)is the original indicator "Ex-factory Price Index of Industrial Products"; Purchasing Price Index for Industrial Producer is the original indicator "Raw Material,Fuel and Power Purchase Price Index" (the same below).

7-2 各种价格定基指数(1978-2012年)
FIXED-BASE PRICE INDICES (1978-2012)

年 份 Year	居民消费价格指数 Consumer Price Index (1978=100)	商品零售价格指数 Retail Price Index (1978=100)	农业生产资料价格指数 Price Index of Agricultural Capital Goods (1978=100)	工业生产者出厂价格指数 Producer Price Index for Industrial Products (1990=100)	工业生产者购进价格指数 Purchasing Price Index for Industrial Producer (1990=100)	固定资产投资价格指数 Price Index for Investment in Fixed Assets (1990=100)
1978	100.0	100.0	100.0			
1979	101.8	101.8	100.0			
1980	107.9	108.6	100.3			
1981	109.3	110.1	100.4			
1982	111.3	112.3	100.5			
1983	111.8	113.0	102.1			
1984	114.3	115.4	112.0			
1985	134.4	136.8	112.9			
1986	143.5	145.9	115.9			
1987	155.8	158.6	128.4			
1988	187.6	193.3	151.0			
1989	219.9	229.1	183.5			
1990	231.8	238.5	187.4	100.0	100.0	100.0
1991	259.4	258.8	192.1	105.8	111.7	107.3
1992	285.1	280.3	199.0	106.8	115.4	120.4
1993	339.3	327.7	217.1	130.0	153.7	152.4
1994	423.8	386.4	260.7	146.8	182.4	177.1
1995	497.1	435.1	347.3	157.5	194.7	201.7
1996	554.8	466.9	370.9	158.6	195.2	218.3
1997	584.2	484.6	372.2	160.4	201.9	224.2
1998	598.2	476.4	381.9	152.5	198.0	226.0
1999	601.8	470.7	359.7	149.0	189.7	225.7
2000	622.9	465.5	365.8	152.7	189.7	228.0
2001	642.2	459.9	366.5	151.8	190.7	229.4
2002	630.6	452.5	377.1	146.6	185.1	230.3
2003	631.9	444.4	371.4	148.8	193.8	235.3
2004	638.2	440.8	424.5	153.3	221.4	245.5
2005	647.8	439.5	430.4	155.3	246.6	247.2
2006	653.6	440.4	446.3	153.9	260.2	248.2
2007	669.3	443.9	496.3	153.5	273.3	255.1
2008	703.4	463.4	582.7	158.6	316.3	275.0
2009	692.8	453.2	618.8	149.8	280.3	266.9
2010	709.4	455.0	661.7	153.1	309.7	273.6
2011	749.1	469.6	709.3	156.6	335.7	289.2
2012	773.8	472.4		154.1	331.3	293.0

7-3 八大类居民消费价格指数(1978-2012年)

(上年=100)

年份 Year	居民消费价格指数 Consumer Price Index	#服务项目价格指数 Service Item Price Index	食品 Food	#粮食 Grain	#油脂 Oil or Fat	#肉禽及其制品 Meat Fowl and Products Thereof	#水产品 Aquatic Products
1978	100.6	100.0	101.2	100.0	100.0		100.6
1979	101.8	101.2	102.2	100.0	100.0		107.2
1980	106.0	95.5	108.2	100.0	100.0		131.3
1981	101.3	100.4	102.9	100.0	100.0		100.0
1982	101.8	100.1	104.2	100.0	100.0		100.0
1983	100.5	100.3	101.5	100.0	100.0		100.0
1984	102.2	103.1	102.8	99.3	100.6		106.6
1985	117.6	108.1	126.6	104.6	116.3		235.3
1986	106.8	107.9	109.6	103.6	132.4		129.7
1987	108.6	107.6	111.3	104.6	103.5		116.1
1988	120.4	106.0	123.9	114.4	120.7		144.9
1989	117.2	104.6	112.5	109.5	129.2		114.5
1990	105.4	118.2	103.7	104.5	101.9		101.7
1991	111.9	142.9	111.2	132.2	137.4		102.0
1992	109.9	122.8	111.5	134.3	110.9		101.8
1993	119.0	133.8	120.7	134.6	111.8		109.3
1994	124.9	136.1	126.7	144.0	133.8	138.2	125.6
1995	117.3	128.3	121.1	135.2	109.0	123.2	111.1
1996	111.6	120.0	107.7	112.2	90.8	101.5	104.5
1997	105.3	117.5	102.2	96.8	100.7	107.0	109.7
1998	102.4	121.3	97.1	96.4	103.3	93.2	94.8
1999	100.6	107.9	97.7	97.9	99.4	92.3	95.5
2000	103.5	116.2	97.9	91.4	85.8	98.4	107.3
2001	103.1	115.9	101.5	95.0	87.5	102.6	96.9
2002	98.2	99.4	98.0	98.5	94.7	98.9	95.7
2003	100.2	100.7	103.2	99.1	114.1	100.9	102.5
2004	101.0	101.8	104.8	120.6	117.0	110.1	107.1
2005	101.5	101.3	104.9	104.6	98.0	103.8	104.7
2006	100.9	101.2	102.8	101.6	101.5	99.4	101.9
2007	102.4	101.3	109.2	107.4	117.3	128.7	108.8
2008	105.1	99.9	116.1	108.9	121.3	125.1	120.1
2009	98.5	94.8	102.4	105.6	83.9	95.2	104.5
2010	102.4	103.7	105.5	109.6	100.9	101.2	110.6
2011	105.6	106.4	110.6	110.8	114.2	121.8	109.5
2012	103.3	104.2	106.6	102.6	104.5	106.7	104.8

EIGHT CATEGORIES OF CPI (1978-2012)

(preceding year=100)

#鲜菜 Fresh Vegetable	#鲜果 Fresh Fruits	烟酒及用品 Tobacco, Liquor and Articles	衣着 Clothing	家庭设备用品及维修服务 Household Equipment, Supplies and Repair Services	医疗保健和个人用品 Healthcare and Personal Commodities	交通和通信 Traffic and Communication	娱乐教育文化用品及服务 Entertainment, Educational, Cultural Commodities and Services	居住 Residence
114.5	101.6		100.0		100.4		100.1	
100.2	99.5		99.3		103.7		104.5	
114.1	106.7		99.5		101.5		100.8	
111.4	100.8		99.4		101.4		100.3	
104.7	94.3		96.7		101.4		100.1	
104.9	119.1		97.0		103.0		98.1	
106.8	112.1		101.2		107.4		100.0	
162.0	148.6		103.0		106.5		101.6	
106.7	121.4		101.3		102.2		100.8	
118.4	124.0		104.0		103.1		103.5	
133.5	124.4		125.1		131.5		114.4	
105.1	112.0		126.2		119.5		133.1	
107.1	98.6		110.3		111.0		93.5	
118.4	111.1		105.7		105.0		94.4	
115.1	104.6		103.3		114.8		92.8	
114.5	109.2		109.2		115.1		99.7	
128.5	114.9		124.7	112.7	113.2	104.9	118.7	124.1
124.3	129.5		117.5	108.3	102.6	100.3	100.8	113.2
113.7	104.6		119.1	104.6	110.1	102.1	110.1	129.2
95.0	94.0		102.9	105.4	105.2	100.3	98.1	121.2
93.9	89.5		105.9	97.5	108.6	99.0	97.8	104.7
106.2	101.4		99.4	96.5	115.8	98.3	98.8	101.0
98.4	88.4		102.6	96.3	113.5	92.3	97.8	117.9
100.2	101.5	101.5	100.4	97.0	98.7	100.8	114.2	104.2
84.7	94.5	100.6	95.9	97.0	100.2	99.5	96.6	101.9
145.4	111.4	100.2	97.1	97.7	100.1	97.8	98.3	101.6
95.0	104.1	101.2	98.9	96.9	99.2	95.7	101.5	101.4
111.9	111.0	100.0	100.1	99.7	98.0	97.5	99.7	105.9
112.8	112.0	99.9	99.7	101.2	101.1	99.3	98.7	101.4
109.9	100.8	101.8	100.0	100.4	100.3	95.7	99.2	103.5
108.1	112.9	106.0	99.1	104.4	102.0	97.6	98.0	103.0
111.9	109.4	102.2	98.4	100.3	99.9	95.9	97.6	89.8
124.0	112.3	101.1	98.4	99.4	101.5	100.8	99.4	105.0
97.3	112.1	102.5	102.7	104.2	103.7	101.5	99.7	108.5
114.5	101.6	102.2	100.9	102.8	101.5	99.1	102.3	103.9

7-4 多基期居民消费价格指数(2012年)
CONSUMER PRICE INDEX WITH MULTIPLE BASE PERIODS (2012)

项目	Item	1978=100	1980=100	1990=100	2000=100	2005=100	2010=100
居民消费价格指数	**Consumer Price Index**	**773.8**	**717.0**	**333.7**	**124.2**	**119.5**	**109.1**
#服务项目价格指数	**Service Item Price Index**	**2908.0**	**2900.5**	**1248.7**	**133.5**	**111.6**	**110.9**
食品	**Food**	**1213.1**	**1098.5**	**440.0**	**187.5**	**166.0**	**117.9**
#粮食	Grain	1176.7	1176.7	797.1	183.0	156.4	113.7
油脂	Oil or Fat	806.6	806.6	316.8	158.2	146.0	119.3
肉禽及其制品	Meat Fowl and Products Thereof	1466.0	1186.3	509.2	234.4	200.3	130.0
水产品	Aquatic Products	2975.7	2113.7	332.1	188.0	176.7	114.8
菜	Vegetable	2931.4	2593.4	713.4	254.8	200.9	109.9
#鲜菜	Fresh Vegetable	3298.2	2886.7	717.3	271.6	207.1	111.4
干菜及菜制品	Dried Vegetable and Vegetable Products	779.5	751.1	361.1	151.5	161.2	116.1
调味品	Flavoring	987.8	1017.0	500.9	143.0	135.8	109.8
干鲜瓜果	Dried and Fresh Melons and Fruits	1275.2	1191.8	327.0	201.5	169.9	113.0
烟酒及用品	**Tobacco, Liquor and Articles**	**452.4**	**452.4**	**206.5**	**120.9**	**116.7**	**104.8**
衣着	**Clothing**	**348.0**	**355.9**	**212.9**	**91.8**	**99.1**	**103.6**
#服装	Garments	363.4	374.9	219.9	92.5	99.8	103.5
衣着材料	Clothing Material	301.4	302.5	213.1	115.3	122.9	118.6
鞋袜帽	Shoes, Socks and Caps	363.5	368.9	215.5	87.0	95.9	103.1
家庭设备用品及维修服务	**Household Equipment, Supplies and Repair Services**	**296.7**	**295.0**	**155.4**	**100.6**	**113.3**	**107.1**
医疗保健和个人用品	**Healthcare and Personal Commodities**	**674.7**	**620.3**	**275.1**	**106.3**	**110.3**	**105.3**
交通和通信	**Traffic and Communication**	**106.3**	**106.3**	**89.6**	**82.6**	**90.1**	**100.6**
娱乐教育文化用品及服务	**Entertainment, Educational, Cultural Commodities and Services**	**218.9**	**213.8**	**112.8**	**104.2**	**94.8**	**102.0**
居住	**Residence**	**681.9**	**916.7**	**671.9**	**133.0**	**114.9**	**112.7**
#住房租金	House Rent	1864.9	2948.7	2925.3	149.6	130.8	114.3
水、电、燃料	Water, Electricity, Fuel	732.3	732.3	603.9	160.6	108.5	102.0

7-5 居民消费价格分类指数(2012年)
CLASSIFIED CONSUMER PRICE INDICES (2012)

项　　目	Item	2011 =100	项　　目	Item	2011 =100
居民消费价格指数	**Consumer Price Index**	**103.3**	家庭服务及加工	Households Service and Manufacuring	115.4
#非食品价格指数	**Non-food Price Index**	**102.0**	维修服务	Upkeep	
#服务项目价格指数	**Price Index of Services**	**104.2**	**医疗保健和个人用品**	**Health Care and Personal Articles**	**101.5**
#消费品价格指数	**Price Index of Consumer Goods**	**102.7**	医疗保健	Health Care	101.4
食　品	**Food**	**106.6**	医疗器具及用品	Medical Apparatuses and Supplies	103.7
粮　食	Grain	102.6	中药材及中成药	Traditional Chinese Medicine	105.6
淀粉及制品	Starches and Their Products	107.0	西　药	Western Medicine	99.7
干豆类及豆制品	Beans and Their Products	103.6	保健器具及用品	Health Care Appliances and Articles	102.8
油　脂	Oil or Fat	104.5	医疗保健服务	Health Care Services	100.0
肉禽及其制品	Meat, Pourtry and Their Products	106.7	个人用品及服务	Personal Articles and Services	101.6
蛋	Eggs	96.9	化妆美容用品	Cosmetics	100.0
水产品	Aquatic Products	104.8	清洁类化妆品	Cosmetics for Cleaning	102.8
菜	Vegetables	112.0	个人饰品	Personal Adornment	98.8
调味品	Flavoring	103.2	个人服务	Personal Services	107.7
糖	Carbohydrate	107.0	**交通和通信**	**Traffic and Communication**	**99.1**
茶及饮料	Tea and Beverages	104.8	交　通	Traffic	100.7
干鲜瓜果	Dried and Fresh Melons and	102.1	交通工具	Transportation Facility	97.1
	Fruits		车用燃料及零配件	Fuels and Parts	102.8
糕点饼干面包	Cake,Biscuit and Bread	106.8	车辆使用及维修费	Using and Upkeeping	109.2
液体乳及乳制品	Liquid Milk and Its Product	102.3	市区公共交通费	Incity Traffic	101.1
在外用膳食品	Outward Dinner	109.9	城市间交通费	Intercity Traffic	90.9
其他食品	Other Foods	105.0	通　信	Communication	95.7
烟酒及用品	**Tobacco, Liquor and Articles**	**102.2**	通信工具	Communication Facility	75.1
			通信服务	Communication Service	100.0
烟　草	Tobacco	100.2	**娱乐教育文化用品**	**Recreation, Education, Culture**	
酒	Liquor	104.4	**及服务**	**Articles and Related Services**	**102.3**
			文娱用耐用	Durable Consumer Goods for Cultural	
衣　着	**Clothing**	**100.9**	消费品及服务	and Recreation Use and Services	91.2
服　装	Garments	100.9	教　育	Education	105.1
衣着材料	Clothing Material	106.2	文化娱乐类	Cultural and Recreational Articles	102.8
鞋袜帽	Shoes, Socks and Caps	100.4	旅　游	Touring	104.2
衣着加工服务费	Clothing Manufacturing Services	106.1	**居　住**	**Residence**	**103.9**
家庭设备用品及	**Households Facilities, Articles**		建房及装修材料	Building and Building Decoration	99.2
维修服务	**and Repairing Services**	**102.8**		Materials	
耐用消费品	Durable Consumer Goods	100.9	住房租金	House-Rent	104.4
室内装饰品	Interior Decorations	99.5	自有住房	Private Housing	105.1
床上用品	Bed Articles	95.2	水、电、燃料	Water, Electricity and Fuels	101.4
家庭日用杂品	Daily Use Household Articles	105.4			

7-6 商品零售价格分类指数(2012年)
CLASSIFIED RETAIL PRICE INDICES (2012)

项目	Item	2011 =100
商品零售价格指数	**Retail Price Index**	**100.6**
食品	**Food**	**106.7**
粮食	Grain	102.6
淀粉及制品	Starches and Their Products	107.0
干豆类及豆制品	Bean and Their Products	103.6
油脂	Oil or Fat	104.5
肉禽及其制品	Meat, Pourtry and Their Products	106.7
食用畜肉及副产品	Meat and Sideline Product	105.8
禽	Pourtry	103.9
加工肉禽	Meat and Pourty Products	110.6
蛋	Eggs	96.9
水产品	Aquatic Products	104.8
鱼	Fish	104.4
其他水产品	Other Aquatic Products	105.1
菜	Vegetables	112.0
调味品	Flavoring	103.2
糖	Carbohydrate	107.0
干鲜瓜果	Dried and Fresh Melons and Fruits	102.1
糕点饼干面包	Cake, Biscuit and Bread	106.8
液体乳及乳制品	Liquid Milk and Its Product	102.3
在外用膳食品	Outward Dinner	109.9
其他食品	Other Foods	105.0
饮料、烟酒	**Beverages,Tobacco and Liquor**	**103.4**
茶及饮料	Tea and Beverages	104.8
茶叶	Tea	101.8
饮料	Beverages	107.1
烟草	Tobacco	100.2
酒	Liquor	104.4
服装、鞋帽	**Garments,Shoes,Hats**	**100.8**
服装	Garments	100.9
男式服装	Clothing for Men	102.6
女式服装	Clothing for Women	100.2
儿童服装	Clothing for Children	94.6
鞋袜帽	Shoes,Socks and Caps	100.4
鞋	Shoes	100.4
袜子	Socks	102.7
帽子	Caps	96.8
其他	Others	99.3
纺织品	**Textiles**	**96.3**
衣着材料	Cloth	106.2

项目	Item	2011 =100
床上用品	Bedding	94.9
家用电器及音像器材	**Household Appliances, Music and Video Equipment**	**95.4**
家庭设备	Household Appliances	100.3
文娱用耐用消费品	Culture and Recreat Durable Consumable	90.2
专业音响器材	Household Appliances and Hifi	98.8
文化办公用品	**Cultural and Office Appliances**	**95.7**
日用品	**Articles for Daily Use**	**102.4**
日用百货	General Merchandise for Daily Use	102.6
日用杂品	Grocery for Daily Use	101.3
洗涤用品	Washing	104.8
其他日用品	Other Daily Use Articles	101.6
体育娱乐用品	**Sports and Recreat Articles**	**104.3**
体育用品	Sports Articles	105.0
娱乐用品	Recreat Articles	101.3
交通、通信用品	**Traffic and Communication Appliances**	**92.7**
交通运输机械	Transportation Equipments	95.8
通信器材	Communication Equipments	76.8
家具	**Furnitures**	**101.6**
化妆品	**Cosmetics**	**102.1**
金银珠宝	**Gold,Silver and Jewelry**	**101.3**
中西药品及医疗保健用品	**Traditional Chinese and Western Medicines and Health Care Articles**	**102.0**
医疗器具及用品	Medical Apparatus and Articles	103.7
中药材及中成药	Traditional Chinese Medicinal Materials and Medicines	105.6
西药	Western Medicines	99.7
保健器具及用品	Health Care Apparatus and Articles	102.8
书报杂志及电子出版物	**Books, Newspapers, Magazines and Electronic Publications**	**102.5**
教材及参考书	Teaching Material and Reference Book	99.9
书报杂志	Books and Magazines	106.2
电子音像制品	Electronic Publications	103.6
燃料	**Fuels**	**102.7**
煤炭及制品	Coal and Coal Products	108.3
石油及制品	Petroleum and Related Products	102.2
建筑材料及五金电料	**Building Materials and Hardware**	**99.2**
建筑装璜材料	Building Decoration Materials	98.8
五金电料	Hardware	102.7

7-7 农产品生产价格指数
INDICES OF PRODUCERS' PRICES FOR FARMING PRODUCTS

(上年=100) (preceding year=100)

项　　目	Item	2012	2011
总指数	**General Price Index**	**104.7**	**110.7**
农业产品	Agricultural Products	107.9	101.6
#粮　食	Grain	105.7	109.5
蔬　菜	Vegetables	108.0	99.5
林业产品	Forestry Products	107.8	109.1
牧业(畜产品)	Animal Husbandry Products	100.7	120.6
#肉　牛	Beef Cattle	114.4	113.9
肉　羊	Sheep and Goats	110.1	120.8
奶产品	Milk Products	99.7	106.3
猪	Hogs	93.5	139.0
肉禽(毛重)	Table Poultry(Gross Weight)	104.8	109.0
禽　蛋	Poultry Eggs	100.5	114.8
渔　业	Fishery	112.6	107.9

7-8 工业生产者出厂价格及购进价格指数(2000-2012年)

(上年=100)

年 份 Year	工业生产者 出 厂 价格指数 Producer Price Index for Industrial Products (PPI)	轻工业 Light Industry	重工业 Heavy Industry	生产资料 Capital Goods	生活资料 Living Goods	工业生产者 购 进 价格指数 Purchasing Price Index for Industrial Producer	燃 料、 动力类 Fuel and Power
2000	102.5	98.0	104.2	103.4	98.8	100.0	104.3
2001	99.4	99.6	99.4	99.4	99.6	100.5	101.7
2002	96.6	97.6	96.4	96.4	97.9	97.1	102.3
2003	101.5	98.0	104.5	102.2	99.1	104.7	109.6
2004	103.0	100.2	105.3	103.7	100.6	114.2	120.0
2005	101.3	98.7	103.3	101.9	99.1	111.4	117.1
2006	99.1	97.9	99.6	99.0	99.3	105.5	113.1
2007	99.7	100.7	99.2	99.3	101.3	105.0	105.1
2008	103.3	101.8	104.0	103.8	101.3	115.8	132.3
2009	94.4	96.2	93.6	93.3	99.1	88.6	85.1
2010	102.2	98.7	103.8	102.7	100.3	110.5	121.3
2011	102.3	104.6	102.0	102.5	101.6	108.4	117.8
2012	98.4	101.1	98.0	97.8	101.0	98.7	99.0

PPI AND PURCHASING PRICE INDICES FOR INDUSTRIAL PRODUCTS (2000-2012)

(preceding year=100)

黑色金属材料类 Ferrous Metals	有色金属材料和电线类 Nonferrous Metals	化工原料类 Raw Chemical Materials	木材及纸浆类 Timber and Paper Pulp	建筑材料及非金属矿类 Construction Materials and Nonmetals	其他工业原材料及半成品类 Other Industrial Materials and Semi-finished Products	农副产品类 Agricultural Products	纺织原料类 Textile Materials
100.5	106.9	103.4	94.8	101.9	98.4	94.5	91.5
100.3	97.9	97.6	98.3	99.5	98.8	103.5	100.6
96.4	96.1	99.3	102.5	97.6	92.3	93.6	97.8
110.9	101.4	107.3	100.6	99.0	95.2	114.3	98.1
124.5	120.9	111.1	100.7	105.8	103.8	122.3	102.8
108.3	123.3	114.9	103.6	101.8	102.8	96.3	106.2
96.7	138.3	104.1	100.3	99.4	98.0	101.3	100.9
115.6	112.2	106.7	101.7	103.5	95.3	138.6	99.2
128.5	97.9	108.3	108.5	115.2	94.9	132.6	101.5
79.8	81.1	82.3	97.0	99.4	95.3	88.2	97.6
115.4	121.6	111.7	104.2	102.7	99.0	106.6	102.8
112.7	115.2	112.7	105.7	103.0	98.9	128.8	108.2
92.2	96.7	102.5	99.0	93.9	98.8	98.5	100.8

7-9 工业生产者出厂价格指数
PRODUCER PRICE INDEX FOR INDUSTRIAL PRODUCTS

(上年=100) (preceding year=100)

项目	Item	2012	2011
总指数	**General Index**	**98.4**	**102.3**
按轻、重工业分	**Group by Light Industry and Heavy Industry**		
轻工业	Light Industry	101.1	104.6
以农产品为原料	Using Farming Products as Raw Materials	102.6	106.6
以非农产品为原料	Using Non-farming Products as Raw Materials	98.7	101.6
重工业	Heavy Industry	98.0	102.0
采　掘	Excavation	93.9	121.2
原　料	Raw Material	101.8	108.6
加　工	Processing	96.6	98.2
按生产、生活资料分	**Group by Capital Goods and Living Goods**		
生产资料	Capital Goods	97.8	102.5
采　掘	Excavation	93.9	121.2
原　料	Raw Material	101.8	108.6
加　工	Processing	96.2	98.6
生活资料	Living Goods	101.0	101.6
食　品	Food	103.3	107.4
衣　着	Clothing	98.8	100.2
一般日用品	Articles for Daily Use	100.2	97.4
耐用消费品	Durable Consumer Goods	99.9	99.9

7-10 工业生产者出厂价格指数(按行业分)
PRODUCER PRICE INDEX FOR INDUSTRIAL PRODUCTS(BY SECTOR)

(上年=100) (preceding year=100)

项目	Item	2012	2011
煤炭开采和洗选业	Mining and Washing of Coal	94.7	121.9
黑色金属矿采选业	Mining and Processing of Ferrous Metal Ores	80.5	113.0
非金属矿采选业	Mining and Processing of Nonmetal Ores	99.5	108.7
农副食品加工业	Processing of Food from Agriculture Products	102.1	115.8
食品制造业	Manufacture of Foods	107.8	105.5
酒、饮料和精制茶制造业	Manufacture of Alcohol, Beverages and refined Tea	101.8	
烟草制品业	Manufacture of Tobacco	100.3	100.0
纺织业	Manufacture of Textile	96.5	102.3
纺织服装、服饰业	Manufacture of Textile Wearing Apparel, Footware and Caps	100.5	101.8
皮革、毛皮、羽毛及其制品和制鞋业	Manufacture of Leather, Furs, Feather (Down) and Related Products	99.9	101.3
木材加工和木、竹、藤、棕、草制品业	Processing of Timber,Manufacture of Wood, Bamboo, Rattan, Palm and Straw Products	102.7	103.0
家具制造业	Manufacture of Furniture	102.2	103.1
造纸和纸制品业	Manufacture of Paper and Paper Products	101.6	101.0
印刷和记录媒介复制业	Printing,Reproduction of Recording Media	99.8	101.6
文教、工美、体育和娱乐用品制造业	Manufacture of Articles for Culture, Education, Arts, Crafts, Sports and Entertainment Activity	99.8	
石油加工、炼焦和核燃料加工业	Processing of Petroleum, Coking, Processing of Nuclear Fuel	103.8	118.2
化学原料和化学制品制造业	Manufacture of Raw Chemical Materials and Chemical Products	94.6	107.3
医药制造业	Manufacture of Medicines	100.3	92.1
化学纤维制造业	Manufacture of Chemical Fibers	99.3	97.5
橡胶和塑料制品业	Manufacture of Rubber and Plastics Products	98.4	
非金属矿物制品业	Manufacture of Non-Metallic Mineral Products	98.0	107.7
黑色金属冶炼和压延加工业	Smelting and Pressing of Ferrous Metals	90.8	113.6
有色金属冶炼和压延加工业	Smelting and Pressing of Non-Ferrous Metals	103.5	216.9
金属制品业	Manufacture of Metal Products	99.9	105.7
通用设备制造业	Manufacture of General Purpose Machinery	99.6	99.7
专用设备制造业	Manufacture of Special Purpose Machinery	100.5	99.5
汽车制造业	Manufacture of Automobile	99.3	
铁路、船舶、航空航天和其他运输设备制造业	Manufacture of Railway Locomotives, Building of Ships and Boats, Manufacture of Air and Spacecrafts and Other Transportation Equipments	98.9	
电气机械和器材制造业	Manufacture of Electrical Machinery and Equipment	95.9	99.7
计算机、通信和其他电子设备制造业	Manufacture of Computer, Communication Equipment and Other Electronic Equipment	92.4	93.0
仪器仪表制造业	Manufacture of Measuring Instruments	99.6	100.4
其他制造业	Other Manufacturing	103.1	
废弃资源综合利用业	Recycling and Disposal of Waste	95.2	113.1
金属制品、机械和设备修理业	Repair of Fabricated Metal Products,Machinery and Equipment	99.3	
电力、热力生产和供应业	Production and Supply of Electric Power and Heat Power	102.2	100.6
燃气生产和供应业	Production and Distribution of Gas	97.8	105.4
水的生产和供应业	Production and Distribution of Water	105.5	105.9

注：根据国家统计局规定，2012年起执行2011年国民经济行业分类标准（GB/T 4754-2011）。受行业划分标准变化影响，有些行业缺少2011年同口径数据。

Note: According to provisions of the National Bureau of Statistics, from 2012 the Standard for Classification of Sectors in National Economy 2011 (GB/T 4754-2011) is implemented. Due to changes in the sector classification standard, there may be no comparable figures in 2011 for some sectors.

7-11 工业生产者购进价格指数
PURCHASING PRICE INDICES FOR INDUSTRIAL PRODUCER

(上年=100) (preceding year=100)

项 目	Item	2012	2011
总指数	**General Index**	**98.7**	**108.4**
燃料、动力类	Fuel and Power	99.0	117.8
黑色金属材料类	Ferrous Metals	92.2	112.7
#钢 材	Steel Products	91.1	110.9
其 他	Others	95.9	119.9
有色金属材料和电线类	Nonferrous Metals	96.7	115.2
化工原料类	Raw Chemical Materials	102.5	112.7
木材及纸浆类	Timber and Paper Pulp	99.0	105.7
建筑材料及非金属矿类	Construction Materials and Nonmetals	93.9	103.0
其他工业原材料及半成品类	Other Industrial Materials and Semi-finished Products	98.8	98.9
农副产品类	Agricultural Products	98.5	128.8
纺织原料类	Textile Materials	100.8	108.2

7-12 固定资产投资价格指数(2012年)
PRICE INDEX FOR INVESTMENT IN FIXED ASSETS (2012)

项 目	Item	1992 =100	1993 =100	1994 =100	2000 =100	2004 =100	2005 =100	2006 =100	2007 =100	2008 =100	2009 =100	2010 =100	2011 =100
总指数	**General Index**	**243.4**	**192.4**	**165.4**	**128.4**	**119.4**	**118.5**	**118.1**	**114.9**	**106.6**	**109.7**	**107.1**	**101.3**
建筑安装工程	Construction and Installation	307.4	234.3	195.5	143.3	124.2	123.6	124.0	119.0	106.5	113.0	108.6	99.0
人工费	Labor Cost	921.6	651.6	450.4	197.7	170.1	163.6	157.2	148.1	135.7	130.2	122.4	109.7
材料费	Costs of Materials	251.5	186.4	158.5	136.5	116.9	117.1	118.8	114.3	101.1	110.2	106.2	96.5
机械使用费	Costs of Machinery Use				121.7	118.3	118.3	116.7	114.9	109.2	108.4	106.6	103.1
设备、工器具购置	Purchase of Equipment,Tools and Instruments	106.6	92.7	90.9	72.8	87.9	89.2	89.6	90.6	92.3	95.5	96.3	97.4
其他费用	Others	202.4	165.8	134.3	127.0	123.4	121.2	119.1	116.5	111.2	110.2	108.2	104.0

注：按国家统计局的有关规定，固定资产投资价格指数从1991年开始计算。

Note: According to rules of National Bureau of Statistics, price index of investment in fixed assets is counted from 1991.

7-13 住宅销售价格指数(2012年各月)
RESIDENTIAL HOUSES SELLING PRICE INDEX(EACH MONTH OF 2012)

(上年同期=100) (preceding year=100)

项 目	Item	1月 JAN	2月 FEB	3月 MAR	4月 APR	5月 MAY	6月 JUN
新建住宅	**New Residential Houses**	**100.1**	**99.6**	**99.2**	**99.0**	**98.8**	**99.0**
#新建商品住宅	New Commercial Residential Houses	100.1	99.5	99.0	98.7	98.4	98.7
90平方米及以下	90sq.m and below	99.6	98.5	98.4	98.6	98.4	98.8
90-144平方米	90-144sq.m	100.5	99.6	98.7	98.3	97.9	98.4
144平方米以上	144sq.m over	100.2	100.1	99.6	99.1	98.8	98.9
二手住宅	**Second-hand Residential Houses**	**96.9**	**96.3**	**96.6**	**96.8**	**96.9**	**97.2**
90平方米及以下	90sq.m and below	97.4	96.8	96.8	96.9	97.3	97.5
90-144平方米	90-144sq.m	96.4	95.8	96.1	96.6	96.5	96.6
144平方米以上	144sq.m over	96.4	96.1	96.7	97.0	96.7	97.4

7-13 续表 continued

(上年同期=100) (preceding year=100)

项 目	Item	7月 JUL	8月 AUG	9月 SEP	10月 OCT	11月 NOV	12月 DEC
新建住宅	**New Residential Houses**	**99.3**	**99.4**	**99.5**	**99.8**	**100.7**	**101.6**
#新建商品住宅	New Commercial Residential Houses	99.0	99.2	99.3	99.7	100.9	102.0
90平方米及以下	90sq.m and below	99.2	99.3	99.4	99.7	100.8	102.2
90-144平方米	90-144sq.m	98.8	99.1	99.2	99.5	100.7	101.9
144平方米以上	144sq.m over	99.1	99.3	99.4	99.8	101.0	102.0
二手住宅	**Second-hand Residential Houses**	**97.5**	**97.7**	**98.2**	**98.8**	**99.8**	**101.6**
90平方米及以下	90sq.m and below	97.4	97.7	98.1	98.7	100.0	101.8
90-144平方米	90-144sq.m	97.1	97.4	97.6	98.4	99.2	101.1
144平方米以上	144sq.m over	98.3	98.4	99.0	99.4	100.0	101.7

主要统计指标解释

居民消费价格指数 是度量消费商品及服务项目价格水平随着时间而变动的相对数，反映居民家庭购买的消费品及服务价格水平的变动情况。居民消费价格指数变动率通常被用来作为反映通货膨胀（或紧缩）程度的指标。

商品零售价格指数 是度量工业、商业、餐饮业和其他零售企业向城乡居民、机关团体出售生活消费品和办公用品价格水平随着时间而变动的相对数，反映市场商品零售价格的变动程度。

工业生产者出厂价格指数 是反映全部工业产品出厂价格总水平变动程度的相对数。其中包括工业企业售给商业、外贸、物资部门的产品，还包括售给工业和其他部门的生产资料以及直接售给居民的生活消费品。通过工业生产价格指数能观察工业产品出厂价格变动对工业总产值的影响。

工业生产者购进价格指数 是反映全部工业原材料、燃料、动力购进价格总水平变动程度的相对数。用其可以观察和研究工业企业原材料价格变动对生产的影响，以及企业对原材料涨价的消化能力和承受能力，为制定价格政策提供依据。

固定资产投资价格指数 是反映固定资产投资额价格变动程度的相对数。固定资产投资额由建筑安装工程投资完成额，设备、工器具购置投资完成额和其他费用投资完成额三部分组成。编制固定资产投资价格指数应首先分别编制上述三部分投资的价格指数，然后采用加权算术平均法求出固定资产投资价格总指数。编制固定资产投资价格指数可以准确地反映固定资产投资中涉及的各类商品和取费项目价格变动幅度，消除按现价计算的固定资产投资指标中的价格变动因素，真实地反映固定资产投资的规模、速度、结构和效益，为国家科学地制定、检查固定资产投资计划，提高宏观调控水平，为完善国民经济核算体系提供科学、可靠的依据。

住宅销售价格指数 是反映住宅销售价格总水平变动趋势和程度的相对数。包括新建住宅销售价格指数和二手住宅销售价格指数。

农产品生产价格指数 是指农产品生产价格总水平变动程度的相对数。农产品生产价格是指农产品生产者第一次出售其产品时的单位产品价格。

农业生产资料价格指数 是反映农村居民用于发展生产所购买的生产资料价格变动程度的综合价格指数。包括生产用种籽、化学肥料、农用薄膜、饲料、生产用电、生产用燃料，大、中、小型农机具等价格变动因素。

Explanatory Notes on Main Statistical Indicators

Consumer Price Index (CPI) is a relative number measuring the changes in consumer goods and service prices over time. It reflects the changes in prices of consumer goods and services purchased by consumers. CPI is an indicator usually used for reflecting the level of inflation (deflation).

Retail Price Index is a relative number measuring the changes in prices of consumer goods and office supplies provided by industrial, commercial, food & drink and other retail businesses over time. It reflects the extent of changes in retail prices of commodities on the market.

Producer Price Index for industrial products (PPI) is a relative number reflecting the degree of changes in general producer prices of all industrial products, including products sold by industrial enterprises to commercial, foreign trade and materials companies, as well as production materials sold to industrial and other enterprises, and consumer goods directly sold to residents. It can be used to analyze the impact of producer prices of industrial products on gross industrial output value.

Purchasing Price Index for Industrial Producer is a relative number reflecting the degree of changes in the overall level of prices of all industrial materials, fuels and power. It can be used to observe and analyze the effect of changes in prices of raw materials in industrial enterprises on their production, as well as the enterprises' capacity of digesting and bearing the rising prices of raw materials, thus proving basis for development of price policies.

Price Index for Investment in Fixed Assets is a relative number reflecting the degree of changes in prices of investment in fixed assets. The investment in fixed assets consists of three components, i.e. the investment in construction and installation, the investment in purchases of equipment and instrument, and the investment in other items. Price index of investment in fixed assets is calculated as the weighted arithmetic mean of the price indices of the three components of investment in fixed assets. Removing the factor of price change in the aggregates of investment at current prices, this indicator shows the changes in the prices of commodities and fees involved in the investment of fixed assets, and can be used to observe the actual size, growth, structure, and efficiency of investment in fixed assets and provides reliable and scientific basis for government planning on and examination of fixed assets investment, improving overall adjustment and controlling skill, and further improving the national accounting system.

House Selling Price Index is a relative number reflecting the trend and degree of changes in the overall level of house selling prices, including new house selling price index and second-hand house selling price index.

Producer Price Index of Agricultural Products is a relative number reflecting the degree of changes in the overall production prices of agricultural products. Producer price of agricultural products means the price of unit product at which the producers of agricultural products sell their products for the first time.

Price Index of Agricultural Capital Goods is a comprehensive price index showing the degree of changes in the prices of capital goods bought by rural residents for production development. It consists of such price change factors as productive seeds, chemical fertilizer, farming film, feedstuff, electricity and fuel for production, small-, medium- and large-sized agricultural machines and tools.

08

北京统计年鉴2013 BEIJING STATISTICAL YEARBOOK

人民生活
PEOPLE'S LIVELIHOOD

简要说明

一、本章资料的主要内容

本章资料反映北京市居民生活现状及变化情况，分为城镇居民生活和农村居民生活两部分。调查内容主要包括家庭现金收支、主要商品购买数量及支出金额、居住状况和耐用消费品的拥有量等。

二、本章资料的数据来源

城乡居民生活状况的数据来源于国家统计局北京调查总队。

三、本章资料的调查方法

城乡居民住户调查方法和方案由国家统计局统一制定。城镇居民生活调查方法为抽样调查，2008 年开始城镇居民生活调查样本为 5000 户，覆盖全市 16 个区县。农村住户调查网点的抽选是以全市所辖行政村为总体，直接抽选调查村，在抽中村中抽选调查户。2008 年开始北京共抽选样本户 3000 户，覆盖 13 个郊区县。

四、五等分组的含义

要客观的反映不同收入层次家庭的收支及生活状况，必须按不同收入水平进行分组来观察和分析。“五等分组”即城镇住户按人均可支配收入、农村住户按人均纯收入从低到高排队分成五等份，有低收入组、中低收入组、中等收入组、中高收入组和高收入组五部分，各组的户数均占总户数的 20%。通过对调查户的分组，可以分别计算各组人均收入、消费性支出的情况，以观察不同收入组之间的差距和存在的问题。

Brief Introduction

I. Main Content

Statistics in this chapter reflect the conditions and changes in the life of residents in Beijing, consisting of two parts, one for urban residents, and the other for rural residents. Figures include household income and payment in cash, purchase quantity and amount of expenditures of main commodities, living status and number of durable consumables in possession.

II. Source of Data

Data of status of urban and rural residents’ life are from National Bureau of Statistics Survey Office in Beijing.

Ⅲ. Method of Survey

Methods and proposals for urban and rural resident households’ statistics are developed by the National Bureau of Statistics. Sample survey method was used for urban and rural residents’ life statistics, with sample size of 5000 households, covering 16 districts and counties from 2008. Sites for rural household’s survey were sampled directly from administrative villages across the city. Households were sampled from sampled villages. 3000 households from 13 suburb counties were selected as samples fro 2008.

Ⅳ. Meaning of Five-level Grouping

It is necessary to have different-level groups for observation and analysis in order to reflect the income and payment and living status of households at different classes. “Five-level grouping” means urban households are divided into five groups in a low-to-high order for the per-capita disposable income, while rural households using net per-capita income of rural households. These five groups are the low-income, middle-low-income, middle-income, middle-high-income and high-income groups. The number of households in each group accounts for 20% of the total. Through grouping of the households under survey, we can calculate the per-capital income and consumptive expenditure of each group so as to observe the difference between different income groups and problems that can be found.

8-1 人民生活基本情况(1978-2012年)
PEOPLE'S LIFE (1978-2012)

年份 Year	城镇居民家庭基本情况 Basic Information on Urban Household Lives							
	人均家庭总收入(元) Per Capita Total Income (yuan)	人均可支配收入(元) Per Capita Disposable Income (yuan)	人均可支配收入实际增长(%) Real Growth Rate of Per Capita Disposable Income (%)	人均消费性支出(元) Per Capita Living Expenditures (yuan)	#食品 Food	城镇居民家庭恩格尔系数(%) Engel Coefficient of Urban Households (%)	每一城镇就业者负担人数(人) Dependents Per Urban Employee (person)	城镇居民人均住房建筑面积(平方米) Per Capita Floor Space of Houses in Urban Areas (sq.m)
1978	450.2	365.4		359.9	211.2	58.7	1.86	
1979	491.5	415.0	11.6	408.7	236.7	57.9	1.83	
1980	599.4	501.4	14.0	490.4	271.0	55.3	1.80	
1981	619.6	514.1	1.2	511.4	295.1	57.7	1.72	
1982	668.1	561.1	7.2	534.8	317.6	59.3	1.66	
1983	716.6	590.5	4.7	574.1	337.7	58.8	1.65	
1984	837.7	693.7	15.0	666.8	379.1	56.8	1.63	
1985	1158.8	907.7	11.3	923.3	466.9	50.6	1.66	
1986	1317.3	1067.5	10.1	1067.4	543.4	50.9	1.66	
1987	1413.2	1181.9	1.9	1147.6	605.0	52.7	1.65	
1988	1767.7	1437.0	1.0	1455.6	743.4	51.1	1.71	
1989	1899.6	1597.1	-5.2	1520.4	841.3	55.3	1.52	
1990	2067.3	1787.1	6.2	1646.1	892.2	54.2	1.52	
1991	2359.9	2040.4	2.1	1860.2	1016.8	54.7	1.47	
1992	2813.1	2363.7	5.4	2134.7	1126.3	52.8	1.43	
1993	3935.4	3296.0	17.1	2939.6	1404.7	47.8	1.42	
1994	5585.9	4731.2	14.9	4134.1	1919.0	46.4	1.41	
1995	6748.7	5868.4	5.7	5019.8	2436.5	48.5	1.41	
1996	7945.8	6885.5	5.1	5729.5	2671.5	46.6	1.41	
1997	8741.7	7813.1	7.8	6531.8	2854.4	43.7	1.43	
1998	10098.2	8472.0	5.9	6970.8	2865.7	41.1	1.40	
1999	10654.8	9182.8	7.8	7498.5	2959.2	39.5	1.41	
2000	12560.3	10349.7	8.9	8493.5	3083.4	36.3	1.41	
2001	13768.8	11577.8	8.5	8922.7	3229.3	36.2	1.39	
2002	13253.3	12463.9	15.6	10285.8	3472.5	33.8	1.41	19.22
2003	14959.3	13882.6	11.2	11123.8	3522.7	31.7	1.39	19.71
2004	17116.5	15637.8	11.5	12200.4	3925.5	32.2	1.44	21.49
2005	19533.3	17653.0	11.2	13244.2	4215.6	31.8	1.39	22.03
2006	22417.0	19978.0	12.2	14825.0	4561.0	30.8	1.40	23.65
2007	24576.0	21989.0	11.2	15330.0	4934.0	32.2	1.40	24.77
2008	27678.0	24725.0	7.0	16460.0	5562.0	33.8	1.40	26.90
2009	30674.0	26738.0	9.7	17893.0	5936.0	33.2	1.40	27.69
2010	33360.0	29073.0	6.2	19934.0	6393.0	32.1	1.40	28.94
2011	37124.0	32903.0	7.2	21984.0	6905.0	31.4	1.50	29.38
2012	41103.0	36469.0	7.3	24046.0	7535.0	31.3	1.40	29.26

注：1. 城镇住户调查的口径范围：2000-2003年是1000户城市居民(城八区)数据；2004-2006年是2000户城市居民(城八区)数据；2007年是3000户城镇居民(十八区县)数据；2008年及以后由3000户调整为5000户，覆盖所有区县。

2. 表内城镇居民人均住房建筑面积为城镇住户抽样调查数据。

Note: a) Urban households investigation specification: figures of 1000 urban households'(in 8 districts) per-capita in 2000-2003; figures of 2000 urban households' per-capita in 2004-2006; figures of 3000 urban households'(in 18 districts and counties)per-capita in 2007; 3000 urban households changed to 5000 from 2008, covering all districts and counties.

b) Figures of per-capita floor space of houses in urban areas are from spot check data of urban households .

8-1 续表 continued

年份 Year	农村居民家庭基本情况 Basic Information on Rural Household Lives								居民储蓄存款余额（亿元） Balance of Saving Deposits (100 million yuan)	人均储蓄（元） Per Capita Saving Deposits (yuan)
	人均纯收入（元） Per Capita Net Income (yuan)	人均纯收入实际增长（%） Real Growth Rate of Per Capita Net Income (%)	人均总支出（元） Per Capita Total Expenditures (yuan)	人均生活消费支出(元) Per Capita Living Expenditures (yuan)	#食品 Food	农村居民家庭恩格尔系数(%) Engel Coefficient of Rural Households (%)	每一农村劳动力负担人数（人） Dependents Per Rural Labor Force (person)	农村人均住房面积（平方米） Rural Per Capita Living Space (sq.m)		
1978	224.8		219.0	185.4	116.7	63.2	2.15	9.20	9.33	110
1979	250.0	10.9	235.0	204.7	131.1	63.9	2.16	9.67	11.07	127
1980	308.1	22.1	290.0	256.8	140.2	54.1	2.13	10.09	14.39	162
1981	361.4	17.1	350.5	307.2	160.6	52.3	2.14	12.35	17.39	193
1982	430.2	17.3	411.2	345.5	181.1	52.4	1.97	13.01	21.77	237
1983	519.5	20.9	498.5	384.4	193.8	50.4	1.82	14.24	29.81	319
1984	664.2	25.7	559.3	435.0	222.5	51.1	1.79	14.22	38.82	411
1985	775.1	14.5	726.0	510.0	240.5	47.1	1.64	16.48	51.70	540
1986	823.1	3.7	857.0	645.3	292.4	45.3	1.66	17.41	68.58	706
1987	916.4	6.5	943.0	705.5	340.9	48.3	1.64	18.38	92.90	940
1988	1062.6	3.1	1246.0	883.3	407.9	46.2	1.63	19.23	111.60	1115
1989	1230.7	2.2	1356.0	976.3	484.3	49.6	1.62	20.09	162.01	1587
1990	1297.1	2.1	1372.0	980.7	497.0	50.7	1.61	20.62	226.62	2196
1991	1422.3	1.7	1585.0	1100.1	537.0	48.8	1.59	21.92	299.23	2879
1992	1568.8	2.0	1684.0	1179.0	573.8	48.7	1.58	22.67	389.79	3730
1993	1854.8	5.1	1714.0	1308.9	611.7	46.8	1.51	23.70	562.54	5351
1994	2422.1	9.1	2175.0	1676.5	824.8	49.2	1.49	24.42	853.21	8036
1995	3208.5	6.3	3080.0	2433.0	1206.0	49.6	1.47	24.74	1253.95	11716
1996	3562.7	4.8	3272.0	2655.5	1233.1	46.4	1.45	25.74	1706.98	15839
1997	3762.4	5.1	3379.0	2795.4	1248.4	44.7	1.48	27.39	1975.26	18197
1998	4028.9	6.7	3617.0	2945.5	1241.9	42.2	1.44	27.64	2287.19	20955
1999	4316.4	7.2	3938.0	3132.5	1253.5	40.0	1.43	28.65	2680.66	24374
2000	4687.0	7.3	4517.9	3441.4	1263.6	36.7	1.51	28.91	2923.21	26395
2001	5274.3	8.7	5098.8	3871.5	1353.2	34.9	1.52	31.01	3536.32	31510
2002	5880.1	12.3	5548.7	4206.0	1386.6	33.0	1.48	32.58	4389.69	38631
2003	6496.3	11.5	5886.6	4655.3	1475.6	31.7	1.45	33.95	5293.53	46079
2004	7172.1	9.2	6275.2	4886.4	1592.3	32.6	1.46	34.21	6122.35	52647
2005	7860.0	8.1	7181.2	5515.0	1807.0	32.8	1.45	36.94	7477.59	49346
2006	8620.0	8.7	7935.0	6061.0	1937.0	32.0	1.42	39.10	8703.29	55453
2007	9559.0	8.2	8866.0	6828.0	2190.0	32.1	1.40	39.54	9113.49	55621
2008	10747.0	6.5	10166.0	7656.0	2629.0	34.3	1.40	39.40	11869.91	68871
2009	11986.0	13.4	11814.0	9141.0	2961.0	32.4	1.39	39.42	14566.30	80233
2010	13262.0	8.1	12805.0	10109.0	3121.0	30.9	1.39	40.62	16876.30	88314
2011	14736.0	7.6	14503.0	11078.0	3593.0	32.4	1.38	48.63	18924.64	95087
2012	16476.0	8.2	15196.0	11879.0	3945.0	33.2	1.40	49.08	21419.28	104794

注：1．本表中“居民储蓄存款余额”为中资金融机构人民币储蓄存款余额。
2．本表中计算“人均储蓄”使用的人口标准，2004年及以前年份使用北京市户籍人口，2005年开始使用北京市年平均常住人口。
3．2011年农村居民人均纯收入及其分组数据按国家统计局方案进行了口径调整，2011年增长速度为同口径增速。

资料来源：表中“居民储蓄存款余额”数据来自中国人民银行营业管理部。

Note: a) In this table, the "balance of saving deposits" is the balance of saving deposits in RMB in China-funded financial institutions.
b) Population figures used for "per capital saving deposits" in this table were the population for household registered in Beijing before 2004, and effective 2005, are the annual permanent population in Beijing.
c) From 2011, standard on figures of per-capita net income of rural households and their grouping are adjusted in accordance with plans of the National Bureau of Statistics. Growth rates 2011 are figures of the same standard.

Source: Balance of Savings Deposits figures in the table come from the Banking Administration Department of the People's Bank of China.

8-2 5000户城镇居民家庭基本情况(按收入水平分)(2012年)
BASIC STATISTICS OF 5000 SAMPLED URBAN HOUSEHOLDS (BY INCOME LEVEL) (2012)

项目		Item		全市平均 Total	低收入户 20% Low Income	中低收入户 20% Medium-Low Income	中等收入户 20% Medium Income	中高收入户 20% Medium-High Income	高收入户 20% High Income
调查户数	(户)	Households Surveyed	(household)	5000	1000	1000	1000	1000	1000
平均每户家庭人口	(人)	Average Persons Per Household	(person)	2.7	3.1	2.9	2.7	2.7	2.4
有收入者人数	(人)	Persons Having Income	(person)	10798	1937	2189	2221	2298	2152
就业人口数	(人)	Employees	(person)	7199	1354	1466	1295	1505	1579
离退休人员数	(人)	Retirees	(person)	3375	443	685	908	777	562
其他有收入者人数	(人)	Others	(person)	224	140	38	18	16	11
无收入者人数	(人)	Persons having no Income	(person)	2928	1141	686	441	377	283
平均每户就业人口数	(人)	Average Employees Per Household	(person)	1.4	1.4	1.5	1.3	1.5	1.6
平均每一就业者负担人数	(人)	Dependents Per Employee	(person)	1.4	2.0	1.5	1.4	1.3	1.2
平均每人年可支配收入	(元)	Annual Disposable Income Per Capita	(yuan)	36469	16386	25506	32196	40846	65966
平均每人年消费性支出	(元)	Annual Living Expenditure Per Capita	(yuan)	24046	14245	19688	21842	25824	37935

8-3 5000户城镇居民家庭平均每人年现金收入(2012年)
ANNUAL CASH INCOME PER CAPITA OF 5000 URBAN HOUSEHOLDS (2012)

单位：元 (yuan)

项目	Item	全市平均 Total	低收入户 20% Low Income	中低收入户 20% Medium-Low Income	中等收入户 20% Medium Income	中高收入户 20% Medium-High Income	高收入户 20% High Income	2012年为2011年% 2012 as % of 2011
家庭总收入	**Familial Gross Income**	**41103**	**18824**	**28982**	**36153**	**45855**	**74096**	**110.7**
#可支配收入	Annual Disposable Income	36469	16386	25506	32196	40846	65966	110.8
工资性收入	Emolument	27962	13041	19293	22409	30775	53150	111.1
工资及补贴收入	Laborage and Allowance Income	27341	12553	18911	22067	30215	51834	110.6
其他劳动收入	Other Income from Work	621	488	382	342	560	1316	138.0
经营净收入	Business Income	1430	387	778	1030	801	4087	120.1
财产性收入	Property Income	718	367	350	439	508	1895	103.0
利息收入	Interest Income	69	15	20	40	53	214	107.8
股息与红利收入	Dividend Income	64	24	45	31	42	176	145.5
保险收益	Insurance Proceeds	4	…	1	1	10	10	57.1
其他投资收入	Other Income from Yield	57		4	13		266	44.5
出租房屋收入	Lease House Income	506	304	259	329	402	1220	114.2
知识产权收入	Sciential Property Right							
其他财产性收入	Other Income from Property	18	24	21	25	1	9	163.6
转移性收入	Transfer Income	10993	5029	8561	12275	13771	14964	109.1
#养老金或离退休金	Annuities and Pension	10102	4422	7968	11581	13069	13122	112.4
社会救济收入	Receiving Special Reilief Income	23	104	6	1	5	2	33.8
辞退金	Resignation Allowances	13		…		5	57	…
保险收入	Insurance Income	5	4	1	…	3	18	125.0
#失业保险金	Unemployment Insurance Income	3	3	1		1	10	75.0
赡养收入	Maintenance Income	137	107	83	150	174	171	87.3
捐赠收入	Gift Income	192	99	163	144	142	404	68.8
提取住房公积金	Draw Money of Housing Accumulation Fund	221	5	45	81	77	881	79.5
记账补贴	Subsidies of Account	261	240	254	273	267	272	96.3
出售财物收入	**Proceeds from Sales of Belongings**	**36**	**17**	**51**	**22**	**23**	**65**	**62.1**
借贷收入	**Credit Income**	**17521**	**9253**	**14211**	**15374**	**19697**	**28464**	**103.1**

注：人均可支配收入实际增长7.3%。
Note: Real growth rate of the per capita annual disposable income is 7.3%.

8-4 5000户城镇居民家庭平均每人年现金支出(2012年)
ANNUAL CASH EXPENDITURES PER CAPITA OF 5000 URBAN HOUSEHOLDS (2012)

单位：元 (yuan)

项目	Item	全市平均 Total	低收入户 20% Low Income	中低收入户 20% Medium-Low Income	中等收入户 20% Medium Income	中高收入户 20% Medium-High Income	高收入户 20% High Income	2012年为2011年% 2012 as % of 2011
家庭总支出	**Familial Gross Expenditures**	**30828**	**17568**	**24371**	**27134**	**33138**	**50963**	**109.1**
消费性支出	Living Expenditures	24046	14245	19688	21842	25824	37935	109.4
#服务性消费支出	Service Living Expenditures	6969	3838	5430	6011	7629	11703	109.4
购房与建房支出	Expenditures on Purchasing and Building Houses	437	255	56	118	341	1392	112.6
购　房	Purchasing Houses	433	252	38	118	341	1392	123.4
建　房	Building Houses	4	3	18				10.8
转移性支出	Transfer Expenditures	2260	855	1402	1556	2433	4944	92.6
缴纳个人所得税	Individual Income-tax	395	10	68	117	314	1435	62.3
捐赠支出	Gift Expenditures	1350	690	988	1099	1558	2361	106.7
购买彩票	Buy Lottery Expenditures	11	6	10	8	14	17	91.7
赡养支出	Support Expenditures	288	78	185	168	301	692	106.7
各种非储蓄性保险支出	Non-saving-deposits Insurance Expenditures	191	65	135	143	211	394	82.3
#车辆保险支出	Automotive Insurance	144	39	90	92	156	334	88.3
其他转移性支出	Others	25	6	16	21	35	45	89.3
财产性支出	Property Expenditures	107	25	71	52	112	269	87.0
社会保障支出	Social Security Expenditures	3978	2188	3154	3566	4428	6423	119.9
个人交纳的养老基金	Annuities	1430	911	1244	1270	1558	2128	119.1
个人交纳的住房公积金	Housing Accumulation Fund	2037	930	1458	1839	2317	3564	120.4
个人交纳的医疗基金	Iatrical Accumulation Fund	464	317	413	414	501	664	121.5
个人交纳的失业基金	Disemployed a Accumulation Fund	46	27	39	43	52	66	115.0
其他社会保障支出	Others	1	3	…	…	…	1	50.0
借贷支出	**Credit Expenditures**	**27652**	**10379**	**18617**	**24268**	**32290**	**51462**	**108.0**
#存入储蓄款	Saving Deposits	27016	10141	18200	23950	31644	49940	110.2
归还借款	Repayment of Loans	102	28	25	35	122	294	69.4
储蓄性保险支出	Saving-purpose Insurance Costs	122	34	87	95	109	278	76.7
购买有价证券	Purchase of Securities	22		3	18	1	84	9.1
归还住房贷款	Repayment of House Loan	235	91	248	82	267	473	71.9
归还汽车贷款	Repayment of Auto Loan	14	5	16	…	10	37	45.2

8-5 5000户城镇居民家庭平均每人年消费性支出(2012年)
ANNUAL LIVING EXPENDITURE PER CAPITA OF 5000 URBAN HOUSEHOLDS (2012)

单位：元 (yuan)

项目	Item	全市平均 Total	低收入户 20% Low Income	中低收入户 20% Medium-Low Income	中等收入户 20% Medium Income	中高收入户 20% Medium-High Income	高收入户 20% High Income	2012年为2011年% 2012 as % of 2011
消费性支出	**Living Expenditures**	**24046**	**14245**	**19688**	**21842**	**25824**	**37935**	**109.4**
食品	Food	7535	5405	6677	7534	8198	9723	109.1
衣着	Clothing	2639	1484	2050	2355	2947	4274	116.5
居住	Housing	1971	1267	1507	1739	1942	3349	102.4
家庭设备用品及服务	Household Appliances and Service	1611	902	1317	1353	1929	2497	103.1
医疗保健	Health Care and Medical Services	1658	1111	1471	1603	1793	2276	108.9
交通和通信	Transport and Communications	3782	1673	3230	3090	3329	7444	107.4
#汽车	Motor Vehicle	1077	287	1050	753	471	2777	106.5
教育文化娱乐服务	Education,Cultural and Recreation Services	3696	2028	2757	3278	4296	5996	111.8
其他商品和服务	Miscellaneous Goods and Services	1154	375	679	890	1390	2376	118.4
#服务	Services	350	131	224	283	411	683	110.8

注：人均消费性支出实际增长5.9%。
Note: Real growth rate of the per capita living expenditure is 5.9%.

8-6 5000户城镇居民家庭消费性支出构成(2012年)
MAKE UP OF ANNUAL LIVING EXPENDITURE 5000 URBAN HOUSEHOLDS (2012)

单位：% (%)

项目	Item	全市平均 Total	低收入户 20% Low Income	中低收入户 20% Medium-Low Income	中等收入户 20% Medium Income	中高收入户 20% Medium-High Income	高收入户 20% High Income	2012年比2011年增、减百分点 2012 Increase or Decrease than 2011
消费性支出	**Living Expenditures**	**100.0**	**100.0**	**100.0**	**100.0**	**100.0**	**100.0**	
食品(恩格尔系数)	Food (Engel Coefficient)	31.3	38.0	33.9	34.5	31.8	25.6	-0.1
衣着	Clothing	11.0	10.4	10.4	10.8	11.4	11.3	0.7
居住	Housing	8.2	8.9	7.7	8.0	7.5	8.8	-0.6
家庭设备用品及服务	Household Appliances and Service	6.7	6.3	6.7	6.2	7.5	6.6	-0.4
医疗保健	Health Care and Medical Services	6.9	7.8	7.5	7.3	6.9	6.0	持平
交通和通信	Transport and Communications	15.7	11.8	16.4	14.1	12.9	19.6	-0.3
教育文化娱乐服务	Education,Cultural and Recreation Services	15.4	14.2	14.0	15.0	16.6	15.8	0.4
其他商品和服务	Miscellaneous Goods and Services	4.8	2.6	3.4	4.1	5.4	6.3	0.3

8-7 5000户城镇居民家庭平均每人年购买食品支出(2012年)
ANNUAL EXPENDITURE OF FOOD PER CAPITA OF 5000 URBAN HOUSEHOLDS (2012)

单位：元 (yuan)

项目	Item	全市平均 Total	低收入户20% Low Income	中低收入户20% Medium-Low Income	中等收入户20% Medium Income	中高收入户20% Medium-High Income	高收入户20% High Income	2012年为2011年% 2012 as % of 2011
食　品	**Food**	**7535**	**5405**	**6677**	**7534**	**8198**	**9723**	**109.1**
粮油类	Grain and Oil	735	612	684	762	781	827	101.4
粮　食	Grain	432	360	401	453	459	483	98.0
淀粉及薯类	Starches and Tubers	52	43	48	55	56	55	94.5
干豆类及豆制品	Bean and Their Products	73	60	68	76	80	82	持平
油脂类	Oil or Fat	178	149	167	178	186	207	114.1
肉禽蛋及水产品类	Meat, Poultry and Related Products	1528	1215	1405	1582	1656	1762	105.7
肉　类	Meat Products	909	749	840	943	984	1019	104.0
禽　类	Poultry Products	176	143	166	182	191	195	102.9
蛋　类	Eggs	147	117	135	155	158	167	持平
水产品类	Aquatic Products	296	206	264	302	323	381	116.5
蔬菜类	Vegetable	583	489	537	606	624	656	108.6
鲜　菜	Fresh Vegetable	521	442	481	541	555	582	108.3
干　菜	Dried Vegetable	35	26	31	36	40	41	106.1
菜制品	Vegetable Products	27	21	25	29	29	33	117.4
调味品	Flavoring	129	101	120	133	142	146	106.6
糖烟酒饮料类	Sugar, Tabacco and Beverage	973	725	892	992	1042	1198	116.0
糖　类	Sugar	81	57	73	81	91	102	105.2
烟草类	Tabacco	301	233	284	307	326	353	119.4
酒　类	Liquor	284	213	256	288	292	364	117.4
饮　料	Beverage	307	222	279	316	333	379	114.6
干鲜瓜果类	Nuts and Fresh Melon and Fruits	773	581	681	800	841	950	109.5
鲜　果	Fresh Fruits	462	341	407	477	500	574	110.0
鲜　瓜	Fresh Melon	83	64	75	86	92	99	122.1
其他干鲜瓜果类及制品	Other Fresh Fruits/Melons and Nuts and Products	228	176	199	237	249	277	104.6
糕点、奶及奶制品	Cake, Milk and Dairy Products	679	490	600	699	749	846	109.7
其他食品	Other	101	79	91	101	106	128	127.8
饮食服务	Catering Service	2034	1113	1667	1859	2257	3210	111.0
食品加工服务费	Food Processing Service	2	1	1	2	3	2	200.0
在外饮食	Dinning Out	2032	1112	1666	1857	2254	3208	110.9

8-8 5000户城镇居民家庭平均每人年购买衣着、居住支出(2012年) ANNUAL PURCHASES OF CLOTHING AND RESIDENCE PER CAPITA OF 5000 URBAN HOUSEHOLDS (2012)

单位：元 (yuan)

项目	Item	全市平均 Total	低收入户20% Low Income	中低收入户20% Medium-Low Income	中等收入户20% Medium Income	中高收入户20% Medium-High Income	高收入户20% High Income	2012年为2011年% 2012 as % of 2011
衣着	**Clothing**	**2639**	**1484**	**2050**	**2355**	**2947**	**4274**	**116.5**
服装	Garments	1815	992	1396	1615	2040	2969	112.6
衣着材料	Cloth	13	10	11	14	17	15	92.9
鞋类	Shoes	706	430	562	636	772	1113	128.1
其他衣着用品	Other	89	45	69	75	101	151	121.9
衣着加工服务费	Clothing Processing Service Charges	16	7	12	15	17	26	持平
居住	**Residence**	**1971**	**1267**	**1507**	**1739**	**1942**	**3349**	**102.4**
住房	House	870	417	535	592	825	1943	109.7
租赁房房租	Rent	258	170	156	185	226	546	86.3
住房装潢支出	Construction Materials	531	195	320	323	516	1275	118.3
维修用建筑材料	Repairs	74	48	56	82	70	110	180.5
其他住房支出	Others	7	4	3	2	13	12	175.0
水电燃料及其他	Fare for Water, Electricity and Fuel	941	766	845	981	962	1142	97.8
水费	Water	112	82	101	115	117	143	96.6
电费	Electricity	387	307	355	424	405	442	97.0
燃料	Fuel	166	182	159	165	157	167	97.1
煤炭	Coal	25	69	27	15	15	8	…
罐装液化石油气	Tanked LPG	19	31	20	19	13	9	90.5
管道液化石油气	Pipeline LPG	2	…	3	2	2	1	持平
管道煤气	Pipeline Gas							
管道天然气	Pipeline Natural Gas	120	82	109	129	127	149	81.1
柴油	Diesel Oil							
其他燃料	Others Fuel							
取暖费	Heating Costs	265	185	219	267	268	380	99.6
其他相关支出	Other Related Expenditure	11	10	11	10	15	10	110.0
居住服务费	Habitation Service Charge	160	84	127	166	155	264	94.7

8-9 5000户城镇居民家庭平均每人年家庭设备用品及服务、医疗保健、交通和通信支出(2012年)

ANNUAL EXPENDITURE OF HOUSEHOLDS ARTICLES AND SERVICES, MEDICINE AND MEDICAL SERVICES AND TRANSPORTATION AND COMMUNICATION PER CAPITA OF 5000 URBAN HOUSEHOLDS (2012)

单位：元 (yuan)

项　目	Item	全市平均 Total	低收入户20% Low Income	中低收入户20% Medium-Low Income	中等收入户20% Medium Income	中高收入户20% Medium-High Income	高收入户20% High Income	2012年为2011年% 2012 as % of 2011
家庭设备用品及服务	**Households Articles and Services**	**1611**	**902**	**1317**	**1353**	**1929**	**2497**	**103.1**
耐用消费品	Durable Consumer Goods	652	316	546	459	858	1048	88.5
家　具	Furniture	293	123	235	211	374	506	93.0
家庭设备	Household Appliances	359	193	311	248	484	542	85.1
室内装饰品	Indoor Ornament	55	23	42	36	78	94	125.0
床上用品	Bedding	184	98	123	172	212	309	148.4
家庭日用杂品	Groceries for Households Daily Use	605	414	533	581	650	832	113.5
家具材料	Furniture Materials	11	2	7	5	26	15	84.6
家庭服务	Household Services	104	49	66	100	105	199	92.9
医疗保健	**Medicine and Medical Services**	**1658**	**1111**	**1471**	**1603**	**1793**	**2276**	**108.9**
医疗器具	Medical Apparatus	18	12	18	16	16	28	112.5
保健器具	Health Care Apparatus	51	32	20	56	74	69	96.2
药品费	Medicine Expenses	768	638	717	783	852	841	108.6
滋补保健品	Tonic	281	98	154	247	324	570	135.7
医疗费	Medical Services	522	322	547	486	506	736	99.2
其他医疗保健支出	Other	18	9	15	15	21	32	128.6
交通和通信	**Transportation and Communication**	**3782**	**1673**	**3230**	**3090**	**3329**	**7444**	**107.4**
交　通	Transportation	2726	957	2289	2096	2221	5947	109.8
家庭交通工具	Means of Transport for Household	1128	323	1096	809	530	2835	107.3
车辆用燃料及零配件	Fuels and Parts	870	312	677	730	949	1641	114.0
交通工具服务支出	Means of Transport Services Expense	262	84	176	169	231	635	106.9
交通费	Transport Fare	466	238	340	388	511	836	109.9
通　信	Communication	1056	716	941	994	1108	1497	101.7
通信工具	Communication Facility	287	167	228	261	306	464	110.0
通信服务	Communication Service	769	549	713	733	802	1033	99.0

8-10 5000户城镇居民家庭平均每人年教育文化娱乐服务、其他商品和服务支出(2012年)

ANNUAL EXPENDITURE OF EDUCATION,CULTURE,RECREATION SERVICES AND MISCELLANEOUS COMMODITIES AND SERVICES PER CAPITA OF 5000 URBAN HOUSEHOLDS (2012)

单位：元 (yuan)

项　　目	Item	全市平均 Total	低收入户 20% Low Income	中低收入户 20% Medium-Low Income	中等收入户 20% Medium Income	中高收入户 20% Medium-High Income	高收入户 20% High Income	2012年为2011年% 2012 as % of 2011
教育文化娱乐服务	**Education, Culture, Recreation Services**	**3696**	**2028**	**2757**	**3278**	**4296**	**5996**	**111.8**
文化娱乐用品	Cultural and Recreational Articles	824	413	612	817	928	1320	94.2
文化娱乐服务	Cultural and Recreation Services	1658	559	924	1390	2039	3296	131.5
教　育	Education	1214	1056	1221	1071	1329	1380	103.7
教　材	Teaching Material	41	46	39	34	38	47	105.1
教育费用	Education Expenses	1173	1010	1182	1037	1291	1333	103.6
#非义务教育学杂费	Tuition for Non-compulsory Education	131	159	168	105	137	87	87.9
义务教育学杂费	Tuition for Compulsory Education	11	15	14	8	12	6	84.6
成人教育费	Tuition of Adult Education	159	105	124	135	201	225	99.4
家教费	Family Education Expenses	124	103	128	118	153	116	129.2
培训班	Training Courses	538	452	541	423	585	680	119.3
学校住宿费	Expenses for Accommodation in School	14	16	16	10	16	10	93.3
其他教育费用	Other Education Costs	50	44	45	73	39	51	49.5
其他商品和服务	**Miscellaneous Commodities and Services**	**1154**	**375**	**679**	**890**	**1390**	**2376**	**118.4**
其他商品	Miscellaneous Commodities	804	244	455	607	979	1693	122.0
其他服务	Services	350	131	224	283	411	683	110.8

8-11 城镇居民家庭每百户主要耐用消费品拥有量(1978-2012年)
PER 100 HOUSEHOLDS POSSESSION OF MAIN DURABLE CONSUMER GOODS OF URBAN HOUSEHOLDS (1978-2012)

年份 Year	淋浴热水器 (台) Shower Heaters (unit)	洗衣机 (台) Washing Machines (unit)	彩色电视机 (台) Color TV Sets (unit)	电冰箱 (台) Refrige-rators (unit)	照相机 (架) Cameras (unit)	空调器 (台) Air-Conditioners (unit)	计算机 (台) Computers (unit)	移动电话 (部) Mobile telephone (unit)	家用汽车 (辆) Motor Vehicle (unit)
1978					8				
1979		…			10				
1980		2		…	11				
1981		12	2	2	13				
1982		19	2	3	17				
1983		29	4	7	21				
1984		42	8	15	29				
1985		58	32	42	35				
1986		76	51	62	47				
1987		83	58	72	56				
1988		86	70	81	60				
1989		90	81	89	62				
1990		93	91	96	67				
1991		93	97	102	73	…			
1992	17	96	101	101	77	1			
1993	23	100	107	101	82	2			
1994	39	103	112	104	85	5			
1995	45	100	114	104	87	12			
1996	52	101	119	105	87	14			
1997	58	101	124	104	88	27	12	1	1
1998	65	102	133	105	95	34	15	3	1
1999	67	100	141	103	95	50	24	13	3
2000	74	103	146	107	96	70	32	28	3
2001	78	102	149	107	101	90	45	62	3
2002	84	99	148	102	100	107	56	94	4
2003	85	99	147	100	103	119	68	134	7
2004	94	102	151	103	100	136	79	165	13
2005	97	105	153	104	109	147	89	190	14
2006	98	107	155	105	113	157	96	206	18
2007	99	102	147	108	99	157	92	207	20
2008	95	99	134	103	82	152	86	191	23
2009	98	100	138	104	89	163	97	213	30
2010	98	100	140	103	92	169	104	221	34
2011	97	100	138	103	85	171	104	215	38
2012	99	101	141	103	90	179	112	226	42

8-12 5000户城镇居民家庭每百户主要耐用消费品拥有量(2012年)
PER 100 HOUSEHOLDS POSSESSION OF MAIN DURABLE CONSUMER GOODS OF 5000 URBAN HOUSEHOLDS (2012)

项目		Item		全市平均 Total	低收入户20% Low Income	中低收入户20% Medium-Low Income	中等收入户20% Medium Income	中高收入户20% Medium-High Income	高收入户20% High Income	2012年为2011年% 2012 as % of 2011
洗衣机	(台)	Washing Machines	(unit)	101	97	101	101	102	103	101.0
电冰箱	(台)	Refrigerators	(unit)	103	102	102	103	104	106	持平
微波炉	(台)	Microwave Stove	(unit)	88	79	86	88	93	92	101.1
空调器	(台)	Air-Conditioners	(unit)	179	149	169	179	187	201	104.7
淋浴热水器	(台)	Showers	(unit)	99	93	98	99	100	103	102.1
消毒碗柜	(台)	Disinfector	(unit)	8	4	5	7	9	12	114.3
洗碗机	(台)	Dishwasher	(unit)	1	…	1	1	2	2	持平
摩托车	(辆)	Motorcyles	(unit)	4	6	4	4	4	2	持平
助力车	(辆)	Powered Bicycle	(unit)	15	19	17	16	13	12	125.0
家用汽车	(辆)	Motor Vehicle	(unit)	42	26	36	37	43	64	110.5
移动电话	(部)	Mobile telephone	(unit)	226	221	227	218	232	230	105.1
#接入互联网的移动电话	(部)	Mobile Phones Accessed to Internet	(unit)	43	32	41	38	41	61	143.3
彩色电视机	(台)	Color TV Sets	(unit)	141	129	137	138	147	151	102.2
#接入有线电视网络的电视机	(台)	TV Sets Accessed to CATV Network	(unit)	123	113	121	121	126	129	108.8
计算机	(台)	Computers	(unit)	112	89	104	106	120	134	107.7
#接入互联网的计算机	(台)	Computers Accessed to Internet	(unit)	95	75	88	91	102	114	115.9
组合音响	(套)	Hi-Fi Systems	(unit)	25	18	23	26	29	30	108.7
摄像机	(架)	Pickup Camera	(unit)	25	9	20	26	27	37	119.0
照相机	(架)	Camera	(unit)	90	60	84	88	97	113	105.9
钢琴	(架)	Piano	(unit)	5	2	4	5	5	8	125.0
其他中高档乐器	(件)	Secondary and Top Grade Musical Instrument	(unit)	8	4	9	8	7	11	133.3
健身器材	(套)	Fitness Equipment	(unit)	8	4	7	6	7	13	133.3

8-13 5000户城镇居民家庭居住构成情况
COMPOSITION OF HOUSING CONDITIONS IN 5000 URBAN HOUSEHOLDS

项 目	Item	构成(%) Composition (%) 2012	2011
调查户数(户)	**Households Surveyed(household)**	**5000**	**5000**
房屋产权情况	**Building Property Right**		
租赁公房	Public House Rented	11.3	11.5
租赁私房	Private House Rented	3.5	4.1
原有私房	Private House Formerly Owned	4.8	5.7
房改私房	Private House from Housing Reform	42.1	41.9
商品房	Commercial House	35.0	33.8
借用房	Borrowed House	0.5	
其 他	Other	2.8	3.0
住宅建筑式样	**Style of House Construction**		
单栋住宅	Individual Storied Building	0.2	0.1
四居室	Four-bedroom	1.3	1.4
三居室	Three-bedroom	25.5	24.0
二居室	Two-bedroom	55.4	55.8
一居室	One-bedroom	8.2	8.3
普通楼房	Ordinary Storied Building	0.7	0.8
平房及其他	Single-story Building and Other	8.7	9.6
饮水情况	**Water Drinking**		
自来水	Tap Water	89.4	90.4
矿泉水	Mineral Water	5.9	5.6
纯净水	Purified Water	4.7	4.0
井、河水	Well-Water and River-Water		
其 他	Other		
用水情况	**Water Using**		
独用自来水	Tap Water for Separate Use	99.4	99.2
公用自来水	Public Tap Water	0.6	0.8
井、河水	Well-Water and River-Water		
其 他	Other		
卫生设备拥有情况	**Grouped by Possession of Sanitary Equipment**		
无卫生设备	No Sanitary Equipment	3.4	3.9
有厕所浴室	Having Bathroom and Lavatory	93.4	92.9
有厕所无浴室	Having Lavatory and No Bathroom	0.8	0.8
公 用	Public Sanitary Equipment	2.4	2.4
取暖设备拥有情况	**Grouped by Possession of Heating Equipment**		
无取暖设备	No Heating Equipment		
空调设备	Air Conditioner	0.4	0.4
暖 气	Central Heating	91.4	91.3
其 他	Other	8.2	8.3
炊用燃料使用情况	**Grouped by Using of Cooking Fuel**		
液化石油气	Liquefied Petroleum Gas		
煤 炭	Coal	0.3	0.4
罐装液化石油气	Tanked LPG	13.3	15.8
管道液化石油气	Pipeline LPG	1.4	1.6
管道煤气	Pipeline Gas		
管道天然气	Pipeline Natural Gas	84.4	81.8
柴 油	Diesel Oil		
其他燃料	Other	0.6	0.4

8-14 城镇居民居住水平(2007-2012年)
RESIDENTIAL CONDITIONS OF URBAN RESIDENTS (2007-2012)

单位：万平方米 (10000 sq.m)

项目	Item	2007	2008	2009	2010	2011	2012
年末实有房屋建筑面积	Floor Space of Houses(year-end)	66918	70993	74715	77772	80986	83510
年末实有住宅建筑面积	Floor Space of Residential Buildings(year-end)	37981	39852	41756	43431	44113	45627

注：数据统计范围为全市国有土地上的全部房屋，其中2011年和2012年数据为房屋全生命周期平台年末时点数据，2007-2010年数据为根据房屋初始备案登记信息调整和修订后的数据。
数据来源：北京市住房和城乡建设委员会。
Note: These statistics cover all houses on state-owned land of Beijing. Of which, figures of 2011 and 2012 were year-end figures on life-cycle platform, and figures of 2007-2010 were adjusted and revised according to the original house registration information.
Source: Beijing Municipal Commission of Housing And Urban-rural Development.

8-15 3000户农民家庭基本情况(按收入水平分)(2012年)
SAMPLING STATISTICS FOR 3000 RURAL HOUSEHOLDS (2012)

项目	Item	全市平均 Total	低收入户20% Low Income	中低收入户20% Low-Medium Income	中等收入户20% Medium Income	中高收入户20% Medium-High Income	高收入户20% High Income	2012年为2011年% 2012 as % of 2011
调查户数 (户)	Households Surveyed (household)	3000	600	600	600	600	600	
常住人口 (人)	Permanent Residents (person)	9512	2017	2012	1924	1876	1683	99.3
平均每户 (人)	Average Per Household (person)	3.17	3.36	3.35	3.21	3.13	2.81	99.4
整半劳动力 (个)	Full-time and Part-time Labors (person)	6781	1348	1348	1362	1381	1342	98.0
平均每户 (个)	Average Per Household (person)	2.26	2.25	2.25	2.27	2.30	2.24	97.8
平均每一劳动力负担人口 (人)	Dependents Per Labor Force (person)	1.40	1.50	1.49	1.41	1.36	1.25	101.4
学龄前儿童人数 (人)	Number of Preschool Children (person)	328	100	82	68	55	23	90.4
家庭经营耕地面积 (公顷)	Cultivated Land Area Runned by Households (hectare)	314.30	87.52	74.14	64.84	50.18	37.61	103.2
家庭经营山地面积 (公顷)	Mountain Land Area Runned by Households (hectare)	79.30	14.75	14.91	12.35	15.77	21.51	97.8
人均生产性固定资产原值 (元)	Original Value of Productive Fixed Assets Per Capita (yuan)	4027	8274	4091	1947	2054	3434	101.8
人均住房面积 (平方米)	Per Capita Living Space (sq.m)	49.08	38.03	42.70	47.41	50.89	69.84	100.9
人均总收入 (元)	Per Capita Total Revenue (yuan)	19132	11569	14683	17158	21372	33275	109.8
#现金收入 (元)	Cash Income (yuan)	18902	11393	14453	16933	21124	32994	110.2
人均纯收入 (元)	Per Capita Net Income (yuan)	16476	7019	12094	15754	20063	29873	111.8
人均生活消费支出 (元)	Per Capita Annual Living Expenditures (yuan)	11879	8050	9574	11386	13457	18027	107.2
#现金支出 (元)	Cash Expenditures (yuan)	11828	7975	9512	11341	13419	17998	107.3
平均每个劳动力创造纯收入 (元)	Average Net Income Per Labor Force (yuan)	19852	9686	16350	19138	22904	29949	114.1
农村居民家庭恩格尔系数 (%)	Engel Coefficient of Rural Hous (%)	33.2	34.4	34.3	33.4	33.7	31.3	

注：1. 人均纯收入实际增长8.2%。
2. 人均生活消费支出实际增长3.8%。
Note: a) Real growth rate of the per capita net income is 8.2%.
b) Real growth rate of the per capita annual living expenditure is 3.8%.

8-16 3000户农民家庭平均每人年纯收入(2012年)
ANNUAL NET INCOME PER CAPITA OF 3000 RURAL HOUSEHOLDS (2012)

单位：元 (yuan)

项目	Item	全市平均 Total	低收入户 20% Low Income	中低收入户 20% Low-Medium Income	中等收入户 20% Medium Income	中高收入户 20% Medium-High Income	高收入户 20% High Income	2012年为2011年% 2012 as % of 2011
合计	**Total**	**16476**	**7019**	**12094**	**15754**	**20063**	**29873**	**111.8**
生产性收入	**Producing Income**	**12161**	**5190**	**9175**	**12018**	**14765**	**21350**	**111.1**
工资性收入	Wage	10843	4737	8019	10989	13439	18480	113.2
在非企业组织中劳动的报酬	From Non-enterprise Organizations	588	30	297	384	554	1877	109.7
在企业劳动得到的报酬	From Enterprises	3552	1199	2135	3604	4819	6596	107.3
在其他单位劳动得到的报酬	From Other Units	6703	3508	5587	7001	8066	10007	116.9
家庭经营纯收入	Net Income from Family Business	1318	453	1156	1029	1326	2870	96.7
从第一产业得到	From Primary Industry	731	488	636	661	762	1181	100.6
#牧业收入	From Animal Husbandry	98	14	80	38	120	263	81.0
从第二产业得到	From Secondary Industry	-40	-528	34	57	22	278	
从第三产业得到	From Tertiary Industry	627	493	486	311	542	1411	93.6
#交通运输业收入	From Transportation	236	174	249	196	166	418	78.7
非生产性收入	**Nonproducing Income**	**4315**	**1829**	**2919**	**3736**	**5298**	**8523**	**113.7**
转移性收入	Transfer Income	2598	1401	2129	2640	3124	3957	115.1
财产性收入	Property Income	1717	428	790	1096	2174	4566	111.7

8-17 3000户农民家庭平均每人年生活消费支出(2012年)
ANNUAL LIVING EXPENDITURES PER CAPITA OF 3000 RURAL HOUSEHOLDS (2012)

单位：元 (yuan)

项目	Item	全市平均 Total	低收入户20% Low Income	中低收入户20% Low-Medium Income	中等收入户20% Medium Income	中高收入户20% Medium-High Income	高收入户20% High Income	2012年为2011年% 2012 as % of 2011
合计	**Total**	**11879**	**8050**	**9574**	**11386**	**13457**	**18027**	**107.2**
食品支出	**Food Expenditure**	**3945**	**2769**	**3279**	**3805**	**4539**	**5648**	**109.8**
#谷物	Corn	351	335	344	342	363	375	101.2
蔬菜及制品	Vegetable and Related Products	367	265	309	368	413	506	107.3
肉、禽、蛋、奶及制品	Meat, Poultry, Egg, Milk and Products	1012	713	869	1008	1159	1381	106.5
衣着支出	**Clothing Expenditure**	**948**	**493**	**648**	**908**	**1125**	**1700**	**109.8**
#服装支出	Garments	603	298	394	582	716	1119	110.0
居住支出	**Residence**	**2200**	**1799**	**2111**	**2060**	**2262**	**2876**	**93.6**
#住房	Housing	1064	1051	1137	987	976	1178	80.8
燃料	Fuels	613	430	578	601	663	832	106.1
家庭设备用品及服务支出	**Household Facilities,Articles and Services**	**773**	**445**	**617**	**686**	**936**	**1272**	**108.1**
#耐用消费品	Durable Consumer Goods	434	219	361	356	527	766	104.1
家庭日用杂品	Daily Use Household Articles	221	155	175	211	253	329	111.1
医疗保健支出	**Medicines and Medical Services**	**1125**	**781**	**1020**	**1226**	**1209**	**1456**	**108.7**
交通和通讯支出	**Transportation and Communications**	**1399**	**881**	**910**	**1336**	**1617**	**2432**	**113.9**
#交通工具	Transportation Means	426	309	188	442	525	724	115.4
通讯工具	Telecommunication Means	135	74	98	122	157	245	127.4
通讯费	Telecommunications	306	208	244	309	335	460	102.7
文教娱乐用品及服务支出	**Cultural, Education and Recreation Articles and Services**	**1153**	**706**	**785**	**1094**	**1352**	**1972**	**114.8**
#文娱用机电消费品	Mechanical and Electric Consumer Goods of Culture and Recreation	207	106	149	185	217	412	103.5
书报杂志	Books, Newspapers and Magazines	17	11	13	19	21	21	100.0
学杂费	Tuition and Incidentals	90	86	72	89	84	120	50.8
文娱费	Recreation	363	140	186	296	441	830	134.9
其他商品及服务支出	**Other Commodity and Services**	**336**	**176**	**204**	**271**	**417**	**671**	**115.9**
#服务性支出	Services Expenditures	80	42	44	66	107	154	123.1

8-18 3000户农民家庭平均每人年粮食收支情况(2012年)
BROUGHT IN, SENT OUT OF GRAIN PER CAPITA OF 3000 RURAL HOUSEHOLDS (2012)

单位：公斤 (kg)

项目	Item	全市平均 Total	低收入户20% Low Income	中低收入户20% Low-Medium Income	中等收入户20% Medium Income	中高收入户20% Medium-High Income	高收入户20% High Income	2012年为2011年% 2012 as % of 2011
年内粮食收入实物量	**Grain Reaped in Kind in This Year**	**331.1**	**331.7**	**445.4**	**253.8**	**245.8**	**377.1**	**96.6**
家庭经营生产	Household Production	147.5	172.6	177.9	139.2	130.0	109.7	89.4
购　买	Purchasing	170.0	145.5	256.2	101.4	102.3	250.4	103.4
其　他	Other	13.6	13.6	11.3	13.2	13.5	17.0	100.0
年内粮食消费及出售量	**Grain Consumed and Sold in This Year**	**325.5**	**332.3**	**437.8**	**251.1**	**232.8**	**371.5**	**99.4**
生活用粮	Living Consumption	102.3	106.4	106.8	97.9	100.8	98.9	96.0
#稻　谷	Rice	40.0	41.5	41.1	38.2	38.8	40.2	94.3
小　麦	Wheat	53.2	54.9	56.2	51.2	53.0	50.2	102.7
出售粮食	Sold	141.2	162.2	165.5	137.5	120.9	113.8	94.4
其　他	Other	82.0	63.7	165.5	15.7	11.1	158.7	114.8

8-19 3000户农民家庭主要生活消费品平均每人消费量(2012年)
PER CAPITA CONSUMPTION OF MAJOR LIVING CONSUMER GOODS OF 3000 RURAL HOUSEHOLDS (2012)

项目	Item	全市平均 Total	低收入户20% Low Income	中低收入户20% Low-Medium Income	中等收入户20% Medium Income	中高收入户20% Medium-High Income	高收入户20% High Income	2012年为2011年% 2012 as % of 2011
粮　食　(公斤)	Grains (kg)	102.3	106.4	106.7	97.9	100.8	98.9	96.0
豆制品　(公斤)	Bean Products (kg)	7.0	6.0	6.5	7.4	7.1	8.1	100.0
蔬　菜　(公斤)	Vegetables (kg)	100.5	85.6	93.2	99.7	106.9	120.7	92.2
植物油　(公斤)	Vegetable Oil (kg)	9.8	9.1	9.5	9.6	10.0	11.0	103.2
猪　肉　(公斤)	Pork (kg)	14.9	12.1	13.4	15.5	16.1	18.1	99.3
牛羊肉　(公斤)	Beef, Mutton (kg)	4.2	2.3	3.2	4.0	5.2	6.9	93.3
家　禽　(公斤)	Poultry (kg)	4.0	3.0	3.4	3.9	4.8	5.0	100.0
蛋　类　(公斤)	Eggs (kg)	11.1	8.9	10.3	11.4	11.6	13.4	102.8
奶及奶制品　(公斤)	Milk and Diary Products (kg)	12.5	8.0	10.1	12.4	14.9	18.3	105.0
水产品　(公斤)	Aquatic Products (kg)	5.3	3.6	4.4	5.2	6.2	7.8	98.1
食　糖　(公斤)	Sugar (kg)	1.2	1.2	1.0	1.1	1.3	1.2	109.1
酒　类　(公斤)	Liquor (kg)	16.1	13.0	15.5	16.9	18.6	17.2	98.2
茶　叶　(公斤)	Tea (kg)	0.6	0.4	0.5	0.5	0.7	0.9	100.0
干鲜瓜果　(公斤)	Melons and Fruits (kg)	46.7	35.1	39.8	46.6	52.4	62.7	105.9
服　装　(件)	Clothing (unit)	4.9	3.5	4.1	5.0	5.4	6.9	90.7

8-20 农民家庭每百户主要耐用消费品拥有量(1978-2012年)
PER 100 HOUSEHOLDS POSSESSION OF MAIN DURABLE CONSUMER GOODS OF RURAL HOUSEHOLDS (1978-2012)

年 份 Year	自行车 (辆) Bicycles (unit)	移动电话 (部) Mobile Telephone (unit)	空调机 (台) Air Conditioner (unit)	影碟机 (台) Video CD (unit)	彩色电视机 (台) Color TV Sets (unit)	家用计算机 (台) Computer (unit)	照相机 (架) Cameras (unit)	洗衣机 (台) Washing Machines (unit)	电冰箱 (台) Refrigerators (unit)	家用汽车 (辆) Motor Vehicle (unit)
1978	109									
1979	98									
1980	123									
1981	135									
1982	141									
1983	167									
1984	187									
1985	182				7		2	23	2	
1986	191				12		4	39	5	
1987	204				15		5	48	9	
1988	218				20		7	56	14	
1989	224				25		8	61	19	
1990	235				29		8	63	23	
1991	232				42		11	69	36	
1992	245				46		14	73	40	
1993	249				56		15	76	47	
1994	254		1		65		17	80	53	
1995	251		2		74		21	81	63	
1996	250		2		79		21	83	67	
1997	248		3		85		25	84	72	
1998	249		5		92		26	85	75	
1999	241		9		101		29	86	81	
2000	220	14	20	23	107	7	26	85	84	3
2001	220	30	27	27	112	12	29	91	86	5
2002	214	52	35	30	116	16	32	94	91	6
2003	210	77	39	34	116	22	32	94	94	6
2004	206	102	47	39	119	27	35	96	96	8
2005	189	139	63	49	129	36	37	97	100	10
2006	182	161	72	50	131	41	38	97	100	10
2007	182	182	78	47	134	46	37	99	104	11
2008	183	201	89	49	137	52	39	101	104	12
2009	181	212	98	50	138	58	42	101	105	12
2010	175	224	107	46	139	64	42	103	107	16
2011	147	231	108	25	134	63	37	99	104	19
2012	147	235	113	26	136	67	37	99	103	21

8-21 3000户农民家庭每百户主要耐用消费品拥有量(2012年)
PER 100 HOUSEHOLDS POSSESSION OF MAIN DURABLE CONSUMER GOODS OF 3000 RURAL HOUSEHOLDS (2012)

项目		Item		全市平均 Total	低收入户20% Low Income	中低收入户20% Low-Medium Income	中等收入户20% Medium Income	中高收入户20% Medium-High Income	高收入户20% High Income	2012年为2011年% 2012 as % of 2011
自行车	(辆)	Bicycles	(unit)	147	131	148	160	151	143	100.0
洗衣机	(台)	Washing Machines	(unit)	99	95	98	99	102	101	100.0
电冰箱	(台)	Refrigerators	(unit)	103	98	102	103	106	106	99.0
摩托车	(辆)	Motorcycles	(unit)	14	17	12	14	15	12	100.0
家用汽车	(辆)	Motor Vehicle	(unit)	21	13	16	19	24	33	110.5
彩色电视机	(台)	Color TV Sets	(unit)	136	128	136	136	139	140	101.5
照相机	(架)	Cameras	(unit)	37	20	26	33	48	56	100.0
抽油烟机	(台)	Range Hoods	(unit)	71	48	63	76	80	88	102.9
吸尘器	(台)	Vacuum Cleaners	(unit)	8	4	3	7	10	16	100.0
微波炉	(台)	Microwave Oven	(unit)	56	36	47	57	67	72	101.8
热水器	(台)	Showers	(unit)	92	79	87	96	99	101	102.2
电话机	(部)	Telephone	(unit)	86	77	83	88	89	92	97.7
移动电话	(部)	Mobile phone	(unit)	235	218	232	242	240	243	101.7
影碟机	(台)	Video CD	(unit)	26	20	20	24	28	36	104.0
家用计算机	(台)	Computer	(unit)	67	43	58	67	78	88	106.3
空调机	(台)	Air Conditioners	(unit)	113	68	92	120	129	154	104.6

8-22 3000户农村居民居住情况
LIVING CONDITIONS Of RURAL HOUSEHOLDS

项目		Item		2012	2011
调查户数	**（户）**	**Households Surveyed**	**(households)**	**3000**	**3000**
年内建房户数比重	(%)	**Of Households Building House within the Year**	**(%)**	**1.3**	**3.4**
户均住房价值	**（元）**	**House Value per Family**	**(yuan)**	**475037**	**319928**
住房类型		**Type Of House**			
楼房面积占比重	(%)	Of Area Of Storied Buildings	(%)	20.2	19.6
砖瓦平房面积占比重	(%)	Of Area Of Single-storey Houses	(%)	79.3	80.1
其他面积占比重	(%)	Of Other Area	(%)	0.5	0.3
饮用水来源情况		**Source Of Drinking Water**			
自来水户数占比重	(%)	Of Tap Water Users	(%)	99.5	99.5
深井水户数占比重	(%)	Of Deep-well Water Users	(%)	0.4	0.4
浅井水户数占比重	(%)	Of Shallow-well Water Users	(%)	0.1	0.1
住房卫生设备使用情况		**Use Of Sanitation Facilities in Living House**			
无厕所户数占比重	(%)	Of Families Without Washroom	(%)	2.1	2.8
使用旱厕户数占比重	(%)	Of Families Using Water-free Washroom	(%)	20.9	23.0
使用卫生厕所户数占比重	(%)	Of Families Using Sanitary Washroom	(%)	77.0	74.2
取暖设备使用情况		**Use Of Heating Device**			
使用火炕户数占比重	(%)	Of Households Using Heatable Brick Bed	(%)	10.5	11.2
使用暖气户数占比重	(%)	Of Households Using Central Heating	(%)	71.8	71.3
使用空调户数占比重	(%)	Of Families Using Air Conditioner	(%)	9.9	9.7
使用其他取暖设备户数占比重	(%)	Of Families Using Other Heating Device	(%)	7.8	7.8
炊事使用的主要能源		**Main Energy Used in Cooking**			
使用液化气的户数占比重	(%)	Of Households Using LPG	(%)	83.9	82.7
使用煤炭的户数占比重	(%)	Of Households Using Coal	(%)	2.6	3.5
使用柴草的户数占比重	(%)	Of Households Using Firewood	(%)	5.6	5.9
使用电的户数占比重	(%)	Of Households Using Electricity	(%)	6.6	6.4
使用其他燃料的户数占比重	(%)	Of Households Using Other Fuel	(%)	1.3	1.5
住宅外道路路面状况		**Status Of Surface Of Road Outside House**			
水泥或柏油路面的户数占比重	(%)	Of Households With Cement or Pitchy Road	(%)	97.0	95.6
沙石或石板等硬质路面的户数占比重	(%)	Of Households with Road Of Hard Surface Such as Sand and Stone or Slate	(%)	3.0	4.2
其它路面的户数占比重	(%)	Of Households with Other Road Surface	(%)		0.2

主要统计指标解释

城镇部分

平均每一就业者负担人数 是由家庭人口数与离退休人口数之差，再除以就业人口数计算得到的。计算公式为：

$$平均每一就业者负担人数=\frac{(家庭人口数-离退休人口数)}{就业人口数}$$

家庭总收入 指调查户中生活在一起的所有家庭成员在调查期得到的工资性收入、经营净收入、财产性收入、转移性收入的总和，不包括出售财物和借贷收入。收入的统计标准以实际发生的数额为准，无论收入是补发还是预发，只要是调查期得到的都应如实计算。

可支配收入 指调查户可用于最终消费支出和其他非义务性支出以及储蓄的总和，即居民家庭可以用来自由支配的收入。它是家庭总收入扣除交纳的个人所得税、个人交纳的社会保障支出以及调查户的记账补贴后的收入。计算公式为：

可支配收入＝家庭总收入－交纳个人所得税－个人交纳的社会保障支出－记账补贴

工资性收入 指就业人员通过各种途径得到的全部劳动报酬，包括所从事主要职业的工资以及从事第二职业、其他兼职和零星劳动得到的其他劳动收入。

工资及补贴收入 指劳动者从工作单位得到的全部劳动报酬和各种福利。

其他劳动收入 指家庭成员从事第二职业、兼职、零星劳动等劳动所得的报酬。

经营净收入 指家庭成员从事生产经营活动所获得的净收入，是全部生产经营收入中扣除生产成本和税金（但不扣除个人所得税）后所得的收入。如当期收入小于生产费用的开支，冲减成本后直接计入即可。

财产性收入 指家庭拥有的动产(如银行存款、有价证券)、不动产(如房屋、土地等)所获得的收入。包括出让财产使用权所获得的利息、租金、专利收入；财产营运所获得的红利收入、财产增值收益等。不包括出售财物获得的收入。

保险收益 指家庭参加储蓄性保险，扣除缴纳的保险本金后，所获得的保险净收益。不包括保险责任人对保险人给予的保险理赔收入。

其他投资收入 指家庭从事股票、保险以外的投资行为所获得的投资收益。如出售艺术品、邮票等收藏品超过原购买价的那部分收入；如投资各种经营活动（自己不参与经营）所获得的利润；财产转让溢价部分收入，包括出售住房增值部分的收入。

知识产权收入 指出让家庭或家庭成员拥有的专利、版权等知识产权所获得的净收入。

转移性收入 指国家、单位、社会团体对居民家庭的各种转移支付和居民家庭间的收入转移。包括政府对个人收入转移的离退休金、失业救济金、赔偿等；单位对个人收入转移的辞退金、保险理赔、住房公积金、家庭间的赠送和赡养等。

保险收入 指参加保险的住户得到的保险收入，包括从保险公司得到的保险理赔款以及其他责任赔款。如人身意外事故赔偿、财产损失赔偿和住院医疗赔偿等。不包括人寿保险返回的年金。

记账补贴 指调查户因承担记账工作从统计部门、工作单位和其他途径所得到的现金。不包括实物部分。

出售财物收入 指调查户出售家庭财物所得到的收入。由于出售财物是家庭财产从实物形态转为货币形态，家庭财产总量不变，因此不计入可支配收入中。

借贷收入 指家庭资产不发生增减的周转性非生产经营性收入。包括提取银行存款、借入款、收回借出款、兑售有价证券、收回投资本金、贷款等。

家庭总支出 指家庭除借贷支出以外的全部实际支出。包括消费性支出、购房与建房支出、转移性支出、财产性支出、社会保障支出。支出统计是以实际购得的商品或服务的总价值填报，不论其付款方式是一次付清、分期付款、还是赊购，只要商品或服务已被消费就要按其总价值计量。如果采用分期付款或赊购形式，则要在借贷收入类相应的项目填入实付款与总的应付款的差额。

消费性支出 指调查户用于满足家庭日常生活消费需要的全部支出，包括食品、衣着、居住、家庭设备用品及服务、医疗保健、交通和通信、教育文化娱乐服务、其他商品和服务等八大类。包括用于赠送的商品或服务。消费性支出构成是按照商品或服务的用途进行分类，如果消费支出的目的与用途不一致时，必须按照用途归入相应类内。

服务性消费支出 指调查户用于本家庭支付社会提供的各种文化和生活方面的非商品性服务费用。包括为别人付款的服务。服务消费与商品消费不同，其特点在于其劳动过程和消费过程在时间与空间上的统一。

购房与建房支出 指调查户购买住房、建房时的全部支出。

转移性支出 指调查户对国家、单位、住户、个人的转移支付。包括交纳的税款、捐赠和赡养支出等。

财产性支出 指家庭购买或维护财产所支付的利息等有关费用。

社会保障支出 指调查户家庭成员参加国家法律、法规规定的社会保障项目中由个人交纳的保障支出。不包括职工所在单位交纳的那部分社会保障金。

现住房总建筑面积 指调查户现住房的总建筑面积。现住房计算总建筑面积时以房屋产权证或租赁证为准，建筑面积也可按使用面积 × 1.333 计算得出。应扣除住房中专门用于出租的建筑面积。

农村部分

平均每一劳动力负担人口 是由调查户常住人口除以整半劳动力计算得到的。计算公式为:

$$平均每一劳动力负担人口=\frac{调查户常住人口}{整半劳动力}$$

农村居民家庭整半劳动力 指农村常住居民家庭成员中有劳动能力并经常参加实际劳动的人员。是生产的基本要素指标之一，是发展生产增加农民家庭收入的重要源泉。按规定，农村男18周岁至50周岁、女18周岁至45周岁为整劳动力；男16周岁至17周岁、51周岁到60周岁，女16周岁到17周岁、46周岁至55周岁为半劳动力。农民家庭整半劳动力既包括在上述规定劳动年龄内和在劳动年龄以外有劳动能力并经常参加实际劳动的男女整半劳动力，也包括农民家庭常住人员中属于职工的劳动力。但不包括在劳动年龄内已丧失劳动能力的人员。

农村居民家庭总收入 指报告期内农村住户和住户成员以各种来源渠道得到的收入总和。按收入的性质分为工资性收入、家庭经营性收入、财产性收入和转移性收入。

纯收入 指农村住户当年从各个来源得到的总收入相应地扣除所发生的费用后的收入总和。纯收入主要用于再生产投入和当年生活消费支出，也可用于储蓄和各种非义务性支出。“农民人均纯收入”是按人口平均的纯收入水平，反映的是一个地区或一个农户农村居民的平均收入水平。计算方法:

纯收入 = 总收入 – 家庭经营费用支出 – 税费支出 –
生产性固定资产折旧 – 农村内部亲友赠送收入

农村居民家庭生活消费支出 指农村住户用于物质生活和精神生活方面的支出。包括食品、衣着、居住、家庭设备用品及服务、医疗保健、交通和通讯、文化教育娱乐用品及服务、其他商品和服务等消费支出。

恩格尔系数 随着家庭和个人收入增加，收入中用于食品方面的支出比例将逐渐减小，这一定律被称为恩格尔定律，反映这一定律的系数被称为恩格尔系数。计算公式为:

$$恩格尔系数=\frac{食品支出总额}{家庭或个人消费支出总额}\times100\%$$

Explanatory Notes on Main Statistical Indicators

Urban Households

Number of Dependents per Urban Employee refers to the difference between number of persons and the number of retired persons, which is divided by the number of employed persons in an urban household. The formula is:

Number of Dependents per Urban Employee = (number of persons - the number of retired persons in an urban household)/ number of employed persons in the household

Familial Gross Income refers to the sum of wage and salary; net business income; income from properties; and income from transfers of all members living together in a household surveyed. Income from selling of properties and income from borrowing are not included. Income is calculated on actual basis. Any income paid in the survey period, no matter it is paid retroactively or prepaid, is included according to the facts.

Annual Disposable Income refers to the actual income at the disposal of members of the households which can be used for final consumption, other non-compulsory expenditure and savings. This equals to total income minus income tax, personal contribution to social security and subsidy for keeping accounts in a sample household. The following formula is used:

Annual Disposable Income = total household income – personal income tax - personal contribution to social security - subsidy for keeping accounts for a sampled household

Emolument refers to income earned by employed persons from labour in all channels, including other earnings from main job, second job, other par-time job, and odd work.

Laborage and Allowance Income s refers to all labor rewards and welfares received by a labor from the employer.

Other Income from Work refers to the rewards received by family members from any second job, part-time job, and odd work.

Business Income refers to the net income of family members from productive and operating activities. It is the income of all productive and operating income deducting the production cost and tax. If the income in the period is smaller than the production cost, the difference is entered in the "Other Expenditure on Lending".

Property Income refers to the income earned from personal estates (such as bank deposits, securities) and real estates (such as house and land) owned by households, including the interest, rent, and patent income gained from transfer of use right of any property; bonus from property operation and property premium; excluding the income from selling of any property.

Insurance Proceeds refers to the net proceeds of insurance gained by households for participating in savings-type insurance after the paid insurance principal is deducted, excluding the income of insurance claim paid by the responsible person under the insurance program to the policyholder.

Other Income from Yield refers to the return on investment earned by households from investment acts other than stock transactions and insurance, such as income from selling artwork, stamps and other collections in excess of their original purchase cots; any profit from investment in operating activities (without personally participating in the operation); premium from property assignment, including the added value earned from house sales.

Income from Intellectual Property Rights refers to the net income from transfer of any intellectual property right such as any patent and copyright owned by a family or any family member.

Transfer Income refers to various transfer payment from the State, enterprises, companies, and social groups to households, along with income transfer between households, including such government's transfer of personal income as retirement pension, unemployment relief payment, and compensations; such transfer of personal income from enterprises and companies as dismissal pay, insurance claim compensation, public accumulation funds for housing, and donation and support between families.

Income from Insurance refers to the insurance income obtained by households participating in insurance programs, including any claim payment and other agreed compensation from an insurance company, such as compensation for personal incidence, compensation for property loss, and compensation for hospitalization costs, excluding annuity paid fro life insurance.

Subsidy for Account Keeping refers to the cash paid by authorities of statistics, employers and other channels to the sample household for its responsibility of accounts keeping, excluding any allowance in kind.

Proceeds from Sales of Belongings refers to the income received by the sample household for selling any household property. As the sale of household property is a conversion of physical form of household property to monetary form, and the total amount of household properties remains unchanged, the income from selling property is not included in the disposable income. The amount of household property, including withdrawal of bank deposits, borrowings, lending repaid, conversion and sale of securities, returned principal of investment, loans, etc.

Credit Income refers to the non-productive and non-operating income which causes no change in the amount of household property, including withdrawal of bank deposits, borrowings, lending repaid, conversion and sale of securities, returned principal of investment, loans, etc.

Familial Gross Expenditures refers to all expenditure of households except expenditure on lending. It includes expenditure on consumption; on purchasing or building houses; on transfers; on properties; and on social security. Expenditure is calculated with the total value of goods and services actually purchased. Whether they are purchased with lump-sum payment, installment, or on credit basis, the goods and services are measured at their total value so long as they are consumed. In the case of installment or credit-based purchase, the difference between the actually made payment and the payables shall be entered in the relevant item of income from borrowing and lending.

Consumption Expenditure of Urban Households refers to total expenditure of households for consumption in daily life, including eight major categories, i.e. expenditure on the food, clothing, housing, household appliances and services, health care and medical services, transport and communications, recreation, education and cultural services; and miscellaneous goods and services. It includes any goods and service for donation. Components of consumption expenditure are classified according to the purpose of goods and services. In the event of any discrepancy in the aim and purpose of consumption expenditure, it must be involved in relevant category according to the purpose of goods and service.

Expenditure of Urban Households on Consumption of Services refers to expenditure of households on various kinds of non-commercial services provided by society, including services paid for other persons. Not like commodity consumption, service consumption is completed in a consistent period and space.

Expenditure on Purchasing or Building Houses refers to all expenditures for purchase and construction of house by the sample household.

Transfer Expenditure refers to the transfer payment made by the sample household to the State, enterprises and companies, households and individuals, including tax payment, donation and support payments, etc.

Property Expenditures refers to relevant costs including interest paid by the sample household for purchasing or maintaining properties.

Social Security Expenditures refers to the personal payment made by members of the sample family for any social security program stated in national laws and regulations, excluding the payment made by employers for social security.

Total Building Area of Current House refers to the total building area of house of investigated household, which is calculated on the basis of the house title or lease certificate. The building area can also be calculated as the usable floor space multiplied by 1.333, which shall deduct the building area of the house specially used for lease.

Rural Households

Number of Dependents per Labour refers to the number of permanent population in the sample household divided by the number of full/semi labours. It is calculated with the following formula:

Number of Dependents per Labour = Number of permanent population in the sample household / number of full/semi labours

Full/Semi Labour Force in Rural Households refers to persons among permanent family members in rural households who are capable of working and work frequently. This is one of the indicators for basic production elements, and an important source for production development and increase of farmer's household income. As stated in regulations, rural males aged 18-50, females aged 18-45 are full labours. Males aged 16-17, and 51-60, females aged 16-17 and 46-55 are semi-labours. Full/Semi Labour Force in Rural Households includes the male and female full/semi labours within the above-mentioned range age as well as those beyond such range of age who are capable of working and work frequently; also include labours among permanent members in rural households who are employees. But it exclude persons who are within the range of labour age but incapable of working.

Total Income of Rural Households refers to the total income earned from various sources by the rural households and their members in the reporting period, and by the nature of income, consists of income from wages and salaries, income from household operations, income from properties and transfer income.

Net Income refers to the total income of rural households from all sources minus all corresponding expenses. Net income is mainly used as input for reinvestment in production and as consumption expenditure of the year, and also used for savings and non-compulsory expenses of various forms. "Per-capita net income of farmers" is the level of net income averaged by population, reflecting the average income level of rural households in a given area. It is calculated as follows:

Net income = total income - household operation expenses - taxes and fees paid - taxes and fees - depreciation of fixed assets for production – income from donation by rural internal relatives and friends

Rural Household Expenditures on Living Consumption refers to spending by rural households on material life and ideological life, including consumption spending on food, clothes, housing, household appliance and service, medical service and health care, transport and communication, cultural, educational and entertainment supplies and services, other goods and services.

Engel's Coefficient Along with the increase in household and personal income, a gradually smaller portion of income is used for purchase of food. This law is called Engel's law, and the coefficient reflecting such law is called Engel's Coefficient. It is calculated as following:

$$\text{Engels Coefficient} = \frac{\text{expenditure on food}}{\text{total consumption expenditure}} \times 100\%$$

09

北京统计年鉴2013　BEIJING STATISTICAL YEARBOOK

城市公用事业
PUBLIC UTILITIES

简要说明

一、本章资料的主要内容

本章资料反映北京市城市公用事业的综合水平，主要内容包括四部分：

1. 历年城市公用事业基本情况；
2. 水、气、热等供应及消费情况；
3. 城市公交、出租车情况；
4. 市政主要设施情况。

二、本章资料的数据来源

本章城市供热、供气情况由北京市市政市容管理委员会提供；自来水情况由北京市水务局提供；城市公交、出租车情况由北京市交通委员会提供；道路及市政主要设施情况由北京市交通委员会、北京市公安交通管理局、北京市路灯管理中心提供。

Brief Introduction

I. Main Content

Statistics in this chapter show the overall level of urban utility services in Beijing, which consist of four parts:

1. Basic statistics for urban utility services in previous years;
2. Water, gas and heat supply and consumption;
3. Urban public transit and taxi;
4. Main public facilities.

II. Source of Data

Data on urban heat and gas supply were provided by Beijing Municipal Administration Committee; data on tap water were provided by Beijing Water Authority; data on urban public transit and taxi were provided by Beijing Municipal Commission of Transport; data on roads and main public facilities were provided by Beijing Municipal Commission of Transport, Beijing Traffic Management Bureau and Street Lighting Administration Center Of Beijing.

9-1 公路、城市道路及桥梁(1978-2012年)
HIGHWAYS, URBAN ROADS AND BRIDGES (1978-2012)

年份 Year	境内道路总里程(公里) Total Length of Highways and Roads (km)	公路里程(公里) Total Length of Highways (km)	#高速公路 Express ways	城市道路里程(公里) Length of Urban Roads (km)	#快速路 Rapid Roads	#主干路 Trunk Roads	城市道路面积(万平方米) Area of Urban Roads (10000 sq.m)	城市道路桥梁(座) Number of Bridges (unit)	#立交桥 Flyovers
1978		6562		2078			1611	351	2
1979		7278		2131			1618	348	2
1980		7487		2185			1664	351	6
1981		7566		2234			1742	342	8
1982		7683		2671			2098	408	9
1983		8058		2820			2265	431	10
1984		8271		2928			2393	440	11
1985		8482		2979			2485	460	16
1986		8995		3038			2559	479	16
1987		9103		3087			2631	510	22
1988		9124		3151			2701	522	23
1989		9371		3235			2815	552	27
1990		9648	35	3276			2905	562	33
1991		10259	63	3308			3134	569	40
1992		10827	71	3189			3212	595	55
1993		11260	99	3285			3398	596	64
1994		11532	112	3316			3470	616	75
1995		11811	113	3194			3494	582	84
1996		12084	114	3665			3807	646	133
1997		12306	144	3637			4061	693	140
1998		12498	190	3721			4214	715	138
1999		12825	230	3753			4353	787	141
2000		13600	268	4126			4921	834	149
2001		13891	335	4312			6062	891	160
2002		14359	463	5444			7645	1051	180
2003	18942	14453	499	3055			5345	848	119
2004	19010	14630	525	4067	219	834	6417	949	271
2005	19015	14696	548	4073	239	922	7437	964	304
2006	25377	20503	625	4419	232	955	7258	1079	376
2007	25765	20754	628	4460	236	960	7632	1230	377
2008	26921	20340	777	6186	242	755	8941	1738	381
2009	27436	20755	884	6247	242	805	9179	1765	393
2010	27907	21114	903	6355	263	874	9395	1855	411
2011	28446	21347	912	6258	263	861	9164	1885	418
2012	28585	21492	923	6271	263	865	9236	1950	413

注：1. 境内道路总里程为全市道路和公路里程之和(剔除道路、公路交叉重复部分)。
2. 道路及桥梁1978年-1981年统计范围为城八区及通县；1982年-2002年统计范围为城八区及14个县城；2003年-2010年统计范围为城八区和北京经济技术开发区。2011年起城市道路及其附属设施统计范围为城六区。
3. 2008年道路数据为北京市城市道路普查数据。

资料来源：北京市交通委员会。

Note: a) Total length of highways and roads means the sum of roads and highways across the city (excluding intersections of roads and highways)
b) Roads and bridge figures covered 8 districts and Tongxian County in 1978-1981; covered 8 districts and 14 counties in 1982-2002; and covered 8 districts and Beijing economic-technological development zones in 2003-2010.From 2011, figures on Urban Roads and Auxiliary Facilities covered 6 districts.
c) Road figures for 2008 were from Beijing Urban Road Census.

Source: Beijing Municipal Communnission of Transport.

9-2 城市公共交通(1978-2012年)
URBAN PUBLIC TRANSIT (1978-2012)

年份 Year	公共交通运营线路长度(公里) Length of Public Transit Lines (km)	公共电汽车 Buses and Trolley Buses	轨道交通 Rail Transit	公共交通运营车辆(辆) Number of Public Transit Vehicles in Operation(unit)	公共电汽车 Buses and Trolley Buses	轨道交通 Rail Transit	公共交通客运量(万人次) Passengers Carried by Public Transit (10000 person-times)	公共电汽车 Buses and Trolley Buses	轨道交通 Rail Transit
1978	1427	1403	24	2743	2627	116	172559	169465	3094
1979	1469	1446	24	2997	2889	108	205703	200918	4785
1980	1479	1455	24	3113	3001	112	236998	231477	5521
1981	1525	1501	24	3375	3259	116	263944	257478	6466
1982	1678	1654	24	3620	3500	120	284175	276922	7253
1983	1820	1797	24	3907	3753	154	302501	294301	8200
1984	1939	1899	40	4221	4037	184	324437	314132	10305
1985	2312	2272	40	4583	4398	185	335227	321264	13963
1986	2574	2534	40	4576	4371	205	328770	312990	15780
1987	2382	2342	40	4776	4524	252	330417	311190	19227
1988	2445	2405	40	4787	4535	252	337094	306396	30698
1989	2525	2485	40	4890	4587	303	306435	275383	31052
1990	2654	2614	40	5160	4857	303	334673	296495	38178
1991	2755	2715	40	5182	4877	305	344525	307438	37087
1992	3379	3338	42	5223	4900	323	348770	305959	42811
1993	3532	3491	42	5213	4890	323	335378	286268	49110
1994	4117	4075	42	5319	4984	335	353289	299993	53296
1995	4538	4497	42	5367	4984	383	371579	315777	55802
1996	7317	7276	42	6828	6427	401	349847	305433	44414
1997	14011	13969	42	10479	10044	435	391182	346676	44507
1998	14929	14888	42	10819	10382	437	418825	372494	46331
1999	16566	16513	54	12509	12018	491	426706	378483	48223
2000	15639	15585	54	14191	13604	587	406691	363213	43478
2001	13180	13126	54	15420	14803	617	449720	402850	46870
2002	15835	15760	75	17580	16939	641	492122	443880	48242
2003	16131	16017	114	17445	16753	692	426628	379380	47248
2004	15247	15133	114	19343	18451	892	499830	439130	60700
2005	18328	18214	114	19471	18503	968	517769	449793	67976
2006	18582	18468	114	20489	19522	967	468225	397919	70306
2007	17495	17353	142	20525	19395	1130	488138	422645	65493
2008	18057	17857	200	23221	21507	1714	592523	470863	121660
2009	18498	18270	228	23730	21716	2014	658785	516517	142268
2010	19079	18743	336	24011	21548	2463	689788	505144	184645
2011	19832	19460	372	24478	21628	2850	722552	503272	219280
2012	19989	19547	442	25831	22146	3685	761578	515416	246162

注：1. 2006年5月1日起，公共交通售票采用刷卡方式，因此，2006年公共电汽车客运量与历史数据不可比。
2. 自2006年5月1日起，公共电汽车、轨道交通售票采取刷卡方式，并陆续进行了票制票价改革，客运量统计口径方法相应调整，因此与历史数据不可比。

资料来源：本表2005年及以后数据来源于北京市交通委员会。

Note: a) From May 1, 2006, public transit tickets were sold by card swiping, so passenger transportation volume in 2006 was incomparable with historical data.
b) From May 1, 2006, buses, trolley buses and rail transit tickets were sold by card swiping, ticket system and prices were also reformed successively, the statistical coverage and method for passenger transportation volume were adjusted accordingly, so these figures were incomparable with historical data.

Source: After 2005,date in this table were provided by Beijing Municipal Commission of Transport.

9-3 城市供水、供气及供热(1978-2012年)
URBAN WATER SUPPLY, GAS SUPPLY AND HEAT SUPPLY (1978-2012)

年份 Year	全市集中供热管道长度(公里) Total Length of Pipelines for Centralized Heating (km)	全市集中供热面积(万平方米) Centralized Heating Area in Beijing (10000 sq.m)	#住宅 Dwelling House	煤气销售量(万立方米) Sales Volume of Coal Gas (10000 cu.m)	液化石油气销售量(吨) Liquefied Petroleum Gas Sales (ton)	天然气销售量(万立方米) Natural Gas Sales (10000 cu.m)
1978				32687	97255	
1979				32113	114350	
1980				34935	128990	
1981				36309	134771	
1982				36748	149805	
1983				37319	150058	
1984				38710	156421	
1985				41678	169720	
1986				44542	182239	
1987				47594	178205	
1988				49595	177112	287
1989				56056	175814	1805
1990		3702		59508	172688	3544
1991		4560		66111	174326	5062
1992		5281		73615	174694	6040
1993		5730		80163	177065	6702
1994		7056		80409	173105	7623
1995		7537		85201	177637	11003
1996		7838		88356	185304	13504
1997		8399		76429	172879	16565
1998		9102		68998	174464	32619
1999		9992		61846	188450	64833
2000		10860		46719	190571	95919
2001		14729		33960	182188	150585
2002		18172		21077	234680	176504
2003		25108		23991	311657	208837
2004		28150	18962	17714	431660	250326
2005	6272	31736	22218	16776	356551	294279
2006	7013	34977	23158	9763	415268	389202
2007	10424	37203	23697		319631	441327
2008	11948	42501	26738		289576	578626
2009	12156	44240	27694		332693	645356
2010	12224	46715	32305		299392	677009
2011	11734	50794	34563		394437	726229
2012	11031	52555	35104		379371	883385

注：1.2006年6月开始全市煤气家庭用户已全部置换为天然气用户，因此2007年以后煤气销售量无数据。
2.自来水2012年相关数据口径调整为城镇公共供水。
资料来源：北京市市政市容管理委员会、北京市水务局。
Note: a) From June 2006, all coal gas users were changed to natual gas users. Therefore, there are no figures of coal gas sales volume since 2007.
b) Relevant tap water figures for 2012 were changed to cover urban public water.
Source: Beijing Municipal Commission of City Administration and Environment. Beijing Water Authority.

9-3 续表 continued

年份 Year	居民燃气用户(万户) Household with Access to Gas (10000 households)	自来水综合生产能力(万立方米/日) Integrated Capacity of Tap Water (10000 cu.m/day)	自来水供水管线长度(公里) Length of Tap Water Supply Pipelines (km)	自来水销售总量(万立方米) Total Sales Volume of Tap Water (10000 cu.m)
1978	65.2	134	2926	32664
1979	76.7	151	3083	36232
1980	80.3	163	3272	38933
1981	85.1	167	3435	41634
1982	88.0	164	4216	41136
1983	90.9	166	4452	42778
1984	96.9	167	4622	43716
1985	102.3	176	4927	45601
1986	153.6	188	5079	46695
1987	160.9	185	5257	47680
1988	165.4	189	5550	50059
1989	172.6	206	5647	50145
1990	176.1	215	5770	52718
1991	184.7	221	5947	56107
1992	192.4	226	6130	58704
1993	197.5	234	6367	60794
1994	210.3	242	6727	67977
1995	219.8	264	6907	67877
1996	188.1	266	6907	69684
1997	243.0	302	6339	79046
1998	254.4	330	6989	75969
1999	259.8	357	7179	78098
2000	291.9	367	7610	75364
2001	310.0	371	8146	69807
2002	336.4	428	8555	79322
2003	406.0	429	9278	71583
2004	438.6	399	9981	82986
2005	462.6	348	9831	71600
2006	540.2	373	11899	74970
2007	556.4	391	13133	77778
2008	591.0	404	14118	80792
2009	600.0	424	14791	86881
2010	634.2	445	16144	89185
2011	644.1	473	16963	94622
2012	713.5	411	14029	93826

9-4 全市集中供热
TOTAL CENTRAL HEAT SUPPLY

项 目	Item	2012	2011	2012年为2011年% 2012 as % of 2011
供热面积 （万平方米）	**Total Heating Area (10000 sq.m)**	**52555**	**50794**	**103.5**
#住 宅	Dwelling House	35104	34563	101.6
供热能力 （兆瓦）	**Supply Capacity (megawatt)**	**38298**	**36805**	**104.1**
热电厂供热	Heating from Thermal Power Plants	7187	6713	107.1
锅炉房供热	Heating from Boiler Houses	31111	30092	103.4
供热总量 （万吉焦）	**Total Heating Supply (10000 giga joules)**	**35222**	**35682**	**98.7**
热电厂供热	Heating from Thermal Power Plants	5752	5170	111.3
锅炉房供热	Heating from Boiler Houses	29470	30512	96.6
供热管道长度 （公里）	**Length of Pipeline (km)**	**11031**	**11734**	**94.0**

资料来源：北京市市政市容管理委员会。
Source: Beijing Municipal Commission of City Administration and Environment.

9-5 液化石油气及天然气
LIQUEFIED PETROLEUM GAS AND NATURAL GAS

项 目	Item	2012	2011	2012年为2011年% 2012 as % of 2011
液化石油气	**Liquefied Petroleum Gas**			
供气总量 （吨）	Gas Supply (ton)	418156	442535	94.5
销售气量 （吨）	Gas Sales (ton)	379371	394437	96.2
#家庭用量 （吨）	for Households (ton)	190975	187132	102.1
家庭用户 （万户）	Household (10000 households)	194.1	170.8	113.6
天然气	**Natural Gas**			
供气总量 （万立方米）	Gas Supply (10000 cu.m)	924763	764915	120.9
销售气量 （万立方米）	Gas Sales (10000 cu.m)	883385	726229	121.6
#家庭用量 （万立方米）	for Households (10000 cu.m)	115401	98894	116.7
家庭用户 （万户）	Household (10000 households)	519.4	473.3	109.7
居民燃气用户 （万户）	**Household with Access to Gas (10000 households)**	**713.5**	**644.1**	**110.8**

注：本表天然气、液化石油气用量中包含燕山石化用气量。
资料来源：北京市市政市容管理委员会、中国石化集团北京燕山石化有限公司。
Note: This table includes the figures of Yanshan Petrochem.
Source: Beijing Municipal Commission of City Administration and Environment,SINOPEC Beijing Yanshan Petrochemical Co., Ltd..

9-6 自来水及自备水源
TAP WATER AND SELF-PROVIDED SOURCE OF WATER

项目		Item		2012	2011
自来水		**Tap Water**			
综合生产能力	(万立方米/日)	General Production Capacity	(10000cu.m/day)	411	473
供水管道长度	(公里)	Length of Water Pipelines	(km)	14029	16963
销售总量	(万立方米)	Tatal Sales in Volume	(10000 cu.m)	93826	94622
#生产运营用	(万立方米)	for Production Use	(10000 cu.m)	12045	12583
公共服务用	(万立方米)	for Public Service Use	(10000 cu.m)	34710	33296
居民家庭用	(万立方米)	for Households Use	(10000 cu.m)	46303	48003
自备井水		**Self-provided Well Water**			
用水量	(万立方米)	Consumption	(10000 cu.m)	46087.8	46483.3
#生产运营用	(万立方米)	for Production Use	(10000 cu.m)	10271.9	10780.3
公共服务用	(万立方米)	for Public Service Use	(10000 cu.m)	12345.9	13183.9
居民家庭用	(万立方米)	for Households Use	(10000 cu.m)	18380.5	17137.1

注：自来水2012年相关数据口径调整为城镇公共供水。自备井用水量为城镇范围用水量。
资料来源：北京市水务局。
Note: Relevant tap water figures for 2012 were changed to cover urban public water. Consumption of self-provided well water is for unban area.
Source: Beijing Water Authority.

9-7 公共交通及客运出租小轿车
PUBLIC TRAFFIC AND TAXIS SERVICE

项目		Item		2012	2011
公共交通		**Public Traffic**			
运营车辆	(辆)	Operating Vehicles (year-end)	(unit)	25831	24478
公共电汽车	(辆)	Buses and Trolley Buses	(unit)	22146	21628
轨道交通	(辆)	Subways	(unit)	3685	2850
运营线路条数	(条)	Number of Operating Routes (year-end)	(line)	795	764
公共电汽车	(条)	Buses and Trolley Buses	(line)	779	749
轨道交通	(条)	Subways	(line)	16	15
运营线路长度	(公里)	Length of Operating Routes (year-end)	(km)	19989	19832
公共电汽车	(公里)	Buses and Trolley Buses	(km)	19547	19460
轨道交通	(公里)	Subways	(km)	442	372
客运量	(万人次)	Passengers Carried	(10000 person-times)	761578	722552
公共电汽车	(万人次)	Buses and Trolley Buses	(10000 person-times)	515416	503272
轨道交通	(万人次)	Subways	(10000 person-times)	246162	219280
客运出租小汽车		**Taxis Service**			
年末运营车辆	(辆)	Operating Vehicles (year-end)	(unit)	66646	66646
客运量	(万人次)	Passengers Carried	(10000 person-times)	69862	69600

资料来源：北京市交通委员会。
Source: Beijing Municipal Commission of Transport.

9-8 市政设施情况
BASIC STATISTICS ON MUNICIPAL ENGINEERING

项　　目		Item		2012	2011
境内道路总里程	(公里)	Total Length of Highways and Roads	(km)	28585	28446
高速公路里程	(公里)	Length of Expressways	(km)	923	912
城市道路里程	(公里)	Length of Urban Roads	(km)	6271	6258
#快速路	(公里)	Rapid Roads	(km)	263	263
#主干路	(公里)	Trunk Roads	(km)	865	861
城市道路面积	(万平方米)	Area of Urban Roads	(10000 sq.m)	9236	9164
#铺装步道	(万平方米)	Paved Roads	(10000 sq.m)	1605	1588
城市道路立交桥数	(座)	Number of Flyovers in City	(unit)	413	418
城市过街天桥数	(座)	Number of Pedestrain Overbridges in City	(unit)	512	489
城市地下通道数	(座)	Number of Underpass in City	(unit)	210	211
备案停车场个数	(个)	Number of Parking Lots Recorded	(unit)	6273	5787
备案停车场车位总数	(个)	Total Capacity of Parking Lots Recorded	(unit)	1611372	1471427
路口电视监视点位	(台)	TV Monitor at Crossings	(unit)	1235	1216
城六区照明线路长度	(公里)	Length of Lighting Lines in 8 Districts	(km)	5948	5839

注：1. 2011年开始本表统计范围为城六区。
2. 表中"备案停车场个数"和"备案停车场车位总数"为原指标"经营性停车场个数"和"经营性停车场车位总数"。
资料来源：北京市交通委员会、北京市公安交通管理局、北京市路灯管理中心。

Note: a) From 2011 roads and bridge figures covered 6 districts .
b) In the table, the "Parking Lots Recorded" and "Total Capacity of Parking Lots Recorded" are the original indicators "Operational Parking Lots" and "Total Capacity of Operational Parking Lots".

Source: Beijing Municipal Communission of Transport, Beijing Administration for Public Security & Traffic, Beijing Street Lamp Administration Center.

主要统计指标解释

自来水综合生产能力　指按供水设施取水、净化、送水、出厂输水干管等环节实际测定计算的综合生产能力。不包括供水高峰阶段，超负荷增加的生产能力。计算时，以四个环节中最薄弱的环节为主确定能力。

自来水供水管道长度　指从送水泵至用户水表之间所有管道的长度。不包括新安装尚未使用的管道。

生产运营用水　指在城市范围内生产、运营的农、林、牧、渔业、工业、建筑业、交通运输业等单位在生产、运营过程中的用水。

公共服务用水　指为城市社会公共生活服务的用水。包括行政事业单位、部队营区和公共设施服务、社会服务业、批发零售贸易业、旅馆饮食业以及社会服务业等单位的用水。

居民家庭用水　指城市范围内所有居民家庭的日常生活用水。包括城市居民家庭、农民家庭、公共供水站用水。

公共交通年末运营车辆　指公交企业（单位）用于运营业务的全部车辆数。

运营线路总长度　指全部运营线路长度之和。计算公式：

$$\text{运营线路长度} = \sum \text{各条运营线路长度}$$

$$= \sum\left[\begin{pmatrix}\text{上行起点至终点里程} + \text{下行起点至终点里程} \\ + \text{上下行终点掉头里程}\end{pmatrix}\right]$$

公路里程　指公路的长度，凡达到《公路工程技术标准（JTGB01-2003）》规定的技术等级的公路，均统计公路里程，包括大、中城市的郊区公路里程，公路通过城镇（指县城、集镇）街道的里程和公路桥梁长度、隧道长度、渡口的宽度以及分期修建的公路已验收交付使用的里程。国道、省道、县道、乡道和专用公路中新增的人工修建的、路基宽度在4.5米以上的等外路里程也纳入公路里程统计。按技术等级公路可分为高速公路、一级公路、二级公路、三级公路、四级公路和等外公路。

道路里程　指道路长度和与道路相通的桥梁、隧道的长度，按车行道中心线计算。城市道路由车行道和人行道两部分组成。在统计时只统计路面宽度在3.5米（含3.5米）以上的各种铺装道路，包括开放型工业区和住宅区道路在内。

道路面积　指道路面积和与道路相通的广场、桥梁、隧道的面积（统计时，将人行道面积单独统计）。人行道面积按道路两侧面积相加计算。包括步行街和广场，不含人车混行的道路。

Explanatory Notes on Main Statistical Indicators

General Production Capacity means the comprehe- nsive production capacity of water supply facilities actually measured for water intake, purifying, outlet, and delivering trunk pipes, excluding additional capacity beyond load at water supply peak hours. It is determined mainly by the weakest one of four sections.

Length of Water Pipelines means the length of all pipes between the water outlet pumps the user's water meters, excluding any pipes newly installed and not used.

Water for Production Use means the water used by entities in sectors of agriculture, forestry, livestock raising, fishery, industry, construction, transportation, which are producing and operating in urban area, in their production and operation.

Water for Public Service Use means the water used for urban public living services, including that used for administrative and public institutions, army camps, public facility services, social service, wholesale and retail trades, hotels and restaurants, and social service organizations.

Water for Households Use means the water used for daily life of all households in urban area, including the water used for urban residents, farmer households, and public water supply stations.

Year-end Public Transit Vehicles in Operation means the number of all vehicles used for operational business in pubic transit enterprises (companies).

Total Length of Public Transit Lines means the sum of all lines in operation. It is calculated with the formula:

Length of Public Transit Lines = ∑ Length of all lines in operation = ∑ [(mileage from the upward starting point to the end point + mileage from the downward starting point to the end point + mileage of double back from upward and downward end points)]

Total Length of Highways means the length of highways. Such statistics apply for any highway reaching the technical grade stated in Highway Engineering Technical Standards (JTGB01-2003), including the mileage of highways in suburbs in middle and large cities, mileage of highways passing through streets in towns (county seats and towns), length of highway bridges, length of tunnels, width of ferries, and mileage of highways constructed in several phases and put into use. The mileage of substandard new highways built manually in national highways, provincial highways, county highways, township highways and special highways, with roadbed width of 4.5m over. In terms of technical grade, highways fall into expressways, first-grade highways, second-grade highways, third-grade highways, fourth-grade highways, and substandard highways.

Mileage of Roads means the length of roads and bridges and tunnels connecting with roads, calculated by the central lines of carriage ways. Urban roads consist of carriageways and pavements. Statistics only apply for laid roads with road surface width of 3.5m (including 3.5m), including roads in open industrial zones and residential zones.

Area of Roads means the area of roads and the area of squares, bridges and tunnels connecting to the roads (the area of pavements is calculated separately). The area of pavements is the sum of area of roads on sides of road, including pedestrian streets and squares, excluding roads for both pedestrians and vehicles.

10

农业及农村经济
AGRICULTURE AND RURAL ECONOMY

简要说明

一、本章资料的主要内容

本章资料反映北京市农业生产和农村经济基本情况，主要包括农村基层组织情况、农村地区人口、从业人员、耕地、农林牧渔业产值及主要农产品生产情况、设施农业、农业观光园、民俗旅游、农村固定资产投资、乡镇企业情况、农村经济收入与分配情况等。

二、本章资料的统计范围

农林牧渔业统计范围包括辖区内全部农林牧渔业生产单位、非农行业单位附属的农林牧渔业生产活动单位以及农户的农业生产活动。军委系统的农林牧渔业生产（除军马外）也应包括在内，但不包括农业科学试验机构进行的农业生产。

1. 农业：指各种农作物的种植活动。包括谷物、豆类、薯类、棉花、油料、糖料、麻类、烟叶、蔬菜、食用菌及花卉盆景园艺产品、水果、坚果、饲料和香料作物、药材及其它作物的种植。

2. 林业：包括林木的栽培(不包括茶园、桑园和果园的栽培、管理和收获等活动)、木材和竹材的采运、林产品的采集。

3. 畜牧业：包括牲畜饲养和放牧、家禽饲养以及野生动物的捕猎和饲养。

4. 渔业：分为淡水养殖和海水养殖，包括水生动物和海藻类植物的养殖和捕捞。

农村社会经济统计范围包括所有乡镇辖区内的社会经济活动。

三、本章资料的数据来源

乡镇企业数据由北京市经济和信息化委员会提供。农村经济收入分配数据由北京市农村经济研究中心农村合作经济经营管理站提供，耕地数据由北京市国土资源局提供，林业数据由北京市园林绿化局提供，水产品数据由北京市农业局提供，农村基层组织资料由北京市民政局提供。其余资料均由北京市统计局、国家统计局北京调查总队提供。

四、本章资料的调查方法和核算方法

根据农业生产特点，农林牧渔业总产值的核算采用“产品法”计算，即用产品产量乘以价格求出各种产品的产值，按产品产值类别分别汇总，计算出农林牧渔各业的产值，各业相加为农林牧渔业总产值。

(1)农业：包括谷物和其他作物；蔬菜、食用菌及花卉盆景园艺产品；水果、坚果、饮料、香料；中药材。

(2)林业：包括林木的培育和种植；木材、竹材采运；林产品的采集。

(3)牧业：包括除渔业养殖以外的一切动物饲养和放牧以及野生动物的捕猎和饲养。

(4)渔业：包括水生动物和海藻类植物的养殖和捕捞。

(5)服务业：产值等于农林牧渔服务业营业收入。

1957 年以前的农业总产值中包括了厩肥和农民自给性手工业（如农民自制衣服、鞋、袜，自己从事粮食初步加工等）。1958 年及以后的农业总产值、林业中增加了村及村以下竹木采伐产值；牧业中取消了厩肥产值；副业中取消了农民自给性手工业产值；渔业中增加了海洋捕捞水产品产值。1980 年及以后的农业总产值，在副业中增加了农民家庭兼营工业商品部分的产值。从 1984 年起村及村以下办工业产值划归工业。从 1993 年起，取消副业。将野生动物的捕猎划入牧业，野生植物采集和农民家庭兼营商品性工业划归农业。从 2003 年起按照新的《国民经济济行业分类》标准取消了“其它农业”；将农林牧渔服务业产值纳入农林牧渔业总产值中；从农林牧渔业总产值中取消了“家庭兼营商品性工业”；将村以上木材和竹材的采运划入了林业；产值计算采用生产者价格，即生产者第一次出售农产品的价格；2004 年国家统计局报表制度规定农林牧渔业总产值增加按可比价计算的产值及发展速度（计算方法：用现价产值的中类数据除以中类缩减指数求得各中类的可比价产值，各中类相加得大类的可比价产值，最后用大类数据相加得农业可比价总产值，可比价产值除以上年现价产值得发展速度）。从 2005 年起，取消了按 1990 年价格计算的农业产值。由于 2006 年农业普查后对农业生产历史数据进行了修订，新修订的农业产值数据只到大类，如果按大类缩减计算农业可比价总产值不符合国家报表制度要求，故 2005 年及以前年度没有按可比价计算的发展速度。2010 年起，根据新的《统计用产品分类目录》将原林业产值中的核桃、栗子、白果、松子等干果产值调整至农业产值中，为同口径对比，将 2009 年年报数据也作了相应调整。

主要粮食播种面积数据通过卫星遥感测量方法取得,粮食产量数据通过抽样调查方法取得。农林牧渔业生产统计采取全面调查方法，村级起报。

五、本章中关于历史数据调整的问题

根据 2006 年第二次农业普查结果，北京市统计局、国家统计局北京调查总队按照国务院农普办要求，依照国际通用做法，已对 1997—2005 年的相关指标历史数据进行了修订。

Brief Introduction

I. Main Content of Statistics

Statistics in this chapter show basic situation of agricultural production and rural economy in Beijing, mainly consisting of figures on rural grass-root organizations, population and employed persons in rural area, arable land, output value of agriculture, forestry, animal husbandry and fishery, production of main agricultural products, facility agriculture, agricultural sightseeing garden, folk custom tour, rural fixed assets investment, township enterprises, rural economic income and allocation.

II. Scope of Statistics

Statistics for agriculture, forestry, animal husbandry and fishery involve all producing entities of agriculture, forestry, animal husbandry and fishery, productive activities entities of agriculture, forestry, animal husbandry and fishery attached to entities in non-agricultural sectors, as well as farmers' agricultural production activities. Production of agriculture, forestry, animal husbandry and fishery in the military committee system shall also be included (warhorses excluded) . The agricultural production conducted in experimental organizations of agricultural science is not included.

1. Agriculture: means planting activities of various agricultural crops, including the planting of grain, beans, potatoes, cottons, oil plants, sugar plants, hemp plants, tobacco leaves, vegetables, edible fungus, flower bonsai and gardening products, fruits, nuts, feedstuff, and flavor crops, herbs, and other crops.

2. Forestry: including the planting of forest (excluding the planting, management, harvest of tea garden, mulberry garden, fruit garden and other activities), felling and transporting of timber and bamboo, collection of forestry products.

3. Animal husbandry: including the raising and grazing of livestock, poultry raising, and hunting and breeding of wildlife.

4. Fishery: divided into fresh water cultivation and seawater cultivation, including cultivation and catching of aquatic animals and seaweed plants.

Statistics for social and economic development in rural areas include social and economic activities within the jurisdiction of all villages and towns.

Ⅲ. Source of Data

Data on township enterprises were provided by Beijing Municipal Commission of Economy and Information Technology. Data on income allocation in rural economy were provided by the Operation and Management State of Rural Cooperative Economy, Beijing Research Center for Rural Economy. Data on arable land were provided by Beijing Municipal Bureau of Land and Resources. Forestry data were provided by Beijing Gardening and Landscaping Bureau. Data on aquatic products were provided by Beijing Municipal Bureau of Agriculture. All other data were provided by Beijing Municipal Bureau of Statistics and National Bureau of Statistics Survey Office in Beijing.

Ⅳ. Method and Calculation of Statistics

Figures on seeded area of main grain were obtained through satellite remote sensing measurement. Data on rural grass-root organizations are from Beijing Municipal Bureau of Civil Affairs. Obtained through complete survey, data on production of agriculture, forestry, animal husbandry and fishery were reported from the minimum level of villages.

According to features of agricultural production, the gross output value of agriculture, forestry, animal husbandry and fishery is calculated with the "product method", namely multiplying the output of each product by its price, summing up the output value of each type of product to get the output value of each sector of agriculture, forestry, animal husbandry and fishery, adding them to get the gross output value of agriculture, forestry, animal husbandry and fishery.

Agriculture: including cereal and other crops; vegetables, edible fungus, flower bonsai and gardening products; fruits, nuts, beverage, flavor, and herbs.

Forestry: including the cultivation and planting of forest trees; felling and transporting of timber and bamboo; and collection of forestry products.

Animal husbandry: including the breeding and grazing of animals other than fish breeding, as well as hunting and breeding of wildlife.

Fishery: including cultivation and catching of aquatic animals and seaweed plants.

Service: the output value is equal to the operating income of services in support of activities of agriculture, forestry, animal husbandry and fishery.

Prior to 1957, China's gross agricultural output value included barnyard manure and handicraft products for self-consumption (clothes, shoes, stockings, and initial grain processing undertaken by peasants). In and after 1958, output value of cutting and felling of bamboo and trees by villages and other cooperative organizations under villages were included in forestry; output value of barnyard manure was from animal husbandry; self consumed handicrafts was not included in sideline product output value; and the output value of aquatic products caught in ocean was added to fishery. For the gross output of agriculture in and after 1980, the output value of industrial commodities operated by farmer households was included in the output value of sideline. Since 1984, industries run by villages and organizations under villages have been included in the sector of industry. Since 1993, the subdivision of sideline has been cancelled, and the hunting of wild animals has been classified as animal husbandry, and the gathering of wild plants and commodity industry run by rural households have been included in farming. A new industrial classification of economic activities was introduced in 2003. Under the new classification, "other agriculture" is cancelled. And the value of services to agriculture, forestry, animal husbandry and fishery is included in the gross output value of agriculture, value of industrial output by households is not included in agriculture, value of wood and bamboo felling and transport is included in forestry; the output value is calculated at producer's price, namely the price at which producers sell their agricultural products for the first time; the Reporting System 2004 of National Bureau of Statistics states that, for incremental gross output value of agriculture, forestry, animal husbandry and fishery, the output value and growth rate can be calculated at comparable price (calculation method: figures of output value at present price for medium categories are divided by the reduction index for medium categories to get the output values at current price for medium categories, which are added together to get the output value at current price for general categories. Finally, figures of general categories are added together to get the gross output value at current price for agriculture. The output value at comparable price is divided by the output value at current price in previous year to get the growth rate). From 2005, the output value at the price 1990 was cancelled. As historical data of agricultural production were revised after the agricultural census in 2006, revised agricultural production output value figures were presented by general categories, it does not meet the requirements of national reporting system to calculate the gross agricultural output value at comparable price. Therefore, there were no growth rates at comparable price in and prior to 2005. Since 2010, the output value of dry fruits such as walnuts, chestnuts, gingko and pine nuts formerly involved in forestry has been included in the output value of agriculture according to the new Directory on Statistical Product Classification. For comparison, data in the annual report 2009 have been adjusted accordingly.

Ⅴ.Adjustment to Historical Data

Based on results of the second agricultural census 2006, Beijing Municipal Bureau of Statistics and National Bureau of Statistics Survey Office in Beijing revised relevant historical data 1997-2005 as required by the Agricultural Census Office of the State Council and in accordance with international universal practice.

10-1 农村基本情况（1978-2012年）
BASIC STATISTICS FOR RURAL AREA (1978-2012)

年份 Year	乡政府 (个) Township Governments (unit)	镇政府 (个) Town Governments (unit)	村民委员会 (个) Villagers Committees (unit)	乡镇及行政村常住户数 (万户) Number of Towns and Administrative Villages (10000 households)	乡镇及行政村常住人口 (万人) Towns and Administrative Population (10000 persons)	乡镇及行政村从业人员 (万人) Number of Persons Employed in Towns and Administrative Villages (10000 persons)
1978				91.9	382.1	165.3
1979				92.9	374.7	165.1
1980				95.0	374.3	167.4
1981				98.9	377.6	172.9
1982				103.2	381.8	179.4
1983				106.6	384.0	184.6
1984				108.9	385.6	188.9
1985	350	15	4394	111.8	387.2	190.0
1986	327	15	4400	113.1	386.9	189.5
1987	324	14	4326	115.7	388.9	189.8
1988	321	13	4111	118.6	389.6	189.2
1989	322	14	4483	121.5	390.0	186.1
1990	252	77	4481	124.5	392.0	184.3
1991	209	77	4480	125.5	390.7	182.1
1992	209	77	4229	126.2	387.6	178.7
1993	192	81	4476	126.5	382.4	176.0
1994	174	92	4464	124.9	376.0	171.6
1995	166	100	4355	125.0	371.5	163.6
1996	166	100	4357	124.6	368.9	164.2
1997	132	108	4348	124.6	365.3	161.2
1998	126	105	4032	125.9	364.4	161.0
1999	125	103	4040	125.9	363.9	165.3
2000	70	142	4039	126.8	363.7	165.8
2001	52	139	4010	127.6	361.6	165.3
2002	51	141	4005	128.0	357.6	165.6
2003	45	142	3985	131.1	360.6	169.6
2004	42	142	3985	132.8	359.9	171.4
2005	43	142	3953	142.2	381.8	184.0
2006	41	142	3957	143.6	501.6	316.9
2007	41	142	3955	176.9	510.0	313.4
2008	40	142	3951	189.8	547.4	321.3
2009	40	142	3950	203.8	572.5	338.7
2010	40	142	3943	216.0	589.4	347.8
2011	38	144	3941	212.4	574.8	338.3
2012	38	144	3940	215.2	582.5	341.7

注：1. 从业人员指标1998年以前为乡村劳动力。
2. 乡政府个数、镇政府个数、村民委员会个数由北京市民政局提供。
3. 2006年乡镇及行政村人口和从业人员为农普数据；2007年以后乡镇及行政村人口和从业人员为农普口径，包含居住半年以上外来人口。
4. 2006年乡镇及行政村户数为农普数据，为自然户口径；2007年以后为居住一年以上的户口径。

Note: a) Employed Persons before 1998 were rural labor force.
b) Number of Township Governments, Town Governments, Villagers Committees are provided by Beijing Civil Affairs Bureau.
c) Number of towns and administrative villages and population in towns and administrative villages were agriculture census data in 2006. These figures are from agriculture census and include non-local population since 2007.
d) Number of households in towns and administrative villages in 2006 was from agricultural census, as natural ones; since 2007, it is from the household living for more than one year at a place.

10-2 农业生产条件(1978-2012年)
PRODUCTIVE CONDITIONS OF AGRICULTURE (1978-2012)

年 份 Year	年末实有耕地面积 (万公顷) Cultivated Area (year-end) (10000 hectares)	有 效 灌溉面积 (千公顷) Irrigated Area (1000 hectares)	农业机械总动力 (万千瓦) Total Power of Agricultural Machinery (10000 kw)	农 村 用电量 (万千瓦小时) Rural Electricity Consumption (10000 kwh)	化 肥 施用量 (万吨) Consumption of Chemical Fertilizers (10000 tons)
1978	42.9	341.7	189.4	58802	11.6
1979	42.7	340.8	212.2	63124	11.3
1980	42.6	340.3	234.6	76753	12.3
1981	42.5	341.3	244.8	91844	11.2
1982	42.4	339.4	242.2	96961	12.0
1983	42.3	343.3	261.8	104608	12.0
1984	42.2	342.6	290.8	119289	10.7
1985	42.1	338.4	320.4	126830	8.2
1986	41.9	337.9	345.5	180640	9.1
1987	41.8	337.9	388.4	159450	10.0
1988	41.6	338.1	399.7	163986	10.6
1989	41.4	338.4	423.9	128414	11.8
1990	41.3	335.1	416.2	122711	14.4
1991	41.1	328.7	384.8	111347	14.4
1992	40.9	331.1	399.8	143963	14.4
1993	40.6	314.7	450.5	169911	14.9
1994	40.2	323.4	459.2	172042	19.8
1995	39.4	292.4	468.1	201731	18.8
1996	34.4	301.9	468.4	275871	18.9
1997	34.2	323.3	433.2	301655	19.7
1998	34.1	323.7	415.5	290859	19.3
1999	33.8	322.1	410.4	330069	19.0
2000	32.9	322.7	399.2	572257	17.9
2001	29.2	322.7	394.9	619806	15.7
2002	27.5	219.7	381.8	414248	14.9
2003	26.0	178.9	366.9	427266	14.3
2004	23.6	186.7	340.3	383954	14.5
2005	23.3	181.5	337.7	421680	14.8
2006	23.3	181.5	325.5	416459	14.8
2007	23.2	173.6	300.5	411238	14.0
2008	23.2	171.8	267.0	427377	13.6
2009		165.2	271.5	439099	13.8
2010		162.6	276.0	443774	13.7
2011		163.1	265.2	454009	13.8
2012		159.2	241.1	473121	13.7

注：1. 化肥施用量为折纯量。
2. 2003年以前农村用电量由原北京市供电局提供。
3. 农业机械总动力数据由北京市农业局提供。
4. 1991-2001年有效灌溉面积由北京市水务局提供。

Note: a) Consumption of chemical fertilizers means that converted into pure.
b) Figures of rural electricity consumption before 2003 were provided by Beijing Electric Power Supply Bureau.
c) Figures of Total Power of Agricultural Machinery are provided by Beijing Agriculture Bureau.
d) Figures of Irrigated Area 1991-2001 were provided by Beijing Water Authority.

10-3 农作物播种面积和造林面积(1978-2012年) SOWN AND AFFORESTATION AREA (1978-2012)

年份 Year	农作物播种面积(万公顷) Sown Area (10000 hectares)	#粮食作物 Grain Crops	#玉米 Corn	#小麦 Wheat	#棉花 Cotton	#油料 Oil-bearing Crops	#蔬菜及食用菌 Vegetables and Edible Mushrooms	#瓜类及草莓 Melon & Strawberry	#饲料 Forage	造林面积(万公顷) Afforestation Area (10000 hectares)
1978	69.1	56.1	16.9	19.2	1.3	3.3	5.6	0.2	2.0	1.4
1979	67.7	56.0	18.2	19.7	0.2	3.0	5.4	0.3	2.0	1.6
1980	65.7	54.9	19.7	18.8	0.2	2.8	5.1	0.4	1.8	2.4
1981	64.4	53.0	19.8	18.4	0.2	2.7	5.5	0.6	1.7	2.7
1982	64.2	52.7	19.7	18.1	0.2	2.4	5.9	0.8	1.6	2.8
1983	63.8	53.0	20.1	18.7	0.3	1.9	5.7	0.5	1.5	3.3
1984	63.3	52.3	20.6	19.5	0.6	1.8	5.8	0.7	1.5	3.2
1985	61.8	51.1	21.7	19.1	0.5	2.0	5.4	0.9	1.3	3.0
1986	60.5	49.9	21.6	18.5	0.3	2.0	5.8	1.1	1.0	1.5
1987	59.8	49.5	22.3	18.3	0.3	1.6	6.0	0.9	1.1	2.0
1988	59.5	48.8	22.2	18.6	0.3	1.5	6.3	1.0	1.2	1.6
1989	58.9	48.3	21.9	18.5	0.3	1.3	6.8	0.8	1.1	0.8
1990	59.0	48.4	22.4	18.8	0.3	1.2	7.0	0.6	1.1	1.3
1991	59.0	48.3	22.3	19.2	0.4	1.2	7.3	0.5	1.0	1.5
1992	58.5	47.7	22.4	19.2	0.5	1.2	7.5	0.5	0.8	1.5
1993	56.5	45.6	21.8	17.8	0.4	1.3	7.8	0.5	0.7	4.8
1994	55.1	43.0	20.6	16.4	0.4	1.2	9.1	0.6	0.6	5.5
1995	55.3	43.4	20.8	17.2	0.3	1.2	9.1	0.5		4.7
1996	53.8	42.7	20.8	17.1	0.3	1.1	8.8	0.5	0.5	4.0
1997	53.6	42.5	20.6	17.1	0.2	1.0	8.9	0.5	0.5	3.8
1998	53.5	42.3	20.8	17.1	0.2	1.0	9.0	0.5	0.5	3.7
1999	52.6	41.0	19.8	16.8	0.2	1.0	9.2	0.5	0.5	3.0
2000	45.4	30.8	13.6	12.2	0.2	1.5	10.4	0.8	1.2	2.6
2001	38.0	21.4	10.0	7.3	0.3	1.4	11.3	0.9	1.9	3.2
2002	33.5	16.9	8.7	4.7	0.3	1.6	11.5	0.9	1.8	4.8
2003	30.1	14.1	7.5	3.6	0.3	1.4	10.8	0.9	1.9	4.7
2004	30.4	15.4	9.4	3.9	0.7	1.1	9.1	0.8	2.8	3.2
2005	30.8	19.2	12.0	5.3	0.2	0.9	7.9	0.8	1.5	1.2
2006	32.0	22.0	13.6	6.3	0.2	0.7	7.1	0.9	0.6	1.3
2007	29.5	19.7	13.9	4.1	0.2	0.7	7.0	0.9	0.4	1.1
2008	32.2	22.6	14.6	6.4	0.1	0.7	6.8	0.8	0.4	0.9
2009	32.0	22.6	15.1	6.1	0.1	0.6	6.8	0.8	0.4	1.8
2010	31.7	22.3	15.0	6.2	…	0.5	6.8	0.8	0.5	1.4
2011	30.3	20.9	14.1	5.8	…	0.5	6.7	0.8	0.5	2.1
2012	28.3	19.4	13.2	5.2	…	0.5	6.4	0.8	0.3	3.6

注：1．蔬菜播种面积2006年为农普衔接数据，1997年-2005年为历史修订数据。
2．造林面积2009年以前为人工造林面积，2009年起调整为荒山荒(沙)地造林面积，包括人工造林、无林地和疏林地新封面积。

Note: a) Figures of vegetable sown area in 2006 were from agricultural census, figures in 1997-2005 were historically revised ones.
b) Afforestation area before 2009 was man-made afforestation area, and changed to afforestation area for barren mountains and barren sand after 2009, including the area of man-made forest, forest-free land and newly enclosed light-forest land.

10-4 农林牧渔业总产值(1978-2012年)
GROSS OUTPUT VALUE OF FARMING, FORESTRY, ANIMAL HUSBANDRY AND FISHERY (1978-2012)

年份 Year	农林牧渔业总产值(亿元) Gross Output Value of Farming, Forestry, Animal Husbandry and Fishery (100 million yuan)						农林牧渔业总产值比上年增长(%) Growth Rate (%)	
		农业 Farming	林业 Forestry	牧业 Animal Husbandry	渔业 Fishery	服务业 Services	按现价计算 calculated at current price	按可比价计算 calculated at constant price
1978	11.5	8.9	0.2	2.4	0.01			
1979	12.3	8.8	0.2	3.3	0.02		7.0	
1980	14.3	9.8	0.5	3.9	0.05		16.3	
1981-1985	**99.4**	**64.6**	**3.9**	**30.1**	**0.8**			
1981	14.9	10.1	0.7	4.1	0.05		4.2	
1982	16.8	11.3	0.7	4.7	0.05		12.8	
1983	19.6	12.7	0.8	6.0	0.1		16.7	
1984	22.2	14.4	0.9	6.7	0.2		13.3	
1985	25.9	16.1	0.8	8.6	0.4		16.7	
1986-1990	**245.7**	**142.1**	**4.1**	**91.6**	**7.9**			
1986	28.1	17.2	0.8	9.4	0.7		8.5	
1987	34.4	20.3	0.8	12.3	1.0		22.4	
1988	52.6	31.4	0.9	18.6	1.7		52.9	
1989	60.4	34.2	0.7	23.3	2.2		14.8	
1990	70.2	39.0	0.9	28.0	2.3		16.2	
1991-1995	**570.1**	**293.2**	**11.2**	**244.6**	**21.1**			
1991	76.5	39.6	1.5	32.8	2.6		9.0	
1992	84.5	43.2	1.6	36.3	3.4		10.5	
1993	100.4	51.1	2.3	42.7	4.3		18.8	
1994	144.3	72.5	3.1	64.0	4.7		43.7	
1995	164.4	86.8	2.7	68.8	6.1		13.9	
1996-2000	**883.4**	**441.8**	**18.2**	**388.5**	**34.9**			
1996	168.9	89.2	2.8	71.1	5.8		2.7	
1997	170.5	86.8	2.9	74.6	6.2		0.9	
1998	174.8	88.3	3.2	75.8	7.5		2.5	
1999	180.6	89.4	4.1	79.5	7.6		3.3	
2000	188.6	88.1	5.2	87.5	7.8		4.4	
2001-2005	**1114.6**	**423.2**	**57.0**	**567.3**	**45.6**			
2001	202.2	84.7	9.0	99.3	9.2		7.2	
2002	213.5	83.5	11.9	108.6	9.5		5.6	
2003	224.7	80.9	12.3	114.3	9.3	7.9	5.2	
2004	234.9	83.1	11.4	124.3	8.9	7.2	4.5	
2005	239.3	91.0	12.4	120.8	8.7	6.4	1.9	
2006-2010	**1459.4**	**648.4**	**87.1**	**643.7**	**51.5**	**28.7**		
2006	240.2	104.5	14.8	105.1	9.8	6.0	0.4	0.9
2007	272.3	115.5	17.8	122.4	10.1	6.5	13.4	0.8
2008	303.9	128.1	20.5	140.5	9.8	5.0	11.6	0.8
2009	315.0	146.1	17.2	136.1	10.3	5.3	3.6	5.5
2010	328.0	154.2	16.8	139.6	11.5	5.9	4.1	-1.7
2011	363.1	163.4	18.9	162.7	11.5	6.6	10.7	0.9
2012	395.7	166.3	54.8	154.2	13.0	7.5	9.0	2.9

注：1. 农林牧渔业总产值绝对数按现价计算，从2003年起执行新《国民经济行业分类标准》，农林牧渔业总产值中含农林牧渔服务业产值。
2. 2003年以后，计算农林牧渔业总产值使用的价格从农产品综合平均价调整为农产品生产价格。
3. 2006年为与农业普查衔接的数据，1997-2005年为历史修订数据。
4. 2010年按照新的《统计用产品分类目录》，将原归属林业产值的核桃、板栗等林产品调整至农业产值，并对2009年数据作了调整。

Note: a) Figures in value terms are at current prices. In the year of 2003, new Classification Standards of National Economy Industries are implemented and Gross output value of farming, forestry, animal husbandry and fishery includes the output value of services of farming forestry, animal husbandry and fishery.
b) After 2003, the prices used for calculating the output value of farming, forestry, animal husbandry and fishery were changed from comprehensive average price of farming products to production price of farming products.
c) Figures for 2006 were from agricultural census, figures in 1997-2005 were historically revised ones.
d) Output value of forest produces such as walnuts and chestnuts was transferred to that of agricultural products in 2010 according to the new Directory of Product Classification Used for Statistics. Figures 2009 were adjusted accordingly.

10-5 主要农业产品产量(1978-2012年)
OUTPUT OF MAJOR AGRICULTURAL PRODUCTS (1978-2012)

单位：万吨 (10000 tons)

年份 Year	粮食 Grain	棉花 Cotton	油料 Oilbearing Crops	蔬菜及食用菌 Vegetables and Edible Mushroom	干鲜果品 Nuts and Fresh Fruit	牛奶 Milk	肉类 Meat	#猪牛羊肉 Pork, Beef and Mutton	禽蛋产量 Poultry Eggs	水产品 Aquatic Products
1978	186.0	0.3	2.6	164.5	17.5	5.4	11.9	11.9	2.1	0.2
1979	172.8	0.1	2.6	181.3	15.8	6.0	13.1	13.2	3.1	0.3
1980	186.0	0.1	3.1	175.9	15.9	6.8	15.1	15.1	3.4	0.4
1981-1985	**1004.8**	**1.4**	**13.1**	**1002.2**	**86.7**	**53.3**	**69.0**	**68.9**	**44.3**	**4.0**
1981	180.7	0.1	2.2	172.8	15.6	7.6	13.2	13.2	3.7	0.4
1982	185.5	0.1	2.3	208.3	13.8	8.9	13.9	13.8	5.4	0.4
1983	201.5	0.2	2.1	199.1	18.2	10.6	14.9	14.9	8.9	0.6
1984	217.4	0.6	2.6	218.0	20.2	12.6	13.4	13.4	12.2	1.0
1985	219.7	0.4	3.9	204.0	18.9	13.5	13.6	13.6	14.1	1.6
1986-1990	**1181.9**	**1.4**	**15.2**	**1422.2**	**119.3**	**89.7**	**90.8**	**78.3**	**103.8**	**18.8**
1986	216.5	0.2	3.0	222.7	18.7	14.6	13.3	13.3	14.7	2.2
1987	227.0	0.3	3.3	241.1	22.5	15.5	12.9	12.9	16.8	3.0
1988	234.6	0.3	3.0	271.3	23.8	18.0	14.5	14.5	21.8	3.9
1989	239.2	0.3	2.8	331.0	26.7	19.9	23.3	17.2	24.7	4.6
1990	264.6	0.3	3.1	356.1	27.6	21.7	26.8	20.4	25.8	5.1
1991-1995	**1354.7**	**1.9**	**17.6**	**1915.9**	**198.5**	**113.7**	**180.7**	**134.0**	**139.3**	**34.7**
1991	279.7	0.3	3.3	368.4	29.3	23.9	33.9	24.8	27.9	5.6
1992	281.9	0.5	3.4	381.4	34.0	24.5	35.9	27.3	30.0	6.4
1993	284.1	0.4	3.8	418.8	39.6	22.5	36.7	28.2	31.4	7.0
1994	249.2	0.4	3.8	350.0	48.8	22.2	34.4	24.8	31.2	7.6
1995	259.8	0.3	3.3	397.3	46.8	20.6	39.8	28.9	28.5	8.1
1996-2000	**1059.4**	**1.1**	**15.0**	**2101.9**	**291.8**	**120.2**	**218.1**	**146.5**	**98.2**	**38.2**
1996	237.4	0.3	2.9	403.2	51.3	21.0	38.2	27.3	24.7	7.8
1997	237.5	0.2	2.7	408.8	54.8	22.2	39.9	27.8	23.8	7.7
1998	239.3	0.2	2.8	403.8	59.5	22.7	43.4	30.3	17.9	7.6
1999	201.0	0.2	2.8	419.8	60.2	24.0	46.1	30.2	15.8	7.6
2000	144.2	0.2	3.8	466.3	66.0	30.3	50.5	30.9	16.0	7.5
2001-2005	**410.3**	**1.9**	**18.5**	**2302.3**	**419.5**	**295.5**	**287.8**	**169.1**	**78.9**	**35.0**
2001	104.9	0.3	4.3	491.0	71.9	42.9	55.9	33.0	15.6	7.4
2002	82.3	0.3	4.6	507.4	78.7	55.1	60.9	35.2	15.2	7.4
2003	58.0	0.3	3.3	486.7	84.1	63.3	60.6	35.2	16.2	7.1
2004	70.2	0.8	2.9	444.1	90.9	70.0	57.4	34.0	15.9	6.7
2005	94.9	0.2	2.5	373.1	93.9	64.2	53.3	31.7	16.0	6.4
2006-2010	**577.3**	**0.6**	**10.0**	**1622.7**	**445.3**	**322.1**	**231.7**	**135.0**	**76.5**	**29.6**
2006	109.2	0.2	2.2	341.2	88.7	61.9	45.3	26.9	15.2	5.4
2007	102.1	0.2	2.2	340.1	91.1	62.2	47.9	27.1	15.6	6.0
2008	125.5	0.1	2.2	321.3	89.8	66.4	45.1	25.9	15.2	6.1
2009	124.8	0.1	1.8	317.1	90.3	67.4	47.2	27.6	15.4	5.8
2010	115.7	…	1.6	303.0	85.4	64.1	46.3	27.5	15.1	6.3
2011	121.8	0.1	1.4	296.9	87.8	64.0	44.4	27.6	15.1	6.1
2012	113.8	…	1.3	279.9	84.3	65.1	43.2	27.3	15.2	6.4

注：1. 蔬菜、干鲜果品、猪牛羊肉产量2006年为农普衔接数据，1997年-2005年为历史修订数据。
2. 肉类产量1988年及以前为猪牛羊肉产量。
3. 2006年及以前水产品产量为淡水鱼产量，2007年以后含远洋捕捞量。水产品数据由北京市农业局提供。

Note: a) Figures of vegetable, nuts and fresh fruit, pork, beef and mutton output in 2006 were from agricultural census, figures in 1997-2005 were historically revised ones.
b) Output of meat in and before 1988 was that of pork, beef and mutton.
c) Output of aquatic products was that of fresh water fish in and before 2006, and included deep-sea fishing amount since 2007. Aquatic product figures were provided by Beijing Agriculture Bureau.

10-6 平均每一从业人员创造农、林、牧、渔业产值(1990-2012年) OUTPUT VALUE OF FARMING, FORESTRY, ANIMAL HUSBANDRY AND FISHERY CREATED BY EACH PERSON (1990-2012)

单位：元 (yuan)

年 份 Year	农林牧渔业总产值 Total Output Value of Farming, Forestry, Animal Husbandry and Fishery	#农 业 Farming	#林 业 Forestry	#畜牧业 Animal Husbandry	#渔 业 Fishery
1990	8507	5537	1540	54837	22729
1991	9523	5722	2807	68268	26442
1992	11329	6678	3826	78905	33689
1993	13859	8271	4558	92901	39518
1994	21002	12461	6507	139136	39182
1995	25110	15760	5750	156332	47266
1996	25250	15504	6741	173404	53133
1997	26101	15605	6886	169541	56211
1998	25817	15653	7724	124279	68379
1999	25396	15621	8398	101869	63684
2000	27061	16454	8416	99481	65223
2001	29772	16838	12287	109151	76321
2002	33313	18193	15209	116799	86784
2003	37770	19579	14634	129862	92879
2004	40569	20934	12376	153518	98619
2005	40834	22700	12496	156911	96184
2006	36559	21147	17398	166889	195867
2007	44276	25892	19324	177359	126998
2008	49175	28405	22031	212910	122318
2009	51750	33061	18507	215008	128750
2010	54579	35130	17886	228814	164441
2011	62556	38613	20344	285988	155637
2012	70258	40585	59852	282916	175234

注：1. 2006年从业人员为农普数据，2007年以后为农普口径，含居住半年以上的外来人口。
2. 2006年农林牧渔业总产值及分行业产值为与农业普查衔接的数据，1997-2005年为历史修订数据。
3. 2010年按照新的《统计用产品分类目录》，将原归属林业产值的核桃、板栗等林产品调整至农业产值，并对2009年数据作了调整。

Note: a) Figures of Employees in 2006 were from agriculture census. These figures are from agriculture census and include non-local population since 2007.
b) Figures for output value of farming,forestry,amimal husbandry and fishery in 2006 were from agricultural census, figures in 1997-2005 were historically revised ones.
c) Output value of forest produces such as walnuts and chestnuts was transferred to that of agricultural products in 2010 according to the new Directory of Product Classification Used for Statistics. Figures 2009 were adjusted accordingly.

10-7 耕地面积(2008年)
ARABLE LAND AREA (2008)

单位：公顷 (hectare)

项　　目	Item	2008	2007
年初耕地总资源	**Year-beginning Total Arable Land Resources**	**232187.3**	**232574.8**
年内增加	**Increased in the Year**	**1984.5**	**2657.2**
#新开荒地	Wasteland Newly Opened Up	785.7	881.7
园地改为耕地	Gardening Land Converted into Arable Land	660.5	609.5
年内减少	**Decreased in the Year**	**2483.6**	**3044.7**
#国家基建占地	Occupied by National Capital Construction	1791.7	2065.6
其它基建占地	Occupied by Other Capital Construction		
退耕还林还草占地	Occupied by Restoration of Forest and Grassland from Cultivated Land		
耕地改为园地	Arable Land Converted into Gardening Land	31.7	41.4
年末耕地总资源	**Year-end Total Arable Land Resources**	**231688.2**	**232187.3**
#水　田	Paddy Field	6870.2	7049.9
水浇地	Irrigable Land	157044.5	157989.9

注：1. 1平方公里=100公顷=1500亩。

2. 由于全国第二次土地调查结果尚未正式发布，本表中土地面积数据截止到2008年。

资料来源：北京市国土资源局。

Note: a) 1sq.km =100 hectare =1500 mu.

b) As the results of national 2nd land investigation haven't been formally released, land area figures in this table were those ending 2008.

Source: Beijing Land Resource Administration.

10-8 农村固定资产投资情况(2012年)
INVESTMENT IN FIXED ASSETS IN RURAL AREAS (2012)

单位：万元、万平方米 (10000 yuan, 10000 sq.m)

项目	Item	合计 Total	非农户 Non-Agricultural	农户 Agricultural
本年固定资产投资完成额	**Investment in Fixed Assets Completed in This Year**	**6097571**	**5635232**	**462339**
按投资方向分	**Investment Completed Grouped by Use of Funds**			
农、林、牧、渔业	Agriculture, Forestry, Animal Production and Hunting, Fishing	882162	808012	74150
采矿业	Mining	16610	16610	
制造业	Manufacturing	627056	627056	
电力、热力、燃气及水生产和供应业	Production and Distribution of Electricity, Heating Power, Gas and Water	92147	92147	
建筑业	Construction	40086	40086	
交通运输、仓储和邮政业	Transport, Storage and Post	341605	338176	3429
信息传输、软件和信息技术服务业	Information Transmission, Software and Information Technology Services	38551	38551	
批发和零售业	Wholesale and Retail Trade	110443	110443	
住宿和餐饮业	Accommodation and Restaurants	235600	235600	
金融业	Finance			
房地产业	Real Estate	1394933	1010839	384094
租赁和商务服务业	Renting and Leasing Activities and Business Services	47692	47692	
科学研究和技术服务业	Scientific Research and Development, Technical sServices	2928	2928	
水利、环境和公共设施管理业	Management of Water Conservancy, Environment and Public Facilities	1470512	1470512	
居民服务、修理和其他服务业	Resident Services, Repair and Other Services	89510	88844	666
教育	Education	152138	152138	
卫生和社会工作	Health Care and Social Works	33784	33784	
文化、体育和娱乐业	Culture, Sports and Entertainment	325356	325356	
公共管理、社会保障和社会组织	Pulic Administration,Social Security and Social Organizations	196458	196458	
上年末结余资金	**Balance of Last Year End**	**554808**	**554808**	
本年资金来源小计	**Total Source of Funds in This Year**	**5321236**	**4930903**	**390333**
国家资金	State Funds	19455	19455	
国内贷款	Domestic Loan	475261	475261	
利用外资	Foreign Funds	23597	23597	
自筹资金	Self-raising Funds	4049987	3661622	388365
其他资金	Other Funds	752936	750968	1968
本年施工房屋面积	**Floor Space of Buildings under Construction in This Year**	**2106**	**1795**	**310**
#住宅	Residential Buildings	848	563	285
本年竣工房屋面积	**Floor Space of Buildings Completed in This Year**	707	384	323
#住宅	Residential Buildings	409	110	299
本年竣工房屋投资完成额	**Investment of Buildings Completed in This Year**	**382224**		**382224**
#住宅	Residential Buildings	364180		364180
本年新增固定资产	**Original Value of Incremental Fixed Assets**	**3769283**	**3340309**	**428974**

注：本表非农户固定资产投资为全面调查；农户固定资产投资为抽样调查。

Note: It is investigated in an all-round way to get Non-Agricultural household's investment in fixed assets; Agricultural household's investment in fixed assets is from sample survey.

10-9 农业生产条件
PRODUCTIVE CONDITIONS OF AGRICULTURE

项目		Item		2012	2011	2012年为2011年% 2012 as % of 2011
主要农业机械拥有量		**Possession of Major Agricultural Machinery**				
农业机械总动力	(万千瓦)	Total Power of Agricultural Machinery	(10000 kw)	241.1	265.2	90.9
大中型拖拉机	(混合台)	Large and Medium Tractors	(unit)	7426	8864	83.8
小型拖拉机	(台)	Mini-Tractors	(unit)	7270	11653	62.4
机引农具	(台)	Towing Farm Machinery	(unit)	20655	23047	89.6
机动喷雾器	(部)	Motorized Sprayer	(unit)	29505	20212	146.0
联合收割机	(台)	Combine Harvester	(unit)	2172	2167	100.2
机动脱粒机	(台)	Motorized Sheller	(unit)	4236	4364	97.1
米面加工机	(台)	Processing Machine of Rice and Flour	(unit)	4620	5237	88.2
机动挤奶器	(台)	Motorized Milker	(unit)	1293	1049	123.3
饲料粉碎机	(台)	Fodder Grinder	(unit)	4368	4416	98.9
载重汽车	(辆)	Truck	(unit)	3804	4712	80.7
农业机械作业面积		**Operation Area with Agricultural Machinery**				
机耕面积	(公顷)	Cultivated Area by Machine	(hectare)	81425	89380	91.1
占全部耕地面积比重	(%)	As Percentage of Total	(%)	82.9	81.5	
机播面积	(公顷)	Sown Area by Machine	(hectare)	183689	206162	89.1
占播种面积比重	(%)	As Percentage of Sown Area	(%)	68.0	68.6	
机收面积	(公顷)	Harvest Area by Machine	(hectare)	157139	151559	103.7
占收获面积比重	(%)	As Percentage of Harvest Area	(%)	56.5	50.4	
农村用电量及小水电		**Rural Electricity Consumption and Small Hydropower Station**				
农村用电量	(万千瓦小时)	Rural Electricity Consumption	(10000 kwh)	473121	454009	104.2
农村小水电站	(处)	Rural Small Hydropower Station	(unit)	19	20	
农村小水电站发电量	(万千瓦小时)	Energy by Generated	(10000 kwh)	422.6	631.9	66.9
农田水利		**Irrigation and Water Conservancy**				
排灌用动力机械	(台)	Power-driven Irrigation Machinery	(unit)	41193	42680	96.5
排灌用动力机械动力	(万千瓦)	Power-driven Irrigation Machinery	(10000 kw)	46.2	48.2	95.9
机(电)井	(眼)	Motor-pumped Well	(unit)	49000	47754	102.6
#已配套	(眼)	Completed Set	(unit)	47000	45610	103.0
扬水站(固定机电排灌站)	(处)	Pumping Station	(unit)	1573	1679	93.7
有效灌溉面积	(公顷)	Irrigated Areas	(hectare)	159236	163091	97.6
化肥施用量(折纯)		**Consumption of Chemical Fertilizer (converted into pure)**				
化肥施用量	(吨)	Consumption of Chemical Fertilizers	(ton)	136707	138472	98.7
#氮　肥	(吨)	Nitrogenous Fertilizer	(ton)	64858	67784	95.7
磷　肥	(吨)	Phosphate Fertilizer	(ton)	7825	8822	88.7
钾　肥	(吨)	Potash Fertilizer	(ton)	7012	7440	94.2

注：1. 农村小水电站是指乡村两级小水电实有数。
2. 主要农业机械拥有量、农业机械作业面积、排灌动力机械数据由北京市农业局提供。
3. 机(电)井和扬水站数据由北京市水务局提供。

Note: a) Figures of rural small hydropower station refer to actual number of small hydropower at township and village level.
b) Figures of Possession of Major Agricultural Machinery,Operation Area with Agricultural Machinery and Power-driven Irrigation Machinery are provided by Beijing Agricultural bureau.
c) Figures of Motor-pumped Well are provided by Beijing Water Authority.

10-10 农林牧渔业总产值
GROSS OUTPUT VALUE OF FARMING, FORESTRY, ANIMAL HUSBANDRY AND FISHERY

单位：万元 (10000 yuan)

项目	Item	总产值 Gross Output Value		2012年为2011年% 2012 as % of 2011
		2012	2011	
合 计	**Total**	**3957128.8**	**3631375.5**	**109.0**
农 业	**Farming**	**1662890.9**	**1633731.8**	**101.8**
谷 物	Cereal	235780	248451.6	94.9
豆 类	Beans	5493.2	6064.7	90.6
经济作物	Cash Crops	12815.3	12572.5	101.9
蔬菜、食用菌	Vegetable and Domestic Fungus	623672	594995.9	104.8
水果（含瓜果类）	Fruits (including melons)	543067.7	482489.5	112.6
其 他	Other	242062.7	289157.6	83.7
林 业	**Forestry**	**548252.5**	**189202.3**	**289.8**
牧 业	**Animal Husbandry**	**1541607.2**	**1627269.9**	**94.7**
牲畜饲养	Animals Breeding	418170.4	394251.8	106.1
养 猪	Hogs	527536	594349.5	88.8
家禽饲养	Poultry Raising	511970.8	520991.9	98.3
#禽 蛋	Poultry Eggs	203250.1	191812.7	106.0
其 他	Others	83930	117676.7	71.3
渔 业	**Fishery**	**129778.2**	**115171.5**	**112.7**
农林牧渔服务业	**Services for Agriculture**	**74600.0**	**66000.0**	**113.0**

10-11 主要农作物播种面积及产量
SOWN AREA AND YIELD OF MAJOR CROPS

项目	Item	2012 播种面积(公顷) Sown Areas (hectare)	2012 单产(公斤/公顷) Unit Yield (kg/hectare)	2012 总产量(吨) Total Yield (ton)	2011 播种面积(公顷) Sown Areas (hectare)	2011 单产(公斤/公顷) Unit Yield (kg/hectare)	2011 总产量(吨) Total Yield (ton)
粮食	**Grain**	**193874.5**	**5868.4**	**1137733.6**	**209381.9**	**5815.7**	**1217700.1**
按季节分	Grouped by Season						
夏粮	Summer Grain	52212.5	5257.5	274507.4	58150.0	4881.8	283876.8
秋粮	Autumn Grain	141662.0	6093.6	863226.2	151231.9	6174.8	933823.3
按品种分	Grouped by Variety						
稻谷	Rice	202.1	6442.9	1302.1	230.7	6533.6	1507.3
冬小麦	Winter Wheat	52183.0	5258.1	274383.4	58104.3	4882.6	283702.8
玉米	Corn	132021.4	6330.9	835814.3	140506.7	6429.6	903402.1
薯类	Tubers	2132.6	5740.7	12242.6	2351.4	5459.9	12838.4
大豆	Soybean	4716.3	1880.8	8870.5	5372.3	2010.1	10798.7
棉花	**Cotton**	**239.3**	**1135.4**	**271.7**	**440.7**	**1168.8**	**515.1**
油料	**Oil-bearing Crops**	**4531.2**	**2958.3**	**13404.6**	**4881.1**	**2852.3**	**13922.2**
#花生	Peanuts	4038.8	3070.3	12400.4	4427.7	2987.6	13228.0
药材	**Drug**	**2465.9**	**852.7**	**2102.7**	**2551.9**	**753.6**	**1923.1**
蔬菜及食用菌	**Vegetables and Edible Mushrooms**	**64090.4**	**43673.0**	**2799019.5**	**66796.9**	**44443.7**	**2968700.9**
瓜类及草莓	**Melon & Strawberry**	**7659.8**	**44415.1**	**340210.7**	**8203.9**	**46076.5**	**378007.0**
#西瓜	Watermelon	6473.7	47843.8	309726.5	7340.7	48350.8	354928.9
饲料	**Forage**	**3388.0**			**4523.7**		
#牧草	Grazing	771.9			1063.9		
花卉	**Flower**	**3412.9**			**2959.7**		

10-12 林业及干鲜果品生产
FORESTRY, NUTS AND FRESH FRUIT PRODUCTION

项目		Item		2012	2011	2012年为2011年% 2012 as % of 2011
林业生产		**Forestry**				
荒山荒(沙)地造林面积	(公顷)	Afforestation Area for Barren Mountains and Barren Sand	(hectare)	35752	20796	171.9
育苗面积	(公顷)	Nursery Garden Area	(hectare)	9744	12015	81.1
#本年新育	(公顷)	New Growing This Year	(hectare)	985	1015	97.0
果类生产		**Fruit**				
干鲜果总产量	(吨)	Output of Nuts and Fresh Fruit	(ton)	842580	878066	96.0
干果	(吨)	Nuts	(ton)	46744	47385	98.6
#核桃	(吨)	Walnut	(ton)	11840	12256	96.6
板栗	(吨)	Chinese Chestnut	(ton)	29737	29347	101.3
鲜果	(吨)	Fresh Fruit	(ton)	795836	830681	95.8
#苹果	(吨)	Apple	(ton)	103017	104626	98.5
梨	(吨)	Pear	(ton)	162632	161712	100.6
葡萄	(吨)	Grape	(ton)	41316	41552	99.4
柿子	(吨)	Persimmon	(ton)	44235	46990	94.1
桃	(吨)	Peach	(ton)	373295	404280	92.3
年末实有果园面积	**(公顷)**	**Actual Orchard Area (year-end)**	**(hectare)**	**62469**	**63458**	98.4

资料来源：林业生产数据由北京市园林绿化局提供。
Source: Data of Forestry are from Beijing Municipal Bureau of Landscape and Forestry.

10-13 牲畜饲养及畜产品产量
NUMBER OF LIVESTOCK AND OUTPUT OF LIVESTOCK PRODUCTS

项目		Item		2012	2011	2012年为2011年% 2012 as % of 2011
畜禽存栏		**Amount of Livestock and Poultry on Hand**				
大牲畜	(万头)	Large Animals on Hand (year-end)	(10000 heads)	22.28	22.28	100.0
#役畜	(万头)	Draught Animals	(10000 heads)	0.40	0.47	85.1
#牛	(万头)	Cattle and Buffaloes	(10000 heads)	21.36	21.09	101.3
猪	(万头)	Pork Pigs on Hand (year-end)	(10000 heads)	187.39	179.34	104.5
羊	(万只)	Sheep on Hand (year-end)	(10000 unit)	58.07	57.77	100.5
山羊	(万只)	Goats	(10000 unit)	16.63	16.03	103.7
绵羊	(万只)	Sheep	(10000 unit)	41.43	41.73	99.3
家禽	(万只)	Livestock on Hand (year-end)	(10000 unit)	2596.35	2662.84	97.5
#产蛋鸡	(万只)	Hens	(10000 unit)	1569.60	1448.16	108.4
肉鸡	(万只)	Chickens	(10000 unit)	685.10	834.61	82.1
鸭	(万只)	Ducks	(10000 unit)	329.08	361.48	91.0
兔	(万只)	Rabbits on Hand(year-end)	(10000 unit)	4.66	4.81	96.9
畜禽出栏		**Amount of Livestock and Poultry Slaughtered**				
牛	(万头)	Beef Cattle Slaughtered in the Whole Year	(10000 heads)	11.88	11.40	104.2
猪	(万头)	Pork Pigs Slaughtered in the Whole Year	(10000 heads)	306.11	312.20	98.0
羊	(万只)	Sheep Slaughtered in the Whole Year	(10000 unit)	71.80	78.62	91.3
畜禽产品产量		**Output of Livestock and Poultry Products**				
肉类产量	(万吨)	Output of Meat	(10000 tons)	43.2	44.4	97.2
#猪肉	(万吨)	Pork	(10000 tons)	23.9	24.2	98.9
牛肉	(万吨)	Beef	(10000 tons)	2.2	2.1	103.5
羊肉	(万吨)	Mutton	(10000 tons)	1.2	1.3	93.5
牛奶产量	(万吨)	Cow Milk	(10000 tons)	65.1	64.0	101.7
禽蛋	(万吨)	Poultry Eggs	(10000 tons)	15.2	15.1	100.6
#鸡蛋	(万吨)	Eggs	(10000 tons)	15.0	14.9	100.5
蜂蜜	(吨)	Honey	(ton)	2554	3270	78.1

10-14 水产品生产
AQUATIC PRODUCTS

项　　目	Item	2012	2011	2012年为2011年% 2012 as % of 2011
渔业水域面积　（公顷）	**Area of Water Surface　(hectare)**	**20789**	**20655**	**100.6**
#淡水养殖面积　(公顷)	Freshwater Area　(hectare)	4364	4860	89.8
#水　库　(公顷)	Large Reservoirs　(hectare)		300	
池　塘　(公顷)	Puddle and Pond　(hectare)	4254	4344	97.9
水产品产量　（吨）	**Output of Freshwater Fish　(ton)**	**63842**	**61228**	**104.3**
#淡水鱼产量　(吨)	Output of Freshwater Fish　(ton)	54262	53696	101.1
#大水库　(吨)	Large Reservoirs　(ton)	2241	2613	85.8
中、小水库　(吨)	Medium and Small Reservoirs　(ton)	1581	1815	87.1
池　塘　(吨)	Puddle and Pond　(ton)	45494	44924	101.3

资料来源：北京市农业局。
Source: Beijing Agriculture Bureau.

10-15 农业观光园、民俗旅游、种业和设施农业(2005-2012年)
AGRICULTURAL SIGHTSEEING GARDENS，FOLK-CUSTOM TOURISM，BREEDING OF SEED AND FACILITY-AGRICULTURE (2005-2012)

项　目	Item	2005	2006	2007	2008
农业观光园	**Agricultural Sightseeing Garden**				
农业观光园个数　(个)	Number of Agricultural Sightseeing Gardei　(unit)	1012	1230	1302	1332
生产高峰期从业人员　(人)	Employed Persons At Production Climax　(person)	40729	52828	51392	49366
接待人次　(万人次)	Visits Received　(10000 person-time)	892.5	1210.6	1446.8	1498.2
经营总收入　(亿元)	Total Operating Income　(100 million yuan)	7.88	10.49	13.15	13.58
民俗旅游	**Folk-Custom Tourism Receiption**				
从事民俗旅游实际经营接待户　(户)	Number of actually operating families in Folk-Custom Tourism Receiption　(household)	7268	8726	10323	9151
从事民俗旅游接待的人数　(人)	Number of Persons Engaged in Folk-Custom Tourism Receiption　(person)	14070	18253	20750	19421
民俗旅游接待人次　(万人次)	Folk-Custom Tourism Receiption Visits　(10000 person-time)	758.9	982.5	1167.6	1205.6
民俗旅游总收入　(亿元)	Total Income of Folk-Custom Tourism　(100 million yuan)	3.14	3.65	4.96	5.29
种　业	**Breeding of Seed**				
种业收入　(亿元)	Income　(100 million yuan)	5.94	7.75	9.91	10.93
设施农业	**Facility-agriculture**				
设施农业实际利用占地面积　(公顷)	Area of Facility-agriculture Utilization　(hectare)	15645	17832	18022	17051
设施农业播种面积　(公顷)	Planting Area of Facility-agriculture　(hectare)			30331	33889
设施农业收入　(亿元)	Income of Facility-agriculture　(100 million yuan)	18.62	21.11	28.12	28.17

10-15 续表 continued

项 目		Item		2009	2010	2011	2012
农业观光园		**Agricultural Sightseeing Garden**					
农业观光园个数	(个)	Number of Agricultural Sightseeing Gardens	(unit)	1294	1303	1300	1283
生产高峰期从业人员	(人)	Employed Persons At Production Climax	(person)	49504	42561	46038	48906
接待人次	(万人次)	Visits Received	(10000 person-time)	1597.4	1774.9	1842.9	1939.9
经营总收入	(亿元)	Total Operating Income	(100 million yuan)	15.24	17.80	21.72	26.88
民俗旅游		**Folk-Custom Tourism Receiption**					
从事民俗旅游实际经营接待户	(户)	Number of actually operating families in Folk-Custom Tourism Receiption	(household)	8705	7979	8396	8367
从事民俗旅游接待的人数	(人)	Number of Persons Engaged in Folk-Custom Tourism Receiption	(person)	19790	16856	18232	18705
民俗旅游接待人次	(万人次)	Folk-Custom Tourism Receiption Visits	(10000 person-time)	1393.1	1553.6	1668.9	1695.8
民俗旅游总收入	(亿元)	Total Income of Folk-Custom Tourism	(100 million yuan)	6.09	7.35	8.68	9.05
种 业		**Breeding of Seed**					
种业收入	(亿元)	Income	(100 million yuan)	12.84	14.57	18.12	16.09
设施农业		**Facility-agriculture**					
设施农业实际利用占地面积	(公顷)	Area of Facility-agriculture Utilization	(hectare)	18762	18323	18616	19059
设施农业播种面积	(公顷)	Planting Area of Facility-agriculture	(hectare)	36203	36811	38006	37797
设施农业收入	(亿元)	Income of Facility-agriculture	(100 million yuan)	33.91	40.72	45.58	51.98

10-16 农业观光园
STATISTICS ON AGRICULTURAL SIGHTSEEING GARDENS

项 目		Item		2012	2011	2012年为2011年% 2012 as % of 2011
农业观光园个数	(个)	Number of Agricultural Sightseeing Gardens	(unit)	1283	1300	98.7
生产高峰期从业人员	(人)	Employed Persons At Production Climax	(person)	48906	46038	106.2
接待人次	(万人次)	Visits Received	(10000 person-time)	1939.9	1842.9	105.3
经营总收入	(万元)	Total Operating Income	(10000 yuan)	268820.9	217151.8	123.8

10-17 民俗旅游
STATISTICS ON FOLK-CUSTOM TOURISM

项　目		Item		2012	2011	2012年为2011年% 2012 as % of 2011
从事民俗旅游实际		Number of actually operating families in				
经营接待户	（户）	Folk-Custom Tourism Receiption	(household)	8367	8396	99.7
期末从业人员	（人）	Number of Engaged Persons	(person)	18705	18232	102.6
民俗旅游接待人次	（万人次）	Folk-Custom Tourism Receiption Visits	(10000 person-time)	1695.8	1668.9	101.6
民俗旅游总收入	（万元）	Total Income of Folk-Custom Tourism	(10000 yuan)	90548.4	86822.2	104.3

10-18 种业生产
STATISTICS ON BREEDING OF SEEDING

项　目		Item		产　量 Output			收　入(万元) Income (10000 yuan)		
				2012	2011	2012年为2011年% 2012 as % of 2011	2012	2011	2012年为2011年% 2012 as % of 2011
合　计		**Total**					**160947.9**	**181189.0**	**88.8**
农　业		**Farming**					**8671.6**	**15844.2**	**54.7**
#小麦种	（公斤）	Wheat Seed	(kg)	5700925	5264445	108.3	1210.9	1100.1	110.1
玉米种	（公斤）	Corn Seed	(kg)	1113903	953318	116.8	606.6	592.9	102.3
蔬菜种	（公斤）	Vegetable Seed	(kg)	200029	530834	37.7	2403.2	9002.2	26.7
林　业		**Forestry**					**8541.5**	**7492.3**	**114.0**
#树　苗	（百株）	Sapling	(100-unit)	29742.0	24440.0	121.7	8000.3	7408.3	108.0
牧　业		**Animal Husbandry**					**136286.3**	**150905.4**	**90.3**
#种猪	（头）	Boar	(Heads)	255546	260656	98.0	54657.7	59225.5	92.3
种雏禽	（万只）	Breeding Bird	(10000-unit)	3429.0	3901.1	87.9	33720.3	39870.0	84.6
种蛋	（万枚）	Breeding Egg	(10000-unit)	35725.5	41573.6	85.9	40128.0	43224.2	92.8
渔　业		**Fishery**					**7448.5**	**6947.1**	**107.2**
#种鱼苗	（万尾）	Breeding Young Fish	(10000-unit)	12180.2	17479.1	69.7	6889.2	6421.1	107.3

10-19 设施农业(2012年)
FACILITY-AGRICULTURE (2012)

项　目	Item	设施农业播种面积（公顷） Planting Area of Facility-agriculture (hectare)	设施农业产量（吨） Output of Facility-agriculture (ton)	设施农业收入（万元） Income of Facility-agriculture (10000 yuan)
合　计	**Total**	**37797**		**519824.2**
温　室	**Hothouse**	**21361**		**364106.9**
蔬菜及食用菌	Vegetables and Edible Mushrooms	18999	717392	255029.8
花　卉	Flowers	957		41264.8
#切　花	Cut Flowers	260	2804	7774.1
盆　花	Potted Flowers	660	8883	33200.3
瓜果类	Melons	949	22008	57540.6
水　果	Fruits	297	4303	5553.1
其　它	Others	159		4718.6
大　棚	**Large Shed**	**11785**		**120163.9**
蔬菜及食用菌	Vegetables and Edible Mushrooms	8582	326373	77227.0
花　卉	Flowers	215		6482.5
#切　花	Cut Flowers	36	662	809.7
盆　花	Potted Flowers	133	2606	5129.8
瓜果类	Melons	2710	126400	32137.0
水　果	Fruits	155	2128	2145.3
其　它	Other	123		2172.1
中小棚	**Medium and Small Shed**	**4651**		**35553.4**
蔬菜及食用菌	Vegetables and Edible Mushrooms	2441	79199	17761.5
花　卉	Flowers	34		550.0
#切　花	Cut Flowers	3	32	31.0
盆　花	Potted Flowers	15	244	484.0
瓜果类	Melons	2105	95052	17157.0
水　果	Fruits			
其　它	Other	72		84.9

注：切花产量的计量单位是万枝，盆花产量的计量单位是万盆。
Note: Cut flowers are measured with 10000 units, and potted flowers, 10000 pots.

10-20 乡镇企业各业基本情况(2012年)
BASIC STATISTICS ON SECTORS OF TOWN AND TOWNSHIP ENTERPRISES (2012)

项 目	Item	企业个数(个) Number of Enterprises (unit)		从业人员(人) Persons Employed (person)		总收入(万元) Total Revenue (10000 yuan)		利润总额(万元) Total Profits (10000 yuan)	
		数 量 Number	构成(%) Composition (%)	数 量 Number	构成(%) Composition (%)	数 量 Number	构成(%) Composition (%)	数 量 Number	构成(%) Composition (%)
合 计	**Total**	**154436**	**100.0**	**1292746**	**100.0**	**49466979**	**100.0**	**2686674**	**100.0**
农 业	Agriculture	2703	1.8	22623	1.7	465673	0.9	41797	1.6
工 业	Industry	21027	13.6	576532	44.6	26140632	52.8	1297956	48.3
建筑业	Construction	4007	2.6	121550	9.4	4928894	10.0	241714	9.0
交通运输业	Transportation	33487	21.7	96160	7.4	3693642	7.5	301794	11.2
批发零售业	Wholesale & Retail	42812	27.7	151190	11.7	8069301	16.3	329332	12.3
住宿及餐饮业	Accomodation and Catering	14140	9.2	80086	6.2	1255227	2.5	105261	3.9
居民服务、其它服务和娱乐业	Household Service, Other Service and Entertainment	21298	13.8	195684	15.1	2941408	5.9	271368	10.1
其 他	Others	14962	9.7	48921	3.8	1972202	4.0	97452	3.6

资料来源：北京市经济和信息化委员会。
Source: Beijing Municipal Commission of Economy and Information Technology.

10-21 农村经济收入与分配
INCOME AND DISTRIBUTION OF RURAL ECONOMY

单位：万元 (10000 yuan)

项目	Item	2012	2011	2012年为2011年% 2012 as % of 2011
营业收入	**Operation Income**	**48129713.4**	**44406685.1**	**108.4**
农业	Agriculture	1162659.8	1068397.9	108.8
#粮食	Grain	305752.2	307972.7	99.3
林业	Forestry	214391.2	184605.0	116.1
牧业	Animal Husbandry	1174299.9	1123251.6	104.5
渔业	Fishery	98683.3	96423.2	102.3
工业	Industry	14226578.0	13099244.1	108.6
建筑业	Construction	5657689.8	4980858.3	113.6
交通运输业	Transportation	2555781.1	2658477.3	96.1
商业、饮食业	Commerce and Catering	9834460.9	9639553.1	102.0
服务业	Services	9411390.7	8316499.7	113.2
其他	Other	3793778.7	3239374.9	117.1
营业成本	**Operation Cost**	**42740806.4**	**39266711.6**	**108.8**
农业	Agriculture	1133488.0	1042167.9	108.8
#粮食	Grain	305721.2	296073.5	103.3
林业	Forestry	210266.7	178220.4	118.0
牧业	Animal Husbandry	1163534.2	1111865.1	104.6
渔业	Fishery	96343.9	93773.4	102.7
工业	Industry	12512204.1	11424047.1	109.5
建筑业	Construction	5052260.9	4446454.7	113.6
交通运输业	Transportation	2477162.4	2558780.3	96.8
商业、饮食业	Commerce and Catering	8981789.8	8735753.3	102.8
服务业	Services	7757250.6	6841528.4	113.4
其他	Other	3356505.8	2834121.0	118.4
营业利润	**Operating Profits**	**1132259.4**	**1140200.1**	**99.3**
利润总额	**Total Profits**	**1623797.3**	**1504394.7**	**107.9**
税后利润	**After-tax Profits**	**1399396.5**	**1313463.7**	**106.5**
可供分配的利润	**Profit to be Divided**	**1733207.7**	**1737142.8**	**99.8**
未分配利润	**Retained Profits**	**1046237.2**	**1177889.6**	**88.8**

资料来源：北京市农村经济研究中心农村合作经济经营管理站。
Source: Beijing Rural Economy Research Center Management Station for Rural Cooperative Economy.

10-22 乡镇企业出口供货情况
GOODS SUPPLIES FOR EXPORT OF TOWN AND TOWNSHIP ENTERPRISES

单位：万元 (10000 yuan)

项目	Item	2012	2011
合计	**Total**	**1452479**	**1635673**
化工	Chemical Products	66813	75240
机械	Machinery	254339	286418
矿产	Mineral Products	13071	14720
轻工	Light Industry	218407	245954
食品	Food	159773	179924
土产畜产	Local Products	31955	35985
纺织服装	Garment	476948	537104
工艺品	Handicraft	33411	37625
其他	Others	197762	222703

资料来源：北京市经济和信息化委员会。
Source: Beijing Municipal Commission of Economy and Information Technology.

主要统计指标解释

农林牧渔业总产值 是以货币表现的农林牧渔业的全部产品总量和对农林牧渔业生产活动进行的各种支持性服务活动的价值。

年末耕地总资源 指能够种植农作物的田地。包括当年实际耕种的熟地；新开荒且已种植的地；“沿海”、“沿湖”地区已围垦利用三年以上的“海涂”、“湖田”；弃耕、休闲不满三年，随时可以复耕的地；因灾害或其他因素，虽然当年内未种植农作物但仍可复耕的地；以种植农作物为主，附带种植桑树、果树和其他林的地；年年进行耕耘种草的地；南方小于1米、北方小于2米宽的沟、渠、路、田埂。不包括：因灾害或其他因素，已不能复耕的地；弃耕、休闲满三年的地，或者虽不满三年，但已经成为荒地的土地；不进行耕耘，种植牧草已成为永久性草地的土地；专业性的桑园、茶园、果园、果木苗圃地、芦苇地、天然草场等；以混凝土等铺设的温室、玻璃室，导致栽培的植物体与地面隔绝的基地。

农作物播种面积 指实际播种或移植有农作物的面积。凡是实际种植有农作物的面积，不论种植在耕地上还是种植在非耕地上，均包括在农作物播种面积中。在播种季节基本结束后，因遭灾而重新改种和补种的农作物面积，也包括在内。

有效灌溉面积 指具有一定的水源，地块比较平整，灌溉工程或设备已经配套，在一般年景下当年能够进行正常灌溉的耕地面积。

设施农业 指以工厂化生产方式，建造人工设施，改变气候条件，提高农作物抵御自然灾害的能力，改良生物特性，使作物实现错季或反季节生产，达到农作物均衡生产的目的。

农业机械总动力 指主要用于农、林、牧、渔业的各种动力机械的动力总和。包括耕作机械、排灌机械、收获机械、农用运输机械、植物保护机械、牧业机械、渔业机械和其他农用机械[内燃机按引擎马力折成瓦（特）计算，电动机按功率折成瓦（特）计算]。不包括专门用于乡、镇、村、组办工业、基本建设、非农业运输、科学实验和教学等非农业生产方面用的动力机械与作业机械。

农村用电量 指本年度内，扣除在农村中的国有经济工业交通、基建等单位的用电量以后的农村生产和生活的全年用电总量（计量单位千瓦小时，按全年累计数统计），即包括国家电网供电，也包括农村自办电站供电量。

农用化肥施用量 指本年度内实际用于农业生产的化学肥料数量，包括氮肥、磷肥、钾肥和复合肥。施用量要求按折纯量计算数量，即各类化学肥料的实际施用数量按其含氮、含五氧化二磷、含氧化钾的比例折成百分之百计算。

折纯量＝实物量×某种化肥有效成份含量的百分比

乡镇及行政村单位常住户数 指长期（一年以上）居住在乡镇（不包括城关镇）行政管理区域内的住户，还包括居住在城关镇所辖行政村范围内的农村住户。户口不在本地而在本地居住一年及以上的住户也包括在本地农村住户内；有本地户口，但举家外出谋生一年以上的住户，无论是否保留承包耕地都不包括在本地农村住户范围内。不包括乡村地区内的国有经济的机关、团体、学校、企业、事业单位的集体户及集中连片的商品住宅小区居民户。

乡镇及行政村常住人口 指乡村地区常住居民户数中的常住人口数，即经常在家或在家居住6个月以上，而且经济和生活与本户连成一体的人口。外出从业人员在外居住时间虽然在6个月以上，但收入主要带回家中，经济与本户连为一体，仍视为家庭常住人口；在家居住，生活和本户连成一体的国家职工、退休人员也为家庭常住人口。但是现役军人、中专及以上（走读生除外）的在校学生、以及常年在外（不包括探亲、看病等）且已有稳定的职业与居住场所的外出从业人员，不应当作家庭常住人口。

乡镇及行政村从业人员 指全部乡镇及行政村人口中16岁以上实际参加生产经营活动并取得实物或货币收入的人员，既包括劳动年龄内经常参加劳动的人员，也包括超过劳动年龄（男16—60岁；女16—55岁）但经常参加劳动的人员。但不包括户口在家的在外学生、现役军人和丧失劳动能力的人，也不包括待业人员和家务劳动者。从业人员按从事主业时间最长（时间相同按收入）分为农业从业人员、工业从业人员、建筑业从业人员、交运仓储及邮电通讯业从业人员、批零贸易及餐饮业从业人员、其它从业人员。

Explanatory Notes on Main Statistical Indicators

Gross Output Value of Agriculture, Forestry, Animal Husbandry and Fishery refers to the monetary value of all products of agriculture, forestry, animal husbandry and fishery, as well as the monetary value of services in support of activities of agriculture, forestry, animal husbandry and fishery.

Year-end Total Resources of Arable Land refers to the plow land on which crops can be planted, including the cultivated land actually tilled in the year; any land which is newly opened up and has been cultivated; sea mudflat and lake field in the area off the sea shore and lake shore, that have been enclosed and utilized for more than three years; any land that has been idle for less than three years, which can be cultivated again at any time; any land which is not planted in the year due to disaster or other factors but can be cultivated again; any land mostly grown with farm plants, together with mulberry trees, fruit trees, and other forest trees; any land tilled and grown with grass every year; channels, dykes, field ridges less than 1m in southern part of China, and less than 2m in northern part of China. Excluding: any land that cannot be cultivated again due to disasters and other factors; any land that has been idle at least for three full years, or any land that has been idle for less than three years but has been waste land; any land that cannot be cultivated, and has been grown with forage grass and become permanent grass land; any land for professional mulberry gardens, tea gardens, fruit gardens, fruit tree nursery, reed, and natural meadow, etc.; any base where greenhouse and glasshouse are built with concrete which causes isolation of plants grown from the ground.

Sown Area of Crops refers to area of land actually sown or transplanted with crops regardless of being in cultivated area or non-cultivated area. Area of land re-sown due to natural disasters is also included after the planting season is over basically.

Irrigated Area refers to area of arable land that are effectively irrigated, i.e. relatively level land, where there are water sources or complete sets of irrigation facilities to irrigate under normal harvest situations.

Facility Agriculture means to build man-made facilities in a manner of factory production in order to change the climate conditions, improve the crops of capability of resisting natural disasters, improve the biological property, and achieve balanced production of crops in all seasons.

Total Power of Agricultural Machinery refers to total power of motive power machines used in agriculture, forestry, animal husbandry and fishery, including machinery for ploughing, irrigation and drainage, harvesting, agricultural transport, plant protection, animal husbandry, fishery and other agricultural machineries (For the power of internal combustion engines, it is converted from its horsepower into watts while for electric motors the output power is converted into watts). Motive power machines and operating machines specially used for industry run by township, towns, villages and teams, capital construction, non-agricultural transport, scientific experiments and teaching and other non-agricultural production, are not included.

Consumption of Chemical Fertilizers refers to the quantity of chemical fertilizers applied in agriculture in the year, including nitrogenous fertilizer, phosphate fertilizer, potash fertilizer, and compound fertilizer. The application amount of chemical fertilizers is calculated in terms of equivalent pure amount by means of converting the gross weight of the respective fertilizers into weight containing effective ingredient (e.g. nitrogen content in nitrogenous fertilizer, phosphorous pentoxide contents in phosphate fertilizer, and potassium oxide contents in potash fertilizer).

Equivalent Pure Amount = physical quantity× content (%) of effective ingredients of certain chemical fertilizer

Towns and Administrative Villages Households refer to households living in the administrative areas in towns and villages (excluding towns just outside city gates) for many years (more than one year), including those living in administrative villages under the jurisdiction of towns just outside city gate. Households with non-local household register but living locally for more than one year are also included in local rural households; households with local household register but staying away for more than one year with all family members are also included in local rural households; excluding collective households in government agencies, groups, schools, enterprises, and public institutions in state economy as well as households in concentrated commercial residential quarters in rural areas.

Towns and Administrative Villages Population refers to the population in permanent households in rural areas, namely those regularly living or living in the household for more than 6 months, and whose economy and life are a part of the household. Employed persons staying out for more than 6 months but taking most of their income to home, whose economy is a part of the household, is still regarded as permanent population of the household; employees and retired persons of the State who live in the household, and whose life is a part of the household is also permanent population of the household. But soldiers in active service, enrolled students (externs excluded) in technical secondary schools, as well as employed persons always staying away (excluding going home to visit their families and see a doctor) and having a stable job and residential place, are not regarded as permanent household population.

Number of Persons Employed in Towns and Administrative Villages refer to persons above 16 in all towns and administrative villages who actually participate in productive and operative activities and earn incomes in kind or cash, including persons within the range of labor age and regularly participating in labor, and persons beyond the range of labor age (16-60 for males, 16-55 for females) but regularly participating in labor, excluding persons waiting for employment and housework laborers. In terms of the length employment period (in terms of income in the event of same employment period), employed persons fall into employees in agricultural, industrial, transport, warehouse storage, post and telecom sectors, wholesale and retail trades, food and drink, and other sectors.

11

北京统计年鉴2013 BEIJING STATISTICAL YEARBOOK

工 业
INDUSTRY

简要说明

一、本章统计的主要内容

本章资料反映北京市工业方面的基本情况，主要包括：按登记注册类型、轻重工业、企业规模、高技术制造业、工业行业大类等分组的主要经济指标，指标包括：单位数、工业总产值、工业增加值、资产总计、负债合计、主营业务收入、主营业务成本、主营业务税金及附加、利润总额、应交增值税、总资产贡献率、资产负债率、成本费用利润率、主要工业产品产量等。

本章还包括国有控股工业企业、股份制工业企业、港澳台及外商投资工业企业、大中型工业企业的主要经济指标，按工业行业大类、轻重工业、企业规模等主要分组数据。

二、本章资料的统计范围

1984 年以前农村的村及村以下办工业归属农业，1984 年以后划归工业。

1999 年以前，工业的统计范围按隶属关系划分为乡及乡以上独立核算工业企业和非独立核算生产单位、村办工业、城镇合作工业、农村合作工业、城镇个体工业、农村个体工业六大部分（1984 年以前村办工业不在工业统计范围内）。

2000 年-2006 年，工业统计调查范围由按隶属关系划分，改变为按企业规模划分。2000 年至 2006 年，分为全部国有及年主营业务收入在 500 万元及以上非国有工业企业（简称“规模以上”）和年主营业务收入在 500 万元以下非国有工业企业和全部个体经营工业单位（简称“规模以下”）两部分。

2007 年-2010 年，分为年主营业务收入在 500 万元及以上法人工业企业（简称“规模以上”）和年主营业务收入在 500 万元以下法人工业企业和全部个体经营工业单位（简称“规模以下”）两部分。

2011 年及以后，分为年主营业务收入在 2000 万元及以上法人工业企业（简称“规模以上”）和年主营业务收入在 2000 万元以下法人工业企业和全部个体经营工业单位（简称“规模以下”）两部分。

三、数据来源和调查方法

本章工业企业统计数据来源于北京市统计局、国家统计局北京调查总队。其中，规模以上数据为全面调查，规模以下数据为抽样调查。

四、有关统计标准的变化说明

（一）关于行业划分：本章资料中工业行业分类 2002-2011 年期间执行 2002 年《国民经济行业分类标准》(GB/T 4754-2002)划分标准，2012 年开始执行 2011 年《国民经济行业分类》(GB/T 4754-2011)划分标准；

（二）关于企业标准划分：2010 年以前企业大中小型划分执行《统计上大中小型企业划分办法（暂行）》标准，自 2011 年开始，大中小微型企业划分标准执行《国家统计局关于印发统计上大中小微型企业划分办法的通知》（国统字[2011]75 号）。

五、本章中关于历史数据调整的问题

按照国家统计局统一要求和统一方法，规模以上工业总产值及增加值历史资料已根据“北京市第一次全国经济普查”的结果采用“趋势离差法”进行了修正。调整历史区间为 1993 年至 2003 年。2004 年为第一次经济普查数据，2008 年为第二次经济普查数据。

Brief Introduction

I. Main Content

Data in this chapter shows the basic situation of industry in Beijing, mainly including: main economic indicators grouped by type of registration, light and heavy industries, enterprise size, high-tech manufacturing, and industrial sectors. Indicators include: gross industrial output value, industrial added value, total assets, total liabilities, main business income, main business cost, main business tax and surtax, total profits, payable VAT, contribution rate of total assets, asset-liability ratio, cost-profit ratio, and output of main industrial products, etc.

This chapter also includes main economic indicators for state-controlled industrial enterprises, joint-stock industrial enterprises, industrial enterprises funded by Hong Kong, Macao, Taiwan and foreign companies, and data grouped by industrial sectors, light and heavy industries and enterprise size.

II . Scope of Statistics

Prior to 1984, the rural industry run by villages and cooperative organizations under village was classified into agriculture. Since 1984, it has been grouped into industry.

Before 1999, industrial statistics covered six parts, i.e. industrial enterprises keeping separate accounts and producers not keeping separate accountings at the township level and above, village-run industrial, urban cooperative industrial, rural cooperative industrial, urban private industrial and rural private industry (village-run industry was not involved in the industrial statistics before 1984).

2000-2006, the scope of industrial statistics was grouped by size instead of by registration status. From 2000 to 2006, industrial enterprises fell into two parts. One part includes all state-owned ones and non-state-owned ones with annual main business income of RMB5 million and above ("above designated size"), the other part includes non-state-owned ones with annual main business income below RMB5 million ("below designated size").

2007-2010, industrial enterprises fell into two parts. One part includes industrial enterprises as legal persons with main business income of RMB5 million and above ("above designated size"), the other part includes industrial enterprises as legal persons with main business income below RMB5 million and all privately-run industrial entities ("below designated size").

In and after2011, industrial enterprises fell into two parts. One part includes industrial enterprises as legal persons with main business income of RMB20 million and above ("above designated size"), the other part includes industrial enterprises as legal persons with main business income below RMB20 million and all privately-run industrial entities ("below designated size").

III. Source of Data and Methods of Survey

Statistical data of industrial enterprises in this chapter are sourced from Beijing Municipal Bureau of Statistics and National Bureau of Statistics Survey Office in Beijing. Data of industrial enterprises above designated size were obtained through complete survey, that below designated size were obtained through sample survey.

IV. Changes in Relevant Statistical Standard

(I) Classification of Industrial Sectors: In this chapter, classification of industrial sectors in 2002-2011 was based on the Standard for Classification of National Economic Sectors 2002 (GB/T 4754-2002). Standard for Classification of National Economic Sectors (GB/T 4754-2011) became effective in 2012;

(II) Classification of Enterprises: Before 2010, the classification of small-, medium- and large-sized enterprises complied with the Measures for Statistical Classification (Provisional) of Small-, Medium- and Large-sized Enterprises. From 2011, the classification of small-, medium- and large-sized enterprises complied with the Notification of National Bureau of Statistics on Printing and Issuing the Measures for Statistical Classification of Mini-, Small-, Medium- and Large-sized Enterprises (GTZ[2011]No.75).

V. Adjustment to Historical Data

In accordance with the uniform requirement and method of the National Bureau of Statistics, data of total output value and added value of industrial enterprises above designated size were adjusted with "trend deviation method", which was according to results from the "first national economic census in Beijing". Data during 1993-2003 were adjusted. Data from the first economic census were used for 2004. And data from the second economic census were used for 2008.

11-1 规模以上工业总产值(1984-2012年)
GROSS OUTPUT VALUE OF INDUSTRY ABOVE DESIGNATED SIZE (1984-2012)

单位：亿元 (100 million yuan)

年份 Year	合计 Total	轻工业 Light Industry	重工业 Heavy Industry	#大中型工业 Medium- and Large-sized Industry
1984	276.2	118.0	158.2	178.7
1985	324.2	135.8	188.4	213.7
1986-1990	**2448.3**	**1039.7**	**1408.6**	**1691.2**
1986	336.5	140.8	195.7	231.6
1987	387.6	160.1	227.5	272.1
1988	495.6	212.5	283.1	345.4
1989	602.7	264.1	338.6	408.3
1990	625.9	262.2	363.7	433.8
1991-1995	**5826.7**	**1936.6**	**3890.1**	**3770.8**
1991	730.2	298.1	432.1	507.4
1992	860.0	306.5	553.5	587.4
1993	1166.6	361.9	804.7	747.6
1994	1576.6	497.9	1078.7	990.7
1995	1493.3	472.2	1021.1	937.7
1996-2000	**10382.8**	**3026.2**	**7356.6**	**5765.7**
1996	1590.6	509.1	1081.5	962.3
1997	1819.7	577.8	1241.9	999.6
1998	1947.0	598.2	1348.8	1059.8
1999	2183.5	621.8	1561.7	1090.9
2000	2842.0	719.3	2122.7	1653.1
2001-2005	**23980.6**	**4911.1**	**19069.5**	**16858.4**
2001	3270.1	842.4	2427.7	2298.4
2002	3620.2	882.4	2737.8	2434.7
2003	4410.8	936.7	3474.1	3183.9
2004	5733.3	1084.7	4648.6	3699.3
2005	6946.2	1164.9	5781.3	5242.1
2006-2010	**53010.4**	**8204.7**	**44805.7**	**40357.2**
2006	8210.0	1258.2	6951.8	6237.9
2007	9648.4	1505.5	8142.9	7365.9
2008	10413.1	1674.3	8738.8	7898.9
2009	11039.1	1766.7	9272.4	8349.3
2010	13699.8	2000.0	11699.8	10505.3
2011	14513.6	2227.2	12286.4	11289.3
2012	15596.2	2402.1	13194.1	12239.6

注：1. 工业总产值按现价计算。

2. 规模以上工业：2000年以前各年为乡及乡以上工业口径；2000-2006年调整为全部国有及年主营业务收入在500万元及以上非国有工业口径；2007年-2010年调整为年主营业务收入500万元及以上的全部法人工业企业；2011年及以后调整为年主营业务收入2000万元及以上的全部法人工业企业(下同)。

3. 自2011年开始，大中型企业划分标准执行《国家统计局关于印发统计上大中小微型企业划分办法的通知》(国统字[2011]75号)(下同)。

Note: a) Gross output value is calculated at current prices.

b) Data in the column "Industry above designated size" covered enterprises at and above the township level before 2000, 2000-2006, covered all State-owned enterprises and non-State-owned enterprises with main business income of over 5 million yuan annually, 2007-2010 covered all industrial enterprises as legal persons with main business income of over 5 million yuan annually,from 2011 covered all industrial enterprises with main business income over 20 million yuan (The same below) .

c) From 2011， the classification of medium- and large-sized enterprises complies with the Notification of National Bureau of Statistics (The same below) .

11-2 规模以上工业企业主要指标(1978-2012年)
MAIN INDICATORS FOR INDUSTRIAL ENTERPRISES ABOVE DESIGNATED SIZE (1978-2012)

年 份 Year	企业单位个数(个) Number of Enterprises (unit)	从业人员平均人数(万人) Average Number of Persons Employed (10000 persons)	资产总计(万元) Total Assets (10000 yuan)	负债合计(万元) Total Liabilities (10000 yuan)	固定资产原价(万元) Original Value of Fixed Assets (10000 yuan)	主营业务收入(万元) Operating Income (10000 yuan)	利润总额(万元) Total Profits (10000 yuan)	利税总额(万元) Total Taxes & Profits (10000 yuan)
1978	4225	114.79			1305271	1098279	370551	501588
1979	3746	116.79	1417223		1371335	1186497	414344	554895
1980	3733	140.91	1547267		1495083	1987967	453147	604241
1981-1985						**12561630**	**2404751**	**3383077**
1981	3778	152.90	1650869		1622035	2054862	440753	599452
1982	3867	158.70	1748915		1750727	2183458	440000	604372
1983	4011	161.98	1846698		1886857	2408893	469364	642437
1984	4291	165.50	2003625		2045344	2728866	505249	707360
1985	4458	165.63	2338194		2337082	3175551	549385	829456
1986-1990						**24054442**	**2924045**	**4825016**
1986	5461	169.85	2720485		2627346	3385055	523961	813979
1987	5746	170.52	3147157		3008917	3935004	570760	885303
1988	5932	170.54	3607173		3412765	5032042	701574	1081370
1989	6175		4343353		3890267	5597829	638385	1087017
1990	6272	173.46	4982746		4382462	6104512	489365	957347
1991-1995						**57731437**	**4241285**	**8051832**
1991	6344	172.39	5672894		5052285	7271529	583381	1106009
1992	6205	175.48	6409037		5754181	8526860	748098	1347058
1993	10320	167.90	15209851		9986886	12822058	1095165	1811556
1994	10889	179.50	19692285		9648050	13207344	961715	1857476
1995	10712	176.16	25826309	15287699	13900296	15903646	852926	1929733
1996-2000						**103617473**	**3188809**	**8655552**
1996	16905	166.63	28755517	17220941	16319878	15801389	330539	1225314
1997	19387	157.52	34083006	20496564	18503218	17070867	405129	1405499
1998	18089	167.11	40129028	24839166	22213387	20345380	484460	1617338
1999	19682	161.10	42540707	25863159	23121446	22186280	697807	1846310
2000	16027	145.60	46127325	26763977	25316408	28213557	1270874	2561091
2001-2005						**233471075**	**13486920**	**23453788**
2001	4356	108.02	44482243	24595592	25036546	30068965	1369794	2795203
2002	4551	107.56	47429487	25278299	26554117	31827790	1655153	3219863
2003	4019	100.81	51779832	27511740	27559571	38856527	2352909	4189859
2004	6872	113.60	120495094	41430793	39221838	59926564	3974076	6417537
2005	6301	117.06	128298350	47067350	44340413	72791229	4134988	6831326
2006-2010						**576103251**	**35550064**	**57599572**
2006	6400	117.36	142444009	55423362	50306165	89141630	5311453	8479249
2007	6398	119.25	162155043	65083476	58148433	104401683	6956067	10552194
2008	7206	123.38	168024206	80850104	65745860	112758173	5569968	9379138
2009	6891	120.41	195407033	98746128	70836396	121730618	7429216	12699472
2010	6885	124.15	227505774	115480740	79360648	148071147	10283360	16489519
2011	3740	117.87	253217462	126486073	86208174	157533565	11294991	18061726
2012	3692	120.15	286131557	148372202	102771932	169051357	12678868	20104385

注：规模以上指:2000年以前统计范围为独立核算工业企业；2000-2006年为全部国有及年主营业务收入500万元及以上非国有企业；2007年-2010年调整为年主营业务收入500万元及以上的全部法人工业企业；2011年及以后调整为年主营业务收入2000万元及以上的全部法人工业企业。

Note: Statistics in this form covered industrial enterprises with independent accounting system before 2000,2000-2006, covered all State-owned enterprises and non-State-owned enterprises with main business income of and over 5 million yuan annually, 2007-2010 covered all industrial enterprises as legal persons with main business income of and over 5 million yuan annually, from 2011, covered all industrial enterprises with main business income over 20 million yuan .

11-3 规模以上工业增加值(1993-2012年)

单位：亿元

年份 Year	增加值 Added Value of Industry	轻工业 Light Industry	重工业 Heavy Industry	#计算机、通信和其他电子设备制造业 Manufacture of computer, communication Equipment and Other Electronic Equipment	#汽车制造业 Manufacture of motor vehicles	#电力、热力生产和供应业 Production and Supply of Electric Power and Heat Power	#黑色金属冶炼和压延加工业 Smelting and Pressing of Ferrous Metals
1993	304.1	98.3	205.8	22.6	28.4	4.6	54.3
1994	374.6	138.0	236.6	30.9	29.7	9.5	56.4
1995	473.1	112.3	360.8	46.7	44.4	33.0	94.9
1996-2000	**3058.8**	**981.7**	**2077.1**	**622.0**	**180.7**	**170.4**	**264.5**
1996	500.2	168.8	331.4	66.6	38.1	-12.1	75.6
1997	558.0	170.1	387.9	75.7	58.0	45.8	62.2
1998	588.2	197.2	391.0	133.8	30.0	41.5	22.4
1999	636.5	200.6	435.9	154.5	25.6	45.4	35.4
2000	776.0	245.0	531.0	191.4	29.0	49.8	68.9
2001-2005	**6153.4**	**1549.4**	**4604.0**	**1078.7**	**505.4**	**564.2**	**696.3**
2001	866.3	265.2	601.0	203.6	39.0	52.4	87.4
2002	960.7	306.6	654.1	177.8	54.8	66.6	71.2
2003	1174.7	304.8	869.9	228.3	126.0	78.3	98.2
2004	1524.7	332.6	1192.1	197.5	144.2	174.4	211.3
2005	1627.0	340.2	1286.8	271.5	141.4	192.5	228.2
2006-2010	**11071.1**	**2366.2**	**8704.9**	**1423.7**	**1329.5**	**1705.0**	**687.9**
2006	1840.2	370.1	1470.1	329.7	155.1	254.6	240.0
2007	2159.4	427.6	1731.9	363.6	194.9	355.2	235.8
2008	2037.6	482.3	1555.3	289.4	211.1	358.4	110.9
2009	2282.2	529.4	1752.8	201.2	310.6	327.3	71.9
2010	2751.7	556.8	2194.8	239.8	457.8	409.5	29.3
2011	2899.1	619.2	2279.9	204.5	562.1	448.8	1.6
2012	3033.3	681.3	2352.0	243.6	512.6	536.0	7.2

注：1. 本表增加值均按生产法计算，2004年以前数据为根据全国第一次经济普查数据调整后的数据。
2. 2012年开始行业划分执行2011年国民经济行业分类标准（GB/T 4754-2011）；表中2012年前，汽车制造业为原“交通运输设备制造业”数据，计算机、通信和其它电子设备制造业为原“通信设备、计算机及其他电子设备制造业”的数据。

ADDED VALUE OF INDUSTRY ABOVE DESIGNATED SIZE (1993-2012)

(100 million yuan)

#化学原料和化学制品制造业 Manufacture of Raw Chemical Materials and Chemical Products	#通用设备制造业 Manufacture of General Purpose Machinery	#专用设备制造业 Manufacture of Special Purpose Machinery	#电气机械和器材制造业 Manufacture of Electrical Machinery and Equipment	#仪器仪表制造业 Manufacture of measuring and Machinery instrument and meter	#医药制造业 Manufacture of Medicines	#非金属矿物制品业 Manufacture of Non-Metallic Mineral Products	#石油加工、炼焦和核燃料加工业 Processing of Petroleum, Coking, Processing of Nuclear Fuel
15.5	13.0	10.0	10.1	3.2	5.5	14.8	12.5
19.7	15.9	26.4	11.6	4.5	5.3	21.2	14.2
28.9	17.2	12.1	9.8	9.0	7.5	17.7	45.9
136.2	**73.1**	**114.5**	**99.5**	**52.6**	**90.3**	**139.4**	**194.5**
26.0	18.1	16.9	15.4	10.6	11.8	28.4	37.9
21.4	13.2	19.3	17.3	7.5	15.6	25.7	42.3
25.3	17.5	22.9	21.0	10.9	12.6	30.9	31.4
24.0	8.2	22.9	19.0	11.1	22.7	19.6	42.3
39.5	16.1	32.5	26.8	12.4	27.6	34.8	40.6
381.2	**200.8**	**263.7**	**257.8**	**142.2**	**225.4**	**230.1**	**215.6**
44.1	25.7	29.2	36.5	17.0	31.0	34.4	35.8
55.3	25.5	56.3	38.7	19.0	47.2	47.2	53.9
76.3	36.6	49.8	54.9	21.6	53.2	48.5	29.6
141.8	56.5	67.7	65.1	38.3	44.7	52.0	19.7
63.7	56.5	60.7	62.6	46.4	49.3	48.0	76.6
331.2	**495.2**	**526.7**	**497.0**	**313.6**	**543.0**	**333.5**	**461.6**
56.9	72.6	86.6	57.1	57.2	57.0	53.5	49.6
72.6	84.7	84.7	85.8	70.6	81.6	52.7	56.9
60.5	99.1	111.9	92.9	58.7	115.3	55.2	-2.3
57.1	97.4	112.3	126.4	61.0	135.8	85.8	172.5
84.1	141.4	131.2	134.8	66.1	153.3	86.3	184.9
77.7	153.1	139.8	137.1	63.6	184.2	80.7	122.8
56.1	130.2	130.4	124.8	59.6	222.2	79.5	126.2

Note: a) Added value in this table is calculated with production method. Figures before 2004 are adjusted according to the national first economic cens

b) The Standard on Classification of Sectors in National Economy 2011 (GB/T 4754-2011) became effective in 2012; in this table, figures of "manufacture of motor vehicles" in 2012 were figures of the former "manufacture of transport equipment", and figures of "manufacture of computer, communication equipment and other electronic equipment" were figures of the former "manufacture of communication equipment, computer and other electronic equipment".

11-4 规模以上工业产品产量(1978-2012年) OUTPUT OF INDUSTRIAL PRODUCTS ABOVE DESIGNATED SIZE (1978-2012)

年份 Year	布(万米) Cloth (10000 m)	机制纸及纸板(万吨) Machine-made Paper and Paperboard (10000 tons)	饮料酒(万千升) Beverage (10000 kl)	乳制品(万吨) Dairy Products (10000 tons)	家用电冰箱(万台) Household Refrigerators (10000 units)	照相机(万台) Camera (10000 units)	家具(万件) Furniture (10000 units)	原煤(万吨) Raw Coal (10000 tons)	原油加工量(万吨) Pressing of Crude Oil (10000 tons)	乙稀(万吨) Ethylene (10000 tons)	发电量(万千瓦时) Electricity (10000 kwh)
1978	25436	12.1	8.4			0.5	137.8	818.7			990750
1979	27297	13.9	9.9		2.0	0.7	171.3	711.1			1042870
1980	28940	14.0	11.6		2.6	1.0	200.2	791.0	591.1		1065060
1981-1985	**142080**	**86.9**	**87.3**	**2.0**	**41.6**	**25.7**	**1348.4**	**4269.1**	**2811.3**	**132.3**	**5101356**
1981	28635	14.5	13.4		3.1	4.2	217.7	788.7	533.5	24.7	993071
1982	29758	15.8	14.9	0.2	4.5	0.9	243.5	811.3	533.5	25.6	1003446
1983	30068	17.1	17.4	0.3	6.4	2.8	254.2	840.5	563.8	27.3	1028826
1984	27621	18.9	20.3	0.6	10.3	5.3	297.9	884.3	589.4	26.9	1038842
1985	25998	20.6	21.3	0.9	17.3	12.5	335.1	944.3	591.1	27.8	1037171
1986-1990	**153032**	**120.5**	**131.4**	**4.7**	**96.4**	**74.6**	**2096.6**	**4745.3**	**3210.5**	**141.8**	**5656282**
1986	27503	21.9	21.5	0.7	18.1	15.9	303.8	917.2	619.0	25.3	1043208
1987	29738	24.1	22.7	0.8	19.4	16.5	283.0	899.8	640.2	27.0	1057493
1988	32262	23.3	23.9	1.0	23.6	15.8	347.1	906.0	645.0	30.3	1110758
1989	32271	25.8	28.7	1.0	24.7	13.5	572.1	1016.8	651.9	29.1	1191269
1990	31258	25.4	34.6	1.2	10.7	12.9	590.6	1005.5	654.4	30.1	1253554
1991-1995	**133994**	**116.5**	**347.3**	**5.9**	**27.0**	**450.8**	**3261**	**4851.0**	**3269.9**	**172.2**	**6772732**
1991	31497	27.2	43.8	1.3	7.1	5.4	602.0	996.5	653.4	31.1	1318000
1992	29717	22.6	56.6	1.2	9.1	4.2	570.0	1015.2	662.5	32.8	1423000
1993	26816	19.1	72.6	1.6	4.2	39.3	729.0	835.4	664.0	27.2	1410900
1994	21440	21.0	83.1	0.3	6.6	158.8	605.0	1008.5	642.0	28.1	1298718
1995	24524	26.6	91.2	1.5		243.1	755.0	995.4	648.0	53.0	1322114
1996-2000	**96005**	**70.0**	**436.6**	**7.3**	**15.9**	**706.5**	**1986.8**	**4360.0**	**3336.5**	**306.0**	**7330814**
1996	22585	15.3	102.2	1.2	6.3	234.3	510.6	1013.7	633.6	57.5	1415555
1997	25185	18.1	...	1.7	...	157.7	469.4	1011.7	657.0	58.0	1464302
1998	21299	13.1		0.9	0.3	177.7	348.5	989.5	602.3	57.0	1566621
1999	14753	13.0	148.8	1.4	5.8	81.6	386.2	792.1	701.9	68.0	1431772
2000	12183	10.6	185.6	2.1	3.6	55.2	272.1	553.0	741.7	65.5	1452564
2001-2005	**38411**	**59.5**	**700.9**	**119.7**	**189.7**	**685.0**	**2036.9**	**4359.5**	**3624.5**	**430.7**	**8369923**
2001	11353	8.8	135.8	3.7	5.9	61.3	370.6	690.2	647.9	54.3	1326588
2002	10314	6.2	138.7	1.4	16.2	220.7	368.3	880.9	695.2	90.4	1419754
2003	8393	7.9	132.8	1.3	22.8	238.3	323.8	822.6	701.1	88.8	1451197
2004	4081	19.6	148.0	56.4	63.1	116.8	567.7	1067.9	783.4	98.2	2038933
2005	4270	17.0	145.6	56.9	81.7	47.9	406.5	897.9	796.9	99.0	2133451
2006-2010	**4508**	**64.0**	**906.9**	**270.8**	**447.0**	**189.1**	**3765.4**	**2971.5**	**5143.2**	**455.6**	**11960020**
2006	930	14.0	170.8	63.5	74.1	49.2	893.4	629.2	828.9	99.1	2136918
2007	536	10.4	189.1	57.9	73.1	34.7	638.8	633.3	915.0	90.9	2278658
2008	1583	14.9	180.0	44.9	79.0	49.0	690.9	567.7	1114.6	85.4	2431255
2009	965	14.1	181.1	52.2	128.7	27.1	719.4	641.3	1161.3	84.1	2424839
2010	495	10.6	185.8	52.3	92.1	29.2	822.8	500.0	1123.4	96.2	2688350
2011	339	10.0	187.0	58.6	73.5	26.6	750.2	500.1	1103.1	89.6	2628331
2012	351	11.3	191.7	56.6	80.4	18.2	720.1	493.1	1075.0	84.0	2908214

11-4 续表 continued

年 份 Year	粗 钢 (万吨) Crude Steel (10000 tons)	钢 材 (万吨) Rolled-steel (10000 tons)	水 泥 (万吨) Cement (10000 tons)	交流电动机 (万千瓦) Alternator (10000 kw)	汽 车 (万辆) Motor Vehicle (10000 units)	#轿 车 Saloon Car	移动通信手持机 (万台) Mobile telephone (10000 units)	微型计算机设备 (万台) Micro-computer (10000 units)	数控金属切削机床 (台) Digitally-controlled Metal Cutting Lathe (unit)	显示器 (万台) Display (10000 units)	集成电路 (亿块) IC (100 million units)
1978	191.0	116.8	191.5	152.5	1.8						
1979	196.5	137.5	196.9	179.7	2.4						
1980	200.9	152.1	217.4	142.7	2.8						
1981-1985	**1114.2**	**907.9**	**1355.7**	**713.0**	**17.2**			**2.0**			
1981	190.3	149.5	225.7	104.0	2.7						
1982	200.4	159.4	249.1	123.3	2.8						
1983	214.1	177.9	270.8	148.3	3.1			0.3			
1984	241.7	200.1	291.6	165.4	3.6			1.2			
1985	267.7	221.0	318.5	172.0	5.0			0.5			
1986-1990	**1837.8**	**1556.7**	**1649.3**	**889.7**	**39.5**			**6.9**			
1986	303.6	255.5	310.5	178.4	5.8			0.5			
1987	335.5	283.4	319.6	196.4	7.4			0.9			
1988	369.0	314.9	334.3	199.5	9.0			3.0			
1989	386.0	327.9	345.9	163.8	8.5			1.3			
1990	443.7	375.0	339.0	151.6	8.8			1.2			
1991-1995	**3411.0**	**2613.9**	**2364.7**	**824.3**	**70.8**			**32.3**			
1991	499.7	402.9	377.6	156.7	11.0			1.7			
1992	575.0	438.3	403.0	174.9	13.8			3.0			
1993	702.7	525.3	477.9	162.3	13.4			4.1			
1994	828.7	617.6	531.7	165.0	14.7			4.3			
1995	804.9	629.8	574.2	165.4	17.9			19.2			
1996-2000	**3937.5**	**3343.3**	**3758.9**	**753.3**	**57.7**			**686.6**	**2238**		**5.4**
1996	794.7	654.3	666.0	151.9	13.4			28.1	326		0.5
1997	801.7	652.4	700.9	148.7	11.0			59.8	433		0.6
1998	803.2	676.1	762.0	149.7	8.5			160.9	430		0.6
1999	734.5	663.8	803.0	142.0	12.3	1.0		180.0	481		1.3
2000	803.4	696.7	827.0	161.0	12.5	0.5	1549.6	257.8	568		2.4
2001-2005	**4113.3**	**4096.9**	**4963.3**	**1169.8**	**179.6**	**45.7**	**21081.2**	**2407.0**	**5783**		**33.0**
2001	824.9	727.3	809.0	175.1	14.3	0.5	2163.4	339.7	1004		2.1
2002	816.9	750.0	884.0	199.3	18.1	0.7	2280.1	415.7	912		2.5
2003	816.4	785.0	882.0	253.1	34.7	7.3	3334.5	469.3	1188		4.7
2004	827.5	868.3	1204.5	279.4	53.9	15.0	4172.1	532.7	1024		11.1
2005	827.6	966.3	1183.8	262.9	58.6	22.2	9131.1	649.6	1655		12.6
2006-2010	**2988.1**	**4267.1**	**5443.8**	**1160.6**	**492.9**	**191.6**	**106256.6**	**4052.3**	**23256**	**3205.7**	**90.2**
2006	818.1	1016.3	1269.4	269.0	68.3	27.0	14068.0	736.1	1875	680.7	11.8
2007	810.8	1030.4	1167.3	281.9	70.7	20.3	22719.9	843.3	2382	513.6	15.7
2008	466.8	656.8	880.8	259.7	76.6	28.3	20725.5	691.7	3108	478.1	19.1
2009	464.9	769.6	1077.4	159.0	127.1	53.8	21355.3	842.7	6125	655.6	18.3
2010	427.5	794.0	1049.0	191.1	150.3	62.2	27388.0	938.6	9766	877.8	25.3
2011	2.9	287.0	911.5	146.0	150.5	67.1	25962.3	1083.7	12537	851.4	32.0
2012	2.6	253.8	874.5	117.1	167.0	78.5	19949.3	1074.5	18887	796.9	31.9

11-5 规模以上工业企业主要经济指标(2012年)

单位: 万元

项目	Item	企业单位个数(个) Number of Enterprises (unit)	#亏损企业 Loss-Suffering Enterprises	工业总产值(当年价格) Gross Output Value of Industry (at current prices)	工业增加值 Added Value of Industry	工业销售产值(当年价格) Sales Value of Industry (at current price)	#出口交货值 Delivery Value of Exports
合　计	**Total**	**3692**	**623**	**155962123**	**30333223**	**154466492**	**15165151**
在合计中:	**Of the Total:**						
中央企业	Central Enterprises	242	29	53748291	10197715	53681057	453768
地方企业	Local Enterprises	3450	594	102213833	20135507	100785435	14711383
在合计中:	**Of the Total:**						
内资企业	Domestic Funded Enterprises	2767	418	97361379	18498001	96478273	2950714
国有企业	State-Owned Enterprises	108	23	19003282	4586815	18962410	40388
集体企业	Collective Owned Enterprises	63	9	383180	106882	375687	11896
股份合作企业	Cooperative Enterprises	77	18	469620	108984	465076	31897
联营企业	Joint Owned Enterprises	3	***	***	***	***	***
有限责任公司	Limited-Liability Corporations	1261	219	46539541	7463587	45988371	1213324
股份有限公司	Share Holding Corporations Ltd.	212	26	22783953	4551032	22776552	1198594
私营企业	Private Enterprises	1043	123	8168287	1676472	7897024	450679
其他企业	Other						
港澳台商投资企业	Enterprises with Funds from Hongkong, Macao and Taiwan	240	53	11232295	1827176	10899577	1584272
港澳台合资经营	Joint Venture	130	26	3680808	969095	3591906	356441
港澳台合作经营	Cooperative	9	3	53648	18357	53380	
港澳台商独资企业	Hongkong, Macao and Taiwan Enterprises	92	22	6441392	715626	6221494	1150221
港澳台商投资股份有限公司	Hongkong, Macao and Taiwan Funded Share Holding Corporations	9	2	1056446	124098	1032796	77610
外商投资企业	Foreign Funded Enterprises	685	152	47368450	10008046	47088643	10630164
中外合资经营	Joint Venture	276	48	28564936	6229668	28443179	7248831
中外合作经营	Cooperative	14	3	219132	84450	224581	61339
外资(独资)企业	Foreign Enterprises	379	98	17752991	3380873	17568077	3251939
外商投资股份有限公司	Foreign Funded Share Holding Corporations	16	3	831391	313054	852807	68056
在合计中:	**Of the Total:**						
#农村企业	Rural Enterprises	97	17	888849	193168	868785	45535
在合计中:	**Of the Total:**						
#国有控股	State-holding Enterprises	790	154	90858999	17721617	90695706	2361982
集体控股	Collective-holding Enterprises	159	24	2852968	611346	2698746	170301
私人控股	Private-holding Enterprises	1960	262	20236517	4604162	19583112	1036045
港澳台控股	HK, Macao, Taiwan-holding Enterprises	178	45	8915281	1310858	8657403	1331853
外商控股	Foreign Investor-holding Enterprises	587	136	32879770	6026540	32601237	10254713
在合计中:	**Of the Total:**						
轻工业	Light Industry	1264	230	24021367	6813352	23162532	1939542
重工业	Heavy Industry	2428	393	131940756	23519871	131303960	13225609
在合计中:	**Of the Total:**						
#大中型企业	Medium-and Large-sized Industry	776	123	122395688	24996215	121322539	13356845

注: 1. 工业增加值按生产法计算。
　　2. 应交税金合计包括应交增值税、应交所得税、营业税金及附加和管理费用中的税金。

MAIN ECONOMIC INDICATORS OF INDUSTRIAL ABOVE DESIGNATED SIZE (2012)

(10000 yuan)

从业人员平均人数（人） Average Number of Persons Employed (person)	资产负债 Assets and Liabilities: 资产总计 Total Assets	流动资产合计 Total Current Assets	#存货 Inventories	#产成品 Stock Inventory of Finished Products	#应收账款 Accounts Receivable (Net)	固定资产合计 Total Fixed Assets	固定资产原价 Total Original Value of Fixed Assets
1201482	**286131557**	**115547666**	**21043667**	**6354841**	**29731328**	**59455870**	**102771932**
220807	136255748	32852330	4820161	1064472	6982965	29442756	53634707
980675	149875809	82695337	16223505	5290370	22748363	30013114	49137225
804243	230302815	79478499	13326525	4157538	19090450	48216944	80326557
65782	104136962	18270042	1190673	179036	2891309	20938933	35961739
10093	424298	301204	95947	51477	68617	90159	160322
11467	557103	404048	132657	64220	132718	116985	175198
397	***	***	***	***	***	***	***
384474	75363708	34013277	6286194	1980612	9606504	20897585	32373806
195236	40375569	19950791	3866360	1236414	4212147	4733014	9528903
136794	9423684	6523147	1750885	643919	2171681	1435956	2117789
98216	13986355	10194350	2305916	564468	3086833	1897468	3650838
46965	3893283	2202662	501249	192198	774645	1200529	2385242
1163	182679	158790	15020	6528	16878	14826	28099
40126	5319968	4128407	778369	247650	940301	582096	1045435
9962	4590425	3704491	1011278	118091	1355009	100018	192062
299023	41842386	25874818	5411226	1632836	7554045	9341458	18794538
135113	21757419	13945438	2848960	806991	3577809	4077038	7885596
6655	316159	235434	62061	8821	75307	60230	141453
145975	17645885	10675359	2367683	785441	3644278	4935398	10245308
11280	2122922	1018587	132521	31583	256652	268793	522180
19085	1001007	719651	212098	100920	262665	209998	364242
530917	215983076	67432219	10448261	2865611	14063003	47518069	80677201
33524	3620768	2677458	651661	241469	1003623	455493	779313
316010	29847593	20849045	4599078	1606330	6737110	3791252	5569049
73450	8318970	6086261	1190535	356290	1565441	1158632	1985363
244431	27888975	18132855	4073463	1269661	6243703	6482136	13671303
380758	31759574	19397967	4900552	2186624	3826510	6388182	12982700
820724	254371982	96149700	16143115	4168218	25904818	53067689	89789232
871473	246357552	89372597	14774724	3999080	21370188	53232691	92727661

Note: a) Added Value of Industry is calculated with production method.
b) Total Tax mainly includes payable VAT,payable income tax, business tax and surtax, and tax in management expenses.

11-5 续表

单位：万元

项目	Item	资产负债 Assets and Liabilities				
		负债合计 Total Liabilities	#流动负债合计 Total Current Liabilities	#应付账款 Accounts Receivable	所有者权益合计 Total Owner's Equity	#实收资本 Paid-up Capital
合　计	**Total**	**148372202**	**92098814**	**31635464**	**137746559**	**69216227**
在合计中：	**Of the Total:**					
中央企业	Central Enterprises	69579315	32850390	8559529	66676432	34250293
地方企业	Local Enterprises	78792887	59248424	23075935	71070127	34965934
在合计中：	**Of the Total:**					
内资企业	Domestic Funded Enterprises	117679930	65035477	19025671	112614257	55290314
国有企业	State-Owned Enterprises	51108410	17270226	3451994	53028408	21310232
集体企业	Collective Owned Enterprises	259612	230804	92018	164684	45971
股份合作企业	Cooperative Enterprises	401395	358517	138495	155676	80799
联营企业	Joint Owned Enterprises	***	***	***	***	***
有限责任公司	Limited-Liability Corporations	42614484	28074514	9598913	32745670	24786018
股份有限公司	Share Holding Corporations Ltd.	17991280	14152284	3805056	22383469	7013633
私营企业	Private Enterprises	5293826	4942248	1937463	4125782	2051384
其他企业	Other					
港澳台商投资企业	Enterprises with Funds from Hongkong, Macao and Taiwan	8334086	7513833	3373949	5648523	2797087
港澳台合资经营	Joint Venture	1999855	1782321	529479	1890118	1106304
港澳台合作经营	Cooperative	21808	19412	7434	160872	44779
港澳台商独资企业	Hongkong, Macao and Taiwan Enterprises	3647600	3528265	1853068	1671942	935631
港澳台商投资股份有限公司	Hongkong, Macao and Taiwan Funded Share Holding Corporations	2664823	2183836	983967	1925591	710373
外商投资企业	Foreign Funded Enterprises	22358186	19549504	9235844	19483779	11128827
中外合资经营	Joint Venture	12278914	11029953	5171765	9478094	5569602
中外合作经营	Cooperative	188206	173258	78396	127953	151408
外资(独资)企业	Foreign Enterprises	9419283	7975204	3837982	8226593	4694405
外商投资股份有限公司	Foreign Funded Share Holding Corporations	471784	371089	147701	1651139	713411
在合计中：	**Of the Total:**					
#农村企业	Rural Enterprises	643822	563657	225949	357184	172479
在合计中：	**Of the Total:**					
#国有控股	State-holding Enterprises	110611809	57792388	16650535	105368509	54059938
集体控股	Collective-holding Enterprises	2105643	1922572	823784	1515123	580706
私人控股	Private-holding Enterprises	15353632	14041343	5070434	14487096	5763194
港澳台控股	HK,Macao,Taiwan-holding Enterprises	5229663	4967565	2381530	3087776	1637754
外商控股	Foreign Investor-holding Enterprises	14890379	13199006	6649399	12998584	7069532
在合计中：	**Of the Total:**					
轻工业	Light Industry	16360084	14147817	4214888	15394953	7986660
重工业	Heavy Industry	132012118	77950997	27420576	122351606	61229567
在合计中：	**Of the Total:**					
#大中型企业	Medium-and Large-sized Industry	126860264	72936260	24267512	119494297	58932707

11-5 continued

(10000 yuan)

损益 Profits and Loss								应交			
营业收入 Business Income	#主营业务收入 Main Business Income	营业成本 Business Cost	#主营业务成本 Main Business Cost	销售费用 Sales Expenses	管理费用 Management Expenses	财务费用 Financial Expenses	利润总额 Total Profits	税金合计 Total Tax	#营业税金及附加 Business Tax and Surtax	#主营业务税金及附加 Main Business Tax and Surtax	#应交增值税 Value Added Tax Payable
172770950	**169051357**	**145958224**	**143074099**	**7558018**	**7682260**	**1974809**	**12678868**	**9628722**	**2665122**	**2635845**	**4557614**
56749105	55729379	51167484	50295503	417585	1426474	1201140	4272484	3206606	1279329	1269798	1217696
116021845	113321977	94790740	92778596	7140433	6255787	773669	8406384	6422116	1385793	1366047	3339918
107468039	105091720	93275247	91408570	2872468	4937282	1693726	8229470	5603282	1686889	1663832	2611501
19483572	19282320	16678535	16535390	154612	369467	921700	3542171	1554731	438133	431429	640570
387715	378288	327247	320999	12493	32702	199	19480	27453	4525	4280	18614
514664	510716	426725	423948	31630	38569	4446	20007	24948	3374	3374	16426
***	***	***	***	***	***	***	***	***	***	***	***
53032472	51855516	48391667	47452118	1010316	2254695	500686	2134589	1541137	193660	181626	931242
25547668	24835066	20650301	20110454	1160595	1547128	208945	2011674	2075355	1012016	1008627	754263
8488561	8216620	6791449	6556349	502405	692924	57698	499790	378469	35081	34405	249615
14899598	14551195	12336570	12089710	1331827	631191	85186	595120	569277	50558	50316	381362
3968400	3848072	3140987	3042537	235632	214692	47478	325515	238738	22905	22816	145571
70809	69411	53300	52337	6476	8730	115	2115	5396	429	429	3614
9519256	9433007	7984523	7959130	1018845	319195	-583	215245	277235	24074	23975	196701
1341134	1200706	1157760	1035706	70875	88574	38175	52245	47907	3150	3096	35477
50403313	49408442	40346407	39575818	3353723	2113788	195897	3854278	3456163	927675	921697	1564751
29441940	29152406	23720378	23534945	1363857	1047895	92412	2553271	2378405	839790	839619	911396
368560	361114	305142	298193	38427	15348	-4239	9914	12031	1022	1022	8059
19646894	19040242	15670675	15176838	1877710	972769	99799	1110219	984264	80869	75245	596329
945919	854681	650212	565842	73730	77775	7925	180875	81463	5995	5812	48967
915531	892921	773497	755453	33372	60169	6968	61468	51740	4180	4083	32604
99800314	97753049	87437871	85840775	2129505	3524177	1675055	7839276	6166533	2361872	2341140	2469420
2899163	2859151	2375801	2352698	142494	228885	12733	172564	148542	19322	18284	90592
21659175	21071274	16393775	15907435	1476493	1861808	153570	1950371	1167583	111726	110253	726512
12094775	11940045	10036868	9957769	1171211	482969	24585	390069	415844	38642	38533	281714
35904120	35025580	29379240	28686045	2613513	1563611	107834	2292033	1713888	132217	126466	980518
27113348	26339336	18890455	18340291	3729737	2003754	216027	2104455	2276962	494727	488090	1303452
145657602	142712020	127067769	124733808	3828281	5678506	1758782	10574414	7351760	2170395	2147755	3254163
136109201	133164274	114956261	112616074	6086465	5409172	1760951	10594600	8135963	2498539	2473020	3665135

11-6 规模以上工业企业主要经济指标(按行业分)(2012年)

单位: 万元

项目	Item	企业单位个数(个) Number of Enterprises (unit)	#亏损企业 Loss-Suffering Enterprises	工业总产值(当年价格) Gross Output Value of Industry (at current prices)	工业增加值 Added Value of Industry
合 计	**Total**	**3692**	**623**	**155962123**	**30333223**
煤炭开采和洗选业	Mining and Washing of Coal	6	1	8114922	649859
石油和天然气开采业	Extraction of Petroleum and Natural Gas	1		***	***
黑色金属矿采选业	Mining of Ferrous Metal Ores	7		1725739	452004
非金属矿采选业	Mining and Processing of Nonmetal Ores	3		***	***
开采辅助活动	Mining Support Service Activities	5		2422379	1259728
农副食品加工业	Processing of Food from Agricultural Products	135	30	3496368	347272
食品制造业	Manufacture of Foods	122	26	2450772	418458
酒、饮料和精制茶制造业	Manufacture of Wines,Beverage and Refined Tea	42	11	2128080	618553
烟草制品业	Manufacture of Cigarettes and Tobacco	1		***	***
纺织业	Manufacture of Textile	35	5	373862	45232
纺织服装、服饰业	Manufacture of Textile Wearing Apparel and Ornament	170	35	1545488	562330
皮革、毛皮、羽毛及其制品和制鞋业	Manufacture of Leather, Fur, Feather and its Products	20	2	118160	18974
木材加工和木、竹、藤、棕、草制品业	Processing of Timbers, Manufacture of Wood, Bamboo, Rattan, Palm, and Straw Products	21	3	116970	18609
家具制造业	Manufacture of Furniture	66	10	692334	168407
造纸和纸制品业	Manufacture of Paper and Paper Products	45	7	628095	190459
印刷和记录媒介复制业	Printing,Reproduction of Recording Media	125	27	1203673	499687
文教、工美、体育和娱乐用品制造业	Manufacture of Articles for Culture,Education, Artwork, Sport and Entertainment Activity	36	6	802247	119849
石油加工、炼焦和核燃料加工业	Processing of Petroleum ,Coking, Processing of Mucleus Fuel	24	1	8863394	1261781
化学原料和化学制品制造业	Manufacture of Chemical Raw Material and Chemical Products	220	31	3458832	561243
医药制造业	Manufacture of Medicines	175	22	5433353	2221856
化学纤维制造业	Manufacture of Chemical Fibres	3		***	***
橡胶和塑料制品业	Manufacture of Rubber and Plastics Products	126	23	1100145	223709
非金属矿物制品业	Manufacture of Non-metallic Mineral Products	266	41	4611240	794990
黑色金属冶炼和压延加工业	Manufacture and Processing of Ferrous Metals	31	8	1621909	72499
有色金属冶炼和压延加工业	Manufacture and Processing of Non-ferrous Metals	43	10	866905	158045
金属制品业	Manufacture of Fabricated Metal Products	238	42	2991437	617907
通用设备制造业	Manufacture of General-purpose Machinery	259	37	5247449	1301908
专用设备制造业	Manufacture of Special-purpose Machinery	302	39	5103239	1304070
汽车制造业	Manufacture of Motor Vehicles	209	39	25214885	5126489
铁路、船舶、航空航天和其他运输业其他运输设备制造业	Manufacture of Railway Locomotives, Building of Ships and Boats, Manufacture of Air and Spacecrafts and Other Transportation Equipments	66	5	2001808	534871
电气机械和器材制造业	Manufacture of Electrical Machinery and Equipment	270	48	6696846	1248404
计算机、通信和其他电子设备制造业	Manufacture of Computer, Communication Equipment and Other Electronic Equipment	300	58	20548734	2436391
仪器仪表制造业	Manufacture of Measuring Instrument and Meter	170	21	2243373	595731
其他制造业	Other Manufacturing	27	5	562451	126300
废弃资源综合利用业	Waste Recycling and Recovery	9	4	78631	19833
金属制品、机械和设备修理业	Repair of Fabricated Metal Products, Machinery and Equipment	13	2	360351	151942
电力、热力生产和供应业	Production and Supply of Electric Power and Heat Power	62	18	30180551	5360431
燃气生产和供应业	Production and Distribution of Gas	20	3	2014071	315608
水的生产和供应业	Production and Distribution of Water	19	3	412161	139492

注: 1. 行业划分执行2011年国民经济行业分类标准(GB/T 4754-2011)。
2. 应交税金合计包括应交增值税、应交所得税、营业税金及附加和管理费用中的税金。

MAIN ECONOMIC INDICATORS OF INDUSTRIAL ABOVE DESIGNATED SIZE (BY SECTOR) (2012)

(10000 yuan)

工业销售产值(当年价格) Sales Value of Industry (at current price)	#出口交货值 Delivery Value of Exports	从业人员平均人数(人) Average Number of Persons Employed (person)	资产负债 Assets and Liabilities: 资产总计 Total Assets	流动资产合计 Total Current Assets	#存货 Inventories	#产成品 Stock Inventory of Finished Products	#应收账款 Accounts Receivable	固定资产合计 Total Fixed Assets	固定资产原价 Total Original Value of Fixed Assets
154466492	**15165151**	**1201482**	**286131557**	**115547666**	**21043667**	**6354841**	**29731328**	**59455870**	**102771932**
8143016	199196	16179	2279872	1104409	107765	106126	395063	68723	198110
***	***	644	***	***	***	***	***	***	***
1719072		21205	19323977	6245976	217263	43701	1051216	3600046	4259559
***	***	283	***	***	***	***	***	***	***
2411905	132152	31552	5929403	3057828	732625	12990	1150392	1383126	2478473
3441284	97682	35132	2959541	2073930	428591	181906	212757	438209	655799
2392163	156539	52310	2969417	1853152	320091	144651	437154	680437	1126567
2105858	4943	33329	3706420	1795134	320911	113535	166624	654113	1279376
***	***	940	***	***	***	***	***	***	***
359189	48814	6278	563732	366531	83110	56404	75766	100459	171418
1410771	353870	55993	1677939	1254828	584519	307008	243309	225827	376003
118670	34954	2811	93001	77444	35082	14733	23338	10705	17145
118014	8202	3001	150724	78364	24001	6082	23677	59386	101850
653605	46897	15734	781900	493775	155868	75016	132922	157963	219140
621889	41637	6222	640992	371884	92643	24226	122453	182038	333957
1210687	13334	28631	1938323	1051159	250711	97611	199963	685948	1466818
808613	94168	8475	917174	734608	432702	318967	52889	89167	151318
8948171		17215	3058428	1534917	939100	203853	161235	846465	2760357
3421718	119519	37494	5512241	2969035	517703	211743	666796	1293195	2599766
5118651	85984	63711	7672222	4830866	1210792	559967	955462	1022169	1647286
***	***	540	***	***	***	***	***	***	***
1094613	127837	21138	1543037	896280	190701	99795	248597	300037	534240
4551401	167659	60753	7849979	5396328	972824	252742	2606836	1167600	2056151
1624865	179238	10496	2704858	647207	240785	67990	159985	917754	2006452
868606	356605	6353	735392	505470	144097	55690	117983	109674	188207
2897248	225483	44646	4179213	2648646	771565	251535	654843	693027	1166203
5161871	834888	58904	7927681	5855984	1811376	553341	1590145	1081225	1747680
4861505	685178	71266	9926109	7006834	1613284	422570	2118354	1258328	1828842
25259437	480021	119618	23124885	12851697	1988142	925399	3138085	4396375	6417450
2035940	10129	33235	4032688	2878068	1167948	109956	843632	617683	1065076
6559476	610842	63411	11344498	9195780	1914721	366388	4068091	830540	3071956
20246340	9763661	140406	25579405	14750633	2530546	595760	4018600	4948400	8790224
2233501	150831	32313	3657379	2777855	733918	123650	833900	284489	494108
477007	25969	8723	1145845	673309	142660	21970	228382	269844	452014
77278		922	123508	55719	9638	4318	18064	54275	72581
397255	79890	6972	454167	245745	79966	1405	107296	184618	321648
30168635	9440	64092	112725281	17055999	119951	5490	2586701	27017032	47088497
2008534		10682	3346977	864970	13071	9655	181378	1212256	1598988
409912		9873	4678592	1042700	14290	396	102849	2446085	3777075

Note: a) Sectors in this table are classified in accordance with the Standard for Classification of National Economic Sectors 2011 (GB/T 4754-2011).
b) Total Tax mainly includes payable VAT,payable income tax, business tax and surtax, and tax in management expenses.

11-6 续表

单位：万元

项目	Item	资产负债 Assets and Liabilities 负债合计 Total Liabilities	#流动负债合计 Total Current Liabilities	#应付账款 Accounts Payable	所有者权益合计 Total Owner's Equity
合计	**Total**	**148372202**	**92098814**	**31635464**	**137746559**
煤炭开采和洗选业	Mining and Washing of Coal	898473	883143	299107	1381398
石油和天然气开采业	Extraction of Petroleum and Natural Gas	***	***	***	***
黑色金属矿采选业	Mining of Ferrous Metal Ores	10679956	2977222	761682	8643629
非金属矿采选业	Mining and Processing of Nonmetal Ores	***	***	***	***
开采辅助活动	Mining Support Service Activities	2665819	2228143	911562	3263584
农副食品加工业	Processing of Food from Agricultural Products	1807924	1588522	228032	1151562
食品制造业	Manufacture of Foods	1994981	1818401	562268	974435
酒、饮料和精制茶制造业	Manufacture of Wines,Beverage and Refined Tea	1788816	1611548	270810	1917605
烟草制品业	Manufacture of Cigarettes and Tobacco	***	***	***	***
纺织业	Manufacture of Textile	300841	236418	114923	262891
纺织服装、服饰业	Manufacture of Textile Wearing Apparel and Ornament	1055843	952455	317813	622095
皮革、毛皮、羽毛及其制品和制鞋业	Manufacture of Leather, Fur, Feather and its Products	58717	57460	18771	34284
木材加工和木、竹、藤、棕、草制品业	Processing of Timbers, Manufacture of Wood, Bamboo, Rattan, Palm, and Straw Products	90364	89794	20970	60360
家具制造业	Manufacture of Furniture	492956	433843	114951	288637
造纸和纸制品业	Manufacture of Paper and Paper Products	318144	295207	104325	322339
印刷和记录媒介复制业	Printing,Reproduction of Recording Media	798834	690519	225757	1139488
文教、工美、体育和娱乐用品制造业	Manufacture of Articles for Culture, Education, Artwork Sport and Entertainment Activity	573195	525901	233012	342536
石油加工、炼焦和核燃料加工业	Processing of Petroleum ,Coking,Processing of Mucleus Fuel	1919799	1915105	691741	1138628
化学原料和化学制品制造业	Manufacture of Chemical Raw Material and Chemical Products	3083106	2483326	435042	2426907
医药制造业	Manufacture of Medicines	3562520	3045167	992498	4109307
化学纤维制造业	Manufacture of Chemical Fibres	***	***	***	***
橡胶和塑料制品业	Manufacture of Rubber and Plastics Products	802936	686979	209945	739195
非金属矿物制品业	Manufacture of Non-metallic Mineral Products	4560403	4200768	1782613	3285960
黑色金属冶炼和压延加工业	Manufacture and Processing of Ferrous Metals	1592089	719807	231679	1112768
有色金属冶炼和压延加工业	Manufacture and Processing of Non-ferrous Metals	299006	259621	98995	436386
金属制品业	Manufacture of Fabricated Metal Products	2170598	1924511	689923	2008568
通用设备制造业	Manufacture of General-purpose Machinery	3716972	3497494	1314735	4210639
专用设备制造业	Manufacture of Special-purpose Machinery	5561998	5137836	1928769	4364093
汽车制造业	Manufacture of Motor Vehicles	13067521	10767678	5326826	10056994
铁路、船舶、航空航天和其他运输设备制造业	Manufacture of Railway Locomotives, Building of Ships and Boats, Manufacture of Air and Spacecrafts and Other Transportation Equipments	2634715	2274754	703551	1397156
电气机械和器材制造业	Manufacture of Electrical Machinery and Equipment	6776818	5916474	2425950	4567290
计算机、通信和其他电子设备制造	Manufacture of Computer, Communication Equipment and Other Electronic Equipment	12772910	10092662	4606930	12805726
仪器仪表制造业	Manufacture of Measuring Instrument and Meter	1921378	1789875	713234	1735569
其他制造业	Other Manufacturing	440337	313243	141030	705508
废弃资源综合利用业	Waste Recycling and Recovery	76877	50404	22756	46631
金属制品、机械和设备修理业	Repair of Fabricated Metal Products, Machinery and Equipment	256479	253539	43254	197688
电力、热力生产和供应业	Production and Supply of Electric Power and Heat Power	56106826	20365715	4810939	56618455
燃气生产和供应业	Production and Distribution of Gas	1149813	942124	113018	2197145
水的生产和供应业	Production and Distribution of Water	1977719	742768	32389	2700873

11-6 continued

(10000 yuan)

#实收资本 Paid-up Capital	损益 Profits and Loss: 营业收入 Business Income	#主营业务收入 Main Business Income	营业成本 Business Cost	#主营业务成本 Main Business Cost	销售费用 Sales Expenses	管理费用 Management Expenses	财务费用 Financial Expenses	利润总额 Total Profits	应交税金合计 Total Tax	#营业税金及附加 Business Tax and Surtax	#主营业务税金及附加 Main Business Tax and Surtax	#应交增值税 Value Added Tax Payable
69216227	**172770950**	**169051357**	**145958224**	**143074099**	**7558018**	**7682260**	**1974809**	**12678868**	**9628722**	**2665122**	**2635845**	**4557614**
593401	8157455	8133256	7742042	7736868	73796	64191	1949	304970	198460	34344	33949	**96768**
***	***	***	***	***	***	***	***	***	***	***	***	***
2839764	5357851	5133982	4912378	4685730	4410	118740	115061	806836	166649	24854	20467	125911
***	***	***	***	***	***	***	***	***	***	***	***	***
2764224	2422543	2404952	2231117	2218280	9665	97903	45233	88854	124281	37831	37696	62890
492624	3861984	3832406	3357886	3339715	204852	145910	35560	109600	122864	46840	46823	48315
963045	3756839	3692191	2481455	2426242	860614	228816	18013	169345	266220	23635	23550	196191
858369	2451571	2285891	1724011	1579565	398365	130524	32819	88764	261163	94192	93803	140696
***	***	***	***	***	***	***	***	***	***	***	***	***
229992	491597	485176	440765	438089	8423	29429	4610	15292	11995	1717	1491	6426
330411	1646616	1627088	1136890	1124468	212122	145881	14907	130374	116512	9179	9134	78504
13593	133897	133071	117684	116908	4162	6454	1104	4586	4302	236	233	2705
70249	133295	130284	118452	117417	8495	8914	553	-1610	5926	639	512	4814
168483	647606	639154	514719	508492	54853	48955	5914	36417	35234	3435	3381	24719
202480	748138	732222	602865	590649	22112	31871	558	103300	57713	3084	3027	26826
707371	1338076	1289169	1007266	978257	39220	165125	1820	125719	107209	9357	9034	69069
213845	981873	963228	885607	879840	30996	48143	9591	17987	35471	2255	1845	27102
103744	9660763	9195391	8581979	8123014	70921	197490	38469	42581	939916	767096	766553	152720
1652397	3795009	3605506	3118602	2965239	293274	275449	57482	41653	185721	21007	20429	119071
1550629	5457596	5257178	2560031	2397364	1470748	501655	69427	861306	674801	53482	53260	449793
***	***	***	***	***	***	***	***	***	***	***	***	***
393975	1340345	1290725	1142713	1106591	45586	82565	13093	57035	55068	4901	4769	35471
1663639	4956125	4868126	4171677	4113501	217210	314310	52627	311417	179845	23250	22402	96341
658397	1755762	1731204	1718473	1701319	46890	34561	26279	-40880	27208	3254	3058	16240
172328	995551	896872	836462	743757	11497	49624	5293	70380	71755	34823	34802	25525
955344	3368343	3224628	2798764	2682878	109592	236308	32493	219045	131542	16117	14627	70991
1794373	5719231	5586852	4494311	4416523	288906	410547	8916	506731	333908	25614	25413	196051
1657185	5922269	5705025	4372957	4254821	358450	631657	45022	560011	369023	38558	37789	230269
4737250	26196219	25689049	21706939	21295333	1017515	994558	99370	2252218	2146849	829347	828815	782072
551052	2220453	2196623	1757850	1743682	47523	230821	20911	179913	105116	8520	8398	65582
2495786	7072123	6675140	5804131	5441470	336580	463626	71679	459491	331873	23821	23304	201803
7480594	24988664	24685294	22031844	21899647	1055505	1145927	58801	921869	540097	61928	54878	291485
622518	2663651	2623272	1916082	1895875	178679	289998	11394	299846	181429	17682	17086	110736
290552	646813	639075	494355	492121	13747	81031	-491	63210	28772	2815	2815	15197
21132	80142	78708	61870	61323	8217	8757	128	6431	5930	530	487	4007
142927	405393	398141	301327	298898	6032	73318	7362	20465	27317	3657	3607	16930
28634237	30332883	30213357	28292513	28216885	7164	176119	1049714	3495108	1398500	210302	207614	662680
574891	2043003	2019620	1828117	1813726	24802	112073	5446	246077	58582	5620	4417	32626
2409003	473047	463855	461746	453815	2629	61153	11864	42068	31468	2906	2390	15330

11-7 规模以上工业企业主要经济效益指标(2012年)

单位: %

项 目	Item	工业经济效益综合指数 Aggregate Index of Industrial Economic Efficiency	企业亏损面 Loss-Making Enterprises as % of Total	总资产贡献率 Ratio of Profits,Taxes and Interest to Average Assets	资产保值增值率 Changing Rate of Net Assets
合 计	**Total**	**253.53**	**16.87**	**7.98**	**109.67**
在合计中:	**Of the Total:**				
中央企业	Central Enterprises	379.08	11.98	6.10	104.54
地方企业	Local Enterprises	227.72	17.22	9.72	114.96
在合计中:	**Of the Total:**				
内资企业	Domestic Funded Enterprises	236.41	15.11	6.48	108.72
国有企业	State-Owned Enterprises	559.28	21.30	5.64	111.95
集体企业	Collective Owned Enterprises	145.45	14.29	10.63	110.69
股份合作企业	Cooperative Enterprises	130.09	23.38	8.37	115.12
联营企业	Joint Owned Enterprises	204.35		15.60	132.05
有限责任公司	Limited Liability Corporations	197.01	17.37	4.94	95.61
股份有限公司	Share Holding Corporations Ltd.	249.83	12.26	10.98	120.96
私营企业	Private Enterprises	173.28	11.79	9.83	130.22
其他企业	Others				
港澳台商投资企业	Enterprises with Funds from Hongkong, Macao and Taiwan	198.45	22.08	8.07	110.06
港澳台合资经营	Joint Venture	244.11	20.00	14.04	112.28
港澳台合作经营	Cooperative	157.59	33.33	3.60	101.19
港澳台商独资企业	Hongkong, Macao and Taiwan Enterprises	188.29	23.91	8.94	119.41
港澳台商投资股份有限公司	Hongkong, Macao and Taiwan Funded Share Holding Corporations	138.30	22.22	2.58	101.89
外商投资企业	Foreign Funded Enterprises	327.04	22.19	16.32	115.40
中外合资经营	Joint Venture	420.03	17.39	21.27	118.17
中外合作经营	Cooperative	153.49	21.43	5.74	100.00
外资(独资)企业	Foreign Enterprises	243.09	25.86	10.86	109.89
外商投资股份有限公司	Foreign Funded Share Holding Corporations	339.77	18.75	12.79	132.19
在合计中:	**Of the Total:**				
#农村企业	Rural Enterprises	149.57	17.53	10.87	108.42
在合计中:	**Of the Total:**				
#国有控股	State-holding Enterprises	302.09	19.49	6.93	106.73
集体控股	Collective-holding Enterprises	200.60	15.09	8.52	108.73
私人控股	Private-holding Enterprises	200.55	13.37	11.01	130.01
港澳台控股	HK, Macao, Taiwan-holding Enterprises	187.73	25.28	9.26	112.37
外商控股	Foreign Investor-holding Enterprises	261.27	23.17	12.76	114.88
在合计中:	**Of the Total:**				
轻工业	Light Industry	221.31	18.20	13.73	112.63
重工业	Heavy Industry	272.64	16.19	7.27	109.31
在合计中:	**Of the Total:**				
#大中型企业	Medium-and Large-sized Industry	276.10	15.85	7.81	108.46

MAIN INDICATORS ON ECONOMIC BENEFIT OF INDUSTRIAL ABOVE DESIGNATED SIZE (2012)

(%)

资产负债率 Ratio of Debts to Assets	流动资产周转率（次） Turnover of Working Capital (times)	成本费用利润率 Ratio of Profits to Industrial Cost	全员劳动生产率（元/人） Overall Labor Productivity (yuan/person)	产品销售率 Proportion of Products Sold	增加值率 Rate of Value Added to Gross Output Value	人均销售收入（元） Sales Revenue Per Capita (yuan)	流动比率（倍） Circulating Assets/ Liquid Liabilities (times)	速动比率（倍） Quick-circulating Assets/Liquid Liabilities (times)
51.85	**1.59**	**7.91**	**252465**	**99.04**	**19.45**	**1407024**	**1.25**	**1.03**
51.07	1.83	8.01	461838	99.87	18.97	2523896	1.00	0.85
52.57	1.50	7.86	205323	98.60	19.70	1155551	1.40	1.12
51.10	1.44	8.16	230005	99.09	19.00	1306716	1.22	1.02
49.08	1.15	19.70	697275	99.78	24.14	2931246	1.06	0.99
61.19	1.35	5.32	105897	98.04	27.89	374802	1.31	0.89
72.05	1.31	4.01	95041	99.03	23.21	445379	1.13	0.76
50.82	1.06	15.20	106504	97.30	31.28	332380	2.32	1.77
56.55	1.65	4.17	194125	98.82	16.04	1348739	1.21	0.99
44.56	1.36	8.74	233104	99.97	19.97	1272054	1.41	1.14
56.18	1.42	6.40	122555	96.68	20.52	600656	1.32	0.97
59.59	1.51	4.21	186036	97.04	16.27	1481550	1.36	1.05
51.37	1.82	9.19	206344	97.58	26.33	819349	1.24	0.95
11.94	0.45	3.13	157845	99.50	34.22	596827	8.18	7.41
68.56	2.61	2.32	178345	96.59	11.11	2350846	1.17	0.95
58.05	0.32	4.24	124571	97.76	11.75	1205286	1.70	1.23
53.43	2.10	8.52	334692	99.41	21.13	1652329	1.32	1.05
56.44	2.29	9.81	461071	99.57	21.81	2157631	1.26	1.01
59.53	1.61	2.85	126897	102.49	38.54	542620	1.36	1.00
53.38	1.95	6.12	231606	98.96	19.04	1304350	1.34	1.04
22.22	1.02	24.94	277530	102.58	37.65	757696	2.74	2.39
64.32	1.33	7.18	101214	97.74	21.73	467865	1.28	0.90
51.21	1.55	8.41	333793	99.82	19.50	1841212	1.17	0.99
58.15	1.12	6.31	182361	94.59	21.43	852867	1.39	1.05
51.44	1.14	10.05	145697	96.77	22.75	666791	1.48	1.16
62.86	2.18	3.35	178469	97.11	14.70	1625602	1.23	0.99
53.39	2.13	6.95	246554	99.15	18.33	1432943	1.37	1.07
51.51	1.46	8.66	178942	96.42	28.36	691761	1.37	1.02
51.9	1.62	7.78	286575	99.52	17.83	1738855	1.23	1.03
51.49	1.62	8.42	286827	99.12	20.42	1528037	1.23	1.02

11-8 规模以上国有控股工业企业主要经济指标(2012年)

单位：万元

项目	Item	企业单位个数(个) Number of Enterprises (unit)	#亏损企业 Loss-Suffering Enterprises	工业总产值(当年价格) Gross Output Value of Industry (at current prices)	工业增加值 Added Value of Industry	工业销售产值(当年价格) Sales Value of Industry (at current price)
合　计	**Total**	**790**	**154**	**90858999**	**17721617**	**90695706**
在合计中：	**Of the Total:**					
中央企业	Central Enterprises	227	28	53561232	10154602	53492712
地方企业	Local Enterprises	563	126	37297767	7567015	37202994
在合计中：	**Of theTotal:**					
轻工业	Light Industry	212	39	7093307	2279905	6901538
重工业	Heavy Industry	578	115	83765692	15441712	83794168
在合计中：	**Of the Total:**					
#大中型企业	Medium-and Large -sized Industry	303	55	77466275	16436154	77315400

11-8 续表

单位：万元

项目	Item	资产负债 Assets and Liabilities				
		负债合计 Total Liabilities	#流动负债合计 Total Current Liabilities	#应付账款 Accounts Payable	所有者权益合计 Total Owner's Equity	#实收资本 Paid-up Capital
合　计	**Total**	**110611809**	**57792388**	**16650535**	**105368509**	**54059938**
在合计中：	**Of the Total:**					
中央企业	Central Enterprises	69491320	32764820	8507134	66611093	34220071
地方企业	Local Enterprises	41120489	25027568	8143401	38757416	19839867
在合计中：	**Of the Total:**					
轻工业	Light Industry	6286669	4850137	914123	7140207	3264367
重工业	Heavy Industry	104325140	52942251	15736412	98228302	50795571
在合计中：	**Of the Total:**					
#大中型企业	Medium-and Large -sized Industry	103378205	51999821	14653814	99364820	50109921

MAIN ECONOMIC INDICATORS OF STATE-OWNED AND STATE-CONTROLLED INDUSTRIAL ABOVE DESIGNATED SIZE (2012)

(10000 yuan)

#出口交货值 Delivery Value of Exports	从业人员平均人数（人） Average Number of Employed Persons (person)	资产负债 Assets and Liabilities: 资产总计 Total Assets	流动资产合计 Total Current Assets	#存货 Inventories	#产成品 Stock Inventory of Finished Products	#应收账款（净额） Accounts Receivable (Net)	固定资产合计 Total Fixed Assets
2361982	**530917**	**215983076**	**67432219**	**10448261**	**2865611**	**14063003**	**47518069**
445806	218083	136102414	32726422	4771998	1044031	6943630	29420655
1916176	312834	79880662	34705797	5676263	1821581	7119373	18097414
186928	107983	13427017	7248596	1829397	818931	977018	2921015
2175054	422934	202556059	60183623	8618864	2046680	13085985	44597054
2000053	464388	202744179	60226026	8767664	2082282	11957836	45196540

11-8 continued

(10000 yuan)

损益 Profits and Loss: 营业收入 Business Income	#主营业务收入 Main Business Income	营业成本 Business Cost	#主营业务成本 Main Business Cost	销售费用 Sales Expenses	管理费用 Management Expenses	财务费用 Financial Expenses	利润总额 Total Profits	应交税金合计 Total Tax	#营业税金及附加 Business Tax and Surtax	#主营业务税金及附加 Main Business Tax and Surtax	#应交增值税 Value Added Tax Payable
99800314	**97753049**	**87437871**	**85840775**	**2129505**	**3524177**	**1675055**	**7839276**	**6166533**	**2361872**	**2341140**	**2469420**
56548604	55537322	51007139	50142586	411137	1411311	1200085	4255642	3194256	1278300	1268784	1210024
43251710	42215727	36430732	35698189	1718368	2112866	474970	3583633	2972276	1083573	1072356	1259396
8076437	7879393	5990540	5856839	560727	634043	72979	673002	882224	372028	366274	379534
91723877	89873657	81447331	79983937	1568778	2890134	1602076	7166273	5284309	1989844	1974866	2089886
85175963	83364327	74168338	72708589	1835510	2967027	1590412	7176183	5732469	2292659	2274196	2228854

11-9 规模以上国有控股工业企业主要经济指标(按行业分)(2012年)

单位: 万元

项 目	Item	企业单位个数(个) Number of Enterprises (unit)	#亏损企业 Loss-Suffering Enterprises	工业总产值(当年价格) Gross Output Value of Industry (at current prices)	工业增加值 Added Value of Industry
合 计	**Total**	**790**	**154**	**90858999**	**17721617**
煤炭开采和洗选业	Mining and Washing of Coal	4		8112907	649662
石油和天然气开采业	Extraction of Petroleum and Natural Gas	1		***	***
黑色金属矿采选业	Mining of Ferrous Metal Ores	4		1657503	428241
开采辅助活动	Mining Support Service Activities	3		***	***
农副食品加工业	Processing of Food from Agricultural Products	24	6	1747733	176039
食品制造业	Manufacture of Foods	16	4	459734	91816
酒、饮料和精制茶制造业	Manufacture of Wines,Beverage and Refined Tea	10	2	677498	265675
烟草制品业	Manufacture of Cigarettes and Tobacco	1		***	***
纺织业	Manufacture of Textile	17	4	127913	18978
纺织服装、服饰业	Manufacture of Textile Wearing Apparel and Ornament	11	3	73005	16981
皮革、毛皮、羽毛及其制品和制鞋业	Manufacture of Leather, Fur, Feather and its Products	3		***	***
木材加工和木、竹、藤、棕、草制品业	Processing of Timbers, Manufacture of Wood, Bamboo, Rattan, Palm, and Straw Products	2	2	***	***
家具制造业	Manufacture of Furniture	5	2	61231	16417
造纸和纸制品业	Manufacture of Paper and Paper Products	4		40618	5400
印刷和记录媒介复制业	Printing,Reproduction of Recording Media	37	9	563947	281775
文教、工美、体育和娱乐用品制造业	Manufacture of Articles for Culture,Education, Artwork, Sport and Entertainment Activity	7	1	342832	60828
石油加工、炼焦和核燃料加工业	Processing of Petroleum ,Coking,Processing of Mucleus Fuel	8	1	8427973	1203116
化学原料和化学制品制造业	Manufacture of Chemical Raw Material and Chemical Products	39	13	1414838	29918
医药制造业	Manufacture of Medicines	34	2	1411537	681996
化学纤维制造业	Manufacture of Chemical fibres	2		***	***
橡胶和塑料制品业	Manufacture of Rubber and Plastics Products	15	2	211488	43750
非金属矿物制品业	Manufacture of Non-metallic Mineral Products	65	14	1471873	259577
黑色金属冶炼和压延加工业	Manufacture and Processing of Ferrous Metals	7	3	992631	-8520
有色金属冶炼和压延加工业	Manufacture and Processing of Non-ferrous Metals	13	4	524612	104502
金属制品业	Manufacture of Fabricated Metal Products	30	6	1095987	238465
通用设备制造业	Manufacture of General-purpose Machinery	45	14	888014	214649
专用设备制造业	Manufacture of Special-purpose Machinery	60	7	1998699	463572
汽车制造业	Manufacture of Motor Vehicles	36	8	16702586	3768003
铁路、船舶、航空航天和其他运输设备制造业	Manufacture of Railway Locomotives, Building of Ships and Boats, Manufacture of Air and Spacecrafts and Other Transportation Equipments	30	3	1651386	426214
电气机械和器材制造业	Manufacture of Electrical Machinery and Equipment	33	7	1520797	64540
计算机、通信和其他电子设备制造业	Manufacture of Computer, Communication Equipment and Other Electronic Equipment	83	12	3428017	638743
仪器仪表制造业	Manufacture of Measuring Instrument and Meter	48	4	883433	205482
其他制造业	Other Manufacturing	11	1	470467	104320
废弃资源综合利用业	Waste Recycling and Recovery	3	1	***	***
金属制品、机械和设备修理业	Repair of Fabricated Metal Products, Machinery and Equipment	2		***	***
电力、热力生产和供应业	Production and Supply of Electric Power and Heat Power	50	14	30072357	5360368
燃气生产和供应业	Production and Distribution of Gas	11	3	268440	23678
水的生产和供应业	Production and Distribution of Water	16	2	379193	121759

注: 1、行业划分执行2011年国民经济行业分类标准(GB/T 4754-2011)。
2、应交税金合计包括应交增值税、应交所得税、营业税金及附加和管理费用中的税金。

MAIN ECONOMIC INDICATORS OF STATE-OWNED AND STATE-CONTROLLED INDUSTIRAL ABOVE DESIGNATED SIZE (BY SECTOR) (2012)

(10000 yuan)

工业销售产值(当年价格) Sales Value of Industry (at current price)	#出口交货值 Delivery Value of Exports	从业人员平均人数(人) Average Number of Employed Persons (person)	资产负债 Assets and Liabilities: 资产总计 Total Assets	流动资产合计 Total Current Assets	#存货 Inventories	#产成品 Stock Inventory of Finished Products	#应收账款 Accounts Receivable	固定资产合计 Total Fixed Assets
90695706	**2361982**	**530917**	**215983076**	**67432219**	**10448261**	**2865611**	**14063003**	**47518069**
8139616	199196	16093	2271552	1096403	105726	104244	393170	68588
***	***	644	***	***	***	***	***	***
1652933		20015	19246596	6203996	200433	40104	1048568	3568484
***	***	30964	***	***	***	***	***	***
1719865	9347	13096	1620277	1215602	197828	98305	73049	188653
446727	10842	12128	646829	252945	34539	9326	79130	148404
687740	3567	13237	2054411	999913	150558	50784	47631	221589
***	***	940	***	***	***	***	***	***
122054	26889	4231	362687	210476	50937	31564	33450	74936
80377	34333	4184	102560	67509	42078	23161	7154	26356
***	***	731	***	***	***	***	***	***
***	***	535	***	***	***	***	***	***
48949	3516	1801	127326	61798	17288	8307	14678	31037
40274		423	73240	50467	13792	2831	18743	11047
563124	1250	13908	979180	499316	116715	51604	65730	367411
367676	9485	2591	535557	450763	277900	223128	26314	40725
8515155		15578	2915884	1424531	899607	192805	140864	826612
1395510	4877	13326	3208642	1445644	236455	96883	168283	824487
1340940	39024	19252	2897507	1693966	574146	270911	262924	352098
***	***	488	***	***	***	***	***	***
206994	41236	4925	268080	154847	44693	24165	36909	78018
1447889	40968	24034	3063450	1929742	278370	103590	916943	550070
998672	116153	5267	2251240	303971	131232	32038	28976	854122
539068	267738	3329	436535	304444	85687	34332	55778	69584
1064924	154532	15423	1707842	848355	248331	57621	181987	335034
897751	45627	16265	2230867	1588482	643432	166121	324017	250802
1911499	82819	29853	4974352	3282710	737950	235262	959610	770649
16829691	249412	71403	16506024	8489762	1240851	588486	1012597	2903507
1666896	6871	28438	3445329	2403776	1062331	89794	662194	557978
1489657	61876	13848	5234366	4529204	872965	31514	2128470	143058
3309732	674447	34216	12268154	4914837	756656	216548	999303	2679630
899364	23377	11496	1112811	875941	267948	45873	248621	105480
385809		6937	1053982	611031	130247	17727	206132	249591
***	***	413	***	***	***	***	***	***
***	***	5980	***	***	***	***	***	***
30070994	9440	62437	112574341	16986340	99489	2725	2582247	26947630
262902		3175	290852	171097	8376	7014	34326	104643
376944		9313	4606659	1004040	11822		93328	2422102

Note: a) Sectors in this table are classified in accordance with the Standard for Classification of National Economic Sectors 2011 (GB/T 4754-2011).
b) Total Tax mainly includes payable VAT,payable income tax, business tax and surtax, and tax in management expenses.

11-9 续表

单位：万元

项目	Item	负债合计 Total Liabilities	#流动负债合计 Total Current Liabilities	#应付账款 Accounts Payable	所有者权益合计 Total Owner's Equity
合计	**Total**	**110611809**	**57792388**	**16650535**	**105368509**
煤炭开采和洗选业	Mining and Washing of Coal	892927	877596	296876	1378625
石油和天然气开采业	Extraction of Petroleum and Natural Gas	***	***	***	***
黑色金属矿采选业	Mining of Ferrous Metal Ores	10641749	2941484	748360	8604847
开采辅助活动	Mining Support Service Activities	***	***	***	***
农副食品加工业	Processing of Food from Agricultural Products	1119156	955357	54792	501121
食品制造业	Manufacture of Foods	355635	280988	57624	291194
酒、饮料和精制茶制造业	Manufacture of Wines,Beverage and Refined Tea	872645	812267	25472	1181767
烟草制品业	Manufacture of Cigarettes and Tobacco	***	***	***	***
纺织业	Manufacture of Textile	184676	121473	44318	178012
纺织服装、服饰业	Manufacture of Textile Wearing Apparel and Ornament	95385	94089	12506	7176
皮革、毛皮、羽毛及其制品和制鞋业	Manufacture of Leather, Fur, Feather and its Products	***	***	***	***
木材加工和木、竹、藤、棕、草制品业	Processing of Timbers, Manufacture of Wood, Bamboo, Rattan, Palm, and Straw Products	***	***	***	***
家具制造业	Manufacture of Furniture	106149	82470	23877	21177
造纸和纸制品业	Manufacture of Paper and Paper Products	38468	28425	12048	34772
印刷和记录媒介复制业	Printing,Reproduction of Recording Media	349549	280654	71138	629630
文教、工美、体育和娱乐用品制造业	Manufacture of Articles for Culture,Education, Artwork, Sport and Entertainment Activity	366176	344857	179805	169380
石油加工、炼焦和核燃料加工业	Processing of Petroleum ,Coking,Processing of Mucleus Fuel	1875894	1871454	666753	1039990
化学原料和化学制品制造业	Manufacture of Chemical Raw Material and Chemical Products	2114789	1595889	201014	1092700
医药制造业	Manufacture of Medicines	1101796	779246	198432	1795571
化学纤维制造业	Manufacture of Chemical Fibres	7152	2648	821	23090
橡胶和塑料制品业	Manufacture of Rubber and Plastics Products	164896	156023	19362	103184
非金属矿物制品业	Manufacture of Non-metallic Mineral Products	1789894	1653370	561788	1272118
黑色金属冶炼和压延加工业	Manufacture and Processing of Ferrous Metals	1271258	420389	126245	979983
有色金属冶炼和压延加工业	Manufacture and Processing of Non-ferrous Metals	129036	117849	41458	307499
金属制品业	Manufacture of Fabricated Metal Products	874700	699904	287413	833142
通用设备制造业	Manufacture of General-purpose Machinery	1268038	1169806	306548	962828
专用设备制造业	Manufacture of Special-purpose Machinery	2810877	2470074	874704	2163470
汽车制造业	Manufacture of Motor Vehicles	9224681	7155036	2997171	7281342
铁路、船舶、航空航天和其他运输设备制造业	Manufacture of Railway Locomotives, Building of Ships and Boats, Manufacture of Air and Spacecrafts and Other Transportation Equipments	2358692	2003771	579062	1086637
电气机械和器材制造业	Manufacture of Electrical Machinery and Equipment	3386512	2801745	1098126	1847854
计算机、通信和其他电子设备制造业	Manufacture of Computer, Communication Equipment and Other Electronic Equipment	4975284	3455109	970572	7292869
仪器仪表制造业	Manufacture of Measuring Instrument and Meter	642207	582306	223732	470603
其他制造业	Other Manufacturing	401663	276702	129386	652319
废弃资源综合利用业	Waste Recycling and Recovery	***	***	***	***
金属制品、机械和设备修理业	Repair of Fabricated Metal Products, Machinery and Equipment	***	***	***	***
电力、热力生产和供应业	Production and Supply of Electric Power and Heat Power	55975285	20279441	4780026	56599056
燃气生产和供应业	Production and Distribution of Gas	142145	129902	20555	148688
水的生产和供应业	Production and Distribution of Water	1947016	715454	30143	2659643

11-9 continued

(10000 yuan)

#实收资本 Paid-up Capital	损益 Profits and Loss: 营业收入 Business Income	#主营业务收入 Main Business Income	营业成本 Business Cost	#主营业务成本 Main Business Cost	销售费用 Sales Expenses	管理费用 Manage-ment Expenses	财务费用 Financial Expenses	利润总额 Total Profits	应交税金: 税金合计 Total Tax	#营业税金及附加 Business Tax and Surtax	#主营业务税金及附加 Main Business Tax and Surtax	#应交增值税 Value Added Tax Payable
54059938	**99800314**	**97753049**	**87437871**	**85840775**	**2129505**	**3524177**	**1675055**	**7839276**	**6166533**	**2361872**	**2341140**	**2469420**
591325	8146472	8122273	7731046	7725871	73585	63913	1869	305405	198166	34309	33914	96509
***	***	***	***	***	***	***	***	***	***	***	***	***
2837699	5289791	5070453	4858615	4636836	3764	111512	114573	802299	159268	22998	18610	121588
***	***	***	***	***	***	***	***	***	***	***	***	***
166218	2017418	2012104	1752043	1750313	112567	60882	23632	38197	89645	44889	44872	31725
206979	530441	517486	397616	388001	99392	36878	6499	3026	24382	1899	1828	17370
202935	849899	790575	612057	562890	60425	45311	19146	49300	142153	76206	75817	56999
***	***	***	***	***	***	***	***	***	***	***	***	***
175019	168888	163152	143295	141142	2462	21213	2387	1706	6249	1238	1022	3046
54863	109121	108407	100588	100158	1711	8077	4032	-5571	5038	552	545	3826
***	***	***	***	***	***	***	***	***	***	***	***	***
***	***	***	***	***	***	***	***	***	***	***	***	***
16057	62991	59534	46205	43589	11947	6847	457	7307	4378	476	441	3301
9685	96141	95139	90310	90145	791	3106	-110	2002	1550	129	77	767
438426	670469	628361	479016	453071	12496	105655	-620	74873	61873	5702	5400	39886
137839	441248	438318	408022	407350	13953	13969	5420	-85	21341	965	942	19729
81887	9222742	8762406	8209270	7754106	48451	186583	37565	13214	922508	764128	763611	145964
1066963	1531529	1422572	1443747	1363959	39112	134470	42715	-132697	36267	5360	5092	25649
584744	1381879	1368728	735680	728150	175919	144443	10096	341906	172176	14676	14542	107801
9200	14481	14189	10953	10737	357	1788	124	1420	1091	87	87	769
84347	294012	282254	247878	243986	8201	22270	2735	13668	12181	1431	1345	7374
753603	1681312	1617001	1437441	1395415	66639	115454	24179	123414	67302	9573	8733	36341
574438	1101338	1080054	1115753	1099778	31159	15652	20800	-53960	9952	1729	1608	5270
112967	639106	545604	530644	442087	5634	24767	3235	50951	61785	33934	33913	19545
416547	1331466	1270816	1140528	1095308	20781	91622	8977	83154	40211	5149	4001	18864
552189	1024150	996013	821502	802022	37535	104222	7503	43705	65796	7209	7100	46008
873676	2533619	2412404	1989172	1892822	118096	249710	31977	168252	142252	15809	15136	93649
3375753	17167500	16934930	13731263	13571591	853970	665025	81795	1716714	1754440	804569	804208	573212
448142	1819674	1802298	1486706	1475634	21347	186203	18898	125298	67984	5739	5618	41009
1021631	1621535	1548515	1467385	1412583	80643	107868	45486	23752	28968	731	637	26839
4634388	4338216	4187143	3666257	3600471	151042	385998	50094	243319	122473	21626	19896	65940
232893	994765	973672	791778	779040	36856	99110	3535	70402	54602	6232	5874	35661
262695	554863	548610	425177	423764	7749	71368	-1235	56522	22929	2147	2147	11819
***	***	***	***	***	***	***	***	***	***	***	***	***
***	***	***	***	***	***	***	***	***	***	***	***	***
28617827	30233106	30113849	28180464	28105400	4742	167701	1048490	3494098	1397104	210151	207464	662472
136559	277414	266813	288246	284017	2365	27602	-1334	5351	13325	1965	1414	8201
2386144	440334	431152	442636	434704	1210	56172	11143	35508	27516	2428	1913	12931

11-10 规模以上股份制工业企业主要经济指标(2012年)

单位：万元

项目	Item	企业单位个数(个) Number of Enterprises (unit)	#亏损企业 Loss-Suffering Enterprises	工业总产值(当年价格) Gross Output Value of Industry (at current prices)	工业增加值 Added Value of Industry	工业销售产值(当年价格) Sales Value of Industry (at current price)	#出口交货值 Delivery Value of Exports
合　计	**Total**	**1473**	**245**	**69323493**	**12014619**	**68764923**	**2411918**
在合计中:	**Of the Total:**						
中央企业	Central Enterprises	157	20	34734901	5432738	34676369	312763
地方企业	Local Enterprises	1316	225	34588592	6581882	34088554	2099156
在合计中:	**Of the Total:**						
轻工业	Light Industry	463	72	8802216	2413859	8437709	230680
重工业	Heavy Industry	1010	173	60521277	9600761	60327214	2181238
在合计中:	**Of the Total:**						
#大中型企业	Medium-and Large -sized Industry	372	61	51021596	9689291	50638469	1914645

11-10 续表

单位：万元

项目	Item	资产负债 Assets and Liabilities					
		固定资产原价 Total Original Value of Fixed Assets	负债合计 Total Liabilities	#流动负债合计 Total Current Liabilities	#应付账款 Accounts Payable	所有者权益合计 Total Owner's Equity	#实收资本 Paid-up Capital
合　计	**Total**	**41902709**	**60605765**	**42226798**	**13403969**	**55129139**	**31799651**
在合计中:	**Of theTotal:**						
中央企业	Central Enterprises	16849679	18348456	15500229	5018576	13880562	12333177
地方企业	Local Enterprises	25053030	42257309	26726569	8385393	41248577	19466474
在合计中:	**Of the Total:**						
轻工业	Light Industry	5505540	7808943	6232284	1467249	7783486	3724851
重工业	Heavy Industry	36397170	52796822	35994514	11936720	47345653	28074799
在合计中:	**Of the Total:**						
#大中型企业	Medium-and Large -sized Industry	37586164	50425141	33053319	9933565	46502952	26998286

MAIN ECONOMIC INDICATORS OF SHARE-HOLDING INDUSTRIAL ABOVE DESIGNATED SIZE (2012)

(10000 yuan)

从业人员平均人数(人) Average Number of Employed Persons (person)	资产负债 Assets and Liabilities					
	资产总计 Total Assets	流动资产合计 Total Current Assets	#存货 Inventories	#产成品 Stock Inventory of Finished Products	#应收账款 Accounts Receivable	固定资产合计 Total Fixed Assets
579710	**115739277**	**53964067**	**10152554**	**3217026**	**13818650**	**25630599**
160236	32229018	15046100	3565373	902972	3928417	8203189
419474	83510259	38917968	6587182	2314054	9890234	17427410
145279	15592503	8868078	2144871	1041176	1373629	3219003
434431	100146775	45095989	8007683	2175850	12445022	22411597
445282	96929315	41372023	7311239	2031847	9814032	22987891

11-10 continued

(10000 yuan)

损益 Profits and Loss								应交税金合计 Total Tax	#营业税金及附加 Business Tax and Surtax	#主营业务税金及附加 Main Business Tax and Surtax	#应交增值税 Value Added Tax Payable
营业收入 Business Income	#主营业务收入 Main Business Income	营业成本 Business Cost	#主营业务成本 Main Business Cost	销售费用 Sales Expenses	管理费用 Management Expenses	财务费用 Financial Expenses	利润总额 Total Profits				
78580140	**76690581**	**69041968**	**67562571**	**2170911**	**3801824**	**709630**	**4146262**	**3616492**	**1205676**	**1190253**	**1685505**
37078413	36287088	34408097	33719933	306425	1004056	246268	689363	1650154	870596	866953	556658
41501727	40403493	34633871	33842639	1864486	2797768	463362	3456900	1966338	335080	323300	1128847
9910729	9747703	7357548	7267304	875212	810717	79801	915625	710097	129510	127564	412196
68669412	66942878	61684419	60295267	1295698	2991107	629829	3230638	2906396	1076166	1062689	1273309
58562022	57012353	51545539	50283336	1589001	2792942	606408	3102005	2929808	1108893	1095662	1298456

11-11 规模以上股份制工业企业主要经济指标(按行业分)(2012年)

单位：万元

项目	Item	企业单位个数(个) Number of Enterprises (unit)	#亏损企业 Loss-Suffering Enterprises	工业总产值(当年价格) Gross Output Value of Industry (at current prices)	工业增加值 Added Value of Industry
合计	**Total**	**1473**	**245**	**69323493**	**12014619**
煤炭开采和洗选业	Mining and Washing of Coal	6	1	8114922	649859
石油和天然气开采业	Extraction of Petroleum and Natural Gas	1		***	***
黑色金属矿采选业	Mining of Ferrous Metal Ores	5		1682836	436073
非金属矿采选业	Mining and Processing of Nonmetal Ores	1		***	***
开采辅助活动	Mining Support Service Activities	3		***	***
农副食品加工业	Processing of Food from Agricultural Products	60	13	2009209	223595
食品制造业	Manufacture of Foods	41	10	631583	124124
酒、饮料和精制茶制造业	Manufacture of Wines,Beverage and Refined Tea	11	5	164056	76591
纺织业	Manufacture of Textile	19	3	245796	25386
纺织服装、服饰业	Manufacture of Textile Wearing Apparel and Ornament	41	7	459978	187617
皮革、毛皮、羽毛及其制品和制鞋业	Manufacture of Leather, Fur, Feather and its Products	8	1	41691	3917
木材加工和木、竹、藤、棕、草制品业	Processing of Timbers, Manufacture of Wood, Bamboo, Rattan, Palm, and Straw Products	6	2	16836	1354
家具制造业	Manufacture of Furniture	18	4	148610	33557
造纸和纸制品业	Manufacture of Paper and Paper Products	16	2	89153	10033
印刷和记录媒介复制业	Printing,Reproduction of Recording Media	40	4	545969	268861
文教、工美、体育和娱乐用品制造业	Manufacture of Articles for Culture,Education, Artwork, Sport and Entertainment Activity	15	1	621280	79676
石油加工、炼焦和核燃料加工业	Processing of Petroleum ,Coking,Processing of Mucleus Fuel Mucleus Fuel	10	1	8335063	1205514
化学原料和化学制品制造业	Manufacture of Chemical Raw Material and Chemical Products	78	13	1472239	120213
医药制造业	Manufacture of Medicines	92	9	2252804	1006389
化学纤维制造业	Manufacture of Chemical fibres	2		***	***
橡胶和塑料制品业	Manufacture of Rubber and Plastics Products	39	9	404776	60586
非金属矿物制品业	Manufacture of Non-metallic Mineral Products	134	17	3122710	496737
黑色金属冶炼和压延加工业	Manufacture and Processing of Ferrous Metals	18	6	1099421	23794
有色金属冶炼和压延加工业	Manufacture and Processing of Non-ferrous Metals	17	6	634351	122071
金属制品业	Manufacture of Fabricated Metal Products	75	14	1385762	297798
通用设备制造业	Manufacture of General-purpose Machinery	84	19	1031149	224032
专用设备制造业	Manufacture of Special-purpose Machinery	108	11	2507860	653339
汽车制造业	Manufacture of Motor Vehicles	66	16	5544227	569826
铁路、船舶、航空航天和其他运输设备制造业	Manufacture of Railway Locomotives, Building of Ships and Boats, Manufacture of Air and Spacecrafts and Other Transportation Equipments	37	3	1241942	284599
电气机械和器材制造业	Manufacture of Electrical Machinery and Equipment	118	19	3364207	499807
计算机、通信和其他电子设备制造业	Manufacture of Computer, Communication Equipment and Other Electronic Equipment	142	19	3691409	808669
仪器仪表制造业	Manufacture of Measuring Instrument and Meter	82	10	1214440	340282
其他制造业	Other Manufacturing	12	2	387966	66705
废弃资源综合利用业	Waste Recycling and Recovery	4	2	33729	7663
金属制品、机械和设备修理业	Repair of Fabricated Metal Products, Machinery and Equipment	5	2	24801	11785
电力、热力生产和供应业	Production and Supply of Electric Power and Heat Power	36	10	13777413	1657415
燃气生产和供应业	Production and Distribution of Gas	10	3	298212	52062
水的生产和供应业	Production and Distribution of Water	13	1	360706	108287

注：1. 行业划分执行2011年国民经济行业分类标准(GB/T 4754-2011)。
2. 应交税金合计包括应交增值税、应交所得税、营业税金及附加和管理费用中的税金。

MAIN ECONOMIC INDICATORS OF SHARE-HOLDING INDUSTRIAL ABOVE DESIGNATED SIZE (BY SECTOR) (2012)

(10000 yuan)

工业销售产值(当年价格) Sales Value of Industry (at current price)	#出口交货值 Delivery Value of Exports	从业人员平均人数(人) Average Number of Employed Persons (person)	资产负债 Assets and Liabilities					
			资产总计 Total Assets	流动资产合计 Total Current Assets	#存货 Inventories	#产成品 Stock Inventory of Finished Products	#应收账款 Accounts Receivable	固定资产合计 Total Fixed Assets
68764923	**2411918**	**579710**	**115739277**	**53964067**	**10152554**	**3217026**	**13818650**	**25630599**
8143016	199196	16179	2279872	1104409	107765	106126	395063	68723
***	***	644	***	***	***	***	***	***
1678204		20272	19271536	6217977	206256	40734	1048706	3576830
***	***	190	***	***	***	***	***	***
***	***	30964	***	***	***	***	***	***
1973022	2259	17471	2257142	1608627	220790	93137	117474	256791
615542	40207	16418	1089713	561669	77896	29762	121238	212774
160681	1477	3928	502505	310482	92599	48534	46116	115117
240119	20432	4227	466245	294692	58236	39965	43857	77957
427947	52653	17709	642820	433348	200325	113884	73984	84839
41019	17887	754	20332	18373	9329	3860	3621	1612
17862		666	45949	24772	7827	1464	4751	11741
136169	6332	4899	243926	136566	47323	26654	34549	51548
89870		1745	98790	54142	14508	4702	19362	37147
542089	3549	11443	846590	420088	113822	45787	58839	327171
635254	14951	4462	725784	577754	339151	251981	31266	70975
8428121		15460	2849416	1389424	860843	152541	141182	807768
1485330	9345	16931	3357820	1717770	237396	90592	274920	642922
2114781	41917	33397	4681590	2642664	643770	267240	460448	629712
***	***	488	***	***	***	***	***	***
401409	55787	7799	825762	421624	88394	46195	66032	120295
3081675	107275	39438	5587049	3921682	660936	166301	1946105	774468
1107134	120362	7555	2369881	378670	160755	46666	42761	878681
635322	284052	4269	541341	349314	102964	40195	73488	84450
1317837	133200	18890	1918648	1114487	335996	101512	241820	328351
1036895	31138	20856	2767725	1850228	483149	172034	477910	326972
2362954	171718	35039	5068697	3643677	891857	270444	1071492	577074
5702488	278976	57745	9894839	4396836	717011	396987	674871	1323536
1268538	8064	20319	2300471	1738733	546111	65205	611820	352166
3213970	52294	28043	5343475	4213207	648108	176977	2101381	393289
3567885	574601	46594	13728364	6135163	974947	306602	1425306	2590909
1187113	35434	17417	2162827	1588689	413375	80234	449488	169664
303569		5543	873192	475754	101161	17973	118927	209215
32457		553	71503	19340	7008	3239	1815	42459
23870		686	59997	38132	6359	129	16388	9584
13767470	9440	40293	12055332	2136034	53148	5490	393533	6681232
298212		1706	165829	113412	970	4	35367	35805
359195		8718	4498815	954220	11122		93158	2373939

Note: a) Sectors in this table are classified in accordance with the Standard for Classification of National Economic Sectors 2011 (GB/T 4754-2011).
b) Total Tax mainly includes payable VAT,payable income tax, business tax and surtax, and tax in management expenses.

11-11 续表

单位：万元

项目	Item	资产负债 Assets and Liabilities 固定资产原价 Total Original Value of Fixed Assets	负债合计 Total Liabilities	#流动负债合计 Total Current Liabilities	#应收账款 Accounts Payable
合计	**Total**	**41902709**	**60605765**	**42226798**	**13403969**
煤炭开采和洗选业	Mining and Washing of Coal	198110	898473	883143	299107
石油和天然气开采业	Extraction of Petroleum and Natural Gas	***	***	***	***
黑色金属矿采选业	Mining of Ferrous Metal Ores	4226669	10649273	2948659	748605
非金属矿采选业	Mining and Processing of Nonmetal Ores	***	***	***	***
开采辅助活动	MiningSsupport Service Activities	***	***	***	***
农副食品加工业	Processing of Food from Agricultural Products	345589	1383002	1180481	106797
食品制造业	Manufacture of Foods	297117	698795	555878	99189
酒、饮料和精制茶制造业	Manufacture of Wines,Beverage and Refined Tea	155452	268021	239715	11786
纺织业	Manufacture of Textile	117763	244025	180773	92868
纺织服装、服饰业	Manufacture of Textile Wearing Apparel and Ornament	147626	346447	324946	105230
皮革、毛皮、羽毛及其制品和制鞋业	Manufacture of Leather, Fur, Feather and its Products	2833	11282	11282	65
木材加工和木、竹、藤、棕、草制品业	Processing of Timbers, Manufacture of Wood, Bamboo, Rattan, Palm, and Straw Products	18961	32045	31847	6672
家具制造业	Manufacture of Furniture	77182	193423	157865	38170
造纸和纸制品业	Manufacture of Paper and Paper Products	48939	57688	55158	22464
印刷和记录媒介复制业	Printing,Reproduction of Recording Media	688844	289247	268908	92154
文教、工美、体育和娱乐用品制造业	Manufacture of Articles for Culture,Education, Artwork, Ssport and Entertainment Activity	118462	475426	428507	193665
石油加工、炼焦和核燃料加工业	Processing of Petroleum ,Coking,Processing of Mucleus Fuel	2704629	1836163	1831468	664849
化学原料和化学制品制造业	Manufacture of Chemical Raw Material and Chemical Products	1528780	2108378	1692976	213250
医药制造业	Manufacture of Medicines	1024246	1953597	1572506	426890
化学纤维制造业	Manufacture of Chemical fibres	***	***	***	***
橡胶和塑料制品业	Manufacture of Rubber and Plastics Products	190515	417991	313275	49007
非金属矿物制品业	Manufacture of Non-metallic Mineral Products	1317325	3396876	3085625	1253656
黑色金属冶炼和压延加工业	Manufacture and Processing of Ferrous Metals	1911262	1353192	496945	141545
有色金属冶炼和压延加工业	Manufacture and Processing of Non-ferrous Metals	145379	209608	175390	59608
金属制品业	Manufacture of Fabricated Metal Products	507262	1077648	906323	341764
通用设备制造业	Manufacture of General-purpose Machinery	517092	1147145	1037588	296719
专用设备制造业	Manufacture of Special-purpose Machinery	886391	2967471	2772832	951927
汽车制造业	Manufacture of Motor Vehicles	1751973	5442081	3649006	1271705
铁路、船舶、航空航天和其他运输设备制造业	Manufacture of Railway Locomotives, Building of Ships and Boats, Manufacture of Air and Spacecrafts and Other Transportation Equipments	605893	1442248	1274888	469429
电气机械和器材制造业	Manufacture of Electrical Machinery and Equipment	616013	3493768	3201787	1092478
计算机、通信和其他电子设备制造业	Manufacture of Computer, Communication Equipment and Other Electronic Equipment	3004427	5166632	3634483	1007267
仪器仪表制造业	Manufacture of Measuring Instrument and Meter	280888	1030113	957462	345167
其他制造业	Other Manufacturing	334594	307670	203702	67612
废弃资源综合利用业	Waste Recycling and Recovery	50951	49306	22942	4907
金属制品、机械和设备修理业	Repair of Fabricated Metal Products, Machinery and Equipment	16334	35156	34430	13041
电力、热力生产和供应业	Production and Supply of Electric Power and Heat Power	11868753	6840724	5007404	1909769
燃气生产和供应业	Production and Distribution of Gas	53143	120240	119869	24417
水的生产和供应业	Production and Distribution of Wwater	3660948	1906959	684021	29948

11-11 continued

(10000 yuan)

所有者权益合计 Total Owner's Equity	#实收资本 Paid-up Capital	损益 Profits and Loss 营业收入 Business Income	#主营业务收入 Main Business Income	营业成本 Business Cost	#主营业务成本 Main Business Cost	销售费用 Sales Expenses	管理费用 Management Expenses	财务费用 Financial Expenses	利润总额 Total Profits	应交税金合计 Total Tax	#营业税金及附加 Business Tax and Surtax	#主营业务税金及附加 Main Business Tax and Surtax	#应交增值税 Value Added Tax Payable
55129139	**31799651**	**78580140**	**76690581**	**69041968**	**67562571**	**2170911**	**3801824**	**709630**	**4146262**	**3616492**	**1205676**	**1190253**	**1685505**
1381398	593401	8157455	8133256	7742042	7736868	73796	64191	1949	304970	198460	34344	33949	96768
***	***	***	***	***	***	***	***	***	***	***	***	***	***
8622263	2839154	5315475	5094949	4877214	4654193	4178	114429	114589	805262	161716	23809	19422	122384
***	***	***	***	***	***	***	***	***	***	***	***	***	***
***	***	***	***	***	***	***	***	***	***	***	***	***	***
874140	310206	2243953	2227922	1894970	1885646	128671	94343	24734	80671	100570	45444	45428	35777
390918	247267	775212	758516	595124	582452	117613	49712	10581	15142	37742	2861	2780	26462
234484	113507	272724	268948	211874	210706	9015	19283	5672	-3673	51365	36297	36234	13261
222220	197514	355374	349070	320336	317727	3571	23644	3229	11258	7220	1280	1054	3334
296373	148826	554153	546078	339611	336543	86981	58672	5327	62664	52822	4389	4350	34834
9049	4520	42622	42560	37594	37558	1974	2017	347	1884	1131	73	69	733
13904	10614	27264	24676	23405	22726	2220	1984	250	-268	1335	225	98	908
50444	38627	151768	148394	120767	118256	17835	13377	2296	8438	9277	819	784	6727
41102	35557	122894	122160	113331	113090	3052	5816	529	-506	2585	209	209	1952
557342	354510	617134	595043	438578	426592	10856	84590	116	83686	57504	4479	4230	36294
250358	186443	799677	782245	736482	731118	21958	34832	7872	8892	27806	1697	1287	22895
1013253	58694	9138558	8674810	8137095	7678942	42812	182418	35652	13235	920280	764196	763679	144046
1248260	1047346	1717726	1600695	1542500	1455294	60584	152109	43807	-79975	55586	6777	6499	36664
2727982	923010	2183084	2160982	1075777	1062545	380117	235923	5281	513273	262647	21145	20973	166763
***	***	***	***	***	***	***	***	***	***	***	***	***	***
407771	182517	551094	533586	476788	467338	15357	31649	8581	20701	17984	1918	1826	10845
2187997	994063	3444764	3379729	2929263	2884250	125993	215866	38284	227367	114100	16819	15996	54948
1016689	589788	1217689	1194330	1214440	1198084	33258	24399	22932	-48722	15665	2292	2096	9375
331733	125988	741992	647814	622888	533226	6901	30130	4217	54040	63504	33926	33905	20779
840999	352450	1441084	1396105	1211658	1177294	26454	99100	15496	95033	57725	8168	7749	29686
1620511	728589	1180483	1141195	906773	882267	64202	131069	927	78243	68475	6254	6133	44085
2101224	857838	2675700	2637843	1953426	1932346	155096	284027	22030	256457	175409	21885	21531	106625
4452757	1885648	6129738	5949044	5563589	5437778	277411	408066	69476	450520	192271	33325	32964	106823
857406	376243	1397822	1383811	1170718	1163944	25719	123011	13107	81259	53064	4666	4563	32474
1849640	1255957	3440713	3284315	2878535	2735133	158050	255697	47060	149912	131909	14029	13527	89668
8561767	4484538	5050481	4905497	3905078	3846755	226619	547100	26489	497562	218614	26248	24295	123935
1132712	381849	1341026	1321755	959510	949527	70997	165542	6606	167325	91425	8832	8688	57923
565522	188436	443664	437454	337995	336601	8913	58432	-1005	43436	22134	2369	2369	12157
22197	17650	32466	32308	29191	29191	663	4791	170	2270	1938	180	180	1434
24841	6215	25796	25646	14889	14887	3143	4379	413	6037	3202	252	252	2220
5214608	7108699	13892310	13832437	13756241	13726853	3556	125903	119716	86521	267629	34969	32801	144929
45571	32390	307253	298585	277026	273382	2498	13968	-190	12472	16066	1903	1610	9542
2591856	2346438	421798	412647	431109	423179	307	50103	11222	34487	25878	2268	1752	11880

11-12 规模以上港澳台及外商投资工业企业主要经济指标(2012年)

单位：万元

项目	Item	企业单位个数(个) Number of Enterprises (unit)	#亏损企业 Loss-Suffering Enterprises	工业总产值(当年价格) Gross Output Value of Industry (at current prices)	工业增加值 Added Value of Industry	工业销售产值(当年价格) Sales Value of Industry (at current price)	#出口交货值 Delivery Value of Exports
合计	**Total**	**925**	**205**	**58600745**	**11835222**	**57988219**	**12214436**
在合计中：	**Of the Total:**						
中央企业	Central Enterprises	23	2	1304761	354647	1339853	102801
地方企业	Local Enterprises	902	203	57295983	11480575	56648367	12111635
在合计中：	**Of the Total:**						
轻工业	Light Industry	338	89	10413095	2989712	10040975	1487697
重工业	Heavy Industry	587	116	48187650	8845509	47947245	10726740
在合计中：	**Of the Total:**						
#大中型企业	Medium-and Large -sized Industry	271	47	50784463	10115882	50274848	11211450

11-12 续表

单位：万元

项目	Item	资产负债 Assets and Liabilities					
		固定资产原价 Total Original Value of Fixed Assets	负债合计 Total Liabilities	#流动负债合计 Total Current Liabilities	#应付账款 Accounts Payable	所有者权益合计 Total Owner's Equity	#实收资本 Paid-up Capital
合计	**Total**	**22445375**	**30692272**	**27063337**	**12609793**	**25132302**	**13925913**
在合计中：	**Of the Total:**						
中央企业	Central Enterprises	1833669	1496874	1212907	301373	1471742	945010
地方企业	Local Enterprises	20611706	29195398	25850429	12308420	23660560	12980904
在合计中：	**Of the Total:**						
轻工业	Light Industry	5484074	5466411	5179037	2022762	4699184	3295626
重工业	Heavy Industry	16961302	25225861	21884299	10587031	20433118	10630287
在合计中：	**Of the Total:**						
#大中型企业	Medium-and Large -sized Industry	19197283	24869278	22112107	10633576	19573654	10558553

MAIN ECONOMIC INDICATORS OF HONGKONG, MACAO, TAIWAN AND FOREIGN FUNDED INDUSTRIAL ABOVE DESIGNATED SIZE (2012)

(10000 yuan)

从业人员平均人数（人） Average Number of Employed Persons (person)	资产负债 Assets and Liabilities					
	资产总计 Total Assets	流动资产合计 Total Current Assets	#存货 Inventories	#产成品 Stock Inventory of Finished Products	#应收账款 Accounts Receivable	固定资产合计 Total Fixed Assets
397239	**55828742**	**36069168**	**7717142**	**2197304**	**10640878**	**11238927**
15105	2968617	1137185	224619	36168	386158	803054
382134	52860125	34931983	7492523	2161135	10254720	10435872
149382	10167894	6989310	1730292	772212	1761936	2031315
247857	45660847	29079858	5986850	1425092	8878942	9207612
317936	44444310	28986662	5945324	1626156	8375751	9340478

11-12 continued

(10000 yuan)

损益 Profits and Loss								应交税金合计 Total Tax			
营业收入 Business Income	#主营业务收入 Main Business Income	营业成本 Business Cost	#主营业务成本 Main Business Cost	销售费用 Sales Expenses	管理费用 Management Expenses	财务费用 Financial Expenses	利润总额 Total Profits		#营业税金及附加 Business Tax and Surtax	#主营业务税金及附加 Main Business Tax and Surtax	#应交增值税 Value Added Tax Payable
65302911	**63959636**	**52682977**	**51665529**	**4685550**	**2744979**	**281083**	**4449398**	**4025440**	**978233**	**972013**	**1946113**
1673901	1570951	1386050	1293082	39266	153446	48069	92221	100077	7648	7543	69101
63629011	62388686	51296928	50372447	4646284	2591533	233013	4357178	3925363	970586	964470	1877012
12168140	11682213	7760193	7396162	2521732	814695	102073	895650	1021947	95230	95147	678441
53134771	52277423	44922785	44269367	2163818	1930284	179009	3553748	3003493	883004	876866	1267673
56580521	55434137	45713728	44830253	4200395	2132743	221182	3754161	3536214	940919	935229	1651610

11-13 规模以上港澳台及外商投资工业企业主要经济指标(按行业分)(2012年)

单位：万元

项目	Item	企业单位个数(个) Number of Enterprises (unit)	#亏损企业 Loss-Suffering Enterprises	工业总产值(当年价格) Gross Output Value of Industry (at current prices)	工业增加值 Added Value of Industry
合计	**Total**	**925**	**205**	**58600745**	**11835222**
开采辅助活动	MiningSsupport Service Activities	2		***	***
农副食品加工业	Processing of Food from Agricultural Products	28	9	601722	83898
食品制造业	Manufacture of Foods	45	12	1586560	244615
酒、饮料和精制茶制造业	Manufacture of Wines,Beverage and Refined Tea	24	6	1432517	362029
纺织业	Manufacture of Textile	9	2	96258	15744
纺织服装、服饰业	Manufacture of textile wearing apparel and ornament	38	11	419568	127131
皮革、毛皮、羽毛及其制品和制鞋业	Manufacture of Leather, Fur, Feather and its Products	2		***	***
木材加工和木、竹、藤、棕、草制品业	Processing of Timbers, Manufacture of Wood, Bamboo, Rattan, Palm, and Straw Products	3	1	***	***
家具制造业	Manufacture of Furniture	13	2	238391	59826
造纸和纸制品业	Manufacture of Paper and Paper Products	17	4	488382	172451
印刷和记录媒介复制业	Printing,Reproduction of Recording Media	25	9	263639	96885
文教、工美、体育和娱乐用品制造业	Manufacture of Articles for Culture,Education, Artwork, Sport and Entertainment Activity	14	4	148354	36043
石油加工、炼焦和核燃料加工业	Processing of Petroleum ,Coking,Processing of Mucleus Fuel	4		395971	53393
化学原料和化学制品制造业	Manufacture of Chemical Raw Material and Chemical Products	53	10	1139072	303054
医药制造业	Manufacture of Medicines	32	6	2720538	1084435
橡胶和塑料制品业	Manufacture of Rubber and Plastics Products	30	9	397915	116140
非金属矿物制品业	Manufacture of Non-metallic Mineral Products	35	7	599503	170762
黑色金属冶炼和压延加工业	Manufacture and Processing of Ferrous Metals	5		462538	48142
有色金属冶炼和压延加工业	Manufacture and Processing of Non-ferrous Metals	7	2	44047	12982
金属制品业	Manufacture of Fabricated Metal Products	41	10	819227	191012
通用设备制造业	Manufacture of General-purpose Machinery	98	12	3437933	870323
专用设备制造业	Manufacture of Special-purpose Machinery	89	19	1590071	380998
汽车制造业	Manufacture of Motor Vehicles	107	20	19376367	4503986
铁路、船舶、航空航天和其他运输设备制造业	Manufacture of Railway Locomotives, Building of Ships and Boats, Manufacture of Air and Spacecrafts and Other Transportation Equipments	9	2	124469	36238
电气机械和器材制造业	Manufacture of Electrical Machinery and Equipment	46	10	2455997	629339
计算机、通信和其他电子设备制造业	Manufacture of Computer, Communication Equipment and Other Electronic Equipment	87	28	16313127	1474254
仪器仪表制造业	Manufacture of Measuring Instrument and Meter	37	7	663024	137078
其他制造业	Other Manufacturing	8	3	33958	8682
金属制品、机械和设备修理业	Repair of Fabricated Metal Products, Machinery and Equipment	5		321211	133082
电力、热力生产和供应业	Production and Supply of Electric Power and Heat Power	4		584404	155506
燃气生产和供应业	Production and Distribution of Gas	7		1639872	281803
水的生产和供应业	Production and Distribution of Water	1		***	***

注：1. 行业划分执行2011年国民经济行业分类标准(GB/T 4754-2011)。
2. 应交税金合计包括应交增值税、应交所得税、营业税金及附加和管理费用中的税金。

FOREIGN FUNDED INDUSTRIAL ABOVE DESIGNATED SIZE (BY SECTOR) (2012)

(10000 yuan)

工业销售产值(当年价格) Sales Value of Industry (at current price)	#出口交货值 Delivery Value of Exports	从业人员平均人数(人) Average Number of Employed Persons (person)	资产负债 Assets and Liabilities: 资产总计 Total Assets	流动资产合计 Total Current Assets	#存货 Inventories	#产成品 Stock Inventory of Finished Products	#应收账款 Accounts Receivable	固定资产合计 Total Fixed Assets
57988219	**12214436**	**397239**	**55828742**	**36069168**	**7717142**	**2197304**	**10640878**	**11238927**
***	***	588	***	***	***	***	***	***
582366	72955	11295	413389	260201	111986	34529	60882	115085
1549100	107800	29610	1674909	1159955	201081	104597	279526	422545
1412023	1376	20166	1514376	732803	138462	44724	104991	364434
88237	28232	1481	73579	51385	20709	13761	18504	19735
380850	233222	16494	400639	340631	146410	67278	76563	44272
***	***	908	***	***	***	***	***	***
***	***	388	***	***	***	***	***	***
220432	24916	4143	197761	141339	48802	24660	47628	43913
480124	41637	3575	419124	266680	69667	17915	82175	121332
273143	5287	5469	411915	251953	40518	17503	66872	131198
139139	65147	3297	142532	120361	85515	63635	9109	13676
395093		1246	112352	88751	29951	7790	17056	14749
1098751	58984	11721	1324678	731605	147476	63117	225942	484884
2573955	35552	23408	2372222	1822836	480513	265908	410097	278016
396241	61353	7421	462461	300368	63171	32546	108444	132621
588693	44171	9970	831279	552199	166273	38962	187925	195140
450254	51835	2120	260460	217785	65437	14532	103338	21828
43485	16069	698	57362	43533	16317	4383	6020	11885
815088	69715	9110	1191979	845512	213310	62776	227642	178002
3413932	746841	27000	4197384	3309160	1176216	322008	813285	641453
1553770	430678	17906	2844431	2079983	413972	72144	548474	245852
19301642	194335	57393	12959905	8275416	1226828	513854	2397678	3015308
125763	2065	948	128050	112640	26693	8502	48080	11967
2483128	548777	22730	4746205	4076718	1080997	104085	1679012	282602
16136405	9169364	84758	11126965	8079900	1436283	249197	2422191	2305134
675101	88638	7073	909203	755381	181167	28557	282320	58813
33263	19169	1088	31842	17664	5892	1517	5531	11085
359194	79890	6053	377549	192716	69239	564	87229	173350
583208		1402	3194182	331609	12281		95569	707646
1639872		7380	3026381	673945	5092	3085	145415	1110072
***	***	400	***	***	***	***	***	***

Note: a) Sectors in this table are classified in accordance with the Standard for Classification of National Economic Sectors 2011 (GB/T 4754-2011).
b) Total Tax mainly includes payable VAT,payable income tax, business tax and surtax, and tax in management expenses.

11-13 续表

单位：万元

项目	Item	资产负债 Assets and Liabilities			
		固定资产原价 Total Original Value of Fixed Assets	负债合计 Total Liabilities	#流动负债合计 Total Current Liabilities	#应付账款 Accounts Payable
合计	**Total**	**22445375**	**30692272**	**27063337**	**12609793**
开采辅助活动	MiningSsupport Service Activities	***	***	***	***
农副食品加工业	Processing of Food from Agricultural Products	210214	269178	261777	86031
食品制造业	Manufacture of Foods	765170	1169179	1141133	418928
酒、饮料和精制茶制造业	Manufacture of Wines,Beverage and Refined Tea	715242	876644	766307	240825
纺织业	Manufacture of Textile	48934	39659	39659	15479
纺织服装、服饰业	Manufacture of Textile Wearing Apparel and Ornament	89531	266892	255544	77367
皮革、毛皮、羽毛及其制品和制鞋业	Manufacture of Leather, Fur, Feather and its Products	***	***	***	***
木材加工和木、竹、藤、棕、草制品业	Processing of Timbers, Manufacture of Wood, Bamboo, Rattan, Palm, and Straw Products	***	***	***	***
家具制造业	Manufacture of Furniture	61284	108728	108238	23607
造纸和纸制品业	Manufacture of Paper and Paper Products	260069	182034	177665	67967
印刷和记录媒介复制业	Printing,Reproduction of Recording Media	282447	119381	110207	29002
文教、工美、体育和娱乐用品制造业	Manufacture of Articles for Culture,Education, Artwork, Sport and Entertainment Activity	24880	65086	65066	25241
石油加工、炼焦和核燃料加工业	Processing of Petroleum ,Coking,Processing of Mucleus Fuel	27283	31548	31548	19748
化学原料和化学制品制造业	Manufacture of Chemical Raw Material and Chemical Products	782212	568752	422182	108462
医药制造业	Manufacture of Medicines	466762	1233050	1158469	456377
橡胶和塑料制品业	Manufacture of Rubber and Plastics Products	260843	237139	234259	103107
非金属矿物制品业	Manufacture of Non-metallic Mineral Products	420951	374046	367660	104234
黑色金属冶炼和压延加工业	Manufacture and Processing of Ferrous Metals	61870	168694	154667	83275
有色金属冶炼和压延加工业	Manufacture and Processing of Non-ferrous Metals	22551	11901	10379	6767
金属制品业	Manufacture of Fabricated Metal Products	364412	483078	453654	156335
通用设备制造业	Manufacture of General-purpose Machinery	1066631	2046362	1953614	826252
专用设备制造业	Manufacture of Special-purpose Machinery	400164	1636285	1473698	590689
汽车制造业	Manufacture of Motor Vehicles	4581981	7454278	6952334	3976206
铁路、船舶、航空航天和其他运输设备制造业	Manufacture of Railway Locomotives, Building of Ships and Boats, Manufacture of Air and Spacecrafts and Other Transportation Equipments	19364	77023	77023	33835
电气机械和器材制造业	Manufacture of Electrical Machinery and Equipment	2257158	2560418	2161324	1109689
计算机、通信和其他电子设备制造业	Manufacture of Computer, Communication Equipment and Other Electronic Equipment	5694161	7286496	6161659	3501928
仪器仪表制造业	Manufacture of Measuring Instrument and Meter	125074	542182	519726	285745
其他制造业	Other Manufacturing	21671	11816	11808	5022
金属制品、机械和设备修理业	Repair of Fabricated Metal Products, Machinery and Equipment	302117	215407	213193	28508
电力、热力生产和供应业	Production and Supply of Electric Power and Heat Power	1569053	1446841	801514	50154
燃气生产和供应业	Production and Distribution of Gas	1413458	991970	796524	86065
水的生产和供应业	Production and Distribution of Water	***	***	***	***

11-13 continued

(10000 yuan)

所有者权益合计 Total Owner's Equity	#实收资本 Paid-up Capital	损益 Profits and Loss: 营业收入 Business Income	#主营业务收入 Main Business Income	营业成本 Business Cost	#主营业务成本 Main Business Cost	销售费用 Sales Expenses	管理费用 Management Expenses	财务费用 Financial Expenses	利润总额 Total Profits	应交税金合计 Total Tax	#营业税金及附加 Business Tax and Surtax	#主营业务税金及附加 Main Business Tax and Surtax	#应交增值税 Value Added Tax Payable
25132302	**13925913**	**65302911**	**63959636**	**52682977**	**51665529**	**4685550**	**2744979**	**281083**	**4449398**	**4025440**	**978233**	**972013**	**1946113**
***	***	***	***	***	***	***	***	***	***	***	***	***	***
144211	130813	686154	673893	589308	580931	50648	33970	7024	7664	14755	1059	1059	8647
505729	675409	2725459	2680497	1673406	1633547	724998	164975	5597	144324	215619	19809	19809	160414
637732	731045	1593977	1488779	1105392	1009962	331026	83306	14576	43400	123024	20528	20528	85937
33920	30060	102046	101929	89887	89820	3349	5060	1192	3017	3285	271	271	2093
133748	92741	454586	448093	335292	329204	45960	36234	5543	29653	20116	1488	1488	12405
***	***	***	***	***	***	***	***	***	***	***	***	***	***
***	***	***	***	***	***	***	***	***	***	***	***	***	***
89032	36340	182204	178576	134487	131700	22039	15243	1537	7806	10170	1253	1253	7771
236581	143406	530488	516831	401556	389957	18088	22083	-245	100664	52746	2721	2721	23624
292534	178598	284692	279663	214360	212513	13571	27079	281	28114	25206	2006	2006	16180
77446	15612	144469	143639	117367	117110	6996	10526	1079	8421	6741	446	446	3559
80804	11673	395865	395458	335004	335000	21137	9047	655	28402	16308	2759	2759	6107
754915	465440	1131420	1119852	768021	760528	197679	73772	8117	73786	99749	11644	11644	63452
1139172	521023	2837521	2663404	1219179	1072138	1036165	195669	63383	296638	373072	29293	29243	255284
224546	155562	458999	432564	373342	350264	20252	31999	3537	28511	28191	2064	2064	18452
455795	271637	600584	592440	475053	470351	30411	41663	6399	50521	40081	4067	4042	25613
91766	47946	470485	469864	439092	438856	11341	7126	1257	12459	10460	839	839	6089
45461	25162	45352	42209	35853	33377	993	3973	364	4240	2240	114	114	1311
708858	266159	1084099	1018686	879857	816675	56422	64719	10836	87619	48436	3440	3437	27490
2151021	920224	3748252	3669754	2987767	2942222	185249	211552	2832	350655	216909	14473	14473	121350
1208142	463754	2095903	1935952	1585128	1496425	129585	204413	14462	190136	121997	8712	8622	77607
5505259	2811819	19800768	19478233	15911416	15628078	733102	568017	27925	1795277	1947273	795250	795214	669848
51026	23879	137745	136370	97745	97151	10316	10647	959	17824	14134	829	829	10058
2185786	889371	2718556	2607068	2146187	2052978	139741	137670	18992	286242	169177	6968	6954	91520
3840465	2866735	19326300	19178926	17703632	17634930	782978	510804	27818	365642	282591	31907	26933	141473
367010	165717	880938	865899	651492	644966	76062	65560	3356	80063	56214	5312	5015	30657
20026	16091	34397	34248	28217	28217	1967	4707	490	-93	1605	169	169	1016
162141	135812	365363	358304	278590	276163	2333	66475	6906	10873	22265	3247	3197	13447
1747340	1236598	587593	583392	490621	487974		29824	35984	153421	51519	2232	2232	34876
2034411	431472	1655922	1643105	1442036	1431550	20269	84050	6832	231575	40305	3405	2725	22269
***	***	***	***	***	***	***	***	***	***	***	***	***	***

11-14 大中型工业企业主要经济指标(2012年)

单位：万元

项　目	Item	企业单位个数(个) Number of Enterprises (unit)	#亏损企业 Loss-Suffering Enterprises	工业总产值(当年价格) Gross Output Value of Industry (at current prices)	工业增加值 Added Value of Industry	工业销售产值(当年价格) Sales Value of Industry (at current price)	#出口交货值 Delivery Value of Exports
合　计	**Total**	**776**	**123**	**122395688**	**24996215**	**121322539**	**13356845**
在合计中:	**Of the Total:**						
中央工业	Central Industry	112	13	47398206	9729187	47323835	412359
地方工业	Local Industry	664	110	74997481	15267028	73998704	12944486
在合计中:	**Of the Total:**						
内资企业	Domestic Funded Enterprises	505	76	71611225	14880333	71047691	2145395
国有企业	State-Owned Enterprises	44	8	18448007	4482038	18412031	39997
集体企业	Collective Owned Enterprises	7		111363	55119	111691	7240
股份合作企业	Cooperative Enterprises	2	1	***	***	***	***
联营企业	Joint Owned Enterprises						
有限责任公司	Limited Liability Corporations	260	43	30036972	5609430	29640582	992963
股份有限公司	Share Holding Corporations Ltd.	112	18	20984625	4079860	20997888	921682
私营企业	Private Enterprises	80	6	1940775	600972	1804218	169589
港澳台商投资企业	Enterprises with Funds from Hongkong, Macao and Taiwan	74	15	9406031	1321823	9092430	1351347
港澳台合资经营	Joint Venture	37	6	2669263	641235	2596158	243293
港澳台合作经营	Cooperative	1	1	***	***	***	***
港澳台商独资企业	Hongkong, Macao and Taiwan Enterprises	28	6	5690836	561757	5471885	1045251
港澳台商投资股份有限公司	Hongkong, Macao and Taiwan Funded Share Holding Corporations	8	2	1038835	117174	1017098	62802
外商投资企业	Foreign Funded Enterprises	197	32	41378432	8794058	41182419	9860103
中外合资经营	Joint Venture	82	9	26138356	5728802	26060246	6934931
中外合作经营	Cooperative	4	2	156515	68493	163484	50000
外资(独资)企业	Foreign Enterprises	102	20	14344974	2699169	14209905	2810910
外商投资股份有限公司	Foreign Funded Share Holding Corporations	9	1	738587	297594	748783	64262
在合计中:	**Of the Total:**						
#农村企业	Rural Enterprises	15	2	376076	82894	367397	27861
在合计中:	**Of the Total:**						
轻工业	Light Industry	286	54	16268225	5017313	15597374	1298810
重工业	Heavy Industry	490	69	106127463	19978902	105725165	12058035
在合计中:	**Of the Total:**						
#大型企业	Large Enterprise	166	24	90946981	18354579	90499246	10671210

MAIN ECONOMIC INDICATORS OF LOCAL MEDIUM AND LARGE-SIZED INDUSTRIAL ENTERPRISES (2012)

(10000 yuan)

从业人员平均人数（人） Average Number of Employed Persons (person)	资产负债 Assets and Liabilities					
	资产总计 Total Assets	流动资产合计 Total Current Assets	#存货 Inventories	#产成品 Stock Inventory of Finished Products	#应收账款 Accounts Receivable	固定资产合计 Total Fixed Assets
871473	**246357552**	**89372597**	**14774724**	**3999080**	**21370188**	**53232691**
203728	132065016	30170554	4060322	613231	6276930	28858951
667745	114292537	59202043	10714402	3385849	15093258	24373741
553537	201913243	60385935	8829400	2372924	12994437	43892213
56943	102488893	17413975	1067460	119092	2690140	20418257
4021	121697	90030	18578	4254	11232	29649
3118	***	***	***	***	***	***
265668	60710435	24131604	3871965	961560	6352148	18581971
179614	36218880	17240419	3439274	1070288	3461883	4405920
44173	2281800	1449521	407332	197210	469025	429062
77887	11115746	8125449	1849371	380887	2490446	1413387
34251	2362226	1153547	306524	117286	416500	890738
404	***	***	***	***	***	***
33446	4178987	3280552	533779	146618	718893	422771
9786	4572703	3689696	1008635	116748	1354101	99702
240049	33328563	20861213	4095953	1245269	5885306	7927091
110216	16854312	11593436	2307765	631114	2870510	3347335
5748	249876	190136	49364	6194	66535	42160
113794	14198958	8134007	1623908	581690	2731976	4278689
10291	2025417	943634	114916	26272	216284	258908
9115	356733	257493	44824	19521	139500	78970
260344	21626847	12520242	2936384	1246239	2308331	4456210
611129	224730705	76852355	11838340	2752841	19061857	48776481
537652	203908585	64356977	9376214	2274734	13487189	45472429

11-14 续表

单位：万元

项目	Item	资产负债 Assets and Liabilities				
		固定资产原价 Total Original Value of Fixed Assets	负债合计 Total Liabilities	#流动负债合计 Total Current Liabilities	#应付账款 Accounts Payable	所有者权益合计 Total Owner's Equity
合　计	**Total**	**92727661**	**126860264**	**72936260**	**24267512**	**119494297**
在合计中:	**Of the Total:**					
中央工业	Central Industry	52517741	67290098	30774040	7826304	64774917
地方工业	Local Industry	40209919	59570165	42162220	16441208	54719381
在合计中:	**Of the Total:**					
内资企业	Domestic Funded Enterprises	73530378	101990986	50824154	13633936	99920643
国有企业	State-Owned Enterprises	35222215	50348175	16728516	3289031	52140717
集体企业	Collective Owned Enterprises	64186	59085	56965	21363	62613
股份合作企业	Cooperative Enterprises	***	***	***	***	***
联营企业	Joint Owned Enterprises					
有限责任公司	Limited Liability Corporations	28506409	33828805	20185887	6545604	26880409
股份有限公司	Share Holding Corporations Ltd.	9079755	16596336	12867432	3387961	19622542
私营企业	Private Enterprises	626576	1102099	960807	378657	1179310
港澳台商投资企业	Enterprises with Funds from Hongkong, Macao and Taiwan	2801239	7006939	6284331	2928426	4107435
港澳台合资经营	Joint Venture	1835829	1282953	1146199	334403	1077911
港澳台合作经营	Cooperative	***	***	***	***	***
港澳台商独资企业	Hongkong, Macao and Taiwan Enterprises	773009	3061645	2956590	1611363	1117342
港澳台商投资股份有限公司	Hongkong, Macao and Taiwan Funded Share Holding Corporations	191431	2661377	2180577	981975	1911316
外商投资企业	Foreign Funded Enterprises	16396044	17862339	15827775	7705150	15466220
中外合资经营	Joint Venture	6669291	9674154	9105930	4535395	7180158
中外合作经营	Cooperative	103781	150631	138166	63119	99245
外资(独资)企业	Foreign Enterprises	9118566	7610486	6256663	2985780	6588468
外商投资股份有限公司	Foreign Funded Share Holding Corporations	504406	427067	327017	120856	1598350
在合计中:	**Of the Total:**					
#农村企业	Rural Enterprises	136680	218242	192519	96814	138491
在合计中:	**Of the Total:**					
轻工业	Light Industry	9801018	10831283	9073772	2574837	10794201
重工业	Heavy Industry	82926643	116028981	63862489	21692676	108700096
在合计中:	**Of the Total:**					
#大型企业	Large Enterprise	79559664	105915653	55259155	18078280	97992928

11-14 continued

(10000 yuan)

#实收资本 Paid-up Capital	损益 Profits and Loss: 营业收入 Business Income	#主营业务收入 Main Business Income	营业成本 Business Cost	#主营业务成本 Main Business Cost	销售费用 Sales Expenses	管理费用 Manage-ment Expenses	财务费用 Financial Expenses	利润总额 Total Profits	应交税金合计 Total Tax	#营业税金及附加 Business Tax and Surtax	#主营业务税金及附加 Main Business Tax and Surtax	#应交增值税 Value Added Tax Payable
58932707	**136109201**	**133164274**	**114956261**	**112616074**	**6086465**	**5409172**	**1760951**	**10594600**	**8135963**	**2498539**	**2473020**	**3665135**
33105199	49817104	48892733	44738454	43928414	289950	1258221	1172214	4045682	3055296	1264416	1255452	1123844
25827508	86292097	84271541	70217807	68687660	5796515	4150952	588738	6548918	5080667	1234123	1217568	2541291
48374154	79528680	77730136	69242532	67785822	1886070	3276429	1539769	6840439	4599750	1557620	1537792	2013525
20977670	18790150	18608759	16108305	15972852	121564	293818	920807	3508759	1522385	434668	428373	620755
12653	117386	113102	92716	88837	2314	13851	-801	7772	14054	1873	1873	10153
***	***	***	***	***	***	***	***	***	***	***	***	***
20878115	35360881	34418711	32647722	31831254	526143	1433046	409212	1417832	1020035	143702	133695	617649
6120171	23201141	22593641	18897817	18452082	1062858	1359896	197195	1684173	1909774	965190	961967	680806
380746	1969462	1907078	1439022	1384284	159996	168124	13250	210682	125325	11544	11241	77756
1936714	12732186	12426579	10674903	10450605	1197439	471300	68193	395215	424022	39602	39548	291709
663865	2841590	2739247	2320545	2230964	153891	128418	33308	193235	149707	16091	16091	86671
***	***	***	***	***	***	***	***	***	***	***	***	***
565208	8559517	8496681	7199353	7186690	973450	256231	-3353	154760	226491	20437	20437	169133
705873	1323790	1183362	1149241	1027187	68986	86245	38239	47271	47294	3018	2964	35435
8621840	43848335	43007558	35038825	34379647	3002956	1661444	152989	3358946	3112192	901317	895681	1359901
3993430	26862048	26627898	21638206	21496046	1236758	863678	65009	2301480	2236443	828212	828127	827117
135774	306556	300174	253576	247440	36358	11130	-4841	2958	7797	757	757	5468
3800640	15850087	15333077	12591905	12160203	1664051	716785	85475	878021	790906	66884	61338	481428
691996	829645	746409	555138	475958	65790	69852	7346	176487	77046	5463	5458	45888
57589	384150	373190	328015	318180	13389	24044	3166	23484	18646	1992	1992	11452
5153186	18394922	17767685	11942616	11481479	3167508	1345300	163702	1554112	1827932	454233	448372	1014641
53779521	117714278	115396589	103013644	101134595	2918957	4063872	1597249	9040488	6308031	2044306	2024649	2650495
43063434	101355471	99566010	86772882	85291045	4390153	3165248	1509852	8076730	6202638	2133694	2116902	2646261

11-15 大中型工业企业主要经济指标(按行业分)(2012年)

单位：万元

项 目	Item	企业单位个数(个) Number of Enterprises (unit)	#亏损企业 Loss-Suffering Enterprises	工业总产值(当年价格) Gross Output Value of Industry (at current prices)	工业增加值 Added Value of Industry
合 计	**Total**	**776**	**123**	**122395688**	**24996215**
煤炭开采和洗选业	Mining and Washing of Coal	1		***	***
石油和天然气开采业	Extraction of Petroleum and Natural Gas	1		***	***
黑色金属矿采选业	Mining of Ferrous Metal Ores	6		1700406	444171
开采辅助活动	MiningSsupport Service Activities	4		2412413	1254225
农副食品加工业	Processing of Food from Agricultural Products	28	9	2265293	249105
食品制造业	Manufacture of Foods	39	8	1846647	280917
酒、饮料和精制茶制造业	Manufacture of Wines,Beverage and Refined Tea	15	4	1872285	550961
烟草制品业	Manufacture of Cigarettes and Tobacco	1		***	***
纺织业	Manufacture of Textile	4	1	27968	3726
纺织服装、服饰业	Manufacture of Textile Wearing Apparel and Ornament	53	14	1038080	453087
皮革、毛皮、羽毛及其制品和制鞋业	Manufacture of Leather, Fur, Feather and its Products	3		***	***
木材加工和木、竹、藤、棕、草制品业	Processing of Timbers, Manufacture of Wood, Bamboo, Rattan, Palm, and Straw Products	3	1	***	***
家具制造业	Manufacture of Furniture	11		386792	118319
造纸和纸制品业	Manufacture of Paper and Paper Products	4		365051	138021
印刷和记录媒介复制业	Printing,Reproduction of Recording Media	23	3	634221	284794
文教、工美、体育和娱乐用品制造业	Manufacture of Articles for Culture,Education, Artwork, Sport and Entertainment Activity	6	1	286008	34818
石油加工、炼焦和核燃料加工业	Processing of Petroleum ,Coking,Processing of Mucleus Fuel	5	1	8672050	1249992
化学原料和化学制品制造业	Manufacture of Chemical Raw Material and Chemical Products	22	4	1578637	328440
医药制造业	Manufacture of Medicines	44	4	4329942	1833038
化学纤维制造业	Manufacture of Chemical fibres	1		***	***
橡胶和塑料制品业	Manufacture of Rubber and Plastics Products	16	3	405376	91614
非金属矿物制品业	Manufacture of Non-metallic Mineral Products	44	4	2528057	510813
黑色金属冶炼和压延加工业	Manufacture and Processing of Ferrous Metals	7	1	1083955	15692
有色金属冶炼和压延加工业	Manufacture and Processing of Non-ferrous Metals	5	1	213255	32463
金属制品业	Manufacture of Fabricated Metal Products	35	3	1550356	349430
通用设备制造业	Manufacture of General-purpose Machinery	47	7	3652583	956615
专用设备制造业	Manufacture of Special-purpose Machinery	50	8	2985581	674195
汽车制造业	Manufacture of Motor Vehicles	61	9	23194368	4748549
铁路、船舶、航空航天和其他运输设备制造业	Manufacture of Railway Locomotives, Building of Ships and Boats, Manufacture of Air and Spacecrafts and Other Transportation Equipments	19	2	1475496	388350
电气机械和器材制造业	Manufacture of Electrical Machinery and Equipment	50	10	4740790	934508
计算机、通信和其他电子设备制造业	Manufacture of Computer, Communication Equipment and Other Electronic Equipment	87	13	18328376	1987208
仪器仪表制造业	Manufacture of Measuring Instrument and Meter	34	2	1145467	308100
其他制造业	Other Manufacturing	8	1	461506	100914
金属制品、机械和设备修理业	Repair of Fabricated Metal Products, Machinery and Equipment	1		***	***
电力、热力生产和供应业	Production and Supply of Electric Power and Heat Power	30	9	29800073	5302508
燃气生产和供应业	Production and Distribution of Gas	3		***	***
水的生产和供应业	Production and Distribution of Water	5		338750	101012

注：1．行业划分执行2011年国民经济行业分类标准(GB/T 4754-2011)。
2．应交税金合计包括应交增值税、应交所得税、营业税金及附加和管理费用中的税金。

MAIN ECONOMIC INDICATORS OF MEDIUM AND LARGE-SIZED INDUSTRIAL ENTERPRISES (BY SECTOR) (2012)

			资产负债 Assets and Liabilities						
工业销售产值（当年价格） Sales Value of Industry (at current price)	#出口交货值 Delivery Value of Exports	从业人员平均人数（人） Average Number of Employed Persons (person)	资产总计 Total Assets	流动资产合计 Total Current Assets	#存货 Inventories	#产成品 Stock Inventory of Finished Products	#应收账款 Accounts Receivable	固定资产合计 Total Fixed Assets	固定资产原价 Total Original Value of Fixed Assets
121322539	**13356845**	**871473**	**246357552**	**89372597**	**14774724**	**3999080**	**21370188**	**53232691**	**92727661**
***	***	15699	***	***	***	***	***	***	***
***	***	644	***	***	***	***	***	***	***
1693800		20948	19299037	6231995	211441	43071	1051078	3591700	4249001
2402413	132152	31439	5916313	3047995	732625	12990	1143003	1380007	2473727
2216946	38770	24103	2194882	1539665	263531	118133	105932	282912	422217
1792044	98822	41710	2149904	1273468	201692	107620	315535	537557	885937
1858346	4404	29292	2990006	1373495	230237	68953	78332	504415	1055797
***	***	940	358481	205986	122229	3630	22197	138908	210797
23532	2984	2262	206742	127481	19308	10411	4231	45703	74129
930724	266800	40010	1063300	800789	355595	197207	146760	135975	231019
***	***	1323	***	***	***	***	***	***	***
***	***	1702	***	***	***	***	***	***	***
355918	24666	9633	427459	229818	56608	31134	65798	108214	137897
363666	3127	1729	263341	170944	48352	10909	29997	65886	163788
640374	8451	15299	927722	461325	129034	50480	72927	377720	825286
270367	33993	4296	243874	145109	57395	36526	19328	57189	99694
8764682		16142	2896407	1430381	873161	151831	150378	810505	2703471
1581812	53511	21492	3123396	1531908	223569	85210	224096	707204	1715457
4081606	61172	45847	5819415	3617842	974182	476040	712184	690020	1141465
***	***	409	***	***	***	***	***	***	***
406588	90296	9876	743196	372298	52207	24405	71728	106545	192325
2479402	137033	35866	4694892	3134863	648044	142815	1424706	672336	1186442
1091299	163656	7595	2328888	360127	149483	38908	46930	867330	1904912
198776	86923	2952	288531	181718	57940	23115	52380	50181	84529
1520510	184172	23349	2471156	1416268	343221	85857	302627	428482	705998
3596036	633377	36454	5540619	4084485	1278286	408727	1071928	805334	1321958
2832722	520061	41677	5712030	4043548	886138	256263	1181333	638359	1056178
23278761	417880	100845	21363042	11556682	1660722	801055	2582408	4096728	5962093
1473228	1377	27310	3143933	2161519	993983	62500	572460	507596	916479
4638947	575223	39829	8416805	7013910	1487368	214268	3275683	518288	2597490
18056412	9454430	113934	21910865	12158738	2008557	408190	3253148	4610544	8225987
1133653	47673	16110	1812795	1319588	347101	61849	367723	153124	287152
377339		6605	1042570	600857	128177	16741	204203	248475	416236
***	***	5909	***	***	***	***	***	***	***
29789637	9440	60602	109748030	16535593	100432	5159	2435386	26380046	45897591
***	***	9626	***	***	***	***	***	***	***
339308		8015	4365600	897427	10068		91634	2322625	3570644

Note: a) Sectors in this table are classified in accordance with the Standard for Classification of National Economic Sectors 2011 (GB/T 4754-2011).
b) Total Tax mainly includes payable VAT,payable income tax, business tax and surtax, and tax in management expenses.

11-15 续表

单位：万元

项　　目	Item	资产负债 Assets and Liabilities			
		负　债 合　计 Total Liabilities	#流　动 负债合计 Total Current Liabilities	#应　付 账　款 Accounts Payable	所有者 权　益 合　计 Total Owner's Equity
合 计	**Total**	**126860264**	**72936260**	**24267512**	**119494297**
煤炭开采和洗选业	Mining and Washing of Coal	***	***	***	***
石油和天然气开采业	Extraction of Petroleum and Natural Gas	***	***	***	***
黑色金属矿采选业	Mining of Ferrous Metal Ores	10672432	2970048	761437	8626214
开采辅助活动	Mining Support Service Activities	2661823	2224148	911581	3254490
农副食品加工业	Processing of Food from Agricultural Products	1281981	1096566	114418	912901
食品制造业	Manufacture of Foods	1397466	1312399	445135	752439
酒、饮料和精制茶制造业	Manufacture of Wines, Beverage and Refined Tea	1486167	1336085	208879	1503840
烟草制品业	Manufacture of Cigarettes and Tobacco	***	***	***	***
纺织业	Manufacture of Textile	85896	24951	5268	120845
纺织服装、服饰业	Manufacture of Textile Wearing Apparel and Ornament	619356	562883	189669	443944
皮革、毛皮、羽毛及其制品和制鞋业	Manufacture of Leather, Fur, Feather and its Products	***	***	***	***
木材加工和木、竹、藤、棕、草制品业	Processing of Timbers, Manufacture of Wood, Bamboo, Rattan, Palm, and Straw Products	***	***	***	***
家具制造业	Manufacture of Furniture	267715	220765	46918	159745
造纸和纸制品业	Manufacture of Paper and Paper Products	123782	123782	42654	139558
印刷和记录媒介复制业	Printing, Reproduction of Recording Media Manufacture	302923	276298	84050	624799
文教、工美、体育和娱乐用品制造业	Manufacture of Articles for Culture,Education, Artwork, Sport and Entertainment Activity	124946	84290	26738	118929
石油加工、炼焦和核燃料加工业	Processing of Petroleum ,Coking,Processing of Mucleus Fuel	1845970	1842430	672953	1050436
化学原料和化学制品制造业	Manufacture of Chemical Raw Material and Chemical Products	1882665	1465774	143489	1238995
医药制造业	Manufacture of Medicines	2752503	2285666	753337	3066911
化学纤维制造业	Manufacture of Chemical fibres	***	***	***	***
橡胶和塑料制品业	Manufacture of Rubber and Plastics Products	369732	273246	62283	372688
非金属矿物制品业	Manufacture of Non-metallic Mineral Products	2547887	2265235	807095	2147005
黑色金属冶炼和压延加工业	Manufacture and Processing of Ferrous Metals	1309654	452755	141751	1019234
有色金属冶炼和压延加工业	Manufacture and Processing of Non-ferrous Metals	91027	82505	41142	197504
金属制品业	Manufacture of Fabricated Metal Products	1179142	984253	363748	1292014
通用设备制造业	Manufacture of General-purpose Machinery	2438791	2254133	856373	3101760
专用设备制造业	Manufacture of Special-purpose Machinery	3574389	3295705	1214034	2137640
汽车制造业	Manufacture of Motor Vehicles	12080404	9820541	4711653	9282638
铁路、船舶、航空航天和其他运输设备制造业	Manufacture of Railway Locomotives, Building of Ships and Boats, Manufacture of Air and Spacecrafts and Other Transportation Equipments	2179617	1842609	498152	964317
电气机械和器材制造业	Manufacture of Electrical Machinery and Equipment	5090137	4527025	1808011	3326667
计算机、通信和其他电子设备制造业	Manufacture of Computer, Communication Equipment and Other Electronic Equipment	11027861	8537226	3900028	10883000
仪器仪表制造业	Manufacture of Measuring Instrument and Meter	971726	872054	325755	841059
其他制造业	Other Manufacturing	394827	269866	128896	647743
金属制品、机械和设备修理业	Repair of Fabricated Metal Products, Machinery and Equipment	***	***	***	***
电力、热力生产和供应业	Production and Supply of Electric Power and Heat Power	54351666	19383322	4672297	55396364
燃气生产和供应业	Production and Distribution of Gas	***	***	***	***
水的生产和供应业	Production and Distribution of Water	1838330	613672	25745	2527270

11-15 continued

(10000 yuan)

#实收资本 Paid-up Capital	营业收入 Business Income	#主营业务收入 Main Business Income	营业成本 Business Cost	#主营业务成本 Main Business Cost	销售费用 Sales Expenses	管理费用 Manage-ment Expenses	财务费用 Financial Expenses	利润总额 Total Profits	应交税金合计 Total Tax	#营业税金及附加 Business Tax and Surtax	#主营业务税金及附加 Main Business Tax and Surtax	#应交增值税 Value Added Tax Payable
58932707	**136109201**	**133164274**	**114956261**	**112616074**	**6086465**	**5409172**	**1760951**	**10594600**	**8135963**	**2498539**	**2473020**	**3665135**
***	***	***	***	***	***	***	***	***	***	***	***	***
***	***	***	***	***	***	***	***	***	***	***	***	***
2838309	5332167	5109485	4893779	4668373	3995	115824	115045	803873	164200	24043	19655	125115
2758525	2413051	2395460	2226728	2213890	9323	96149	45239	85943	123664	37672	37538	62890
346693	2489089	2476464	2106946	2100521	152236	99779	26965	78016	106499	45860	45845	39444
781669	3046915	2993981	1932934	1886800	803067	169678	11959	132602	223922	20569	20498	167238
586724	2082128	1927619	1430617	1294247	366043	111821	30082	69821	232515	86300	85949	128033
***	***	***	***	***	***	***	***	***	***	***	***	***
90747	44123	40407	33539	32880	342	9748	649	-931	3098	714	532	1649
190589	1073865	1059068	661320	651314	166356	103527	10614	125303	96101	7277	7271	63071
***	***	***	***	***	***	***	***	***	***	***	***	***
***	***	***	***	***	***	***	***	***	***	***	***	***
52420	331087	324563	248234	242794	34509	28313	3247	31263	24299	2459	2424	17063
49292	398791	386571	289085	278575	14248	13302	-646	94847	43860	2473	2473	17030
392240	698001	664069	524950	503594	14924	98906	-381	59911	56462	4899	4633	37651
79013	362605	352905	328307	327676	8177	25547	4041	6689	7614	1099	713	3519
59895	9464447	9006442	8415039	7961521	59437	186239	36080	38790	934337	766550	766033	149014
916976	1716581	1571391	1362420	1244482	189815	152825	33301	-35475	104520	14450	14030	68797
1008509	4377756	4190589	1940326	1785281	1311059	351263	70334	696411	566113	45216	45023	377068
***	***	***	***	***	***	***	***	***	***	***	***	***
139942	448085	435531	371543	361339	15877	30610	7514	21399	21676	1740	1707	13921
868131	2800348	2741970	2315846	2274103	107789	178758	30986	203243	116920	17389	16887	62863
597314	1190501	1170095	1181095	1165344	40144	22769	22692	-48003	13783	2292	2216	7737
73258	222016	212841	186664	179055	4284	17274	1316	13814	5182	668	668	2380
513354	1839174	1745499	1499427	1422954	57867	136283	20658	153781	74668	7456	6360	38235
1241015	3913167	3826119	3097328	3038627	180266	231387	2215	385800	246134	18181	18105	143725
922814	3484992	3307475	2635896	2536571	206946	368861	32768	280458	201131	20822	20444	128142
4350809	24021451	23582391	19855839	19501801	973013	870524	92045	2107216	2044351	822961	822596	724852
380738	1618242	1601642	1330291	1319437	16566	168711	16065	103013	56063	4799	4719	33391
1628816	4948853	4701507	4028676	3805117	252041	279358	54522	400408	247505	15247	14890	144528
6554893	22388049	22114692	19941479	19824680	940860	876732	46186	769554	432449	49835	43046	223404
290921	1357338	1341119	982593	973315	94410	135022	7357	153755	96189	9592	9427	56808
260917	542868	536614	416346	414933	7205	69192	-1226	55941	22087	2033	2033	11274
***	***	***	***	***	***	***	***	***	***	***	***	***
27729802	29918450	29818096	27919430	27845393	3595	153018	1017513	3363526	1366057	207866	205183	646981
***	***	***	***	***	***	***	***	***	***	***	***	***
2299924	398243	392002	405352	399581	307	46495	11335	34967	25877	2121	1713	12029

11-16 规模以上工业企业主要工业产品生产能力(2012年)
CAPACITY OF MAIN INDUSTRIAL PRODUCTS IN INDUSTRIAL ABOVE DESIGNATED SIZE (2012)

主要工业产品名称		Name of Main Industrial Product		年末生产能力 Year-end Capacity
原油加工能力	（吨）	Crude Oil Processing Capacity	(ton)	14000000
硅酸盐水泥熟料	（吨）	Portland Cement Chamotte	(ton)	7166000
发电设备容量总计	（万千瓦）	Total Capacity of Power Generation Equipment	(10000 KW)	707
火电设备容量	（万千瓦）	Capacity of Thermal Power Equipment	(10000 KW)	591
水电设备容量	（万千瓦）	Capacity of Hydropower Equipment	(10000 KW)	101
风电设备容量	（万千瓦）	Capacity of Wind Power Equipment	(10000 KW)	15
原　煤	（吨）	Raw Coal	(ton)	5200000
卷　烟	（万支）	Cigarette	(10000 units)	4023000
棉纺锭	（锭）	Cotton Spindle (Ring Spindle Spinning)	(unit)	19360
气流纺锭	（头）	Air Spinning Spindle (Rotating-cup Spinning)	(unit)	1656
棉布织机	（台）	Cotton Cloth Weaver	(unit)	66
水　泥	（吨）	Cement	(ton)	10200000
钢　材	（吨）	Rolled Steel	(ton)	2433156
金属切削机床	（台）	Metal-Cutting Machine Tools	(unit)	23683
汽　车	（辆）	Motor Vehicle	(unit)	2314500
#基本型乘用车(轿车)	（辆）	Basic-type Passenger Vehicles (Sedans)	(unit)	725000
家用电冰箱	（台）	Household Refrigerators	(unit)	1500000
移动通信手持机(手机)	（台）	Mobile Telephone	(unit)	215500000
微型计算机设备	（台）	Micro-computer	(unit)	21528000

11-17 主要工业产品产量(2012年)
OUTPUT OF MAIN INDUSTRIAL PRODUCTS (2012)

工业产品名称		Name of Main Industrial Product		2012
单晶硅	(千克)	Monocrystalline Silicon	(kg)	119321.7
中成药	(万吨)	Prepared Chinese Medicine	(10000 ton)	3.7
沥青和改性沥青防水卷材	(万平方米)	Asphalt and Modified Asphalt Waterproof Roofing	(10000 sq.m)	5077.6
纤维增强塑料制品	(万吨)	Fiber-reinforced Plastic Products	(10000 ton)	2.2
耐火材料制品	(万吨)	Products Made from Fire-resistant Materials	(10000 ton)	49.6
冷轧薄宽钢带	(万吨)	Cold-rolled Thin Broad Steel Bands	(10000 ton)	102.1
单一稀土金属	(千克)	Single Rare Earth Metals	(kg)	161148.0
发动机	(万千瓦)	Engines	(10000 KW)	2894.9
气动元件	(万件)	Pneumatic Components	(10000 unit)	17573.1
数控金属切削机床	(台)	Digital Metal Cutting Tools	(unit)	18887
机床数控装置	(套)	Lathe Digital Controllers	(unit)	71202
工业电炉	(台)	Industrial Electric Cookers	(unit)	298
环境污染防治专用设备	(台套)	Special Equipment for Prevention and Control of Environmental Pollution	(set)	91342
汽 车	(万辆)	Automobiles	(10000 unit)	167.0
#基本型成用车(轿车)	(万辆)	Including: Basic-type Passenger Vehicles (Sedans)	(10000 unit)	78.5
运动型多用途乘用车(SUV)	(万辆)	Sport Multi-purpose Vehicles(SUV)	(10000 unit)	19.8
载货汽车	(万辆)	Freight Trucks	(10000 unit)	60.0
改装汽车	(万辆)	Refitted Automobiles	(10000 unit)	1.5
风力发电机组	(万千瓦)	Wind Power Generator Units	(10000 KW)	334.9
锂离子电池	(万只)	Lithiums Ion Batteries	(10000 unit)	9519.9
移动通信手持机(手机)	(万台)	Mobile Communication Handsets	(10000 unit)	19949.3
微型计算机设备	(台)	Micro-computer Equipment	(unit)	10745377
服务器	(台)	Servers	(unit)	99843
液晶显示模组	(万套)	Liquid Crystal Display Modules	(10000 unit)	3468.8
显示器	(万台)	Displays	(10000 unit)	796.9
集成电路	(亿块)	Integrated Circuits	(100 million pieces)	31.9
彩色电视机	(台)	Color TV Sets	(unit)	543533

11-18 规模以上高技术制造业主要经济指标(2012年)
GROSS OUTPUT VALUE OF HIGH-TECH MANUFACTURING IN INDUSTRIAL ABOVE DESIGNATED SIZE (2012)

单位：亿元 (100 million yuan)

项目	Item	工业总产值 Gross Output Value of Industry	主营业务收入 Main Business Income	利润总额 Total Profits	应交税金 Tax Payable
合计	**Total**	**3031.6**	**3460.0**	**236.0**	**148.6**
按登记注册类型分	**Grouped by Registration Status**				
内资	Domestic Funded Enterprises	970.0	1099.1	148.4	72.8
国有	State-owned	52.8	52.6	5.9	2.6
集体	Collective-owned	0.8	0.9		
股份合作企业	Cooperative Enterprises	3.9	4.6	0.1	0.3
联营企业	Joint Owned Enterprises	0.6	0.6	0.1	0.1
有限责任公司	Limited-Liability Corporations	467.7	500.9	46.1	26.2
股份有限公司	Share Holding Corporations Ltd.	313.8	403.4	81.4	33.9
私营企业	Private Enterprises	130.3	136.1	14.8	9.7
其他	Others				
港澳台商投资	Enterprises with Funds from Hongkong, Macao and Taiwan	550.9	832.0	22.5	21.7
外商投资	Foreign-funded	1510.7	1528.9	65.0	54.1
按高技术领域分	**Grouped by the High-tech Field Technology**				
信息化学品制造	Information Chemicals Manufacturing	0.5	0.4	0.2	0.1
医药制造业	Pharmaceutics	543.3	525.7	86.1	67.5
航空航天器制造	Aircraft Manufacturing	74.7	72.2	6.8	0.9
电子及通信设备制造业	Electronic and Communication Equipment Manufacturing	1627.7	1731.1	81.3	39.6
电子计算机及办公设备制造业	Electronic Computer and Office Equipment Manufacturing	455.1	766.9	12.7	15.1
医疗设备及仪器仪表制造业	Medical Equipment, Apparatus and Instrument Manufacturing	329.2	362.6	48.8	25.4
其他	Others	1.0	1.0	0.2	

注：应交税金合计包括应交增值税、应交所得税、营业税金及附加和管理费用中的税金。
Note: Total Tax mainly includes payable VAT,payable income tax, business tax and surtax, and tax in management expenses.

11-19 规模以下工业主要指标(2012年)
MAJOR INDICATORS FOR INDUSTRIAL ENTERPRISES BELOW DESIGNATED SIZE (2012)

项目	Item	单位个数(个) Number of Enterprises (unit)	从业人员平均人数(人) Average Number of Persons Employed(person)	工业总产值(当年价格，万元) Gross Output Value (at current prices, 10000 yuan)
合计	**Total**	**28108**	**319971**	**7091233**
法人工业企业	Corporation Unit	18838	270799	6696755
个体经营工业单位	Individual Unit	9270	49172	394478

注：规模以下工业企业指年主营业务收入2000万元以下的法人工业企业和全部个体经营工业单位。
Note: Industrial enterprises below designed size refers to enterprises with main business income below 20 million yuan and all individual industrial units.

主要统计指标解释

工业 指从事自然资源的开采，对采掘品和农产品进行加工和再加工的物质生产部门。具体包括：（1）对自然资源的开采，如采矿、晒盐、森林采伐等（但不包括禽兽捕猎和水产捕捞）；（2）对农副产品的加工、再加工，如粮油加工、食品加工、扎花、纺织、制革等；（3）对采掘品的加工、再加工，如炼铁、炼钢、化工生产、石油加工、机器制造、木材加工等，以及电力、自来水、煤气的生产和供应等；（4）对工业品的修理、翻新，如机器设备的修理。

轻工业 指主要提供生活消费品和制作手工工具的工业。按其所使用的原料不同，可分为两大类：（1）以农业为原料的轻工业，是指直接或间接以农产品为基本原料的轻工业。主要包括食品制造、饮料制造、烟草加工、纺织、缝纫、皮革和毛皮制作、造纸以及印刷等工业；（2）以非农产品为原料的轻工业，是指以工业品为原料的轻工业。主要包括文教体育用品、化学药品制造、合成纤维制造、日用化学制品、日用玻璃制品、日用金属制品、手工工具制造、医疗器械制造、文化和办公用机械制造等工业。

重工业 是指为国民经济各部门提供物质技术基础的主要生产资料的工业。按其生产性质和产品用途，可以分为下列三类：（1）采掘（伐）工业，是指对自然资源的开采，包括石油开采、煤炭开采、金属矿开采、非金属矿开采和木材采伐等工业；（2）原材料工业，指向国民经济各部门提供基本材料、动力和燃料的工业。包括金属冶炼及加工、炼焦及焦炭化学、化工原料、水泥、人造板以及电力、石油和煤炭加工等工业；（3）加工工业，是指对工业原材料进行再加工制造的工业。包括装备国民经济各部门的机械设备制造工业、金属结构、水泥制品等工业，以及为农业提供的生产资料如化肥、农药等工业。

根据上述划分原则，修理业中以重工业产品为修理作业对象的划为重工业，反之划为轻工业。

工业总产值 指工业企业在报告期内生产的以货币形式表现的工业最终产品和提供工业劳务活动的总价值量。它包括：在本企业内不再进行加工，经检验、包装入库（规定不需包装的产品除外）的成品价值，对外加工费收入，自制半成品、在制品期末期初差额价值。工业总产值采用“工厂法”计算，即以工业企业作为一个整体，按企业生产活动的最终成果来计算，企业内部不允许重复计算，不能把企业内部各个车间（分厂）生产的成果相加。但在企业之间、行业之间、地区之间存在着重复计算。

轻重工业总产值的划分也是按“工厂法”计算的，即一个工业企业在正常情况下生产的主要产品的性质属于轻工业，则该企业的全部总产值作为轻工业总产值；一个工业企业生产的主要产品的性质属于重工业，则该企业的全部总产值作为重工业总产值。

工业增加值 是指工业企业在报告期内以货币形式表现的工业生产活动的最终成果，反映企业生产过程中新创造的价值。

工业销售产值 是以货币形式表现的，工业企业在报告期内销售的本企业生产的工业产品或提供工业性劳务价值的总价值量。包括企业在报告期内实际销售（包括本期生产和非本期生产）的全部成品、半成品的总价值，报告期内完成的对外承接的工业品加工的加工费收入，对外工业品修理作业可获取的加工费收入和对内非工业部门提供的加工修理、设备安装等收入。已销售的成品、半成品不论是本期生产的、还是非本期生产的，只要是本期销售出去的均包括在内。企业为本单位基本建设部门、生活福利部门等提供的产品和工业性作业及自制设备也应视同销售，这部分也应作为销售统计。

工业销售产值的计算价格和计算方法与工业总产值一致，但两者计算的基础不同，工业销售产值计算的基础是产品销售总量，工业总产值计算的基础是工业产品生产总量。工业销售产值不包括自制半成品、在制品期末期初差额价值，而工业总产值包括这部分内容。

资产总计 指企业过去的交易或者事项形成的、由企业拥有或者控制的、预期会给企业带来经济利益的资源。资产一般按流动性分为流动资产和非流动资产。其中流动资产可分为货币资金、交易性金融资产、应收票据、应收账款、预付款项、其他应收款、存货等；非流动资产可分为长期股权投资、固定资产、无形资产及其他非流动资产等。

（1）流动资产合计 资产满足以下条件之一应归为流动资产：①预计在一个正常营业周期中变现、出售或耗用，主要包括存货、应收账款等；②主要为交易目的而持有；③预计在资产负债表日起一年内（含一年）变现；④自资产负债表日起一年内，交换其他资产或清偿负债的能力不受限制的现金或现金等价物。包括货币资金、应收票据、应收账款、存货等项目。

（2）固定资产合计 指企业为生产商品、提供劳务、出租或经营管理而持有的，使用寿命超过一个会计年度的有形资产。包括使用期限超过一年的房屋、建筑物、机器、机械、运输工具以及其他与生产、经营有关的设备、器具、工具等。固定资产合计是时点指标，表示固定资产经过扣减折旧、减值准备等后的期末余额。

负债合计 指企业过去的交易或者事项形成的，预期会导致经济利益流出企业的现时义务。负债一般按偿还期长短分为流动负债和非流动负债。

（1）流动负债合计 负债满足下列条件之一的应归为流动负债：①预计在一个正常营业周期中清偿；②主要为交易目的而持有；③自资产负债表日起一年内到期应予清偿；④企业无权自主地将清偿推迟至资产负债表日后一年以上。包括短期借款、应付票据、应付账款、应付职工薪酬、应交税费等项目。

（2）非流动负债合计 指流动负债之外的负债。包括长期借款、应付债券等。

所有者权益合计 指企业资产扣除负债后由所有者享有的剩余权益。公司的所有者权益又称股东权益。包括实收资本、资本公积、盈余公积、未分配利润等。

实收资本 指企业各投资者实际投入的资本（或股本）总额，包括货币、实物、无形资产等各种形式的投入。实收资本按投资主体可分为国家资本、集体资本、法人资本、个人资本、港澳台资本和外商资本。

主营业务收入 指企业确认的销售商品、提供劳务等主营业务的收入。

主营业务成本 指企业经营主要业务所发生的成本总额。

主营业务税金及附加 指企业经营主要业务应负担的营业税、消费税、城市维护建设税、教育费附加等。

营业利润 指企业从事生产经营活动所取得的利润。

利润总额 指企业在一定会计期间的经营成果，是生产经营过程中各种收入扣除各种耗费后的盈余，反映企业在报告期内实现的亏盈总额。

应交增值税 指企业按税法规定，从事货物销售或提供加工、修理修配劳务等增加货物价值的活动本期应交纳的税金。

应交增值税=销项税额-（进项税额-进项税额转出）-出口抵减内销产品应纳税额-减免税款+出口退税

应交增值税不含期初未抵扣税额。

工业产品销售率 指报告期工业销售产值与工业总产值之比。计算公式：

$$工业产品销售率(\%)=\frac{报告期现价工业销售产值}{报告期现价工业总产值}\times100\%$$

工业增加值率 指报告期工业增加值占工业总产值的比重，反映降低中间消耗的经济效益。计算公式：

$$工业增加率(\%)=\frac{报告期现价工业增加值}{报告期现价工业总产值}\times100\%$$

工业成本费用利润率 指在一定时期内实现的利润与成本费用之比，是反映工业生产成本及费用投入的经济效益指标，同时也是反映降低成本的经济效益的指标。计算公式：

$$工业成本费用利润率(\%)=\frac{利润总额}{成本费用总额}\times100\%$$

工业全员劳动生产率 指根据产品的价值量指标计算的平均每一个职工在单位时间内创造的工业生产最终成果。是考核企业经济活动的重要指标，是企业生产技术水平、经济管理水平、职工技术熟练程度和劳动积极性的综合表现。

$$工业全员劳动生产率（元/人）=\frac{工业增加值（现价）}{从业人员平均人数}$$

流动资产周转次数 指在一定时期内流动资产完成的周转次数，反映流动资产的周转速度。计算公式：

$$流动资产周转次数(次)=\frac{产品销售收入}{流动资产平均余额}$$

流动比率 是反映企业每百元流动负债中，有多少元流动资产作后盾。计算公式：

$$流动比率(倍)=\frac{流动资产总额}{流动负债总额}$$

速动比率 是衡量企业流动资产中可以立即用于偿付流动负债的能力。计算公式：

$$速动比率(倍)=\frac{流动资产总额-存货}{流动负债总额}$$

资产负债率 反映在企业资产总额中有多少资产是通过借债而得的，也可以用于衡量企业利用债权人提供资金进行经营活动的能力以及企业在清算时保护债权人利益的程度。计算公式：

$$资产负债率=\frac{负债总额}{资产总额}\times100\%$$

总资产贡献率 反映企业全部资产的获利能力，是企业经营业绩和管理水平的集中体现，是评价和考核企业盈利能力的核心指标。计算公式为：

$$总资产贡献率=(利润总额+税金总额+利息支出)\div平均资产总额\times100\%$$

其中：税金总额为主营业务税金及附加、管理费用中的税金与应交增值税之和；平均资产总额为期初期末资产总计的算术平均值。

资本保值增值率 反映企业净资产的变动状况，是企业发展能力的集中体现。计算公式为：

$$资本保值增值率=\frac{报告期期末所有者权益}{上年同期期末所有者权益}\times100\%$$

高技术制造业 在高技术产业中扣除软件开发业以外的全部行业。

Explanatory Notes on Main Statistical Indicators

Industry refers to the material production sector which is engaged in extraction of natural resources and processing and reprocessing of minerals and agricultural products, including (1) extraction of natural resources, such as mining, salt production, logging (but not including hunting and fishing); (2) processing and reprocessing of farm and sideline produces, such as cereal and oil processing, foodstuff processing, cotton ginning, textile, and leather making; (3) manufacture of industrial products, such as steel making, iron smelting, chemicals manufacturing, petroleum processing, machine building, timber processing; water and gas production and electricity generation and supply; (4) repairing of industrial products such as the repairing of machinery and means of transport (including cars).

Light Industry refers to the industry that produces consumer goods and hand tools. It consists of two categories, depending on the materials used:

(1) Industries using farm products as raw materials. These are branches of light industry which directly or indirectly use farm products as basic raw materials, including the manufacture of food and beverages, tobacco processing, textile, clothing, fur and leather manufacturing, paper making, printing, etc.

(2) Industries using non-farm products as raw materials. These are branches of light industry which use manufactured goods as raw materials, including the manufacture of cultural, educational articles and sports goods, chemicals, synthetic fiber, chemical products for daily use, glass products for daily use, metal products for daily use, hand tools, medical apparatus and instruments, and the manufacture of cultural and clerical machinery.

Heavy Industry refers to the industry which produces capital goods, and provides various sectors of the national economy with necessary material and technical basis. It consists of the following three branches according to the purpose of production or the use of products:

(1) Mining, quarrying and logging industry refers to the industry that extracts natural resources, including extraction of petroleum, coal, metal and non-metal ores and logging.

(2) Raw materials industry refers to the industry that provides various sectors of the national economy with raw materials, fuels and power. It includes smelting and processing of metals, coking and coke chemistry, chemical materials and building materials such as cement, plywood, and power, petroleum refining and coal dressing.

(3) Manufacturing industry refers to the industry that processes raw materials. It includes machine building industry which equips sectors of the national economy, industries of metal structure and cement products, industries producing means of agricultural production, such as chemical fertilizers and pesticides.

According to the above principle of classification, the repairing trades which are engaged primarily in repairing products of heavy industry are classified into heavy industry while these engaged in repairing products of light industry are classified into light industry.

Gross Output Value of Industry is the total value of final industrial products made and industrial labor service provided by industrial enterprises in the year. It includes the value of the finished products, which are not to be further processed in the enterprises and have been inspected, packed and put in storage (with the exception of products not to be packaged as stated), the value of industrial services rendered to other units, and the changes in the value of the semi-finished products and products in process between the beginning and end of the period. The gross industrial output value is calculated with "factory method". No double calculations are to be made within the same enterprise. However, double counting does occur among different enterprises.

Output value of light and heavy industries is also classified with the "factory" method. Under normal conditions, if the major products of an industrial enterprise belong to light industry products, the gross output value of that enterprise is classified wholly into light industry; the same principle applies to heavy industry.

Added Value of Industry refers to the final results of industrial production of industrial enterprises in money terms in the reporting period.

Sales Value of Industry refers to the total value of industrial products sold or labor service provided by an industrial enterprise in the year in money terms. It includes the total value of all finished and semi-finished products actual sold by the enterprise(including current period and non current period production), income of charges for processing external industrial products, income of charges for repairing external industrial products, along with income from processing, repairing, and equipment installation for internal non-industrial departments in the reporting period. Finished and semi-finished products that have been sold, whether produced in the current period or in the previous period, are included as long as they are sold in the current period. Provision of production, industrial operation and self-made equipment by the enterprise for its capital construction departments and life welfare departments is also regarded as sale, and shall be included in the industrial sales value.

Sales value of industry is calculated at the same price and with the same method as gross output value of industry. But they are calculated on different bases. The calculation of sales value of industry is based on the total sales volume of products, and that of gross industrial output value, on the total output of industrial products. The sales value of industry does not cover the difference between beginning and ending self-made semi-finished products and in-process products, while the gross industrial output value covers such value.

Total Assets refer to resources formed by previous transactions or matters of an enterprise, owned or controlled by the enterprise, and expected to bring economic benefit to the enterprise. Classified by the fluidity, total assets fall into current assets and non-current assets. Of which, current assets include monetary capital, transaction financial assets, notes receivable, accounts receivable, prepayment, other receivables, and inventory, etc.; non-current assets include long-term equity investment, fixed assets, intangible assets, and other non-current assets, etc.

(1)Total Current Assets Any assets that satisfy any of the following conditions are categorized as current assets: (1) assets that will be cashed in, sold or consumed in a normal operating cycle, mainly including inventory and accounts receivable, etc.; (2) assets that are held mainly for transaction purpose; (3) assets that will be cashed in within one year (including one year) from the balance sheet date; (4) cash or cash equivalents of which the capacity of exchanging other assets or paying off debts is not restricted within one year from the balance sheet date. Including monetary capital, notes receivable, accounts receivable, inventory, and other items.

(2)Total Fixed Assets refer to tangible assets held by an enterprise for producing commodities, rendering services, leasing or management, with service life exceeding one fiscal year. They include houses and buildings, machines, machinery, transport tools as well as other equipment, apparatus and tools in relation to production and operation, which have a service life exceeding one year. Total Fixed Assets is a time point indicator, showing the ending balance of fixed assets after deduction and discount, and impairment provision, etc.

Total Liabilities refer to the present obligations formed by previous transactions or matters of an enterprise, expected to lead to the flow of economic benefit out of the enterprise. By the term of payment, liabilities generally include current liabilities and non-current liabilities.

(1) Total Current liabilities Any liabilities that satisfy any of the following conditions are categorized as current liabilities: (1) assets expected to be paid off within one normal operating cycle; (2) held mostly for the purpose of transaction; (3) to due and paid off within one year from the balance sheet date; (4) that the enterprise has no right to delay the payment to more than one year after the balance sheet date on its own responsibility. They include short-term loans, notes payable, accounts payable, wages payable, taxes and fees payable and other items.

(2) Total Non-current Liabilities refer to liabilities other than current liabilities, including long-term borrowings, and bonds payable, etc.

Total Owner's Equity refers to the remaining equity of assets in an enterprise owned by owners after deducting the liabilities. Owner's equity of a company is also called shareholders' equity, including paid-up capital, accumulation of capital, operating surplus and non-distributed profits, etc.

Paid-up Capital refers to the capital actually contributed by investors to an enterprise, including investment in various forms, such as money, material objects, and intangible assets. Categorized by investor, paid-up capital includes state capital, collective capital, corporate capital, individual capital, capital from Hong Kong, Macao and Taiwan, and foreign capital.

Main Business Income refers to the income from main business of selling commodities and rendering services recognized by the enterprise.

Main Business Cost refers to the total cost incurred by the enterprise during its operation of main business.

Main Business Tax and Surtax refers to the business tax, excise, urban maintenance and construction tax, educational surcharge to be levied against the main business operated by an enterprise.

Operating Profits refers to the profits reaped by an enterprise from its productive and operating activities. For an enterprise implementing the Accounting Standard for Business Enterprise 2006, its operating profits are equal to the operating income minus the operating cost, operating tax and surtax, sales expenses, management expenses, financial expenses, assets impairment loss, plus earnings from changes in fair value and return on investment. For an enterprise not implementing the Accounting Standard for Business Enterprise 2006, its operating profits are the amount of the main business income minus the main business cost, main business tax and surtax, plus the profit from other business, and minus sales expenses, management expenses, and financial expenses.

Total Profits refers to the operating results of an enterprise during certain account period, representing the surplus of various incomes from production and operation deducting various expenses, reflecting the total gains and losses realized in the enterprise in the reporting period. It is reported according to the current amount of the item "Total Profits" in the accounting "Profit Statement".

VAT Payable refers to the tax payable by an enterprise in current period according to provisions in Law of Tax for its activities adding value to goods, including sales of goods, provision of labor service such as processing, repair and replacement. Based on the accumulated amount of credit of relevant accounting subject, it is reported by using the expression below:

VAT Payable = Sales-related Tax – (Purchase-related Tax – Transfer-out of Purchase-related Tax) – Taxable Amount of Exports Deducting Domestically Sold Products – Tax Concession +Export Rebate

The VAT Payable excludes the beginning tax amount not deducted.

Rate of Sales of Industrial Products refers to the rate of industrial sales output value to the gross output value of industry .It is calculated as follows:

Rate of Sales of Industrial Products (%) = sales value of industry at present value in the reporting period / gross output value of industry at present value in the reporting period × 100%

Rate of Added Value of Industry refers to the rate of added value of industry to the gross output value of industry in the reporting period. It indicates the economic benefit from reduction of intermediate consumption. It is calculated as follows:

Rate of Added Value of Industry = added value of industry at present value in the reporting period / gross output value of industry at present value in the reporting period × 100%

Rate of Profits to Total Industrial Costs refers to the ratio of profits realized in a given period to the total costs in the sameperiod, which reflects the economic efficiency of input Rate of Added Value of Industry refers to the rate of added value of industry to the gross output value of industry in the reporting period. It indicates the economic benefit from reduction of intermediate consumption. It is calculated as follows: Rate of Added Value of Industry = added value of industry at present value in the reporting period / gross output value of industry at present value in the reporting period × 100%

Rate of Profits to Total Industrial Costs refers to the ratio of profits realized in a given period to the total costs in the same period, which reflects the economic efficiency of input cost and is calculated as follows:

Rate of Profits to Total Industrial Cost(%)=(Total Profits/ Total Costs)×100%

Overall Labor Productivity of Industry refers to the final result of industrial production created by each employee in value terms of products within a unit time, measured with the value of products. It is an important indicator measuring the economic activities of an enterprise, and reflects the level of production technology, level of economic management, employees' skill and labor enthusiasm of the enterprise.

Overall Labor Productivity of Industry (RMB/person) = added value of industry (at present value) / average number of all employees

Turnovers of Current Assets refer to the number of turnovers of current assets within a given period of time. It reflects the turnover velocity of current assets. It is calculated as follows:

Turnovers of Current Assets (Nos.) = product sales / average balance of current assets

Liquidity Ratio indicates how much money of current assets is supporting the current liabilities of RMB100 in an enterprise. It is calculated as follows:

Liquidity Ratio (Times) = total current assets / total current liabilities

Quick Ratio indicates the capacity of current assets in an enterprise that can be used instantly for paying off current liabilities.

Quick Ratio = (total current assets – inventory)/total liabilities

Ratio of Liabilities to Assets reflects that how many assets of the total assets in an enterprise are obtained from liabilities.

It can be used for measuring the enterprise's capability of carrying out operating activities by using the funds provided by creditors, and to what extent the enterprise protects the creditors' interest during liquidation. It is calculated as follows:

Ratio of Liabilities to Assets = total liabilities / total assets × 100%

Contribution Rate of Total Assets indicates the profitability of all assets in an enterprise, reflecting the operating performance and management skill of the enterprise, service as a core indicator measuring the enterprise's profitability. It is calculated with the following formula:

Contribution Rate of Total Assets = (total profit + total tax + total interest) ÷average total assets × 100%

Where, the total tax is the sum of tax and surtax on main business, tax in management expenses, and payable VAT; average total assets is the arithmetic mean of beginning and ending total assets.

Rate of Capital Value Preservation and Appreciation reflects the changes in the net assets of an enterprise. It is a concentrated materialization of enterprise growth capacity. The formula for calculation is:

Rate of Capital Value Preservation and Appreciation = owner's equity at the end of the reporting period / owner's equity at the end of the same period in the previous year × 100%

High-tech Manufacturing means all sectors in the high-tech industry other than public software services (including basic software service and application software service).

12

北京统计年鉴2013　BEIJING STATISTICAL YEARBOOK

建筑业
CONSTRUCTION

简要说明

一、本章资料的主要内容

本章资料主要反映北京市建筑业企业基本情况和生产经营情况。主要指标包括企业个数、从业人员、建筑业总产值、建筑业企业房屋建筑面积、利润、税金等。

二、本章资料的统计范围

建筑业统计范围从 2004 年起，由原具有建筑业资质等级四级及四级以上的独立核算的建筑业企业调整为具有施工总承包、专业承包资质的所有法人建筑业企业。

三、本章资料的数据来源及调查方法

本章建筑业企业统计数据根据国家统计局制定的《建筑业统计报表制度》整理汇总。建筑业统计数据采取全面调查的方法。资料由北京市统计局、国家统计局北京调查总队提供。

四、有关统计标准的变化说明

本章资料中建筑业行业分类2002-2011 年期间执行 2002 年《国民经济行业分类标准》(GB/T 4754-2002)划分标准，2012 年开始执行 2011 年《国民经济行业分类》(GB/T 4754-2011)划分标准。

五、本章中关于历史数据调整的问题

由于 2004 年开展了“北京市第一次全国经济普查”，按照国家统计局统一要求和统一方法，历史资料要根据普查结果进行修正。本章中 1993 至 2003 年的建筑业总产值数据采用“趋势离差法”进行了调整，2004 年为第一次经济普查数据，2008 年为第二次经济普查数据。

Brief Introduction

I. Main Content

Figures in this chapter reflect the basic situation and operation of building enterprises in Beijing. Main indicators include number of enterprises, employees, total output value of building sector, house building area of enterprises in building sector, profit, tax etc.

II. Scope of Statistics

From 2004, figures of statistics for building sector cover all building enterprises with qualification of general and specialized contracting of construction, compared with previous building enterprises keeping separate accounts at and above class-4 building sector qualification.

III. Source of Data and Method of Survey

Statistical data of building sector were summarized according to Statistical Statement System for Building Sector developed by the National Bureau of Statistics, which were gained from complete survey. They are from Beijing Bureau of Statistics and National Bureau of Statistics Survey Office in Beijing.

IV. Changes in Relevant Statistical Standards

In this chapter, classification of building sectors in 2002-2011 was based on the Standard for Classification of National Economic Sectors 2002 (GB/T 4754-2002). Standard for Classification of National Economic Sectors (GB/T 4754-2011) became effective in 2012.

V. Adjustment to Historical Data

As “The First National Economic Census in Beijing” was conducted in 2004, in accordance with the uniform requirement and method of the National Bureau of Statistics, historical data must be corrected according to the census result. Data of total output value of building sector in 1993-2003 were adjusted with “trend deviation method”. Data from the first economic census were used for 2004. And data from the second economic census were used for 2008.

12-1 建筑业企业基本情况(1978-2012年)

BASIC STATISTICS ON CONSTRUCTION ENTERPRISES WITH INDEPENDENT ACCOUNTING SYSTEM (1978-2012)

年份 Year	建筑施工企业单位数(个) Construction Enterprises (unit)	建筑施工企业年末从业人员(万人) Employed Persons (year-end) (10000 persons)	建筑施工企业总产值(亿元) Gross Output Value (100 million yuan)	主营业务收入(亿元) Settled Project Income (100 million yuan)	建筑施工企业利润总额(亿元) Total Profits (100 million yuan)	建筑施工企业房屋建筑面积(万平方米) Floor Space of Buildings (10000 sq.m)	
						施工面积 Floor Space under Construction	竣工面积 Floor Space Completed
1978	64	25.4	10.5		0.7		
1979	70	26.4	12.7		0.9		
1980	71	27.8	14.7		1.5		
1981	71	27.0	14.5		1.6		
1982	91	30.7	17.3		1.7		
1983	116	37.2	22.6		2.5		
1984	2765	53.0	33.4		3.2		
1985	2549	63.9	43.9		3.9		
1986	2361	61.3	51.3		3.3		
1987	2292	64.4	67.0		4.1		
1988	1659	64.2	81.6		3.9		
1989	1545	60.0	89.0		3.8		
1990	994	60.2	94.7		3.4		
1991	922	60.3	99.6		2.8	2495	1172
1992	976	62.7	122.6		3.1	2774	1227
1993	1098	75.9	215.5	205.5	6.1	3499	1428
1994	1259	73.4	336.0	289.4	9.4	4035	1437
1995	1332	82.6	426.6	337.6	7.8	4602	1593
1996	1292	82.5	494.7	431.3	8.9	5328	1967
1997	1297	80.3	556.4	481.1	10.4	5801	2117
1998	1482	75.6	678.6	579.3	12.4	6525	2225
1999	1588	62.0	750.6	645.8	13.6	6824	2632
2000	1697	56.6	812.5	706.8	16.4	7247	2809
2001	1811	57.8	1055.4	906.9	18.7	8919	3198
2002	2122	57.0	1211.3	1094.0	24.7	10241	3827
2003	2419	59.1	1521.2	1329.9	31.5	12160	4486
2004	2623	51.2	1659.8	1936.0	40.0	14424	5258
2005	2752	67.2	1894.0	2206.9	67.3	15418	4862
2006	2800	66.9	2167.9	2666.2	112.8	16202	4786
2007	2845	51.7	2576.8	3351.3	115.7	18225	4946
2008	3527	47.0	3066.2	3856.8	84.5	19537	4803
2009	3556	56.2	4059.7	5081.1	217.4	22721	5225
2010	3594	59.9	5196.0	6545.0	265.2	29440	5933
2011	3667	49.6	6046.3	7565.9	219.6	36507	6456
2012	3572	49.2	6588.3	8125.2	293.0	41660	8414

注：1. 1996-2003年全部指标的统计口径为四级及四级以上的法人建筑施工企业。
2. 2004-2011年全部指标的统计口径为建筑施工总承包、专业承包的建筑业企业。
3. 建筑施工企业房屋建筑面积包括在本市和外省完成的施工、竣工面积。

Note: a) All figures from 1996 to 2003 covered the construction enterprises as legal persons at Grade IV and above.
b) All figures from 2004 to 2011 covered the general contracting and specialized contracting construction enterprises.
c) Building area of houses completed by construction enterprises included the construction and Completion area completed both inside and outside the city.

12-2 建筑业施工企业基本情况(2012年)
BASIC INFORMATION ON PROFESSIONAL CONTRACTING BUILDING CONSTRUCTION ENTERPRISES (2012)

项目	Item	建筑施工企业单位数（个）Construction Enterprises (unit)	总产值（万元）Gross Output Value (10000 yuan)	年末从业人员（人）Employed Persons (year-end) (person)	年末自有机械设备 Machines and Equipment Owned (year-end) 净值(万元) Net Value (10000 yuan)	总台数(台) Total Number (set)	总功率(千瓦) Total Power (kw)
合计	**Total**	**3572**	**65882953**	**492182**	**1019164**	**124665**	**3769012**
按企业登记注册类型分	**Grouped by Registration Status of Enterprises**						
内资企业	Domestic Funded Enterprises	3479	64378972	473962	1008423	122831	3718519
国有企业	State-Owned Enterprises	115	3723101	29743	53158	9453	283462
集体企业	Collective Owned Enterprises	132	1186006	15830	7466	5021	65806
私营企业	Private Enterprises	1828	5410048	90328	106506	25334	465065
联营企业	Joint Owned Enterprises	2	2063	50			
股份有限公司	Share Holding Corporations Ltd.	68	6022999	22505	85912	6527	336576
有限责任公司	Limited-Liability Corporations	1263	47648556	307723	746374	72434	2522330
股份合作企业	Cooperative Enterprises	71	386199	7783	9007	4062	45280
其他企业	Others						
外商投资企业	Foreign Funded Enterprises	42	513051	6328	3417	770	33910
港、澳、台商投资企业	Enterprises with Funds from Hongkong, Macao and Taiwan	51	990930	11892	7324	1064	16583
按隶属关系分	**Grouped by Administrative Relationship**						
中央	Central	211	34675231	181289	542449	35545	1678066
地方	Local	3361	31207722	310893	476715	89120	2090946
按行业分	**Grouped by Sector**						
房屋建筑业	Construction of Building	621	35522350	190616	303668	44520	1258830
土木工程建筑业	Civil engineering Construction	565	18838477	128433	581501	40299	1901426
建筑安装业	Construction Installation	817	5552966	90362	57105	19541	327454
建筑装饰和其他建筑业	Building Completion, Finishing and Other Construction	1569	5969160	82771	76890	20305	281302

注：1. 统计范围为施工总承包、专业承包的法人建筑业企业（下表同）。
2. 行业划分执行2011年国民经济行业分类标准（GB/T 4754-2011）。

Note: a) Statistics covers general contracting and specialized contracting construction enterprises as legal persons (same to the following table).
b) Sectors in this table are classified in accordance with the Standard for Classification of National Economic Sectors 2011 (GB/T 4754-2011).

12-3 建筑业施工企业主要财务指标(2012年)

单位：万元

项目	Item	企业单位个数(个) Number of Enterprises (unit)	资产负债 Assets and Liabilities 资产总计 Total Assets	流动资产合计 Total Current Assets	#应收账款 Accounts Receivable	固定资产合计 Total Fixed Assets	固定资产原价 Total Original Value of Fixed Assets	负债合计 Total Liabilities	#流动负债合计 Total Current Liabilities
合　计	**Total**	**3572**	**136059059**	**90569123**	**18525957**	**4464594**	**6890113**	**91722512**	**79092897**
按企业登记注册类型分	**Grouped by Registration Status of Enterprises**								
内资企业	Domestic Funded Enterprises	3479	134201235	88841680	18024933	4410456	6789288	90321055	77703483
国有企业	State-Owned Enterprises	115	7687783	5354628	1042678	472223	800464	4633080	4170305
集体企业	Collective Owned Enterprises	132	1687283	1370422	95895	82878	133553	1397737	1390526
私营企业	Private Enterprises	1828	6217098	5115359	1159516	580450	828420	3661290	3554626
联营企业	Joint Owned Enterprises	2	1099	1035	449	64	200	1327	1327
股份有限公司	Share Holding Corporations Ltd.	68	43076417	15521144	1772609	390569	530758	18724256	11362954
有限责任公司	Limited-Liability Corporations	1263	75004957	61021415	13893450	2845588	4426296	61546184	56887991
股份合作企业	Cooperative Enterprises	71	526598	457677	60336	38684	69597	357181	335754
其他企业	Other								
外商投资企业	Foreign Funded Enterprises	42	832669	773822	194624	24142	48612	611100	603321
港、澳、台商投资企业	Enterprises with Funds from Hongkong, Macao and Taiwan	51	1025155	953621	306400	29996	52213	790357	786093
按隶属关系分	**Grouped by Administrative Relationship**								
中　央	Central	211	90790636	56035064	10758173	2155300	3250694	58556717	49045047
地　方	Local	3361	45268423	34534059	7767784	2309294	3639419	33165795	30047850
按行业分	**Grouped by Sector**								
房屋建筑业	Construction of Building	621	59247197	44666908	10580812	1639764	2710911	43112114	38576864
土木工程建筑业	Civil engineering Construction	565	61317422	33097943	5149457	1695010	2821384	37411317	29755466
建筑安装业	Construction Installation	817	8934295	7608120	1460039	510985	723890	6734732	6540019
建筑装饰和其他建筑业	Building Completion, Finishing and Other Construction	1569	6560145	5196152	1335649	618835	633928	4464349	4220548

注：1. 行业划分执行2011年国民经济行业分类标准(GB/T 4754-2011)。
2. 应交税金合计包括应交增值税、应交所得税、营业税金及附加和管理费用中的税金。

MAIN FINANCIAL INDICATORS ON CONSTRUCTION ENTERPRISES (2012)

(10000 yuan)

	损 益 Profits and Loss									应交税金合计		
#应付账款 Accounts Payable	所有者权益合计 Total Owner's Equity	#实收资本 Paid-up Capital	营业收入 Business Income	#主营业务收入 Main Business Income	营业成本 Business Cost	#主营业务成本 Main Business Cost	管理费用 Management Expenses	财务费用 Financial Expenses	利润总额 Total Profits	Total Tax	#营业税金及附加 Business Tax and Surtax	#主营业务税金及附加 Main Business Tax and Surtax
27639502	**44336547**	**20795766**	**81944529**	**81252285**	**74833219**	**74208635**	**3149750**	**534680**	**2930261**	**2629922**	**2090497**	**2048042**
27081432	43880181	20543896	79823585	79167763	72942644	72349510	3049959	534789	2849671	2552928	2036791	1995854
916992	3054703	1415376	5532928	5448366	5090680	4992608	206968	-1587	176720	165448	133141	132245
249350	289547	186708	1303609	1298114	1186050	1152294	99792	-2880	15892	45453	38960	38318
1182565	2555808	2164938	5909947	5815821	5071613	4950787	422586	15100	106670	228619	186385	182093
209	-228	700	2051	2051	1807	1807	381		-224	60	50	50
3102894	24352161	8068081	7777612	7700270	7136355	7089562	274150	159697	1185529	210764	153076	151158
21571283	13458773	8607288	58878301	58494844	54083789	53799489	2027138	364709	1350063	1884779	1511137	1478221
58139	169417	100805	419137	408297	372350	362963	18944	-250	15021	17805	14042	13769
199333	221569	119200	968864	943495	841599	821691	51507	245	39129	39345	24532	24099
358737	234797	132670	1152080	1141027	1048976	1037434	48284	-354	41461	37649	29174	28089
18789777	32233920	13060505	46598908	46308399	43150782	42901558	1456270	234479	2203970	1364506	1055673	1038241
8849725	12102627	7735261	35345621	34943886	31682437	31307077	1693480	300201	726291	1265416	1034824	1009801
15601491	16135082	7883625	40267875	39980039	37214018	36978170	1177103	334407	1152746	1275176	1042850	1025699
8909152	23906106	9816690	26892517	26715067	24669339	24519689	1096214	181374	1331676	808625	642606	622462
1836232	2199563	1437551	7860477	7724811	6933320	6764554	481251	-1261	234131	270355	193719	190035
1292627	2095796	1657900	6923660	6832368	6016542	5946222	395182	20160	211708	275766	211322	209846

Note: a) Sectors in this table are classified in accordance with the Standard for Classification of National Economic Sectors 2011 (GB/T 4754-2011).
b) Total Tax mainly includes payable VAT,payable income tax, business tax and surtax, and tax in management expenses, etc.

12-3 续表 continued

项目	Item	#应交所得税 Value Income Tax Payable	#应交增值税 Value Added Tax Payable	流动比率(倍) Current Ratio (times)	速动比率(倍) Quick Ratio (times)	资产负债率(%) Assets-Liabilities Ratio (%)	资本金利润率(%) Profit-Capital Ratio (%)
合计	**Total**	**417675**	**73630**	**1.15**	**0.92**	**67.4**	**14.1**
按企业登记注册类型分	**Grouped by Registration Status of Enterprises**						
内资企业	Domestic Funded Enterprises	401754	67550	1.14	0.92	67.3	13.9
国有企业	State-Owned Enterprises	23558	5576	1.28	1.08	60.3	12.5
集体企业	Collective Owned Enterprises	4581	344	0.99	0.56	82.8	8.5
私营企业	Private Enterprises	28161	6398	1.44	1.18	58.9	4.9
联营企业	Joint Owned Enterprises	2	7	0.78	0.43	120.7	-32.0
股份有限公司	Share Holding Corporations Ltd.	40124	12645	1.37	1.24	43.5	14.7
有限责任公司	Limited-Liability Corporations	301807	42569	1.07	0.84	82.1	15.7
股份合作企业	Cooperative Enterprises	3521	11	1.36	0.85	67.8	14.9
其他企业	Others						
外商投资企业	Foreign Funded Enterprises	8344	5662	1.28	1.14	73.4	32.8
港、澳、台商投资企业	Enterprises with Funds from Hongkong, Macao and Taiwan	7577	418	1.21	0.94	77.1	31.3
按隶属关系分	**Grouped by Administrative Relationship**						
中央	Central	251050	40949	1.14	0.94	64.5	16.9
地方	Local	166625	32681	1.15	0.90	73.3	9.4
按行业分	**Grouped by Sector**						
房屋建筑业	Construction of Building	195522	16764	1.16	0.93	72.8	14.6
土木工程建筑业	Civil engineering Construction	125309	27045	1.11	0.92	61.0	13.6
建筑安装业	Construction Installation	53530	15755	1.16	0.89	75.4	16.3
建筑装饰和其他建筑业	Building Completion,Finishing and Other Construction	43314	14066	1.23	0.98	68.1	12.8

12-4 建筑业施工企业竣工率
PROJECT COMPLETION RATE OF PROFESSIONAL CONTRACTING BUILDING CONSTRUCTION ENTERPRISES

单位：% (%)

项目	Item	产值竣工率 Completion Rate by Output Value		面积竣工率 Completion Rate by Floor Space	
		2012	2011	2012	2011
合计	**Total**	**49.8**	**43.6**	**20.2**	**17.7**
按企业登记注册类型分	**Grouped by Registration Status of Enterprises**				
内资企业	Domestic Funded Enterprises	49.4	43.5	20.3	17.9
国有企业	State-Owned Enterprises	59.8	44.5	19.2	16.1
集体企业	Collective Owned Enterprises	64.1	72.9	26.0	26.3
私营企业	Private Enterprises	60.1	66.4	28.2	29.2
联营企业	Joint Owned Enterprises		56.4		
股份有限公司	Share Holding Corporations Ltd.	33.3	26.7	22.8	11.2
有限责任公司	Limited-Liability Corporations	48.7	42.1	19.7	18.2
股份合作企业	Cooperative Enterprises	96.8	66.4	37.2	22.3
其他企业	Others				
外商投资企业	Foreign Funded Enterprises	46.5	67.9	15.5	39.0
港、澳、台商投资企业	Enterprises with Funds from Hongkong, Macao and Taiwan	80.5	41.2	16.0	5.6
按隶属关系分	**Grouped by Administrative Relationship**				
中央	Central	43.2	32.4	16.8	13.2
地方	Local	57.2	56.7	25.7	24.1
按行业分	**Grouped by Sector**				
房屋建筑业	Construction of Building	55.0		20.2	
土木工程建筑业	Civil engineering Construction	37.5		20.6	
建筑安装业	Construction Installation	54.6		20.2	
建筑装饰和其他建筑业	Building Completion, Finishing and Other Construction	53.4		14.3	

注：根据国家统计局规定，2012年起执行2011年国民经济行业分类标准（GB/T 4754-2011）。受行业划分标准变化影响，按行业分缺少2011年同口径数据。

Note: According to provisions of the National Bureau of Statistics, from 2012 the Standard for Classification of Sectors in National Economy 2011 (GB/T 4754-2011) is implemented. Due to changes in the sector classification standard, there may be no comparable figures in 2011 for some sectors.

主要统计指标解释

建筑业总产值 是以货币表现的建筑业企业在一定时期内生产的建筑产品和服务的总和。它包括建筑工程产值、设备安装工程产值、其他产值三部分内容。

(1)建筑工程产值 指列入建筑工程预(概)算内的各种工程价值。

(2)安装工程产值 指为设备安装而发生的安装工程费用，在设备安装产值中，不得包括被安装设备本身价值。

(3)其他产值 建筑业总产值中除建筑工程、安装工程以外的产值，包括房屋构筑物修理产值、非标准设备制造产值、总包企业向分包企业收取的管理费，以及不能明确划分的施工活动所完成的产值。

年末从业人员 指年末最后一日24小时在本单位工作，并取得工资或其他形式劳动报酬的人员数。该指标为时点指标，不包括最后一日当天及以前与单位解除劳动合同关系的人员，是在岗职工、劳务派遣人员及其他从业人员之和。

房屋施工面积 指报告期内施过工的全部房屋建筑面积，包括：本期新开工的房屋面积、上期施工跨入本期继续施工的房屋面积、上期停缓建本期复工的房屋面积、本期开工又停缓建和本期竣工的房屋面积。

房屋竣工面积 指在报告期内房屋建筑按照设计要求已全部完工，达到了住人和使用条件，经检验验收鉴定合格或达到竣工验收标准，可正式移交使用的房屋建筑面积。

自有机械设备净值 指本企业(或单位)自有机械设备经过使用、磨损后实际存在的价值，即原值减去累计折旧后的净额。

自有机械设备年末总台数 指年末本企业(或单位)自有的直接用于工程施工的各种机械设备的台数。不包括附属辅助生产机械设备、运输机械设备、生产试验机械设备的台数。

自有机械设备年末总功率 指年末本企业(或单位)自有的直接用于工程施工的各种机械设备年末总功率，按设定能力或查定能力计算。包括施工机械本身的动力和为该机械服务的单独动力设备，如电动机等。但不包括附属辅助生产机械设备、运输机械设备、生产试验机械设备的功率。计量单位用千瓦，动力换算可按1马力＝0.735千瓦折合成千瓦数。电焊机、变压器、锅炉不计算动力。

主营业务收入 指企业确认的销售商品、提供劳务等主营业务的收入。

主营业务成本 指企业经营主要业务所发生的成本总额。

主营业务税金及附加 指企业经营主要业务应负担的营业税、消费税、城市维护建设税、教育费附加等。

主营业务利润 指企业经营主要业务实现的利润。

利润总额 指企业在一定会计期间的经营成果，是生产经营过程中各种收入扣除各种耗费后的盈余，反映企业在报告期内实现的亏盈总额。

Explanatory Notes on Main Statistical Indicators

Gross Output Value of Construction refers to total of construction products and services, expressed in money terms, completed by construction and installation enterprises during a given period of time. It includes: output value of construction works, output value of installation works and other output value.

Output Value of Construction Works means the value of works involved in project budgets.

Output Value of Installation Works means the costs of installation works incurred for equipment installation. The calculation is based on the construction targets of construction enterprises, instead of the industrial sector of construction enterprises.

Other Output Value means, of the total output value of construction, the output value other than that of construction and installations works. It includes the repair output value of houses and structures, manufacturing output value of non-standard equipment, management charges collected by general contracting enterprises from subcontracting enterprises, as well as the output value of construction activities falling in no specific categories.

Employed Persons mean the actual ending number of persons receiving labor remuneration or income in the enterprise. Year-end employed person include foreigners and persons from Hong Kong, Macao and Taiwan, part-time persons, re-employed retired persons, workers temporarily transferred from other entities, and second-job workers who work in an enterprise, but exclude those employees who have left the entity with their labor relationship remained.

House Construction Area means the building area of all houses in the reporting period, including: the area of houses newly started in current period, area of houses built in the previous period and continued in current period, area of houses suspended in the previous period and restarted in current period, area of houses started and suspended in current period, and area of houses completed in current period.

Area of Houses Completed means the area of houses and buildings entirely completed in line with requirements of design, meeting conditions of use, satisfactorily accepted by relevant authorities in the reporting period.

Net Value of Machinery and Equipment Owned means the actual value of machinery and equipment owned by an enterprise (or entity) after use and wear, i.e. the net amount of original value minus the accumulated depreciation. Leased equipment for operation is not included as construction machinery and equipment owned. Leased equipment for financing is included as construction machinery and equipment owned by a construction enterprise.

Year-end Total Number of Machinery and Equipment Owned means the number of various machines and equipment owned by an enterprise (or entity) directly used for project construction. It excludes the number of auxiliary productive machines and equipment, transport machines and equipment, production test machines and equipment. Leased equipment for operation is not included as construction machinery and equipment owned. Leased equipment for financing is included as construction equipment owned by a construction enterprise.

Year-end Total Power of Machinery and Equipment Owned means the total power of machinery and equipment owned by an enterprise (entity) at the year end and directly used for project construction, calculated at the verified capacity, including the power of construction machines themselves and the power of any separate equipment serving the machine, such as motors, but excluding the power of auxiliary productive machines and equipment, transport machines and equipment, production test machines and equipment. machinery and equipment for construction, production and transportation. The unit used for the calculation of power is kilowatt, with horsepower converted to kilowatt by 1 horsepower=0.735 kilowatt. The power of welders, transformers and boilers is not included. Leased equipment for operation is not included as construction machinery and equipment owned. Leased equipment for financing is included as construction equipment owned by a construction enterprise.

Income from Main Business means the income recognized by an enterprise from main business such as sale of commodities and rendering of service.

Cost of Main Business means the total cost incurred in an enterprise for the operation of main business.

Tax and Surtax on Main Business means the sales tax, excise, urban maintenance and construction tax, educational surcharge, etc. to be paid by an enterprise for the operation of main business.

Profit of Main Business means the profit reaped by an enterprise in its operation of main business.

Total Profits mean the operating result of an enterprise in certain accounting period. It is the surplus of all revenues deducting all costs in its production and operation, reflecting its total profit and loss realized in the reporting period.

13

交通运输邮电
TRANSPORT, POST AND TELECOMMUNICATON SERVICES

简要说明

一、本章资料的主要内容

本章资料反映北京市交通运输业和邮政电信业发展的基本状况。

交通运输业资料主要包括：铁路、公路、民航、管道四种运输方式的线路条数、里程、总运量及周转量、主要技术经济指标（不含管道）；机动车拥有情况。

邮政电信业资料主要包括：邮电业务完成情况、邮政电信发展水平等资料。

二、各部分资料的调查范围及数据来源

1. 铁路资料：主要是国家铁路运营情况，不含地方铁路、合资铁路和军用铁路及由厂矿企事业单位自建的铁路专用线和专用铁道资料来源于北京铁路局。

2. 公路资料：(1)公路里程为年末通车里程数，不含在建和未正式投入使用的公路里程；(2)公路运输统计范围包括在北京市注册从事公路货运的全部企事业单位和私人(包括个体联户)，资料来源于北京市交通委员会。

3. 管道运输资料：包括输送原油、成品油、天然气以及其他气体的管线长度、输送能力及完成的运输量。管道运输统计数据主要来源于中石油北京天然气管道有限公司和中国石油化工股份有限公司、北京燕山分公司所属的管道运输企业，由两家集团公司分别负责收集审核本部门统计数据。

4. 民航运输资料：不包括在京运输飞行的外省市及外国航空公司。统计范围为各航空公司从事国内运输、港澳台运输、国际运输的定期航班航线条数及里程、运输量等。2009年及以前数据主要来源于中国国际航空公司、新华航空有限责任公司，2010年起为北京地区的民航运输法人单位。

5. 邮政电信资料：包括邮政和电信运营企业为社会公众提供的各类邮政和电信服务，不含专用网业务资料。邮电业务量按业务种类分为邮政业务量和电信业务量。数据主要来源于北京市邮政公司、中国联合网络通信有限公司北京市分公司、中国移动通信集团北京有限公司、中国铁通集团有限公司北京分公司、中国电信股份有限公司北京分公司等单位。

6. 民用汽车拥有量：民用汽车指在公安交通管理部门已注册登记领有民用车辆牌照的全部汽车数量。民用汽车根据汽车结构分为载客汽车、载货汽车及其他汽车；根据汽车所有者不同分为私人汽车、单位汽车。民用汽车数据来自于北京市公安局公安交通管理局。

Brief Introduction

I. Main Content

Figures in this chapter show the basic situation of development of transportation, post and telecommunication in Beijing.

Transport statistics include the number of lines, kilometers, total volume of transport, and turnover for four transport forms, i.e. railway, highway, civil aviation, and pipeline, main technological and economic indicators (excluding pipelines); possession of mobile vehicles.

Post and telecommunication statistics include: performance of post and telecom services; development level of post and telecom, and so on.

II. Scope of Survey and Source of Data

1. Data on railways: operation of national railways, excluding local railways, joint venture railways, military railways, as well as dedicated lines and railways built by factories, mines, enterprises and public institutions. These data are from Beijing Railway Bureau.

2. Data on highways: (1) highway kilometers mean those open to traffic at the year end, excluding those under construction and not put into formally use; (2) highway transport statistics cover all enterprises and public institutions as well as individuals (including self-employed) registered in Beijing for highway cargo transportation. These data are from Beijing Municipal Commission of Transport.

3. Pipeline transport data: including the length, capacity and completed traffic of pipelines for transport of crude oil, product oil, natural gas, and other gas. These data are mainly from Beijing Huayou Natural Gas Co., Ltd. and pipeline transport enterprises attached to Beijing Yanshan Branch of SINOPEC. Each of these two corporations was responsible for collecting and reviewing statistical data in its own system.

4. Civil aviation data: not covering non-local and foreign airlines flying and operating in Beijing. Statistics consist of the number, mileage, and traffic volume of regular flight lines of airlines for domestic transport, transport from and to Hong Kong, Macao and Taiwan, and international transport. Data for 2009 and earlier are sourced from Air China and Xinhua Airline. From 2010, they are sourced from corporate entities of civil aviation transport in Beijing area.

5. Post and telecom data: including those on postal and telecom services offered by post and telecom operators, excluding data on services of dedicated networks. Traffic falls into postal service traffic and telecom traffic. Data are mainly sourced from Beijing Post and Telecom Company, Beijing Branch of China Unicom, China Mobile Beijing Company, Beijing Branch of China Tietong, Beijing Branch of China Telecom.

6. Data on possession of civil automobiles: civil automobiles include all mobiles registered with traffic administration and granted license plates. In terms of mobile structure, civil automobiles consist of passenger automobiles, cargo automobiles, and others; in terms of owners, they include private and company ones. These data are sourced from Beijing Traffic Management Bureau.

13-1 交通运输邮电业基本情况(1978-2012年)
TRANSPORTATION, POSTS AND TELECOMMUNICATIONS (1978-2012)

年 份 Year	铁路里程(公里) Railway Operating Length (km)	公路里程(公里) Highway Operating Length (km)	客运量(万人) Passenger Traffic (10000 persons)	铁 路 Railway	公 路 Highway	民 航 Civil Aviation	货运量(万吨) Freight Traffic (10000 tons)	铁 路 Railway	公 路 Highway	民 航 Civil Aviation	管 道 Pipeline
1978	699	6562	4431	2264	2120	47	7394	3370	4023	1	
1979	700	7278	4777	2504	2220	53	7764	3485	4277	2	
1980	707	7487	5285	2762	2465	58	7571	3356	4213	2	
1981-1985			**33230**	**17688**	**15058**	**484**	**45456**	**15425**	**29063**	**14**	**954**
1981	858	7566	5877	2982	2824	71	8546	3046	5498	2	
1982	858	7683	6215	3205	2931	79	9097	3065	5812	2	218
1983	860	8058	6662	3546	3038	78	9403	3152	6016	3	232
1984	864	8271	7273	3877	3287	109	9671	3133	6301	3	234
1985	876	8482	7203	4078	2978	147	8739	3029	5436	4	270
1986-1990			**38506**	**21290**	**16160**	**1056**	**121771**	**15518**	**104929**	**41**	**1283**
1986	876	8995	7337	4106	3059	172	22121	3030	18794	6	291
1987	876	9103	7763	4418	3117	228	23068	3125	19734	8	201
1988	876	9124	8491	4782	3460	249	24749	3168	21308	9	264
1989	876	9371	7434	4214	3034	186	25184	3144	21767	8	265
1990	876	9648	7480	3770	3490	220	26648	3051	23326	10	262
1991-1995			**40918**	**20615**	**18010**	**2292**	**147385**	**14923**	**131956**	**79**	**427**
1991	876	10259	7704	4036	3378	289	26804	2983	23739	11	71
1992	875	10827	8158	4196	3593	369	27707	2912	24700	14	80
1993	875	11260	7607	4374	2781	452	29865	3048	26730	17	70
1994	875	11532	8537	3992	4008	537	30825	3006	27700	19	99
1995	875	11811	8913	4017	4250	646	32184	2974	29087	17	106
1996-2000			**62554**	**19683**	**38888**	**3983**	**154376**	**13491**	**140455**	**125**	**304**
1996	922	12084	8801	3650	4395	756	32907	2851	29960	18	78
1997	924	12306	9263	3613	4902	748	32351	2883	29360	20	87
1998	924	12498	11228	3762	6704	762	30127	2563	27490	22	52
1999	997	12825	14866	4201	9878	788	28275	2583	25635	30	27
2000	997	13600	18396	4458	13009	929	30717	2612	28010	35	60
2001-2005			**191964**	**25350**	**157061**	**9553**	**156702**	**11053**	**144049**	**277**	**1323**
2001	987	13891	22469	4750	16630	1090	30607	2505	28007	38	57
2002	987	14359	28384	5032	22103	1249	30961	2348	28375	44	194
2003	964	14453	30520	4352	24940	1228	30925	2265	28361	45	254
2004	964	14630	49750	5437	41463	2850	31700	1959	29256	73	412
2005	966	14696	60841	5779	51925	3137	32509	1976	30050	77	406
2006-2010			**435377**	**37892**	**376377**	**21107**	**121931**	**8820**	**106451**	**508**	**6151**
2006	962	20503	12276	6269	2482	3525	33547	1956	30953	89	549
2007	962	20754	20040	6915	9275	3850	20770	1925	17872	98	875
2008	956	20340	128525	7644	117118	3763	21885	1733	18689	93	1369
2009	956	20755	133872	8161	121373	4339	22017	1635	18753	98	1531
2010	956	21114	140663	8903	126130	5630	23712	1572	20184	130	1827
2011	1067	21347	145773	9755	129918	6100	26849	1380	23276	132	2061
2012	1115	21492	149037	10315	132333	6389	28650	1232	24925	134	2359

注：1. 铁路数据为北京市市辖范围，2005年以前取自北京铁路分局，2005年及以后取自北京铁路局。
2. 从2006年开始，公路里程包括村道数据。
3. 2006-2007年公路客运量为持有道路运输经营许可证的客运车辆发生的旅客运输量；从2008年开始，公路客运量根据交通运输部《公路水路运输量专项调查方案》调整旅客运输量统计口径,调整后包括旅游客运、省际客运企业、郊区客运和市郊公交的运输量。
4. 从2007年开始,公路货物运输为营业性运量。
5. 民航统计范围为北京地区的民航运输法人单位，不包括在京运输飞行的外省市及外国航空公司。

Note: a) Railway figures are statistics for Beijing's jurisdiction. Those figures for years before 2005 were from Beijing Railway Branch,those for 2005 and after were from Beijing Railway Bureau.
b) From 2006, road length includes figures of rural roads.
c) In 2006 and 2007, passenger traffic by highway was that by passenger transportation vehicles holding road transportation license ; From 2008, passenger traffic by highway included suburb road passenger traffic, traffic by buses of numbers beginning with "9" and taxes according to Special Survey Program for Highway and Water Way Transportation Volume of the Ministry of Traffic and Transportation.
d) From 2007, freight traffic by highway is operational traffic.
e) Civil aviation covers judicial entities of civil aviation in Beijing, excluding airlines of other provinces and other countries which fly and transport in Beijing.

13-1 续表 1 continued

年份 Year	旅客周转量(万人公里) Total Passenger-Kilometers (10000 passengers-km)	铁路 Railway	公路 Highway	民航 Civil Aviation	货物周转量(万吨公里) Total Freight Ton-Kilometers (10000 ton-km)	铁路 Railway	公路 Highway	民航 Civil Aviation	管道 Pipeline
1978			59367				92247		
1979			64033				97616		
1980			73692				93899		
1981-1985			**498768**				**540035**		
1981			81879				93254		
1982	755815	641550	90092	24173	3451037	3329450	106767	13530	1290
1983	853655	723200	103742	26713	3794223	3666600	110118	16099	1406
1984	968481	821431	113871	33179	4309798	4171789	115740	20896	1373
1985	1089919	936300	109184	44435	4719663	4576400	114156	27437	1670
1986-1990	**6333894**	**2608550**	**649210**	**3076133**	**13703344**	**11007906**	**2496086**	**191715**	**7637**
1986	1133620	496288	119065	518267	2569579	2133836	405645	28281	1817
1987	1281763	534720	133735	613308	2792589	2282106	471393	37966	1124
1988	1503508	588947	141625	772936	2887270	2344684	498391	42612	1583
1989	1216981	521263	122435	573283	2765660	2179878	546022	38194	1566
1990	1198022	467332	132350	598339	2688246	2067402	574635	44662	1547
1991-1995	**8690001**	**2645880**	**842807**	**5201314**	**15220745**	**11382191**	**3488944**	**346841**	**2769**
1991	1383465	506431	139041	737993	2799731	2153176	591187	54929	439
1992	1666810	531574	161735	973501	2938746	2230406	642200	65614	527
1993	1656130	551392	127461	977277	3143512	2301941	767790	73216	565
1994	1906718	547488	180030	1179200	3107722	2303265	725740	78142	575
1995	2076879	508995	234540	1333344	3231034	2393403	762027	74940	663
1996-2000	**12752549**	**2649587**	**1744526**	**8358436**	**14987253**	**10458031**	**3918017**	**609517**	**1688**
1996	2219196	459514	250488	1509194	3176234	2311011	784888	79983	352
1997	2272177	477538	261204	1533435	3129097	2263274	769190	96202	431
1998	2419787	505554	304592	1609641	2846652	1952602	783237	110470	343
1999	2701471	579759	400597	1721115	2838857	1929269	754264	155171	153
2000	3139918	627222	527645	1985051	2996414	2001875	826438	167691	410
2001-2005	**27318106**	**3454437**	**5282581**	**18581088**	**18786284**	**12470145**	**4130198**	**1121536**	**1064404**
2001	3462571	677146	529776	2255649	3159848	2167201	826437	165832	378
2002	3961623	642676	603510	2715437	3405498	2213728	835873	195792	160105
2003	3933077	619631	693100	2620346	3620777	2409620	789952	208058	213147
2004	7580057	738956	1582441	5258660	4022791	2571459	822992	270182	358158
2005	8380778	776028	1873754	5730996	4577370	3108137	854944	281672	332617
2006-2010	**53738139**	**4632513**	**10259436**	**38846188**	**22812698**	**12714298**	**4414583**	**1906235**	**3777583**
2006	8254536	890691	791947	6571898	4231243	2625719	885991	335693	383840
2007	9603464	908438	1474249	7220776	4490390	2684862	792883	376074	636572
2008	10419977	902281	2409604	7108091	4542168	2535249	840878	356744	809297
2009	11464758	935596	2677144	7852018	4412317	2293902	878887	355257	884271
2010	13995404	995507	2906492	10093405	5136580	2574567	1015944	482467	1063602
2011	15286501	1086609	3036655	11163237	6169272	3113203	1323259	474856	1257955
2012	15957877	1163833	3047757	11746287	6383052	3076143	1397736	489845	1419328

13-1 续表 2 continued

年份 Year	机动车拥有量(万辆) Possession of Motor Vehicles (10000 unit)	#民用汽车拥有量 Possession of Civil Motor Vehicles	#私人 Private	邮电业务总量(万元) Business Volum of Post and Telecommunication Service (10000 yuan)	年末固定电话用户数(万户) Number of Fixed Telephone subscribers (10000 units)	年末移动电话用户数(万户) Number of Mobile Telephone subscribers (10000 units)	固定电话主线普及率(线/百人) Popularization Rate of Telephone (lines/100 persons)	移动电话普及率(户/百人) Popularization Rate of Mobile Telephone (sets/100 persons)	互联网宽带接入用户数(万户) Broad Band Subscribers of Internet(10000 subscribers)
1978		6.1		24114	7.3		0.8		
1979		7.0		26724	7.8		0.9		
1980		8.1		30047	8.4		0.9		
1981-1985				**204839**					
1981		8.9		31907	9.2		1.0		
1982		9.3		34777	9.8		1.1		
1983		9.8		38525	10.9		1.2		
1984		12.1		45629	12.1		1.3		
1985		16.0		54002	13.6		1.4		
1986-1990				**434582**					
1986		18.6		62079	16.5		1.6		
1987		19.3	0.7	71152	19.5		1.9		
1988		22.2	1.3	84331	23.8		2.2		
1989		24.8	2.4	98124	27.8		2.6		
1990		27.1	2.8	118896	33.3	0.3	3.1	0.03	
1991-1995				**1664508**					
1991		29.7	3.5	157418	39.5	0.7	3.6	0.1	
1992		34.1	4.9	215769	48.0	1.2	4.4	0.1	
1993		41.6	6.7	311251	66.5	3.2	6.0	0.3	
1994		48.1	8.5	418774	100.4	7.7	8.9	0.7	
1995		58.9	12.8	561296	150.5	16.9	12.0	1.4	
1996-2000				**6756754**					
1996		62.2	17.4	729022	195.7	31.0	15.5	2.5	
1997		78.4	29.8	930137	251.2	62.0	20.3	5.0	
1998		89.8	40.7	1290967	313.3	104.2	25.1	8.4	
1999		95.1	44.7	1659133	376.3	186.2	29.9	14.8	
2000	157.8	104.1	49.4	2147496	451.2	347.2	33.1	25.5	
2001-2005				**15331552**					
2001	169.9	114.5	62.4	2182782	525.7	629.4	38.0	45.4	
2002	189.9	133.9	81.1	2540454	585.5	919.5	41.1	64.6	
2003	212.4	163.1	107.1	3040327	682.7	1109.0	46.9	76.1	
2004	229.6	187.1	129.8	3438376	847.4	1340.7	56.8	89.8	
2005	258.3	214.6	154.0	4129614	943.5	1459.8	61.3	94.9	228.9
2006-2010				**40044606**					
2006	287.6	244.1	181.0	5046014	905.2	1571.1	56.5	98.1	281.2
2007	312.8	277.8	212.1	6726273	914.5	1598.3	54.6	95.4	347.2
2008	350.4	318.1	248.3	8008147	884.9	1616.2	50.0	91.3	382.7
2009	401.9	372.1	300.3	9175072	893.1	1825.4	48.0	98.1	451.7
2010	480.9	452.9	374.4	11089100 (4284217)	885.6	2129.8	45.1	108.6	545.6
2011	498.3	473.2	389.7	4878792	883.9	2575.9	43.8	127.6	523.4
2012	520.0	495.7	407.5	5464681	883.1	3168.0	42.7	153.1	572.0

注：1. 邮电业务总量2000年及以前按1990年不变价格计算，2001-2010按2000年不变价格计算，2011年开始按2010年不变价格计算。表内2010年邮电业务总量是按2000年价格计算,()内数据是按2010年价格计算。

2. 2006-2010年主线普及率和移动电话普及率根据第六次人口普查数据进行了调整。

Note: a) Business volumes of post and telecommunications before 2000 were calculated at 1990's constant prices, and 2001-2010 were calculated at 2000's constant prices,from 2011 they were calculated at 2010's constant prices. In this table, the volume of post & telecom service in 2010 was calculated at 2000's price, and figures in () were calculated at 2010's price.

b) Date of Popularization Rate of Telephone and Popularization Rate of Mobile Telephone for 2006-2010 were adjusted from the 6th population census .

13-2 社会客货运总量(换算周转量)
PASSENGER AND FREIGHT TRAFFIC (CONVERTED INTO TURNOVER VOLUME)

单位：万吨公里 (10000 ton-km)

项 目	Item	2012	2011	2012年为2011年% 2012 as % of 2011	构 成(%) Composition(%)	
					2012	2011
运输总量	**Total**	**8895413.6**	**8553100.8**	**104.0**	**100.0**	**100.0**
铁 路	Railway	4239975.4	4199812.0	101.0	47.7	49.1
公 路	Highway	1702511.3	1626924.5	104.6	19.1	19.0
民 航	Civil Aviation	1533598.7	1468409.8	104.4	17.2	17.2
管 道	Pipelines	1419328.1	1257954.5	112.8	16.0	14.7

13-3 运输线路
TRANSPORTATION ROUTES

项 目	Item	条 数 (条) Number (line)		长 度 (公里) Length (km)	
		2012	2011	2012	2011
铁 路	Railway	56	51	1115.1	1067
公 路	Highway	10145	10065	21491.8	21347.1
民 航	Civil Aviation				
#中国国际航空公司	Air China	284	282		
中国新华航空有限责任公司	China Xinhua Airlines	327	294		
管 道	Pipeline	15	15	3496.9	3496.5

注：铁路长度为营业里程，管道长度为管输里程。
Note: Railway length means operating kilometers, pipeline length means pipe transportation kilometers.

13-4 铁路、民航主要技术经济指标
MAIN TECHNICAL AND ECONOMIC INDICATORS OF RAILWAY AND CIVIL AVIATION

项　目	Item	2012	2011	2012年为2011年% 2012 as % of 2011
铁　路	**Railway**			
内燃机车每万吨公里耗柴油（千克）	Diesel Consumption of Internal-Combustion Engine Per 10000 Ton-km (kg)	34.3	33.6	102.0
电力机车每万吨公里耗电（千瓦小时）	Electricity Consumption of Electric Power Engine Per 10000 Ton-km (kwh)	92.9	91.6	101.5
民　航	**Civil Aviation**			
每吨公里耗航空油（千克）	Aviation-oil Consumption Per Ton-km (kg)	0.24	0.29	83.9

13-5 机动车拥有量
POSSESSION OF CIVIL MOTOR VEHICLES

单位：万辆　　(10000 units)

项　目	Item	2012	2011	2012年为2011年% 2012 as % of 2011
机动车	**Motor Vehicles**	**520.0**	**498.3**	**104.4**
#民用汽车	Civil Automobiles	495.7	473.2	104.8
#载货汽车	Trucks	23.7	21.5	110.2
载客汽车	Passanger Cars	464.9	444.2	104.7
#私人汽车	Private Cars	407.5	389.7	104.6
#轿　车	Sedans	298.2	286.2	104.2

资料来源：北京市公安局公安交通管理局。
Source: Beijing Traffic Management Bureau.

13-6 邮电业务主要指标
MAIN INDICATORS OF POST AND TELECOMMUNICATION SERVICES

项 目		Item		2012	2011	2012年为2011年% 2012 as % of 2011
邮电业务量	**(万元)**	**Sales Revenue of Posts and Telecommunications**	**(10000 yuan)**			
(2010年不变价)		**(at 2010 constant prices)**		**5464681**	**4878792**	**112.0**
邮 政		Posts		584535	515951	113.3
电 信		Telecommunications		4880146	4362841	111.9
邮电业务总量		**Business Volume of Post and Telecommunication Service**				
函 件	(万件)	Number of Letters	(10000 pcs)	67219	70828	94.9
包 件	(万件)	Parcels	(10000 pcs)	597	615	97.1
特快专递	(万件)	EMS	(10000 pcs)	3984	3257	122.3
汇 票	(万件)	Postal Money Order	(10000 pcs)	763	854	89.4
订销报纸累计	(万份)	Newspaper	(10000 copies)	83133	77549	107.2
订销杂志累计	(万份)	Magazines	(10000 copies)	6076	5336	113.9
邮政储蓄期末余额	(亿元)	Post Savings Deposit Balance	(100 million yuan)	713.8	628.9	113.5
长途电话通话量(固定)	(亿分钟)	Length of Long-distance Calls of Fixed Telephone	(101 million minutes)	44.0	49.6	88.8
本地电话通话量(固定)	(亿次)	Local Calls(Stationary)	(100 million times)	142.5	173.8	82.0
移动电话通话量	(亿分钟)	Length of Calls of Mobile Telephone	(100 million minutes)	1478.5	1346.4	109.8
移动短信业务量	(亿条)	Short Message Services	(100 million messages)	447.9	410.1	109.2
年末移动电话用户	(万户)	Mobile Telephone Subscribers	(10000 subscribers)	3168.0	2575.9	123.0
#3G移动电话用户数	(万户)	3G Mobile Phone Subscribers	(10001 subscribers)	855.5	464.7	184.1
年末固定电话用户	(万户)	Fixed Telephone Subscribers	(10000 subscribers)	883.1	883.9	99.9
#住宅电话用户	(万户)	Household Telephone Subscribers	(10001 subscribers)	563.8	568.1	99.2
长途光缆纤芯长度	(芯公里)	Fiber Length of Long Distance Optic Cables	(core-km)	172857.0	165387.0	104.5
长途电话交换机容量	(万路端)	Capacity of Long Distance Telephone Exchanges	(10000 roadheads)	55.1	55.1	100.0
局用交换机容量	(万门)	Capacity of Office Telephone Exchange	(10000 units)	1581.1	1324.8	119.3
移动电话交换机容量	(万户)	Capacity of Mobile Telephone Exchange	(10000 subscribers)	4734	4474	105.8
固定电话主线普及率	(线/百人)	Widespreading Rate of Main Line	(lines/100 persons)	42.7	43.8	
移动电话普及率	(户/百人)	Widespreading Rate of Mobile Telephone	(sets/100 persons)	153.1	127.6	
互联网宽带接入用户数	(万户)	Broad Band Subscribers of Internet	(10000 subscribers)	572.0	523.4	109.3
互联网上网人数	(万人)	Number of Internet Users	(10000 persons)	1458.0	1379.0	105.7

注：1. 固定电话用户包括市内电话用户和农村电话用户。
2. "互联网上网人数"来源于中国互联网络信息中心（CNNIC)发布的《中国互联网络发展状况统计报告》。

Note: a) Data of fixed telephone subscribers included urban and rural areas.
b) "Number of Internet Users" was sourced from the Statistic Report on Internet Development Status in China issued by CNNIC.

主要统计指标解释

货（客）运量 指在一定时期内，各种运输工具实际运送的货物（旅客）数量。是反映运输业为国民经济和人民生活服务的数量指标，也是制定和检查运输生产计划，研究运输发展规模和速度的重要指标。货运按吨计算，客运按人计算。货物不论运输距离长短，货物类别，均按实际重量统计；旅客不论行程远近或票价多少，均按一人一次作为客运量统计。半价票、小孩票也按一人统计。

货物（旅客）周转量 指在一定时期内，由各种运输工具运送的货物（旅客）数量与其相应运输距离的乘积之总和，是反映运输业生产总成果的重要指标，也是编制和检查运输生产计划、计算运输效率、劳动生产率以及核算运输单位的主要基础资料。计算货物周转量通常按发出站与到达站之间的最短距离，也就是计费距离计算。

邮电业务总量 是以货币形式表示的邮政电信企业为社会提供各类邮政通信服务的总数量。计算公式为：

$$邮电业务总量=\sum\left(各类邮政通信业务量\times不变单价\right)+出租代维及其他业务收入$$

函件 是指邮政部门为用户传递以书面信息为主的邮件，包括信件、印刷品和邮送广告。

包件 指符合包裹准寄范围，通过邮政渠道寄递的物品。包括国内普通包裹、国内快递包裹、国际及港澳台包裹。

长途电话交换机容量 是指用于接入长途电话网的电话交换机的设备额定容量。

局用交换机容量 是指安装在本地电信企业内用于接续本地固定电话的电话交换机容量。包括现用和备用的人工或自动交换机（含远端模块）的全部容量，包括接入网设备容量。

移动电话交换机容量 分为 GSM、CDMA 两种。指移动电话交换机根据一定话务模型和交换机处理能力计算出来的最大同时服务用户的数量。

主线普及率 是指报告期行政区域常住人口中，平均每百人拥有的固定电话主线数。计算公式为：

$$主线普及率=\frac{电话主线数(本地电话用户)}{行政区域常住人口数}$$

移动电话普及率 是指报告期行政区域常住人口中，平均每百人拥有的移动电话的用户数。计算公式为：

$$移动电话普及率=\frac{移动电话用户总数}{行政区域常住人口数}$$

互联网宽带接入用户数 指报告期末在电信企业登记注册，通过 xDSL、FTTx+LAN 以及其他宽带接入方式和普通专线接入公众互联网的用户。

Explanatory Notes on Main Statistical Indicators

Freight (Passenger) Traffic refers to the volume of freight (passenger) transported with various means. It is a quantitative measure to show how the transport industry serves the national economy and people, and is also an important indicator for planning the transport industry and for studying the development scale and speed of the transport industry. Freight transport is calculated in tons and passenger traffic is calculated in the number of persons. Despite the type of freight and travelling distance, the freight transport is calculated in the actual weight of the goods: and despite the travelling distance and ticket price, the passenger traffic is calculated by the principle that one person can be counted only once in one travel. The passenger who travels with a half price ticket or a child ticket is also calculated as one person.

Freight Ton-kilometers (Passenger-kilometers) refer to the sum of the products of the volume of transported cargo (passengers) multiplying by the transport distance, usually using ton-kilometer and passenger-kilometer as units for measurement. This is an important indicator to show the total results of the transport industry, also serving as main basic data for preparing and examining the transport plan and measuring the efficiency, the labor productivity and the unit cost of transport. Freight Ton-kilometers are usually calculated by the shortest distance between the delivering station and the arrival station, namely the charging distance.

Business Volume of Post and Telecommunications refers to the total amount of post and telecommunications services, expressed in currency form, provided by the post and telecommunications departments for the society. The formula is as follows:

Business Volume of Post and Telecommunications

=∑(Transaction of Post and Telecommunication Service x Constant Price) + Income from Leasing, Maintenance and other Services

Correspondences mean mails mainly in the form of written information delivered by post and telecom offices, including letters, prints and delivered advertisements.

Parcels means articles permitted for mailing, and mailed through postal channels, including domestic express parcels, international parcels, and parcels from and to Hong Kong, Macao and Taiwan.

Capacity of Long-distance Phone Exchangers means the rated capacity of phone exchangers used for connecting to the long-distance phone network.

Capacity of Local Exchangers means the capacity of phone exchangers installed in local telecom businesses and used for linking local fixed telephones. It includes all capacity of existing and backup manual or automatic exchangers (including far-end modules), including the capacity of network access equipment.

Capacity of Mobile Phone Exchangers falling into GSM and CDMA, means the maximum number of users receiving services simultaneously from mobile phone exchangers, calculated for given talking model and exchanger processing capacity.

Popularization Rate of Telephone means the number of fixed phone main lines owned by one hundred persons of permanent population in administrative areas in the reporting period. It is calculated with the following formula:

Popularization Rate of Telephone= Number of Main Lines of Telephone (Local Phone Users) / Number of Permanent Population in Administrative Areas

Popularization Rate of Mobile Telephone means the number of mobile phones owned by 100 persons among permanent population in administrative areas in the reporting period. It is calculated with the following formula:

Popularization Rate of Mobile Telephone = Total Number of Mobile Phone Users / Permanent Population in Administrative Areas

Subscribers Connected with Internet through Broadband means subscribers registered at telecom companies to connect with public Internet through xDSL, FTTx+LAN as well as other broadband connections and general special lines at the end of reporting period.

Explanatory Notes on Main Statistical Indicators

14

北京统计年鉴2013　BEIJING STATISTICAL YEARBOOK

批发和零售业、住宿和餐饮业
WHOLESALE, RETAIL, HOUSING AND CATERING

简要说明

一、本章资料的主要内容

本章资料反映北京市商品流通市场发展及批发和零售业、住宿和餐饮业经营情况。主要内容有社会消费品零售总额；批发和零售业商品购进、销售、库存总值、商品分类销售情况及主要商品销售情况；机动车销售情况；限额以上批发和零售业、住宿业、餐饮业财务状况；连锁企业基本情况；商品交易市场基本情况、成交额及主要商品的成交量；消费者投诉处理情况。

二、本章的统计范围

社会消费品零售总额指标1993年、1997年和2003年做了较大调整。1993年起不再包括对农民的农业生产资料；1997年起不再包括居民购买住房；2003年起不再包括由各种经济类型的制造业法人企业、产业活动单位直接售给城乡居民（包括本企业职工）和社会集团的商品以及农民对非农业居民的零售额。

限额以上批发和零售业、餐饮业统计限额标准。2008年前为批发业年销售额2000万元及以上；零售业年销售额500万元及以上；住宿业为星级饭店和星级以外年营业收入500万元及以上；餐饮业年营业额200万元及以上。2008年调整，调整后为批发业年主营业务收入2000万元及以上；零售业年主营收入500万元及以上；住宿业为星级饭店和星级以外年主营业务收入200万元及以上；餐饮业年主营业务收入200万元及以上。

三、本章的资料来源

本章资料由北京市统计局、国家统计局北京调查总队提供。

四、本章的统计调查方法

限额以上批发和零售业、住宿和餐饮业单位采用全面调查的方法；连锁企业、商品交易市场采取全数调查；限额以下批发和零售业、住宿和餐饮业法人单位及个体户采用抽样调查方法。

五、有关统计标准的变化说明

2010年以前企业大中小型划分执行2003年《统计上大中小型企业划分办法（暂行）》标准；自2011年开始，大中微型企业划分标准执行《国家统计局关于印发统计上大中小微型企业划分办法的通知》（国统字[2011]75号）。

本章中行业分类2002-2011年期间执行2002年《国民经济行业分类标准》（GB/T 4754-2002）划分标准，2012年开始执行2011年《国民经济行业分类》（GB/T 4754-2011）划分标准。

六、本章中关于历史数据调整的问题

按照国家统计局统一要求和统一方法，本章中1978年至2003年的社会消费品零售额数据，根据2004年第一次经济普查结果，采用“速度推算法”进行了修正。2004年数据为第一次经济普查数据。2005-2007年数据根据2008年第二次经济普查结果，采用“趋势离差法”进行了修正。2008年数据为第二次经济普查数据。

Brief Introduction

I. Main Content

Statistics in this chapter show the development of commodity circulation market and the operating performance of wholesale and retail trades, accommodation and catering. Figures are mainly for consumer goods retails, total value of commodity purchase, sale and inventory in wholesale and retail trades, sales of commodities by categories, and sales of main commodities; sales of mobile vehicles; financial status of wholesale, retail, accommodation and catering enterprises above designated size; chain businesses; basic situation of commodity transaction markets, transaction volume, and transaction volume of main commodities; and settlement of consumer complaints.

II. Scope of Statistics

Greater adjustment was made to the indicator of Retail Sales of Consumer Goods for 1993, 1997 and 2003. From 1993, this indicator does not cover agricultural capital goods for farmers any loner; from 1997, it does not cover houses bought by residents any longer; from 2003, it does not cover goods sold by manufacturing corporate enterprises and industrial activity entities of various economic types to urban and rural residents (including enterprises' own employees) and social groups as well as retail sales by farmers to non-agricultural residents any longer.

Standard for designated size of wholesale and retail trades, and catering industry. Before 2008, for whole sale trades, the designated size was annual sales of RMB 20 million and over; for retail trades, annual sales of RMB 5 million and over; for accommodation industry, star-level hotels and non-star-level hotels with annual business income of RMB 5 million and over; for catering industry, annual turnover of RMB 2 million and over. Adjustment was made in 2008. After adjustment, the designated size is, for whole sale trades, annual sales of RMB 20 million and over; for retail trades, annual sales of RMB 5 million and over; for accommodation industry, star-level hotels and non-star-level hotels with annual main business income of RMB 2 million and over; for catering industry, annual main business income of RMB 2 million and over.

III. Source of Data

Data in this chapter are sourced from Beijing Municipal Bureau of Statistics and NBS Survey Office in Beijing.

IV. Method of Statistics

The method of complete survey was used for statistics for wholesale and retail trades, accommodation, catering service enterprises above designated size; total survey was used for chain businesses, commodity trading markets; method of sample survey was used for wholesale and retail trades, accommodation, catering service enterprises as legal persons below designated size as well as self-employed operators.

Ⅴ. Changes in Relevant Statistical Standards

Before 2010，the classification of small-, medium- and large-sized enterprises complied with the standard of Measures for Statistical Classification of Small-, Medium- and Large-sized Enterprises (Temporary) 2003; From 2011, the classification of mini-, medium- and large-sized enterprises complies with the Notification of National Bureau of Statistics on Printing and Issuing the Measures for Statistical Classification of Mini-, Small-, Medium- and Large-sized Enterprises (GTZ[2011]No.75).

In this chapter, classification of building sectors in 2002-2011 was based on the Standard for Classification of National Economic Sectors 2002 (GB/T 4754-2002). Standard for Classification of National Economic Sectors (GB/T 4754-2011) became effective in 2012.

Ⅵ.Adjustment to Historical Data

In accordance with the uniform requirement and method of the National Bureau of Statistics, 1978-2003 data of retail sales of consumer goods were adjusted with the "speed calculation method" according to the first economic census results in 2004. Data 2004 are those from the first economic census. Data for 2005-2007 were corrected with the "trend deviation method" in accordance with results from the second economic census 2008. Data 2008 are those from the second economic census.

14-1 历年社会消费品零售总额(1978-2012年)
TOTAL RETAIL SALES OF CONSUMER GOODS (1978-2012)

单位：亿元 (100 million yuan)

年份 Year	社会消费品零售总额 Retail Sales of Consumer Goods	按商品类别分 By Category of Commodity			
		吃类商品 Food	穿类商品 Clothing	用类商品 Daily Supplies	烧类商品 Fuels
1978	44.2	18.0	8.9	16.0	1.3
1979	53.3	20.8	11.3	19.7	1.5
1980	62.8	24.9	13.4	22.9	1.6
1981-1985	**472.7**	**180.9**	**85.1**	**196.2**	**10.5**
1981	70.7	28.0	14.5	26.5	1.7
1982	75.4	29.7	13.7	30.3	1.7
1983	86.4	34.0	15.7	34.8	1.9
1984	105.8	39.6	18.7	45.2	2.3
1985	134.4	49.6	22.5	59.4	2.9
1986-1990	**1239.8**	**494.9**	**166.7**	**551.8**	**26.4**
1986	155.0	60.7	22.8	68.0	3.5
1987	188.9	77.4	27.4	80.2	3.9
1988	256.0	100.6	36.0	114.9	4.5
1989	294.8	119.4	34.9	134.1	6.4
1990	345.1	136.8	45.6	154.6	8.1
1991-1995	**3239.5**	**1261.4**	**481.3**	**1422.2**	**74.6**
1991	408.3	158.2	53.7	187.6	8.8
1992	503.0	193.6	66.9	230.5	12.0
1993	611.2	220.7	96.5	277.6	16.4
1994	766.6	283.2	125.3	338.6	19.5
1995	950.4	405.7	138.9	387.9	17.9
1996-2000	**6811.7**	**2177.0**	**858.9**	**3576.5**	**199.3**
1996	1061.6	427.5	152.5	461.8	19.8
1997	1208.5	447.9	161.6	565.6	33.4
1998	1373.6	399.8	167.2	764.2	42.4
1999	1509.3	430.4	178.8	852.9	47.2
2000	1658.7	471.4	198.8	932.0	56.5
2001-2005	**11671.8**	**3061.2**	**1218.6**	**6722.7**	**669.3**
2001	1831.4	528.7	221.9	1016.9	63.9
2002	2005.2	540.2	219.9	1167.4	77.7
2003	2296.9	596.4	252.3	1356.4	91.8
2004	2626.6	644.9	242.1	1538.3	201.3
2005	2911.7	751.0	282.4	1643.7	234.6
2006-2010	**23315.2**	**5343.5**	**2107.9**	**14019.4**	**1844.4**
2006	3295.3	818.8	314.7	1852.6	309.2
2007	3835.2	940.4	359.3	2205.2	330.3
2008	4645.5	1073.3	411.7	2799.4	361.1
2009	5309.9	1180.0	473.8	3278.2	377.9
2010	6229.3	1331.0	548.4	3884.0	465.9
2011	6900.3	1561.4	665.2	4080.1	593.6
2012	7702.8	1679.1	718.0	4678.4	627.3

注：1978-2003年社会消费品零售额按2004年第一次经济普查数据进行了修订，2004年为第一次经济普查数据，2005-2007年数据按第二次经济普查进行了修订，2008年数据为第二次经济普查数据。

Note: Total retail sales of consumer goods for 1978-2003 were revised according to the first economic cencus statistics.Figures for 2004 were from the first economic census. Figures for 2005-2007 were revised from the second economic census. Figures for 2008 were from the second economic census.

14-2 社会消费品零售总额(2009-2012年)
TOTAL RETAIL SALES OF CONSUMER GOODS (2009-2012)

单位：亿元 (100 million yuan)

项目	Item	2009	2010	2011	2012	2012年为2011年% 2012 as % of 2011
社会消费品零售总额	**Retail Sales of Consumer Goods**	**5309.9**	**6229.3**	**6900.3**	**7702.8**	**111.6**
按商品类别分	**By Category of Commodity**					
吃类商品	Food	1180.0	1331.0	1561.4	1679.1	107.5
穿类商品	Clothing	473.8	548.4	665.2	718.0	107.9
用类商品	Daily Supplies	3278.3	3884.0	4080.1	4678.4	114.7
烧类商品	Fuel	377.9	465.9	593.6	627.3	105.7
按销售单位所在地分	**By Location of Seller**					
城镇	Towns and Cities	5221.7	6128.8	6789.6	7580.4	111.6
农村	Countryside	88.1	100.5	110.7	122.4	110.5
按消费品形态分	**By Form of Consumer Goods**					
餐饮收入	Food & Drink Income	590.3	666.6	765.9	824.4	107.6
商品零售额	Retail Sales of Commodities	4719.6	5562.7	6134.4	6878.4	112.1

14-3 按登记注册类型分限额以上批发和零售企业商品零售额
RETAIL SALES OF GOODS IN WHOLESALE AND RETAIL ENTERPRISES ABOVE DESIGNATED SIZE BY REGISTRATION STATUS

单位：万元 (10000 yuan)

项目	Item	2012	2011	2012年为2011年% 2012 as % of 2011
总计	**Total**	**63934235**	**54791370**	**116.7**
内资企业	Domestic Funded Enterprises	51824866	43591525	118.9
#国有	State-owned Enterprises	1424528	1319965	107.9
集体	Collective-owned Enterprises	536640	507371	105.8
股份有限公司	Share Holding Corporations Ltd.	8329566	8392615	99.2
港澳台商投资企业	Enterprises with Funds from Hongkong, Macao and Taiwan	3440600	3053455	112.7
外商投资企业	Foreign Funded Enterprises	8668770	8146390	106.4

注：限额以上批发和零售企业是指年主营业务收入2000万元及以上批发企业和年主营业务收入500万元及以上零售企业。

Note: Above designated size of wholesale and retail trades include annual main business income are 20 million yuan or above for wholesale trade; 5 million yuan or above for retail trade.

14-4 批发和零售业商品购进、销售、库存总额
TOTAL VALUE OF PURCHASES, SALES AND INVENTORY OF COMMODITIES IN WHOLESALE AND RETAIL TRADES

单位：万元 (10000 yuan)

项目	Item	2012	2011	2012年为2011年% 2012 as % of 2011
商品购进额	**Total Purchases of Goods**	**501985637**	**435099097**	**115.4**
市内购进额	In the City	102283271	91271411	112.1
市外购进额	From Outside Beijing	316570502	270405615	117.1
进口	Imported	83131864	73422071	113.2
商品销售额	**Total Sales**	**536925945**	**469243196**	**114.4**
批发额	**Wholesale**	**467294051**	**407904488**	**114.6**
市内批发额	In the City	106488128	88113346	120.9
市外批发额	To Outside	342804730	304296747	112.7
出口	Exported	18001193	15494395	116.2
零售额	**Retail**	**69631894**	**61338708**	**113.5**
期末商品库存额	**Inventory (year-end)**	**47904492**	**42928314**	**111.6**

注：本表统计范围为批发和零售业法人单位和个体经营户，不包括其他行业购进、销售、库存数据。
Note: Figures in this table cover corporate entities, self-employed operators in wholesale and retail trades, excluding figures on purchase, sales and inventory in other sectors.

14-5 批发和零售业法人单位商品购进、销售、库存总额
TOTAL VALUE OF PURCHASES, SALES AND INVENTORY IN WHOLESALE AND RETAIL CORPORATE ENTITIES

单位：万元 (10000 yuan)

项目	Item	2012	2011	2012年为2011年% 2012 as % of 2011
商品购进额	**Total Purchases of Goods**	**493506629**	**424575734**	**116.2**
市内购进额	In the City	96919822	84694640	114.4
市外购进额	From Outside Beijing	313454943	266459023	117.6
进口	Imported	83131864	73422071	113.2
商品销售额	**Total Sales**	**529580077**	**458123720**	**115.6**
批发额	**Wholesale**	**464332399**	**401935742**	**115.5**
市内批发额	In the City	104701434	84060344	124.6
市外批发额	To Outside	341629772	302381003	113.0
出口	Exported	18001193	15494395	116.2
零售额	**Retail**	**65247678**	**56187978**	**116.1**
期末商品库存额	**Inventory (year-end)**	**47807195**	**42838226**	**111.6**

14-6 批发和零售业法人单位商品分类销售(2012年)
SALES BY CATEGORY IN WHOLESALE AND RETAIL ENTERPRISES(2012)

单位：万元 (10000 yuan)

项目	Item	合计 Total			#大中型企业 Medium-and Large Enterprises		
		商品销售额 Total Sales	批发额 Wholesale	零售额 Retail	商品销售额 Total Sales	批发额 Wholesale	零售额 Retail
合　计	**Total**	**529580077**	**464332399**	**65247678**	**454085693**	**396608664**	**57477028**
粮油、食品、饮料、烟酒类	Food,Beverages,Tobacco and Liquor	33774783	27297573	6477210	30613734	24417168	6196566
粮油、食品类	Food	23191662	18353224	4838438	20880707	16210591	4670116
#粮油类	Grain and Oil	10323310	9600169	723141	9270466	8600305	670161
肉禽蛋类	Meat,Poultry and Eggs	1647189	944714	702476	1451278	763153	688125
饮料类	Beverages	2770121	2182146	587975	2571886	2016961	554925
烟酒类	Tobacco and Liquor	7813000	6762203	1050797	7161141	6189616	971525
服装鞋帽、针、纺织品类	Clothing,Shoes,Hats and Textiles	11180260	4470033	6710227	9724966	3364207	6360759
服装类	Clothing	7336812	2236324	5100488	6584783	1739958	4844825
鞋帽类	Shoes and Hats	2262666	1079365	1183302	2026757	896756	1130001
针、纺织品类	Knitwear and Textiles	1580782	1154344	426437	1113426	727493	385932
化妆品类	Cosmetics	2420059	881943	1538116	2302685	820840	1481845
金银珠宝类	Gold, Silver and Jewelry	12002009	8832152	3169857	11311740	8253076	3058664
日用品类	Articles for Daily Use	5626852	2840790	2786062	4786709	2320980	2465728
#洗涤用品类	Washing Articles	946844	588236	358608	863067	519024	344043
儿童玩具类	Children Toys	137721	34081	103640	125966	25632	100334
五金、电料类	Hardware and Electrical Materials	1431951	1227162	204790	632791	565750	67041
体育、娱乐用品类	Sports and Recreation Articles	5639710	4758220	881490	5251699	4485693	766006
书报、杂志类	Newspapers and Magazines	1981014	927044	1053971	1658300	710998	947302
电子出版物及音像制品类	E-Journal and Video Products	491088	260556	230533	370813	177021	193792
家用电器和音像器材类	Household Appliances and Video Appliances	11234467	8467508	2766959	10352530	7887030	2465500
中西药品类	Traditional Chinese and Western Medicines	13198724	6733315	6465409	11350147	6013194	5336954
#西药类	Western Medicines	9412452	4862356	4550096	8487842	4544077	3943766
中草药及中成药类	Traditional Chinese Medicines	2140415	968079	1172336	1958129	880317	1077812
文化、办公用品类	Cultural and Official Goods	17069794	13340715	3729078	13073992	10293055	2780938
家具类	Furniture	970702	164992	805710	882840	133871	748970
通讯器材类	Communication Appliances	27735877	24024175	3711702	21791598	18615069	3176529
煤炭及制品类	Coal and Related Products	39524982	39502404	22578	32566367	32549378	16989
木材及制品类	Wood and Wooden Products	1188401	1188401		915710	915710	
石油及制品类	Petroleum and Related Products	64338219	58575287	5762933	51839436	47194826	4644611
化工材料及制品类	Raw Chemical Materials	53086473	53086473		46171803	46171803	
#化肥类	Fertilizer	11049538	11049538		10438972	10438972	
金属材料类	Metal Materials	104778655	104778655		88186483	88186483	
建筑及装潢材料类	Building and Decoration Materials	3257122	3012595	244527	2133441	1977942	155499
机电产品及设备类	Electric-mechanic Products and Equipments	23822846	23167258	655588	19401397	19101040	300358
#农机类	Agricultural Machinery	368652	368652		292552	292552	
汽车类	Automobile	73912277	57230141	16682136	71537143	56131715	15405429
种子饲料类	Seed and Feedstuff	960234	960234		735663	735663	
棉麻类	Cotton, Hemp	3572179	3570894	1285	2842185	2842185	
其他类	Others	16381399	15033880	1347519	13651522	12743970	907551

注：行业划分执行2011年国民经济行业分类标准（GB/T 4754-2011）。
Note: Sectors in this table are classified in accordance with the Standard for Classification of National Economic Sectors 2011 (GB/T 4754-2011).

14-7 限额以上批发和零售企业商品销售情况(2012年)
COMMODITY SALES OF WHOLESALE AND RETAIL ENTERPRISES ABOVE DESIGNATED SIZE (2012)

项目		Item		商品销售总量 Total Sales	批发量 Wholesale Trade	零售量 Retail Trade
大米(稻米)	(百公斤)	Rice	(100 kg)	31654747	30403589	1251158
白面(小麦面)	(百公斤)	Flour	(100 kg)	3690503	2990712	699791
杂　粮	(百公斤)	Coarse Cereals	(100 kg)	26985470	26784931	200539
食用植物油	(百公斤)	Edible Vegetable Oil	(100 kg)	61848980	60854835	994146
猪　肉	(百公斤)	Pigs and Pork	(100 kg)	2564764	1842486	722279
牛　肉	(百公斤)	Cattle and Beef	(100 kg)	267930	93761	174169
羊　肉	(百公斤)	Goat,Sheep and Mutton	(100 kg)	170643	35361	135281
禽　肉	(百公斤)	Poultry	(100 kg)	1445570	1164444	281126
鲜　蛋	(百公斤)	Fresh Eggs	(100 kg)	631543	119000	512543
鲜　菜	(百公斤)	Fresh Vegetable	(100 kg)	3796160	1336650	2459510
鲜瓜果	(百公斤)	Fresh Melons and Fruits	(100 kg)	3049140	1179100	1870040
水产品	(百公斤)	Aquatic Products	(100 kg)	1304250	931020	373230
食　糖	(百公斤)	Sugar	(100 kg)	21245140	20854980	390160
卷　烟	(万支)	Cigarettes	10000 units)	9154428	8695774	458655
酒	(百升)	Liquor Wine	(100 liter)	13549919	12619067	930852
#白　酒	(百升)	Distilled Spirit	(100 liter)	1544277	1208975	335302
啤　酒	(百升)	Beer	(100 liter)	7413693	7041900	371793
茶　叶	(百公斤)	Tea	(100 kg)	203960	132560	71400
各种服装	(百件)	Clothing	(100 units)	3817306	1872641	1944665
鞋	(百双)	Shoe	(100 pairs)	1117470	626070	491400
数码照相机	(台)	Digital Camera	(unit)	15933449	14580367	1353082
自行车	(辆)	Bicycle	(unit)	718251	532398	185853
彩色电视机	(台)	Color TV Set	(unit)	8913087	7310208	1602879
摄像机	(台)	Pickup Camera	(unit)	1617074	1513275	103799
家用电风扇	(台)	Electrical Fans	(unit)	1172940	907231	265709
电冰箱（家用电冰箱）	(台)	Household Refrigerators	(unit)	2159845	1347894	811951
洗衣机（家用洗衣机）	(台)	Household Washing Machine	(unit)	7251335	6490577	760758
家用空调器（房间空调器）	(台)	Room Air Conditioners	(unit)	8400038	7203056	1196982
微波炉	(台)	Microwave Oven	(unit)	1969455	1536261	433194

14-7 续表 continued

项目		Item		商品 销售总量 Total Sales	批发量 Wholesale Trade	零售量 Retail Trade
热水淋浴器	（台）	Showers	(unit)	990057	471873	518184
吸尘器	（台）	Dust Catcher	(unit)	1188456	1031929	156527
抽油烟机	（台）	Exhauster	(unit)	523002	275493	247509
电脑（微型计算机）	（台）	Micro Computers	(unit)	16362197	12966429	3395768
移动电话机	（部）	Mobile phone	(unit)	173631602	161949209	11682393
煤 炭	（吨）	Coal	(ton)	483453804	483110436	343368
汽 油	（吨）	Gasoline	(ton)	10072240	5836732	4235508
煤 油	（吨）	Kerosene	(ton)	12910346	12909642	704
柴 油	（吨）	Diesel Oil	(ton)	17789068	16368386	1420682
钢 材	（吨）	Steel Products	(ton)	116212116	116212116	
水 泥	（吨）	Cement	(ton)	32416508	32211979	204529
汽 车	（辆）	Motor Vehicles	(unit)	2220517	1539626	680891
#轿 车	（辆）	Cars	(unit)	1236045	709106	526939
化学肥料	（吨）	Chemical Fertilizer	(ton)	39814996	39814996	
化学农药	（吨）	Chemical Pesticide	(ton)	91216	91216	
铜	（吨）	Copper	(ton)	1780431	1780431	
铝	（吨）	Aluminium	(ton)	2910476	2910476	

14-8 机动车销售情况(2001-2012年)
SALES OF MOTOR VEHICLE (2001-2012)

单位：万辆 (10000 units)

项目	Item	2001	2002	2003	2004	2005	2006	2007	2008	2009	2010	2011	2012
机动车销售量	**Motor Vehicles Sold**	**22.9**	**26.0**	**40.8**	**44.7**	**57.0**	**71.4**	**79.8**	**87.8**	**114.8**	**143.2**	**79.7**	**128.5**
#轿 车	Car	11.4	15.1	25.2	27.2	38.0	46.2	52.7	54.5	70.6	92.4	49.0	83.2
新 车	**New Car**	**16.4**	**17.7**	**29.3**	**30.4**	**37.2**	**39.1**	**44.3**	**49.3**	**70.2**	**91.6**	**40.0**	**58.6**
#轿 车	Car	10.0	12.0	19.7	20.6	27.7	30.3	34.8	34.9	50.6	66.6	26.2	39.4
旧 车	**Second-hand Vehicles Traded**	**6.6**	**8.3**	**11.5**	**14.3**	**19.8**	**32.3**	**35.5**	**38.5**	**44.6**	**51.6**	**39.7**	**69.9**
#轿 车	Car	1.4	3.0	5.6	6.6	10.2	15.9	17.9	19.5	19.9	25.8	22.8	43.8

资料来源：北京市工商行政管理局。
Source: Beijing Administration For Industry & Commerce.

14-9 限额以上批发和零售企业财务状况(2012年)
FINANCIAL INDICATORS OF WHOLESALE AND RETAIL ENTERPRISES ABOVE DESIGNATED SIZE (2012)

单位：万元 (10000 yuan)

项目	Item	企业单位个数(个) Number of Enterprises (unit)	资产负债 Assets and Liabilities 资产总计 Total Assets	流动资产合计 Total Current Assets	#应收账款 Accounts Receivable	固定资产合计 Total Fixed Assets	固定资产原价 Total Original Value of Fixed Assets
合计	**Total**	**8100**	**280573556**	**209295622**	**37850372**	**8317712**	**12716033**
按企业登记注册类型分	**Grouped by Registration Status of Enterprises**						
内资	Domestic Funded Enterprises	7571	228748225	170078393	32723812	6816690	10008331
国有	State-Owned Enterprises	321	32131687	22436408	2613306	964386	1330794
集体	Collective Owned Enterprises	112	1391691	938759	40371	83412	132014
股份合作	Cooperative Enterprises	108	318218	244314	69390	47071	57528
联营	Joint Owned Enterprises	9	28335	26822	5893	1430	2778
有限责任公司	Limited-Liability Corporation	2534	140261572	107494330	23605617	3846301	5597605
股份有限公司	Share Holding Corporations Ltd.	124	33324073	19766252	1772355	1109530	1693217
私营	Private Enterprises	4363	21292649	19171508	4616880	764561	1194394
其他	Others						
港澳台商投资	Enterprises with Funds from Hongkong, Macao and Taiwan	179	8220635	6120546	895175	353804	550599
外商投资	Foreign Funded Enterprises	350	43604696	33096683	4231385	1147217	2157103
按国民经济行业分	**Grouped by Sectors**						
批发业	Wholesale Trade	5379	243878422	181100879	34730452	5322740	8050508
农、林、牧产品批发	Agricultural or Livestock Products	78	13004070	6545873	310039	280442	355127
食品、饮料及烟草制品批发	Foods, Beverage and Tobaccos	389	14799184	11975005	794856	387245	570765
纺织、服装及家庭日用品批发	Textile, Clothes and Household Commodities	488	10189151	7817580	1185423	250683	374603
文化、体育用品及器材批发	Products and Equipment of Culture or Sports	286	7711134	5500794	870855	298562	424778
医药及医疗器材批发	Medicine and Medical Appliance	351	6932295	5542013	2086639	179050	307606
矿产品、建材及化工产品批发	Mineral,Construction Material, Chemical Products	1742	108398903	78729197	13784973	2336091	3274617
机械设备、五金交电及电子产品批发	Machinery, Hardware, Electrical Appliance and Electronic Product	1901	58558719	45245794	8077344	1331380	2351249
贸易经纪与代理	Trade and Deputy	68	18155712	15799008	7306603	155479	210598
其他批发	Others	76	6129256	3945615	313719	103809	181165
零售业	Retail	2721	36695134	28194743	3119920	2994972	4665525
综合零售	Total Retail	229	10903769	7403353	235453	1201612	2013361
食品、饮料及烟草制品专门零售	Food, Beverage and Tobacoo	119	586857	407630	22852	139750	201400
纺织、服装及日用品专门零售	Textile, Garments and Daily Use Goods	260	1670699	1279085	203379	139467	212153
文化、体育用品及器材专门零售	Products and Equipment of Culture or Sports	224	1964615	1660342	184745	155163	195521
医药及医疗器材专门零售	Medicine and Medical Appliance	381	3665675	2387546	1124909	97637	149811
汽车、摩托车、燃料及零配件专门零售	Automobile, Motorcycle, Elding and Spares or Fittings	734	8107796	6268709	414613	1021728	1517947
家用电器及电子产品专门零售	Household Appliances and Electronic Product	463	7132425	6667233	529743	75105	117746
五金、家具及室内装修材料专门零售	Hardware, Electrical Appliance Furniture and Interior Decoration Material	115	614391	417514	28546	87076	136688
货摊、无店铺及其他零售业	Stand Retail, Retail Without Shops and other Retail	196	2048908	1703331	375682	77435	120897
按规模划分	**Grouped by Size**						
#大中型企业	Medium-and Large Enterprises	2958	241672771	179108134	31992797	6863181	10765627

注：1. 限额以上批发和零售企业是指年主营业务收入2000万元及以上批发企业和年主营业务收入500万元及以上的零售企业。
2. 行业划分执行2011年国民经济行业分类标准（GB/T 4754-2011）。
3. 自2011年开始，大中型企业划分标准执行《国家统计局关于印发统计上大中小微型企业划分办法的通知》(国统字[2011]75号)

Note: a) Above designated size of wholesale and retail trades include the corporations meeting the following criteria: annual sales are 20 million yuan
b) Sectors in this table are classified in accordance with the Standard for Classification of National Economic Sectors 2011 (GB/T 4754-2011).
c) From 2011, the classification of medium- and large-sized enterprises complies with the Notification of National Bureau of Statistics

14-9 续表 1 continued

单位：万元 (10000 yuan)

项　目	Item	负债合计 Total Liabilities	#流动负债合计 Total Current Liabilities	#应付账款 Accounts Payable	所有者权益合计 Total Owner's Equity	#实收资本 Paid-up Capital
		资产负债 Assets and Liabilities				
合　计	**Total**	**201154961**	**181033094**	**55832540**	**79418595**	**39818228**
按企业登记注册类型分	**Grouped by Registration Status of Enterprises**					
内　资	Domestic Funded Enterprises	168665252	150482617	44907285	60082973	31418974
国　有	State-Owned Enterprises	22146136	19013719	2685758	9985552	4406834
集　体	Collective Owned Enterprises	1136127	815819	111432	255564	62764
股份合作	Cooperative Enterprises	254962	248873	88958	63257	55266
联　营	Joint Owned Enterprises	24824	24824	19643	3511	2269
有限责任公司	Limited-Liability Corporation	108796124	98194519	34431000	31465448	19555506
股份有限公司	Share Holding Corporations Ltd.	19100598	15169193	2476248	14223475	4038568
私　营	Private Enterprises	17206482	17015670	5094247	4086166	3297768
其　他	Others					
港澳台商投资	Enterprises with Funds from Hongkong, Macao and Taiwan	5632074	4846919	1549758	2588562	1338343
外商投资	Foreign Funded Enterprises	26857635	25703558	9375498	16747061	7060911
按国民经济行业分	**Grouped by Sectors**					
批发业	Wholesale Trade	172528312	153975066	48549248	71350110	34345225
农、林、牧产品批发	Agricultural or livestock products	8952719	7290590	1001917	4051350	1217052
食品、饮料及烟草制品批发	Foods, beverage and tobaccos	9896075	9605875	1692852	4903109	1944336
纺织、服装及家庭日用品批发	Textile, clothes and household commodities	6339239	6063960	2181413	3849912	2201314
文化、体育用品及器材批发	Products and Equipment of Culture or Sports	5705452	4529937	822085	2005681	976213
医药及医疗器材批发	Medicine and Medical Appliance	4899816	4503731	2193816	2032479	1013202
矿产品、建材及化工产品批发	Mineral,Construction Material, Chemical Products	78276206	68572138	17016258	30122697	17377653
机械设备、五金交电及电子产品批发	Machinery,Hardware,Electrical Appliance and Electronic product	38363643	35316913	11799839	20195076	7789424
贸易经纪与代理	Trade and Deputy	15109403	14730631	11335905	3046309	1377506
其他批发	Others	4985759	3361291	505163	1143497	448526
零售业	Retail	28626649	27058027	7283292	8068486	5473003
综合零售	Total Retail	7364597	6681126	2288820	3539172	1605135
食品、饮料及烟草制品专门零售	Food,Beverage and Tobacoo	269661	265162	81803	317196	120697
纺织、服装及日用品专门零售	Textile,Garments and Daily Use Goods	1524258	1485568	848530	146441	380286
文化、体育用品及器材专门零售	Products and Equipment of Culture or Sports	1505365	1413856	493905	459250	294593
医药及医疗器材专门零售	Medicine and Medical Appliance	2776564	2523191	893004	889111	347712
汽车、摩托车、燃料及零配件专门零售	Automobile,Motorcycle, Elding and Spares or Fittings	6221086	5911339	564197	1886709	1492402
家用电器及电子产品专门零售	Household Appliances and Electronic product	6389669	6372992	1067412	742756	520870
五金、家具及室内装修材料专门零售	Hardware,Electrical Appliance Furniture and Interior Decoration Material	490335	401930	81314	124056	138015
货摊、无店铺及其他零售业	Stand Retail, Retail Without Shops and Other Retail	2085113	2002864	964308	-36205	573294
按规模划分	**Grouped by Size**					
#大中型企业	Medium-and Large Enterprises	173619140	156522910	48144004	68053631	30631706

14-9 续表 2

单位：万元

项目	Item	损益 营业收入 Business Income	#主营业务收入 Main Business Income	营业成本 Business Cost	#主营业务成本 Main Business Cost
合计	**Total**	**449966772**	**441776324**	**419164456**	**413785221**
按企业登记注册类型分	**Grouped by Registration Status of Enterprises**				
内资	Domestic Funded Enterprises	364667433	357792057	346744302	341590983
国有	State-Owned Enterprises	46143911	45933854	43906315	43861522
集体	Collective Owned Enterprises	1423173	1396180	1328003	1323611
股份合作	Cooperative Enterprises	1043436	1037969	999000	998306
联营	Joint Owned Enterprises	75911	75557	66029	65980
有限责任公司	Limited-Liability Corporation	238970263	233119207	229038341	224199112
股份有限公司	Share Holding Corporations Ltd.	32412352	32051575	30286992	30215778
私营	Private Enterprises	44598387	44177715	41119623	40926674
其他	Others				
港澳台商投资	Enterprises with Funds from Hongkong, Macao and Taiwan	11017237	10842718	8919112	8882256
外商投资	Foreign Funded Enterprises	74282102	73141549	63501041	63311982
按国民经济行业分	**Grouped by Sectors**				
批发业	Wholesale Trade	388568644	381825774	365355331	360207324
农、林、牧产品批发	Agricultural or livestock products	9429764	9397778	9064345	9057512
食品、饮料及烟草制品批发	Foods, beverage and tobaccos	16377099	16222934	14317585	14257071
纺织、服装及家庭日用品批发	Textile, clothes and household commodities	14624738	14443659	12030753	11961702
文化、体育用品及器材批发	Products and Equipment of Culture or Sports	12620810	12499450	11735571	11687905
医药及医疗器材批发	Medicine and Medical Appliance	10198762	10078101	8846188	8831702
矿产品、建材及化工产品批发	Mineral,Construction Material, Chemical Products	222207080	220908240	217594184	216468454
机械设备、五金交电及电子产品批发	Machinery,Hardware,Electrical Appliance and Electronic product	94979551	90271062	84699488	80895296
贸易经纪与代理	Trade and Deputy	3921632	3831342	3292605	3288228
其他批发	Others	4209208	4173210	3774613	3759455
零售业	Retail	61398127	59950549	53809125	53577897
综合零售	Total Retail	15443186	14580681	12459495	12420646
食品、饮料及烟草制品专门零售	Food,Beverage and Tobacoo	819946	800894	569983	565261
纺织、服装及日用品专门零售	Textile,Garments and Daily Use Goods	2759830	2697483	1877483	1866794
文化、体育用品及器材专门零售	Products and Equipment of Culture or Sports	2053110	1997763	1635488	1623081
医药及医疗器材专门零售	Medicine and Medical Appliance	3997021	3967993	3466461	3463269
汽车、摩托车、燃料及零配件专门零售	Automobile,Motorcycle, Elding and Spares or Fittings	22778461	22562234	21390186	21333043
家用电器及电子产品专门零售	Household Appliances and Electronic product	8917396	8782386	8179234	8158054
五金、家具及室内装修材料专门零售	Hardware,Electrical Appliance Furniture and Interior Decoration Material	571326	559771	363535	361322
货摊、无店铺及其他零售业	Stand retail, Retail Without Shops and Other Retail	4057852	4001343	3867261	3786428
按规模划分	**Grouped by Size**				
#大中型企业	Medium-and Large Enterprises	388627070	384822491	360661203	359396666

注：应交税金合计包括应交增值税、应交所得税、营业税金及附加和管理费用中的税金。

14-9 continued 2

(10000 yuan)

Profits and Loss				应交税金合计 Total Tax				
销售费用 Sales Expenses	管理费用 Management Expenses	财务费用 Financial Expenses	利润总额 Total Profits		#营业税金及附加 Business Tax and Surtax	#主营业务税金及附加 Main Business Tax and Surtax	#应交增殖税 Value Added Tax Payable	#应交所得税 Income Tax Payable
15372786	**7916906**	**1813578**	**9428650**	**6960773**	**889077**	**834912**	**3671294**	**2188968**
8621054	4792531	1764314	5638545	4480040	641419	597597	2376383	1309712
729088	588825	217963	994711	506265	139384	134037	146132	201264
49031	43277	28979	7433	16218	2909	2567	10504	1318
20572	18826	2472	2930	11320	1098	960	9053	737
7978	1004	137	532	1576	72	69	1347	138
4926359	2525464	1147155	2497490	2816896	320789	301571	1580994	819428
983686	458747	174818	1934579	460909	98957	85573	171049	170947
1904340	1156387	192790	200870	666855	78210	72820	457303	115881
1186383	490663	65715	344019	462874	47533	43965	264185	144105
5565349	2633712	-16452	3446086	2017859	200125	193351	1030727	735150
10741759	5816137	1523264	8801280	5347243	654208	621494	2676690	1846237
156479	174185	209489	231093	55850	8477	7486	6532	35164
1281273	328668	44468	558818	557461	135527	134949	283429	129473
1809704	562217	2916	450110	416438	41595	40437	278970	85150
442431	253603	94352	108469	157962	20248	20016	72787	58647
723079	281675	29123	353029	276903	24064	23132	164746	81841
1842661	1280992	930660	2388772	1736035	196459	180843	1007514	462167
4198470	2678682	140825	4026017	1883041	191005	178921	804069	832333
135527	149870	23682	505182	155196	27812	27590	9387	113755
152135	106245	47751	179789	108357	9020	8123	49257	47708
4631027	2100769	290314	627370	1613530	234870	213419	994604	342731
1673837	690570	77118	601920	612448	118922	104585	314763	161454
136171	44068	1656	65123	64691	5873	5804	39317	18388
705538	205037	10287	-70315	154768	18383	16228	112490	21418
235913	135619	11595	41635	71344	11437	10745	40188	16948
237192	145631	52348	114694	135658	13047	12586	93308	26803
722554	447614	119756	106436	345198	31838	29456	239577	65897
506568	205830	5720	17508	139095	20891	19943	98690	16141
122865	46151	6951	39003	34880	6453	6287	15855	10844
290391	180248	4882	-288634	55449	8028	7785	40417	4839
14055081	6890441	1591961	9136824	6044272	793745	750221	3067807	1997945

Note: Total Tax mainly includes payable VAT,payable income tax, business tax and surtax, and tax in management expense.

14-10 限额以上住宿业企业财务状况(2012年)

单位：万元

项目	Item	企业单位个数(个) Number of Enterprises (unit)	资产负债 Assets and Liabilities							
			资产总计 Total Assets	流动资产合计 Total Current Assets	#应收账款 Accounts Receivable	固定资产合计 Total Fixed Assets	固定资产原价 Total Original Value of Fixed Assets	负债合计 Total Liabilities	#流动负债合计 Total Current Liabilities	#应付账款 Accounts Payable
合计	**Total**	**1154**	**11364379**	**3610293**	**130342**	**4562182**	**7784700**	**8275079**	**5661205**	**444192**
按登记注册类型分	**Grouped By Registration Status of Enterprises**									
内资	Domestic Investment Enterprises	1086	8293823	2633069	105712	3509453	5374579	6361662	4649503	388789
国有	State-Owned Enterprises	293	2288516	535140	36295	1125163	1832148	1493788	984742	92475
集体	Collective-Owned Enterprises	55	326995	97299	3081	187630	289333	246985	129600	9471
股份合作	Private Enterprises	38	86745	36980	3005	39769	71259	60804	42703	3606
联营	Joint-Owned Enterprises	3	11384	6833	-279	1385	5528	12762	12362	312
有限责任公司	Limited-Liabilities Corporations	397	4579582	1459516	41907	1864648	2742737	3589903	2718260	182395
股份有限公司	Share Holding Corporations Ltd.	14	285272	155328	2078	86857	131583	240944	150075	14752
私营	Private Enterprises	286	715329	341974	19626	204000	301991	716477	611760	85779
其他	Others									
港澳台商投资	Enterprises with Funds from Hongkong, Macao and Taiwan	40	2050018	520726	18849	653952	1520677	1195180	669722	37374
外商投资	Foreign Funded Enterprises	28	1020538	456498	5782	398777	889443	718237	341980	18030
按行业划分	**By Sectors**									
旅游饭店	Tourism Hotels	681	9956803	3063224	110662	4184668	7210194	7383126	4905687	377058
一般旅馆	Common Inns	452	1332183	528287	19236	341580	526152	820262	684268	63608
其他住宿服务	Other Accomodation Service	21	75393	18782	444	35934	48354	71691	71251	3527

注：1. 限额以上住宿业企业是指年主营业务收入200万元及以上的住宿业法人企业。

2. 应交税金合计包括应交增值税、应交所得税、营业税金及附加和管理费用中的税金。

FINANCIAL STATUS OF ACCOMODATION ENTERPRISES ABOVE DESIGNATED SIZE(2012)

(10000 yuan)

		损益 Profits and Loss												
所有者权益合计 Total Owner's Equity	#实收资本 Paid-up Capital	营业收入 Business Income	#主营业务收入 Main Business Income	营业成本 Business Cost	#主营业务成本 Main Business Cost	销售费用 Sales Expenses	管理费用 Management Expenses	财务费用 Financial Expenses	利润总额 Total Profits	应交税金合计 Total Tax	营业税金及附加 Business Tax and Surtax	#主营业务税金及附加 Main Business Tax and Surtax	#应交增值税 Value Added Tax Payable	#应交所得税 Income Tax Payable
3089300	**3423979**	**3788254**	**3765526**	**1013826**	**1008229**	**1108292**	**1266471**	**146692**	**38902**	**340350**	**208301**	**207522**	**2695**	**60184**
1932161	2326084	2793242	2773724	765108	761440	887813	961715	101377	-111248	221981	154000	153226	1953	20262
794728	805675	814798	807783	232421	230592	256483	299108	20086	-34407	62446	44717	44369	661	3722
80010	54598	103756	103142	20878	20851	21726	50198	400	4718	9500	5691	5691	60	1347
25941	20089	43261	43172	10440	10420	17967	12187	853	-298	3174	2333	2329	18	400
-1378	4022	6776	6748	1801	1778	2636	2569	22	-663	417	385	383		
989679	1303865	1359545	1350412	360745	359179	412294	476825	65610	-70253	116005	75046	74840	1112	13325
44328	44126	69234	69003	36178	36175	8994	13460	7627	-473	4718	3753	3753	39	192
-1148	93711	395873	393464	102645	102445	167714	107369	6779	-9872	25721	22077	21861	64	1278
854838	799868	654318	653475	190520	190349	142560	181218	24734	109351	75954	35468	35464	569	26121
302301	298026	340694	338327	58199	56440	77919	123537	20582	40800	42415	18833	18833	173	13801
2573677	2985050	3172850	3156843	851938	847383	888955	1085433	132359	856	292725	173926	173565	2363	53259
511921	419998	587108	580461	152513	151472	210466	171026	10446	42252	45393	32855	32436	322	6904
3702	18931	28295	28223	9376	9374	8871	10013	3888	-4206	2231	1521	1521	9	21

Note: a) Above designated size of accomodation includes annual sales are 2 million yuan or above for hotels.

b) Total Tax mainly includes payable VAT,payable income tax, business tax and surtax, and tax in management expenses.

14-11 限额以上餐饮业企业财务状况(2012年)

单位：万元

项目	Item	企业单位个数(个) Number of Enterprises (unit)	资产负债 Assets and Liabilities 资产总计 Total Assets	流动资产合计 Total Current Assets	#应收账款 Accounts Receivable	固定资产合计 Total Fixed Assets	固定资产原价 Total Original Value of Fixed Assets	负债合计 Total Liabilities	#流动负债合计 Total Current Liabilities	#应付账款 Accounts Payable
合　计	**Total**	**1949**	**4079056**	**2220375**	**128201**	**641724**	**1079255**	**3180076**	**2729302**	**491539**
按登记注册类型分	**Grouped By Registration Status of Enterprises**									
内　资	Domestic Investment Enterprises	1803	3073158	1730658	109316	444814	740436	2531363	2155101	388010
国　有	State-Owned Enterprises	34	40191	24752	1082	7375	14521	21029	16465	2562
集　体	Collective-Owned Enterprises	38	14584	8755	1279	1967	5941	12888	12675	2061
股份合作	Private Enterprises	56	25211	15945	977	3689	6996	22100	20976	2434
联　营	Joint-Owned Enterprises									
有限责任公司	Limited-Liabilities Corporations	489	1322910	721439	49352	212952	325996	1164167	961425	155063
股份有限公司	Share Holding Corporations Ltd.	37	500178	234864	3485	62355	106470	222961	111855	13365
私　营	Private Enterprises	1149	1170084	724903	53140	156476	280513	1088219	1031706	212524
其　他	Others									
港澳台商投资	Enterprises with Funds from Hongkong, Macao and Taiwan	66	436790	289244	5300	59190	100405	286443	229236	49300
外商投资	Foreign Funded Enterprises	80	569109	200473	13584	137719	238414	362270	344965	54229
按行业划分	**Grouped by Sectors**									
正　餐	Restaurant	1739	3126168	1785402	100045	492740	812552	2475165	2179047	388030
快　餐	Snack Counter	131	585176	247255	12992	127177	228316	364236	346632	74936
饮料及冷饮	Beverage and Cold Drink	29	76755	49393	2049	10282	17527	47633	47084	8131
其他餐饮业	Other	50	290958	138326	13115	11525	20861	293042	156539	20441

注：1. 限额以上餐饮业企业是指年主营业务收入200万元及以上的餐饮业法人企业。
2. 应交税金合计包括应交增值税、应交所得税、营业税金及附加和管理费用中的税金。

FINANCIAL STATUS OF CATERING ENTERPRISES ABOVE DESIGNATED SIZE (2012)

(10000 yuan)

		损益 Profits and Loss								应交税金合计 Total Tax				
所有者权益合计 Total Owner's Equity	#实收资本 Paid-up Capital	营业收入 Business Income	#主营业务收入 Main Business Income	营业成本 Business Cost	#主营业务成本 Main Business Cost	销售费用 Sales Expenses	管理费用 Management Expenses	财务费用 Financial Expenses	利润总额 Total Profits	应交税金合计 Total Tax	#营业税金及附加 Business Tax and Surtax	#主营业务税金及附加 Main Business Tax and Surtax	#应交增值税 Value Added Tax Payable	#应交所得税 Income Tax Payable
898980	**776795**	**5469273**	**5435674**	**2386576**	**2378783**	**1965690**	**632015**	**54324**	**150928**	**380171**	**299536**	**298215**	**4209**	**68596**
541794	511051	3613062	3591041	1600979	1596795	1265217	459234	46029	68527	244824	197854	196664	2842	37514
19162	7460	49931	44375	20603	19708	17739	6998	43	1743	4169	3085	2835	459	495
1696	4901	27708	27694	14803	14780	8339	3641	130	-626	1519	1430	1429		73
3111	3600	50406	50285	28232	28164	15096	3551	423	288	3018	2825	2824	10	101
158744	203785	1415769	1407197	606933	605411	500115	184146	13379	41425	101652	76956	76451	955	20772
277216	83285	260377	257939	95465	95439	88168	36386	10587	31896	21275	13679	13677	546	6328
81866	208020	1808871	1803551	834944	833293	635760	224513	21466	-6199	113191	99880	99447	872	9746
150347	117362	603898	600981	233721	233447	232178	65588	6386	33203	47285	32917	32888	465	12991
206839	148383	1252313	1243651	551876	548542	468295	107193	1909	49199	88062	68766	68663	902	18091
651002	612216	3941944	3926401	1720730	1717090	1375741	496987	50978	101761	275052	218022	216964	1822	48489
220940	114767	1274860	1256834	531735	527582	508183	104487	1820	56359	88650	69422	69159	836	17431
29121	20289	103702	103695	32093	32093	51753	12252	13	2647	7809	5354	5354	144	2241
-2083	29523	148768	148743	102018	102018	30014	18289	1513	-9839	8660	6738	6738	1408	435

Note: a) Above designated size of accomodation includes annual sales are 2 million yuan or above for hotels.
b) Total Tax mainly includes payable VAT,payable income tax, business tax and surtax, and tax in management expense.

14-12 连锁企业基本情况(2001-2012年)
STATISTICS FOR CHAIN ENTERPRISES (2001-2012)

年份 Year	连锁总店(个) Number of Head Offices of Chain Stores (unit)	门店总数(个) Number of Chain Stores (unit)	从业人员年末人数(人) Year-end Employed Persons (person)	营业面积(平方米) Operational Area (sq.m)	商品销售总额(营业额)(万元) Total Revenue of Sales (10000 yuan)	#零售额 Retail Sales
2001	129	2123	139470	1605808	4831168	2186540
2002	146	3523	109089	2356266	6621975	6487185
2003	153	4519	132030	3405562	8404232	7601221
2004	196	5432	153942	3783507	8603560	8337829
2005	188	5973	166598	4376383	10612658	9507168
2006	205	6730	170007	5546003	11229026	9514297
2007	210	7645	185114	6677266	13890913	11573838
2008	240	8611	223954	6745802	15720473	12954839
2009	240	8928	218024	6995047	17366414	13816796
2010	234	9299	228292	7268786	21329783	16255496
2011	233	9845	280798	7953891	25742536	19507890
2012	220	10014	287975	8339674	26758403	20140433

14-13 连锁企业基本情况(按登记注册类型、经营业态分)(2012年)
STATISTICS FOR CHAIN ENTERPRISES (GROUPED BY REGISTRATION STATUS OF ENTERPRISES AND INDUSTRIES)(2012)

指标	Item	门店总数(个) Number of Chain Stores (unit)	从业人员年末人数(人) Year-end Employed Persons (person)	营业面积(平方米) Operational Area (sq.m)	商品销售总额(营业额)(万元) Total Revenue of sales (10000 yuan)	#零售额 Retail Sales
合计	**Total**	**10014**	**287975**	**8339674**	**26758403**	**20140433**
按登记注册类型分	**Grouped by Registration Status of Enterprises**					
内资	Domestic Funded Enterprises	7070	167684	6456863	21725469	15443353
国有	State-Owned Enterprises	41	687	10995	26440	24408
集体	Collective Owned Enterprises	306	1406	93195	124818	123306
股份合作	Cooperative Enterprises	7	198	5410	4312	4312
联营	Joint Ownership Units	5	37	928	833	833
有限责任公司	Limited-Liability Corporations	2966	84585	3078054	9409166	6446214
股份有限公司	Share Holding Corporations Ltd.	1529	57365	2735474	11356347	8068481
私营	Private Enterprises	2216	23406	532807	803553	775799
其他	Others					
港、澳、台商投资	Enterprises with Funds from Hongkong,Macao and Taiwan	1089	28572	418749	1118012	951553
外商投资	Foreign Funded Enterprises	1855	91719	1464062	3914921	3745527
按经营业态分	**Grouped by Industries**					
零售业态	**Chain Retail**	**6810**	**149657**	**6680540**	**24209886**	**17697345**
便利店	Convenient Store	920	3948	94481	191403	189570
折扣店	Discount Store	116	1688	78873	198781	191274
超市	Supermarket	1483	50763	1822760	4470414	3157110
大型超市	Supermarket	104	26297	980762	2216110	2179912
仓储会员店	Storage Store	7	2683	130869	378715	378715
百货店	Department Store	59	15359	1754065	3114446	3114446
专业店	Professional Shop	1903	26809	1227659	4488594	4051771
加油站	Gas Station	672	8852	337550	8061120	3554123
专卖店	Regie Shop	1544	12467	201521	911308	701430
家居建材商店	Fitment Store	2	791	52000	178995	178995
餐饮业态	**Chain Catering Services**	**3079**	**134859**	**1650968**	**2446423**	**2440428**
中式正餐	Chinese Restaurant	660	49410	958705	955587	952057
中式快餐	Chinese Snack Counter	1074	19243	223944	423345	423049
外国风味正餐	Foreign-flavoring Restaurant	377	27060	145092	304318	304318
外国风味快餐	Foreign-flavoring Snack Counter	780	36781	292025	675874	673705
茶馆	Tea shop	9	40	910	577	577
咖啡店	Cafe	146	1838	27394	73615	73615
其他	Other	33	487	2898	13107	13107
住宿业态	**Chain Accomodation Sector**	**125**	**3459**	**8166**	**102094**	**2660**
旅游饭店	Tourism Hotels	57	1942	3596	51233	903
一般旅馆	Common Inns	68	1517	4570	50861	1757

注:本表登记注册类型分数据口径有所调整。其中国有只包括国有企业，集体只包括集体企业，联营包括国有联营、集体联营、国有与集体联营企业，有限责任公司包括国有独资公司、其他有限责任公司企业，其他项目未做调整。

Note: In this table, figures were adjusted. After adjusted, state-owned enterprises include state-owned enterprises only; collective enterprises include collectively enterprises only; jointly-run enterprises inlcude state-owned, collective and state-collective jointly-run enterprises; limited liability companies include wholly state-funded companies, and corporate limited liaibility companies. The coverage of other items was not changed.

14-14 商品交易市场基本情况(2012年)
STATISTICS FOR COMMODITY TRANSACTION MARKETS (2012)

单位：个 (unit)

项目	Item	全市 Total	各区 Districts	各县 Counties
商品交易市场总数	**Total Number of Commodity Transaction Markets**	**835**	**793**	**42**
#亿元市场	Million-yuan Markets	143	138	5
一、综合市场	**Comprehensive Markets**	**397**	**366**	**31**
综合贸易市场	**Comprehensive Trade Market**	**397**	**366**	**31**
生产资料综合市场	Comprehensive Market of Capital Goods	2	2	
工业消费品综合市场	Comprehensive Market of Industrial Consumables	62	60	2
农产品综合市场	Comprehensive Market of Agricultural Products	231	222	9
其他综合市场	Other Comprehensive Markets	102	82	20
二、专业市场	**Special Markets**	**438**	**427**	**11**
生产资料市场	**Market of Capital Goods**	**52**	**51**	**1**
农业生产用具市场	Market of Agricultural Production Tools			
农用生产资料市场	Market of Agricultural Production Means	1	1	
煤炭市场	Coal Market			
木材市场	Timber Market	2	2	
建材市场	Building Materials Market	44	43	1
化工材料及制品市场	Chemical Materials and Products Market			
金属材料市场	Metal Materials Market	3	3	
机械设备市场	Mechanical Equipment Market	1	1	
其他生产资料市场	Other Production Means Market	1	1	
农产品市场	**Agricultural Products Market**	**77**	**76**	**1**
粮油市场	Foodstuff and Oil Market	5	5	
肉禽蛋市场	Meat, Poultry and Egg Market	8	8	
水产品市场	Aquatic Product Market	3	3	
蔬菜市场	Vegetable Market	17	16	1
干鲜果品市场	Fried and Fresh Fruits Market	3	3	
棉麻土畜、烟叶市场	Cotton, Linen,Local and Livestock Product, and Tobacco Leaf Market			
其他农产品市场	Other Agricultural Product Market	41	41	
食品、饮料及烟酒市场	**Food, Beverage, Tobacco and Wine Market**	**21**	**19**	**2**
食品饮料市场	Food & Beverage Market	8	7	1
茶叶市场	Tea Market	6	6	
烟酒市场	Tobacco and Wine Market			
其他食品饮料及烟酒市场	Other Food, Beverage, Tobacco and Wine Market	7	6	1
纺织、服装、鞋帽市场	**Textile, Costume, Shoes and Caps Market**	**82**	**80**	**2**
布料及纺织品市场	Cloth and Textile Market	11	11	
服装市场	Costume Market	57	56	1
鞋帽市场	Shoes and Caps Market	2	2	
其他纺织服装鞋帽市场	Other Textile, Costume, Shoes and Caps Market	12	11	1
日用品及文化用品市场	**Daily-use Articles and Cultural Articles Market**	**14**	**14**	
小商品市场	Small Commodities Market	6	6	

14-14 续表 continued

单位：个 (unit)

项目	Item	全市 Total	各区 Districts	各县 Counties
箱包市场	Case and Bag Market			
玩具市场	Toys Market			
文具市场	Stationary Market	1	1	
图书、报刊杂志市场	Books, Newspapers, Periodicals and Journals Market	1	1	
音像制品及电子出版物市场	Audio/visual Products, Electronic Publications Market	1	1	
体育用品市场	Sports Article Market			
其他日用品及文化用品市场	Other Daily-use Articles and Cultural Articles Market	5	5	
黄金、珠宝、玉器等首饰市场	**Market of Gold, Jewelry, Jade**	**13**	**13**	
电器、通讯器材、电子设备市场	**Market of Electrical Appliance, Communication Apparatus, Electronic Equipment**	**21**	**21**	
家电市场	Household Appliances Market	2	2	
通讯器材市场	Communication Apparatus Market	5	5	
照相、摄像器材市场	Photography and Camera Shot Apparatus Market	2	2	
计算机及辅助设备市场	Computer and Peripheral Equipment Market	7	7	
其他电器、通讯器材、电子设备市场	Other Electrical Appliance, Communication Apparatus and Electronic Equipment Market	5	5	
医药、医疗用品及器材市场	**Medicine, Medial Articles and Equipment Market**			
中药材市场	Chinese Herb Market			
其他医药、医疗用品及器材市场	Other Medicine, Medial Articles and Equipment Market			
家具、五金及装饰材料市场	**Furniture, Hardware, and Decoration Materials Market**	**77**	**74**	**3**
家具市场	Furniture Market	34	33	1
装饰材料市场	Decoration Materials Market	21	21	
灯具市场	Lamps and Lanterns Market	4	4	
厨具、盥洗设备市场	Kitchen and Washroom Equipment Market			
五金材料市场	Hardware Market	13	13	
其他装修市场	Other Fitment Market	5	3	2
汽车、摩托车及零配件市场	**Automobile, Autobike,Parts and Fittings Market**	**26**	**26**	
汽车市场	Automobile Market	10	10	
摩托车市场	Autobike Market			
机动车零配件市场	Motor Vehicle Parts and Fittings Market	16	16	
花、鸟、鱼、虫市场	**Flowers, Birds, Fish and Insects Market**	**19**	**19**	
花卉市场	Flower Market	18	18	
鸟市场	Bird Market			
观赏鱼市场	Fish Market			
其他花鸟鱼虫市场	Other Flowers, Birds, Fish and Insects Market	1	1	
旧货市场	**Used Goods Market**	**14**	**14**	
古玩、古董、字画市场	Curio, Antique, Calligraphy and Paintings Market	5	5	
邮票、硬币市场	Stamps and Coins Market	1	1	
其他旧货市场	Other Used Goods Market	8	8	
其他专业市场	**Other Specialized Market**	**22**	**20**	**2**

14-15 商品交易市场成交额(2012年)
TRANSACTION VALUE OF COMMODITY TRANSACTION MARKETS (2012)

单位：万元 (10000 yuan)

项目	Item	全市 Total	各区 Districts	各县 Counties
商品交易市场总计	**Total Number of Commodity Transaction Markets**	**31737204**	**31424597**	**312607**
#亿元市场	Million-yuan Markets	30457075	30196117	260958
一、综合市场	**Comprehensive Markets**	**13614353**	**13392421**	**221932**
综合贸易市场	**Comprehensive Trade Market**	**13614353**	**13392421**	**221932**
生产资料综合市场	Comprehensive Market of Capital Goods	9988	9988	
工业消费品综合市场	Comprehensive Market of Industrial Consumables	959581	959149	432
农产品综合市场	Comprehensive Market of Agricultural Products	10337966	10153790	184176
其他综合市场	Other Comprehensive Markets	2306818	2269494	37324
二、专业市场	**Special Markets**	**18122851**	**18032176**	**90675**
生产资料市场	**Market of Capital Goods**	**730117**	**680687**	**49430**
农业生产用具市场	Market of Agricultural Production Tools			
农用生产资料市场	Market of Agricultural Production Means	455	455	
煤炭市场	Coal Market			
木材市场	Timber Market	11176	11176	
建材市场	Building Materials Market	463600	414170	49430
化工材料及制品市场	Chemical Materials and Products Market			
金属材料市场	Metal Materials Market	29218	29218	
机械设备市场	Mechanical Equipment Market	145000	145000	
其他生产资料市场	Other Production Means Market	80668	80668	
农产品市场	**Agricultural Products Market**	**5887123**	**5861701**	**25422**
粮油市场	Foodstuff and Oil Market	1437857	1437857	
肉禽蛋市场	Meat, Poultry and Egg Market	67072	67072	
水产品市场	Aquatic Product Market	1464691	1464691	
蔬菜市场	Vegetable Market	1533562	1508140	25422
干鲜果品市场	Fried and Fresh Fruits Market	190337	190337	
棉麻土畜、烟叶市场	Cotton, Linen,Local and Livestock Product, and Tobacco Leaf Market			
其他农产品市场	Other Agricultural Product Market	1193604	1193604	
食品、饮料及烟酒市场	**Food, Beverage, Tobacco and Wine Market**	**61275**	**60829**	**446**
食品饮料市场	Food & Beverage Market	10872	10827	45
茶叶市场	Tea Market	44959	44959	
烟酒市场	Tobacco and Wine Market			
其他食品饮料及烟酒市场	Other Food, Beverage, Tobacco and Wine Market	5444	5043	401
纺织、服装、鞋帽市场	**Textile, Costume, Shoes and Caps Market**	**579471**	**574999**	**4472**
布料及纺织品市场	Cloth and Textile Market	40452	40452	
服装市场	Costume Market	466122	465387	735
鞋帽市场	Shoes and Caps Market	5149	5149	
其他纺织服装鞋帽市场	Other Textile, Costume, Shoes and Caps Market	67748	64011	3737
日用品及文化用品市场	**Daily-use Articles and Cultural Articles Market**	**489604**	**489604**	
小商品市场	Small Commodities Market	301200	301200	

14-15 续表 continued

单位：万元 (10000 yuan)

项　　目	Item	全市 Total	各区 Districts	各县 Counties
箱包市场	Case and Bag Market			
玩具市场	Toys Market			
文具市场	Stationary Market	159300	159300	
图书、报刊杂志市场	Books, Newspapers, Periodicals and Journals Market	18823	18823	
音像制品及电子出版物市场	Audio/visual Products, Electronic Publications Market	3597	3597	
体育用品市场	Sports Article Market			
其他日用品及文化用品市场	Other Daily-use Articles and Cultural Articles Market	6684	6684	
黄金、珠宝、玉器等首饰市场	**Market of Gold, Jewelry, Jade**	**278588**	**278588**	
电器、通讯器材、电子设备市场	**Market of Electrical Appliance, Communication Apparatus, Electronic Equipment**	**1025591**	**1025591**	
家电市场	Household Appliances Market	1763	1763	
通讯器材市场	Communication Apparatus Market	9260	9260	
照相、摄像器材市场	Photography and Camera Shot Apparatus Market	40079	40079	
计算机及辅助设备市场	Computer and Peripheral Equipment Market	840893	840893	
其他电器、通讯器材、电子设备市场	Other Electrical Appliance, Communication Apparatus and Electronic Equipment Market	133596	133596	
医药、医疗用品及器材市场	**Medicine, Medial Articles and Equipment Market**			
中药材市场	Chinese Herb Market			
其他医药、医疗用品及器材市场	Other Medicine, Medial Articles and Equipment Market			
家具、五金及装饰材料市场	**Furniture, Hardware, and Decoration Materials Market**	**1249409**	**1242152**	**7257**
家具市场	Furniture Market	554369	552048	2321
装饰材料市场	Decoration Materials Market	302216	302216	
灯具市场	Lamps and Lanterns Market	25856	25856	
厨具、盥洗设备市场	Kitchen and Washroom Equipment Market			
五金材料市场	Hardware Market	41991	41991	
其他装修市场	Other Fitment Market	324977	320041	4936
汽车、摩托车及零配件市场	**Automobile, Autobike,Parts and Fittings Market**	**7628025**	**7628025**	
汽车市场	Automobile Market	7080104	7080104	
摩托车市场	Autobike Market			
机动车零配件市场	Motor Vehicle Parts and Fittings Market	547921	547921	
花、鸟、鱼、虫市场	**Flowers, Birds, Fish and Insects Market**	**35399**	**35399**	
花卉市场	Flower Market	35339	35339	
鸟市场	Bird Market			
观赏鱼市场	Fish Market			
其他花鸟鱼虫市场	Other Flowers, Birds, Fish and Insects Market	60	60	
旧货市场	**Used Goods Market**	**55774**	**55774**	
古玩、古董、字画市场	Curio, Antique, Calligraphy and Paintings Market	12990	12990	
邮票、硬币市场	Stamps and Coins Market	11235	11235	
其他旧货市场	Other Used Goods Market	31549	31549	
其他专业市场	**Other Specialized Market**	**102475**	**98827**	**3648**

14-16 商品交易市场主要商品成交量
TRANSACTION VOLUME OF COMMODITY TRANSACTION MARKETS

项目		Item		2012	2011	2012年为2011年% 2012 as % of 2011
粮食	(吨)	Grain	(ton)	2813912	3363393	83.7
食用植物油	(吨)	Edible Vegetable Oil	(ton)	397602	524003	75.9
猪肉	(吨)	Hog and Pork	(ton)	455655	388695	117.2
牛肉	(吨)	Oxes and Beef	(ton)	109845	97402	112.8
羊肉	(吨)	Goat, Sheep and Mutton	(ton)	96173	83127	115.7
家禽	(吨)	Poultry	(ton)	74766	71226	105.0
鲜蛋	(吨)	Fresh Eggs	(ton)	319657	412210	77.5
鲜菜	(吨)	Fresh Vegetable	(ton)	13363912	13680882	97.7
鲜瓜果	(吨)	Fresh Melon and Fruit	(ton)	8159415	8866411	92.0
水产品	(吨)	Aquatic Products	(ton)	946622	968393	97.8
新、旧机动车	(辆)	New and Old Automobiles	(unit)	753558	442872	170.2
钢材	(吨)	Rolled Steel	(ton)	104258	123573	84.4
煤炭	(吨)	Coal	(ton)	34290	35110	97.7

14-17 消费者投诉与处理
CONSUMER'S COMPLAINTS AND HANDLING

单位：件 (unit)

项目	Item	2012		2011	
		受理投诉件数 Complaints Accepted	构成(%) Composition (%)	受理投诉件数 Complaints Accepted	构成(%) Composition (%)
合计	**Total**	**16892**	**100.0**	**16362**	**100.0**
按行业分	**Grouped by Sector**				
家用电器类	Household Appliances	2866	17.0	3414	20.9
#电视机	TV Sets	298	1.8	269	1.6
空调类	Air Conditioners	286	1.7	202	1.2
洗衣机类	Washing Machines	80	0.5	88	0.5
电冰箱(柜)	Refrigerators	119	0.7	127	0.8
厨房电器及设备	Cookroom Appliances	178	1.1	215	1.3
通讯类	Communication Product	1313	7.8	1569	9.6
计算机类	Computer	410	2.4	543	3.3
家用机械类	Household Machines	562	3.3	626	3.8
#汽车	Automobile	323	1.9	305	1.9
热水器	Showers	100	0.6	104	0.6
百货类	General Merchandise	3763	22.3	3644	22.3
#家具类	Furniture	492	2.9	529	3.2
服装鞋帽	Garments,Shoes and Hats	1238	7.3	1181	7.2
日用杂品	Articles of Daily Use	362	2.1	325	2.0
食品	Food	975	5.8	752	4.6
房屋及装修建材	Tenement and Fitment	525	3.1	478	2.9
#房屋	Tenement	141	0.8	88	0.5
装饰材料	Fitment	334	2.0	317	1.9
农用生产资料	Materials for Agricultural Use	26	0.2	302	1.8
服务类	Service	8905	52.8	7581	46.3
#美容美发	Hairdressing	596	3.5	597	3.6
食宿娱乐庆典	Room Entertainment and Celebration	657	3.9	549	3.4
洗衣业	Wash Clothers	416	2.5	365	2.2
装修物业	Fitment and Realty	167	1.0	115	0.7
教育或培训	Education or Training	453	2.7	385	2.4
咨询中介	Consultation Agency	1675	9.9	1413	8.6
其他商品类	Others	245	1.5	317	1.9
按内容分	**Grouped by Content**				
#质量	Quality	9161	54.2	9504	58.1
安全	Safety	59	0.3	57	0.3
价格	Price	306	1.8	321	2.0
计量	Measure	36	0.2	25	0.2
广告	False Advertisements	95	0.6	87	0.5
假冒	Counterfeit Goods	56	0.3	52	0.3
虚假品质表示	Inveracious Quality	82	0.5	151	0.9
营销合同	Manage and Sell Contract	5025	29.7	2892	17.7
人格尊严	Personality and Dignity	37	0.2	51	0.3

注：总解决率为98.8%。
资料来源：北京市消费者协会。
Note: Total rate of settlement is 98.8%.
Source: Beijing Customer Institution.

主要统计指标解释

社会消费品零售总额　指企业（单位、个体户）通过交易直接售给个人、社会集团非生产、非经营用的实物商品金额，以及提供餐饮服务所取得的收入金额。个人包括城乡居民和入境人员，社会集团包括机关、社会团体、部队、学校、企事业单位、居委会或村委会等。

批发和零售业单位　指在流通环节主要从事商品批发活动和零售活动的单位。

商品购进额　指从本企业（单位）以外的单位和个人购进(包括从国外直接进口)作为转卖或加工后转卖的商品金额（含增值税）。本指标反映批发和零售从国内外市场上购进商品的总价。

商品销售额　指对本企业以外的单位和个人出售的商品金额（包括售给本单位消费用的商品，含增值税）。在批发和零售业中，本指标反映在国内市场上销售商品以及出口商品的总量。

期末商品库存额　对于批发和零售业法人企业和个体经营户，是指取得所有权的全部商品金额（含增值税）；对于批发和零售业产业活动单位，是指期末实际在库且归属法人具有所有权的全部商品金额（含增值税）。这个指标反映批发和零售业的商品库存情况，以及对市场商品供应的保证程度。

连锁总店（总部）　负责连锁企业资源（商号、商誉、经营模式、服务标准、管理模式等）的开发、配置、控制或使用等功能的企业核心管理机构。连锁经营是指经营同类商品或服务，使用统一商号的若干店铺，在同一总店(总部）的管理下，采取统一采购或特许经营等方式,实现规模效益的组织形式，包括直营连锁、特许连锁和自愿连锁三种形式。直营连锁是指连锁店铺由连锁公司全资或控股开设，在总部的直接控制下，开展统一经营的连锁经营形式；特许连锁是指拥有注册商标、企业标志、专利、专有技术等经营资源的企业（特许人），以合同形式将其拥有的经营资源许可其他经营者（被特许人）使用，被特许人按合同约定在统一的经营模式下开展经营，并向特许人支付特许经营费用的连锁经营形式；自愿连锁是指若干个店铺或企业自愿组合起来，在不改变各自资产所有权关系的情况下，以同一个品牌形象面对消费者，以共同进货为纽带开展的连锁经营形式。

连锁门店　在连锁企业经营管理的基础上，按照总店（总部）的指示和服务规范要求，承担日常销售业务的店铺，称连锁门店，包括直营店（控股店）和加盟店。

（1）直营店（控股店）　是指由连锁企业总部投资开设，按连锁经营管理模式，由总部统一管理的店铺。

（2）加盟店　是指在特许连锁中，被特许人获得特许人授权后，使用其商标、商号、经营模式、专利和专有技术等经营资源建立的店铺，也包括自愿连锁的成员店。

门店总数　指该连锁企业所拥有的全部门店（包括直营店和加盟店，下同）数量，既包括本市门店也包括外埠门店。其中，总店（如果总公司有门店的话）作为一个直营店处理。此外，控股店按直营店统计。

批发业及零售业大中型企业的划分标准按照《2011 统计上大中小微型企业划分标准》执行。

批发业:

大型企业: 年营业收入 40000 万元及以上，且从业人员 200 人及以上;

中型企业: 年营业收入 5000-40000 万元及以上，且从业人员 20-200 人。

零售业:

大型企业: 年营业收入 20000 万元及以上，且从业人员 300 人及以上;

中型企业: 年营业收入 500-20000 万元及以上，且从业人员 50-300 人。

餐饮业企业　指在一定场所，专门从事对食物进行现场烹饪、调制，并出售给顾客主要供现场消费服务活动的企业。如各种饭馆、中西餐厅、酒馆、茶馆和火车餐车、车站食堂、飞机场餐厅等。

住宿业企业　指有偿为顾客提供临时住宿服务活动的单位。如旅游饭店、宾馆、酒店和旅馆、旅店等。

商品交易市场　指经有关部门和组织批准设立，有固定场所、设施，有经营管理部门和监管人员，若干市场经营者入内，常年或实际开业三个月以上，集中、公开、独立地进行生活消费品、生产资料等现货商品交易以及提供相关服务的交易场所，包括各类消费品市场，生产资料市场等。

Explanatory Notes on Main Statistical Indicators

Total Retail Sales of Consumer Goods refer to the amount of commodities in kind sold by enterprises (entities or self-employed operators) through transaction directly to individuals and social groups to be used for non-productive and non-operating purposes, as well as the amount of income from provision of food and drink services. Individuals include urban and rural residents and overseas personnel entering China. Social groups include government agencies, social organizations, armies, schools, enterprises and public institutions, residents' committee or villagers' committee, and so on.

Wholesale and Retail Establishments refer to establishments engaged in commodity wholesale and retail activities on the circulation link.

Total Purchases of Commodities refer to the total value (including value added tax) of purchases (including direct imports from foreign countries) of commodities by the establishments (entities) from other establishments or individuals for the purpose of re-selling, either with or without further processing of the commodities purchased. This indicator is used to show the total value of purchases of commodities by wholesale and retail establishments from domestic and overseas markets.

Total Sales of Commodities refer to value of commodities sold by the establishments to other establishments and individuals (including sold to this establishment, including value added tax). This indicator is used to show the total value of commodities sold in domestic markets and exported commodities in the wholesale and retail trades.

Inventory (year-end) refer to, for wholesale and retail enterprises as legal persons and self-employed operators, the value of all commodities with ownership gained (VAT included); for wholesale and retail establishments, refer to the value of all commodities with ownership, actually in storage at the end of a period, and owned by the legal person (VAT included). This indicator shows the commodity stocks in wholesale and retail trades, and to what extent the commodities are ensured to supply to markets.

Head Chain Store (Headquarters) means a core management organization in an enterprise, responsible for the development, deployment, control or use and other functions of resources (trade name, goodwill, operating mode, service standards, and management mode, etc.) of the chain enterprise. Chain operation means an organization form in which several stores using uniform trade name operate the same commodities or provide the same services through uniform purchase or franchise operation under the management of the same head store (headquarters) to achieve large-scale benefit. Chain operation falls into direct subordinate chain, franchise chain and voluntary chain. Direct subordinate chain is a form of chain operation that chain stores are wholly funded or controlled by chain companies, carrying out uniform operation under the direct control of headquarters; franchise chain is a form of chain operation that

any enterprise (the franchiser) owning such operating resources as trademark, logo, patent and know-how grants license of use of such operating resources to any other operator (the franchisee) by using a contract, and the franchisee operates under uniform operating mode as stated in the contract, and pays franchise fees to the franchiser; voluntary chain is a form of chain operation that several stores or enterprises combine together voluntarily to face consumers with the same brand image without changing their own assets ownership relations, and linking together through joint purchase.

Chain Stores Based on the operation and management of chain enterprises, stores carrying out daily sales business by following the head store's (headquarters) instruction and required service standards are called chained stores. They include direct subordinate stores (controlled stores) and franchise stores.

Direct Subordinate Stores (Controlled Stores) refer to stores opened with funds from the headquarters of chain enterprises, operating in chain operation and management mode, and under the uniform management of the headquarters.

Franchise Stores refer to, in franchise chains, stores established after the franchisee is authorized by the franchisor to use its trademark, trade name, operating mode, patent and know-how and other operating resources, including member stores on voluntary chains.

Total Number of Stores refers to the number of all stores owned by the chain enterprise (including direct subordinate stores and franchise stores). Of which, the head store (if the parent company has stores) is regarded as a direct subordinate store. In addition, controlled stores are listed separately in some areas, which are regarded as direct subordinate stores.

Standards for classification of large- and medium-sized enterprises of wholesale and retail sales trades complies with the 2011 Statistical Standards for Classification of Large-, Medium-, Small- and Mini-sized Enterprises.

Wholesale trades:

Large-sized Enterprises: those with annual sales of RMB400 million, and 200 and more employees.

Medium-sized Enterprises: those with annual sales of RMB50-400 million, and 20-200 employees.

Retail trades:

Large-sized Enterprises: those with annual sales of

RMB200 million and more, and 300 and more employees;

Medium-sized Enterprises: those with annual sales of RMB5-200 million, and 50-300 employees.

Catering Enterprises refer to enterprises specializing in food cooking and preparing for selling to clients for on-site consumption at a specific site, such as various restaurants, Chinese food and Western food restaurants, pubs, tea houses, dining compartments on trains, eateries at railway stations, and restaurants at airports.

Accommodation Enterprises refer to entities providing clients with temporary accommodation services, such as tourist hotels, guest houses, rest houses and inns.

Commodity Transaction Markets refer to transaction sites approved by relevant authorities and organizations, provided with fixed place and facilities, with operation management departments and regulating personnel, where several market operators stay, always opening or actually opening for more than three months, conducting transactions of on-hand commodities such as living consumables and production goods, and offering relevant services in a concentrated, open and independent manner.

15

对外经济贸易
FOREIGN ECONOMY AND TRADE

简要说明

一、本章资料的主要内容

本章资料综合反映北京市对外贸易、利用外资、对外经济合作的历年概况，以及对外友好交往情况，重点反映对外经济贸易的发展状况。

二、本章资料的统计范围和数据来源

1.对外贸易部分

对外贸易统计的主要内容包括：北京地区进出口总值；主要产品进出口数量等。

对外贸易统计范围：凡能引起北京市海关境内物质资源存量增加或减少的进出口货物，除制度另有规定者外，均列入该项统计。

对外贸易统计的资料来源于中华人民共和国北京海关，调查方法采用全面调查。

2.口岸运营情况

口岸运营情况统计范围包括：北京首都国际机场空港口岸、北京丰台货运口岸、北京朝阳口岸、北京西站铁路口岸、北京平谷国际陆港、北京天竺综合保税区。

口岸运营情况来源于北京市人民政府口岸办公室。

3.利用外资

利用外资统计的主要内容包括外商直接投资，外商投资企业登记注册情况，外商投资企业经营情况。

统计范围：凡经工商行政管理机关核准登记，在中华人民共和国北京地域内所有使用外资（包括港澳台地区投资）的单位和部门，经批准设立的中外合资经营企业、合作经营企业、外资企业、外商投资股份制企业、合作开发项目等具有法人资格的独立核算企业(包括港澳台地区投资企业)，在华从事经营活动的外国及港澳台地区企业及外国公司在中国境内设立的分支机构。

利用外资统计的资料主要来源于北京市商务委员会(原北京市商务局)、北京市工商行政管理局，调查方法采用全面调查；外商投资企业投产开业及经营情况调查范围为限额以上企业，调查方法采用全面调查，数据来源于北京市统计局。

4.对外经济合作

主要内容包括对外承包工程、劳务合作和设计咨询。

统计范围为经各级商务部门批准的从事对外承包、劳务合作和设计咨询业务并具有法人资格的对外承包劳务企业；调查方法采用全面调查，数据来源于北京市商务委员会(原北京市商务局)。

5.友好城市

主要内容包括与北京市建立友好关系的城市名录。数据来源于北京市人民政府外事办公室。

Brief Introduction

I. Main Content

Data in this chapter show the general situation of foreign trade, foreign capital utilization, and foreign economic cooperation in Beijing in previous years, as well as foreign intercourse, with focus on the development of foreign economy and trade..

II. Method of Survey and Source of Data

1. Foreign trade

Foreign trade data include those of: total value of import and export in Beijing, and quantity of main imported and exported products, etc.

Foreign trade statistics apply for: any imports and exports that lead to increase or decrease in the stock of physical resources at the customs of Beijing, except for those otherwise stated in regulations.

Foreign trade data are from Beijing Customs, P.R.C., and were obtained through complete survey.

2. Data of performance of port operation

Data of performance of port operation include those of: Port of Beijing Capital International Airport, Beijing Chaoyang Transport Port, Railway Port at Beijing West Railway Station, Beijing Pinggu International Land Port , Beijing Tianzhu Comprehensive Bonded Zone.

Data of performance of port operation are from Beijing Port Office of the People's Government of Beijing.

3. Foreign capital utilization

Foreign capital utilization data include those of foreign direct investment, registration of foreign-funded enterprises, and operation of foreign-funded enterprises.

Scope of statistics: all entities and organizations registered with administration for industry and commerce upon approval, and using foreign capital (including that from Hong Kong, Macao and Taiwan) within the jurisdiction of Beijing, P.R.C, Sino-foreign joint ventures, cooperative enterprises and foreign-funded enterprises, foreign-funded joint-stock enterprise, cooperative development projects, and all other enterprises as legal persons keeping separate accounts (including enterprises funded by companies of Hong Kong, Macao and Taiwan), enterprises of foreign countries and Hong Kong, Macao and Taiwan conducting operations in China as well as branch offices opened by foreign companies in China.

Foreign capital utilization data are mainly sourced from Beijing Municipal Commission of Commerce (former Beijing Municipal Bureau of Commerce), Beijing Administration for Industry and Commerce. These data were obtained through complete survey; survey for the opening and operation of foreign-funded enterprises covers enterprises above designated size. Complete survey method was used. Data are sourced from Beijing Municipal Bureau of Statistics.

4. Foreign economic cooperation

Foreign economic cooperation statistics apply for: foreign contracting project, labor cooperation and design consulting.

Statistics cover foreign labor service enterprises as legal persons engaged in foreign contracting, labor cooperation and design consulting with approval by departments of commerce at different levels. Complete survey method was used. Data are sourced from Beijing Municipal Commission of Commerce (former Beijing Municipal Bureau of Commerce).

5. Sister cities

Data are from the Foreign Affairs Office of the People's Government of Beijing Municipality, showing the detailed list of sister cities of our city.

15-1 北京地区对外经济贸易(1980-2012年)
FOREIGN TRADE (1980-2012)

年份 Year	进出口总值(万美元) Total Value of Imports and Exports (USD 10000)	出口 Exports	#高新技术产品 High-tech Products	#机电产品 Mechanical and Electrical Products	进口 Imports	#高新技术产品 High-tech Products	#机电产品 Mechanical and Electrical Products
1980							
1981-1985							
1981							
1982							
1983	3059926	1468740			1591186		
1984	3559284	1751704			1807580		
1985	3254341	437398			2816943		
1986-1990	**13945243**	**1865234**			**12080009**		
1986	3060236	371282			2688954		
1987	2670466	354374			2316092		
1988	2988576	395887			2592689		
1989	2861489	302343			2559146		
1990	2364476	441348			1923128		
1991-1995	**14305670**	**3547263**			**10758405**		
1991	2424137	457114			1967023		
1992	2498241	561037		157835	1937204	271005	731359
1993	2791700	669930		151133	2121769	302965	885074
1994	2888079	834205		194937	2053873	421071	1121082
1995	3703513	1024977		281810	2678536	407176	1225200
1996-2000	**17397285**	**5011639**		**1609152**	**12385646**	**2242338**	**5049210**
1996	2931833	811975		254450	2119858	240903	733641
1997	3038852	961103		271119	2077749	346166	766288
1998	3050608	1051293		325390	1999315	347556	909222
1999	3435951	990352		320852	2445599	567687	1213857
2000	4940041	1196916	226549	437341	3743125	740026	1426202
2001-2005	**39258570**	**9270820**	**2525916**	**4291246**	**29987748**	**5318558**	**10501427**
2001	5149809	1177236	263382	477568	3972572	992797	1883151
2002	5250529	1261386	314174	570971	3989142	916363	1701504
2003	6850017	1688682	396489	715359	5161335	990357	1949077
2004	9457572	2056926	580929	970117	7400647	1053395	2271805
2005	12550643	3086590	970942	1557231	9464052	1365646	2695890
2006-2010	**113918161**	**24817747**	**8781469**	**14861935**	**89100414**	**11589524**	**25107110**
2006	15803663	3795398	1388925	2170700	12008265	1704997	3786847
2007	19299976	4892639	1797751	2862301	14407337	2360093	4477646
2008	27169290	5749961	1906381	3354179	21419329	2417936	4987666
2009	21479103	4835807	1751571	3080447	16643296	2357239	5194072
2010	30166129	5543942	1936840	3394308	24622187	2749258	6660878
2011	38958314	5899770	1811744	3523452	33058544	3145224	7667795
2012	40810735	5963212	1901750	3737918	34847523	2987939	7217809

注：进出口总值为海关统计的北京地区进出口数据(包括中央单位)。

资料来源：北京市商务委员会、中华人民共和国北京海关。

Note: Figures of "total value of imports and exports" were imports and exports of Beijing counted by Beijing Customs (including central businesses).

Source: Beijing Municipal Commission of Commerce , Beijing Customs District People's Republic of China.

15-1 续表 continued

年份 Year	外商直接投资项目(合同)个数(个) Number of Foreign Direct Investment Projects (Contracts) (unit)	实际利用外商直接投资额(万美元) Foreign Capital Actually Used (USD10000)
1980	4	
1981-1985	**124**	
1981	3	
1982	4	
1983	5	
1984	29	
1985	83	
1986-1990	**709**	
1986	63	
1987	72	9534
1988	148	50278
1989	185	31846
1990	241	27696
1991-1995	**10912**	**410896**
1991	724	24482
1992	2208	34984
1993	3753	66693
1994	2675	144460
1995	1552	140277
1996-2000	**4100**	**989794**
1996	868	155290
1997	790	159286
1998	651	206415
1999	644	223004
2000	1147	245799
2001-2005	**7821**	**1231631**
2001	1147	177000
2002	1370	178964
2003	1362	214675
2004	1806	308354
2005	2136	352638
2006-2010	**9232**	**2818387**
2006	2106	455191
2007	2177	506572
2008	1897	608172
2009	1423	612094
2010	1629	636358
2011	1345	705447
2012	1360	804160

15-2 北京地区海关进出口贸易总值(按登记注册类型、贸易方式分)
TOTAL VALUE OF IMPORTS AND EXPORTS AT CUSTOMS OF BEIJING (BY TYPE OF REGISTRATION AND COMPOSITION)

项目	Item	金额(万美元) Value (USD 10000)		2012年为2011年% 2012as % of 2011	构成(%) Composition(%)	
		2012	2011		2012	2011
出口	**Local Exports**	**5963212**	**5899770**	**101.1**	**100.00**	**100.00**
按登记注册类型分	**Grouped by registration status**					
内资企业	Domestic Funded Enterprises	3828499	3735189	102.5	64.20	63.31
国有企业	State-owned Enterprises	3207836	3163470	101.4	53.79	53.62
集体企业	Collective-owned Enterprises	12306	11080	111.1	0.21	0.19
其他	Others	608357	560639	108.5	10.20	9.50
外商投资企业	Foreign Funded Enterprises	2134714	2164581	98.6	35.80	36.69
中外合资	Joint Venture	1294838	1365925	94.8	21.71	23.15
中外合作	Cooperative	8276	10259	80.7	0.14	0.17
外商独资	Foreign Enterprises	831600	788397	105.5	13.95	13.36
按贸易方式分	**Grouped by Composition**					
#一般贸易	General Trade	2861663	2987627	95.8	47.99	50.64
来料加工装配贸易	Trade of Processing & Assembling Supplied Materials	457138	385414	118.6	7.67	6.53
进料加工贸易	Trade of Processing Imported Materials	1777013	1678342	105.9	29.80	28.45
对外承包工程货物	Goods for Contracted Foreign Projects	503388	530291	94.9	8.44	8.99
出料加工贸易	Trade of Processing Exported Materials	1488	337	441.0	0.02	0.01
进口	**Local Imports**	**34847523**	**33058544**	**105.4**	**100.00**	**100.00**
按登记注册类型分	**Grouped by registration status**					
内资企业	Domestic Funded Enterprises	29534324	27543311	107.2	84.75	83.32
国有企业	State-owned Enterprises	25392602	23507822	108.0	72.87	71.11
集体企业	Collective-owned Enterprises	148699	142259	104.5	0.43	0.43
其他	Others	3993022	3893230	102.6	11.46	11.78
外商投资企业	Foreign Funded Enterprises	5313199	5515232	96.3	15.25	16.68
中外合资	Joint Venture	1045059	1185970	88.1	3.00	3.59
中外合作	Cooperative	4950	7038	70.3	0.01	0.02
外商独资	Foreign Enterprises	4263190	4322224	98.6	12.23	13.07
按贸易方式分	**Grouped by Composition**					
#一般贸易	General Trade	31140187	29758806	104.6	89.36	90.02
来料加工装配贸易	Trade of Processing & Assembling Supplied Materials	1009828	868622	116.3	2.90	2.63
进料加工贸易	Trade of Processing Imported Materials	661672	622921	106.2	1.90	1.88
外商投资企业进口设备、物品	Equipment and Goods Imported by Foreign-funded Enterprises	41633	105837	39.3	0.12	0.32
租赁贸易	Leasing Trade	244142	148119	164.8	0.70	0.45

资料来源：中华人民共和国北京海关。
Source: Beijing Customs District People's Republic of China.

15-3 北京地区海关进出口贸易总值(按国别、地区分)
TOTAL VALUE OF IMPORTS AND EXPORTS AT CUSTOMS OF BEIJING (GROUPED BY COUNTRY AND REGION)

项 目	Item	金 额 (万美元) Value (USD 10000)		2012年为2011年% 2012as % of 2011	构 成 (%) Composition(%)	
		2012	2011		2012	2011
出口合计	**Local Exports**	**5963212**	**5899770**	**101.1**	**100.00**	**100.00**
按国别(地区)分	**Grouped by Country (Region)**					
#中国香港	Hongkong,China	478361	458932	104.2	8.02	7.78
中国澳门	Macao,China	34788	28513	122.0	0.58	0.48
中国台湾	Taiwan,China	116659	124868	93.4	1.96	2.12
日 本	Japan	473689	544131	87.1	7.94	9.22
新加坡	Singapore	119907	128983	93.0	2.01	2.19
韩 国	Korea	200287	295974	67.7	3.36	5.02
越 南	Viet Nam	182520	156322	116.8	3.06	2.65
伊 朗	Iran	113798	170014	66.9	1.91	2.88
印 度	India	253408	286989	88.3	4.25	4.86
印度尼西亚	Indonesia	157064	149885	104.8	2.63	2.54
英 国	United Kingdom	89216	85003	105.0	1.50	1.44
德 国	Germany	153649	170328	90.2	2.58	2.89
法 国	France	88877	81498	109.1	1.49	1.38
意大利	Italy	57159	56045	102.0	0.96	0.95
匈牙利	Hungary	64445	129271	49.9	1.08	2.19
俄罗斯联邦	Russia Union	155925	127119	122.7	2.61	2.15
美 国	United States	499105	491284	101.6	8.37	8.33
澳大利亚	Australia	76280	106035	71.9	1.28	1.80
进口合计	**Local Imports**	**34847523**	**33058544**	**105.4**	**100.00**	**100.00**
按国别(地区)分	**Grouped by Country (Region)**					
#中国香港	Hongkong,China	476084	473831	100.5	1.37	1.43
日 本	Japan	1382380	1679045	82.3	3.97	5.08
新加坡	Singapore	191048	209930	91.0	0.55	0.64
韩 国	Korea	1436414	1515742	94.8	4.12	4.59
沙特阿拉伯	Saudi Arabia	3085971	3250811	94.9	8.86	9.83
英 国	United Kingdom	344132	279459	123.1	0.99	0.85
德 国	Germany	2009873	2102093	95.6	5.77	6.36
法 国	France	285006	275954	103.3	0.82	0.83
意大利	Italy	166330	191059	87.1	0.48	0.58
瑞 士	Switzerland	854275	1522584	56.1	2.45	4.61
比利时	Belgium	78587	78653	99.9	0.23	0.24
俄罗斯联邦	Russia Union	1039310	785882	132.2	2.98	2.38
加拿大	Canada	413133	368721	112.0	1.19	1.12
美 国	United States	2914011	2251284	129.4	8.36	6.81
澳大利亚	Australia	1781719	1233772	144.4	5.11	3.73
阿 曼	Oman	1236702	1065132	116.1	3.55	3.22
安哥拉	Angola	2894101	2030226	142.6	8.31	6.14

资料来源：中华人民共和国北京海关。
Source: Beijing Customs District People's Republic of China.

15-4 北京地区海关主要商品进口量及金额(2012年)
VOLUME & VALUE OF MAJOR COMMODITIES IMPORTED AT CUSTOMS OF BEIJING (2012)

项 目		Item		进口数量 Import Volume	进口金额 (万美元) Import Value (USD 10000)
粮 食	(万吨)	Grain	(10000 tons)	1408	608839
食用植物油	(万吨)	Edible Vegetable Oil	(10000 tons)	133	166613
食 糖	(万吨)	Sugar	(10000 tons)	226	141599
酒 类	(万升)	Wine	(10000 liters)	7365	20090
合成橡胶(包括胶乳)	(万吨)	Synthetic Rubber (including latex)	(10000 tons)	3	11936
纸 浆	(万吨)	Paper Pulp	(10000 tons)	74	47901
羊 毛	(万吨)	Wool	(10000 tons)	4	22760
棉 花	(万吨)	Cotton	(10000 tons)	152	369975
纺织用合成纤维	(万吨)	Synthetic Fibre for Textile	(10000 tons)	5	12659
铁矿砂及其精矿	(万吨)	Iron Sand and Iron Ore Concentrate	(10000 tons)	10911	1407836
原 油	(万吨)	Crude Oil	(10000 tons)	19599	15878010
成品油	(万吨)	Product Oil	(10000 tons)	1060	869459
液化石油气及其他烃类气	(万吨)	LPG and Other Hydrocarbon	(10000 tons)	679	630799
医药品	(万吨)	Medicine	(10000 tons)	1	254461
肥 料	(万吨)	Fertilizer	(10000 tons)	539	266919
非泡沫塑料的板、片、膜、箔	(万吨)	Non-foamed Plastic Plate, Slice, Film and Foil	(10000 tons)	2	14021
纸及纸板(未切成形的)	(万吨)	Paper and Pressboard (not shaped by cutting)	(10000 tons)	18	28490
纺织纱线、织物及制品		Textile Yarn, Fabric and Products			125707
服装及衣着附件		Costume and Clothing Attachments			32886
钢 材	(万吨)	Steel Products	(10000 tons)	73	124680
建筑及采矿用机械及零件		Building and Mining Machinery and Parts			50522
印刷、装订机械及零件		Printing and Binding Machinery and Parts			112024
自动数据处理设备及其部件		Automatic Data Processing Equipment and Their Components			233329
电动机及发电机	(万台)	Electric Motors and Generators	(10000 sets)	1064	37281
变压、整流、电感器及零件		Transformers, Rectifiers, Inducers and Parts			101368
电视摄像机、数字照相机及视频摄录一体机	(万台)	Television Camera, Digital Camera and Integrated Video Camera and Recorder	(10000 sets)	1729	246615
印刷电路	(万块)	Printed Circuit	(10000 pieces)	72964	23714
集成电路	(万个)	Integrated Circuit	(10000 units)	688842	427767
电线和电缆	(万吨)	Wires and Cables	(10000 tons)	1	20116
汽 车		Car			2319595
汽车零件		Auto Parts			289387
飞 机		Plan			404751
船 舶		Boat			21775
医疗仪器及器械		Medical Instruments and Apparatus			178574
计量检测分析自控仪器及器具		Automatically-controlled Measuring, Testing and Analyzing Instruments			459162

资料来源：中华人民共和国北京海关。
Source: Beijing Customs District People's Republic of China.

15-5 北京地区海关主要商品出口量及金额(2012年)
VOLUME & VALUE OF MAIN COMMODITIES EXPORTED AT CUSTOMS OF BEIJING(2012)

品名		Item		出口数量 Export Volume	出口金额 Export Value (万美元) (USD 10000)
粮食	(万吨)	Grain	(10000 tons)	48	31974
果蔬汁	(万吨)	Fruit and Vegetable Juice	(10000 tons)	10	20771
肥料	(万吨)	Fertilizer	(10000 tons)	376	152055
煤	(万吨)	Coal	(10000 tons)	392	56731
焦炭、半焦炭	(万吨)	Coke and Semi-coke	(10000 tons)	27	11323
原油	(万吨)	Crude Oil	(10000 tons)	54	58805
成品油	(万吨)	Product Oil	(10000 tons)	622	599188
医药品	(万吨)	Medicine	(10000 tons)	1	27320
纺织纱线、织物及制品		Textile Yarn, Fabric and Products			65331
铁合金	(万吨)	Ferroalloy	(10000 tons)	2	45386
钢材	(万吨)	Steel Products	(10000 tons)	304	290102
未锻造的铝及铝材	(万吨)	Non-forged Aluminum and Aluminum Products	(10000 tons)	2	9079
纺织机械及零件		Textile Machinery and Parts			17698
金属加工机床	(万台)	Metal Processing Lathe	(10000 sets)	1	13283
自动数据处理设备及其部件		Automatic Data Processing Equipment and Their Components			17993
液晶显示板	(万个)	LCD Plates	(10000 units)	1846	50355
电动机及发电机	(万台)	Electric Motors and Generators	(10000 sets)	201	11732
变压器	(万个)	Transformers	(10000 units)	98	17662
蓄电池	(万个)	Storage Cells	(10000 units)	5353	20771
电话机	(万台)	Telephone Sets	(10000 sets)	15074	1011293
二极管及类似半导体器件	(万个)	Diode and Similar Semiconductor Devices	(10000 units)	74721	40662
集成电路	(万个)	Integrated Circuit	(10000 units)	371979	159246
电线和电缆	(万吨)	Wires and Cables	(10000 tons)	4	32023
汽车(包括整套散件)	(万辆)	Automobiles (including complete set of spare parts)	(10000 sets)	4	95548
汽车零件		Auto Parts			84966
船舶		Watercraft			234338
医疗仪器及器械		Medical Instrument and Apparatus			50585
家具及其零件		Furniture and Their Parts			23365
服装及衣着附件		Costume and Clothing Attachments			185014
鞋类	(万吨)	Shoes	(10000 tons)	2	20444
塑料制品	(万吨)	Plastic Products	(10000 tons)	4	17415

资料来源：中华人民共和国北京海关。
Source: Beijing Customs District People's Republic of China.

15-6 北京口岸运营情况
STATISTICS ON PORT OPERATION IN BEIJING

项目		Item		2012	2011	2012年为2011年% 2012 as % of 2011
北京首都国际机场空港口岸		**Port of Beijing Capital International Airport**				
旅客吞吐量	(万人次)	Passenger Throughout	(10000 person-times)	8192.93	7867.51	104.1
进出境人员	(万人次)	Entering/Exiting Visitors	(10000 person-times)	2034.70	1861.01	109.3
#外籍人员进出境	(万人次)	Entering/Exiting Foreign Visitors	(10000 person-times)	892.50	881.43	101.3
货邮运量	(万吨)	Cargos Carried	(10000 tons)	174.50	163.26	106.9
飞机起降	(架次)	Takeoff and Landing of Airplanes	(unit)	557168	533257	104.5
#进出境飞机起降	(架次)	Takeoff and Landing of Airplanes Entering/Exiting	(unit)	121507	114242	106.4
海关监管货物	(万吨)	Cargos under Customs Regulating	(10000 tons)	51.25	50.73	101.0
海关征收关税及代征税	(万元)	Duties Levied and Withheld by Customs	(10000 yuan)	3342931	3156308	105.9
北京丰台货运口岸		**Beijing Fengtai Cargo Transport Port**				
海关监管货物	(吨)	Cargos under Customs Regulating	(ton)	9263	5922	156.4
海关征收关税及代征税	(万元)	Duties Levied and Withheld by Customs	(10000 yuan)	3756	3110	120.8
北京朝阳口岸		**Beijing Chaoyang Transport Port**				
海关监管货物	(标箱)	Cargos under Customs Regulating	(standard containers)	56367	55741	101.1
海关监管货物	(吨)	Cargos under Customs Regulating	(ton)	867860	990825	87.6
海关征收关税及代征税	(万元)	Duties Levied and Withheld by Customs	(10000 yuan)	1418290	1251048	113.4
北京西站铁路口岸		**Railway Port at Beijing West Railway Station**				
进出境人员	(人次)	Entering/Exiting Visitors	(person-times)	116563	132738	87.8
#外籍人员进出境	(人次)	Entering/Exiting Foreign Visitors	(person-times)	7438	7546	98.6
北京平谷国际陆港		**Beijing Pinggu International Land Port**				
海关监管货物	(标箱)	Cargos under Customs Regulating	(standard containers)	21260	7649	277.9
海关监管货物	(吨)	Cargos under Customs Regulating	(ton)	152821	67668	225.8
海关征收关税及代征税	(万元)	Duties Levied and Withheld by Customs	(10000 yuan)	170992	77086	221.8
北京天竺综合保税区		**Beijing Tianzhu Comprehensive Bonded Zone**				
实际进出货物	(吨)	Cargos under Customs Regulating		31271	35915	87.1
海关征收关税及代征税	(万元)	Duties Levied and Withheld by Customs		644270	277475	232.2

资料来源：北京市人民政府口岸办公室。
Source: Beijing People's Government Port Office.

15-7 外商投资企业实际利用外资情况(2006-2012年)
FOREIGN CAPITAL ACTURLLY USED OF FOREIGN FUNDED ENTERPRISES(2006-2012)

单位：万美元 (USD 10000)

项　　目	Item	2006	2007	2008	2009	2010	2011	2012
实际利用外商直接投资额	**Amount of Foreign Capital Actually Used**	**455191**	**506572**	**608172**	**612094**	**636358**	**705447**	**804160**
按登记注册类型分	**Grouped by Investment Manner**							
合资经营	Joint Venture	80570	77887	90916	91049	91335	78983	191944
合作经营	Cooperative Operation	33039	18037	21372	32249	22890	15068	14184
独资经营	Foreign Funded Enterprises	341367	408754	490252	448912	516766	594890	592310
外商投资股份制	Foreign Funded Joint-Stock	215	1894	5632	39884	5367	16506	5722
按产业分	**Grouped by Industry**							
第一产业	Primary Industry	544	4774	2032	3833	1246	214	733
第二产业	Secondary Industry	109380	93391	162515	88536	71899	80798	112326
第三产业	Tertiary Industry	345267	408407	443625	519725	563213	624435	691101
按行业分	**Grouped by Sector**							
农、林、牧、渔业	Farming, Forestry, Animal Husbandry and Fishery	544	4774	2032	3833	1246	214	733
制造业	Manufacturing	105590	89618	150056	75364	68496	63303	86378
建筑业	Construction	1254	878	1715	2493	411	2343	383
信息传输、计算机服务和软件业	Information Transmission,Computer Services and Software	44341	78470	105396	94752	95453	109246	135121
批发与零售业	Wholesale and Retail Trade	24378	33318	34677	55411	66032	115437	74311
住宿和餐饮业	Hotel and Restaurants	1882	5824	3357	8427	3525	1705	2877
房地产业	Real Estate	72242	119476	78787	79682	141728	112539	87739
租赁和商务服务业	Leasing and Business Services	174342	92896	132541	225888	175580	190363	161595
其他行业	Other Sectors	30618	81318	99611	66244	83887	110297	255023
按外商国别(地区)分	**Grouped by Country(Region) of Foreign Partner**							
#中国香港	Hongkong,China	86600	149291	173292	270295	312863	323041	440357
英属维尔京群岛	Virgin Islands	78445	104154	125045	123201	76255	112981	28882
开曼群岛	Cayman Islands	27596	68646	75463	41389	45209	35982	59320
日　本	Japan	67580	30386	47174	23905	40692	77196	59022
韩　国	Korea	35357	24420	27841	17601	14725	22372	70959
美　国	United States	20043	18280	17888	18628	21370	30221	21097
新加坡	Singapore	17616	15328	10520	12600	24888	12898	31656
巴巴多斯	Barbados	7278	13789	15803	2384	941	821	200
德　国	Germany	47797	11476	26654	14308	22344	17939	25763
毛里求斯	Mauritius	10166	8068	7780	5615	7179	1311	1392
百慕大	Bermuda	1658	7540	1699	4441	4860	813	1483
萨摩亚	Samoan	1483	6189	2468	1310	1705	893	1163
荷　兰	Netherlands	4610	4876	28520	4906	10639	3677	8542
法　国	France	3578	3824	2583	6349	3700	6642	2286
英　国	United Kingdom	2977	3304	4897	4242	1120	6245	3828

资料来源：北京市商务委员会。
Source: Beijing Municipal Commission of Commerce.

15-8 外商投资企业基本情况
STATISTICS FOR OPENING OF FOREIGN FUNDED ENTERPRISES

项 目	Item	企业单位数（个） Number of Enterprises (unit) 2012	2011	从业人员平均人数(人) Average Number of Employed Persons (person) 2012	2011
合 计	**Total**	**4334**	**4191**	**1298578**	**1218094**
按登记注册类型分	**Grouped by Registration Status**				
港澳台商投资企业	Enterprises with Funds from Hongkong,Macao and Taiwan	1567	1481	479876	443648
与港澳台商合资	Joint Venture	527	515	152096	145619
与港澳台商合作	Cooperative	136	142	23269	25423
港澳台商独资	Hongkong,Macao and Taiwan Enterprises	874	788	248026	214654
港澳台商投资股份有限公司	Hongkong,Macao and Taiwan Funded Share Holding Company	30	36	56485	57952
其他港澳台投资企业	Others				
外商投资企业	Foreign Funded Enterprises	2767	2710	818702	774446
中外合资	Joint Venture	818	822	290606	280611
中外合作	Cooperative	118	120	20040	20010
外商独资	Foreign Enterprises	1781	1707	476056	448635
外商投资股份有限公司	Foreign Funded Share Holding Company	49	61	27638	25190
其他外商投资企业	Others	1		4362	
按行业分	**Grouped by Sector**				
农、林、牧、渔业	Agriculture,Forestry,Animal Husbandry and Fishery				
制造业	Manufacturing	911	942	387469	383949
建筑业	Construction	93	97	17247	18330
批发与零售业	Wholesale and Retail Trade	529	510	188558	173837
住宿和餐饮业	Hotel and Restaurants	214	221	94453	89781
信息传输、软件和信息技术服务业	Information Transmission, Software and Iinformation Technology Services	598	587	203680	188148
房地产业	Real Estate	428	443	63785	65065
租赁和商务服务业	Leasing and Business Services	749	670	110729	100086
其他行业	Other Sectors	812	721	232657	198898
按三次产业分	**Grouped by Industry**				
第一产业	Primary Industry				
第二产业	Secondary Industry	1011	1054	407845	411227
第三产业	Tertiary Industry	3323	3137	890733	806867

注：1. 本表统计范围为限额以上法人企业。
2. 行业划分执行2011年国民经济行业分类标准(GB/T 4754-2011)。

Note: a) The range of Statistics were for corporative enterprises above designated size.
b) Sectors in this table are classified in accordance with the Standard for Classification of National Economic Sectors 2011 (GB/T 4754-2011).

15-8 续表 continued

单位：万元 (10000 yuan)

项 目	Item	主营业务收入 Operating Income		利润总额 Total Profits		应交税金合计 Total Taxes Paid	
		2012	2011	2012	2011	2012	2011
合 计	**Total**	**215074562**	**208764236**	**25055724**	**20156809**	**7743904**	**7549636**
按登记注册类型分	**Grouped by Registration Status**						
港澳台商投资企业	Enterprises with Funds from Hongkong,Macao and Taiwan	56774419	53825836	5239482	5239500	2425660	1906580
与港澳台商合资	Joint Venture	11182539	10937201	1059468	1155521	520910	436642
与港澳台商合作	Cooperative	3408334	2006568	822650	257005	552196	139551
港澳台商独资	Hongkong,Macao and Taiwan Enterprises	32598098	30121059	2625229	2345408	1140283	1012368
港澳台商投资股份有限公司	Hongkong,Macao and Taiwan Funded Share Holding Company	9585448	10761008	732134	1481566	212271	318020
其他港澳台投资企业	Others						
外商投资企业	Foreign Funded Enterprises	158300144	154938399	19816242	14917309	5318244	5643056
中外合资	Joint Venture	50233264	51491839	5198304	5137742	2272252	2210549
中外合作	Cooperative	1493559	1464511	200260	252203	90360	97305
外商独资	Foreign Enterprises	105186514	100598758	14260113	9459349	2852320	3215840
外商投资股份有限公司	Foreign Funded Share Holding Company	1320074	1383291	161724	68015	100786	119363
其他外商投资企业	Others	66733		-4159		2527	
按行业分	**Grouped by Sector**						
农、林、牧、渔业	Agriculture,Forestry,Animal Husbandry and Fishery						
制造业	Manufacturing	61596575	60797284	4051768	4743505	2685055	2465283
建筑业	Construction	2084522	1964181	80590	41936	61073	59013
批发与零售业	Wholesale and Retail Trade	83984267	85750515	3790105	6379445	1601477	2226905
住宿和餐饮业	Hotel and Restaurants	2836435	2620622	232552	247874	182712	175137
信息传输、软件和信息技术服务业	Information Transmission, Software and Iinformation Technology Services	16636743	15359345	8709491	2121761	845363	787384
房地产业	Real Estate	6340299	5377178	2057550	1151373	1008262	644511
租赁和商务服务业	Leasing and Business Services	21473819	18574875	1884459	1661029	655025	554560
其他行业	Other Sectors	20121903	18320236	4249209	3809886	704937	636844
按三次产业分	**Grouped by Three Industry**						
第一产业	Primary Industry						
第二产业	Secondary Industry	65564311	64561991	4508446	5090719	2794063	2567161
第三产业	Tertiary Industry	149510251	144202244	20547279	15066090	4949841	4982475

注：应交税金合计不含所得税。
Note: Total taxes paid exclude income tax.

15-9 境外投资情况(2003-2011年)
STATISTICS ON OVERSEAS INVESTMENT IN PREVIOUS YEARS (2003-2011)

单位：万美元 (USD 10000)

年份 Year	中方投资额 Mount of Investment by China Side	截至到各年期末直接投资存量 FDI Stock by Year End
2003	30054	44844
2004	15739	70086
2005	11306	92940
2006	5612	91873
2007	15295	159195
2008	47299	251019
2009	45185	375865
2010	76614	480882
2011	117503	603380

资料来源：北京市商务委员会。
Source: Beijing Municipal Commission of Commerce.

15-10 对外经济合作(1984-2012年)
STATISTICS ON FOREIGN ECONOMIC COOPERATION (1984-2012)

年份 Year	合同数(份) Number of Contracts (unit)	#对外承包工程 Foreign Contracted Works	合同额(万美元) Contract Value (USD 10000)	#对外承包工程 Foreign Contracted Works	完成营业额(万美元) Turnover Realized (USD 10000)	#对外承包工程 Foreign Contracted Works	年末在外人数(人) Year-end Workers Staying Abroad (persons)	对外承包工程 Foreign Contracted Works	对外劳务合作 Foreign LaborService Cooperation
1984	9	2	2801	2768	502	331	541	163	378
1985	12	2	852	736	2083	355	2401	18	2383
1986	30	7	446	319	1535	90	837	71	766
1987	37	5	547	354	696	186	690	20	670
1988	46	5	885	344	802	281	819	104	715
1989	111	7	1685	235	1018	459	600	83	517
1990	105	16	3756	2253	1056	625	336	25	311
1991	114	9	3202	1671	1897	1469	980	306	674
1992	130	16	8889	7762	3140	2543	952	264	688
1993	143	48	29397	27625	9748	8871	1555	532	1023
1994	114	34	15715	15089	18783	17822	2720	1694	1026
1995	116	35	15613	14014	12789	12156	2604	1297	1307
1996	116	49	67689	62945	43057	38124	2516	1559	957
1997	107	37	35640	23374	29629	17945	3122	1993	1129
1998	180	48	25526	19292	31009	24930	3647	2239	1408
1999	90	28	25232	18715	26167	19690	3476	2199	1277
2000	104	54	16285	9936	19799	13543	3205	1660	1545
2001	105	54	21439	14758	18628	11680	3494	2141	1353
2002	73	42	27949	19376	23160	14453	2134	1112	1022
2003	117	99	48271	30761	34926	17334	2097	1270	827
2004	128	116	81185	51136	59630	29241	2552	1629	923
2005	272	238	93732	56709	71281	35554	4424	2528	1896
2006	232	166	176752	160328	83518	70062	8962	6760	2202
2007	317	143	236881	211560	94077	71727	11299	7060	4239
2008	486	197	558714	520973	168416	131686	11422	6366	5056
2009	190	182	336223	296851	226893	185017	17121	11805	5316
2010	199	170	286179	251114	259794	222514	22499	17145	5354
2011	229	229	264019	262078	252951	249146	17821	12393	5428
2012	340	340	405885	403475	295639	289902	16747	12143	4604

注：1984-2008年，对外承包工程统计中含对外设计咨询统计数据。
资料来源：北京市商务委员会。
Note: In 1984-2008, statistics on foreign contracted works included statistics on foreign design consulting.
Source: Beijing Municipal Commission of Commerce.

15-11 外国及港澳地区企业驻京代表机构
REPRESENTATIVE OFFICES IN BEIJING OF FOREIGN, HONGKONG AND MACAO ENTERPRISES

项 目	Item	数 量(个) Number(unit)		构 成 (%) Composition(%)	
		2012	2011	2012	2011
合 计	**Total**	**8911**	**13792**	**100.0**	**100.0**
#日 本	Japan	482	746	5.4	5.4
中国香港	Hongkong, China	2023	3178	22.7	23.0
中国澳门	Macao, China	15	30	0.2	0.2
美 国	United States	1641	2655	18.4	19.3
德 国	Germany	393	614	4.4	4.5
法 国	France	190	278	2.1	2.0
英 国	United Kingdom	433	563	4.9	4.1
意大利	Italy	144	232	1.6	1.7
瑞 士	Switzerland	117	157	1.3	1.1
瑞 典	Sweden	60	91	0.7	0.7
加拿大	Canada	330	503	3.7	3.6
澳大利亚	Australia	267	391	3.0	2.8
比利时	Belgium	36	62	0.4	0.4
新加坡	Singapore	213	371	2.4	2.7
荷 兰	Holland	90	139	1.0	1.0
奥地利	Austria	41	69	0.5	0.5

资料来源：北京市工商行政管理局。
Source: Beijing Administration for Industry & Commerce.

15-12 北京市市级友好城市
MUNICIPAL-LEVEL SISTER CITIES OF BEIJING

顺序 No.	城市	City	国家	Contury	所属洲	Continent	缔结日期 Date of Conclusion
1	东京都	Tokyo	日本	Japan	亚洲	Asia	1979.03.14
2	纽约市	New York	美国	USA	北美洲	North America	1980.02.25
3	贝尔格莱德市	Belgrade	塞尔维亚	Serbia	欧洲	Europe	1980.10.14
4	利马市	Lima	秘鲁	Peru	南美洲	South America	1983.11.21
5	华盛顿特区	Washington, DC	美国	USA	北美洲	North America	1984.05.15
6	马德里市	Madrid	西班牙	Spain	欧洲	Europe	1985.09.16
7	里约热内卢市	Rio De Janeiro	巴西	Brazil	南美洲	South America	1986.11.24
8	巴黎大区	Greater Parisian Region	法国	France	欧洲	Europe	1987.07.02
9	科隆市	Cologne	德国	Germany	欧洲	Europe	1987.09.14
10	安卡拉市	Ankara	土耳其	Turkey	亚洲	Asia	1990.06.20
11	开罗省	Cairo	埃及	Egypt	非洲	Africa	1990.10.28
12	雅加达省	Jakarta	印度尼西亚	Indonesia	亚洲	Asia	1992.08.04
13	伊斯兰堡市	Islamabad	巴基斯坦	Pakistan	亚洲	Asia	1992.10.08
14	曼谷市	Bangkok	泰国	Thailand	亚洲	Asia	1993.05.26
15	布宜诺斯艾利斯市	Buenos Aires	阿根廷	Argentina	南美洲	South America	1993.07.13
16	首尔特别市	Seoul Special City	韩国	South Korea	亚洲	Asia	1993.10.23
17	基辅市	Kiev	乌克兰	Ukraine	欧洲	Europe	1993.12.13
18	柏林市	Berlin	德国	Germany	欧洲	Europe	1994.04.05
19	布鲁塞尔大区	Greater Brussels Region	比利时	Belgium	欧洲	Europe	1994.09.22
20	河内市	Ha noi	越南	Viet Nam	亚洲	Asia	1994.10.06
21	阿姆斯特丹市	Amsterdam	荷兰	Holland	欧洲	Europe	1994.10.29
22	莫斯科市	Moscow	俄罗斯	Russia	欧洲	Europe	1995.05.16
23	巴黎市	Paris	法国	France	欧洲	Europe	1997.10.23
24	罗马市	Rome	意大利	Italy	欧洲	Europe	1998.05.28
25	豪登省	Gauteng	南非	South Africa	非洲	Africa	1998.12.06
26	渥太华市	Ottawa	加拿大	Canada	北美洲	North America	1999.10.18
27	首都地区	The Capital Region	澳大利亚	Australia	大洋洲	Oceania	2000.09.14
28	马德里自治区	Madrid Autonomous Region	西班牙	Spain	欧洲	Europe	2005.01.17
29	雅典市	Athens	希腊	Greek	欧洲	Europe	2005.05.10
30	布达佩斯市	Budapest	匈牙利	Hungary	欧洲	Europe	2005.06.16
31	布加勒斯特市	Bucharest	罗马尼亚	Rumania	欧洲	Europe	2005.06.21
32	哈瓦那市	Havana	古巴	Cuba	南美洲	South America	2005.09.24
33	马尼拉市	Manila	菲律宾	Philippines	亚洲	Asia	2005.11.14
34	伦敦市	London	英国	UK	欧洲	Europe	2006.04.11
35	亚的斯亚贝巴市	Addis Abeba	埃塞俄比亚	Ethiopia	非洲	Africa	2006.04.17
36	惠灵顿市	Wellington	新西兰	New Zealand	大洋洲	Oceania	2006.05.10
37	赫尔辛基市	Helsinki	芬兰	Finland	欧洲	Europe	2006.07.14
38	阿斯塔纳市	Astana	哈萨克斯坦	Kazakstan	亚洲	Asia	2006.11.16
39	特拉维夫市	Tel Aviv	以色列	Israel	亚洲	Asia	2006.11.21
40	首都大区	The Greater Capital Region	智利	Chile	南美洲	South America	2007.08.06
41	里斯本市	Lisbon	葡萄牙	Portugal	欧洲	Europe	2007.10.22
42	地拉那市	Tirana	阿尔巴尼亚	Albania	欧洲	Europe	2008.03.21
43	多哈市	Doha	卡塔尔	Qatar	亚洲	Asia	2008.06.23
44	圣何塞市	San Jose	哥斯达黎加	Costarica	北美洲	North America	2009.10.17
45	墨西哥城	Mexican City	墨西哥	Mexico	北美洲	North America	2009.10.19
46	都柏林市	Dublin	爱尔兰	Ireland	欧洲	Europe	2011.06.02
47	哥本哈根市	Copenhagen	丹麦	Denmark	欧洲	Europe	2012.06.28
48	新南威尔士州	New South Wales	澳大利亚	Australia	大洋洲	Oceania	2012.08.03

资料来源：北京市人民政府外事办公室。
Sourse: Foreign Affairs Office of the People's Government of Beijing Municipality.

主要统计指标解释

进出口总值 海关进出口总值指实际进、出我国海关并能引起我国境内物质资源增加或减少的进出口货物总金额。包括我国境内法人和其他组织以一般贸易、易货贸易、加工贸易、补偿贸易、寄售代销贸易等方式进出口的货物、租赁期一年及以上的租赁进出口货物、边境小额贸易货物、国际援助物资或捐赠品、保税区和保税仓库进出口货物等的金额合计。进出口总值用以观察一个国家在对外贸易方面的总规模。我国规定出口货物按离岸价格统计，进口货物按到岸价格统计。

一般贸易 指我国境内有进出口经营权的企业单边进口或单边出口的货物。

来料加工装配贸易 指由外商提供全部或部分原材料、辅料、零部件、元器件、配套件和包装物料，必要时提供设备，由我方按对方的要求进行加工装配，成品交对方销售，我方收取工缴费，对方提供的作价设备价款，我方用工缴费偿还的交易形式。

进料加工贸易 指我方用外汇购买进口的原料、材料、辅料、元器件、零部件、配套件和包装物料，加工成品或半成品后再外销出口的交易形式。

旅客吞吐量 指乘国内、国际航班，出入首都机场空港口岸的所有人员数量。

货邮运量 指国内、国际航班经首都机场起降运输的货物和邮件量的总和。

飞机起降 指在首都机场起飞和降落的所有航班数量。

海关征收关税及代征税 指海关依法实际征收的关税和代征环节税的总和。

外商直接投资项目（合同）个数 指外商直接投资中批准设立的外商投资企业个数、批准的合作开发项目个数。

实际使用外商直接投资额 指批准的合同外资金额的实际执行数，外国投资者根据批准外商投资企业的合同（章程）的规定实际缴付的出资额和企业投资总额内外国投资者以自己的境外自有资金实际直接向企业提供的贷款。

对外承包工程 指企业按照国际通行做法，在国（境）外承揽和实施各类工程项目的经济活动。企业承揽的我国对外经济援助项目、我国驻外使（领）馆等建设项目视同对外承包工程项目。

对外劳务合作 指企业按照与国（境）外政府有关机构、团体、企业、私人雇主所签合同规定，向国（境）外派遣各类劳务人员的经济活动。企业自带设备以提供技术服务的形式在国（境）外承揽的项目视同对外劳务合作项目。

外国及港澳台地区企业常驻代表机构 指外国及港澳台企业在中国境内设立的开展与本企业业务有关的联络活动的办事机构。

Explanatory Notes on Main Statistical Indicators

Total Imports and Exports at Customs refer to the total value of goods actually imported and exported through China's customs, which lead to increase or decrease in the physical resources in China, including goods imported/exported by China domestic legal persons and other organizations in such manners as general trade, barter trade, processing trade, compensation trade, commission-based sales trade, leased imports/exports with a lease period of one year and more, goods in small-sum border trade, international aid goods and donations, imports/exports in bonded zones and bonded warehouses. The indicator of the total imports and exports at customs can be used to observe the total size of foreign trade in a country. In accordance with the stipulation of the Chinese government, imports are calculated at CIF, while exports are calculated at FOB.

General Trade means any domestic enterprise which has import/export rights imports or exports any goods unilaterally.

Processing Trade is a form of transaction all or part of raw materials, auxiliary materials, parts and components, elements, fittings, and packaging materials, and equipment if necessary are provided by the foreign party, processed or assemble by Chinese party pursuant to requirements of the foreign party, with the finished products sold by the foreign party. Chinese party receives processing charges and pays the money of equipment provided by the foreign party with processing charges.

Feeding Processing Trade is a form of transaction that Chinese party purchases raw materials, auxiliary materials, parts and components, elements, fittings, and packaging materials with foreign exchange, processing them into finished or semi-finished products and export them.

Passenger Throughput means the number of all persons passing through the port of Beijing Capital Airport by domestic and international flights.

Cargo and Mail Transport means the sum of cargoes and mails transported by domestic and international flights taking off from and touching down at Beijing Capital Airport.

Aircraft Taking-off and Touching-down means the number of all flights taking off from and touching down at Beijing Capital Airport.

Customs Duties and Withheld Duties means the sum of duties actually levied and duties withheld at customs.

Number of Direct Foreign-funded Enterprises means the number of foreign-funded enterprises and cooperative development projects approved in foreign direct investment (FDI).

Foreign Direct Investment Actually Utilized means the value of approved contractual foreign investment actually performed, the amount of actual capital contribution by foreign investors according to the contract (articles of incorporation) of the foreign-funded enterprise approved and, in the total investment of an enterprise, the amount of loans provided directly by foreign investor with its own overseas money.

Foreign Contracted Projects refer to economic activities in which enterprises undertake and implement various projects in foreign (overseas) countries in line with international practice. Foreign economic aid projects and construction projects of Chinese embassies (consulates) undertaken by enterprises are deemed as foreign contracted projects.

Foreign Labor Service Cooperation means any economic activity in which enterprises dispatch labors to foreign (overseas) countries as stated in contracts signed with foreign (overseas) government agencies, groups, enterprises, and private employers. Projects undertaken by enterprise in foreign (overseas) countries in a manner of providing technical service with their own equipment are deemed as foreign labor service cooperation projects.

Standing Representative Offices of Enterprises from Foreign Countries, Hong Kong, Macao and Taiwan refer to liaison offices opened in mainland of China by enterprises from foreign Countries, Hong Kong, Macao and Taiwan which are related to their business.

16

旅游业
TOURISM

简要说明

一、本章资料的主要内容和统计范围

本章内容主要包括来京旅游者人数及其在京花费情况、星级饭店经营及接待住宿者情况、旅行社接待及出境旅游情况、A 级及以上重点旅游景区活动情况等。

统计范围包括国际旅游和国内旅游。

二、本章资料的数据来源

本章中的旅游外汇收入、国内旅游者人数、国内旅游收入、在京旅游花费情况资料来源于北京市旅游发展委员会。入境旅游者人数根据北京市统计局的星级饭店、限额以上非星级饭店全面调查、限额以下饭店抽样调查，以及北京市旅游发展委员会的其他住宿设施抽样调查结果汇总得出。星级饭店、旅行社、A 级以上和重点旅游景区有关数据通过全面调查取得，由北京市统计局、国家统计局北京调查总队提供。

Brief Introduction

I. Main Content and Scope of Statistics

This chapter includes statistics for the number and spending of tourists to Beijing, operation and occupancy of star-level hotels, reception and exiting tourists of travel services, activities in key scenic spots at class A and above, and so on.

Statistics apply for international and domestic tours.

II. Source of Data

Data of foreign exchange income from tourism, number of domestic tourists, domestic tourism income, spending of tourists in Beijing are from Beijing Municipal Commission of Tourism Development. The number of entering tourists are summed from the results of complete survey of star-level hotels and non-star-level hotels above designated size, sample survey of hotels below designated size conducted by Beijing Municipal Bureau of Statistics, as well as the results of sample survey of other accommodation facilities conducted by Beijing Municipal Commission of Tourism Development. Data concerning star-level hotels, travel services, key scenic spots at class A and above were obtained through complete survey, and provided by Beijing Municipal Bureau of Statistics and NBS Survey Office in Beijing.

16-1 国际、国内旅游情况(1978-2012年)
STATISTICS ON INTERNATIONAL AND DOMESTIC TOURISM (1978-2012)

年份 Year	来京旅游者人数(万人次) Number of Tourists to Beijing (10000 person-times)	入境旅游者人数 International Tourists	国内旅游者人数 Domestic Tourists	旅游外汇收入总额(万美元) Tourism Foreign Exchange Earnings (USD 10000)	国内旅游收入(亿元) Earnings Created by Domestic Tourists (100 million yuan)
1978		18.7		10000	
1979		25.2		9000	
1980		28.6		12000	
1981-1985		**295.4**		**94000**	
1981		39.4		12000	
1982		45.7		13000	
1983		50.9		14000	
1984		65.7		23000	
1985		93.7		32000	
1986-1990		**492.0**		**280901**	
1986		99.0		46000	
1987		108.1		55000	
1988		120.4		67000	
1989		64.5		47195	
1990		100.0		65706	
1991-1995		**919.6**		**735519**	
1991		132.0		85001	
1992		174.8		107286	
1993		202.8		124128	
1994	6913.0	203.0	6710.0	200904	298.0
1995	6527.0	207.0	6320.0	218200	352.6
1996-2000	**45284.7**	**1203.3**	**44081.4**	**1214800**	**2388.4**
1996	7901.9	218.9	7683.0	225200	359.6
1997	8450.8	229.8	8221.0	224800	391.3
1998	8951.5	220.1	8731.4	238400	424.5
1999	9512.4	252.4	9260.0	249600	530.0
2000	10468.1	282.1	10186.0	276800	683.0
2001-2005	**57116.7**	**1459.7**	**55657.0**	**1475000**	**4968.7**
2001	11292.8	285.8	11007.0	295000	887.7
2002	11810.4	310.4	11500.0	311000	930.0
2003	8885.1	185.1	8700.0	190000	706.0
2004	12265.5	315.5	11950.0	317000	1145.0
2005	12862.9	362.9	12500.0	362000	1300.0
2006-2010	**77925.4**	**2107.4**	**75818.0**	**2247000**	**9712.9**
2006	13590.3	390.3	13200.0	402600	1482.7
2007	14715.5	435.5	14280.0	458000	1753.6
2008	14560.0	379.0	14181.0	446000	1907.0
2009	16669.5	412.5	16257.0	436000	2144.5
2010	18390.1	490.1	17900.0	504400	2425.1
2011	21404.4	520.4	20884.0	541600	2864.3
2012	23134.6	500.9	22633.7	514900	3301.3

资料来源：旅游外汇收入总额、国内旅游者人数、国内旅游收入来源于北京市旅游发展委员会。

Source: Data of "Tourism Foreign Exchange Earnings, Domestic Tourists, Earnings Created by Domestic Tourists " were provided by Beijing Municipal Commission of Tourism Development.

16-2 按客源地分入境旅游者人数(1978-2012年)
NUMBER OF OVERSEA VISITOR ARRIVALS BY COUNTRY/REGION(1978-2012)

单位：万人次 (10000 person-times)

年 份 Year	入境旅游者人数 Number of International Tourists	港澳台同胞 Hongkong, Macao and Taiwan Chinese	外国人 Foreigner	#香港 Hongkong	#日本 Japan	#韩国 Korea	#美国 United States	#英国 United Kingdom	#法国 France	#德国 Germany	#俄罗斯 Russia
1978	18.7	3.3	15.4								
1979	25.2	4.1	21.1								
1980	28.6	5.8	21.7		6.0		3.7	1.3	0.9	0.9	
1981-1985	**295.4**	**47.5**	**233.0**		**68.3**		**47.1**	**10.1**	**9.2**	**10.6**	
1981	39.4	6.8	31.3		5.3		3.8	1.1	1.1	1.0	
1982	45.7	8.2	35.9		8.2		6.6	1.3	1.3	1.4	
1983	50.9	8.9	39.7		10.0		9.4	1.5	1.5	1.7	0.1
1984	65.7	10.0	52.1		17.2		12.5	2.3	2.1	2.5	0.1
1985	93.7	13.6	74.0		27.6		14.8	3.9	3.2	4.0	0.2
1986-1990	**492.0**	**117.7**	**357.0**		**110.0**		**63.8**	**18.1**	**15.7**	**22.4**	**3.8**
1986	99.0	15.8	79.0		25.5		14.7	4.1	3.1	4.6	0.3
1987	108.1	21.8	81.7		26.3		16.5	4.5	4.3	5.1	0.3
1988	120.4	28.8	86.5		27.8		16.7	4.2	4.2	5.4	0.7
1989	64.5	16.6	46.0		12.2		7.3	2.4	2.1	3.3	1.0
1990	100.0	34.7	63.8	11.4	18.2		8.6	2.9	2.0	4.0	1.5
1991-1995	**919.6**	**217.9**	**683.4**	**122.7**	**188.0**	**47.2**	**68.9**	**25.2**	**30.1**	**45.9**	**27.4**
1991	132.0	38.2	91.4	17.6	27.6	4.3	9.5	4.3	3.7	6.0	3.5
1992	174.8	51.2	120.5	24.6	37.6	5.6	12.3	4.4	6.6	9.4	5.1
1993	202.8	52.8	145.0	29.4	39.3	7.3	14.3	5.3	6.9	12.0	7.7
1994	203.0	39.4	160.0	25.7	41.1	12.7	15.4	5.4	6.7	9.7	4.9
1995	207.0	36.3	166.5	25.4	42.4	17.3	17.4	5.8	6.2	8.8	6.2
1996-2000	**1203.3**	**206.2**	**984.3**	**128.3**	**229.4**	**92.6**	**118.6**	**43.8**	**37.5**	**53.0**	**28.1**
1996	218.9	38.6	176.2	25.5	43.0	18.0	18.5	7.5	6.6	10.0	6.9
1997	229.8	40.3	186.9	26.3	43.0	19.4	21.7	9.0	6.5	9.1	6.5
1998	220.1	39.1	178.2	25.0	43.5	8.2	23.2	8.8	6.9	11.3	6.2
1999	252.4	44.1	205.0	26.5	45.6	19.2	24.1	8.8	7.9	10.5	4.6
2000	282.1	44.1	238.0	25.0	54.3	27.8	31.1	9.7	9.6	12.1	3.9
2001-2005	**1459.7**	**220.9**	**1238.8**	**133.2**	**233.7**	**182.9**	**173.8**	**57.8**	**51.7**	**56.9**	**33.2**
2001	285.8	45.9	239.9	26.9	50.7	32.7	33.1	11.1	10.2	12.3	4.9
2002	310.4	43.9	266.5	25.5	56.5	38.0	37.4	12.9	11.3	12.2	5.2
2003	185.1	32.4	152.7	21.7	29.2	24.5	19.4	8.1	5.5	6.3	5.2
2004	315.5	47.4	268.1	27.7	52.3	42.4	37.4	11.8	11.1	11.5	8.2
2005	362.9	51.3	311.6	31.4	45.0	45.3	46.5	13.9	13.6	14.6	9.7
2006-2010	**2107.4**	**286.2**	**1821.1**	**174.4**	**248.2**	**207.9**	**291.8**	**82.4**	**72.3**	**85.7**	**85.2**
2006	390.3	52.0	338.3	30.3	50.6	42.4	49.8	14.8	14.2	15.3	15.0
2007	435.5	52.9	382.6	31.3	58.8	44.4	60.3	17.0	16.4	17.5	18.3
2008	379.0	43.3	335.7	28.1	40.0	35.3	53.8	17.5	14.5	16.0	17.9
2009	412.5	69.6	342.9	44.4	46.2	35.2	57.9	16.3	12.9	16.8	15.0
2010	490.1	68.4	421.6	40.3	52.6	50.6	70.0	16.8	14.3	20.1	19.0
2011	520.4	73.0	447.4	43.4	51.0	53.4	78.9	18.8	15.0	22.2	20.5
2012	500.9	66.5	434.4	37.6	43.7	44.2	75.1	18.5	15.1	24.5	20.0

注：1．1980-1999年的入境旅游者人数由外国游客、港澳台游客、华侨三部分组成。
2．1990-1999年香港游客人数为香港、澳门合计。

Note: a) The "number of international tourists" in 1980-1999 consisted of foreign visitors, visitors from Hong Kong, Macao and Taiwan, and overseas Chinese.

b) Tourists from Hong Kong in 1990-1999 were total tourists from Hong Kong and Macao.

16-3 来京旅游者人数
NUMBER OF TOURISTS TO BEIJING

单位：万人次 (10000 person-times)

项　目	Item	2012	2011	2012年为2011年% 2012 as % of 2011
合　计	**Total**	**23134.6**	**21404.4**	**108.1**
国内旅游人数	**Number of Domestic Tourists**	**22633.7**	**20884.0**	**108.4**
外地来京旅游者人数	Number of Tourists to Beijing from Outside Beijing	13620.2	12818.0	106.3
市民在京游人数	Number of Beijing Citizen Touring in Beijing	9013.6	8066.0	111.7
入境旅游者人数	**Number of International Tourists**	**500.9**	**520.4**	**96.2**
港澳台同胞	Hongkong,Macao and Taiwan Chinese	66.5	73.0	91.1
中国香港	Hongkong,China	37.6	43.4	86.5
中国澳门	Macao,China	1.4	1.3	111.4
中国台湾	Taiwan,China	27.4	28.3	97.0
外国人	Foreigner	434.4	447.4	97.1
亚　洲	Asia	171.4	184.9	92.7
#日　本	Japan	43.7	51.0	85.7
韩　国	Korea	44.2	53.4	82.8
菲律宾	Philippines	2.6	3.4	77.6
印度尼西亚	Indonesia	6.7	6.3	106.5
马来西亚	Malaysia	16.1	13.9	116.6
新加坡	Singapore	15.4	14.4	107.4
泰　国	Thailand	6.4	6.2	103.6
印　度	India	7.1	7.4	95.8
蒙　古	Mongolia	7.3	7.6	96.4
美　洲	America	101.6	105.3	96.4
#美　国	United States	75.1	78.9	95.2
加拿大	Canada	17.2	18.2	94.5
欧　洲	Europe	130.7	128.8	101.5
#英　国	United Kingdom	18.5	18.8	98.5
法　国	France	15.1	15.0	100.4
德　国	Germany	24.5	22.2	110.3
意大利	Italy	8.2	7.6	108.4
西班牙	Spain	5.2	5.7	91.6
瑞　典	Sweden	5.8	6.2	94.1
瑞　士	Switzerland	3.6	2.7	131.2
俄罗斯	Russia	20.0	20.5	97.6
大洋洲	Oceania	19.8	17.8	111.4
#澳大利亚	Australia	16.9	15.3	110.6
新西兰	New Zealand	2.5	2.0	124.3
非　洲	Africa	8.6	6.8	125.5
其　他	Others	2.4	3.8	62.8

资料来源：表中“国内旅游人数”的相关资料来自北京市旅游发展委员会。
Source: Data related to "Number of Domestic Tourists" in the table were provided by Beijing Municipal Commission of Tourism Development.

16-4 在京旅游花费构成情况(2005-2012年)
COMPOSITION OF EXPENDITURES FOR TOURISM IN BEIJING (2005-2012)

单位：% (%)

项目	Item	2005	2006	2007	2008	2009	2010	2011	2012
入境旅游者花费构成	**Compositition of Expenditures for International Tourists**	**100.0**	**100.0**	**100.0**	**100.0**	**100.0**	**100.0**	**100.0**	**100.0**
长途交通费	Long-distance Transportation Expenses	35.3	30.0	29.0	31.1	37.4	28.1	26.4	28.0
民航	Air	30.9	29.6	24.4	25.3	27.1	19.8	20.5	22.3
铁路	Railway	1.1	0.3	3.0	3.6	5.5	5.3	3.4	3.3
公路	Highway	3.3	0.1	1.6	2.2	4.8	3.0	2.5	2.4
市内交通费	Local Transportation Expenses	1.1	1.7	2.6	2.4	2.7	3.4	3.5	3.5
住宿	Accommodation	17.3	32.0	16.9	16.4	14.5	14.4	15.5	16.5
餐饮	Food and Beverage	9.2	11.7	8.7	8.7	7.5	8.7	6.8	7.4
购物	Shopping	19.9	15.9	22.5	19.1	20.4	25.1	25.3	23.5
邮电通讯	Posts and Telecommunications	3.4	0.8	2.7	3.8	2.7	3.2	2.0	2.2
景区游览	Scenic Spots Sightseeing	4.7	2.3	4.2	4.8	3.9	4.7	4.2	5.0
文化娱乐	Culture and Entertainment	4.6	3.2	5.0	4.5	4.6	5.0	6.0	5.4
其他	Others	4.5	2.4	8.4	9.2	6.3	7.4	10.3	8.5
外地来京游客花费构成	**Compositition of Expenditures for Tourists from Outside Beijing**	**100.0**	**100.0**	**100.0**	**100.0**	**100.0**	**100.0**	**100.0**	**100.0**
长途交通费	Long-distance Transportation Expenses	12.8	15.1	16.3	15.4	12.9	12.8	13.5	15.5
民航	Air		8.0	9.2	9.1	6.6	6.0	6.2	7.7
铁路	Railway		6.1	6.4	4.5	1.3	5.8	6.9	7.5
公路	Highway		1.1	0.7	1.8	5.0	1.0	0.3	0.3
市内交通费	Local Transportation Expenses	5.7	5.1	5.5	5.6	4.9	5.0	4.5	4.0
住宿	Accommodation	17.2	14.9	17.3	15.1	17.7	19.6	20.0	19.8
餐饮	Food and Beverage	19.8	18.7	20.5	23.2	21.8	20.2	20.9	21.4
购物	Shopping	24.1	22.2	25.8	32.7	34.5	34.5	34.3	32.1
邮电通讯	Posts and Telecommunications	1.0	1.2	1.8	1.0	0.6	0.5	0.3	0.2
景区游览	Scenic Spots Sightseeing	9.1	9.5	7.2	4.5	6.1	6.2	5.7	6.1
文化娱乐	Culture and Entertainment	3.1	2.5	1.9	1.6	1.2	1.0	0.8	0.7
其他	Others	7.1	10.8	3.7	0.9	0.3	0.2	0.1	0.1

资料来源：北京市旅游发展委员会。
Source: Beijing Municipal Commission of Tourism Development.

16-5 旅游服务设施情况(1978-2012年)
STATISTICS ON TOURISM SERVICE FACILITIES (1978-2012)

年 份	饭店个数(个) Number of Hotels (unit)	五星 5-star	四星 4-star	三星 3-star	二星 2-star	一星 1-star	饭店客房数(万间) Number of Hotel Guest Rooms (10000 rooms)	旅行社家数(个) Number of Travel Agencies (unit)	#国际社 Int'l Agencies	A级及以上景区个数(个) Number of Scenic Spots at Grade-A and Above(unit)	5A	4A	3A	2A	1A
1978	11						0.39								
1979	13						0.44								
1980	20						0.49								
1981	35						0.69								
1982	39						1.00								
1983	41						1.03								
1984	50						1.30								
1985	63						1.66								
1986	80						2.10								
1987	97						2.40								
1988	96						2.80	30							
1989	101						3.50	77							
1990	122						3.95	77							
1991	213						4.40	69							
1992	226						5.20	69							
1993	226						5.20	55							
1994	175	14	20	32	72	37	5.40	297	113						
1995	197	15	25	43	79	35	5.90	310	125						
1996	204	15	25	46	82	36	6.10	349	128						
1997	248	16	26	60	109	37	6.80	350	130						
1998	258	16	32	65	113	32	7.00	380	135						
1999	268	17	32	71	117	31	7.20	419	144						
2000	409	21	34	132	176	46	8.40	456	150						
2001	506	21	43	154	230	58	9.30	490	160	47		17	4	22	4
2002	572	26	56	175	252	63	10.30	505	161	86		25	9	43	9
2003	614	30	62	195	267	60	10.90	530	165	93		28	9	46	10
2004	613	34	70	207	260	42	9.10	585	170	93		28	9	46	10
2005	652	36	79	224	267	46	10.97	714	196	124		36	26	50	12
2006	700	37	91	228	292	52	11.20	790	212	124		36	26	50	12
2007	806	42	114	257	338	55	13.00	844	239	154	4	41	35	54	20
2008	836	52	127	272	334	51	13.40	860	266	158	4	44	36	54	20
2009	757	54	129	268	269	37	12.95	888	265	179	4	55	53	51	16
2010	729	64	139	262	237	27	13.05	819		201	4	66	72	44	15
2011	598	63	127	207	181	20	11.64	919		211	6	63	80	46	16
2012	612	62	130	207	191	22	11.71	1021		203	8	64	78	40	13

注：1. 1993年及以前饭店数为涉外饭店口径,1994-2011年为星级饭店口径。

2. 1994-1996年国际旅行社为一、二类旅行社合计。从2010年起，旅行社不再按国际旅行社和国内旅行社分组。

资料来源：北京市旅游发展委员会。

Note: a) Number of hotels in 1993 and before was the number of foreign-related hotels,and in 1994-2011,the number of star-level hotels.

b) International travel agencies were the total number of travel agencies of categories I and II in 1994-1996.From 2010, statistics of travel agencies were no more grouped into international and domestic angencies.

Source: Beijing Municipal Commission of Tourism Development.

16-6 星级饭店接待及经营情况(1995-2012年)
RECEPTION AND OPERATION OF STAR-LEVEL HOTELS (1995-2012)

年 份 Year	企业个数(个) Number of Enterprises (unit)	接待住宿人数(万人次) Tourists Received (10000 person-time)	接待住宿人天数(万人天) Vistor-Days Received (10000 person-day)	出租率(%) Renting Rate (%)	平均房价(元/间天) Average Price (yuan/room.day)	营业收入(万元) Business Revenue (10000 yuan)	利润总额(万元) Total Profits (10000 yuan)	从业人员平均人数(人) Average Persons Employed (person)
1995	191	484.6	1843.4	67	491	1136136	188095	98535
1996-2000		**3168.1**	**10110.0**			**5388348**	**286868**	
1996	207	485.3	1691.6	63	483	1132827	153145	94352
1997	235	541.8	1801.4	59	463	1145884	104918	103255
1998	262	605.0	1867.7	55	397	1038991	-24239	104391
1999	263	681.5	1918.6	57	352	970907	22383	103827
2000	294	854.5	2830.6	61	394	1099739	30661	96115
2001-2005		**5931.5**	**14152.9**			**7243160**	**316031**	
2001	363	1038.5	3191.7	62	384	1202746	50466	105792
2002	390	1071.2	2437.6	62	392	1307094	27212	107091
2003	441	1007.4	2497.2	52	389	1227956	-33471	105994
2004	464	1270.8	2798.9	65	409	1654198	117541	107386
2005	594	1543.6	3227.5	62	425	1851166	154283	126817
2006-2010		**8761.5**	**17721.0**			**11799293**	**650440**	
2006	597	1578.5	3284.5	61	460	2055300	194460	126430
2007	638	1664.2	3403.6	60	494	2369964	219891	129523
2008	694	1566.1	3206.6	52	605	2504849	232746	130609
2009	815	1827.3	3652.8	49	430	2261411	-76121	134159
2010	729	2125.4	4173.5	56	450	2607769	79464	130050
2011	598	2111.1	4119.6	60	482	2853358	162374	128609
2012	612	2101.0	4085.2	60	523	3031116	179495	122379

注：1．表中企业个数为全市星级宾馆饭店数，其余指标1995-1999年为涉外饭店数据，2000年及以后为星级宾馆饭店数据。

2．2011年,北京市旅游发展委员会对全市星级饭店进行了重新评定，对未达标饭店取消星级(16-6和16-7表同此)。

Note: a) Number of Enterprises means the number of star-level hotels in Beijing. Other indicators covered foreign-related hotels for 1995-1999, and star-level hotels after 2000.

b) In 2011, Beijing Tourism Development Commission made a new evaluation for star-level hotels across the city, cancelling the star level for hotels not meeting the standard (This is the same in Tables 16-6 and 16-7).

16-7 星级饭店经营情况
STATISTICS FOR STAR-LEVEL HOTELS

项 目	Item	企业个数(个) Number of Enterprises (unit)		出租率(%) Renting Rate (%)		平均房价(元/间天) Average Price (yuan/room.day)	
		2012	2011	2012	2011	2012	2011
合 计	**Total**	**612**	**598**	**60**	**60**	**523**	**482**
四星、五星合计	**Hotels of 4 and 5 Star Grade**	**192**	**190**	**63**	**63**	**670**	**619**
五 星	5 Star	62	63	64	64	871	792
四 星	4 Star	130	127	63	63	500	473
一星至三星合计	**Hotels of 1 to 3 Star Grade**	**420**	**408**	**57**	**56**	**323**	**305**
三 星	3 Star	207	207	57	58	362	340
二 星	2 Star	191	181	56	52	239	219
一 星	1 Star	22	20	38	38	260	244

16-7 续表 continued

项 目	Item	营业收入(万元) Business Revenue (10000 yuan)		利润总额(万元) Total Profits (10000 yuan)		从业人员平均人数(人) Average Persons Employed (person)	
		2012	2011	2012	2011	2012	2011
合 计	**Total**	**3031116**	**2853358**	**179495**	**162374**	**122379**	**128609**
四星、五星合计	**Hotels of 4 and 5 Star Grade**	**2264272**	**2088082**	**186966**	**177118**	**79764**	**81406**
五 星	5 Star	1316408	1216507	133711	140834	39278	42330
四 星	4 Star	947864	871575	53255	36284	40486	39076
一星至三星合计	**Hotels of 1 to 3 Star Grade**	**766844**	**765276**	**-7471**	**-14744**	**42615**	**47203**
三 星	3 Star	618315	624862	-8730	-13485	33871	37416
二 星	2 Star	143089	133930	956	-1447	8337	9288
一 星	1 Star	5440	6484	303	187	407	499

16-8 星级饭店接待住宿者情况(按住宿者类别分)
STATISTICS FOR RECEPTION OF STAR GRADE HOTELS (GROUP BY TOURISTS)

项目	Item	2012 接待量 Reception	2012 构成(%) Composition (%)	2011 接待量 Reception	2011 构成(%) Composition (%)	2012年为2011年% 2012 as % of 2011
接待住宿人数 （万人次）	**Tourists Received (10000 person-times)**	**2101.0**	**100.0**	**2111.1**	**100.0**	**99.5**
国内住宿者	Domestic Tourists	1811.3	86.21	1799.6	85.25	100.6
外国人	Foreigners	255.8	12.17	272.6	12.91	93.8
香港同胞	Compatriots from Hongkong, China	20.7	0.99	24.6	1.17	84.2
澳门同胞	Compatriots from Macao, China	0.7	0.03	0.6	0.03	100.7
台湾同胞	Compatriots from Taiwan, China	12.6	0.60	13.6	0.65	92.5
接待住宿人天数（万人天）	**Person-day Received (10000 person-day)**	**4085.2**	**100.0**	**4119.6**	**100.0**	**99.2**
国内住宿者	Domestic Tourists	3407.6	83.41	3361.3	81.59	101.4
外国人	Foreigners	599.2	14.67	666.7	16.18	89.9
香港同胞	Compatriots from Hongkong, China	46.7	1.14	56.5	1.37	82.7
澳门同胞	Compatriots from Macao, China	1.7	0.04	2.0	0.05	82.1
台湾同胞	Compatriots from Taiwan, China	30.0	0.74	33.0	0.80	91.0

16-9 星级饭店接待住宿者情况(按饭店星级分)
STATISTICS FOR RECEPTION OF STAR GRADE HOTELS (GROUP BY STAR GRADE)

单位：万人次　　(10000 person-times)

项目	Item	2012 接待量 Reception	2012 构成(%) Composition (%)	2011 接待量 Reception	2011 构成(%) Composition (%)	2012年为2011年% 2012 as % of 2011
接待住宿人数	**Tourists Received**	**2101.0**	**100.0**	**2111.1**	**100.0**	**99.5**
五星级	5 Star	543.5	25.9	524.3	24.8	103.7
四星级	4 Star	633.5	30.2	589.0	27.9	107.6
三星级	3 Star	640.4	30.5	704.2	33.4	90.9
二星级	2 Star	270.1	12.9	278.3	13.2	97.1
一星级	1 Star	13.6	0.6	15.4	0.7	88.4
接待入境住宿人数	**Tourists Received From Abroad**	**289.7**	**100.0**	**311.5**	**100.0**	**93.0**
五星级	5 Star	158.8	54.8	167.7	53.9	94.7
四星级	4 Star	98.6	34.0	104.8	33.6	94.0
三星级	3 Star	23.8	8.2	29.0	9.3	82.2
二星级	2 Star	8.5	2.9	9.8	3.1	86.7
一星级	1 Star	0.1	0.04	0.2	0.1	71.2

16-10 旅行社接待及经营情况(1990-2012年)
RECEPTION AND OPERATION OF TRAVEL SERVICES (1990-2012)

年份 Year	企业个数(个) Number of Enterprises (unit)	外联(组团)人数(万人次) Overseas Persons Contacted(Organized) (10000 person-times)	接待人数(万人次) Tourists Received (10000 person-times)	国内居民出境人数(万人次) Persons of Chinese Outbound Visitors (10000 person-times)	营业收入(万元) Business Revenue (10000 yuan)	利润总额(万元) Total Profits (10000 yuan)	从业人员平均人数(人) Average Persons Employed (person)
1990		32.5	54.7				
1991-1995		**355.6**	**451.7**				
1991		53.3	69.1				
1992		61.2	100.7				
1993		71.3	103.6				
1994		84.1	91.0	1.0			
1995	100	85.7	87.4	1.2	290987.9	107654.6	
1996-2000		**487.1**	**417.5**	**37.9**	**2187374.9**	**106167.0**	
1996	105	88.0	78.6	2.7	351634.7	13520.8	
1997	110	87.3	76.0	3.8	386254.1	16009.6	
1998	131	85.0	69.0	6.6	387562.7	21319.9	
1999	120	103.1	92.9	11.1	485678.8	26572.0	
2000	127	123.7	101.0	13.7	576244.6	28744.7	6280
2001-2005		**986.2**	**919.6**	**185.4**	**4453919.0**	**51899.5**	
2001	140	143.4	130.1	21.9	700529.0	18682.5	8259
2002	151	179.4	176.3	28.5	823551.0	23362.0	9350
2003	147	80.2	82.4	31.9	553787.0	-11829.0	8382
2004	147	274.8	252.6	51.4	1059989.0	11444.0	7760
2005	147	308.4	278.2	51.7	1316063.0	10240.0	8752
2006-2010		**2036.3**	**1852.4**	**515.9**	**11530195.8**	**82083.6**	
2006	147	343.9	315.7	79.2	1610265.0	7012.0	8659
2007	189	424.1	377.9	100.2	2101874.5	28409.2	11597
2008	245	359.6	310.1	102.0	2166898.1	18121.6	14369
2009	265	370.6	306.6	84.9	2134058.8	5904.6	15262
2010	819	538.1	542.2	149.6	3517099.4	22636.2	21454
2011	919	593.9	552.3	184.3	4436713.3	20879.2	23871
2012	1021	684.5	519.1	272.5	5415692.9	35274.4	28022

注：1．本表2009年及以前为国际旅行社口径，从2010年起，调整为全部旅行社口径。
2．国内居民出境人数为旅行社组织出境游客的实际人次数，不重复统计。

Note: a) Figures in this table were for international travel service in and before 2009, and are for all travel services after 2010.
b) Number of Domestic Residents Going Abroad is the actual number of tourists going abroad who were organized by travel services. They were not calculated repeatedly.

16-11 旅行社外联(组团)及接待情况
STATISTICS ON OVERSEAS TOURISTS CONTACTED (ORGANIZED) AND RECEIVED BY TRAVEL SERVICES

项目	Item	2012	2011	2012年为2011年% 2012 as % of 2011
外联(组团)人数 (万人次)	**Overseas Persons Contacted(Organized) (10000 person-times)**	**684.5**	**593.9**	**115.3**
国内旅游者	Domestic Tourists	473.6	446.4	106.1
港澳同胞	Compatriots from Hongkong and Macao, China	6.5	9.1	71.6
台湾同胞	Compatriots from Taiwan, China	5.1	4.2	121.7
外国人	Foreigners	199.3	134.2	148.6
接待人数 (万人次)	**Tourists Received (10000 person-times)**	**519.1**	**552.3**	**94.0**
国内旅游者	Domestic Tourists	350.7	383.8	91.4
港澳同胞	Compatriots from Hongkong and Macao, China	7.9	12.3	64.1
台湾同胞	Compatriots from Taiwan, China	3.3	4.5	73.4
外国人	Foreigners	157.2	151.7	103.6
外联(组团)人天数 (万人天)	**Person-days of Contacted(Organized) (10000 person-day)**	**2979.0**	**2740.7**	**108.7**
国内旅游者	Domestic Tourists	1956.6	1858.4	105.3
港澳同胞	Compatriots from Hongkong and Macao, China	28.3	39.5	71.6
台湾同胞	Compatriots from Taiwan, China	28.2	23.5	120.0
外国人	Foreigners	965.9	819.3	117.9
接待人天数 (万人天)	**Person-day of Received (10000 person-day)**	**1975.8**	**2770.1**	**71.3**
国内旅游者	Domestic Tourists	1224.7	1359.7	90.1
港澳同胞	Compatriots from Hongkong and Macao, China	33.1	48.7	68.0
台湾同胞	Compatriots from Taiwan, China	17.9	24.4	73.4
外国人	Foreigners	700.1	1337.3	52.4

16-12 旅行社组织国内居民出境旅游情况
STATISTICS FOR DOMESTIC TOURISTS TRAVELLING ABROAD ORGANIZED BY TRAVEL SERVICES

项 目	Item	2012	2011	2012年为2011年% 2012 as % of 2011
国内居民出境人数 （万人次）	**Number of Domestic Residents Going Abroad (10000 person-times)**	**272.5**	**184.3**	**147.9**
前往国别及地区 （万人次）	**Travelling to Other Countries and Regions (10000 person-times)**			
#中国香港	Hongkong, China	30.7	26.4	116.0
中国澳门	Macao, China	12.7	10.6	119.1
中国台湾	Taiwan, China	14.6	9.2	159.1
泰 国	Thailand	40.5	20.9	194.1
新加坡	Singapore	23.6	14.3	165.7
马来西亚	Malaysia	17.6	11.7	150.5
菲律宾	Philippines	2.3	1.9	118.4
韩 国	Korea	28.4	17.9	158.9
日 本	Japan	21.4	11.5	186.5
澳大利亚	Australia	9.6	10.6	90.9
新西兰	New Zealand	5.8	6.1	95.0

注：1．本表统计范围为有特许经营出境旅游业务权的212家旅行社。
2．国内居民出境人数为旅行社组织出境游客的实际人次数，不重复统计。
3．前往国别及地区统计中，游客一次出境旅游去往多个国家及地区的，分别计入前往国家及地区。

Note: a) Figures in this table are for 212 travel services with right of franchised business of tour abroad.
b) Number of Domestic Residents Going Abroad is the actual number of tourists going abroad who were organized by travel services. They were not calculated repeatedly.
c) In the statistics for "Travelling to Other Countries and Regions", if a tourist went to several countries and regions, he/she was involved in each country and region.

16-13 旅行社经营情况
BUSINESS OF TRAVEL SERVICES

单位：万元 (10000 yuan)

项　　目	Item	2012	2011	2012年为2011年% 2012 as % of 2011
企业个数　(个)	Number of Enterprises　(unit)	1021	919	111.1
营业收入	Business Revenue	5415692.9	4436713.3	122.1
主营业务成本	Operating Cost	5064662.7	4143876.1	122.2
营业费用	Business Expenses	153000.6	125728.3	121.7
主营业务税金及附加	Operating Tax and Extra Charges	21098.7	17029.2	123.9
主营业务利润	Operating Profits	326800.4	271446.9	120.4
管理费用	Overhead Expenses	174599.4	146524.5	119.2
营业利润	Business Profits	26962.9	15197.7	177.4
利润总额	Total Profits	35274.4	20879.2	168.9
从业人员平均人数　(人)	Average Employed Persons　(person)	28022	23871	117.4

16-14 A级以上及重点旅游景区活动情况
STATISTICS ON KEY SIGHT SPOTS ABOVE GRADE A

项　　目	Item	2012	2011	2012年为2011年% 2012 as % of 2011
A级以上及重点旅游景区数　(个)	Number of key sight spots above grade A　(unit)	217	206	105.3
收入合计　(万元)	Total Revenue　(10000 yuan)	586395	552330	106.2
门票收入	Ticket Revenue	380993	367641	103.6
商品销售收入	Commodity Sales	15454	14136	109.3
其他收入	Other Revenue	189948	170553	111.4
接待人数　(万人次)	Tourists Received　(10000 person-times)	24276	24255	100.1
#入境旅游者人数	International Tourists	1055	1030	102.5

主要统计指标解释

入境旅游者 指来中国（大陆）观光、度假、探亲访友、就医疗养、购物、参加会议或从事经济、文化、体育、宗教活动，且在中国（大陆）的旅游住宿设施内至少停留一夜的外国人、港澳台同胞等游客。入境旅游者不包括以下人员：（1）应邀来华访问的政府部长以上官员及其随行人员；（2）外国驻华使领馆官员、外交人员以及随行的家庭服务人员和受赡养者；（3）常住我国一年以上的外国专家、留学生、记者、商务机构人员等；（4）乘坐国际航班过境不需要通过护照检查进入我国口岸的中转旅客；(5) 边境地区往来的边民；（6）回大陆定居的港澳台同胞。

国内旅游者 指中国（大陆）居民离开惯常居住地在境内其他地方的旅游住宿设施内至少停留一夜，最长不超过十二个月的国内游客。

旅游外汇收入 入境游客在中国（大陆）境内旅行、游览过程中用于交通、参观游览、住宿、餐饮、购物、娱乐等全部花费。

国内旅游收入 指国内游客在国内旅行、游览过程中用于交通、参观游览、住宿、餐饮、购物、娱乐等全部花费。

外联（组团）入境旅游者人数 指报告期内旅行社自组外联的入境旅游者人数，反映旅行社对外招徕的能力。旅行社按以下要求统计外联人数：入境游客不论其停留时间多少、旅游线路长短，只统计一次；旅行社只统计本社自主外联团的实到人数，不包括非本社外联、仅由本社接受委托办理签证的人数。

接待入境旅游者人数 指报告期内本旅行社派地陪接待的入境人数。

出境旅游总人数 指中国（大陆）公民因公或因私出境前往其他国家、中国香港特别行政区、澳门特别行政区和台湾省观光、度假、探亲访友、就医疗养、购物、参加会议或从事经济、文化、体育、宗教活动的人数。统计时，出境游客按每出境一次统计1人次。

Explanatory Notes on Main Statistical Indicators

International Tourists refer to tourists from foreign countries, Hong Kong, Macao and Taiwan to (mainland of) China for sightseeing, holiday, visiting relatives and friends, medical service and recuperation, shopping, conferences, or economic, cultural, sports and religious activities, and staying in a tour accommodation facility in (mainland of) China for at least one night. They do not include: (1) officials above the rank of governmental ministers, and their accompanying persons who visit China upon invitation; (2) officials in foreign embassies and consulates in Beijing, diplomatic agents, and their accompanying family service personnel and dependents; (3) foreign experts, foreign students, reporters, and personnel in business institutions who have been in China for more than one year; (4) transit passengers via China by international flights without passport checking; (5) people living on the frontier who pass through borders; (6) compatriots from Hong Kong, Macao and Taiwan who settle down in mainland of China.

Domestic Tourists refer to domestic visitors as residents in (mainland of) China who leave their regular dwelling place to stay at least one night, at most 12 months in a travel accommodation facility in other places.

Tourism Foreign Exchange Earnings means the total spending of international tourists on traffic, tour, accommodation, food and drink, shopping, entertainment and so on during their tour and travel in (mainland of) China.

Earnings Created by Domestic Tourists means the total spending of domestic tourists on traffic, tour, accommodation, food and drink, shopping, entertainment and so on during their tour and travel in China.

Number of International Tourists Organized by Travel Services means the number of international tourists organized by travel services in the reporting period. It shows the capacity of travel services in soliciting international tourists; travel services shall count the tourists so organized: an international tourist is regarded as one visit regardless of the duration and distance of tour route; only the actual tourists organized by a travel service are included. Those organized by other travel services who execute visa formalities through the travel service on commission basis are not included.

Number of International Tourists Received means the number of international tourists received by local guides dispatched by a travel service.

Total Number of Tourists Going Abroad means the number of citizens from (mainland of) China who visit other countries, Hong Kong Special Administrative Area of PRC, Macao Special Administrative Area of PRC, and Taiwan for sightseeing, holiday, visiting relatives and friends, medical service and recuperation, shopping, conferences, or economic, cultural, sports and religious activities for official or private purpose. One visit is calculated as one person-time.

17

北京统计年鉴2013　　BEIJING STATISTICAL YEARBOOK

金融和保险
BANKING AND INSURANCE

简要说明

一、本章资料的主要内容

本章反映北京地区金融业发展情况。主要包括以下四个部分：

1. 金融机构信贷收支情况；
2. 证券市场交易情况；
3. 保险业务情况；
4. 上市公司基本情况。

二、本章资料的数据来源

1. 信贷收支数据统计范围包括中国人民银行营业管理部、政策性银行北京分行、各国有商业银行北京市分行、各股份制商业银行在京营业机构、北京银行、北京农村商业银行、信托投资公司、财务公司、外资银行北京市分行和村镇银行。资料来源于中国人民银行营业管理部。

2. 证券市场交易量数据来源于北京市统计局。

3. 银行、保险系统机构及人员数据来源于北京市统计局。

4. 反映保险业务情况的资料来源于中国保险监督管理委员会北京监管局。

5. 反映上市公司基本情况的数据来源于中国证券监督管理委员会北京证监局。

Brief Introduction

I. Main Content

This chapter reflects the development of situation of finance in Beijing, consisting of four parts:

1. Credit income and payment in financial institutions;
2. Transactions in securities market;
3. Insurance business;
4. Basic information on listed companies.

II. Source of Data

1. Figures of credit income and payment are for Banking Management Department of the People's Bank of China, Beijing branches of policy banks, Beijing branches of state-owned commercial banks, banking departments of joint-stock commercial banks in Beijing, Bank of Beijing, Beijing Rural Commercial Bank, trust investment companies, financial companies, Beijing branches of foreign-funded banks, and village and town banks. Data are from the Banking Management Department of the People's Bank of China.

2. Data of transactions in securities market are from Beijing Municipal Bureau of Statistics.

3. Data of banks, insurance institutions and personnel are from Beijing Municipal Bureau of Statistics.

4. Data about insurance business are from Beijing Regulatory Bureau of China Insurance Regulatory Commission.

5. Data about basic information of listed companies are from Beijing Securities Regulatory Bureau of China Securities Regulatory Commission.

17-1 北京市金融机构(含外资)存贷款余额(2000-2012年)
DEPOSIT AND LOAN BALANCE OF FINANCIAL INSTITUTIONS (INCLUDE FOREIGN BANKS)(2000-2012)

单位: 亿元 (100 million yuan)

项　　目	Item	2000	2001	2002	2003	2004	2005
金融机构本外币存款余额	**Balance of Savings Deposit in Standard and Foreign Currencies in Financial Institutions**	**11526.0**	**14109.2**	**17438.4**	**20476.0**	**23781.3**	**28969.9**
#储蓄存款	Savings Deposit		4599.8	5559.5	6441.4	7154.3	8315.8
定　期	Fixed			3884.1	4361.9	4758.4	5586.8
活　期	Current			1675.4	2079.5	2395.9	2729.0
#中资金融机构	Chinese Financial Institutions						
人民币	RMB	9759.8	12223.4	15392.7	18321.9	21625.9	26731.3
#储蓄存款	Savings Deposit	2923.2	3536.3	4389.7	5293.5	6122.3	7477.6
定　期	Fixed	2096.1	2404.3	2875.8	3413.0	3966.1	4957.0
活　期	Current	827.1	1132.0	1513.9	1880.5	2156.2	2520.6
外　汇(亿美元)	Foreign Exchange(USD 100 million)	205.6	219.8	238.9	250.9	248.1	256.4
外资银行	Foreign-funded Financial Bank						
人民币	RMB						54.6
外　汇(亿美元)	Foreign Exchange(USD 100 million)	…	7.3	8.3	9.4	12.3	14.2
金融机构本外币贷款余额	**Balance of Loan in Standard and Foreign Currencies in Financial Institutions**	**6407.9**	**7612.2**	**9704.3**	**12057.7**	**13577.7**	**15335.5**
#中资金融机构	Chinese Financial Institutions						
人民币	RMB	6008.2	7202.9	9230.8	11314.7	12600.2	13792.2
外　汇(亿美元)	Foreign Exchange (USD 100 million)	27.7	37.4	44.9	68.8	86.0	149.2
外资银行	Foreign-funded Financial Bank						
人民币	RMB						42.3
外　汇(亿美元)	Foreign Exchange(USD 100 million)	9.0	10.8	12.1	20.9	32.0	36.8

资料来源：中国人民银行营业管理部。
Source: Banking Management Department of People's Bank of China.

17-1 续表 continued

单位：亿元 (100 million yuan)

项 目	Item	2006	2007	2008	2009	2010	2011	2012
金融机构本外币存款余额	**Balance of Savings Deposit in Standard and Foreign Currencies in Financial Institutions**	**33793.3**	**37700.3**	**43980.7**	**56960.1**	**66584.6**	**75001.9**	**84837.3**
#储蓄存款	Savings Deposit	9515.0	9743.5	12538.1	15329.2	17585.2	19690.6	22298.6
定 期	Fixed	6265.0	6029.4	8440.9	9960.8	11052.0		
活 期	Current	3250.0	3714.1	4097.3	5368.3	6533.2		
#中资金融机构	Chinese Financial Institutions							
人民币	RMB	31179.2	35014.1	41500.0	53428.8	63025.2	70985.1	79620.6
#储蓄存款	Savings Deposit	8703.3	9113.5	11869.9	14566.3	16876.3	18924.6	21419.3
定 期	Fixed	5704.0	5646.4	7997.1	9466.4	10604.5		
活 期	Current	2999.3	3467.1	3872.8	5099.9	6271.8		
外 汇(亿美元)	Foreign Exchange(USD 100 million)	295.2	283.8	233.3	348.0	282.7	322.8	476.5
外资银行	Foreign-funded Financial Bank							
人民币	RMB	134.5	355.6	607.5	846.6	1428.7	1670.3	1769.1
外 汇(亿美元)	Foreign Exchange(USD 100 million)	22.4	35.2	40.8	45.2	39.0	49.6	72.0
金融机构本外币贷款余额	**Balance of Loan in Standard and Foreign Currencies in Financial Institutions**	**18131.6**	**19861.5**	**23010.7**	**31052.9**	**36479.6**	**39660.5**	**43189.5**
#中资金融机构	Chinese Financial Institutions							
人民币	RMB	15486.9	17360.2	19431.1	24805.1	28748.1	32434.6	35441.7
外 汇(亿美元)	Foreign Exchange (USD 100 million)	274.7	231.9	399.4	783.0	997.2	948.4	1017.9
外资银行	Foreign-funded Financial Bank							
人民币	RMB	145.8	452.3	554.0	616.7	815.6	932.5	999.6
外 汇(亿美元)	Foreign Exchange(USD 100 million)	45.3	48.6	43.3	41.7	47.1	50.4	55.7

资料来源：中国人民银行营业管理部。
Source: Banking Management Department of People's Bank of China.

17-2 北京市中资金融机构存贷款余额(1978-2012年)
DEPOSIT AND LOAN BALANCE OF CHINA-FUNDED FINANCIAL INSTITUTIONS(1978-2012)

单位：亿元 (100 million yuan)

年份 Year	中资金融机构本外币存款 Balance of Savings Deposit in Standard Foreign Currencies in Chinese Financial Institutions	#单位存款 Deposits by Enterprises	#储蓄存款 Savings Deposit	#人民币存款 RMB	#储蓄存款 Savings Deposit	定期 Fixed	活期 Current
1978				114.7	9.3	7.8	1.5
1979				139.1	11.1	9.2	1.9
1980				168.0	14.4	11.5	2.9
1981				220.5	17.4	14.1	3.3
1982				279.2	21.8	17.7	4.1
1983				321.3	29.8	23.9	5.9
1984				375.5	38.8	30.7	8.1
1985				411.0	51.7	40.5	11.2
1986				508.8	68.6	54.8	13.8
1987				610.8	92.9	74.6	18.3
1988				609.9	111.6	91.6	20.0
1989				717.6	162.0	141.2	20.8
1990				893.9	226.6	201.6	25.0
1991				1244.1	299.2	268.3	30.9
1992				1528.3	389.8	342.7	47.1
1993				1873.1	562.5	489.5	73.0
1994				2677.3	853.2	742.6	110.6
1995				3527.2	1254.0	1109.1	144.9
1996				4378.9	1707.0	1501.7	205.3
1997				5228.0	1975.3	1682.5	292.8
1998				6666.8	2287.2	1851.7	435.5
1999				8267.2	2680.7	2060.5	620.2
2000				9759.8	2923.2	2096.1	827.1
2001	14042.1			12223.4	3536.3	2404.3	1132.0
2002	17369.9	9328.0	5555.2	15392.7	4389.7	2875.8	1513.9
2003	20398.2	10834.2	6432.9	18321.9	5293.5	3413.0	1880.5
2004	23679.3	13183.8	7137.8	21625.9	6122.3	3966.1	2156.2
2005	28800.9	16234.3	8297.4	26731.3	7477.6	4957.0	2520.6
2006	33484.1	18968.0	9472.0	31179.2	8703.3	5704.0	2999.3
2007	37087.5	21645.5	9639.7	35014.1	9113.5	5646.4	3467.1
2008	43094.4	23686.3	12383.6	41500.0	11869.9	7997.1	3872.8
2009	55804.8	29632.0	15149.0	53428.8	14566.3	9466.4	5099.9
2010	64897.6	30989.1	17398.8	63025.2	16876.3	10604.5	6271.8
2011	73018.9	45309.0	19420.6	70985.1	18924.6		
2012	82615.9	49671.1	21988.4	79620.6	21419.3		

注：1．表中1990年及以前为银行数据，1991年及以后为中资金融机构数据。
2．2011年开始人民银行系统不再提供定期、活期储蓄存款以及信托存贷款数据。
资料来源：中国人民银行营业管理部。

Note: a) Figures in and before 1990 were for banks. Figures in and after 1991 were for China-funded financial institutions.
b) From 2011, the people's bank system do not provide data on fixed, current savings deposit, trust deposits and loans any longer.
Source: Banking Management Department of People's Bank of China.

17-2 续表 continued

单位：亿元 (100 million yuan)

年 份 Year	中资金融机构本外币贷款 Balance of Loan in Standard and Foreign Currencies in China-funded Financial Institutions	#人民币贷款 RMB	#中长期贷款 Medium-term &Long-term Loans	#短期贷款 Short-term Loans
1978		53.9		
1979		74.2		
1980		87.3		
1981		91.3		
1982		109.1		
1983		149.5		
1984		174.3		
1985		249.8		
1986		299.2		
1987		346.1		
1988		415.7		
1989		487.1		
1990		573.1		
1991		735.8		
1992		894.7		
1993		1128.1		
1994		1429.0		
1995		1779.1		
1996		2082.8		
1997		2720.7		
1998		3326.6		
1999		4007.8		
2000		6008.2		
2001	7514.9	7202.9		
2002	9602.6	9230.8	4985.0	3760.9
2003	11884.4	11314.7	6281.0	4510.3
2004	13312.3	12600.2	7387.4	4906.1
2005	14996.6	13792.2	8473.4	5039.6
2006	17631.7	15486.9	10929.9	5202.4
2007	19053.9	17360.2	11910.8	6042.1
2008	22160.5	19431.1	14285.0	6712.8
2009	30151.6	24805.1	20759.3	7146.7
2010	35352.0	28748.1	25718.3	8062.2
2011	38410.3	32434.6	24439.5	10595.5
2012	41839.8	35441.7	25825.7	12153.1

17-3 北京市金融机构(含外资)本外币信贷收支表
DEPOSITS AND LOANS OF FINANCIAL INSTITUTIONS (INCLUDE FOREIGN BANKS)

单位：万元，汇率：6.2855　　(10000 yuan , exchange rate 6.2855)

项目	Item	余额 Balance 2012	2011	2012年为2011% 2012 as % of 2011	比年初增减额(+、-) Increase or Decrease than Year-beginning 2012	2011
各项存款	**Total Deposits**	**848373099**	**750019148**	**113.1**	**98438114**	**86212967**
单位存款	Deposits by Enterprises	515808083	470157622	109.7	44305791	39428130
#活期存款	Current Deposits	182988565	179322426	102.0	6500816	9886074
定期存款	Fixed Deposits	191436352	170417816	112.3	21018639	14916482
个人存款	Personal Deposits	250463256	213918119	117.1	36545139	36939563
#储蓄存款	Savings Deposit	222986186	196905778	113.2	26080411	22652646
财政性存款	Fiscal Deposits	13618685	10703077	127.2	2915584	54840
临时性存款	Provisional Deposits	985822	1029183	95.8	-43362	-595835
委托存款	Entrusted Deposits	5287999	3412057	155.0	1875969	1928146
其他存款	Other Deposits	62209254	50799090	122.5	12838993	8458122
各项贷款	**Total Loans**	**431895276**	**396605082**	**108.9**	**35080493**	**33691815**
境内贷款	Domestic Loans	403437235	369580546	109.2	33765350	42294613
短期贷款	Short-term Loans	128081061	111990543	114.4	16384672	20829674
中长期贷款	Medium-term&Long-term Loans	263335138	248862617	105.8	14087028	22109725
融资租赁	Financial Lease	504856	467883	107.9	36973	222431
票据融资	Notes Financing	11457861	8186888	140.0	3270973	-863149
各项垫款	Advances	58319	72616	80.3	-14296	-4068
境外贷款	Over Loans	28458041	27024536	105.3	1315144	-8602798

资料来源：中国人民银行营业管理部。
Source: Banking Management Department of People's Bank of China.

17-4 银行、保险系统机构及人员(2012年)
INSTITUTIONS AND PERSONNEL OF BANK AND INSURANCE SYSTEM (2012)

项目	Item	银行系统 Bank System 机构(个) Institution(unit)	人员(人) Personnel(person)	保险系统 Insurance System 机构(个) Institution(unit)	人员(人) Personnel(person)
全市	**Total**	**3437**	**161279**	**602**	**111884**
城区	Urban Districts	701	90898	161	38575
郊区	Suburban Districts	2607	68230	417	71067
各县	Counties	129	2151	24	2242

注：1. 本表口径为在北京地区经营的银行、保险公司的总行(总公司)、分行(分公司)及所属分支机构。
2. 保险系统人员构成中含营销员。

Note: a) Figures in this table cover the headquarters(head offices), branches banks (branch companies) and subsidiaries of banks and insurance companies operating in Beijing.
b) Personnel of Insurance System included marketing personnel.

17-5 证券市场交易量情况(1994-2012年)
SECURITIES MARKET TRADING VOLUME (1994-2012)

单位: 亿元 (100 million yuan)

年份 Year	证券市场交易量 Trading Volume of Securities Market	股票交易 Treasury Bonds	基金交易 Fund Transaction	债券交易 Securities Transaction	权证交易 Warrant Transaction	其他交易 Other Transaction	股市开户数(万户) Tatal Investors (10000 household)
1994	183.26	135.51		47.75			
1995	1619.04	520.48		152.31		946.25	
1996	5224.77	2900.63		2324.06		0.07	
1997	7934.42	3900.93		3844.82		188.67	
1998	10241.50	3426.37	187.02	6435.43		192.68	
1999	10694.46	5268.19	341.74	5005.52		79.01	88.93
2000	14456.98	9136.52	346.02	4825.91		148.53	115.18
2001	12596.50	5339.61	400.61	6729.69		126.60	148.95
2002	12565.91	3788.22	485.77	8216.53		75.39	154.99
2003	23369.83	5041.40	110.45	18048.37		169.60	162.39
2004	18512.92	7247.72	78.94	10928.92		257.33	166.21
2005	9322.49	4343.65	91.30	4567.28		320.26	169.83
2006	19557.06	14851.55	298.27	2075.20		2332.04	189.37
2007	97978.66	77487.83	1534.96	2060.09	9756.74	7139.04	314.92
2008	62773.56	46231.27	1389.37	4052.52	9587.51	1512.89	373.62
2009	92148.02	78339.50	2253.54	1791.32	8823.82	939.84	426.10
2010	87575.38	79843.07	1714.94	3384.28	2287.76	345.33	475.14
2011	79103.13	61743.17	1494.81	15275.31	437.86	151.98	521.53
2012	85412.95	44993.38	2355.87	37388.61		675.07	551.50

17-6 上市公司基本情况(1993-2012年)
LISTED COMPANIES (1993-2012)

年份 Year	境内上市公司 (家) Companies Listed at Home (unit)	股票总发行股本 (万股) Total Issued Capital (10000 Shares)	股票首发数量 (万股) Initial Issued Shares (10000 Shares)	股票筹资额 (万元) Amount of Fund Raised by Stocks (10000 yuan)
1993	2	10814	1900	39780
1994	6	90121	19000	113737
1995	6			27048
1996-2000		**1542276**	**396463**	**4060434**
1996	13	99575	18013	111254
1997	27	237503	68700	546787
1998	34	195512	52750	518179
1999	45	489880	109000	767286
2000	58	519806	148000	2116928
2001-2005		**10774652**	**755200**	**4664942**
2001	65	9355826	342500	1964590
2002	69	94199	23800	317099
2003	76	1259132	367600	1843666
2004	83	65495	21300	508452
2005	83			31135
2006-2010		**160295150**	**11318172**	**86820080**
2006	91	63036411	2667911	11343486
2007	103	49890423	2305303	27326555
2008	109	3376142	698853	8705788
2009	126	6626871	2048990	15081487
2010	164	37365303	3597115	24362764
2011	194	2131793	440920	12968165
2012	217	1934216	214252	19693834

资料来源：中国证券监督管理委员会北京证监局。
Source: Beijing Regulatory Bureau of China Securities Regulatory Commission.

17-7 保险业务情况(1997-2012年)
INSURANCE BUSINESS (1997-2012)

单位：亿元 (100 million yuan)

年份 Year	原保险保费收入 Premiums Income	人身险 Personal Insurance	财产险 Property Insurance	赔付支出 Indemnity Payment	人身险 Personal Insurance	财产险 Property Insurance
1997	102.5					
1998	88.6					
1999	91.8			29.9		
2000	93.4			28.4		
2001	141.3			32.0		
2002	234.1			46.9		
2003	282.5			48.0		
2004	279.3			55.3		
2005	498.2			75.4		
2006	411.5	327.2	84.4	84.0	45.1	38.9
2007	498.1	386.3	111.8	135.4	85.7	49.7
2008	585.9	451.8	134.1	188.9	121.0	67.9
2009	697.6	533.2	164.4	196.0	110.6	85.4
2010	966.5	754.2	212.3	199.7	105.9	93.7
2011	820.9	588.4	232.6	232.8	113.8	119.0
2012	923.1	656.1	267.0	286.2	133.9	152.3

资料来源：中国保险监督管理委员会北京监管局。
Source: Beijing Regulatory Bureau of China Insurance Regulatory Commission.

17-8 保险业务情况
STATISTICS FOR INSURANCE

单位：亿元 (100 million yuan)

项　目	Item	原保险保费收入 Premiums Income		赔付支出 Indemnity Payment	
		2012	2011	2012	2011
合　计	**Total**	**923.1**	**820.9**	**286.2**	**232.8**
人身险业务小计	**Subtotal of Personal Insurance**	**656.1**	**588.4**	**133.9**	**113.8**
人寿保险	Life Insurance	554.3	505.8	100.2	84.4
非分红产品	Non-melon-cutting Products	46.6	38.7	24.0	16.7
分红产品	Melon-Cutting Products	503.6	463.2	75.3	66.7
投资连接产品	Investment Products	0.5	0.5	0.2	0.4
万能产品	Omnipotence Products	3.6	3.4	0.6	0.6
意外伤害保险	Accidental Injury Insurance	21.7	16.2	5.0	3.9
健康保险	Health Insurance	80.1	66.3	28.7	25.5
财产险业务小计	**Subtotal of Property Insurance**	**267.0**	**232.6**	**152.3**	**119.0**
#企业财产保险	Enterprise Property Insurance	30.2	28.8	12.3	8.0
家庭财产保险	Family Property Insurance	0.6	0.5	0.3	0.1
机动车辆及第三者责任保险	Motor Vehicle and Third-Party Responsibility	183.0	158.7	119.6	97.0
货物运输保险	Freight Transport Insurance	12.6	13.2	4.0	2.8
责任保险	Liability Insurance	15.2	10.6	4.4	3.4
工程险	Engineering Insurance	5.6	5.7	2.5	3.5

资料来源：中国保险监督管理委员会北京监管局。
Source: Beijing Regulatory Bureau of China Insurance Regulatory Commission.

主要统计指标解释

存款 企业、机关、团体或居民根据可以收回的原则，把货币资金存入银行或其他信用机构保管并取得一定利息的一种信用活动形式。根据存款对象的不同可划分为企业存款、财政存款、机关团体存款、储蓄存款、农业存款等科目。它是银行信贷资金的主要来源。

贷款 银行或其他信用机构根据必须归还的原则，按一定利率，为企业、个人等提供资金的一种信用活动形式。我国银行贷款分为短期贷款、中长期贷款、委托及信托类贷款、其他类贷款等。

原保险保费收入 是指保险企业确认的原保险合同保费收入。是投保人根据保险合同的有关规定，为被保险人取得因约定危险事故发生所造成的经济损失补偿（或给付）权利，付给保险人的代价。包括财产险和人身险收入。

保险赔付支出 公司按保险合同约定支付给被保险人（或受益人）的赔款、保险金、给付等。包括赔款支出、死伤医疗给付、满期给付和年金给付。

股票交易额 指投资者在市场买卖各种股票的总金额。包括A股、B股。不含认购新股及认购中签。

基金交易额 指投资者在市场买卖各种基金的总金额。包括封闭式基金、开放式基金等。

债券交易额 指投资者在市场买卖各种债券的总金额。包括债券现货、债券回购。

债券现货交易额 指投资者在市场买卖各种债券现货的总金额。包括国债、金融债、企业债、可转债等。

债券回购额 指投资者在市场债券回购的总金额。包括国债回购、企业债回购等。回购交易只记录单边交易额。

权证交易额 指投资者在市场买卖各种权证的总金额。

Explanatory Notes on Main Statistical Indicators

Deposit is a form of credit activity that enterprises, public institutions, groups or residents saves their monetary fund, on reclaimable basis, in banks or other credit institutions and receive certain interest. In terms of target of deposit, it consists of enterprise deposit, fiscal deposit, government agency deposit, savings deposit, agricultural deposit and so on. It serves as a main source of credit funds in banks.

Loan is a form of credit activity that banks or other credit institutions provide funds for enterprise and individuals at a given interest rate, which must be repaid. In China, bank loans are composed of short-term loan, medium & long-term loan, commission and trust loan, and other loan.

Premium Income means the income of insurance premium of confirmed original insurance contracts in insurance companies. It is the cost of police holder paid to the insurer for the right to receive compensation (claim settlement) for any economic loss caused by agreed dangerous accidents pursuant to relevant provisions in the insurance contract. It includes property insurance and person insurance incomes.

Indemnity Payment means any indemnity, insurance money, and claim settlement, etc. paid by the insurance company to the insurant (beneficiary) as agreed in the insurance contract. It consists of payment of indemnity, claim settlement for medical costs for death and injury, maturity money and annuity payment.

Shares Transaction Amount means the total amount of shares traded by investors in market. This includes A shares and B shares, excluding the amount of IPO subscription and subscription lot winning.

Fund Transaction Amount means the total amount of funds traded by investors in market, including closed and open fund, etc.

Bonds Transaction Amount means the total amount of bonds traded by investors in market, including stock bonds and bonds repurchase.

Bonds Stock Transaction Amount means the total amount of stock bonds traded by investors in market, including national bonds, financial bonds, enterprise bonds and convertible bonds, etc.

Bonds Repurchase Amount means the total amount of bonds repurchased by investors in market. It includes the repurchase of national bonds and enterprise bonds. Only unilateral transaction amount is involved in the repurchase amount.

Warrants Transaction Amount means the total amount of warrants traded by investors in market.

18

教育、文化
EDUCATION AND CULTURE

简要说明

一、教育部分的主要内容和资料来源

教育统计资料包括高等教育（研究生教育、普通本专科教育、成人本专科、其他各类高等学历教育）、中等教育(高中阶段、初中阶段)、小学教育、学前教育、特殊教育(盲聋哑和弱智儿童学校等)、工读学校等资料。主要指标包括学校数、在校学生数、招生数、毕业生数、教职工数、专任教师数和教育收支情况等。

教育统计资料由北京市教育委员会提供。

二、文化部分的主要内容和资料来源

文化部分主要包括专业艺术剧团、公共图书馆、博物馆、文化馆、档案馆、文化站、广播、电影、电视以及新闻等文化单位的机构、人员、经费和业务活动情况。

文化部分数据中，艺术事业、图书馆事业和群众文化事业的资料主要来自北京市文化局；档案馆资料来自北京市档案局；文物资料来自北京市文物局；广播、电影和电视资料来自北京市广播电影电视局及国家广播电影电视总局。

Brief Introduction

I. Main Content and Source of Data for the Part of Education

Educational statistics include those for higher education (postgraduate education, undergraduate and junior college education, undergraduate and junior college education for adults, and other kinds of higher-diploma education); middle education (senior high school, junior high school); primary education; preschool education; special education (schools for blinds, deaf and mutes, and weak-intelligence children, etc.); work-study schools for delinquent children. Main indicators include the number of schools, number of enrolled students, number of new students, number of faculty, number of full-time teachers, and educational income and payment, etc.

Educational data were provided by Beijing Municipal Commission of Education.

II. Main Content and Source of Data for the Part of Culture

Cultural statistics include the number, personnel, funds, and activities of professional artistic performance groups, artistic performance sites, public libraries, museums, cultural centers, archives, radio, film, television and press organizations.

Cultural data were processed with statistic statements of departments. Data of art, libraries, and mass culture are from Beijing Municipal Bureau of Culture; data of archives are from Beijing Municipal Bureau of Archives; cultural relics data are from Beijing Municipal Administration of Cultural Heritage; radio, film and television data are from Beijing Municipal Bureau of Radio, Film, and Television and the National Administration for Radio, Film, and Television.

18-1 教育基本情况(1978-2012年)
BASIC STATISTICS ON EDUCATION (1978-2012)

年份 Year	全市各类学校数(个) Total Number of Various Schools (unit)	#普通高等学校 Colleges & Universities	#普通中等学校 Middle Schools	#高中 Senior Middle Schools	#小学 Primary Schools	全市各类学校在校学生数(人) Enrolled Students in Various Schools (person)	#普通高等学校 Colleges & Universities	#普通中等学校 Middle Schools	#高中 Senior Middle Schools	#小学 Primary Schools
1978		35			4666		48618		415612	937336
1979		48			4534		55073		299974	968723
1980		50			4485		83032		312188	951763
1981		51			4445		98044		175180	900350
1982		51			4381		93878		92401	854516
1983		54			4269		90894		88657	838078
1984		57			4168		102962		110916	763204
1985		61			4059		122791		119876	733605
1986		66			3995		129647		109862	749101
1987		67			3875		136694		109023	777982
1988		67			3793		145134		108106	850577
1989		67			3703		141625		110745	934696
1990		67			3611		139646		100669	995831
1991	8496	67	1168	282	3482	2142085	136940	565357	93728	1013268
1992	8052	67	1150	279	3306	2194268	139978	617847	82894	1001762
1993	7789	66	1145	280	3190	2266932	158906	679821	78261	1022166
1994	7574	67	1150	280	3035	2348406	175203	758310	86584	1024503
1995	7158	65	1170	286	2867	2380096	182173	834903	102522	1007301
1996	7121	65	1189	296	2780	2388002	189953	881912	118476	999740
1997	6858	65	1181	288	2696	2361438	195842	887644	133461	977323
1998	6456	63	1190	282	2511	2325043	212984	895042	145966	919531
1999	5807	64	1182	275	2352	2297673	234033	931029	161473	836655
2000	5458	59	1159	302	2169	2299433	282585	972930	179002	743109
2001	4873	61	1111	289	1960	2297107	340284	988985	194283	664443
2002	4447	62	998	325	1824	2294947	398573	984117	220667	594241
2003	4158	74	977	329	1652	2299416	458898	968035	250959	546530
2004	3971	77	945	338	1504	2291594	500245	919178	274803	516042
2005	3782	79	917	335	1403	2264004	536724	859132	278358	494482
2006	3751	82	888	335	1310	2910228	554702	799074	259414	473275
2007	3593	83	863	328	1235	3195763	567875	839038	243818	666617
2008	3508	82	838	325	1202	3208704	575639	782866	219163	659500
2009	3425	88	804	305	1160	3214354	577154	740396	203477	647101
2010	3330	89	779	289	1104	3299555	577828	727741	198415	653255
2011	3367	89	769	290	1090	3426025	578633	711130	195072	680457
2012	3314	91	760	289	1081	3568273	581844	732224	193505	718655

注：1. 从2007年开始，普通中学、小学、工读学校、特殊教育、学前教育在校学生数包括外省市户口借读学生。
2. 1991-2005年，普通中等学校包括普通中专、技工学校、职业中学、普通中学和工读学校。2006年及以后普通中等学校为中等教育口径，包括普通中专、成人中专、技工学校、职业高中和普通中学。

资料来源：北京市教育委员会。

Note: a) From 2007, enrolled students in general high schools, primary schools, work-study schools for delinquent children, special education schools, and pre-school education included those from outside Beijing and studying in Beijing on temporary basis.
b) In 1991-2005, middle schools included special secondary schools, technician training schools, vocational schools, general high schools, and work-study schools. In and after 2006, middle schools included special secondary schools, special secondary schools for adults, technician training schools, vocational senior high schools and general high schools.

Source: Beijing Municipal Commission of Education.

18-1 续表 continued

年份 Year	全市各类学校招生数(人) New Enrollments in Various Schools (person)	#普通高等学校 Colleges & Universities	#普通中等学校 Middle Schools	#高中 Senior Middle Schools	#小学 Primary Schools	学龄儿童入学率(%) Enrollment Rate of Children at School-age (%)	专任教师数(人) Full-time Teachers (person)	平均每一专任教师负担学生数(人) Average Number of Students Instructed by a Full-time Teacher(person) 高等学校 Institutions of Higher Education	普通中学 Regular Secondary Schools	小学 Primary Schools
1978		17445		161288	199076	99.00			19.9	20.7
1979		15848		160340	154809	98.50			16.1	21.3
1980		17972		131961	138751	98.70			14.8	21.7
1981		17921		54296	121744	98.90			13.4	19.7
1982		21936		35212	104357	98.90			12.3	19.5
1983		27988		40282	96028	99.10			11.5	19.6
1984		31805		47068	103482	99.30			13.2	18.2
1985		40670		35265	135048	99.10			13.9	17.4
1986		35390		27863	160513	99.50			14.1	17.3
1987		41163		41186	156954	99.50			12.8	16.8
1988		42187		35429	184516	99.50			11.4	17.6
1989		33557		33254	184609	99.70			11.0	19.1
1990		36275		30596	161742	99.50			10.1	18.6
1991	571685	37700	205107	28589	148300	99.17	168485		10.5	18.0
1992	622142	41517	232765	25790	157145	99.65	169249		11.3	17.4
1993	651729	52205	242274	26275	175853	99.88	170361		12.1	17.4
1994	704933	51884	287642	34704	186315	99.92	175025		13.1	16.9
1995	691972	52868	308786	40803	168903	99.93	176591		13.6	16.5
1996	628772	55269	289612	42603	156898	99.93	178006		13.7	16.1
1997	581091	56884	289719	49566	124231	99.95	179080		13.2	15.7
1998	581786	62264	308157	52956	100415	99.96	178210		12.8	14.9
1999	603332	78354	320731	56998	94358	99.95	175496	12.0	13.2	13.7
2000	635328	99397	324862	65890	92002	99.95	167040	14.0	14.1	12.8
2001	641432	116344	313257	69195	91230	99.62	168080	17.0	14.3	12.1
2002	671956	128320	326835	84679	86406	99.63	166490	19.0	14.2	11.2
2003	662877	143483	302071	94894	82631	99.95	166510	19.0	13.7	11.0
2004	635842	147298	271396	93519	73577	99.92	172055	17.1	12.9	10.6
2005	630515	156124	259133	88605	71020	99.90	174589	17.0	11.8	10.3
2006	851808	154969	234524	76375	73138	99.96	191365	17.0	10.8	9.8
2007	927144	156222	252709	71590	109203	100.00	195568	15.4	11.5	13.8
2008	938891	157238	236714	68397	110440	100.00	199114	17.1	10.9	13.5
2009	962648	158992	240937	65983	102414	100.00	203825	16.5	10.0	13.0
2010	1002141	155228	238954	65649	113728	99.96	206602	16.6	10.2	13.2
2011	1050131	157543	243754	64146	132719	99.99	199789	17.1	9.8	13.4
2012	1108574	162042	254790	63381	141738	99.99	204812	17.0	9.7	13.7

18-2 幼儿园基本情况(1978－2012年)
BASIC STATISTICS FOR KINDERGARTENS (1978-2012)

单位：人 (person)

年份 Year	园数(所) Number of Kindergartens (unit)	班数(个) Number of Classes (unit)	离园人数 Leaving Children	入园人数 Entering Children	在园人数 Children Enrollment	教职工数 Teachers Staff and Workers	#专任教师 Full-time Teachers
1978	5074				235923	39982	8369
1979	4623				237037	40424	8777
1980	3991				219407	38475	7765
1981	3888				233089	38832	8814
1982	3849				254458	42663	9271
1983	1999				306975	48666	8234
1984	3682				295427	47721	9499
1985	2955				316024	47033	10523
1986	3503				342824	52654	12690
1987	3732				364011	54211	14449
1988	3563				354367	52105	14705
1989	3509				344394	50280	17208
1990	3798				372555	49587	17972
1991	3761		133788	172884	402699	49472	18788
1992	3510		158740	181299	404779	48007	18513
1993	3369		165963	170580	372368	44741	18114
1994	3301		113652	167267	352979	42118	17413
1995	3024		103355	148272	315277	38549	16084
1996	3056		135376	112449	271752	33586	14792
1997	2892		110345	95140	253478	32811	14596
1998	2662		99279	93819	245046	30362	13841
1999	2180		91996	89463	237055	29367	13216
2000	2047		85301	91724	229012	27257	12595
2001	1719	8259	85842	87892	217521	26106	12479
2002	1540	8494	79447	91092	213794	25402	12127
2003	1430	7733	76879	86465	199390	26324	13056
2004	1422	8087	71677	86672	205532	28326	14208
2005	1358	8148	71926	83485	202301	28026	14813
2006	1361	8051	70400	68299	197546	28958	15632
2007	1306	8132	70681	83969	214423	30465	17013
2008	1266	8382	72119	85938	226681	32535	18176
2009	1253	9036	65684	89761	247778	34973	17952
2010	1245	9883	68135	105048	276994	37227	21677
2011	1305	11213	76790	115539	311417	44458	24170
2012	1266	11882	79131	115248	331524	48080	26330

资料来源：北京市教育委员会。
Source: Beijing Municipal Commission of Education.

18-3 各类学校基本情况
BASIC STATISTICS FOR SCHOOLS

单位：人 (person)

项目	Item	校数(所) Number of Schools (unit)		教职工数 Teachers and Staff		专任教师 Full-time Teachers	
		2012	2011	2012	2011	2012	2011
合计	**Total**	**3314**	**3367**	**346555**	**335604**	**204812**	**199789**
高等教育	**Higher Education**	**179**	**176**	**146801**	**140527**	**64052**	**63025**
研究生培养机构(不计校数)	Institutions Providing Postgraduate Programs(Schools Excluded)	(135)	(130)			(45052)	(42039)
高等学校	Colleges & Universities	(56)	(52)			(36539)	(29737)
科研机构	Research Institutes	(79)	(78)			(8513)	(12302)
普通高等学校	Regular Institutions of Higher Education	91	89	137277	130056	60004	58735
成人高等学校	Adult Institutions of Higher Education	19	19	3407	3409	1527	1507
民办的其他高等教育机构	Non-state Institutions of Higher Education	69	68	6117	7062	2521	2783
中等教育	**Secondary Education**	**760**	**769**	**94433**	**94351**	**66537**	**65838**
高中阶段教育	Senior Secondary	419	427	94433	94351	46569	46114
普通高中	Regular Schools	289	290	78730	77282	37411	36315
中等职业教育	Secondary Vocational Schools	130	137	15703	17069	9158	9799
普通中专	Regular Technical Secondary Schools	31	35	3738	4717	1984	2460
成人中专	Adult Technical Secondary Schools	11	11	592	637	342	330
职业高中	Vocational High Schools	54	56	7834	7978	4928	4997
技工学校	Technical Schools	34	35	3539	3737	1904	2012
初中阶段教育	Junior Secondary Education	341	342			19968	19724
小学教育	**Primary Schools**	**1081**	**1090**	**55710**	**54781**	**46783**	**45684**
工读学校	**Work-Study School for Delinquent Children**	**6**	**6**	**300**	**328**	**212**	**210**
特殊教育	**Special Education**	**22**	**21**	**1231**	**1159**	**898**	**862**
学前教育	**Pre-school Education**	**1266**	**1305**	**48080**	**44458**	**26330**	**24170**

注：1. 普通高中的教职工数中包含普通初中的教职工数。
2. 表中带()数据不计入“校数”的合计数据中。
资料来源：北京市教育委员会。

Note: a) Number of "Teachers and Staff" in regular senior high schools includes those in junior high schools.
b) In this table data with () was not be calculated in the total schools.
Source: Beijing Municipal Commission of Education.

18-3 续表 continued

单位：人 (person)

项目	Item	毕业生数 Graduates		招生数 New Enrollment		在校学生数 Total Enrollment	
		2012	2011	2012	2011	2012	2011
合计	**Total**	**881804**	**838521**	**1108574**	**1050131**	**3568273**	**3426025**
高等教育	**Higher Education**	**466202**	**434104**	**595309**	**556789**	**1777024**	**1714259**
研究生	Postgraduates	70491	63196	87044	83002	252175	240735
高等学校	Colleges & Universities	66438	55288	81613	72302	236926	208460
科研机构	Research Institutes	4053	7908	5431	10700	15249	32275
普通本专科	Regular University and Junior College	152980	151277	162042	157543	581844	578633
中央部委属高校	Under the Jurisdication of Central Ministries and Commissions	71152	70460	77825	76436	299717	295258
市属高校	Under the Jurisdication of Municipal Government	81828	80817	84217	81107	282127	283375
公办高校	Public Colleges and Universities	59410	57727	63691	61076	214448	213433
民办高校	Civilian-run Colleges and Universities	22418	23090	20526	20031	67679	69942
成人本专科	Adult University and Junior College	94728	97601	107082	106365	265049	264109
成人高等学校	Adult Institutions of Higher Education	9664	11968	10024	10424	24605	25528
普通高等学校	Regular Institutions of Higher Education	85064	85633	97058	95941	240444	238581
在职人员攻读	Employees Enrolled in Graduate Programes						
硕士学位	Leading to Master Degrees			19140	19247	70076	65132
网络本专科生	Online University and Junior College Students	148003	122030	220001	190632	607880	565650
中等教育	**Secondary Education**	**224938**	**223955**	**254790**	**243754**	**732224**	**711130**
高中阶段教育	Senior Secondary	129156	126368	146657	143118	426714	408861
普通高中	Regular Senior	55657	58275	63381	64146	193505	195072
#北京市户籍	Domicile in Beijing	52208	54813	55728	57449	174089	177855
中等职业教育	Secondary Vocational Schools	73499	68093	83276	78972	233209	213789
普通中专	Regular Technical Secondary School	16111	17896	14753	15186	59895	63107
成人中专	Adult Technical Secondary School	23523	12365	27398	24688	64858	41802
职业高中	Vocational High Schools	19281	20851	21925	21633	64987	64073
技工学校	Technical School	14584	16981	19200	17465	43469	44807
初中阶段教育	Junior Secondary Education	95782	97587	108133	100636	305510	302269
#北京市户籍	Domicile in Beijing	79250	81940	71109	68465	212437	221506
小学教育	**Primary Schools**	**109492**	**101678**	**141738**	**132719**	**718655**	**680457**
#北京市户籍	Domicile in Beijing	71313	68077	74550	74412	394472	391325
工读学校	**Work-study School for Delinquent Children**	**294**	**303**	**299**	**281**	**728**	**725**
特殊教育	**Special Education Schools**	**1747**	**1691**	**1190**	**1049**	**8118**	**8037**
学前教育	**Preschool Education**	**79131**	**76790**	**115248**	**115539**	**331524**	**311417**

18-4 全市高等教育学生情况(2012年)
PUPILLARY STATISTICS FOR INSTITUTION OF HIGHER EDUCATION (2012)

单位：人 (person)

项目	Item	毕(结)业生人数 Graduates	招生数 New Enrollment	在校学生数 Enrolled Students
普通本科、专科生	Regular Undergraduates and College Students	152980	162042	581844
专科	Enrolled in Specialized Courses Education	41448	38792	108313
本科	Enrolled in Full Undergraduate Courses	111532	123250	473531
成人本科、专科生	Adult Undergraduates and College Students	94728	107082	265049
专科	Enrolled in Specialized Courses	44939	47845	108283
本科	Enrolled in Full Undergraduate Courses	49789	59237	156766
网络本科、专科生	Students Enrolled in Internet-based Courses	148003	220001	607880
专科	Enrolled in Specialized Courses	86721	130256	328273
本科	Enrolled in Full Undergraduate Courses	61282	89745	279607
研究生	Postgraduates	70491	87044	252175
硕士	Master's Degree	57020	69581	183463
博士	Doctor's Degree	13471	17463	68712
在职人员攻读硕士学位	Employees Enrolled in Graduate Programes Leading to Master Degrees		19140	70076
自考助学班	Classes for Self-Learning Programs	4401		8018
普通预科生	College Preparatory Courses			2534
研究生课程进修班	Postgraduate Courses for Advanced Study	12782		18013
进修及培训	In-Service Training Courses	573313		381838
留学生	Overseas Students	25570	29165	40549

资料来源：北京市教育委员会。
Source: Beijing Municipal Commission of Education.

18-5 普通高等学校本专科基本情况(2012年)
BASIC STATISTICS ON COLLEGES AND UNIVERSITIES (2012)

单位：人 (person)

项目	Item	校数(所) Number of Schools (unit)	毕业生数 Graduates	招生数 New Enrollment	在校学生数 Enrolled Students	教职工数 Teachers and Staff	#专任教师 Full-time Teachers
合计	**Total**	**91**	**152980**	**162042**	**581844**	**137277**	**60004**
#女性	Female		78809	84084	299314	66494	28131
综合大学	Comprehensive Universities	5	20314	21013	73353	26560	7450
理工院校	Science and Engineering	31	62061	67287	241560	49873	25660
农业院校	Agriculture	3	6741	6333	23686	4498	2401
林业院校	Forestry	1	3160	3352	13218	1750	1147
医药院校	Medicine	4	3022	3527	12765	17048	2999
师范院校	Teacher Training	2	4436	4966	19236	5806	3388
语文院校	Literature	9	11171	11797	42484	7317	4002
财经院校	Finance and Economics	16	23167	23537	83904	10879	6108
政法院校	Politics and Law	8	10081	10789	35611	6365	2835
体育院校	Physical Culture	3	2588	3001	10958	1696	980
艺术院校	Art	8	3502	3628	13808	3599	1951
民族院校	Minorities Colleges	1	2737	2812	11261	1886	1083

资料来源：北京市教育委员会。
Source: Beijing Municipal Commission of Education.

18-6 全市分学科研究生情况(2012年)
NUMBER OF POSTGRADUATE BY SUBJECT OF STUDY (2012)

单位：人 (person)

项目	Item	毕业生 Graduates			招生数 New Enrollment			在校学生数 Enrolled Students		
		合计 Total	硕士 Master's Degree	博士 Doctor's Degree	合计 Total	硕士 Master's Degree	博士 Doctor's Degree	合计 Total	硕士 Master's Degree	博士 Doctor's Degree
合计	**Total**	**70491**	**57020**	**13471**	**87044**	**69581**	**17463**	**252175**	**183463**	**68712**
#女性	Female	34245	29092	5153	42258	35651	6607	118165	93303	24862
学术型学位	**Academic Degree**	**56361**	**43411**	**12950**	**60950**	**43851**	**17099**	**193344**	**126252**	**67092**
哲学	Philosophy	631	416	215	703	463	240	2256	1349	907
经济学	Economics	4185	3467	718	4130	3200	930	11510	8052	3458
法学	Law	4879	3924	955	4884	3701	1183	14919	10416	4503
教育学	Education	1874	1565	309	1661	1322	339	5549	4308	1241
文学	Literature	3804	3238	566	3868	3147	721	11582	8805	2777
历史学	History	597	428	169	591	404	187	1960	1243	717
理学	Science	6437	3807	2630	9106	5373	3733	27917	14784	13133
工学	Engineering	21856	17278	4578	23632	17311	6321	78661	51404	27257
农学	Agriculture	1765	1196	569	2080	1345	735	6370	3806	2564
医学	Medicine	3147	2120	1027	3470	2331	1139	10307	6684	3623
军事学	Military	29	17	12	43	32	11	125	78	47
管理学	Management	5221	4271	950	5023	3768	1255	16317	10566	5751
艺术学	Art	1936	1684	252	1759	1454	305	5871	4757	1114
专业学位	**Professional Degree**	**14130**	**13609**	**521**	**26094**	**25730**	**364**	**58831**	**57211**	**1620**

资料来源：北京市教育委员会。
Source: Beijing Municipal Commission of Education.

18-7 高等教育外国留学生情况(2012年)
STATISTICS FOR FOREIGN STUDENTS STUDYING IN BEIJING OF HIGHER EDUCATION (2012)

单位：人 (person)

项目	Item	毕(结)业生数 Graduates	授予学位人数 Number of Students Conferred with Degree	招生数 New Enrollment	在校学生数 Enrolled Students
合计	**Total**	**25570**	**4455**	**29165**	**40549**
#女性	Female	12690	1912	14435	18356
按学历划分	**By Educational Background**				
专科	Enrolled in Specialized Courses	102		123	171
本科	Enrolled in Full Undergraduate Courses	3486	2886	4237	14389
硕士	Master's Degree	1487	1344	2108	4557
博士	Doctor's Degree	387	225	604	1988
培训	Training	20108		22093	19444
按地区划分	**By Region**				
亚洲	Asia	13756	3443	16829	26601
非洲	Africa	999	341	1379	2261
欧洲	Europe	5946	339	6222	6699
北美洲	North America	3720	221	3532	3498
南美洲	South America	382	70	443	589
大洋洲	Oceania	767	41	760	901
按经费来源	**By Sources of Funds**				
国际组织资助	From International Organizations	52	13	85	116
中国政府资助	From Chinese Government	2801	977	3444	5759
本国政府资助	From the Government of the Student's Own Country	270	76	371	783
学校间交换	Interscholastic Exchange	2637	84	2622	2198
自费	Self Funding	19810	3305	22643	31693

资料来源：北京市教育委员会。
Source: Beijing Municipal Commission of Education.

18-8 普通中专分科情况(2012年)
SPECIALIZED SECONDARY SCHOOLS BY MAJOR (2012)

单位：人 (person)

项　　目	Item	毕业生数 Graduates	招生数 New Enrollment	在校学生数 Enrolled Students
合　计	**Total**	**16111**	**14753**	**59895**
#女　生	Female	8063	6849	28761
按类别分	**By Category**			
农林牧渔类	Agriculture, Forestry, Animal Husbandry and Fishery	294	159	615
资源环境类	Resource and Environment		110	306
能源与新能源类	Energy and New Energy	351	168	1408
土木水利类	Construction and Water Conservancy	789	838	3290
加工制造类	Processing and Manufacturing	2285	1328	6126
石油化工类	Petroleum and Chemicals	110		150
轻纺食品类	Light Industry, Textile and Food	79	124	372
交通运输类	Transportation	2028	2607	9413
信息技术类	IT	1320	1167	4163
医药卫生类	Medicine and Health	2856	2870	12684
休闲保健类	Relaxation and Health Care			
财经商贸类	Business and Trade	2361	1707	6483
旅游服务类	Tourism Service	427	129	1010
文化艺术类	Culture and Art	1616	1752	8022
体育与健身	Sports and Fitness	553	566	1755
教育类	Education	284	556	1409
司法服务类	Judicial Service	242	246	654
公共管理与服务类	Public Management and Service	152	182	688
其　他	Others	364	244	1347

资料来源：北京市教育委员会。
Source: Beijing Municipal Commission of Education.

18-9 职业高中分科情况(2012年)
VOCATIONAL SCHOOLS BY MAJOR (2012)

单位：人 (person)

项目	Item	毕业生数 Graduates	招生数 New Enrollment	在校学生数 Enrolled Students
合计	**Total**	**19281**	**21925**	**64987**
#女生	Female	9318	10858	33080
按类别分	**By Category**			
农林牧渔类	Agriculture, Forestry, Animal Husbandry and Fishery	251	304	920
资源环境类	Resource and Environment			
能源与新能源类	Energy and New Energy	7	2	2
土木水利类	Construction and Water Conservancy	99	110	401
加工制造类	Processing and Manufacturing	1386	1136	3474
石油化工类	Petroleum and Chemicals			
轻纺食品类	Light Industry, Textile and Food	70	116	360
交通运输类	Transportation	2626	2536	6798
信息技术类	IT	3479	3489	10293
医药卫生类	Medicine and Health	605	478	1665
休闲保健类	Relaxation and Health Care	277	950	2604
财经商贸类	Business and Trade	3734	3878	11365
旅游服务类	Tourism Service	2428	2860	8636
文化艺术类	Culture and Art	1786	2503	8409
体育与健身	Sports and Fitness	200	313	893
教育类	Education	1823	2718	7664
司法服务类	Judicial Service	71	245	360
公共管理与服务类	Public Management and Service	372	287	1048
其他	Others	67		95

资料来源：北京市教育委员会。
Source: Beijing Municipal Commission of Education.

18-10 校外教育情况(2012年)
STATISTICS OF AFTER-SCHOOL EDUCATION (2012)

单位：人 (person)

项目	Item	单位数(个) Number of Organizations(unit)	活动小组数(个) Activity Groups(unit)	参加小组学生数 Participating Students	教职工人数 Teachers and Staff	#专职辅导员 Full-time Coaches	兼职辅导员 Part-time Coaches
合计	**Total**	**555**	**8208**	**376521**	**2308**	**1370**	**1833**
少年宫	Children's Palace	21	5829	210767	1380	834	748
少年科技馆	Children's Scientific Museums	7	480	27430	204	153	45
少年之家	Children's Home	29	1067	111383	372	228	420
少年活动站	Children's Club	498	832	26941	352	155	620

资料来源：北京市教育委员会。
Source: Beijing Municipal Commission of Education.

18-11 幼儿园基本情况(2012年)
STATISTICS FOR KINDERGARTENS (2012)

单位：人 (person)

项目	Item	总计 Total	#女 Female	城区 In City	镇区 In Counties and Towns	乡村 In Villages
园数 (所)	Number of Kind (unit)	1266		922	179	165
班数 (个)	Number of Class (unit)	11882		9821	1272	789
在园幼儿数	Children Enrollment	331524	157203	275250	37044	19230
教职工数	Teachers,Staff and Workers	48080	44130	42041	4321	1718
#园长	Headmaster	1892	1812	1557	202	133
专任教师	Teachers	26330	25785	22669	2540	1121
保健医	Health Workers	1748	1715	1566	134	48

注：从2007年开始,基础教育(普通中小学、工读学校、特殊教育、学前教育)的城乡划分按照国家统计局新的标准进行统计。
资料来源：北京市教育委员会。
Note: From 2007, statistics for urban and rural division of fundamental education (general primary and high shcools,work-study schools for delinquent, special education and pre-school education) is made in line with the new standard of National Statistics Bureau.
Source: Beijing Municipal Commission of Education.

18-12 高等教育自学考试情况
STATISTICS FOR HIGHER EDUCATION SELF-STUDY EXAMINATION

项 目	Item	2012	2011
报考人次 (人次)	Number of Person-times Registered (person-times)	136864	266393
报考科次 (科次)	Number of Major-times Registered (subject-times)	399989	738226
发出专科毕业证书 (个)	Number of Junior College Diploma Issued (unit)	8866	6284
发出本科毕业证书 (个)	Number of Regular College Diploma Issued (unit)	4753	4580
开考专业 (个)	Number of Majors Examined (unit)	113	111

资料来源：北京市教育委员会。
Source: Beijing Municipal Commission of Education.

18-13 特殊教育情况(2012年)
STATISTICS FOR SPECIAL EDUCATION (2012)

单位：人 (person)

项 目	Item	毕业生 Graduates	招生数 New Enrollment	在校学生数 Enrolled Students
合 计	**Total**	**1747**	**1190**	**8118**
#女 性	Female	633	414	2899
特殊教育学校	Special Education Schools	394	485	2923
小学附设特教班	Primary Schools Adnascent Special Classes	14	10	164
小学随班就读	Study In Primary Schools	678	148	2919
普通(职业)初中随班就读	Study In Reguar Junior Secondary (Vocational) Classes	661	547	2112

资料来源：北京市教育委员会。
Source: Beijing Municipal Commission of Education.

18-14 职业技术培训机构基本情况(2012年)
BASIC STATISTICS ON VOCATIONAL TECHNOLOGY TRAINING INSTITUTIONS(2012)

项目	Item	学校数(所) Schools (unit)	教学班(点、个) Teaching Classes (site,unit)	结业生数(人次) Students Completing Courses (person-time)	
				合计 Total	#女性 Female
合计	**Total**	**3711**	**40644**	**2640055**	**1330821**
#少数民族	National Miniority			29536	6986
按培训机构分	**Group by Training Institutions**				
职工技术培训学校(机构)	**Technical Training Schools (Institutions) for Employees**	**86**	**2127**	**83290**	**31840**
教育部门和集体办	Run by Education Dept. and Collective	1	1	12759	8293
其他部门办	Run by Other Dept.	8	176	11331	5047
民办	Run by Private	77	1950	59200	18500
农村成人文化技术培训学校(机构)	**Cultural & Technical Training Schools (Institutions) for Rural Adults**	**2107**	**8519**	**804835**	**416577**
#教育部门和集体办	Run by Education Dept. and Collective	2102	8497	801936	415145
县办	Run by County	29	2879	189071	110485
乡办	Run by Township	641	3443	388745	195198
村办	Run by Village	1432	2175	224120	109462
其他培训机构(含社会培训机构)	**Other Training Institutions (Incld. Social Training Institutions)**	**1518**	**29998**	**1751930**	**882404**
教育部门和集体办	Run by Education Dept. and Collective	84	41	87527	47858
其他部门办	Run by Other Dept.	192	180	628189	350933
民办	Run by Private	1242	29777	1036214	483613
按培训时间分	**Group by Training Duration**				
一个月以内	1 month below			1285807	636504
一个月至三个月以内	1 month to 3 months below			412950	232446
三个月至半年以内	3 month to 6 months below			605485	291483
半年至一年以内	6 months to 1 year			217728	106248
一年及以上	1 year over			118085	64140
按培训形式分	**Group by Form of Training**				
#资格证书培训	Qualification Certificate Training			426202	214443
岗位证书培训	Job Post Certificate Training			352492	161423

资料来源：北京市教育委员会。
Source: Beijing Municipal Commission of Education.

18-14 续表 continued

单位：人 (person)

项　目	Item	注册学生数 Enrolled Students 合　计 Total	#女 性 Female	教职工数 Teachers and Staff 合　计 Total	#专任教师 Full-time Teachers	聘请校外教　师 External Teachers Retained
合　计	**Total**	**2543507**	**1283416**	**58613**	**19306**	**19934**
#少数民族	National Miniority			162	61	64
按培训机构分	**Group by Training Institutions**					
职工技术培训学校(机构)	**Technical Training Schools (Institutions) for Employees**	**38332**	**24301**	**1025**	**705**	**496**
教育部门和集体办	Run by Education Dept. and Collective	4740	3081	83	73	55
其他部门办	Run by Other Dept.	8572	3120	123	70	61
民　办	Run by Private	25020	18100	819	562	380
农村成人文化技术培训学校(机构)	**Cultural & Technical Training Schools (Institutions) for Rural Adults**	**451245**	**255569**	**1640**	**815**	**2868**
#教育部门和集体办	Run by Education Dept. and Collective	451245	255569	1631	809	2851
县　办	Run by County	188382	109532	180	36	701
乡　办	Run by Township	184305	103139	595	394	731
村　办	Run by Village	78558	42898	856	379	1419
其他部门办	Run by Other Dept.			9	6	17
其他培训机构(含社会培训机构)	**Other Training Institutions (Incld. Social Training Institutions)**	**2053930**	**1003546**	**55948**	**17786**	**16570**
教育部门和集体办	Run by Education Dept. and Collective	106478	57751	3566	1007	1463
其他部门办	Run by Other Dept.	869853	442491	17417	3388	5409
民　办	Run by Private	1077599	503304	34965	13391	9698
按培训时间分	**Group by Training Duration**					
一个月以内	1 month below	961206	464502			
一个月至三个月以内	1 month to 3 months below	529200	283224			
三个月至半年以内	3 month to 6 months below	703258	351177			
半年至一年以内	6 months to 1 year	215368	119715			
一年及以上	1 year over	134475	64798			
按培训形式分	**Group by Form of Training**					
#资格证书培训	Qualification Certificate Training	369814	179115			
岗位证书培训	Job Post Certificate Training	316427	146907			

18-15 民办教育基本情况(2012年)
STATSTICS FOR NON-STATE EDUCATION (2012)

单位：人 (person)

项目	Item	校数(所) Number of Schools (unit)	毕业生数 Numer of Students Graduated	招生数 New Enrollment	在校学生数 Enrolled Students	教职工数 Teachers and Staff	#专任教师 Full-time Teachers	聘请校外教师数 Substitutive and Part-time Teachers
合计	**Total**	**669**	**62338**	**82577**	**276753**	**42921**	**22563**	**4874**
一、民办高等教育	**Civilian-run Higher Education**	**84**	**22418**	**20526**	**67679**	**13024**	**6010**	**4403**
普通高校	General Universities & Colleges	15	22418	20526	67679	6907	3489	2158
民办高等教育机构	Other Higher Education Institutions Run by Civilian	69				6117	2521	2245
二、民办中等教育	**Civilian-run Secondary Education**	**94**	**12125**	**18405**	**52127**	**8996**	**5636**	**285**
(一)高中阶段教育	Senior High School Education	77	5081	9402	26410	8996	5636	285
1.民办普通高中	Civilian-run Senior High Schools	55	3543	7315	19675	7808	5017	53
2.民办中等职业教育	Civilian-run Secondary Vocational Education	22	1538	2087	6735	1188	619	232
(二)初中阶段教育	Junior High School Education	17	7044	9003	25717			
三、民办小学	**Civilian-run Primary Schools**	**40**	**5350**	**10899**	**51426**	**1852**	**1302**	**9**
四、民办幼儿园	**Civilian-run Kindergartens**	**451**	**22445**	**32747**	**105521**	**19049**	**9615**	**177**
补充资料:	Supplementary Data: Civilian-run							
民办职业技术培训机构	Vocational Technical Training Institutions	1242	1036214		1077599	34965	13391	9698

注：普通中学教职工数、专任教师及聘请校外教师数为初中高中合计数。
资料来源：北京市教育委员会。
Note: Number of teachers,staff,full-time teachers,substitutive and part-time teachers in regular secondary schools includes those in junior and senior middle schools.
Source: Beijing Municipal Commission of Education.

18-16 高校办学条件(2012年)

RUNNING CONDITIONS OF INSTITUTIONS OF HIGHER EDUCATION (2012)

项目		Item		合计 Total	中央 Central	市属市管 Municipal
普通高校		**Institutions of Regular Higher Education**				
校舍建筑面积	(平方米)	Floor Space of Schoolhouses	(sq.m)	32835079	22918996	9916083
占地面积	(平方米)	Land Area	(sq.m)	41081319	26063900	15017419
图书	(万册)	Books	(10000 volumes)	10347	6627	3720
电子图书藏量	(千兆字节)	Electro-books Reserved	(Gigabyte)	610923	428270	182653
拥有教学用计算机	(台)	Computers for Teaching	(unit)	372272	189619	182653
语言实验室座位数	(个)	Language Laboratory Seating	(unit)	46009	22442	23567
多媒体教室座位数	(个)	Multimedia Laboratory Seating	(unit)	953056	493807	459249
上网课程数	(门)	Number of Online Courses	(sort)	50646	32146	18500
成人高校		**Institutions of Adult Higher Education**				
校舍建筑面积	(平方米)	Floor Space of Schoolhouses	(sq.m)	867943	236280	631663
占地面积	(平方米)	Land Area	(sq.m)	1521957	302865	1219092
图书	(万册)	Books	(10000 volumes)	217	41	176
电子图书藏量	(千兆字节)	Electro-books Reserved	(Gigabyte)	65654	57871	7783
拥有教学用计算机	(台)	Computers for Teaching	(unit)	9410	1137	8273
语言实验室座位数	(个)	Language Laboratory Seating	(unit)	1226	188	1038
多媒体教室座位数	(个)	Multimedia Laboratory Seating	(unit)	29390	2978	26412
上网课程数	(门)	Number of Online Courses	(sort)	2292	1019	1273

资料来源：北京市教育委员会。
Source: Beijing Municipal Commission of Education.

18-17 基础教育办学条件(2012年)
SCHOOL CONDITIONS OF BASIC EDUCATION (2012)

单位：平方米 (sq.m)

项目	Item	普通中学 Regular Secondary Schools	小学 Primary Schools
学校占地面积	Areas of Schools	21985020	13670667
校舍建筑面积	Floor Space of Schoolhouses	11512899	5891766
#当年新增	New adding In those Years	383197	250059
#危房面积	Areas of Dangerous Building	3182	276
教学及辅助用房	Teaching and Auxiliary Houses	4152472	2784326
普通教室	Senior Room	2395280	2186583
实验室	Laboratory	729959	198788
图书室	Library	311595	134606
微机室	Computer Room	181032	130320
语音室	Language Laboratory Seating	35614	15817
体育馆	Areas of Stadiums and Gymnasiums	498992	118212
行政办公用房	Administrative Houses	1279012	725811
生活用房	Houses for Life	3203347	1000207
其他用房	Houses for Other Purpose of Use	2878068	1381422
计算机 (台)	Computers (unit)	223413	178776
图书藏量 (册)	Books Collections (volume)	26612626	25600500
电子图书藏量 (千兆字节)	Electronics Collections (Gigabyte)	156804	116473

资料来源：北京市教育委员会。
Source: Beijing Municipal Commission of Education.

18-18 外省市、外籍学生就读情况(2012年)
STATISTICS ON STUDENTS FROM OTHER PROVINCES, MUNICIPALITIES AND AUTONOMOUS REGIONS ALONG WITH OTHER COUNTRIES (2012)

单位：人 (person)

项目	Item	非本市户籍学生数 Students from Other Provinces, Municipalities and Autonomous Regions	#民办学校 Non-state Education	外国留学生 Foreign Students	#民办学校 Non-state Education
合计	**Total**	**588533**	**109985**	**7385**	**3010**
普通中学	Regular Secondary Schools	112489	20027	3024	913
初中	Junior Secondary Schools	93073	13956	1289	318
高中	Senior Secondary Schools	19416	6071	1735	595
中等职业教育	Vocational Secondary Schools	66869	6431	90	
小学	Primary Schools	324183	43988	2705	936
特殊教育	Special Education Schools	790	35	3	
幼儿园	Kindergartens	84202	39504	1563	1161

资料来源：北京市教育委员会。
Source: Beijing Municipal Commission of Education.

18-19 图书馆、文化馆、档案馆情况(1978-2012年)
LIBRARIES, CULTURAL CENTERS AND ARCHIVING INSTITUTION (1978-2012)

年份 Year	公共图书馆 Public Libraries				群众艺术馆、文化馆 Mass Art Stations, Cultural Centers		档案馆 Archiving Institution			
	个数 (个) Number (unit)	总藏数 (万册、万件) Total Collections (10000 volumes)	建筑面积 (万平方米) Floor Space of Building (10000 sq.m)	书刊文献外借人次 (万人次) Person-times of Books,Periodicals, Literature Lent (10000 person-times)	个数 (个) Number (unit)	组织文艺活动 (次) Art Activities Organized (times)	个数 (个) Number (unit)	建筑面积 (平方米) Floor Space of Building (10000 sq.m)	利用档案资料人次 (万人次) Persons of Using Files (10000 person-times)	案卷 (万卷件) Records (10000 rolls)
1978	18	1423		168.5	19	516				
1979	21	1502		173.7	19	1033				
1980	20	1606	1.8	210.4	19	778				
1981	21	1614	1.9	211.0	19	1131				
1982	21	1676	2.0	228.4	20	1334				
1983	21	1733	1.9	243.0	20	1015				
1984	22	1824	2.3	223.7	22	489				
1985	22	1860	3.0	219.9	23	469				
1986	23	1874	6.0	219.9	23	883				
1987	23	1959	20.6	169.8	23	1067	20	10695	1.30	86.13
1988	23	2050	23.4	300.4	23	647	20	21472	1.46	115.98
1989	23	2128	24.5		23	1411	20	31280	1.48	156.28
1990	23	2205	25.0		23	1429	20	23618	2.51	167.37
1991	23	2281	25.3		23	1128	20	33491	3.24	177.45
1992	23	2397	25.4	147.0	23	978	20	35950	2.64	181.31
1993	23	2461	25.5	212.0	23	764	20	37650	1.73	192.39
1994	23	2548	23.8	383.8	23	1034	20	42641	1.50	192.35
1995	23	2629	24.1	139.3	23	1127	20	65489	1.42	204.06
1996	22	2652	25.3	145.6	23	2277	20	62994	3.03	223.70
1997	23	2789	25.7	188.0	23	1875	20	64147	2.69	227.42
1998	24	2848	25.6	189.0	23	2554	20	67759	2.71	240.78
1999	24	2934	26.4	607.0	23	1490	20	72597	2.52	259.50
2000	26	3020	27.0	283.0	23	1809	20	72596	3.01	278.29
2001	26	3133	31.4	287.7	23	1822	20	72730	4.17	297.02
2002	26	3248	30.7	337.5	20	1817	20	72946	4.53	328.42
2003	26	3355	30.9	334.8	20	2023	20	81519	6.27	358.95
2004	26	3451	30.9	405.0	22	1826	20	83162	7.03	379.13
2005	26	3626	31.7	480.0	22	3697	20	84656	6.97	404.69
2006	25	3776	31.0	515.0	21	2200	20	93773	10.59	436.70
2007	25	3940	31.5	479.0	21	4752	20	93463	9.51	461.67
2008	25	4100	33.4	450.0	20	3007	20	97605	9.00	495.70
2009	25	4368	41.9	471.0	20	3470	20	97605	9.88	523.84
2010	25	4613	42.4	441.0	20	3564	18	97611	13.45	557.99
2011	25	5049	42.1	333.0	20	3401	18	97976	12.30	582.92
2012	25	5556	47.6	317.0	20	3848	18	98879	12.37	602.54

注：1978-1981年，群众艺术馆、文化馆数据不包括群众艺术馆。

资料来源：北京市文化局、国家图书馆、北京市档案局。

Note: In 1978-1981, the data of mass art stations and cultural centers didn't include mass art stations.

Source: Beijing Municipal Bureau of Culture,National Library of China,Beijing Municipal Bureau of Archives.

18-20 博物馆情况(1982-2012年)
STATISTICS ON MUSEUMS(1982-2012)

年份 Year	北京地区博物馆数 (个) Number of Museums in Beijing	文物藏品数 (万件) Cultural Relic Collections (10000 unit)	博物馆及其他文物保护机构(文物局系统内) Museums and Other CulturalRelic Protection & Administration Organizationunder (under the jurisdiction of Beijing Municipal Administration) 个数 (个) Number (unit)	#博物馆 Museum	文物藏品数 (万件) Cultural Relic Collections (10000 unit)	#一级品 (件) Grade-I Collections (unit)	参观人次 (万人次) Visitors (10000 person-time)
1982			28		8.4	294	9.7
1983			29		4.0		58.0
1984							
1985			32		9.0		20.0
1986			39	7	21.0		905.0
1987							
1988			42	11	21.0		1098.0
1989			46	12	14.0		992.0
1990							
1991			46	12	11.7	2901	6629.1
1992							
1993			50	16	17.4	479	2423.4
1994			51	17	16.7	447	955.0
1995			51	17	16.7	447	2100.3
1996			51	17	18.0	443	2009.3
1997			54	24	18.2	443	935.8
1998			56	26	18.3	387	697.8
1999			54	26	18.5	374	5641.8
2000			53	25	18.2	367	702.7
2001			58	26	17.3	366	99.1
2002			48	27	20.1	716	170.8
2003			55	27	112.4	716	119.2
2004			66	31	370.4	656	599.9
2005			73	34	115.1	620	1370.9
2006			70	33	115.5	643	1416.7
2007			69	34	113.5	439	1493.0
2008	148	331	71	37	116.0	678	1368.4
2009	151	331	76	40	117.0	722	1647.9
2010	156	332	79	41	117.0	725	1712.1
2011	162	430	78	41	117.0	852	1373.4
2012	165	430	78	41	117.0	903	1887.9

资料来源：北京市文物局。
Source: Beijing Municipal Administration of Cultural Heritage.

18-21 博物馆及其他文物保护管理机构情况(2012年)
STATISTICS ON MUSEUMS AND OTHER CULTURAL RELIC PROTECTION & ADMINISTRATION ORGANIZATIONS (2012)

项 目		Item		合 计 Total	市 属 Under the Jurisdiction of the City	区县属 Under the Jurisdiction of a District/County
全市按行业管理登记的博物馆		**Museums of the City**				
博物馆数	(个)	Museum	(unit)	165	42	42
#免费开放的博物馆数	(个)	Museum Open for Free	(unit)	48	19	14
文物藏品数	(万件)	Cultural Relic Collections	(10000 units)	430		
参观人次	(万人次)	Visitors	(10000 person-times)	3500		
文物古迹个数	(处)	Historic Sites	(unit)	3550		
文物拍卖机构数	(个)	Organizations of Cultural Relic Auctions	(unit)	115		
举办文物艺术品拍卖场次	(场)	Times of Cultural Relic Auctions	(times)	215		
文物拍卖标的数	(件、套)	Cultural Relic Auctions	(unit)	170659		
文物拍卖标的成交金额	(万元)	Turnover of cultural relics auction	(10000 yuan)	2403472		
文物局系统内博物馆及文物保护管理机构	(个)	**Museums and Cultural Relic Protection & Administration Organizations of the Cultural Bureau System**	(unit)	**78**	**31**	**47**
#博物馆	(个)	Museum	(unit)	41	17	24
博物馆按类别分		Grouped by Category				
综合性	(个)	Comprehensive	(unit)	11	2	9
历史性	(个)	Historic	(unit)	17	7	10
艺术性	(个)	Art	(unit)	6	5	1
自然科技类	(个)	Natural,Science & Technology	(unit)	2	1	1
其他类	(个)	Other	(unit)	5	2	3
从业人员	(人)	Employment	(person)	4988	1416	3572
文物藏品数	(万件)	Cultural Relic Collections	(10000 units)	117	113	4
#一级品	(件)	Grade-I Collections	(unit)	903	609	294
参观人次	(万人次)	Visitors	(10000 person-times)	1887.9	346.1	1541.8
本年收入	(万元)	Revenues in the Year	(10000 yuan)	233696	112939	120757
#财政收入	(万元)	Fiscal Revenue	(10000 yuan)	160682	92439	68243
门票收入	(万元)	Ticket Revenue	(10000 yuan)	51243	1776	49467
本年支出	(万元)	Expenditure in the Year	(10000 yuan)	185599	82175	103424

注：全市博物馆数为北京地区按行业管理登记的博物馆数。
资料来源：北京市文物局。
Note: Number of Museums of the City means the number of museums registered by industrial administration in Beijing.
Source: Beijing Municipal Administration of Cultural Heritage.

18-22 公共图书馆(2012年)
PUBLIC LIBRARIES (2012)

项目		Item		合计 Total	中央属 Under Central Jurisdiction	市属 Under the Jurisdiction of the City	区县属 Under the Jurisdiction of a District/County
个数	(个)	Number	(unit)	25	1	1	23
从业人员	(人)	Employment	(person)	2684	1426	380	878
总藏数	(万册、万件)	Total Collections	(10000 volumes)	5556	3473	654	1429
#图书	(万册、万件)	Books	(10000 volumes)	2743	1050	507	1186
建筑面积	(万平方米)	Floor Space of Building	(10000 sq.m)	47.6	25.4	9.4	12.8
阅览座席	(个)	Seating Capacity of Reading Rooms	(unit)	17917	4392	2109	11416
总流通人次	(万人次)	Total Number of Visitors	(10000 person-times)	1243	378	287	578
#书刊文献外借人次	(万人次)	Person-times of Books, Periodicals, Literature Lent	(10000 person-times)	317		64	253
#书刊文献外借册次	(万册次)	Copy-times of Volumes of Books, Periodicals, Literature Lent	(10000 person-times)	819		178	641

资料来源：北京市文化局、国家图书馆。
Source: Beijing Municipal Bureau of Culture,National Library of China.

18-23 群众艺术馆、文化馆和文化站情况(2012年)
STATISTICS ON MASS ART STATIONS, CULTURAL CENTERS AND CULTURAL STATIONS(2012)

项目		Item		合计 Total	群众艺术馆 Mass Art Stations	文化馆 Cultural Centers	文化站 Cultural Stations
个数	(个)	Number	(unit)	343	1	19	323
从业人员	(人)	Employment	(person)	2321	60	787	1474
举办展览个数	(个)	Exhibitions Held	(unit)	2144	6	292	1846
组织文艺活动	(次)	Art Activities Organized	(times)	29076	249	3599	25228

资料来源：北京市文化局。
Source: Beijing Municipal Bureau of Culture.

18-24 档案事业基本情况(2012年)
BASIC STATISTICS ON ARCHIVING INSTITUTION (2012)

项目		Item		合计 Total	市属 Under the Jurisdiction of the City	区县属 Under the Jurisdiction of a District/County
档案馆个数	**(个)**	**Number of National Archives**	**(unit)**	**18**	**2**	**16**
建筑面积	**(平方米)**	**Floor Space of Building**	**(sq.m)**	**98879**	**30962**	**67917**
馆藏档案情况		**Files Colllected in Archives**				
全宗	(个)	Full Archives	(unit)	3001	633	2368
案卷	(万卷件)	Records	(10000 rolls)	602.54	278.87	323.67
建国前档案	(万卷件)	Files Prior to Foundation of PRC	(10000 rolls)	100.44	98.84	1.59
建国后档案	(万卷件)	Files After Foundation of PRC	(10000 rolls)	502.11	180.03	322.08
录音、录像、影片档案	(盘)	Tape, Video, and Film Files	(piece)	43170	34600	8570
照片档案	(张)	Photo Files	(disc)	623248	300592	322656
缩微胶片		Microfiche				
平片、开窗卡	(张)	Flat and Window-open Microfich	(disc)	288817	288817	
卷片	(万幅)	Rolled Microfiche	(10000 rolls)	5353	5303	50
档案利用情况		**File Utilization**				
本年利用档案人次	(人次)	Persons Using Files in the Year	(person-times)	123073	13148	109925
本年利用档案	(万卷件次)	Files Used in the Year	(10000 roll.times)	18.11	4.10	14.01
本年利用资料册次	(册次)	Datum Used in the Year	(volume-times)	5844	461	5383
本年利用资料人次	(人次)	Persons Using Data in the Year	(person-times)	629	119	510
本年编研档案、资料	(万字)	Files and Data Prepared and Studied in the Year	(10000 Chinese characters)	715.2	133.7	581.5
档案馆网站来访IP次数	**(万次)**	**Archive Website Visiting IP**	**(10000 times)**	**96.26**	**42.21**	**54.05**

资料来源：北京市档案局。
Source: Beijing Municipal Bureau of Archives.

18-25 专业艺术剧团、艺术表演场所情况(1978-2012年)
PROFESSIONAL ART TROUPES AND ART PERFORMANCE VENUES (1978-2012)

年 份 Year	专业艺术剧团 Professional Art Troupes 个 数(个) Number (unit)	从业人员(人) Perons Employed (person)	演出场次(场次) Perfor-mances (times)	#国内演出场 次 Domestic Performances	国 内 观众人数(万人次) Domestic Spectator (10000 person-times)	艺术表演场所 Art Performance Venues 个 数(个) Number (unit)	从业人员(人) Perons Employed (person)	演出场次(场次) Perfor-mances (times)	#艺术演出场 次 Art Shows	观众人数(万人次) Audience (10000 person-times)
1978						35	933		3430	
1979						29	792		3354	
1980	42	10035		16544	2092.0	30	850		4106	
1981	42	10150		16298	1860.0	33	887	25963	3234	
1982	43	10674		16656	1721.0	31	833	24367	3641	
1983	41	10424		13997	1596.0	32	849	28603	3680	
1984	41	10645		13470	1443.0	32	898	32460	3407	
1985	42	10390		11380	1105.0	32	892	36021	2883	
1986	42	10871		10907	1086.0	32	1085	33582	3001	2362.8
1987	42	10752		10652	1035.0	26	765	29695	2840	1866.5
1988	41	10228		8194	889.0	25	809	34731	2633	2044.3
1989	43	9865		7544	756.0	25	813	37030	1340	1913.9
1990	43	9847		7527	839.0	25	833	49444	1331	1782.4
1991	44	10116		6623	1612.0	25	849	44846	1147	1463.2
1992	43	9734		6850	682.0	25	810	49259	1195	1070.5
1993	42	9701		6538	529.0	25	831	37406	989	615.9
1994	42	9182		7290	554.0	23	745	30468	895	525.9
1995	43	8925		6728	447.0	23	724	28316	720	429.9
1996	38	7679		7615	638.0	24	761	33356	1411	371.2
1997	38	8090		8426	696.0	22	709	32412	1851	352.3
1998	37	5388		8105	495.0	22	720	32218	1800	270.4
1999	37	6959		8564	1275.0	24	784	32666	2294	264.7
2000	31	5089		7610	926.0	24	739	25922	2088	272.9
2001	37	6786		8466	1668.9	23	709	20373	2302	237.1
2002	36	6911		9528	678.7	24	715	18434	2950	257.8
2003	36	6965		8797	586.1	24	698	13956	2461	216.2
2004	36	6939		8731	846.4	36	1223	24310	7085	538.3
2005	36	6986	11059	8934	758.7	39	1313	26931	7160	542.9
2006	33	7363	10929	9790	866.0	42	1291	31408	8253	504.2
2007	33	7364	11720	10076	720.0	43	1803	34946	9288	553.3
2008	33	7146	11417	10663	877.0	54	2245	45014	11293	750.0
2009	35	7504	10131	9684	863.0	73	1798	59464	14061	791.0
2010	35	7415	10983	10483	1108.0	73	2879	54376	16941	1035.0
2011	35	6713	11757	11069	1173.0	68	2954	54905	16625	931.0
2012	35	7826	12672	11675	1204.0					

注：1. 专业艺术剧团包括中央、市属及区县属专业院团。
2. 1978年艺术表演场所范围含中央属；1979—2003年包括文化部门主管直属剧场；2004—2011年包括全行业主要剧场。

资料来源：北京市文化局。

Note: a) Professional art troupes include professional troupes at the central, municipal, district and county levels.
b) In 1978, art performance venues included central ones; in 1979-2003 they included theaters directly under the Ministry of Culture; in 2004-2011 they included main theaters across the sector.

Source: Beijing Municipal Bureau of Culture.

18-26 专业艺术剧团(2012年)
PROFESSIONAL ART TROUPES (2012)

项目	Item	个数 (个) Number (unit)	从业人员 (人) Perons Employed (person)	演出场次 (场次) Perfor-mances (times)	#国内演出场次 Domestic Performances	#农村演出场次 Rural Per-formances	国内观众人数 (万人次) Domestic Spectator (10000 person-times)	演出收入 (万元) Performances Revenue (10000 yuan)
合　计	**Total**	**35**	**7826**	**12672**	**11675**	**1699**	**1204**	**53770**
按隶属关系分组	**Grouped by Administrative Relationship**							
中央属	Central	17	5376	3997	3698	704	762	35193
市　属	Municipal	11	2254	7831	7153	995	416	17914
区县属	District and County	7	196	844	824		26	663
按剧种分	**Grouped by Art Troupes**							
话剧、儿童剧团、滑稽剧团	Stage Play, Children's Drama, and Farce Troupes	4	1103	1940	1901	51	131	7208
歌剧、舞剧、歌舞剧团	Opera, Ballet and Dance Troupes	2	898	477	456	15	130	6405
歌舞团、轻音乐团	Song and Dance Troupes and Light Music Troupes	4	1348	2215	2155	373	249	11266
乐团、合唱团	Philharmonic Troupes and Glee Club	4	746	538	512	5	55	8941
戏曲剧团	Local Opera Troupes	10	1640	2795	2573	581	131	6348
曲、杂、木、皮影剧团	Recitation and Ballad Troupes,Acrobatics and Circus Troupes,Puppet Show Troupes and Shadow Play Troupes	5	478	3654	3089	37	133	5251
综合艺术表演团体	General Art Performance Groups	6	1613	1053	989	637	375	8351

资料来源：北京市文化局。
Source: Beijing Municipal Bureau of Culture.

18-27 电影电视、广播电台情况(1978-2012年)

年 份 Year	电影 Film					电视 TV		
	电 影 单位数 (个) Number (unit)	放映场次 (万场次) Show Times (10000 Times)	观众人次 (万人次) Spectators (10000 Person-times)	票款收入 (亿元) Ticket Revenue (100 million yuan)	发行收入 (万元) Publishing Income (10000 yuan)	电视节目 套 数 (套) Number of TV Programs (unit)	平均每日电视 节目播出时间 (小时) Daily Show Hours of TV Programs (hour)	电视综合 覆 盖 率 (%) Comprehensive Coverage Rate of TV (%)
1978	2904	31.9	29924.1		1137.4			
1979	3077	35.5	34626.0		1450.6			
1980	3192	33.1	31189.5		1294.0	1	4.25	
1981	2951	31.9	30067.0		1340.5	1	5.46	100.00
1982	2701	32.8	28743.5		1374.9	1	6.85	91.00
1983	2714	30.1	27345.5		1403.2	1	7.07	90.00
1984	2524	27.8	23966.7		1537.0	1	7.15	98.00
1985	2166	23.0	18875.0		1688.6	1	7.54	98.00
1986	1905	20.6	15904.4		1697.9	2	19.07	98.00
1987	1522	19.0	13517.7		1743.6	2	13.64	98.00
1988	1479	19.2	13269.4		1925.7	2	19.39	98.00
1989	1216	21.5	14492.6		2126.6	4	25.43	98.00
1990	1216	20.7	12771.2		2202.4	4	29.43	98.00
1991	1004	21.3	12558.3		2492.1	4	27.79	98.00
1992	955	22.1	11587.4		2439.3	6	45.02	98.00
1993	955	11.9	5369.8		1948.5	7	58.18	98.00
1994	961	10.6	2166.5	0.51		9	77.79	98.30
1995	339	9.2	1598.6	0.93		12	98.36	98.30
1996	323	11.5	1644.1	1.07		12	101.01	98.81
1997	333	12.6	1742.3	1.17		12	111.00	99.12
1998	189	12.3	1443.5	1.28		12	110.68	99.60
1999	226	11.7	964.7		2923.4	12	118.36	99.80
2000	236	12.2	873.2		3359.8	12	122.45	99.80
2001	213	12.6	804.7	0.92		16	200.15	99.91
2002	192	12.3	827.4	1.09		18	329.40	99.82
2003	214	11.8	683.0	1.35		19	259.32	99.90
2004	172	18.1	814.4	1.86		24	244.17	99.50
2005	160	22.6	873.8	2.29		25	329.81	99.99
2006		28.0	1221.0	3.02		25	294.23	99.99
2007		38.0	1711.0	3.70		25	309.12	99.99
2008		46.8	1767.3	5.37		24	309.06	99.99
2009		62.4	2451.5	8.19		26	319.13	99.99
2010		74.3	2923.3	11.81		26	319.24	99.99
2011		97.4	3235.9	13.52		25	334.22	100.00
2012		120.0	3954.6	16.23		26	343.68	100.00

资料来源：北京市广播电影电视局。

FILM, TELEVISION, BROADCAST, AND RADIO STATIONS (1978-2012)

电视 TV				广播电台 Broadcasting Stations			
农村电视综合覆盖率 (%) Comprehensive Coverage Rate of TV in Rural Area (%)	无线电视综合覆盖率 (%) Comprehensive Coverage Rate of Wireless TV (%)	有线电视注册用户数 (万户) Access Subscnbers of CATV (10000 households)	有线广播电视入户率 (%) Access Rate of CATV (%)	广播节目套数 (套) Number of Radio Programs (unit)	平均每日广播节目播出时间 (小时) Daily Show Hours of Radio Programs (hour)	广播综合覆盖率 (%) Comprehensive Coverage Rate of Broadcast (%)	广告收入 (万元) Advertising Income (10000 yuan)
				4	56.08		
				4	57.22	100.00	139
				4	59.37	98.00	166
				5	61.97	98.00	117
				5	73.67	98.00	668
				5	65.87	98.00	645
				5	66.17	98.00	555
				6	68.75	98.00	771
				6	76.33	98.00	964
				7	78.67	98.00	1668
				7	77.87	98.00	2885
				7	77.87	98.00	5115
				10	94.75	98.00	9680
				12	134.75	98.00	15225
		52.71		12	134.85	98.00	26480
		82.21		13	148.25	91.00	45398
		182.97		13	150.25	96.97	93428
		202.75		15	156.05	98.44	100546
		230.97		16	174.67	99.98	106773
		165.78	43.24	16	178.20	99.96	115072
		175.71	45.80	16	188.90	97.7	149661
		205.95	51.76	16	192.43	99.91	136451
		231.24	57.05	16	197.43	99.88	154317
		243.00	58.39	16	197.86	99.91	157210
	97.57	265.50	62.09	16	229.55	100.00	212091
	99.99	282.00	64.12	17	281.88	100.00	236334
99.97	94.90	319.58	70.75	17	282.88	100.00	240146
99.97	93.13	345.06	74.43	17	288.92	99.98	317437
99.97	93.19	383.13	81.00	17	297.40	99.98	385231
99.97	94.38	413.50	85.90	18	316.58	99.99	453932
99.97	98.72	448.12	91.68	18	324.82	99.99	613672
100.00	99.74	475.92	95.90	18	329.56	100.00	796113
100.00	99.75	495.70	99.13	25	471.69	100.00	1081857

Source: Beijing Municipal Bureau of Radio,Film and Television.

18-28 电影、电视剧、电视动画片制作情况
PRODUCTION OF FILMS, TV PLAYS AND TV CARTOONS

项目		Item		2012 全国 National Total	2012 北京 Local	2012 占全国比重(%) As % of National Total	2011 全国 National Total	2011 北京 Local	2011 占全国比重(%) As % of National Total
生产故事片	(部)	Feature Films	(Piece)	893	243	27.2	558	306	54.8
制作电视剧	(部)	TV Plays	(Piece)	506	98	19.4	469	87	18.6
	(集)		(Episode)	17703	3408	19.3	14942	2721	18.2
制作电视动画片	(部)	TV Cartoons	(Piece)	395	23	5.8	435	20	4.6
	(分钟)		(Minute)	222938	9952	4.5	261224	11168	4.3
电视剧出口量部	(部)	TV Plays Exported	(Piece)	326	98	30.1	298	62	20.8
	(集)		(Episode)	15329	3253	21.2	14001	2340	16.7
电视剧出口额	(万元)	Value of TV Plays Exported	(10000 yuan)	15020	2549	17.0	14649	2338	16.0

资料来源：北京市广播电影电视局
Source: Beijing Municipal Bureau of Radio, Film and Television

18-29 电影放映单位情况(2012年)
STATISTICS ON MOVIE SHOW ORGANIZATIONS (2012)

项目	Item	放映单位数(个) Number of Show Organizations (unit)	总银幕数(块) Total Screens (Pieces)	#3D银幕数 3D Screens	#IMAX巨幕数 IMAX Large Screens	放映场次(万场次) Show Times (10000 Times)	观影人次(万人次) Spectators (10000 Person-times)	票房收入(亿元) Ticket Revenue (100 million yuan)
合　计	**Total**	**135**	**726**	**244**	**5**	**119.99**	**3954.56**	**16.23**
院线影院	Cinema Chain	135	726	244	5	119.87	3752.61	16.21
二级市场	Secondary Market					0.12	201.95	0.02

资料来源：北京市广播电影电视局。
Source: Beijing Municipal Bureau of Radio,Film and Television.

18-30 电视台情况
BASIC STATISTICS ON TELEVISION STATIONS

项目		Item		2012 中央 Central	2012 地方 Local	2011 中央 Central	2011 地方 Local
基本情况		**Basic Statistics**					
电视台	(座)	Television Stations	(unit)	1	1	1	1
公共节目套数	(套)	Programs	(unit)	32	26	30	25
全年公共节目播出时间	(小时)	Program Hours Per Year	(hour)	268458	125444	251908	113232
播放节目情况		**Shows of TV Programs**					
新闻咨询类节目	(小时)	News Consulting Programs	(hour)	67995	22112	68594	17916
专题服务类节目	(小时)	Special Service Programs	(hour)	92092	50093	80497	47217
综艺益智类节目	(小时)	General Entertainment Art Programs	(hour)	40538	8893	40246	8109
影视剧类节目	(小时)	Movie and TV Play Programs	(hour)	56371	23314	53450	21067
广告类节目	(小时)	Advertisement Programs	(hour)	9301	11767	9120	10580
其他类节目	(小时)	Other Programs	(hour)	2158	9262		8341

注：电视台数不包括区县电视台。
资料来源：国家广播电影电视总局、北京市广播电影电视局。
Note: Number of television stations excludes TV stations of districts and counties.
Source: National Administration for Radio, Film and Television, Beijing Municipal Bureau of Radio, Film and Television.

18-31 广播电台情况
BASIC STATISTICS ON BROADCASTING STATIONS

项目		Item		2012 中央 Central	2012 地方 Local	2011 中央 Central	2011 地方 Local
基本情况		**Basic Statistics**					
电台数	(座)	Number of Broadcasting Station:	(unit)	2	1	2	1
公共节目套数	(套)	Programs	(unit)	27	25	26	18
全年公共节目播出时间	(小时)	Program Hours Per Year	(hour)	292062	172170	274574	120291
播放节目情况		**Shows of TV Programs**					
新闻咨询类节目	(小时)	News Consulting Programs	(hour)	91255	18950	85455	19718
专题服务类节目	(小时)	Special Service Programs	(hour)	111099	39666	104759	39233
综艺类节目	(小时)	General Art Programs	(hour)	64294	73536	57677	19796
广播剧类节目	(小时)	Broadcast Plays	(hour)	2815	8535	2111	7807
广告类节目	(小时)	Commercial Programs	(hour)	14984	14753	15734	16442
其他类节目	(小时)	Other Programs	(hour)	7614	16728	8836	17294

注：1. 广播电台数不包括区县电台。
2. 公共节目套数中含县级广播电视台的广播节目套数。
资料来源：国家广播电影电视总局、北京市广播电影电视局
Note: a) Number of broadcasting stations excluded those of districts and counties.
b) Programs included broadcast programs of radio stations at county levels.
Source: National Administration for Radio, Film and Television,Beijing Municipal Bureau of Radio,Film and Television.

18-32 广播电视综合覆盖率(2012年)
COMPREHENSIVE COVERAGE RATE OF BROADCAST/TV(2012)

项目		Item		2012
广播综合覆盖率	(%)	Comprehensive Coverage Rate of Broadcast	(%)	100.0
农村广播综合覆盖率	(%)	Comprehensive Coverage Rate of Broadcast in Rural Area	(%)	100.0
无线广播综合覆盖率	(%)	Comprehensive Coverage Rate of Radio	(%)	100.0
电视综合覆盖率	(%)	Comprehensive Coverage Rate of TV	(%)	100.0
农村电视综合覆盖率	(%)	Comprehensive Coverage Rate of TV in Rural Area	(%)	100.0
无线电视综合覆盖率	(%)	Comprehensive Coverage Rate of Wireless TV	(%)	99.75
有线广播电视入户率	(%)	Access Rate of CATV	(%)	99.13
有线电视注册用户数	(万户)	Access Subscnbers of CATV	(10000 households)	495.7
#高清交互数字电视用户数	(万户)	Digital Broadcast/TV Subscribers	(10000 households)	310.9
付费电视用户数	(万户)	Pay Broadcast/TV Subscribers	(10000 households)	0.94
农村有线广播电视用户数	(万户)	Cable Broadcast/TV Subscribers in Rural Area	(10000 households)	70.51

资料来源：北京市广播电影电视局。
Source: Beijing Municipal Bureau of Radio,Film and Television.

18-33 报纸、期刊、图书出版情况(1978-2012年)
NEWSPAPER,MAGAZINES AND BOOK PUBLISHING (1978-2012)

年份 Year	报纸出版 Newspaper Publications 种数(种) Number (kind)	平均期印数(万份) Average Printed Copies Per Issue (10000 copies)	总印数(亿份) Total Printed Copies (100 million copies)	总印张(亿印张) Total Paper Capacity (100 million pieces)	期刊出版 Magazines Publications 种数(种) Number (kind)	平均期印数(万册) Average Printed Copies Per Issue (10000 copies)	总印数(亿册) Total Printed Copies (100 million copies)	总印张(亿印张) Total Paper Capacity (100 million pieces)	图书出版 Books Publications 种数(种) Number (kind)	总印数(亿册、亿张) Total Printed Copies (100 million copies)	总印张(亿印张) Total Paper Capacity (100 million pieces)
1978	11		68.50		468		4.50		5253	5.12	
1979	16		81.60		697		5.92		6723	5.91	
1980	41		84.50		839		5.80		9534	6.28	
1981	55		83.10		886		6.69		11139	7.84	
1982	57		78.30		882		6.67		13862	8.71	
1983	61		79.90		940		6.84		14384	8.49	
1984	73		83.00		987		7.89		15636	8.43	
1985	99		86.00		1098		8.21		17178	9.01	
1986	126		82.00		1206		7.95		19362	5.82	
1987	129		86.00		1409		8.24		21843	6.94	
1988	151		87.00		1514		8.23		23689	7.28	
1989	161		66.00		1580		6.24		25980	6.31	
1990	148		68.00		1415		5.90		27345	6.17	
1991	157		76.70		1499		6.83		29609	7.05	
1992	164	3886	81.38	88.39	1594	6043	7.79	22.30	31320	7.83	58.67
1993	170	3965	81.70	87.71	1597	6037	7.80	22.36	34393	8.60	70.96
1994	233	3759	69.98	92.59	1854	5328	6.29	19.11	38498	8.28	71.71
1995	240	3823	72.92	108.32	1884	5018	6.38	19.62	38819	8.33	70.15
1996	242		70.52		2129		6.13		41572	9.45	
1997	242	3624	71.80	122.17	2162	5396	6.61	22.87	45775	9.93	78.62
1998	247	3561	71.70	130.01	2274	5797	7.28	26.54	50155	10.95	86.05
1999	247	3520	71.65	144.65	2273	6116	8.04	35.18	54783	11.34	93.38
2000	240	3343	68.67	149.58	2352	5909	7.91	32.96	57821	9.63	92.98
2001	243	3339	69.35	153.22	2374	5761	8.09	32.61	63928	10.27	105.06
2002	247	3364	71.02	169.87	2377	5708	8.23	34.34	73836	12.16	127.48
2003	250	3393	72.45	190.35	2382	5702	8.18	34.25	85244	13.82	140.77
2004	253	3405	70.40	206.53	2791	5233	7.97	35.53	98312	15.22	157.17
2005	255	3169	66.16	227.22	2809	4957	7.72	40.80	108152	17.07	180.51
2006	256	3651	74.01	240.39	2809	5077	8.29	47.39	113232	17.19	186.10
2007	256	3454	73.09	218.55	2809	5340	9.17	54.21	125412	18.68	195.30
2008	259	3328	73.21	241.27	2898	5392	9.36	55.39	136284	20.78	220.00
2009	260	3232	71.63	232.50	3030	5373	9.70	59.35	144211	21.04	220.21
2010	262	3406	77.54	275.62	3063	5519	10.03	69.61	155209	21.45	251.18
2011	254	3453	83.07	293.72	3044	5991	10.19	76.74	167942	22.60	243.05
2012	257	3725	89.49	300.17	3064	5940	10.31	76.68	179634	22.54	250.70

注：1991年及以前，报纸、期刊、图书为出版数；1992年及以后均为总印数。

资料来源：中华人民共和国新闻出版总署、北京市新闻出版局。

Note: Figures on newspaper, magazines and books before 1991 were published figures; after 1992, they were total printed copies.

Source: The General Administration of Press and Publication of the P.R.China,Beijing Municipal Bureau of Press and Publication.

18-34 报纸出版情况
NEWSPAPER PUBLICATION

项目	Item	种数(种) Number of Publications (kind)		平均期印数(万份) Average Printed Copies Per Issue (10000 copies)		总印数 (亿份) Total Printed Copies (100 million copies)		总印张 (亿印张) Total Paper Capacity (100 million pieces)	
		2012	2011	2012	2011	2012	2011	2012	2011
合 计	**Total**	**257**	**254**	**3725**	**3453**	**89.5**	**83.1**	**300.2**	**293.7**
综合报	Comprehensive	30	33	1382	1357	46.0	45.2	178.2	187.0
专业报	Professional	227	221	2343	2096	43.5	37.9	121.9	106.7

资料来源：中华人民共和国新闻出版总署、北京市新闻出版局。
Source: The General Administration of Press and Publication of the P.R.China,Beijing Municipal Bureau of Press and Publication.

18-35 期刊出版情况
MAGAZINES PUBLICATION

项目	Item	种数 (种) Number of Publications (kind)		平均期印数 (万册) Average Copies Per Issue (10000 copies)		总印数 (亿册) Total Copies (100 million copies)		总印张 (亿印张) Total Paper Capacity (100 million pieces)	
		2012	2011	2012	2011	2012	2011	2012	2011
合 计	**Total**	**3064**	**3044**	**5940**	**5991**	**10.31**	**10.19**	**76.68**	**76.74**
综 合	Comprehensive	70	130	167	165	0.40	0.39	3.19	2.96
哲学、社会科学	Philosophy and Social Sciences	906	869	3484	3361	6.20	5.84	32.82	30.83
自然科学技术	Natural Sciences and Technology	1580	1548	1335	1347	1.88	1.91	19.92	20.39
文化、教育	Culture and Education	369	362	761	922	1.46	1.65	18.14	19.95
文学、艺术	Literature and Art	139	135	193	196	0.38	0.40	2.61	2.62

资料来源：中华人民共和国新闻出版总署、北京市新闻出版局。
Source: The General Administration of Press and Publication of the P.R.China,Beijing Municipal Bureau of Press and Publication.

18-36 图书出版情况
BOOKS PUBLICATION

项目	Item	出版图书种数合计(种) Number of Publications (kind) 2012	2011	#新书 New Publications 2012	2011	总印数(万册、万张) Total Copies (10000 volumes, 10000 pieces) 2012	2011	总印张(万印张) Total Print Sheets (10000 print sheets) 2012	2011
合计	**Total**	**179634**	**167942**	**107013**	**96689**	**225411**	**225969**	**2506987**	**2430527**
书籍合计	**Books**	**179569**	**167827**	**106971**	**96600**	**223445**	**223931**	**2490769**	**2421430**
马列主义、毛泽东思想	Maxism-Leninism -Mao Zedong Thought	318	309	203	196	969	1294	18408	25366
哲学	Philosophy	4993	5485	3561	4251	3388	3983	51042	61286
社会科学总论	General Social Sciences	3140	3376	1974	2171	1923	2016	34300	34415
政治、法律	Politics and Law	12239	10982	9464	8690	11407	10161	155462	148069
军事	Military	760	695	603	540	542	518	7452	8297
经济	Economics	20775	20752	13635	13210	11360	12122	194531	206304
文化、科学、教育、体育	Culture,Science,Education and Sports	34881	31427	17958	14222	121643	124143	942051	900036
语言、文字	Languages	11979	11061	5853	5445	12809	13435	222689	217573
文学	Literature	13938	9949	10559	7186	14615	11605	193013	148840
艺术	Art	7408	6114	5065	4116	4732	4445	62674	39411
历史、地理	History and Geography	8029	6741	6112	5255	6282	5441	78955	74994
自然科学总论	General Natural Sciences	296	322	157	207	202	211	2589	3056
数学科学、化学	Mathematics and Chemistry	4736	4718	1870	1717	2885	3008	50102	50683
天文学、物理科学	Astronomy and Physics	1434	1365	972	877	598	569	7375	6919
生物科学	Biology	1516	1516	882	821	997	919	12474	13678
医药、卫生	Medicine and Health Care	10483	9778	6078	5549	7948	7216	126241	128458
农业科学	Agricultural Science	3453	3261	1997	1870	2060	2506	21294	24034
工业技术	Industrial Technology	33321	34273	16609	17093	15520	16235	261673	277705
交通运输	Transportation	3334	3271	1664	1585	2059	1939	28466	26953
航空、航天	Aeronautics and Aerospace	301	244	212	166	113	110	1565	1517
环境科学	Environmental Science	1269	1265	883	911	566	705	7299	8044
综合性图书	General Books	966	923	660	522	827	1350	11116	15795
图片及小件印品合计	**Pictures**	**65**	**115**	**42**	**89**	**1966**	**2038**	**16218**	**9097**

资料来源：中华人民共和国新闻出版总署、北京市新闻出版局。
Source: The General Administration of Press and Publication of the P.R.China,Beijing Municipal Bureau of Press and Publication.

18-37 录音制品出版情况
PUBLICATION OF AUDIO PRODUCTS

项 目 Item	录音带 Audio-tapes				激光唱盘 CDs				高密度激光唱盘 DVD-A			
	种数(种) Kind (kind)		数量(万盒) Volume (10000 cassettes)		种数(种) Kind (kind)		数量(万张) Volume (10000 pieces)		种数(种) Kind (kind)		数量(万张) Volume (10000 pieces)	
	2012	2011	2012	2011	2012	2011	2012	2011	2012	2011	2012	2011
合 计 Total	**1267**	**1541**	**13904.0**	**15424.6**	**2014**	**1744**	**1345.1**	**1511.6**	**965**	**1106**	**1070.8**	**954.8**
#市 属 Municipal	17	212	4.2	63.2	56	26	59.3	51.3	44	20	12.4	4.8

资料来源：中华人民共和国新闻出版总署、北京市新闻出版局。
Source: The General Administration of Press and Publication of the P.R.China, Beijing Municipal Bureau of Press and Publication.

18-38 录像制品出版情况
PUBLICATION OF VIDEO PRODUCTS

项 目 Item	录像带 Videotapes				激光视盘 VCD				高密度激光视盘 DVD-V			
	种数(种) Kind (kind)		数量(万盒) Volume (10000 cassettes)		种数(种) Kind (kind)		数量(万张) Volume (10000 pieces)		种数(种) Kind (kind)		数量(万张) Volume (10000 pieces)	
	2012	2011	2012	2011	2012	2011	2012	2011	2012	2011	2012	2011
合 计 Total	**46**	**75**	**20.3**	**37.2**	**964**	**1439**	**3261.7**	**4009.3**	**3282**	**2530**	**3421.8**	**2990.4**
#市 属 Municipal		2		2.8	4	24	0.5	22.9	124	133	133.4	289.9

资料来源：中华人民共和国新闻出版总署、北京市新闻出版局。
Source: The General Administration of Press and Publication of the P.R.China, Beijing Municipal Bureau of Press and Publication.

18-39 电子出版物出版情况(2012年)
PUBLICATION OF E-PUBLICATIONS (2012)

项目	Item	只读光盘CD-ROM		交互式光盘CD-I		高密度只读光盘DVD-ROM	
		种数(种) Kind (kind)	数量(万盒) Volume (10000 cassettes)	种数(种) Kind (kind)	数量(万张) Volume (10000 pieces)	种数(种) Kind (kind)	数量(万张) Volume (10000 pieces)
合计	**Total**	**4646**	**13966.4**	**718**	**894.8**	**2619**	**3827.8**
#市属	Municipal	32	31.31	35	1.7	20	11

资料来源：中华人民共和国新闻出版总署、北京市新闻出版局。
Source: The General Administration of Press and Publication of the P.R.China,Beijing Municipal Bureau of Press and Publication.

18-40 引进版权量情况
AMOUNT OF IMPORTED COPYRIGHTS

项目	Item	2012	2011
引进版权量 (件)	**Amount of Imported Copyrights (set)**	**9587**	**8232**
软件和电子出版物 (件)	Software and E-Publications (set)	233	313
图书 (件)	Books (set)	9354	7919

注：2012年引进图书版权量含期刊。
Note: The date of amount of inported copyrights include magzines.
资料来源：北京市新闻出版局。
Source: Beijing Municipal Bureau of Press and Publication.

主要统计指标解释

教　育

研究生培养机构　指经国家批准按国家计划招收和培养硕士、博士和其他研究生的高等学校和科学研究机构。

普通高等学校　指按国家规定的设置标准和审批程序批准举办的，通过国家统一招生考试，招收高中毕业生为主要培养对象，实施高等教育的全日制大学、独立设置的学院和高等专科学校、短期职业大学。

成人高等学校　指按国家规定的设置标准和审批程序批准举办的，通过全国成人高等教育统一招生考试，招收具有高中毕业或同等学历的人员为主要培养对象，利用函授、业余、脱产等多种形式对其实施高等学历教育的学校。包括：职工高等学校、农民高等学校、管理干部学院、教育学院、独立函授学院、广播电视大学和其他机构。

高等教育机构　指经省、自治区、直辖市教育行政部门审批并颁发办学许可证，不具有颁发学历文凭资格的实施高等教育的单位。

民办学校　指经有关主管部门批准，公民个人、社会团体及其他社会组织等利用非国家财政性教育经费，面向社会举办的学校及其他教育机构。

学历文凭考试机构　经教育行政部门专门批准，进行全日制高等教育的民办其他高等教育机构。

专科教育　应当使学生掌握本专业必备的基础理论、专门应用技术知识，具有从事本专业实际工作的基本技能和技术应用能力。全日制专科教育的基本修业年限为二至三年。

本科教育　应当使学生比较系统地掌握本学科、专业必需的基础理论、基本知识，掌握本专业必要的基本技能、方法和相关知识，具有从事本专业实际工作和研究工作的初步能力。全日制本科教育的基本修业年限为四至五年。

硕士研究生教育　应当使学生掌握本学科坚实的基础理论、系统的专业知识，掌握相应的技能、方法和相关知识，具有从事本专业实际工作和科学研究工作的能力。硕士研究生教育的基本修业年限为二至三年。

博士研究生教育　应当使学生掌握本学科坚实宽广的基础理论、系统深入的专业知识、相应的技能和方法，具有独立从事本学科创造性科学研究工作和实际工作的能力。博士研究生教育的基本修业年限为三至四年。

网络学生　指经教育部批准的现代远程教育试点学校设立的网络教育学院，基于互联网上实施高等学历教育所招收的普通和成人本科、专科学生。

在职人员攻读博士、硕士学位学生　指经国务院学位委员会批准的，为提高在职人员业务水平，通过攻读博士、硕士学位入学全国联考所招收的学生。培养的学生只有学位没有学历。

证书教育　指由各类高等教育机构举办的，招收具有高中毕业文化程度，从事专业技术工作或专业性较强的管理工作人员，经过学校学习及考试合格，取得达到岗位要求的专业知识水平证明的非学历教育。证书教育形式包括单科班和专业证书班。

单科班　指学生在学校只学一个科目中的一门或几门课程，考试合格可获得单科结业证书。

专业证书班　学生在学校学习8至10门课程，考试合格可获得岗位要求的大专层次专业知识水平的证书。

岗位培训　指由各类高等教育机构举办的，以提高本职工作能力为目的的非学历教育和培训活动。接受培训的各类人员按要求经考核合格，颁发岗位合格证书和上岗任职聘任书。岗位培训形式包括资格性培训和适应性培训。

资格性培训　指学生按照岗位规范要求取得上岗(在岗)、转岗、晋升等资格的培训。

适应性培训　指学生根据本岗位工作的发展需要而进行各种适应性的培训。

进修及培训　指对具有大学专科以上学历和中级以上职称的专业人员和管理人员进行扩展知识，提高技能的非学历教育。

外国留学生　指接受来中国学习的外籍学生。

毕业生数　指上学年度内，具有学籍的学生学完教学计划规定的全部课程，考试及格，取得毕业证书，实际毕业的学生数。不包括结业生和肄业生数。

招生数　指新学年开始时，按照国家计划实际招收入学的新生数。不包括留级生和复读学生数。

在校学生数　指学年初开学以后，具有学籍的注册学生数。

结业生数　指具有学籍的学生学习期满，有一门以上主要课程(包括毕业论文或毕业设计)不及格或其他方面不合格，未予毕业而发给结业证书的学生数。不包括短训班和单科结业学生。

教职工数　指在学校(机构)工作并由学校(机构)支付工资的教职工人数。教职工数包括校本部教职工、科研机构人员、校办企业职工、其他附设机构人员。

教师　指专职从事教学工作的人员，包括临时调去帮助做其他工作的人员，不包括调离教学岗位担负行政领导工作的原教学人员。

专任教师　指主要从事教育工作的人员。包括临时（一年以内）调去帮助做其他工作的教学人员。不包括调离教学岗位，担任行政领导工作或其他工作的原教学人员；不包括兼任教师和代课教师。

特殊教育学校　指招收盲聋哑青少年进行初中等教育的学校。

校舍建筑面积　指产权归学校所有，已经使用的各种用房的建筑面积。不包括尚未竣工的在建工程和借用、租用的房舍或临时搭用的棚舍。

危房面积　指年久失修、结构构件受到严重损坏，有倒塌危险，经房管部门鉴定属于危房的面积。

学校占地面积　指学校校园内的土地面积，不包括校园外学校拥有的农场、林场及校办工厂等的土地面积。

文　化

公共图书馆藏书　指各级文化部门举办的面向社会服务的独立的图书馆（不包括文化馆的图书室，也不包括文化系统以外的图书馆）藏书数量。

艺术剧团　指从事戏曲、音乐、舞蹈、杂技等专业艺术表演，有独立账户、实行独立核算的团体。不包括半工半艺和民间职业剧团。

艺术表演观众人数（人次）　指售票、包场演出或民族地区免费演出的艺术表演观众人次数。不包括彩排审查和内部 观摩演出的观众人次数。

广播电视

广播综合覆盖率　根据国家广电总局制定的《广播电视人口覆盖率统计技术标准和方法》进行统计调查的，在对象区内能接收到广播节目的覆盖人口数占本行政区域内人口总数的比率。

农村广播综合覆盖率　根据国家广电总局制定的《广播电视人口覆盖率统计技术标准和方法》进行统计调查的，在对象区内能接收到广播节目的农村人口数占本行政区域内农村人口总数的比率。农村是指经国家批准设立的乡镇人民政府的乡和农村建制镇所辖区，不包括县政府驻地镇。

无线广播综合覆盖率　根据国家广电总局制定的《广播电视人口覆盖率统计技术标准和方法》进行统计调查的，在对象区内能接收到用中、短波、调频等无线传输技术发射转播的广播节目的人口数占本行政区域内人口总数的比率。包括中央、省、地市、县四级无线广播综合覆盖人口。

电视综合覆盖率　根据国家广电总局制定的《广播电视人口覆盖率统计技术标准和方法》进行统计调查的，在对象区内能接收到电视节目的人口数占本行政区域内人口总数的比率，包括中央、省、地市、县电视节目综合覆盖人口。

农村电视综合覆盖率　根据国家广电总局制定的《广播电视人口覆盖率统计技术标准和方法》进行统计调查的，在对象区内能接收到电视节目的农村人口数占本行政区域内农村人口总数的比率，包括中央、省、地市、县电视节目综合覆盖农村人口。农村是指经国家批准设立的乡镇人民政府的乡和农村建制镇所辖区，不包括县政府驻地镇。

无线电视综合覆盖率　根据国家广电总局制定的《广播电视人口覆盖率统计技术标准和方法》进行统计调查的，在对象区内能接收到用中、短波、调频等无线传输技术发射转播的电视节目的人口数占本行政区域内人口总数的比率。包括中央、省、地市、县四级无线电视综合覆盖人口。

有线电视入户率　指通过广播电视有线传输网收看电视节目的家庭用户数（包括接收模拟信号和接收数字信号的有线电视用户数，不包括宾馆、单位、写字楼等集体用户）与本行政区域内总户数的比率。

数字电视用户数　指通过广播电视有线传输网收看数字信号电视节目的家庭用户数。

付费电视用户数　指通过广播电视有线传输网收看数字信号的电视节目，并交纳收看费的有线电视家庭用户数。

Explanatory Notes on Main Statistical Indicators

Education

Postgraduate Education Institutions refer to colleges and universities, research institutions recruiting and educating postgraduates of master's degree, doctor's degree and other degree upon approval by the government and under the State Plan.

Regular Institutions of Higher Education refer to educational establishments set up according to the government evaluation and approval procedures, recruiting graduates from senior secondary schools as the main target by National Matriculation Test. They include full-time universities, independent colleges and higher professional schools, short-term vocational colleges.

Adult Institutions of Higher Education refer to educational establishments, set up in line with relevant rules approved by the government, recruiting personnel with senior high school or equivalent educational diploma through national college entrance test for adults, and providing higher education courses in many forms of correspondence, spare-time, or full-time teaching for adults. Institutions of higher learning for adults include schools of higher education for staff and workers, schools of higher education for farmers, colleges for management cadres, pedagogical colleges, independent correspondence colleges, Radio and TV universities and other educational establishments.

Higher Education Institutions refer to institutions offering higher education upon examination and approval by administrative departments in charge of education in provinces, autonomous regions and municipalities, with an education license, which are not eligible for conferring diploma.

Civilian-run Schools refer to schools and other educational institutions run by individuals, social groups and other social organizations upon approval by relevant competent authorities, by using educational funds not from state revenues.

Diploma Test Institutions refer to other civilian-run higher education institutions offering full-time higher education upon special approval by educational administration.

Undergraduate Education shall enable students to understand necessary basic theories and knowledge of a subject or specialty, have necessary basic skills, methodology and relevant knowledge of the specialty, and have preliminary skills for practical work and research of the specialty. Full-time undergraduate education offers a basic study term of 4-5 years.

Secondary Technical Education shall enable students to understand necessary basic theories and special knowledge on applied technologies of a specialty, have basic skills and technical application ability for practice of the specialty. Full-time secondary technically education offers a basic study term of 2-3 years.

Master's-degree Postgraduate Education shall enable students to understand solid basic theories, systematic professional knowledge of a subject, have relevant skills, methodology and relevant knowledge of the specialty, and have preliminary skills for practical work and research of the specialty. Master's-degree postgraduate education offers a basic study term of 2-3 years.

Doctor's-degree Postgraduate Education shall enable students to understand solid and extensive basic theories, systematic and in-depth professional knowledge, relevant skills and methodology of a subject, have relevant skills, methodology and relevant knowledge of the specialty, and have preliminary skills for independent creative research and practical work of the specialty. Doctor's-degree postgraduate education offers a basic study term of 3-4 years.

Online Students refer to students for Internet-based general higher courses, undergraduate courses for adults, and secondary technical courses recruited in online education colleges opened in schools as modern remote education pilots approved by the Ministry of Education.

Employees Enrolled in Graduate Programs refer to students recruited through national joint test for studies of Doctor's and Master's degrees approved by the Academic Degree Commission of the State Council, in order to improve the practical skills of on-the-job personnel. Graduated students will be conferred academic degree only, without academic credentials.

Certificate Education refers education not for academic credentials, run by various higher education institutions that recruit management personnel who are graduated from senior high schools and engaged in professional technical work or strongly professional management work, and receive a certificate for professional knowledge level meeting the requirements of their job position after studying in the school and pass the test. It consists of single-subject program and professional certificate program.

Single-subject Program means that students study only one or more courses of one subject, and will be awarded a certificate of completion of single subject.

Professional Certificate Program means that students study 8-10 courses in the school, and will be awarded a certificate for professional knowledge at junior college level required for their job.

Occupational Training refers to educational and training activities not for academic credentials, aiming to improve the competence, run by various higher education institutions. Various trainees will be awarded Occupational Incumbency

Certification and Engagement Certification. The occupational training is in the form of qualification training and adaptability training.

Qualification Training means any training for students to become qualified for being employed (reemployed) on a job, transfer of job, and promotion as required by job criterion.

Adaptability Training means that students receive training for adaptability in line with needs of their own job.

Advanced Studies and Trainings means education not for academic credentials, offered for professional and managers with educational background of college and above, and technical title above middle rank, to expand their knowledge and improve their skill.

Foreign Students Studying in China refers to foreign students who study in China.

Number of Graduated Students means the number of enrolled students who are actually graduated after passing all exams and receiving a diploma upon completing all courses stated in the teaching plan within the last academic year. This does not include the number of students completing all courses with any one course not passed, and students not completing all courses or discontinuing their schooling.

Number of New Students refers to the number of students actually recruited at the beginning of an academic year in line with State plan, excluding the number of students failing to go up to the next grade and those resuming their interrupted studies.

Number of Enrolled Students means the number of students enrolled at the beginning of a new academic year.

Number of Students Completing Courses means the number of enrolled students completing their schooling with one and more courses not passed (including the graduation paper or graduation design) or other aspects not passed, who are not granted for graduation and awarded a certificate of completion, excluding the number of students completing short-term training courses and single-subject programs.

Faculty Number means the number of faculty working in and paid by schools (institutions). It includes the number of teachers and workers in the principal campus, in research institutions, school-run enterprises and other subsidiaries.

Teachers refer to full-time teaching personnel, including persons temporarily transferred to other jobs, excluding persons transferred from teaching to administrative leadership.

Full-time Teachers refer to personnel mainly engaged in teaching, including persons temporarily (within one year) transferred to other jobs, excluding persons transferred from teaching to administrative leadership or other jobs; excluding part-time teachers and teachers taking over a class for absent teachers.

Schools for Special Education mean schools recruiting blind, deaf and mute teenagers for primary and secondary education.

Floor Space of Schoolhouse refers to the building area of various houses of which the property right is owned by the school and which have been used, excluding houses not completed and under construction, borrowed and rented, or temporarily built sheds and houses.

Area of Dilapidated Houses refers to the area of those houses that have not been repaired for many years, have seriously damaged components, are at the risk of collapse, and are identified by the house administration authority as dilapidated houses.

Area of Land Occupied by School means the area of land within campus, excluding the area of land for farms and forest land outside schools and school-run factories.

Culture

Collection of Books in Public Libraries means the number of books collected in independent libraries open to the public and run by all-level cultural bodies (excluding book rooms in culture centers, and books collected in libraries not included in the cultural system).

Art Troupes refer to groups engaged drama and opera, music, dancing, acrobatics, and other professional art performance, keeping independent accounts. They exclude spare-time and folk vocational art performance troupes.

Audience refer to visitors to art performance for which tickets are sold, as well as free performance provided on performance sites or in ethical group areas, excluding visitors to rehearsal review and internal performance.

Radio and Television

Comprehensive Coverage Rate of Broadcast means the share of population who can receive broadcasting programs in the target area, calculated in line with Statistical Standard and Method on Television and Radio Coverage of Population established by the State Administration of Broadcasting, Film and Television, of the total population in the administrative area.

Comprehensive Coverage Rate of Broadcast in Rural Area means the share of rural population who can receive broadcasting programs in the target area, calculated in line with Statistical Standard and Method on Television and Radio Coverage of Population established by the National Administration of Broadcasting, Film and Television, of the total rural population in the administrative area. Rural area means villages of towns with people's governments approved by the State and areas under the jurisdiction of rural towns with organizational system, excluding towns where people's governments of counties are located.

Comprehensive Coverage Rate of Radio means the share of population who can receive broadcasting programs transmitted with short-wave, medium-wave, FM and other radio transmission technologies in the target area, calculated in line with Statistical Standard and Method on Television and Radio Coverage of Population established by the National Administration of Broadcasting, Film and Television, of the total population in the administrative area, including the population covered by broadcasting programs from central, provincial, prefectural cities and county radio stations.

Comprehensive Coverage Rate of TV means the share of

population who can receive TV programs in the target area, calculated in line with Statistical Standard and Method on Television and Radio Coverage of Population established by the National Administration of Broadcasting, Film and Television, of the total population in the administrative area, including the population covered by TV programs from central, provincial, prefectural cities and county TV stations.

Comprehensive Coverage Rate of TV in Rural Area means the share of rural population who can receive TV programs in the target area, calculated in line with Statistical Standard and Method on Television and Radio Coverage of Population established by the National Administration of Broadcasting, Film and Television, of the total rural population in the administrative area, including the population covered by TV programs from central, provincial, prefectural cities and county TV stations. Rural area means villages of towns with people's governments approved by the State and areas under the jurisdiction of rural towns with organizational system, excluding towns where people's governments of counties are located.

Comprehensive Coverage Rate of Wireless TV means the share of population who can receive TV programs transmitted with short-wave, medium-wave, FM and other radio transmission technologies in the target area, calculated in line with Statistical Standard and Method on Television and Radio Coverage of Population established by the National Administration of Broadcasting, Film and Television, of the total population in the administrative area, including the population covered by radio television programs from central, provincial, prefectural cities and county TV stations.

Access Rate of CATV refers to the percentage of households which can watch television programs by cable broadcasting and television transmission network (including cable TV households receiving analog signals and digital signals, excluding collective subscribers such as hotels, companies and entities, office buildings), to the total households in the administrative area).

Number of Digital Broadcast/TV Subscribers means the number of households watching digital-signal TV programs through the TV and radio cable transmission network.

Number of Pay TV Subscribers means the number of cable TV households watching digital-signal TV programs through the TV and radio cable transmission network and paying fees for watching.

19

科　技
SCIENCE AND TECHNOLOGY

简要说明

一、本章资料的主要内容

本章主要包括：科技活动及专利情况、研究与试验发展（R&D）人员情况、研究与试验发展（R&D）经费情况、研究与试验发展（R&D）项目（课题）情况、研究机构情况、规模以上工业企业R&D活动基本情况、限额以上信息传输、软件和信息技术服务业企业研究与试验发展(R&D)活动基本情况、高等学校科技活动情况、研究与开发机构研发活动、专利申请及授权情况等。

二、本章资料的统计范围

国民经济中研究与试验发展（R&D）活动相对密集行业的法人单位。2012年主要数据包括：农、林、牧、渔业，采矿业，制造业，电力、热力、燃气及水的生产和供应业，建筑业，交通运输、仓储和邮政业，信息传输、软件和信息技术服务业，金融业，租赁和商务服务业，科学研究和技术服务，水利、环境和公共设施管理业，教育，卫生和社会工作，文化、体育和娱乐业，公共管理、社会保障和社会组织等。

三、本章资料的数据来源

本章由北京市统计局、北京市科学技术委员会、北京市教育委员会、北京市经济和信息化委员会、北京市人力资源和社会保障局、北京市知识产权局、北京市质量技术监督局、北京市科学技术协会、北京技术市场管理办公室等部门负责提供。

四、有关统计标准的变化说明

（一）关于行业划分。根据国家统计局规定，自2012年开始执行《国民经济行业分类》GB/T 4754-2011标准。

（二）关于三次产业划分。根据国家统计局《三次产业划分规定》(国统字[2012]108号)，该规定对三次产业的范围进行了调整。其中第一产业是指农、林、牧、渔业（不含农、林、牧、渔服务业）；第二产业是指采矿业（不含开采辅助活动），制造业（不含金属制品、机械和设备修理业），电力、热力、燃气及水生产和供应业，建筑业；第三产业是指除第一产业、第二产业以外的其他行业。2012年本章数据根据此规定进行了调整。

Brief Introduction

I. Main Content

Data in this chapter reflect the situation of scientific and technological activities and patents, R&D activity personnel, R&D funds payment, R&D projects (tasks), research institutions, basic information on R&D activities in industrial enterprises above designated size, basic information on R&D activities of information situation of scientific and technological activities in colleges and universities, scientific research institutions and personnel, patent application and authorization, etc.

II. Scope of Statistics

Included in this chapter are the corporate entities in sectors with relatively intensive R&D activities in national economy, such as agriculture, forestry, animal production and hunting, fishing, mining, and quarrying, manufacturing, production and distribution of electricity, heating power, gas and water, construction, transport, storage and post, scientific research and development, technical services, information transmission, software and information technology services, finance, renting and leasing activities and business services, management of water conservancy, environment and public facilities, education, health care and social works, culture, sports and entertainment, pulic administration, social security and social organizations, International organizations, etc.

III. Source of Data

Data in this chapter are from Beijing Municipal Bureau of Statistics, Beijing Municipal Science & Technology Commission, Beijing Municipal Commission of Education, Beijing Municipal Commission of Economy and Information Technology, Beijing Human Resource and Social Security Bureau, Beijing Intellectual Property Bureau Beijing Municipal Bureau of Quality and Technology Supervision, Beijing Municipal Association of Science and Technology, and Beijing Management Office of Technological Market, etc.

Ⅳ. Changes in Relevant Statistical Standards

(I) Classification of Sectors. According to relevant provisions of National Bureau of Statistics, the Standard for Classification of National Economic Sectors (GB/T4754-200) became effective in 2012.

(II) Classification of Three Industries. According to the provision of National Bureau of Statistics on Classification of Three Industries (GTZ[2012]No.108), the scope of three industries has changed. The primary industry means agriculture, forestry, animal husbandry and fishery (excluding agricultural, forestry, animal husbandry and fishery services); the secondary industry means mining (excluding auxiliary activities), manufacturing (excluding metal products, machinery and equipment repair), electrical power, thermal power, fuel gas and water production and service sectors, and construction industry; the tertiary industry means industries other than the primary and secondary industries. In this chapter, figures for 2012 were adjusted according to this provision.

19-1 科技活动及专利情况(1985-2012年)
SCIENCE AND TECHNOLOGY ACTIVITIES AND PATENTS (1985-2012)

年份 Year	科技活动人员(人) Personnel Engaged in Science and Technology (person)	研究与试验发展(R&D)人员折合全时当量(人年) Full-time Personnel Equivalent R&D Personnel (person-years)	研究与试验发展(R&D)经费内部支出(万元) Internal R&D Expenditure (10000 yuan)	研究与试验发展(R&D)经费内部支出相当于地区生产总值比例(%) R&D Expenditures as Percentage of GDP (%)
1985				
1986-1990				
1986				
1987				
1988				
1989				
1990				
1991-1995				
1991	228167			
1992	247525			
1993	252811			
1994	240386			
1995	252232			
1996-2000			**4307457**	
1996	265552	84793	418614	2.34
1997	273161	84913	532257	2.56
1998	237127	86602	861138	3.62
1999	229584	85740	938437	3.50
2000	261113	98723	1557011	4.92
2001-2005			**13434129**	
2001	240609	95255	1711696	4.62
2002	257326	114919	2195402	5.09
2003	270921	110358	2562518	5.12
2004	301202	152132	3169064	5.25
2005	383153	177765	3795450	5.45
2006-2010			**30706037**	
2006	382756	168875	4329878	5.33
2007	450331	204668	5270591	5.35
2008	450147	200080	6200983	5.58
2009	529985	191779	6686351	5.50
2010	529811	193718	8218234	5.82
2011	605980	217255	9366440	5.76
2012	651003	235493	10633640	5.95

资料来源：北京市统计局、北京市科学技术委员会、北京市教育委员会、北京市经济和信息化委员会、北京市知识产权局。
Source: Beijing Municipal Bureau of Statistics,Beijing Municipal Science & Technology Commission, Beijing Municipal Commission of Education, Beijing Municipal Commission of Economy and Information Technology，Beijing Intellectual Property Office of Bureau.

19-1 续表 continued

年 份 Year	专利申请量(件) Applications for Patents (unit)	发 明 Invention	实用新型 Utility Model	外观设计 Design	专利授权量(件) Grants for Patents (unit)	发 明 Invention	实用新型 Utility Model	外观设计 Design
1985	1540	754	720	66				
1986-1990	**15087**	**3332**	**11003**	**752**	**6700**	**737**	**5614**	**349**
1986	1692	535	1091	66	491	43	408	40
1987	2425	523	1796	106	776	102	630	44
1988	3342	702	2494	146	1376	169	1147	60
1989	3344	742	2408	194	1789	207	1497	85
1990	4284	830	3214	240	2268	216	1932	120
1991-1995	**31126**	**6604**	**21787**	**2736**	**19379**	**1801**	**15835**	**1743**
1991	4624	1023	3324	277	2369	263	1917	189
1992	6316	1340	4493	483	3265	312	2724	229
1993	6972	1483	4931	558	5806	530	4780	496
1994	6852	1506	4666	680	3914	368	3245	301
1995	6362	1252	4372	738	4025	328	3169	528
1996-2000	**37296**	**10344**	**20395**	**6557**	**22156**	**2483**	**14836**	**4837**
1996	6595	1441	4255	899	3295	246	2563	486
1997	6313	1678	3667	968	3327	281	2340	706
1998	6321	1754	3444	1123	3800	309	2522	969
1999	7723	2062	4045	1616	5829	573	3948	1308
2000	10344	3409	4984	1951	5905	1074	3463	1368
2001-2005	**83993**	**39312**	**30960**	**13721**	**39944**	**10960**	**20019**	**8965**
2001	12174	4984	5114	2076	6246	946	3600	1700
2002	13842	5785	5920	2137	6345	1061	3721	1563
2003	17003	7833	6665	2505	8248	2261	4244	1743
2004	18402	8608	6321	3473	9005	3216	3956	1833
2005	22572	12102	6940	3530	10100	3476	4498	2126
2006-2010	**209275**	**124175**	**62237**	**22863**	**100371**	**35532**	**48350**	**16489**
2006	26555	14226	8200	4129	11238	3864	5490	1884
2007	31680	18763	8819	4098	14954	4824	7364	2766
2008	43508	28394	11157	3957	17747	6478	8776	2493
2009	50236	29326	15424	5486	22921	9157	10141	3623
2010	57296	33466	18637	5193	33511	11209	16579	5723
2011	77955	45057	26615	6283	40888	15880	19628	5380
2012	92305	52720	32609	6976	50511	20140	24672	5699

19-2 研究与试验发展(R&D)活动人员情况

项目	Item	研究与试验发展(R&D)人员(人) R&D Personnel (person)	
		2012	2011
合计	**Total**	**322417**	**296990**
按执行部门分	**Group by Administer Department**		
企业	Enterprise	138601	125358
工业企业	Industrial Enterprises	75543	67421
非工业企业	Non-industrial Enterprises	63058	57937
科研机构	Scientific Research Institutions	103017	96058
高等学校	Institutions of Higher Education	69615	64946
事业单位	Public Institutions	11184	10628
按隶属关系分	**Group by Administrative Relationship**		
中央	Central	193523	179214
地方	Local	128894	117776
按行业门类分	**Grouped by Sector**		
#制造业	Manufacturing	70458	62418
信息传输、软件和信息技术服务业	Information Transmission, Software and Information Technology Services	30944	29180
科学研究和技术服务业	Scientific Research and Development, Technical Services	121502	110630
教育	Education	69951	65282

注：行业划分执行2011年国民经济行业分类标准（GB/T 4754-2011）。

资料来源：北京市统计局、北京市科学技术委员会、北京市教育委员会、北京市经济和信息化委员会。

RESEARCH AND DEVELOPMENT PERSONNEL

#本科及以上学历 Above Undergraduate		研究与试验发展(R&D)人员折合全时当量(人年) Full-time Personnel Equivalent R&D Personnel (person-year)		基础研究 Basic Research		应用研究 Applied Research		试验发展 Experimental Development	
2012	2011	2012	2011	2012	2011	2012	2011	2012	2011
218303	**203362**	**235493**	**217255**	**34603**	**31734**	**57824**	**54739**	**143066**	**130782**
60098	56257	105506	97717	499	354	4169	3202	100838	94161
26659	26110	53510	49829	163	170	1198	374	52149	49285
33439	30147	51996	47888	336	184	2971	2828	48689	44876
88739	83316	92577	83796	21309	18514	33325	32672	37943	32610
64161	58935	31239	30178	11878	12055	18276	16825	1085	1298
5305	4854	6171	5564	917	811	2054	2040	3200	2713
153798	143135	146005	132795	30407	27501	47026	45854	68572	59440
64505	60227	89488	84460	4196	4233	10798	8885	74494	71342
25925	25481	49616	47030	116	163	528	364	48972	46503
12173	11620	27032	25282	57	13	881	967	26094	24302
105082	96469	108027	96265	21883	18874	35285	34375	50859	43016
64493	59267	31438	30377	11941	12117	18340	16890	1157	1370

Note: Sectors in this table are classified in accordance with the Standard for Classification of National Economic Sectors 2011 (GB/T 4754-2011).
Source: Beijing Municipal Bureau of Statistics,Beijing Municipal Science & Technology Commission, Beijing Municipal Commission of Education, Beijing Municipal Commission of Economy and Informatization.

19-3 研究与试验发展(R&D)经费情况

单位：万元

项目	Item	研究与试验发展(R&D)经费内部支出 Internal R&D Expenditure		按活动类型分 Group by Type of Activity			
				基础研究 Basic Research		应用研究 Applied Research	
		2012	2011	2012	2011	2012	2011
合计	**Total**	**10633640**	**9366440**	**1258199**	**1085317**	**2418132**	**2280063**
按执行部门分	**Group by Administer Department**						
企业	Enterprise	4213920	3655260	20833	18236	208350	175171
工业企业	Industrial Enterprises	1973442	1648538	1883	8635	28952	15973
非工业企业	Non-industrial Enterprises	2240478	2006722	18950	9601	179398	159198
科研机构	Scientific Research Institutions	4885351	4343010	750378	683625	1404913	1294634
高等学校	Institutions of Higher Education	1369404	1233547	467476	367159	767061	774704
事业单位	Public Institutions	164965	134623	19512	16297	37808	35554
按隶属关系分	**Group by Administrative Relationship**						
中央	Central	7592953	6672918	1193367	1020651	2154411	2057595
地方	Local	3040687	2693522	64832	64666	263721	222468
按行业门类分	**Grouped by Sector**						
#制造业	Manufacturing	1880965	1579309	1180	8613	20759	15922
信息传输、软件和信息技术服务业	Information transmission,software and information technology services	1117841	1010618	1264	235	57578	54776
科学研究和技术服务业	Scientific research and development, technical services	5753870	5054656	778661	700370	1523888	1393958
教育	Education	1375309	1239451	469415	369099	768834	776477

注：行业划分执行2011年国民经济行业分类标准（GB/T 4754-2011）。

资料来源：北京市统计局、北京市科学技术委员会、北京市教育委员会、北京市经济和信息化委员会。

RESEARCH AND EXPERIMENTAL DEVELOPMENT FUNDS

(10000 yuan)

试验发展 Expenditure Development		按支出用途分 Group by Purpose of Payment							
		日常性支出 Routine Expenses		#人员劳务费 Labor Cost		资产性支出 Payment for Assets		#仪器和设备 Instruments and Equipment	
2012	2011	2012	2011	2012	2011	2012	2011	2012	2011
6957309	**6001060**	**8967244**	**7678574**	**2806947**	**2373410**	**1666396**	**1687866**	**1239551**	**1228386**
3984737	3461853	3797012	3243974	1705844	1480539	416908	411286	383855	359139
1942607	1623930	1870499	1512981	729277	562110	102943	135557	102007	132193
2042130	1837923	1926513	1730993	976567	918429	313965	275729	281848	226946
2730060	2364751	3879542	3276558	882732	700260	1005809	1066452	642531	688552
134867	91684	1150016	1036571	170283	153456	219388	196976	189532	172760
107645	82772	140674	121471	48088	39155	24291	13152	23633	7935
4245175	3594672	6210491	5241108	1492357	1197795	1382462	1431810	960681	979004
2712134	2406388	2756753	2437466	1314590	1175615	283934	256056	278870	249382
1859026	1554773	1782478	1452686	702954	546263	98487	126622	97613	123496
1058999	955607	972055	905361	587117	585493	145786	105257	145315	104119
3451321	2960328	4618021	3867009	1167692	919773	1135849	1187647	747487	764103
137060	93875	1155921	1042476	171487	154660	219388	196975	189532	172760

Note: Sectors in this table are classified in accordance with the Standard for Classification of National Economic Sectors 2011 (GB/T 4754-2011).

Source: Beijing Municipal Bureau of Statistics,Beijing Municipal Science & Technology Commission, Beijing Municipal Commission of Education, Beijing Municipal Commission of Economy and Informatization.

19-3 续表 continued

单位：万元 (10000 yuan)

项目	Item	按资金来源分 Group by Fund Source							
		政府资金 Governmental		企业资金 Enterprises		国外资金 Foreign		其他资金 Others	
		2012	2011	2012	2011	2012	2011	2012	2011
合计	**Total**	**5659921**	**4978522**	**3686332**	**3229608**	**478994**	**460907**	**808393**	**697403**
按执行部门分	**Group by Administer Department**								
企业	Enterprise	386104	307150	3226816	2790586	433438	404940	167562	152584
工业企业	Industrial Enterprises	178377	123444	1736105	1467823	8983	9071	49977	48200
非工业企业	Non-industrial Enterprises	207727	183706	1490711	1322763	424455	395869	117585	104384
科研机构	Scientific Research Institutions	4208980	3739393	75393	78456	15298	24843	585680	500318
高等学校	Institutions of Higher Education	929647	818121	378033	354634	29157	30244	32567	30548
事业单位	Public Institutions	135190	113858	6090	5932	1101	880	22584	13953
按隶属关系分	**Group by Administrative Relationship**								
中央	Central	5297809	4652718	1480270	1298639	46089	57298	768785	664263
地方	Local	362112	325804	2206062	1930969	432905	403609	39608	33140
按行业门类分	**Grouped by Sector**								
#制造业	Manufacturing	169302	121186	1652919	1401369	8767	9071	49977	47683
信息传输、软件和信息技术服务业	Information transmission,software and information technology services	38008	37808	758512	671992	307552	290278	13769	10539
科学研究和技术服务业	Scientific research and development, technical services	4440143	3925400	475917	397395	132190	130202	705620	601659
教育	Education	931744	820217	379175	355776	29157	30244	35233	33214

19-4 单位内部办研发机构情况
STATISTICS FOR IN-HOUSE RESEARCH INSTITUTIONS

项目	Item	机构数 (个) Number of Institutions (unit)		机构研究与试验发展(R&D)人员 (人) R&D Persons in Insitutions (Person)		机构研究与试验发展(R&D)经费支出 (万元) Payment of R&D Fundss in Institutions (10000 yuan)	
		2012	2011	2012	2011	2012	2011
合　计	**Total**	**2482**	**2297**	**175322**	**175740**	**7460008**	**6606446**
按机构所属学科分	**Gouped by Suject of Instituion**						
自然科学	Natural Science	142	135	27394	26350	969224	866903
农业科学	Agricultural Science	68	62	5088	4721	194797	168383
医药科学	Mecidine Science	99	93	8686	8206	234875	207541
工程与技术科学	Engineering and Technology Science	1807	1685	124002	127614	5885848	5225365
人文与社会科学	Humanism and Social Science	366	322	10152	8849	175264	138254
按机构组成类型分	**Grouped by Type of Institution Composition**						
政府部门办	Run by Government Agency	531	518	116778	108641	5485454	4878306
与国内高校合办	Jointly Run with Domestic Colleges and Universities	38	29	809	637	30436	20015
与国内独立研究机构合办	Jointly Run with Domestic Independent Research Institutions	8	5	112	42	574	220
与境外机构合办	Jointly Run with Overseas Institutions	7	4	78	45	801	510
与境内注册外商独资企业合办	Jointly Run with Wholly-Foreign-Funded Enterprises Domestically Registered						
与境内注册其他企业合办	Jointly Run with Other Enterprises Domestically Registered	56	57	904	992	35412	31842
单位自办	Self Run	1837	1680	56532	65305	1907047	1675148
其　他	Other	5	4	109	78	284	405

资料来源：北京市统计局、北京市科学技术委员会、北京市教育委员会、北京市经济和信息化委员会。
Source: Beijing Municipal Bureau of Statistics,Beijing Municipal Science & Technology Commission, Beijing Municipal Commission of Education, Beijing Municipal Commission of Economy and Informatization.

19-5 研究与试验发展(R&D)项目(课题)情况
TASKS OF R&D PROJECTS

项　目	Item	项目(课题)数(项) Number of Projects (unit)		项目(课题)人员折合全时当量(人年) Project Personnel Full Time Equivalent (person-year)		项目(课题)经费内部支出(万元) Internal Payment of All Project Funds (10000 yuan)	
		2012	2011	2012	2011	2012	2011
合　计	**Total**	**109514**	**103526**	**217963**	**195369**	**8427518**	**6618502**
按项目(课题)来源分	**Group by Source of Project (Task)**						
国家科技项目	National Science and Technology Projects	48100	43949	99000	85445	4553968	3174360
地方科技项目	Local Science and Technology Projects	9743	8740	9789	9050	167292	162769
企业委托科技项目	Science and Technology Projects Entrusted by Enterprise	24731	24395	16463	15535	574382	614545
自选科技项目	Self-chosen Science and Technology Projects	21991	21760	71691	67044	2030674	1707828
来自国外的科技项目	Science and Technology Projects from Foreign Countries	2050	2100	9982	8718	585921	520446
其它科技项目	Other Science and Technology Projects	2899	2582	11038	9577	515281	438554
按项目(课题)合作形式分	**Group by Form of Cooperation of Project (Task)**						
与境外机构合作	Cooperated with Overseas Institutions	1618	1598	6961	7255	325760	275052
与国内高校合作	Cooperated with Domestic Colleges and Universities	5843	5218	14702	12559	582329	426235
与国内独立研究机构合作	Cooperated with Domestic Independent Research Institutions	7921	7621	19050	17543	779987	719888
与境内注册外商独资企业合作	Cooperated with Wholly-Foreign-Funded Enterprises Domestically Registered	231	214	584	415	43102	10294
与境内注册其他企业合作	Cooperated with Other Enterprises Domestically Registered	6124	6905	13413	16464	460438	554555
独立完成	Completed Independently	84992	79504	157504	134440	6026612	4296783
其　他	Other	2785	2466	5749	6693	209290	335695
按项目(课题)活动类型分	**Group by Type of Project (Task) Activity**						
基础研究	Basic Research	35704	31777	32564	28157	927333	718523
应用研究	Applied Research	52504	51617	54607	52306	1813321	1659643
试验发展	Experimental Development	21306	20132	130792	114906	5686864	4240336
按项目(课题)社会经济目标分	**Group by Social and Economic Objective of Project (Task)**						
#环境保护及污染防治	Environmental Protection and Pollution Prevention and Control	4541	4148	5483	5758	171020	171925
促进能源的生产、分配和合理利用	Promotion of Production, Allocation and Reasonable Utilization of Energy	6195	5979	10848	9970	404666	394286
促进卫生事业的发展	Promotion of Development of Health Career	6893	6138	14884	13535	194113	177453
促进教育事业的发展	Promotion of Development of Education Career	8916	7190	2714	2520	39841	37848
基础设施以及城市和农村规划	Infrastructures,Urban and Rural Planning	6672	6865	11042	10157	418050	341632

注：本表统计范围为限额以上R&D项目(课题)。
资料来源：北京市统计局、北京市科学技术委员会、北京市教育委员会、北京市经济和信息化委员会。
Note: Figures in this table cover Tasks of R&D projects of above designated size.
Source: Beijing Municipal Bureau of Statistics,Beijing Municipal Science & Technology Commission, Beijing Municipal Commission of Education, Beijing Municipal Commission of Economy and Informatization.

19-5 续表 continued

项 目	Item	项目(课题)数 (项) Number of Projects (unit)		项目(课题)人员折合全时当量 (人年) Project Personnel Full Time Equivalent (person-year)		项目(课题)经费内部支出 (万元) Internal Payment of All Project Funds (10000 yuan)	
		2012	2011	2012	2011	2012	2011
社会发展和社会服务	Social Development and Social Service	14832	14712	14024	35180	308029	1073526
地球和大气层的探索和利用	Exploration and Exploitation of Earth and Aerosphere	2865	2877	5022	4442	157189	129439
民用空间的探测及开发	Exploration and Exploitation of Civil Space	930	736	1747	1156	73494	41760
促进农林牧渔业发展	Promotion of Development of Agriculture, Forestry, Animal Husbandry and Fishery	5609	5939	7076	6330	231423	182248
促进工商业发展	Promotion of Development of Industry and Commerce	21662	18644	82659	52608	2941252	1635161
非定向研究	Non-finite Research	22357	21052	20463	19983	655626	569724
按项目(课题)服务的国民经济行业分	**Group by Sector of National Economy Served by the Project (Task)**						
农、林、牧、渔业	Farming,Forestry,Animal Husbandry and Fishery	4926	3364	6082	1163	194268	68924
采矿业	Mining	2932	1381	6741	3438	240969	62755
制造业	Manufacturing	20395	15128	58466	45084	2123530	1464501
电力、热力、燃气及水生产和供应业	Production and Distribution of Electricity,Gas and Water	1549	1016	2113	985	64070	29626
建筑业	Construction	2893	2854	6738	6017	161132	162841
批发和零售业	Wholesale and Retail Trade	121	186	59	53	1037	1006
交通运输、仓储和邮政业	Transport, Storage and Post	2968	2398	3206	1446	137945	54100
住宿和餐饮业	Accommodation and Restaurants	243	36	109	12	2938	117
信息传输、软件和信息技术服务业	Information Transmission,Software and Information Technology Services	3591	3990	27281	24590	1057285	902059
金融业	Finance	981	712	364	247	6006	3599
房地产业	Real Estate	413	169	123	53	1751	935
租赁和商务服务业	Tenancy and Commercial Servecis	2448	4320	4232	4743	105375	128929
科学研究和技术服务业	Scientific Research and Development, Technical Services	38487	47262	77989	93143	3946028	3571778
水利、环境和公共设施管理业	Water, Environment and Municipal Engineering Conservancy	3630	1497	3911	804	121078	33069
居民服务、修理和其他服务业	Resident Services and Other Services	1694	433	557	152	10215	6163
教 育	Education	7703	7754	2400	2594	50486	41165
卫生和社会工作	Health Care and Social Works	4603	4401	10039	7569	119774	44948
文化、体育和娱乐业	Culture, Sports and Entertainment	5737	3640	4611	1562	35154	22719
公共管理、社会保障和社会组织	Pulic Administration,Social Security and Social Organizations	4062	2844	2904	1669	47872	18741
国际组织	International Organization	138	141	38	42	605	531

注：行业划分执行2011年国民经济行业分类标准（GB/T 4754-2011）。
Note: Sectors in this table are classified in accordance with the Standard for Classification of National Economic Sectors 2011 (GB/T 4754-2011).

19-6 规模以上工业企业研究与试验发展(R&D)活动基本情况(2012年)

项 目	Item	企业数(个) Number of Enterprises (unit)	#有研究与试验发展(R&D)活动的企业数 Enterprises with R&D Activities	研究与试验发展(R&D)人员(人) Scientific Research Persons (person)	研究与试验发展(R&D)人员折合全时当量(人年) Full-time Personnel Equivalent R&D Personnel (person-year)	研究与试验发展(R&D)经费内部支出(万元) Internal R&D Expenditure (10000 yuan)
合 计	**Total**	**3692**	**984**	**75543**	**53510**	**1973442**
按企业规模分	**By Size of Enterprise**					
#大中型企业	Medium- and Large-sized	776	360	58558	41534	1637096
按隶属关系分	**By Administrative Relationship**					
中 央	Central	242	126	14706	10925	567547
地 方	Local	3450	858	60837	42585	1405895
按登记注册类型分	**By Registration Status**					
内资企业	Domestic Investment Economy	2767	788	59213	42154	1425456
#国有企业	State-owned Units	108	34	4034	3533	94702
港澳台商投资企业	Units with Funds from Hongkong, Macao and Taiwan	240	63	4755	3283	188051
外商投资企业	Foreign Funded Units	685	133	11575	8073	359935
按重点产业分	**By Key Sector**					
#高技术制造业	High-tech Manufacturing	764	398	27925	20488	923079
#现代制造业	Modern Manufacturing	1466	572	47248	33493	1386300

BASIC INFORMATION ON R&D ACTIVITIES OF INDUSTRIAL ENTERPRISES ABOVE DESIGNATED SIZE (2012)

				专利				
政府资金 Govern-mental	企业资金 Enterprises	国外资金 Foreign	其他资金 Others	申请数(件) Applications for Patents (unit)	#发明专利 Invention	新产品产值(万元) New Product Value (10000 yuan)	新产品销售收入(万元) New Product Income (10000 yuan)	#出口 Exports
178377	**1736105**	**8983**	**49977**	**20189**	**10318**	**33606799**	**33176311**	**5572510**
155326	1431451	8006	42313	16226	8799	23865490	23455417	5191638
88054	439153	1163	39178	4646	2280	8254649	8363196	105677
90323	1296953	7820	10799	15543	8038	25352150	24813115	5466833
165615	1211344	1234	47263	15267	6979	20683031	20298150	931065
11325	79464		3912	2162	910	830685	818359	10172
5173	182698	94	86	2832	2236	4681772	4611787	543630
7589	342063	7654	2629	2090	1103	8241997	8266373	4097815
126618	752696	262	43503	9994	6330	13340115	13178206	4398926
116285	1213688	8103	48225	14063	7575	20973916	20282813	4673711

19-7 规模以上工业企业研究与试验发展(R&D)活动基本情况(按行业分)(2012年)

项　目	Item	企业数(个) Number of Enterprises (unit)	有研究与试验发展(R&D)活动的企业数 Enterprises with R&D Activities	研究与试验发展(R&D)人员(人) Scientific Research Persons (person)
合　计	**Total**	**3692**	**984**	**75543**
采矿业	**Mining**	**22**	**10**	**4344**
煤炭开采和洗选业	Mining and Washing of Coal	6	4	3054
石油和天然气开采业	Extraction of Petroleum and Natural Gas	1	1	125
黑色金属矿采选业	Mining and Processing of Ferrous Metal Ores	7	1	93
有色金属矿采选业	Mining and Processing of Non-Ferrous Metal Ores			
非金属矿采选业	Mining and Processing of Nonmetal Ores	3		
开采辅助活动	Mining Support Service Activities	5	4	1072
其他采矿业	Mining of Other Ores			
制造业	**Manufacturing**	**3569**	**968**	**70458**
农副食品加工业	Processing of Food from Agriculture Products	135	19	840
食品制造业	Manufacture of Foods	122	18	685
酒、饮料和精制茶制造业	Manufacture of Wines,Beverage and Refined Tea	42	4	1540
烟草制品业	Manufacture of Tobacco	1	1	26
纺织业	Manufacture of Textile	35	5	82
纺织服装、服饰业	Manufacture of Textile Wearing Apparel and Ornament	170	4	209
皮革、毛皮、羽毛及其制品和制鞋业	Manufacture of Leather, Fur, Feather and its Products	20		
木材加工和木、竹、藤、棕、草制品业	Processing of Timber, Manufacture of Wood, Bamboo, Rattan, Palm, and Straw Products	21	1	10
家具制造业	Manufacture of Furniture	66	2	413
造纸和纸制品业	Manufacture of Paper and Paper Products	45		
印刷和记录媒介复制业	Printing, Reproduction of Recording Media	125	10	482
文教、工美、体育和娱乐用品制造业	Manufacture of Articles for Culture,Education, Artwork, Sport and Entertainment Activity	36	3	39
石油加工、炼焦和核燃料加工业	Processing of Petroleum, Coking, Processing of Nuclear Fuel	24	5	248
化学原料和化学制品制造业	Manufacture of Raw Chemical Materials and Chemical Products	220	62	1729
医药制造业	Manufacture of Medicines	175	88	5458
化学纤维制造业	Manufacture of Chemical Fibers	3	3	129
橡胶和塑料制品业	Manufacture of Rubber and Plastics Products	126	22	956
非金属矿物制品业	Manufacture of Non-Metallic Mineral Products	266	47	3138
黑色金属冶炼和压延加工业	Smelting and Pressing of Ferrous Metals	31	4	263
有色金属冶炼和压延加工业	Smelting and Pressing of Non-Ferrous Metals	43	15	1145
金属制品业	Manufacture of Metal Products	238	28	1098
通用设备制造业	Manufacture of General Purpose Machinery	259	90	5413
专用设备制造业	Manufacture of Special Purpose Machinery	302	133	7138
汽车制造业	Manufacture of Motor Vehicles	209	28	10392
铁路、船舶、航空航天和其他运输设备制造业	Manufacture of Railway Locomotives, Building of Ships and Boats, Manufacture of Air and Spacecrafts and Other Transportation Equipments	66	33	4020
电气机械和器材制造业	Manufacture of Electrical Machinery and Equipment	270	86	6053
计算机、通信和其他电子设备制造业	Manufacture of Computer, Communication Equipment and Other Electronic Equipment	300	151	13372
仪器仪表制造业	Manufacture of Measuring Instrument and Meter	170	93	3868
其他制造业	Other Manufacturing	27	8	558
废弃资源综合利用业	Recycling and Disposal of Waste	9	2	35
金属制品、机械和设备修理业	Repair of Fabricated Metal Products, Machinery and Equipment	13	3	229
电力、热力、燃气及水的生产和供应业	**Production and Distribution of Electricity, Heating Power, Gas and Water**	**101**	**6**	**741**
电力、热力生产和供应业	Production and Supply of Electric Power and Heat Power	62	1	18
燃气生产和供应业	Production and Distribution of Gas	20	2	306
水的生产和供应业	Production and Distribution of Water	19	3	417

注：行业划分执行2011年国民经济行业分类标准（GB/T 4754-2011）。

BASIC INFORMATION ON R&D ACTIVITIES OF INDUSTRIAL ENTERPRISES ABOVE DESIGNATED SIZE (BY SECTOR)(2012)

R&D人员全时当量(人年) Full-time Equivalent R&D Personnel (person-year)	R&D经费内部支出(万元) Internal R&D Expenditure (10000 yuan)	政府资金 Governmental	企业资金 Enterprises	国外资金 Foreign	其他资金 Others	专利申请数(件) Applications for Patents (unit)	#发明专利 Invention	新产品产值(万元) New Product Value (10000 yuan)	新产品销售收入(万元) New Product Income (10000 yuan)	#出口 Exports
53540	**1973442**	**178377**	**1736105**	**8983**	**49977**	**20189**	**10318**	**33606799**	**33176311**	**5572510**
3336	**83709**	**7880**	**75613**	**216**		**552**	**301**	**4636345**	**4636345**	
2487	18085		18085			15	9	4636345	4636345	
41	7457	6351	984	122		4	3			
43	1979		1979			310	223			
765	56188	1529	54565	94		223	66			
48616	**1880965**	**169302**	**1652919**	**8767**	**49977**	**17596**	**9177**	**28939137**	**28511621**	**5572510**
634	19195	923	18272			192	140	261233	260397	4810
570	19969	894	19075			86	40	230525	223186	27066
147	15828	190	15638			15		266722	304490	2707
26	1866		1866			5	2	38232	36694	
46	1422	16	1310		96	37	21	93610	131836	1160
123	2665	84	2581			11		149318	149821	240
1	99		99			11				
141	2583		2583			17		39430	41128	15
293	12702	2	12700			28	6	144398	149427	4508
25	861		861			13		20586	17466	2024
113	3170		3170			50	38	309265	504915	
1262	31116	1526	29481		109	352	261	640014	611644	63047
4027	98914	4966	92557		1391	367	259	1304226	1270708	27267
62	838	9	829			4	3	2135	2454	
622	12245	165	11795		285	77	30	264393	269201	27724
1821	52849	5262	47123		464	576	234	1291447	1290450	102642
122	4329	614	3715			13	5	169018	167915	981
865	20475	2078	18174		223	93	76	355158	365544	199528
1492	31834	2304	29456	2	72	327	141	609770	610408	65158
3733	126661	7354	119146		161	791	160	1976639	2052011	390482
4912	179008	12762	165282	664	300	1755	734	2182156	2062879	199757
6007	255079	2550	251767	51	711	1678	387	3029629	2592263	15125
3264	210819	58763	114986	243	36827	532	251	721279	727383	2690
5048	163245	5036	149686	7788	735	1774	728	3281423	3182184	119538
9585	509395	57061	445519	19	6796	7860	5233	10422412	10336066	4260456
2876	66785	5161	59868		1756	805	376	1039518	1059564	52240
353	34077	1509	32517		51	95	48	90303	86676	3345
32	758	73	685			9	3	6298	4911	
87	2178		2178			23	1			
558	**8768**	**1195**	**7573**			**2041**	**840**	**31317**	**28345**	
12	100		100			1990	824			
161	2848	20	2827			10	3	13480	13480	
385	5821	1175	4646			41	13	17837	14865	

Note: Sectors in this table are classified in accordance with the Standard for Classification of National Economic Sectors 2011 (GB/T 4754-2011).

19-8 限额以上信息传输、软件和信息技术服务业企业研究与试验发展(R&D)活动基本情况(2012年)

项目	Item	企业数(个) Number of Enterprises (unit)	#有研究与试验发展(R&D)活动的企业数 Enterprises with R&D Activities	研究与试验发展(R&D)人员(人) Scientific Research Persons (person)	研究与试验发展(R&D)人员折合全时当量(人年) Full-time Personnel Equivalent R&D Personnel (person-year)	研究与试验发展(R&D)经费内部支出(万元) Internal R&D Expenditure (10000 yuan)
合计	**Total**	**2767**	**283**	**29891**	**25245**	**1085034**
按隶属关系分	**By Administrative Relationship**					
中央	Central	154	31	3418	2626	83645
地方	Local	2613	252	26473	22619	1001389
按登记注册类型分	**By Registration Status**					
内资企业	Domestic Investment Economy	2171	232	16031	12430	392651
#国有企业	State-owned Units	41	9	871	578	27500
港澳台商投资企业	Units with Funds from Hongkong, Macao and Taiwan	174	13	1085	721	24970
外商投资企业	Foreign Funded Units	422	38	12775	12094	667413
按行业分	**By Sector**					
电信、广播电视和卫星传输服务	Telecommunications, Broadcasting, Television and Satellite Transmission services	255	36	6015	5524	355026
互联网和相关服务	Internet and Related Services	239	12	4066	3692	141902
软件和信息技术服务业	Software and Information Technology Services	2273	235	19810	16029	588106

注：行业划分执行2011年国民经济行业分类标准（GB/T 4754-2011）。

BASIC INFORMATION ON R&D ACTIVITIES OF INFORMATION TRANSMISSIOM,SOFTWARE AND INFORMATION TECHNICIAL SEVICES ENTERPRISES ABOVE DESIGNATED SIZE (2012)

政府 资金 Govern-mental	企业 资金 Enterprises	国外 资金 Foreign	其他 资金 Others	专利申请数（件） Applications Applications for Patents (unit)	#发明专利 Invention
37538	**726295**	**307552**	**13649**	**8224**	**6912**
9520	71274		2851	2266	2134
28018	655021	307552	10798	5958	4778
34322	351576		6753	6648	5485
898	25703		899	1621	1563
1156	19286		4528	501	423
2060	355433	307552	2368	1075	1004
7130	225364	120227	2305	1177	1093
1621	139688		593	2229	2079
28787	361243	187325	10751	4818	3740

Note: Sectors in this table are classified in accordance with the Standard for Classification of National Economic Sectors 2011 (GB/T 4754-2011).

19-9 研究与开发机构研发活动情况(2007-2012年)

项目		Item		2007
研究与开发机构基本情况		**Basic Information on R&D Institutions**		
机构数	(个)	Number	(unit)	265
中央	(个)	Central	(unit)	221
地方	(个)	Local	(unit)	44
研究与试验发展(R&D)投入情况		**R&D Input**		
R&D人员	(万人)	R&D Personnel	(10000 person)	4.6
按隶属关系分		Grouped by Administrative Relationship		
中央	(万人)	Central	(10000 person)	4.4
地方	(万人)	Local	(10000 person)	0.2
R&D人员折合全时当量	(万人年)	R&D Personnel Full-time Equivalent	(10000 person year)	3.8
基础研究	(万人年)	Fundamental Research	(10000 person year)	1.2
应用研究	(万人年)	Applied Research	(10000 person year)	1.6
试验发展	(万人年)	Development	(10000 person year)	1
R&D经费内部支出	(亿元)	Internal Spending of R&D Fund	(100 million yuan)	103.1
按隶属关系分		Grouped by Administrative Relationship		
中央	(亿元)	Central	(100 million yuan)	99
地方	(亿元)	Local	(100 million yuan)	4.1
按活动类型分		Grouped by Type of Activity		
基础研究	(亿元)	Fundamental Research	(100 million yuan)	26.4
应用研究	(亿元)	Applied Research	(100 million yuan)	45.2
试验发展	(亿元)	Development	(100 million yuan)	31.5
按资金来源分		Grouped by Source of Fund		
政府资金	(亿元)	Fund from Government	(100 million yuan)	88.6
企业资金	(亿元)	Fund from Enterprise	(100 million yuan)	3.2
境外资金	(亿元)	Overseas Fund	(100 million yuan)	1.3
其他资金	(亿元)	Other Fund	(100 million yuan)	10
研究与试验发展(R&D)项目(课题)情况		**R&D Projects (Tasks)**		
R&D项目(课题)数	(项)	Number of R&D Projects (Tasks)	(unit)	15079
R&D项目(课题)人员折合全时当量	(万人年)	R&D Personnel Full-time Equivalent	(10000 person year)	2.2
R&D项目(课题)经费内部支出	(亿元)	Internal Spending of R&D Project (Task) Fund	(100 million yuan)	57.1
科技产出及成果情况		**Science & Technology Output and Achievement**		
发表科技论文	(篇)	Published Articles on Science and Technology	(unit)	37232
#国外发表	(篇)	Published Abroad	(unit)	9005
出版科技著作	(种)	Published Writings on Science and Technology	(Sort)	1489
专利申请数	(件)	Number of Patents Applied for	(Nos.)	1993
#发明专利	(件)	Invention Patent	(Nos.)	1784
专利授权数	(件)	Number of Patents Granted	(Nos.)	985
#发明专利	(件)	Invention Patent	(Nos.)	752

注：研究与开发机构范围是北京市政府部门属的科学研究与技术开发机构、科技情报与文献机构。
资料来源：北京市科学技术委员会。

STATISTICS ON R&D ACTIVITIES IN R&D INSTITUTIONS (2007-2012)

2008	2009	2010	2011	2012
266	275	281	280	288
225	228	231	231	238
41	47	50	49	50
4.8	5.2	5.7	5.9	6.3
4.5	4.9	5.4	5.6	5.9
0.3	0.3	0.3	0.3	0.4
3.9	4.2	4.6	4.7	5.3
1.3	1.4	1.5	1.6	1.8
1.6	1.7	2.0	2.1	2.2
1.0	1.1	1.1	1.0	1.3
123.8	150.3	187.0	195.1	222.0
117.4	143.9	178.9	185.1	211.5
6.4	6.4	8.1	10.0	10.5
28.3	39.2	49.9	58.5	65.1
49.0	61.5	78.0	84.0	92.0
46.5	49.6	59.1	52.6	64.9
106.6	126.3	164.4	168.0	192.6
4.0	4.4	3.6	6.6	6.5
1.8	2.0	1.5	2.5	1.5
11.4	17.6	17.5	18.0	21.4
16383	17816	19545	20333	22842
2.3	3.8	4.1	4.3	4.9
70.9	87.1	107.2	115.0	142.7
37149	39380	39384	41442	44218
9184	12011	11696	13361	14003
1636	1873	1601	1828	1670
2488	3182	3879	4880	5456
2119	2772	3450	4373	4798
1146	1574	1879	2260	3251
922	1299	1455	1756	2635

Note: R&D institutions cover scientific research and technological development institutions, scientific and technological information institutions subordinate to government authorities of Beijing.

Source: Beijing Municipal Science & Technology Commission.

19-10 高等学校研发活动情况
STATISTICS ON R&D ACTIVITIES IN COLLEGES & UNIVERSITIES

项目		Item		2012	2011
高等学校基本情况		**Basic Information of Colleges & Universities**			
学校数	(个)	Number of Collecges and Universities	(unit)	93	87
#理工农医	(个)	Colleges & Universities of Science, Enginee	(unit)	64	62
#人文社科	(个)	Colleges & Universities of Arts and Social Science	(unit)	64	59
研究与试验发展(R&D)机构数	(个)	Number of R&D Institutions	(unit)	767	679
研究与试验发展(R&D)投入情况		**R&D Input**			
R&D人员	(万人)	R&D Personnel	(10000 person)	6.96	6.49
R&D人员折合全时当量	(万人年)	Full-time Equivalent of R&D Personnel	(10000 person year)	3.12	3.02
基础研究	(万人年)	Basic Research	(10000 person year)	1.19	1.06
应用研究	(万人年)	Applied Research	(10000 person year)	1.83	1.82
试验发展	(万人年)	Development	(10000 person year)	0.11	0.13
R&D经费内部支出	(亿元)	Internal Expenditure of R&D Funds	(100 million yuan)	136.94	123.35
按活动类型分		By Type of Activity			
基础研究	(亿元)	Basic Research	(100 million yuan)	46.75	36.72
应用研究	(亿元)	Applied Research	(100 million yuan)	76.71	77.47
试验发展	(亿元)	Development	(100 million yuan)	13.49	9.17
按资金来源分		By Source of Funds			
#政府资金	(亿元)	Funds from Government	(100 million yuan)	92.96	81.81
企业资金	(亿元)	Funds from Enterprise	(100 million yuan)	37.80	35.46
研究与试验发展(R&D)项目(课题)情况		**R&D Projects (Topics)**			
R&D项目(课题)数	(项)	Number of R&Dprojects (Topics)	(unit)	69557	68025
R&D项目(课题)人员折合全时当量	(万人年)	Full-time Equivalent of R&D Personnel	(10000 person year)	3.12	3.02
R&D项目(课题)经费内部支出	(亿元)	Internal Expenditure of R&D Funds	(100 million yuan)	113.48	98.45
科技产出及成果情况		**Research Outputs and Results**			
发表科技论文	(篇)	Science and Technology Papers Delivered	(unit)	112949	108838
#国外发表	(篇)	Delivered in Foreign Countries	(unit)		
出版科技著作	(种)	Science and Technology Writings Published	(Sort)	5431	5621
专利申请数	(件)	Number of Patents Applied for	(unit)	10327	9413
#发明专利	(件)	Invention Patents	(unit)	8755	8132
专利授权数	(件)	Granted Patents	(unit)	7132	5444
#发明专利	(件)	Invention Patents	(unit)	5667	4298

资料来源：北京市教育委员会。
Source: Beijing Municipal Commission of Education.

19-11 科学技术协会及所属学会工作情况(2012年)
STATISTICS OF SCIENCE AND TECHNOLOGY ASSOCIATION AND SUBORDINATE INSTITUTES (2012)

项目		Item		合计 Total	市科协 Municipal Science and Technology Association	市级学会 Institutes at Municipal Level
基本情况		**Basic Information**				
机构数	(个)	Number of Institutions	(unit)	163	1	162
机构从业人员	(人)	Number of Persons Employed in the Institutions	(person)	228152	52	228100
学术交流活动		**Academic Exchange Activities**				
国内学术会议	(次)	Domestic Academic Meetings	(times)	1121	20	1101
参加人数	(人次)	Number of Participants	(person times)	135965	2854	133111
交流论文	(篇)	Number of Papers Exchagned	(unit)	20091	428	19663
境内国际学术会议	(次)	International Academic Meetings Held Abroad	(times)	103		103
参加人数	(人次)	Number of Participants	(person times)	15101		15101
交流论文	(篇)	Number of Papers Exchagned	(unit)	2951		2951
港澳台地区学术会议	(次)	Academic Meetings Held at Kong Kong, Macao and Taiwan	(times)	19		19
参加人数	(人次)	Number of Participants	(person times)	2766		2766
交流论文	(篇)	Number of Papers Exchagned	(unit)	271		271
科技期刊		**Science & Technology Periodicals**				
主办科技期刊种数	(种)	Types of Science & Technology Periodicals Sponsored	(sort)	33	3	30
科技期刊总印数	(万册)	Number of Total Impression of Science & Technology Periodicals	(10000 copies)	375.3	276.0	99.3
科技期刊发表论文数	(篇)	Papers Published on Science & Technology Periodicals	(unit)	5651	32	5619
科普活动		**Activities to Popularize Scientific Knowledge**				
举办科普宣讲活动	(次)	Holding Scientific Knowledge Teaching Activities	(times)	2985	1047	1938
播放科技广播、影视节目	(分钟)	Playing Radio, Film and TV Programs on Science & Technology	(minutes)	4905	9	4896
举办实用技术培训	(次)	Holding Practical Technology Trainings	(times)	3246	232	3014
推广新技术、新品种	(项)	Promoting New Technologies and New Breeds	(unit)	137	47	90
参加活动科技人员总数	(人次)	Total Number of Participating Science and Technology Workers	(person times)	39530	15478	24052
参加活动的学会、协会、研究会	(个次)	Participating Socieities, Associations and Research Institutes	(unit)	1044	679	365
科技传播		**Science & Technology Dissemination**				
主办科技报纸种数	(种)	Types of Science & Technology Newspaper Sponsored	(sort)	1	1	
制作科普挂图种数	(种)	Types of Scientific Knowlede Flip Charts Produced	(sort)	89	10	79
制作科技广播、影视节目套数	(套)	Science & Technology Raido, Film & TV Programs Produced	(unit)	7		7
制作科技光盘种数	(种)	Types of Science & Technology CD-ROMs Produced	(sort)	30	2	28
制作科普动漫作品套数	(套)	Scientific Knowledge Animation Works Produced	(unit)	2715	2701	14
主办科技网站	(个)	Science & Technology Websites Sponsored	(unit)	48	11	37
科技开放与交流		**Science & Technology Opening-up and Exchange**				
加入国际民间科技组织	(个)	International Cilvilian Science & Technology Organizations Joined	(unit)	1		1
促成科技合作项目	(项)	Scientific & Technological Cooperation Projects Enabled	(unit)	2		2
参加国外科技活动人数	(人次)	Number of Persons Participating Foreign Science & Technology Activities	(person times)	488	220	268
参加港澳台地区科技活动人数	(人次)	Number of Persons Participating Science & Technology Activities in Hong Kong, Macao and Taiwan	(person times)	303	43	260
接待国外专家学者	(人次)	Foreign Experts and Scholars Received	(person times)	426	143	283
接待港澳台地区专家学者	(人次)	Experts and Scholars from Kong Kong, Macao and Taiwan Received	(person times)	381	146	235
科技服务		**Science and Technology Service**				
提供决策咨询报告	(篇)	Providing Decision Consulting Reports	(unit)	151	13	138
举办决策咨询活动	(次)	Holding Decision Consulting Activities	(times)	154	12	142

注：本表统计范围是北京市科学技术协会所属学会、研究会。
资料来源：北京市科学技术协会。
Note: Figures in this table cover societies and research institutes of Beijing Municipal Science and Technology Association.
Source: Beijing Municipal Science and Technology Association

19-12 公有经济企事业单位专业技术人员(2012年)
NUMBER OF PORFESSIONAL TECHNICAL PERSONNEL IN LOCAL STATE-OWNED ENTERPRISES AND INSTITUTIONS (2012)

单位：人 (person)

项 目	Item	合 计 Total	#高 级 Senior	#中 级 Middle	#初 级 Junior
合 计	Total	478874	59931	164378	183250
工程技术人员	Engineering Technicians	112968	11674	28821	38433
农业技术人员	Agricultural Technicians	4600	459	1268	2331
科学研究人员	Science Research Personnel	6723	1671	2567	1069
卫生技术人员	Medical Technicians	90446	9658	29370	47399
教学人员	Teaching Personnel	160863	29242	75890	52028
经济人员	Economic Personnel	46175	2669	10790	15709
会计人员	Accountants	27261	1357	6243	13793
统计人员	Statisticians	3449	108	695	1554

注：公有经济是指北京市属国有和集体企事业单位,不包含在京中央属企事业单位。
资料来源：北京市人力资源和社会保障局。
Note: Public sector means state-owned and collective enterprises and institutions in Beijing, excluding Central enterprises and institutions located in Beijing.
Source: Beijing Human Resource and Social Security Bureau.

19-13 技术合同成交情况(1990-2012年)

STATISTICS FOR SIGNING OF TECHNOLOGICAL CONTRACTS (1990-2012)

年份 Year	合同数(项) Number of Contracts (unit)	技术合同成交总额(亿元) Total Amount of Technological Contracts Signed (100 million yuan)	技术交易额 Technological Transaction Amount	流向外省市技术合同额 Technological Transaction Amount Outside Beijing	实现合同总金额(亿元) Total Amount of Contracts Achieved (100 million yuan)	技术交易实现金额 Amount of Technological Transactions Achieved
1990	18588	20.3	10.5		15.4	8.4
1991-1995	**93970**	**167.7**	**120.0**		**115.4**	**83.8**
1991	18547	22.4	13.1		15.3	9.1
1992	23395	31.3	22.2		20.0	14.4
1993	20461	35.6	25.6		24.9	17.6
1994	15220	37.2	26.9		26.9	20.4
1995	16347	41.2	32.2		28.4	22.3
1996-2000	**91421**	**414.2**	**375.9**		**206.7**	**188.1**
1996	14850	45.8	39.2		29.6	25.4
1997	13866	54.3	48.1		31.1	27.8
1998	20724	81.6	73.9		42.1	37.6
1999	20711	92.2	88.5		43.6	41.0
2000	21270	140.3	126.3	65.5	60.3	56.3
2001-2005	**156114**	**1443.8**	**1217.2**	**688.9**	**669.5**	**628.1**
2001	23921	191.0	164.8	85.4	97.6	93.0
2002	27037	221.1	181.0	100.4	101.9	97.2
2003	32173	265.5	226.8	132.4	119.9	113.9
2004	35478	331.8	294.3	165.8	148.7	143.4
2005	37505	434.4	350.4	204.9	201.4	180.6
2006-2010	**256074**	**5422.8**	**3984.7**	**2372.7**	**2226.7**	**2006.7**
2006	51575	697.3	572.6	325.3	349.5	319.7
2007	50972	882.6	660.3	407.4	418.1	353.5
2008	52742	1027.2	778.1	487.0	406.2	375.0
2009	49938	1236.2	906.9	498.2	516.8	452.9
2010	50847	1579.5	1066.7	654.8	536.0	505.6
2011	53552	1890.3	1268.3	635.9	580.4	563.3
2012	59969	2458.5	2048.6	1385.0	739.8	707.0

资料来源：北京技术市场管理办公室。

Source: Beijing Technical Market Management Office.

19-14 技术合同成交情况
CONCLUSION OF TECHNICAL CONTRACTS

项目	Item	合同数(项) Number of Contracts (unit)		成交额(万元) Amount of Transaction Concluded (10000 yuan)	
		2012	2011	2012	2011
合计	**Total**	**59969**	**53552**	**24585033.6**	**18902752.0**
按合同类别分类	**Grouped by Type of Contract**				
技术开发合同	Technological Development	22965	17377	5916931.8	3540996.1
技术转让合同	Technology Transfer	2015	1470	1731277.5	563910.5
技术咨询合同	Technical Consultation	4364	4245	385822.3	433815.0
技术服务合同	Technical Service	30625	30460	16551002.1	14364030.5
按合同卖方类别分类	**Grouped by Type of Seller**				
机关法人	Establishment Juridical Person	17	7	4800.3	1082.2
事业法人	Insitution Juridical Person	10575	9823	989849.9	691861.5
社团法人	Juridical Association	32	45	879.5	1996.4
企业法人	Enterprise Juridical Person	49286	43521	23563262.9	18163635.9
自然人	Natural Person	42	40	4037.1	7418.9
其他组织	Other Organizaiton	17	116	22204.0	36757.2
按合同买方类别分类	**Grouped by Type of Buyer**				
机关法人	Establishment Juridical Person	4664	4206	1065051.0	756420.0
事业法人	Insitution Juridical Person	8648	8419	1308925.3	2541376.5
社团法人	Juridical Association	240	277	19143.5	14470.0
企业法人	Enterprise Juridical Person	45600	39526	20751332.9	14098524.6
自然人	Natural Person	306	549	24745.0	7219.1
其他组织	Other Organizaiton	511	575	1415835.8	1484741.8
按服务社会经济目标分类	**Grouped by Social and Economic Service Objective**				
农业、林业和渔业的发展	Development of Farming, Forestry and Fishery	703	660	79450.2	989735.9
促进工业的发展	Promoting Industrial Development	6201	6208	2119161.2	1177465.1
能源的生产和合理利用	Production and Reasonable Utilization of Energy	4739	5069	5611694.8	4872590.2
基础设施的发展	Development of Infrastructures	6786	5154	6057361.2	5395982.8
环境治理与保护	Environmental Control & Protection	1860	1707	1390700.8	316446.2
卫生(不包括污染)	Health (Exclude Pollution)	1345	1811	248148.4	263610.0
社会发展和社会服务	Social Development and Service	18906	15331	5776773.1	3682940.5
地球和大气层的探索与利用	Exploration of Earth and Aerosphere and Utilization	138	133	30783.4	27412.4
知识的发展	Development of Knowledge	2449	2794	351444.1	252000.5
民用空间	Civil Space	966	816	170219.4	106876.0
国防	National Defence	1830	1677	340648.1	220802.9
其他	Others	14046	12192	2408649.1	1596889.5
按技术流向分类	**Grouped by Spread Area of Technology**				
流向本市	Inside Beijing	26264	23814	6556372.1	4712657.5
流向外省市	Outside Beijing	32433	28627	13850055.3	6359413.3
技术出口	Export	1272	1111	4178606.2	7830681.3

资料来源：北京技术市场管理办公室。
Source: Beijing Technical Market Management Office.

19-15 科技成果及获奖情况(2001-2012年)
STATISTICS FOR SCIENTIFIC ACHIEVEMENTS AND AWARDS (2001-2012)

单位：项 (unit)

年 份 Year	科技成果登记数 Registered Number of Scientific Achievements	#国家技术发明奖 National Award of Technical Invention	#国家科学技术进步奖 National Award of Scientific Technical Advancement
2001-2005	**3063**	**25**	**233**
2001	326	1	38
2002	275	5	48
2003	468	5	52
2004	976	6	43
2005	1018	8	52
2006-2010	**5081**	**56**	**257**
2006	1002	12	64
2007	1010	9	44
2008	1016	13	42
2009	1023	11	54
2010	1030	11	53
2011	1035	5	56
2012	1040	22	53

资料来源：北京市科学技术委员会。
Source: Beijing Municipal Science & Technology Commission.

19-16 专利申请及授权情况
APPLICATIONS AND GRANTS FOR PATENTS

单位：件 (unit)

项目	Item	申请量 Applications for Patents 2012	2011	授权量 Grants for Patents 2012	2011
合计	Total	92305	77955	50511	40888
按种类分	Grouped by Type				
发明	Invention	52720	45057	20140	15880
实用新型	Utility Model	32609	26615	24672	19628
外观设计	Design	6976	6283	5699	5380
按对象分	Grouped by Applicator				
工矿企业	Industrial Enterprises	54727	43747	29983	22887
大专院校	Universities and Colleges	11842	10499	6841	5698
科研单位	Scientific Research Institutes	10773	9840	5311	4413
机关团体	Organizations	953	1039	1098	495
个人	Individuals	14010	12830	7278	7395

资料来源：北京市知识产权局。
Source: Beijing Intellectual Property Office of Bureau.

19-17 有效发明专利情况
STATISTICS ON EFFECTIVE INVENTION PATENTS

单位：件 (unit)

项目	Item	2012	2011
合计	Total	69554	52522
按对象分	By Object		
工矿企业	Industrial and Mining Enterprises	33601	23984
大专院校	Junior Colleges	16874	13124
科研单位	Research Institutes	13260	9910
机关团体	Government Bodies and Groups	571	448
个人	Individuals	5248	5056

资料来源：北京市知识产权局。
Source: Beijing Intellectual Property Office of Bureau.

主要统计指标解释

科技活动人员 指报告年度调查单位直接从事科技活动，以及从事科技活动管理和为科技活动提供直接服务的人员。直接从事科技活动人员包括：在单位办的研究室、实验室、技术开发中心及中试车间（基地）等机构中从事科技活动的人员；虽不在上述机构工作，但编入科技活动项目（课题）组的人员等。从事科技活动管理和为科技活动提供直接服务的人员包括：与科技活动相关的行政管理人员，以及直接为科技活动提供资料文献、材料供应、设备维护等服务的人员。

研究与试验发展（R&D） 指在科学技术领域，为增加知识总量，以及运用这些知识去创造新的应用而进行的系统的创造性的活动，包括基础研究、应用研究、试验发展三类活动。

研究与试验发展（R&D）人员 指单位内部从事基础研究、应用研究和试验发展三类活动的人员。包括直接参加上述三类项目活动的人员以及这三类项目的管理人员和直接服务人员。为研发活动提供直接服务的人员包括直接为研发活动提供资料文献、材料供应、设备维护等服务的人员。

研究与试验发展（R&D）人员折合全时当量 由参加R&D项目人员的全时当量及应分摊在R&D项目的管理和直接服务人员的全时当量两部分相加计算。

研究与试验发展（R&D）内部支出 指调查单位在报告年度用于内部开展R&D活动（基础研究、应用研究和试验发展）的实际支出。包括用于R&D项目（课题）活动的直接支出，以及间接用于R&D活动的管理费、服务费、与R&D有关的基本建设支出以及外协加工费等。不包括生产性活动支出、归还贷款支出以及与外单位合作或委托外单位进行R&D活动而转拨给对方的经费支出。

专业技术人员 指从事专业技术工作的人员以及从事专业技术管理工作且已在1983年以前评定了专业技术职称或在1984年以后聘任了专业技术职务的人员。从事专业技术工作的人员具体指工程技术人员，农业技术人员，科学研究人员（含自然科学研究及实验技术人员），卫生技术人员，教学人员（含高等院校、中等专业学校、技工学校、中学、小学），民用航空飞行技术人员，船舶技术人员，经济专业人员，会计人员，统计人员，翻译人员，图书资料、档案、文博人员，新闻、出版人员，律师、公证人员，广播电视播音人员，工艺美术人员，体育人员，艺术人员及企业政治思想工作人员。从事专业技术管理工作的人员是指企业、事业单位领导，企业、事业单位下设的职能机构，企业的生产车间的辅助车间（或附属辅助生产单位）中从事生产、技术、经济管理和政治工作的人员。按照公务员管理或参照公务员管理的人员不统计为专业技术人员。

专利 是专利权的简称，是对发明人的发明创造经审查合格后，由专利局依据专利法授予发明人和设计人对该项发明创造享有的专有权。包括发明、实用新型和外观设计。

发明专利 指专利法及其实施细则所称的发明，指对产品、方法或者改进所提出的新的技术方案。

实用新型专利 指专利法及其实施细则所称的实用新型，指对产品的形状、构造或者其结合所提出的适于实用的新的技术方案。

外观设计专利 指专利法及其实施细则所称的外观设计，指对产品的形状、图案、色彩或者其结合所做出的富有美感并适于工业上应用的新设计。

Explanatory Notes on Main Statistical Indicators

Science and Technology Activity Persons refer to persons directly engaged in science and technology activities as well as persons engaged in science and technology management and persons offering direct services for science and technology activities in the investigated entity in the reporting year. Persons directly engged in science and technology activities include: persons engaged in science and technology activities in the such institutions as research room, laboratory, technical development cener and middle-stage test workshop (base); persons not working in the foregoing institutions but included in the science and technology activity project (task) team, etc. persons engaged in science and technology management and persons offering direct services for science and technology activities include administrative persons related to science and technology activity, as well as persons directly providing information and literature, supply of material, equipment maintenance and other services.

R&D means any systematic and creative activity carried out in the field of science and technology to increase the total knowledge, and apply such knowledge to create new applications, including three kinds of activities, i.e. basic research, application research, and development.

R&D Persons refer to persons in the investigated entity who are engaged in three kinds of activities, i.e. basic research, application research, and development. They include those who participate in the foregoing three kinds of activities directly and managerial persons and direct service persons for these activities. Persons providing direct service include those who provide information and literature, supply of material, equipment maintenance and other services.

R&D Persons Full Time Equivalent is the sum of the full time equivalent of personnel participating in R&D projects plus the full time equivalent of management and direct service personnel that should be allocated to R&D projects.

Internal R&D Expenditure means the actual disbursement of investigated entities on internal R&D in the reporting year, including direct spending on R&D project (task) activities, and management expenses and service fees indirectly spent on R&D, R&D related capital construction spending, and external assisting processing charges, etc.

Professional Technicians refer to persons carrying out professional technological work and professional technological management whose professional technological titles were assessed before 1983 or who have been retained at professional technological positions after 1984. Persons carrying out professional technological work refer tp engineering technicians, agricultural technicians, research personnel (including natural science research and experiment technicians), medical technicians, teaching personnel (including those in colleges and universities, technical secondary schools, vocational schools, high schools, and elementary schools), civil aviation flight technicians, watercraft technicians, professionals in economics, accountants, statisticians, translators and interpreters, personnel on books, files, archives and museums, press and publication personnel, lawyers, notaries, TV and radio broadcasting personnel, personnel on arts and crafts, personnel on sports, personnel on art, as well as personnel on political ideology work in enterprises.. Persons carrying out professional technological management refer to leaders of enterprises and public institutions; persons engaged in management of production, technology and economy as well as political work in functional bodies under enterprises and public institutions, auxiliary workshops (or affiliated and auxiliary production entities) of production workshops of enterprises; persons managed as civil servants or by referring to civil servants are not calculated as professional technicians.

Patent is a short name of patent right, referring to the exclusive right granted by patent authorities upon review of the inventor's invention and creation to the inventor and designer with regard to the invention, including invention, utility model and appearance design.

Invention means the invention mentioned in the Patent Law and its detailed rules for implementation, i.e. the new technological scheme presented for the product, methodology, or improvement.

Utility Model means the utility model mentioned in the Patent Law and its detailed rules for implementation, i.e. the new technological scheme presented for the product shape, structure or combination of them, which is suitable for practical use.

Appearance Design means the appearance design mentioned in the Patent Law and its detailed rules for implementation, i.e. the new design of product shape, pattern, color or combination of them, which is artistic and suitable for industrial application.

20

卫生、体育
HEALTH AND SPORTS

简要说明

一、本章资料的主要内容

本章主要反映卫生、体育的发展情况。

卫生部分主要内容包括卫生总费用、卫生机构、卫生技术人员、床位数，医院诊疗人次及入院人数，主要疾病死亡原因及构成，全市主要健康指标等情况。体育部分主要包括群众体育活动情况、体育场地情况、运动员获奖情况、体育彩票情况等。

二、本章资料的数据来源

卫生部分的资料由北京市卫生局提供，体育部分的资料由北京市体育局提供。

Brief Introduction

I. Main Content

This chapter mainly reflects the development situation of health and sports.

Health statistics include the total health costs, the number of health institutions, health technicians, ward beds, medical service visitors and hospitalized persons, the death reason and composition of main diseases, main health indicators in Beijing, and so on. Sports statistics include public sports and sports fields, awards received by athletes, and sports lottery tickets, etc.

II. Source of Data

Health data are from Beijing Municipal Health Bureau. Sports data are from Beijing Municipal Sports Bureau.

20-1 卫生事业基本情况(1978-2012年)
BASIC STATISTICS ON HEALTH (1978-2012)

年 份 Year	卫生机构 (个) Health Care Institutions (unit)	#医院(卫生院) Hospitals (Township)	#医 院 Hospitals	#疾病预防控制中心(防疫站) Epidemic Prevention Station	#妇幼保健院(所、站) Maternity and Child Care Hospitals(station)	#社区卫生服务中心(站) Health Service Centers (Stations) for Community
1978	3263	389		22	15	
1979	3614	387		22	17	
1980	3818	393		22	19	
1981	4135	403		22	19	
1982	4389	413		22	18	
1983	4312	412		22	19	
1984	4173	423		22	18	
1985	4248	376		22	18	
1986	4483	371		22	20	
1987	4744	398		22	19	
1988	4342	445		22	17	
1989	4398	470		22	17	
1990	4953	512		22	17	
1991	4970	525	337	22	17	
1992	4868	535	345	22	16	
1993	4962	548	364	32	16	
1994	4958	629	387	33	16	
1995	4955	629	387	33	15	
1996	6470	645	405	33	13	
1997	6577	673	435	33	13	
1998	5723	676	449	32	11	
1999	5990	686	460	32	8	
2000	6176	674	458	30	8	
2001	5969	673	458	30	9	
2002	4998	647	461	24	19	35
2003	5075	646	459	29	19	36
2004	4835	657	503	29	19	43
2005	4818	692	519	28	18	93
2006	4878	705	541	28	18	90
2007	6189	686	535	31	18	1126
2008	6523	660	537	31	19	1282
2009	6603	638	522	31	19	1395
2010	6539		550	31	19	1587
2011	9699		569	32	19	1744
2012	9974		608	32	19	1897

注：1. 2010年及以前，本表不包含村卫生室及驻京部队医院情况。2011年开始，卫生机构中包含村卫生室。2012年卫生机构数中包含驻京部队医院。
2. 2010年开始，原卫生院数据并入到社区卫生服务中心(站)等其他卫生机构。
3. 表中每千人口拥有执业(助理)医师数、每千人口拥有注册护士数、每千人口拥有医院床位数按年末户籍人口计算。2012年上述指标按年末常住人口计算分别为3.97人、4.60人和4.48张。

资料来源：北京市卫生局。

Note: a) Before 2010, health care institutions in this table unclude village health centers. From 2011 health institutions included health care clinics in villages.From 2012, health institutions included health care clinics in villages and hospitals of troops stationed in Beijing.
b) From 2010, data on health centers were involved into other health institutions such as community health service centers (stations).
c) The data of "Certified Physicians per 1000 Persons", "Registered Nurses per 1000 Persons", "Beds per 1000 Persons" were calculated by year end registered population.These indicators for 2012 calculated by year end permanent population were 3.97 persons,4.60 persons and 4.48 units.

Source: Beijing Municipal Health Bureau.

20-1 续表 continued

年 份 Year	卫生机构人员(人) Employed Persons in Health Care Institution (person)	#卫生技术人员 Medical Technical Personnel	#执业(助理)医师 Certified (Assistant) Physicians	#注册护士 Registered Nurses	实有床位数(张) Beds (unit)	#医院(卫生院) Hospitals (Township)	#医院 Hospitals	每千人口拥有执业(助理)医师数(人) Certified Physicians Per 1000 Persons(person)	每千人口拥有注册护士数(人) Registered Nurses Per 1000 Persons(person)	每千人口拥有医院床位数(张) Beds Per 1000 Persons (unit)
1978	90174	65943	28435	16085	29767	26432		3.35	1.89	3.11
1979	97942	72131	31842	17398	30231	26808		3.66	1.87	3.08
1980	102601	74753	34365	17492	32453	28495		3.88	1.97	3.22
1981	110774	81183	37886	20025	33666	29783		4.20	2.20	3.30
1982	114420	83843	39385	20389	34574	30940		4.30	2.23	3.40
1983	119222	86593	41216	21181	35987	32242		4.40	2.26	3.50
1984	124664	89362	42112	22286	38580	34602		4.40	2.33	3.70
1985	127771	90831	42216	23782	41603	38180		4.44	2.48	3.99
1986	132865	94433	43403	25383	43956	40903		4.47	3.72	4.21
1987	142556	101829	46007	27786	47538	44407		4.66	2.81	4.49
1988	145362	105237	48216	30250	53078	48711		4.82	3.02	4.87
1989	150062	108108	49361	32056	55623	51877		4.83	3.14	5.08
1990	156304	111614	50934	34565	59036	55474		4.93	3.35	5.37
1991	161103	114342	52309	35714	61744	58744	54888	5.03	3.44	5.65
1992	164213	115825	53254	36768	63230	59833	55858	5.10	3.52	5.73
1993	165170	116173	53906	36687	65621	62340	58605	5.13	3.49	5.93
1994	164867	116818	53865	36608	67112	64416	60661	5.07	3.45	6.07
1995	164436	115967	54114	36719	66925	64211	60337	5.06	3.43	6.00
1996	164981	116849	54091	37712	66760	64902	60997	5.02	3.50	6.02
1997	167090	119256	54909	38630	67946	65826	61865	5.06	3.56	6.06
1998	162609	115976	51902	38883	69095	66954	63144	4.76	3.56	6.13
1999	161823	116597	52646	39625	69465	67684	63660	4.79	3.60	6.15
2000	160258	115510	51570	39900	71245	69183	65138	4.66	3.60	6.25
2001	158185	115935	52100	40537	73053	70837	66537	4.64	3.61	6.31
2002	144021	109564	47236	38879	75188	71967	67750	4.18	3.44	6.46
2003	148406	112212	47887	39912	74298	71173	66990	4.21	3.51	5.89
2004	153154	116610	48988	41547	77359	73811	69850	4.25	3.60	6.54
2005	157133	119874	50617	42897	79067	76031	72329	4.32	3.66	6.65
2006	166278	126904	52795	45647	81440	78588	74762	4.41	3.84	6.77
2007	182475	139275	54989	50890	83736	80158	76915	4.53	4.19	6.34
2008	193799	149916	58773	55349	86196	81937	79089	4.78	4.50	6.43
2009	208156	160435	62348	61604	90100	84896	82471	5.00	4.94	6.62
2010	219762	171093	65954	67308	92871		85935	5.24	5.35	6.83
2011	235708	181938	69749	72812	94735		87596	5.46	5.70	6.85
2012	276654	219714	82192	95202	100167		92610	6.33	7.34	7.14

20-2 卫生总费用(2000-2011年)
TOTAL HEALTH EXPENDITURES(2000-2011)

年份 Year	卫生总费用(亿元) Total Health Expenditure (100 million yuan)	政府卫生支出 Health Expenditures by Governments		社会卫生支出 Social Health Expenditures		个人现金卫生支出 Health Expenditures in Cash by Individuals		卫生总费用占GDP比重(%) Total Health Expenditure As % of GDP Total
		绝对数(亿元) Expenditure (100 million yuan)	占卫生总费用比重(%) As % of Total	绝对数(亿元) Expenditure (100 million yuan)	占卫生总费用比重(%) As % of Total	绝对数(亿元) Expenditure (100 million yuan)	占卫生总费用比重(%) As % of Total	
2000	166.72	34.70	20.81	61.78	37.05	70.25	42.13	5.27
2001	201.12	45.28	22.52	73.18	36.39	82.65	41.10	5.42
2002	262.36	48.51	18.49	99.61	37.97	114.23	43.54	6.08
2003	314.16	65.80	20.94	132.04	42.03	116.33	37.03	6.27
2004	357.19	69.35	19.41	150.72	42.20	137.12	38.39	5.92
2005	432.80	85.73	19.81	187.84	43.40	159.22	36.79	6.21
2006	497.41	115.89	23.30	208.00	41.82	173.52	34.88	6.13
2007	523.20	142.03	27.15	212.00	40.52	169.17	32.33	5.31
2008	668.52	180.01	26.93	271.26	40.58	217.25	32.50	6.01
2009	689.60	201.14	29.17	296.25	42.96	192.21	27.87	5.67
2010	814.74	226.84	27.84	385.10	47.27	202.80	24.89	5.77
2011	977.26	275.48	28.19	453.16	46.37	248.62	25.44	6.01

资料来源：北京市卫生局。
Source: Beijing Municipal Health Bureau.

20-3 卫生机构基本情况
BASIC STATISTICS ON INSTITUTIONS OF PUBLIC HEALTH

项目	Item	2012	2011	构成(%) Composition(%) 2012	2011
卫生机构 (个)	**Health Care Institutions (unit)**	**9974**	**9699**	**100.0**	**100.0**
#医院	Hospitals	608	569	6.1	5.9
社区卫生服务中心(站)	Health Service Centers (Stations) for Community	1897	1744	19.0	18.0
门诊部	Clinics	890	836	8.9	8.6
妇幼保健院(所、站)	Maternity and Child Care Hospitals	19	19	0.2	0.2
疾病预防控制中心(防疫站)	Prevent a Disease Control Center (Epidemic Prevention Station)	32	32	0.3	0.3
专科疾病防治院(所、站)	Specialized Disease Prevention & Treatment Institutions	28	28	0.3	0.3
诊所、卫生所、医务室、护理站	Clinics,Health Centers, Infirmaris, Nursing Stations	3373	3335	33.8	34.4
床位 (张)	**Beds (unit)**	**100167**	**94735**	**100.0**	**100.0**
#医院	Hospitals	92610	87596	92.5	92.5
社区卫生服务中心(站)	Health Service Centers (Stations) for Community	4745	4423	4.7	4.7
妇幼保健院(所、站)	Maternity and Child Care Hospitals	1770	1671	1.8	1.8
专科疾病防治院(所、站)	Specialized Disease Prevention & Treatment Institutions	565	568	0.6	0.6
卫生技术人员 (人)	**Medical Technical Personnel (person)**	**219714**	**181938**	**100.0**	**100.0**
#医院	Hospitals	162783	128644	74.1	70.7
社区卫生服务中心(站)	Health Service Centers (Stations) for Community	24003	22601	10.9	12.4
妇幼保健院(所、站)	Maternity and Child Care Hospitals	4336	3888	2.0	2.1
专科疾病防治院(所、站)	Specialized Disease Prevention &Treatment Institutions	602	500	0.3	0.3
#执业(助理)医师	Certified Doctors	82192	69749	37.4	38.3
注册护士	Registered Nurses	95202	72812	43.3	40.0

注：2012年卫生机构、卫生技术人员、执业(助理)医师、注册护士数据中包含驻京部队医院。
资料来源：北京市卫生局。
Note: From 2012, health institutions ,medical technical Personnel and certified doctors included health care clinics in villages and hospitals of troops stationed in Beijing.
Source: Beijing Municipal Health Bureau.

20-4 全市医院基本情况(2012年)
BASIC STATISTICS ON HOSPITALS (2012)

项目	Item	医院数(个) Hospitals (unit)	床位数(张) Beds (unit)	职工人数(人) Staff and Workers (person)	#卫生技术人员 Medical Technical Personnel	#执业医师 Certified Doctors	#中医 Doctors of Chinese Medicine
合计	**Total**	**608**	**92610**	**201344**	**162783**	**54884**	**7684**
按隶属关系分	**Group by Administrative Relationship**						
#市	Municipal	28	20632	42867	34509	10990	712
区县	District and County	98	28716	48879	39279	13660	2421
按专业分	**Group by Specialty**						
综合医院	General Hospitals	328	56632	141337	116979	39645	2216
中医医院	Hospital Specialized in Traditional Chinese Medicine	126	11814	21583	17274	6759	4626
中西医结合医院	Hospitals Which Integrate Traditional Chinese Therapeutics with Western Therapeutics in Practice	11	3585	3569	2772	1021	382
民族医院	Ethnologic Hospitals	3	120	452	336	189	71
口腔医院	Stomatology Hospitals	13	276	3550	2793	1061	
眼科医院	Ophthalmology Hospitals	10	465	689	420	126	6
肿瘤医院	Tumor Hospitals	6	2668	4400	3437	1032	47
心血管病医院	Hospitals for Cardiovascular Diseases	2	1026	2725	2227	608	7
胸科医院	Thorax Hospitals	1	533	815	608	158	1
妇(产)科医院	Hospitals for Gynecology and Obstetrics	8	757	2524	1928	600	25
儿童医院	Children's Hospitals	7	1625	4425	3511	901	42
精神病医院	Mental Hospitals	22	7675	5729	4096	852	40
传染病医院	Infectious Disease Hospitals	3	1338	2637	2049	639	38
骨科医院	Hospitals of Orthopedics	9	646	847	548	144	37
整形外科医院	Orthopaedics Hospitals	1	328	680	463	148	
其他专科医院	Other Specialized Hospitals	33	2330	3468	2414	734	104
护理院	Nursing Hospitals	5	70	25	18	5	1

资料来源：北京市卫生局。
Source: Beijing Municipal Health Bureau.

20-4 续表 continued

单位：人 (person)

项 目	Item	#执业助理医师 Certified Assistant Doctors	#中医 Doctors of Chinese Medicine	#注册护士 Registered Nurses	#药师(士) Pharmacist (Assistant Pharmacist)	#技师(士) Technician (Assistant Technician)	#检验师(士) Laboratorian (Assistant Laboratorian)
合 计	**Total**	**1445**	**297**	**79375**	**7649**	**7112**	**4538**
按隶属关系分	**Group by Administrative Relationship**						
#市	Municipal	102	5	16726	1682	1692	1086
区 县	District and County	499	74	17888	2385	1967	1340
按专业分	**Group by Specialty**						
综合医院	General Hospitals	842	123	59318	4659	4874	3038
中医医院	Hospital Specialized in Traditional Chinese Medicine	265	129	6204	1768	872	588
中西医结合医院	Hospitals Which Integrate Traditional Chinese Therapeutics with Western Therapeutics in Practice	53	18	1165	141	103	77
民族医院	Ethnologic Hospitals	14	3	84	17	22	13
口腔医院	Stomatology Hospitals	19		1116	30	68	19
眼科医院	Ophthalmology Hospitals	9	1	201	17	15	13
肿瘤医院	Tumor Hospitals	6	1	1605	146	164	81
心血管病医院	Hospitals for Cardiovascular Diseases	3		1203	59	67	44
胸科医院	Thorax Hospitals			349	31	50	23
妇(产)科医院	Hospitals for Gynecology and Obstetrics	21	2	1044	66	113	95
儿童医院	Children's Hospitals	4		1601	200	246	175
精神病医院	Mental Hospitals	92	1	2295	182	124	93
传染病医院	Infectious Disease Hospitals	2		1105	103	142	119
骨科医院	Hospitals of Orthopedics	18	5	253	31	28	17
整形外科医院	Orthopaedics Hospitals			246	9	15	7
其他专科医院	Other Specialized Hospitals	62	8	1142	142	156	98
护理院	Nursing Hospitals	1		9	2	1	1

20-5 医院工作情况(2012年)
WORKS OF HOSPITALS (2012)

项目	Item	诊疗人次数(千人次) Patients Treated (1000 person times)	#门诊 Out-patients	健康检查人数(千人次) Health Check (1000 person times)	平均开放病床数(张) Beds in Use (unit)	入院人数(千人次) In-patients (1000 person times)	出院人数(千人次) Leaving Hospital (1000 person times)
合计	**Total**	**132787.2**	**111123.2**	**3020.4**	**88421.4**	**2115.8**	**2553.8**
综合医院	General Hospitals	91850.7	72010.4	2561.0	54130.8	1484.9	1924.8
中医医院	Hospital Specialized in Traditional Chinese Medicine Medicine	24325.7	23389.3	317.9	11114.4	207.7	207.8
中西医结合医院	Hospitals Which Integrate Traditional Chinese Therapeutics with Western Therapeutics in Practice	2627.9	2435.9	56.4	3423.2	33.0	32.7
民族医院	Ethnologic Hospitals	86.9	86.9	0.8	115.1	0.8	0.8
口腔医院	Stomatology Hospitals	2018.9	1937.4	11.0	273.8	7.2	7.2
眼科医院	Ophthalmology Hospitals	204.2	203.4	31.0	406.1	8.8	8.8
肿瘤医院	Tumor Hospitals	1134.8	1120.6	15.1	2656.6	94.0	93.7
心血管病医院	Hospitals for Cardiovascular Diseases	572.4	546.5	0.9	1028.8	46.5	46.5
胸科医院	Thorax Hospitals	193.1	187.9		534.5	9.2	9.2
妇(产)科医院	Hospitals for Gynecology and Obstetrics	1293.5	1267.0	7.5	649.7	35.6	36.0
儿童医院	Children's Hospitals	5215.9	4801.1	11.4	1575.0	78.9	77.7
精神病医院	Mental Hospitals	1012.0	1001.2	3.9	7550.4	14.9	15.0
传染病医院	Infectious Disease Hospitals	865.8	811.3		1341.7	38.3	38.4
骨科医院	Hospitals of Orthopedics	202.5	191.8	0.2	618.9	8.1	8.1
整形外科医院	Orthopaedics Hospitals	90.0	88.4	0.2	328.9	9.8	9.9
其他专科医院	Other Specialized Hospitals	770.1	721.6	3.1	1976.9	28.4	27.8
护理院	Nursing Centers	3.7	3.7		70.0	0.1	

注：诊疗人次数据中包含驻京部队医院。
资料来源：北京市卫生局。
Note:.The date of patients treated included troops stationed in Beijing.
Source: Beijing Municipal Health Bureau.

20-5 续表 continued

项 目	Item	病死率 (%) Rate of Death of Illness (%)	病床周转次数 (次) Turnover Beds (times)	病床使用率 (%) Utilization Rate of Beds (%)	出院者平均住院日 (日) Average Hospitalization Period (day)
合 计	**Total**	**1.34**	**23.87**	**84.29**	**11.30**
综合医院	General Hospitals	1.44	27.37	83.48	11.02
中医医院	Hospital Specialized in Traditional Chinese Medicine Medicine	1.63	18.70	76.17	14.37
中西医结合医院	Hospitals Which Integrate Traditional Chinese Therapeutics with Western Therapeutics in Practice	2.17	9.55	79.72	19.51
民族医院	Ethnologic Hospitals	1.75	6.96	49.24	25.79
口腔医院	Stomatology Hospitals		26.41	64.91	9.00
眼科医院	Ophthalmology Hospitals		21.57	58.03	7.60
肿瘤医院	Tumor Hospitals	0.51	35.29	99.17	10.34
心血管病医院	Hospitals for Cardiovascular Diseases	0.29	45.20	102.37	8.28
胸科医院	Thorax Hospitals	1.59	17.23	100.50	21.44
妇(产)科医院	Hospitals for Gynecology and Obstetrics	0.02	55.45	85.45	5.55
儿童医院	Children's Hospitals	0.14	49.33	101.01	7.34
精神病医院	Mental Hospitals	1.07	1.98	99.57	227.16
传染病医院	Infectious Disease Hospitals	2.53	28.60	104.43	13.49
骨科医院	Hospitals of Orthopedics	0.25	13.08	46.82	12.93
整形外科医院	Orthopaedics Hospitals		30.06	83.70	9.94
其他专科医院	Other Specialized Hospitals	2.36	14.07	68.96	15.81
护理院	Nursing Centers	75.00	0.51	94.13	104.17

20-6 全市居民前十位死因顺位、死亡率及构成(2012年)
DEATH RATE AND COMPOSITION OF 10 MAJOR DISEASE (2012)

顺 位 No.	死因名称	Cause of Death	死亡率(1/10万) Death Rate (1/100 thousands)	构 成(%) Composition(%)
	全 市	**Total**		
1	恶性肿瘤	Malignant Tumour	160.97	26.76
2	心脏病	Heart Trouble	150.84	25.08
3	脑血管病	Cerebrovasular Disease	129.01	21.45
4	呼吸系统疾病	Disease of the Respiratory System	59.39	9.87
5	损伤和中毒	Trauma and Toxicosis	22.78	3.79
6	内分泌、营养、代谢及免疫疾病	Endocrine, Nutrition, Metabolite and Immunity Disease	17.40	2.89
7	消化系统疾病	Disease of the Gigestive System	16.42	2.73
8	神经系统疾病	Neuropathy	7.45	1.24
9	泌尿生殖系统疾病	Disease of the Genitourinary System	4.61	0.77
10	传染病	Infection Disease	4.85	0.81
	男 性	**Male**		
1	恶性肿瘤	Malignant Tumour	191.31	28.47
2	心脏病	Heart Trouble	159.15	23.69
3	脑血管病	Cerebrovasular Disease	143.45	21.35
4	呼吸系统疾病	Disease of the Respiratory System	67.05	9.98
5	损伤和中毒	Trauma and Toxicosis	28.83	4.29
6	消化系病	Disease of the Gigestive System	19.24	2.86
7	内分泌、营养、代谢及免疫疾病	Endocrine, Nutrition, Metabolite and Immunity Disease	16.10	2.40
8	神经系统疾病	Neuropathy	6.34	0.94
9	传染病	Infection Disease	8.15	1.21
10	泌尿生殖系统疾病	Disease of the Genitourinary System	5.08	0.76
	女 性	**Female**		
1	心脏病	Heart Trouble	142.46	26.86
2	恶性肿瘤	Malignant Tumour	130.33	24.58
3	脑血管病	Cerebrovasular Disease	114.42	21.58
4	呼吸系统疾病	Disease of the Respiratory System	51.65	9.74
5	内分泌、营养、代谢及免疫疾病	Endocrine, Nutrition, Metabolite and Immunity Disease	18.70	3.53
6	损伤和中毒	Trauma and Toxicosis	16.69	3.15
7	消化系病	Disease of the Gigestive System	13.56	2.56
8	神经系统疾病	Neuropathy	6.74	1.27
9	泌尿生殖系统疾病	Disease of the Genitourinary System	4.60	0.87
10	肌肉骨骼和结缔组织疾病	Muscle, Skeleton and Connective Tissue Disease	3.00	0.57

资料来源：北京市卫生局。
Source: Beijing Municipal Health Bureau.

20-7 全市主要健康指标情况(1978-2012年)
MAJOR HEALTH INDICATIONS OF BEIJING(1978-2012)

年 份 Year	婴 儿 死亡率 (‰) Infant Mortality (‰)	城 郊 District	远 县 County	新生儿 死亡率 (‰) Newborn Baby Mortality (‰)	城 郊 District	远 县 County	孕产妇 死亡率 (1/10万) Pregnant & Lying-in Women Mortality (1/100000)	城 郊 District	远 县 County	甲乙类传染 病发病率 (1/10万) Incidence Rate of First and Second (1/100000)
1978	17.11	10.34	21.15	12.21	7.35	15.60	31.00	5.00	53.00	
1979	16.97	12.81	19.43	10.08	8.00	12.77	34.70	13.10	41.30	1584.25
1980	14.79	10.40	17.73	10.24	7.12	12.81	26.30	12.50	34.60	2165.23
1981	13.84	9.69	17.26	9.22	6.00	11.85	48.50	18.70	76.10	2225.71
1982	12.97	9.95	15.19	8.02	6.20	9.76	24.50	21.70	32.60	2193.16
1983	13.79	10.54	17.24	8.78	6.22	11.84	28.10	24.30	45.10	1904.55
1984	10.98	10.33	12.49	7.78	6.72	9.20	16.80	11.40	41.50	1666.68
1985	13.94	10.02	18.85	10.41	6.40	15.97	22.90	24.30	35.10	1335.23
1986	16.05	13.42	19.24	12.13	8.97	15.41	30.50	22.90	43.10	1120.19
1987	15.56	12.63	18.23	11.08	8.01	14.02	26.60	14.80	33.30	826.51
1988	14.98	11.71	17.92	10.48	7.96	13.20	24.80	25.40	32.40	640.98
1989	14.96	11.59	18.30	10.53	8.08	13.23	34.50	3.90	55.80	547.61
1990	11.66	10.12	12.55	8.49	7.43	9.38	25.00	13.00	30.50	509.55
1991	12.46	11.94	13.11	8.56	7.83	9.47	24.00	23.80	24.20	448.23
1992	12.12	10.81	14.43	8.93	7.72	11.18	30.10	30.20	29.80	385.98
1993	10.38	10.68	9.93	7.21	7.28	7.10	16.50	21.10	9.60	356.66
1994	10.93	12.09	9.43	7.29	7.57	6.94	18.94	21.02	16.26	374.31
1995	11.45	14.23	8.20	7.52	8.91	5.90	22.27	23.89	20.36	309.99
1996	10.05	11.57	8.13	6.97	7.61	6.17	15.32	11.45	20.19	340.24
1997	9.45	10.49	8.05	6.36	6.75	5.83	23.69	25.25	21.60	294.41
1998	7.58	9.07	5.75	5.53	6.46	4.39	10.46	10.87	9.97	306.37
1999	7.95	7.78	8.38	5.94	5.74	6.45	17.53	15.69	22.06	308.10
2000	5.36	6.29	4.05	3.70	4.26	2.91	9.70	7.10	13.38	301.19
2001	6.01	6.26	5.62	4.05	4.16	3.89	11.71	13.85	8.45	276.85
2002	5.56	5.57	5.54	3.70	3.65	3.77	15.12	16.24	13.29	282.95
2003	5.89	5.91	5.83	3.83	3.56	4.33	15.60	6.92	31.35	228.00
2004	4.61	4.51	4.79	3.49	3.42	3.62	15.19	17.69	10.66	408.03
2005	4.35	4.08	4.84	3.29	3.03	3.79	15.91	7.33	31.95	445.91
2006	4.66	3.96	6.04	3.42	2.99	4.26	7.87	7.12	9.36	448.70
2007	3.89	3.50	4.72	2.65	2.31	3.39	16.74	18.92	12.10	421.02
2008	3.70	3.49	4.21	2.45	2.41	2.52	18.52	15.86	24.76	312.99
2009	3.49	3.28	4.02	2.47	2.37	2.73	14.55	12.56	19.49	339.89
2010	3.29	2.95	4.25	2.06	1.94	2.42	12.14	8.95	21.23	268.99
2011	2.84	2.62	3.43	1.88	1.77	2.17	9.09	9.99	6.67	226.76
2012	2.87	2.48	3.87	1.91	1.65	2.60	6.05	4.20	10.82	174.45

注：城郊包括东城区、西城区、朝阳区、丰台区、石景山区、海淀区、门头沟区、房山区；远县包括通州区、昌平区、顺义区、大兴区、怀柔区、平谷区、密云县、延庆县。

资料来源：北京市卫生局。

Note: Districts include Dongcheng, Xicheng, Chaoyang, Fengtai, Shijingshan, Haidian, Mentougou, and Fangshan districts.Counties include Tongzhou, Changping, Shunyi, Daxing, Huairou, Pinggu, Miyun and Yanqing Counties.

Source: Beijing Municipal Health Bureau.

20-8 主要年份体育场地情况
SITUATION OF THE GYMNASIUMS AND STADIUMS IN MAIN YEAR

单位：个 (unit)

年 份 Year	合 计 Total	#体育场 Palaestra	#体育馆 Gymnasium	#游泳场馆 Natatorium	#室 内 Indoor	#各种训练房 Exercise Rooms
1950	19	1				2
1955	61	1			2	10
1960	124	2		4	3	19
1970	188	2	2	8	3	24
1975	234	3	2	11	4	28
1980	293	3	2	12	4	32
1985	405	4	2	20	8	54
1990	780	12	12	49	26	153
1995	1381	18	18	88	56	291
2000	2815	35	24	214	161	863
2001	3500	42	27	283	216	1101
2002	4176	57	33	334	263	1358
2003	6100	93	36	443	371	1729
2004	6104	93	36	443	371	1729
2005	6112	93	36	446	374	1731
2006	6122	93	36	446	374	1734
2007	6146	94	37	446	374	1736
2008	6149	94	37	446	374	1739
2009	6149	94	37	446	374	1739
2010	6151	94	37	446	374	1741
2011	6151	94	37	446	374	1741
2012	6156	94	37	447	375	1742

资料来源：北京市体育局。
Source: Beijing Municipal Sports Bureau.

20-9 群众体育活动情况
ACTIVITIES OF MASS SPORTS

项 目		Item		2012	2011
晨晚练辅导站	（个）	Instruction Stations of Morning and Evening Exercise	(unit)	6622	5500
青少年体育俱乐部数	（个）	Number of Teenager Sport Clubs	(unit)	203	159
社会体育指导员	（人）	Social Sport Instructors	(person)	30814	36553
专项球类场地设施	（个）	Special ball game venue facilities	(unit)	280	231
社区健身俱乐部	（个）	Community fitness clubs	(unit)	117	102
体育生活化社区	（个）	Life-oriented sports communities	(unit)	821	189

资料来源：北京市体育局。
Source: Beijing Municipal Sports Bureau.

20-10 运动员、裁判员情况
ATHLETES,TRAINERS AND UMPIRE

单位：人 (person)

项　　目	Item	2012	#女　性 Female	2011	#女　性 Female
分等级运动员发展人数	**Number of Certified Athletes Admitted**	**1880**	**744**	**1763**	**692**
国际级运动健将	International Master	11	6	19	4
国家级运动健将	National Master	106	38	145	56
一　级	First Grade Athletes	426	175	422	171
二　级	Second Grade Athletes	1337	525	1177	461
分等级裁判员发展人数	**Number of Certified Referees Admitted**	**1135**	**289**	**907**	**228**
国家级	National Grade Referees	32	13	22	10
一　级	First Grade Referees	152	67	467	127
二　级	Second Grade Referees	951	209	418	91

资料来源：北京市体育局。
Source: Beijing Municipal Sports Bureau.

20-11 运动员获奖牌情况(2012年)
STATISTICS ON MEDALS WON (2012)

单位：块 (piece)

项　　目	Item	金　牌 Gold	银　牌 Silver	铜　牌 Copper
合　　计	**Total**	**68**	**51**	**50**
国际比赛	International Competitions	28	10	8
国内比赛	Domestic Competitions	40	41	42

资料来源：北京市体育局。
Source: Beijing Municipal Sports Bureau.

20-12 体育彩票
SPORT LOTTERY

项　　目		Item		2012	2011
电脑体育彩票销售个数	(个)	Number of Computer Sport Lottery Tickets Sold	(unit)	2420	2383
体育彩票发行额	(万元)	Circulation of Sport Lottery	(10000 yuan)	382996	386417
#足　彩	(万元)	Football Lottery	(10000 yuan)	187998	209744
体育彩票公益金提取额	(万元)	Public Welfare Funds Drawn from Sport Lottery	(10000 yuan)	93566	95648
#足　彩	(万元)	Football Lottery	(10000 yuan)	41515	46144

资料来源：北京市体育局。
Source: Beijing Municipal Sports Bureau.

主要统计指标解释

卫 生

卫生机构 指从卫生行政部门取得《医疗机构执业许可证》，或从民政、工商行政、机构编制管理部门取得法人单位登记证书，为社会提供医疗保健、疾病控制、卫生监督服务或从事医学科研和教育等工作的单位。

卫生技术人员 指由卫生机构支付工资的全部固定职工和合同制职工中现任职务为卫生技术工作的专业人员，不包括从事管理工作的人员。

执业医师和注册护士 指领取医师执业证书和注册护士证书的人员，不包括从事管理工作的医师和护士。与2002年以前年鉴中的医生和护（师）士口径基本相同。

死亡率（死因死亡率） 是指某种原因（如疾病）所致的死亡人数占户籍人口比重。

婴儿死亡率 指某地区一年内每1000名活产婴儿与未满1岁的婴儿死亡人数之比。婴儿死亡率可以衡量一个国家或地区经济文化、居民健康状况和卫生保健事业发展情况，同时也是人口平均期望寿命研究的重要内容。

5岁以下儿童死亡率 指某地区一年内每1000名活产婴儿与未满5岁儿童死亡人数之比。5岁以下儿童死亡率是目前国际上公认的反映儿童生存状况的重要指标。

孕产妇死亡率 指某年某地每十万活产中的孕产妇死亡比例。同婴儿死亡率一样，孕产妇死亡率是评价某一地区社会发展状况的重要指标，它的高低与社会经济状况、孕产妇社会环境及卫生保健服务有直接的联系。

体 育

体育场地 指专门用于体育训练、比赛和健身活动的，有一定投资的公益性或经营性体育建筑设施。

晨晚练辅导站 是指本市公民自愿参加，在本市体育场馆、公园、街道、街心花园等公共场所设立的，利用早晚时间，以开展健身活动为目的的群众体育健身场所。

青少年体育俱乐部数 指创建单位利用自己所拥有的体育场馆、人才等资源建立起来的具有社会主义公益性的新型社会化青少年体育组织。

社会体育指导员 指在竞技体育、学校体育、部队体育以外的群众性体育活动中从事技能传授、锻炼指导和组织管理的工作人员。

专项球类活动场地 为满足不同人群特别是青少年的健身需求，而建设的专项球类活动场地，分篮球广场、笼式多功能球场、乒乓球长廊三种类型。

社区体育健身俱乐部 社区体育健身俱乐部是指“城市社区居民根据共同的目的和兴趣自愿组成的，以辖区内特定的体育场地设施为依托，经常开展体育活动，且隶属于街道办事处或社区居委会的公益性群众体育组织。”

等级运动员人数 指经考核正式批准授予等级运动员称号的人数。运动员等级分为国际级运动健将、国家级运动健将、一级运动员、二级运动员、三级运动员、少年级运动员。

等级裁判员人数 指经考核正式批准授予等级裁判员称号的人数。裁判员等级分为国际级裁判、国家级裁判、一级裁判、二级裁判、三级裁判。

运动员获奖牌情况 指当年我市运动员在世界比赛、亚洲比赛、全国比赛中获得金、银、铜牌的数量。

Explanatory Notes on Main Statistical Indicators

Health

Health Institutions refer to institutions granted with License for Medical Institution by the health administration authority, or granted with certificate of corporate unit by the civil affair, administration for industry and commerce, management authority of institutional organization, and providing medical service and healthcare, disease control, health supervision service or carrying out medical research and education, and so on.

Medical Technicians refer to all fixed employees and of contract-based employees, professional personnel in health technology, who receive pays from health institutions, excluding personnel engaged in management.

Certified Physicians and Registered Nurses refer to personnel who have received a physician practicing certificate and certified nurse certificate, excluding physicians and nurses engaged in management. The statistical range is basically the same as that in the yearbook 2002.

Death Rate (Cause-specific Death Rate) means the proportion of persons dead due to certain cause (such as disease) in the permanent population.

Infant Death Rate means the rate of dead infants under 1 year old to 1000 live infants. Infant death rate measures the development of economy, culture, citizen health and health care in a country or region. It is also an important component of study on average life expectancy of population.

Death Rate of Children under 5 means the rate of dead children under 5 years old to 1000 live infants. This is an important indicator now internationally recognized to reflect the survival status of children.

Death Rate of Pregnant and Lying-in Women refers to the rate of dead pregnant and lying-in women to 100,000 live pregnant and lying-in women in an area in a year. This is an important indicator to evaluate the social development status in an area. The figure of this indicator is directly related to the social and economic status, social environment and health care service for pregnant and lying-in women.

Sports

Sports Venues refer to sports building facilities for public welfare or operating purpose, specially used for sports training, games and fitness activities, and with certain investment.

Instruction Station of Morning and Evening Exercise refer to public sports and fitness sites located in sports gyms and stadiums, parks, streets, street parks and other public sites in a city, where the citizens in the city participate in voluntarily fitness activities in the morning or evening.

Number of Teenager Sports Clubs means the number of new-type social sports organizations for teenagers in the nature of socialistic public welfare, which are established by the builder with its own resources such as sports gyms and stadiums and human resource.

Social Sports Instructors refer to working personnel who carry out skill teaching, exercise instruction, organization and management in mass sports activities other than athletic sports, school sports, and army sports.

Special Ball Game Venue Facilities are special venues for ball activities built to meet the fitness need of different population, especially teenagers, consisting of three types, i.e. basketball squares, multi-purpose cage-shaped courts, and table tennis corridors.

Community Fitness Clubs refer to "mass sports organizations in the nature of public welfare, which are formed by residents in urban communities voluntarily according to their common purpose and interest, based on specific sports venue facilities in the jurisdiction, for frequent sports activities, and under the jurisdiction of sub-district administrative office or community neighborhood committee."

Number of Graded Athletes means the number of athletes formally granted with the title of graded athlete upon examination. Grades of athletes include international master sportsman, national maser sportsman, grade-I athlete, grade-II athlete, grade-III athlete, and juvenile athlete.

Number of Graded Referees means the number of referees formally granted with the title of graded referees upon examination. Grades of referees include international referee, national referee, grade-I referee, grade-II referee, and grade-III referee.

Medals Won by Athletes mean the number of gold, silver and copper medals won by athletes of Beijing in world games, Asian games and national games.

21

北京统计年鉴2013　BEIJING STATISTICAL YEARBOOK

社会福利、社区、政法及其他

SOCIAL WELFARE, COMMUNITY, POLITICS AND LAW AND OTHERS

简要说明

一、本章资料的主要内容

本章主要包括社会活动参与、公检法司、民政事业、劳动保障、残疾人事业、妇女及儿童发展规划监测情况等内容。

二、本章资料的数据来源

1.社会活动参与的内容主要包括历届北京市人大代表和政协委员人数及议案情况、妇联组织和工会组织情况等。资料分别由北京市人民代表大会常务委员会、中国人民政治协商会议北京市委员会、北京市妇女联合会和北京市总工会依据部门统计报表制度整理提供。

2.公检法司的资料主要包括公安机关的刑事案件立案情况和治安案件查处情况，交通、火灾事故情况，检察机关的办案情况，人民法院审理案件和收结案情况，以及司法局提供的律师、公证、调解工作等情况。资料分别由北京市公安局、北京市高级人民法院、北京市人民检察院和北京市司法局依据部门统计报表制度整理提供。

3.民政事业和劳动保障统计资料主要包括社会福利企事业机构、人员、优抚和社会救济情况、婚姻登记情况。资料分别由北京市民政局、北京市人力资源和社会保障局依据部门统计报表制度整理提供。

4.残疾人资料主要包括残疾人康复、教育、就业、扶贫和残联组织建设等情况。资料由北京市残疾人联合会提供。

5.妇女与儿童发展规划监测资料主要包括妇女参与决策和管理、就业、教育、健康、法律保护等情况；儿童的健康、教育、法律保护社会生活环境等情况。资料分别由北京市统计局、北京市人力资源和社会保障局、北京市教育委员会、北京市卫生局、北京市人民代表大会常务委员会、北京市公安局和北京市司法局依据部门统计报表制度整理提供。

6.安全生产情况由北京市行政工商管理局、北京市药品监督管理局、北京市公安交通管理局、北京市安全生产监督管理局提供。

Brief Introduction

I. Main Content

This chapter consists of statistics for social activity participation, public security organs, civil affairs, labor security, disables' undertaking, women and children development planning and monitoring.

II. Source of Data

1. Statistics for social activity participation cover the number of delegates and proposals at people's congress and political consulting conferences of Beijing in previous years, organizations of women's federation, and trade unions. Data were provided respectively by the Standing Committee of Beijing Municipal People's Congress, Beijing Committee of CPPCC, Beijing Women's Federation, and Beijing Federation of Labor Unions in accordance with statistic reporting system of different departments.

2. Statistics for public security organs cover criminal cases put on the record of public security organs as well as public security investigation and punishments, traffic accidents and fires, case settlements in prosecutorial organizations, case trial and settlement in people's courts, information on lawyers, notary, intermediation provided by juridical bureaus. Data were provided by Beijing Municipal Public Security Bureau, The People's High Court of Beijing, The People's Procuratorate of Beijing, and Beijing Justice Bureau in accordance with statistic reporting system of different departments.

3. Statistics for civil affairs and labor security mainly consist of social welfare institutions, personnel, social relief, preferential treatment and bereaved family comforting and compensating, and marriage register. Data were provided by Beijing Civil Affairs Bureau, Beijing Human Resource and Social Security Bureau in accordance with statistic reporting system of different departments.

4. Statistics for disables mainly include information on rehabilitation, education, employment and poverty reduction of disables, and building of disables' federations, etc. Data were provided by Beijing Disabled Persons Federation.

5. Data on women and children development and planning monitoring are composed of women's participation in decision making and management, employment, education, health, legal protection, and so on; children's health, education, legal protection, social living environment, etc. Data were provided respectively by Beijing Bureau of Statistics, Beijing Human Resource and Social Security Bureau, Beijing Municipal Commission of Education, Beijing Municipal Health Bureau, Standing Committee of Beijing Municipal People's Congress, Beijing Municipal Public Security Bureau, and Beijing Justice Bureau of Justice in accordance with statistic reporting system of different departments.

6. Safe production data were provided by Beijing Administration For Industry & Commerce, Beijing Drug Administration, Beijing Municipal Traffic Management Bureau, Beijing Administration of Work Safety.

21-1 优抚及主要救助对象情况
STATISTICS FOR PERSONS RECEIVING SPECIAL PENSIONS AND RELIEF

单位：人 (person)

项目	Item	人数 Number of Persons 2012	2011	2012年为2011年% 2012 as % of 2011
抚恤、补助优抚对象总人数	**Total Persons Receiving Pensions, Subsidies, and Special Care**	**42556**	**40621**	**104.8**
定期抚恤人数	Persons Receiving Regular Pensions	1829	2171	84.2
定期补助人数	Persons Receiving Regular Subsidies	29816	27448	108.6
伤残人数	Total Number of Disabled Persons	10911	11002	99.2
医疗救助人次数	**Total Persons Receiving Medical Assistance**	**112925**	**85420**	**132.2**
城市医疗救助人次数	Total Urban Persons Receiving Medical Assistance	80534	34474	233.6
农村医疗救助人次数	Total Rural Persons Receiving Medical Assistance	32391	50946	63.6
社会救助对象总人数	**Total Persons Receiving Special Relief**	**176825**	**191567**	**92.3**
城市居民最低生活保障人数	Number of Persons Receiving Lowest Cost-of-Living in Urban Area	109743	117286	93.6
农村居民最低生活保障人数	Number of Persons Receiving Lowest Cost-of-Living in Rural Area	62979	70146	89.8
农村五保供养人数	Rural Personnel Enjoying Five Guarantees	4103	4135	99.2
农村集中五保供养人数	Collective Rural Personnel Enjoying Five Guarantees	2097	2146	97.7
农村分散五保供养人数	Scattered Rural Personnel Enjoying Five Guarantees	2006	1989	100.9

注："农村最低生活保障人数"不含"农村五保供养人数"。

资料来源：北京市民政局。

Note: Number of Persons Receiving Lowest Cost-of-Living in Rural Area excludes "Rural Personnel Enjoying Five Guarantees".

Source: Beijing Civil Affairs Bureau.

21-2 北京市历年参加社会保障情况(1995-2012年)

单位：万人

年 份 Year	参加基本养老保险人数 Number of People Participating in Basic Pension Insurance	参加基本医疗保险人数 Number of People Participating in Basic Medical Care Insurance	参加失业保险职工人数 Number of People Participating in Unemployment Insurance	参加工伤保险职工人数 Number of People Participating in Work Injury Insurance	参加生育保险职工人数 Number of People Participating in Maternity Insurance
1995	261.1		219.8		
1996	252.0		214.5		
1997	264.3		214.0		
1998	359.2		222.9		
1999	379.0		289.0		
2000	391.6		287.8	212.0	
2001	425.9	210.2	287.2	212.7	
2002	436.2	353.8	299.5	221.0	
2003	448.5	436.1	306.6	242.9	
2004	460.0	484.0	308.0	259.0	
2005	520.0	574.8	394.6	328.9	226.1
2006	604.1	679.5	482.2	465.3	263.3
2007	671.7	783.0	535.3	609.2	290.6
2008	758.1	871.0	614.3	666.5	324.1
2009	827.7	938.4	675.7	747.1	346.8
2010	982.5	1063.7	774.2	823.8	372.2
2011	1091.9	1188.0	881.0	862.4	395.3
2012	1206.4	1279.7	1006.7	897.2	844.7

注：1. 2001年开始设置基本医疗保险指标，以前年份称为大病统筹，2000年参加大病统筹人数为232.6万人。
2. 2005年7月1日《北京市企业职工生育保险规定》开始实施。全市农村社会养老保险1992年试点，1996年全市正式实施。
3. 从2006年起，农村最低生活保障人数不含农村五保供养人员。
4. 农村居民参加城乡居民养老保险人数在2007年及以前为参加农村社会养老保险人数口径；2008年为参加新型农村社会养老保险人数；2009年及以后为参加城乡居民养老保险人数中农村参保人数。
5. 农民养老保险参保率2008年及以前为农村养老保险覆盖率。

资料来源：城乡居民享受最低生活保障人数来源于北京市民政局；参加农村新型医疗人数和参合率来源于北京市卫生局；其他资料来源于北京市人力资源和社会保障局。

SOCIAL SECURITY PARTICIPATION(1995-2012)

(10000 persons)

农村居民参加城乡居民养老保险人数 Number of People Participating in Rural Basic Pension Insurance	参加新型农村合作医疗人数 Number of People Participating in New-type Rural cooperative medicare	城市居民最低生活保障人数 Number of Persons Receiving Lowest Cost-of-Living in Urban Area	农村最低生活保障人数 Number of Persons Receiving Lowest Cost-of-Living in Rural Area	农民养老保险参保率(%) Coverage Rate of Rural Pension Insurance	新型农村合作医疗参合率(%) Percentage of Persons Participating in New-type Rural Cooperative Medicare
29.2		0.9			
37.4		0.9			
41.2		2.8			
34.4		4.3	1.2		
38.5		6.7	1.6		
34.7		7.6	1.8		
32.0		12.0	5.4		
33.6		16.1	6.7		
36.8	234.0	16.1	7.5		71.9
40.6	250.4	15.5	7.8	25.0	80.3
44.8	261.0	15.2	7.6	29.3	86.9
49.1	268.5	14.8	7.8	36.6	88.9
127.5	272.5	14.5	7.9	85.0	92.9
153.9	274.9	14.7	8.0	90.0	95.7
159.3	278.5	13.7	7.7	92.0	96.7
163.7	276.8	11.7	7.0		97.7
167.0	267.5	11.0	6.3		98.1

Note: a) The basic medicare indicator was offered from 2001, before which it was called general health care program for major diseases.It's 2.3 million people in 2000.

b) Regulations of Beijing on Maternity Insurance for Enterprise Employees were effective from July 1st, 2005. Experiment was made for social pension program in rural area of Beijing in 1992. The program was formally effective in 1996 in Beijing.

c) Rural persons receiving lowest cost-of-living excluded rural persons enjoying five guarantees from 2006.

d) In and before 2007, the number of rural people participating in urban and rural pension insurance covered the people participating in rural social pension insurance; in 2008, this figure covered the people participating in new-type rural social pension insurance; since 2009, this figure covered the rural people of those participating in the urban and rural pension insurance.

e) In and before 2008, the coverage rate of farmer pension insurance was the coverage rate of rural pension insurance.

Source: Figures on persons receiving lowest cost-of-living in urban and rural areas are from Beijing Civil Affairs Bureau; Figures on persons participating in new-type rural medicare and percentage of these persons are from Beijing Municipal Health Bureau; other data are from Beijing Human Resource and Social Security Bureau.

21-3 北京市历年社会保障相关待遇标准(1994-2012年)
HISTORICAL SOCIAL WELFARE TREATMENT STANDARD IN BEIJING (1994-2012)

单位：元/月 (yuan/month)

标准 Standard / 年份 Year		职工最低工资 Lowest Wage of Staff and Workers	失业保险金最低标准 Lowest Cost of Unemployment Insurance	城市居民最低生活保障标准 Urban Lowest Cost-of-living	基本养老金平均增加水平 Average Increased Standard of Basic Old-age Pension	企业退休人员基本养老金最低标准 Lowest Pensions of Retired Persons	企业退职人员基本养老金最低标准 Lowest Pensions of Persons Withdraw	企业退养人员基本养老金最低标准 Lowest Pensions of Persons Withdraw
1994		210						
1995		240	174					
1996		270	189	170		263	202	170
1997		290	203	190	55	293	232	200
1998		310	217	200	50	336	265	233
1999年第一次	First-time in 1999	320	224	210	40			
1999年第二次	Second-time in 1999	400	291	273	80	396	335	288
2000		412	300	280	30	421	360	308
2001		435	305	285	40	441	380	317
2002		465	326	290	70	466	405	367
2003		465	326	290	62	466	405	367
2004年第一次	First-time in 2004	495						
2004年第二次	Second-time in 2004	545	347	290	70	510	443	402
2005		580	382	300	120	563	488	443
2006		640	392	310	120	620	537	487
2007		730	422	330	150	675	592	527
2008		800	502	390	200	775	682	607
2009		800	562	410	200	900	800	700
2010		960	632	430	200	1000	900	800
2011		1160	782	500		1100	1000	900
2012		1260	842	520		1210	1100	1000

资料来源：城市居民最低生活保障标准由北京市民政局提供，本表其他资料由北京市人力资源和社会保障局提供。

Source: Data of urban lowest cost-of-living was provided by Beijing Civil Affairs Bureau,others were provided by Beijing Human Resource and Social Security Bureau.

21-4 社会保险情况(2012年)
GENERAL SOCIAL SECURITY INSURANCE PROGRAM (2012)

项目	Item	基本养老保险 Basic Endowment Insurance Funds		基本医疗保险 Basic Medical Care Insurance Funds	
		单位个数 (个) Number of Units (unit)	人数 (人) Number of Persons (person)	单位个数 (个) Number of Units (unit)	人数 (人) Number of Persons (person)
合　计	**Total**	**347752**	**12063791**	**317537**	**12797358**
按登记注册类型分	**Grouped by Registration Status**				
国　有	State-Owned	8839	2032931	7964	1991222
集　体	Collective-Owned	8552	283906	7326	272336
其　他	Other	330361	9746954	302247	10533800
按隶属关系划分	**Grouped by Administrative Relationship**				
中央单位	Central Units	8253	1800345	7639	1712384
地方单位	Local Units	339499	10263446	309898	11084974

资料来源：北京市人力资源和社会保障局。
Source: Beijing Human Resource and Social Security Bureau.

21-4 续表 continued

项目	Item	失业保险 Unemployment Insurance		工伤保险 Industrial Injury Insurance		生育保险 Maternity Insurance	
		单位个数 (个) Number of Units (unit)	人数 (人) Number of Persons (person)	单位个数 (个) Number of Units (unit)	人数 (人) Number of Persons (person)	单位个数 (个) Number of Units (unit)	人数 (人) Number of Persons (person)
合　计	**Total**	**348590**	**10067391**	**358752**	**8971812**	**346571**	**8446904**
按登记注册类型分	**Grouped by Registration Status**						
国　有	State-Owned	8521	1081705	8714	1086753	8480	1020800
集　体	Collective-Owned	8445	151659	8794	156206	8603	139106
其　他	Other	331624	8834027	341244	7728853	329488	7286998
按隶属关系划分	**Grouped by Administrative Relationship**						
中央单位	Central Units	8087	1469657	8410	1377295	7986	1162090
地方单位	Local Units	340503	8597734	350342	7594517	338585	7284814

资料来源：北京市人力资源和社会保障局。
Source: Beijing Human Resource and Social Security Bureau.

21-5 社会福利事业情况
STATISTICS ON SOCIAL WELFARE

项目		Item		2012	2011	2012年为2011年% 2021 as % of 2011
社区服务设施数	(个)	Number of Service Facilities in Urban Communities	(unit)	6244	5411	115.4
#社区服务中心	(个)	Substreet Community Service Centers	(unit)	186	180	103.3
社区服务设施从业人员数	(人)	Employees in Urban Community Service Facilities	(person)	31921	20658	154.5
社区服务志愿者组织数	(个)	Number of Community Service Volunteer Organizations	(unit)	9751	8012	121.7
城镇便民利民服务网点数	(个)	Number of Urban Convenient Service Outlets	(unit)	11169	12354	90.4
社会福利企业单位数	(个)	Number of Social Welfare Enterprises	(unit)	664	670	99.1
社会福利企业年末职工人数	(人)	Year-end Employees in Social Welfare Enterprises	(person)	31260	32042	97.6
#残疾职工	(人)	Disabled Employees	(person)	12078	12570	96.1

资料来源：北京市民政局。
Source: Beijing Civil Affairs Bureau.

21-6 收养性单位情况(2012年)
STATISTICS ON ADOPTING SOCIAL UNIT (2012)

项目		Item		合计	#光荣院 Honor Institution	#社会福利院 Social Welfare Institution	#儿童福利院 Children's Welfare Institution	#福利类精神病院和医院 Social Welfare of Mental Diseases Hospital	#城市养老服务机构 Urban Pension Service Institutions	#农村养老服务机构 Rural Pension Service Institutions
单位数	(个)	Institutions	(unit)	437	10	8	12	2	133	267
职工人数	(人)	Employees	(person)	11149	223	1150	509	343	4108	4630
床位数	(张)	Beds	(unit)	79178	798	3341	1444	564	26772	44719
收养人数	(人)	Persons Adopted	(person)	33507	213	2987	1121	482	12035	16328
#自　费	(人)	Self-supported	(person)	28547	31	2228	17	464	11776	13695

资料来源：北京市民政局。
Source: Beijing Civil Affairs Bureau.

21-7 离婚、青少年刑事案犯情况
STATISTICS ON DIVORCE AND TEENAGER CRIMINAL CASES

项目		Item		2012	2011
婚姻家庭纠纷案件数(结案)	(件)	Household Marriage Disputes (Ended)	(case)	35201	35149
#离婚案件数	(件)	Divorce Cases	(case)	20825	20872
#调离、判离案件数	(件)	Cases of Divorce Reconciled or Judged	(case)	10332	10522
建立少年法庭个数	(个)	Juvenile Courts Established	(unit)	20	22
青少年罪犯人数	(人)	Teenager Offenders	(person)	8209	7790
#18岁以下青少年罪犯人数	(人)	Teenager Offenders under 18	(person)	1223	1372
青少年刑事案犯占全部刑事案犯的比重	(%)	Teenager Criminal Offenders as % of Total Criminal Offenders	(%)	34.21	38.03
男　性	(%)	Male	(%)	87.62	88.82
女　性	(%)	Female	(%)	12.38	11.18

资料来源：北京市高级人民法院。
Source: The People's High Court of Beijing.

21-8 婚姻登记(1981-2012年)
BASIC STATISTICS ON MARRIAGE AND DIVORCE REGISTRATIONS (1981-2012)

年份 Year	结婚对数(对) Registered Marriages (couple)	#涉外及华侨、港澳台居民登记结婚对数 Registered Marriages with Foreigner and the Citizen of Hongkong, Macao and Taiwan	初婚总人数(人) First Marriages (person)	离婚对数(对) Registered Divorces (couple)	#民政部门登记离婚对数 Registered Divorces with Civil Affair Authorities
1981	200352		392855	5170	1780
1982	141253		265834	5359	1581
1983	117976			5322	1465
1984	113362		218009	5654	1387
1985	134462		258256	5874	1746
1986	143105		273634	7541	2474
1987	149952		285803	8916	3218
1988	113333		212070	10664	4198
1989	103829		190978	12515	5174
1990	92988		168304	14748	5791
1991	91979		166579	15287	6483
1992	89095		159588	15567	6477
1993	89938		160127	17829	7589
1994	90379		161972	19928	8327
1995	85511		149878	20160	8096
1996	86803		147855	20716	8225
1997	84208		145099	22257	8628
1998	85534		148026	23708	9381
1999	83312		141740	23922	8502
2000	80212		135620	26616	6384
2001	79385	873	133259	27683	5425
2002	76136	606	126371	27691	5810
2003	93526	761	158729	30637	10142
2004	126436	974	214443	32657	21013
2005	96596	937	158736	34244	23991
2006	171286	1172	294223	35505	24954
2007	117926	991	193387	36622	26432
2008	147516	1165	246309	37619	27277
2009	181771	1176	305803	41299	29998
2010	138104	1085	222269	43970	32595
2011	173238	1260	288406	43521	32999
2012	174114	1242	287436	48575	38243

注：离婚对数包括在民政部门登记的对数和经法院调离和判离的对数。

资料来源：北京市民政局、北京市高级人民法院。

Note: Registered divorces include those registered with civil affair authorities and those mediated and judged in courts.

Source: Beijing Civil Affairs Bureau,The People's High Court of Beijing.

21-9 婚姻登记情况
BASIC STATISTICS ON MARRIAGE AND DIVORCE REGISTRATIONS

项目		Item		2012	2011	2012年为2011年% 2012 as % of 2011
登记结婚对数	**(对)**	**Registered Marriages**	**(couple)**	**174114**	**173238**	**100.5**
按婚前状况分		**Grouped by pre-marriage status**				
初婚人数	(人)	First Marriages	(person)	287436	288406	99.7
再婚人数	(人)	Remarriages	(person)	60792	58070	104.7
#女性	(人)	Female	(person)	28368	27071	104.8
按居住地分		**Grouped by living area**				
内地居民登记结婚对数	(对)	Registered Marriages of Mainland	(couple)	172872	171978	100.5
涉外及华侨、港澳台居民登记结婚对数	(对)	Registered Marriages with Foreigner and the Citzen of Hongkong, Macao and Taiwan	(couple)	1242	1260	98.6
内地居民	(人)	Mainland Residents	(person)	1160	1171	99.1
#女性	(人)	Female	(person)	854	859	99.4
香港居民	(人)	Hongkong Compatriots	(person)	67	64	104.7
澳门居民	(人)	Macao Compatriots	(person)	10	10	100.0
台湾居民	(人)	Taiwan Compatriots	(person)	128	120	106.7
华侨	(人)	Overseas Chinese	(person)	51	61	83.6
外国人	(人)	Foreigner	(person)	1068	1094	97.6
离婚登记对数	**(对)**	**Registered Divorces**	**(couple)**	**38243**	**32999**	**115.9**
内地居民登记离婚对数	(对)	Mainland Residents	(couple)	38080	32850	115.9
涉外及华侨、港澳台居民登记离婚对数	(对)	Overseas Chinese,Hongkong,Macao, Taiwan Compatriots	(couple)	163	149	109.4

注：离婚对数不含法院判离数。
资料来源：北京市民政局。
Note: Number of Registered Divorces exclude Judged by Court.
Source: Beijing Civil Affairs Bureau.

21-10 残疾人事业基本情况
BASIC INFORMATION ON UNDERTAKING FOR DISABLED PERSONS

项　目		Item		2012	2011
康　复		**Rehabilitation**			
白内障复明手术	(例)	Sight-Rrestoring Cataract Surgeries	(case)	10356	10122
人工晶体植入率	(%)	Artificial Intra-ocular Lens Implantation Rate	(%)	96	96
低视力配用助视器	(人)	Vision-aids Provided for Individuals with Low-vision	(person)	362	129
聋儿康复		Rehabilitation of Children with Hearing Disability			
年收训聋儿	(人)	Hearing and Speech Training	(person)	332	239
聋儿入普幼普小率	(%)	Enrollment Rate of Trained Children to Ordinary Kindergartens and Primary Schools	(%)	80	90
培训家长	(人)	Parents Trained	(person)	498	247
精神病防治康复		Prevention and Treatment of Psychiatric Diseases			
开展精神病防治康复工作区县数	(个)	Counties Carried on the Works of Prevention and Treatment of Psychiatric Diseases	(unit)	16	16
综合防治康复精神病人数	(人)	Prevention and Treatment Provided for Patients with Severe Psychiatric Diseases	(person)	29642	25841
监护率	(%)	Guardianship Rate	(%)	99.79	88.05
显好率	(%)	Significant Improvement Rate	(%)	63.74	70.85
社会参与率	(%)	Social Involvement Rate	(%)	39.47	54.05
肇事率	(%)	Violent Events Rate	(%)	0.03	0.06
康复训练与服务		Rehabilitation Training and Service			
肢体残疾康复训练人次	(人次)	Function Training Provided to Persons with Physical Disability	(person times)	5142	6057
智残儿童康复训练人次	(人次)	Rehabilitation Training Provided to Children with Intellectual Disability	(person times)	361	609
脑瘫儿童康复训练人次	(人次)	Rehabilitation Training Provided to Children with Cerebral Palsy	(person times)	262	184
教　育		**Education**			
未入学适龄残疾儿童少年	(人)	School-age Disabled Children Without Schooling	(person)	419	651
职业教育与培训机构数	(个)	Vocational Education and Training Facilities	(unit)	45	66
教育与培训人数	(人次)	Number of Educated and Trained	(person times)	4111	5533
就　业		**Employment**			
城镇残疾人就业状况		Employment of Urban Handicappeds			
当年安排就业人数	(人)	Persons Employed in the Year	(person)	2907	3911
#按比例就业人数	(人)	Employed by Quota Scheme	(person)	1181	1146
集中就业人数	(人)	Disalbed Persons Employed in Concentrated Way	(person)	285	215
个体就业人数	(人)	Self-employed	(person)	803	2550
残疾人就业服务机构数	(个)	Employment Placement Service Facilities for Disabled Jobseekers	(unit)	17	18
盲人按摩		Massage by Persons with Visual Disability			
保健按摩机构	(家)	Healthcare Massage Institutions	(unit)	498	916
医疗按摩机构	(家)	Medical Massage Institutions	(unit)	2	2
保健按摩员培训人次	(人次)	Massage Therapists Training	(person times)	509	314
医疗按摩员培训人次	(人次)	Keep-fit Massager Training	(person times)	98	98
扶　贫		**Poverty Alleviation**			
享受城镇廉租住房的残疾人户数	(户)	Number of Disabled Families Granted Low-cost Urban House Leasing	(household)	1540	2145
扶持农村残疾人数	(人)	Number of Disabled Persons that Can be Supported in Rural Area	(person)	5064	6319
社会保障		**Social Securtity**			
城　镇		urban			
已纳入最低生活保障范围人数	(人)	With Disabilities Covered by the Basic Living System	(person)	47477	
集中供养人数	(人)	Covered by Concentrated Supporting	(person)	302	
享受生活补助的重残人数	(人)	Severely Disabled Persosn Qualified for Living Subsidies	(person)	17236	
其他救助救济人数	(人)	With Others Aid	(person)	5036	
农　村		Rural Areas			
已纳入最低生活保障范围人数	(人)	With Disabilities Covered by the Basic Living System	(person)	23414	
五保供养人数	(人)	Supported by Five Guarantees	(person)	859	
享受生活补助的重残人数	(人)	Severely Disabled Persosn Qualified for Living Subsidies	(person)	24447	
其他救助救济人数	(人)	With Others Aid	(person)	14022	
残联组织建设		**Organization Building of Disabled Persons'Federation**			
残疾人工作者数	(人)	Workers for Handicappeds	(person)	1432	1942

资料来源：北京市残疾人联合会。
Source: Beijing Disabled Persons Federation.

21-11 残疾人就业、维权援助情况
STATISTICS ON EMPLOYMENT AND AID FOR RIGHT SAFEGUARD OF DISABLED PERSONS

项　　目		Item		2012	2011
残疾人职业培训人数	(人)	Number of Disabled Persons Trained for Employment	(person)	11763	10049
#女　性	(人)	Female	(person)	6859	4377
新安置残疾人员就业人	(人)	Additional Employed of Disabled Person	(person)	4384	5779
#女　性	(人)	Female	(peoson)	1422	1933
维权信访咨询件数	(件)	Cases of Right Safeguard	(case)	16627	14625
维权法律服务件数	(件)	Cases of Right Legal Aid	(case)	4955	4492

资料来源：北京市残疾人联合会。
Source: Beijing Disabled Persons Federation.

21-12 律师工作
STATISTICS ON LAWYERS

项　　目		Item		2012	2011	2012年为2011年% 2012 as % of 2011
律师事务所	(个)	Law Offices	(unit)	1672	1609	103.9
执业律师	(人)	Number of Practicing Lawyers	(person)	22796	22100	103.1
专职律师	(人)	Full-time Lawyers	(person)	21419	20757	103.2
兼职律师	(人)	Part-time Lawyers	(person)	1056	1034	102.1
公司律师	(人)	Company Lawyers	(person)	243	246	98.8
公职律师	(人)	Government Lawyers	(person)	17	20	85.0
法律援助律师	(人)	Law Aid Lawyers	(person)	61	43	141.9
担任法律顾问	(家)	Acting As Counselor-at-law	(unit)	21907	22171	98.8
民事诉讼代理	(件)	Civil Case Litigation Agency	(case)	66341	79172	83.8
行政诉讼代理	(件)	Administrative Case Litigation Agency	(case)	4031	3424	117.7
刑事诉讼辩护及代理	(件)	Criminal Case Litigation Agency	(case)	18174	15631	116.3
非诉讼法律事务	(件)	Off-court Case	(case)	73352	68749	106.7

资料来源：北京市司法局。
Source: Beijing Justice Bureau.

21-13 调解工作
MEDIATION

项　　目		Item		2012	2011	2012年为2011年% 2012 as % of 2011
人民调解委员会个数	(个)	People's Mediation Committees	(unit)	7770	8146	95.4
调解员人数	(万人)	Members of the Mediation Institution	(10000 persons)	7.48	12.35	60.5
调解各类纠纷件数	(万件)	Disputes Mediated	(10000 cases)	23.11	26.32	87.8
#调解各类纠纷成功件数	(万件)	Succeed Disputes Mediated	(10000 cases)	22.26	25.52	87.2
防止民间纠纷激化件数	(件)	Prevent Intensification of Civil Disputes	(case)	1742	821	212.2
防止民间纠纷激化人数	(人)	Prevent Intensification of Civil Disputes	(person)	38420	18146	211.7

资料来源：北京市司法局。
Source: Beijing Justice Bureau.

21-14 公证工作
NOTARIZATIONS

项　　目		Item		2012	2011	2012年为2011年% 2012 as % of 2011
公证处个数	(个)	Notary Offices	(unit)	25	25	100.0
执业公证员人数	(人)	Certified Notaries	(person)	275	259	106.2
办理国内民事公证件数	(件)	Notarized Domestic Civil Affairs	(case)	165885	185887	89.2
办理国内经济公证件数	(件)	Notarized Domestic Economic Affairs	(case)	117110	108590	107.8
办理涉外公证件数	(件)	Notarized Foreign Affairs	(case)	344911	336127	102.6
办理涉台、港、澳公证件数	(件)	Notarized Taiwan,Hongkong,Macao Affairs	(case)	6057	6274	96.5

资料来源：北京市司法局。
Source: Beijing Justice Bureau.

21-15 法律援助工作情况
STATISTICS ON LEGAL AID

项目		Item		2012	2011	2012年为2011年% 2012 as % of 2011
法律援助机构个数	(个)	Number of Legal Aid Bodies	(unit)	26	26	100.0
法律援助机构人员数	(人)	Number of Legal Aid Persons	(person)	209	237	88.2
承办民事法律援助案件数	(件)	Civil Legal Aid Cases	(case)	13804	11688	118.1
承办刑事法律援助案件数	(件)	Penal Legal Aid Cases	(case)	3587	3357	106.9
承办行政法律援助案件数	(件)	Administrative Legal Aid Cases	(case)	28	21	133.3
法律援助机构接待咨询人次	(万人次)	Legal Aid Bodies Consultation	(10000 person-times)	26.0	22.6	114.9
得到法律援助机构援助的妇女人数	(人)	Women Receiving Aid from Legal Aid Bodies	(person)	3370	2645	127.4
得到法律援助机构援助的儿童人数	(人)	Children Receiving Aid from Legal Aid Bodies	(person)	1175	937	125.4

资料来源：北京市司法局。
Source: Beijing Justice Bureau.

21-16 司法鉴定工作情况
STATISTICS ON JUDICIAL APPRAISAL

项目		Item		2012	2011
司法鉴定机构个数	(个)	Judicial Appraisal Organization	(unit)	109	105
司法鉴定人员数	(人)	Judicial Appraisal Personnel	(person)	1675	1618
司法鉴定业务量	(件)	Judicial Appraisal Proceeding	(case)	36451	34636

注：本表中司法鉴定机构数为"北京市司法局审核登记的全部司法鉴定机构"个数。
资料来源：北京市司法局。
Note: In the table, the number of judicial appraisal organizations is the number of "all judicial appraisal organizations approved by and registered with Beijing Justice Bureau".
Source: Beijing Justice Bureau.

21-17 公安、法院、检察院收案、结案情况(2005-2012年)
CASES ACCEPTED AND SETTLED BY PUBLIC SECURITY DEPARTMENT, COURTS AND PROCURATORATES (2005-2012)

项　目		Item		2005	2006	2007
公安部门侦破刑事案件		**Criminal Cases Detected by Public Security Departments**				
立　案	(起)	Cases Put on File	(case)	107988	120554	127446
破　案	(起)	Cases Settled	(case)	59035	66399	74232
法院刑事案件收、结案情况		**Criminal Cases in Courts and Settlement Thereof**				
收　案	(件)	Cases Accepted	(case)	17488	17725	19592
结　案	(件)	Cases Settled	(case)	17624	17701	19536
法院婚姻家庭、继承纠纷案件收、结案情况		**Marriage and Inheritance Dispute Cases in Courts**				
收　案	(件)	Cases Accepted	(case)	26739	27860	28089
结　案	(件)	Cases Settled	(case)	27002	27845	27916
法院合同纠纷案件收、结案情况		**Contract Dispute Cases in Courts and Settlement Thereof**				
收　案	(件)	Cases Accepted	(case)	133534	141485	135099
结　案	(件)	Cases Settled	(case)	135612	141439	134829
法院权属、侵权纠纷及其他民事案件收、结案情况		**Ownership, Infringement Dispute and Other Civil Cases in Courts and Settlement Thereof**				
收　案	(件)	Cases Accepted	(case)	42690	44890	46892
结　案	(件)	Cases Settled	(case)	43166	45005	46372
检察机关办理反贪污贿赂案件		**Anti-Corruption and Bribery Cases Handled by Procuratorates**				
受　案	(件)	Cases Accepted	(case)	1202	1330	1276
立　案		Cases Put on File				
件　数	(件)	Number of Cases	(case)	292	321	322
人　数	(人)	Number of Persons Involved	(person)	356	363	372
挽回经济损失	(万元)	Economic Losses Redeemed	(10000 yuan)	30701	29545	14703
检察机关办理渎职侵权案件		**Misconduct and Infringement Cases Handled by Procuratorates**				
受　案	(件)	Cases Accepted	(case)	218	162	205
立　案		Cases Put on File				
件　数	(件)	Number of Cases	(case)	37	30	34
人　数	(人)	Number of Persons Involved	(person)	38	31	36
挽回经济损失	(万元)	Economic Losses Redeemed	(10000 yuan)	1320	458	71

资料来源：北京市公安局、北京市人民检察院、北京市高级人民法院。
Source: Beijing Municipal Public Security Bureau,The People's Procuratorate of Beijing,The People's High Court of Beijing.

21-17 续表 continued

项 目		Item		2008	2009	2010	2011	2012
公安部门侦破刑事案件		**Criminal Cases Detected by Public Security Departments**						
立 案	(起)	Cases Put on File	(case)	90045	98750	104327	142835	145724
破 案	(起)	Cases Settled	(case)	63294	71950	80401	89156	101776
法院刑事案件收、结案情况		**Criminal Cases in Courts and Settlement Thereof**						
收 案	(件)	Cases Accepted	(case)	20024	18819	19824	19574	22168
结 案	(件)	Cases Settled	(case)	20004	18773	19870	19423	22084
法院婚姻家庭、继承纠纷案件收、结案情况		**Marriage and Inheritance Dispute Cases in Courts**						
收 案	(件)	Cases Accepted	(case)	30402	33056	36799	35251	35418
结 案	(件)	Cases Settled	(case)	29499	32902	37160	35149	35201
法院合同纠纷案件收、结案情况		**Contract Dispute Cases in Courts and Settlement Thereof**						
收 案	(件)	Cases Accepted	(case)	144948	153766	148655	144433	145017
结 案	(件)	Cases Settled	(case)	140512	152128	153130	144766	143153
法院权属、侵权纠纷及其他民事案件收、结案情况		**Ownership, Infringement Dispute and Other Civil Cases in Courts and Settlement Thereof**						
收 案	(件)	Cases Accepted	(case)	53864	58057	64379	65972	62736
结 案	(件)	Cases Settled	(case)	51668	57135	65763	66405	62235
检察机关办理反贪污贿赂案件		**Anti-Corruption and Bribery Cases Handled by Procuratorates**						
受 案	(件)	Cases Accepted	(case)	1060	1113	1138	988	1070
立 案		Cases Put on File						
件 数	(件)	Number of Cases	(case)	282	319	356	343	379
人 数	(人)	Number of Persons Involved	(person)	333	369	418	425	459
挽回经济损失	(万元)	Economic Losses Redeemed	(10000 yuan)	21148	62542	14634	36469	29955
检察机关办理渎职侵权案件		**Misconduct and Infringement Cases Handled by Procuratorates**						
受 案	(件)	Cases Accepted	(case)	150	206	213	193	351
立 案		Cases Put on File						
件 数	(件)	Number of Cases	(case)	29	48	57	55	77
人 数	(人)	Number of Persons Involved	(person)	31	53	60	66	94
挽回经济损失	(万元)	Economic Losses Redeemed	(10000 yuan)	3019	25	16	58	735

21-18 法院行政案件收、结案情况(2012年)
STATISTICS ON ADMINISTRATIVE CASES ACCEPTED AND SETTLED BY COURT (2012)

单位：件 (case)

项 目	Item	收 案 Cases Accepted	结 案 Cases Settled	判 决 Judgment	裁 定 Mediation
合 计	**Total**	**5697**	**5695**	**3855**	**1840**
公 安	Public Security	211	213	128	84
资 源	Resource	92	89	47	42
城 建	City Construction	569	583	219	364
工 商	Industry and Commerce	61	66	42	24
专 利	Patent	726	681	618	63
劳动和社会保障	Labor and Social Security	91	90	55	35
教 育	Education	9	6	1	5
其 他	Other	3938	3967	2745	1223

资料来源：北京市高级人民法院。
Source: The People's High Court of Beijing.

21-19 法院刑事案件收、结案情况(2012年)
STATISTICS ON CRIMINAL CASES ACCEPTED AND SETTLED BY COURT (2012)

项 目	Item	收 案（件） Cases Accepted (case)	结 案（件） Cases Settled (case)	判决发生法律效力 Judgment with Legal Force	
				件 数（件） Number of Cases (case)	人 数（人） Number of Persons (person)
合 计	**Total**	**22168**	**22084**	**18446**	**23993**
#危害公共安全罪	Offences against Public Security	1667	1665	1373	1449
破坏社会主义市场经济秩序罪	Offences against the Socialism Market Economy Order	3128	3107	2174	2941
侵犯公民人身权利、民主权利罪	Offences against Civil Personal Rights and Democratic Rights	4312	4371	3955	4688
侵犯财产罪	Offences against Property	7258	7169	6499	8346
妨害社会管理秩序罪	Offences against Social Management of Order	4800	4793	4127	6125
危害国防利益罪	Offences against National Defense Interest	40	41	32	37
贪污贿赂罪	Offences on Corruption and Bribery Crime	302	300	232	308
渎职罪	Offences on Abuse and Dereliction of Duty	21	23	17	21

资料来源：北京市高级人民法院。
Source: The People's High Court of Beijing.

21-20 法院婚姻家庭、继承纠纷案件收、结案情况(2012年)
STATISTICS ON MARRIAGE AND FAMILY AND INHERITABLE DISPUTE CASE (2012)

单位：件 (case)

项　　目	Item	收案 Cases Accepted	结案 Cases Settled	#判决 Judgment	#调解 Mediation
合　计	**Total**	**35418**	**35201**	**10723**	**13854**
婚姻家庭纠纷	**Marriage and Family Dispute**	**28963**	**28804**	**8952**	**10925**
离　婚	Divorce	20919	20825	6354	7971
解除非法同居关系	Relieving the Relation of Lawless Cohabitation	310	311	112	110
抚养、扶养关系纠纷	Upbringing Disputes	1050	1049	257	529
抚育费纠纷	Upbinging Fee Disputes	1203	1205	537	361
赡养纠纷	Support Disputes	1254	1252	460	402
分家析产	Family property division	2014	1958	467	914
其　他	Others	2213	2204	765	638
继承纠纷	**Inheritance Dispute**	**6455**	**6397**	**1771**	**2929**
法定继承	Legal Inheritance	4007	3997	938	2059
遗嘱继承	Testament Inheritance	705	689	291	239
继承权确认纠纷	Inherited Dispute				
其　他	Others	1743	1711	542	631

资料来源：北京市高级人民法院。
Source: The People's High Court of Beijing.

21-21 法院合同纠纷案件收、结案情况(2012年)
STATISTICS ON CONTRACT CASES ACCEPTED AND CLOSED BY COURT (2012)

单位：件 (case)

项　　目	Item	收案 Cases Accepted	结案 Cases Settled	#判决 Judgment	#调解 Mediation
合　计	**Total**	**145017**	**143153**	**48464**	**31137**
#买卖合同纠纷	Trade Contracts	16566	16349	5898	4131
房地产开发经营合同纠纷	Real Estate Development & Operation Contracts	6264	6244	3257	1209
供用电、水、气、热力合同纠纷	Electricity, Water, Gas, Heating Supply contracts	19259	19246	1590	4736
借款合同纠纷	Loan Contracts	14130	13835	5701	3190
租赁合同纠纷	Lease Contracts	10424	10330	4140	1884
建设工程合同纠纷	Construction Contracts	4143	4012	1614	855
承揽合同纠纷	Contracts for Work	3177	3192	825	1101
运输合同纠纷	Transportation Contracts	810	807	299	195
经营合同纠纷	Management Contracts	1191	1185	505	188
农村承包合同纠纷	Rural Contract	158	156	44	20
劳动争议	Work Disputes	20553	19707	9486	5071

资料来源：北京市高级人民法院。
Source: The People's High Court of Beijing.

21-22 法院权属、侵权纠纷及其他民事案件收、结案情况(2012年)
STATISTICS ON OWNERSHIP AND TORTIOUS DISPUTE CASES ACCEPTED AND CLOSED BY COURT (2012)

单位：件 (case)

项目	Item	收案 Cases Accepted	结案 Cases Closed	#判决 Judgment	#调解 Mediation
合计	**Total**	**62736**	**62235**	**27104**	**11304**
所有权及与所有权相关权利纠纷	Ownership and Related Rights	16933	16871	6338	3666
票据、证券权益纠纷	Disputes of Bill & Securities	299	298	102	72
股东权纠纷	Shareholder's Right	1060	1021	430	95
不正当竞争纠纷	Unfair Competition	130	133	59	17
人身权纠纷	Personal Rights	9229	9307	4675	2121
特殊侵权纠纷	Disputes of Special Infringement of Right	20926	20533	12486	3532
适用特别程序案件	Special Proceedings	4766	4773	799	
其他	Others	9393	9299	2215	1801

资料来源：北京市高级人民法院。
Source: The People's High Court of Beijing.

21-23 检察机关办理各类案件情况(2012年)
STATISTICS ON CASES HANDLED BY PROCURATORIAL ORGAN (2012)

项目	Item	受案(受理) Cases Accepted		审结案合计 Cases Closed	
		件 Cases	人 Persons	件 Cases	人 Persons
审查批捕	**Examine for Arrest**	**18563**	**25984**	**18644**	**26102**
批准逮捕	Approved			14349	19021
不批准逮捕	Disapproved			4295	7081
审查起诉	**Examine Law Suits**	**23553**	**31504**	**21980**	**28888**
起诉	Sue			20965	27361
不起诉	Immunity from Suit			1015	1527
举报案件	**Reported Law Cases**	**4111**		**4112**	
控告申诉案件	**Complaints**	**4930**		**4928**	
民事、行政案件	**Civil and Administrative Cases**	**1933**		**2003**	
民事案件	Civil Cases	1798		1884	
行政案件	Administrative Cases	135		119	

资料来源：北京市人民检察院。
Source: The People's Procuratorate of Beijing.

21-24 反贪污贿赂、渎职侵权案件情况(2012年)
STATISTICS ON CASE THAT COMBAT CORRUPTION TO BRIBE AND MALFEASANCE ENCROACHES RIGHT (2012)

项目	Item	反贪污贿赂案件 Anti-curruption and Bribe Cases	贪污案 Corruption Cases	贿赂案 Bribe Cases	挪用公款案 Misappro-priation of Public Funds	其他 Others	渎职侵权案件 Malpractice and Infringement Cases
受案 （件）	**Cases Accepted (case)**	**1070**	**448**	**541**	**58**	**23**	**351**
立案	**Cases Registered**						
件数 （件）	Cases Registered (case)	379	102	239	33	5	77
人数 （人）	Persons involved (person)	459	145	269	35	10	94
重特大案件 （件）	**Heavy and Extraordinarily Serious Case (case)**						
5万元至不满10万元	50000-100000 Yuan	47	17	30			
10万元至不满50万元	100000-500000 Yuan	133	37	85	9	2	
50万元至不满100万元	500000-1000000 Yuan	41	9	28	4		
100万元以上	Over 1000000 Yuan	78	16	42	17	3	
侦结	**Cases Closed**						
件数 （件）	Number of Cases (case)	338	94	210	28	6	60
人数 （人）	Number of Persons (person)	412	126	244	30	12	78
#移送起诉	Hand over to Law Suit						
件数 （件）	Number of Cases (case)	322	93	198	26	5	58
人数 （人）	Number of Persons (person)	388	125	227	28	8	76
#移送不起诉	Hand over yet Immunity from Suit						
件数 （件）	Number of Cases (case)	6		5		1	2
人数 （人）	Number of Persons (person)	11		7		4	2
挽回经济损失 （万元）	**Retrieved Economic Losses (10000 yuan)**	**29955**	**6596**	**18461**	**4700**	**198**	**735**

资料来源：北京市人民检察院。
Source: The People's Procuratorate of Beijing.

21-25 刑事案件情况
STATISTICS ON CRIMINAL CASES

单位：起 (case)

项目	Item	2012	2011	2012年为2011年% 2012 as % of 2011
刑事案件	**Criminal Cases**			
立案	Cases Registered	145724	142835	102.0
破案	Cases Solved	101776	89156	114.2

资料来源：北京市公安局。
Source: Beijing Municipal Public Security Bureau.

21-26 消防建设情况(1996-2012年)
STATISTICS ON FIRE CONTROL (1996-2012)

年份 Year	公安消防队数 (队) Number of Public Security Fire Stations (unit)	公安消防车辆 (辆) Number of Public Security Fire Engine (unit)	企业专职消防队队数 (个) Number of Full-time Fire Stations in Enterprises (unit)	企业专职消防队人数 (人) Persons of Full-time Fire Stations in Enterprises (person)
1996	36	180	101	1865
1997	38	190	104	1885
1998	41	210	108	1993
1999	44	236	120	2447
2000	47	259	120	2447
2001	50	266	120	2447
2002	52	296	112	2228
2003	56	303	112	2147
2004	57	381	120	2477
2005	57	342	120	2477
2006	64	357	109	2269
2007	69	401	109	2269
2008	77	558	109	2269
2009	86	572	109	2269
2010	91	664	109	2269
2011	98	604	87	1766
2012	107	670	76	1405

资料来源：北京市公安局消防局。
Source: Beijing Municipal Public Security Bureau of Fire Protection.

21-27 火灾及损失
FIRE ACCIDENTS AND LOSSES

项目	Item	数量 Number 2012	数量 Number 2011	直接经济损失(万元) Direct Pecuniary Losses (10000 yuan) 2012	直接经济损失(万元) Direct Pecuniary Losses (10000 yuan) 2011
火灾起数 (起)	**Fire Accidents (case)**	**3418**	**4044**	**2968.8**	**5035.0**
特别重大火灾	Extraordinarily Serious				
重大火灾	Serious		1		286.2
较大火灾	Big Fire	1	1	47.5	3146.2
一般火灾	Relatively Big Fire	3417	4042	2921.3	1602.5
起火原因	**Cause of Fire**				
电气	Electric	1237	1274	1572.7	4216.3
生产作业	Violation of Operation	112	142	113.2	113.6
生活用火不慎	Carelessness in Fire Use	541	797	475.3	250.7
吸烟	Smoking	148	260	32.7	23.2
玩火	Fire Playing	111	163	71.6	14.5
自燃	Spontaneous Combustion	126	81	76.1	20.2
雷击	Thunderstroke	2	6	0.2	3.9
静电	Static	1	2	0.2	9.0
放火	Incendiarism	71	103	52.4	13.0
其他	Others	1069	1216	574.4	253.3
受伤人数 (人)	**Number of Injuries (person)**	**6**	**41**		
死亡人数 (人)	**Number of Deaths (person)**	**26**	**30**		

资料来源：北京市公安局消防局。
Source: Beijing Municipal Public Security Bureau of Fire Protection.

21-28 交通事故及损失
STATISTICS ON TRAFFIC ACCIDENTS AND LOSSES

项目	Item	2012	2011	2012年为2011年% 2012 as % of 2011
交通事故	**Traffic Accidents**			
交通事故发生数 (起)	Number of Traffic Accidents (case)	3196	3934	81.2
受伤人数 (人)	Number of Injuries (person)	3615	4503	80.3
死亡人数 (人)	Number of Deaths (person)	918	924	99.4
机动车事故	**Motor Vehicle Accidents**			
机动车事故发生数 (起)	Number of Motor Vehicle Accidents (case)	2556	3195	80.0
受伤人数 (人)	Number of Injuries (person)	3006	3769	79.8
死亡人数 (人)	Number of Deaths (person)	781	803	97.3
直接经济损失 (万元)	**Direct Pecuniary Losses (10000 yuan)**	**3017.9**	**1946.8**	**155.0**
每万辆机动车死亡人数 (人)	**Died Per 10000 Motor Vehicles (person)**	**1.77**	**1.85**	

资料来源：北京市公安局公安交通管理局。
Source: Beijing Traffic Management Bureau.

21-29 安全生产情况
STATISTICS ON SAFE PRODUCTION

项　　目	Item	2012	2011
亿元地区生产总值生产安全事故死亡率 (人／亿元)	Death Date of Work Accidents Per 100 million yuan GDP (person/100 million yuan)	0.060	0.067
工矿商贸企业从业人员10万人生产安全事故死亡率 (人/10万人)	Death Rate of Work Accidents in the Mining, Commercial and Trade Industries Per 100000 Population (1/100000)	0.98	1.04
煤矿百万吨死亡率 (人／百万吨)	The Death Rate of Coal Mines Per Million Tons (Person/million tons)	0.41	
道路交通万车死亡率 (人／万车)	Road Traffic Death Toll Per 10000 Vehicles (person/10000 vehicles)	1.77	1.85
食品安全监测抽查合格率（含烟酒等） (%)	Food Security Monitor Spot Check Up-to-standard Rate (tobacco and wine include((%)	95.29	95.51
药品抽验合格率 (%)	Drug Spot Check Up-to-standard Rate (%)	99.71	99.32

数据来源：北京市行政工商管理局、北京市药品监督管理局、北京市公安交通管理局、北京市安全生产监督管理局。
Source: Beijing Administration For Industry & Commerce,Beijing Drug Administration,Beijing Municipal Traffic Management Bureau, Beijing Administration of Work Safety.

21-30 地震应急避难场所情况
EMERGENT EARTHQUAKE REFUGES

项　　目	Item	2012	2011
地震应急避难场所累计个数 (个)	Emergent Earthquake Refuges Accumulated (unit)	81	71
地震应急避难场所累计面积 (万平方米)	Accumulated Area of Emergent Earthquake Refuges (10000 sq.m)	1521	1406

资料来源：北京市地震局。
Source: Beijing Earthquake Bureau.

21-31 妇联组织状况
STATISTICS ON WOMAN FEDERATION ORGANIZATIONS

单位：个，人 (unit,person)

项　　目	Item	2012	2011	2012年为2011年% 2012 as % of 2011
妇联组织状况	**Status of Women's Federation Organizations**			
区妇联数	Number of Women's Federations in Districts	14	14	100.0
县妇联数	Number of Women's Federations in Counties	2	2	100.0
乡、镇妇联组织数	Number of Women's Federations in Townships	181	183	98.9
街妇联组织数	Number of Women's Federations in Subdistricts	140	137	102.2
妇联干部状况	**Status of Cadres in Women's Federation**			
区妇联干部数	Cadres in Women's Federations in Districts	253	190	133.2
县妇联干部数	Cadres in Women's Federations in Counties	28	19	147.4
乡、镇、街妇联干部数	Cadres in Women's Federations in Townships, Towns and Subdistricts	321	323	99.4
妇联基层妇代会组织个数	**Number of Grass-root Women Congress of Women's Federations**			
城　市	Urban	2646	2646	100.0
农　村	Rural	3944	3944	100.0
各类妇女联谊组织数	**Women's Sodalities**	**30**	**28**	**107.1**

资料来源：北京市妇女联合会。
Source: Beijing Women's Federation.

21-32 工会组织建设情况(2012年)
STATISTICS ON LABOR UNIONS (2012)

项　目	Item	基层工会组织(个) Grass-root Labor Unions (unit)	职工人数(人) Number of Staff and Workers (person)	会员人数(人) Number of Members (person)
合　计	**Total**	**29623**	**4422691**	**4007753**
按单位类别划分	**Grouped by Registration Status of Enterprises**			
国有企业	State-owned	1483	593617	566801
集体企业	Collective-owned	1556	136471	122043
股份合作企业	Share Holding Cooperative	812	118655	108423
联营企业	Joint-owned	40	1788	1685
国有独资公司	Enterprises with exclusively State Investment	403	150878	146802
其他有限责任公司	Limited-Liability Company	7786	917084	775217
国有控股公司	State-owned Holding Company	429	329176	318646
其他股份有限公司	Other Share Holding Coporations	847	167326	136609
私营企业	Private Owned	6581	502005	433167
其他内资企业	Other Domestic Investment Enterprises	104	11680	10263
港澳台商投资企业	Hongkong,Macao and Taiwan Funded	334	86356	79196
外商投资企业	Foreign Funded Enterprises	807	244551	219764
事业单位	Institutions	4145	618006	580329
机　关	Governmental Agencies and Organizations	1419	220755	213796
其　他	Other	2877	324343	295012
按系统分	**By System**			
工业国防工会	Labor Unions for Industry and National Defence	727	356690	342516
工　业	Industry	710	344527	330493
国　防	National Defence	17	12163	12023
建筑工会	Construction	1339	681744	544911
本　市	Local	483	209170	199148
市　外	Non-local	856	472574	345763
服务业工会	Services	748	233269	220358
交通运输工会	Transportation	192	273835	273343
机关事业部	Governmental Institutions	300	105139	102410
教育工会	Education	89	144282	130998
金融工会	Finance	63	113632	109265
市直机关工会	Institutions under Direct Municipal Leadership	389	42992	40330
区县工会	Labor Unions in Districts and Counties	25776	92227	2243622

资料来源：北京市总工会。
Source: Beijing Federation of Labor Unions.

21-33 北京市妇女发展规划监测统计资料
SUPERVISORY STATISTICS FOR WOMEN DEVELOPMENT PROGRAM OF BEIJING

项目		Item		2012	2011
城镇单位就业人员数	(万人)	Employed Persons in Urban Units	(10000 persons)	717.4	685.9
#女性		Female		287.6	270.8
城镇登记失业人员总数	(万人)	Urban Registeration Unemployment	(10000 persons)	27.4	29.3
#女性		Female		10.6	11.3
城镇登记失业人员就业人数	(万人)	Employed Persons from Urban Registration Unemployment	(10000 persons)	19.0	20.0
#女性		Female		7.6	8.0
女性接受再就业技能培训后合格率	(%)	The Employment Rate of Women Recommend Pass Rate after Training	(%)	96.9	95.5
参加基本养老保险人数	(万人)	Number of Participants in Endowment Funds	(10000 persons)	1206.4	1091.9
#女性		Female		546.9	493.1
参加基本医疗保险人数	(万人)	Number of Participants in Basic Medical Insurance	(10000 persons)	1279.7	1188.0
#女性		Female		588.0	542.4
参加失业保险人数	(万人)	Number of Participants in Unemployment Insurance Funds	(10000 persons)	1006.7	881.0
#女性		Female		442.1	385.5
参加工伤保险人数	(万人)	Number of Participants in Work Injury Insurance	(10000 persons)	897.2	862.4
#女性		Female		376.5	360.5
城乡居民养老保险参保人数	(万人)	Number of People Participating Endowment Insurance for Urban & Rural Residents		177.3	173.4
#女性		Female		91.2	89.3
城镇居民基本医疗保险参保人数	(万人)	Number of People Participating Basic Medicare for Urban & Rural Residents		151.9	159.8
#女性		Female		81.0	85.1
市人大女代表领衔提出的议案数	(件)	Number of Heads the Proposal to Put Forward with The Women Deputy of Beijing Municipal People's Congress(BMPC)	(case)	12	20
市政协女委员提出的提案数	(件)	Number of Heads the Porposal to Put Forward with the Women Deputy of Beijing Committee, Chinese People's Political Consultative Conference	(case)	597	480
普通高校在校学生人数	(万人)	Number of Higher Education	(10000 persons)	58.2	57.9
#女生		Female		29.9	29.6
在读研究生人数	(万人)	Number of Students that Pursuing Master Degree	(10000 persons)	25.2	24.1
#女生		Female		11.8	11.3
成人本专科在校生人数	(万人)	Students Enrollment of Adult Higher Education	(10000 persons)	26.5	26.4
#女生		Female		15.2	15.2
妇科病普查率	(%)	Gynaopathy General Survey Rate	(%)	29.4	16.8
乳腺癌检出率	(1/10万)	Detection Rate of Breast Cancer	(1/100000)	13.6	13.2
宫颈癌检出率	(1/10万)	Detection Rate of Cervical Cancer	(1/100000)	4.5	2.0
高危孕产妇住院分娩率	(%)	Giving Birth Rate of Endanger Pregnant Lying in Hospital	(%)	100.0	100.0
已婚育龄妇女综合避孕率	(%)	Practising Contraception Rate Synthetically of Married Women of Child Bearing Age	(%)	82.7	83.6
抓获刑事作案成员中女性比例	(%)	Share of Female in Criminal Suspects	(%)	18.5	17.4
得到法律援助机构援助的妇女人数	(人)	Number of Women Getting the Aid from Law Aid Institution	(person)	3370	2645

21-34 北京市儿童发展规划监测统计资料
SUPERVISORY STATISTICS ON CHILDREN DEVELOPMENT IN BEIJING

项目		Item		2012	2011
婚前医学检查率	(%)	Rate of Premarital Medical Check	(%)	7.1	7.3
新生儿遗传代谢性疾病筛查	(%)	Screening Rate of Genic Metabolic Diseases for Newborn	(%)	98.4	98.7
出生缺陷监测率	(%)	Monitoring Rate of Birth Deficiency	(%)	100.0	100.0
新生儿听力筛查率	(%)	Screening Rate of Hearing for Newborn	(%)	96.09	96.17
出生缺陷发生率	(‰)	Outbreak Rate of Birth Deficiency	(‰)	14.83	14.54
0-6岁儿童保健覆盖率	(%)	Coverage of Health Care for Children 0-6 Years Old	(%)	97.92	97.42
0-6个月婴儿纯母乳喂养率	(%)	Exclusive Breast Breeding Rate of Infants 0-6 Months	(%)	68.38	66.59
婴儿死亡率	(‰)	Death Rate of Infant	(‰)	2.87	2.84
5岁以下儿童死亡率	(‰)	Death Rate of Children below 5-year-old	(‰)	3.29	3.41
中小学生肥胖检出率	(‰)	Detection Rate of Obesity in Students in Elementary and High Schoools	(‰)	20.74	20.67
中小学生龋齿率	(‰)	Decayed Teeth Rate of Students in Elementary and High Sch	(‰)	11.23	18.60
卡介苗疫苗接种率	(%)	Rate of Inoculation of BCG Vaccine	(%)	99.90	100.00
脊髓灰质炎疫苗接种率	(%)	Rate of Inoculation of Poliomyelities Polio Vaccine	(%)	99.98	99.87
百白破疫苗接种率	(%)	Rate of Inoculation of Pertussis,Diphtheria and Tetanus Vaccine	(%)	99.99	99.87
麻疹疫苗接种率	(%)	Rate of Inoculation of Measles Vaccine	(%)	99.97	98.59
孕产妇系统管理率	(%)	Rate of Gravida and Puerpera in Systematic Management	(%)	97.74	97.72
城市		Urban		97.45	97.79
农村		Rural		98.30	97.58
孕产妇健康教育普及率	(%)	Widespreading Rate of Health Education for Gravida and Puerpera	(%)	99.93	99.91
孕产妇住院分娩率	(%)	Rate of Parturition in Hospital	(%)	100.00	99.99
孕产妇死亡率	(1/10万)	Death Rate of Gravida and Puerpera	(1/100000)	6.05	9.09

21-35 北京市历届人代会代表人数性别构成及议案、建议数
NUMBER AND SEX COMPOSITION OF DEPUTIES AT HISTORICAL PEOPLE'S CONGRESS OF BEIJING ALONG WITH NUMBER OF PROPOSALS AND SUGGESTIONS

单位：人、%、件 (person,%,case)

项目 Item	代表人数 Number of Deputies			性别比例 Sex Percentage		议案立案数 Number of Cases Registered of Proposal	建议数 Suggestions
	合计 Total	女性 Female	男性 Male	女性 Female	男性 Male		
第一届 1st	564	106	458	18.8	81.2		
第二届 2nd	619	142	477	22.9	77.1		
第三届 3rd	618	162	456	26.2	73.8		
第四届 4th	745	202	543	27.1	72.9		
第五届 5th	751	203	548	27.0	73.0		
第七届 7th	1195	325	870	27.1	72.9		
第八届 8th	973	252	721	25.9	74.1	55	6644
第九届 9th	880	217	663	24.7	75.3	86	7921
第十届 10th	885	224	661	25.3	74.7	156	7281
第十一届 11th	763	197	566	25.8	74.2	166	9717
第十二届 12th	762	235	527	30.8	69.2	276	9859
第十三届 13th	779	237	542	30.4	69.6	153	7576
第十四届 14th	771	257	514	33.3	66.7	22	1297

注：1. 北京市人大常委会是经北京市七届三次人民代表大会选举成立的，故一至七届人代会无议案及建议数。
2. 代表人数为届首选举数，议案及建议数均是本届五年会上及平时议案及建议的合计数。
3. 第十四届议案立案及建议数截止到2013年6月底。

资料来源：北京市人民代表大会常务委员会。

Note: a) Standing Committee of Beijing People's Congress was established upon election at the 3rd Session of Beijing 7th People's Congress. As a result, there were no proposals and suggestions at the 1st-7th People's Congresses.
b) Deputies were those first elected for that term. Proposals and suggestions at other terms of Congress included those at the meeting of the said term and/or at ordinary times.
c) Data of Proposal and Advice of 14th Congress was that up to Jun of 2013.

Source: Standing Committee of Beijing Municipal People's Congress(BMPC).

21-36 北京市历届政协会委员人数及提案立案数
NUMBER OF MEMBERS AND PROPOSALS AT HISTORICAL BEIJING CPPCC

单位：人、件 (person,case)

届别 Term	起止年月 Beginning-ending Month	委员人数 Number of Commissaries 合计 Total	女性 Female	男性 Male	提案立案数 Number of Proposals Put on Record
第一届 1st	1955.04-1959.09	270	40	230	37
第二届 2nd	1959.09-1962.12	463	84	379	13
第三届 3rd	1962.12-1965.09	519	92	427	884
第四届 4th	1965.09-1977.11	529	88	441	23
第五届 5th	1977.11-1983.03	779	161	618	1610
第六届 6th	1983.03-1988.01	766	168	598	3122
第七届 7th	1988.01-1993.01	703	179	524	4276
第八届 8th	1993.01-1998.01	740	185	555	4975
第九届 9th	1998.01-2003.01	782	203	579	6240
第十届 10th	2003.01-2008.01	824	226	598	6871
第十一届 11th	2008.01-2013.01	737	233	504	5354

资料来源：中国人民政治协商会议北京市委员会。
Source: The Chinese People's Political Consultative Conference Beijing Committe.

主要统计指标解释

优抚对象 依照法律和政策的规定，享受国家、社会和群众抚恤优待的人员，包括中国人民解放军（包括中国人民武装警察部队）现役军人、革命伤残人员、复员退伍军人、革命烈士家属、因公牺牲军人家属、病故军人家属、现役军人家属。

社会救助对象总人数 指在报告期末生活在当地规定的最低生活保障线以下的家庭人员及国家规定由民政部门救济的特殊人员和60年代精简退职老职工救济人员等。

城市居民最低生活保障人数 指报告期末家庭平均收入在当地规定的最低生活保障线以下的城镇居民数。包括“三无”对象、失业人员和在职、下岗、退休人员等。

农村最低生活保障人数 指报告期末在建立农村最低生活保障制度的地区，得到当地政府或集体给予最低生活保障的农业人口家庭人数。

参加基本养老保险人数 指报告期末按照国家法律、法规和有关政策规定参加基本养老保险并在社保经办机构已建立缴费记录档案的职工人数，包括中断缴费但未终止养老保险关系的职工人数和参加基本养老保险的离休、退休和退职人员的人数。不包括只登记未建立缴费记录档案的人数。

参加基本医疗保险人数 指报告期末按国家有关规定参加基本医疗保险的人数。包括参加保险的职工人数和退休人员数。

参加失业保险人数 指报告期末按照国家法律、法规和有关政策规定参加了失业保险的城镇企业事业单位的职工及地方政府规定参加失业保险的其他人员的人数。参加失业保险人数为参加失业保险的人数。

参加工伤保险人数 指报告期末参加工伤保险的人数。

参加生育保险人数 指报告期末参加生育保险的人数。

农村居民参加城乡居民养老保险人数 指截止报告期末参加城乡居民养老保险的农村居民人数。

参加农村新型合作医疗人数 指截止报告期末乡镇已参加农村新型合作医疗的总人数。农村新型合作医疗制度是由政府组织、引导、支持，农民自愿参加，集体、个人和政府多方筹资，以大病统筹为主的农民医疗互助共济制度。

社区服务设施数 指报告期末城镇(街道办事处、居委会）设立的以非盈利为目的，为本社区居民服务，特别是为老年人、残疾人、儿童服务的社区服务中心、活动站、服务站、养老院、老年公寓（托老所)、残疾儿童日托所、家务服务站、婚姻介绍所等福利性设施以及职工社会保险管理服务的机构数。几种不同类型的社区服务单位，共用一个场所的，只能统计为一个社区服务设施。成为社区服务设施的条件(1)是独立核算单位；(2)有固定的从业人员；(3)有一定的服务项目；(4)有一定的服务场所。

律师 指受聘参加律师事务所工作，提任法律顾问、刑（民）事代理人、刑事辩护人，办理非诉讼事件、解答法律询问，代写法律事务文书等主要从事律师业务的专职法律工作者和兼职律师。

公证人员 指在国家公证机关依法办理公证事务的司法人员。包括公证员、助理公证员和在公证处工作的其他人员。

办理公证文书 指公证处在一定时期内办结的公证文书件数。公证文书系按司法部规定或批准的格式制作。包括国内公证和涉外公证两部分。其中国内公证分为经济公证和民事法律关系公证两大类。

调解人员 指人民调解委员会担负调解民间一般民事纠纷和轻微违法行为所引起的纠纷的工作人员。包括调解委员会的委员和调解小组调解员。

调解民间纠纷 指调解委员会依照法律规定，根据自愿原则，用说服教育的方法调解民间发生的有关民事权利和义务的争执，促成当事双方达到协议和谅解，解决纠纷。包括婚姻家庭纠纷，财产权益纠纷等。不包括法院受理调解的民事案件数。

地震应急避难场所 指适用于地震等自然灾害，也适用于其他事件应急状态下，供居民紧急疏散的公园、公共绿地、城市广场、体育场、学校运动场等场地数量。

Explanatory Notes on Main Statistical Indicators

Key Entitled Groups refer to persons receiving special treatment from the country, society and the public in accordance with provisions in laws and policies, including active servicemen of PLA (including the People's Armed Policy Army), persons wounded and disabled due to revolution, veterans, dependents of revolutionary martyrs, dependents of servicemen who sacrificed on business, dependents of servicemen who died of illness, dependents of active servicemen.

Total Number of Persons Receiving Social Relief refer to the number of family members living under the minimum living standard guarantee line stated by local government, special persons receiving relief by civil affair authorities in line with national regulations, as well as old employees retired in the 1960s, at the end of reporting period.

Number of Persons Receiving Lowest Cost-of-Living in Urban Area refers to the number of urban residents whose average family income is below locally stated minimum living standard guarantee line, including elders, psychotic patients and disables who have no statutory guardian, no fixed pocketbook, no labor ability, unemployed person, on-the-job persons, laid-off persons, and retired person, etc.

Number of Persons Receiving Lowest Cost-of-Living in Rural Area refers to the number of persons in agricultural families covered by minimum living standard guarantee of local government or collective in an area where rural minimum living standard guarantee system is established, at the end of reporting period.

Number of People Participating in Basic Pension Insurance refers to the number of employees participating in basic endowment insurance and keeping insurance premium payment records with social security organizations in accordance with provisions in national laws, rules and relevant policies at the end of reporting period, including the number of employees suspending the payment of insurance premium without terminating the endowment insurance relation as well as retired employees participating in basic endowment insurance, excluding the number of persons only registered but having no insurance premium payment records.

Number of People Participating in Basic Medical Care Insurance means the number of persons participating in medical care insurance program at the end of reporting period in accordance with relevant national regulations, including the number of employees and retired persons participating in the insurance.

Number of People Participating in Unemployment Insurance means the number of employees in urban enterprises and public institutions participating in unemployment insurance program at the end of reporting period in accordance with provisions in national laws, rules and relevant policies, as well as other persons specified by local governments to participate in unemployment insurance. The number of persons participating in unemployment insurance program is the number of persons who participate in unemployment insurance.

Number of People Participating in Work Injury Insurance means the number of persons participating in work injury insurance program at the end of reporting period.

Number of People Participating in Maternity Insurance means the number of persons participating in maternity insurance program at the end of reporting period.

Number of People Participating in Rural Basic Pension Insurance means the number of rural residents who had participated in urban and rural old-age insurance program by the end of reporting period.

Number of People Participating in New-type Rural Cooperative Medicare means the total number of persons who had participated in the rural new-type cooperative medical service by the end of reporting period. The rural new-type cooperative medical service system is a mutual aid medical system for farmers, with focus on general health care program for major diseases, organized, guided and supported by government, with farmers' voluntary participation.

Number of Service Facilities in Urban Community means the number of welfare facilities established in cities and towns (by sub-district office and community neighborhood committees) such as community service centers, activity stations, service stations, rest homes, elders' apartments, the disables' work treatment stations, disabled children's daily kindergarten, housework service stations and marriage service centers serving for residents in the community, especially serving elders, the disables and children for non-profit purpose, and institutions for employees' social security management at the end of reporting period. Several community service organizations in different types using one common site are calculated as on community service facility. To be a community service facility: it must (1) be a organization keeping independent accounts, (2) have fixed employees, (3) have fixed service items; (4) have certain service site.

Lawyer mean a full-time law worker and part-time lawyer joining a law firm, serving as a legal consultant, criminal (civil) proxy, criminal counsel, handling non-lawsuit events, answering legal questions, writing legal documents for others, and other lawyer business.

Notary means any judicial person handling notarization matters in national notarization agencies according to law, including notaries, assistant notaries, and other personnel working in notarization offices.

Notarization Documents Executed means the number of notarization documents executed at notarization offices within a given period of time. Notarization documents are prepared in the format specified or approved by the Ministry of Justice. Notarization includes domestic notarization and foreign notarization. Domestic notarization falls into economic notarization and civil legal relation notarization.

Mediation Personnel mean working personnel responsible for mediating general civil disputes as well as disputes caused by slightly illegal acts in any people's mediation committee, including members of people's mediation committees and mediators of mediation teams.

Mediation of Civil Disputes means the mediation of disputes against civil rights and obligations by mediation committees on voluntary basis and in accordance with provisions in laws in order to urge both parties to reach an agreement and understanding and resolve the dispute, including marriage and family dispute, property rights and interests dispute, etc., excluding the number of civil cases accepted by courts.

Emergent Earthquake Refuges refer to the number of parks, public green land, city squares, gyms, school playgrounds for residents' emergent evacuation in the event of natural disaster such as earthquake, and under the condition state of other emergent events.

22

北京统计年鉴2013　BEIJING STATISTICAL YEARBOOK

第三产业
TERTIARY INDUSTRY

简要说明

一、本章资料的主要内容

本章主要内容包括：第三产业主要指标、规模以上第三产业主要指标、规模以上第三产业企业财务状况、北京地区服务贸易、文化创意产业、物流业、会展活动和体育及相关产业活动情况等。

二、本章资料的数据来源

本章除北京地区服务贸易情况由北京市商务委员会提供外，其他资料由北京市统计局、国家统计局北京调查总队提供。

三、本章资料的统计范围

本章规模以上第三产业是指除国际组织以外的各行业限额以上的法人单位。2012 年具体为金融业、房地产开发业的全部法人单位；批发业年主营业务收入 2000 万元及以上的企业；零售业年主营业务收入 500 万元及以上的企业；住宿业为星级饭店和星级以外年主营业务收入 200 万元及以上企业；餐饮业年主营业务收入 200 万元及以上的企业；其余行业为年营业收入或收入合计 500 万元及以上的法人单位。

文化创意产业资料根据文化创意产业法人单位调查资料测算取得。

物流业统计范围包括限额（规模）以上交通（货物）运输、仓储和邮政业、包装服务业、批发业、零售业和制造业企业。

会展业统计对象涉及会展活动的举办服务单位和接待单位。具体包括星级宾馆饭店及年主营业务收入 200 万元及以上的宾馆饭店；从事各种会展活动的场馆；大型会展活动的主办单位（名单由北京市公安局提供）以及为会展活动提供各类专业服务的单位。本统计调查为年度统计调查，由于每年的调查单位范围不完全相同（有新增和消亡单位），为保持数据的可比性，调查时，同时采集调查对象本年和上年数据。

体育及相关产业情况根据“北京市体育产业专项调查”和统计年报资料汇总计算，执行国家体育总局、国家统计局颁布的《体育及相关产业分类（试行）》标准。

四、有关统计标准的变化说明

（一）关于行业划分。根据国家统计局规定，自 2012 年开始执行《国民经济行业分类》GB/T 4754-2011 标准。

（二）关于三次产业划分。根据国家统计局《三次产业划分规定》（国统字[2012]108 号），该规定对三次产业的范围进行了调整。其中第一产业是指农、林、牧、渔业（不含农、林、牧、渔服务业）；第二产业是指采矿业（不含开采辅助活动），制造业（不含金属制品、机械和设备修理业），电力、热力、燃气及水生产和供应业，建筑业；第三产业是指除第一产业、第二产业以外的其他行业。2012 年本章数据根据此规定进行了调整。

Brief Introduction

I. Main Content

This chapter includes: main indicators for the tertiary industry, main indicators for tertiary industry above designated size, financial status of tertiary industry above designated size, service trade, cultural creation industry, logistics, MICE, sports and activities in related sectors in Beijing area.

II. Source of Data

Except for the data on service trade in Beijing area, which are sourced from Beijing Municipal Commission of Commerce, other data are sourced from Beijing Municipal Bureau of Statistics, and NBS Survey Office in Beijing.

III. Scope of Statistics

As stipulated in the *Provisions on Division of Three Industries* National Bureau of Statistics, the tertiary industry covers: transport, storage and postal service, computer service and software, wholesale and retail trades, accommodation and catering, finance, real estate, leasing and business service, scientific research, technological service, geological survey, water conservancy, environment and public facilities management, residents service and other service, education, health, social security and social welfare, culture, sports and entertainment, public management, social organizations and international organizations.

In this chapter, the tertiary industry above designated size means corporate enterprises above designated size other than international organizations, in details including all corporate enterprises in finance and real estate development sectors; enterprises with annual main business income of RMB20 million and more in wholesale sector; enterprises with annual main business income of RMB5 million and more in retail sector star-level and off-star-level enterprises with annual main business income of RMB2 million and more in accommodation sector; enterprises with annual main business income of RMB2 million and more in catering sector; and in other sectors, corporate enterprises with annual business income or total income of RMB5 million and more.

Data on cultural creation were obtained from investigation to corporate enterprises in cultural creation sector.

Statistics for logistics apply for enterprises in (cargo) transport, storage and postal service, packaging service, wholesale trades, retail trades and manufacturing sectors above designated size.

Target of MICE statistics covers service companies and reception companies holding the MICE, in details, including: star-level hotels and those hotels with annual main business income of RMB2 million and more; venues for MICE; sponsors of large MICEs (with the list provided by Beijing Municipal Bureau of Public Security) together with organizations providing various professional services for MICEs. Such survey is conducted on yearly basis. As the scope of companies under survey is not completely the same (there companies newly added and companies died out), data in both the current year and previous year are collected from the surveyed companies to keep the data comparable.

Data on sports industry were calculated according to the “Special Survey on Sports Industry in Beijing” and the annual statistical report. As for the scope of statistics, the standards in the Classification of Sports Industry (Tryout) issued by the State Administration for Sports and National Bureau of Statistics were applied.

Ⅳ. Changes in Relevant Statistical Standards

(I) Classification of Sectors. According to relevant provisions of National Bureau of Statistics, the Standard for Classification of National Economic Sectors (GB/T4754-200) became effective in 2012.

(II) Classification of Three Industries. According to the provision of National Bureau of Statistics on Classification of Three Industries (GTZ[2012]No.108), the scope of three industries has changed. The primary industry means agriculture, forestry, animal husbandry and fishery (excluding agricultural, forestry, animal husbandry and fishery services); the secondary industry means mining (excluding auxiliary activities), manufacturing (excluding metal products, machinery and equipment repair), electrical power, thermal power, fuel gas and water production and service sectors, and construction industry; the tertiary industry means industries other than the primary and secondary industries. In this chapter, figures for 2012 were adjusted according to this provision.

22-1 第三产业主要指标及占全市比重(2000-2012年)

项目	Item	2000	2001	2002	2003	2004
增加值 (亿元)	Gross Domestic Product (100 million yuan)	2049.1	2484.8	2982.6	3435.9	4092.2
占全市比重 (%)	Percentage of the Total (%)	64.8	67.0	69.1	68.6	67.8
劳动生产率 (元/人)	Overall Labor Productivity (yuan/person)	61525	73082	83069	86864	83977
相当于全市比例 (%)	Percentage of the Total (%)	120.4	123.0	125.9	119.9	108.4
从业人员年末人数 (万人)	Year-end Employed Persons (10000 persons)	338.2	341.8	376.3	414.8	559.8
占全市比重 (%)	Percentage of the Total (%)	54.6	54.4	55.4	59.0	65.5
固定资产投资 (亿元)	Investment in Fixed Assets (100 million yuan)	510.3	1367.9	1621.8	1875.4	2112.7
占全市比重 (%)	Percentage of the Total (%)	39.3	89.3	89.4	86.9	83.6
实际利用外资金额 (亿美元)	Amount of Foreign Capital Actually Used (USD 100 million)	22.2	12.8	12.5	14.0	19.2
占全市比重 (%)	Percentage of the Total (%)	90.5	72.4	69.8	65.3	62.4
能源消费总量 (万吨标准煤)	Energy Consumption (10000 tons of SCE)	1080.9	1196.2	1334.5	1391.0	1638.0
相当于全市比例 (%)	Percentage of the Total (%)	26.1	28.3	30.1	29.9	31.9

MAIN INDICATORS OF THE TERTIARY SECTOR AND THEIR PERCENTAGES OF BEIJING'S TOTAL (2000-2012)

2005	2006	2007	2008	2009	2010	2011	2012
4854.3	5837.6	7236.1	8375.8	9179.2	10600.8	12363.1	13669.9
69.6	71.9	73.5	75.4	75.5	75.1	76.1	76.5
84828	95800	112388	122794	126872	140968	158613	167852
105.4	106.1	106.3	106.3	103.3	101.4	102.5	102.2
584.7	634.0	653.7	710.5	736.5	767.5	791.4	837.4
66.6	68.9	69.3	72.4	73.8	74.4	74.0	75.6
2405.6	2993.8	3465.8	3434.4	4389.5	4922.3	5101.3	5597.5
85.1	88.8	87.4	89.2	90.3	89.6	86.3	86.6
23.0	34.5	40.8	44.4	52.0	56.3	62.4	69.1
65.2	75.8	80.6	72.9	84.9	88.5	88.5	85.9
1918.7	2129.3	2389.5	2610.5	2760.3	2897.4	3100.5	3252.1
34.7	36.1	38.0	41.3	42.0	41.7	44.3	45.3

22-2 北京地区服务贸易情况(2003-2012年)
STATISTICS ON SERVICE TRADE(2003-2012)

单位：亿美元 (USD 100 million)

项 目	Item	2003	2004	2005	2006	2007	2008	2009	2010	2011	2012
服务贸易总额	**Total Turnover of Service Trade**	**162.24**	**235.70**	**300.74**	**393.23**	**503.06**	**691.92**	**644.10**	**798.29**	**895.40**	**1000.20**
运 输	Transportation	42.73	66.79	80.06	107.29	110.96	144.38	140.50	177.11	196.30	223.21
旅 游	Travel	30.87	48.60	54.93	68.22	94.13	88.66	92.90	108.68	136.10	155.48
通讯服务	Communication Service	8.71	7.41	8.55	11.49	18.39	24.28	17.20	17.62	21.50	26.15
建筑服务	Construction Service	10.66	11.90	19.56	23.69	46.28	79.56	74.30	87.16	92.40	85.23
保险服务	Insurance Service	8.91	11.90	14.91	19.85	23.54	72.85	58.60	92.22	133.10	132.14
金融服务	Financial	0.53	0.47	0.53	0.53	1.79	1.93	4.70	8.09	11.70	22.16
计算机和信息服务	Computer and Information	9.00	9.76	11.60	18.32	24.74	29.25	28.80	39.83	52.00	60.19
专利使用费和特许费	Fees for Patent or Royalty	5.27	7.38	9.40	14.39	16.80	20.38	16.40	21.11	22.60	28.40
咨 询	Consultation	12.22	18.94	28.33	43.28	57.91	84.38	81.10	89.47	99.10	116.36
广告、宣传	Advertisement and Publicity	3.19	5.16	6.26	7.40	10.02	12.90	10.80	13.19	17.80	19.61
电影、音像	Movies and Audio-video Products	0.74	1.33	1.95	1.82	3.85	5.51	2.70	3.56	3.40	4.91
其他商业服务	Other Commercial Service	29.41	46.06	64.66	76.95	94.65	127.82	116.00	140.27	109.50	126.36

资料来源：北京市商务委员会。
Source: Beijing Municipal Commission of Commerce .

22-3 北京地区服务贸易情况
STATISTICS ON SERVICE TRADE

单位：亿美元 (USD 100 million)

项 目	Item	服务贸易总额 Total Turnover of Service Trade		外汇收入 Forex Income		外汇支出 Forex Payment		顺(逆)差 Surplus (Deficit)	
		2012	2011	2012	2011	2012	2011	2012	2011
合 计	**Total**	**1000.20**	**895.40**	**445.11**	**415.00**	**555.09**	**480.40**	**-109.98**	**-65.40**
运 输	Transportation	223.21	196.30	57.22	53.90	165.99	142.50	-108.76	-88.60
旅 游	Travel	155.48	136.10	51.49	54.20	103.99	81.90	-52.50	-27.70
通讯服务	Communication Service	26.15	21.50	13.56	12.90	12.59	8.70	0.97	4.20
建筑服务	Construction Service	85.23	92.40	64.80	72.40	20.43	20.00	44.36	52.40
保险服务	Insurance Service	132.14	133.10	19.71	16.50	112.43	116.50	-92.72	-100.00
金融服务	Financial	22.16	11.70	4.63	7.10	17.53	4.60	-12.90	2.50
计算机和信息服务	Computer and Information	60.19	52.00	49.08	41.00	11.11	11.00	37.97	30.00
专利使用费和特许费	Fees for Patent or Royalty	28.40	22.60	5.73	2.90	22.66	19.70	-16.93	-16.80
咨 询	Consultation	116.36	99.10	88.71	75.10	27.65	24.00	61.06	51.10
广告、宣传	Advertisement and Publicity	19.61	17.80	12.73	11.60	6.88	6.20	5.86	5.40
电影、音像	Movies and Audio-video Products	4.91	3.40	0.76	0.70	4.15	2.70	-3.38	-2.00
其他商业服务	Other Commercial Service	126.36	109.50	76.68	66.80	49.68	42.60	26.99	24.20

资料来源：北京市商务委员会。
Source: Beijing Municipal Commission of Commerce .

22-4 规模以上第三产业主要指标(2004-2012年)
MAIN INDICATORS OF TERTIARY INDUSTRY ENTERPRISES ABOVE DESIGNATED SIZE (2004-2012)

项　目		Item		2004	2005	2006	2007	2008
单位数	(个)	Enterprises	(unit)	25725	23661	24921	25651	34820
从业人员平均		Average Number of						
人数	(万人)	Employed Persons	(10000 persons)	301.4	323.3	340.4	373.5	443.6
资产总计	(亿元)	Total Assets	(100 million yuan)	184985.5	274180.3	336485.9	422458.7	579095.5
收入合计	(亿元)	Total Incomes	(100 million yuan)	21467.2	24444.6	29468.7	38361.8	47524.3
应交税金合计	(亿元)	Total Tax	(100 million yuan)	908.1	1004.0	1376.0	2360.9	1855.2
企业利润总额	(亿元)	Total Profits	(100 million yuan)	1544.8	2696.1	2967.2	4511.2	4577.6

注：应交税金合计主要包括应交增值税、应交所得税、营业税金及附加和管理费用中的税金等。
Note: Total Tax mainly includes payable VAT,payable income tax, business tax and surtax, and tax in management expenses, etc.

22-4 续表 continued

项　目		Item		2009	2010	2011	2012
单位数	(个)	Enterprises	(unit)	36177	36064	36102	36616
从业人员平均		Average Number of					
人数	(万人)	Employed Persons	(10000 persons)	472.1	487.9	509.9	545.0
资产总计	(亿元)	Total Assets	(100 million yuan)	712313.4	798485.4	909953.5	1022849.7
收入合计	(亿元)	Total Incomes	(100 million yuan)	55390.3	69106.8	79246.0	92138.2
应交税金合计	(亿元)	Total Tax	(100 million yuan)	2560.8	3122.4	4018.9	4652.8
企业利润总额	(亿元)	Total Profits	(100 million yuan)	10540.8	10236.3	11413.1	14248.4

22-5 规模以上第三产业单位主要经济指标(2012年)
MAIN INDICATORS OF TERTIARY INDUSTRY ENTERPRISES ABOVE DESIGNATED SIZE (2012)

项　目	Item	单位数 (个) Enter-prises (unit)	从业人员平均人数 (万人) Average Number of Employed Persons (10000 persons)	资产总计 (亿元) Total Assets (100 million yuan)	收入合计 (亿元) Total Incomes (100 million yuan)	应交税金合计 (亿元) Total Tax (100 million yuan)	利润总额 (亿元) Total Profits (100 million yuan)
第三产业合计	**Total**	**36616**	**545.0**	**1022849.7**	**92138.2**	**4652.8**	**14248.4**
按隶属关系分	**Grouped by Administrative Relationship**						
中央	Central	4225	122.5	806631.9	40857.6	2284.9	9594.9
地方	Local	32391	422.5	216217.9	51280.6	2367.9	4653.5
按行业分	**Grouped by Sector**						
批发和零售业	Wholesale and Retail Trade	8100	71.6	28057.4	44996.7	696.1	942.9
交通运输、仓储和邮政业	Transport, Storage and Post	1078	59.1	11459.3	3684.0	127.8	114.2
住宿和餐饮业	Accommodation and Restaurants	3103	40.8	1544.3	925.8	72.1	19.0
信息传输、软件和信息技术服务业	Information Transmission,Software and Information Technology Services	2813	57.5	24500.4	4629.0	273.0	1319.0
金融业	Financial Intermediation	1559	34.7	821958.4	14233.2	2260.4	8435.7
房地产业	Real Estate	4619	38.8	37375.6	3851.7	606.5	754.7
租赁和商务服务业	Leasing and Business Services	5860	62.8	74589.7	7194.7	304.7	2116.5
科学研究和技术服务业	Scientific Research and Technical Services	3283	51.7	11951.1	5655.4	203.2	419.4
水利、环境和公共设施管理业	Management of Water Conservancy, Environment and Public Facilities	539	8.7	1344.0	367.1	12.2	20.3
居民服务、修理和其他服务业	Resident Services, Repair and Other Services	476	8.3	170.6	183.8	9.4	3.7
教　育	Education	1558	37.7	2792.2	1387.6	13.1	10.7
卫生和社会工作	Health Care and Social Works	604	20.9	1003.4	1135.8	1.7	5.2
文化、体育和娱乐业	Culture, Sports and Entertainment	1262	15.5	2655.1	1232.3	68.8	87.1
公共管理、社会保障和社会组织	Pulic Administration,Social Security and Social Organizations	1762	36.8	3448.2	2661.1	3.9	
按登记注册类型分	**Grouped by Registration Status**						
内　资	Domestic Investment Economy	33305	456.5	982566.4	76282.4	3897.2	12197.2
国　有	State-owned Units	6622	154.8	284936.7	14773.9	256.1	1864.5
集　体	Collective-owned Units	618	7.8	1837.9	647.6	28.2	19.8
股份合作	Share Holding	423	3.3	477.8	172.2	5.3	5.2
联　营	Joint Ownership Units	40	0.4	30.5	18.2	0.5	0.6
有限责任公司	Limited-Liability Corporations	11572	153.0	155942.3	40513.0	1313.8	6622.3
股份有限公司	Share Holding Corporations Ltd.	893	52.3	531433.1	12789.5	2055.0	3458.0
私　营	Private Units	12788	79.8	7387.0	7157.2	235.1	222.9
其　他	Others	349	5.2	521.0	210.8	3.2	3.9
港澳台商投资	Units with Funds from Hongkong, Macao and Taiwan	1276	37.3	12624.2	4244.0	304.2	460.2
外商投资	Foreign Funded Units	2035	51.2	27659.1	11611.8	451.4	1591.0

注：1. 行业划分执行2011年国民经济行业分类标准(GB/T 4754-2011)。
　　2. 应交税金合计主要包括应交增值税、应交所得税、营业税金及附加和管理费用中的税金等。

Note: a) Sectors in this table are classified in accordance with the Standard for Classification of National Economic Sectors 2011 (GB/T 4754-2011).
b) Total Tax mainly includes payable VAT,payable income tax, business tax and surtax, and tax in management expenses, etc.

22-6 规模以上第三产业企业财务状况(2012年)
FINANCIAL STATUS OF TERTIARY INDUSTRY ENTERPRISES ABOVE DESIGNATED SIZE (2012)

单位：万元 (10000 yuan)

项目	Item	企业单位个数(个) Number of Enterprises (unit)	资产负债 资产总计 Total Assets	流动资产合计 Total Current Assets	#应收账款 Accounts Receivable
合计	**Total**	**31463**	**8178112278**	**936284136**	**85186865**
按隶属关系分	**Grouped by Administrative Relationship**				
中央	Central	2685	6061363275	345385958	33156824
地方	Local	28778	2116749003	590898178	52030041
按登记注册类型分	**Grouped by Registation Status of Enterprises**				
内资企业	Domestic Funded Enterprises	28157	7775319870	783145875	65744280
国有企业	State-Owned Enterprises	1943	811890853	145916393	7042797
集体企业	Collective Owned Enterprises	533	11104900	6653550	408688
股份合作企业	Share Holding Enterprises	414	4732139	3158338	307017
联营企业	Joint Owned Enterprises	31	273131	121142	11088
有限责任公司	Limited-Liability Corporations	11566	1558806023	443401523	41185246
股份有限公司	Share Holding Corporations Ltd.	892	5314330295	126760925	7698510
私营企业	Private Enterprises	12740	73673518	56731778	9069208
其他企业	Others	38	509011	402226	21726
港澳台商投资企业	Enterprises with Funds from Hongkong, Macao and Taiwan	1276	126242314	62811177	6038928
外商投资企业	Foreign Funded Enterprises	2030	276550094	90327083	13403657
按国民经济行业分	**Grouped by Sector**				
批发和零售业	**Wholesale Trade and Retail Trade**	**8100**	**280573556**	**209295622**	**37850372**
批发业	Wholesale Trade	5379	243878422	181100879	34730452
零售业	Retail Trade	2721	36695134	28194743	3119920
交通运输、仓储和邮政业	**Transportation,Storage and Post**	**1078**	**114592533**	**33968429**	**3317268**
铁路运输业	Railway Transport	17	47024341	4418852	761076
道路运输业	Road Transport	564	16663623	4822268	518456
水上运输业	Water Transport	6	54479	19879	5285
航空运输业	Air Transport	19	21586713	2766838	685968
管道运输业	Transport Via Pipelines	1	2768601	181298	13009
装卸搬运和运输代理业	Loading, unloading, Portage and Other Transport Services	322	5667861	3484983	883351
仓储业	Storage	122	16589800	15791134	56501
邮政业	Posts	27	4237115	2483176	393621
住宿和餐饮业	**Hotel and Restaurants**	**3103**	**15443435**	**5830668**	**258543**
住宿业	Hotels	1154	11364379	3610293	130342
餐饮业	Restaurants	1949	4079056	2220375	128201
信息传输、软件和信息技术服务业	**Information Transmission,Software and Iinformation Technology Services**	**2767**	**243423259**	**90508391**	**11314654**
电信、广播电视和卫星传输服务	Telecommunications,Broadcasting,Television and Satellite Transmission Services	254	195479249	55417086	2227190
互联网和相关服务	Internet and Related Services	240	7504269	5347918	659317
软件和信息技术服务业	Software and Information Technology Services	2273	40439741	29743387	8428148

注：行业划分执行2011年国民经济行业分类标准(GB/T 4754-2011)。
Note: Sectors in this table are classified in accordance with the Standard for Classification of National Economic Sectors 2011 (GB/T 4754-2011).

22-6 续表 1 continued

单位：万元 (10000 yuan)

项目	Item	企业单位个数(个) Number of Enterprises (unit)	资产负债 资产总计 Total Assets	流动资产合计 Total Current Assets	#应收账款 Accounts Receivable (Net)
金融业	**Finance Intermediation**	**1530**	**6294580073**	**26962572**	**3600016**
货币金融服务	Monetary Financial Services	429	5236073768	7047426	2673240
资本市场服务	Capital Market Services	405	318036743	2333850	82875
保险业	Insurance	410	264916458	549700	56683
其他金融业	Other financial Services	286	475553105	17031596	787218
房地产业	**Real Estate**	**4598**	**373499443**	**293341100**	**7041724**
租赁和商务服务业	**Leasing and Business Services**	**5552**	**739798820**	**207999832**	**11540662**
租赁业	Leasing	132	2148780	654490	128579
商务服务业	Business Services	5420	737650039	207345342	11412083
科学研究和技术服务业	**Scientific Studies and Technical Services**	**2711**	**86878162**	**53664422**	**8668220**
研究和试验发展	Research and Experimental Development	270	12291357	7987051	802759
专业技术服务业	Professional Technical Services	1477	53195370	32801964	5137832
科技推广和应用服务业	Technique Generalization and Application Services	964	21391435	12875407	2727629
水利、环境和公共设施管理业	**Water,Environment and Municipal Engineering Conservancy**	**320**	**11678110**	**3561110**	**591956**
水利管理业	Management of Water Conservancy	17	652145	130312	16710
生态保护和环境治理业	Ecological Protection and Environmental Control	43	1631296	976426	238826
公共设施管理业	Management of Public Facilities	260	9394670	2454371	336419
居民服务、修理和其他服务业	**Resident Services, Repair and Other Services**	**423**	**1322078**	**988663**	**150914**
居民服务业	Services to Households	128	466214	336814	21018
机动车、电子产品和日用产品修理业	Repair of Motor Vehicles, Electronics and Household Appliances	133	462012	368431	54289
其他服务业	Other Services	162	393852	283419	75607
教育	**Education**	**197**	**1543469**	**1026010**	**58757**
卫生和社会工作	**Health Care and Social Works**	**126**	**712914**	**401564**	**64767**
卫生	Health	122	681165	388862	64765
社会工作	Social Work Activities	4	31749	12702	3
文化、体育和娱乐业	**Culture,Sports and Entertainment**	**958**	**14066426**	**8735754**	**729012**
新闻和出版业	Journalism and Publishing Activites	455	7849790	5363336	398142
广播、电视、电影和影视录音制作业	Radio Broadcasting, Television, Movies, Videos and Sound Recording	180	3894041	2293018	263701
文化艺术业	Cultural and Art Activities	91	470115	271040	23982
体育	Sports Activities	133	1406539	560545	35515
娱乐业	Entertainment	99	445940	247816	7672

22-6 续表 2 continued

单位：万元 (10000 yuan)

项目	Item	资产负债 Assets and Liabilities				
		固定资产合计 Total Fixed Assets	固定资产原价 Total Original Value of Fixed Assets	负债合计 Total Liabilities	#流动负债合计 Total Current Liabilities	#应付账款 Accounts Payable
合计	**Total**	**146889060**	**204026499**	**6310557998**	**730210244**	**111230235**
按隶属关系分	**Grouped by Administrative Relationship**					
中央	Central	61485441	86801117	4642318766	276509279	44654607
地方	Local	85403619	117225381	1668239232	453700965	66575629
按登记注册类型分	**Grouped by Registation Status of Enterprises**					
内资企业	Domestic Funded Enterprises	120217584	158727335	6075955969	613434003	88954940
国有企业	State-Owned Enterprises	28200365	38143888	471466823	96907448	8556041
集体企业	Collective Owned Enterprises	1774993	2288380	7696120	6332528	448327
股份合作企业	Share Holding Enterprises	678637	907563	3360097	2818134	304030
联营企业	Joint Owned Enterprises	61713	104693	143514	132575	22983
有限责任公司	Limited-Liability Corporations	45028608	64168725	890925004	359131132	61017687
股份有限公司	Share Holding Corporations Ltd.	39798913	46160755	4647906937	98317560	8865416
私营企业	Private Enterprises	4599504	6850110	54132289	49490041	9706580
其他企业	Others	74852	103222	325185	304585	33876
港澳台商投资企业	Enterprises with Funds from Hongkong, Macao and Taiwan	20164168	34127892	85224149	47385573	7327209
外商投资企业	Foreign Funded Enterprises	6507308	11171272	149377880	69390669	14948086
按国民经济行业分	**Grouped by Sector**					
批发和零售业	**Wholesale Trade and Retail Trade**	**8317712**	**12716033**	**201154961**	**181033094**	**55832540**
批发业	Wholesale Trade	5322740	8050508	172528312	153975066	48549248
零售业	Retail Trade	2994972	4665525	28626649	27058027	7283292
交通运输、仓储和邮政业	**Transportation, Storage and Post**	**62236682**	**80406109**	**63615112**	**37770608**	**6384860**
铁路运输业	Railway Transport	35335086	42221187	17288729	6835665	2513975
道路运输业	Road Transport	10128611	13430155	9986241	4954452	480211
水上运输业	Water Transport	16866	49191	31157	20357	3512
航空运输业	Air Transport	13316432	19146697	14204360	5449243	1589151
管道运输业	Transport Via Pipelines	2053630	3318476	1403616	533616	340411
装卸搬运和运输代理业	Loading, Unloading, Portage and Other Transport Services	504117	772457	2686720	2392789	954287
仓储业	Storage	439946	628464	16033561	15675753	174270
邮政业	Posts	441994	839481	1980728	1908735	329044
住宿和餐饮业	**Hotel and Restaurants**	**5203906**	**8863955**	**11455155**	**8390507**	**935731**
住宿业	Hotels	4562182	7784700	8275079	5661205	444192
餐饮业	Restaurants	641724	1079255	3180076	2729302	491539
信息传输、软件和信息技术服务业	**Information Transmission, Software and Information Technology Services**	**12112801**	**24935065**	**65632608**	**53732838**	**9334815**
电信、广播电视和卫星传输服务	Telecommunications, Broadcasting,Television and Satellite Transmission Services	8374892	18051008	42331159	31722147	3420212
互联网和相关服务	Internet and Related Services	889801	1603492	3864227	3616763	630879
软件和信息技术服务业	Software and Information Technology Services	2848108	5280565	19437222	18393928	5283724

22-6 续表 3 continued

单位：万元 (10000 yuan)

项目	Item	资产负债 Assets and Liabilities 固定资产合计 Total Fixed Assets	固定资产原价 Total Original Value of Fixed Assets	负债合计 Total Liabilities	#流动负债合计 Total Current Liabilities	#应付账款 Accounts Payable
金融业	**Finance Intermediation**	**16724386**	**19512230**	**5306762973**	**19262865**	**975577**
货币金融服务	Monetary Financial Services	10861531	14205615	4797244136	7322051	377888
资本市场服务	Capital Market Services	855331	1233749	132975289	1245874	22601
保险业	Insurance	3975930	2457745	200118457	203465	45655
其他金融业	Other financial Services	1031594	1615121	176425091	10491474	529432
房地产业	**Real Estate**	**14289997**	**19443604**	**289368381**	**218112160**	**15781959**
租赁和商务服务业	**Leasing and Business Services**	**17768369**	**22947819**	**304435338**	**158022880**	**10606083**
租赁业	Leasing	802292	1180333	1518178	792945	65445
商务服务业	Business Services	16966077	21767486	302917160	157229935	10540638
科学研究和技术服务业	**Scientific Studies and Technical Services**	**5460457**	**8394143**	**51828545**	**44199235**	**9499333**
研究和试验发展	Research and Experimental Development	932066	1491408	7827723	6245488	730561
专业技术服务业	Professional Technical Services	3162828	4908663	31437133	26661330	5867864
科技推广和应用服务业	Technique Generalization and Application Services	1365563	1994072	12563689	11292416	2900908
水利、环境和公共设施管理业	**Water,Environment and Municipal Engineering Conservancy**	**2103549**	**2553824**	**7988010**	**2508716**	**540739**
水利管理业	Management of Water Conservancy	138823	215829	326737	143700	14474
生态保护和环境治理业	Ecological Protection and Environmental Control	299740	406810	1068703	764975	195680
公共设施管理业	Management of Public Facilities	1664986	1931185	6592571	1600041	330585
居民服务、修理和其他服务业	**Resident Services, Repair and Other Services**	**171682**	**298214**	**1001963**	**942986**	**139661**
居民服务业	Services to Households	58930	110153	388274	368156	44480
机动车、电子产品和日用产品修理业	Repair of Mmotor Vehicles, Electronics and Household Appliances	70864	115997	344057	337505	50804
其他服务业	Other Services	41888	72063	269632	237325	44376
教育	**Education**	**290206**	**478379**	**997266**	**930258**	**68508**
卫生和社会工作	**Health care and social works**	**176151**	**330366**	**353456**	**326490**	**129498**
卫生	Health	157120	293860	339929	312962	129498
社会工作	Social Work Activities	19030	36507	13527	13527	
文化、体育和娱乐业	**Culture,Sports and Entertainment**	**2033164**	**3146759**	**5964230**	**4977609**	**1000930**
新闻和出版业	Journalism and Publishing Activites	1063735	1616303	2703721	2316461	639350
广播、电视、电影和影视录音制作业	Radio Broadcasting, Television,Movies,Videos and Sound Recording	349378	547772	1388272	1199221	252461
文化艺术业	Cultural and Art Activities	67389	102131	254536	243131	24626
体育	Sports Activities	446062	711683	1332503	1033723	56813
娱乐业	Entertainment	106601	168871	285199	185073	27680

22-6 续表 4 continued

单位：万元

项目	Item	资产负债 Assets and Liabilities 所有者权益合计 Total Owner's Equity	#实收资本 Paid-up Capital
合计	**Total**	**1867554280**	**993797421**
按隶属关系分	**Grouped by Administrative Relationship**		
中央	Central	1419044509	756876629
地方	Local	448509771	236920792
按登记注册类型分	**Grouped by Registation Status of Enterprises**		
内资企业	Domestic Funded Enterprises	1699363901	929617647
国有企业	State-Owned Enterprises	340424031	172997762
集体企业	Collective Owned Enterprises	3408780	686949
股份合作企业	Share Holding Enterprises	1372042	611599
联营企业	Joint Owned Enterprises	129617	156421
有限责任公司	Limited-Liability Corporations	667881019	464292943
股份有限公司	Share Holding Corporations Ltd.	666423357	277933793
私营企业	Private Enterprises	19541229	12921228
其他企业	Others	183826	16951
港澳台商投资企业	Enterprises with Funds from Hongkong, Macao and Taiwan	41018166	30390363
外商投资企业	Foreign Funded Enterprises	127172213	33789411
按国民经济行业分	**Grouped by Sector**		
批发和零售业	**Wholesale Trade and Retail Trade**	**79418595**	**39818228**
批发业	Wholesale Trade	71350110	34345225
零售业	Retail Trade	8068486	5473003
交通运输、仓储和邮政业	**Transportation,Storage and Post**	**50977421**	**43754218**
铁路运输业	Railway Transport	29735612	31427674
道路运输业	Road Transport	6677382	5202055
水上运输业	Water Transport	23322	15868
航空运输业	Air Transport	7382353	2769885
管道运输业	Transport Via Pipelines	1364985	1024000
装卸搬运和运输代理业	Loading, Unloading, Portage and Other Transport Services	2981141	1575366
仓储业	Storage	556239	375272
邮政业	Posts	2256387	1364099
住宿和餐饮业	**Hotel and Restaurants**	**3988280**	**4200774**
住宿业	Hotels	3089300	3423979
餐饮业	Restaurants	898980	776795
信息传输、软件和信息技术服务业	**Information Transmission,Software and Information Technology Services**	**177790651**	**75299588**
电信、广播电视和卫星传输服务	Telecommunications, Broadcasting,Television and Satellite Transmission Services	153148090	65241849
互联网和相关服务	Internet and Related Services	3640042	1303576
软件和信息技术服务业	Software and Information Technology Services	21002519	8754163

22-6 续表 5 continued

单位：万元 (10000 yuan)

项目	Item	损益 Profits and Loss 营业收入 Business Income	#主营业务收入 Main Business Income	营业成本 Business Cost	#主营业务成本 Main Business Cost
合计	**Total**	**847594383**	**833507484**	**656602625**	**648277301**
按隶属关系分	**Grouped by Administrative Relationship**				
中央	Central	367375208	364320596	274110181	272771846
地方	Local	480219176	469186889	382492445	375505455
按登记注册类型分	**Grouped by Registation Status of Enterprises**				
内资企业	Domestic Funded Enterprises	689064636	677158030	536973234	529223851
国有企业	State-Owned Enterprises	79969775	78113990	71815126	71228930
集体企业	Collective Owned Enterprises	2604014	2418833	1928425	1838314
股份合作企业	Share Holding Enterprises	1659742	1631632	1271881	1268201
联营企业	Joint Owned Enterprises	130697	127280	89184	88324
有限责任公司	Limited-Liability Corporations	404994410	396757303	315541544	309562648
股份有限公司	Share Holding Corporations Ltd.	127893975	126997606	88138505	87337918
私营企业	Private Enterprises	71433777	70738589	57993183	57706478
其他企业	Others	378246	372798	195387	193038
港澳台商投资企业	Enterprises with Funds from Hongkong, Macao and Taiwan	42439728	41914344	28784564	28495732
外商投资企业	Foreign Funded Enterprises	116090020	114435110	90844828	90557719
按国民经济行业分	**Grouped by Sector**				
批发和零售业	**Wholesale Trade and Retail Trade**	**449966772**	**441776324**	**419164456**	**413785221**
批发业	Wholesale Trade	388568644	381825774	365355331	360207324
零售业	Retail Trade	61398127	59950549	53809125	53577897
交通运输、仓储和邮政业	**Transportation,Storage and Post**	**36839796**	**36149043**	**31835762**	**30942947**
铁路运输业	Railway Transport	10434421	9998310	9663238	8873612
道路运输业	Road Transport	4278059	4190716	4661054	4621220
水上运输业	Water Transport	35222	35211	23334	23334
航空运输业	Air Transport	10343515	10267308	8423173	8374570
管道运输业	Transport Via Pipelines	918137	917544	368741	367865
装卸搬运和运输代理业	Loading, Unloading, Portage and Other Transport Services	6933100	6895281	6027212	6021362
仓储业	Storage	1636224	1620278	1439303	1436230
邮政业	Posts	2261120	2224395	1229708	1224755
住宿和餐饮业	**Hotel and Restaurants**	**9257527**	**9201200**	**3400402**	**3387012**
住宿业	Hotels	3788254	3765526	1013826	1008229
餐饮业	Restaurants	5469273	5435674	2386576	2378783
信息传输、软件和信息技术服务业	**Information Transmission, Software and Information Technology Services**	**45688633**	**44989184**	**28742846**	**28292741**
电信、广播电视和卫星传输服务	Telecommunications, Broadcasting,Television and Satellite Transmission Services	9761808	9486569	6285925	6070302
互联网和相关服务	Internet and Related Services	5862601	5845346	2910961	2907308
软件和信息技术服务业	Software and Information Technology Services	30064223	29657269	19545960	19315130

注：执行《2006年会计准则》的银行、证券、保险业企业，其“主营业务收入”用“业务收入”代替，“营业成本”和“主营业务成本”用“营业支出-营业税金及附加”代替。

Note: For entities implementing accounting <2006 Accountant Systems > for financial and insurance industries, the indicator "Main Business Income" is replaced with "Business Income"; "Business Cost" and "Main Business Cost" are replaced with "Business Cost - Business Tax and Surtax".

22-6 续表 6 continued

单位：万元 (10000 yuan)

项目	Item	所有者权益合计 Total Owner's Equity	#实收资本 Paid-up Capital	损益 Profits and Loss: 营业收入 Business Income	#主营业务收入 Main Business Income	营业成本 Business Cost	#主营业务成本 Main Business Cost
金融业	**Finance Intermediation**	**987817101**	**560298858**	**142020825**	**141651322**	**54181332**	**54022232**
货币金融服务	Monetary Financial Services	438829631	186906166	55066240	55058578	25765624	25765612
资本市场服务	Capital Market Services	185061454	176700852	20330521	20317291	2552851	2551931
保险业	Insurance	64798001	25694893	30555482	30553618	23010966	23008905
其他金融业	Other financial Services	299128014	170996947	36068582	35721835	2851891	2695785
房地产业	**Real Estate**	**84131062**	**51322524**	**38443570**	**37407137**	**22180599**	**21807206**
租赁和商务服务业	**Leasing and Business Services**	**435363481**	**196780050**	**70254432**	**68183455**	**55239258**	**54661768**
租赁业	Leasing	630602	313311	604583	589311	384509	381391
商务服务业	Business Services	434732879	196466739	69649849	67594144	54854749	54280378
科学研究和技术服务业	**Scientific Studies and Technical Services**	**35049618**	**16859985**	**43089681**	**42733038**	**34259168**	**34148944**
研究和试验发展	Research and Experimental Development	4463634	2398043	3999852	3936520	3013360	2988042
专业技术服务业	Professional Technical Services	21758237	10155429	26773239	26639088	21168975	21124433
科技推广和应用服务业	Technique Generalization and Application Services	8827746	4306513	12316591	12157430	10076833	10036470
水利、环境和公共设施管理业	**Water,Environment and Municipal Engineering Conservancy**	**3690100**	**1252336**	**2343906**	**2315018**	**1739933**	**1728534**
水利管理业	Management of Water Conservancy	325408	202665	68105	66920	43947	43915
生态保护和环境治理业	Ecological Protection and Environmental Control	562593	444028	528901	527119	361250	360997
公共设施管理业	Management of Public Facilities	2802099	605643	1746899	1720979	1334736	1323623
居民服务、修理和其他服务业	**Resident Services, Repair and Other Services**	**320115**	**280907**	**1618675**	**1370443**	**1034779**	**815503**
居民服务业	Services to Households	77940	69972	372486	360069	141528	138604
机动车、电子产品和日用产品修理业	Repair of Mmotor Vehicles, Electronics and Household Appliances	117955	102648	800226	567948	611911	397238
其他服务业	Other Services	124220	108286	445964	442426	281340	279662
教育	**Education**	**546204**	**233527**	**1116826**	**1101879**	**545057**	**539735**
卫生和社会工作	**Health care and social works**	**359458**	**232467**	**765389**	**763017**	**501445**	**499277**
卫生	Health	341237	231728	759235	758065	498262	496094
社会工作	Social Work Activities	18221	739	6155	4952	3183	3183
文化、体育和娱乐业	**Culture,Sports and Entertainment**	**8102195**	**3463960**	**6188352**	**5866426**	**3777591**	**3646181**
新闻和出版业	Journalism and Publishing Activites	5146070	1664122	3613525	3385892	2152297	2071863
广播、电视、电影和影录音制作业	Radio Broadcasting, Television, Movies, Videos and Sound Recording	2505769	1257151	1685128	1612985	1151251	1109871
文化艺术业	Cultural and Art Activities	215579	93252	259868	253673	166056	163637
体育	Sports Activities	74035	325441	430546	416212	202965	195972
娱乐业	Entertainment	160742	123995	199285	197664	105022	104839

注：执行《2006年会计准则》的银行、证券、保险业企业，其“主营业务收入”用“业务收入”代替，“营业成本”和“主营业务成本”用“营业支出-营业税金及附加”代替。

Note: For entities implementing accounting <2006 Accountant Systems > for financial and insurance industries, the indicator "Main Business Income" is replaced with "Business Income"; "Business Cost" and "Main Business Cost" are replaced with "Business Cost - Business Tax and Surtax".

22-6 续表 7 continued

单位：万元

项目	Item	损益 Profits and Loss 销售费用 Sales Expenses	管理费用 Management Expenses	财务费用 Financial Expenses	利润总额 Total Profits
合计	**Total**	**34595070**	**39454926**	**10398599**	**142484100**
按隶属关系分	**Grouped by Administrative Relationship**				
中央	Central	5336407	11109009	4961689	95949380
地方	Local	29258663	28345917	5436910	46534720
按登记注册类型分	**Grouped by Registation Status of Enterprises**				
内资企业	Domestic Funded Enterprises	20560484	27923695	9518343	121972352
国有企业	State-Owned Enterprises	1589896	5906503	1887398	18645193
集体企业	Collective Owned Enterprises	152300	358795	2724	198406
股份合作企业	Share Holding Enterprises	138504	207961	-12478	52151
联营企业	Joint Owned Enterprises	18757	22620	487	5994
有限责任公司	Limited-Liability Corporations	10737769	12931157	5257196	66222817
股份有限公司	Share Holding Corporations Ltd.	2498334	3275702	1925973	34579885
私营企业	Private Enterprises	5355366	5153362	460214	2229324
其他企业	Others	69560	67595	-3171	38584
港澳台商投资企业	Enterprises with Funds from Hongkong, Macao and Taiwan	4199961	3850427	622676	4602119
外商投资企业	Foreign Funded Enterprises	9834625	7680804	257580	15909629
按国民经济行业分	**Grouped by Sector**				
批发和零售业	**Wholesale Trade and Retail Trade**	**15372786**	**7916906**	**1813578**	**9428650**
批发业	Wholesale Trade	10741759	5816137	1523264	8801280
零售业	Retail Trade	4631027	2100769	290314	627370
交通运输、仓储和邮政业	**Transportation,Storage and Post**	**1708809**	**2429646**	**1504649**	**1142496**
铁路运输业	Railway Transport	3880	784628	855977	-845468
道路运输业	Road Transport	214715	497132	355403	221756
水上运输业	Water Transport	2793	5874	624	1701
航空运输业	Air Transport	707257	326208	243112	692905
管道运输业	Transport Via Pipelines	24224	16405	34178	453645
装卸搬运和运输代理业	Loading, unloading, portage and other transport services	285169	426743	5260	274749
仓储业	Storage	60227	84476	10358	59447
邮政业	Posts	410543	288180	-263	283761
住宿和餐饮业	**Hotel and Restaurants**	**3073982**	**1898485**	**201016**	**189830**
住宿业	Hotels	1108292	1266471	146692	38902
餐饮业	Restaurants	1965690	632015	54324	150928
信息传输、软件和信息技术服务业	**Information transmission,software and information technology services**	**5408136**	**6789119**	**-270001**	**13189761**
电信、广播电视和卫星传输服务	Telecommunications, broadcasting,television and satellite transmission services	1383698	1513249	-215002	8823240
互联网和相关服务	Internet and related services	820569	858842	-48776	1225656
软件和信息技术服务业	Software and information technology services	3203870	4417029	-6224	3140865

22-6 续表 8 continued

单位：万元

项目	Item	损益 Profits and Loss 销售费用 Sales Expenses	管理费用 Management Expenses	财务费用 Financial Expenses	利润总额 Total Profits
金融业	**Finance Intermediation**	**246922**	**888408**	**206527**	**84357044**
货币金融服务	Monetary Financial Services	34918	113343	108060	26414464
资本市场服务	Capital Market Services	20277	143086	38019	17503842
保险业	Insurance	37475	125720	-1381	7230435
其他金融业	Other Financial Services	154252	506259	61829	33208303
房地产业	**Real Estate**	**1740503**	**3916568**	**1960483**	**7547043**
租赁和商务服务业	**Leasing and Business Services**	**4241842**	**9493784**	**4786055**	**21165347**
租赁业	Leasing	63071	67172	34804	49498
商务服务业	Business Services	4178770	9426612	4751251	21115848
科学研究和技术服务业	**Scientific Studies and Technical Services**	**1392254**	**4079941**	**177247**	**4193709**
研究和试验发展	Research and Experimental Development	164586	642742	-33058	439700
专业技术服务业	Professional Technical Services	817092	2443295	96548	2725205
科技推广和应用服务业	Technique generalization and application services	410575	993905	113757	1028804
水利、环境和公共设施管理业	**Water, Environment and Municipal Engineering Conservancy**	**80622**	**279453**	**38351**	**202649**
水利管理业	Management of Water Conservancy	323	28603	9949	10056
生态保护和环境治理业	Ecological protection and environmental control	23956	56103	12146	69883
公共设施管理业	Management of Public Facilities	56342	194747	16256	122710
居民服务、修理和其他服务业	**Resident services, repair and other services**	**289533**	**213862**	**8180**	**37430**
居民服务业	Services to Households	123770	70579	4128	17336
机动车、电子产品和日用产品修理业	Repair of motor vehicles, electronics and household appliances	101706	63527	3500	13045
其他服务业	Other Services	64057	79756	553	7048
教育	**Education**	**194459**	**239719**	**-7701**	**107302**
卫生和社会工作	**Health care and social works**	**81253**	**132519**	**1011**	**52239**
卫生	Health	81188	126694	1444	53302
社会工作	Social work activities	65	5825	-433	-1064
文化、体育和娱乐业	**Culture,Sports and Entertainment**	**763972**	**1176517**	**-20794**	**870601**
新闻和出版业	Journalism and Publishing Activites	435810	782290	-29742	572139
广播、电视、电影和影视录音制作业	Radio broadcasting, television,movies,videos and sound recording	125821	189611	-6118	324057
文化艺术业	Cultural and Art Activities	30044	46439	1885	24075
体育	Sports Activities	122152	122172	9252	-47350
娱乐业	Entertainment	50146	36006	3930	-2320

22-6 续表 9 continued

单位：万元 (10000 yuan)

项目	Item	应交税金合计 Total Tax	#营业税金及附加 Business Tax and Surtax	#主营业务税金及附加 Main Business Tax and Surtax	#应交所得税 Income Tax Payable
合计	**Total**	**46058172**	**12225503**	**11899377**	**26714520**
按隶属关系分	**Grouped by Administrative Relationship**				
中央	Central	22456312	3391786	3234361	17382357
地方	Local	23601860	8833718	8665016	9332163
按登记注册类型分	**Grouped by Registation Status of Enterprises**				
内资企业	Domestic Funded Enterprises	38502339	9758825	9472200	24080423
国有企业	State-Owned Enterprises	2267548	1164866	1062998	878809
集体企业	Collective Owned Enterprises	125892	57139	54270	39905
股份合作企业	Share Holding Enterprises	53365	24021	23294	10821
联营企业	Joint Owned Enterprises	5092	2032	1894	976
有限责任公司	Limited-Liability Corporations	13138189	4742487	4610734	5545480
股份有限公司	Share Holding Corporations Ltd.	20549747	2779153	2743364	17100272
私营企业	Private Enterprises	2347401	977145	963780	501955
其他企业	Others	15107	11982	11868	2205
港澳台商投资企业	Enterprises with Funds from Hongkong, Macao and Taiwan	3042325	1387659	1372538	1065898
外商投资企业	Foreign Funded Enterprises	4513507	1079020	1054639	1568199
按国民经济行业分	**Grouped by Sector**				
批发和零售业	**Wholesale Trade and Retail Trade**	**6960773**	**889077**	**834912**	**2188968**
批发业	Wholesale Trade	5347243	654208	621494	1846237
零售业	Retail Trade	1613530	234870	213419	342731
交通运输、仓储和邮政业	**Transportation,Storage and Post**	**1277937**	**743139**	**720771**	**693447**
铁路运输业	Railway Transport	548555	318886	307170	219337
道路运输业	Road Transport	186152	102164	97961	47391
水上运输业	Water Transport	1888	808	808	869
航空运输业	Air Transport	379922	179854	177092	175959
管道运输业	Transport Via Pipelines	148566	21833	21799	113276
装卸搬运和运输代理业	Loading, Unloading, Portage and Other Transport Services	144075	48053	47203	51703
仓储业	Storage	-275191	14368	13447	5694
邮政业	Posts	143971	57175	55291	79218
住宿和餐饮业	**Hotel and Restaurants**	**720520**	**507837**	**505737**	**128780**
住宿业	Hotels	340350	208301	207522	60184
餐饮业	Restaurants	380171	299536	298215	68596
信息传输、软件和信息技术服务业	**Information Transmission, Software and Information Technology Services**	**2723935**	**904821**	**886579**	**635104**
电信、广播电视和卫星传输服务	Telecommunications, Broadcasting,Television and Satellite Transmission Services	346602	261387	248363	-21955
互联网和相关服务	Internet and Related Services	494819	230470	229960	187778
软件和信息技术服务业	Software and Information Technology Services	1882515	412964	408256	469281

22-6 续表 10 continued

单位：万元 (10000 yuan)

项　目	Item	应交税金合计 Total Tax	#业务税金及附加 Business Tax and Surtax	#主营业务税金及附加 Main Business Tax and Surtax	#应交所得税 Income Tax Payable
金融业	**Finance Intermediation**	**22604052**	**3243868**	**3221204**	**19182384**
货币金融服务	Monetary Financial Services	19563386	2643915	2643797	16834825
资本市场服务	Capital Market Services	1213945	159441	159273	1030903
保险业	Insurance	870148	234139	233549	595868
其他金融业	Other Financial Services	956573	206372	184586	720788
房地产业	**Real Estate**	**6064625**	**3973130**	**3907880**	**1782238**
租赁和商务服务业	**Leasing and Business Services**	**3005161**	**1049254**	**929744**	**1196629**
租赁业	Leasing	37418	24161	24020	9447
商务服务业	Business Services	2967743	1025092	905724	1187181
科学研究和技术服务业	**Scientific Studies and Technical Services**	**1940741**	**623520**	**610163**	**698649**
研究和试验发展	Research and Experimental Development	193376	39638	37919	76994
专业技术服务业	Professional Technical Services	1235709	467423	462447	454985
科技推广和应用服务业	Technique Generalization and Application Services	511656	116459	109797	166670
水利、环境和公共设施管理业	**Water，Environment and Municipal Engineering Conservancy**	**114399**	**57255**	**56675**	**40070**
水利管理业	Management of Water Conservancy	3267	712	587	1098
生态保护和环境治理业	Ecological Protection and Environmental Control	28199	7560	7482	11539
公共设施管理业	Management of Public Facilities	82934	48983	48606	27433
居民服务、修理和其他服务业	**Resident Services, Repair and Other Services**	**91837**	**42370**	**41551**	**18529**
居民服务业	Services to Households	24941	15683	15661	6670
机动车、电子产品和日用产品修理业	Repair of Motor Vehicles, Electronics and Household Appliances	38767	7636	7252	7519
其他服务业	Other Services	28129	19052	18638	4340
教　育	**Education**	**77097**	**40097**	**39887**	**30523**
卫生和社会工作	**Health care and social works**	**13084**	**1078**	**1056**	**10831**
卫　生	Health	12909	1023	1001	10830
社会工作	Social Work Activities	175	55	55	1
文化、体育和娱乐业	**Culture,Sports and Entertainment**	**464012**	**150056**	**143219**	**108368**
新闻和出版业	Journalism and Publishing Activites	279780	61813	59414	41972
广播、电视、电影和影视录音制作业	Radio Broadcasting, Television, Movies ,Videos and Sound Recording	115557	41122	39307	54162
文化艺术业	Cultural and Art Activities	15848	7290	7194	4983
体　育	Sports Activities	34229	24909	22435	5025
娱乐业	Entertainment	18598	14923	14869	2226

注：1. 应交税金合计主要包括应交增值税、应交所得税、营业税金及附加和管理费用中的税金。
　　2. 执行《2006年会计准则》的银行、证券、保险业企业，其"主营营业税金及附加"用"营业税金及附加"代替。

Note: a) Total Tax mainly includes payable VAT,payable income tax, business tax and surtax, and tax in management expenses.
　　b) For banking, securities and insurance companies implementing the Accounting Standard 2006, their Main Business Tax and Surtax is replaced with "Business Tax and Surtax".

22-7 文化创意产业活动单位基本情况
STATISTICS ON UNITS IN CULTURAL AND CREATIVE INDUSTRY

单位：亿元 (100 million yuan)

项　目	Item	资产总计 Total Assets		收入合计 Total Income		从业人员平均人数（万人） Average Number of Employed Persons (10000 persons)	
		2012	2011	2012	2011	2012	2011
合　计	**Total**	**15575.2**	**12942.6**	**10313.6**	**9012.2**	**152.9**	**140.9**
文化艺术	Cultural and Artistic	551.2	470.8	237.0	217.0	7.2	7.4
新闻出版	Journalism and Publication	1514.6	1260.4	883.0	755.6	15.6	15.1
广播、电视、电影	Broadcast,TV and Film	1570.7	1326.0	680.3	553.5	6.0	5.5
软件、网络及计算机服务	Software, Network & Computer Service	6529.0	5436.5	3888.1	3342.5	69.8	61.3
广告会展	Advertisements & Exhibitions	1050.0	1002.2	1256.8	1154.9	12.5	11.5
艺术品交易	Transaction of Artwork	817.5	464.4	705.6	492.2	2.8	2.5
设计服务	Design Service	1163.7	920.0	443.0	369.9	11.9	10.1
旅游、休闲娱乐	Touring,Relaxation and Amusement	934.5	713.9	849.0	706.6	11.1	10.6
其他辅助服务	Other Auxiliary Service	1444.0	1348.4	1370.8	1420.0	16.0	16.9

22-8 物流业活动情况
STATISTICS FOR LOGISTICS ACTIVITY

项 目		Item		2012	2011	2012年为2011年% 2012 as % of 2011
物流业务收入	**(亿元)**	**Business Income of Logistics Sector**	**(100 million yuan)**	**2104.4**	**1891.1**	**111.3**
运输收入		Transportation Income		1517.2	1467.6	103.4
保管收入		Storage Income		562.4	406.3	138.4
一体化物流业务收入		Integrated Logistics Income		24.8	17.1	144.7
限额以上企业物流基础设施情况		**Logistics Infrastructure in Enterprises above the Designated Size**				
自有仓库和货场面积	(万平方米)	Area of Self-owned and Goods Yard Warehouses	(10000 sq.m)	3208.8	3055.9	105.0
货运车辆数	(辆)	Number of Transportation Vehicles	(unit)	42907	42074	102.0
普通货车数		Number of Genreal Trucks		32988	31673	104.2
专业货车数		Number of Special Trucks		9919	10401	95.4
装卸设备台数	(台)	Number of Loading Equipment	(unit)	39844	35998	110.7
社会物流总额	**(亿元)**	**Total Amount of Social Logistics**	**(100 million yuan)**	**65851.1**	**59624.5**	**110.4**
农产品		Agricultural Products		337.8	310.2	108.9
工业品		Industrial Products		13008.6	12327.9	105.5
进口货物		Imported Goods		21984.3	21344.4	103.0
再生资源		Renewable Resource		67.0	105.4	63.6
外省市流入物品		Goods from Other Provinces and Cities		30284.2	25387.0	119.3
单位与居民物品		Entities and Residents' Goods		169.2	149.6	113.1
物流业从业人员平均人数	**(万人)**	**Employed Person in Logistics Sector**	**(10000 persons)**	**51.9**	**50.6**	**102.6**
交通运输、邮政、仓储业		Transportation, Post, Storage		35.0	33.9	103.4
采掘业、制造业、批发和零售业		Excavation, Manufacturing, Wholesale, Retail		16.8	16.7	100.6

注：表中物流业增加值增速按现价计算。

Note: The growth rates for Added value of Logistics Sector were calculated at current prices.

22-9 会展业活动情况
STATISTICS ON THE MICE INDUSTRY IN BEIJING

项目	Item	2012	2011	2012年为2011年% 2012 as % of 2011
人员情况	**Employed Persons**			
从业人员年末人数 (万人)	Year-end Employed Persons (10000 person)	22.48	21.97	102.3
设施情况	**Facilities**			
接待场所会议室个数 (个)	Number of Meeting Rooms (unit)	5720	5693	100.5
#座位数超过500座的会议室 (个)	Number of Meeting Rooms with more than 500 Seats (unit)	195	198	98.5
接待场所会议室使用面积 (万平方米)	Floorage of Meeting Rooms (10000 sq.m)	81.6	80.4	101.5
接待场所会议室可容纳人数 (万人)	Capacity of Meeting Rooms (10000 person)	49.2	48.7	100.9
展览场馆展厅使用面积 (万平方米)	Usable Area of Exhibition Halls (10000 sq.m)	39.9	40.1	99.5
展览场馆室外可使用展览面积 (万平方米)	Usable Exhibition Area Outside Exhibition Halls (10000 sq.m)	27.2	24.9	109.1
会议情况	**Meetings**			
接待会议个数 (个)	Number of Meetings Held in Beijing (unit)	277487	283453	97.9
#国际会议 (个)	International Meetings (unit)	7403	7993	92.6
接待会议人数 (万人次)	Number of Meeting Participants (10000 person-times)	1882.8	1947.0	96.7
#国际会议 (万人次)	International Meeting Participants (10000 person-times)	73.7	70.5	104.5
展览情况	**Exhibitions**			
接待展览个数 (个)	Number of Exhibitions Held in Beijing (unit)	1059	1313	80.7
#国际展览 (个)	International Exhibitions (unit)	281	322	87.3
#展览面积1万(不含)平方米以下的展览个数 (个)	Number of Exhibitions with Exhibition Area under 10000sq.m (10000sq.m excluded) (unit)	865	1140	75.9
展览面积1万(含)-5万(不含)平方米的展览个数 (个)	Number of Exhibitions with Exhibition Area of 10000(10000sq.m included)-50000sq.m (50000sq.m excluded) (unit)	171	158	108.2
展览面积5万平方米及以上的展览个数 (个)	Number of Exhibitions with Exhibition Area of 50000sq.m and over (unit)	23	15	153.3
接待展览累计面积(含室外展览面积) (万平方米)	Accumulative Exhibition Area (including outdoor exhibition area) (10000 sq.m)	745.8	685.2	108.8
#国际展览累计面积 (万平方米)	International Exhibition Area (10000 sq.m)	378.1	356.7	106.0
接待展览观众人数 (万人次)	Number of Exhibition Visitors (10000 person-times)	575.3	466.7	123.3
#国际展览观众人数 (万人次)	International Exhibition Visitors (10000 person-times)	201.8	193.8	104.1
奖励旅游情况	**Incentives**			
服务奖励旅游项目个数 (个)	Number of Incentive Projects (unit)	12147	12591	96.5
服务奖励旅游人数 (万人次)	Number of Incentive Tourists (10000 person-times)	38.3	41.2	93.0
收入情况	**Revenues**			
会展收入 (万元)	Total Revenues from MICE Industry (10000 yuan)	2507206.1	2229634.8	112.4
会议收入 (万元)	Revenues from Meetings (10000 yuan)	1378457.9	1253964.1	109.9
#国际会议收入 (万元)	Revenues from International Meetings (10000 yuan)	100469.2	96245.9	104.4
展览收入 (万元)	Revenues from Exhibitions (10000 yuan)	959336.5	832870.5	115.2
#国际展览收入 (万元)	Revenues from International Exhibition (10000 yuan)	421151.5	351955.1	119.7
奖励旅游收入 (万元)	Revenues from Incentives (10000 yuan)	169411.7	142800.2	118.6

22-10 体育及相关产业情况
STATISTICS ON SPORTS INDUSTRY

项 目	Item	增加值 (亿元) Added Value (100 million yuan)		收入合计 (亿元) Total Income (100 million yuan)		从业人员平均人数 (万人) Average Number of Employed Persons (10000 persons)	
		2012	2011	2012	2011	2012	2011
合 计	**Total**	**144.2**	**129.2**	**777.0**	**680.1**	**12.3**	**11.9**
体育组织管理活动	Sports Organizational Management Activities	33.1	28.0	108.3	98.2	1.6	1.5
体育场馆管理活动	Gym Management Activities	8.6	8.8	18.7	16.1	0.7	0.7
体育健身休闲活动	Sports Body Building and Entertainment Activities	14.0	13.4	41.2	38.0	3.0	3.0
体育中介活动	Sports Agency Activities	5.0	4.2	21.8	20.6	0.4	0.4
其他体育活动	Other Sports Activities	19.8	14.3	77.7	62.7	1.2	1.2
体育用品、服装、鞋帽及相关体育产品的制造	Manufacturing of Sports Supplies, Clothes, Shoes and Caps, and Related Products	12.9	12.0	61.7	47.1	0.9	1.0
体育用品、服装、鞋帽及相关体育产品的销售	Sales of Sports Supplies, Clothes, Shoes and Caps, and Related Products	50.2	45.0	436.5	372.0	4.3	3.9
体育场馆建筑活动	Gymnasium Building Activities	0.9	3.4	11.2	26.1	0.1	0.3

主要统计指标解释

物流业务收入 指通过物流业务活动取得的收入。包括企业完成运输、存储、装卸、搬运、包装、流通加工、配送、信息等物流业务取得的收入之和。反映物流相关行业物流活动的总规模。

物流业从业人员 指企业中直接或间接从事物流活动的人数。直接从事物流活动的人员包括在企业中从事运输、配送、装卸搬运、仓储保管等物流活动并取得劳动报酬的从业人员；间接从事物流活动的人员包括在企业中从事物流管理活动并取得劳动报酬的从业人员，包括采购、销售部门的主管人员，但不包括采购、销售部门内部办事人员。

社会物流总额 指第一次进入市内需求领域，产生从供应地向接受地实体流动的物品的价值总额。包括六个方面的内容：进入需求领域的农产品物流总额、工业品物流总额、进口货物物流总额、外省市调入物品物流总额、再生资源物流总额、单位与居民物品物流总额。.

接待会议个数 指报告期内，接待的各种类型会议的个数。包括国际会议和国内会议。

接待国际会议个数 指报告期内，接待的国际会议的个数。国际会议是指在我国境内举办的，与会者来自 3 个或 3 个以上中国大陆以外国家和地区（含港、澳、台地区）的会议、论坛、研讨会、报告会、交流会等。

接待展览个数 指报告期内，接待的各种类型展览的个数。包括国际展览和国内展览。

接待国际展览个数 指报告期内，接待的国际展览的个数。国际展览指中国大陆以外国家和地区（含港、澳、台地区）的参展商参展面积达到该次展出面积 20%以上的展览个数。

服务奖励旅游项目个数 指报告期内，服务奖励旅游项目个数的总和。奖励旅游指作为对员工的奖励或鼓励单位通过全面或部分资助的任何形式的旅程安排。

服务奖励旅游人数 指报告期内，服务的奖励旅游人数的总和。

服务贸易 服务贸易包括跨境提供、境外消费、商业存在和自然人移动等内容。

跨境提供 是指服务提供者从中国境内向任何其他国家或地区的服务消费者提供服务以及服务提供者从其他国家或地区向中国境内的服务消费者提供服务。

境外消费 是指在中国境内向其他国家或地区的服务消费者提供服务以及在其他国家或地区向中国境内的服务消费者提供服务。

商业存在 是指中国境内的服务提供者通过在任何其他国家或地区设立的企业或分支机构提供服务以及其他国家或地区的服务提供者通过在中国境内设立企业或分支机构提供服务。

自然人移动 是指中国境内的服务提供者通过在其他国家或地区的自然人提供服务以及其他国家或地区的服务提供者通过在中国境内的自然人提供服务。

体育组织管理活动 指专门为社会公众提供比赛、训练、辅导和管理的组织的活动，如群众性体育组织、专项性体育管理组织的活动。

体育场馆管理活动 指为社会公众提供观赏比赛和专业训练的体育场馆管理活动，如综合性体育场馆，训练用场地的管理活动。

体育健身休闲活动 指社会公众提供的可供参与和选择的各种健身休闲活动场所的管理活动。

体育中介活动 指为社会公众提供的体育中介活动，如各种体育商务代理、经纪、咨询活动。

其他体育活动 指为社会公众提供的其他体育服务活动。包括体育培训服务、体育科研服务、体育彩票服务、体育传媒服务、体育展览服务、体育市场管理服务、体育场馆设计服务、体育场所保洁服务和体育文物及文化保护服务。

体育用品、服装、鞋帽及相关体育产品的制造 指提供体育服务所必须的体育用品、服装、鞋帽及相关体育产品的制造活动。

体育用品、服装、鞋帽及相关体育产品的销售 指提供体育服务所必须的体育用品、服装、鞋帽及相关体育产品的销售活动。

体育场馆管理活动 指提供体育服务所必须的体育场馆建筑活动。

Explanatory Notes on Main Statistical Indicators

Income of Logistics Sector means the income earned from logistics business activities, which is equal to the sum of incomes from such logistics operations completed by enterprises as transportation, storage, loading and unloading, handling, package, circulation and processing, delivery, and information. It reflects the overall scale of logistics activities in logistics related sector.

Employees in Logistics Sector means the number of persons directly and indirectly engaged in logistics activities in enterprises. Persons directly engaged in logistics activities are included in employees engaged in logistics activities such as transportation, delivery, loading and unloading, handling, storage and warehouse keeping in enterprises and receiving labor remuneration; persons indirectly engaged in logistics activities are included in employees engaged in management activities in enterprises and receiving labor remuneration, including executives in purchase and sales departments, but excluding clerks in purchase and sales departments.

Total Amount of Social Logistics means the total value of goods entering the demand area in the city for the first time and having physical flow from the supply place to the receiving place, consisting of value on six aspects: total logistics amount of agricultural products, total logistics amount of industrial products, total logistics amount of imported goods, total logistics amount of goods transferred from other provinces and cities, total logistics amount of recycled resources, and total logistics amount of corporate and household supplies entering the demand field.

Number of Conferences Received means the number of various types of conference received in the reporting period, including international and domestic conferences.

Number of International Conferences Received means the number of international conferences received in the reporting period. International conference means any conference, forum, seminar, report conference, and workshops, etc. held in our country, with participants coming from 3 or more countries and regions (including Hong Kong, Macao and Taiwan) outside mainland of China.

Number of Exhibitions Received means the number of various types of exhibitions received in the reporting period, including international and domestic exhibitions.

Number of International Exhibitions Received means the number of international exhibitions received in the reporting period. International exhibition means any exhibition with participants from countries and regions (including Hong Kong, Macao and Taiwan) outside mainland of China whose exhibition floorage accounts for more than 20% of the exhibition.

Number of Incentive Projects means the sum of incentive tour projects served in the reporting period. Incentive tourism means a tour arrangement in any form fully or partially financed by an enterprise as incentive or encouragement to its employee.

Number of Incentive Tourists means the sum of persons of incentive tour served in the reporting period.

Service Trade includes overseas provision, overseas consumption, commercial existence, movement of natural person, and so on.

Overseas Provision means any service provider provides service within China for service consumers in any other country or region, and any service provider provides service in any other country or region to service consumers within China.

Overseas Consumption means provision of service in China for service consumers in any other country or region, and provision of service in any other country or region for service consumers in China.

Commercial Existence means that any service provider in China provides service through its business or branch set up in any other country or region, and any service provider in any other country or region provides service through its business or branch set up in China.

Movement of Natural Person means that any service provider in China provides service through any natural person in any other country or region, and any service provider in any other country or region provides service through any natural person in China.

Sports Organizational Management Activities mean activities organized specially for providing games, training, coach and management for the public, such as activities organized for mass sport organizations and special sport management.

Gym Management Activities mean management activities in gym providing games for view and special trainings for the public, such as management activities in comprehensive sports venues and training fields and courts.

Sports Body Building and Entertainment Activities mean management activities provided for the public at Sports bodybuilding and entertainment sites, which are to be participated in and chosen.

Sports Agency Activities mean sport agency activities provided for the public, such as various sports business agency, broker and consulting activities.

Other Sports Activities mean activities of other sports service provided for the public, including sports training service, sports research service, sports lottery service, sports communication service, sports exhibition service, sports market management service, sports venue design service, sports site cleaning service, sports cultural relics and cultural protection service.

Manufacturing of Sports Supplies, Clothes, Shoes and Caps, and Related Sports Products means manufacturing of sports supplies, clothes, shoes and caps, and related sports products necessary for provision of sports service.

Sales of Sports Supplies, Clothes, Shoes and Caps, and Related Sports Products means sales of sports supplies, clothes, shoes and caps, and related sports products necessary for provision of sports service.

Gymnasium Building Activities mean activities of construction of sports venues necessary for provision of sports service.

23

企业景气指数、消费者信心指数

PROSPERITY INDEX ON ENTERPRISES,CONSUMER CONFIDENCE INDEX

简要说明

一、本章资料的主要内容

本章资料包括企业景气调查和消费者信心指数调查。

二、本章资料的统计范围和调查方法

2012年企业景气调查包括工业，建筑业，批发和零售业，交通运输、仓储和邮政业，住宿和餐饮业，信息传输、软件和信息技术服务业，房地产业，社会服务业等行业的具有法人资格的企业及其负责人（如厂长、总经理等）以及依照法人单位进行统计的产业活动单位及其负责人。

消费者信心指数调查采用计算机辅助电话方式调查，调查对象为居住在北京市半年以上18-65周岁的城镇居民，调查范围覆盖全市16个区县。

三、本章资料的数据来源

本章资料由国家统计局北京调查总队提供。

四、有关统计标准的变化说明

（一）关于行业划分。根据国家统计局规定，自2012年开始执行《国民经济行业分类》GB/T 4754-2011标准。

（二）关于三次产业划分。根据国家统计局《三次产业划分规定》（国统字[2012]108号），该规定对三次产业的范围进行了调整。其中第一产业是指农、林、牧、渔业（不含农、林、牧、渔服务业）；第二产业是指采矿业（不含开采辅助活动），制造业（不含金属制品、机械和设备修理业），电力、热力、燃气及水生产和供应业，建筑业；第三产业是指除第一产业、第二产业以外的其他行业。2012年本章数据根据此规定进行了调整。

Brief Introduction

I. Main Content of Statistics

This chapter consists of survey on enterprise prosperity index and consumer confidence index.

II. Scope of Statistics

In 2012 survey on enterprise climate index covers enterprises as legal persons and their responsible persons (e.g. factor director, general manager), as well as industrial activity entities under statistics as corporate entities and their responsible persons in such sectors as industry, building, wholesale and retail trades, traffic and transportation, warehouse storage and postal service, accommodation and estaurants,information transmission, computer service and software, real estate, social service.

Data on consumer confidence index were obtained through computer-aided phone calls to urban residents at 18-65 who have been living in Beijing for more than half a year. The survey covers 16 districts and counties in the City.

III. Source of Data

Data in this chapter are from NBS Survey Office in Beijing.

III. Changes in Relevant Statistical Standards

(I) Classification of Sectors. According to relevant provisions of National Bureau of Statistics, the Standard for Classification of National Economic Sectors (GB/T4754-2011) became effective in 2012.

(II) Classification of Three Industries. According to the provision of National Bureau of Statistics on Classification of Three Industries (GTZ[2012]No.108), the scope of three industries has changed. The primary industry means agriculture, forestry, animal husbandry and fishery (excluding agricultural, forestry, animal husbandry and fishery services); the secondary industry means mining (excluding auxiliary activities), manufacturing (excluding metal products, machinery and equipment repair), electrical power, thermal power, fuel gas and water production and service sectors, and construction industry; the tertiary industry means industries other than the primary and secondary industries. In this chapter, figures for 2012 were adjusted according to this provision.

23-1 企业景气指数、企业家信心指数(1999-2012年)
PROSPERITY INDEX ON ENTERPRISES AND INDEXS OF CONFIDENCE ON MACRO ECONOMY BY ENTERPRISERS(1999-2012)

年份 Year	企业景气指数 Prosperity Index on Enterprises				企业家信心指数 Index of Confidence on Macro Economy by Enterprises			
	一季度 Frist Quarter	二季度 Second Quarter	三季度 Third Quarter	四季度 Fourth Quarter	一季度 Frist Quarter	二季度 Second Quarter	三季度 Third Quarter	四季度 Fourth Quarter
1999	111.0	114.7	112.4	121.0	98.0	97.4	102.4	104.4
2000	113.7	130.0	132.9	138.1	107.7	120.6	123.5	118.6
2001	112.6	123.5	117.7	115.8	124.0	116.1	118.7	111.9
2002	117.6	126.9	128.2	131.8	125.4	125.3	124.9	128.8
2003	124.8	100.9	134.5	137.6	132.5	108.0	136.7	136.1
2004	132.7	135.1	134.0	138.0	136.7	127.2	130.0	129.5
2005	129.5	132.9	131.8	127.9	131.4	128.0	126.2	125.1
2006	131.6	138.9	143.4	150.0	136.7	137.5	134.3	140.4
2007	145.8	153.8	158.5	158.7	138.4	142.6	142.3	136.1
2008	152.0	144.7	128.7	108.9	152.9	138.7	117.4	85.5
2009	110.3	115.4	127.9	133.3	91.5	104.0	121.7	126.2
2010	133.2	138.1	141.5	143.8	131.5	130.1	136.7	141.1
2011	131.6	140.0	139.4	138.8	134.4	137.8	132.7	123.0
2012	127.6	127.5	125.9	128.1	124.0	121.5	116.1	122.9

23-2 企业景气指数(2012年)

项目	Item	一季度 First Quarter 本期实际 Real Index in This Period	一季度 First Quarter 比上年同期增减 Change over Same Period of Previous Year
企业景气指数	**Prosperity Index on Enterprises**	**127.6**	**-4.0**
按登记注册类型分	**Grouped by Registration Status**		
国有企业	State-owned Enterprises	125.0	-4.1
集体企业	Collective-owned Enterprises	79.0	-34.2
股份合作企业	Cooperative Enterprises	116.7	
有限责任公司	Limited-Liability Corporations	128.7	0.5
股份有限公司	Share Holding Corporations Ltd.	132.2	-6.3
私营企业	Private Enterprises	111.3	-7.4
港、澳、台投资企业	Enterprises with Funds from Hogkong, Macao and Taiwan	138.5	-4.7
外商投资企业	Foreign Funded Enterprises	125.9	-14.3
按行业分	**Grouped by Sector**		
工　业	Industry	113.3	-15.9
建筑业	Construction	123.3	-3.6
批发和零售业	Wholesale and Retail Trade	129.0	-13.6
交通运输、仓储和邮政业	Transport, Storage, Posts	114.2	-6.9
住宿和餐饮业	Hotels and Restaurants	150.7	16.6
信息传输、软件和信息技术服务业	Information Transmission, Software and Information Technology Services	158.2	36.3
房地产业	Real Estate	115.6	-9.8
社会服务业	Social Services	137.9	-4.8
按企业规模分	**Grouped by Size of Enterprises**		
大　型	Large-sized	140.6	-13.6
中　型	Medium-sized	127.9	-2.5
小　型	Small-sized	114.4	6.0
微　型	mini-sized	76.7	
按单项指标分	**Grouped by Monomial Indicator**		
生产总量	Gross Production	90.9	-11.3
盈利(亏损)变化	Changes of Profit(Loss)	84.9	-6.7
流动资金	Working Capital	108.8	-8.4
货款拖欠	Payment for Goods in Arrears	105.6	-0.2
劳动力需求	Demand on Labors	112.7	-3.3
固定资产投资	Investment in Fixed Assets	95.2	-8.4
产品订货	Order Products	91.7	-12.0
企业融资	Financing	94.8	-1.9

注：1. 本表中的企业规模划分标准，依照《国家统计局关于印发统计上大中小微型企业划分办法的通知》〔国统字(2011)75号〕中关于《统计上大中小微型企业划分标准》规定。
2. 行业划分执行2011年国民经济行业分类标准（GB/T 4754-2011）。

PROSPERITY INDEX ON ENTERPRISES (2012)

二季度 Second Quarter		三季度 Third Quarter		四季度 Fourth Quarter	
本期实际 Real Index in This Period	比上年同期增减 Change over Same Period of Previous Year	本期实际 Real Index in This Period	比上年同期增减 Change over Same Period of Previous Year	本期实际 Real Index in This Period	比上年同期增减 Change over Same Period of Previous Year
127.5	**-12.5**	**125.9**	**-13.5**	**128.1**	**-10.7**
127.6	-4.9	122.5	-14.4	132.2	-3.1
80.2	-38.6	96.9	-15.9	106.8	-2.6
133.3	33.3	108.3		116.7	8.4
129.2	-11.9	129.3	-12.6	134.7	-0.1
127.1	-17.0	125.9	-3.3	117.6	-24.5
115.9	-6.2	120.6	0.1	114.7	-13.2
122.2	-32.2	122.6	-28.9	133.4	-3.7
127.8	-4.7	124.2	-17.0	116.8	-21.9
111.8	-21.3	113.3	-13.3	117.0	-16.3
133.3	-12.2	130.8	-13.7	137.1	-4.3
127.1	-12.2	123.1	-20.9	124.7	-9.7
115.4	-12.7	112.3	-19.1	129.8	1.5
151.7	4.2	149.7	-9.5	143.3	
162.4	-10.5	159.1	-4.8	152.7	-19.3
116.8	-5.1	112.0	-8.6	117.6	3.1
131.9	-6.4	133.2	-14.7	129.7	-16.7
138.9	-19.2	138.4	-19.6	144.1	-12.1
129.3	-8.2	126.4	-11.1	125.0	-14.0
111.0	-2.4	111.4	-4.1	108.9	-2.0
90.0		83.1		93.2	
123.4	-12.6	117.0	-8.6	115.9	-6.2
85.4	-35.1	86.7	-32.1	88.4	-28.1
108.5	-4.9	109.4	-2.1	108.3	-9.7
101.1	-0.1	99.9	-3.2	102.8	0.4
109.6	-8.1	110.3	-4.7	105.7	-4.7
110.7	-5.1	109.4	-3.1	111.9	-1.8
112.3	-11.0	108.3	-9.9	110.7	-2.8
98.2	2.7	98.1	2.3	99.6	4.3

Note: a) In this table, enterprise size is identified in accordance with the provisions concerning the Statistical Division Standards of Mini-, Small-, Mediume- and Large-sized Enterprises in the Notice of the National Bureau of Statistics Concerning Printing and Issuing Measures for Statistical Division of Mini-, Small-, Mediume- and Large-sized Enterprises (GTZ (2011)No.75).

b) Sectors in this table are classified in accordance with the Standard for Classification of National Economic Sectors 2011 (GB/T 4754-2011).

23-3 企业家信心指数(2012年)

项目	Item	一季度 First Quarter 本期实际 Real Index in This Period	一季度 First Quarter 比上年同期增减 Change over Same Period of Previous Year
企业家信心指数	**Index of Confidence by Enterprisers**	**124.0**	**-10.4**
按登记注册类型分	**Grouped by Registration Status**		
国有企业	State-owned Enterprises	126.8	-6.9
集体企业	Collective-owned Enterprises	101.2	-6.1
股份合作企业	Cooperative Enterprises	125.0	16.7
有限责任公司	Limited-Liability Corporations	122.7	-9.1
股份有限公司	Share Holding Corporations Ltd.	120.7	-17.5
私营企业	Private Enterprises	116.8	-15.5
港、澳、台投资企业	Enterprises with Funds from Hogkong, Macao and Taiwan	117.9	-27.3
外商投资企业	Foreign Funded Enterprises	127.7	-11.7
按行业分	**Grouped by Sector**		
工业	Industry	114.3	-21.0
建筑业	Construction	125.6	-10.5
批发和零售业	Wholesale and Retail Trade	125.8	-20.8
交通运输、仓储和邮政业	Transport, Storage, Posts	115.2	-13.3
住宿和餐饮业	Hotels and Restaurants	156.5	8.8
信息传输、软件和信息技术服务业	Information Transmission, Software and Information Technology Services	155.0	23.4
房地产业	Real Estate	81.0	-15.5
社会服务业	Social Services	139.8	-6.3
按企业规模分	**Grouped by Size of Enterprise**		
大型	Large-sized	140.8	-9.1
中型	Medium-sized	119.5	-18.5
小型	Small-sized	110.6	-4.8
微型	mini-sized	78.3	

注：1. 本表中的企业规模划型标准，依照《国家统计局关于印发统计上大中小微型企业划分办法的通知》〔国统字(2011)75号〕中关于《统计上大中小微型企业划分标准》规定。
2. 行业划分执行2011年国民经济行业分类标准（GB/T 4754-2011）。

INDEX OF CONFIDENCE ON MACRO ECONOMY BY ENTERPRISERS (2012)

二 季 度 Second Quarter		三 季 度 Third Quarter		四 季 度 Fourth Quarter	
本期实际 Real Index in This Period	比上年同期增减 Change over Same Period of Previous Year	本期实际 Real Index in This Period	比上年同期增减 Change over Same Period of Previous Year	本期实际 Real Index in This Period	比上年同期增减 Change over Same Period of Previous Year
121.5	**-16.3**	**116.1**	**-16.6**	**122.9**	**-0.1**
118.2	-12.5	115.0	-10.7	123.0	18.3
95.7	-5.6	96.9	-4.8	94.5	1.8
125.0	16.7	91.7	-8.3	108.3	-8.4
126.7	-15.8	122.5	-12.7	126.5	-0.4
109.1	-20.0	113.1	-9.7	114.4	5.1
115.0	-7.3	108.2	-10.6	122.9	1.5
110.2	-23.7	92.4	-45.5	114.0	-13.9
123.5	-19.7	112.3	-28.1	114.9	-18.5
109.2	-24.5	103.9	-21.1	111.8	-7.8
123.8	-14.9	119.4	-3.6	114.5	-12.0
119.3	-25.5	102.3	-46.2	114.2	-3.8
105.5	-17.4	101.2	-28.6	123.0	13.8
161.2	6.6	154.2	-0.7	154.9	5.1
156.8	-7.7	160.9	2.3	161.0	-4.3
97.8	1.1	99.4	8.6	109.5	37.1
131.0	-13.6	127.4	-5.0	126.3	-7.9
133.6	-16.3	121.1	-27.3	128.9	-2.9
119.2	-22.7	118.3	-13.2	122.8	-3.1
109.3	-5.2	106.8	-5.4	111.1	5.5
85.0		81.4		93.2	

Note: a) In this table, enterprise size is identified in accordance with the provisions concerning the Statistical Division Standards of Mini-, Small-, Mediume- and Large-sized Enterprises in the Notice of the National Bureau of Statistics Concerning Printing and Issuing Measures for Statistical Division of Mini-, Small-, Mediume- and Large-sized Enterprises (GTZ (2011)No.75).

b) Sectors in this table are classified in accordance with the Standard for Classification of National Economic Sectors 2011 (GB/T 4754-2011).

23-4 北京消费者信心指数(2012年)
BEIJING CONSUMER CONFIDENCE INDEX(2012)

项 目	Item	一季度 Frist Quarter	二季度 Second Quarter	三季度 Third Quarter	四季度 Fourth Quarter
消费者信心指数	**Consumer Confidence Index**	**108.1**	**108.8**	**107.7**	**114.2**
消费者满意指数	**Consumer Satisfaction Index**	**108.1**	**110.1**	**109.3**	**111.6**
宏观经济满意指数	Index of Satisfaction with Macroeconomy	111.7	116.4	116.6	119.9
就业状况满意指数	Index of Satisfaction with Employment Status	102.3	103.5	104.4	105.6
家庭收入状况满意指数	Index of Satisfaction with Household Income Status	100.7	98.3	95.7	98.2
家庭物质生活水平满意指数	Index of Satisfaction with Physical Living Standard	117.6	122.2	120.4	122.6
消费者预期指数	**Consumer Expectation Index**	**108.0**	**107.9**	**106.7**	**115.9**
宏观经济预期指数	Index of Expectation for Macroeconomy	117.4	117.1	114.7	130.1
就业状况预期指数	Index of Expectation for Employment Status	111.9	108.8	109.4	117.6
家庭收入状况预期指数	Index of Expectation for Household Income Status	98.8	99.6	98.2	105.0
家庭物质生活水平预期指数	Index of Expectation for Household Physical Living Standard	104.1	106.3	104.5	111.0

主要统计指标解释

企业景气调查 也称为经济周期调查或短期经济观测调查，是以企业家为调查对象，采用问卷方式，定期收集有关宏观经济和企业生产经营景气状况变动判断的一种统计调查。简言之，企业景气调查就是调查企业家对宏观经济态势，对企业生产经营状况所做出的判断和预期。调查采用重点调查和抽样调查相结合的方法，2012 年调查范围覆盖国民经济八个主要行业，即：工业，建筑业，批发和零售业，交通运输、仓储和邮政业，住宿和餐饮业，信息传输、软件和信息技术服务业，房地产业，社会服务业。

景气指数 又称景气度，是对企业景气调查中定性经济指标的定量描述，以直观地反映经济所处的状态。指数的数值介于 0 和 200 之间，100 为临界值。指数大于 100 时，表明经济状况趋于上升或改善，处于景气状态；指数小于 100 时，表明经济状况趋于下降或恶化，处于不景气状态。

企业家信心指数 亦称宏观经济景气指数，是根据企业决策者对本行业发展状况的判断及其未来走势的预期（选择“乐观”、“一般”、“不乐观”）而编制的指数，反映企业决策者对国家宏观经济发展的信心和预期，是企业决策者对当前宏观经济状况及未来走势的一种感受、体验和期望。

企业景气指数 亦称企业综合生产经营景气指数，是根据企业决策者对本企业当前生产经营状况的判断及未来企业生产经营状况的预期（选择“良好”、“一般”、“不佳”）而编制的指数，是企业决策者对企业生产经营现状及未来景气动向的一种综合评价和判断。

消费者信心指数 是综合反映并量化消费者对当前经济形势评价和对经济前景、收入水平、收入预期以及消费心理状态的主观感受，是预测经济走势和消费趋向的一个先行指标，是监测经济周期变化不可缺少的依据。消费者信心指数由消费者满意指数和消费者预期指数构成。其中消费者满意指数反映了消费者对当前经济生活的评价；消费者预期指数反映了消费者对未来一段时期经济发展变化的预期。

指数值的含义：指数取值介于 0 和 200 之间，100 为指数强弱临界点。指数超过 100，表明消费者信心处于强信心区，数值由 100 趋近 200，表明消费者信心逐渐增强；反之，指数小于 100 时，表示消费者信心处于弱信心区，数值由 100 趋近 0，表明消费者信心逐渐减弱。

Explanatory Notes on Main Statistical Indicators

Enterprise Prosperity Index Survey also known as economic cycle survey or short-term economic observation survey. Targeting at entrepreneurs, the survey is conducted in a manner of questionnaires. It is a statistical survey to collect information on judgment of macro-economy and enterprise business climate changes. To be brief, enterprise prosperity survey is to investigate entrepreneurs' judgment and expectation on macro-economic dynamics and enterprise production and business status. The survey covers 8 major national economic sectors, i.e. industry, building, wholesale and retail trades, traffic and transportation, warehouse storage and postal service, accommodation and estaurants,information transmission, computer service and software, real estate, social service.

Prosperity Index also called prosperity degree, is a quantitative description of qualitative indicators in enterprise climate survey, aiming to visualize the status of economy. The value of index ranges from 0 to 200, with 100 as the critical value. When the index is greater than 100, it indicates that the economic status is rising or improving, and in a prosperous state; when the index is 100, it shows the economic status is declining or deteriorating, and in a non-prosperous state.

Index of Confidence by Enterprisers also known as Macroeconomic Climate Index, which is indexed according to the enterprise decision makers' opinions and expectations (with choices of "optimistic", "moderate" and "non-optimistic") on the development status of the sector and its future trend. It reflects the enterprise decision makers' confidence about and expectation on the national macroeconomic development. It serves as the enterprise decision makers' feeling, experience and expectation about current macroeconomic status and its trend.

Prosperity Index on Enterprises also known as Business Climate Index, which is indexed according to estimations and expectations of enterprise decision makers' opinions and expectation on the enterprise's current and future production and operation status (choice of "good", "moderate" and "bad"). It represents the enterprise decision makers' comprehensive evaluation and judgment on the current situation and future trend of the enterprise production and operation.

Consumer Confidence Index is an indicator reflecting and quantifying the consumers' evaluation on current economic situation, and their personal feeling about the economic prospect, income level, income expectation, and psychological state of consumption. It serves as a leading indicator predicting the trend of economy tendency of consumption, and an essential basis for monitoring the changes in economic cycle. and other conditions as well as expectation on the economic prospect in a future period of time. Consumer Confidence Index consists of consumer satisfaction index and consumer expectation index. Of which, consumer satisfaction index reflects consumers' evaluation on current economic life; consumer expectation index reflects consumers' expectation on the development and changes in the economic prospect in a future period of time.

Meaning of index values: Values of the index range from 0 to 200. 100 represents a critical point between strong and weak confidence. An index greater than 100 indicates the consumers' confidence is in a strong area of confidence. An index going toward 200 from 100 shows the consumers' confidence is becoming strong gradually; in contrary, an index smaller than 100 means the consumers' confidence is in a area of weak confidence. When the index value going toward 0 from 100, it means the consumers' confidence is weakening gradually.

24

开发区
DEVELOPMENT ZONES

简要说明

一、本章资料的主要内容

本章资料包括北京市 19 家开发区的基本情况，重点介绍了北京经济技术开发区及中关村国家自主创新示范区的主要情况。本章所指开发区包括北京市级及国家级开发区。其中，中关村亦庄园在中关村国家自主创新示范区与北京经济技术开发区中为重叠部分。

二、本章资料的数据来源

本章资料由北京市统计局提供，其中 24-7 表由北京经济技术开发区统计局、调查队提供。

Brief Introduction

I. Main Content

Data in this chapter show the basic condition of 19 development zones in Beijing, mainly describing the situation of Beijing Economic and Technological Development Zone and Zhongguancun National Innovation Demonstration Zone. Development Zones mentioned herein are development zones at municipal level and national level. Of which, Zhongguancun Yizhuang Park is overlapped in Zhongguancun National Innovation Demonstration Zone and Beijing Economic and Technological Development Zone.

II. Source of Data

Data in this chapter are sourced from Beijing Municipal Bureau of Statistics. Of which, data for Table 24-7 are sourced from the Statistics Bureau and Survey Team of Beijing Economic and Technological Development Zone.

24-1 北京市开发区基本情况(2005-2012年)
STATISTICS ON DEVELOPMENT ZONES OF BEIJING (2005-2012)

项目		Item		2005	2006	2007
开发区个数	(个)	Number of Development Zones	(unit)	28	19	19
区规划总面积	(平方公里)	Layout Area of Development Zones	(sq.km)	204.60	319.23	326.67
累计实际征用土地面积	(平方公里)	Accumulated Area of Actual Land Acquisition	(sq.km)	108.74	126.59	139.41
累计土地开发施工面积	(平方公里)	Accumulated Area of Actual Land Development Construction	(sq.km)	93.89	103.62	115.28
累计土地开发完工面积	(平方公里)	Accumulated Area of Land Development Complet	(sq.km)	88.47	94.82	107.38
累计出让转让土地使用权签定合同土地面积	(平方公里)	Accumulated Area of Land with a Land Use Right Transfer Contract	(sq.km)	52.28	60.86	58.17
#三资企业	(平方公里)	Foreign Funded Enterprises	(sq.km)	15.18	16.11	14.33
累计招商项目企业个数	(个)	Accumulated Number of Enterprises Inviting Business	(unit)	30474	32669	30942
累计招商项目总投资	(亿元)	Accumulative Total Investment of Inviting Business	(100 million yuan)	5367.5	6129.6	6403.7
累计招商项目注册资本	(亿元)	Accumulative Registered Capital of Inviting Business	(100 million yuan)	3849.6	4411.1	4958.4
#三资企业	(亿元)	Foreign Funded Enterprises	(100 million yuan)	1100.3	1282.4	1533.9
累计招商项目合同外资金额	(亿美元)	Accumulative Contracted Foreign Capital of Inviting Business	(USD 100 million)	111.6	134.5	166.4
累计招商项目外商实际投资	(亿美元)	Accumulated Actual Foreign Investment of Inviting Business	(USD 100 million)	80.6	94.9	110.4
总收入	(亿元)	Total Revenue Completed	(100 million yuan)	6573.8	8792.6	11495.2
工业总产值(当年价格)	(亿元)	Gross Output Value(at current prices)	(100 million yuan)	3748.0	4746.1	5260.5
应缴税金	(亿元)	Total Taxes Payable	(100 million yuan)	289.1	389.1	522.1
利润总额	(亿元)	Total Profits Completed	(100 million yuan)	379.8	516.2	908.5

注：1. 本表所指开发区包括北京市级及国家级开发区情况。
2. 表内"累计"指自开始年份至本年末的累计数。

Note: a) Development Zones referred to in this table include those at Beijing municipal level and State level.
b) Accumulative data of this table refer to that from the beginning to the end of this year.

24-1 续表 continued

项 目		Item		2008	2009	2010	2011	2012
开发区个数	(个)	Number of Development Zones	(unit)	19	19	19	19	19
区规划总面积	(平方公里)	Layout Area of Development Zones	(sq.km)	335.74	338.94	344.98	346.21	393.12
累计实际征用土地面积	(平方公里)	Accumulated Area of Actual Land Acquisition	(sq.km)	153.25	168.74	172.19	179.21	185.52
累计土地开发施工面积	(平方公里)	Accumulated Area of Actual Land Development Construction	(sq.km)	119.69	126.59	132.91	138.91	144.47
累计土地开发完工面积	(平方公里)	Accumulated Area of Land Development Completed	(sq.km)	111.07	115.92	121.89	124.87	127.62
累计出让转让土地使用权		Accumulated Area of Land with a Land						
签定合同土地面积	(平方公里)	Use Right Transfer Contract	(sq.km)	60.62	74.08	79.51	81.54	82.80
#三资企业	(平方公里)	Foreign Funded Enterprises	(sq.km)	14.38	15.41	17.69	17.64	17.45
累计招商项目企业个数	(个)	Accumulated Number of Enterprises Inviting Business	(unit)	32362	36044	39031	42974	46940
累计招商项目总投资	(亿元)	Accumulative Total Investment of Inviting Business	(100 million yuan)	6756.4	7172.8	8254.6	9472.8	10786.6
累计招商项目注册资本	(亿元)	Accumulative Registered Capital of Inviting Business	(100 million yuan)	5259.3	5612.5	6434.7	7469.6	8642.3
#三资企业	(亿元)	Foreign Funded Enterprises	(100 million yuan)	1620.0	1705.2	1817.5	1967.7	1963.2
累计招商项目合同外资金额	(亿美元)	Accumulative Contracted Foreign Capita of Inviting Business	(USD 100 million)	216.6	213.8	227.6	253.4	261.5
累计招商项目外商实际投资	(亿美元)	Accumulated Actual Foreign Investment of Inviting Business	(USD 100 million)	156.9	160.8	169.3	192.4	207.2
总收入	(亿元)	Total Revenue Completed	(100 million yuan)	13162.5	15108.9	18401.4	23173.1	29434.3
工业总产值(当年价格	(亿元)	Gross Output Value(at Current Prices)	(100 million yuan)	5209.1	5127.7	6169.5	7277.0	8108.3
应缴税金	(亿元)	Total Taxes Payable	(100 million yuan)	616.6	713.4	943.8	1093.8	1639.8
利润总额	(亿元)	Total Profits Completed	(100 million yuan)	868.0	1232.3	1451.4	1733.4	1952.0

24-2 北京市开发区基本情况(2012年)
STATISTICS ON DEVELOPMENT ZONES OF BEIJING (2012)

项目		Item		合计 Total	国家级 Of State	市级 Of City
开发区个数	(个)	Number of Development Zones	(unit)	19	3	16
区规划总面积	(平方公里)	Layout Area of Development Zones	(sq.km)	393.12	305.50	87.62
累计实际征用土地面积	(平方公里)	Accumulated Area of Actual Land Acquisition	(sq.km)	185.52	123.39	62.13
累计土地开发施工面积	(平方公里)	Accumulated Area of Actual Land Development Construction	(sq.km)	144.47	95.46	49.01
累计土地开发完工面积	(平方公里)	Accumulated Area of Land Development Complet	(sq.km)	127.62	83.38	44.24
累计出让转让土地使用权签定合同土地面积	(平方公里)	Accumulated Area of Land with a Land Use Right Transfer Contract	(sq.km)	82.80	44.70	38.10
#三资企业	(平方公里)	Foreign Funded Enterprises	(sq.km)	17.45	10.73	6.72
累计招商项目企业个数	(个)	Accumulated Number of Enterprises Inviting Business	(unit)	46940	34583	12357
累计招商项目总投资	(亿元)	Accumulative Total Investment of Inviting Business	(100 million yuan)	10786.6	8622.5	2164.1
累计招商项目注册资本	(亿元)	Accumulative Registered Capital of Inviting Business	(100 million yuan)	8642.3	7466.8	1175.5
#三资企业	(亿元)	Foreign Funded Enterprises	(100 million yuan)	1963.2	1626.0	337.2
累计招商项目合同外资金额	(亿美元)	Accumulative Contracted Foreign Capital of Inviting Business	(USD 100 million)	261.5	207.0	54.5
累计招商项目外商实际投资	(亿美元)	Accumulated Actual Foreign Investment of Inviting Business	(USD 100 million)	207.2	150.8	56.4

注：1. 本表所指开发区包括北京市级及国家级开发区情况。
2. 表内“累计”指自开始至年末的累计数。

Note: a) Development Zones referred to in this table include those at Beijing municipal level and State level.
b) Accumulative data of this table refer to that from the beginning to the end of this year.

24-3 北京市开发区主要指标完成情况
ACCOMPLISHMENT OF MAJOR INDICATORS ON DEVELOPMENT ZONE OF BEIJING

项目	Item	2012	2011	2012年为2011年% 2012 as % of 2011
固定资产投资 (亿元)	Investment in Fixed Assets Completed (100 million yuan)	759.0	615.8	123.3
新增固定资产 (亿元)	Increased Fixed Assets (100 million yuan)	339.3	232.9	145.7
房屋建筑施工面积 (万平方米)	Floor Space of Buildings under Construction (10000 sq.m)	2544.6	1987.5	128.0
房屋建筑竣工面积 (万平方米)	Floor Space of Buildings Completed (10000 sq.m)	274.8	369.5	74.4
总收入 (亿元)	Total Revenue Completed (100 million yuan)	29434.3	23173.1	127.0
工业总产值(当年价格) (亿元)	Gross Output Value(at current prices) (100 million yuan)	8108.3	7277.0	111.4
工业销售产值(当年价格) (亿元)	Sales Value of Industry (at current price) (100 million yuan)	8008.4	7164.9	111.8
利润总额 (亿元)	Total Profits Completed (100 million yuan)	1952.0	1733.4	112.6
应缴税金 (亿元)	Total Taxes Payable (100 million yuan)	1639.8	1093.8	149.9

注：本表所指开发区包括北京市级及国家级开发区情况。

Note: Development Zones referred to in this table include those at Beijing municipal level and State level.

24-4 北京市开发区土地开发情况(2012年)

LAND EXPLOITATION OF DEVELOPMENT ZONES OF BEIJING(2012)

单位：公顷 (hectare)

名 称 Name	规划总面积 Total Area of Layout Land	累计国家批准征用土地面积 Area of Land Approved by the State for Acquisition	累计实际征用土地面积 Total Area of Land Actually Expropriated	累计土地开发施工面积 Total Construction Area of Land Exploitation	累计土地开发完工面积 Total Completed Area of Land Exploitation
北京经济技术开发区	4650.00	3980.00	4924.00	3891.00	3700.00
中关村国家自主创新示范区	27983.13	10704.68	9916.17	7982.94	6966.63
中关村示范区海淀园	13306.00	2103.35	2103.35	1788.77	1483.74
中关村示范区丰台园	818.00	436.33	436.33	327.72	327.72
中关村示范区昌平园	5140.00	1119.00	1108.11	862.78	757.72
中关村示范区电子城科技园	1809.00	1809.00	1471.00	542.49	147.11
中关村示范区亦庄园	2678.00	2678.00	2678.00	2678.00	2678.00
中关村示范区德胜园	1000.00				
中关村示范区雍和园	290.30				
中关村示范区石景山园	345.00	56.00	56.00	56.00	56.00
中关村示范区通州园	1490.50	1450.00	1208.85	1208.85	1055.94
中关村示范区大兴生物工程与医药产业基地	1106.33	1053.00	854.53	518.33	460.40
北京天竺综合保税区	594.40	594.40	177.42	349.50	349.50
北京石龙经济开发区	231.50	231.50	150.00	184.44	150.00
北京良乡经济开发区	240.00	118.03	109.50	109.50	109.50
北京大兴经济开发区	412.30	239.72	239.72	235.99	232.75
北京通州经济开发区	761.88	478.15	478.15	401.80	288.50
北京雁栖经济开发区	1096.00	733.83	733.83	733.83	733.83
北京兴谷经济开发区	978.79	474.29	470.45	299.82	257.92
北京密云经济开发区	1240.17	1240.17	1240.17	923.97	841.07
北京林河经济开发区	416.00	247.00	247.00	157.00	157.00
北京天竺空港经济开发区	965.05	944.43	944.43	559.60	559.60
北京八达岭经济开发区	480.79	317.95	258.55	234.44	234.44
北京永乐经济开发区	459.81	235.08	235.08	235.08	79.87
北京延庆经济开发区	303.53	111.96	111.96	111.96	111.96
北京昌平小汤山工业园区	257.34	257.34	257.34	111.24	111.24
北京采育经济开发区	355.01	306.23	306.23	306.23	306.23
北京房山工业园区	218.52	218.52	218.52	141.90	141.90
北京马坊工业园区	345.58	211.91	211.91	154.56	108.09

注：1. 本表所指开发区包括北京市级及国家级开发区情况。
2. 中关村示范区亦庄园数据在中关村国家自主创新示范区与北京经济技术开发区中为重叠部分。

Note: a) Development Zones referred to in this table include those at Beijing municipal level and State level.
b) Data on Yizhuang Park of Zhongguancun Demonstration Zone are overlapped in Zhongguancun National Innovation Demonstration Zone and Beijing Economic & Technological Development Zone.

24-5 各类开发区招商、入资情况(2012年)
STATISTICS ON BUSINESS INVITATION AND INVESTMENT IN DEVELOPMENT ZONES (2012)

名称 Name	自开始至报告期累计 Accumulative Number from Beginning					
	招商项目企业个数(个) Number of Inviting Business (unit)	项目总投资(万元) Total Investment (10000 yuan)	注册资本(万元) Registered Capital (10000 yuan)	#三资企业 Foreign Partner	合同外资金额(万美元) Contracted Foreign Capital (USD 10000)	外商实际投资(万美元) Actual Foreign Investment (USD 10000)
北京经济技术开发区	5684	23060218	16317134	5546049	728282	559746
中关村国家自主创新示范区	29344	75158479	63820775	14500687	1624250	1235939
中关村示范区海淀园	18743	35563518	32391484	8059934	1091502	718353
中关村示范区丰台园	4368	10570142	10570142	227253	26905	33239
中关村示范区昌平园	1698	5112239	4934615	571416	46386	46386
中关村示范区电子城科技园	1225	6819067	6819067	1153778	96679	96679
中关村示范区亦庄园	564	13126385	5942095	4046110	322539	291826
中关村示范区德胜园	283	663115	662914		43	43
中关村示范区雍和园	151	485882	485882	72716	1678	1796
中关村示范区石景山园	2153	1436073	1508981	203504	31308	34210
中关村示范区通州园	99	1005652	273129	142776	2460	8657
中关村示范区大兴生物工程与医药产业基地	60	376405	232465	23200	4750	4750
北京天竺综合保税区	119	1132262	472243	259942	39948	4533
北京石龙经济开发区	4468	1569914	1566914	41265	7997	6423
北京良乡经济开发区	1695	1252852	1252852	17185	2728	2728
北京大兴经济开发区	748	463940	355388	135143	10675	9491
北京通州经济开发区	336	2798564	579931	215495	39358	36196
北京雁栖经济开发区	1262	2498593	882502	460489	240471	252780
北京兴谷经济开发区	250	909717	420061	222669	50021	38870
北京密云经济开发区	227	2177100	452173	117117	23807	39099
北京林河经济开发区	94	828008	515863	113882	13382	8312
北京天竺空港经济开发区	540	5589373	3639833	1959875	142683	155842
北京八达岭经济开发区	1074	657317	461634	19981	60	60
北京永乐经济开发区	25	193769	47139			1487
北京延庆经济开发区	725	1238484	1065034	7497	5857	6494
北京昌平小汤山工业园区	78	52800	34731	6242	989	655
大兴采育经济开发区	57	662972	110404	6981	1735	780
北京房山工业园区	721	370991	270923			
北京马坊工业园区	57	376818	99656	47940	5000	4850

注：中关村示范区亦庄园数据在中关村国家自主创新示范区与北京经济技术开发区中为重叠部分。

Note: Data on Yizhuang Park of Zhongguancun Demonstration Zone are overlapped in Zhongguancun National Innovation Demonstration Zone and Beijing Economic & Technological Development Zone.

24-6 各类开发区投资、生产情况(2012年)
INVESTMENT AND PRODUCTION OF DEVELOPMENT ZONES (2012)

名称 Name	自年初累计 Accumulative Number from Year-beginning						
	固定资产投资(万元) Investment in Fixed Assets (10000 yuan)	新增固定资产(万元) Increased Fixed Assets (10000 yuan)	房屋建筑施工面积(平方米) Floor Space of Buildings under Construction (sq.m)	房屋建筑竣工面积(平方米) Floor Space of Buildings Completed (sq.m)	总收入(万元) Total Revenues Reaped (10000 yuan)	利润总额(万元) Total Profits (10000 yuan)	应缴税金合计(万元) Total Taxes Payable (10000 yuan)
北京经济技术开发区	3399375	897700	13674395	712774	44281638	2183072	2681226
中关村国家自主创新示范区	2970859	1651691	7291310	1097750	250249575	17885600	14457699
中关村示范区海淀园	800044	786797	1809123	340971	106657471	8223570	4230918
中关村示范区丰台园	555000		1270000	416500	29384764	976582	754281
中关村示范区昌平园	506447	188068	962800	80883	23441944	1128281	782604
中关村示范区电子城科技园	430000	115585	2559539	152075	38451875	3665153	5410362
中关村示范区亦庄园					28696461	2020725	2303660
中关村示范区德胜园	8597	27204	104879	26800	7648834	1137139	378646
中关村示范区雍和园	502206	483394	46998		3794778	188757	147652
中关村示范区石景山园	3138	3087			9094780	484727	290334
中关村示范区通州园					2415391	-11160	108928
中关村示范区大兴生物工程与医药产业基地	165427	47556	537971	80521	663278	71826	50314
北京天竺综合保税区	51256	19459	448921		816694	33779	43430
北京石龙经济开发区	34502	34502	344428		1065725	189575	235440
北京良乡经济开发区	30000	25000	38500	31500	2001761	31894	90266
北京大兴经济开发区	37067	19641	238747	87349	1747960	59067	62849
北京通州经济开发区	201243	38730	432400	93009	1773439	61582	83935
北京雁栖经济开发区	48849	34098	345697	39778	2554078	224472	176446
北京兴谷经济开发区	101210	67700	217728	60590	2177563	193163	133836
北京密云经济开发区	176297	146015	600599	195339	2864675	145824	178427
北京林河经济开发区	26166	66203	121406	103906	1463552	66993	73584
北京天竺空港经济开发区	208031	165049	1130988	60445	8917910	354564	254812
北京八达岭经济开发区	61373	61373			932606	93811	88597
北京永乐经济开发区	40322	40322	83000		55858	3885	12180
北京延庆经济开发区	59813		79051		1164601	13621	108474
北京昌平小汤山工业园区					369708	9153	5121
大兴采育经济开发区	39617	39082	164881	144364	322723	-7726	4491
北京房山工业园区	18076	807	42446	2317	122742	2770	5181
北京马坊工业园区	85608	85608	191304	119125	156487	-4271	5166

注：中关村示范区亦庄园数据在中关村国家自主创新示范区与北京经济技术开发区中为重叠部分。

Note: Data on Yizhuang Park of Zhongguancun Demonstration Zone are overlapped in Zhongguancun National Innovation Demonstration Zone and Beijing Economic & Technological Development Zone.

24-7 北京经济技术开发区主要经济指标
MAIN ECONOMIC INDICATORS FOR BEIJING ECONOMIC-TECHNOLOGICAL DEVELOPMENT ZONES

项目		Item		2012	2011	2012年为2011年% 2012 as % of 2011
规划面积	(公顷)	Area Planned	(hectare)	4650.0	4650.0	100.0
累计征用土地面积	(公顷)	Accumulative Land Area Requisitioned	(hectare)	4924.0	4924.0	100.0
开发区生产总值	(亿元)	Gross Output Value of Development Zones	(100 million yuan)	827.7	782.5	105.8
工业总产值	(亿元)	Gross Output Value of Industry	(100 million yuan)	2187.9	2284.7	95.8
(当年价格)		(at current price)				
#高新技术企业	(亿元)	High-tech Industry Enterprises	(100 million yuan)	1993.7	2087.3	95.5
销售(营业)收入	(亿元)	Sales(Business)Revenue	(100 million yuan)	4328.5	4141.1	104.5
利润总额	(亿元)	Total Profits	(100 million yuan)	212.1	339.8	62.4
进出口总值	(亿美元)	Total Imports and Exports Value	(USD 100 million)	213.4	252.5	84.5
出　口	(亿美元)	Exports	(USD 100 million)	105.8	110.5	95.7
进　口	(亿美元)	Imports	(USD 100 million)	107.7	142.0	75.8
财政收入(含免抵)	(亿元)	Financial Revenue(Including Exempted and Set-off Revenue)	(100 million yuan)	335.5	269.1	124.7
税收(含免抵)	(亿元)	Tax(Including Exempted and Set-off Tax)	(100 million yuan)	268.1	245.4	109.3
土地收入	(亿元)	Land Revenue	(100 million yuan)	67.4	23.7	283.9
财政支出	(亿元)	Financial Expenditure	(100 million yuan)	129.3	109.4	118.3
批准企业个数	(个)	Number of Enterprises Ratified	(unit)	1210	1038	116.6
入区企业投资额	(亿美元)	Investment of Enterprises Entered	(USD 100 million)	60.1	63.6	94.6
注册资本	(亿美元)	Registered Capital	(USD 100 million)	43.3	57.3	75.4
合同外资金额	(亿美元)	Contracted Foreign Capital	(USD 100 million)	7.3	17.1	42.5
实际利用外资	(亿美元)	Foreign Capital Actually Used	(USD 100 million)	6.7	6.4	103.8
固定资产投资	(亿元)	Investment in Fixed Assets	(100 million yuan)	339.9	320.2	106.2
从业人员期末人数	(人)	Number of Employed Persons	(person)	275219	253934	108.4
从业人员工资总额	(万元)	Total Wages of Laboreo	(10000 yuan)	2297846	1904412	120.7

资料来源：北京经济技术开发区统计局、调查队。
Source: Beijing Economic & Technological Development Zone Bureau of Statistics.

24-8 中关村国家自主创新示范区企业经营及科技活动情况(2008-2012年)
OPERATING ACTIVITIES AND SCIENCE ACTIVITIES OF ENTERPRISES IN ZHONGGUANCUN NATIONAL INNOVATION DEMONSTRATION ZONE (2008-2012)

项　目		Item		2008	2009	2010	2011	2012
总收入	**(亿元)**	**Total Income**	**(100 million yuan)**	**10222.4**	**13004.6**	**15940.2**	**19646.0**	**25025.0**
技术收入	(亿元)	Technology Income	(100 million yuan)	1693.4	2093.6	2478.3	2845.9	3403.1
产品销售收入	(亿元)	Products Sales Income	(100 million yuan)	5229.2	5923.6	6889.6	7809.4	8741.2
#新产品销售收入	(亿元)	New Product Sales Income	(100 million yuan)	3327.0	3203.7	3949.2	3405.1	3352.1
商品销售收入	(亿元)	Commodity Sales Income	(100 million yuan)	2398.9	3689.4	5032.2	7161.9	10077.4
其他收入	(亿元)	Other Revenue	(100 million yuan)	900.9	1298.0	1540.1	1828.9	2803.4
出口总额	(亿美元)	Foreign Exchange Created by Export	(USD 100 million)	207.4	208.2	227.4	237.3	261.7
实缴税费总额	(亿元)	Total Taxes Paid	(100 million yuan)	504.0	658.7	767.2	925.8	1445.8
利润总额	(亿元)	Total Profits Completed	(100 million yuan)	726.3	1122.4	1298.9	1533.9	1788.6
研究与试验发展人员	(人)	R&D Personnel	(person)	174797	152168	96699	111685	125429
研究与试验发展经费内部支出	(亿元)	Internal R&D Expenditure	(100 million yuan)	324.5	235.4	260.4	313.5	381.3
获奖成果情况		**Statistics on Prize-winning Achievements**						
获奖成果个数	(个)	Number of Prize-winning Achievements	(unit)	1448	1909	1811	2329	2509
#国家级	(个)	National	(unit)	282	276	256	323	377
省部级	(个)	Provincial	(unit)	641	1044	1015	1351	1318
专利情况		**Statistics on Patent**						
专利申请数	(件)	Number of Patents Applied	(unit)	17219	17226	18515	24894	34192
拥有有效发明专利数	(件)	Number of Patents in Force	(unit)	9836	11611	13988	15232	23198
专利授权数	(件)	Certified	(unit)	9050	10512	13151	12951	17969

24-9 中关村国家自主创新示范区企业经营活动情况
OPERATING ACTIVITIES OF ENTERPRISES IN ZHONGGUANCUN NATIONAL INNOVATION DEMONSTRATION ZONE

单位：亿元 (100 million yuan)

项　　目	Item	2012	2011
工业总产值(当年价格)	Gross Output Value of Industry (at current prices)	6494.7	5831.6
工业销售产值(当年价格)	Sales Value of Industry (at current price)	6420.5	5729.8
#出口交货值	Delivery Value of Exports	910.0	932.1
总收入	Total Income	25025.0	19646.0
技术收入	Technology Income	3403.1	2845.9
产品销售收入	Products Sales Income	8741.2	7809.4
#出口收入	Export Revenue	1021.1	997.5
商品销售收入	Commodity Sales Income	10077.4	7161.9
其他收入	Other Income	2803.4	1828.9
实缴税费总额	Total Taxes Paid	1445.8	925.8
#增值税	Value Added Tax	443.4	400.0
营业税	Business Tax	148.2	148.4
所得税	Corporate Income Tax	340.2	256.5
本年实缴关税	Duties	290.5	55.9
减免税总额	Total Tax Reduced and Exempted	169.1	160.9
#增值税	Value Added Tax	49.3	36.0
营业税	Business Tax	15.5	19.1
所得税	Corporate Income Tax	97.7	103.8
应交增值税	Value Added Tax Payable	444.3	875.5
出口总额　　(亿美元)	Foreign Exchange Created by Export　　(USD100 million)	261.7	237.3

24-10 中关村国家自主创新示范区企业科技活动情况
SCIENCE ACTIVITIES OF ENTERPRISES IN ZHONGGUANCUN NATIONAL INNOVATION DEMONSTRATION ZONE

项目	Item	2012	2011
科技活动情况	**Statistics on science and technology activities**		
科技活动人员合计 (人)	Total of Personnel Engaged in Science and Technology (person)	402330	359475
#全时人员	Full-time	357559	316127
#研究与试验发展(R&D)人员	R&D Personnel	125429	111685
企业内部用于科技活动的经费支出 (亿元)	Total Expenditures on Research Activities Inside Organizations (100 million yuan)	811.9	682.7
#人员人工费(包括各种补贴)	Labor Cost (Including Wages)	431.4	348.1
原材料费	Cost of Raw Materials	129.6	124.7
#研究与试验发展(R&D)经费内部支出	R&D Expenditure	381.3	313.5
委托外单位开展科技活动经费支出 (亿元)	Expenditures for Science Activities Conducted by External Institutes Entrusted (100 million yuan)	106.3	98.3
#对境内研究机构及高等学校的支出	Payment to Domestic Research Institutes	68.3	60.0
对境外支出	Domesticn Other Corporation	3.0	1.7
本年度R&D项目情况	**R&D Projects in the year**		
R&D项目数 (项)	Number of R&D Projects (unit)	12124	10826
项目人员折合全时当量 (人年)	Total Participants in R&D Projects (person-years)	77153	73016
研究与试验发展(R&D)项目经费支出 (亿元)	Expenditure fo R&D Programs (100 million yuan)	296.9	244.4
企业科技活动产出情况	**Science and Technologh Output**		
获奖成果情况	**Statistics on Prize-winning Achievements**		
获奖成果个数 (个)	Number of Prize-winning Achievements (unit)	2509	2329
#国家级 (个)	National (unit)	377	323
省部级 (个)	Provincial (unit)	1318	1351
地市级 (个)	Prefecture- and City-level (unit)	785	595
专利情况	**Statistics on Patent**		
专利申请数 (件)	Number of Patents Applied (case)	34192	24894
#发明专利 (件)	Invention Patents (case)	20914	14505
拥有有效发明专利数 (件)	Number of Patents in Force (case)	23198	15232
专利授权数 (件)	Certified (case)	17969	12951
论文、著作情况	**Statistics on Papers and Writings**		
发表科技论文篇数 (篇)	Scientific Papers Published (unit)	10197	8827
技术改造和技术获取情况	**Technical Rennovation and Acquisition**		
技术改造经费支出 (亿元)	Payment for Technical Rennovation Expenses (100 million yuan)	17.7	34.3
引进国外技术经费支出 (亿元)	Payment for Technical Introduction Expenses (100 million yuan)	12.8	14.4
引进技术的消化吸收经费支出 (亿元)	Payment for Digest and Absorption Expenses (100 million yuan)	4.3	0.7
购买国内技术经费支出 (亿元)	Payment for Purchase Cost of Domestic Technology (100 million yuan)	9.9	11.3

24-11 中关村国家自主创新示范区企业人力资源情况
HUMAN RESOURCE IN ENTERPRISES IN ZHONGGUANCUN NATIONAL INNOVATION DEMONSTRATION ZONE

单位：人 (person)

项　　目	Item	2012	2011
企业人力资源情况	**Statistics on Human Resource**		
从业人员年末人数	**Year-end Empolyed Persons**	**1585950**	**1384821**
#工程技术人员	Engineering Technician	472496	389899
#留学归国人员	Returned Students Studying Abroad	16102	13704
#在岗长期职工	Fully Employed Staff and Workers	1427907	1248163
按文化程度分	**Group by Educational Background**		
博士及以上	Doctor Degree and Above	15193	14058
#留学归国人员	Returned Students Studying Abroad	1890	1748
硕　士	Masters	156736	132382
#留学归国人员	Returned Students Studying Abroad	10529	8390
大　本	Undergraduates	614973	533580
大　专	Junior College	321269	276863
按技术职称分	**Grouped by Technical Post**		
高　级	Senior	83488	70501
中　级	Middle	154997	138500
初　级	Junior	173594	145800
按年龄分	**Group by Age**		
29岁及以下	Age 29 and Below	762377	695727
30-39岁	30-39	507631	427637
40-49岁	40-49	215710	179855
50岁及以上	Age 50 and Over	100232	81602
从业人员平均人数	**Average Number of Empolyed Persons**	**1562830**	**1303190**
在岗职工参加社会保险人数	**Number of Take Part in the Social Insurance**	**1311960**	**1134881**

24-12 中关村国家自主创新示范区企业财务状况
FINANCIAL STATUS OF ENTERPRISES IN ZHONGGUANCUN NATIONAL INNOVATION DEMONSTRATION ZONE

单位：亿元 (100 million yuan)

项　　目	Item	2012	2011
资产总计	Total Assets	40386.9	29191.1
流动资产合计	Total Current Assets	22958.8	17444.1
固定资产合计	Total Fixed Assets	4980.9	2512.6
固定资产原价	Original Value of Fixed Assets	7164.2	4036.9
累计折旧	Accumulative Depreciation	2026.6	1549.6
负债合计	Total Liabilities	22393.1	16075.7
所有者权益合计	Owner's Equity	17982.2	13115.4
实收资本	Paid-up Capital	9340.1	6684.1
主营业务收入	Operating Income	24588.2	19300.8
主营业务成本	Operating Cost	20228.4	15700.1
主营业务税金及附加	Operating Tax and Extra Charges	239.5	226.5
利润总额	Total Profits	1788.6	1533.9

主要统计指标解释

累计实际征用土地面积 指自开始至报告期末累计实际完成征用的土地面积合计。

累计土地开发施工面积 指自开始至报告期末累计进行“七通”（道路、上水、供电、供气、供热、电信、下水）“一平”（场地平整一进行地上物拆除）施工的土地开发面积。

累计土地开发完工面积合计 指自开始至报告期末累计已具备“七通一平”条件的土地开发面积。

累计出让转让土地使用权签订合同土地面积 指自开始至报告期末累计出让转让土地使用权，签订正式出让转让土地使用权合同的土地面积合计。包括科技园区、开发区和工业小区自行建设占用的土地面积。

累计招商项目企业个数 指自开始至报告期末累计招商入区，并经工商管理机关注册取得法人营业执照的企业个数。

累计招商项目总投资 指自开始至报告期末累计批准的合同（章程）规定的投资总额。

累计招商项目注册资本 指自开始至报告期末累计为设立经营企业在工商行政管理机关注册的资本总额。

累计招商项目合同外资金额 指自开始至报告期末累计批准的合同（章程）中，外商和港、澳、台商的出资额。

累计招商项目外商实际投资 指自开始至报告期末累计按合同规定的外方和港、澳、台方以现金、实物、工业产权及专有技术的计价实缴资本投资额。

总收入 指企业全年的生产产品销售收入、技术性收入和与本企业产品相关的商品的销售收入、其它收入等各种收入的总和，总收入等于主营业务收入加上其他业务收入。总收入应按不含增值税的价格计算，不包括补贴收入、营业外收入、投资收益。

出口总额 指出售给外贸部门或直接出售给外商的产品或商品的总金额。包括来料加工装配出口，境外技术合同实现金额及在国内以外汇计价的商品出售和技术服务的总额等。

留学归国人员 指出国学习，取得学位的归国人员。

Explanatory Notes on Main Statistical Indicators

Accumulated Area of Actual Land Acquisition means total area of land actually expropriated from the beginning to the end of the reporting period.

Accumulated Area of Actual Land Development and Construction means total development area of land on which construction works of road, water supply, electric power supply, gas, heating, telecom, and drainage, as well as site leveling – removal of matters on the ground, are carried out from the beginning to the end of the reporting period.

Accumulated Area of Land Development Completed means the total area of land development that is provided with conditions of available road, water supply, electric power supply, gas, heating, telecom, and drainage, as well as site leveling from the beginning to the end of the reporting period.

Accumulated Area of Land with a Land Use Right Transfer Contract means the total area of land under transfer contracts from the beginning to the end of the reporting period, including the area of land built and occupied by development zones.

Accumulated Number of Enterprises Inviting Business means the total number of enterprises invited to development zones and awarded with business licenses for legal persons from the administration for industry and commerce from the beginning to the end of the reporting period.

Accumulative Total Investment of Inviting Business means the total investment of contracts (articles of incorporation) approved from the beginning to the end of the reporting period.

Accumulative Registered Capital of Inviting Business means the total capital registered with the administration for industry and commerce for the purpose of establishment of operating enterprises from the beginning to the end of the reporting period.

Accumulative Contracted Foreign Capital of Inviting Business means the cumulative capital contribution of investors from foreign countries, Hong Kong, Macao and Taiwan as approved in contracts (articles of incorporation) from the beginning to the end of the reporting period.

Accumulated Actual Foreign Investment of Inviting Business means the cumulative amount of paid-up capital contribution investors from foreign countries, Hong Kong, Macao and Taiwan made in cash, in kind, industrial property right and know-how, as stated in contracts, from the beginning to the end of the reporting period.

Total Revenue Completed means the sum of income earned by enterprises from sales of their own products, technological income, and income from selling commodities related to their own products, and other income. Total income is the sum of main business income and other business income. Total income shall be calculated at VAT-excluded prices, and exclude subsidies, non-operating income and return on investment across the year.

Total Value of Export means the total amount of products or commodities sold to foreign trade organizations or directly sold to foreign traders. It includes the value of export of investor’s raw materials processed, the value of technical contracts completed at home and abroad, and the total value of domestic commodity sales and technical services measured in foreign currency.

Returned Students Studying Abroad mean persons who have come home after studying abroad and been conferred with academic degrees.